CENSUS OF INDIA 1931

Census of India 1871-1951, 9 Sets In 384 Bindings (9788121258876) Rs. 700000

Census of India 1931, 28 Vols. In 52 Bindings (9788121271233) Rs. 102000

1. India - Report (9788121276153) Rs. 2820 (Vol. I, Pt. 1)
2. India - Imperial Tables (9788121276139) Rs. 3210 (Vol. I, Pt. 2)
3. India - Ethnographical and Administration Report (9788121276115) Rs. 2900 (Vol. I, Pt. 3 & 5)
4. The Andaman And Nicobar Islands - Report, Tables (9788121276078) Rs. 720 (Vol. II, Pt. 1, Pt. 2)
5. Assam - Report (9788121276054) Rs. 1340 (Vol. III, Pt. 1)
6. Assam - Tables and Administrative Report (9788121276030) Rs. 1830 (Vol. III, Pt. 2 & 3)
7. Baluchistan - Report, Imeprial and Provincial Tables and Administrative Report (9788121276016) Rs. 2320 (Vol. IV, Pt. 1 & 2 & 3)
8. Bengal & Sikkim - Report (9788121275972) Rs. 2860 (Vol. V, Pt. 1)
9. Bengal & Sikkim - Tables (9788121275958) Rs. 1660 (Vol. V, Pt. 2)
10. Calcutta (9788121275910) Rs. 960 (Vol. VI, Pt. 1 & 2)
11. Bengal, Sikkim And Calcutta - Administrative Report (9788121275934) Rs. 580 (Vol. V & VI, Pt. 3)
12. Bihar And Orissa - Report (9788121275897) Rs. 1780 (Vol. VII, Pt. 1)
13. Bihar And Orissa - Tables and Administrative Report (9788121275873) Rs. 1190 (Vol. VII, Pt. 2 & 3)
14. Bombay Presidency - General Report (9788121275835) Rs. 3620 (Vol. VIII, Pt. 1)
15. Bombay - Statistical tables (9788121275811) Rs. 3060 (Vol. VIII, Pt. 2)
16. Bombay Presidency Aden - report and tables and Administrative report (9788121275798) Rs. 520 (Vol. VIII, Pt. 3 & 4)
17. Cities of the Bombay Presidency Report & Statistical tables (9788121275750) Rs. 2020 (Vol. IX, Pt. 1 & 2)
18. The Western India States Agency, In Two Parts - The Report & The Statistical Tables (9788121275736) Rs. 2560 (Vol. X, Pt. 1 & 2)
19. Burma - Report (9788121275712) Rs. 1860 (Vol. XI, Pt. 1)
20. Burma - Tables and Administrative Report (9788121275699) Rs. 1690 (Vol. XI, Pt. 2 & 3)
21. Central Provinces & Berar - Report (9788121275651) Rs. 2340 (Vol. XII, Pt. 1)
22. Central Provinces & Berar - Tables and Administrative Report (9788121275637) Rs. 3120 (Vol. XII, Pt. 2 & 3)
23. Coorg - Report And Tables and Madras - Report (9788121275613) Rs. 2680 (Vol. XIV, Pt. 1)
24. Madras - Imperial And Provincial Tables and The Administration Report (9788121275576) Rs. 1950 (Vol. XIV, Pt. 2 & 4)
25. North - West Frontier Province - Report & Tables (9788121275538) Rs. 2300 (Vol. XV, Pt. 1 & 2)
26. Delhi - Report & Tables (9788121275514) Rs. 1180 (Vol. XVI, Pt. 1 & 2)
27. Punjab - Report (9788121275491) Rs. 2070 (Vol. XVII, Pt. 1)
28. Punjab - Tables (9788121275477) Rs. 1690 (Vol. XVII, Pt. 2)
29. United Provinces of Agra And Oudh - Report (9788121275453) Rs. 3380 (Vol. XVIII, Pt. 1)
30. United Provinces of Agra And Oudh - Imperial And Provincial Tables and Administrative (9788121275439) Rs. 3600 (Vol. XVIII, Pt. 2 & 3)
31. Baroda - Report (9788121275415) Rs. 2800 (Vol. XIX, Pt. 1)
32. Baroda - Tables (9788121275392) Rs. 730 (Vol. XIX, Pt. 2)
33. Baroda - Administrative (9788121275378) Rs. 780 (Vol. XIX, Pt. 3)
34. Central India Agency - Report (9788121275354) Rs. 1690 (Vol. XX, Pt. 1)
35. Central India Agency - Tables and Administrative Volume (9788121275330) Rs. 2260 (Vol. XX, Pt. 2 & 3)
36. Cochin - Report & Tables (9788121275293) Rs. 2460 (Vol. XXI, Pt. 1 & 2 - A & B.)
37. Gwalior - Report (9788121275279) Rs. 1470 (Vol. XXII, Pt. 1)
38. Gwalior - Tables (9788121275255) Rs. 980 (Vol. XXII, Pt. 2)
39. H. E. H. The Nizam's Dominions (Hyderabad State) - Report (9788121275231) Rs. 1540 (Vol. XXIII, Pt. 1)
40. H. E. H. The Nizam's Dominions (Hyderabad State) - Tables (9788121275217) Rs. 1510 (Vol. XXIII, Pt. 2)
41. Jammu & Kashmir State - Report (9788121275194) Rs. 2060 (Vol. XXIV, Pt. 1)
42. Jammu & Kashmir State - Imperial & State Tables (9788121275170) Rs. 1940 (Vol. XXIV, Pt. 2 & 3)
43. Mysore - Report (9788121275156) Rs. 1950 (Vol. XXV, Pt. 1)
44. Mysore - Tables (9788121275132) Rs. 1380 (Vol. XXV, Pt. 2)
45. Ajmer-Merwara - Report And Tables (9788121275118) Rs. 780 (Vol. XXVI)
46. Rajputana Agency And Ajmer-Merwara - Report and Tables and Administrative (9788121275095) Rs. 2380 (Vol. XXVII, Pt. 1 & 2)
47. Travancore - Report (9788121276092) Rs. 2960 (Vol. XXVIII, Pt. 1)
48. Travancore - Tables & Administrative (9788121275996) Rs. 1360 (Vol. XXVIII, Pt. 2 & 4)
49. Jaipur State- Report (9788121275859) Rs. 1280 (Pt. 1)
50. Jaipur State- Tables (9788121275774) Rs. 2030 (Pt. 2)
51. Mayurbhanj state- Report (9788121275675) Rs. 3180 (Pt. 1)
52. Mayurbhanj state- Tables (9788121275552) Rs. 3070 (Pt. 2)

Owing to the antiquity and rarity of this book, certain pages are regrettably absent, and readability is compromised due to the blurring of the original text. If you possess any insights regarding the availability of these missing sections, kindly inform us. Your assistance is crucial in ensuring the completion of this significant work for the benefit of future generations.

CENSUS OF INDIA, 1931

BOOK - 28: VOLUME - XVII

PUNJAB

PART II - TABLES

KHAN AHMAD HASAN KHAN

GYAN

Published by

Gyan Publishing House
5, Ansari Road
Daryaganj, New Delhi-110002
Phone: 011-47034999, 9811692060
E-mail: books@gyanbooks.com

Distribution Network
gyanbooks.com
India, USA, Canada, UK, Australia

ISBN: 978-81-212-7123-3 (Set) 28 Vols. In 52 Bindings

ISBN: 978-81-212-7547-7 (PB) Vol. XVII, Pt. II

First Published, 1933

2nd Impression 2024

Printed at: Gyan Press, Delhi.

CENSUS OF INDIA 1931

CENSUS OF INDIA, 1931

VOLUME XVII.

PUNJAB.

PART II.

TABLES

BY

KHAN AHMAD HASAN KHAN, M.A., K.S.,

SUPERINTENDENT OF CENSUS OPERATIONS,
PUNJAB & DELHI.

Lahore:

PRINTED AT THE "CIVIL AND MILITARY GAZETTE" PRESS.

1933.

Agents for the Sale of Punjab Government Publications.

The General Manager, "The Qaumi Daler" and The Union Press, Amritsar.

Messrs. D. B. Taraporewala, Sons & Co., Bombay.

Messrs. W. Newman & Co., Ltd., Calcutta.

Messrs. Thacker Spink & Co., Calcutta.

Messrs. Rama Krishna & Sons, Lahore.

The Secretary, Punjab Religious Book Society, Lahore.

The Manager, University Book Agency, Lahore.

L. Ram Lal Suri, Proprietor, "The Students' Own Agency," Lahore.

L. Dewan Chand, Proprietor, The Mercantile Press, Lahore.

The Manager, Mufid-i-'Am Press, Lahore.

The Proprietor, Punjab Law Book Mart, Lahore.

Mr. D. Pestonji, Stockists' Representative Lahore.

The Managing-Proprietor, The Commercial Book Company, Lahore.

R. S. Jaura, Esq., B.A., B.T., The Students' Popular Depôt, Anarkali, Lahore.

Messrs. Thacker Spink & Co., Simla.

The Manager, The English Book Depôt, Taj Road, Agra.

The Managing-Partner, The Bombay Book Depôt, Booksellers and Publishers, Girgaon, Bombay.

The Proprietor, The Book Company, Calcutta.

Messrs. Chatterji & Co., Booksellers, 204, Cornwallis Street, Calcutta.

The Manager, Standard Book Depôt, Lahore.

The Proprietor, Aftab Punjab General Law Book Agency, Lahore.

The Manager, Oxford Book and Stationery Co., The Mall, Lahore.

The Proprietor, City Book Co., Post Box No. 283, Madras.

The Manager, The New Book Depôt, No. 79, The Mall, Simla.

TABLE OF CONTENTS.

TABLE I.

AREA, HOUSES AND POPULATION.

1. This Table shows for each District and State the area, the number of towns and villages, the number of occupied houses, and the total urban and rural population, male and female. The Districts are arranged, in this and other Tables, in the order of Administrative Divisions, with the only exception that the figures of Delhi Province have not been shown in this Volume, a separate Volume for that Province being prepared on the present occasion.

2. " *Houses* " in colums 6 to 8 means census houses. For a discussion of the definition of this term, see the closing paragraphs of Chapter I of the Report Volume. Briefly, the census house is the dwelling-place of the commensal family ; but any non-residential building which contained a single individual on the Census night was also reckoned as a " *House.* "

3. The differences between some of the areas shown in this Table and those given in the corresponding Table of 1921 are due to territorial transfers. The recent Survey figures as communicated by the Department of Survey of India for Rohtak, Gujrat, Shahpur and Sheikhupura Districts have been entered after adjustment for subsequent changes ; in the case of other Districts those supplied by the Survey of India and reported in the Tables of Agricultural Statistics of the Punjab for the year 1929-30 have been adopted without alteration.

4. The territorial transfers that have occurred since the last Census are :—

(*a*) Inter-District transfers in the Ferozepore, Lahore, Sialkot, Sheikhupura, Montgomery, Lyallpur and Multan Districts.

(*b*) A transfer of one square mile from Ferozepore District to Bikaner State.

(*c*) A transfer of two square miles from Kangra District to Mandi State.

(*d*) A transfer of less than one square mile from Bulandshahr District (U. P.) to Gurgaon District and *vice versa,* caused by alluvion and diluvion.

(*e*) A transfer of less than one square mile from Muzaffarnagar District (U. P.) to Karnal District caused by alluvion and diluvion.

5. In the case of Indian States, the figures of 1921 have been repeated, as figures from Survey Department were received too late for adoption.

6. " Biloch Trans-Frontier " is the hilly tract across the border of the Dera Ghazi Khan District proper. It is administered by Tumandars (Tribal Chiefs) under the control of a Political Assistant to the Deputy Commissioner. The tract has not yet been regularly surveyed and the area given in the last Census Report has been repeated.

Note.—The population statistics for tahsils will be found in Provincial Tables I and II at the end of this Volume.

Note.—The figures in italics below the District figures relate to Cantonments.

TABLE I.—AREA, HOUSES AND POPULATION.

Serial No.	District or State.	Area in square miles.	Towns.	Villages.	Occupied Houses. Total.	Occupied Houses. In Towns.	Occupied Houses. In Villages.	Population. Persons. Total.	Persons. Urban.	Persons. Rural.	Males. Total.	Males. Urban.	Males. Rural.	Females. Total.	Females. Urban.	Females. Rural.	Serial No.
1	2	3	4	5	6	7	8	9	10	11	12	13	14	15	16	17	18
	PUNJAB	136,261	222	50,691	5,943,652	714,299	5,229,353	28,490,857	3,521,449	24,969,408	15,561,194	2,065,249	13,495,945	12,929,663	1,456,200	11,473,463	
					44,966	*44,966*		*220,974*	*220,974*		*146,318*	*146,318*		*74,656*	*74,656*		
	BRITISH TERRITORY	99,200	177	34,630	4,894,035	607,281	4.286,754	23,580,852	3,067,464	20,513,388	12,880,510	1,805,872	11,074,638	10,700,342	1,261,592	9,438,750	
					44,966	*44,966*		*220,974*	*220,974*		*146,318*	*146,318*		*74,656*	*74,656*		
	AMBALA DIVISION	15,055	40	6,348	861,413	116,682	744.731	4,077,565	532,855	3,544,710	2,226,856	303,787	1,923,069	1,850,709	229,068	1,621,641	
					13,023	*13,023*		*55,486*	*55,486*		*33,962*	*33,962*		*21,524*	*21,524*		
1	Hissar	5,213	6	963	177,076	23,928	153,148	899,479	114,198	785,281	485,690	63,661	422,029	413,789	50,537	363,252	1
2	Rohtak	2,471	7	722	158,522	18,024	140,498	805,621	91,481	714,140	432,855	50,532	382,323	372,766	40,949	331,817	2
3	Gurgaon	2,263	8	1,358	157,736	15,756	141,980	740,163	71,805	668,268	398,513	39,471	359,042	341,650	32,424	309,226	3
4	Karnal	3,125	6	1,380	185,560	21,299	164,261	852,614	101,999	750,615	469,870	56,781	413,089	382,744	45,218	337,526	4
5	Ambala	1.882	8	1,723	171,248	29,475	141,773	742,902	131,764	611,138	416,411	77,598	338,813	326,491	54,166	272,325	5
					12,072	*12,072*		*52,220*	*52,220*		*31,959*	*31,959*		*20,261*	*20,261*		
6	Simla	101	5	202	11,271	8,200	3,071	36,786	21,518	15,268	23,517	15,744	7,773	13,209	5,774	7,495	6
					951	*951*		*3,266*	*3,266*		*2,003*	*2,003*		*1,263*	*1,263*		
	JULLUNDUR DIVISION	19,396	29	6,380	976,259	98,543	877,716	4,606,446	472,595	4,133.851	2,491,638	274,347	2,217,291	2,114,808	198,248	1,916,560	
					8,291	*8,291*		*47,415*	*47,415*		*30,530*	*30,530*		*16,885*	*16,885*		
7	Kangra	9.076	1	713	177,159	1,071	176,088	801,312	6,359	794,953	415,288	4,154	411,134	386,024	2,205	383,819	7
					151	*151*		*2,383*	*2,383*		*1,527*	*1,527*		*856*	*856*		
8	Hoshiarpur	2.247	6	2,099	233,614	13,362	220,252	1,032,187	57,295	974,892	551,867	31,542	520,325	480,320	25,753	454,567	8
9	Jullundur	1,431	8	1,210	184,728	27,771	156,957	943,721	140,424	803,297	512,667	79,134	433,533	431,054	61,290	369,764	9
					2,342	*2,342*		*14,735*	*14,735*		*9,798*	*9,798*		*4,937*	*4,937*		
10	Ludhiana	1,452	4	851	144,598	23,259	121,339	672,494	114,059	558.435	375,560	67,803	307,757	296,934	46,256	250,678	10
11	Ferozepore	4,290	10	1,507	236,160	33,080	203,080	1,156,732	154,458	1,002,274	636,256	91,714	544,542	520,476	62,744	457,732	11
					5,798	*5,798*		*30,297*	*30,297*		*19,205*	*19,205*		*11,092*	*11,092*		
	LAHORE DIVISION	12,353	40	8.716	1,168,312	218,921	949,391	5,879,075	1,191,113	4,687,962	3,277,661	720,237	2,557.424	2,601,414	470,876	2,130,538	
					9,729	*9,729*		*51,244*	*51,244*		*35,403*	*35,403*		*15,841*	*15,841*		
12	Lahore	2,682	8	1,121	290,740	110,404	180,336	1,378,570	531,480	847,090	794,389	333,553	460,836	584,181	197,927	386,254	12
					5,907	*5.907*		*29,672*	*29,672*		*20,741*	*20,741*		*8,931*	*8,931*		
13	Amritsar	1,593	5	1,036	212,771	42,561	170,210	1,117,120	296,112	821,008	621,040	176,382	444,658	496,080	119,730	376,35[illegible]	13
					508	*508*		*1,630*	*1,630*		*1,162*	*1,162*		*468*	*468*		
14	Gurdaspur	1,889	9	2.243	193.676	15,306	178.370	970,898	74,658	896,240	531,935	42,672	489,263	438,963	31,986	406,97[illegible]	14
					1,076	*1,076*		*4,091*	*4,091*		*2,705*	*2,705*		*1,386*	*1,386*		
15	Sialkot	1,578	6	2,066	186,758	20,247	166,511	979,617	134,847	844,770	537,301	78,286	459,015	442,316	56,561	385,755	15
					2,238	*2,238*		*15,851*	*15,851*		*10,795*	*10,795*		*5,056*	*5,056*		
16	Gujranwala	2,309	7	1.219	148,857	21,357	127,500	736,138	115,912	620,226	408,606	66,502	342,104	327,532	49,410	278,122	16
17	Sheikhupura	2,302	5	1.031	135.510	9,046	126,464	696,732	38,104	658,628	384,390	22,842	361,548	312,342	15,262	297,080	17
	RAWALPINDI DIVISION	21.347	35	5.480	884,981	81,455	803,526	3.914.849	424,025	3,490,824	2,092,622	248,389	1,844,233	1,822,227	175,686	1,646,591	
					11,897	*11,897*		*55,723*	*55,723*		*39,104*	*39,104*		*16,619*	*16,619*		
18	Gujrat	2,250	5	1,440	203,660	11,612	192,048	922,427	57,272	865,155	498,336	31,388	466,948	424,091	25,884	398,207	18
19	Shahpur	4.789	13	973	171,922	22,090	149,832	821,490	107,595	713,895	445,836	60,878	384,958	375,654	46,717	328,937	19
20	Jhelum	2,773	4	884	134,222	9,301	124,921	541,076	48,899	492,177	282,714	29,611	253,103	258,362	19,288	239,074	20
					917	*917*		*6,233*	*6,233*		*5,312*	*5,312*		*921*	*921*		
21	Rawalpindi	2,023	2	1,170	145,093	24,757	120,336	634,357	121,264	513,093	342,771	77,487	265,284	291,586	43,777	247,809	21
					9,906	*9,906*		*43.967*	*43,967*		*30,273*	*30,273*		*13,694*	*13,694*		
22	Attock	4,117	7	615	139,622	8,919	130,703	583,960	50,858	533,102	306,949	28,118	278,831	277,011	22,740	254,271	22
					1.074	*1,074*		*5,523*	*5,523*		*3,519*	*3,519*		*2,004*	*2,004*		
23	Mianwali	5,395	4	398	90.462	4,776	85,686	411,539	38,137	373,402	216,016	20,907	195,109	195,523	17,230	178,293	23
	MULTAN DIVISION	31,049	33	7,706	1,003,070	91,680	911.390	5,102,917	446,876	4,656,041	2.791,733	259.112	2,532,621	2,311,184	187,764	2,123,420	
					2,026	*2,026*		*11,106*	*11.106*		*7,319*	*7.319*		*3,787*	*3,787*		
24	Montgomery	4,518	4	1,958	187,596	11,199	176,397	999,772	52,574	947,198	552,456	33,640	518,816	447,316	18,934	428,382	24
25	Lyallpur	3,224	6	1,241	201,351	15,609	185,742	1.151,351	85,249	1,066,102	630,749	53,529	577,220	520,602	31,720	488,882	25
26	Jhang	3,452	5	981	135,537	15,182	120,355	664,833	76,963	587,870	355,671	41,199	314,472	309,162	35,764	273,398	26
27	Multan	5,892	3	1,916	238,413	29,225	209.188	1,174,900	137,280	1,037,620	646,025	79,065	566,960	528,875	58,215	470,660	27
					2,026	*2.026*		*11,106*	*11,106*		*7,319*	*7,319*		*3,787*	*3,787*		
28	Muzaffargarh	6,052	6	862	128,009	7,108	121,891	591,375	30,898	560,477	320,674	16,663	304,011	270,701	14,235	256,466	28
29	Dera Ghazi Khan	5,325	9	739	104,312	13,367	90,955	491,044	63,912	427,132	269,341	35,016	234,325	221,703	28,896	192,8[illegible]7	29
	Biloch trans-frontier tract	2,586	..	9	6,862	..	6,862	29,642	..	29,642	16,817	..	16,817	12,825	..	12,825	

No.	State																No.
	PUNJAB STATES ..	37,061	45	16,061	1,049,617	107,018	942,599	4,910,005	453,985	4,456,020	2,680,684	259,377	2,421,307	2,229,321	194,608	2,034,718	
	A.—Having Political Relations with the Punjab Government.	5,820	4	2,610	95,112	3,368	91,744	437,787	14,534	423,253	229,290	7,907	221,383	208,497	6,627	201,870	
1	Dujana	91	1	32	5,676	443	5,233	28,216	1,561	26,655	14,537	816	13,721	13,679	745	12,934	1
2	Pataudi	52	1	40	4,040	797	3,243	18,873	3,667	15,206	9,922	1,882	8,040	8,951	1,785	7,166	2
3	Kalsia	188	2	173	13,469	2,128	11,341	59,848	9,306	50,542	33,306	5,209	28,097	26,542	4,097	22,445	3
4	SIMLA HILL STATES	5,469	..	2,365	71,927	..	71,927	330,850	..	330,850	171,525	..	171,525	159,325	.	159,325	4
	Total Bashahr	3,881	..	85	17,066	..	17,066	104,389	..	104,389	51,593	..	51,593	52,796	..	52,796	
	Bashahr Proper	3,820	..	70	16,219	..	16,219	100,192	.	100,192	49,515	..	49,515	50,677	..	50,677	
	Feudatories { Khaneti ..	19	..	9	527	..	527	2,797	..	2,797	1,368	..	1,368	1,429	..	1,429	
	Feudatories { Delath ..	42	..	6	320	..	320	1,400	..	1,400	710	..	710	690	..	690	
	Nalagarh	256	..	617	12,100	..	12,100	50,015	..	50,015	26,635	..	26,635	23,380	..	23,380	
	Total Keonthal	359	..	457	12,384	..	12,384	48,093	..	48,093	25,734	..	25,734	22,359	..	22,359	
	Keonthal Proper	116	..	215	6,558	..	6,558	25,560	..	25,560	13,582	..	13,582	11,978	.	11,978	
	Feudatories { Koti	50	..	10	2,810	..	2,810	8,785	..	8,785	5,030	..	5,030	3,755	..	3,755	
	Feudatories { Theog ..	144	.	169	1,546	..	1,546	6,912	..	6,912	3,613	..	3,613	3,299	..	3,299	
	Feudatories { Madhan ..	9	..	34	931	..	931	4,315	..	4,315	2,201	..	2,201	2,114	..	2,114	
	Feudatories { Ghund ..	28	..	17	397	..	397	1,963	..	1,963	999	..	999	964	..	964	
	Feudatories { Ratish ..	12	..	12	142	..	142	558	..	558	309	..	309	249	..	249	
	Baghal	124	..	416	6,145	..	6,145	26,352	..	26,352	13,457	..	13,457	12,895	..	12,895	
	Total Jubbal .. .	320	..	35	5,286	..	5,286	27,172	..	27,172	14,507	..	14,507	12,665	..	12,665	
	Jubbal Proper	288	..	21	5,043	..	5,043	26,021	..	26,021	13,908	..	13,908	12,113	..	12,113	
	Feudatories { Rawain ..	7	..	12	186	..	186	939	..	939	493	..	493	446	..	446	
	Feudatories { Dhadi .	25	..	2	57	..	57	212	..	212	106	..	106	106	..	106	
	Baghat	36	..	133	2,810	..	2,810	9,725	..	9,725	5,744	..	5,744	3,981	..	3,981	
	Kumharsain . ..	90	..	11	2,297	..	2,297	12,781	..	12,781	6,425	..	6,425	6,356	..	6,356	
	Bhajji	96	.	179	5,689	..	5,689	15,413	..	15,413	7,943	..	7,943	7,470	.	7,470	
	Mahlog	43	.	184	2,012	..	2,012	8,155	..	8,155	4,299	..	4,299	3,856	..	3,856	
	Balsan	51	..	37	1,464	..	1,464	6,864	..	6,864	3,603	..	3,603	3,261	..	3,261	
	Dhami	26	..	107	1,150	..	1,150	5,232	..	5,232	2,693	..	2,693	2,539	..	2,539	
	Kuthar	20	..	6	918	..	918	3,760	..	3,760	2,023	..	2,023	1,737	..	1,737	
	Kunihar	80	..	16	504	..	504	2,061	..	2,061	1,035	..	1,035	1,026	..	1,026	
	Mangal	12	..	15	276	..	276	1,248	.	1,248	680	..	680	568	..	568	
	Bija	4	..	46	319	..	319	994	..	994	579	..	579	415	..	415	
	Darkoti	8	..	13	106	..	106	531	..	531	257	..	257	274	..	274	
	Tharoch	67	..	3	731	..	731	4,568	..	4,568	2,521	..	2,521	2,047	..	2,047	
	Sangri	16	..	5	670	..	670	3,497	.	3,497	1,797	..	1,797	1,700	..	1,700	
	B.—Having Political Relations with the Government of India.	31,241	41	13,451	954,505	103,650	850,855	4,472,218	439,451	4,032,767	2,451,394	251,470	2,199,924	2,020,824	187,981	1,832,843	
5	Loharu	222	1	70	4,193	445	3,748	23,338	2,956	20,382	12,326	1,572	10,754	11,012	1,384	9,628	5
6	Sirmoor	1,198	2	965	32,204	1,827	30,377	148,568	7,808	140,760	82,384	4,584	77,800	66,184	3,224	62,960	6
7	Bilaspur	448	1	940	23,825	561	23,264	100,994	2,387	98,607	53,154	1,427	51,727	47,840	960	46,880	7
8	Mandi	1,202	2	3,606	45,388	3,147	42,241	207,465	13,501	193,964	107,876	9,143	98,733	99,589	4,358	95,231	8
9	Suket	420	1	87	12,634	577	12,057	58,408	2,401	56,007	30,851	1,362	29,489	27,557	1,039	26,518	9
10	Kapurthala	598	3	617	69,644	9,730	59,914	316,757	40,865	275,892	171,529	23,152	148,377	145,228	17,713	127,515	10
11	Maler Kotla	167	3	111	21,223	8,334	12,889	83,072	31,465	51,607	45,883	17,779	28,104	37,189	13,686	23,503	11
12	Faridkot	638	2	171	33,168	6,558	26,610	164,364	33,261	131,103	91,163	19,585	71,578	73,201	13,676	59,525	12
13	Chamba	3,216	1	53	30,665	1,352	29,313	146,870	6,219	140,651	76,059	3,605	72,454	70,811	2,614	68,197	13
14	Phulkian States { Patiala .	5,942	11	3,528	343,998	39,533	304,465	1,625,520	169,339	1,456,181	900,597	95,729	804,868	724,923	73,610	651,313	14
15	Phulkian States { Jind ..	1,259	4	439	64,327	8,306	56,021	324,676	39,029	285,647	176,383	22,620	153,763	148,293	16,409	131,884	15
16	Phulkian States { Nabha ..	928	6	492	61,774	10,385	51,389	287,574	47,043	240,531	158,086	26,410	131,676	129,488	20,633	108,855	16
17	Bahawalpur	15,003	4	2,372	211,462	12,895	198,567	984,612	43,177	941,435	545,103	24,502	520,601	439,509	18,675	420,834	17

TABLE II.

VARIATION IN POPULATION DURING THE LAST FIFTY YEARS.

1. In this Table the figures of the present census are compared with those of previous censuses.

2 The territorial transfers (*a*) inter-District and (*b*) with the United Provinces have affected the population of the following Districts :-

Gurgaon. Karnal, Ferozepore, Lahore, Sialkot, Sheikhupura, Montgomery, Lyallpur and Multan.

3. The population of areas transferred has been taken into account and the figures of former censuses adjusted accordingly. The total population of the Province in 1881, 1891, 1901, 1911 and 1921 has been increased by 402, 412, 488, 474 and 454 persons respectively on account of transfer of area from the United Provinces of Agra and Oudh.

TABLE II.—VARIATION IN POPULATION DURING THE LAST FIFTY YEARS.

District or State.	Persons. 1931.	1921.	1911.	1901.	1891.	1881.	Variation: Increase (+), Decrease (—). 1921 to 1931.	1911 to 1921.	1901 to 1911.	1891 to 1901.	1881 to 1891.
1	2	3	4	5	6	7	8	9	10	11	12
PUNJAB ..	**28,490,857**	**25,101,514**	**23,791,841**	**24,367,113**	**22,915,894**	**20,800,995**	**+3,389,343**	**+1,309,673**	**—575,272**	**+1,451,219**	**+2,114,899**
BRITISH TERRITORY.	**23,580,852**	**20,685,478**	**19,579,047**	**19,942,715**	**18,652,614**	**16,939,312**	**+2,895,374**	**+1,106,431**	**363,668**	**+1,290,101**	**+1,713,302**
AMBALA DIVISION.	**4,077,565**	**3,827,069**	**3,780,327**	**4,199,528**	**4,079,366**	**3,897,604**	**-250,496**	**+46,742**	**-419,201**	**+120,162**	**+181,762**
1. Hissar ..	*899,479*	816,810	804,889	781,580	775,896	672,513	+82,669	+11,921	+23,300	+5,693	+103,383
2. Rohtak ..	*805,621*	772,272	714,834	834,010	779,875	740,444	+33,349	+57,438	—119,176	+54,135	+39,431
3. Gurgaon ..	*740,163*	682,361	730,204	842,932	760,226	761,906	+57,802	—47,843	—112,728	+82,706	—1,770
4. Karnal ..	*862,614*	828,822	801,110	884,722	862,548	855,966	+23,792	+27,712	-83,612	+22,174	+6,582
5. Ambala ..	*742,902*	681,477	690,854	816,808	864,719	831,450	+61,425	—9,377	—125,954	—47,911	+33,269
6. Simla ..	*36,786*	45,327	38,436	39,467	36,102	35,235	—8,541	+6,891	—1,031	+3,365	+867
JULLUNDUR DIVISION.	**4,606,446**	**4,182,516**	**3,968,271**	**4,306,273**	**4,216,878**	**3,788,069**	**+423,930**	**+214,245**	**—338,002**	**+89,395**	**+428,809**
7. Kangra ..	*801,312*	766,065	770,386	768,124	763,030	730,845	+35,247	—4,321	+2,262	+5,094	+32,185
8. Hoshiarpur ..	*1,032,187*	927,419	918,569	989,738	1,011,465	901,044	+104,768	+8,850	—71,169	—21,727	+110,421
9. Jullundur ..	*943,721*	822,544	801,920	917,587	907,583	789,555	+121,177	+20,624	—115,667	+10,004	+118,028
10. Ludhiana ..	*672,494*	567,622	517,192	673,097	648,722	618,835	+104,872	+50,430	—155,905	+24,375	+29,887
11. Ferozepore ..	*1,156,732*	1,098,866	960,204	957,727	886,078	747,790	+57,866	+138,662	+2,477	+71,649	+138,288
LAHORE DIVISION.	**5,879,075**	**5,047,437**	**4,734,894**	**5,164,454**	**4,859,836**	**4,295,072**	**+831,638**	**+312,543**	**—429,560**	**+304,618**	**+564,764**
12. Lahore ..	*1,378,570*	1,129,839	999,521	1,003,862	898,790	767,831	+248,731	+130,318	—4,341	+105,072	+130,959
13. Amritsar ..	*1,117,120*	929,374	880,796	1,023,985	992,850	893,380	+187,746	+48,578	—143,189	+31,135	+99,470
14. Gurdaspur ..	*970,898*	852,192	836,771	940,334	943,922	823,695	+118,706	+15,421	—103,563	—3,588	+120,227
15. Sialkot ..	*979,617*	877,867	871,650	933,205	961,600	880,684	+101,750	+6,217	—61,555	—28,395	+80,916
16. Gujranwala ..	*736,138*	623,581	605,582	739,546	661,223	579,258	+112,557	+17,999	—133,964	+78,323	+81,965
17. Sheikhupura ..	*696,732*	634,584	540,574	523,522	401,451	350,224	+62,148	+94,010	+17,052	+122,071	+51,227
RAWALPINDI DIVISION.	**3,914,849**	**3,460,710**	**3,353,052**	**3,106,771**	**3,067,947**	**2,782,847**	**+454,139**	**+107,658**	**+246,281**	**+38,824**	**+285,100**
18. Gujrat ..	*922,427*	824,046	787,999	792,159	806,382	727,044	+98,381	+36,047	—4,160	—14,223	+79,338
19. Shahpur ..	*821,490*	719,918	645,001	488,149	478,289	383,652	+101,572	74,917	156,852	+9,860	+94,637
20. Jhelum ..	*541,076*	477,068	511,575	501,424	514,090	494,499	+64,008	—34,507	+10,151	—12,666	+19,591
21. Rawalpindi ..	*634,357*	569,224	547,827	558,699	533,740	471,079	+65,133	+21,397	—10,872	+24,959	+62,661
22. Attock ..	*583,960*	512,249	519,273	464,430	448,420	444,307	+71 711	—7,024	+54,843	+16,010	+4,113
23. Mianwali ..	*411,539*	358,205	341,377	301,910	287,026	262,266	+53,334	+16,828	+39,467	+14,884	+24,760
MULTAN DIVISION.	**5,102,917**	**4,167,746**	**3,742,503**	**3,165,689**	**2,428,587**	**2,175,720**	**+935,171**	**+425,243**	**+576,814**	**+737,102**	**+252,867**
24. Montgomery ..	*999,772*	685,690	481,965	429,674	416,559	348,312	+314,082	+203,725	+52,291	+13,115	+68,247
25. Lyallpur ..	*1,151,351*	957,881	824,470	576,939	46,926	53,832	+193,470	+133,411	+247,531	+530,013	—6,906
26. Jhang ..	*664,833*	570,559	524,803	426,225	402,341	390,630	+94,274	+45,756	+98,578	+23,884	+11,711
27. Multan ..	*1,174,900*	889,328	813,357	709,297	634,538	555,516	+285,572	+75,971	+104,060	+74,759	+79,022
28. Muzaffargarh ..	*591,375*	568,478	569,461	527,681	403,914	441,217	+22,897	—983	+41,780	+33,767	+52,697
29. Dera Ghazi Khan	*491,044*	469,052	499,860	471,786	428,375	386,213	+21,992	—30,808	+28,074	+43,411	+42,162
29. Biloch trans-frontier tract.	*29,642*	23,758	28,587	24,087	5,934	..	+2,884	—1,829	+4,500	+18,153	+5,934

TABLE II.—VARIATION IN POPULATION DURING THE LAST FIFTY YEARS—*continued*

Net variation in Period 1881-1931. Increase (+). Decrease (—).	Males.						Females.					
	1931.	1921	1911.	1901.	1891.	1881.	1931.	1921.	1911.	1901.	1891.	1881.
13	14	15	16	17	18	19	20	21	22	23	24	25
+7,689,862	**15,561,194**	**13,732,290**	**13,093,893**	**13,144,341**	**12,380,786**	**11,279,489**	**12,929,663**	**11,369,224**	**10,697,948**	**11,222,772**	**10,535,108**	**9,521,506**
+6,641,540	**12,880,510**	**11,306,507**	**10,770,985**	**10,734,532**	**10,056,695**	**9,167,186**	**10,700,342**	**9,378,971**	**8,808,062**	**9,208,183**	**8,595,919**	**7,772,126**
+179,961	**2,226,856**	**2,088,882**	**2,070,936**	**2,262,250**	**2,198,201**	**2,112,569**	**1,850,709**	**1,738,187**	**1,709,391**	**1,937,278**	**1,881,165**	**1,785,035**
+226,966	485,690	435,362	438,458	418,089	414,841	364,113	413,789	381,248	366,431	363,500	361,055	308,400
+65,177	432,855	417,379	385,401	443,680	416,306	397,700	372,766	354,893	320,433	390,360	363,569	342,744
—21,833	398,513	367,984	389,739	442,967	399,821	404,183	341,650	314,377	340,465	399,965	360,405	357,813
—3,352	460,870	453,695	438,455	479,776	468,485	462,927	382,744	375,127	362,655	404,946	394,003	393,039
—88,548	416,411	383,802	394,600	452,129	470,421	461,121	320,491	297,675	296,164	364,679	388,298	370,329
+1,551	23,517	30,460	24,193	25,639	22,327	22,525	13,269	14,867	14,243	13,828	13,775	12,710
+818,377	**2,491,638**	**2,276,464**	**2,184,717**	**2,314,926**	**2,269,607**	**2,044,043**	**2,114,808**	**1,906,052**	**1,783,554**	**1,991,347**	**1,947,271**	**1,744,026**
+70,467	415,288	393,615	401,109	399,106	397,061	380,867	386,024	372,450	369,277	369,018	365,969	349,978
+131,143	551,867	498,662	501,510	525,831	539,952	481,344	480,320	428,757	417,059	463,907	471,513	419,700
+154,166	512,667	455,174	449,876	496,690	492,877	431,435	431,054	367,370	352,044	420,897	414,706	358,120
+53,659	375,560	318,845	293,531	369,165	354,409	339,598	296,934	248,777	223,661	303,932	294,313	279,237
+408,942	636,256	610,168	538,691	524,134	485,308	410,799	520,476	488,698	421,513	433,593	400,770	336,991
+1,584,003	**3,277,661**	**2,816,070**	**2,664,617**	**2,803,347**	**2,646,558**	**2,233,658**	**2,601,414**	**2,231,367**	**2,070,277**	**2,361,107**	**2,213,278**	**1,961,414**
+610,739	794,389	645,372	575,081	554,382	496,178	424,839	584,181	484,467	424,440	449,480	402,612	342,992
+223,740	621,040	519,146	496,618	559,933	543,161	490,751	496,080	410,228	384,178	464,032	449,680	402,629
+147,203	531,935	470,465	469,243	509,951	513,429	445,798	438,963	381,727	367,528	430,383	430,493	377,807
+98,933	537,301	477,368	482,326	489,593	510,494	466,645	442,316	400,499	389,324	443,612	451,106	414,039
+156,880	408,606	348,695	337,538	398,121	361,565	312,375	327,532	274,886	268,044	341,425	299,658	266,853
+346,508	384,390	355,024	303,811	291,367	221,731	193,250	312,342	279,560	236,763	232,155	179,720	166,974
+1,132,002	**2,092,622**	**1,838,598**	**1,795,555**	**1,619,005**	**1,622,614**	**1,485,668**	**1,822,227**	**1,622,112**	**1,557,497**	**1,487,766**	**1,445,333**	**1,297,179**
+195,383	498,336	438,550	425,117	413,445	426,767	384,038	424,091	385,496	362,882	378,714	379,615	343,006
+437,838	445,836	392,086	352,365	252,342	248,507	199,839	375,654	327,832	292,636	236,807	229,782	183,813
+46,577	282,714	241,380	268,621	253,058	268,006	263,732	258,362	235,682	242,954	248,366	245,184	230,707
163,278	342,771	311,636	296,518	299,893	292,657	258,953	291,586	257,588	251,309	258,806	241,083	212,126
+139,653	306,949	264,919	273,037	242,398	234,475	240,050	277,011	247,330	246,236	222,032	213,945	201,257
+149,273	216,016	190,021	179,897	157,869	151,302	139,056	195,523	168,184	161,480	144,041	135,724	123,210
+2,927,197	**2,791,733**	**2,286,493**	**2,055,160**	**1,735,004**	**1,319,715**	**1,191,248**	**2,311,184**	**1,881,253**	**1,687,343**	**1,430,685**	**1,108,872**	**984,472**
+651,460	552,456	378,615	264,288	232,336	225,186	190,811	447,316	307,075	217,677	197,338	191,373	157,501
+1,097,519	630,749	533,700	467,690	332,459	25,080	28,920	520,602	424,181	356,780	244,480	21,846	24,912
+274,203	355,671	303,483	282,397	226,207	214,656	211,855	309,162	265,076	242,406	200,018	187,085	178,775
+619,384	646,025	487,562	443,854	387,827	348,814	306,424	528,875	401,766	369,503	321,470	285,724	249,092
+150,158	320,674	308,605	308,350	285,976	267,574	240,180	270,701	259,873	261,111	241,705	226,310	201,037
+104,831	269,341	257,386	272,409	256,740	234,668	213,058	221,703	211,666	227,451	215,046	193,707	173,155
+29,642	16,817	15,142	16,172	13,459	3,737	..	12,825	11,616	12,415	10,628	2,197	..

TABLE II.—VARIATION IN POPULATION DURING THE LAST FIFTY YEARS—*continued*.

District or State.	Persons. 1931.	1921.	1911.	1901.	1891.	1881.	Variation: Increase (+). Decrease (—). 1921 to 1931.	1911 to 1921.	1901 to 1911.	1891 to 1901.	1881 to 1891.
1	2	3	4	5	6	7	8	9	10	11	12
PUNJAB STATES	4,910,005	4,416,036	4,212,794	4,424,398	4,263,280	3,861,688	+493,969	-203,242	-211,604	161,118	-401,597
A.—Having Political Relations with the Punjab Government	437,787	408,019	412,173	411,764	392,525	360,423	-29,768	-4,154	-409	19,239	32,102
1. Dujana ..	*28,216*	25,833	25,485	24,174	26,450	23,416	+2,383	+348	1,311	-2,276	-3,034
2. Pataudi .	*18,873*	18,097	19,543	21,933	19,002	17,847	+ 776	1,446	-2,390	+2,931	1,155
3. Kalsia .	*59,848*	57,371	55,909	67,181	68,633	67,708	+2,477	1,462	11,272	−1,452	+925
4. *SIMLA HILL STATES*	330,850	306,718	311,236	298,476	278,440	251,452	-24,132	4,518	12,760	+20,036	-26,988
Bashahr	*104,389*	90,366	93,203	84,636	75,727	64,345	+14,023	2,837	+8,567	+8,909	11,382
Nalagarh ..	*50,015*	46,868	49,230	52,551	54,032	53,373	-3,147	−2,362	−3,321	1,481	-659
Keonthal ..	*48,093*	47,455	46,224	42,192	37,320	31,154	+638	1,231	4,032	4,872	-6,166
Baghal .	*26,352*	25,009	26,008	25,720	24,545	20,633	+1,253	− 909	-288	1,175	+3,912
Jubbal ..	*27,172*	25,752	24,620	22,242	21,412	20,118	+1,420	+1,132	-2,378	+830	1,294
Baghat .	*9,725*	9,505	8,797	9,490	8,668	8,339	-220	708	−693	+822	-329
Kumharsain .	*12,781*	12,227	12,219	11,735	10,416	9,515	+554	-8	+484	+1,319	+901
Bhajji ..	*15,413*	14,263	14,972	13,309	12,205	12,106	+1,150	709	+ 1,663	+1,104	+99
Mahlog ..	*8,156*	8,206	8,663	8,968	9,329	9,169	− 141	-367	−305	−361	+100
Balsan ..	*6,864*	6,137	6,225	6,704	5,496	5,190	+727	—88	-479	1,208	+306
Dhami ..	*5,232*	4,786	4,484	4,505	3,985	3,322	+446	+302	−21	+520	−663
Kuthar ..	*3,760*	3,841	4,016	4,195	3,947	3,648	—81	—175	-179	+248	+299
Kunihar ..	*2,061*	1,945	2,208	2,168	1,957	1,923	+116	—263	+40	+211	-34
Mangal ..	*1,248*	1,193	1,267	1,227	1,091	1,060	+55	—74	+ 40	+136	31
Bija ..	*994*	943	1,064	1,131	1,171	1,158	+51	— 121	—67	—40	13
Darkoti ..	*531*	610	521	518	595	590	—79	+80	+3	− 77	+5
Tharoch ..	*4,568*	4,219	4,493	4,411	3,938	3,216	+349	−274	+82	473	722
Sangri .	*3,497*	3,213	3,022	2,774	2,606	2,593	+284	+191	+248	168	+13
B.—Having Political Relations with the Government of India.	4,472,218	4,008,017	3,800,621	4,012,634	3,870,755	3,501,260	+464,201	+207,396	-212,013	+141,879	+369,495
5. Loharu ..	*23,338*	20,621	18,597	15,229	20,139	13,754	+2,717	+2,024	+3,368	−4,910	-6,385
6. Sirmoor ..	*148,568*	140,448	138,520	135,687	124,134	112,371	+8,120	+1,928	-2,833	11,553	+11,763
7. Bilaspur ..	*100,994*	98,000	93,107	90,873	91,760	86,546	+2,994	+4,893	+2,234	—887	+5,214
8. Mandi ..	*207,465*	185,048	181,110	174,045	166,923	147,017	+22,417	+3,938	-7,065	+ 7,122	+19,906
9. Suket ..	*58,408*	54,328	54,928	54,676	52,403	52,484	+4,080	−600	+252	+2,273	−81
10. Kapurthala ..	*316,757*	284,275	268,133	314,351	299,690	252,617	+32,482	16,142	−46,218	+14,661	+47,073
11. Maler Kotla .	*83,072*	80,322	71,144	77,506	75,755	71,051	+2,750	+9,178	−6,362	+1,751	+4,704
12. Faridkot ..	*164,364*	150,661	130,294	124,912	115,040	97,034	+13,703	-20,367	+5,382	+9,872	+18,006
13. Chamba ..	*146,870*	141,867	135,873	127,834	124,032	115,773	+5,003	+5,994	-8,039	+ 3,802	8,259
14 Patiala } Phulkian States. ..	*1,625,520*	1,499,739	1,407,659	1,596,692	1,583,521	1,467,433	+125,781	+92,080	−189,033	13,171	116,088
15. Jind } Phulkian States. ..	*324,676*	308,183	271,728	282,003	284,560	249,862	+16,493	+36,455	−10,275	−2,557	+34,698
16. Nabha } Phulkian States. ..	*287,574*	263,334	248,887	297,949	282,756	261,824	+24,240	+14,447	−49,062	+15,193	+20,932
17. Bahawalpur ..	*984,612*	781,191	780,641	720,877	650,042	573,494	+203,421	+550	+59,764	+70,835	+76,548

TABLE II.—VARIATION IN POPULATION DURING THE LAST FIFTY YEARS—*concluded.*

Net variation in Period 1881-1931. Increase (+). Decrease (−).	Males.						Females.					
	1931.	1921.	1911.	1901.	1891.	1881.	1931.	1921.	1911.	1901.	1891.	1881.
13	14	15	16	17	18	19	20	21	22	23	24	25
+1,048,322	**2,680,684**	**2,425,783**	**2,322,908**	**2,409,809**	**2,324,091**	**2,112,303**	**2,229,321**	**1,990,253**	**1,889,886**	**2,014,589**	**1,939,189**	**1,749,380**
+77,364	**229,290**	**215,633**	**216,853**	**217,794**	**209,124**	**194,597**	**208,497**	**192,386**	**195,320**	**193,970**	**183,401**	**165,826**
+4,800	14,537	13,538	13,388	12,481	13,771	12,525	13,679	12,295	12,097	11,693	12,679	10,891
+1,026	9,922	9,560	10,150	11,311	9,953	9,510	8,951	8,537	9,393	10,422	9,049	8,337
—7,860	33,306	32,573	31,297	36,980	37,620	36,896	26,542	24,798	24,612	30,201	31,013	30,812
+79,398	**171,525**	**159,962**	**162,018**	**156,822**	**147,780**	**135,666**	**159,325**	**146,756**	**149,218**	**141,654**	**130,660**	**115,786**
+40,044	51,593	44,688	46,208	42,066	39,104	33,019	52,796	45,678	46,995	42,570	36,623	31,326
—3,358	26,635	24,665	26,458	28,425	29,185	29,082	23,380	22,203	22,772	24,126	24,847	24,291
+16,939	25,734	26,054	24,314	22,575	19,803	17,329	22,359	21,401	21,910	19,617	17,517	13,825
+5,719	13,457	12,742	13,429	13,772	12,960	11,036	12,895	12,357	12,579	11,948	11,585	9,597
+7,054	14,507	14,090	13,126	11,853	11,741	11,129	12,665	11,662	11,494	10,389	9,671	8,989
+1,386	5,744	5,662	5,072	5,671	5,041	4,937	3,981	3,843	3,725	3,819	3,627	3,382
+3,266	6,425	6,220	6,105	5,949	5,271	4,920	6,356	6,007	6,114	5,786	5,145	4,595
+3,307	7,943	7,369	8,296	6,884	6,337	6,720	7,470	6,894	6,676	6,425	5,808	5,386
—1,014	4,299	4,394	4,614	4,766	4,973	4,966	3,856	3,902	4,049	4,202	4,356	4,203
+1,674	3,603	3,280	3,345	3,556	2,988	2,878	3,261	2,857	2,880	3,148	2,508	2,312
+1,910	2,693	2,377	2,279	2,435	2,125	1,776	2,539	2,409	2,205	2,070	1,860	1,546
+112	2,023	2,061	2,146	2,258	2,092	2,020	1,737	1,780	1,870	1,937	1,855	1,628
+138	1,035	950	1,166	1,123	1,014	1,017	1,020	995	1,042	1,045	943	906
+188	680	645	697	659	604	583	568	548	570	508	487	477
—164	579	522	568	628	636	649	415	421	496	503	535	509
−59	257	327	246	253	285	295	274	283	275	265	310	295
+1,352	2,521	2,271	2,406	2,470	2,232	1,850	2,047	1,948	2,087	1,941	1,706	1,366
+904	1,797	1,645	1,543	1,479	1,389	1,440	1,700	1,568	1,479	1,295	1,217	1,153
+970,958	**2,451,394**	**2,210,150**	**2,106,055**	**2,192,015**	**2,114,967**	**1,917,706**	**2,020,824**	**1,797,867**	**1,694,566**	**1,820,619**	**1,755,788**	**1,583,554**
+9,584	12,326	10,955	9,980	8,160	11,010	7,539	11,012	9,666	8,617	7,069	9,129	6,215
+36,197	82,384	77,003	76,044	75,461	69,268	63,305	66,184	63,445	62,476	60,226	54,866	49,066
+14,448	53,154	52,306	50,009	49,384	49,595	47,133	47,840	45,694	43,098	41,489	42,165	39,413
+60,448	107,876	95,191	93,678	90,896	86,344	75,588	99,589	89,857	87,432	83,149	80,579	71,429
+5,924	30,851	28,642	29,014	28,964	27,768	29,280	27,557	25,686	25,914	25,712	24,635	23,204
+64,140	171,529	156,530	150,220	169,797	163,373	138,638	145,228	127,745	117,913	144,554	136,317	113,979
+12,021	45,883	46,950	40,602	41,915	40,746	38,550	37,189	33,372	30,542	35,591	35,009	32,501
+67,330	91,163	84,206	73,836	69,321	63,909	53,848	73,201	66,455	56,458	55,591	51,131	43,186
+31,097	76,059	74,230	70,612	66,474	64,561	60,382	70,811	67,637	65,261	61,360	59,471	55,391
+158,087	900,597	837,479	792,540	877,197	871,467	806,984	724,923	662,260	615,119	719,495	712,054	660,449
+74,814	176,383	169,658	149,947	153,376	155,948	136,909	148,293	138,525	121,781	128,627	128,612	112,953
+25,750	158,086	146,910	139,319	165,386	155,825	145,155	129,488	116,424	109,568	132,563	126,931	116,869
+411,118	545,103	430,090	430,254	395,684	355,153	314,395	439,509	351,101	350,387	325,193	294,889	259,099

TABLE III.

TOWNS AND VILLAGES CLASSIFIED BY POPULATION.

1. This Table has been prepared from the Village Tables, every revenue estate being treated as one unit. When, however, one or more villages are included in a Town, City or Cantonment, the latter has been taken as one unit. According to revenue records the total number of villages in the British Territory is 36,861, of which 34,852 are inhabited. The total number of inhabited villages, towns and cities according to this Table comes to 34,819, the difference being due to some revenue estates being included in towns, cities, etc. In some of the Indian States, which have not been surveyed, the unit for collection of revenue has been treated as a village.

2. For the purposes of India Tables, figures of Cantonments are shown in smaller type in the proper class, and this accounts for an excess of 12 in the number of cities, towns and villages in this Table as compared with Table I, in which the 12 Cantonments adjoining towns and cities, are shown as forming part of them. Civil Lines have been included in towns which they adjoin except two (Hidayatpur Chhauni and Sanawar), which are isolated units.

3. Villages, whose homesteads lie in one block so that no line can be drawn to distinguish the population of one village from that of the other, were at the time of enumeration treated as a single unit. In compilation, however, the total population of such villages has been divided equally between the component villages and each village treated as a separate unit.

4. The total number of travellers enumerated in encampments, boats and trains, etc., has been shown separately in this Table. In Tables IV and V the number has been included in the population of the towns within whose limits the enumeration took place.

TABLE III.- TOWNS AND VILLAGES CLASSIFIED BY POPULATION.

Serial No.	District or State.	Total number of inhabited Cities, Towns and Villages.	Under 500.		500 to 1,000.		1,000 to 2,000.		2,000 to 5,000.		5,000 to 10,000.		10,000 to 20,000.		20,000 to 50,000.		50,000 to 100,000.		100,000 and over.		Encampments, boat and railway population, unclassed.	Serial No.
			Population.	Number.	Population.	Number.	Population.	Number.	Population.	Number.	Population.	Number.	Population.	Number.	Population.	Number.	Population.	Number.	Population.	Number.	Population.		
	1	2	3	4	5	6	7	8	9	10	11	12	13	14	15	16	17	18	19	20	21	22	
	PUNJAB ..	50,925 19	28,490,857 220,974	34,351 2	6,545,406 920	9,901 1	7,001,541 852	4,924 4	6,703,544 6,252	1,454 4	4,145.166 12,171	194 1	1,296,066 6,233	60 3	769,205 41,692	31 4	805,811 152,854	7	436,786	3	773,311	14,021	
	BRITISH TERRITORY ..	34,819 19	23,580,852 220,974	20,950 2	4,927,920 920	8,237 1	5,839,984 852	4,139 4	5,643,902 6,252	1,237 4	3,524,563 12,171	171 1	1,145,769 6,233	50 3	635,404 41,692	26 1	694,598 152,854	6	381,657	3	773,311	13,749	
	AMBALA DIVISION .	6,390	4,077,565 65,186	4,150 1	931,264 470	1,257	884,058	667 2	915,581 2,796	265 1	749,127 2,852	31	208,079	11	143,519	9 1	242,724 49,368	..	..	..	..	3,213	
1	Hissar	971	899,479	404	105,977	303	217,780	194	273,533	57	164,590	6	38,610	3	30,661	3	67,824	..	..	..	..	504	1
2	Rohtak	729	805,621	256	76,635	214	156,728	167	230,906	82	226,827	6	40,427	3	38,431	1	35,535	..	..	..	..	138	2
3	Gurgaon .. .	1,366	740,163	949	224,408	268	181,943	92	123,353	50	137,449	5	33,639	1	12,649	1	26,575	..	.	..	.	147	3
4	Karnal	1,386	852,614	937	202,480	234	163,888	143	193,565	58	164,977	11	70,451	2	30,000	1	27,165	..	..	..	.	88	4
5	Ambala	1,732 2	742,902 52,220	1,401	306,448	237	163,189	69	91,434	18 1	55,284 2,852	3	24,952	1	13,638	: 1	85,625 49,368	.		..	..	2,332	5
6	Simla .. .	207 3	36,786 3,206	203 1	15,316 470	1	530	2 2	2,796 2,796	..	.	..	..	1	18,140	.	..	..	.	.	..	4	6
	JULLUNDUR DIVISION ..	6,412 3	4,606,446 47,415	3,615	855,120	1,635	1,164,567	846	1,162,017	259 1	732,426 2,383	38	254,920	13 1	163,027 14,735	3 1	75,688 30,297	3	193,772	..	..	4,909	
7	Kangra	715 1	801,312 2,383	285	71,087	195	140,842	135	191,803	78	228,133 2,383	19	129,671	3	39,776	..	..	..	..	.	..	..	7
8	Hoshiarpur	2,105	1,032,187	1,455	330,205	419	291,589	181	244,091	45	120,192	4	24,435	..	..	1	21,357	..	..	..	..	318	8
9	Jullundur	1,218 1	943,721 14,737	618	105,939	380	268,157	166	232,518	42	125,106	8	56,504	3 1	36,613 14,735	..	..	1	58,714	..	..	170	9
10	Ludhiana	855	672,494	434	107,576	254	179,155	126	173,887	36	94,917	2	11,809	1	11,810	1	24,034	1	65,274	..	..	4,032	10
11	Ferozepore .. .	1,519 1	1,156,732 30,297	823	180,313	387	284,824	238	319.718	58	164,078	5	32,501	6	74,828	1 1	30,297 30,297	1	69,784	..	..	389	11
	LAHORE DIVISION ..	8,758 5	5,879,075 51,244	5,729	1,408,181	1,864 1	1,306,557 852	875 1	1,215,866 1,630	242 1	704,154 3,239	30	208,233	9 1	119,304 15,851	5 1	134,921 29,672	2	113,676	2	664,960	3,223	
12	Lahore	1,130 1	1,378,570 29,672	561	139,262	311	224,360	174	241,797	70	204,951	7	51,233	3	39,203	3 1	77,683 29,672	..	..	1	398,564	1,511	12
13	Amritsar .. .	1,042 1	1,117,120 1,630	460	126,683	317	228,436	200 1	285,448 1,630	59	170,598	4	28,496	1	10,103	.	..	.	..	1	266,396	960	13
14	Gurdaspur	2,252 2	970,898 4,001	1,721	392,116	375 1	254,727 852	119	158,861	29 1	77,208 3,239	6	39,291	1	12,226	1	36,288	..	..	..	..	181	14
15	Sialkot .. .	2,072 1	979,617 15,851	1,586	397,286	365	251,688	110	156,758	25	72,870	4	31,317	1 1	15,851 15,851	..	..	1	54,825	.	.	22	15
16	Gujranwala	1,226	736,138	819	208,137	263	180,749	109	150,526	30	89,567	2	12,804	1	14,510	1	20,950	1	58,851	..	..	44	16
17	Sheikhupura	1,036	696,732	602	144,697	233	166,591	103	223,476	29	88,960	7	45,092	2	27,411	..	..	.	..	..	.	505	17
	RAWALPINDI DIVISION ..	5,519 5	3,914,849 55,728	3,242 1	775,238 450	1,316	925,474	651 1	903,594 1,828	256 1	752,822 3,607	42 1	282,400 6,233	8	103,821	3 1	95,882 43,517	1	74,209	.	.	1,409	
18	Gujrat	1,445	922,427	870	223,479	346	245,391	171	239,995	53	152,550	3	22,024	1	13,323	1	25,604	.	..	..	.	61	18
19	Shahpur .. .	987	821,490	458	118,048	344	243,068	109	145,287	62	190,533	10	63,339	3	34,001		26,761	..	..	..	.	453	19
20	Jhelum	889 1	541,076 6,233	563	131,678	197	138,896	92	132,857	31	88,636	6 1	31,633 6,233	1	17,374	..	..	..	..	..	..	2	20
21	Rawalpindi	1,173 2	634,357 43,967	858 1	182,053 450	196	133,185	88	120,717	27	69,976	2	10,700	.	..	1 1	43,517 43,517	1	74,209	.	..	..	21
22	Attock	623 2	583,960 5,523	286	77,080	150	107,643	128 1	176,903 1,828	49 1	143,654 3,607	8	54,986	2	22,080	..	..	.	..	..	.	714	22
23	Mianwali .. .	402	411,539	207	42,900	83	57,291	63	87,835	34	107,473	14	99,718	1	16,143	.	..		..		..	179	23

CLASSIFIED BY POPULATION—*concluded.*

No.	State or District																						No.
	MULTAN DIVISION	7 740	5,102,917	4,214	958,117	2,165	1,559,328	1,100	1,446,844	215	586,034	30	192,137	9	105,733	6	145,378	..	..	1	108,351	995	
			11,10											1	11,106								
24	Montgomery ..	1 962	999,779	1,224	309,352	575	396,831	135	174,825	24	63,014	1	6,303	2	23,167	1	26,164	..	..	..	..	122	24
25	Lyallpur ..	1,24	1,151,351	2,301	75,549	571	132,917	398	504,008	22	33,568	4	28,785	1	13,220	2	42,922	..	..	..	..	382	25
26	Jhang ..	986	664,833	546	122,666	267	191,544	135	178,876	33	92.725	2	12,391	1	13,631	2	52,824	..	..	..	..	176	26
27	Multan ..	1,919	1,174,900	1,219	26 ,965	427	306,067	200	267,896	63	161,111	7	43,594	2	22,6'8	..	..	..	..	1	108,351	2?8	27
		1	11,10											1	11,106								
28	Muzaffargarh ..	868	591,375	486	100,2'5	194	140,337	142	195,703	39	109,367	7	15,763	..	..	..	..	..	..	..	..	..	28
29	{ Dera Ghazi Khan ..	7.8	191,044	185	87,438	131	91,632	89	123,690	32	94.306	8	49.828	2	20,656		23,468	..	..	..	..	17	29
	{ Biloch trans frontier tract ..	9	29,612	4	932	..	..	1	1,837	2	8,943	1	5,483	1	12,447	..	..	..	..	..	..	..	
	PUNJAB STATES ..	**16,106**	**4,910,005**	**13,401**	**1,617,486**	**1,664**	**1,161,557**	**785**	**1,059,642**	**217**	**620,603**	**23**	**150,297**	**10**	**133,801**	**5**	**111,218**	**1**	**55,129**	..	..	**272**	
	A. HAVING POLITICAL RELATIONS WITH THE PUNJAB GOVERNMENT.	**2,614**	**437,787**	**2,433**	**207.706**	**92**	**66,159**	**69**	**100,931**	**19**	**57,867**	**1**	**5,124**	..	..	..	..	..	..	..	..	..	
1	Dujana ..	33	28,216	10	3,058	14	9,127	7	9,157	2	6,574	..	..	..	..	..	..	..	..	..	..	..	1
2	Pataudi ..	41	18,873	30	5,826	7	1,117	2	2,130	2	6,200	..	..	..	..	..	..	..	..	..	..	..	2
3	Kalsia ..	175	59,848	147	29,057	21	11,175	1	1,022	2	7,470	1	6,124	..	..	..	..	..	..	..	..	..	3
4	***SIMLA HILL STATES*** ..	**2,365**	**330,850**	**2,246**	**169,765**	**47**	**35,140**	**59**	**88,322**	**13**	**37,623**	..	..	..	..	..	..	..	..	..	..	..	4
	Bashahr ..	85	104,389	17	1,556	22	17,255	37	56,995	9	25,583	..	..	..	..	..	..	..	..	..	..	..	
	Nalagarh ..	617	50,015	617	50,015	..	..	..	..	..	..	..	..	..	..	..	..	..	..	..	..	..	
	Keonthal ..	457	48,09..	447	38,587	7	5,112	3	4,394	..	..	..	..	..	..	..	..	..	..	..	..	..	
	Baghal ..	416	26,352	413	23,957	2	1,236	1	1,159	..	..	..	..	..	..	..	..	..	..	..	..	..	
	Jubbal ..	35	27,172	20	3,153	5	4,014	7	9,698	3	10,007	..	..	..	..	..	..	..	..	..	..	..	
	Baghat	133	9,725	131	7,735	1	572	1	1,418	..	..	..	..	..	..	..	..	..	..	..	..	..	
	Kumharsain ..	11	12,781	3	1,112	1	775	6	8,861	1	2,033	..	..	..	..	..	..	..	..	..	..	..	
	Bhajji ..	179	15,417	178	14,721	1	692	..	..	..	..	..	..	..	..	..	..	..	..	..	..	..	
	Mahlog ..	184	8,155	184	8,155	..	..	..	..	..	..	..	..	..	..	..	..	..	..	..	..	..	
	Balsan ..	37	6,864	37	6,864	..	..	..	..	..	..	..	..	..	..	..	..	..	..	..	..	..	
	Dhami ..	107	5,232	107	5,232	..	..	..	..	..	..	..	..	..	..	..	..	..	..	..	..	..	
	Kuthar ..	6	3,760	2	625	3	1,906	1	1,229	..	..	..	..	..	..	..	..	..	..	..	..	..	
	Kunihar	16	2,061	15	1,535	1	526	..	..	..	..	..	..	..	..	..	..	..	..	..	..	..	
	Mangal ..	15	1,218	15	1,218	..	..	..	..	..	..	..	..	..	..	..	..	..	..	..	..	..	
	Bija ..	46	994	46	994	..	..	..	..	..	..	..	..	..	..	..	..	..	..	..	..	..	
	Darkot ..	13	531	13	531	..	..	..	..	..	..	..	..	..	..	..	..	..	..	..	..	..	
	Tharoch ..	3	4,568	..	..	..	..	3	4,568	..	..	..	..	..	..	..	..	..	..	..	..	..	
	Sangri ..	5	3,497	1	445	4	3,052	..	..	..	..	..	..	..	..	..	..	..	..	..	..	..	
	B. HAVING POLITICAL RELATIONS WITH THE GOVERNMENT OF INDIA.	**13,492**	**4,472,218**	**10,966**	**1,409,780**	**1,572**	**1,095,398**	**716**	**958,711**	**198**	**562,736**	**22**	**145,173**	**10**	**133,801**	**5**	**111,218**	**1**	**55,129**		..	**272**	
5	Loharu ..	71	23,338	61	13,810	9	6,572	..	..	1	2,956	..	..	..	..	..	..	..	..	..	..	..	5
6	Sirmoor ..	967	118,568	930	113,547	30	20,999	6	7,075	..	..	1	6,917	..	..	..	..	..	..	..	..	..	6
7	Bilaspur ..	941	100,994	923	86,310	15	10,159	2	2,138	1	2,387		..	..	..	..	..	..	..	..	..	..	7
8	Mandi	3,608	207,465	3,599	192,797	1	2,681	5	3,910	1	2,114		5,963				..	..			..	..	8
9	Suket	88	58,408	62	11,610	10	?,875	7	10,942	9	27,951	..	..	..	..	..	..	..	..	..	..	..	9
10	Kapurthala ..	620	316,757	442	101,200	113	76,172	50	65,525	1?	1,756	1	8,606	1	13,139	1	20,?9	..	..	..	..	..	10
11	Maler Kotla ..	114	83,072	74	20,656	29	19,860	7	8,466	3	8,850	..	..	..	..	..	25,?40	..	..	..	..	..	11
12	Faridkot ..	173	161,364	72	20,970	36	46,895	34	48,692	9	21,146	..	..	2	3?,26	..	..	..	..	..	..	..	12
13	Chamba	54	116,870	..	..	7	6,564	10	15,631	33	103,316	4	22,359	..	..	..	..	..	..	..	..	..	13
14	Phulkian States { Patiala ..	3,539	1,625,520	2,555	446,757	603	413,002	293	398,032	75	210,701	7	46,939	3	3?,194	2	14,076	1	55,129	..	..	..	14
15	{ Jind ..	445	324,676	225	70,721	137	96,555	65	88,323	12	30,048	2	13,128	2	25,600	..	..	..	..	..	..	..	15
16	{ Nabha ..	498	287,574	326	86,122	120	82,839	39	54,258	9	25,105	3	22,899	1	17,311	..	..	..	..	..	..	40	16
17	Bahawalpur ..	2,376	984,612	1,699	277,150	439	312,225	200	255,719	33	90,016	3	18,031	1	10,296	1	20,943	..	..	..	..	232	17

TABLE IV.

TOWNS CLASSIFIED BY POPULATION WITH VARIATION FOR FIFTY YEARS.

1. For Census purposes a town has been defined to include every Municipality, every Cantonment, all the Civil Lines not included in municipal limits, and every other continuous collection of houses inhabited by not less than 5,000 persons, which though not a Municipality possesses urban characteristics

2. The question whether a collection of residential houses should or should not be classed under the last category was determined by the Superintendent of Census Operations in correspondence with local officers before the Census with reference to the probable population and consequently in many cases the limit of 5,000 was not reached. On the other hand many places with more than 5,000 inhabitants were omitted as they had not urban characteristics. The headquarters of all Punjab States, except the Simla Hill States, have been included in this Table irrespective of their population.

3. No attempt has been made to adjust the figures affected by changes in the area of towns during the last decade, and the figures given in the previous Census have been repeated.

4. The first five lines in the Table give the urban population of the Punjab, and in regard to the past five Censuses they do not represent the aggregate of the items that appear below them.

5. The Table below shows the changes that have taken place in the urban population of the province:—

Changes in the urban population from Census to Census.	1891.	1901.	1911.	1921.	1931.
1	2	3	4	5	6
1. (a) Number of towns at the next preceding Census which ceased to be towns at each Census since 1881 ..	72	23	63	11	4
(b) Population ..	252,609	247,148	260,979	48,883	11,223
2. (a) Number of new towns added at each Census ..	9	10	12	24	37
(b) Population ..	24,273	42,[illegible]11	74,672	123,145	189,778
3. Variation in population due to difference in number of towns. (Increase +, Decrease -) ..	−228,336	−205,037	−186,307	-74,262	178,55[illegible]
4. Net variation in urban population at each Census	+218,387	−124,162	−35,784	187,971	+746,216

6. No attempt has been made to show the population for past Censuses of places treated as towns for the first time, as it is deemed to have been rural.

7. The summer population of Simla, as ascertained at a special Census held on the 30th June 1931, is as follows :—

Towns.	Persons.	Males.	Females.
1	2	3	4
Simla ..	51,706	37,157	14,54[illegible]
Kasumpti ..	727	47[illegible]	256
Jutogh ..	1,516	1,165	35[illegible]
Total ..	**53,949**	**38,793**	**15,156**

8. In this Table as well as Table V, Civil Lines and Cantonments have been included in towns or cities which they adjoin, except in cases in which they are isolated units such as Jutogh, Dagshai, Sabathu, etc. Separate figures have, however, been given for them under those of the cities and towns concerned. The abbreviations used are :—

M=Municipality. C. L.=Civil Lines.

Cantt.=Cantonment. U.=Urban.

S.=Suburban.

TABLE IV.—TOWNS CLASSIFIED BY POPULATION WITH VARIATION FOR FIFTY YEARS—*continued*.

No.	Name of Town.	District or State.	Description of Cities, Towns, (Municipalities, Suburbs, Cantonments etc.)	Population. 1931.	1921.	1911.	1901.	1891.	1881.	Variation; Increase (+), Decrease (—). 1921 to 1931.	1911 to 1921.	1901 to 1911.	1891 to 1901.	1881 to 1891.	Variation in period 1881 to 1931 Increase (+) Decrease (—).	Males. 1931.	1921.	1911.	Females. 1931.	1921.	1911.
	1	2	3	4	5	6	7	8	9	10	11	12	13	14	15	16	17	18	19	20	21
	PUNJAB	..	222	3,521,449	2,596,678	2,334,445	2,580,798	2,454,901	2,475,929	+924,771	262,233	-246,353	+125,897	--21,028	+1,045,520	2,065,249	1,510,853	1,341,449	1,456,200	1,085,825	992,996
	BRITISH TERRITORY.	..	177	3,067,464	2,212,191	1,979,127	2,116,892	1,998,357	2,042,833	+855,273	+233,064	—137,765	+118,535	--44,476	+1,024,631	1,805,872	1,292,335	1,139,283	1,261,592	919,856	839,844
	PUNJAB STATES	..	45	453,985	384,487	355,318	463,906	456,544	433,096	+69,498	+29,169	—108,588	+7,362	+23,448	+20,889	259,377	218,518	202,166	194,608	165,969	153,152
	A.—Having Political Relations with the Punjab Government.	..	4	14,534	15,561	8,482	25,061	21,669	29,170	—1,027	+7,079	—16,579	+3,392	—7,501	—14,636	7,907	8,272	4,591	6,627	7,289	3,891
	B—Having Political Relations with the Government of India.	..	41	439,451	368,926	346,836	438,845	434,875	403,926	+70,525	+22,090	—92,009	+3,970	+30,940	+35,525	251,470	210,246	197,575	187,981	158,680	149,261
								CLASS I.—100,000 AND OVER.													
1	Lahore ..	.. Lahore ..	Total ..	429,747	281,781	228,687	202,964	176,854	149,309	+147,966	+53,094	+25,723	+26,110	+27,485	+280,378	274,587	179,350	143,249	155,160	102,431	85,438
			M U. ..	*179,263*	*131,354*	*198,692*	*186,881*	*159,597*	*130,960*	*+142,780*	*+47,024*	*+23,387*	*+27,287*	*28,637*	*--269,115*	*106,546*	*74,997*	*122,097*	*72,717*	*56,357*	*76,595*
			M S. ..	*220,812*	*125,941*	*11,579*										*147,300*	*86,058*	*7,416*	*73,512*	*39,883*	*4,163*
			Cantt. ..	*29,672*	*24,486*	*18,416*	*16,080*	*17,257*	*18,409*	*+5,186*	*+6,070*	*+2,336*	*- 1,177*	*—1,152*	*+11,263*	*20,741*	*18,295*	*13,736*	*8,931*	*6,191*	*4,680*
2	Amritsar	.. Amritsar ..	Total ..	264,840	160,218	152,756	162,429	136,766	151,896	+104,622	+7,462	—9,673	+25,663	- 15,130	+112,944	158,985	95,106	88,879	105,855	65,112	63,877
			M. ..	*263,210*	*157,031*	*151,339*	*161,039*	*135,401*	*150,665*	*+106,179*	*+5,692*	*—9,700*	*+25,638*	*- 15,264*	*+112,545*	*157,823*	*92,437*	*87,828*	*105,387*	*64,594*	*63,511*
			Cantt. ..	*1,630*	*3,187*	*1,417*	*1,390*	*1,365*	*1,231*	*—1,557*	*+1,770*	*+27*	*+25*	*+134*	*+399*	*1,162*	*2,669*	*1,051*	*468*	*518*	*366*
3	Multan ..	.. Multan ..	Total ..	119,457	84,806	99,243	87,394	74,562	68,674	+34,651	—14,437	+11,849	+12,832	+5,888	+50,783	68,119	48,180	56,280	51,338	36,626	42,963
			M. ..	*108,351*	*74,270*	*85,747*	*74,627*	*64,265*	*57,471*	*+34,081*	*—11,477*	*+11,120*	*+10,362*	*+6,794*	*+50,880*	*60,800*	*40,975*	*46,987*	*47,551*	*33,295*	*38,760*
			Cantt. ..	*11,106*	*10,536*	*13,496*	*12,767*	*10,297*	*11,203*	*+570*	*—2,960*	*+729*	*+2,470*	*--906*	*--97*	*7,319*	*7,205*	*9,293*	*3,787*	*3,331*	*4,203*
4	Rawalpindi	.. Rawalpindi.	Total ..	119,284	101,142	86,483	87,688	73,795	52,975	+18,142	+14,059	—1,205	+13,893	+20,820	+66,309	75,971	70,180	57,451	43,313	30,962	29,032
			M. ..	*75,767*	*55,251*	*46,642*	*47,077*	*35,925*	*26,785*	*+20,516*	*+8,609*	*—435*	*+11,152*	*+9,140*	*48,982*	*46,086*	*35,493*	*28,948*	*29,681*	*19,758*	*17,694*
			Cantt. ..	*43,517*	*45,891*	*39,841*	*40,611*	*37,870*	*26,190*	*—2,374*	*- 6,050*	*--770*	*+2,741*	*+11,680*	*+17,327*	*29,885*	*34,687*	*28,503*	*13,632*	*11,204*	*11,338*
5	Sialkot ..	.. Sialkot ..	Total ..	100,973	70,619	64,869	57,956	55,087	45,762	+30,354	+5,750	+6,913	+2,869	+9,325	+55,211	59,894	41,026	38,130	41,079	29,594	26,739
			M. ..	*85,093*	*55,911*	*48,595*	*44,789*	*39,612*	*33,850*	*+29,182*	*+7,316*	*+3,806*	*+5,177*	*+5,762*	*+51,243*	*49,071*	*30,771*	*26,651*	*36,022*	*25,140*	*21,944*
			C. L. ..	*29*	*107*	..	*585*	..	..	*—78*	..	..	..	..	..	*28*	*92*	..	*1*	*15*	..
			Cantt. ..	*15,851*	*14,601*	*16,274*	*12,582*	*15,475*	*11,912*	*+1,250*	*—1,673*	*+3,692*	*—2,893*	*+3,563*	*+3,939*	*10,795*	*10,162*	*11,419*	*5,056*	*4,439*	*4,795*
								CLASS II.—50,000 TO 100,000.													
6	Jullundur	.. Jullundur ..	Total ..	89,030	71,008	69,318	67,735	66,202	52,119	+18,022	+1,690	+1,583	+1,533	+14,083	+36,011	51,119	40,593	39,816	37,911	30,415	20,502
			M. ..	*74,295*	*59,085*	*55,354*	*54,455*	*50,375*	*42,651*	*+15,210*	*+3,731*	*+899*	*+4,080*	*+7,724*	*+31,644*	*41,321*	*33,062*	*30,539*	*32,074*	*26,023*	*24,815*
			Cantt. ..	*14,735*	*11,923*	*13,964*	*13,280*	*15,827*	*9,468*	*+2,812*	*—2,041*	*+684*	*—2,547*	*+6,359*	*+5,267*	*9,798*	*7,531*	*9,277*	*4,937*	*4,392*	*4,687*
7	Ambala ..	.. Ambala ..	Total ..	86,592	76,326	80,131	78,638	79,294	67,463	+10,266	—3,805	+1,493	—056	+11,831	+19,129	51,523	45,795	49,204	35,069	30,531	30,927
			M. ..	*35,193*	*27,287*	*24,493*	*26,744*	*26,856*	*26,159*	*+7,906*	*+2,794*	*—2,251*	*—112*	*+697*	*+9,034*	*20,045*	*15,298*	*13,589*	*15,148*	*11,989*	*10,904*
			C. L. ..	*2,031*	*1,294*	*1,415*	*1,456*	*1,422*	*618*	*+737*	*—121*	*—41*	*+34*	*+804*	*+1,413*	*1,487*	*806*	*1,169*	*544*	*488*	*246*
			Cantt. ..	*49,368*	*47,745*	*51,223*	*50,438*	*51,016*	*40,686*	*+1,623*	*—6,478*	*+3,785*	*—578*	*+10,330*	*+8,682*	*29,991*	*29,691*	*34,446*	*19,377*	*18,054*	*19,777*
8	Ludhiana	.. Ludhiana ..	Total ..	68,586	51,880	44,170	48,649	46,334	44,163	+16,706	+7,710	—4,470	+2,315	+2,171	+24,423	40,032	30,273	25,517	28,554	21,607	18,653
			M. .	*66,098*	*50,312*	*43,152*	*48,211*	*46,024*	..	*+15,786*	*+7,160*	*—5,059*	*+2,187*	..	..	*38,218*	*29,061*	*24,765*	*27,880*	*21,251*	*18,387*
			C. L. ..	*2,488*	*1,568*	*1,018*	*438*	*310*	..	*+920*	*+550*	*+580*	*+128*	..	..	*1,814*	*1,212*	*752*	*674*	*356*	*266*
9	Ferozepore	.. Ferozepore	Total ..	64,634	54,351	30,836	49,341	50,437	39,570	+10,283	+3,515	+1,495	—1,096	+10,867	+25,064	38,884	32,684	31,459	25,750	21,667	19,377
			M. ..	*34,337*	*29,695*	*24,678*	*23,475*	*25,337*	*20,870*	*+4,642*	*+5,017*	*+1,203*	*—1,862*	*+4,467*	*+13,467*	*19,679*	*17,022*	*13,930*	*14,658*	*12,673*	*10,748*
			Cantt. ..	*30,297*	*24,656*	*26,158*	*25,806*	*25,100*	*18,700*	*+5,641*	*—1,502*	*+292*	*+766*	*+6,400*	*+11,597*	*19,205*	*15,662*	*17,529*	*11,092*	*8,994*	*8,629*
10	Gujranwala	.. Gujranwala	M. ..	58,716	37,887	29,472	20,224	26,785	22,884	+20,829	+8,415	+248	+2,439	+3,901	+35,832	34,216	21,728	16,271	24,500	16,159	13,201
11	Patiala	.. Patiala ..	M. ..	55,129	47,531	46,974	53,545	55,856	53,629	+7,598	+557	—6,571	—2,311	+2,227	+1,500	33,139	28,476	28,663	21,990	19,055	18,311

CLASS III.—20,000 TO 50,000.

Town	District																			
12 KASUR	Lahore	M.	46,815	31,018	24,783	22,022	20,290	17,336	+15,797	+6,235	+2,761	+1,732	+2,954	+29,479	28,067	17,125	13,769	18,748	13,893	11,014
13 LYALLPUR	Lyallpur	M.	42,022	28,136	19,578	9,171	..	..	+14,786	+8,558	+10,407	..	..	..	27,489	18,875	13,353	15,433	9,261	6,225
14 JHANG MAGHIANA	Jhang	M.	36,035	30,139	25,014	24,382	23,290	21,629	-5,896	+4,225	+1,532	+1,092	1,661	+14,406	19,275	15,714	13,212	16,760	14,425	12,702
15 BHIWANI	Hissar	M.	35,866	33,270	31,100	35,917	35,487	33,762	-2,596	+2,170	4,817	+430	+1,725	-2,104	19,135	17,746	16,249	16,731	15,524	14,851
16 ROHTAK	Rohtak	Total	35,235	25,240	20,361	20,323	16,702	15,699	+9,995	4,879	+38	+3,621	+1,003	+19,536	20,838	14,036	11,035	14,397	10,604	9,326
		M.	34,112	24,701	19,862	19,700	16,191	15,160	+9,411	4,839	+96	+3,575	+1,031	+18,952	19,907	14,199	10,622	14,205	10,502	9,240
		C. L.	1,123	539	499	551	511	539	+584	+40	-58	+46	-28	+584	931	437	413	192	102	86
17 BATALA	Gurdaspur	M.	33,204	26,122	26,430	27,365	27,223	24,281	7,082	-308	-935	+142	+2,942	+8,923	18,102	13,929	14,180	15,102	12,193	12,250
18 PANIPAT	Karnal	M.	32,915	27,343	26,342	26,914	27,547	25,022	5,572	-1,001	572	-633	-2,525	+7,893	18,010	14,606	13,554	14,005	12,677	12,786
19 JAGRAON	Ludhiana	M.	27,108	17,731	15,039	8,760	18,116	16,873	9,377	+2,692	-3,721	+644	1,243	+10,235	17,151	9,771	8,128	9,957	7,960	6,911
20 SARGODHA	Shahpur	M.	26,761	17,728	8,849	..	..	..	+9,033	8,879	.	..	..	..	16,498	11,602	6,180	10,263	6,126	2,669
21 HOSHIARPUR	Hoshiarpur	Total	26,730	21,286	17,449	17,549	21,552	21,363	5,445	-3,836	100	-4,003	189	+5,367	15,249	12,160	9,875	11,481	9,125	7,574
		M.	25,925	20,413	16,980	17,037	21,099	20,638	-5,512	3,433	57	-4,062	+461	+5,287	14,689	11,536	9,576	11,236	8,877	7,404
		C. L.	805	872	469	512	453	725	-67	+403	-43	-59	-272	+80	560	624	299	245	248	170
22 KARNAL	Karnal	Total	26,610	22,845	21,961	23,559	21,963	23,133	-3,765	884	-1,598	+1,596	-1,170	+3,477	15,241	12,798	11,959	11,369	10,047	10,002
		M.	25,371	21,841	21,018	22,703	21,530	22,528	+3,530	-823	-1,685	+1,173	-998	+2,843	14,314	12,054	11,233	11,057	9,787	9,[illegible]85
		C. L.	1,239	1,004	943	856	433	605	+235	-61	-87	+423	172	+634	927	744	726	312	260	21[illegible]
23 GUJRAT	Gujrat	Total	26,511	21,974	19,090	19,410	18,050	18,743	+4,537	+2,884	-320	+1,360	-693	+7,768	14,691	11,916	9,981	11,820	10,058	9,109
		M.	25,004	21,274	18,692	19,048	17,671	18,162	+4,330	+2,582	356	+1,377	491	+7,442	13,956	11,384	9,657	11,648	9,890	9,035
		C. L.	907	700	398	362	379	581	207	+302	36	17	202	326	735	532	324	172	168	74
24 REWARI	Gurgaon	M.	26,269	23,129	24,780	27,295	27,934	23,972	-3,140	1,651	-2,515	-639	3,962	+2,297	14,383	12,586	12,885	11,886	10,543	11,895
25 MONTGOMERY	Montgomery	M.	26,164	14,601	8,129	6,602	5,159	3,178	+11,563	+6,472	1,527	+1,443	+1,981	+22,986	17,392	10,011	5,773	8,772	4,590	2,356
26 CHINIOT	Jhang	M.	25,841	17,613	14,085	15,685	13,476	10,731	+8,328	+3,428	1,600	+2,209	2,745	+15,110	14,027	9,008	7,073	11,814	8,505	7,012
27 MALER KOTLA	Maler Kotla	Total	25,240	21,564	23,880	21,122	21,754	20,621	+676	+684	+2,758	-632	1,133	+4,619	14,173	14,466	13,538	11,007	10,098	10,342
		M.	22,396	..	..	..	..	..	..	..	..	.	..	..	12,230	..	..	10,166	..	..
		C. L.	1,014	.	..	..	..	..	..	..	..	.	..	.	748	..	..	266	.	..
		Cantt.	1,830	..	..	..	..	..	..	..	..	.	..	..	1,195	.	..	635	..	..
28 HISSAR	Hissar	M.	25,179	21,415	17,102	17,64[illegible]	16,854	14,167	+3,764	4,253	485	793	2,687	11,012	15,065	1[illegible],326	9,710	10,114	9,089	7,452
29 JHELUM	Jhelum	Total	23,499	18,060	19,678	14,951	12,878	21,107	+5,439	-1,618	4,727	+2,073	8,229	[illegible]2,392	15,973	11,900	13,745	7,526	6,160	5,933
		M.	17,266	14,422	12,298	11,703	9,711	16,634	+2,844	-2,124	595	+1,992	6,923	+632	10,661	8,840	7,352	6,605	5,582	4,946
		Cantt.	6,233	3,638	7,380	3,248	3,167	4,473	+2,595	-3,742	+4,132	81	-1,306	1,760	5,312	3,060	6,393	921	578	987
30 DERA GHAZI KHAN	Dera Ghazi Khan.	M.	23,468	20,731	18,466	23,731	27,886	22,309	+2,737	+2,265	-5,265	-1,155	-5,577	+1,159	12,759	11,380	10,428	10,709	9,345	8,028
31 BHATINDA	Patiala		22,771	20,154	15,087	13,185	8,530	5,084	+2,617	+5,117	+1,852	-4,649	+3,452	+17,687	13,575	12,484	9,232	9,196	7,670	5,865
32 NARNAUL	Patiala		21,905	20,410	21,350	19,489	21,159	20,052	1,495	-940	1,861	1,670	+1,107	+1,853	11,270	10,536	10,985	10,635	9,874	10,365
33 BAHAWALPUR	Bahawalpur		20,943	18,494	18,414	18,546	18,716	13,635	+2,449	+80	-132	-170	-5,081	+7,308	11,809	10,520	10,493	9,134	7,974	7,921
34 WAZIRABAD	Gujranwala	M.	20,707	18,645	17,146	18,069	13,786	16,462	+2,062	+1,499	-923	+2,283	-676	+4,245	11,778	10,478	9,456	8,929	8,167	7,090
35 KAPURTHALA	Kapurthala	M.	20,210	16,242	16,367	18,519	16,747	15,237	+3,968	125	-2,152	1,772	1,510	+4,973	11,772	9,340	9,485	8,438	6,902	6,882

CLASS IV.—10,000 TO 20,000.

Town	District																			
36 BHERA	Shahpur	M.	19,741	17,027	15,202	18,680	17,428	15,165	+2,714	-1,825	-3,478	+1,252	2,263	+4,576	10,860	8,809	7,950	8,881	8,218	7,262
37 KAITHAL	Karnal	M.	19,418	15,477	12,912	14,408	15,768	14,754	+3,941	+2,565	-1,496	-1,360	1,014	+4,664	10,745	8,113	6,552	8,673	7,364	6,360
38 SIRSA	Hissar	M.	18,909	16,241	14,629	15,800	16,415	12,292	+2,668	+1,612	-1,171	-615	4,123	+6,617	10,710	9,049	8,047	8,199	7,192	6,582
39 FAZILKA	Ferozepore	M.	18,463	13,829	10,985	8,605	7,503	6,851	-4,634	-2,844	+2,480	+942	+712	+11,612	10,789	7,846	6,555	7,674	5,983	4,430
40 HANSI	Hissar	M.	18,356	15,425	14,576	16,623	15,190	12,036	+2,931	+849	1,947	1,333	2,534	+5,700	9,943	8,157	7,586	8,413	7,268	6,991
41 SIMLA	Simla	M.	18,144	26,149	18,934	13,960	13,034	12,305	-8,005	+7,215	+4,974	+926	+729	+5,839	13,667	19,955	13,767	4,477	6,194	5,167
42 MOGA	Ferozepore	M.	17,581	14,145	..	6,725	6,569	6,430	+3,436	..	..	+156	+139	+11,151	10,454	8,848	..	7,127	5,297	..
43 NABHA	Nabha		17,311	14,750	13,620	18,468	17,108	17,116	+2,561	+1,130	4,848	+1,360	-8	+195	10,055	8,674	7,915	7,256	6,076	5,705
44 FARIDKOT	Faridkot	M	16,759	12,304	11,673	10,405	8,319	6,593	+4,455	+631	+1,268	+2,086	-1,726	+10,166	10,151	7,020	6,777	6,608	5,284	4,896
45 KOT KAPURA	Faridkot		16,502	14,063	10,644	9,519	7,730	6,196	+2,439	+3,419	+1,125	+1,789	1,534	+10,306	9,434	8,401	6,304	7,068	5,662	4,340
46 MIANWALI	Mianwali	Total	15,412	9,115	7,064	..	..	—	+6,297	+2,051	..	..	..	..	8,804	5,160	4,061	6,608	3,955	3,003
		M.	14,107	8,395	6,224	..	..	..	+5,712	+2,171	..	.	.	..	7,695	4,580	3,386	6,412	3,815	2,838
		C. L.	1,305	720	840	..	..	..	+585	-120	..	..	..	..	1,109	580	675	196	140	166

TABLE IV.—TOWNS CLASSIFIED BY POPULATION WITH VARIATION FOR FIFTY YEARS—*continued.*

No.	Name of Town.	District or State.	Description of Cities, Towns, (Municipalities, Suburbs, Cantonments etc.)	Population. 1931.	1921.	1911.	1901.	1891.	1881.	Variation; Increase (+), Decrease (—). 1921 to 1931.	1911 to 1921.	1901 to 1911.	1891 to 1901.	1881 to 1891.	Variation in period 1881 to 1931 Increase (+) Decrease (—).	Males. 1931.	1921.	1911.	Females. 1931.	1921.	1911.
	1	2	3	4	5	6	7	8	9	10	11	12	13	14	15	16	17	18	19	20	21
47	Sonipat	Rohtak	M.	15,050	12,981	12,014	12,096	12,611	13,077	+2,069	+967	—976	- 379	-466	+1,973	8,274	7,002	6,192	6,776	5,979	5,822
48	Muktsar	Ferozepur	M.	14,839	10,539	8,834	6,389	5,271	3,125	+4,300	+1,705	+2,445	+1,118	+2,146	+11,714	8,544	6,296	5,202	6,295	4,243	3,632
49	Hafizabad	Gujranwala	..	14,431	8,854	..	4,597		2,453	+5,577	..	..	..	..	+11,978	8,702	5,132	..	5,729	3,722	..
50	Khushab	Shahpur	M.	14,194	10,009	10,159	11,403	9,832	8,989	+4,185	—150	—1,244	+1,571	+843	+5,205	8,055	5,325	5,333	6,139	4,684	4,826
51	Abohar	Ferozepur	M.	14,035	8,916	9,492	..	..	..	+5,119	—576	..	..	..	..	8,431	5,405	5,665	5,604	3,421	3,827
52	Sangrur	Jind	M.	13,901	10,799	9,041	11,852	8,820	9,139	+3,102	+1,758	—2,811	+3,032	—319	+4,762	8,564	6,653	5,615	5,337	4,146	3,420
53	Baghbanpura (cum Bhogiwal)	Lahore	M.	13,805	10,251	..	..	..	..	+3,554	..	..	..	..	..	7,854	5,820	..	5,951	4,431	..
54	Jagadhri	Ambala	M.	13,268	11,514	12,045	13,462	13,029	12,300	+1,724	-501	—1,417	+433	+729	-968	7,450	6,272	6,691	5,818	5,272	5,354
55	Kamalia	Lyallpur	M.	13,220	8,916	8,237	6,976	7,490	7,594	+4,304	+679	+1,261	—514	- 104	+5,626	7,280	4,551	4,225	5,934	4,365	4,012
56	Basi	Patiala	..	12,970	11,560	11,125	13,738	13,810	12,896	+1,419	+435	—2,613	- 72	+914	+83	6,868	6,119	5,995	6,111	5,441	5,130
57	Patti	Lahore	M.	12,882	10,439	7,987	8,187	7,495	6,407	+2,443	+2,452	-200	+692	+1,088	+6,475	7,003	5,886	4,368	5,879	4,553	3,619
58	Jalalpur Jattan	Gujrat	M.	12,507	10,792	11,615	10,640	11,065	12,839	+1,715	—823	+975	—425	-1,774	-332	6,771	5,622	6,171	5,736	5,170	5,444
59	Shahabad	Karnal	M.	12,293	11,329	11,054	11,009	11,473	10,218	+964	+275	+45	—464	+1,255	+2,075	6,736	6,207	5,735	5,557	5,122	5,310
60	Jhajjar	Rohtak	M.	12,232	10,800	10,617	12,227	11,881	11,650	+1,432	+183	—1,610	+346	+231	+582	6,266	5,364	5,182	5,906	5,436	5,436
61	Sheikhupura	Sheikhupura	..	12,166	3,487	..	..	..	..	+8,679	..	..	..	..	..	7,666	2,182	..	4,500	1,305	..
62	Gurdaspur	Gurdaspur	Total	12,094	8,906	6,248	5,764	5,857	4,706	+3,188	+2,658	+484	—93	+1,151	+7,388	7,330	5,331	3,897	4,764	3,575	2,351
			M.	*11,116*	*7,852*	*5,133*	*4,903*	*5,189*	*4,513*	*+3,264*	*+2,719*	*+230*	*—286*	*+676*	*+6,603*	*6,597*	*4,501*	*2,983*	*4,519*	*3,351*	*2,150*
			C. L.	*978*	*1,054*	*1,115*	*861*	*668*	*193*	*—76*	*—61*	*+254*	*+193*	*+475*	*+785*	*733*	*830*	*914*	*245*	*224*	*201*
63	Phagwara	Kapurthala	M.	12,049	11,395	11,779	14,108	12,331	10,627	+654	—384	—2,329	+1,777	+1,704	+1,422	6,741	6,526	6,832	5,308	4,869	4,947
64	Rai Kot	Ludhiana	M.	11,810	8,379	7,510	10,131	9,381	9,219	+3,431	+869	—2,621	+750	+162	+2,591	6,530	4,553	4,073	5,280	3,828	3,437
65	Jind	Jind		11,699	10,840	8,783	8,047	8,116	7,136	+859	+2,057	+736	—69	+980	+4,563	6,610	6,367	4,805	5,089	4,473	3,978
66	Campbellpur	Attock	Total	11,694	9,850	4,022	3,036	2,556	1,467	+1,844	+5,828	+986	+480	+1,089	+10,227	7,216	6,980	2,034	4,478	2,870	1,388
			M.	*7,997*	*3,669*	*665*	..	..	..	*+4,328*	*+3,004*	..	..	..	..	*5,029*	*2,296*	*540*	*2,968*	*1,373*	*125*
			Cantt.	*3,697*	*6,181*	*3,357*	*3,036*	*2,556*	*1,467*	*—2,484*	*+2,824*	*+321*	*+480*	*+1,089*	*+2,230*	*2,187*	*4,684*	*2,094*	*1,510*	*1,497*	*1,263*
67	Pakpattan	Montgomery	M.	11,311	7,218	7,912	6,192	6,522	5,993	+4,093	—694	+1,720	—330	+529	+5,318	6,472	3,835	4,467	4,839	3,383	3,445
68	Khanewal	Multan	..	11,205	5,647	..	..	..	..	+5,558	..	..	..	..	..	7,523	3,938	..	3,682	1,709	..
69	Palwal	Gurgaon	M.	10,807	9,352	9,485	12,830	11,227	10,635	+1,455	—133	—3,345	+1,603	+592	+172	5,893	5,049	5,044	4,914	4,303	4,441
70	Okara	Montgomery	..	10,712	..	..	..	..	..	..	..	..	..	..	..	6,925	..	..	3,787	..	..
71	Sunam	Patiala	..	10,652	8,265	7,329	10,069	10,869	12,223	+2,387	+936	—2,740	—800	—1,354	—1,571	6,132	4,747	4,161	4,520	3,518	3,108
72	Sumana	Patiala	..	10,563	9,685	9,273	10,209	10,035	9,495	+878	+412	—936	+174	+540	+1,068	5,610	5,149	4,913	4,953	4,536	4,360
73	Pindi Gheb	Attock	M.	10,506	9,419	9,045	8,452	8,462	8,583	+1,087	+374	+593	—10	—121	+1,023	5,326	4,642	4,548	5,180	4,777	4,497
74	Ahmadpur Sharqi	Bahawalpur	..	10,296	8,255	9,472	9,928	9,844	9,853	+2,041	—1,217	—456	+84	—9	+443	5,525	4,378	5,000	4,771	3,877	4,472
75	Tarn Taran	Amritsar	..	10,103	5,988	4,260	4,428	3,900	3,210	+4,115	+1,728	—168	+528	+690	+6,893	5,795	3,418	2,443	4,308	2,570	1,817
	CLASS V.—5,000 TO 10,000																				
76	Kartarpur	Jullundur	M.	9,878	8,512	8,631	10,840	10,441	9,260	+1,366	—119	—2,209	+399	+1,181	+618	5,290	4,592	4,631	4,588	3,920	4,000
77	Pind Dadan Khan	Jhelum	M.	9,832	9,919	10,590	13,770	15,065	16,724	—87	—671	—3,180	—1,285	—1,609	—6,892	5,424	5,209	5,537	4,408	4,710	5,053
78	Gojra	Lyallpur	M.	9,779	7,622	5,417	..	..	..	+2,157	+2,205	..	..	..	..	6,165	5,174	3,800	3,614	2,448	1,617
79	Pathankot	Gurdaspur	M.	9,763	7,353	7,007	6,091	4,749	4,344	+2,410	+346	+916	+1,342	+405	+5,419	5,798	4,326	4,181	3,965	3,027	2,826
80	Nakodar	Jullundur	M.	9,584	9,434	8,859	9,958	9,740	8,486	+150	+575	—1,099	+218	+1,254	+1,098	5,147	5,110	4,780	4,437	4,324	4,079
81	Leiah	Muzaffargrah	M.	9,578	8,476	8,173	7,546	7,437	5,899	+1,102	+303	+627	+109	+1,538	+3,679	5,014	4,270	4,265	4,564	4,206	3,908
82	Chakwal	Jhelum	..	9,542	7,425	6,400	6,520	6,070	5,717	+2,117	+1,025	—120	+450	+353	+3,825	5,170	3,794	3,228	4,366	3,631	3,172
83	Urmurtanda	Hoshiarpur	..	9,510	8,362	7,016	10,247	11,632	10,295	+1,148	+1,346	—3,231	—1,385	+1,337	—785	5,085	4,422	3,775	4,425	3,940	3,241
84	Jampur	D. G. Khan	M.	9,430	7,317	6,517	5,928	5,815	4,697	+2,113	+800	+589	+113	+1,118	+4,733	5,163	4,001	3,420	4,267	3,316	3,097

WITH VARIATION FOR FIFTY YEARS—*continued.*

85	MAHINDARGARH	Patiala ..	..	—	9,194	8,580	9,761	9,984	10,847	10,398	+614	−1,181	−223	−863	+449	−1,204	4,552	4,194	4,754	4,642	4,386	5,007
86	HAZRO ..	Attock ..	M.	..	9,155	8,408	9,950	9,799	7,580	6,533	+747	−1,542	+151	+2,219	+1,047	+2,622	4,880	4,359	5,270	4,275	4,049	4,680
87	NANKANA SAHIB	Sheikhupura	..		9,155	..	..	..	..	..	..	..	..	..	..	..	5,429	..	..	3,726	..	..
88	MEHAM ..	Rohtak ..	..		9,079	7,820	..	7,824	7,600	7,315	+1,259	..	..	+224	+285	+1,764	4,718	3,906	..	4,361	3,914	..
89	BARNALA ..	Patiala ..	..		8,915	7,714	5,341	6,905	6,612	5,449	+1,201	+2,373	−1,564	+293	+1,163	+3,460	5,182	4,703	3,189	3,733	3,011	2,152
90	JANDIALA ..	Amritsar ..	M.	..	8,888	7,464	6,959	7,750	7,732	6,535	+1,424	+505	−791	+18	+1,197	+2,353	4,809	4,019	3,822	4,079	3,445	3,137
91	RUPAR ..	Ambala ..	M.	..	8,764	7,606	6,935	8,888	8,693	10,326	+1,158	+671	−1,953	+195	−1,633	−1,562	4,943	4,246	3,816	3,821	3,360	3,119
92	HARDO DASKA ..	Sialkot	..		8,636	6,283	6,046	6,655	3,070	5,525	+2,353	+237	−609	+3,585	−2,455	+3,111	4,861	3,369	3,320	3,775	2,914	2,726
93	SULTANPUR ..	Kapurthala	M.	..	8,606	8,141	6,492	9,004	8,986	8,217	+465	+1,649	−2,512	+18	+769	+389	4,639	4,318	3,453	3,967	3,823	3,039
94	JAITU ..	Nabha ..	..		8,542	7,912	7,694	..	..	..	+630	+218	..	..	..	..	4,832	4,566	4,806	3,710	3,346	2,888
95	BUDHLADA ..	Hissar ..	..		8,369	..	..	..	..	..	..	..	..	..	..	..	4,839	..	..	3,530	..	..
96	KALA BAGH ..	Mianwali ..	..		8,333	8,455	6,654	5,824	6,702	6,036	−102	+1,801	+830	−878	+646	+2,297	4,476	4,644	3,402	3,877	3,811	3,252
97	CHUNIAN ..	Lahore ..	M.	..	8,269	7,642	7,151	8,939	10,339	8,122	+627	+491	−1,808	−1,380	+2,217	+147	4,505	3,940	3,752	3,764	3,702	3,399
98	MANDI PATTOKI	Lahore ..	..		8,016	..	..	..	..	..	..	..	..	..	..	..	5,158	..	..	2,858	..	..
99	KALKA ..	Ambala ..	..		7,937	7,635	4,532	7,045	..	..	+302	+3,103	−2,513	..	..	..	5,002	5,060	2,803	2,935	2,575	1,639
100	PASRUR ..	Sialkot	M.	..	7,905	6,909	7,564	8,335	9,200	8,378	+996	−655	−771	−865	+822	−473	4,146	3,490	4,021	3,759	3,419	3,543
101	BERI ..	Rohtak ..	M.	..	7,877	7,454	7,798	9,723	9,825	9,695	+423	−344	−1,925	−102	+130	−1,818	4,001	3,875	3,958	3,876	3,579	3,840
102	SADHAURA ..	Ambala	M.	..	7,769	7,630	7,774	9,812	10,445	10,794	+139	−144	−2,038	−633	−349	−3,025	4,171	4,058	4,107	3,598	3,572	3,667
103	SAHIWAL ..	Shahpur ..	M.	..	7,762	6,582	7,658	9,163	9,210	8,880	+1,180	−1,076	−1,505	−47	+330	−1,118	4,028	3,270	3,858	3,734	3,312	3,800
104	JALALABAD ..	Ferozepore	..		7,703	3,833	5,096	..	..	..	+3,870	−1,263	..	..	..	..	5,160	2,190	2,837	2,543	1,643	2,259
105	MANDI NAGAR ..	Mandi ..	M	..	7,538	6,870	7,896	8,144	6,889	5,030	+668	−1,026	−248	+1,255	+1,859	+2,508	4,551	4,052	4,878	2,987	2,818	3,018
106	DHANAULA ..	Nabha	..		7,521	6,886	6,094	7,443	7,095	7,264	+635	+792	−1,349	+348	−160	+257	4,084	3,781	3,387	3,437	3,105	2,707
107	TOHANA ..	Hissar ..	..		7,519	..	..	..	..	4,155	..	..	..	..	..	+3,364	3,969	..	..	3,550	..	..
108	ISA-KHEL ..	Mianwali ..	..		7,515	6,172	6,868	7,630	7,600	6,692	+1,343	−696	−762	+30	+908	+823	3,876	3,116	3,441	3,639	3,056	3,427
109	TAUNSA .	D. G. Khan	..		7,506	5,103	5,965	..	..	..	+2,403	−862	..	..	..	..	4,324	2,716	3,203	3,182	2,387	2,762
110	EMINABAD ..	Gujranwala	M.	..	7,329	5,816	5,526	6,494	5,841	5,886	+1,513	+290	−968	+653	−45	+1,443	3,937	3,064	2,832	3,392	2,752	2,694
111	JARANWALA ..	Lyallpur ..	..		7,320	..	..	..	..	..	..	..	..	..	..	..	4,778	..	..	2,542	..	..
112	DADRI ..	Jind ..	..		7,260	6,582	5,713	7,009	7,604	7,837	+678	+869	−1,296	−595	−233	−577	3,815	3,370	2,833	3,445	3,212	2,880
113	HODAL ..	Gurgaon ..	M.	.	7,258	5,854	5,468	8,142	9,601	6,453	+1,404	+386	−2,674	−1,459	+3,148	+805	3,883	3,189	2,898	3,375	2,665	2,570
114	HIDAYATPUR CHHAUNI. ..	Gurgaon .	C. L.	..	7,208	5,107	5,461	4,765	4,083	3,990	+2,101	−354	+696	+682	+93	+3,218	4,212	2,906	3,084	2,996	2,201	2,377
115	NAWAN SHAHR ..	Jullundur ..	..		7,153	5,316	4,475	5,641	5,601	4,960	+1,837	+841	−1,166	+40	+641	+2,193	4,133	2,975	2,517	3,020	2,341	1,958
116	KUNJAH ..	Gujrat ..	M.	..	7,152	7,240	7,090	6,431	5,474	5,709	−88	+150	+659	+957	−325	+1,353	3,690	3,700	3,633	3,462	3,540	3,457
117	TALAGANG ..	Attock ..	..		7,146	6,438	6,746	..	..	6,236	+708	−308	..	..	..	+910	3,599	3,133	3,300	3,547	3,305	3,446
118	NAROWAL ..	Sialkot ..	M.	..	7,095	..	..	4,422	4,898	4,558	..	..	..	−476	+340	+2,537	3,948	..	..	3,147	..	..
119	NUR MAHAL ..	Jullundur ..	M.	..	7,079	6,845	7,178	8,706	8,520	8,161	+234	−333	−1,528	+186	+359	−1,082	3,742	3,628	3,798	3,337	3,217	3,380
120	DINGA ..	Gujrat ..	M.	..	7,068	6,014	5,351	5,412	5,424	5,015	+1,054	+663	−61	−12	+409	+2,033	3,924	3,235	2,925	3,144	2,779	2,426
121	BAHADURGARH ..	Rohtak ..	M.	..	6,963	5,955	4,990	5,974	6,103	6,674	+1,008	+965	−984	−129	−371	+289	3,736	3,306	2,579	3,227	2,649	2,411
122	KHEM KARAN ..	Lahore ..	M.	..	6,898	6,152	5,732	6,083	5,935	5,516	+746	+420	−351	+148	+419	+1,382	3,598	3,121	2,974	3,300	3,031	2,758
123	NAHAN ..	Sirmoor ..	M.	..	6,859	5,756	6,341	6,256	6,121	5,253	+1,103	−585	+85	+135	+868	+1,606	3,976	3,240	3,636	2,883	2,516	2,705
124	BHAKKAR ..	Mianwali ..	..		6,857	6,193	5,388	5,312	5,210	4,402	+664	+805	+76	+102	+808	+2,455	3,751	3,363	2,890	3,106	2,830	2,498
125	SANAUR ..	Patiala ..	..		6,846	6,532	6,307	8,580	8,678	9,128	+314	+225	−2,273	−98	−450	−2,282	3,664	3,479	3,455	3,182	3,053	2,852
126	PHUL ..	Nabha ..	..		6,836	4,943	4,515	4,964	5,188	..	+1,893	+428	−449	−224	..	..	3,915	2,783	2,566	2,021	2,160	1,949
127	SHORKOT ..	Jhang ..	..		6,826	5,317	..	..	..	2,283	+1,509	..	..	..	..	+4,513	3,585	2,653	..	3,241	2,664	..
128	DHARMKOT ..	Ferozepore	..		6,779	5,960	5,859	6,731	6,725	6,007	+819	+101	−872	+6	+718	+772	3,600	3,217	3,163	3,179	2,743	2,696
129	MAJITHA ..	Amritsar ..	..		6,709	5,664	5,223	6,403	6,417	6,053	+1,045	+441	−1,180	−14	+364	+636	3,713	2,964	2,852	2,996	2,700	2,371
130	BAHAWALNAGAR	Bahawalpur	..		6,707	..	..	..	..	..	..	..	..	..	..	..	4,166	..	..	2,541	..	..
131	RAHON .	Jullundur ..	M.	..	6,692	5,947	6,292	8,651	10,067	11,736	+745	−345	−2,359	−2,016	−1,069	−5,044	3,640	3,207	3,437	3,052	2,740	2,855
132	SHUJABAD ..	Multan ..	M.	..	6,618	6,730	6,334	5,880	6,329	6,458	−112	+396	+454	−449	−129	+160	3,423	3,517	3,318	3,195	3,213	3,016
133	KHANNA KALAN ..	Ludhiana ..	..		6,555	..	3,319	3,838	3,877	3,088	..	..	−519	−39	−111	+2,567	4,090	..	1,842	2,465	..	1,477
134	SANGLA ..	Sheikhupura	..		6,478	..	..	..	..	..	..	..	..	..	..	..	4,049	..	..	2,429	..	..
135	MIANI .	Shahpur ..	M.	..	6,472	5,965	5,819	7,220	7,149	8,069	+507	+146	−1,401	+71	−920	−1,597	3,265	2,980	2,849	3,207	2,985	2,970
136	CHAWINDA ..	Sialkot ..	..		6,411	..	4,695	..	..	..	..	..	..	..	..	..	3,395	..	2,475	3,016	..	2,220
137	DHARAMSALA ..	Kangra .	Total	.	6,359	4,904	6,923	6,971	6,181	5,322	+1,455	−2,019	−48	+787	862	+1,037	4,154	2,996	4,705	2,205	1,908	2,128
			M.	.	*3,976*	*3,065*	*3,223*	*3,288*	*2,778*	*3,839*	*+911*	*−158*	*−65*	*+510*	*−1,061*	*+137*	*2,627*	*1,981*	*2,087*	*1,349*	*1,084*	*1,136*
			Cantt.	..	*2,383*	*1,839*	*3,700*	*3,683*	*3,406*	*1,483*	*+544*	*−1,861*	*+17*	*+277*	*+1,923*	*+900*	*1,527*	*1,015*	*2,708*	*856*	*824*	*992*

TABLE IV.—TOWNS CLASSIFIED BY POPULATION WITH VARIATION FOR FIFTY YEARS *concluded.*

No.	Name of Town.	District or State.	Description of Cities, Towns, (Municipalities, Suburbs, Cantonments, etc.)	Population. 1931.	1921.	1911.	1901.	1891.	1881.	Variation; Increase (+), Decrease (—). 1921 to 1931.	1911 to 1921.	1901 to 1911.	1891 to 1901.	1881 to 1891.	Variation in period 1881 to 1931, Increase (+), Decrease (—).	Males. 1931.	1921.	1911.	Females. 1931.	1921.	1911.
	1	2	3	4	5	6	7	8	9	10	11	12	13	14	15	16	17	18	19	20	21
138	Bhadaur	Patiala	..	6,282	5,577	5,465	7,710	7,177	6,912	+705	+112	—2,245	+533	+265	—630	3,488	3,104	3,111	2,794	2,473	2,354
139	Chamba	Chamba	..	6,219	5,668	5,523	6,000	5,905	5,218	+551	+145	—477	+95	+687	+1,001	3,605	3,265	3,217	2,614	2,403	2,306
140	Dajal	D. G. Khan	M.	6,186	5,775	6,893	6,213	6,085	5,952	+411	—1,118	+680	+128	+133	+234	3,349	3,107	3,666	2,837	2,668	3,227
141	Safidan	Jind	..	6,169	5,199	..	4,832	4,593	4,160	+970	..	..	+239	+433	+2,009	3,631	2,964	..	2,538	2,235	..
142	Muzaffargarh	Muzaffargarh	Total	6,110	5,386	4,387	4,018	3,642	2,720	+724	+999	+369	+376	+922	+3,390	3,616	3,286	2,592	2,494	3,100	1,795
			M.	*5,853*	*4,587*	*4,119*	*3,737*	*3,058*	*2,679*	*+1,266*	*+468*	*+382*	*+679*	*+379*	*+3,174*	*3,439*	*2,607*	*2,368*	*2,414*	*1,980*	*1,751*
			C. L.	*257*	*799*	*268*	*281*	*584*	*41*	*—542*	*+531*	*—13*	*—303*	*+543*	*+216*	*177*	*679*	*224*	*80*	*120*	*44*
143	Tandlianwala	Lyallpur	..	6,105	..	..	..	..	..	..	..	..	..	..	..	3,951	..	..	2,154	..	..
144	Bhaun	Jhelum	..	6,026	5,572	..	5,340	5,196	5,080	+454	..	..	+144	+116	+946	3,038	2,821	..	2,988	2,751	..
145	Hariana	Hoshiarpur	..	5,971	5,205	5,395	6,005	7,066	6,472	+766	-190	—610	—1,061	+594	—501	3,242	2,736	2,916	2,729	2,469	2,479
146	Jogindarnagar	Mandi	..	5,963	..	..	..	..	..	..	..	..	..	..	..	4,592	.	.	1,371	..	..
147	Toba Tek Singh	Lyallpur	..	5,903	5,041	..	..	..	..	+862	..	..	..	..	..	3,860	3,349	..	2,043	1,692	..
148	Banga	Jullundur	M.	5,840	5,089	4,602	4,697	5,010	4,565	+751	+487	—95	—313	+445	+1,275	3,210	2,850	2,552	2,630	2,239	2,050
149	Gharaunda	Karnal	..	5,731	..	..	..	..	..	..	..	..	..	..	..	3,059	..	..	2,672	..	..
150	Hasan Abdal	Attock	..	5,682	..	..	..	..	..	.	..	..	..	..	..	3,191	..	.	2,491	..	..
151	Sohna	Gurgaon	..	5,667	4,758	5,138	6,024	5,990	7,374	+909	-380	—886	+34	—1,384	—1,707	3,052	2,491	2,618	2,615	2,267	2,520
152	Sultanwind	Amritsar	..	5,572	5,572	..	..	..	..	.	..	..	..	..	..	3,080	3,065	..	2,492	2,507	..
153	Garhshankar	Hoshiarpur	..	5,561	..	4,923	5,803	6,064	5,275	..	..	—880	-261	+789	+286	2,883	..	2,601	2,078	..	2,322
154	Akalgarh	Gujranwala	..	5,483	..	3,943	4,961	4,262	4,312	..	..	-1,018	+699	—50	+1,171	3,052	..	2,071	2,431	..	1,872
155	Ferozpur Jhirka	Gurgaon	M.	5,390	4,542	5,719	7,278	6,848	6,878	+848	—1,177	—1,559	+430	—30	—1,488	2,875	2,353	2,918	2,515	2,189	2,801
156	Zira	Ferozepore	M.	5,318	4,622	4,378	4,001	4,356	3,492	+696	+244	+377	—355	+864	+1,826	2,863	2,519	2,465	2,455	2,103	1,913
157	Shahpur Shahr	Shahpur	..	5,280	..	8,739	9,386	9,233	7,752	..	..	—647	+153	+1,481	-2,472	2,768	..	4,760	2,512	..	3,979
158	Shahdara	Sheikhupura	..	5,249	4,908	..	..	..	..	+251	..	..	..	..	..	2,961	2,951	..	2,288	2,047	..
159	Khanpur	Bahawalpur	..	5,231	4,213	9,192	8,611	7,494	7,189	+1,018	—4,979	+581	+1,117	+305	—1,958	3,002	2,363	5,326	2,229	1,850	3,866
160	Dera Baba Nanak	Gurdaspur	M.	5,176	4,333	4,556	5,118	5,750	5,956	+843	-223	-562	—632	—206	-780	2,815	2,278	2,501	2,361	2,056	2,055
161	Phillaur	Jullundur	M.	5,168	4,696	5,224	6,986	6,957	7,107	+472	-528	—1,762	+29	—150	—1,939	2,853	2,505	2,870	2,315	2,191	2,354
162	Faridabad	Gurgaon	M.	5,134	4,337	4,487	5,310	5,929	7,427	+797	-150	—823	—619	—1,498	-2,293	2,880	2,310	2,384	2,254	2,027	2,103
163	Miani	Hoshiarpur	..	5,125	..	4,870	6,118	6,649	6,499	..	..	—1,248	—531	+150	-1,374	2,697	..	2,546	2,428	..	2,324
164	Chachrauli	Kalsia	M.	5,124	4,202	4,246	5,520	5,674	5,389	+922	—44	—1,274	154	+285	—265	2,986	2,427	2,285	2,138	1,775	1,961
165	Dinanagar	Gurdaspur	M.	5,114	4,047	4,154	5,191	5,454	5,589	+1,067	—107	1,037	—263	- 135	—475	2,825	2,146	2,264	2,289	1,901	1,890
166	Jhawarian	Shahpur	..	5,095	4,559	..	..	..	..	+536	..	..	..	..	..	2,695	2,433	..	2,400	2,126	..
167	Sharakpur	Sheikhupura	M.	5,056	4,127	4,482	4,474	4,924	4,595	+929	355	+8	—450	+329	+461	2,737	2,231	2,450	2,319	1,896	2,032
168	Jubhra	Lahore	..	5,048	3,584	..	..	..	..	+1,464	..	..	..	..	..	2,781	1,994	..	2,267	1,590	..
169	Gohana	Rohtak	M.	5,045	5,107	5,438	6,567	7,690	7,444	—62	—331	—1,129	—1,123	+246	—2,399	2,699	2,665	2,752	2,346	2,442	2,686
170	Ahmadpur	Jhang	..	5,045	4,045	..	..	..	2,338	+1,000	..	..	..	..	+2,707	2,603	2,112	..	2,442	1,933	..
171	Thanesar	Karnal	M.	5,032	4,226	4,719	5,066	6,111	6,005	+806	—493	—347	—1,045	+106	—973	2,990	2,392	2,692	2,042	1,834	2,027
	CLASS VI.—UNDER 5,000.																				
172	Bawal	Nabha	..	4,944	5,137	5,332	5,739	5,091	4,781	-193	—195	—407	+648	+310	+163	2,448	2,669	2,609	2,496	2,468	2,663
173	Kot Adu	Muzaffargarh	..	4,925	..	..	..	..	2,574	..	..	..	..	..	+2,351	2,648	..	..	2,277	..	..
174	Fatehjang	Attock	..	4,849	..	..	..	..	4,875	..	..	..	..	..	-26	2,574	..	..	2,275	..	..
175	Ramnagar	Gujranwala	..	4,768	4,632	5,250	7,121	6,592	6,830	+136	—624	—1,865	+529	-238	—2,062	2,457	2,443	2,778	2,311	2,189	2,478
176	Mitha Tiwana	Shahpur	..	4,713	4,158	..	..	..	..	+555	..	..	..	..	..	2,397	2,078	..	2,316	2,080	..
177	Nurpur	Shahpur	..	4,619	5,117	..	..	..	..	-498	..	..	..	..	..	2,252	2,537	..	2,307	2,580	

178	RAJANPUR	.. D. G. Khan	M.		4 510	3,904	3,704	3,017	4,073	4,932	+546	+260	-213	-1,056	+41	-429	2,533	2,185	1,855	1,977	1,779	1,849
179	PINDI BHATTIAN	. Gujranwala	..		4,478	..	..	..	..	3,528	..	..	.	..	..	+950	2,360	..	..	2,118	..	..
180	ROJHAN	.. D. G. Khan	..		4,424	4,363	9,624	.	..	..	-61	-5,261	..	..	..		2,477	2,330	5,297	1,947	2,033	4,327
181	UNA	.. Hoshiarpur	..		4 398	.	.	4,746	4,483	1,389	..	..	..	+263	+94	+9	2,386	..	..	2,012	..	..
182	CHICHAWATNI	.. Montgomery	..		1,387																	
183	DHARIWAL	. Gurdaspur	..		4,186	..	..	..	..	..	..	..	..	..	..	..	2,851	..	..	1,536	..	..
184	DERA BASSI	.. Kalsia ..	M.	..	4,182	3,890	4,236	4,641	4,966	1,907	292	-346	+05	-325	59	-725	2,435	..	..	1,751	..	..
185	BALLABGARH	.. Gurgaon ..	M.	..	4,162	3,72?	4,053	4,506	4,474	3,8??	441	-332	-453	+32	-1,347	-1,659	2,223	2,077	2,306	1,959	1,813	1,930
																	2,293	2,013	2,176	1,869	1,708	1,877
186	BHALWAL	.. Shahpur ..	..		4,153	4,082					71	..	..	..	..	..	2,602	2,631	..	1,551	1,451	..
187	SIRHIND	.. Patiala ..	..		4,103	4,064	3,843	5,415	5,254	5,40	+39	221	-1,572	161	147	-1,298	2,249	2,198	2,166	1,854	1,866	1,677
188	MALAKWAL	. Gujrat ..	..		4,034	..	..	..	..	..	..	..	..	..	..	..	2,312	..	..	1,722	..	..
189	ALIPUR	.. Muzaffargarh	M	..	3,931	3,431	3,3??	?788	2,?52	2,555	497	122	524	-236	-3	+1,376	2,046	1,804	1,774	1,885	1,630	1,538
190	SAMBARIAL	.. Sialkot .	..		3,827	3,324	6,285	..	..	..	+503	2,961	..	..	..	..	2,042	1,798	3,450	1,785	1,526	2,835
191	PATAUDI	.. Pataudi ..	M.	..	3,667	3,342	..	4,171	3,861	4,052	+325	..	..	-310	191	-385	1,882	1,708	..	1,785	1,634	..
192	MANDI GIDDARBAHA.	Ferozepore	..		3,636	..	..	..	..	..	..	..	..	..	..	..	2,134	..	..	1,502	..	..
193	BURIA	.. Ambala ..	M.	..	3,494	3,574	4,272	5,86?	6,809	7,411	-80	608	-1,593	-944	-602	-3,917	1,848	1,878	2,261	1,646	1,696	2,011
194	KAROR	.. Muzaffargarh	M.	.	3,49?	3,539	3,703	3,24?	2,833	2,723	48	36	260	410	116	+768	1,813	1,781	1,782	1,678	1,758	1 721
195	AHMADGARH	.. Maler Kotla	M.	..	3,283	..	..	..	..	..	..	..	..	..	..	..	2,035	..	..	1,248	..	..
196	SHAHPUR CHHAWANI.	Shahpur ..	..		3,265	..	..	..	..	..	..	..	..	..	..	..	1,976	..	..	1,289	..	..
197	BAKLOH	.. Gurdaspur	Cant.	..	3,239	4,430	3,566	3,642	2,503	1,479	191	-136	+624	+539	1,024	1,760	2,114	2,173	2,668	1,125	1,257	898
198	LALIAN	.. Jhang .	..		3,216	..	..	..	..	..	..	..	..	..	..	.	1,709	..	..	1,507	..	..
199	VEHOA	.. D. G. Khan	..		3,089	..	..	..	..	..	..	..	..	..	..	..	1,602	..	..	1,487	-	..
200	PHULERWAN	.. Shahpur ..	..		2,957	1,926	..	..	.	..	1,031	..	..	..	..	..	1,871	1,342	..	1,086	584	..
201	LOHARU	.. Loharu ..	..		2,956	2,339	2,343	2,17?	2,431	2,038	+617	-4	+168	-256	+393	+918	1,572	1,205	1,217	1,384	1 134	1,126
202	JAMALPUR	.. Maler Kotla	M.	..	2,942	..	..	..	..	..	..	..	..	..	..	..	1,571	..	..	1,371	..	..
203	KHANGARH	.. Muzaffargarh	M.	..	2,863	3,184	3,349	3,6?1	3,505	3,417	-321	165	-272	+116	88	-554	1,526	1,683	1,791	1,337	1,501	1,558
204	KASAULI	.. Ambala ..	Cantt.	..	2,852	3,212	3,194	2,192	1,977	2,807	360	+18	+1,002	+215	-830	45	1,968	2,249	2,249	884	963	945
205	MITHANKOT	.. D. G. Khan	M.	..	2,680	3,204	2,589	3,487	3,624	3,353	-524	-615	-898	-137	271	-673	1,399	1,911	1,357	1,281	1,293	1,232
206	KOT CHHUTTA	.. D. G. Khan	..		2,619	..	..	..	..	..	..	..	..	..	..	..	1,410	..	..	1,209	..	..
207	SILLANWALI	.. Shahpur ..	..		2,583	2,205	..	..	..	..	+378	..	..	..	..	..	1,611	1,373	..	972	832	..
208	SUNDARNAGAR	.. Suket ..	..		2,401	..	..	..	..	..	..	..	..	..	..	+1,706	1,362	..	..	1,039	..	..
209	BILASPUR	.. Bilaspur ..	..		2,387	..	..	3,192	3,260	..	..	..	..	--68	..	..	1,427	..	..	960	..	..
210	MURREE	.. Rawalpindi	Total	.	1,980	3,292	1,705	1,844	1,768	2,489	1,312	+1,587	-139	-76	-72	-509	1,516	2,522	1,239	464	770	466
			M.	..	*1,530*	2,397	1,36	1,517	1,459	1,821	-867	+1,030	-150	+58	362	-291	*1,128*	1,715	948	*402*	382	413
			Cantt.	..	*450*	*895*	*344*	*327*	*309*	*668*	*-445*	*+551*	*+17*	*+18*	*359*	*-218*	*388*	807	291	*62*	88	53
211	AMLOH	.. Nabha ..	..		1,889	1,543	..	..	..	..	+346	..	..	..	..	..	1,076	867	..	813	676	..
212	ATTOCK CANTT.	.. Attock ..	Cantt.	..	1,826	170	630	497	419	120	+1,656	-466	133	+78	+299	+1,706	1,332	153	551	494	17	79
213	DUJANA	Dujana ..	..		1,561	4,127	..	5,445	5,738	5,314	-2,566	..	..	-103	424	-3,753	816	2,060	-	745	2,067	..
214	MANDI GURU-HAR SAHAI.	Ferozepore	..		1,470	..	..	..	..	..	..	..	..	..	..	..	855	..	..	615	..	..
215	DAGSHAI	.. Simla ..	Cantt.	..	1,409	1,745	2,032	2,150	2,569	3,642	276	-287	-127	-410	-1,073	2,173	923	1,103	1,266	546	642	766
216	SABATHU	.. Simla ..	Cantt.	..	1,327	1,587	1,847	2,177	2,171	2,329	254	-266	-330	6	-158	-1,002	748	908	1,097	579	673	750
217	SANAWAR	.. Ambala ..	C. L.	..	1,088	899	884	..	..	..	189	-15	..	..	..	..	693	551	525	395	548	359
218	DALHOUSIE	.. Gurdaspur	M.	..	1,030	1 457	938	808	807	870	-427	+519	+130	+1	-63	+160	662	922	593	368	535	345
219	SHAMSHERPUR	.. Sirmoor ..	..		949	..	..	..	..	..	..	..	..	..	..	..	608	..	..	341	..	..
220	BALUN	.. Gurdaspur	Cantt.	..	852	948	644	308	425	740	-96	+304	+136	+83	-315	+112	591	716	460	261	232	184
221	JUTOGH	.. Simla ..	Cantt.	..	470	1,064	47?	375	557	953	-394	-593	+96	-182	-396	-483	332	850	340	138	214	131
222	KASUMPTI	.. Simla ...	M.	..	108	28?	..	170	245	..	-173	..	..	-75	..	..	74	202	..	34	79	..

TABLE V.

TOWNS ARRANGED TERRITORIALLY WITH POPULATION BY RELIGION.

1. In the case of Municipalities with Cantonments or Civil Lines adjoining them, the whole area has been treated as a single town but separate figures have been given below the total in smaller type for the Municipalities, Cantonments, etc.

2. Persons returned under the head " Others " have been classified and thrown into religious as noted on the title page of Table XVI.

3. The abbreviations used in this Table are :—

M.=Municipality. C. L.=Civil Lines.

Cantt.=Cantonment.

4. The figures of Aryas and Brahmos have been included in those of Hindus.

5. The Civil and Military population of Cantonments appears below :—

Name of Cantonment.	Population.		Name of Cantonment.	Population.	
	Military.	Civil.		Military.	Civil.
1. Ambala ..	7,069	42,299	11. Balun ..	157	695
2. Kasauli ..	400	2,452	12. Bakloh ..	2,237	1,002
3. Jutogh ..	41	429	13. Sialkot ..	6,990	8,861
4. Dagshai ..	21	1,448	14. Jhelum ..	3,784	2,449
5. Subathu ..	12	1,315	15. Rawalpindi ..	9,043	34,474
6. Dharamsala ..	2,057	326	16. Murree ..	25	425
7. Jullundur ..	4,745	9,990	17. Campbellpur ..	1,826	1,871
8. Ferozepore ..	10,065	20,232	18. Attock ..	1,430	396
9. Lahore ..	10,038	19,634	19. Multan ..	3,173	7,933
10. Amritsar ..	664	966	Total ..	63,777	157,197

Note The Military figures represent those obtained from the Census of the strictly Military area, and the figures for Civil population may contain a certain number that should properly be reckoned Military.

TABLE V.—TOWNS ARRANGED TERRITORIALLY WITH POPULATION BY RELIGION.

Serial No.	District or State.	Towns, Municipalities, Suburbs, Cantonments, etc.	Population.			Hindu.			Ad-Dharmi.			Sikh.			Jain.			Buddhist.			Zoroastrian.			Muslim.			Christian.			Jew.			Serial No.
			Persons.	Males.	Females.	Persons.	Males.	Females.	Persons.	Males.	Females.	Persons.	Males.	Females.	Persons.	Males.	Females.	Persons.	Males.	Females.	Persons.	Males.	Females.	Persons.	Males.	Females.	Persons.	Males.	Females.	Persons.	Males.	Females.	
	1	2	3	4	5	6	7	8	9	10	11	12	13	14	15	16	17	18	19	20	21	22	23	24	25	26	27	28	29	30	31	32	
		PUNJAB ..	3,521,449	2,065,249	1,456,200	1,325,645	782,858	542,787	19,491	11,209	8,282	255,590	158,114	97,476	25,463	13,647	11,816	41	32	9	528	329	199	1,827,935	1,058,679	769,256	66,745	40,376	26,369	11	5	6	
		BRITISH TERRITORY.	3,067,464	1,805,872	1,261,592	1,126,247	667,944	458,303	18,060	10,379	7,681	205,681	126,992	78,689	21,620	11,584	10,036	39	30	9	511	315	196	1,629,660	948,892	680,768	65,636	39,731	25,905	10	5	5	
1	Hissar ..	Hissar .. M.	25,179	15,065	10,114	13,846	8,501	5,345	..	..	..	336	279	57	749	403	346	..	..	..	1	1	..	10,128	5,836	4,292	119	45	74	..	..	..	1
2		Tohana	7,519	3,969	3,550	3,134	1,667	1,467	..	..	..	38	31	7	315	160	155	..	..	..	..	..	..	3,909	2,092	1,907	33	19	14	..	..	..	2
3		Budhlada	8,369	4,839	3,530	3,558	2,139	1,419	8	8	..	1,426	820	606	145	71	74	..	..	..	..	..	..	2,980	1,660	1,320	252	141	111	..	..	..	3
4		Hansi .. M.	18,356	9,943	8,413	8,629	4,812	3,817	1	..	1	31	16	15	930	456	474	..	..	..	..	..	..	8,742	4,641	4,101	23	18	5	..	..	..	4
5		Bhiwani .. M.	35,866	19,135	16,731	27,906	14,836	13,070	..	..	..	8	6	2	274	140	134	..	..	..	..	..	..	7,567	4,102	3,465	111	51	60	..	..	..	5
6		Sirsa .. M.	18,909	10,710	8,199	10,470	5,945	4,525	..	..	..	2,010	1,109	901	297	173	124	..	..	..	1	1	..	5,998	3,404	2,594	133	78	55	..	..	..	6
7	Rohtak ..	Rohtak	35,235	20,838	14,397	16,891	10,553	6,338	..	..	..	282	156	126	1,325	729	596	..	..	..	..	..	..	16,581	9,311	7,270	156	89	67	..	..	..	7
		" .. M.	34,112	19,907	14,205	16,238	10,003	6,235	...	...	...	240	130	110	1,325	729	596	...	...	...	...	...	...	16,180	8,976	7,205	129	70	59	..	..	..	
		" .. C. L.	1,123	931	192	653	550	103	...	...	...	42	26	10	...	...	...	...	...	...	...	...	...	401	336	65	27	19	8	..	..	..	
8		Jhajjar .. M.	12,232	6,266	5,966	5,863	3,106	2,757	..	..	..	78	41	37	102	45	57	..	..	..	..	..	..	6,179	3,069	3,110	10	5	5	..	..	..	8
9		Bahadurgarh M.	6,963	3,736	3,227	4,059	2,259	1,800	..	..	..	2	2	..	98	46	52	..	..	..	..	..	..	2,740	1,403	1,337	64	35	29	..	..	..	9
10		Beri .. M.	7,877	4,001	3,876	7,003	3,547	3,456	..	..	..	22	10	12	10	6	4	..	..	..	..	..	..	842	438	404	..	..	..	..	..	..	10
11		Gohana .. M.	5,045	2,699	2,346	1,155	674	481	..	..	..	6	5	1	678	337	341	..	..	..	..	..	..	3,201	1,679	1,522	5	4	1	..	..	..	11
12		Meham	9,079	4,718	4,361	3,936	2,097	1,839	..	..	..	3	1	2	26	14	12	..	..	..	..	..	..	5,113	2,605	2,508	1	1	..	..	..	..	12
13		Sonepat .. M.	15,050	8,274	6,776	6,101	3,515	2,586	..	..	.	11	10	1	765	411	354	..	..	..	..	..	..	8,060	4,251	3,809	113	87	26	..	..	..	13
14	Gurgaon ..	Hidayatpur Chhauni .. C. L.	7,208	4,212	2,996	3,940	2,316	1,624	..	..	..	21	15	6	173	90	83	..	..	..	..	..	..	2,875	1,679	1,196	199	112	87	..	..	..	14
15		Sohna	5,667	3,052	2,615	2,624	1,445	1,179	..	..	..	67	36	31	..	..	..	..	..	..	..	..	..	2,947	1,554	1,393	29	17	12	..	..	..	15
16		Firozpur Jhirka M.	5,390	2,875	2,515	2,038	1,103	955	..	..	..	..	..	..	252	119	133	..	..	..	..	..	..	3,080	1,653	1,427	..	..	..	..	..	..	16
17		Palwal .. M.	10,807	5,893	4,914	6,724	3,660	3,064	..	..	..	10	7	3	64	41	23	..	..	..	2	1	1	3,943	2,142	1,801	64	42	22	..	..	..	17
18		Hodal .. M.	7,258	3,883	3,375	5,397	2,872	2,525	..	..	..	..	..	..	6	3	3	..	..	..	2	2	..	1,852	1,005	847	1	1	..	..	..	..	18
19		Rewari .. M.	26,269	14,383	11,886	13,201	7,362	5,839	..	..	..	13	7	6	632	324	308	..	..	..	..	..	..	12,224	6,588	5,636	199	102	97	..	..	..	19
20		Ballabgarh .. M.	4,162	2,293	1,869	3,057	1,716	1,341	..	..	..	6	6	..	41	23	18	..	..	..	..	..	..	1,058	548	510	..	..	..	..	..	..	20
21		Faridabad .. M.	5,134	2,880	2,254	3,438	1,946	1,492	..	..	..	11	9	2	..	..	..	..	..	..	..	..	..	1,677	919	758	8	6	2	..	..	..	21
22	Karnal ..	Karnal	26,610	15,241	11,369	13,908	8,020	5,888	..	..	..	183	122	61	184	96	80	..	..	..	..	..	..	12,206	6,940	5,266	129	64	65	..	..	..	22
		" .. M.	25,371	14,314	11,057	13,251	7,519	5,732	...	...	...	137	85	52	182	93	80	...	...	...	...	...	...	11,729	6,578	5,151	72	39	33	..	..	..	
		" .. C. L.	1,239	927	312	657	501	156	...	...	...	46	37	9	2	2	...	...	...	...	...	...	...	477	362	115	57	25	32	..	..	..	
23		Gharaunda	5,731	3,059	2,672	3,324	1,764	1,560	..	..	..	9	5	4	32	15	17	..	..	..	..	..	..	2,364	1,274	1,090	2	1	1	..	..	..	23
24		Panipat .. M.	32,916	18,010	14,905	8,003	4,616	3,387	..	..	..	71	46	25	860	458	402	..	..	..	..	..	..	23,930	12,861	11,069	51	29	22	..	..	..	24
25		Kaithal .. M.	19,418	10,745	8,673	9,566	5,338	4,228	..	..	..	327	188	139	119	60	59	..	..	..	..	..	..	9,356	5,139	4,217	50	20	30	..	..	..	25
26		Thanesar .. M.	5,032	2,990	2,042	3,367	1,990	1,377	..	..	..	196	140	56	18	9	9	..	..	..	..	..	..	1,449	850	599	2	1	1	..	..	..	26
27		Shahabad .. M.	12,293	6,736	5,557	3,191	1,891	1,300	429	246	183	535	281	254	1	1	..	..	..	..	..	..	..	8,102	4,296	3,806	35	21	14	..	..	..	27
28	Ambala ..	Ambala	86,592	51,623	35,069	39,945	23,894	16,051	..	..	..	4,143	2,845	1,298	1,269	694	575	5	3	2	2	2	..	38,080	21,981	16,108	3,138	2,103	1,035	1	1	..	28
		" ... M.	35,190	20,045	15,145	11,716	7,057	4,659	..	...	..	1,898	1,139	759	760	412	[illegible]	..	..				..	20,816	11,436	9,380	3	1	2	..	..	..	
		" C. L.	2,031	1,487	544	880	631	226			..	264	224	40	...									708	577	131	199	52	147	..	..	..	
		Cantt.	49,365	29,991	19,377	27,369	16,203	11,166				1,981	1,482	499	509	282	227	5	3	2	2	2		16,556	[illegible]	[illegible]	2,936	2,050	886	1	1	..	

29	AMBALA	Sanawar	C.L.	*1*	693	395	106	287	118	..	..	..	87	68	19	10	8	2	1	1	..	..	..	..	48	36	12	635	370	265	29
30		Kasauli	Cant.	*2,852*	1,36[illegible]	884	1,8[illegible]	,32	179	..	..	..	425	267	1,8	56	30	26	..	..	..	..	..	..	587	391	196	367	179	188	30
31		Kalka	..	*,937*	5,02	2,935	4,47	2,839	1,638	..	..	..	171	115	56	101	55	46	..	..	..	..	..	..	2,784	1,749	1,035	202	124	78	31
32		Jagadhri	M.	*13,268*	7,450	5,818	8,914	4,082	3,932	..	..	..	87	49	38	54	23	31	..	..	..	..	..	..	4,002	2,263	1,739	80	35	45	32
33		Buria	M.	*3,494*	,848	1,646	1,130	620	510	..	..	..	314	187	127	323	179	144	..	..	..	..	..	..	2,220	1,155	1,065	3	1	2	33
34		Sadhaura	M.	*7,769*	,171	3,598	2,693	1,463	1,230	..	..	..	716	488	228	252	137	115	..	..	..	..	..	..	4,433	2,338	2,09[illegible]	6	4	2	34
35		Rupar	M.	*8,764*	4,943	3,821	3,003	1,746	1,257	..	..	..	..	..	..	..	..	..	..	..	..	..	..	..	4,697	2,518	2,179	96	54	42	35
36	SIMLA	Simla	M.	*18,144*	13,667	4,477	11,491	8,805	2,686	..	..	..	614	452	162	..	..	..	..	..	..	..	..	..	4,800	3,770	1,030	1,239	640	599	36
37		Kasumpti	M.	*108*	74	34	92	61	28	..	..	..	1	1	..	..	..	..	..	..	..	..	..	..	12	8	4	3	1	2	37
38		Jutogh	Cant.	*470*	332	138	316	215	100	..	..	..	2	2	..	..	..	..	..	..	..	..	..	..	119	93	26	34	22	12	38
39		Dagshai	Cant.	*1,469*	923	546	994	640	354	..	..	..	44	27	17	..	..	..	..	..	..	..	..	..	327	201	126	104	55	49	39
40		Subathu	Cant.	*1,327*	748	579	824	501	323	..	..	..	79	40	39	..	..	..	..	..	..	..	..	..	363	179	184	61	28	33	40
41	KANGRA	Dharmsala	..	*6,359*	4,[illegible]5	3,205	5,365	3,482	1,883	..	..	..	8	58	23	..	..	..	..	..	..	2	2	.	858	579	279	53	33	20	41
		"	M.	3,07[illegible]	2,027	1,31[illegible]	3,10[illegible]	2,055	1,05[illegible]	..	..	..	.	55	20	..	..	..	..	..	..	2	2	.	784	492	292	37	23	1	
		"	Cant.	2,58[illegible]	1,52[illegible]	80	2,37	1,2[illegible]	0	..	..	..	6	3	3	..	..	..	..	..	..	..	..	..	104	87	17	16	10	6	
42	HOSHIARPUR	Hoshiarpur	..	*26,730*	15,249	11,481	11,341	6,762	4,779	601	371	250	1,188	761	427	173	272	201	..	..	..	..	..	..	12,907	7,028	5,879	220	75	145	42
		"	M.	25,925	14,6[illegible]	11,236	1,097	6,[illegible]	4,5[illegible]	512	346	246	1,097	679	418	472	271	201	..	..	..	..	..	..	12,609	7,801	5,808	78	30	2	
		"	C.L.	805	590	215	244	900	1	90	5	..	91	82	9	1	1	..	..	..	..	..	..	..	298	227	71	162	45	117	
43		Hariana	..	*5,971*	3,249	2,729	3,074	1,662	1,412	106	66	40	418	238	180	..	..	..	..	..	..	..	..	..	2,300	1,233	1,067	73	43	30	43
44		Urmar Tanda	..	*9,510*	5,085	4,42[illegible]	2,881	1,554	1,327	277	157	120	285	148	137	137	82	55	..	..	..	..	..	..	5,922	3,138	2,784	8	6	2	44
45		Miani	..	*5,125*	2,697	2,428	717	387	330	72	45	27	3	3	..	27	14	13	..	..	..	..	..	..	4,302	2,246	2,056		2	2	45
46		Garhshankar	..	*5,561*	2,883	2,678	1,524	806	718	459	268	191	184	98	86	..	..	..	..	..	..	..	..	..	3,387	1,706	1,681	7	5	2	46
47		Una	..	*4,398*	2,386	2,012	3,297	1,78[illegible]	1,5[illegible]7	149	91	58	419	225	194	..	..	..	..	..	..	..	..	..	533	290	243	..	..	..	47
48	JULLUNDUR	Jullundur	..	*89,030*	51,119	37,911	27,946	15,734	12,206	2,893	1,613	1,280	3,003	2,148	855	1,014	515	499	..	..	..	70	44	26	52,577	28,878	23,699	1,533	1,187	346	48
		"	M.	74,295	41,321	32,971	20,756	11,888	8,868	2,492	1,381	1,111	2,107	1,480	687	802	458	4[illegible]	..	..	..	..	..	..	47,798	26,01[illegible]	21,781	190	97	93	
		"	Cantt.	14,735	9,798	4,937	7,184	1,810	2,388	401	232	169	[illegible]36	668	168	122	3	85	..	..	..	70	44	26	4,779	2,861	1,918	1,343	1,090	253	
49		Kartarpur	M.	*9,878*	5,290	4,588	4,161	2,186	1,975	856	457	399	1,169	664	505	..	..	..	..	..	..	..	..	..	3,692	1,983	1,709	..	..	..	49
50		Nawanshahr	..	*7,153*	4,133	3,020	3,649	2,116	1,533	706	385	315	482	288	194	37	24	13	..	..	..	..	..	..	2,279	1,317	962	6	3	3	50
51		Banga	M.	*5,840*	3,21[illegible]	2,630	2,721	1,513	1,208	394	212	182	1,417	785	632	109	66	43	..	..	..	..	..	..	1,196	632	564	3	[illegible]	1	51
52		Rahon	M.	*6,692*	3,646	3,052	2,143	1,168	975	377	198	179	84	59	25	30	19	11	..	..	..	..	..	..	4,033	2,179	1,854	25	17	8	52
53		Phillaur	M.	*5,168*	2,853	2,315	1,569	911	658	..	..	..	337	214	123	..	..	..	..	..	..	..	..	..	3,226	1,706	1,520	36	22	14	53
54		Nurmahal	M.	*7,079*	3,742	3,337	3,014	1,376	1,438	..	..	..	328	187	141	..	..	..	..	..	..	..	..	..	3,733	1,977	1,756	4	2	2	54
55		Nakodar	M.	*9,584*	5,147	4,437	3,516	1,828	1,682	329	178	151	276	167	109	112	60	52	..	..	..	..	..	..	5,351	2,911	2,440	6	3	3	55
56	LUDHIANA	Ludhiana	..	*65,586*	[illegible]	28,55[illegible]	20,364	12,20[illegible]	8,161	394	241	153	3,445	2,321	1,124	344	172	172	4	4	..	5	4	1	42,981	24,704	18,277	1,049	386	663	56
		"	M.	[illegible],088	[illegible],218	27,880	19,275	[illegible]	7,871	[illegible]	212	138	[illegible],870	1,84[illegible]	1,03[illegible]	334	167	167	4	..	..	1	1	..	42,254	24,238	18,016	1,011	[illegible]	645	
		"	C.L.	2,[illegible]88	1,811	67	1,10[illegible]	6	268		29	5	606	475	91	10	5	5	..	..	..	4	..	1	727	[illegible]	261	38	[illegible]	18	
57		Jagraon	M.	*[illegible],108*	1,151	[illegible],957	6,851	4,[illegible]63	2,688	2,000	1,241	759	3,785	2,880	905	228	125	103	..	..	..	..	..	..	14,175	8,690	5,485	69	52	17	57
58		Raikot	M.	*11,810*	6,530	[illegible],280	2,030	1,[illegible]32	898	734	390	344	755	424	331	377	208	169	..	..	..	..	..	..	7,890	4,363	3,527	24	13	11	58
59		Khanna Kalan	..	*6,655*	4,[illegible]	2,465	4,344	[illegible],34	1,610	..	..	..	580	374	206	13	9	4	..	..	..	..	..	..	1,594	957	637	24	16	8	59
60	FEROZEPORE	Ferozepore	..	*64,634*	38,88[illegible]	25,[illegible]50	26,936	16,129	10,8[illegible]7	[illegible],317	786	531	4,439	2,809	1,541	511	263	248	1	1	..	24	16	8	28,464	16,760	11,704	2,942	2,040	902	60
		"	M.	[illegible],[illegible]17	[illegible]9,679	[illegible],658	1,[illegible]087	[illegible]	5,[illegible]	[illegible]	39[illegible]	17	4,044	1,330	1,204	108	51	54	..	..	..	..	..	..	1,128	[illegible]	7,468	344	183	161	
		"	Cantt.	30,297	[illegible],20	1,[illegible]092	1[illegible],2[illegible]	[illegible],206	5,01	[illegible],2[illegible]4	[illegible]	314	1,106	1,082	936	408	20[illegible]	191	1	1	..	24	16	8	11,[illegible]36	[illegible],200	4,236	2,[illegible]8	1,857	741	
61		Zira	M.	*5,318*	2,863	2,455	1,585	831	754	100	60	49	349	207	142	292	131	141	..	..	..	..	..	..	2,975	1,609	1,366	8	5	3	61
62		Dharmkot	..	*6,[illegible]79*	3,600	3,179	1,8[illegible]	943	897	438	219	219	1,291	730	561	..	..	..	..	..	..	..	..	..	3,208	1,707	1,501	2	1	1	62
63		Moga	M.	*17,581*	10,454	7,127	6,341	3,963	2,378	626	332	294	5,309	3,168	2,141	26	15	11	..	..	..	..	..	..	4,964	2,756	2,208	316	220	96	63
64		Muktsar	M.	*14,839*	8,544	6,295	6,985	[illegible],046	2,940	570	320	250	3,195	1,879	1,316	91	49	42	..	..	..	..	..	..	3,947	2,217	1,730	51	34	17	64
65		Jalalabad	..	*7,703*	5,160	2,543	2,520	1,582	938	83	55	28	440	352	88	..	..	..	..	..	..	..	..	..	4,613	3,150	1,463	47	21	26	65
66		Mandi Guru Har Sahai.		*1,470*	855	615	590	362	228	..	..	..	579	322	257	17	12	5	..	..	..	..	..	..	284	139	125	..	..	..	66
67		Mandi Giddarbaha	..	*3,636*	2,134	1,502	2,680	1,555	1,125	120	69	51	394	246	148	92	55	37	..	..	..	..	..	..	350	209	141	..	..	..	67
68		Fazilka	M.	*18,463*	10,789	7,674	11,536	6,709	4,847	55	32	23	568	362	206	70	41	29	..	..	..	..	..	..	6,181	3,630	2,551	33	15	18	68
69		Abohar	M.	*14,035*	8,43[illegible]	5,604	10,415	6,291	4,194	120	75	45	385	257	128	..	..	..	..	..	..	..	..	..	3,104	1,802	1,302	11	6	5	69

TABLE V.—TOWNS ARRANGED TERRITORIALLY WITH POPULATION BY RELIGION—*continued.*

Serial No.	District or State.	Towns, Municipalities, Suburbs, Cantonments, etc.	Population. Persons.	Population. Males.	Population. Females.	Hindu. Persons.	Hindu. Males.	Hindu. Females.	Ad-Dharmi. Persons.	Ad-Dharmi. Males.	Ad-Dharmi. Females.	Sikh. Persons.	Sikh. Males.	Sikh. Females.	Jain. Persons.	Jain. Males.	Jain. Females.	Buddhist. Persons.	Buddhist. Males.	Buddhist. Females.	Zoroastrian. Persons.	Zoroastrian. Males.	Zoroastrian. Females.	Muslim. Persons.	Muslim. Males.	Muslim. Females.	Christian. Persons.	Christian. Males.	Christian. Females.	Jew. Persons.	Jew. Males.	Jew. Females.	Serial No.
	1	2	3	4	5	6	7	8	9	10	11	12	13	14	15	16	17	18	19	20	21	22	23	24	25	26	27	28	29	30	31	32	
70	LAHORE	Lahore ..	*429,747*	274,587	155,160	139,125	91,667	47,458	..	..	..	23,477	15,526	7,951	791	442	349	14	11	3	150	87	63	249,315	156,486	92,829	16,875	10,368	6,507	..	..	..	70
		" .. M	400,075	253,846	146,229	127,016	83,592	43,424	..	..	..	20,010	13,802	7,208	725	404	321	10	7	3	128	76	52	238,033	148,708	89,325	13,153	7,257	5,896	..	..	..	
		" .. Cantt.	29,672	20,741	8,931	12,109	8,075	4,034	..	..	..	3,467	1,724	743	66	38	28	4	4	..	22	11	11	11,282	7,778	3,504	3,722	3,111	611	..	..	..	
71		Ichhra ..	*5,048*	2,781	2,267	680	378	302	..	..	..	198	99	99	..	..	..	..	..	..	..	..	..	4,000	2,216	1,784	170	88	82	..	..	..	71
72		Baghbanpura Cum Bhogiwal .. M.	*13,805*	7,854	5,951	1,171	735	436	..	..	..	476	287	189	..	..	..	..	..	..	..	..	..	11,881	6,689	5,192	277	143	134	..	..	..	72
73		Chunian .. M.	*8,269*	4,505	3,764	3,390	1,852	1,538	..	..	..	441	283	158	21	10	11	..	..	..	..	..	..	4,380	2,340	2,040	37	20	17	..	..	..	73
74		Mandi Pattoki ..	*8,016*	5,158	2,858	4,753	3,075	1,678	..	..	..	743	455	288	..	..	..	..	..	..	..	..	..	2,392	1,558	834	128	70	58	..	..	..	74
75		Kasur .. M.	*46,815*	28,067	18,748	8,245	5,003	3,242	6	6	..	1,529	1,052	477	144	72	72	..	..	..	6	4	2	36,658	21,825	14,833	227	105	122	..	..	..	75
76		Khem Karan .. M.	*6,898*	3,598	3,300	1,223	619	604	..	..	..	904	495	409	..	..	..	..	..	..	..	..	..	4,404	2,288	2,116	367	196	171	..	..	..	76
77		Patti .. M.	*12,882*	7,003	5,879	2,545	1,483	1,062	..	..	..	908	533	375	402	207	195	..	..	..	..	..	..	8,909	4,764	4,235	28	16	12	..	..	..	77
78	AMRITSAR ..	Amritsar ..	*264,840*	158,985	105,855	97,837	59,544	38,293	164	101	63	32,009	18,721	13,288	604	329	275	..	..	..	41	24	17	132,362	79,324	53,038	1,819	941	878	4	1	3	78
		" .. M	263,210	157,823	105,387	96,975	58,890	38,085	164	101	63	31,855	18,627	13,228	604	329	275	..	..	..	41	24	17	132,016	79,118	52,898	1,555	734	821	..	..	..	
		" .. Cantt.	1,630	1,162	468	862	654	208	...	...	...	154	94	60	..	..	...	..	..	..	..	..	..	346	206	140	264	207	57	4	1	3	
79		Jandiala .. M.	*8,888*	4,800	4,079	2,206	1,197	1,009	..	..	..	846	472	374	534	290	244	..	..	..	..	..	..	5,274	2,839	2,435	28	11	17	..	..	..	79
80		Majitha	*6,709*	3,713	2,996	1,811	1,011	800	..	..	..	1,389	769	620	32	12	20	..	..	..	..	..	..	3,452	1,904	1,548	25	17	8	..	..	..	80
81		Sultanwind	*5,572*	3,080	2,492	859	502	357	..	..	..	1,952	1,069	883	..	..	..	..	..	..	..	..	..	2,754	1,506	1,248	7	3	4	..	..	..	81
82		Tarn Taran	*10,103*	5,795	4,308	2,067	1,615	1,052	..	..	..	3,242	1,926	1,316	..	..	..	..	..	..	..	..	..	4,056	2,198	1,858	138	56	82	..	..	..	82
83	GURDASPUR	Gurdaspur ..	*12,094*	7,330	4,764	4,260	2,626	1,634	..	..	..	1,274	826	448	..	..	..	..	..	..	..	..	..	5,982	3,583	2,399	578	295	283	..	..	..	83
		" ... M.	11,116	6,597	4,519	3,928	2,386	1,542	..	...	...	1,101	671	430	..	..		..	..	..	..	..	..	5,576	3,293	2,283	511	247	264	..	..	..	
		" ... C. L.	978	733	245	332	240	92			...	173	155	18	..	...		..	..	..	..	..	..	406	290	116	67	48	19	..	..	..	
84		Dinanagar .. M.	*5,114*	2,825	2,289	2,231	1,243	988	..	..	..	158	98	60	..	..	..	..	..	..	..	..	..	2,562	1,400	1,162	163	84	79	..	..	..	84
85		Dhariwal	*4,186*	2,435	1,751	1,451	832	619	..	..	..	490	288	202	..	..	..	..	..	..	..	..	..	1,843	1,078	765	402	237	165	..	..	..	85
86		Batala .. M.	*33,204*	18,102	15,102	9,149	5,052	4,097	97	74	23	1,327	740	587	..	..	..	2	2	..	..	..	..	22,323	12,060	10,263	306	174	132	..	..	..	86
87		Dera Baba Nanak M.	*5,176*	2,815	2,361	1,849	974	875	..	..	..	1,051	582	469	2	2	..	..	..	..	..	..	..	2,140	1,181	959	134	76	58	..	..	..	87
88		Pathankot .. M.	*9,763*	5,798	3,965	3,631	2,270	1,361	99	54	45	352	208	144	6	3	3	..	..	..	..	..	..	5,353	3,121	2,232	322	142	180	..	..	..	88
89		Dalhousie .. M.	*1,030*	662	368	619	388	231	..	..	..	24	15	9	..	..	..	..	..	..	..	..	..	347	244	103	40	15	25	..	..	..	89
90		Balun .. Cantt.	*852*	591	261	240	179	61	..	..	..	33	20	13	..	..	..	..	..	..	..	..	..	441	335	106	138	57	81	..	..	..	90
91		Bakloh .. Cantt.	*3,239*	2,114	1,125	2,935	1,920	1,015	..	..	..	14	12	2	1	1	.	..	..	..	..	..	..	260	162	98	29	19	10	..	..	..	91
92	SIALKOT ..	Sialkot	*100,973*	59,894	41,079	18,644	11,098	7,546	26	5	21	4,931	3,338	1,593	1,670	858	712	..	..	..	7	4	3	69,700	40,605	29,095	6,095	3,986	2,109	..	..	..	92
		" M.	85,093	49,071	30,022	13,273	7,744	5,531	26	5	21	3,201	1,997	1,206	1,632	841	691	..	..	..	..	..	..	64,713	37,317	27,396	2,344	1,267	1,077	..	..	..	
		" .. C. L.	29	28	1	2	2	..		..	..	2	2	...	..	...	..	..	..	..	..	..	..	25	24	1	.	...	..	..	..	..	
		" ... Cantt.	15,851	10,795	5,056	5,367	3,352	2,015	...	..	..	1,726	1,339	387	38	17	21	..	..	..	7	4	3	4,962	3,264	1,698	3,751	2,719	1,032	..	..	..	
93		Pasrur .. M.	*7,905*	4,146	3,759	1,159	636	523	..	..	..	241	128	113	345	201	144	..	..	..	..	..	..	5,629	2,911	2,718	531	270	261	..	..	..	93
94		Chawinda	*6,411*	3,395	3,016	937	504	433	..	..	..	682	378	304	..	..	..	..	..	..	..	..	..	4,515	2,370	2,145	277	143	134	..	..	..	94
95		Narowal .. M.	*7,095*	3,948	3,147	1,636	942	694	..	..	..	593	356	237	178	91	87	..	..	..	..	..	..	4,247	2,289	1,958	441	270	171	..	..	..	95
96		Sambarial	*3,827*	2,042	1,785	1,046	560	486	..	..	..	309	194	115	..	..	..	..	..	..	..	..	..	2,263	1,178	1,085	209	110	99	..	..	..	96
97		Hardo Daska ..	*8,636*	4,861	3,775	1,874	1,067	807	..	..	..	1,544	828	716	13	9	4	..	..	..	..	..	..	4,706	2,655	2,051	499	302	197	..	..	..	97

98	GUJRANWALA	Gujranwala	M	8,[illegible]	[illegible]	24,[illegible]	16,958	10,03[illegible]	6,927	..	..	..	5,870	3,440	2,439	978	543	435	..	..	..	..	..	..	,241	19,265	3,976	,660	937	723	..	..	..	98
99		Eminabad	..	7,329	[illegible]	3,392	1,515	[illegible]22	69[illegible]	..	..	..	296	224	72	..	..	..	..	..	..	..	..	..	5,293	2,768	[illegible]	225	123	102	..	..	..	99
100		Wazirabad	M.	20,707	11,[illegible]77	8,929	4,674	2,714	1,960	2	2	..	1,206	699	507	16	7	9	..	..	..	..	..	..	14,4[illegible]	8,13[illegible]	6,292	385	224	161	..	..	..	100
101		Ramnagar	..	4,768	[illegible]457	2,311	1,133	553	580	..	..	..	224	127	97	7	5	2	..	..	..	..	..	..	3,300	1,717	1,58[illegible]	104	55	49	..	..	..	101
102		Akalgarh	..	5,483	3,052	2,431	2,083	1,214	869	..	..	..	303	160	143	..	..	..	..	..	..	..	..	..	2,89[illegible]	1,581	1,31[illegible]	205	97	108	..	..	..	102
103		Hafizabad	..	14,431	8,702	5,729	6,176	3,949	2,227	..	..	..	1,096	671	425	2	1	1	..	..	..	..	..	..	6,702	3,835	2,867	455	246	209	..	..	..	103
104		Pindi Bhattian	..	4,478	2,360	2,118	1,545	809	736	..	..	..	199	106	93	..	..	..	..	..	..	..	..	..	2,734	1,445	1,289	..	..	..	..	..	..	104
105	SHEIKHUPURA	Sheikhupura	..	12,166	7,666	4,500	4,241	2,728	1,513	14	10	4	1,615	1,008	607	..	..	..	..	..	..	..	..	..	5,716	3,569	2,147	580	351	229	..	..	..	105
106		Sangla	..	6,478	4,049	2,429	2,528	1,605	923	1	1	..	740	445	295	..	..	..	..	..	..	..	..	..	2,678	1,708	970	531	290	241	..	..	..	106
107		Nankana Sahib	..	9,155	5,429	3,726	3,412	2,048	1,364	773	423	350	2,604	1,382	1,022	..	1	..	..	..	..	..	..	..	2,230	1,307	923	135	68	67	..	..	..	107
108		Sharakpur	M.	5,056	2,737	2,319	593	332	261	..	..	..	112	90	52	..	..	..	..	..	..	..	..	..	4,193	2,242	1,957	128	73	55	..	..	..	108
109		Shahdara	..	5,249	2,961	2,288	713	408	305	..	..	..	278	165	113	..	..	..	..	..	..	2	2	..	4,132	2,319	1,813	124	67	57	..	..	..	109
110	GUJRAT	Gujrat	..	26,511	14,691	11,820	5,984	3,586	2,398	..	..	..	659	437	222	..	..	..	..	..	..	..	..	..	[illegible]	[illegible],069	8,813	386	190	1[illegible]7	..	..	..	110
		"	M.	25,604	13,956	11,648	5,772	3,225	2,547	..	..	..	587	374	213	..	..	..	..	..	..	..	..	..	18,[illegible]	10,1[illegible]	[illegible],11	9[illegible]	1[illegible]	14[illegible]	..	..	..	
		"	C. L.	907	73[illegible]	1,[illegible]	212	[illegible]1	61	..	..	..	72	63	9	..	..	..	..	..	..	..	..	..	[illegible]	72	72	79	[illegible]9	[illegible]0	..	..	..	
111		Jalalpur Jattan	M	12,507	6,771	5,736	2,45[illegible]	[illegible]79	1,172	..	..	..	108	71	37	..	..	..	..	..	..	..	..	..	9,773	5,304	4,469	175	17	58	..	..	..	111
112		Kunjah	M.	7,152	3,690	3,162	1,417	740	677	..	..	..	4[illegible]	249	204	21	13	8	..	..	..	..	..	..	[illegible],1[illegible]	2,6[illegible]2	2,[illegible]00	105	82	73	..	..	..	112
113		Dinga	M.	7,068	3,924	3,144	2,678	1,460	1,218	..	..	..	758	451	307	..	..	..	..	..	..	..	..	..	3,[illegible]30	2,033	1,617	2	..	2	..	..	..	113
114		Malakwal	..	4,034	2,312	1,722	1,619	927	692	..	..	..	173	109	64	..	..	..	..	..	..	..	..	..	2,222	1,204	1,0[illegible]8	20	12	8	..	..	..	114
115	SHAHPUR	Sahiwal	M.	7,762	4,028	3,734	2,687	1,366	1,321	..	..	..	792	417	375	..	..	..	..	..	..	..	..	..	4,2[illegible]	2,245	2,038	..	..	..	..	..	..	115
116		Shahpur Chhawani	..	3,265	1,976	1,289	852	501	351	..	..	..	12[illegible]	86	39	..	..	..	..	..	..	..	..	..	2,[illegible]	[illegible],37[illegible]	872	18	11	7	..	..	..	116
117		Shahpur Shahr	..	5,280	2,768	2,512	1,811	931	88	..	..	..	361	206	155	1	..	1	..	..	..	..	..	..	3,107	1,63[illegible]	1,476	..	..	..	..	..	..	117
118		Jhawarian	..	5,096	2,695	2,400	[illegible]28	369	359	..	..	..	154	71	83	..	..	..	..	..	..	..	..	..	4,2[illegible]3	2,255	1,958	..	..	..	..	..	..	118
119		Khushab	M.	14,194	8,055	6,139	2,212	1,906	1,006	..	..	..	448	247	201	..	..	..	..	..	..	..	..	..	11,514	6,589	4,925	20	13	7	..	..	..	119
120		Mitha-Tiwana	..	4,713	2,397	2,316	929	441	488	..	..	..	606	344	262	..	..	..	..	..	..	..	..	..	3,178	1,612	1,566	..	..	..	..	..	..	120
121		Bhera	M.	19,741	10,860	8,881	4,794	2,508	2,286	..	..	..	363	210	153	..	..	..	..	..	..	..	..	..	14,570	8,137	6,433	14	5	9	..	..	..	121
122		Miani	M.	6,472	3,265	3,207	2,826	1,383	1,443	..	..	..	40	73	67	..	..	..	..	..	..	..	..	..	3,506	1,809	1,697	..	..	..	..	..	..	122
123		Nurpur	..	4,619	2,252	2,367	1,821	851	970	..	..	..	483	239	244	..	..	..	..	..	..	..	..	..	2,3[illegible]	1,162	1,153	..	..	..	..	..	..	123
124		Bhalwal	..	4,153	2,602	1,551	2,140	1,330	810	..	..	..	569	344	225	..	..	..	..	..	..	..	..	..	1,410	908	502	34	20	14	..	..	..	124
125		Phularwan	..	2,957	1,871	1,086	1,976	1,203	773	..	..	..	263	165	98	..	..	..	..	..	..	..	..	..	715	501	214	3	2	1	..	..	..	125
126		Sargodha	M.	26,761	16,498	10,263	11,674	7,021	4,653	30	16	19	5,201	3,333	1,868	1	1	..	..	..	..	..	..	..	9,146	5,780	3,366	704	341	363	..	..	..	126
127		Sillanwali	..	2,58[illegible]	1,6[illegible]1	972	1,161	709	452	..	..	..	686	397	289	..	..	..	..	..	..	..	..	..	7[illegible]9	499	22[illegible]	17	6	11	..	..	..	127
128	JHELUM	Jhelum	..	23,499	1[illegible],973	7,[illegible]26	6,3[illegible]4	4,181	2,123	..	..	..	2,58[illegible]	1,830	7[illegible]1	[illegible]	41	35	..	..	..	..	..	..	1[illegible],98[illegible]	9,608	4,372	565	320	45[illegible]	..	..	..	128
		"	M.	17,[illegible]	10,[illegible]	[illegible]	4,60[illegible]	2,773	1,[illegible]15	..	..	..	1,[illegible]56	961	594	6	4	3	..	..	..	..	..	..	10,682	[illegible],604	[illegible]	2	100	153	..	..	..	
		"	Cantt.	6,233	[illegible],312	[illegible]21	1,606	[illegible],108	2[illegible]	..	..	..	1,02[illegible]	869	157	..	..	..	..	..	..	..	..	..	[illegible],2[illegible]8	[illegible],91[illegible]	38[illegible]	21[illegible]	221	92	..	..	..	
129		Pind Dadan Khan	M	9,832	5,424	4,408	2,765	1,479	1,286	..	..	..	227	129	98	18	13	5	..	..	..	..	..	..	6,821	3,802	3,019	1	1	..	..	..	..	129
130		Chakwal	..	9,542	5,176	4,366	2,461	1,303	1,158	..	..	..	1,466	805	661	..	..	..	..	..	..	..	..	..	5,585	3,051	2,534	30	17	13	..	..	..	130
131		Bhaun	..	6,026	3,038	2,988	1,319	578	741	..	..	..	559	273	286	..	..	..	..	..	..	..	..	..	4,145	2,186	1,959	3	1	2	..	..	..	131
132	RAWALPINDI	Rawalpindi	..	119,284	75,971	43,313	40,161	24,669	15,492	..	..	..	15,532	9,399	6,133	1,[illegible]25	563	62	9	6	3	65	37	28	55,63[illegible]	36,[illegible]32	18,905	6,850	4,562	2,288	5	3	2	132
		"	M.	[illegible],767	46,056	[illegible],661	[illegible],80	11,549	[illegible]	..	..	..	12,[illegible]88	7,327	[illegible],961	971	..	4[illegible]1	..	2	..	..	..	..	36,36[illegible]	23,120	13,54[illegible]	[illegible]	[illegible]	375	..	..	..	
		"	Cantt.	1[illegible],517	29,8[illegible]	1[illegible],632	[illegible],385	10,120	[illegible],2[illegible]	..	..	..	3,144	2,072	1,072	[illegible]	30	2[illegible]	6	1	2	6	..	28	18,9[illegible]1	1[illegible],62[illegible]	5,36[illegible]	[illegible],01[illegible]	4,007	1,010	5	3	2	
133		Murree	..	1,980	1,516	464	41[illegible]	293	12[illegible]	..	..	..	2[illegible]7	198	[illegible]9	..	..	..	..	..	..	..	..	..	1,2[illegible]	981	221	103	44	59	..	..	..	133
		"	M.	1,530	[illegible],128	402	[illegible]11	231	110	..	..	..	215	157	58	..	..	..	..	..	..	..	..	..	941	726	196	63	1[illegible]	38	..	..	..	
		"	Cantt.	450	38[illegible]	62	[illegible]	32	15	..	..	..	42	41	1	..	..	..	..	..	..	..	..	..	2[illegible]1	25[illegible]	25	50	2[illegible]	21	..	..	..	
134	ATTOCK	Campbellpur	..	11,694	7,216	1,478	3,031	1,725	1,306	..	..	..	2,009	1,112	897	..	..	..	..	..	..	..	..	..	6,24[illegible]	4,076	2,170	409	303	106	..	..	..	134
		"	M.	7,097	4,029	2,968	2,012	1,157	855	..	..	..	1,711	940	771	..	..	..	..	..	..	..	..	..	4,1[illegible]7	2,[illegible]88	1,20[illegible]	87	43	44	..	..	..	
		"	Cantt.	3,09[illegible]	2,187	1,510	[illegible]88	5[illegible]	120	..	..	..	298	172	126	..	..	..	..	..	..	..	..	..	2,08[illegible]	1,187	902	322	260	62	..	..	..	
135		Hazro	M.	9,155	4,880	4,275	2,347	1,243	1,104	..	..	..	1,017	523	494	..	..	..	..	..	..	..	..	..	5,778	3,107	2,671	13	7	6	..	..	..	135
136		Hasanabdal	..	5,682	3,191	2,491	1,200	660	540	..	..	..	387	223	164	..	..	..	..	..	..	..	..	..	4,034	2,277	1,757	61	31	30	..	..	..	136
137		Attock	Cantt.	1,826	1,352	494	420	393	27	..	..	..	208	201	7	..	..	..	1	1	..	..	..	..	1,172	720	452	25	17	8	..	..	..	137
138		Pindigheb	M.	10,506	5,326	5,180	2,438	1,129	1,309	..	..	..	832	454	378	..	..	..	..	..	..	..	..	..	7,230	3,739	3,491	6	4	2	..	..	..	138
139		Talagang	..	7,146	3,599	3,547	1,494	748	746	..	..	..	767	378	389	..	..	..	..	..	..	..	..	..	4,882	2,472	2,410	3	1	2	..	..	..	139
140		Fatehjang	..	4,849	2,574	2,275	1,367	688	679	..	..	..	442	231	211	..	..	..	..	..	..	..	..	..	3,030	1,649	1,381	10	6	4	..	..	..	140
141	MIANWALI	Mianwali	..	15,412	8,804	6,608	5,946	3,255	2,691	..	..	..	429	256	173	4	2	2	..	..	..	..	..	..	8,84[illegible]	5,198	3,[illegible]47	188	93	95	..	..	..	141
		"	M.	1[illegible],107	7,[illegible]	[illegible],112	5,717	3,006	2,[illegible]71	..	..	..	303	202	161	4	2	2	..	..	..	..	..	..	7,[illegible]10	4,30[illegible]	[illegible]	18[illegible]	90	9[illegible]	..	..	..	
		"	L.	1,705	1,109	[illegible]	1[illegible]9	130	[illegible]	..	..	..	66	54	12	..	..	..	..	..	..	..	..	..	1,[illegible]	[illegible]0	142	5	3	2	..	..	..	
142		Bhakkar	..	6,857	3,751	3,106	3,[illegible]	[illegible]	[illegible]	..	..	..	60	27	92	..	..	..	..	..	..	..	..	..	3,161	1,703	1,368	..	..	..	..	..	..	142

TABLE V.—TOWNS ARRANGED TERRITORIALLY WITH POPULATION BY RELIGION—*concluded*.

Serial No.	District or State.	Towns, Municipalities, Suburbs, Cantonments, etc.	Population.			Hindu.			Ad-Dharami.			Sikh.			Jain.			Buddhist.			Zoroastrian.			Muslim.			Christian.			Jew.			Serial No.
			Persons.	Males.	Females.	Persons.	Males.	Females.	Persons.	Males.	Females.	Persons.	Males.	Females.	Persons.	Males.	Females.	Persons.	Males.	Females.	Persons.	Males.	Females.	Persons.	Males.	Females.	Persons.	Males.	Females.	Persons.	Males.	Females.	
	1	2	3	4	5	6	7	8	9	10	11	12	13	14	15	16	17	18	19	20	21	22	23	24	25	26	27	28	29	30	31	32	
143	MIANWALI	Isakhel	*7,515*	3,876	3,639	1,393	692	701	..	..	..	228	110	118	..	..	..	..	..	..	..	..	..	5,868	3,058	2,810	26	16	10	..	..	..	143
144		Kalabagh	*8,353*	4,476	3,877	1,151	594	557	..	..	..	59	36	23	13	7	6	..	..	..	..	..	..	7,096	3,821	3,275	34	18	16	..	..	..	144
145	MONTGOMERY	Montgomery M.	*26,164*	17,392	8,772	11,014	7,142	3,872	27	15	12	3,356	2,342	1,014	13	11	2	2	1	1	3	2	1	11,168	7,570	3,598	581	309	272	..	..	..	145
146		Chichawatni	*4,387*	2,851	1,536	2,144	1,406	738	226	148	78	440	286	154	1	1	..	..	..	..	..	..	..	1,538	992	546	38	18	20	..	..	..	146
147		Okara	*10,712*	6,925	3,787	5,218	3,500	1,718	50	30	20	1,604	983	621	..	..	..	..	..	..	3	3	..	3,666	2,324	1,342	171	85	86	..	..	..	147
148		Pakpattan .. M.	*11,311*	6,472	4,839	4,878	2,807	2,071	..	..	..	430	289	141	10	6	4	..	..	..	1	1	..	5,972	3,353	2,619	20	16	4	..	..	..	148
149	LYALLPUR ..	Lyallpur .. M.	*42,922*	27,489	15,433	19,992	12,880	7,112	155	95	60	5,181	3,243	1,938	65	47	18	..	..	..	7	7	..	15,534	10,115	5,419	1,988	1,102	886	..	..	..	149
150		Tandlianwala .	*6,105*	3,951	2,154	3,430	2,261	1,179	242	144	98	733	469	264	..	..	..	..	..	..	..	..	..	1,677	1,072	605	23	15	8	..	..	..	150
151		Toba Tek Singh ..	*5,903*	3,860	2,043	2,650	1,717	933	46	36	10	593	363	230	9	4	5	..	..	..	..	..	..	2,284	1,556	728	321	184	137	..	..	..	151
152		Gojra . M.	*9,779*	6,165	3,614	4,403	2,804	1,599	114	85	29	1,320	858	462	5	4	1	..	..	..	..	..	..	3,050	1,940	1,110	887	474	413	..	..	..	152
153		Kamalia .. M.	*13,220*	7,286	5,934	5,625	2,898	2,727	..	..	..	1,646	1,016	630	..	..	..	..	..	..	..	..	..	5,940	3,365	2,575	9	7	2	..	..	..	153
154		Jaranwala	*7,320*	4,778	2,542	3,921	2,573	1,348	61	38	23	1,008	667	341	1	1	..	..	..	..	..	..	..	2,216	1,432	784	113	67	46	..	..	..	154
155	JHANG ..	Jhang Maghiana M.	*36,035*	19,275	16,760	16,724	8,594	8,130	..	..	..	1,243	684	559	..	..	..	..	..	..	..	..	..	18,042	9,984	8,058	26	13	13	..	..	..	155
156		Chiniot .. M.	*25,841*	14,027	11,814	8,711	4,903	3,808	9	8	1	208	139	69	..	..	..	..	..	..	..	..	..	16,913	8,977	7,936	..	..	..	..	..	..	156
157		Lalian	*3,216*	1,709	1,507	1,363	707	656	6	3	3	59	36	23	..	..	..	..	..	..	..	..	..	1,778	960	818	10	3	7	..	..	..	157
158		Shorkot . ..	*6,826*	3,585	3,241	2,228	1,116	1,112	..	..	..	40	30	10	..	..	..	..	..	..	..	..	..	4,555	2,438	2,117	3	1	2	..	..	..	158
159		Ahmadpur .. .	*5,045*	2,603	2,442	2,038	987	1,051	..	..	..	47	28	19	..	..	..	..	..	..	..	..	..	2,960	1,588	1,372	..	..	..	..	..	..	159
160	MULTAN ..	Multan	*119,457*	68,119	51,338	40,424	22,585	17,839	1,575	925	650	2,960	1,828	1,132	424	211	213	..	..	..	117	71	46	72,134	41,221	30,913	1,823	1,278	545	..	..	..	160
		" .. M.	108,351	60,800	47,551	37,113	20,486	16,627	973	560	413	2,228	1,265	963	371	186	185	..	..	..	31	13	18	67,131	38,023	29,108	504	267	237	..	..	..	
		" . Cant.	11,106	7,319	3,787	3,311	2,099	1,212	602	365	237	732	563	169	53	25	28	..	..	..	86	58	28	5,003	3,198	1,805	1,319	1,011	308	..	..	..	
161		Shujabad .. M.	*6,618*	3,423	3,195	3,890	1,994	1,896	..	..	..	292	153	139	..	..	..	..	..	..	..	..	..	2,436	1,276	1,160	..	..	..	..	..	..	161
162		Khanewal	*11,205*	7,523	3,682	5,224	3,532	1,692	115	65	50	1,177	795	382	7	4	3	..	..	..	..	..	..	4,298	2,905	1,393	384	222	162	..	..	..	162
163	MUZAFFARGARH.	Muzaffargarh ..	*6,110*	3,616	2,494	2,505	1,464	1,041	..	..	..	337	205	132	..	..	..	..	..	..	..	..	..	3,111	1,865	1,246	157	82	75	..	..	..	163
		" . M.	5,853	3,439	2,414	2,452	1,431	1,021	..	..	.	332	200	132	..	..	...	..	..	.	..	...	...	2,938	1,740	1,198	131	68	63	..	..	..	
		" C. L.	257	177	80	53	33	20	...	..	..	5	5	...	..	..	..	..	...	..	..	.	...	173	125	48	26	14	12	..	..	..	
164		Khangarh .. M.	*2,863*	1,526	1,337	1,655	859	796	..	..	..	10	5	5	..	..	..	..	..	..	..	..	..	1,183	651	532	15	11	4	..	..	..	164
165		Alipur .. M.	*3,931*	2,046	1,885	2,290	1,166	1,124	..	..	..	6	3	3	..	..	..	..	..	..	..	..	..	1,635	877	758	..	..	..	..	..	..	165
166		Kot Adu	*4,925*	2,648	2,277	2,997	1,549	1,448	..	..	..	78	48	30	..	..	..	..	..	..	..	..	..	1,821	1,034	787	29	17	12	..	..	..	166
167		Leiah .. M.	*9,578*	5,014	4,564	3,952	2,014	1,938	..	..	..	11	8	3	..	..	..	..	..	..	..	..	..	5,615	2,992	2,623	..	..	..	..	..	..	167
168		Karor .. M.	*3,491*	1,813	1,678	1,912	983	929	..	..	..	37	18	19	..	..	..	..	..	..	..	..	..	1,542	812	730	..	..	..	..	..	..	168
169	*DERA GHAZI KHAN.	Dera Ghazi Khan M.	*23,468*	12,759	10,709	9,284	4,845	4,439	..	..	..	91	56	35	125	71	54	..	..	..	..	..	..	13,953	7,777	6,176	15	10	5	..	..	..	169
170		Kot Chhutta	*2,619*	1,410	1,209	1,320	687	633	..	..	..	5	4	1	..	..	..	..	..	..	..	..	..	1,294	719	575	..	..	..	..	..	..	170
171		Vehoa .. .	*3,089*	1,602	1,487	1,114	537	577	..	..	..	..	..	..	..	..	..	..	..	..	..	..	..	1,975	1,065	910	..	..	..	..	..	..	171
172		Taunsa	*7,506*	4,324	3,182	1,177	643	534	..	..	..	..	..	..	..	..	..	..	..	..	..	..	..	6,329	3,681	2,648	..	..	..	..	..	..	172
173		Rajanpur .. M.	*4,510*	2,533	1,977	1,505	761	744	..	..	..	37	26	11	..	..	..	..	..	..	..	..	..	2,967	1,745	1,222	1	1	..	..	..	..	173
174		Mithan Kot M.	*2,680*	1,399	1,281	1,172	581	591	..	..	..	6	3	3	.	..	..	..	..	..	..	..	..	1,502	815	687	..	..	..	..	..	..	174
175		Rojhan .. .	*4,424*	2,477	1,947	1,745	896	849	..	..	.	1	1	..	..	..	..	..	..	..	..	..	..	2,678	1,580	1,098	..	..	..	..	..	..	175
176		Jampur .. M.	*9,430*	5,163	4,267	3,424	1,743	1,681	..	..	..	36	20	16	..	..	..	..	..	..	..	..	..	5,955	3,392	2,563	15	8	7	..	..	..	176
177		Dajal .. M.	*6,186*	3,349	2,837	2,596	1,328	1,268	..	..	..	1	..	1	..	..	..	..	..	..	..	..	..	3,589	2,021	1,568	..	..	..	..	..	..	177

No.	State	Town																																No.
		PUNJAB STATES.		453,985	259,277	194,608	199,398	114,914	84,484	1,431	830	601	49,909	31,122	18,787	3,843	2,063	1,780	2	2	..	17	14	3	198,275	109,787	88,488	1,109	645	464	1	.	1	
		A.—HAVING POLITICAL RELATIONS WITH THE PUNJAB GOVERNMENT		14,534	7,907	6,627	7,718	4,227	3,491	..	..	..	475	278	197	207	107	100	..	..	..	..	..	..	6,125	3,289	2,836	9	6	3	..	..	..	
178	DUJANA ..	Dujana ..	..	1,561	816	745	1,549	809	740	..	..	..	..	..	..	..	..	..	..	..	..	..	..	..	12	7	5	..	..	..	..	..	..	178
179	PATAUDI ..	Pataudi ..	M.	3,667	1,882	1,785	1,689	856	833	..	..	..	1	1	..	69	32	37	..	..	..	..	..	..	1,905	991	914	3	2	1	..	..	..	179
180	KALSIA ..	Chachrauli	M.	5,124	2,986	2,138	2,890	1,719	1,171	..	..	..	247	152	95	22	12	10	..	..	..	..	..	..	1,959	1,099	860	6	4	2	..	..	..	180
181		Dera Bassi	M.	4,182	2,223	1,959	1,590	843	747	..	..	..	227	125	102	116	63	53	..	..	..	..	..	..	2,249	1,192	1,057	..	..	..	..	..	..	181
		B.—HAVING POLITICAL RELATIONS WITH THE GOVERNMENT OF INDIA.		439,451	251,470	187,981	191,680	110,687	80,993	1,431	830	601	49,434	30,844	18,590	3,636	1,956	1,680	2	2	..	17	14	3	192,150	106,498	85,652	1,100	639	461	1	..	1	
182	LOHARU ..	Loharu ..	..	2,956	1,572	1,384	1,299	711	588	..	..	..	2	2	..	13	5	8	..	..	..	..	..	..	1,641	854	787	1	..	1	..	..	..	182
183	SIRMOOR ..	Nahan ..	M.	6,859	3,976	2,883	5,056	2,979	2,077	..	..	..	249	146	103	48	36	12	..	..	..	..	..	..	1,466	797	669	40	18	22	..	..	..	183
184		Shamsherpur	..	949	608	341	842	543	299	..	..	..	3	3	..	..	..	..	..	..	..	..	..	..	97	59	38	7	3	4	..	..	..	184
185	BILASPUR ..	Bilaspur ..	..	2,387	1,427	960	2,194	1,319	875	..	..	..	9	5	4	..	..	..	..	..	..	..	..	..	178	101	77	6	2	4	..	..	..	185
186	MANDI ..	Mandi Nagar	M.	7,538	4,551	2,987	6,880	4,186	2,694	..	..	..	87	51	36	..	..	..	2	2	..	..	..	..	560	310	250	9	2	7	..	..	..	186
187		Jogindarnagar	..	5,963	4,592	1,371	3,774	2,744	1,030	..	..	..	364	268	96	..	..	..	..	..	..	..	..	..	1,734	1,518	216	90	62	28	1	..	1	187
188	SUKET ..	Sundar Nagar	..	2,401	1,362	1,039	2,306	1,305	1,001	..	..	..	19	14	5	..	..	..	..	..	..	..	..	..	75	42	33	1	1	..	..	..	..	188
189	KAPURTHALA	Kapurthala	M.	20,210	11,772	8,438	6,261	3,632	2,629	69	46	23	1,916	1,336	580	27	15	12	..	..	..	..	..	..	11,902	6,720	5,182	35	23	12	..	..	..	189
190		Sultanpur ..	M.	8,606	4,639	3,967	2,852	1,537	1,315	5	3	2	328	203	125	..	..	..	..	..	..	..	..	..	5,412	2,891	2,521	9	5	4	..	..	..	190
191		Phagwara ..	M.	12,049	6,741	5,308	6,379	3,612	2,767	545	310	235	1,090	627	463	..	..	..	..	..	..	..	..	..	4,032	2,190	1,842	3	2	1	..	..	..	191
192	MALERKOTLA	Malerkotla	..	25,240	14,173	11,067	5,246	3,018	2,228	..	..	..	269	196	73	1,240	674	566	..	..	..	..	..	..	18,449	10,261	8,188	36	24	12	..	..	..	192
		"	M.	22,396	12,230	10,166	4,601	2,637	1,964	...	...	...	202	137	65	1,236	670	566	...	...	...	...	...	...	16,326	8,765	7,561	31	21	10	..	...		
		"	C. L.	1,014	748	266	295	188	107		...	...	38	30	8	4		4	...	...	...	...	...	...	673	521	152	4	2	2	...	...	...	
		"	Cantt.	1,830	1,195	635	350	193	157	...	...		29	29	...	...	...	...	...	...	...	...	...	...	1,450	972	478	1	1	..	...	...	...	
193		Ahmadgarh ..	M.	3,283	2,035	1,248	2,222	1,343	879	..	..	..	355	251	104	45	25	20	..	..	..	..	..	..	625	394	231	36	22	14	..	..	..	193
194		Jamalpura ..	M.	2,942	1,571	1,371	361	192	169	..	..	..	272	136	136	..	..	..	..	..	..	..	..	..	2,309	1,243	1,066	..	..	..	..	..	..	194
195	FARIDKOT ..	Faridkot	M.	16,759	10,151	6,608	3,591	2,136	1,455	239	146	93	3,865	2,569	1,296	434	230	204	..	..	..	..	..	..	8,605	5,059	3,546	25	11	14	..	..	..	195
196		Kot Kapura	..	16,502	9,434	7,068	5,906	3,602	2,304	180	99	81	4,015	2,260	1,755	31	16	15	..	..	..	..	..	..	6,343	3,440	2,903	27	17	10	..	..	..	196
197	CHAMBA ..	Chamba	..	6,219	3,605	2,614	4,716	2,794	1,922	..	..	..	50	27	23	..	..	..	..	..	..	..	..	..	1,372	735	637	81	49	32	..	..	..	197
198	PATIALA ..	Patiala ..	M.	55,129	33,139	21,990	22,764	13,416	9,348	..	..	..	10,462	7,087	3,375	183	92	91	..	..	..	2	1	1	21,591	12,465	9,126	127	78	49	..	..	..	198
199		Sanaur ..	..	6,846	3,664	3,182	2,390	1,274	1,116	..	..	..	607	350	257	..	..	..	..	..	..	..	..	..	3,849	2,040	1,809	..	..	..	..	..	..	199
200		Sirhind ..	..	4,103	2,249	1,854	1,319	716	603	42	23	19	524	284	240	..	..	..	..	..	..	..	..	..	2,218	1,226	992	..	..	..	..	..	..	200
201		Basi ..	..	12,979	6,868	6,111	3,456	1,891	1,565	17	9	8	796	466	330	..	..	..	..	..	..	..	..	..	8,690	4,495	4,195	20	7	13	..	..	..	201
202		Sumana ..	..	10,563	5,610	4,953	2,728	1,447	1,281	..	..	..	39	36	3	214	123	91	..	..	..	..	..	..	7,561	3,994	3,567	21	10	11	..	..	..	202
203		Sunam ..	..	10,652	6,132	4,520	5,295	3,127	2,168	..	..	..	1,311	805	506	25	14	11	..	..	..	..	..	..	4,016	2,185	1,831	5	1	4	..	..	..	203
204		Barnala ..	..	8,915	5,182	3,733	4,125	2,419	1,706	150	77	73	2,402	1,438	964	96	48	48	..	..	..	..	..	..	2,135	1,195	940	7	5	2	..	..	..	204
205		Bhadaur ..	..	6,282	3,488	2,794	1,252	688	564	41	22	19	2,897	1,652	1,245	57	30	27	..	..	..	..	..	..	2,002	1,079	923	33	17	16	..	..	..	205
206		Bhatinda ..	..	22,771	13,575	9,196	11,026	6,553	4,473	115	74	41	3,598	2,255	1,343	60	35	25	..	..	..	..	..	..	7,743	4,523	3,220	229	135	94	..	..	..	206
207		Narnaul ..	..	21,905	11,270	10,635	12,605	6,662	5,943	..	..	..	52	39	13	238	122	116	..	..	..	..	..	..	9,002	4,440	4,562	8	7	1	..	..	..	207
208		Mohindargarh	..	9,194	4,552	4,642	5,029	2,600	2,429	..	..	..	14	10	4	35	14	21	..	..	..	..	..	..	4,110	1,928	2,188	..	..	..	..	..	..	208
209	JIND ..	Sangrur ..	M	13,901	8,564	5,337	6,412	4,030	2,382	..	..	..	2,390	1,579	820	115	61	54	..	..	..	..	..	..	4,911	2,853	2,058	64	41	23	..	..	..	209
210		Jind ..	.	11,699	6,610	5,089	6,604	3,818	2,786	..	..	..	131	85	46	227	123	104	..	..	..	..	..	..	4,596	2,507	2,089	141	77	64	..	..	..	210
211		Safidon ..	..	6,169	3,631	2,538	3,950	2,381	1,569	..	..	..	15	10	5	120	73	47	..	..	..	..	..	..	2,080	1,166	914	4	1	3	..	..	..	211
212		Dadri .	..	7,260	3,815	3,445	4,703	2,538	2,165	..	..	..	6	5	1	204	107	97	..	..	..	..	..	..	2,347	1,165	1,182	..	..	..	..	..	..	212
213	NABHA ..	Amloh ..	..	1,889	1,076	813	1,107	625	482	..	..	..	153	96	57	..	..	..	..	..	..	..	..	..	629	355	274	..	..	..	..	..	..	213
214		Nabha ..	.	17,311	10,055	7,256	7,225	4,206	3,019	6	6	..	2,771	1,787	984	180	90	90	..	..	..	..	..	..	7,124	3,962	3,162	5	4	1	..	..	..	214
215		Phul ..	..	6,836	3,915	2,921	3,806	2,177	1,629	..	..	..	1,967	1,129	838	..	..	..	..	..	..	..	..	..	1,063	609	454	..	..	..	..	..	..	215
216		Jaitu ..		8,542	4,832	3,710	3,998	2,282	1,716	..	..	..	2,674	1,516	1,158	42	21	21	..	..	..	..	..	..	1,827	1,012	815	1	1	..	..	..	..	216
217		Dhanaula .	..	7,521	4,084	3,437	1,765	962	803	..	..	..	3,264	1,793	1,471	..	..	..	..	..	..	..	..	..	2,492	1,329	1,163	..	..	..	..	..	..	217
218		Bawal ..	..	4,944	2,448	2,496	3,120	1,649	1,471	..	..	..	16	9	7	..	..	..	..	..	..	..	..	..	1,800	787	1,013	8	3	5	..	..	..	218
219	BAHAWALPUR	Bahawalnagar	.	6,707	4,166	2,541	3,433	2,056	1,377	22	15	7	318	223	95	2	2	..	..	..	..	13	11	2	2,910	1,855	1,055	9	4	5	..	..	..	219
220		Bahawalpur	.	20,943	11,809	9,134	7,166	4,030	3,136	..	..	.	29	26	3	..	..	..	..	..	..	1	1	..	13,735	7,745	5,990	12	7	5	..	..	..	220
221		Ahmadpur Sharqi		10,296	5,625	4,771	4,097	2,137	1,960	..	..	.	44	31	13	..	..	..	..	..	..	1	1	..	6,154	3,356	2,798	.	..	..	..	..	..	221
222		Khanpur ..	..	5,231	3,002	2,229	2,420	1,350	1,070	.	.	..	52	39	13	..	..	..	..	..	..	..	..	..	2,759	1,613	1,146	..	..	..	..	..	..	222

TABLE VI.

BIRTH-PLACE.

1. This Table is divided into four parts. Part A, the Provincial Summary, contains statistics of birth-place for the Province as a whole, as well as for British Territory and Punjab States. Part B gives the same information, for each District and State. Part C gives statistics of birth-place by Districts and States within the Province for the colony Districts of Gujranwala, Sheikhupura, Shahpur, Montgomery, Lyallpur, Jhang and Multan, and Bahawalpur State. Part D gives the information as in Part B, for selected towns and cities.

2. Throughout this Table the phrase " within British DOMINIONS," should be taken to mean, " within the British Empire and Mandated Territories except Iraq."

TABLE VI.—BIRTH-PLACE.

PROVINCIAL SUMMARY—PART A.

WHERE ENUMERATED.

WHERE BORN.	PUNJAB PROVINCE.			BRITISH TERRITORY.			PUNJAB STATES.		
	Persons.	Males.	Females.	Persons.	Males.	Females.	Persons.	Males.	Females.
PUNJAB ..	**28,490,857**	**15,561,194**	**12,929,663**	**23,580,852**	**12,880,510**	**10,700,342**	**4,910,005**	**2,680,684**	**2,229,321**
A. Born in India ..	**28,447,614**	**15,528,901**	**12,918,713**	**23,541,725**	**12,851,277**	**10,690,448**	**4,905,889**	**2,677,624**	**2,228,265**
PUNJAB ..	**27,816,705**	**15,217,586**	**12,599,119**	**23,021,126**	**12,588,397**	**10,432,729**	**4,795,579**	**2,629,189**	**2,166,390**
British Territory .	23,188,747	12,669,159	10,519,588	22,685,305	12,465,876	10,219,429	503,442	203,283	300,159
State ..	4,627,937	2,548,414	2,079,523	335,800	122,508	213,292	4,292,137	2,425,906	1,866,23
Punjab Unspecified ..	21	13	8	21	13	8	.	..	.
(a) BRITISH TERRITORY	**346,716**	**179,225**	**167,491**	**311,103**	**159,903**	**151,200**	**35,613**	**19,322**	**16,291**
Delhi .	*37,119*	13,616	23,503	33,065	11,873	21,192	4,054	1,743	2,311
Baluchistan ..	*4,063*	2,576	1,487	3,898	2,454	1,444	165	122	43
N. W. F. Province ..	*52,773*	33,151	19,622	50,046	31,331	18,715	2,727	1,820	907
U. P. of Agra and Oudh	*231,122*	118,054	113,068	205,839	104,344	101,495	25,283	13,710	11,573
Ajmere Merwara ..	*931*	447	484	753	386	367	178	61	117
Andamans & Nicobars	*106*	69	36	104	69	35	1	..	1
Assam .	*314*	146	168	306	141	165	8	5	3
Bengal .	*4,618*	2,445	2,173	4,320	2,286	2,034	298	159	139
Bihar and Orissa ..	*1,275*	558	717	1,150	482	668	125	76	49
Bombay ..	*8,503*	4,994	3,509	6,419	3,789	2,630	2,084	1,205	879
Aden ..	*17*	*7*	*10*	*16*	*7*	*9*	*1*	..	*1*
Burma ..	*2,047*	1,167	880	1,852	1,039	813	195	128	67
C. P. and Berar ..	*2,288*	994	1,294	1,904	768	1,136	384	226	158
Madras ..	*1,558*	1,008	550	1,447	941	506	111	67	44
(b) STATES ..	**283,318**	**131,662**	**151,656**	**208,654**	**102,571**	**106,083**	**74,664**	**29,091**	**45,573**
Baluchistan States .	*2*	2	..	.	..	..	2	2	..
U. P. States .	*990*	465	525	698	298	400	292	167	125
Jammu and Kashmir State ..	*79,691*	46,342	33,349	75,028	42,797	32,231	4,663	3,545	1,118
Rajputana Agency ..	*199,214*	83,125	116,089	130,154	58,100	72,054	69,060	25,025	44,035
Assam States ..	*8*	2	6	7	2	5	1	..	1
Baroda State ..	*143*	83	60	127	74	53	16	9	7
Bihar & Orissa States.	*6*	3	3	6	3	3	..	.	.
Bombay States .	*108*	73	35	84	49	35	24	24	.
C. I. Agency ..	*331*	185	146	228	114	114	103	71	32
C. P. States .	*131*	61	70	129	59	70	2	2	.
Gwalior State ..	*1,560*	736	824	1,182	541	641	378	195	183
Hyderabad State ..	*797*	373	424	707	332	375	90	41	49
Madras States ..	44	12	32	14	12	32	..	.	..
Travancore State ..	*1*	..	*1*	*1*	..	*1*	..	..	.
Mysore State .	*293*	200	93	260	190	70	33	10	23
INDIA UNSPECIFIED ..	**842**	**405**	**437**	**831**	**401**	**430**	**11**	**4**	**7**
FRENCH SETTLEMENT	**1**	..	**1**	..	..	..	**1**	.	**1**
PORTUGUESE SETTLEMENT.	**32**	**23**	**9**	**11**	**5**	**6**	**21**	**18**	**3**
B. Asia Beyond India ..	**24,916**	**18,522**	**6,394**	**21,261**	**15,710**	**5,551**	**3,655**	**2,812**	**843**
Inside British Dominions. ..	*205*	116	89	184	98	86	21	18	3
Outside British Dominions. ..	*24,665*	18,396	6,269	21,073	15,611	5,462	3,592	2,785	807
Asia Unspecified ..	*46*	10	36	4	1	3	42	9	33
C. Europe ..	**16,989**	**13,110**	**3,879**	**16,832**	**13,022**	**3,810**	**157**	**88**	**69**
Inside British Dominions. ..	*15,589*	12,450	3,139	15,450	12,370	3,080	139	80	59
Outside British Dominions. ..	*193*	113	80	175	105	70	18	8	10
Europe Unspecified ..	*1,207*	547	660	1,207	547	660	.	.	..
D. Africa ..	**657**	**366**	**291**	**631**	**350**	**281**	**26**	**16**	**10**
Outside British Dominions. .	*38*	25	13	38	25	13	..	..	
Africa Unspecified ..	*619*	341	278	593	325	268	26	16	10
E. America .	**319**	**126**	**193**	**298**	**112**	**186**	**21**	**14**	**7**
Inside British Dominions. .	*25*	8	17	23	7	16	2	1	1
Outside British Dominions. ..	*9*	..	9	9	..	9	..	..	..
America Unspecified ..	*285*	118	167	266	105	161	19	13	6
F. Australasia ..	**121**	**45**	**76**	**105**	**39**	**66**	**16**	**6**	**10**
Inside British Dominions. ..	*121*	45	76	105	39	66	16	6	10
Birth-Place Not Returned ..	**241**	**124**	**117**	..	..	..	**241**	**124**	**117**

TABLE VI.—BIRTH-PLACE.—PART B.

PROVINCE, DISTRICT OR STATE WHERE ENUMERATED.

District, State, Province or Country where born	Population of Province or State. Persons.	Males.	Females.	Hissar. Persons.	Males.	Females.	Rohtak. Persons.	Males.	Females.	Gurgaon. Persons.	Males.	Females.	Karnal. Persons.	Males.	Females.	Ambala. Persons.	Males.	Females.	Simla. Persons.	Males.	Females.
1	2	3	4	5	6	7	8	9	10	11	12	13	14	15	16	17	18	19	20	21	22
A.—DISTRICTS OR STATES WITHIN THE PROVINCE																					
(I) BRITISH TERRITORY ..	*23,188,747*	12,669,159	10,519,588	830,199	461,356	368,843	747,956	418,098	329,858	654,471	376,999	277,472	795,543	450,643	344,900	677,627	386,484	291,143	26,720	16,153	10,567
District of Enumeration ..	*20,443,989*	11,314,478	9,129,511	787,006	445,881	341,125	705,816	407,734	298,082	642,188	373,191	268,997	746,371	433,620	312,751	621,243	360,294	260,949	19,508	10,643	8,865
(II) PUNJAB STATES ..	*4,627,937*	2,548,414	2,079,523	34,677	9,986	24,691	22,056	4,513	17,543	8,332	1,600	6,732	26,773	7,333	19,440	29,626	10,550	19,076	4,023	2,583	1,440
State of Enumeration ..	*4,107,902*	2,366,341	1,741,561																		
(III) PUNJAB UNSPECIFIED	*21*	13	8	21	13	8	.	..	.	..	.	.	..	..	.	.	..	..	..	..	..
TOTAL A. ..	**27,816,705**	**15,217,586**	**12,599,119**	**864,897**	**471,355**	**393,542**	**770,012**	**422,611**	**347,401**	**662,803**	**378,599**	**284,204**	**822,316**	**457,976**	**364,340**	**707,253**	**397,034**	**310,219**	**30,743**	**18,736**	**12,007**
B.—PROVINCES OR STATES IN INDIA BEYOND THE PROVINCE.																					
(a).—Provinces or States adjacent to the Province																					
(I)—BRITISH TERRITORY																					
Delhi ..	*37,119*	13,616	23,503	1,103	533	570	14,314	3,424	10,890	6,295	2,077	4,218	1,478	606	872	1,047	542	505	131	80	51
Baluchistan ..	*4,063*	2,576	1,487	11	8	3	33	22	11	30	27	3	16	13	3	69	46	23	16	7	9
N. W. F. Province ..	*52,773*	33,151	19,622	35	25	10	62	45	17	40	25	15	99	78	21	777	596	181	58	34	24
U. P. of Agra and Oudh ..	*231,122*	118,054	113,068	4,005	2,049	1,956	16,890	5,382	11,508	33,548	8,203	25,345	26,935	10,158	16,777	27,910	14,108	13,808	3,204	2,553	651
Total (I) ..	**325,077**	**167,397**	**157,680**	**5,154**	**2,615**	**2,539**	**31,299**	**8,873**	**22,426**	**39,913**	**10,332**	**29,581**	**28,528**	**10,855**	**17,673**	**29,809**	**15,292**	**14,517**	**3,409**	**2,674**	**735**
(II)—FEUDATORY STATES																					
Baluchistan States ..	*21*	2	.	..	..	..	..	..	..	..	.	..	..	.	..	..	..	..	..	..	..
United Provinces States ..	*990*	465	525	20	3	17	..	..	..	..	..	..	..	..	..	47	44	3	..	..	..
Jammu & Kashmir State ..	*79,691*	46,342	33,349	22	15	7	6	3	3	12	11	1	27	21	6	385	289	96	1,004	971	33
Rajputana Agency ..	*199,214*	83,125	116,089	28,875	11,422	17,453	3,947	1,182	2,765	36,415	9,166	27,249	1,413	822	591	1,925	1,278	647	60	43	17
Jaisalmer ..	*5,216*	2,802	2,414	..	..	..	..	..	..	..	..	..	..	..	..	.	..	.	.	.	..
Bikaner ..	*33,819*	17,851	15,968	..	..	..	..	..	..	..	..	..	..	..	..	..	..	.	.	..	..
Alwar ..	*21,135*	7,947	13,188	..	..	..	..	..	..	..	..	..	..	.	..	.	.	.	..	..	..
Jaipur ..	*43,808*	19,087	24,721	..	..	..	..	..	..	..	..	..	..	.	..	3	.	3	..	..	..
Bharatpur ..	*942*	521	421	..	..	..	..	..	..	..	..	..	..	.	..	2	1	r	..	..	..
Other States ..	*94,294*	34,917	59,377	28,875	11,422	17,453	3,947	1,182	2,765	36,415	9,166	27,249	1,413	822	591	2	1	1	..	..	..
																1,918	1,276	642	60	43	17
Total (II) ..	**279,897**	**129,934**	**149,963**	**28,917**	**11,440**	**17,477**	**3,953**	**1,185**	**2,768**	**36,427**	**9,177**	**27,250**	**1,440**	**843**	**597**	**2,357**	**1,611**	**746**	**1,064**	**1,014**	**50**
TOTAL (a) ..	**604,974**	**297,331**	**307,648**	**34,071**	**14,055**	**20,016**	**35,252**	**10,058**	**25,194**	**76,340**	**19,509**	**56,831**	**29,968**	**11,698**	**18,270**	**32,166**	**16,903**	**15,263**	**4,473**	**3,688**	**785**
(b).—Other Provinces and States in India.																					
(I) BRITISH TERRITORY																					
Ajmer Marwara ..	*931*	447	484	82	46	36	28	12	16	225	87	138	3	3	.	35	19	16	..	.	..
Andamans and Nicobars ..	*105*	69	36	1	1	..	1	1	..	.	..	..	1	.	1	4	3	1	..	..	..
Assam ..	*314*	146	168	16	5	11	.	..	.	1	..	1	1	..	1	2	1	1	7	6	1
Bengal ..	*4,618*	2,445	2,173	103	55	48	40	20	20	45	23	22	68	43	25	297	189	108	290	171	119
Bihar and Orissa ..	*1,275*	558	717	33	16	17	25	8	17	17	10	7	5	5	..	61	27	34	37	22	15

Bombay	8,503	4,994	3,509	96	58	38	63	39	24	137	81	56	35	23	12	316	189	127	118	82	36
Aden	17	7	10	1		..		..	6	4	2	1		1	1		1		..	..	..
Burma	2,047	1,167	880	16	7	9	10	6	4	17	11	6	4	2	2	66	42	24	12	6	6
Central Provinces and Berar	2,288	991	1,294	11	8	3	38	14	24	245	43	202	13	6	7	120	70	50	11	3	8
Madras	1,558	1,008	550	4	2	2	4	3	1	61	34	27	6	1	5	92	52	40	59	30	29
Total (I)	21,639	11,828	9,811	362	198	164	209	108	106	748	289	459	136	83	53	993	592	401	534	320	214
(II) FEUDATORY STATES																					
Assam States	8	2	6	..	..	..	..	..	..	..	..	..	..	..	..	..	..	..	..	..	..
Baroda State	143	83	60	10	7	3	1	..	1	6	5	1	1	1	..	13	5	8	..	..	..
Bihar and Orissa States	6	3	3	..	..	..	..	..	..	..	..	..	..	..	..	..	..	..	..	..	..
Bombay States	108	73	35	..	..	..	..	..	..	..	..	..	..	..	..	2	..	2	..	..	..
Central India Agency	331	185	146	9	3	6	25	15	10	27	8	19	28	10	18	14	4	10	11	11	..
Central Provinces States	131	61	70	3	3	..	..	..	..	..	..	..	..	..	..	..	..	..	..	..	..
Gwalior State	1,560	736	824	41	9	32	31	15	16	170	58	112	56	34	22	91	61	30	19	15	4
Hyderabad State	797	373	424	12	7	5	26	9	17	20	13	7	32	13	19	37	21	16	3	2	1
Madras States (Including Cochin and Travancore).	44	12	32	..	..	..	..	..	..	..	..	..	..	..	..	..	..	..	..	..	..
Travancore State	1	1																			
Mysore State	293	200	93	2	1	1	..	..	..	..	..	..	5	5	..	20	9	11	6	4	2
Total (II)	3,421	1,728	1,693	77	30	47	83	39	44	223	84	139	122	63	59	177	100	77	39	32	7
TOTAL (*b*)	25,060	13,556	11,504	439	228	211	292	142	150	971	373	598	258	146	112	1,170	692	478	573	352	221
(c) INDIA UNSPECIFIED	842	405	437	..	..	..	..	..	..	3	3	..	..	..	..	90	35	55	..	..	..
(d) FRENCH AND PORTUGUESE SETTLEMENTS — French	1	..	1	..	..	..	..	..	..	..	..	..	..	..	..	..	..	..	..	..	..
(d) FRENCH AND PORTUGUESE SETTLEMENTS — Portuguese	32	23	9	..	..	..	..	..	..	..	..	..	..	..	..	..	..	..	..	..	..
TOTAL B.	630,909	311,315	319,594	34,510	14,283	20,227	35,544	10,200	25,344	77,314	19,885	57,429	30,226	11,844	18,382	33,426	17,630	15,796	5,046	4,040	1,006
Total A and B (Born in India)	28,447,614	15,528,901	12,918,713	899,407	485,638	413,769	805,556	432,811	372,745	740,117	398,484	341,633	352,542	469,820	382,722	740,679	414,664	326,015	35,789	22,776	13,013
C.—COUNTRIES IN ASIA BEYOND INDIA.																					
(I) INSIDE BRITISH DOMINIONS.																					
Ceylon	63	39	14	1	1	..	2	2	..	1	1	..	1	1	..	1	..	1	3	1	2
Hong Kong	13	6	7	..	..	..	1	1	..	..	..	..	..	..	..	..	..	..	..	..	..
Straits Settlements and Malaya	139	71	68	1	1	..	..	..	..	..	..	..	..	..	..	..	..	..	..	..	..
Total (I)	205	116	89	2	2	..	3	3	..	1	1	..	1	1	..	1	..	1	3	1	2
(II) OUTSIDE BRITISH DOMINIONS.																					
Afghanistan	14,854	11,020	3,834	19	18	1	18	17	1	9	8	1	16	14	2	36	30	6	64	54	..
Arabia	372	289	83	11	11	..	..	..	..	5	3	2	..	..	..	24	16	8	3	1	2
Bhotan	20	10	10	..	..	..	..	..	..	..	..	..	..	..	..	..	..	..	..	..	..
China	963	559	404	3	..	3	..	..	..	..	..	..	..	..	..	8	6	2	..	..	..
French Indo-China	1	..	1	..	..	..	..	..	..	..	..	..	..	..	..	..	..	..	..	..	..
Iraq	49	38	11	..	..	..	..	..	..	..	..	..	..	..	..	..	..	..	..	..	..
Japan	17	16	1	..	..	..	..	..	..	..	..	..	..	..	..	1	..	1	2	..	2
Java	14	7	7	..	..	..	..	..	..	..	..	..	1	1	..	..	..	..	..	..	..
Nepal	6,922	5,364	1,558	14	13	1	15	13	2	2	1	1	32	23	9	148	127	21	74	64	10
Persia	441	301	140	..	..	..	1	1	..	1	1	..	..	..	..	6	4	2	1	..	1
Philippine Islands	1	1	..	..	..	..	..	..	..	..	..	..	..	..	..	..	..	..	..	..	..
Russia in Asia	2	1	1	..	..	..	..	..	..	..	..	..	..	..	..	..	..	..	..	..	..
Russian Turkistan	3	2	1	..	..	..	..	..	..	..	..	..	..	..	..	..	..	..	..	..	..
Siam	4	2	2	..	..	..	..	..	..	..	..	..	..	..	..	..	..	..	1	..	1

TABLE VI.—BIRTH-PLACE.—PART B—*continued.*

PROVINCE, DISTRICT OR STATE WHERE ENUMERATED.

District, State, Province or Country where born.	Population of Province or State.			Hissar.			Rohtak.			Gurgaon.			Karnal.			Ambala.			Simla.		
	Persons.	Males.	Females.	Persons.	Males.	Females.	Persons.	Males.	Females.	Persons.	Males.	Females.	Persons.	Males.	Females.	Persons.	Males.	Females.	Persons.	Males.	Females.
1	2	3	4	5	6	7	8	9	10	11	12	13	14	15	16	17	18	19	20	21	22
Sumatra	*14*	11	3	..	..	..	..	..	..	..	..	..	..	..	..	..	..	..	..	..	..
Syria	*1*	1	..	..	..	..	..	..	..	..	..	..	..	..	..	..	..	..	..	..	..
Tibet	*878*	682	196	..	..	..	..	..	..	..	..	..	..	..	..	5	5	..	433	381	52
Turkey in Asia	*90*	77	13	..	..	..	..	..	..	..	..	..	..	..	..	1	1	..	..	..	..
Turkistan Unspecified	*19*	15	4	..	..	..	1	1	..	..	..	..	..	..	..	..	..	..	..	..	..
Total (II)	24,665	18,396	6,269	47	42	5	35	32	3	17	13	4	49	38	11	229	189	40	568	500	68
(III) ASIA UNSPECIFIED	*46*	10	36	..	..	..	3	..	3	..	..	..	..	..	..	..	..	..	..	..	..
TOTAL C.	24,916	18,522	6,394	49	44	5	41	35	6	18	14	4	50	39	11	230	189	41	571	501	70
D.—COUNTRIES IN EUROPE																					
(I) INSIDE BRITISH DOMINIONS.																					
England and Wales	*14,430*	11,705	2,725	15	6	9	5	2	3	20	9	11	17	9	8	1,767	1,450	317	328	193	135
Gibraltar	*4*	..	4	..	..	..	..	..	..	..	..	..	..	..	..	4	..	4	..	..	..
Irish Free States	*35*	27	8	..	..	..	..	..	..	..	..	..	..	..	..	22	17	5	..	..	..
Malta	*4*	2	2	..	..	..	..	..	..	..	..	..	..	..	..	2	..	2	..	..	..
Northern Ireland	*563*	376	187	..	..	..	3	..	3	2	1	1	..	..	..	23	14	9	31	18	13
Scotland	*550*	339	211	3	..	3	2	2	..	..	..	..	2	1	1	85	34	51	25	12	13
United Kingdom Unspecified	*3*	1	2	..	..	..	..	..	..	..	..	..	..	..	..	..	..	..	..	..	..
Total (I)	15,589	12,450	3,139	18	6	12	10	4	6	22	10	12	19	10	9	1,903	1,515	388	384	223	161
(II) OUTSIDE BRITISH DOMINIONS.																					
Austria	*1*	1	..	..	..	..	..	..	..	..	..	..	..	..	..	..	..	..	..	..	..
Belgium	*45*	24	21	..	..	..	..	..	..	..	..	..	..	..	..	5	3	2	..	..	..
Denmark	*1*	1	..	..	..	..	..	..	..	..	..	..	..	..	..	..	..	..	..	..	..
France	*34*	10	24	..	..	..	..	..	..	..	..	..	..	..	..	2	..	2	..	..	..
Germany	*38*	21	17	..	..	..	..	..	..	..	..	..	..	..	..	8	3	5	..	..	..
Greece	*1*	1	..	..	..	..	..	..	..	..	..	..	..	..	..	..	..	..	..	..	..
Holland	*2*	..	2	..	..	..	..	..	..	..	..	..	..	..	..	..	..	..	..	..	..
Italy	*5*	2	3	..	..	..	..	..	..	..	..	..	..	..	..	1	1	..	..	..	..
Latvia	*1*	1	..	..	..	..	..	..	..	..	..	..	..	..	..	..	..	..	..	..	..
Norway	*1*	..	1	..	..	..	..	..	..	..	..	..	..	..	..	..	..	..	..	..	..
Portugal	*8*	6	2	..	..	..	..	..	..	1	1	..	..	..	..	..	..	..	..	..	..
Rumania	*2*	1	1	..	..	..	..	..	..	..	..	..	..	..	..	..	..	..	..	..	..
Russian Union	*7*	4	3	..	..	..	..	..	..	..	..	..	..	..	..	..	..	..	..	..	..
Spain	*4*	3	1	..	..	..	..	..	..	..	..	..	..	..	..	..	..	..	..	..	..
Sweden	*3*	..	3	..	..	..	..	..	..	..	..	..	..	..	..	..	..	..	..	..	..
Switzerland	*3*	3	..	..	..	..	..	..	..	..	..	..	..	..	..	..	..	..	..	..	..
Turkey in Europe	*37*	35	2	..	..	..	..	..	..	..	..	..	..	..	..	..	..	..	..	..	..
Total (II)	193	113	80	..	..	..	..	..	..	1	1	..	..	..	..	16	7	9	..	..	..

(III) EUROPE UNSPECIFIED	*1,207*	547	660	.	..	..	..	..	..	..	..	..	..	..	..	..	..	..	15	7	8
TOTAL D. ..	**16,989**	**13,110**	**3,879**	**18**	**6**	**12**	**10**	**4**	**6**	**23**	**11**	**12**	**19**	**10**	**9**	**1,919**	**1,522**	**397**	**399**	**230**	**169**
E.—COUNTRIES IN AFRICA																					
(I) OUTSIDE BRITISH DOMINIONS.																					
Egypt ..	*38*	25	13	..	..	..	..	..	..	..	..	..	..	..	..	13	8	5	..	..	..
(II) AFRICA UNSPECIFIED	*619*	341	278	1	1	..	11	4	7	1	1	..	1	1	..	23	11	12	8	2	6
TOTAL E. ..	**657**	**366**	**291**	**1**	**1**	..	**11**	**4**	**7**	**1**	**1**	..	**1**	**1**	..	**36**	**19**	**17**	**8**	**2**	**6**
F.—COUNTRIES IN AMERICA																					
(I) INSIDE BRITISH DOMINIONS.																					
British Guiana ..	*1*	..	1	..	..	..	..	..	..	..	..	..	1	..	1	..	..	..	..	..	..
Canada ..	*24*	8	16	..	.	..	..	..	..	..	..	..	..	..	..	2	..	2	..	..	..
Total (I) ..	25	8	17	..	..	..	..	..	..	..	..	..	1	..	1	2	..	2	..	..	..
(II) OUTSIDE BRITISH DOMINIONS.																					
United States ..	*9*	..	9	..	..	..		..	..	..	..	..	..	..	..	..	..	..	..	..	..
(III) AMERICA UNSPECIFIED.	*285*	118	167	4	1	3	2	..	2	4	3	1	1	..	1	20	13	7	6	3	3
TOTAL F. ..	**319**	**126**	**193**	**4**	**1**	**3**	**2**	..	**2**	**4**	**3**	**1**	**2**	..	**2**	**22**	**13**	**9**	**6**	**3**	**3**
G.—COUNTRIES IN AUSTRALASIA																					
(I) INSIDE BRITISH DOMINIONS.																					
Australia ..	*83*	33	50	.	..	..	1	1	..	..	..	..	..	..	..	4	2	2	13	5	8
Fiji Islands ..	*21*	8	13	..	..	..	..	..	..	..	..	..	..	..	..	1	.	1	..	..	..
New Zealand ..	*15*	4	11	..	..	..	..	..	..	..	..	..	..	..	..	11	2	9	..	..	..
Elsewhere in British Australasia	*2*	..	2	..	..	..	..	..	..	..	..	..	..	..	..	..	..	..	..	..	..
Total (I)	**121**	**45**	**76**	..	..	..	**1**	**1**	..	..	..	..	..	..	..	**16**	**4**	**12**	**13**	**5**	**8**
TOTAL G. ..	**121**	**45**	**76**	..	..	..	**1**	**1**	..	..	..	..	..	..	.	**16**	**4**	**12**	**13**	**5**	**8**
TOTAL RETURNED ..	**28,490,616**	**15,561,070**	**12,929,546**	**899,479**	**485,690**	**413,789**	**805,621**	**432,855**	**372,766**	**740,163**	**398,513**	**341,650**	**852,614**	**469,870**	**382,744**	**742,902**	**416,411**	**326,491**	**36,786**	**23,517**	**13,269**
Birth-place not Returned ..	**241**	**124**	**117**	..	..	..	..	..	..	..	..	..	..	..	..	..	..	..	..	..	..
TOTAL POPULATION. ..	**28,490,857**	**15,561,194**	**12,929,663**	**899,479**	**485,690**	**413,789**	**805,621**	**432,855**	**372,766**	**740,163**	**398,513**	**341,650**	**852,614**	**469,870**	**382,744**	**742,902**	**416,411**	**326,491**	**36,786**	**23,517**	**13,269**

TABLE VI.—BIRTH-PLACE.—PART B—*continued*.

District, State, Province or Country where born.	Kangra. Persons. 23	Kangra. Males. 24	Kangra. Females. 25	Hoshiarpur. Persons. 26	Hoshiarpur. Males. 27	Hoshiarpur. Females. 28	Jullundur. Persons. 29	Jullundur. Males. 30	Jullundur. Females. 31	Ludhiana. Persons. 32	Ludhiana. Males. 33	Ludhiana. Females. 34	Ferozepore. Persons. 35	Ferozepore. Males. 36	Ferozepore. Females. 37	Lahore. Persons. 38	Lahore. Males. 39	Lahore. Females. 40	Amritsar. Persons. 41	Amritsar. Males. 42	Amritsar. Females. 43
	Province, District or State where Enumerated.																				
A.—Districts or States within the Province																					
(I) BRITISH TERRITORY ..	*784,984*	406,150	378,834	1,020,901	548,055	472,846	915,817	503,346	412,471	613,083	354,621	258,462	1,055,069	589,324	465,745	1,297,261	736,520	560,741	1,090,283	605,065	485,218
District of Enumeration ..	*767,164*	398,042	369,122	967,464	530,397	437,067	840,965	476,571	364,394	551,698	325,335	226,363	969,093	545,585	423,508	1,072,220	605,230	466,990	989,036	565,507	423,529
(II) PUNJAB STATES ..	*11,379*	5,763	5,616	8,205	2,476	5,729	21,656	5,850	15,806	51,878	16,629	35,249	57,141	21,317	35,824	6,957	4,425	2,532	12,907	7,468	5,439
State of Enumeration ..	..	..	..	..	..	..	..	..	..	..	..	..	..	..	..	..	..	..	..	..	..
(III) PUNJAB UNSPECIFIED	..	..	..	..	..	..	..	..	..	..	..	..	..	..	..	..	..	..	..	..	..
TOTAL A. ..	**796,363**	**411,913**	**384,450**	**1,029,106**	**550,531**	**478,575**	**937,473**	**509,196**	**428,277**	**864,961**	**371,250**	**493,711**	**1,112,210**	**610,641**	**501,569**	**1,304,218**	**740,945**	**563,273**	**1,103,190**	**612,533**	**490,657**
B.—Provinces or States in India beyond the Province.																					
(a).—Provinces or States Adjacent to the Province																					
(I)—BRITISH TERRITORY																					
Delhi ..	*45*	15	30	285	95	190	308	68	240	366	153	213	661	350	311	2,963	1,784	1,179	219	54	165
Baluchistan ..	*8*	4	4	63	31	32	86	38	48	16	10	6	14	10	4	415	301	114	141	84	57
N. W. F. Province ..	*215*	186	29	177	113	64	350	196	154	286	222	64	3,109	1,688	1,421	7,788	5,455	2,333	1,214	639	575
U. P. of Agra and Oudh ..	*585*	437	148	1,275	461	814	2,509	1,272	1,237	4,449	2,685	1,764	10,524	6,453	4,071	31,889	23,023	8,866	7,157	4,480	2,677
Total (I) ..	853	642	211	1,800	700	1,100	3,253	1,574	1,679	5,117	3,070	2,047	14,308	8,501	5,807	43,055	30,563	12,492	8,761	5,257	3,504
(II)—FEUDATORY STATES																					
Baluchistan States ..	..	..	..	..	..	..	..	..	..	..	..	..	..	..	..	..	..	..	..	..	..
United Provinces States ..	*28*	11	17	6	5	1	7	..	7	35	23	12	..	..	..	314	128	186	1	1	..
Jammu & Kashmir State ..	*1,691*	1,130	561	313	178	135	381	267	114	135	74	61	308	240	68	9,075	7,621	1,454	587	452	135
Rajputana Agency ..	*230*	*138*	*92*	*324*	*155*	*169*	*360*	*162*	*198*	*827*	*446*	*381*	27,415	15,232	12,183	10,194	6,880	3,314	1,403	985	418
Jaisalmer ..	..	..	..	..	..	..	..	..	..	44	..	44	..	..	..	27	1	26	..	..	..
Bikaner ..	2	2	..	135	40	95	68	30	38	279	149	130	13,510	7,129	6,381	514	279	235	258	212	46
Alwar ..	7	4	3	14	7	7	29	14	15	60	33	27	3,350	1,802	1,548	1,481	1,060	421	..	..	..
Jaipur ..	125	75	50	111	61	50	3	3	..	137	58	79	5,810	3,462	2,348	7,358	5,112	2,246	46	45	1
Bharatpur ..	9	9	..	3	1	2	4	1	3	43	16	27	31	6	25	108	57	51	17	16	1
Other States ..	87	48	39	61	46	15	256	114	142	264	190	74	4,714	2,833	1,881	706	371	335	1,082	712	370
Total (II) ..	1,949	1,279	670	643	338	305	748	429	319	997	543	454	27,723	15,472	12,251	19,583	14,629	4,954	1,991	1,433	558
TOTAL (a) ..	2,802	1,921	881	2,443	1,038	1,405	4,001	2,003	1,998	6,114	3,613	2,501	42,031	23,973	18,058	62,638	45,192	17,446	10,752	6,695	4,057
(b).—Other Provinces and States in India.																					
(I) BRITISH TERRITORY																					
Ajmer Marwara ..	7	5	2	..	..	..	10	5	5	4	..	4	6	..	6	176	117	59	50	27	23
Andamans and Nicobars ..	2	1	1	1	..	1	..	..	..	..	..	..	5	4	1	26	19	7	21	13	8
Assam ..	*5*	3	2	3	2	*1*	9	3	6	97	13	84	..	..	..	65	48	17	41	16	25
Bengal ..	*30*	19	11	73	24	49	225	67	158	117	44	73	164	52	112	1,311	885	426	409	129	280
Bihar and Orissa ..	2	2	..	10	3	7	7	2	5	47	23	24	51	25	26	117	91	26	216	48	168

Bombay	*38*	20	18	173	86	87	172	82	90	139	70	69	256	168	88	1,634	1,074	560	544	346	198
Aden	*1*	1	..	..	..	..	..	..	..	..	..	..	..	..	..	1	..	1	..	..	..
Burma	*24*	11	13	72	40	32	153	52	101	216	129	87	175	123	52	203	124	79	278	159	119
Central Provinces and Berar	*14*	7	7	56	7	49	101	42	59	74	17	57	29	24	5	233	165	68	274	49	225
Madras	*21*	19	2	6	2	4	43	21	22	226	188	38	59	44	15	462	308	154	46	25	17
Total (I)	143	87	56	394	164	230	720	274	446	920	484	436	745	440	305	4,227	2,831	1,396	1,879	816	1,063
(II) FEUDATORY STATES																					
Assam States	..	..	..	..	..	..	..	..	..	..	..	..	..	..	..	7	2	5	..	..	..
Baroda State	..	..	..	4	2	2	..	..	..	..	..	..	2	2	..	40	27	13	9	3	6
Bihar and Orissa States	..	..	..	..	..	..	..	..	..	..	..	..	..	..	..	1	1	..	..	..	..
Bombay States	..	..	..	1	..	1	..	..	..	..	..	..	..	..	..	46	31	15	..	..	..
Central India Agency	*1*	1	..	..	..	..	1	..	1	..	..	..	6	1	5	26	24	2	15	13	2
Central Provinces States	..	..	..	33	12	21	4	..	4	29	14	15	..	..	..	51	23	28	..	..	..
Gwalior State	*13*	6	7	57	11	46	21	10	11	48	21	27	124	50	74	165	102	63	49	25	24
Hyderabad State	*2*	2	..	11	6	5	132	43	89	46	15	31	55	26	29	157	100	57	33	16	17
Madras States (Including Cochin and Travancore).	..	..	..	..	..	..	..	..	..	30	4	26	..	..	..	13	8	5	..	..	..
Travancore State	..	..	..	..	..	..	..	..	..	..	..	..	..	..	..	..	..	..	..	..	..
Mysore State	*1*	..	1	..	..	..	2	2	..	42	31	11	..	..	..	131	118	13	4	4	..
Total (II)	17	9	8	106	31	75	160	55	105	195	85	110	187	79	108	637	436	201	110	61	49
TOTAL (*b*)	160	96	64	500	195	305	880	329	551	1,115	569	546	932	519	413	4,864	3,267	1,597	1,989	877	1,112
(c) INDIA UNSPECIFIED	*3*	..	3	..	..	..	10	10	..	..	..	..	..	..	..	125	116	9	..	..	..
(*d*) FRENCH AND PORTUGUESE SETTLEMENTS — French	..	..	..	..	..	..	..	..	..	..	..	..	..	..	..	..	..	..	..	..	..
(*d*) FRENCH AND PORTUGUESE SETTLEMENTS — Portuguese	..	..	..	..	..	..	..	..	..	..	..	..	..	..	..	11	5	6	..	..	..
TOTAL B.	2,965	2,017	948	2,943	1,233	1,710	4,891	2,342	2,549	7,229	4,182	3,047	42,963	24,492	18,471	67,638	48,580	10,058	12,741	7,572	5 169
Total A and B (Born in India)	799,328	413,930	385,398	1,032,049	551,764	480,285	942,364	511,538	430,826	672,190	375,432	296,758	1,155,172	635,133	520,040	1,371,856	789,525	582,331	1,115,981	620,105	495 826
C.—COUNTRIES IN ASIA BEYOND INDIA.																					
(I) INSIDE BRITISH DOMINIONS.																					
Ceylon	*1*	1	..	..	..	..	1	..	1	..	..	..	2	..	2	27	26	1	1	1	..
Hong Kong	..	..	..	..	..	..	..	..	..	..	..	.	4	1	3	..	.	..	..	..	..
Straits Settlements and Malaya	..	..	..	1	1	..	9	4	5	44	7	37	41	29	12	10	5	5	13	5	8
Total (I)	1	1	..	1	1	..	10	4	6	44	7	37	47	30	17	37	31	6	14	6	8
(II) OUTSIDE BRITISH DOMINIONS.																					
Afghanistan	*34*	33	1	62	61	1	14	12	2	15	12	3	50	43	7	1,020	735	285	159	145	14
Arabia	..	..	..	..	..	..	15	6	9	12	12	..	2	2	..	111	97	14	4	3	1
Bhotan	*17*	8	9	..	..	..	..	..	..	..	..	..	1	1	..	2	1	1	..	..	..
China	*17*	8	9	3	1	2	19	11	8	43	23	20	108	58	50	117	71	40	315	181	134
French Indo-China	..	..	..	..	..	..	..	..	..	..	..	..	..	..	..	..	..	..	..	.	..
Iraq	..	..	..	..	..	..	1	..	1	..	..	..	..	..	..	29	27	2	..	..	.
Japan	..	..	..	..	..	..	..	..	..	..	..	..	..	..	..	15	15	..	.	..	..
Java	..	..	..	5	3	2	6	4	2	..	..	..	..	..	..	..	..	..	..	..	..
Nepal	*1,714*	1,148	566	35	22	13	60	57	3	41	18	23	156	152	4	224	173	51	401	348	53
Persia	..	..	..	..	..	..	13	5	8	5	..	9	2	1	1	101	68	33	11	3	8
Philippine Islands	*1*	1	..	..	..	..	..	..	..	..	.	..	..	..	..	..	..	..	..	..	..
Russia in Asia	*2*	1	*1*	..	..	..	..	..	..	..	..	..	..	..	..	..	..	..	..	..	..
Russian Turkistan	*1*	..	1	2	2	..	..	..	..	..	..	..	..	..	..	..	..	..	..	..	..
Siam	..	..	..	..	..	..	..	..	..	..	..	..	..	..	..	2	2	..	..	..	.

TABLE VI.—BIRTH-PLACE.—PART B—*continued.*

District, State, Province or Country where born.	Kangra. Persons. 23	Males. 24	Females. 25	Hoshiarpur. Persons. 26	Males. 27	Females. 28	Jullundur. Persons. 29	Males. 30	Females. 31	Ludhiana. Persons. 32	Males. 33	Females. 34	Ferozepore. Persons. 35	Males. 36	Females. 37	Lahore. Persons. 38	Males. 39	Females. 40	Amritsar. Persons. 41	Males. 42	Females. 43
	PROVINCE, DISTRICT OR STATE WHERE ENUMERATED.																				
Sumatra	..	..	..	..	..	..	..	..	..	..	..	..	1	..	..	..	..	..	5	4	1
Syria	..	..	..	..	..	..	..	..	..	..	..	..	..	..	..	..	..	..	..	..	..
Tibet	139	130	9	..	..	..	..	..	..	..	..	..	..	..	..	4	4	..	..	..	..
Turkey in Asia	..	..	..	1	1	..	..	..	..	..	..	..	..	..	..	..	..	..	71	70	1
Turkistan Unspecified	..	..	..	..	..	..	..	..	..	5	3	2	..	..	..	..	..	..	..	..	..
Total (II)	1,925	1,329	596	108	90	18	128	95	33	125	68	57	319	257	62	1,625	1,193	432	966	754	212
(III) ASIA UNSPECIFIED	..	..	..	..	..	..	..	..	..	..	..	..	..	..	—	..	..	..	..	..	..
TOTAL C.	1,926	1,330	596	109	91	18	138	99	39	169	75	94	366	287	79	1,662	1,224	438	980	760	220
D.—COUNTRIES IN EUROPE																					
(I) INSIDE BRITISH DOMINIONS.																					
England and Wales	30	20	10	..	..	..	1,095	960	135	4	2	2	1,003	700	303	3,423	2,812	611	169	155	14
Gibraltar	..	..	..	..	..	..	..	..	..	..	..	..	..	..	..	..	..	..	..	..	..
Irish Free States	..	..	..	..	..	..	..	..	..	..	..	..	..	..	..	..	..	..	..	..	..
Malta	..	..	..	..	..	..	..	..	..	..	..	..	..	..	..	..	..	..	..	..	..
Northern Ireland	8	..	8	..	..	..	21	21	..	..	..	..	80	80	..	100	53	47	..	..	..
Scotland	5	2	3	1	1	..	8	7	1	..	..	..	64	32	32	138	93	45	1	..	1
United Kingdom Unspecified	..	..	..	..	..	..	..	..	..	..	..	..	..	..	..	..	..	..	..	..	..
Total (I)	43	22	21	1	1	..	1,124	988	136	4	2	2	1,147	812	335	3,661	2,958	703	170	155	15
(II) OUTSIDE BRITISH DOMINIONS.																					
Austria	..	..	..	..	..	..	..	..	..	..	..	..	..	..	..	..	..	..	..	..	..
Belgium	..	..	..	..	..	..	..	..	..	..	..	..	..	..	..	..	..	..	..	..	..
Denmark	1	1	..	..	..	..	..	..	..	..	..	..	..	..	..	..	..	..	..	..	..
France	..	..	..	..	..	..	..	..	..	..	..	..	10	7	3	2	2	..	2	1	1
Germany	..	..	..	..	..	..	1	1	..	3	2	1	..	..	..	1	..	1	1	1	..
Greece	..	..	..	..	..	..	..	..	..	..	..	..	..	..	..	..	..	..	..	..	..
Holland	..	..	..	..	..	..	..	..	..	..	..	..	..	..	..	..	..	..	..	..	..
Italy	..	..	..	..	..	..	1	1	..	..	..	..	..	..	..	..	..	..	..	..	..
Latvia	1	1	..	..	..	..	..	..	..	..	..	..	..	..	..	..	..	..	..	..	..
Norway	..	..	..	..	..	..	..	..	..	..	..	..	..	..	..	..	..	..	..	..	..
Portugal	..	..	..	..	..	..	..	..	..	..	..	..	..	..	..	..	..	..	..	..	..
Rumania	2	1	1	..	..	..	..	..	..	..	..	..	..	..	..	..	..	..	..	..	..
Russian Union	..	..	..	..	..	..	1	..	1	..	..	..	..	..	..	..	..	..	..	..	..
Spain	..	..	..	..	..	..	..	..	..	..	..	..	..	..	..	..	..	..	..	..	..
Sweden	..	..	..	..	..	..	..	..	..	..	..	..	..	..	..	..	..	..	..	..	..
Switzerland	..	..	..	..	..	..	..	..	..	..	..	..	..	..	..	..	..	..	..	..	..
Turkey in Europe	..	..	..	..	..	..	..	..	..	..	..	..	1	1	..	36	34	2	..	..	..
Total (II)	4	3	1	..	..	..	3	2	1	3	2	1	11	8	3	39	36	3	3	2	1

(III) *EUROPE UNSPECIFIED*	..	..	..	.	..	..	..	..	.	.	..	..	.	.	..	1,130	507	623	5	3	2
TOTAL D. ..	47	25	22	1	1	..	1,127	990	137	7	4	3	1,158	820	338	4,830	3,501	1,329	178	160	18
E.—COUNTRIES IN AFRICA																					
(I) OUTSIDE BRITISH DOMINIONS.																					
Egypt ..	..	..	..	..	..	..	1	1	.	..	.	..	.	..	..	..	..	..	.	..	..
(II) AFRICA UNSPECIFIED	..	..	..	15	6	9	66	32	34	95	36	59	16	12	4	139	94	45	28	15	13
TOTAL E. ..	..	..	..	15	6	9	67	33	34	95	36	59	16	12	4	139	94	45	28	15	13
F.—COUNTRIES IN AMERICA																					
(I) INSIDE BRITISH DOMINIONS.																					
British Guiana ..	..	..	..	..	..	..	..	..	..	.	.	..	..	.	..	..	..	..	..	..	..
Canada ..	6	2	4	..	..	..	4	..	4	..	..	..	..	.	..	5	5	..	..	.	.
Total (I) ..	6	2	4	..	..	..	4	..	4	.	.	.	..	..	..	5	5	..	..	.	.
(II) OUTSIDE BRITISH DOMINIONS.																					
United States ..	..	..	..	..	..	..	..	..	..	..	..	..	..	.	.	.	.	.	..	..	..
(III) AMERICA UNSPECIFIED.	2	1	1	1	..	1	10	7	3	27	9	18	17	4	13	61	31	30	2	..	2
TOTAL F. ..	8	3	5	1	.	1	14	7	7	27	9	18	17	4	13	66	36	30	2	..	2
G.—COUNTRIES IN AUSTRALASIA.																					
(I) INSIDE BRITISH DOMINIONS.																					
Australia ..	2		2	1	1	..	5	..	5	6	4	2	2	..	2	14	8	6	1	..	1
Fiji Islands ..	1	..	1	9	4	5	6	..	6	..	..	..	..	.	.	.	..	..	..	..	..
New Zealand ..	..	..	..	..	..	..	..	..	..	..	..	..	..	.	.	3	1	2	..	..	..
Elsewhere in British Australasia	..	..	..	2	.	2	.	..	..	..	..	..	..	..	..	..	..	..	.	.	..
Total (I) ..	3	..	3	12	5	7	11	..	11	6	4	2	2	.	2	17	9	8	1	..	1
TOTAL G. ..	3	..	3	12	5	7	11	..	11	6	4	2	2	.	2	17	9	8	1	.	1
TOTAL RETURNED ..	801,312	415,288	386,024	1,032,187	551,867	430,320	943,721	512,667	431,054	672,494	375,560	296,934	1,156,732	636,256	520,476	1,378,570	794,389	584,181	1,117,120	621,040	496,080
Birth-Place not Returned.	.	..	..	..	..	..	.	.	.	..	.	..	.	.	.	.	.	..	.	..	..
TOTAL POPULATION	801,312	415,288	386,024	1,032,187	551,867	480,320	943,721	512,667	431,054	672,494	375,560	296,934	1,156,732	636,256	520,476	1,378,570	794,389	584,181	1,117,120	621,040	496,080

TABLE VI.—BIRTH-PLACE.—PART B—*continued.*

District, State, Province or Country where born.	Gurdaspur.			Sialkot.			Gujranwala.			Sheikhupura.			Gujrat.			Shahpur.			Jhelum.		
	Persons. 44	Males. 45	Females. 46	Persons. 47	Males. 48	Females. 49	Persons. 50	Males. 51	Females. 52	Persons. 53	Males. 54	Females. 55	Persons. 56	Males. 57	Females. 58	Persons. 59	Males. 60	Females. 61	Persons. 62	Males. 63	Females. 64
A.—DISTRICTS OR STATES WITHIN THE PROVINCE																					
(I) BRITISH TERRITORY ..	*953,120*	523,949	429,171	961,733	530,089	431,644	727,397	402,073	325,324	686.195	377,537	308,658	905,772	489,833	415,939	803,220	433,891	369,329	533,992	278,824	255,168
District of Enumeration ..	*894,807*	500,330	394,477	908,239	507,206	401,033	646,069	361,275	284,794	490,837	273,369	217,468	849,481	460,996	388,485	683,369	365,327	318,042	518,843	272,503	246,340
(II) PUNJAB STATES ..	*2,366*	975	1,391	62	41	21	377	290	87	2,759	1,603	1,156	428	285	143	1,464	840	624	191	117	74
State of Enumeration ..	..	..	..	..	..	..	..	..	..	..	..	..	..	..	..	..	..	..	..	..	..
(III) PUNJAB UNSPECIFIED	..	..	..	..	..	..	..	..	..	..	..	..	..	..	..	..	..	..	..	..	..
TOTAL A. ..	**955,486**	**524,924**	**430,562**	**961,795**	**530,130**	**431,665**	**727,774**	**402,363**	**325,411**	**688,954**	**379,140**	**309,814**	**906,200**	**490,118**	**416,082**	**804,684**	**434,731**	**369,953**	**534,183**	**278,941**	**255,242**
B.—PROVINCES OR STATES IN INDIA BEYOND THE PROVINCE.																					
(a).—Provinces or States adjacent to the Province																					
(I)—BRITISH TERRITORY																					
Delhi ..	*317*	95	222	281	103	178	344	173	171	494	280	214	143	92	51	144	83	61	61	21	40
Baluchistan ..	*125*	49	76	119	75	44	84	59	25	106	24	82	63	44	19	153	81	72	87	37	50
N. W. F. Province ..	*468*	343	125	579	426	153	307	147	160	829	421	408	965	603	362	2,926	1,795	1,131	915	525	390
U. P. of Agra and Oudh ..	*1,347*	646	701	879	416	463	1,835	1,546	289	1,973	1,501	472	3,292	2,068	1,224	6,117	3,933	2,184	892	486	406
Total (I) ..	**2,257**	**1,133**	**1,124**	**1,858**	**1,020**	**838**	**2,570**	**1,925**	**645**	**3,402**	**2,226**	**1,176**	**4,468**	**2,807**	**1,656**	**9,340**	**5,892**	**3,448**	**1,955**	**1,069**	**886**
(II)—FEUDATORY STATES																					
Baluchistan States ..	..	..	..	..	..	..	..	..	..	..	..	..	..	..	..	..	..	..	..	..	..
United Provinces States ..	..	..	..	..	..	..	..	..	..	12	..	12	..	..	..	140	6	134	4	3	1
Jammu & Kashmir State ..	*9,640*	3,863	5,777	12,653	3,505	9,148	3,523	2,547	976	2,073	1,372	701	9,662	4,003	5,659	2,879	2,164	715	3,637	1,916	1,721
Rajputana Agency ..	*428*	234	194	288	173	115	1,134	890	244	1,157	798	359	587	380	207	751	515	236	85	55	30
Jaisalmer ..	..	..	..	..	..	..	..	..	..	..	..	..	..	..	..	..	..	..	..	..	..
Bikaner ..	*2*	..	2	38	15	23	159	85	74	187	124	63	54	37	17	49	33	16	4	2	2
Alwar ..	*1*	1	..	..	..	..	141	135	6	327	204	123	66	38	28	100	81	19	..	..	..
Jaipur ..	*38*	1	37	..	..	..	786	633	153	418	283	135	291	233	58	354	223	131	33	23	10
Bharatpur ..	*1*	..	1	..	..	..	..	..	..	14	12	2	13	2	11	43	41	2	3	1	2
Other State ..	*386*	232	154	250	158	92	48	37	11	211	175	36	163	70	93	205	137	68	45	29	16
Total (II) ..	10,068	4,097	5,971	12,941	3,678	9,263	4,657	3,437	1,220	3,242	2,170	1,072	10,249	4,883	5,866	3,770	2,685	1,085	3,726	1,974	1,752
TOTAL (a) ..	12,325	5,230	7,095	14,799	4,698	10,101	7,227	5,362	1,865	6,644	4,396	2,248	14,712	7,190	7,522	13.110	8,577	4,533	5,681	3,043	2,638
(b).—Other Provinces and States in India.																					
(I) BRITISH TERRITORY																					
Ajmer Marwara ..	*1*	..	1	4	1	3	7	6	1	13	1	12	2	..	2	52	31	21	4	2	2
Andamans and Nicobars ..	*2*	2	..	3	2	1	..	..	..	..	..	..	5	1	4	7	6	1	5	4	1
Assam ..	*9*	3	6	1	1	..	11	9	2	1	1	..	17	17	..	1	1	..	3	1	2
Bengal	*260*	42	218	213	158	55	11	5	6	18	16	2	63	40	23	14	6	8	46	22	24
Bihar and Orissa	*185*	50	135	35	11	24	58	6	52	26	14	12	50	17	33	3	1	2	5	3	2

PROVINCE, DISTRICT OR STATE WHERE ENUMERATED.

TABLE VI.—BIRTH-

Bombay	*156*	75	81	72	40	32	29	23	6	41	26	15	105	113	82	97	65	32	148	74	74
Aden	..	..	..	..	..	..	..	..	3	..	3	..	..	..	..	..	..	..	..	..	..
Burma	*84*	39	45	46	30	16	10	5	5	7	2	5	84	55	29	31	17	14	98	57	41
Central Provinces and Berar	*134*	24	110	63	34	29	13	10	3	9	1	8	108	52	56	47	27	20	25	16	9
Madras	*8*	8	..	49	31	18	3	..	3	8	4	4	7	1	6	5	2	3	21	11	10
Total (I)	839	243	596	486	308	178	142	64	78	128	65	58	531	296	235	257	156	101	355	190	165
(II) FEUDATORY STATES.																					
Assam States	..	..	..	..	..	..	..	..	..	..	..	..	..	..	..	..	..	..	..	..	..
Baroda State	*1*	..	1	2	..	2	..	..	..	..	..	..	..	..	..	..	..	..	..	..	..
Bihar and Orissa States	..	..	..	..	..	..	..	..	..	..	..	..	3	3	..	..	..	..	..	..	..
Bombay States	..	..	..	..	..	..	..	..	..	..	..	..	..	..	..	5	2	3	..	..	..
Central India Agency	*12*	5	7	1	1	..	..	..	..	..	..	..	..	..	..	6	4	2	..	..	..
Central Provinces States	*1*	1	..	..	..	..	..	..	..	..	..	..	15	5	10	20	5	15	..	..	..
Gwalior State	*33*	9	24	4	..	4	1	1	..	1	1	..	..	..	..	5	5	..	2	1	1
Hyderabad State	*12*	7	5	12	..	12	1	..	1	3	3	..	32	26	6	29	14	15	18	9	9
Madras States (Including Cochin and Travancore).	..	..	..	..	..	..	..	..	..	..	..	..	..	..	..	4	2	2	5	4	1
Travancore State	..	..	..	..	..	..	..	..	..	..	..	..	..	..	..	..	..	..	..	..	..
Mysore State	*6*	1	5	..	..	..	..	..	..	..	..	..	9	1	8	..	..	..	4	3	1
Total (II)	65	23	42	19	1	18	2	1	1	4	4	..	59	35	24	69	32	37	29	17	12
TOTAL (b)	904	266	638	505	309	198	144	65	79	127	69	58	590	331	259	326	188	138	384	207	177
(c) INDIA UNSPECIFIED	..	..	..	..	..	..	9	6	3	25	..	25	24	..	24	..	..	..	..	..	..
(d) FRENCH AND PORTUGUESE SETTLEMENTS — French	..	..	..	..	..	..	..	..	..	..	..	..	..	..	..	..	..	..	..	..	..
(d) FRENCH AND PORTUGUESE SETTLEMENTS — Portuguese	..	..	..	..	..	..	..	..	..	..	..	..	..	..	..	..	..	..	..	..	..
TOTAL B.	13,229	5,496	7,733	15,304	5,007	10,297	7,380	5,433	1,947	6,796	4,465	2,331	15,326	7,521	7,805	13,436	8,765	4,671	6,065	3,250	2,815
Total A and B (Born in India)	968.715	530,420	438,295	977,099	535,137	441,962	735,154	407,796	327,358	695,750	383,605	312,145	921,526	497,639	423,887	818,120	443,496	374,624	540,248	282,191	25[illegible],057
C.—COUNTRIES IN ASIA BEYOND INDIA.																					
(I) INSIDE BRITISH DOMINIONS.																					
Ceylon	*2*	1	1	1	..	1	..	..	..	..	..	..	..	..	..	..	..	..	..	..	..
Hong Kong	..	..	..	..	..	..	..	..	..	..	..	..	..	..	..	..	..	..	..	..	..
Straits Settlements and Malaya	..	..	..	..	..	..	..	..	..	..	..	..	4	2	2	1	1	..	..	..	..
Total (I)	2	1	1	1	..	1	..	..	..	..	..	..	4	2	2	1	1	..	..	..	..
(II) OUTSIDE BRITISH DOMINIONS.																					
Afghanistan	*130*	97	33	205	185	20	807	736	162	914	744	170	691	567	124	3,111	2,125	986	622	398	224
Arabia	*7*	2	5	10	7	3	..	..	..	2	..	2	15	4	11	11	11	..	3	..	3
Bhotan	..	..	..	..	..	..	..	..	..	..	..	..	..	..	..	..	..	..	..	..	..
China	*36*	8	28	3	3	..	6	5	1	11	5	6	41	33	8	8	5	3	12	5	4
French Indo-China	..	..	..	1	..	1	..	..	..	..	..	..	..	..	..	..	..	..	..	..	..
Iraq	..	..	..	..	..	..	..	..	..	..	..	..	..	..	..	..	..	..	..	..	..
Japan	..	..	..	..	..	..	..	..	..	..	..	..	..	..	..	..	..	..	..	..	..
Java	..	..	..	..	..	..	..	..	..	..	..	..	..	..	..	..	..	..	..	..	..
Nepal	*1,731*	1,280	451	2	1	1	76	68	8	20	20	..	69	59	10	26	23	3	20	14	6
Persia	*10*	4	6	26	19	7	..	..	..	..	..	..	13	5	8	151	140	11	10	4	6
Philippine Islands	..	..	..	..	..	..	..	..	..	..	..	..	..	..	..	..	..	..	..	..	..
Russia in Asia	..	..	..	..	..	..	..	..	..	..	..	..	..	..	..	..	..	..	..	..	..
Russian Turkistan	..	..	..	..	..	..	..	..	..	..	..	..	..	..	..	..	..	..	..	..	..
Siam	..	..	..	..	..	..	..	..	..	..	..	..	..	..	..	..	..	..	..	..	..

TABLE VI.—BIRTH-PLACE.—PART B—*continued.*

PROVINCE, DISTRICT OR STATE WHERE ENUMERATED.

District, State, Province or Country where born.	Gurdaspur.			Sialkot.			Gujranwala.			Sheikhupura.			Gujrat.			Shahpur.			Jhelum.		
	Persons. 44	Males. 45	Females. 46	Persons. 47	Males. 48	Females. 49	Persons. 50	Males. 51	Females. 52	Persons. 53	Males. 54	Females. 55	Persons. 56	Males. 57	Females. 58	Persons. 59	Males. 60	Females. 61	Persons. 62	Males. 63	Females. 64
Sumatra ..	7	7	..	..	..	..	..	..	..	2	..	2	..	..	..	..	..	..	..	..	..
Syria ..	..	..	..	..	..	..	..	..	..	..	..	..	..	..	..	..	..	..	..	..	..
Tibet ..	*28*	20	8	1	1	..	..	..	..	..	..	..	..	..	..	..	..	..	..	..	..
Turkey in Asia ..	..	..	..	13	1	12	..	..	..	..	..	..	..	..	..	..	..	..	..	..	..
Turkistan Unspecified ..	*3*	2	1	..	..	..	..	..	..	..	..	..	2	1	1	..	..	..	6	6	..
Total (II) ..	**1,952**	**1,420**	**532**	**261**	**217**	**44**	**979**	**808**	**171**	**949**	**769**	**180**	**831**	**669**	**162**	**3,307**	**2,304**	**1,008**	**673**	**430**	**243**
(III) ASIA UNSPECIFIED ..	..	..	..	..	..	..	..	..	..	..	..	..	..	..	..	..	..	..	..	..	..
TOTAL C. ..	**1,954**	**1,421**	**533**	**262**	**217**	**45**	**979**	**808**	**171**	**949**	**769**	**180**	**835**	**671**	**164**	**3,308**	**2,305**	**1,008**	**673**	**430**	**243**
D.—COUNTRIES IN EUROPE																					
(I) INSIDE BRITISH DOMINIONS.																					
England and Wales ..	*136*	55	81	2,144	1,865	279	2	1	1	9	5	4	15	4	11	19	16	3	93	57	36
Gibraltar ..	..	..	..	..	..	..	..	..	..	..	..	..	..	..	..	..	..	..	..	..	..
Irish Free States ..	..	..	..	..	..	..	..	..	..	..	..	..	..	..	..	..	..	..	..	..	..
Malta ..	..	..	..	..	..	..	..	..	..	..	..	..	..	..	..	..	..	..	..	..	..
Northern Ireland ..	*7*	6	1	30	23	7	..	..	..	..	..	..	2	..	2	..	..	..	1	1	..
Scotland ..	*12*	7	5	13	11	2	..	..	..	..	..	..	8	1	7	..	..	..	7	6	1
United Kingdom Unspecified ..	..	..	..	..	..	..	..	..	..	..	..	..	..	..	..	..	..	..	..	..	..
Total (I) ..	**155**	**68**	**87**	**2,187**	**1,899**	**288**	**2**	**1**	**1**	**9**	**5**	**4**	**25**	**5**	**20**	**19**	**16**	**3**	**101**	**64**	**37**
(II) OUTSIDE BRITISH DOMINIONS.																					
Austria ..	..	..	..	..	..	..	..	..	..	..	..	..	..	..	..	..	..	..	..	..	..
Belgium ..	*7*	2	5	4	4	..	..	..	..	2	2	..	..	..	..	..	..	..	3	3	..
Denmark ..	..	..	..	..	..	..	..	..	..	..	..	..	..	..	..	..	..	..	..	..	..
France ..	*3*	..	3	..	..	..	..	..	..	1	..	1	..	..	..	..	..	..	1	..	1
Germany ..	*1*	..	1	..	..	..	..	..	..	5	2	3	..	..	..	..	..	..	..	..	..
Greece ..	..	..	..	..	..	..	..	..	..	..	..	..	..	..	..	..	..	..	..	..	..
Holland ..	*1*	..	1	..	..	..	..	..	..	..	..	..	..	..	..	..	..	..	..	..	..
Italy ..	..	..	..	..	..	..	..	..	..	..	..	..	..	..	..	..	..	..	..	..	..
Latvia ..	..	..	..	..	..	..	..	..	..	..	..	..	..	..	..	..	..	..	..	..	..
Norway ..	..	..	..	..	..	..	..	..	..	..	..	..	..	..	..	..	..	..	..	..	..
Portugal ..	..	..	..	..	..	..	..	..	..	..	..	..	..	..	..	..	..	..	..	..	..
Rumania ..	..	..	..	..	..	..	..	..	..	..	..	..	..	..	..	..	..	..	..	..	..
Russian Union ..	*1*	1	..	..	..	..	..	..	..	..	..	..	..	..	..	..	..	..	..	..	..
Spain ..	*1*	..	1	..	..	..	..	..	..	..	..	..	1	1	..	..	..	..	..	..	..
Sweden ..	*1*	..	1	..	..	..	..	..	..	..	..	..	..	..	..	..	..	..	..	..	..
Switzerland ..	..	..	..	..	..	..	..	..	..	..	..	..	..	..	..	..	..	..	..	..	..
Turkey in Europe ..	..	..	..	..	..	..	..	..	..	..	..	..	..	..	..	..	..	..	..	..	..
Total (II) ..	**15**	**3**	**12**	**4**	**4**	..	..	..	..	**8**	**4**	**4**	**1**	**1**		..	..	..	**4**	**3**	**1**

(III) EUROPE UNSPECIFIED	..	..	..	19	18	1	..	..	..	..	..	..	..	..	..	30	12	18	1	..	1
TOTAL D. ..	170	71	99	2,210	1,921	289	2	1	1	17	9	8	26	6	20	49	28	21	106	67	39
E.—COUNTRIES IN AFRICA																					
(I) OUTSIDE BRITISH DOMINIONS.																					
Egypt ..	4	1	3	..	..	..	..	..	..	..	..	..	..	..	..	..	..	..	..	..	..
(II) AFRICA UNSPECIFIED	45	19	26	14	13	1	2	..	2	1	..	1	38	20	18	10	7	3	34	23	11
TOTAL E. ..	49	20	29	14	13	1	2	..	2	1	..	1	38	20	18	10	7	3	34	23	11
F.—COUNTRIES IN AMERICA.																					
(I) INSIDE BRITISH DOMINIONS.																					
British Guiana ..	..	..	..	..	..	..	..	..	..	..	..	..	..	..	..	..	..	..	..	..	..
Canada ..	..	..	..	..	..	..	..	..	..	..	..	..	..	..	..	..	..	..	..	..	..
Total (I) ..	..	..	..	..	..	..	..	..	..	..	..	..	..	..	..	..	..	..	..	..	..
(II) OUTSIDE BRITISH DOMINIONS.																					
United States ..	..	..	..	..	..	..	..	..	..	..	..	..	..	..	..	..	..	..	7	..	7
(III) AMERICA UNSPECIFIED.	10	3	7	31	13	18	1	1	..	14	6	8	..	..	..	3	..	3	6	2	4
TOTAL F. ..	10	3	7	31	13	18	1	1	..	14	6	8	..	..	..	3	..	3	13	2	11
G.—COUNTRIES IN AUSTRALASIA																					
(I) INSIDE BRITISH DOMINIONS.																					
Australia ..	..	..	..	..	..	..	..	..	..	..	..	..	..	..	..	..	..	..	..	..	..
Fiji Islands ..	..	..	..	1	..	1	..	..	..	..	..	..	..	..	..	..	..	..	..	..	..
New Zealand ..	..	..	..	..	..	..	..	..	..	..	..	..	2	..	2	..	..	..	2	1	1
Elsewhere in British Australasia	..	..	..	..	..	..	..	..	..	1	1	..	..	..	..	..	..	..	..	..	..
Total (I) ..	..	..	..	1	..	1	..	..	..	1	1	..	2	..	2	..	..	..	2	1	1
TOTAL G. ..	..	..	..	1	..	1	..	..	..	1	1	..	2	..	2	..	..	..	2	1	1
TOTAL RETURNED ..	970,898	531,935	438,963	979,617	537,301	442,316	736,138	408,606	327,532	696,732	384,390	312,342	922,427	498,336	424,091	821,490	445,836	375,654	541,076	282,714	258,362
Birth-Place not Returned ..	..	..	..	..	..	..	..	..	..	..	..	..	..	..	..	..	..	..	..	..	..
TOTAL POPULATION ..	970,898	531,935	438,963	979,617	537,301	442,316	736,138	408,606	327,532	696,732	384,390	312,342	922,427	498,336	424,091	821,490	445,836	375,654	541,076	282,714	258,362

TABLE VI.—BIRTH-PLACE.—PART B—*continued.*

PROVINCE, DISTRICT OR STATE WHERE ENUMERATED.

District, State, Province or Country where born	Rawalpindi Persons 65	Rawalpindi Males 66	Rawalpindi Females 67	Attock Persons 68	Attock Males 69	Attock Females 70	Mianwali Persons 71	Mianwali Males 72	Mianwali Females 73	Montgomery Persons 74	Montgomery Males 75	Montgomery Females 76	Lyallpur Persons 77	Lyallpur Males 78	Lyallpur Females 79	Jhang Persons 80	Jhang Males 81	Jhang Females 82	Multan Persons 83	Multan Males 84	Multan Females 85
A.—DISTRICTS OR STATES WITHIN THE PROVINCE																					
(I) BRITISH TERRITORY ..	*598,073*	318,015	280,058	575,652	301,776	273,876	405,250	212,549	192,701	972,183	535,410	436,773	1,129,377	618,702	510,675	662,765	354,204	308,561	1,154,614	633,018	521,596
District of Enumeration ..	*555,095*	291,637	263,458	563,991	295,020	268,971	398,591	208,619	189,972	748,915	405,057	343,852	752,709	405,685	347,024	644,880	341,170	300,690	1,122,624	554,222	468,402
(II) PUNJAB STATES ..	*302*	216	86	69	45	24	91	68	23	13,319	7,594	5,725	11,165	5,741	5,424	147	111	36	5,535	3,056	2,479
State of Enumeration ..	..	..	..	..	..	..	..	..	..	..	..	..	..	..	..	..	..	..	..	..	..
(III) PUNJAB UNSPECIFIED	..	..	..	..	..	..	..	..	..	..	..	..	..	..	..	..	..	..	..	..	..
TOTAL A. ..	598,375	318,231	280,144	575,721	301,821	273,900	405,341	212,617	192,724	985,502	543,004	442,498	1,140,542	624,443	516,099	662,912	354,315	308,597	1,160,149	636,074	524,075
B.—PROVINCES OR STATES IN INDIA BEYOND THE PROVINCE.																					
(a).—PROVINCES OR STATES ADJACENT TO THE PROVINCE																					
(I)—BRITISH TERRITORY																					
Delhi .	*316*	190	126	80	63	17	78	50	28	420	273	147	492	276	216	45	21	24	568	337	211
Baluchistan .	*270*	144	126	69	60	9	42	28	14	25	7	18	167	117	50	482	406	70	377	228	149
N. W. F. Province .	*11,855*	7,801	4,054	5,847	3,395	2,452	4,930	2,618	2,312	970	626	344	1,484	918	566	490	263	227	2,730	1,745	985
U. P. of Agra and Oudh ..	*5,582*	3,733	1,849	652	420	232	385	263	122	4,491	3,151	1,340	2,670	1,443	1,227	196	105	91	4,321	3,160	1,161
Total (I) ..	18,023	11,868	6,155	6,648	3,938	2,710	5,435	2,959	2,476	5,906	4,057	1,849	4,813	2,754	2,059	1,213	795	418	7,996	5,490	2,506
(II)—FEUDATORY STATES																					
Baluchistan States .	.			.		..	.	.	..		..	.	.	.	.	.		.	..		..
United Provinces States .	*40*	39	1	10	3	7	1	1	. .	.	..	..	.	.	..	29	29		2		2
Jammu & Kashmir Stat .	*11,687*	8,462	3,225	458	381	77	79	50	29	1,351	1,041	310	2,376	1,369	1,007	326	306	20	602	130	172
Rajputana Agency .	*467*	287	180	38	33	5	25	17	8	4,685	2,654	2,031	2,296	1,302	994	249	160	89	3,475	2,060	1,415
Jaisalmer .			.		.	..	..			..				.		.	.		.	..	..
Bikaner ..	*11*		4	2	2		2		2	1,833	1,091	742	544	283	261	5	4		358	202	136
Alwar ..	*36*	33	2	1	1	..	2	2	.	713	484	229	308	173	135	50	32	18	150	111	39
Jaipur ..	*215*	121	94	5	6				..	1,337	584	733	497	340	157	138	102	36	277	214	63
Bharatpur ..	*1*		1	8	18		.	.		149	125	24	.	.	.	4		4	8	7	1
Other State ..	*205*	126	79	12	7	5	21	15	6	653	470	283	947	506	441	52	22	30	2,682	1,526	1,156
Total (II) ..	12,194	8,788	3,406	506	417	89	105	68	37	6,036	3,695	2,341	4,672	2,671	2,001	604	495	109	4,079	2,490	1,589
TOTAL (a) ..	30,217	20,656	9,561	7,154	4,355	2,799	5,540	3,027	2,513	11,942	7,752	4,190	9,485	5,425	4,060	1,817	1,290	527	12,075	7,980	4,095
(b).—OTHER PROVINCES AND STATES IN INDIA.																					
(I) BRITISH TERRITORY																					
Ajmer Marwara .	3	3	.	2	2	..	1	..	1	10	6	4	5	3	2	.	.	.	16	3	1
Andamans and Nicobars .	6	4	2	3	1	2	.	..	..	1	1	.	10	6	4	.	.	.	..	..	.
Assam ..	2	.	2	..	..	..	..	..	..	..	..	.	13	10	3		.	..	1	1	..
Bengal ..	*294*	175	119	21	12	9	10	6	4	37	16	21	58	21	37	20	10	10	78	33	45
Bihar and Orissa ..	*51*	36	15	4	4	..	1	1	..	31	26	5	18	5	13	.	..		45	25	20

PLACE.—PART B.

	1	2	3	4	5	6	7	8	9	10	11	12	13	14	15	16	17	18	19	20	21
Bombay	505	277	228	58	45	8	75	49	26	249	102	147	328	174	154	22	5	17	582	310	[illegible]72
Aden	1	1										1	1								
Burma	121	54	67	36	14	22	..	..	.	33	16	17	40	26	14	.	..	.	15	12	3
Central Provinces and Berar	89	14	75	16	12	4	12	21	10	67	56	11	35	9	26	44	35	9	19	18	1
Madras	[illegible]	100	72	7	4	3	13	8	5	13	8	5	16	6	10	1	1	..	33	22	11
Total (I)	1,244	664	580	142	94	48	112	66	46	441	231	210	523	260	263	87	51	36	789	426	[illegible]63
(II) FEUDATORY STATES.																					
Assam States																					
Baroda State	21	10	11	8	5	3	1	1	..	2	1	1		..	..	..	..	.	3	2	1
Bihar and Orissa States																					
Bombay States																					
Central India Agency	8	2	6							17	10	7	10	2	8						
Central Provinces States										9	6	3									
Gwaliar State	104	28	76										1		1						
Hyderabad State	28	22	6							14	8	6	29	12	17	1	1	.	26	11	16
Madras States (Including Cochin							6	3	3	20	8	12	5	3	2				38		38
and Travancore).													1		1						
Travancore State												1		1							
Mysore State	3	2	1	3		3	7	4	3	13	5	8	2		2						
Total (II)	164	64	100	11	5	6	14	8	6	75	38	37	48	17	31	1			67	13	54
TOTAL (b)	1,408	728	680	153	99	54	126	74	52	516	269	247	571	277	294	88	2	36	856	439	417
(c) INDIA UNSPECIFIED	478	196	282	34	19	15	3	2	1	5	3	2	7	4	3	..			..	..	..
(d) FRENCH AND PORTUGUESE SETTLEMENTS — French																					
Portuguese																					
TOTAL B.	32,108	21,580	10,523	7,341	4,473	2,868	5,669	3,103	2,566	12,463	8,024	4,439	10,063	5,706	4,357	1,905	1,342	563	12,981	8,419	4,512
Total A and B (Born in India)	680,478	389,811	290,667	583,062	306,294	276,768	411,010	215,720	195,290	997,965	551,[illegible]28	446,937	1,150,605	630,149	520,456	664,817	355,657	309,160	1,173,080	644,493	528,587
C.—COUNTRIES IN ASIA BEYOND INDIA.																					
(I) INSIDE BRITISH DOMINIONS.																					
Ceylon	3	1	2	1	.	1	.	.	.	1	1	.	..	..	..	.	.	.	2	1	1
Hong Kong				1		1															
Straits Settlements and Malaya													3	3							
Total (I)	3	1	2	2		2	..	.	..	1	1	.	3	3	.		.	.	2	1	1
(II) OUTSIDE BRITISH DOMINIONS.																					
Afghanistan	392	243	149	438	290	148	493	270	223	1,690	1,358	332	638	541	97	..	.	.	736	577	169
Arabia	72	69	3	1		1	3	2	1	4	..	4	13	6	7	2	2		38	33	5
Bhotan																					
China	25	13	12	12	4	8	1		1	8	6	2	10	9	1				24	22	2
French Indo-China																					
Iraq										3	3										
Japan													1		1						
Java				3		3															
Nepal	140	114	26	125	107	18	16	16		14	6	8	5	4	1	1	1		50	43	7
Persia	10	3	7	12	4	8	7	2	6	1	..	1	2		2	8	7	1	32	19	13
Philippine Islands																					
Russia in Asia																					
Russian Turkistan																					
Siam				1		1															

TABLE VI.—BIRTH-PLACE.—PART B—*continued.*

PROVINCE, DISTRICT OR STATE WHERE ENUMERATED.

District, State, Province or Country where born.	Rawalpindi.			Attock.			Mianwali.			Montgomery.			Lyallpur.			Jhang.			Multan.		
	Persons.	Males.	Females.	Persons.	Males.	Females.	Persons.	Males.	Females.	Persons.	Males.	Females.	Persons.	Males.	Females.	Persons.	Males.	Females.	Persons.	Males.	Females.
	65	66	67	68	69	70	71	72	73	74	75	76	77	78	79	80	81	82	83	84	85
Sumatra	..	..	..	..	..	..	..	..	..	..	..	..	..	..	..	..	..	..	..	..	..
Syria	..	..	..	..	..	..	..	..	..	..	..	..	1	1	..	..	..	..	..	..	..
Tibet	7	7	..	..	..	..	..	..	..	..	..	..	..	..	..	3	3	..	..	..	..
Turkey in Asia	..	..	..	2	2	..	..	..	..	2	2	..	..	..	..	..	..	..	..	..	..
Turkistan Unspecified	1	1	..	..	..	..	..	..	..	..	..	..	..	..	..	..	..	..	..	..	..
Total (II)	647	450	197	594	407	187	520	290	230	1,722	1,375	347	670	561	109	14	13	1	880	694	186
(III) ASIA UNSPECIFIED	1	1	..	..	..	..	..	..	..	..	..	..	..	..	..	..	..	..	..	..	..
TOTAL C.	651	452	199	596	407	189	520	290	230	1,723	1,376	347	673	564	109	14	13	1	882	695	187
D.—COUNTRIES IN EUROPE																					
(I) INSIDE BRITISH DOMINIONS.																					
England and Wales	2,797	2,242	555	260	223	37	8	5	3	50	31	19	33	19	14	..	..	..	866	791	75
Gibraltar	..	..	..	..	..	..	..	..	..	..	..	..	..	..	..	..	..	..	..	..	..
Irish Free States	..	..	..	..	..	..	..	..	..	..	..	..	13	10	3	..	..	..	..	..	..
Malta	2	2	..	..	..	..	..	..	..	..	..	..	..	..	..	..	..	..	..	..	..
Northern Ireland	210	132	78	14	8	6	..	..	..	4	4	..	..	..	..	..	..	..	13	9	4
Scotland	128	95	33	15	11	4	1	1	..	8	5	3	1	..	1	2	1	1	10	10	..
United Kingdom Unspecified	..	..	..	..	..	..	..	..	..	..	..	..	..	..	..	..	..	..	..	..	..
Total (I)	3,137	2,471	666	289	242	47	9	6	3	62	40	22	47	29	18	2	1	1	889	810	79
(II) OUTSIDE BRITISH DOMINIONS.																					
Austria	..	..	..	1	1	..	..	..	..	..	..	..	..	..	..	..	..	..	..	..	..
Belgium	..	..	..	..	..	..	..	..	..	3	3	..	15	5	10	..	..	..	6	2	..
Denmark	..	..	..	..	..	..	..	..	..	..	..	..	..	..	..	..	..	..	..	..	..
France	8	..	8	..	..	..	..	..	..	..	..	..	..	..	..	..	..	..	..	..	..
Germany	15	10	5	1	..	1	..	..	..	..	..	..	..	..	..	..	..	..	..	..	..
Greece	1	1	..	..	..	..	..	..	..	..	..	..	..	..	..	..	..	..	..	..	..
Holland	1	..	1	..	..	..	..	..	..	..	..	..	..	..	..	..	..	..	..	..	..
Italy	..	..	..	..	..	..	..	..	..	..	..	..	..	..	..	..	..	..	..	..	..
Latvia	..	..	..	..	..	..	..	..	..	..	..	..	..	..	..	..	..	..	..	..	..
Norway	..	..	..	..	..	..	..	..	..	..	..	..	..	..	..	..	..	..	..	..	..
Portugal	..	..	..	..	..	..	..	..	..	2	2	..	..	..	..	..	..	..	..	..	..
Rumania	..	..	..	..	..	..	..	..	..	..	..	..	..	..	..	..	..	..	..	..	..
Russian Union	..	..	..	2	..	2	..	..	..	..	..	..	..	..	..	..	..	..	..	..	..
Spain	..	..	..	2	2	..	..	..	..	..	..	..	..	..	..	..	..	..	..	..	..
Sweden	2	..	2	..	..	..	..	..	..	..	..	..	..	..	..	..	..	..	..	..	..
Switzerland	..	..	..	..	..	..	..	..	..	..	..	..	..	..	..	..	..	..	..	..	..
Turkey in Europe	..	..	..	..	..	..	..	..	..	..	..	..	..	..	..	..	..	..	3	3	..
Total (II)	27	11	16	6	3	3	..	..	..	5	5	..	15	5	10	..	..	..	9	5	4

	(1)	(2)	(3)	(4)	(5)	(6)	(7)	(8)	(9)	(10)	(11)	(12)	(13)	(14)	(15)	(16)	(17)	(18)	(19)	(20)	(21)
(III) EUROPE UNSPECIFIED	1		1																6		6
TOTAL D.	3,165	2,482	683	295	245	50	9	6	3	67	45	22	62	34	28	2	1	1	904	815	89
E.—COUNTRIES IN AFRICA																					
(I) OUTSIDE BRITISH DOMINIONS.																					
Egypt	1		1	1		1													18	15	3
(II) AFRICA UNSPECIFIED	28	22	6	6	3	3							7	2	5				3	1	2
TOTAL E.	29	22	7	7	3	4							7	2	5				21	16	5
F.—COUNTRIES IN AMERICA																					
(I) INSIDE BRITISH DOMINIONS.																					
British Guiana																					
Canada	5																				
Total (I)	5		5																		
(II) OUTSIDE BRITISH DOMINIONS.																					
United States	2		2																		
(III) AMERICA UNSPECIFIED.	26	4	22							12	2	10	4		4				2	2	
TOTAL F.	33	4	29							12	2	10	4		4				2	2	
G.—COUNTRIES IN AUSTRALASIA.																					
(I) INSIDE BRITISH DOMINIONS																					
Australia	1		1							1	1								11	4	7
Fiji Islands										4	4										
New Zealand																					
Elsewhere in British Australasia																					
Total (I)	1		1							5	5								11	4	7
TOTAL G.	1		1							5	5								11	4	7
TOTAL RETURNED	634,357	342,771	291,586	583,960	306,949	277,011	411,539	216,016	195,523	999,772	552,456	447,316	1,151,351	630,749	520,602	664,833	355,671	309,162	1,174,900	646,025	528,875
Birth-Place not Returned																					
TOTAL POPULATION	634,357	342,771	291,586	583,960	306,949	277,011	411,539	216,016	195,523	999,772	552,456	447,316	1,151,351	630,749	520,602	664,833	355,671	309,162	1,174,900	646,025	528,875

TABLE VI.—BIRTH-PLACE.—PART B—*continued.*

PROVINCE, DISTRICT OR STATE WHERE ENUMERATED.

District, State, Province or Country where born.	Muzaffargarh. Persons.	Muzaffargarh. Males.	Muzaffargarh. Females.	Dera Ghazi Khan. Persons.	Dera Ghazi Khan. Males.	Dera Ghazi Khan. Females.	Dujana. Persons.	Dujana. Males.	Dujana. Females.	Pataudi. Persons.	Pataudi. Males.	Pataudi. Females.	Kalsia. Persons.	Kalsia. Males.	Kalsia. Females.	Bashahr. Persons.	Bashahr. Males.	Bashahr. Females.	Nalagarh. Persons.	Nalagarh. Males.	Nalagarh. Females.	Keonthal. Persons.	Keonthal. Males.	Keonthal. Females.
	86	87	88	89	90	91	92	93	94	95	96	97	98	99	100	101	102	103	104	105	106	107	108	109
A.—DISTRICTS OR STATES WITHIN THE PROVINCE																								
(I) BRITISH TERRITORY ..	*588,018*	318,573	269,445	518,030	284,619	233,411	4,681	868	3,813	4,107	1,178	2,929	13,863	5,114	8,749	289	207	82	4,073	1,423	2,650	2,191	1,497	694
District of Enumeration ..	*570,423*	308,037	262,386	515,364	282,995	232,369	..	..	..	..	..	..	..	..	..	..	..	..	..	..	..	..	..	..
(II) PUNJAB STATES ..	*966*	553	412	950	480	470	22,743	13,542	9,201	12,921	8,407	4,514	44,127	27,426	16,701	103,903	51,266	52,637	45,851	25,160	20,691	44,908	23,522	21,386
State of Enumeration ..	.	..	.	.	..	.	20,498	13,189	7,309	12,541	8,309	4,232	41,045	26,058	14,387	103,752	51,222	52,530	43,941	24,580	19,361	39,388	21,015	18,373
(III) PUNJAB UNSPECIFIED		..	.	.	.	..	..	..	..	..	..	..	..	..	..	..	..	..	..	..	..	.	..	..
TOTAL A. ..	588,983	319,126	269,857	518,980	285,099	233 881	27,424	14,410	13,014	17,028	9,585	7,448	57,990	32,540	25,450	104,192	51,473	52,719	49,924	26,583	23,341	47,099	25,019	22,060
B.—PROVINCES OR STATES IN INDIA BEYOND THE PROVINCE.																								
(a).—Provinces or States Adjacent to the Province.																								
(I)—BRITISH TERRITORY																								
Delhi ..	*33*	14	19	4	1	3	93	15	78	196	63	133	25	9	16	..	..	..	12	5	7	4	3	1
Baluchistan ..	*242*	141	101	569	353	216	..	..	..	..	..	..	3	3	..	1	1	..	..	..	..	..	..	..
N. W. F. Province ..	*507*	378	129	34	25	9	1	1	..	2	1	1	1	1	..	..	..	..	3	2	1	10	6	4
U. P. of Agra and Oudh ..	*231*	163	68	90	46	44	78	18	60	564	66	498	1,704	675	1,029	21	19	2	57	32	25	255	179	76
Total (I) ..	1,013	696	317	697	425	272	172	34	138	762	130	632	1,733	688	1,045	22	20	2	72	39	33	269	188	81
(II)—FEUDATORY STATES.																								
Baluchistan States ..	..	..	..	..	..	..	..	..	..	..	..	..	..	..	..	..	..	..	..	..	..	..	..	..
United Provinces States .	2	2	..	..	..	..	..	..	..	..	..	..	8	5	3	..	..	..	2	2	..	109	55	64
Jammu & Kashmir State ..	*101*	91	10	33	25	10	..	..	..	..	..	..	3	1	2	154	82	72	5	2	3	163	145	20
Rajputana Agency ..	*1,047*	605	442	54	26	28	608	87	521	1,047	195	852	33	15	18	5	5	..	1	1	..	3	3	..
Jaisalmer ..	*144*	77	67	2	..	2	..	..	..	..	..	..	..	..	..	..	..	..	..	..	..	..	..	..
Bikaner ..	*98*	55	43	17	9	8	..	..	..	..	..		..	..	..	..	..	..	..	..	..	..	..	..
Alwar ..	*135*	77	58		..	..	..	..	..	..	..	..	..	..	..	..	..	..	..	..	..	..	..	..
Jaipur ..	*434*	275	159		..	..	.	.	..	..	..	..	..	..	..	..	..	..	..	..	..	..	..	..
Bharatpur ..	*33*	23	10		..	..	..	..	..	..	..	..	..	..	..	..	..	..	..	..	..	..	..	..
Other States ..	*203*	98	105	35	17	18	608	87	521	1,047	196	852	33	15	18	5	5	..	1	1	..	3	3	..
Total (II) ..	1,150	698	452	89	51	38	608	87	521	1,047	195	852	44	21	23	159	87	72	8	5	3	277	203	74
TOTAL (a) ..	2,163	1,394	769	786	476	310	780	121	659	1,809	325	1,484	1,777	709	1,068	181	107	74	80	44	36	546	391	155
(b).—Other Provinces and States in India.																								
(I) BRITISH TERRITORY.																								
Ajmer Marwara ..	*6*	5	1	1	..	1	1	..	1	9	2	7	..	..	..	..	..	..	..	..	..	..	..	..
Andamans and Nicobars ..	..	..	..	..	..	..	..	..	..	1	..	1	..	..	..	..	..	..	..	..	..	..	..	..
Assam ..	..	..	..	..	..	..	..	..	..	..	..	..	..	..	.	..	..	..	..	..	..	..	..	..
Bengal ..	*1*	1	..	4	2	2	1	..	1	3	1	2	1	..	1	..	..	..	1	..	1	7	6	1
Bihar and Orissa ..	*4*	1	3	6	..	6	..	..	..	..	..	..	7	4	3	..	..	..	..	..	..	2	2	..

Bombay ..	92	52	40	54	41	13	..	..	..	8	1	7	3	1	2	..	..	..	2	..	2	4	1	3
Aden ..	..	..	..	..	..	..	..	..	..	..	..	..	..	..	..	..	..	..	..	..	1	..	1	
Burma ..	1	..	1	..	..	..	..	..	..	..	..	..	1	..	1	..	..	..	..	..	..	1	1	..
Central Provinces and Berar ..	..	..	..	4	3	1	.	..	..	..	..	..	1	..	1	..	..	..	..	..	..	..	..	..
Madras ..	1	1	..	..	..	..	1	1	..	..	..	.		..	..	..	..	..	..	..	..	9	4	5
Total (I) ..	105	60	45	69	46	23	3	1	2	21	4	17	13	5	8	..	..	..	3	..	3	23	14	9
(II) FEUDATORY STATES																								
Assam States ..	..	..	..	..	..	..	..	..	..	..	..	..	..	..	..	..	..	..	..	..	..	..	..	..
Baroda State ..	..	..	..	..	..	..	..	..	..	..	..	..	1	..	1	..	..	..	..	..	..	2	2	..
Bihar and Orissa States ..	..	..	..	..	..	..	..	..	..	..	..	..	..	..	..	..	..	..	..	..	..	..	..	..
Bombay States ..	2	2	..	..	..	..	..	..	..	..	..	..	..	..	..	..	..	..	..	..	..	..	..	..
Central India Agency ..	..	..	..	..	..	..	1	1	..	..	..	..	..	..	..	..	..	..	..	..	..	1	..	1
Central Provinces States ..	..	..	..	..	..	..	..	..	..	..	..	..	..	..	..	..	..	..	..	..	..	..	..	..
Gwalior State ..	..	..	..	5	4	1	1	..	1	10	6	4	2	..	2	..	..	..	..	..	..	1	1	..
Hyderabad State ..	6	6	..	1	1	..	4	3	1	2	..	2	4	..	4	..	..	..	..	..	..	..	..	..
Madras States (Including Cochin and Travancore)	..	..	..	..	..	..	..	..	..	..	..	..	..	..	..	..	..	..	..	..	..	..	..	..
Travancore State ..	..	..	..	..	..	..	..	..	..	..	..	..	..	..	..	..	..	..	..	..	..	..	..	..
Mysore State ..	..	..	..	..	..	..	..	..	..	..	..	..	..	..	..	..	..	..	..	..	..	..	..	..
Total (II) ..	8	8	..	6	5	1	6	4	2	12	6	6	7	..	7	..	..	..	..	..	..	4	3	1
TOTAL (*b*) ..	113	68	45	75	51	24	9	5	4	33	10	23	20	5	15	..	..	..	3	..	3	27	17	10
(*c*) INDIA UNSPECIFIED ..	15	7	8	..	..	..	..	..	..	..	..	..	..	..	..	..	..	..	..	..	..	11	4	7
(*d*) FRENCH AND PORTUGUESE SETTLEMENTS — French ..	..	..	..	..	..	..	..	..	..	..	..	..	..	..	..	..	..	..	..	..	..	..	..	..
(*d*) FRENCH AND PORTUGUESE SETTLEMENTS — Portuguese	..	..	..	..	..	..	..	..	..	..	..	..	..	..	..	..	..	..	..	..	..	1	..	1
TOTAL B. ..	2,291	1,469	822	861	527	334	789	126	663	1,842	335	1,507	1,797	714	1,083	181	107	74	83	44	39	585	412	173
Total A and B (Born in India) ..	591,274	320,595	270,879	519,541	285,626	234,215	28,213	14,586	13,677	18,870	9,920	8,950	59,787	33,254	26,533	104,378	51,580	52,793	50,007	26,627	23,380	47,684	25,431	22,258
C.—COUNTRIES IN ASIA BEYOND INDIA.																								
(I) INSIDE BRITISH DOMINIONS.																								
Ceylon ..	..	..	..	..	..	..	..	..	..	..	..	..	..	..	..	..	..	..	..	..	..	..	..	..
Hong Kong ..	..	..	..	..	..	..	..	..	..	..	..	..	..	..	..	..	..	..	..	..	..	..	..	..
Straits Settlements and Malaya ..	..	..	..	..	..	..	..	..	..	..	..	..	..	..	..	..	..	..	..	..	..	..	..	..
Total (I) ..	..	..	..	..	..	..	..	..	..	..	..	..	..	..	..	..	..	..	..	..	..	..	..	..
(II) OUTSIDE BRITISH DOMINIONS.																								
Afghanistan ..	33	66	17	839	520	310	..	..	..	..	..	..	2	2	..	1	1	..	1	1	..	259	259	..
Arabia ..	1	1	..	..	..	..	..	..	..	..	..	..	..	..	..	..	..	..	..	..	..	1	..	1
Bhotan ..	..	..	..	..	..	..	..	..	..	..	..	..	..	..	..	..	..	..	..	..	..	..	..	..
China ..	..	..	..	..	..	..	..	..	..	..	..	..	4	3	1	..	..	..	..	..	..	18	8	5
French Indo-China ..	..	..	..	..	..	..	..	..	..	..	..	..	..	..	..	..	..	..	..	..	..	..	..	..
Iraq ..	..	..	..	..	..	..	..	..	..	..	..	..	..	..	..	..	..	..	..	..	..	..	..	..
Japan ..	..	..	..	..	..	..	..	..	..	..	..	..	..	..	..	..	..	..	..	..	..	..	..	..
Java ..	..	..	..	..	..	..	..	..	..	..	..	..	..	..	..	..	..	..	..	..	..	..	..	..
Nepal ..	5	4	1	..	..	..	..	..	..	..	..	..	55	47	8	3	3	..	7	7	..	29	23	6
Persia ..	5	4	1	..	..	..	..	..	..	1	..	1	..	..	..	..	..	..	..	..	..	..	..	..
Philippine Islands ..	..	..	..	..	..	..	..	..	..	..	..	..	..	..	..	..	..	..	..	..	..	..	..	..
Russia in Asia ..	..	..	..	..	..	..	..	..	..	..	..	..	..	..	..	..	..	..	..	..	..	..	..	..
Russian Turkistan ..	..	..	..	..	..	..	..	..	..	..	..	..	..	..	..	..	..	..	..	..	..	..	..	..
Siam ..	..	..	..	..	..	..	..	..	..	..	..	..	..	..	..	..	..	..	..	..	..	..	..	..

TABLE VI.—BIRTH-PLACE.—PART B—*continued.*

District, State, Province or Country where born.	PROVINCE, DISTRICT OR STATE WHERE ENUMERATED.																							
	Muzaffargarh.			Dera Ghazi Khan.			Dujana.			Pataudi.			Kalsia.			Bashahr.			Nalagarh.			Keonthal.		
	Persons.	Males.	Females.	Persons.	Males.	Females.	Persons.	Males.	Females.	Persons.	Males.	Females.	Persons.	Males.	Females.	Persons.	Males.	Females.	Persons.	Males.	Females.	Persons.	Males.	Females.
	86	87	88	89	90	91	92	93	94	95	96	97	98	99	100	101	102	103	104	105	106	107	108	109
Sumatra	..	..	..	..	..	..	..	..	..	..	..	..	..	..	..	..	..	..	..	..	..	..	..	..
Syria	..	..	..	..	..	..	..	..	..	..	..	..	..	..	..	..	..	..	..	..	..	..	..	..
Tibet	..	..	..	..	..	..	..	..	..	..	..	..	..	..	..	12	9	3	..	..	..	97	11	86
Turkey in Asia	..	..	..	..	..	..	..	..	..	..	..	..	..	..	..	..	..	..	..	..	..	..	..	..
Turkistan Unspecified	..	..	..	..	..	..	..	..	..	..	..	..	..	..	..	..	..	..	..	..	..	..	..	..
Total (II)	94	75	19	839	529	310	..	..	..	1	..	1	61	52	9	16	13	3	8	8	..	399	301	98
(III) ASIA UNSPECIFIED	..	..	..	..	..	..	..	..	..	..	..	..	..	..	..	..	..	..	..	..	..	..	..	..
TOTAL C.	94	75	19	839	529	310	..	..	..	1	..	1	61	52	9	16	13	3	8	8	..	399	301	98
D.—COUNTRIES IN EUROPE																								
(I) INSIDE BRITISH DOMINIONS.																								
England and Wales	3	2	1	6	3	3	..	..	..	2	2	..	..	..	..	..	..	..	..	..	..	6	2	4
Gibraltar	..	..	..	..	..	..	..	..	..	..	..	..	..	..	..	..	..	..	..	..	..	..	..	..
Irish Free States	..	..	..	..	..	..	..	..	..	..	..	..	..	..	..	..	..	..	..	..	..	..	..	..
Malta	..	..	..	..	..	..	..	..	..	..	..	..	..	..	..	..	..	..	..	..	..	..	..	..
Northern Ireland	..	..	..	..	..	..	..	..	..	..	..	..	..	..	..	..	..	..	..	..	..	..	..	..
Scotland	2	2	..	..	..	..	..	..	..	..	..	..	..	..	..	..	..	..	..	..	..	2	..	2
United Kingdom Unspecified	..	..	..	..	..	..	3	1	2	..	..	..	..	..	..	..	..	..	..	..	..	..	..	..
Total (I)	5	4	1	6	3	3	3	1	2	2	2	..	..	..	..	..	..	..	..	..	..	8	2	6
(II) OUTSIDE BRITISH DOMINIONS.																								
Austria	..	..	..	..	..	..	..	..	..	..	..	..	..	..	..	..	..	..	..	..	..	..	..	..
Belgium	..	..	..	..	..	..	..	..	..	..	..	..	..	..	..	..	..	..	..	..	..	..	..	..
Denmark	..	..	..	..	..	..	..	..	..	..	..	..	..	..	..	..	..	..	..	..	..	..	..	..
France	1	..	1	..	..	..	..	..	..	..	..	..	..	..	..	..	..	..	..	..	..	..	..	..
Germany	..	..	..	..	..	..	..	..	..	..	..	..	..	..	..	..	..	..	..	..	..	1	..	1
Greece	..	..	..	..	..	..	..	..	..	..	..	..	..	..	..	..	..	..	..	..	..	..	..	..
Holland	..	..	..	..	..	..	..	..	..	..	..	..	..	..	..	..	..	..	..	..	..	..	..	..
Italy	..	..	..	..	..	..	..	..	..	..	..	..	..	..	..	..	..	..	..	..	..	..	..	..
Latvia	..	..	..	..	..	..	..	..	..	..	..	..	..	..	..	..	..	..	..	..	..	..	..	..
Norway	..	..	..	..	..	..	..	..	..	..	..	..	..	..	..	..	..	..	..	..	..	..	..	..
Portugal	..	..	..	..	..	..	..	..	..	..	..	..	..	..	..	..	..	..	..	..	..	1	..	1
Rumania	..	..	..	..	..	..	..	..	..	..	..	..	..	..	..	..	..	..	..	..	..	..	..	..
Russian Union	..	..	..	..	..	..	..	..	..	..	..	..	..	..	..	..	..	..	..	..	..	..	..	..
Spain	..	..	..	..	..	..	..	..	..	..	..	..	..	..	..	..	..	..	..	..	..	..	..	..
Sweden	..	..	..	..	..	..	..	..	..	..	..	..	..	..	..	..	..	..	..	..	..	..	..	..
Switzerland	..	..	..	..	..	..	..	..	..	..	..	..	..	..	..	..	..	..	..	..	..	..	..	..
Turkey in Europe	..	..	..	..	..	..	..	..	..	..	..	..	..	..	..	..	..	..	..	..	..	..	..	..
Total (II)	1	..	1	..	..	..	..	..	..	..	..	..	..	..	..	..	..	..	..	..	..	2	..	2

TABLE VI.—BIRTH-PLACE.—PART B

Birth-place																								
Austria	..	..	..	..	..	..	..	..	..	..	..	..	..	..	..	..	..	..	..	..	..	..	..	..
Belgium	..	..	..	..	..	..	..	..	..	..	..	..	..	..	..	..	..	..	..	..	..	..	..	..
Denmark	..	..	..	..	..	..	..	..	..	..	..	..	..	..	..	..	..	..	..	..	..	..	..	..
France	1	..	1	..	..	..	..	..	..	..	..	..	..	..	..	..	..	..	..	..	..	1	..	1
Germany	..	..	..	..	..	..	..	..	..	..	..	..	..	..	..	..	..	..	..	..	..	..	..	..
Greece	..	..	..	..	..	..	..	..	..	..	..	..	..	..	..	..	..	..	..	..	..	..	..	..
Holland	..	..	..	..	..	..	..	..	..	..	..	..	..	..	..	..	..	..	..	..	..	..	..	..
Italy	..	..	..	..	..	..	..	..	..	..	..	..	..	..	..	..	..	..	..	..	..	..	..	..
Latvia	..	..	..	..	..	..	..	..	..	..	..	..	..	..	..	..	..	..	..	..	..	..	..	..
Norway	..	..	..	..	..	..	..	..	..	..	..	..	..	..	..	..	..	..	..	..	..	1	..	1
Portugal	..	..	..	..	..	..	..	..	..	..	..	..	..	..	..	..	..	..	..	..	..	..	..	..
Rumania	..	..	..	..	..	..	..	..	..	..	..	..	..	..	..	..	..	..	..	..	..	..	..	..
Russian Union	..	..	..	..	..	..	..	..	..	..	..	..	..	..	..	..	..	..	..	..	..	..	..	..
Spain	..	..	..	..	..	..	..	..	..	..	..	..	..	..	..	..	..	..	..	..	..	..	..	..
Sweden	..	..	..	..	..	..	..	..	..	..	..	..	..	..	..	..	..	..	..	..	..	..	..	..
Switzerland	..	..	..	..	..	..	..	..	..	..	..	..	..	..	..	..	..	..	..	..	..	..	..	..
Turkey in Europe	..	..	..	..	..	..	..	..	..	..	..	..	..	..	..	..	..	..	..	..	..	..	..	..
Total (II)	1	..	1	..	..	..	..	..	..	..	..	..	..	..	..	..	..	..	..	..	..	2	..	2
(III) EUROPE UNSPECIFIED	..	..	..	..	..	..	..	..	..	..	..	..	..	..	..	..	..	..	..	..	..	..	..	..
TOTAL D.	6	4	2	6	3	3	3	1	2	2	2	..	..	..	..	..	..	..	..	..	..	10	2	8
E.—COUNTRIES IN AFRICA																								
(I) OUTSIDE BRITISH DOMINIONS.																								
Egypt	..	..	..	..	..	..	..	..	..	..	..	..	..	..	..	..	..	..	..	..	..	..	..	..
(II) AFRICA UNSPECIFIED	1	..	1	..	..	..	..	..	..	..	..	..	..	..	..	..	..	..	..	..	..	..	..	..
TOTAL E.	1	..	1	..	..	..	..	..	..	..	..	..	..	..	..	..	..	..	..	..	..	..	..	..
F.—COUNTRIES IN AMERICA																								
(I) INSIDE BRITISH DOMINIONS.																								
British Guiana	..	..	..	..	..	..	..	..	..	..	..	..	..	..	..	..	..	..	..	..	..	..	..	..
Canada	..	..	..	..	..	..	..	..	..	..	..	..	..	..	..	..	..	..	..	..	..	..	..	..
Total (I)	..	..	..	..	..	..	..	..	..	..	..	..	..	..	..	..	..	..	..	..	..	..	..	..
(II) OUTSIDE BRITISH DOMINIONS.																								
United States	..	..	..	..	..	..	..	..	..	..	..	..	..	..	..	..	..	..	..	..	..	..	..	..
(III) AMERICA UNSPECIFIED.	..	..	..	..	..	..	..	..	..	..	..	..	..	..	..	..	..	..	..	..	..	..	..	..
TOTAL F.	..	..	..	..	..	..	..	..	..	..	..	..	..	..	..	..	..	..	..	..	..	..	..	..
G.—COUNTRIES IN AUSTRALASIA																								
(I) INSIDE BRITISH DOMINIONS.																								
Australia	..	..	..	..	..	..	..	..	..	..	..	..	..	..	..	..	..	..	..	..	..	..	..	..
Fiji Islands	..	..	..	..	..	..	..	..	..	..	..	..	..	..	..	..	..	..	..	..	..	..	..	..
New Zealand	..	..	..	..	..	..	..	..	..	..	..	..	..	..	..	..	..	..	..	..	..	..	..	..
Elsewhere in British Australasia	..	..	..	..	..	..	..	..	..	..	..	..	..	..	..	..	..	..	..	..	..	..	..	..
Total (I)	..	..	..	..	..	..	..	..	..	..	..	..	..	..	..	..	..	..	..	..	..	..	..	..
TOTAL G.	..	..	..	..	..	..	..	..	..	..	..	..	..	..	..	..	..	..	..	..	..	..	..	..
TOTAL RETURNED	591,375	320,674	270,701	520,686	286,158	234,528	28,216	14,537	13,679	18,873	9,922	8,951	59,848	33,306	26,542	104,389	51,593	52,796	50,015	26,635	23,380	48,093	25,734	22,359
Birth-Place not Returned	..	..	..	..	..	..	..	..	..	..	..	..	..	..	..	..	..	..	..	..	..	..	..	—
TOTAL POPULATION	591,375	320,674	270,701	520,686	286,158	234,528	28,216	14,537	13,679	18,873	9,922	8,951	59,848	33,306	26,542	104,389	51,593	52,796	50,015	26,635	23,380	48,093	25,734	22,359

TABLE VI.—BIRTH-PLACE.—PART B—*continued.*

PROVINCE, DISTRICT OR STATE WHERE ENUMERATED.

District, State, Province or Country where born.	Baghal.			Jubbal.			Other Simla Hill States.			Loharu.			Sirmoor.			Bilaspur.			Mandi.			Suket.			Kapurthala.		
	Persons.	Males.	Females.	Persons.	Males.	Females.	Persons.	Males.	Females.	Persons.	Males.	Females.	Persons.	Males.	Females.	Persons.	Males.	Females.	Persons.	Males.	Females.	Persons.	Males.	Females.	Persons.	Males.	Females.
	110	111	112	113	114	115	116	117	118	119	120	121	122	123	124	125	126	127	128	129	130	13	132	133	134	135	136
A.—DISTRICTS OR STATES WITHIN THE PROVINCE																											
(I) BRITISH TERRITORY ..	*296*	136	160	407	246	101	2,798	1,529	1,269	1,913	618	1,265	8,920	5,349	3,571	3,299	915	2,384	8,500	5,209	3,291	1,149	691	458	43,942	10,042	33,900
District of Enumeration ..	..	..	..	..	..	..	..	..	..	..	..	..	..	..	..	..	..	..	..	..	..	..	..	..	..	..	..
(II) PUNJAB STATES ..	*25,999*	13,284	12,715	26,424	14,114	12,310	71,139	37,526	33,613	18,380	10,942	7,437	136,661	75,170	61,491	97,667	52,217	45,450	195,230	99,356	95,874	56,804	29,808	26,996	271,948	161,110	110,838
State of Enumeration .	*24,516*	12,845	11,671	24,256	13,487	10,769	64,639	35,049	29,590	17,420	10,607	6,813	135,426	74,583	60,843	93,672	50,967	42,705	192,424	98,527	93,897	55,768	29,381	26,387	271,789	161,045	110,744
(III) PUNJAB UNSPECIFIED	..	..	..	..	..	..	..	..	..	..	..	..	..	..	..	..	..	..	..	..	..	..	..	..	..	..	..
TOTAL A. .	**26,295**	**13,420**	**12,875**	**26,831**	**14,360**	**12,471**	**73,937**	**39,055**	**34,882**	**20,293**	**11,591**	**8,702**	**145,581**	**80,519**	**65,062**	**100,966**	**53,132**	**47,834**	**203,730**	**104,565**	**99,165**	**57,953**	**30,499**	**27,454**	**315,890**	**171,152**	**144,738**
B.—PROVINCES OR STATES IN INDIA BEYOND THE PROVINCE.																											
(a).—Provinces or States Adjacent to the Province.																											
(I) BRITISH TERRITORY.																											
Delhi ..	..	..	..	..	..	..	27	16	11	20	5	15	17	12	5	2	1	1	19	14	5	..	.	..	137	44	93
Baluchistan .	..	..	.	..	.	..	8	8	..	..	..	..	6	6	.	..	..	..	..	..	..	3	3	..	9	4	5
N. W. F. Province ..	..	.	..	..	..	..	7	7	..	..	.	.	12	12	.	..	..	.	311	284	27	1	1	.	16	12	4
U. P. of Agra and Oudh ..	*29*	21	8	226	68	158	440	215	225	33	20	13	2,198	1,224	974	11	7	4	489	373	116	288	249	39	553	257	296
Total (I) ..	**29**	**21**	**8**	**226**	**68**	**158**	**482**	**246**	**236**	**53**	**25**	**28**	**2,233**	**1,254**	**979**	**13**	**8**	**5**	**819**	**671**	**148**	**292**	**253**	**39**	**715**	**317**	**398**
(II)—FEUDATORY STATES.																											
Baluchistan States ..	..	..	..	.	..	..	..	..	..	..	..	..	..	..	..	.	..	..	..	..	..	..	..	..	.	..	..
United Provinces States ..	*10*	1	9	40	28	12	75	45	30	..	..	..	47	31	16	..	..	.	..	..	..	..	..	..	.	.	..
Jammu & Kashmir State ..	*11*	10	1	55	34	21	80	60	20	.	..	..	110	89	21	2	1	1	..	..	..	..	..	..			..
Rajputana Agency ..	..	..	..	1	1	..	7	6	1	2,981	708	2,272	157	140	17	2	2	..	1,814	1,707	107	110	59	51	2	2	..
Jaisalmer ..	..	..	..	..	..	..	..	..	..	..	..	..	..	..	..	..	..	..	19	7	12	..	..	..	32	10	22
Bikaner ..	..	..	..	..	..	..	1	..	1	..	..	..	..	..	..	..	..	..	..	..	..	..	..	..	..	..	..
Alwar ..	..	..	..	..	..	..	..	.	..	..	..	..	..	..	..	..	..	..	..	..	..	..	..	..	15	5	10
Jaipur ..	..	..	..	..	..	..	..	..	.	..	..	..	..	..	..	..	..	..	..	..	..	..	..	..	..	..	..
Bharatpur ..	..	..	..	.	..	..	..	..	..	..	..	..	..	..	.	.	..	..	..	..	..	..	..	..	5	5	..
Other States ..	..	..	..	1	1	..	6	6	..	2,981	708	2,273	157	140	17	2	2	..	19	7	12	..	..	..	12	..	12
Total (II) ..	**21**	**11**	**10**	**96**	**63**	**33**	**162**	**111**	**51**	**2,981**	**708**	**2,273**	**314**	**260**	**54**	**4**	**3**	**1**	**1,833**	**1,714**	**119**	**110**	**59**	**51**	**34**	**12**	**22**
TOTAL (a) ..	**50**	**32**	**18**	**322**	**131**	**191**	**644**	**357**	**287**	**3,034**	**733**	**2,301**	**2,547**	**1,514**	**1,033**	**17**	**11**	**6**	**2,652**	**2,385**	**267**	**402**	**312**	**90**	**749**	**329**	**420**
(b).—Other Provinces and States in India.																											
(I) BRITISH TERRITORY.																											
Ajmer Marwara ..	..	..	..	.	..	.	..		..	..	.	..	3	1	2	..	..	..	2	1	1	..	..	.	..	..	..
Andamans and Nicobars ..	.	.	..	.	..	..		.	.	..	.	..	..	..	..	..	..	..	..	..	..	..	..	..	..	..	..
Assam ..	.	..	.	.	..	..	.	..	..	.	..	..	.	..	..	..	..	.	..	..	..	..	..	..	.	..	..
Bengal ..	*3*	1	2	..	..	..	19	13	6	2	..	2	4	4	.	2	2	..	21	12	9	..	..	..	14	2	12
Bihar and Orissa ..	..	..	..	4	4	.	12	5	7	1	.	1	4	3	1	..	..	.	3	1	2	..	..	.	..	..	..

TABLE VI.—BIRTH-

Bombay	..	..	..	..	..	..	25	14	11	1	1	..	6	4	2	..	..	..	19	13	6	..	..	..	6	3	3
Aden	..	..	..	..	..	..	..	..	..	..	..	..	..	..	..	..	..	..	..	..	..	..	..	..	..	..	..
Burma	..	..	..	..	..	..	..	..	..	..	..	..	1	1	..	..	..	..	..	..	..	..	..	..	14	4	10
Central Provinces and Berar	..	..	..	1	1	..	1	1	..	..	..	..	20	12	8	..	..	..	94	60	34	..	..	..	36	17	19
Madras	..	..	..	..	..	..	4	1	3	..	..	..	5	4	1	..	..	..	19	15	4	..	..	..	..	..	..
Total (I)	3	1	2	5	5	..	61	34	27	4	1	3	48	29	14	2	2	..	158	102	56	..	..	..	70	26	44
(II) FEUDATORY STATES.																											
Assam States	..	..	..	..	..	..	..	..	..	..	..	..	..	..	..	..	..	..	..	..	..	..	..	..	..	..	..
Baroda State	..	..	..	..	..	..	..	..	..	..	..	..	..	..	..	..	..	..	1	1	..	..	..	..	..	..	..
Bihar and Orissa States	..	..	..	..	..	..	..	..	..	..	..	..	..	..	..	..	..	..	..	..	..	..	..	..	..	..	..
Bombay States	..	..	..	..	..	..	..	..	..	..	..	..	..	..	..	..	..	..	..	..	..	..	..	..	..	..	..
Central India Agency	..	..	..	..	..	..	2	2	..	..	..	..	10	6	4	..	..	..	..	..	..	..	..	..	2	1	1
Central Provinces States	..	..	..	..	..	..	..	..	..	..	..	..	..	..	..	2	2	..	..	..	..	..	..	..	..	..	..
Gwalior State	..	..	..	..	..	..	..	..	..	6	1	5	1	1	..	1	1	..	..	..	..	..	..	..	1	..	1
Hyderabad State	..	..	..	..	..	..	..	..	..	..	..	..	..	..	..	..	..	..	..	..	..	..	..	..	..	..	..
Madras States (Including Cochin and Travancore).	..	..	..	..	..	..	..	..	..	..	..	..	..	..	..	..	..	..	..	..	..	..	..	..	..	..	..
Travancore State	..	..	..	..	..	..	..	..	..	..	..	..	..	..	..	..	..	..	..	..	..	..	..	..	..	..	..
Mysore State	..	..	..	..	..	..	8	2	6	..	..	..	1	..	1	..	..	..	22	8	14	..	..	..	..	..	..
Total (II)	..	..	..	..	..	..	10	4	6	6	1	5	12	7	5	3	3	..	23	9	14	..	..	..	3	1	2
TOTAL (*b*)	3	1	2	5	5	..	71	38	33	10	2	8	55	36	19	5	5	..	181	111	70	..	..	..	73	27	46
(c) INDIA UNSPECIFIED	..	..	..	..	..	..	..	..	..	..	..	..	..	..	..	..	..	..	..	..	..	..	..	..	..	..	..
(d) FRENCH AND PORTUGUESE SETTLEMENTS — French	..	..	..	..	..	..	..	..	..	..	..	..	..	..	..	..	..	..	..	..	..	..	..	..	1	..	1
(d) FRENCH AND PORTUGUESE SETTLEMENTS — Portuguese	..	..	..	..	..	..	..	..	..	..	..	..	..	..	..	..	..	..	..	..	..	..	..	..	6	6	..
TOTAL B.	53	33	20	327	136	191	715	395	320	3,044	735	2,309	2,602	1,550	1,052	22	16	6	2,833	2,496	337	402	312	90	829	362	467
Total A and B (Born in India.)	26,348	13,453	12,895	27,158	14,496	12,662	74,652	39,450	35,202	23,337	12,326	11,011	148,183	82,069	66,114	100,988	53,148	47,840	206,563	107,061	99,502	58,355	30,811	27,544	316,719	171,514	145,205
C.—COUNTRIES IN ASIA BEYOND INDIA.																											
(I) INSIDE BRITISH DOMINIONS.																											
Ceylon	..	..	..	..	..	..	..	..	..	..	..	..	..	..	..	..	..	..	2	1	1	..	..	..	..	..	..
Hong Kong	..	..	..	..	..	..	..	..	..	..	..	..	..	..	..	..	..	..	..	..	..	..	..	..	..	..	..
Straits Settlements and Malaya	..	..	..	..	..	..	..	..	..	..	..	..	..	..	..	..	..	..	..	..	..	..	..	..	..	1	1
Total (I)	..	..	..	..	..	..	..	..	..	..	..	..	..	..	..	..	..	..	2	1	1	..	..	..	2	1	1
(II) OUTSIDE BRITISH DOMINIONS.																											
Afghanistan	..	..	..	..	..	..	11	8	3	..	..	..	7	7	..	5	5	..	8	8	..	..	..	..	..	..	..
Arabia	..	..	..	..	..	..	..	..	..	..	..	..	..	..	..	..	..	..	..	..	..	..	..	..	..	..	..
Bhotan	..	..	..	..	..	..	..	..	..	..	..	..	..	..	..	..	..	..	..	..	..	..	..	..	..	..	..
China	..	..	..	..	..	..	5	4	1	..	..	..	7	2	5	..	..	..	..	..	..	14	8	6	4	..	1
French Indo-China	..	..	..	..	..	..	..	..	..	..	..	..	..	..	..	..	..	..	..	..	..	..	..	..	..	..	..
Iraq	..	..	..	..	..	..	..	..	..	..	..	..	..	..	..	..	..	..	..	..	..	..	..	..	..	..	..
Japan	..	..	..	..	..	..	..	..	..	..	..	..	..	..	..	..	..	..	..	..	..	..	..	..	..	..	..
Java	..	..	..	..	..	..	..	..	..	..	..	..	..	..	..	..	..	..	..	..	..	..	..	..	..	..	..
Nepal	2	2	..	8	5	3	114	98	16	..	..	..	351	287	64	1	1	..	779	738	41	39	32	7	3	..	1
Persia	..	..	..	..	..	..	..	..	..	..	..	..	..	..	..	..	..	..	1	..	1	..	..	..	..	..	..
Philippine Islands	..	..	..	..	..	..	..	..	..	..	..	..	..	..	..	..	..	..	..	..	..	..	..	..	..	..	..
Russia in Asia	..	..	..	..	..	..	..	..	..	..	..	..	..	..	..	..	..	..	..	..	..	..	..	..	..	..	..
Russian Turkistan	..	..	..	..	..	..	..	..	..	..	..	..	..	..	..	..	..	..	..	..	..	..	..	..	..	..	..
Siam	..	..	..	..	..	..	..	..	..	..	..	..	..	..	..	..	..	..	..	..	..	..	..	..	..	..	..

TABLE VI.—BIRTH-PLACE—PART B—*continued.*

PROVINCE, DISTRICT OR STATE WHERE ENUMERATED.

District, State, Province or Country where born.	Baghal. Persons.	Baghal. Males.	Baghal. Females.	Jubbal. Persons.	Jubbal. Males.	Jubbal. Females.	Other Simla Hill States. Persons.	Other Simla Hill States. Males.	Other Simla Hill States. Females.	Loharu. Persons.	Loharu. Males.	Loharu. Females.	Sirmoor. Persons.	Sirmoor. Males.	Sirmoor. Females.	Bilaspur. Persons.	Bilaspur. Males.	Bilaspur. Females.	Mandi. Persons.	Mandi. Males.	Mandi. Females.	Suket. Persons.	Suket. Males.	Suket. Females.	Kapurthala. Persons.	Kapurthala. Males.	Kapurthala. Females.
	110	111	112	113	114	115	116	117	118	119	120	121	122	123	124	125	126	127	128	129	130	131	132	133	134	135	136
Sumatra	..	..	..	..	..	..	..	..	..	..	..	..	..	..	..	..	..	..	..	..	..	..	..	..	..	..	..
Syria	..	..	..	..	..	..	..	..	..	..	..	..	..	..	..	..	..	..	..	..	..	..	..	..	..	..	..
Tibet	2	2	..	6	6	..	39	33	6	..	..	..	18	18	..	..	..	..	62	30	32	..	..	..	..	..	..
Turkey in Asia	..	..	..	..	..	..	..	..	..	..	..	..	..	..	..	..	..	..	..	..	..	..	..	..	..	..	..
Turkistan Unspecified	..	..	..	..	..	..	..	..	..	..	..	..	..	..	..	..	..	..	..	..	..	..	..	..	..	..	..
Total (II)	4	4	..	14	11	3	169	143	26	..	..	..	383	314	69	6	6	..	850	776	74	53	40	13	7	5	2
(III) ASIA UNSPECIFIED	..	..	..	..	..	..	2	2	..	..	..	..	..	..	..	..	..	..	..	..	..	..	..	..	..	..	..
TOTAL C.	4	4	..	14	11	3	171	145	26	..	..	..	383	314	69	6	6	..	852	777	75	53	40	13	9	6	3
D.—COUNTRIES IN EUROPE.																											
(I) INSIDE BRITISH DOMINIONS.																											
England and Wales	..	..	..	..	..	..	3	2	1	..	..	..	1	1	..	..	..	..	38	27	11	..	..	..	5	3	2
Gibraltar	..	..	..	..	..	..	..	..	..	..	..	..	..	..	..	..	..	..	..	..	..	..	..	..	..	..	..
Irish Free States	..	..	..	..	..	..	..	..	..	..	..	..	..	..	..	..	..	..	..	..	..	..	..	..	..	..	..
Malta	..	..	..	..	..	..	2	2	..	1	..	1	..	..	..	..	..	..	..	..	..	..	..	..	1	..	1
Northern Ireland	..	..	..	..	..	..	..	..	..	..	..	..	..	..	..	..	..	..	3	2	1	..	..	..	..	..	..
Scotland	..	..	..	..	..	..	1	..	1	..	..	..	..	..	..	..	..	..	..	..	..	..	..	..	..	..	..
United Kingdom Unspecified	..	..	..	..	..	..	..	..	..	..	..	..	..	..	..	..	..	..	..	..	..	..	..	..	..	..	..
Total (I)	..	..	..	..	..	..	6	4	2	1	..	1	1	1	..	..	..	..	41	29	12	..	..	..	6	3	3
(II) OUTSIDE BRITISH DOMINIONS.																											
Austria	..	..	..	..	..	..	..	..	..	..	..	..	..	..	..	..	..	..	..	..	..	..	..	..	..	..	..
Belgium	..	..	..	..	..	..	..	..	..	..	..	..	..	..	..	..	..	..	..	..	..	..	..	..	..	..	..
Denmark	..	..	..	..	..	..	..	..	..	..	..	..	..	..	..	..	..	..	..	..	..	..	..	..	..	..	..
France	..	..	..	..	..	..	..	..	..	..	..	..	1	..	1	..	..	..	..	..	..	..	..	..	..	..	..
Germany	..	..	..	..	..	..	..	..	..	..	..	..	..	..	..	..	..	..	..	..	..	..	..	..	..	..	..
Greece	..	..	..	..	..	..	..	..	..	..	..	..	..	..	..	..	..	..	..	..	..	..	..	..	..	..	..
Holland	..	..	..	..	..	..	..	..	..	..	..	..	..	..	..	..	..	..	..	..	..	..	..	..	..	..	..
Italy	..	..	..	..	..	..	..	..	..	..	..	..	..	..	..	..	..	..	..	..	..	..	..	..	3	..	3
Latvia	..	..	..	..	..	..	..	..	..	..	..	..	..	..	..	..	..	..	..	..	..	..	..	..	..	..	..
Norway	..	..	..	..	..	..	..	..	..	..	..	..	..	..	..	..	..	..	..	..	..	..	..	..	..	..	..
Portugal	..	..	..	..	..	..	..	..	..	..	..	..	..	..	..	..	..	..	..	..	..	..	..	..	1	1	..
Rumania	..	..	..	..	..	..	..	..	..	..	..	..	..	..	..	..	..	..	..	..	..	..	..	..	..	..	..
Russian Union	..	..	..	..	..	..	..	..	..	..	..	..	..	..	..	..	..	..	3	3	..	..	..	..	..	..	..
Spain	..	..	..	..	..	..	..	..	..	..	..	..	..	..	..	..	..	..	..	..	..	..	..	..	..	..	..
Sweden	..	..	..	..	..	..	..	..	..	..	..	..	..	..	..	..	..	..	..	..	..	..	..	..	..	..	..
Switzerland	..	..	..	..	..	..	..	..	..	..	..	..	..	..	..	..	..	..	..	..	..	..	..	..	..	..	..
Turkey in Europe	..	..	..	..	..	..	..	..	..	..	..	..	..	..	..	..	..	..	..	..	..	..	..	..	..	..	..
Total (II)	..	..	..	..	..	..	..	..	..	..	..	..	1	..	1	..	..	..	3	3	..	..	..	..	4	1	3

PLACE.—PART B.

(III) EUROPE UNSPECIFIED	..	..	..	..	..	..	..	..	..	..	..	..	..	..	..	..	..	..	..	..	..	..	..	..	..	..	..
TOTAL D.	..	..	..	..	..	..	6	4	2	1	..	1	2	1	1	..	..	..	44	32	12	..	..	..	10	4	6
E.—COUNTRIES IN AFRICA.																											
(I) OUTSIDE BRITISH DOMINIONS.																											
Egypt	..	..	..	..	..	..	..	..	..	..	..	..	..	..	..	..	..	..	..	..	..	..	..	..	..	..	..
(II) AFRICA UNSPECIFIED	..	..	..	..	..	..	..	..	..	..	..	..	..	..	..	..	..	..	..	..	..	..	..	..	5	..	5
TOTAL E.	..	..	..	..	..	..	..	..	..	..	..	..	..	..	..	..	..	..	..	..	..	..	..	..	5	..	5
F.—COUNTRIES IN AMERICA.																											
(I) INSIDE BRITISH DOMINIONS.																											
British Guiana	..	..	..	..	..	..	..	..	..	..	..	..	..	..	..	..	..	..	..	..	..	..	..	..	..	..	..
Canada	..	..	..	..	..	..	..	..	..	..	..	..	..	..	..	..	..	..	..	..	..	..	..	..	..	..	..
Total (I)	..	..	..	..	..	..	..	..	..	..	..	..	..	..	..	..	..	..	..	..	..	..	..	..	..	..	..
(II) OUTSIDE BRITISH DOMINIONS.																											
United States	..	..	..	..	..	..	..	..	..	..	..	..	..	..	..	..	..	..	..	..	..	..	..	..	..	..	..
(III) AMERICA UNSPECIFIED.	..	..	..	..	..	..	..	..	..	..	..	..	..	..	..	..	..	..	..	..	..	..	..	..	5	5	..
TOTAL F.	..	..	..	..	..	..	..	..	..	..	..	..	..	..	..	..	..	..	..	..	..	..	..	..	5	5	..
G.—COUNTRIES IN AUSTRALASIA.																											
(I) INSIDE BRITISH DOMINIONS.																											
Australia	..	..	..	..	..	..	..	..	..	..	..	..	..	..	..	..	..	..	6	6	..	..	..	..	9	..	9
Fiji Islands	..	..	..	..	..	..	..	..	..	..	..	..	..	..	..	..	..	..	..	..	..	..	..	..	..	..	..
New Zealand	..	..	..	..	..	..	..	..	..	..	..	..	..	..	..	..	..	..	..	..	..	..	..	..	..	..	..
Elsewhere in British Australasia	..	..	..	..	..	..	..	..	..	..	..	..	..	..	..	..	..	..	..	..	..	..	..	..	..	..	..
Total (I)	..	..	..	..	..	..	..	..	..	..	..	..	..	..	..	..	..	..	6	6	..	..	..	..	9	..	9
TOTAL G.	..	..	..	..	..	..	..	..	..	..	..	..	..	..	..	..	..	..	6	6	..	..	..	..	9	..	9
TOTAL RETURNED	26,352	13,457	12,895	27,172	14,507	12,665	74,829	39,599	35,230	23,338	12,326	11,012	148,568	82,384	66,184	100,994	53,154	47,840	207,465	107,876	99,589	58,408	30,851	27,557	316,757	171,529	145,228
Birth-Place not Returned	..	..	..	..	..	..	..	..	..	..	..	..	..	..	..	..	..	..	..	..	..	..	..	..	..	..	..
	[illegible]	[illegible]	[illegible]	[illegible]	[illegible]	[illegible]	[illegible]	[illegible]	35,230	23,338	12,326	11,012	148,568	82,384	66,184	100,994	53,154	47,840	207,465	107,876	99,589	58,408	30,851	27,557	316,757	171,529	145,228

TABLE VI.—BIRTH-PLACE.—PART B—*continued.*

PROVINCE, DISTRICT OR STATE WHERE ENUMERATED.

District, State, Province or Country where born.	Malerkotla. Persons.	Males.	Females.	Faridkot. Persons.	Males.	Females.	Chamba. Persons.	Males.	Females.	Patiala. Persons.	Males.	Females.
	137	138	139	140	141	142	143	144	145	146	147	148
A.—DISTRICTS OR STATES WITHIN THE PROVINCE												
(I) BRITISH TERRITORY ..	*11,531*	6,851	4,680	41,537	13,925	27,612	2,139	1,205	934	170,112	61,717	108,395
District of Enumeration ..	..	..	..	..	..	..	..	..	..	..	..	..
(II) PUNJAB STATES ..	*70,792*	38,704	32,088	119,725	75,204	44,521	142,686	73,618	69,068	1,415,712	824,270	591,442
State of Enumeration ..	*62,069*	37,302	24,767	113,189	72,466	40,723	142,446	73,404	69,042	1,356,168	806,105	550,063
(III) PUNJAB UNSPECIFIED	..	..	..	..	..	..	..	..	..	..	..	..
TOTAL A. ..	**82,323**	**45,555**	**36,768**	**161,262**	**89,129**	**72,133**	**144,825**	**74,823**	**70,002**	**1,585,824**	**885,987**	**699,837**
B.—PROVINCES OR STATES IN INDIA BEYOND THE PROVINCE.												
(a).—Provinces or States adjacent to the Province.												
(I).—BRITISH TERRITORY.												
Delhi ..	*126*	78	48	259	160	99	2	1	1	1,297	462	835
Baluchistan ..	..	..	..	..	..	..	4	3	1	.	.	.
N. W. F. Province ..	*7*	4	3	7	7	..	13	10	3	186	134	52
U. P. of Agra and Oudh ..	*362*	182	180	578	433	145	78	48	30	10,250	5,640	4,610
Total (I) ..	**495**	**264**	**231**	**844**	**600**	**244**	**97**	**62**	**35**	**11,733**	**6,236**	**5,497**
(II).—FEUDATORY STATES.												
Baluchistan States ..	..	..	.	..	..	.	..	.	..	..	..	..
United Provinces States ..	..	..	..	..	..	.	..	..	..	..	..	..
Jammu & Kashmir State ..	*1*	.	1	6	2	4	1,626	944	682	252	203	49
Rajputana Agency ..	*27*	17	10	2,104	1,331	773	6	5	1	26,529	7,497	19,032
Jaisalmer ..	..	..	..	..	..	..	..	..	..	2	1	1
Bikaner ..	..	..	..	700	492	208	.	..	.	2,856	1,488	1,368
Alwar ..	..	..	..	384	231	153	.	..	..	6,338	1,855	4,483
Jaipur ..	..	..	..	957	560	397	..	.	..	16,763	3,853	12,910
Bharatpur ..	..	..	..	3	3		..	..	..	223	114	109
Other States ..	27	17	10	60	45	15	6	5	1	347	186	161
Total (II) ..	**28**	**17**	**11**	**2,110**	**1,333**	**777**	**1,632**	**949**	**683**	**26,781**	**7,700**	**19,081**
TOTAL (*a*) ..	**523**	**281**	**242**	**2,954**	**1,933**	**1,021**	**1,729**	**1,011**	**718**	**38,514**	**13,936**	**24,578**
(b).—Other Provinces and States in India.												
(I) BRITISH TERRITORY.												
Ajmer Marwara ..	..	..	..	..	..	..	.	..	..	113	34	79
Andamans and Nicobars ..	..	..	..	..	..	..	..	..	..	..	..	..
Assam ..	..	..	..	..	..	.	1	..	1	5	5	.
Bengal ..		4	.	4	..	.	8	7	1	151	86	65
Bihar and Orissa ..	..	..	..	.	.	.	..	..	..	61	39	22

District, State, Province or Country where born.	Jind. Persons.	Males.	Females.	Nabha. Persons.	Males.	Females.	Bahawalpur. Persons.	Males.	Females.
	149	150	151	152	153	154	155	156	157
A.—DISTRICTS OR STATES WITHIN THE PROVINCE									
(I) BRITISH TERRITORY ..	47,556	14,738	32,818	24,063	8,084	15,979	106,076	61,711	44,365
District of Enumeration ..	..	..	..	..	..	..	..	..	..
(II) PUNJAB STATES ..	267,665	158,259	109,406	251,898	147,068	104,830	848,954	465,932	383,022
State of Enumeration ..	242,370	149,364	93,006	209,693	134,938	74,755	840,892	461,298	379,594
(III) PUNJAB UNSPECIFIED	..	..	.	..	.	..	..	..	..
TOTAL A. ..	**315,221**	**172,997**	**142,224**	**275,961**	**155,152**	**120,809**	**955,030**	**527,643**	**427,387**
B.—PROVINCES OR STATES IN INDIA BEYOND THE PROVINCE.									
(a).—Provinces or States adjacent to the Province.									
(I).—BRITISH TERRITORY.									
Delhi ..	568	195	373	254	97	157	996	563	433
Baluchistan ..	15	12	3	1	1	..	115	81	34
N. W. F. Province ..	31	19	12	27	18	9	2,092	1,301	791
U. P. of Agra and Oudh ..	3,530	1,745	1,785	1,347	707	640	2,192	1,532	660
Total (I) ..	**4,144**	**1,971**	**2,173**	**1,629**	**823**	**806**	**5,395**	**3,477**	**1,918**
(II).—FEUDATORY STATES.									
Baluchistan States ..	.	..	..	..	..	..	2	2	..
United Provinces States ..	..	.	.	1	..	1	..	..	.
Jammu & Kashmir State ..	7	6	1	34	28	6	226	170	56
Rajputana Agency ..	5,069	1,275	3,794	9,565	1,911	7,654	20,864	11,809	9,055
Jaisalmer ..	..	..	..	..	..	..	4,997	2,723	2,274
Bikaner ..	1,203	188	1,015	560	280	280	10,355	5,608	4,747
Alwar ..	461	180	281	6,252	892	5,360	727	497	230
Jaipur ..	3,227	829	2,398	2,583	682	1,901	1,858	1,304	554
Bharatpur ..	77	25	52	114	29	85	21	14	7
Other States ..	101	53	48	56	28	28	2,906	1,663	1,243
Total (II) ..	**5,076**	**1,281**	**3,795**	**9,600**	**1,939**	**7,661**	**21,092**	**11,981**	**9,111**
TOTAL (*a*) ..	**9,220**	**3,252**	**5,968**	**11,229**	**2,762**	**8,467**	**26,487**	**15,458**	**11,029**
(b).—Other Provinces and States in India.									
(I) BRITISH TERRITORY.									
Ajmer Marwara ..	11	4	7	13	4	9	26	15	11
Andamans and Nicobars ..	..	..	..	..	..	..	..	.	..
Assam ..	..	..	..	2	..	2	..	..	..
Bengal ..	26	15	11	14	1	13	17	9	8
Bihar and Orissa ..	11	8	3	2	1	1	18	9	9

TABLE VI.—BIRTH-

Bombay	146	27	11	..	..	..	..	..	..	138	89	49	30	15	15	25	10	15	1,671	1,026	645
Aden	..	..	..	..	..	..	..	..	..	..	..	..	..	..	..	..	..	..	..	..	..
Burma	11	6	5	1	1	..	1	1	..	136	96	40	8	3	5	17	12	5	4	3	1
Central Provinces and Berar	3	1	2	141	96	45	1	..	1	45	19	26	3	2	1	17	4	13	21	13	8
Madras	..	..	..	..	..	..	2	..	2	51	29	22	9	6	3	1	..	1	10	7	3
Total (I)	**164**	**34**	**130**	**142**	**97**	**45**	**13**	**8**	**5**	**700**	**397**	**303**	**98**	**53**	**45**	**91**	**32**	**59**	**1,767**	**1,082**	**685**
(II) FEUDATORY STATES.																					
Assam States	..	..	..	..	..	..	..	..	..	..	..	..	1	..	1	..	..	..	..	..	..
Baroda State	..	..	..	..	..	..	..	..	..	4	1	3	7	4	3	..	..	..	1	1	..
Bihar and Orissa States	..	..	..	..	..	..	..	..	..	..	..	..	..	..	..	..	..	..	..	..	..
Bombay States	..	..	..	..	..	..	..	..	..	..	..	..	..	..	..	..	..	..	24	24	..
Central India Agency	..	..	..	..	..	..	5	5	..	45	34	11	6	2	4	9	2	7	22	18	4
Central Provinces States	..	..	..	..	..	..	..	..	..	..	..	..	..	..	..	..	..	..	..	..	..
Gwalior State	2	..	2	..	..	..	..	..	..	113	39	74	35	15	20	16	3	13	189	128	61
Hyderabad State	2	..	2	..	..	..	..	..	..	50	21	29	20	15	5	7	1	6	1	1	..
Madras States (Including Cochin and Travancore).	..	..	..	..	..	..	..	..	..	..	..	..	..	..	..	..	..	..	..	..	..
Travancore State	..	..	..	..	..	..	..	..	..	..	..	..	..	..	..	..	..	..	..	..	..
Mysore State	..	..	..	..	..	..	..	..	..	..	..	..	2	..	2	..	..	..	..	..	..
Total (II)	4	..	4	..	..	..	5	5	..	212	95	117	71	36	35	32	6	26	237	172	65
TOTAL (*b*)	168	34	134	142	97	45	18	13	5	912	492	420	169	89	80	123	38	85	2,004	1,254	750
(*c*) INDIA UNSPECIFIED	..	..	..	..	..	..	..	..	..	..	..	..	..	..	..	..	..	..	..	..	..
(*d*) FRENCH AND PORTUGUESE SETTLEMENTS — French	..	..	..	..	..	..	..	..	..	..	..	..	..	..	..	..	..	..	..	..	..
Portuguese	..	..	..	..	..	..	..	..	..	..	..	..	14	12	2	..	..	..	..	..	..
TOTAL B.	**691**	**315**	**376**	**3,096**	**2,030**	**1,066**	**1,747**	**1,024**	**723**	**39,426**	**14,428**	**24,998**	**9,403**	**3,353**	**6,050**	**11,352**	**2,800**	**8,552**	**28,491**	**16,712**	**11,779**
Total A and B (Born in India)	**83,014**	**45,870**	**37,144**	**164,358**	**91,159**	**73,199**	**146,572**	**75,847**	**70,725**	**1,625,250**	**900,415**	**724,835**	**324,624**	**176,350**	**148,274**	**287,313**	**157,952**	**129,361**	**983,521**	**544,355**	**439,166**
C.—COUNTRIES IN ASIA BEYOND INDIA.																					
(I) INSIDE BRITISH DOMINIONS.																					
Ceylon	..	..	..	..	..	..	..	..	..	..	..	..	..	..	..	..	..	..	..	..	..
Hong Kong	..	..	..	..	..	..	..	..	..	..	..	..	..	..	..	..	..	..	..	..	..
Straits Settlements and Malaya	..	..	..	..	..	..	..	..	..	15	15	..	2	1	1	..	..	..	..	..	..
Total (I)	..	..	..	..	..	..	..	..	..	15	15	..	2	1	1	..	..	..	..	..	..
(II) OUTSIDE BRITISH DOMINIONS.																					
Afghanistan	..	..	..	..	..	..	12	11	1	94	78	16	7	4	3	2	2	..	1,060	727	333
Arabia	..	..	..	..	..	..	..	..	..	..	..	..	..	..	..	2	1	1	..	..	..
Bhotan	..	..	..	..	..	..	..	..	..	..	..	..	..	..	..	..	..	..	..	..	..
China	2	2	..	3	3	..	1	1	..	68	40	28	..	..	..	12	5	7	..	..	..
French Indo-China	..	..	..	..	..	..	..	..	..	..	..	..	..	..	..	..	..	..	..	..	..
Iraq	..	..	..	..	..	..	..	..	..	..	..	..	..	..	..	..	..	..	13	8	5
Japan	..	..	..	..	..	..	..	..	..	..	..	..	..	..	..	..	..	..	..	..	..
Java	..	..	..	..	..	..	..	..	..	..	..	..	..	..	..	..	..	..	..	..	..
Nepal	8	1	7	..	..	..	262	177	85	2	8	18	12	10	2	4	2	2	3	2	1
Persia	1	1	..	..	..	..	..	..	..	..	..	..	..	..	..	..	..	..	6	6	..
Philippine Islands	..	..	..	..	..	..	..	..	..	..	..	..	..	..	..	..	..	..	..	..	..
Russia in Asia	..	..	..	..	..	..	..	..	..	..	..	..	..	..	..	..	..	..	..	..	..
Russian Turkistan	..	..	..	..	..	..	..	..	..	..	..	..	..	..	..	..	..	..	..	..	..
Siam	..	..	..	..	..	..	..	..	..	..	..	..	..	..	..	..	..	..	..	..	..

TABLE VI.—BIRTH-PLACE.—PART B—*concluded.*

District, State, Province or Country where born.	Mallerkotla. Persons. 137	Males. 138	Females. 139	Faridkot. Persons. 140	Males. 141	Females. 142	Chamba. Persons. 143	Males. 144	Females. 145	Patiala. Persons. 146	Males. 147	Females. 148	Jind. Persons. 149	Males. 150	Females. 151	Nabha. Persons. 152	Males. 153	Females. 154	Bahawalpur. Persons. 155	Males. 156	Females. 157
	Province, District or State where enumerated.																				
Sumatra	..	..	..	..	..	..	..	..	..	..	..	..	..	..	..	..	..	..	..	..	..
Syria	..	..	..	..	..	..	..	..	..	..	..	..	..	..	..	..	..	..	..	..	..
Tibet	..	..	..	..	..	..	22	22	..	..	..	..	..	..	..	..	..	..	..	..	..
Turkey in Asia	..	..	..	..	..	..	..	..	..	..	..	..	..	..	..	..	..	..	..	..	..
Turkistan Unspecified	..	..	..	..	..	..	1	1	..	..	..	..	..	..	..	..	..	..	..	..	..
Total (II)	11	4	7	3	3	..	298	212	86	188	126	62	19	14	5	20	10	10	1,082	743	339
(III) ASIA UNSPECIFIED	40	7	33	..	..	..	..	..	..	..	..	..	..	..	..	..	..	..	..	..	..
TOTAL C.	51	11	40	3	3	..	298	212	86	203	141	62	21	15	6	20	10	10	1,082	743	339
D.—COUNTRIES IN EUROPE.																					
(I) INSIDE BRITISH DOMINIONS.																					
England and Wales	..	..	..	2	1	1	..	..	..	27	14	13	20	11	9	..	..	..	9	5	4
Gibraltar	..	..	..	..	..	..	..	..	..	..	..	..	..	..	..	..	..	..	..	..	..
Irish Free States	..	..	..	..	..	..	..	..	..	..	..	..	..	..	..	..	..	..	..	..	..
Malta	..	..	..	..	..	..	..	..	..	..	..	..	..	..	..	..	..	..	..	..	..
Northern Ireland	..	..	..	1	..	1	..	..	..	3	2	1	4	2	2	..	..	..	..	..	..
Scotland	..	..	..	..	..	..	..	..	..	5	3	2	..	..	..	..	..	..	..	..	..
United Kingdom Unspecified	..	..	..	..	..	..	..	..	..	..	..	..	..	..	..	..	..	..	..	..	..
Total (I)	..	..	..	3	1	2	..	..	..	35	19	16	24	13	11	..	..	..	9	5	4
(II) OUTSIDE BRITISH DOMINIONS.																					
Austria	..	..	..	..	..	..	..	..	..	..	..	..	..	..	..	..	..	..	..	..	..
Belgium	..	..	..	..	..	..	..	..	..	..	..	..	..	..	..	..	..	..	..	..	..
Denmark	..	..	..	..	..	..	..	..	..	..	..	..	..	..	..	..	..	..	..	..	..
France	..	..	..	..	..	..	..	..	..	2	..	2	..	..	..	..	..	..	..	..	..
Germany	..	..	..	..	..	..	..	..	..	1	1	..	1	1	..	..	..	..	..	..	..
Greece	..	..	..	..	..	..	..	..	..	..	..	..	..	..	..	..	..	..	..	..	..
Holland	..	..	..	..	..	..	..	..	..	..	..	..	..	..	..	..	..	..	..	..	..
Italy	..	..	..	..	..	..	..	..	..	..	..	..	..	..	..	..	..	..	..	..	..
Latvia	..	..	..	..	..	..	..	..	..	..	..	..	..	..	..	..	..	..	..	..	..
Norway	..	..	..	..	..	..	..	..	..	..	..	..	..	..	..	..	..	..	..	..	..
Portugal	..	..	..	..	..	..	..	..	..	..	..	..	4	2	2	..	..	..	..	..	..
Rumania	..	..	..	..	..	..	..	..	..	..	..	..	..	..	..	..	..	..	..	..	..
Russian Union	..	..	..	..	..	..	..	..	..	..	..	..	..	..	..	..	..	..	..	..	..
Spain	..	..	..	..	..	..	..	..	..	..	..	..	..	..	..	..	..	..	..	..	..
Sweden	..	..	..	..	..	..	..	..	..	..	..	..	..	..	..	..	..	..	..	..	..
Switzerland	..	..	..	..	..	..	..	..	..	..	..	..	..	..	..	..	..	..	..	..	..
Turkey in Europe	..	..	..	..	..	..	..	..	..	..	..	..	..	..	..	..	..	..	..	..	..
Total (II)	..	..	..	..	..	..	..	..	..	3	1	2	5	3	2	..	..	..	..	..	..

(III) EUROPE UNSPECIFIED	..	..	..	..	..	..	..	..	..	..	..	..	..	..	..	..	..	..	..	..	..
TOTAL D. ..	..	..	..	3	1	2	..	..	..	38	20	18	29	16	13	..	..	..	9	5	4
E.—COUNTRIES IN AFRICA.																					
(I) OUTSIDE BRITISH DOMINIONS.																					
Egypt ..	..	..	..	..	..	..	..	..	..	..	..	..	..	..	..	..	..	..	..	..	..
(II) AFRICA UNSPECIFIED.	2	..	..	3	..	..	..	..	..	17	15	2	1	1	..	..	..	..	..	..	..
TOTAL E. ..	3	..	..	3	..	..	..	..	..	17	15	2	1	1	..	..	..	..	..	..	..
F.—COUNTRIES IN AMERICA																					
(I) INSIDE BRITISH DOMINIONS.																					
British Guiana ..	..	..	..	..	..	..	..	..	..	..	..	..	..	..	..	..	..	..	..	..	..
Canada ..	..	..	..	..	..	..	..	..	..	1	..	1	1	1	..	..	..	..	..	..	..
Total (I) ..	..	..	..	..	..	..	..	..	..	1	..	1	1	1	..	..	..	..	..	..	..
(II) OUTSIDE BRITISH DOMINIONS.																					
United States ..	..	..	..	..	..	..	..	..	..	..	..	..	..	..	..	..	..	..	..	..	..
(III) AMERICA UNSPECIFIED.	4	2	2	..	..	..	..	..	..	10	6	4	..	..	..	..	..	..	..	..	..
TOTAL F. ..	4	2	2	..	..	..	..	..	..	11	6	5	1	1	..	..	..	..	..	..	..
G.—COUNTRIES IN AUSTRALASIA.																					
(I) INSIDE BRITISH DOMINIONS.																					
Australia ..	..	..	..	..	..	..	..	..	..	1	..	1	..	..	..	..	..	..	..	..	..
Fiji Islands ..	..	..	..	..	..	..	..	..	..	..	..	..	..	..	..	..	..	..	..	..	..
New Zealand ..	..	..	..	..	..	..	..	..	..	..	..	..	..	..	..	..	..	..	..	..	..
Elsewhere in British Australasia	..	..	..	..	..	..	..	..	..	..	..	..	..	..	..	..	..	..	..	..	..
Total (I) ..	..	..	..	..	..	..	..	..	..	1	..	1	..	..	..	..	..	..	..	..	..
TOTAL G. ..	..	..	..	..	..	..	..	..	..	1	..	1	..	..	..	..	..	..	..	..	..
TOTAL RETURNED ..	83,072	45,883	37,189	164,364	91,163	73,201	146,870	76,059	70,811	1,625,520	900,597	724,923	324,676	176,383	148,293	287,333	157,962	129,371	984,612	545,103	439,509
Birth-Place not Returned ..	..	..	..	..	..	..	..	..	..	..	..	..	..	..	..	241	124	117	..	..	..
TOTAL POPULATION ..	83,072	45,883	37,189	164,364	91,163	73,201	146,870	76,059	70,811	1,625,520	900,597	724,923	324,676	176,383	148,293	287,574	158,086	129,488	984,612	545,103	439,509

TABLE VI.

BIRTH-PLACE—PART C.

DISTRICT OR STATE WHERE ENUMERATED.

Serial No.	District or State where born.	Gujranwala. Persons.	Gujranwala. Males.	Gujranwala. Females.	Sheikhupura. Persons.	Sheikhupura. Males.	Sheikhupura. Females.	Shahpur. Persons.	Shahpur. Males.	Shahpur. Females.	Montgomery. Persons.	Montgomery. Males.	Montgomery. Females.
	1	2	3	4	5	6	7	8	9	10	11	12	13
	BRITISH TERRITORY ..	**727,397**	**402,073**	**325,324**	**686,195**	**377,537**	**308,658**	**803,220**	**433,891**	**369,329**	**972,188**	**535,410**	**436,778**
	AMBALA DIVISION	**1,464**	**839**	**625**	**3,335**	**2,074**	**1,261**	**2,643**	**1,694**	**949**	**9,544**	**5,513**	**4,031**
1	Hissar	*358*	209	149	748	446	302	552	326	226	3,402	2,052	1,350
2	Rohtak ..	*374*	209	165	491	290	201	630	402	228	1,836	1,038	798
3	Gurgaon	*377*	269	108	873	633	240	437	308	129	1,735	865	870
4	Karnal . .	*72*	27	45	115	70	45	423	248	175	291	167	124
5	Ambala	*271*	118	153	1,069	604	465	578	396	182	2,259	1,379	880
6	Simla	*12*	7	5	39	31	8	23	14	9	21	12	9
	JULLUNDUR DIVISION	**3,414**	**2,210**	**1,204**	**26,571**	**15,960**	**10,611**	**6,618**	**4,040**	**2,573**	**70,744**	**41,913**	**28,831**
7	Kangra . ..	*281*	202	79	204	161	43	242	208	34	454	301	153
8	Hoshiarpur	*1,090*	787	303	8,606	5,272	3,334	2,450	1,551	899	17,531	10,969	6,562
9	Jullundur	*1,010*	618	392	13,584	7,653	5,931	2,022	1,194	828	28,537	17,132	11,405
10	Ludhiana	*278*	157	121	930	554	376	1,101	631	470	6,842	3,980	2,862
11	Ferozepore	*755*	446	309	3,247	2,320	927	798	456	342	17,380	9,531	7,849
	LAHORE DIVISION ..	**697,241**	**385,818**	**311,423**	**621,859**	**341,809**	**280,050**	**38,872**	**22,142**	**16,730**	**84,899**	**49,610**	**35,089**
12	Lahore	*3,307*	1,637	1,670	19,435	9,225	10,210	2,354	1,138	1,216	29,875	16,948	12,927
13	Amritsar	*2,712*	1,501	1,211	25,629	13,981	11,648	4,790	2,847	1,943	19,964	11,925	8,039
14	Gurdaspur .. .	*1,674*	1,117	557	14,774	8,193	6,581	2,387	1,479	908	12,893	7,763	5,130
15	Sialkot	*31,011*	14,492	16,519	29,868	15,258	14,610	21,552	12,582	8,970	13,055	7,946	5,109
16	Gujranwala	*646,069*	361,275	284,794	41,316	21,783	19,533	7,027	3,669	3,358	3,279	2,009	1,270
17	Sheikhupura	*12,468*	5,796	6,672	490,837	273,369	217,468	762	427	335	5,633	3,019	2,614
	RAWALPINDI DIVISION	**18,589**	**9,711**	**8,878**	**10,117**	**5,263**	**4,854**	**730,602**	**392,164**	**338,438**	**18,053**	**11,253**	**6,800**
18	Gujrat	*14,101*	7,023	7,078	6,084	2,961	3,123	22,613	12,198	10,415	3,702	2,206	1,496
19	Shahpur	*2,414*	1,400	1,014	1,383	804	579	683,369	365,327	318,042	4,382	2,492	1,890
20	Jhelum	*866*	527	339	1,118	649	469	16,534	9,967	6,567	4,586	3,031	1,555
21	Rawalpindi	*826*	511	315	1,002	539	463	1,603	1,027	576	3,921	2,586	1,335
22	Attock	*236*	122	114	325	171	154	2,403	1,417	986	795	499	296
23	Mianwali	*146*	128	18	205	139	66	4,080	2,228	1,852	667	439	228
	MULTAN DIVISION ..	**6,689**	**3,495**	**3,194**	**24,313**	**12,431**	**11,882**	**24,490**	**13,851**	**10,639**	**789,143**	**427,121**	**362,022**
24	Montgomery	*543*	242	301	4,167	2,245	1,922	197	110	87	748,915	405,057	343,858
25	Lyallpur	*3,620*	1,898	1,722	18,280	9,153	9,127	2,586	1,493	1,093	26,958	14,282	12,676
26	Jhang	*2,019*	1,050	969	1,162	676	486	20,605	11,612	8,993	4,484	2,538	1,916
27	Multan	*344*	186	158	534	263	271	753	391	362	6,800	3,911	2,889
28	Muzaffargarh	*123*	101	22	100	58	42	217	153	64	1,522	1,079	443
29	Dera Ghazi Khan ..	*40*	18	22	80	46	34	132	92	40	461	254	210

Serial No.	District or State where born.	Lyallpur. Persons.	Lyallpur. Males.	Lyallpur. Females.	Jhang. Persons.	Jhang. Males.	Jhang. Females.	Multan. Persons.	Multan. Males.	Multan. Females.	Bahawalpur State. Persons.	Bahawalpur State. Males.	Bahawalpur State. Females.
	1	14	15	16	17	18	19	20	21	22	23	24	25
	BRITISH TERRITORY ..	**1,129,377**	**618,702**	**510,675**	**662,765**	**354,204**	**308,561**	**1,154,614**	**633,018**	**521,596**	**106,076**	**61,711**	**44,365**
	AMBALA DIVISION	**15,811**	**9,031**	**6,780**	**284**	**145**	**89**	**2,725**	**1,802**	**923**	**14,592**	**8,621**	**5,971**
1	Hissar	1,400	782	618	20	8	12	450	292	158	10,827	6,202	4,625
2	Rohtak ..	447	247	200	14	11	3	393	272	121	1,033	656	377
3	Gurgaon	474	321	153	12	7	5	745	487	258	1,302	880	422
4	Karnal . .	644	342	302	43	32	11	291	211	80	477	298	179
5	Ambala	12,799	7,303	5,496	44	86	58	800	514	286	923	566	357
6	Simla	47	36	11	1	1	..	46	26	20	30	19	11
	JULLUNDUR DIVISION	**106,482**	**60,477**	**46,005**	**1,282**	**839**	**443**	**22,690**	**14,038**	**8,652**	**35,976**	**19,972**	**16,004**
7	Kangra . ..	308	160	148	24	24		418	344	74	99	83	16
8	Hoshiarpur	29,546	16,554	12,992	409	259	150	7,064	4,752	2,312	2,708	1,742	966
9	Jullundur	48,116	27,836	20,280	519	355	164	8,818	5,194	3,624	9,624	5,425	4,199
10	Ludhiana	19,969	11,343	8,626	177	138	39	2,357	1,387	970	1,953	1,124	829
11	Ferozepore	8,543	4,584	3,959	153	63	90	4,033	2,361	1,672	21,592	11,598	9,994
	LAHORE DIVISION ..	**151,724**	**84,761**	**66,963**	**4,661**	**2,732**	**1,929**	**36,425**	**22,141**	**14,284**	**14,475**	**8,929**	**5,546**
12	Lahore	10,820	6,045	4,775	404	221	183	7,259	4,318	2,941	2,429	1,490	939
13	Amritsar	43,617	25,004	18,613	335	202	133	11,093	6,835	4,258	2,849	1,737	1,112
14	Gurdaspur .. .	27,287	15,338	11,949	275	161	114	6,109	3,522	2,587	2,390	1,403	987
15	Sialkot	44,584	24,782	19,802	688	430	258	7,715	4,616	3,099	2,956	2,024	932
16	Gujranwala	11,876	6,826	5,050	2,587	1,516	1,071	2,957	2,062	895	2,342	1,382	960
17	Sheikhupura	13,540	6,766	6,774	372	202	170	1,292	788	504	1,509	893	616
	RAWALPINDI DIVISION	**26,196**	**14,534**	**11,662**	**6,518**	**3,586**	**2,932**	**17,360**	**10,305**	**7,055**	**8,108**	**4,895**	**3,213**
18	Gujrat	10,675	5,959	4,716	1,044	701	343	2,196	1,434	762	2,096	1,319	777
19	Shahpur	4,732	2,546	2,186	3,824	2,007	1,817	3,308	1,931	1,377	2,922	1,652	1,270
20	Jhelum	3,110	1,920	1,190	546	311	235	2,949	1,864	1,085	1,266	769	497
21	Rawalpindi	2,026	1,211	815	163	89	74	1,326	935	391	684	433	251
22	Attock	811	520	291	303	187	116	2,786	1,575	1,211	201	156	45
23	Mianwali	4,842	2,378	2,464	638	291	347	4,795	2,566	2,229	939	566	373
	MULTAN DIVISION ..	**829,164**	**449,899**	**379,265**	**650,070**	**346,902**	**303,168**	**1,075,414**	**584,732**	**490,682**	**32,925**	**19,294**	**13,631**
24	Montgomery	31,784	17,633	14,151	309	201	108	6,782	3,378	3,404	11,276	6,004	5,272
25	Lyallpur	752,709	405,685	347,024	2,198	1,226	972	7,883	4,423	3,460	3,155	1,686	1,469
26	Jhang	35,827	20,981	14,846	644,860	344,170	300,690	22,194	12,718	9,476	1,918	1,139	779
27	Multan	6,907	4,334	2,573	1,878	905	973	1,022,624	554,222	468,402	11,842	7,284	4,558
28	Muzaffargarh	1,493	980	513	698	341	357	2,058	[illegible]250	4,808	2,323	1,703	620
29	Dera Ghazi Khan ..	444	286	158	127	59	68	3,873	2,741	1,132	2,411	1,478	933

PUNJAB STATES ..	377	290	87	2,759	1,603	1,156	1,464	840	624	13,319	7,594	5,725	11,165	5,741	5,424	147	111	36	5,535	3,056	2,479	848,954	465,932	383,022
(A) HAVING POLITICAL RELATIONS WITH THE PUNJAB GOVERNMENT ..	..	..	..	21	15	6	12	7	5	153	16	137	62	30	32	18	18	..	4	3	1	16	11	5
1 Dujana	..	..	..	..	..	..	..	..	..	4	4	..	3	3	..	..	..	..	..	..	..	5	3	2
2 Pataudi	..	..	..	..	..	..	..	..	..	132	..	132	..	..	..	..	..	..	..	..	..	..	..	..
3 Kalsia	..	..	..	..	..	..	12	7	5	8	7	1	43	26	17	1	1	..	2	1	1	11	8	3
4 *SIMLA HILL STATES* ..	..	..	..	21	15	6	..	..	..	9	5	4	16	1	15	17	17	..	2	2	..	..	..	..
Bashahr	..	..	..	..	..	..	..	..	..	..	..	..	4	..	4	1	1	..	..	..	..	..	..	..
Nalagarh	..	..	..	..	..	..	..	..	..	1	1	..	10	..	10	..	..	..	..	..	..	..	..	..
Keonthal	..	..	..	2	2	..	..	..	..	4	2	2	..	..	..	..	..	..	..	..	..	..	..	..
Baghal	..	..	..	..	..	..	..	..	..	..	..	..	1	..	1	..	..	..	..	..	..	..	..	..
Jubbal	..	..	..	..	..	..	..	..	..	..	..	..	..	..	..	..	..	..	..	..	..	..	..	..
Other Simla Hill States..	..	..	..	19	13	6	..	..	..	4	2	2	1	1	..	16	16	..	2	2	..	..	..	..
(B) HAVING POLITICAL RELATIONS WITH THE GOVERNMENT OF INDIA ..	377	290	87	2,738	1,588	1,150	1,452	883	619	13,166	7,578	5,588	11,103	5,711	5,392	129	93	86	5,531	3,053	2,478	848,938	465,921	383,017
5 Loharu	..	..	..	..	..	..	..	..	..	1	..	1	1	..	1	..	..	..	..	..	..	17	12	5
6 Sirmoor	..	..	..	..	..	..	..	..	..	4	1	3	20	6	14	5	5	..	1	1	..	..	..	..
7 Bilaspur	..	..	..	..	..	..	24	14	10	2	1	1	..	..	..	8	8	..	1	..	1	..	..	..
8 Mandi	1	1	..	2	1	1	..	..	..	1	1	..	1	1	..	2	2	..	..	..	..	3	2	1
9 Suket	..	..	..	..	..	..	..	..	..	..	..	..	..	..	..	..	..	..	..	..	..	..	..	..
10 Kapurthala	39	25	14	1,489	841	648	164	85	79	1,913	1,019	894	3,026	1,475	1,551	13	12	1	397	239	158	1,011	575	436
11 Maler Kotla	25	25	..	43	23	20	59	39	20	173	105	68	394	183	211	..	..	..	10	8	2	108	69	30
12 Faridkot	16	14	2	114	58	56	40	19	21	325	210	115	363	202	161	..	..	..	65	37	28	2,258	1,202	1,056
13 Chamba	4	4	..	4	2	2	1	1	..	2	..	2	2	..	2	..	..	..	6	4	2	..	..	..
14 Patiala (Phulkian States)	127	91	36	665	406	259	847	505	342	3,370	2,244	1,126	5,330	2,805	2,525	37	21	16	690	429	261	3,390	1,957	1,433
15 Jind (Phulkian States)	15	13	2	86	69	17	84	50	34	714	398	316	167	107	60	4	3	1	115	78	37	543	348	195
16 Nabha (Phulkian States)	71	67	4	142	94	48	151	89	62	404	274	130	865	419	446	22	22	..	141	87	54	716	458	258
17 Bahawalpur	79	50	29	193	94	99	82	31	51	6,257	3,325	2,932	934	513	421	38	20	18	4,105	2,170	1,935	840,892	461,298	379,594

TABLE VI.—BIRTH-PLACE—PART D.

CITY AND TOWN WHERE ENUMERATED.

District, State, Province or Country where Born.	Lahore City. Persons.	Lahore City. Males.	Lahore City. Females.	Amritsar City. Persons.	Amritsar City. Males.	Amritsar City. Females.	Multan City. Persons.	Multan City. Males.	Multan City. Females.	Rawalpindi Town. Persons.	Rawalpindi Town. Males.	Rawalpindi Town. Females.	Sialkot Town. Persons.	Sialkot Town. Males.	Sialkot Town. Females.	Ambala Town. Persons.	Ambala Town. Males.	Ambala Town. Females.	Jullundur Town. Persons.	Jullundur Town. Males.	Jullundur Town. Females.	Ferozepore Town. Persons.	Ferozepore Town. Males.	Ferozepore Town. Females.
1	2	3	4	5	6	7	8	9	10	11	12	13	14	15	16	17	18	19	20	21	22	23	24	25
A:—DISTRICTS OR STATES WITHIN THE PROVINCE.																								
(I):—BRITISH TERRITORY.	*361,896*	225,105	136,790	249,635	148,512	101,123	112,457	63,097	49,360	95,075	58,133	36,942	96,999	56,566	40,433	67,329	39,712	27,617	83,920	48,098	35,822	50,849	30,747	20,102
(II):—PUNJAB STATES ..	*4,151*	2,882	1,269	7,121	5,073	2,048	850	618	232	251	179	72	..	..	..	3,114	1,625	1,489	1,979	839	1,140	1,357	849	508
TOTAL A. ..	**366,046**	**227,987**	**138,059**	**256,756**	**153,585**	**103,171**	**113,307**	**63,715**	**49,592**	**95,326**	**58,312**	**37,014**	**96,999**	**56,566**	**40,433**	**70,443**	**41,337**	**29,106**	**85,899**	**48,937**	**36,962**	**52,206**	**31,596**	**20,610**
B:—PROVINCES OR STATES IN INDIA BEYOND THE PROVINCE.																								
(a):—PROVINCES OR STATES ADJACENT TO THE PROVINCE.																								
(I):—BRITISH TERRITORY.																								
Delhi ..	*2,416*	1,527	889	..	..	..	236	165	71	292	177	115	106	74	32	616	320	296	79	32	47	270	176	94
Baluchistan ..	*385*	278	107	23	11	12	73	47	26	203	101	102	53	42	11	28	16	12	12	4	8	..	..	..
N. W. F. Province ..	*7,060*	4,969	2,091	954	467	487	828	549	279	6,451	4,721	1,730	245	212	33	601	439	162	154	85	69	2,888	1,508	1,380
U. P. of Agra and Oudh ..	*28,806*	21,083	7,723	4,883	3,231	1,652	2,413	1,759	654	4,767	3,309	1,458	228	146	82	10,883	6,492	4,391	1,083	675	408	5,639	3,312	2,327
TOTAL (I) ..	**38,667**	**27,857**	**10,810**	**5,860**	**3,709**	**2,151**	**3,550**	**2,520**	**1,030**	**11,713**	**8,308**	**3,405**	**632**	**474**	**158**	**12,128**	**7,267**	**4,861**	**1,328**	**796**	**532**	**8,797**	**4,996**	**3,801**
(II):—FEUDATORY STATES.																								
United Provinces States ..	*310*	126	184	..	.	..	30	30	..	39	38	1	..	..	..	41	41	..	..	..	..	..	..	..
Jammu & Kashmir State ..	*8,469*	7,165	1,304	..	..	..	190	163	27	6,688	5,587	1,101	808	665	143	212	156	56	219	177	42	226	174	52
Rajputana Agency	*5,603*	3,875	1,728	1,072	772	300	702	448	254	360	192	168	9	5	4	1,051	704	347	95	44	51	1,637	917	720
Jaisalmer ..	*1*	1	..	..	..	..	..	..	..	..	.	..	..	..	..	..	..	..	..	..	..	..	..	..
Bikaner ..	*110*	67	43	249	203	46	..	..	..	4	..	4	..	..	..	..	..	..	6	2	4	253	165	88
Alwar ..	*994*	747	247	..	..	..	.	.	..	34	32	2	..	..	..	..	..	..	23	10	13	330	70	260
Jaipur ..	*4,227*	[illegible]	[illegible]	..	..	..	..	..	..	193	110	83	..	..	..	..	..	..	..	..	..	860	520	340
Bharatpur ..	*72*	44	28	.	..	..	..	..	..	1	..	1	..	..	..	..	..	..	1	1	..	4	4	..
Other States ..	*199*	107	92	823	569	254	702	448	254	128	50	78	9	5	4	1,051	704	347	65	31	34	190	158	32
TOTAL (II) ..	**14,382**	**11,166**	**3,216**	**1,072**	**772**	**300**	**922**	**641**	**281**	**7,087**	**5,817**	**1,270**	**817**	**670**	**147**	**1,304**	**901**	**403**	**314**	**221**	**93**	**1,863**	**1,091**	**772**
TOTAL (a) ..	**53,049**	**39,023**	**14,026**	**6,932**	**4,481**	**2,451**	**4,472**	**3,161**	**1,311**	**18,800**	**14,125**	**4,675**	**1,449**	**1,144**	**305**	**13,432**	**8,168**	**5,264**	**1,642**	**1,017**	**625**	**10,660**	**6,087**	**4,573**

(b):—OTHER PROVINCES AND STATES IN INDIA.																								
(I):—BRITISH TERRITORY.																								
Ajmer Merwara	*154*	103	51	2	..	2	6	2	4	3	3	..	..	..	..	18	6	12	..	..	..	..	..	..
Andamans and Nicobars	*20*	17	3	3	3	..	..	..	..	3	2	1	..	..	..	..	..	..	..	..	..	..	..	..
Assam	*49*	37	12	6	3	3	1	1	..	2	..	2	..	..	..	1	1	..	4	..	4	..	..	..
Bengal	*1,255*	856	399	98	63	35	45	17	28	259	153	106	175	146	29	155	80	75	55	36	19	126	51	75
Bihar and Orissa	*110*	90	20	3	2	1	35	18	17	47	32	15	1	1	..	32	15	17	..	..	..	14	4	10
Bombay	*1,564*	1,028	526	300	230	79	432	220	212	443	251	192	15	14	1	251	148	103	54	13	41	127	77	50
Aden	*29*	28	1	..	..	..	..	..	..	1	..	1	..	..	..	1	..	1	..	..	..	..	..	..
Burma	*121*	81	40	10	8	2	4	3	1	43	24	19	14	7	7	34	21	13	22	12	10	55	40	15
Central Provinces and Berar	*195*	145	50	66	15	51	13	13	..	78	9	69	39	31	8	66	26	40	16	12	4	13	13	..
Madras	*455*	307	148	19	13	6	30	19	11	158	95	63	36	24	12	72	40	32	39	21	18	58	43	15
TOTAL (I)	**3,913**	**2,664**	**1,249**	**516**	**337**	**179**	**566**	**293**	**273**	**1,036**	**569**	**467**	**280**	**228**	**57**	**629**	**337**	**292**	**190**	**94**	**96**	**393**	**228**	**165**
(II):—FEUDATORY STATES.																								
Baroda State	*37*	27	10	1	..	1	2	1	1	18	10	8	..	..	..	11	3	8	..	..	..	..	..	..
Bihar and Orissa States	*1*	1	..	..	..	..	..	..	..	..	..	..	..	..	..	..	..	..	..	..	..	..	..	..
Bombay States	*42*	27	15	..	..	..	..	..	..	..	..	..	..	..	..	2	..	2	..	..	..	..	..	..
Central India Agency	*23*	23	..	..	..	..	..	..	..	2	1	1	..	..	..	..	..	..	1	..	1	..	..	..
Central Provinces States	*41*	18	23	..	..	..	..	..	..	..	..	..	..	..	..	..	..	..	..	..	..	..	..	..
Gwalior State	*143*	92	51	4	1	3	26	11	15	101	26	75	..	..	..	69	45	24	10	7	3	108	48	60
Hyderabad State	*136*	90	46	11	8	3	38	..	38	23	18	5	..	..	..	21	15	6	117	35	82	38	14	24
Madras States	*13*	8	5	..	..	..	..	..	..	..	..	..	..	..	..	..	..	..	..	..	..	..	..	..
Mysore State	*128*	118	10	2	2	..	..	..	..	2	2	..	..	..	..	19	9	10	..	..	..	..	..	..
TOTAL (II)	**564**	**404**	**160**	**18**	**11**	**7**	**66**	**12**	**54**	**146**	**57**	**89**	..	..	..	**122**	**72**	**50**	**128**	**42**	**86**	**146**	**62**	**84**
TOTAL (b)	**4,477**	**3,068**	**1,409**	**534**	**348**	**186**	**632**	**305**	**327**	**1,182**	**626**	**556**	**280**	**228**	**57**	**751**	**409**	**342**	**318**	**136**	**182**	**539**	**290**	**249**
(c):—INDIA UNSPECIFIED.	*125*	116	9	..	..	..	..	..	..	475	196	279	..	..	..	88	35	53	..	..	..	1	1	..
(d):—FRENCH AND PORTUGUESE SETTLEMENTS. French	..	..	..	..	..	..	..	..	..	..	..	..	..	..	..	..	..	..	..	..	..	..	..	..
Portuguese	*11*	5	6	..	..	..	..	..	..	..	..	..	..	..	..	..	..	..	..	..	..	..	..	..
TOTAL B.	57,662	42,212	15,450	7,466	4,829	2,637	5,104	3,466	1,638	20,457	14,947	5,510	1,729	1,367	362	14,271	8,612	5,659	1,960	1,153	807	11,200	6,378	4,822
(C):—COUNTRIES IN ASIA BEYOND INDIA.																								
(I):—INSIDE BRITISH DOMINIONS.																								
Ceylon	*27*	26	1	1	1	..	2	1	1	3	1	2	..	..	..	1	..	1	..	..	..	2	2	..
Straits Settlements and Malaya.	*7*	4	3	..	..	..	..	..	..	..	..	..	..	..	..	..	..	..	1	..	1	..	..	..
TOTAL (I	**34**	**30**	**4**	**1**	**1**	..	**2**	**1**	**1**	**3**	**1**	**2**	..	..	..	**1**	..	**1**	**1**	..	**1**	**2**	**2**	..

TABLE VI.—BIRTH-PLACE—PART D.—*concluded.*

CITY AND TOWN WHERE ENUMERATED.

District, State, Province or Country where Born.	Lahore City. Persons.	Males.	Females.	Amritsar City. Persons.	Males.	Females.	Multan City. Persons.	Males.	Females.	Rawalpindi Town. Persons.	Males.	Females.	Sialkot Town. Persons.	Males.	Females.	Ambala Town. Persons.	Males.	Females.	Jullundur Town. Persons.	Males.	Females.	Ferozepore Town. Persons.	Males.	Females.
1	2	3	4	5	6	7	8	9	10	11	12	13	14	15	16	17	18	19	20	21	22	23	24	25
(II) :—OUTSIDE BRITISH DOMINIONS.																								
Afghanistan ..	*507*	347	160	38	37	1	26	22	3	138	74	64	13	13	..	1	1	..	7	7	..	..	..	..
Arabia ..	*109*	95	14	3	3	.	33	33	..	71	68	3	9	7	2	16	16	..	11	5	6	1	1	..
Bhotan ..	*2*	1	1	..	..	..	..	..	..	..	..	..	..	..	..	..	..	..	..	..	..	..	..	..
China ..	*49*	40	9	1	1	..	19	19	..	20	12	8	3	3	..	2	1	1	2	2	..	..	..	..
Iraq .	*27*	27	..	..	.	..	..	..	..	..	..	..	..	..	..	..	..	..	..	..	..	..	..	..
Japan ..	*17*	15	2	..	..	..	..	..	..	..	..	..	..	..	..	..	..	..	..	..	..	..	..	..
Java ..	..	..	..	..	..	..	..	..	..	..	..	..	..	.	..	..	..	..	3	1	2	..	..	..
Nepal ..	*191*	152	39	330	300	30	36	31	5	108	91	17	..	..	..	75	61	14	31	51	..	112	112	..
Persia ..	*72*	65	7	9	2	7	9	9	..	5	1	4	14	14	..	1	1	..	5	2	3	..	..	.
Siam ..	*28*	2	26	..	..	..	..	..	..	..	..	..	.	..	..	..	..	..	..	..	..	..	..	..
Tibet ..	*4*	4	..	..	..	..	..	..	..	6	6	..	..	..	..	..	..	..	..	..	..	..	..	..
Turkey in Asia ..	..	..	..	..	..	..	..	..	..	..	..	..	..	..	..	1	1	..	..	..	..	..	..	..
Turkistan Unspecified ..	..	..	..	68	68	..	—	..	..	..	..	..	..	..	..	..	..	..	..	..	..	..	..	..
Total (II) ..	**1,006**	**748**	**258**	**449**	**411**	**38**	**123**	**115**	**8**	**348**	**252**	**96**	**39**	**37**	**2**	**96**	**81**	**15**	**79**	**68**	**11**	**113**	**113**	..
(III) :—ASIA UNSPECIFIED.	..	..	..	..	..		..	..	..	1	1	..	..	..	..	..	..	..	..	..	..	..	..	..
TOTAL C. ..	**1,040**	**778**	**262**	**450**	**412**	**38**	**125**	**116**	**9**	**352**	**254**	**98**	**39**	**37**	**2**	**97**	**81**	**16**	**80**	**68**	**12**	**115**	**115**	..
D :—COUNTRIES IN EUROPE.																								
(I) :—INSIDE BRITISH DOMINIONS.																								
England and Wales ..	*3,389*	2,795	594	159	154	5	854	780	74	2,742	2,206	536	2,139	1,863	276	1,641	1,409	232	1,038	921	117	960	678	282
Gibraltar ..	..	..	..	..	..	..	..	.	..	..	..	..	..	..	..	4	..	4	..	..	..	..	..	..
Irish Free States ..	..	..	..	..	..	..	..	..	..	..	..	..	..	..	..	20	17	3	..	..	..	..	..	..
Malta ..	..	..	..	..	..	..	..	..	..	2	2	..	..	..	..	..	..	..	..	..	..	..	..	..
Northern Ireland ..	*100*	53	47	..	..	..	12	9	3	208	132	76	29	23	6	21	12	9	21	21	..	77	77	..
Scotland ..	*138*	93	45	.	..	..	10	10	..	119	89	30	9	9	..	43	30	13	8	7	1	56	25	31
Total (I) ..	**3,627**	**2,941**	**686**	**159**	**154**	**5**	**876**	**799**	**77**	**3,071**	**2,429**	**642**	**2,177**	**1,895**	**282**	**1,729**	**1,468**	**261**	**1,067**	**949**	**118**	**1,093**	**730**	**313**
(II) :—OUTSIDE BRITISH TERRITORY.																								
Belgium ..	..	..	..	..	..	..	6	2	4	..	..	..	..	..	..	4	3	1	..	..	..	..	..	..
France ..	2	2	..	..	..	..	..	..	..	8	..	8	..	..	..	2	..	2	..	..	..	10	7	3
Germany ..	*1*	..	1	1	1	..	..	..	..	15	10	5	..	..	..	7	2	5	1	1	..	..	..	..

Greece ..	..	..	..	..	..	..	.	..	..	1	1	..	..	..	..	..	..	..	..	.	..	.	..	..
Holland ..	..	..	..	..	..	..	..	..	..	1	..	1	..	..	..	..	..	..	..	..	..	..	..	..
Italy ..	..	..	..	..	..	..	..	..	..	..	..	..	..	..	..	1	1	..	1	1	..	..	..	..
Russian Union ..	..	..	..	..	..	..	..	..	..	..	..	..	..	..	..	..	..	..	1	..	1	..	..	..
Sweden ..	..	..	..	..	..	..	..	..	..	2	..	2	..	..	..	..	..	..	..	..	..	..	..	..
Turkey in Europe ..	32	32	..	..	..	1	.	..	..	..	..	..	..	..	..	..	..	..	..	..	..	..	..	..
TOTAL (II). ..	35	34	1	2	1	1	6	2	4	27	11	16	..	..	..	14	8	8	3	2	1	10	7	3
(III):—EUROPE UNSPECIFIED. ..	*1,130*	507	623	..	..	..	6	..	6	1	..	1	15	15	..	..	..	..	..	..	..	..	..	..
TOTAL D. ..	4,792	3,482	1,310	161	155	6	388	801	87	3,099	2,440	659	2,192	1,910	282	1,743	1,474	269	1,070	951	119	1,103	787	316
E:—COUNTRIES IN AFRICA.																								
(I):—OUTSIDE BRITISH DOMINIONS.																								
Egypt ..	..	..	..	.	..	..	18	15	3	1	..	1	..	..	..	12	7	5	..	..	..	..	..	..
(II):—AFRICA UNSPECIFIED. ..	*128*	86	42	6	4	2	3	1	2	18	14	4	12	12	..	6	1	5	15	9	6	8	8	..
TOTAL E. ..	128	86	42	6	4	2	21	16	5	19	14	5	12	12	..	18	8	10	15	9	6	8	8	..
F:—COUNTRIES IN AMERICA.																								
(I):—INSIDE BRITISH DOMINIONS.																								
Canada ..	5	5	..	..	..	..	..	..	..	5	..	5	.	..	..	2	..	2	..	..	..	..	..	—
(II):—AMERICA UNSPECIFIED. ..	*58*	28	30	..	..	..	1	1	..	25	4	21	2	2	..	15	10	5	2	1	1	..	..	..
TOTAL F. ..	63	33	30	..	..	..	1	1	..	30	4	26	2	2	..	17	10	7	2	1	1	..	..	..
G:—COUNTRIES IN AUSTRALASIA.																								
(I):—INSIDE BRITISH DOMINIONS.																								
Australia ..	*13*	8	5	1	..	1	11	4	7	1	..	1	..	..	..	3	1	2	..	..	..	2	..	2
Fiji Islands ..	..	..	..	..	..	..	..	..	..	..	..	..	..	..	..	..	..	..	4	..	4	..	..	..
New Zealand ..	3	1	2	..	..	..	..	..	..	..	..	..	..	..	..	..	..	..	..	..	..	..	..	..
TOTAL (I) ..	16	9	7	1	..	1	11	4	7	1	..	1	..	..	.	3	1	2	4	..	4	2	..	2
TOTAL G.	16	9	7	1	..	1	11	4	7	1	..	1	..	..	..	3	1	2	4	..	4	2	..	2
TOTAL RETURNED AND POPULATION.	429,747	274,587	155,160	264,840	158,985	105,855	119,457	68,119	51,338	119,284	75,971	43,313	100,973	59,894	41,079	86,592	51,528	35,069	89,030	51,119	37,911	64,634	38,884	25,750

TABLE VII.

AGE, SEX AND CIVIL CONDITION.

1. The age at this Census was recorded according to the nearest birthday. At the last Census, age meant the number of years completed. Each age-group includes the persons who have attained the ages represented by the years constituting the group except the top year. For example, the age-group 5-10 includes all persons whose age is either 5, 6, 7, 8 or 9 years; persons whose age is 10 go into the next higher group, 10-15.

2. This Table is divided into three parts. Part A shows the distribution for the Punjab as a whole of the total population and for each main religion by age, sex and civil condition. Figures for Ad-Dharmis have been shown separately for the first time. Part B shows the distribution for British Territory, for Punjab States (both groups), and for each District and State, of the total population and of the five principal religions (Hindu, Muslim, Christian, Jain and Sikh). The age-groups in Part B are quinary, as in Part A, up to the age of 20 and thereafter decennial down to 60, the final group being 60 and over. Part C gives similar details, with the addition of the figures of "Others" (other religions which include Buddhist, Zoroastrian, Jew and Ad-Dharmi) for cities and selected towns to which Lyallpur, Ludhiana and Sargodha have been added on the present occasion.

Note 1. The age statistics for places treated as towns for Census purposes are given in Part III. The age statistics for selected Tahsils have not been tabulated.

Note 2. Age statistics for Delhi Province appear in a separate Report.

TABLE VII—AGE, SEX
PART A.—PROVINCIAL SUMMARY.

PUNJAB.

Religion and Age.	Population. Persons.	Population. Males.	Population. Females.	Unmarried. Persons.	Unmarried. Males.	Unmarried. Females.	Married. Persons.	Married. Males.	Married. Females.	Widowed. Persons.	Widowed. Males.	Widowed. Females.
1	2	3	4	5	6	7	8	9	10	11	12	13
ALL RELIGIONS ..	**28,490,857**	**15,561,194**	**12,929,663**	**13,843,073**	**8.420,307**	**5.422.766**	**11,959,323**	**5.964,546**	**5.994.777**	**2.688.461**	**1.176,341**	**1,512,120**
0—1 ..	1,050,734	530,770	519,964	1,050,425	530,623	519,802	284	136	148	25	11	14
1—2 ..	793,450	400,213	393,237	792,791	399,948	392,843	619	244	375	40	21	19
2—3 ..	885,394	448,472	436,922	883,625	447,781	435,844	1,703	649	1,054	66	42	24
3—4 ..	892,129	457,208	434,921	887,290	455,571	431,719	4,695	1,573	3,122	144	64	80
4—5 ..	858,453	447,565	410,888	850,601	444,985	405,616	7,446	2,415	5,031	406	165	241
Total 0—5 ..	4,480,160	2,284,228	2,195,932	4,464,732	2,278,908	2,185,824	14,747	5,017	9,730	681	303	378
5—10 ..	3,765,322	2,025,061	1,740,261	3,565,773	1,970,817	1,594,956	195,586	52,347	143,239	3,963	1,897	2,066
10—15 ..	3,428,151	1,888,698	1,539.453	2,921,224	1,748,302	1,172,922	497,166	135,622	361,544	9,761	4,774	4,987
15—20 ..	2,656,926	1,456,871	1,200,055	1,227,207	953,009	274,198	1,388,717	482,031	906,686	41,002	21,831	19,171
20—25 ..	2,662,458	1,438,529	1,223,929	768,050	664,161	103,889	1,818,932	732,816	1,086,116	75,476	41,552	33,924
25—30 ..	2,304,045	1,266,773	1,037.272	319,897	290,284	29,613	1,845,951	902,332	943,619	138,197	74,157	64,040
30—35 ..	2,038,337	1,148,899	889,438	202,907	183,454	19,453	1,659,517	875,841	783,676	175,913	89,604	86,309
35—40 ..	1,582,797	887,353	695,444	110,785	98,355	12,430	1,235,420	684,527	550,893	236,592	104,471	132,121
40—45 ..	1,363,393	758,970	604,423	81,303	71,997	9,306	1,014,458	574,545	439,913	267,632	112,428	155,204
45—50 ..	1,154,958	654,992	499,966	57,200	50,663	6,537	766,758	471,314	295,444	331,000	133,015	197,985
50—55 ..	932,216	529,978	402,238	42,940	37,927	5,013	577,530	365,870	211.660	311,746	126,181	185,565
55—60 ..	701,540	403,129	298,411	28,739	25,795	2,944	365,759	251,710	114,049	307,042	125,624	181,418
60—65 ..	587,556	338,284	249,272	22,969	20,639	2,330	280,640	200,838	79,802	283,947	116,807	167,140
65—70 ..	325,317	192,277	133,040	11,829	10,588	1,241	133,180	101,514	31,666	180,308	80,175	100,133
70 and over ..	507,681	287,152	220,529	17,518	15,408	2,110	164,962	128,222	36,740	325,201	143,522	181,679
HINDU ..	**8,599,720**	**4,685,705**	**3,914,015**	**3,892,353**	**2.410.063**	**1,482,290**	**3,750,730**	**1,877.260**	**1.873.470**	**956,637**	**398,382**	**558,255**
0—1 ..	303,116	152,691	150,425	302,998	152,622	150,376	115	67	48	3	2	1
1—2 ..	227,634	114,019	113,615	227,405	113,891	113,514	221	125	96	8	3	5
2—3 ..	253,191	126,597	126,594	252,651	126,326	126,325	523	260	263	17	11	6
3—4 ..	253,273	128,058	125,215	251,537	127,476	124,061	1,691	567	1,124	45	15	30
4—5 ..	239,863	124,081	115,782	236,897	123,170	113,727	2,825	860	1,965	141	51	90
Total 0—5 ..	1,277,077	645,446	631,631	1,271,488	643,485	628,003	5,375	1,879	3,496	214	82	132
5—10 ..	1,085,926	578,259	507,667	1,001,650	555,364	446,286	82,648	22,166	60,482	1,628	729	899
10—15 ..	1,028,197	561,173	467,024	820,503	501,982	318,521	203,628	57,291	146,337	4,066	1,900	2,166
15—20 ..	835,009	456,924	378,085	328,462	272,292	56,170	490,361	176,703	313,658	16,186	7,929	8,257
20—25 ..	820,521	442,543	377,978	197,781	181,861	15,920	593,892	246,494	347,398	28,848	14,188	14,660
25—30 ..	705,247	387,633	317,614	86,269	80,753	5,516	565,940	281,857	284,083	53,038	25,023	28,015
30—35 ..	633,254	356,912	276,342	59,633	55,548	4,085	504,940	270,292	234,648	68,681	31,072	37,609
35—40 ..	502,047	281,767	220,280	34,886	32,606	2,280	373,485	211,149	162,336	93,676	38,012	55,664
40—45 ..	431,706	242,303	189,403	27,150	25,435	1,715	301,042	175,746	125,296	103,514	41,122	62,392
45—50 ..	360,541	205,603	154,938	20,377	19,153	1,224	218,638	138,971	79,667	121,526	47,479	74,047
50—55 ..	292,495	167,565	124,930	15,375	14,439	936	164,385	108,347	56,038	112,735	44,779	67,956
55—60 ..	218,189	125,565	92,624	10,364	9,783	581	100,742	72,690	28,052	107,083	43,092	63,991
60—65 ..	181,281	103,434	77,847	8,390	7,948	442	75,379	56,235	19,144	97,512	39,251	58,261
65—70 ..	95,164	56,042	39,122	4,358	4,126	232	33,413	26,710	6,703	57,393	25,206	32,187
70 and over ..	133,066	74,536	58,530	5,667	5,288	379	36,862	30,730	6,132	90,537	38,518	52,019
AD-DHARAMI ..	**418,789**	**228,509**	**190,280**	**179,408**	**108,725**	**70,683**	**203,668**	**101,431**	**102,237**	**35,713**	**18,353**	**17,360**
0—1 ..	16,580	8,517	8,063	16,576	8,516	8,060	4	1	3	..	..	..
1—2 ..	11,929	5,971	5,958	11,920	5,969	5,951	9	2	7	..	..	..
2—3 ..	13,273	6,708	6,565	13,245	6,699	6,546	26	8	18	2	1	1
3—4 ..	13,699	7,047	6,652	13,510	6,995	6,515	187	51	136	2	1	1
4—5 ..	13,158	6,868	6,290	12,777	6,761	6,016	368	101	267	13	6	7
Total 0—5 ..	68,639	35,111	33,528	68,028	34,940	33,088	594	163	431	17	8	9
5—10 ..	58,910	31,996	26,914	48,346	28,116	20,230	10,464	3,833	6,631	100	47	53
10—15 ..	51,337	30,028	24,309	35,464	22,640	12,824	18,645	7,263	11,382	228	125	103
15—20 ..	38,908	21,060	17,848	11,393	9,048	2,345	26,909	11,590	15,319	606	422	184
20—25 ..	37,595	20,432	17,163	6,760	5,786	974	29,797	13,892	15,905	1,038	754	284
25—30 ..	32,019	17,685	14,334	3,394	2,979	415	26,847	13,458	13,389	1,778	1,248	530
30—35 ..	27,885	15,615	12,270	2,346	2,104	242	23,320	12,042	11,278	2,219	1,469	750
35—40 ..	21,780	12,176	9,604	1,184	1,001	183	17,756	9,580	8,176	2,840	1,595	1,245
40—45 ..	18,673	10,349	8,324	883	721	162	14,630	7,955	6,675	3,160	1,673	1,487
45—50 ..	15,681	8,853	6,828	549	458	91	11,057	6,418	4,639	4,075	1,977	2,098
50—55 ..	12,281	6,825	5,456	349	301	48	8,182	4,759	3,423	3,750	1,765	1,985
55—60 ..	9,806	5,542	4,264	248	221	27	5,595	3,515	2,080	3,963	1,806	2,157
60—65 ..	8,710	5,055	3,655	228	201	27	4,619	3,104	1,515	3,863	1,750	2,113
65—70 ..	5,208	3,081	2,127	104	88	16	2,383	1,719	664	2,721	1,274	1,447
70 and over ..	8,357	4,701	3,656	132	121	11	2,870	2,140	730	5,355	2,440	2,915
SIKH ..	**4,071,624**	**2,270,946**	**1,800,678**	**2,001,173**	**1,256,861**	**744,312**	**1,677,781**	**828,073**	**849,708**	**392,670**	**186,012**	**206,658**
0—1 ..	151,214	77,660	73,554	151,163	77,635	73,528	42	22	20	9	3	6
1—2 ..	108,866	55,789	53,077	108,766	55,763	53,003	89	22	67	11	4	7
2—3 ..	117,589	60,788	56,801	117,389	60,741	56,648	190	43	147	10	4	6
3—4 ..	117,855	61,652	56,203	117,510	61,541	55,969	332	105	227	13	6	7
4—5 ..	113,340	60,092	53,248	112,763	59,885	52,878	527	184	343	50	23	27
Total 0—5 ..	608,864	315,981	292,883	607,591	315,565	292,026	1,180	376	804	93	40	53
5—10 ..	519,294	284,604	234,690	499,308	279,191	220,117	19,600	5,217	14,383	386	196	190
10—15 ..	487,357	273,106	214,251	425,478	255,623	169,855	60,901	16,953	43,948	978	530	448
15—20 ..	381,145	215,989	165,156	181,958	141,810	40,148	194,643	71,346	123,297	4,544	2,833	1,711
20—25 ..	370,995	208,318	162,677	111,592	99,188	12,404	251,272	104,055	147,217	8,131	5,075	3,056
25—30 ..	309,008	174,389	134,619	50,760	48,013	2,747	243,138	117,369	125,769	15,110	9,007	6,103
30—35 ..	277,189	159,892	117,297	37,249	35,162	2,087	219,509	113,086	106,423	20,431	11,644	8,787
35—40 ..	224,311	126,936	97,375	23,417	22,073	1,344	171,133	89,992	81,141	29,761	14,871	14,890
40—45 ..	201,437	112,341	89,096	18,317	17,216	1,101	147,589	78,267	69,322	35,531	16,858	18,673
45—50 ..	180,826	103,012	77,814	14,033	13,218	815	119,200	68,510	50,690	47,593	21,284	26,309
50—55 ..	149,519	85,979	63,540	10,696	10,128	568	92,277	54,836	37,441	46,546	21,015	25,531
55—60 ..	116,040	67,507	48,533	7,365	7,016	349	60,809	39,252	21,557	47,866	21,239	26,627
60—65 ..	97,330	56,501	40,829	5,874	5,561	313	46,349	31,126	15,223	45,107	19,814	25,293
65—70 ..	58,477	35,000	23,477	3,219	3,026	193	23,332	17,060	6,272	31,926	14,914	17,012
70 and over ..	89,832	51,391	38,441	4,316	4,071	245	26,849	20,628	6,221	58,667	26,692	31,975

AND CIVIL CONDITION (BY RELIGION).
PART A.—PROVINCIAL SUMMARY—*continued.*

PUNJAB.—(*contd*).

Religion and Age.	Population.			Unmarried.			Married.			Widowed.		
	Persons.	Males.	Females.	Persons.	Males.	Females.	Persons.	Males.	Females.	Persons.	Males.	Females.
1	2	3	4	5	6	7	8	9	10	11	12	13
JAIN ..	**43,140**	**22,962**	**20,178**	**20,861**	**12,329**	**8,532**	**16,738**	**8,284**	**8,454**	**5,541**	**2,349**	**3,192**
0—1 ..	*1,564*	782	782	1,562	781	781	2	1	1	..	..	..
1—2 ..	*1,179*	588	591	1,177	587	590	2	1	1	..	..	..
2—3 ..	*1,368*	674	694	1,367	674	693	1	..	1	..	..	..
3—4 ..	*1,259*	634	625	1,259	634	625	..	..	..	..	..	..
4—5 ..	*1,231*	632	605	1,229	629	600	6	3	3	2	..	2
Total 0—5 ..	*6,607*	*3,310*	*3,297*	*6,594*	*3,305*	*3,289*	*11*	*5*	*6*	*2*	..	*2*
5—10 ..	*5,465*	2,861	2,604	5,330	2,816	2,514	124	39	85	11	6	5
10—15 ..	*5,203*	2,755	2,448	4,617	2,597	2,020	571	152	419	15	6	9
15—20 ..	*4,303*	2,274	2,029	1,836	1,369	467	2,375	870	1,505	92	35	57
20—25 ..	*4,091*	2,142	1,949	958	850	108	2,961	1,226	1,735	172	66	106
25—30 ..	*3,400*	1,816	1,584	428	395	33	2,626	1,282	1,344	346	139	207
30—35 ..	*3,067*	1,692	1,375	327	299	28	2,299	1,206	1,093	441	187	254
35—40 ..	*2,522*	1,401	1,121	213	192	21	1,712	960	752	597	249	348
40—45 ..	*2,270*	1,267	1,003	183	159	24	1,429	829	600	658	279	379
45—50 ..	*1,899*	1,068	831	132	121	11	1,025	632	393	742	315	427
50—55 ..	*1,510*	852	658	98	91	7	742	473	269	670	288	382
55—60 ..	*1,046*	595	451	61	56	5	407	283	124	578	256	322
60—65 ..	*799*	435	364	37	35	2	272	190	82	490	210	280
65—70 ..	*430*	237	193	18	18	..	115	85	30	297	134	163
70 and over ..	*528*	257	271	29	26	3	69	52	17	430	179	251
BUDDHIST ..	**7,753**	**3,770**	**3,983**	**4,124**	**2,067**	**2,057**	**3,095**	**1,532**	**1,563**	**534**	**171**	**363**
0—1 ..	*178*	97	81	178	97	81	..	..	..	..	..	..
1—2 ..	*124*	62	62	124	62	62	..	..	..	..	..	..
2—3 ..	*168*	89	79	166	87	79	2	2	..	..	..	..
3—4 ..	*163*	84	79	163	84	79	..	..	..	..	..	..
4—5 ..	*169*	80	89	164	79	85	2	..	2	3	1	2
Total 0—5 ..	*802*	*412*	*390*	*795*	*409*	*386*	*4*	*2*	*2*	*3*	*1*	*2*
5—10 ..	*789*	393	396	778	386	392	9	7	2	2	..	2
10—15 ..	*810*	412	398	783	394	389	26	17	9	1	1	..
15—20 ..	*774*	364	410	612	296	316	158	66	92	4	2	2
20—25 ..	*733*	351	382	456	226	230	272	122	150	5	3	2
25—30 ..	*619*	292	327	191	99	92	410	186	224	18	7	11
30—35 ..	*531*	243	288	126	65	61	387	172	215	18	6	12
35—40 ..	*530*	252	278	96	53	43	403	187	216	31	12	19
40—45 ..	*512*	245	267	86	43	43	389	189	200	37	13	24
45—50 ..	*446*	218	228	55	25	30	335	181	154	56	12	44
50—55 ..	*386*	187	199	41	21	20	290	155	135	55	11	44
55—60 ..	*269*	135	134	29	17	12	163	96	67	77	22	55
60—65 ..	*233*	113	120	24	11	13	133	80	53	76	22	54
65—70 ..	*123*	61	62	22	8	14	55	33	22	46	20	26
70 and over ..	*196*	92	104	30	14	16	61	39	22	105	39	66
ZOROASTRIAN ..	**569**	**358**	**211**	**284**	**192**	**92**	**246**	**140**	**106**	**39**	**26**	**13**
0—1 ..	*17*	10	7	17	10	7	..	..	..	..	..	..
1—2 ..	*9*	4	5	9	4	5	..	..	..	..	..	..
2—3 ..	*11*	7	4	10	6	4	1	1	..	..	..	..
3—4 ..	*5*	5	..	5	5	..	..	..	..	..	..	..
4—5 ..	*20*	11	9	19	11	8	1	..	1	..	..	..
Total 0—5 ..	*62*	*37*	*25*	*60*	*36*	*24*	*2*	*1*	*1*	..	..	..
5—10 ..	*54*	34	20	46	29	17	6	3	3	2	2	..
10—15 ..	*47*	30	17	36	23	13	10	6	4	1	1	..
15—20 ..	*47*	31	16	27	22	5	18	7	11	2	2	..
20—25 ..	*56*	33	23	32	26	6	24	7	17	..	..	..
25—30 ..	*69*	41	28	33	25	8	35	15	20	1	1	..
30—35 ..	*55*	33	22	20	13	7	32	18	14	3	2	1
35—40 ..	*44*	29	15	9	6	3	32	20	12	3	3	..
40—45 ..	*40*	26	14	6	4	2	27	19	8	7	3	4
45—50 ..	*33*	22	11	6	4	2	22	15	7	5	3	2
50—55 ..	*25*	18	10	4	2	2	19	13	6	5	3	2
55—60 ..	*15*	12	3	3	2	1	8	7	1	4	3	1
60—65 ..	*9*	6	3	1	..	1	6	6	..	2	..	2
65—70 ..	*5*	3	2	..	..	..	2	1	1	3	2	1
70 and over ..	*5*	3	2	1	..	1	3	2	1	1	1	..

TABLE VII—AGE, SEX

PART A.—PROVINCIAL SUMMARY.

PUNJAB—(concld.)

Religion and Age.	Population. Persons.	Population. Males.	Population. Females.	Unmarried. Persons.	Unmarried. Males.	Unmarried. Females.	Married. Persons.	Married. Males.	Married. Females.	Widowed. Persons.	Widowed. Males.	Widowed. Females.
1	2	3	4	5	6	7	8	9	10	11	12	13
MUSLIM ..	**14,929,896**	**8,116,383**	**6,813,513**	**7,513,873**	**4,492,722**	**3,020,651**	**6,149,749**	**3,068,096**	**3,081,653**	**1,266,774**	**555,565**	**711,209**
0—1 ..	560,692	282,268	278,424	560,562	282,219	278,343	118	43	75	12	6	6
1—2 ..	430,695	217,225	213,470	430,378	217,118	213,260	296	93	203	21	14	7
2—3 ..	485,577	246,401	239,176	484,594	246,049	238,545	947	327	620	36	25	11
3—4 ..	491,837	252,584	239,253	489,286	251,700	237,586	2,471	845	1,626	80	39	41
4—5 ..	477,236	248,874	228,362	473,376	247,547	225,829	3,673	1,250	2,423	187	77	110
Total 0—5 ..	*2,446,037*	*1,247,352*	*1,198,685*	*2,438,196*	*1,244,633*	*1,193,563*	*7,505*	*2,558*	*4,947*	*336*	*161*	*175*
5—10 ..	2,036,821	1,095,547	941,274	1,953,174	1,073,811	879,363	81,850	20,837	61,013	1,797	899	898
10—15 ..	1,800,325	992,593	807,732	1,586,156	937,254	648,902	209,755	53,155	156,600	4,414	2,184	2,230
15—20 ..	1,356,081	737,411	618,670	679,386	511,250	168,136	657,559	215,814	441,745	19,136	10,347	8,789
20—25 ..	1,386,184	740,322	645,862	433,688	362,427	71,261	916,136	357,028	559,108	36,360	20,867	15,493
25—30 ..	1,218,585	664,484	554,101	171,939	152,018	19,921	980,376	474,850	505,526	66,270	37,616	28,654
30—35 ..	1,067,635	597,963	469,672	100,014	87,680	12,334	885,584	466,451	419,133	82,037	43,832	38,205
35—40 ..	810,642	452,935	357,707	49,677	41,474	8,203	653,969	363,208	290,761	106,996	48,253	58,743
40—45 ..	691,096	382,538	308,558	33,794	27,801	5,993	535,466	303,662	231,804	121,836	51,075	70,761
45—50 ..	581,014	327,960	253,054	21,507	17,332	4,175	406,095	250,330	155,765	153,412	60,298	93,114
50—55 ..	464,644	262,119	202,525	15,985	12,694	3,291	303,911	192,547	111,364	144,748	56,878	87,870
55—60 ..	347,841	198,909	148,932	10,426	8,533	1,893	193,288	132,709	60,579	144,127	57,667	86,460
60—65 ..	292,152	168,548	123,604	8,219	6,747	1,472	150,257	107,533	42,724	133,676	54,268	79,408
65—70 ..	161,943	95,550	66,393	4,020	3,272	748	72,145	54,624	17,521	85,778	37,654	48,124
70 and over ..	268,896	152,152	116,744	7,192	5,796	1,396	95,853	72,790	23,063	165,851	73,566	92,285
CHRISTIAN ..	**419,353**	**232,556**	**186,797**	**231,488**	**137,345**	**94,143**	**157,314**	**79,729**	**77,585**	**30,551**	**15,482**	**15,069**
0—1 ..	17,373	8,745	8,628	17,369	8,743	8,626	3	2	1	1	..	1
1—2 ..	13,013	6,555	6,458	13,011	6,554	6,457	2	1	1	..	..	.
2—3 ..	14,217	7,208	7,009	14,203	7,199	7,004	13	8	5	1	1	
3—4 ..	11,038	7,144	6,894	14,020	7,136	6,884	14	5	9	4	3	1
4—5 ..	13,430	6,927	6,503	13,376	6,903	6,473	44	17	27	10	7	
Total 0—5 ..	*72,071*	*36,579*	*35,492*	*71,979*	*36,535*	*35,444*	*76*	*33*	*43*	*16*	*11*	*5*
5—10 ..	58,062	31,367	26,695	57,140	31,104	26,036	885	245	640	37	18	19
10—15 ..	51,873	28,601	23,272	48,185	27,789	20,396	3,630	785	2,845	58	27	31
15—20 ..	40,656	22,817	17,839	23,530	16,921	6,609	16,694	5,635	11,059	432	261	171
20—25 ..	42,282	24,387	17,895	16,782	13,796	2,986	24,578	9,992	14,586	922	599	323
25—30 ..	35,096	20,432	14,664	6,882	6,001	881	26,578	13,315	13,263	1,636	1,116	520
30—35 ..	28,720	16,549	12,171	3,192	2,583	609	23,446	12,574	10,872	2,082	1,392	690
35—40 ..	20,921	11,857	9,064	1,303	950	353	16,930	9,431	7,499	2,688	1,476	1,212
40—45 ..	17,659	9,901	7,758	884	618	266	13,886	7,878	6,008	2,889	1,405	1,484
45—50 ..	14,517	8,255	6,262	541	352	189	10,385	6,256	4,129	3,591	1,647	1,944
50—55 ..	11,352	6,432	4,920	392	251	141	7,724	4,740	2,984	3,236	1,441	1,795
55—60 ..	8,334	4,864	3,470	243	167	76	4,747	3,158	1,589	3,344	1,539	1,805
60—65 ..	7,042	4,192	2,850	196	136	60	3,625	2,564	1,061	3,221	1,492	1,729
65—70 ..	3,967	2,303	1,664	88	50	38	1,735	1,282	453	2,144	971	1,173
70 and over ..	6,801	4,020	2,781	151	92	59	2,395	1,841	554	4,255	2,087	2,168
JEW ..	**13**	**5**	**8**	**9**	**3**	**6**	**2**	**1**	**1**	**2**	**1**	**1**
0—1 ..	..	..	..	..	..	..	..	..	..	..	..	..
1—2 ..	1	..	1	1	..	1	..	..	..	..	..	..
2—3 ..	..	..	..	..	..	..	..	..	..	..	..	..
3—4 ..	..	..	..	..	..	..	..	..	..	..	..	..
4—5 ..	..	..	..	..	..	..	..	..	..	..	..	..
Total 0—5 ..	*1*	..	*1*	*1*	..	*1*	..	..	..	..	..	..
5—10 ..	1	..	1	1	..	1	..	..	..	..	..	..
10—15 ..	2	..	2	2	..	2	..	..	..	..	..	..
15—20 ..	3	1	2	3	1	2	..	..	..	..	..	..
20—25 ..	1	1	..	1	1	..	..	..	..	..	..	..
25—30 ..	2	1	1	1	1	..	1	..	1	..	..	..
30—35 ..	1	..	1	..	..	..	..	..	..	1	..	1
35—40 ..	..	..	..	..	..	..	..	..	..	..	..	..
40—45 ..	..	..	..	..	..	..	..	..	..	..	..	..
45—50 ..	1	1	..	..	..	..	1	1	..	..	..	..
50—55 ..	1	1	..	..	..	..	..	..	..	1	1	..
55—60 ..	..	..	..	..	..	..	..	..	..	..	..	..
60—65 ..	..	..	..	..	..	..	..	..	..	..	..	..
65—70 ..	..	..	..	..	..	..	..	..	..	..	..	..
70 and over ..	..	..	..	..	..	..	..	..	..	..	..	..

AND CIVIL CONDITION (BY RELIGION).
PART A.—PROVINCIAL SUMMARY.—*continued.*

BRITISH TERRITORY.

Religion and Age.	Population.			Unmarried.			Married.			Widowed.		
	Persons.	Males.	Females.	Persons.	Males.	Females.	Persons.	Males.	Females.	Persons.	Males.	Females.
1	2	3	4	5	6	7	8	9	10	11	12	13
ALL RELIGIONS ..	**23,580,852**	**12,880,510**	**10,700,342**	**11,579,625**	**7,019,221**	**4,560,404**	**9,807,806**	**4,897,276**	**4,910,530**	**2,193,421**	**964,013**	**1,229,408**
0—1 ..	*877,522*	443,644	433,878	877,289	443,551	433,738	208	82	126	25	11	14
1—2 ..	*661,227*	333,732	327,495	660,744	333,579	327,165	445	133	312	38	20	18
2—3 ..	*737,801*	374,302	363,499	736,440	373,815	362,625	1,299	448	851	62	39	23
3—4 ..	*745,547*	382,577	362,970	741,783	381,351	360,432	3,644	1,171	2,473	120	55	65
4—5 .	*718,452*	374,923	343,529	712,389	372,989	339,400	5,730	1,797	3,933	333	137	196
Total 0—5 ..	*3,740,549*	*1,909,178*	*1,831,371*	*3,728,645*	*1,905,285*	*1,823,360*	*11,326*	*3,631*	*7,695*	*578*	*262*	*16*
5—10 ..	*3,143,832*	1,691,328	1,452,504	2,985,952	1,648,441	1,337,511	154,743	41,369	113,374	3,137	1,518	1,619
10—15 ..	*2,851,094*	1,571,550	1,279,544	2,448,603	1,460,509	988,094	394,701	107,179	287,522	7,790	3,862	3,928
15—20 ..	*2,190,257*	1,203,432	986,825	1,036,054	798,242	237,812	1,121,133	387,440	733,693	33,070	17,750	15,320
20—30 ..	*4,094,513*	2,233,334	1,861,179	915,024	796,282	118,742	3,004,096	1,341,439	1,662,657	175,393	95,613	79,780
30—40 ..	*2,982,008*	1,677,452	1,304,556	257,130	228,656	28,474	2,388,153	1,289,378	1,098,775	336,725	159,418	177,307
40—50 ..	*2,065,331*	1,156,766	908,565	110,047	95,845	14,202	1,469,130	861,086	608,044	486,154	199,835	286,319
50—60 ..	*1,337,026*	761,208	575,818	56,290	49,207	7,083	779,484	507,682	271,802	501,252	204,319	296,933
60 and over ..	*1,176,242*	676,262	493,980	41,880	36,754	5,126	485,040	358,072	126,968	649,322	281,436	367,88
HINDU ..	**6,328,588**	**3,465,534**	**2,863,054**	**2,912,517**	**1,804,266**	**1,108,251**	**2,711,682**	**1,363,236**	**1,348,446**	**704,389**	**298,032**	**406,357**
0—1 ..	*227,208*	114,908	112,300	227,149	114,886	112,263	56	20	36	3	2	1
1—2 ..	*169,832*	85,275	84,557	169,740	85,245	84,495	85	27	58	7	3	4
2—3 ..	*187,998*	94,330	93,668	187,734	94,221	93,513	247	98	149	17	11	6
3—4 .	*187,896*	95,344	92,552	186,896	95,064	91,832	966	267	699	34	13	21
4—5 ..	*177,341*	92,103	85,238	175,580	91,640	83,940	1,665	428	1,237	96	35	61
Total 0—5 ..	*950,275*	*481,960*	*468,315*	*947,099*	*481,056*	*466,043*	*3,019*	*840*	*2,179*	*157*	*64*	*9*
5—10 ..	*806,808*	430,878	375,930	747,717	414,939	332,778	57,029	15,405	42,524	1,162	534	628
10—15 ..	*765,555*	419,127	346,428	616,873	376,709	240,164	145,756	41,019	104,737	2,926	1,399	1,527
15—20 ..	*617,594*	340,821	276,773	249,751	206,123	43,628	356,115	128,896	227,219	11,728	5,802	5,926
20—30 ..	*1,124,392*	617,735	506,657	214,772	198,251	16,521	848,514	390,049	458,465	61,106	29,435	31,67
30—40 ..	*830,166*	471,030	359,136	69,963	65,017	4,946	638,579	353,680	284,899	121,624	52,333	69,291
40—50 ..	*574,817*	325,980	248,891	34,708	32,455	2,253	372,919	226,806	146,113	167,250	66,725	100,525
50—60 ..	*366,132*	210,240	155,892	18,318	17,192	1,126	187,023	127,683	59,340	160,791	65,365	95,426
60 and over .	*292,789*	167,757	125,032	13,316	12,524	792	101,828	78,858	22,970	177,645	76,375	101,270
SIKH ..	**3,064,144**	**1,703,584**	**1,360,560**	**1,515,573**	**945,221**	**570,352**	**1,256,825**	**620,358**	**636,467**	**291,746**	**138,005**	**153,741**
0—1 ..	*114,701*	59,058	55,643	114,655	59,036	55,619	37	19	8	9	3	6
1—2 ..	*82,515*	42,301	40,214	82,421	42,280	40,141	84	18	66	10	3	7
2—3 ..	*88,954*	46,017	42,937	88,782	45,980	42,802	166	36	130	6	1	5
3—4 ..	*89,781*	47,050	42,731	89,518	43,959	42,559	254	88	166	9	3	6
4—5 .	*86,988*	46,221	40,767	86,566	46,052	40,514	377	149	228	45	20	25
Total 0—5 ..	*462,939*	*240,647*	*222,292*	*461,942*	*240,307*	*221,635*	*918*	*310*	*608*	*79*	*30*	*49*
5—10 ..	*395,365*	217,179	178,186	382,094	213,356	168,738	13,003	3,697	9,306	268	126	142
10—15 ..	*366,576*	205,771	160,805	323,353	193,472	129,881	42,529	11,934	30,595	694	365	329
15—20 ..	*280,813*	158,524	122,289	135,840	104,994	30,846	141,619	51,451	90,168	3,354	2,079	1,275
20—30 ..	*506,100*	282,598	223,502	121,406	108,791	12,615	367,195	163,336	203,859	17,499	10,471	7,028
30—40 ..	*377,324*	214,145	163,179	44,793	41,557	3,236	295,151	152,994	142,157	37,380	19,594	17,786
40—50 ..	*286,264*	160,204	126,060	23,049	21,233	1,816	202,712	111,194	91,518	60,503	27,777	32,726
50—60 ..	*199,066*	114,592	84,474	13,067	12,195	872	117,572	71,660	45,912	68,427	30,737	37,690
60 and over .	*189,697*	109,924	79,773	10,029	9,316	713	76,126	53,782	22,344	103,542	46,826	56,716
JAIN ..	**35,284**	**18,751**	**16,533**	**17,167**	**10,172**	**6,995**	**13,564**	**6,675**	**6,889**	**4,553**	**1,904**	**2,649**
0—1 ..	*1,274*	644	630	1,272	643	629	2	1	1	..	..	.
1—2 ..	*964*	487	477	962	486	476	2	1	1	..	..	.
2—3 ..	*1,107*	548	559	1,106	548	558	1	..	1	..	..	..
3—4 ..	*1,033*	520	513	1,033	520	513	..	..	..	..	..	..
4—5 ..	*996*	509	487	990	507	483	4	2	2	2	.	2
Total 0—5 ..	*5,374*	*2,708*	*2,666*	*5,363*	*2,704*	*2,659*	*9*	*4*	*5*	*2*	..	*2*
5—10 ..	*4,473*	2,352	2,121	4,376	2,323	2,053	89	25	64	8	4	4
10—15 ..	*4,267*	2,265	2,002	3,821	2,154	1,667	437	109	328	9	2	7
15—20 ..	*3,506*	1,860	1,646	1,548	1,154	394	1,891	683	1,208	67	23	44
20—30 ..	*6,158*	3,233	2,925	1,184	1,054	130	4,552	2,014	2,538	422	165	257
30—40 ..	*4,622*	2,540	2,082	429	384	45	3,325	1,796	1,529	868	360	508
40—50 ..	*3,411*	1,906	1,505	251	220	31	1,998	1,197	801	1,162	489	673
50—60 ..	*2,058*	1,151	907	128	116	12	902	594	308	1,028	441	587
60 and over ..	*1,415*	736	679	67	63	4	361	253	108	987	420	567
MUSLIM ..	**13,332,460**	**7,241,612**	**6,090,848**	**6,731,109**	**4,018,185**	**2,712,924**	**5,473,378**	**2,730,337**	**2,743,041**	**1,127,973**	**493,090**	**634,883**
0—1 ..	*501,246*	252,222	249,024	501,128	252,177	248,951	106	39	67	12	6	6
1—2 ..	*383,606*	193,471	190,135	383,322	193,373	189,949	263	84	179	21	14	7
2—3 ..	*432,902*	219,831	213,071	432,022	219,511	212,511	844	295	549	36	25	11
3—4 ..	*439,692*	225,786	213,906	437,397	224,990	212,407	2,224	761	1,463	71	35	36
4—5 ..	*427,042*	222,569	204,473	423,603	221,398	202,205	3,275	1,103	2,172	164	68	96
Total 0—5 ..	*2,184,488*	*1,113,879*	*1,070,609*	*2,177,472*	*1,111,449*	*1,066,023*	*6,712*	*2,282*	*4,430*	*304*	*148*	*156*
5—10 ..	*1,822,654*	978,898	843,756	1,748,584	959,886	788,698	72,504	18,223	54,281	1,566	789	777
10—15 ..	*1,610,827*	887,055	723,772	1,422,712	838,825	583,887	184,232	46,286	137,946	3,883	1,944	1,939
15—20 ..	*1,210,478*	659,280	551,198	614,302	460,345	153,957	579,267	189,759	389,508	16,909	9,176	7,733
20—30 ..	*2,313,917*	1,248,498	1,065,419	513,943	459,860	84,083	1,678,843	736,712	942,131	91,131	51,926	39,205
30—40 ..	*1,672,901*	934,945	737,956	133,945	115,135	18,810	1,371,671	738,455	633,216	167,285	81,355	85,930
40—50 ..	*1,135,475*	632,068	503,407	49,117	39,778	9,339	842,505	493,953	348,552	243,853	98,337	145,516
50—60 .	*728,691*	411,986	316,705	23,509	18,748	4,761	448,131	291,835	156,296	257,051	101,403	155,648
60 and over ..	*653,029*	375,003	278,026	17,525	14,159	3,366	289,513	212,832	76,681	345,991	148,012	197,979
CHRISTIAN ..	**414,788**	**230,018**	**184,770**	**229,244**	**136,014**	**93,230**	**155,288**	**78,667**	**76,621**	**30,256**	**15,337**	**14,919**
0—1 ..	*17,215*	8,661	8,554	17,211	8,659	8,552	3	2	1	1	..	1
1—2 ..	*12,876*	6,482	6,394	12,874	6,481	6,393	2	1	1	..	..	..
2—3 ..	*14,066*	7,124	6,942	14,053	7,115	6,938	12	8	4	1	1	..
3—4 ..	*13,911*	7,074	6,837	13,893	7,066	6,827	14	5	9	4	3	1
4—5 ..	*13,285*	6,847	6,438	13,231	6,823	6,408	44	17	27	10	7	3
Total 0—5 ..	*71,353*	*36,188*	*35,165*	*71,262*	*36,144*	*35,118*	*75*	*33*	*42*	*16*	*11*	*5*
5—10 ..	*57,473*	31,061	26,412	56,577	30,804	25,773	861	240	621	35	17	18
10—15 ..	*51,367*	28,333	23,034	47,741	27,538	20,203	3,568	768	2,800	58	27	31
15—20 ..	*40,249*	22,604	17,645	23,339	16,781	6,558	16,486	5,565	10,921	424	258	166
20—30 ..	*76,534*	44,350	32,184	23,453	19,627	3,826	50,550	23,026	27,524	2,531	1,697	834
30—40 ..	*48,991*	28,030	20,961	4,439	3,492	947	39,838	21,701	18,137	4,714	2,837	1,877
40—50 ..	*31,730*	17,893	13,837	1,395	950	445	23,928	13,923	10,005	6,407	3,020	3,387
50—60 ..	*19,433*	11,137	8,296	610	404	206	12,307	7,782	4,525	6,516	2,951	3,565
60 and over ..	*17,658*	10,422	7,236	428	274	154	7,676	5,629	2,046	9,555	4,519	5,036

TABLE VII.—AGE, SEX

PART A.—PROVINCIAL SUMMARY.

PUNJAB STATES.

Religion and Age.	Population.			Unmarried.			Married.			Widowed.		
	Persons.	Males.	Females.	Persons.	Males.	Females.	Persons.	Males.	Females.	Persons.	Males.	Females.
1	2	3	4	5	6	7	8	9	10	11	12	13
ALL RELIGIONS ..	**4,910,005**	**2,680,684**	**2,229,321**	**2,263,448**	**1,401,086**	**862,362**	**2,151,517**	**1,067,270**	**1,084,247**	**495,040**	**212,328**	**282,712**
0—1 .	173,212	87,126	86,086	173,136	87,072	86,064	76	54	22	..	.	.
1—2 .	132,223	66,481	65,742	132,047	66,369	65,678	174	111	63	2	1	
2—3 ..	147,593	74,170	73,423	147,185	73,966	73,219	404	201	203	4	3	1
3—4 .	146,582	74,631	71,951	145,507	74,220	71,287	1,051	402	649	24	9	15
4—5 .	140,001	72,642	67,359	138,212	71,996	66,216	1,716	618	1,098	73	28	45
Total 0—5 .	739,611	375,050	364,561	736,087	373,623	362,464	3,421	1,386	2,035	103	41	[illegible]
5—10 ..	621,490	333,733	287,757	579,821	322,376	257,445	40,843	10,978	29,865	826	379	[illegible]
10—15 ..	[illegible]	317,148	259,909	472,621	287,793	184,828	102,465	28,443	74,022	1,971	912	[illegible]
15—20 ..	466,669	253,439	213,230	191,153	151,767	36,386	267,584	94,591	172,993	7,932	4,081	3,851
20—30 .	871,990	471,968	400,022	172,923	158,163	14,760	660,787	293,709	367,078	38,280	20,096	18,184
30—40 .	639,126	358,800	280,326	56,562	53,153	3,409	506,784	270,990	235,794	75,780	34,657	41,123
40—50 ..	453,020	257,196	195,824	28,456	26,815	1,641	312,086	184,773	127,313	112,478	45,608	66,870
50—60 ..	296,730	171,899	124,831	15,389	14,515	874	163,805	109,898	53,907	117,536	47,48[illegible]	70,050
60 and over ..	244,312	141,451	102,861	10,436	9,881	555	93,742	72,502	21,240	140,134	59,068	81,066
HINDU ..	**2,271,182**	**1,220,171**	**1,050,961**	**979,836**	**605,797**	**374,039**	**1,039,048**	**514,024**	**525,024**	**252,248**	**100,350**	**151,898**
0—1 ..	75,908	37,783	38,125	75,849	37,736	38,113	59	47	12	..	.	
1—2 .	57,802	28,744	29,058	57,665	28,646	29,019	136	98	38	1	.	1
2—3 ..	65,193	32,267	32,926	64,917	32,105	32,812	276	162	114	..	.	.
3—4 ..	65,377	32,714	32,633	64,641	32,412	32,229	725	300	425	11	2	
4—5 ..	62,522	31,978	30,544	61,317	31,530	29,787	1,160	432	728	45	16	29
Total 0—5 ..	326,802	163,486	163,316	324,389	162,429	161,960	2,356	1,039	1,317	57	18	39
5—10 ..	279,118	147,381	131,737	253,933	140,425	113,508	24,719	6,761	17,958	466	195	271
10—15 .	262,642	142,046	120,596	203,630	125,273	78,357	57,872	16,272	41,600	1,140	501	639
15—20 ..	217,415	116,103	101,312	78,711	66,169	12,542	134,246	47,807	86,439	4,458	2,127	2,331
20—30 ..	401,376	212,441	188,935	69,278	64,363	4,915	311,318	138,302	173,016	20,780	9,776	[illegible]
30—40 ..	305,135	167,649	137,486	24,556	23,137	1,419	239,846	127,761	112,085	40,733	16,751	[illegible]
40—50 ..	217,370	121,920	95,450	12,819	12,133	686	146,761	87,911	58,850	57,790	21,876	35,914
50—60 ..	144,552	82,890	61,662	7,421	7,030	391	78,104	53,354	24,750	59,027	22,50[illegible]	36,521
60 and over ..	116,722	66,255	50,467	5,099	4,838	261	43,826	34,817	9,009	67,797	26,600	41,197
SIKH ..	**1,007,480**	**567,862**	**440,118**	**485,600**	**311,640**	**173,960**	**420,956**	**207,715**	**213,241**	**100,924**	**48,007**	**52,917**
0—1 ..	36,513	18,602	17,911	36,508	18,599	17,909	5	3	2	..	..	..
1—2 ..	[illegible]	13,488	12,863	26,345	13,483	12,862	5	4	1	1	1	..
2—3 ..	28,635	14,771	13,864	28,607	14,761	13,846	24	7	17	4		1
3—4 ..	28,074	14,602	13,472	27,992	14,582	13,410	78	17	61	4	3	1
4—5 ..	26,352	13,871	12,481	26,197	13,833	12,364	150	35	115	5	4	2
Total 0—5 ..	145,925	75,334	70,591	145,649	75,258	70,391	262	66	196	14	10	4
5—10 ..	123,929	67,425	56,504	117,214	65,835	51,379	6,597	1,520	5,077	118	70	48
10—15 ..	120,781	67,335	53,446	102,125	62,151	39,974	18,372	5,019	13,353	284	165	119
15—20 ..	100,332	57,465	42,867	46,118	36,816	9,302	53,024	19,895	33,129	1,190	754	436
20—30 .	173,903	100,109	73,794	40,946	38,410	2,536	127,215	58,088	69,127	5,742	3,611	2,131
30—40 .	124,176	72,683	51,493	15,873	15,678	195	95,491	57,084	45,407	12,812	6,921	5,891
40—50 ..	95,999	55,149	40,850	9301	9,201	100	64,077	35,583	28,494	22,621	10,365	12,256
50—60 ..	66,493	38,894	27,599	4,994	4,949	45	35,514	22,428	13,086	25,985	11,517	14,468
60 and over ..	55,942	32,968	22,974	3,380	3,342	38	20,404	15,032	5,372	32,158	14,594	17,564
JAIN ..	**7,856**	**4,211**	**3,645**	**3,694**	**2,157**	**1,537**	**3,174**	**1,609**	**1,565**	**988**	**415**	**543**
0—1 .	290	138	152	290	138	152	..	..	..	..	..	.
1—2 .	215	101	114	215	101	114	..	..	..	..	..	.
2—3 ..	261	126	135	261	126	135	..	..	.	..	..	
3—4 ..	226	114	112	226	114	112	..	..	..	..	..	
4—5 .	241	123	118	239	122	117	2	1	1	..	..	.
Total 0—5 ..	1,233	602	631	1,231	601	630	2	1	1	..	.	..
5—10 ..	992	500	483	954	493	461	35	14	21	3	2	1
10—15 ..	936	490	446	796	443	353	134	43	91	6	4	2
15—20 ..	797	414	383	288	215	73	484	187	297	25	12	13
20—30 .	1,333	725	608	202	191	11	1,035	494	541	96	40	56
30—40 ..	967	553	414	111	107	4	686	370	316	170	76	94
40—50 ..	758	429	329	64	60	4	456	264	192	238	105	133
50—60 ..	498	296	202	31	31	..	247	162	85	220	103	117
60 and over .	342	193	149	17	16	1	95	74	21	230	103	127
MUSLIM ..	**1,597,436**	**874,771**	**722,665**	**782,264**	**474,537**	**307,727**	**676,371**	**337,759**	**338,612**	**138,801**	**62,475**	**76,326**
0—1 ..	59,446	30,046	29,400	59,434	30,042	29,392	12	4	8	..	..	.
1—2 ..	47,089	23,754	23,335	47,056	23,745	23,311	33	9	24	..	..	.
2—3 ..	52,676	26,570	26,105	52,572	26,538	26,034	103	32	71	..	..	.
3—4 ..	52,145	26,798	25,347	51,889	26,710	25,179	247	84	163	9	4	5
4—5 .	50,194	26,305	23,889	49,773	26,149	23,624	398	147	251	23	9	14
Total 0—5	261,549	133,473	128,076	260,724	133,184	127,540	793	276	517	32	13	19
5—10 .	214,167	116,649	97,518	204,590	113,925	90,665	9,346	2,614	6,732	231	110	121
10—15 .	189,498	105,538	83,960	163,441	98,429	65,015	25,523	6,869	18,654	531	[illegible]	[illegible]
15—20 ..	145,603	78,131	67,472	65,084	50,905	14,179	78,292	26,055	52,237	2,227	1,171	[illegible]
20—30 .	290,852	156,308	134,544	61,684	54,585	7,099	217,669	95,166	122,503	11,499	6,557	4,942
30—40 ..	205,376	15,953	89,423	15,746	14,019	1,727	167,882	91,204	76,678	21,748	10,730	1,018
40—50 ..	136,635	78,430	58,205	6,184	5,355	829	99,056	60,039	39,017	31,395	13,03[illegible]	[illegible]
50—60 .	83,794	49,042	34,752	2,902	2,479	423	49,068	33,421	15,647	31,824	13,142	8,682
60 and over ..	69,962	41,247	28,715	1,906	1,656	250	28,742	22,115	6,627	39,314	17,476	[illegible]
CHRISTIAN .	**4,565**	**2,538**	**2,027**	**2,244**	**1,331**	**913**	**2,026**	**1,062**	**964**	**295**	**145**	**150**
0—1 ..	158	84	74	158	84	74	..	..	..	..	..	..
1—2 ..	137	73	64	[illegible]	73	64	..	..	..	..	..	.
2—3 ..	151	84	67	150	84	66	1	..	1	..	..	.
3—4 ..	127	70	57	127	70	57	..	..	..	..	..	..
4—5 .	145	80	65	145	80	65	..	..	..	..	..	..
Total 0—5 .	[illegible]	391	327	717	391	326	1	.	1	..	..	.
5—10 .	589	306	283	563	300	263	24	5	19	2	1	
10—15 ..	506	268	238	444	251	193	62	17	45	..	..	..
15—20 ..	407	213	194	191	140	51	208	70	138	8	3	5
20—30 ..	844	469	375	211	170	41	606	281	325	27	18	9
30—40 ..	657	376	274	56	41	15	538	304	234	56	3	25
40—50 ..	446	263	183	30	20	10	343	211	132	73	32	41
50—60 ..	253	159	94	25	14	11	164	110	48	64	29	35
60 and over .	152	93	59	7	4	3	80	58	22	65		34

AND CIVIL CONDITION (BY RELIGION).

PART A.- PROVINCIAL SUMMARY.- *continued.*

PUNJAB STATES—(*contd.*)—(A.—Having Political relations with the Punjab Government).

Religion and Age.	Population.			Unmarried.			Married.			Widowed.		
	Persons.	Males.	Females.	Persons.	Males.	Females.	Persons.	Males.	Females.	Persons.	Males.	Females.
1	2	3	4	5	6	7	8	9	10	11	12	13
ALL RELIGIONS ..	**437,787**	**229,290**	**208,497**	**174,461**	**103,208**	**71,253**	**214,915**	**107,046**	**107,869**	**48,411**	**19,086**	**29,375**
0—1 ..	*13,392*	6,630	6,762	13,390	6,630	6,760	2	..	2	.	..	..
1—2 ..	*9,988*	4,937	5,051	9,988	4,937	5,051	.	.	..	..	..	.
2—3 .	*11,123*	5,383	5,740	11,120	5,382	5,738	3	1	2	..	..	.
3—4 ..	*11,482*	5,613	5,869	11,433	5,598	5,835	49	15	34	..	..	..
4—5 ..	*11,287*	5,618	5,669	11,159	5,577	5,582	122	37	85	6	4	2
Total 0—5 ..	*57,272*	*28,181*	*29,091*	*57,090*	*28,124*	*28,966*	*176*	*53*	*123*	*6*	*4*	*2*
5—10 ..	*50,210*	25,975	24,235	45,766	24,816	20,950	4,355	1,120	3,235	89	39	50
10—15 ..	*47,466*	25,198	22,268	36,059	22,108	14,551	10,542	2,986	7,556	265	104	161
15—20 ..	*39,635*	20,436	19,199	14,429	11,226	3,203	24,269	8,739	15,530	937	471	466
20—30 ...	*76,699*	38,91	37,785	12,484	10,354	2,130	60,228	26,494	33,734	3,987	2,066	1,921
30—40 ..	*64,327*	34,059	30,268	4,209	3,502	707	52,642	27,236	25,406	7,476	3,321	4,155
40—50 .	*46,070*	25,284	20,786	2,017	1,636	381	33,506	19,746	13,760	10,547	3,902	6,645
50—60 ..	*31,575*	17,615	13,960	1,080	860	220	18,907	12,650	6,257	11,588	4,105	7,483
60 and over ..	*24,533*	13,628	10,905	727	582	145	10,290	8,022	2,268	13,516	5,024	8,492
HINDU ..	**383,883**	**199,991**	**183,892**	**150,336**	**88,483**	**61,853**	**190,993**	**95,203**	**95,790**	**42,554**	**16,305**	**26,249**
0—1 ..	*11,453*	5,664	5,789	11,451	5,664	5,787	2	..	2	..	..	..
1—2 ..	*8,516*	4,188	4,328	8,516	4,188	4,328	..	..	..	..	..	..
2—3 ..	*9,558*	4,587	4,971	9,555	4,586	4,969	3	1	2	..	..	..
3—4 .	*9,960*	4,831	5,129	9,919	4,818	5,101	41	13	28	..	.	..
4—5 .	*9,780*	4,831	4,949	9,677	4,796	4,881	98	31	67	5	4	1
Total 0—5 ..	*49,267*	*24,101*	*25,166*	*49,118*	*24,052*	*25,066*	*144*	*45*	*99*	*5*	*4*	*1*
5—10 ..	*43,244*	22,235	21,009	39,497	21,286	18,211	3,673	919	2,754	74	30	44
10—15 ..	*40,818*	21,577	19,241	31,186	18,953	12,533	9,105	2,537	6,568	227	87	140
15—20 ..	*34,441*	17,639	16,802	12,401	9,657	2,744	21,224	7,576	13,648	816	406	410
20—30 ..	*67,531*	34,023	33,508	10,865	8,933	1,932	53,165	23,301	29,864	3,501	1,789	1,712
30—40 ..	*57,479*	30,269	27,210	3,658	3,001	657	47,214	24,403	22,811	6,607	2,865	3,742
40—50 .	*41,127*	22,442	18,685	1,738	1,377	361	30,116	17,760	12,356	9,273	3,305	5,968
50—60 .	*28,265*	15,674	12,591	939	728	211	17,108	11,441	5,667	10,218	3,505	6,713
60 and over .	*21,711*	12,031	9,680	634	496	138	9,244	7,221	2,023	11,833	4,314	7,519
SIKH ..	**10,854**	**6,124**	**4,730**	**4,859**	**3,142**	**1,717**	**4,603**	**2,309**	**2,294**	**1,392**	**673**	**719**
0—1 ..	*356*	167	189	356	167	189	.	..	..	.	..	..
1—2 ..	*281*	144	137	281	144	137	.	..	..	..	..	..
2—3 ..	*275*	147	128	275	147	128	..	..	..	..	.	.
3—4 ..	*269*	143	126	268	143	125	1	..	1	..	.	.
4—5 ..	*285*	154	131	282	154	128	3	..	3	..	..	.
Total 0—5 ..	*1,466*	*755*	*711*	*1,462*	*755*	*707*	*4*	..	*4*	..	..	.
5—10 .	*1,311*	728	583	1,218	704	514	91	23	68	2	1	1
10—15 .	*1,274*	72	553	1,025	642	383	239	76	163	10	3	7
15—20 ..	*1,079*	609	463	420	342	78	617	246	371	35	21	14
20—30 ..	*1,835*	1,048	787	369	342	27	1,350	642	708	116	64	52
30—40 ..	*1,393*	795	598	168	162	6	1,022	521	501	203	112	91
40—50 ..	*1,090*	633	457	96	95	1	694	393	301	300	145	155
50—60 ..	*742*	447	295	58	57	1	362	243	119	322	147	175
60 and over ..	*671*	388	283	43	43	..	224	165	59	404	180	224
JAIN ..	**408**	**218**	**190**	**195**	**112**	**83**	**132**	**70**	**62**	**81**	**36**	**45**
0—1 ..	*10*	4	6	10	4	6	..	..	..	..	..	..
1—2 ..	*10*	5	5	10	5	5	..	.	..	..	..	..
2—3 .	*9*	3	6	9	3	6	..	..	..	..	..	..
3—4 ..	*6*	3	3	6	3	3	..	..	.	..	..	..
4—5 ..	*14*	7	7	14	7	7	..	.	..	..	..	..
Total 0—5 .	*49*	*22*	*27*	*49*	*22*	*27*	..	..	..	..	..	..
5—10 ..	*49*	24	25	49	24	25	..	..	.	..	..	..
10—15 ..	*49*	22	27	46	22	24	3	..	3	.	..	..
15—20 ..	*41*	22	19	19	13	6	21	8	13	1	1	..
20—30 ..	*69*	40	29	14	14	..	44	21	23	11	5	6
30—40 ..	*55*	35	20	8	8	..	32	20	12	15	7	8
40—50 ..	*39*	19	20	5	4	1	16	11	5	18	4	14
50—60 ..	*32*	17	15	2	2	.	10	6	4	20	9	11
60 and over .	*25*	17	8	3	3	..	6	4	2	16	10	6
MUSLIM ..	**40,845**	**22,071**	**18,774**	**18,173**	**11,048**	**7,125**	**18,402**	**9,045**	**9,357**	**4,270**	**1,978**	**2,292**
0—1 .	*1,539*	776	763	1,539	776	763	..	.	..	..	..	..
1—2 ..	*1,151*	588	563	1,151	588	563	..	.	..	..	..	..
2—3 ..	*1,245*	625	620	1,245	625	620	..	..	.	..	..	..
3—4 .	*1,213*	616	597	1,206	614	592	7	2	5	..	.	.
4—5 ..	*1,159*	599	560	1,138	593	545	20	6	14	1	.	1
Total 0—5 ..	*6,307*	*3,204*	*3,103*	*6,279*	*3,196*	*3,083*	*27*	*8*	*19*	*1*	..	*1*
5—10 ..	*5,409*	2,885	2,524	4,808	2,701	2,107	588	176	412	13	8	5
10—15 ..	*5,140*	2,788	2,352	3,923	2,405	1,518	1,'89	369	820	28	14	14
15—20 ..	*3,909*	2,094	1,815	1,460	1,163	297	2,366	889	1,477	83	42	41
20—30 ..	*6,936*	3,656	3,280	1,.02	1,012	90	5,479	2,438	3,041	355	206	149
30—40	*5,140*	2,830	2,310	330	311	19	4,175	2,187	1,988	635	332	303
40—50 ..	*3,604*	2,076	1,528	159	152	7	2,509	1,486	1,023	936	438	498
50—60 .	*2,385*	1,397	988	71	70	1	1,311	891	420	1,003	436	567
60 and over ..	*2,015*	1,141	874	41	38	3	758	601	157	1,216	502	714
CHRISTIAN ..	**206**	**100**	**106**	**118**	**56**	**62**	**76**	**40**	**36**	**12**	**4**	**8**
0—1 ..	*4*	4	..	4	4	..	..	..	..	..	..	..
1—2 .	*6*	3	3	6	3	3	..	..	.	.	..	..
2—3 ..	*6*	4	2	6	4	2	..	..	..	..	..	.
3—4 ..	..	..	.	..	..	..	..	..	.	..	..	..
4—5 ..	*9*	7	2	9	7	2	..	..	.	..	..	..
Total 0—5 ..	*25*	*18*	*7*	*25*	*18*	*7*	..	..	..	..	..	..
5—10 .	*23*	11	12	22	11	11	1	..	1	..	..	..
10—15 ..	*17*	9	8	17	9	8	..	..	..	..	..	..
15—20 ..	*18*	5	13	10	4	6	7	1	6	1	..	1
20—30 ..	*41*	18	23	20	8	12	20	10	10	1	..	1
30—40 ..	*34*	16	18	8	3	5	22	12	10	4	1	3
40—50 ..	*24*	11	13	7	1	6	15	9	6	2	1	1
50—60 .	*16*	8	8	5	1	4	9	6	3	2	1	1
60 and over ..	*8*	4	4	4	1	3	2	2	..	2	1	1

TABLE VII.—AGE, SEX AND CIVIL CONDITION (BY RELIGION).

PART A.—PROVINCIAL SUMMARY.—*concluded.*

PUNJAB STATES (*concld.*)—(B. **Having Political relations with the Government of India**).

RELIGION AND AGE.	POPULATION.			UNMARRIED.			MARRIED.			WIDOWED.		
	Persons.	Males.	Females.	Persons.	Males.	Females.	Persons.	Males.	Females.	Persons.	Males.	Females.
1	2	3	4	5	6	7	8	9	10	11	12	13
ALL RELIGIONS ..	**4,472,218**	**2,451,394**	**2,020,824**	**2,088,987**	**1,297,878**	**791,109**	**1,936,602**	**960,224**	**976,378**	**446,629**	**193,292**	**253,337**
0—1 ..	*159,820*	80,496	79,324	159,746	80,4[illegible]	79,304	74	54	20	.	.	..
1—2 ..	*122,235*	61,544	60,[illegible]91	122,[illegible]	61,432	60,627	174	111	63	2	1	1
2—3 ..	*136,470*	68,787	67,683	136,[illegible]	[illegible]	67,481	40[illegible]	206	201	4	3	1
3—4 ..	*135,100*	69,018	66,082	134,[illegible]	68,622	65,452	1,002	387	615	24	9	15
4—5 ..	*128,714*	67,024	61,690	127,05[illegible]	[illegible]	60,634	1,594	551	1,043	67	24	43
Total 0—5 ..	*682,339*	*346,857*	*335,4[illegible]*	*678,99[illegible]*	*[illegible]5,495*	*333,495*	*3,245*	*1,3[illegible]*	*1,91[illegible]*	*9[illegible]*	*37*	*60*
5—10 ..	*571,280*	307,758	263,522	531,[illegible]	29[illegible]	231,495	38,188	9,808	28,6[illegible]	75	[illegible]	397
10—15 ..	*529,591*	291,950	2[illegible]	435,9[illegible]	[illegible]	170,277	[illegible],923	25,457	66,[illegible]	1,706	808	898
15—20 ..	*427,034*	235,002	191,[illegible]	173,7[illegible]	[illegible]	33,[illegible]85	[illegible]3,3[illegible]	55,802	15[illegible],4[illegible]	[illegible],[illegible]5	3,610	3,385
20—30 ..	*795,291*	433,054	362,287	[illegible],13[illegible]	47,8[illegible]	2,[illegible]	500,559	267,9[illegible]	33[illegible],[illegible]	34,293	18,030	16,263
30—40 ..	*574,799*	324,741	250,058	[illegible]2,355	49,[illegible]	2,70[illegible]	454,[illegible]2	2[illegible],754	210,38[illegible]	68,304	31,335	36,968
40—50 ..	*406,950*	231,912	175,038	[illegible]6,43[illegible]	[illegible]78	[illegible],2[illegible]	2[illegible],550	1[illegible],027	[illegible]	10[illegible],93[illegible]	[illegible]1,706	60,225
50—60 ..	*265,155*	154,284	110,871	[illegible]4,309	3,655	654	[illegible]44,898	9[illegible],248	47,6[illegible]	[illegible]05,94[illegible]	43,38[illegible]	62,567
60 and over ..	*219,779*	127,823	91,956	[illegible],709	9,299	410	83,452	[illegible]4,180	18,9[illegible]2	126,8[illegible]	[illegible]4,041	7[illegible],37
HINDU ..	**1,887,249**	**1,020,180**	**867,069**	**829,500**	**517,314**	**312,186**	**848,055**	**418,82[illegible]**	**429,234**	**209,694**	**84,045**	**125,649**
0—1 ..	*64,455*	32,119	32,336	6[illegible],[illegible]95	32,072	32,326	57	4[illegible]	[illegible]0		.	..
1—2 ..	*49,286*	24,555	24,730	49,149	24,458	24,691	136	[illegible]	38			1
2—3 ..	*55,635*	27,680	27,955	55,36[illegible]	27,[illegible]19	27,843	273	[illegible]8	[illegible]1[illegible]		.	
3—4 ..	*55,417*	27,883	27,534	54,7[illegible]2	27,594	27,128	684	287	397	11	–	9
4—5 ..	*52,742*	27,147	25,595	5[illegible]	26,734	24,906	[illegible],062	401	661	[illegible]	2	28
Total 0—5 ..	*277,535*	*139,385*	*138,150*	*2[illegible]*	*13[illegible],3[illegible]*	*136,[illegible]4*	*2,212*	*994*	*1,218*	*52*	*11*	*38*
5—10 ..	*236,871*	127,143	110,798	214,156	119,[illegible]39	95,29[illegible]	21,0[illegible]	5,842	15,204	392	165	227
10—15 ..	*221,824*	120,469	101,355	172,[illegible]1	106,320	65,824	48,737	13,735	35,032	913	4[illegible]4	499
15—20 ..	*182,974*	98,464	84,510	[illegible]8[illegible]3	56,51[illegible]	9,798	[illegible]13,0[illegible]	[illegible],231	72,791	3,642	1,721	1,921
20—30 ..	*333,845*	178,418	155,427	[illegible]8,4[illegible]	55,430	2,983	258,[illegible]53	15,001	143,15[illegible]	[illegible],279	7,987	9,292
30—40 ..	*247,656*	137,380	110,276	[illegible],595	2[illegible],[illegible]36	702	[illegible]32,632	[illegible]3,37[illegible]	89,27[illegible]	34,126	[illegible]3,886	20,240
40—50 ..	*176,243*	99,478	76,765	11,08[illegible]	[illegible],[illegible]56	325	11[illegible],[illegible]45	7[illegible],[illegible]	[illegible],494	48,51[illegible]	[illegible]8,[illegible]7	29,946
50—60 ..	*116,287*	67,2[illegible]6	49,07[illegible]	[illegible],[illegible]82	[illegible],[illegible]02	[illegible]80	60,[illegible]96	[illegible],[illegible]15	[illegible],[illegible]08	48,8[illegible]	19,0[illegible]	29,808
60 and over ..	*95,011*	5[illegible],22[illegible]	[illegible],787	[illegible],[illegible]85	1,312	123	3[illegible],[illegible]82	27,596	6,[illegible]80	[illegible],964	22,28[illegible]	33,6[illegible]
SIKH ..	**996,626**	**561,238**	**435,388**	**480,741**	**308,498**	**172,243**	**416,353**	**205,406**	**210,947**	**99,532**	**47,334**	**52,198**
0—1 ..	*36,157*	18,435	17,722	36,[illegible]52	18,432	17,720	3	3	2			.
1—2 ..	*26,070*	13,344	12,72[illegible]	26,064	[illegible]3,336	12,725	5	4			1	.
2—3 ..	*28,360*	14,624	13,736	28,332	14,614	13,718	24	7	17	[illegible]	3	1
3—4 ..	*27,805*	14,459	13,346	27,724	14,439	13,285	77	17	[illegible]	4	3	1
4—5 ..	*26,067*	13,717	12,350	2[illegible],9[illegible]	13,679	12,236	1[illegible]	35	112	[illegible]	3	2
Total 0—5 ..	*144,459*	*74,579*	*69,880*	*144,[illegible]*	*74,603*	*69,684*	*2[illegible]*	*66*	*192*	*14*	*10*	*4*
5—10 ..	*122,618*	66,697	55,921	115,[illegible]96	65,131	50,865	6,506	1,497	[illegible],009	1[illegible]6	69	47
10—15 ..	*119,507*	66,614	52,893	[illegible]01,[illegible]00	61,[illegible]0[illegible]	39,591	18,[illegible]33	4,94[illegible]	13,190	274	162	112
15—20 ..	*99,260*	56,856	42,404	45,[illegible]98	3[illegible],474	9,224	52,407	19,649	32,75[illegible]	[illegible],156	733	422
20—30 ..	*172,068*	99,[illegible]6[illegible]	73,007	40,577	38,068	2,509	125,865	57,446	68,419	5,626	3,547	2,079
30—40 ..	*122,783*	71,888	50,895	15,705	15,516	189	94,469	49,563	44,906	12,609	6,809	5,800
40—50 ..	*94,909*	54,516	40,393	9,205	9,106	99	63,383	35,19[illegible]	28,193	22,321	10,220	12,101
50—60 ..	*65,751*	38,447	27,304	4,936	[illegible],892	44	35,[illegible]52	22,185	12,967	25,663	1[illegible],370	14,293
60 and over ..	*55,271*	32,580	22,691	3,337	3,299	38	20,180	14,86[illegible]	5,313	31,754	14,114	17,340
JAIN ..	**7,448**	**3,993**	**3,455**	**3,499**	**2,045**	**1,454**	**3,042**	**1,539**	**1,503**	**907**	**409**	**498**
0—1 ..	*280*	134	146	280	134	146	.	..	..	.	.	
1—2 ..	*205*	96	109	205	96	109	..	.	..	.	..	..
2—3 ..	*252*	123	129	252	123	[illegible]9	..	..	.	.	.	.
3—4 ..	*220*	111	109	220	111	109	..	..	..		..	.
4—5 ..	*227*	116	1[illegible]1	225	115	110	2	.	.		.	.
Total 0—5 ..	*1,184*	*580*	*604*	*1,182*	*579*	*603*	..	*1*	*1*	.	..	
5—10 ..	*913*	485	458	905	469	436	30	14	2	3	2	1
10—15 ..	*887*	468	419	750	421	329	131	47	[illegible]8	6	4	2
15—20 ..	*756*	392	364	269	202	67	463	179	[illegible]51	21	1	13
20—30 ..	*1,264*	685	579	188	177	11	991	473	518	85	35	50
30—40 ..	*91[illegible]*	518	394	103	99	4	[illegible]54	350	304	155	69	86
40—50 ..	*719*	410	309	59	56	.	440	253	187	220	101	119
50—60 ..	*466*	279	187	29	29	..	237	156	81	200	94	106
60 and over ..	*317*	176	141	14	13	1	89	70	19	21	93	121
MUSLIM ..	**1,556,591**	**852,700**	**703,891**	**764,091**	**463,489**	**300,602**	**657,969**	**328,714**	**329,255**	**134,531**	**60,497**	**74,034**
0—1 ..	*57,907*	29,270	28,637	57,895	29,266	28,629	[illegible]2	4	8	..		.
1—2 ..	*45,938*	23,166	22,772	45,905	23,157	22,748	33	9	24	..		..
2—3 ..	*51,430*	25,945	25,485	51,327	25,913	25,414	103	32	71	..	.	..
3—4 ..	*50,932*	26,182	24,750	50,683	26,096	24,587	240	82	158	9	4	5
4—5 ..	*49,035*	25,706	23,329	48,635	25,556	23,079	378	141	237	22	9	13
Total 0—5 ..	*255,242*	*130,269*	*124,973*	*251,445*	*129,988*	*124,457*	*766*	*268*	*498*	*31*	*13*	*18*
5—10 ..	*208,758*	113,764	94,994	199,782	111,224	88,558	8,758	2,438	6,320	2[illegible]8	102	116
10—15 ..	*184,358*	102,750	81,608	159,521	96,024	63,497	24,334	6,500	17,834	503	226	277
15—20 ..	*141,694*	76,037	65,657	63,624	49,742	13,882	75,926	25,166	50,760	2,144	1,129	[illegible],0[illegible]5
20—30 ..	*283,916*	152,652	131,264	60,582	53,573	7,009	212,190	92,728	119,462	11,144	6,35[illegible]	4,793
30—40 ..	*200,236*	113,123	87,113	15,416	13,708	1,708	163,707	89,01[illegible]	74,690	2[illegible],113	10,398	[illegible]0,715
40—50 ..	*133,031*	76,354	56,677	6,025	5,203	822	96,547	58,553	37,994	30,459	12,598	[illegible]7,861
50—60 ..	*81,409*	47,645	33,764	2,831	2,409	422	47,757	32,530	15,227	30,821	12,706	18,115
60 and over ..	*67,947*	40,106	27,841	1,865	1,618	247	27,984	21,514	6,470	38,098	16,974	2[illegible],124
CHRISTIAN ..	**4,359**	**2,438**	**1,921**	**2,126**	**1,275**	**851**	**1,950**	**1,022**	**928**	**283**	**141**	**142**
0—1 ..	*154*	80	74	154	80	74	..	..	..	..	..	..
1—2 ..	*131*	70	61	131	70	61	..	.	..	..	..	..
2—3 ..	*145*	80	65	144	80	64	1	..	1	..	..	..
3—4 ..	*127*	70	57	127	70	57	.	..	..	..	..	
4—5 ..	*136*	73	63	136	73	63	..	..	.	.	..	.
Total 0—5 ..	*693*	*373*	*320*	*692*	*373*	*319*	*1*	..	*1*	.	..	.
5—10 ..	*566*	295	271	541	289	252	23	5	18	2	1	1
10—15 ..	*439*	259	230	427	242	185	62	17	45	..	..	..
15—20 ..	*389*	208	181	181	136	45	201	69	132	7	3	4
20—30 ..	*803*	451	352	191	162	29	586	271	315	26	18	8
30—40 ..	*616*	360	256	48	38	10	516	292	224	52	30	22
40—50 ..	*422*	252	170	23	19	4	328	202	126	71	31	40
50—60 ..	*237*	151	86	20	13	7	155	110	45	62	28	34
60 and over ..	*144*	89	55	3	3	..	78	56	22	63	30	33

TABLE VII.—AGE, SEX AND CIVIL CONDITION (BY RELIGION).

PART B.—DETAILS FOR DISTRICTS AND STATES—*continued.*

HISSAR DISTRICT.

Religion and Age.	Population. Persons.	Population. Males.	Population. Females.	Unmarried. Persons.	Unmarried. Males.	Unmarried. Females.	Married. Persons.	Married. Males.	Married. Females.	Widowed. Persons.	Widowed. Males.	Widowed. Females.
1	2	3	4	5	6	7	8	9	10	11	12	13
ALL RELIGIONS	**899,479**	**485,690**	**413,789**	**423,027**	**257,568**	**165,464**	**391,568**	**192,684**	**198,884**	**84,884**	**35,443**	**49,441**
0–1	33,609	16,763	16,846	33,585	16,756	16,829	24	7	17		.	.
1–2	26,028	12,969	13,059	25,998	12,960	13,038	30	9	21	.		
2–3	28,789	14,437	14,352	28,739	14,423	14,316	50	14	36			.
3–4	27,931	14,226	13,705	27,699	14,171	13,528	225	52	73	7	3	4
4–5	25,544	13,329	12,215	25,123	13,227	11,896	401	92	309	20	10	10
Total 0–5	*141,901*	*71,724*	*70,177*	*141,144*	*71,537*	*69,607*	730	*174*	556	27	13	*14*
5–10	129,440	68,570	56,870	109,789	60,804	48,985	10,488	2,642	7,846	213	124	89
10–15	116,373	62,723	54,150	92,351	55,724	36,627	24,041	6,740	17,301	481	259	222
15–20	93,746	51,323	42,423	37,274	30,013	7,261	51,920	20,488	31,432	552	822	730
20–30	151,777	81,997	69,780	27,593	25,322	2,271	117,930	53,628	64,302	6,254	3,047	3,207
30–40	110,758	60,041	50,717	7,466	7,060	406	87,435	47,658	39,777	12,887	5,323	7,564
40–50	79,866	44,673	35,193	4,054	3,848	206	55,176	32,750	22,426	20,536	8,066	12,470
50–60	50,084	28,506	21,578	2,051	1,964	87	27,368	[illegible]	[illegible]	20,665	8,326	12,339
60 and over	37,104	21,133	15,971	1,355	1,291	64	13,480	10,379	[illegible]	22,269	[illegible]	12,806
HINDU	**583,420**	**315,578**	**267,842**	**263,687**	**162,110**	**101,577**	**260,555**	**128,467**	**132,088**	**59,178**	**25,001**	**34,177**
0–1	21,647	10,826	10,821	21,630	10,823	10,807	17	3	14	.		
1–2	16,470	8,210	8,260	16,449	8,206	8,243	21	4	17	.	.	
2–3	18,268	9,140	9,128	18,237	9,134	9,103	31	6	25			.
3–4	17,792	9,066	8,726	17,648	9,039	8,609	139	26	113	5		4
4–5	16,279	8,483	7,796	16,020	8,432	7,588	247	47	200	12		8
Total 0–5	*90,456*	*45,725*	*44,731*	*89,984*	*45,634*	*44,350*	*455*	*86*	*369*	*1*		*12*
5–10	77,166	40,608	36,558	69,450	38,628	30,822	7,563	1,893	5,670	153	87	66
10–15	75,327	40,368	34,957	57,175	35,111	22,064	17,792	5,068	12,724	358	89	169
15–20	61,135	33,594	27,541	21,066	17,948	3,118	38,934	15,055	23,879	1,135	53	[illegible]
20–30	98,244	53,204	45,040	15,370	14,594	776	78,420	36,505	41,915	4,454	2,105	2,349
30–40	70,644	39,526	31,118	4,998	4,763	235	56,411	31,003	25,408	9,235	3,760	5,475
40–50	52,347	29,663	23,184	3,076	2,851	125	35,365	21,016	14,349	14,506	5,796	8,710
50–60	33,583	19,046	14,537	1,590	1,541	49	17,348	11,511	5,837	14,425	5,974	8,451
60 and over	24,240	13,864	10,376	1,078	1,040	38	8,267	6,330	1,937	14,895	6,494	8,401
SIKH	**55,169**	**30,542**	**24,627**	**28,154**	**17,669**	**10,485**	**22,875**	**10,847**	**11,528**	**4,640**	**2,026**	**2,614**
0–1	1,975	1,016	959	1,974	1,015	959	1	1	.		.	.
1–2	1,491	767	724	1,490	766	724	1	1	.	.	.	
2–3	1,625	847	778	1,624	847	777	1	..		.		
3–4	1,619	861	758	1,610	858	752	9	3	6	.	.	
4–5	1,488	808	678	1,465	801	664	20	6	14	1		
Total 0–5	*8,196*	*4,299*	*3,897*	*8,163*	*4,287*	*3,876*	*32*	*11*	*21*	*1*	*1*	
5–10	7,187	3,841	3,346	6,769	3,761	3,008	414	79	335	4	1	3
10–15	7,011	3,805	3,206	6,129	3,704	2,519	876	95	781	12	6	6
15–20	5,600	3,197	2,403	3,033	2,296	737	2,524	877	1,647	43	24	19
20–30	9,362	5,303	4,059	2,569	2,293	276	6,543	2,871	3,672	250	39	[illegible]
30–40	6,620	3,801	2,819	804	771	33	5,249	2,742	2,507	567	288	279
40–50	5,102	2,876	2,226	407	391	16	3,659	2,017	642	1,036	468	568
50–60	3,424	1,942	1,482	184	171	13	2,033	1,274	759	1,207	[illegible]	710
60 and over	2,667	1,478	1,189	102	95	7	1,045	781	264	1,520	602	918
JAIN	**5,988**	**3,137**	**2,851**	**2,976**	**1,729**	**1,247**	**2,300**	**1,138**	**1,162**	**712**	**270**	**442**
0–1	228	102	126	226	101	125	2	1	1		.	
1–2	174	85	89	173	85	88	1	.	1	.	.	.
2–3	199	103	96	199	103	96	.		..	.		
3–4	181	91	90	181	91	90	.		..	.	.	
4–5	163	82	81	163	82	81	.	.	..	.		
Total 0–5	*945*	*463*	*482*	*942*	*462*	*480*	*3*	*1*	*2*	.		
5–10	789	404	385	782	401	382	6	2	4	1	1	
10–15	767	381	386	707	369	308	59	12	47	1	.	
15–20	615	342	273	265	210	55	339	128	211	11	4	7
20–30	1,027	525	502	172	158	14	783	341	442	72	26	46
30–40	771	407	364	61	54	7	561	305	256	149	48	101
40–50	551	303	248	28	26	2	341	210	131	182	67	115
50–60	341	178	163	13	13	..	155	99	56	173	66	107
60 and over	182	104	78	6	6	.	53	40	13	23	58	65
MUSLIM	**253,784**	**135,840**	**117,944**	**127,598**	**75,706**	**51,892**	**105,901**	**52,017**	**53,884**	**20,285**	**8,117**	**12,168**
0–1	9,717	4,795	4,922	9,713	4,793	4,920	4	2	2	..		
1–2	7,855	3,885	3,970	7,848	3,881	3,967	7	4	3	.		
2–3	8,660	4,328	4,332	8,642	4,320	4,322	18	8	10	.		.
3–4	8,304	4,189	4,115	8,225	4,164	4,061	77	23	54	2	2	.
4–5	7,576	3,935	3,641	7,437	3,892	3,545	132	38	94	7	5	2
Total 0–5	*42,112*	*21,132*	*20,980*	*41,865*	*21,050*	*20,815*	238	75	*163*	9		2
5–10	35,131	18,628	16,503	32,577	17,926	14,651	2,499	667	1,832	55	35	20
10–15	33,619	18,055	15,564	28,213	16,531	11,682	5,296	1,460	3,836	110	64	46
15–20	26,294	14,141	12,153	12,854	9,524	3,330	13,077	4,414	8,663	363	203	160
20–30	42,952	22,873	20,079	9,432	8,248	1,184	32,049	13,851	18,198	1,471	774	697
30–40	29,615	16,233	13,382	1,590	1,463	127	25,100	13,547	11,553	2,925	1,223	1,702
40–50	21,176	11,776	9,400	637	577	60	15,748	9,474	6,274	4,791	1,725	3,066
50–60	12,910	7,337	5,573	261	237	24	7,803	5,315	2,488	4,846	1,785	3,061
60 and over	9,975	5,665	4,310	169	150	19	4,091	3,214	877	5,715	2,301	3,414
CHRISTIAN	**1,107**	**583**	**524**	**609**	**346**	**263**	**430**	**208**	**222**	**68**	**29**	**39**
0–1	42	24	18	42	24	18	.	.	..	..		
1–2	38	22	16	38	22	16	.	.	..	..		.
2–3	37	19	18	37	19	18	.	..	.	..	.	.
3–4	35	19	16	35	19	16	.	..	..	..	.	.
4–5	39	21	19	37	19	18	2	1	1	..		.
Total 0–5	*191*	*104*	*87*	*189*	*103*	*86*	2	*1*	*1*		.	..
5–10	165	87	78	160	87	73	5	..	5	.	.	..
10–15	149	82	67	133	79	51	16	3	13	.	.	.
15–20	101	48	53	55	34	21	46	14	32	..	..	..
20–30	191	91	100	50	29	21	134	59	75	7	3	4
30–40	135	72	63	13	9	4	112	59	53	10	4	6
40–50	90	55	35	6	3	3	63	42	21	21	10	11
50–60	46	23	23	3	2	1	29	17	12	14	4	10
60 and over	39	21	18	..		..	23	13	10	16	8	8

TABLE VII.—AGE, SEX

PART B.—DETAILS FOR DISTRICTS AND STATES.

ROHTAK DISTRICT.

Religion and Age.	Population. Persons.	Population. Males.	Population. Females.	Unmarried. Persons.	Unmarried. Males.	Unmarried. Females.	Married. Persons.	Married. Males.	Married. Females.	Widowed. Persons.	Widowed. Males.	Widowed. Females.
1	2	3	4	5	6	7	8	9	10	11	12	13
ALL RELIGIONS ..	**805,621**	**432,855**	**372,766**	**334,058**	**203,071**	**130,987**	**381,239**	**186,951**	**194,288**	**90,324**	**42,833**	**47,491**
0- -1 ..	*30,747*	15,509	15,238	30,743	15,507	15,236	4	2	2	..	..	..
1- -2 ..	*23,333*	11,741	11,592	23,316	11,736	11,580	17	5	12	..	..	..
2- -3 ..	*25,377*	12,865	12,512	25,329	12,857	12,472	47	7	40	1	1	..
3- -4 ..	*24,556*	12,603	11,953	24,263	12,508	11,755	286	90	196	7	5	2
4—5 ..	*22,318*	11,643	10,675	21,788	11,458	10,330	514	175	339	16	10	6
Total 0- -5 .	*126,331*	*64,361*	*61,970*	*125,439*	*64,066*	*61,373*	*868*	*279*	*589*	*24*	*16*	*8*
5- -10 ..	*106,225*	57,298	48,927	90,224	51,205	39,019	15,749	5,918	9,831	252	175	77
10- -15 ..	*104,902*	57,690	47,212	69,631	43,658	25,973	34,685	13,618	21,067	586	414	172
15- -20 ..	*83,996*	44,685	39,311	20,245	17,257	2,988	61,933	26,287	35,646	1,818	1,141	677
20—30 ..	*140,181*	72,767	67,414	15,098	14,125	973	117,020	54,109	62,911	8,063	4,533	3,530
30- -40 ..	*101,482*	55,834	45,648	6,197	5,846	351	78,835	42,167	36,668	16,450	7,821	8,629
40—50 ..	*68,975*	38,452	30,523	4,099	3,927	172	42,535	24,547	17,988	22,341	9,978	12,363
50- -60 ..	*42,610*	24,096	18,514	1,877	1,781	96	20,164	13,072	7,092	20,569	9,243	11,326
60 and over .	*30,919*	17,672	13,247	1,248	1,206	42	9,450	6,954	2,496	20,221	9,512	10,709
HINDU ..	**655,963**	**353,935**	**302,028**	**269,860**	**165,192**	**104,668**	**310,335**	**152,224**	**158,111**	**75,768**	**36,519**	**39,249**
0- -1 ..	*24,780*	12,483	12,297	24,777	12,482	12,295	3	1	2	..	..	..
1- -2 ..	*18,658*	9,429	9,229	18,650	9,426	9,224	8	3	5	..	..	..
2—3 ..	*20,321*	10,374	9,947	20,297	10,369	9,928	23	4	19	1	1	..
3- -4 ..	*19,716*	10,162	9,554	19,506	10,088	9,418	203	69	134	7	5	2
4 -5 ..	*17,834*	9,319	8,515	17,442	9,175	8,267	378	134	244	14	10	4
Total 0- -5 ..	*101,309*	*51,767*	*49,542*	*100,672*	*51,540*	*49,132*	*615*	*211*	*404*	*22*	*16*	*6*
5- 10 ..	*86,002*	46,591	39,411	72,780	41,424	31,356	13,012	5,016	7,996	210	151	59
10- 15 .	*85,597*	47,352	38,245	56,080	35,322	20,758	29,040	11,686	17,354	477	344	133
15- -20 ..	*68,614*	36,694	31,920	15,772	13,570	2,202	51,368	22,195	29,173	1,474	929	545
20- -30 ..	*114,160*	59,536	54,624	12,278	11,546	732	95,150	44,195	50,955	6,732	3,795	2,937
30- 40 ..	*83,305*	45,983	37,322	5,555	5,301	254	63,661	33,906	29,755	14,089	6,776	7,313
40- -50 ..	*56,626*	31,641	24,985	3,809	3,689	120	33,847	19,295	14,552	18,970	8,657	10,313
50 -60 ..	*35,202*	19,872	15,330	1,741	1,664	77	16,133	10,275	5,858	17,328	7,933	9,395
60 and over .	*25,148*	14,499	10,649	1,173	1,136	37	7,509	5,445	2,064	16,466	7,918	8,548
SIKH ..	**596**	**328**	**268**	**261**	**185**	**126**	**301**	**175**	**126**	**34**	**18**	**16**
0- 1 ..	*27*	7	20	27	7	20	.	..	..	..	.	..
1- -2 ..	*21*	7	14	21	7	14	..	..	..	..	..	..
2- 3 ..	*19*	8	11	19	8	11	..	..	..	..	..	..
3- -4 ..	*20*	8	12	20	8	12	..	..	..	..	..	..
4 -5 ..	*22*	10	12	22	10	12	..	.	.	..	..	
Total 0- -5 ..	*109*	*40*	*69*	*109*	*40*	*69*	..	..	..	..	.	
5- -10 .	*76*	40	36	70	36	34	6	4	2	..	.	.
10- -15 ..	*62*	34	28	44	26	18	18	8	10	..		..
15- -20 ..	*62*	33	29	18	16	2	43	17	26	1	..	1
20- -30 ..	*122*	75	47	13	11	2	104	61	43	5	3	2
30- 40 ..	*87*	55	32	6	5	1	73	47	26	8	3	5
40- -50 ..	*42*	26	16	1	1	..	36	23	13	5	2	3
50- 60 .	*24*	17	7	..	..	..	14	10	4	10	7	3
60 and over ..	*12*	8	4	..	.	..	7	5	2	5	3	2
JAIN ..	**6,375**	**3,320**	**3,055**	**2,760**	**1,610**	**1,150**	**2,608**	**1,288**	**1,320**	**1,007**	**422**	**585**
0- 1 ..	*217*	116	101	217	116	101	..	..	..	..	..	.
1- -2 ..	*161*	77	84	161	77	84	..	..	..	..	..	.
2- -3 ..	*191*	89	102	191	89	102	..	..	..	..	..	..
3- -4 ..	*179*	84	95	179	84	95	..	..	..	..	..	..
4- 5 ..	*164*	81	83	164	81	83	..	..	..	..	..	..
Total 0- -5 .	*912*	*447*	*465*	*912*	*447*	*465*	..	..	..	..	..	.
5- 10 ..	*763*	390	373	736	382	354	25	7	18	2	1	1
10- 15 ..	*754*	390	364	621	347	274	130	42	88	3	1	2
15- 20 ..	*635*	329	306	205	158	47	417	165	252	13	6	7
20 -30 ..	*1,110*	582	528	148	143	5	872	402	470	90	37	53
30- 40 ..	*875*	493	382	71	67	4	621	342	279	183	84	99
40- -50 ..	*642*	363	279	42	41	1	351	201	150	249	121	128
50 -60 ..	*383*	214	169	19	19	..	146	95	51	218	100	118
60 and over ..	*301*	112	189	6	6	..	46	34	12	249	72	177
MUSLIM ..	**137,880**	**72,820**	**65,060**	**59,359**	**35,081**	**24,278**	**65,425**	**32,070**	**33,355**	**13,096**	**5,669**	**7,427**
0- -1 ..	*5,526*	2,792	2,734	5,525	2,791	2,734	1	1	..	..	..	..
1- -2 ..	*4,331*	2,141	2,190	4,322	2,139	2,183	9	2	7	..	..	..
2- -3 ..	*4,661*	2,303	2,358	4,638	2,300	2,338	23	3	20	..	..	..
3- -4 ..	*4,458*	2,265	2,193	4,380	2,244	2,136	78	21	57	..	..	..
4 5 .	*4,143*	2,160	1,983	4,014	2,120	1,894	127	40	87	2	..	2
Total 0- 5 .	*23,119*	*11,661*	*11,458*	*22,879*	*11,594*	*11,285*	*238*	*67*	*171*	*2*	..	*2*
5- -10 .	*18,673*	9,902	8,771	16,150	9,084	7,066	2,488	798	1,690	35	20	15
10 15 ..	*17,816*	9,547	8,269	12,569	7,751	4,818	5,148	1,732	3,416	99	64	35
15 -20 ..	*14,203*	7,395	6,808	4,173	3,450	723	9,710	3,746	5,964	320	199	121
20- -30 ..	*24,013*	12,210	11,803	2,610	2,384	226	20,206	9,152	11,054	1,197	674	523
30- -40 ..	*16,642*	9,033	7,609	554	466	88	13,986	7,633	6,353	2,102	934	1,168
40- -50 ..	*11,307*	6,234	5,073	240	192	48	8,047	4,885	3,162	3,020	1,157	1,863
50- -60 ..	*6,793*	3,879	2,914	116	97	19	3,760	2,621	1,139	2,917	1,161	1,756
60 and over ..	*5,314*	2,959	2,355	68	63	5	1,842	1,436	406	3,404	1,460	1,944
CHRISTIAN ..	**4,807**	**2,452**	**2,355**	**1,818**	**1,053**	**765**	**2,570**	**1,194**	**1,376**	**419**	**205**	**214**
0—1 ..	*197*	111	86	197	111	86	..	..	..	..	..	.
1- -2 ..	*162*	87	75	162	87	75	..	.	..	..	..	
2- -3 ..	*185*	91	94	184	91	93	1	..	1	.	..	
3—4 ..	*183*	84	99	178	84	94	5	..	5	..	..	
4- -5 .	*155*	73	82	146	72	74	9	1	8		..	
Total 0—5 ..	*882*	*446*	*436*	*867*	*445*	*422*	*15*	*1*	*14*	.	..	.
5- -10 ..	*711*	375	336	488	279	209	218	93	125	5	3	2
10—15 ..	*673*	367	306	317	212	105	340	150	190	7	5	2
15- -20 ..	*482*	234	248	77	63	14	395	164	231	10	7	3
20- -30 ..	*776*	364	412	49	41	8	688	299	389	39	24	15
30- 40 ..	*573*	270	303	11	7	4	494	239	255	68	24	44
40- -50 ..	*358*	188	170	7	4	3	254	143	111	97	41	56
50 -60 ..	*208*	114	94	1	1	..	111	71	40	96	42	54
60 and over ..	*144*	94	50	1	1		46	34	12	97	59	[illegible]

AND CIVIL CONDITION (BY RELIGION).

PART B.—DETAILS FOR DISTRICTS AND STATES—*continued.*

GURGAON DISTRICT.

Religion and Age.	Population.			Unmarried.			Married.			Widowed.		
	Persons.	Males.	Females.	Persons.	Males.	Females.	Persons.	Males.	Females.	Persons.	Males.	Females.
1	2	3	4	5	6	7	8	9	10	11	12	13
ALL RELIGIONS ..	**740,163**	**398,513**	**341,650**	**327,720**	**200,393**	**127,327**	**330,734**	**160,776**	**169,958**	**81,709**	**37,344**	**44,365**
0—1 ..	*28,472*	14,391	14,081	28,468	14,389	14,079	4	2	2	..	..	..
1—2 ..	*20,738*	10,317	10,421	20,728	10,312	10,416	10	5	5	..	..	..
2—3 ..	*23,715*	11,799	11,916	23,690	11,792	11,898	25	7	18	..	..	..
3—4 ..	*23,699*	12,031	11,668	23,568	11,992	11,576	127	37	90	4	2	2
4—5 ..	*22,012*	11,525	10,487	21,777	11,455	10,322	227	66	161	8	4	4
Total 0—5 ..	*118,636*	*60,063*	*58,573*	*118,231*	*59,940*	*58,291*	*393*	*117*	*276*	*12*	*6*	*6*
5—10 ..	*99,545*	54,344	45,201	90,915	52,093	38,822	8,472	2,161	6,311	158	90	68
10—15 ..	*93,492*	52,295	41,197	71,858	45,778	26,080	21,184	6,260	14,924	450	257	193
15—20 ..	*71,800*	38,638	33,162	22,906	19,604	3,301	47,272	18,039	29,233	1,623	995	628
20—30 ..	*131,401*	68,514	62,887	15,789	15,113	676	108,022	49,131	58,891	7,590	4,270	3,320
30—40 ..	*97,372*	53,331	44,041	4,443	4,349	94	78,070	42,048	36,022	14,859	6,934	7,925
40—50 ..	*62,223*	34,378	27,845	1,929	1,891	38	40,314	24,062	16,252	19,980	8,425	11,555
50—60 ..	*38,265*	21,202	17,063	995	977	18	18,111	12,108	6,003	19,159	8,117	11,042
60 and over ..	*27,429*	15,748	11,681	655	648	7	8,896	6,850	2,046	17,878	8,250	9,628
HINDU ..	**493,174**	**266,641**	**226,533**	**217,705**	**133,459**	**84,246**	**217,242**	**106,862**	**110,880**	**58,227**	**26,820**	**31,407**
0—1 ..	*18,428*	9,298	9,130	18,428	9,298	9,130	..	..	..	..	..	..
1—2 ..	*13,406*	6,704	6,702	13,405	6,703	6,702	1	1	..	..	..	..
2—3 ..	*15,563*	7,765	7,798	15,558	7,763	7,795	5	2	3	..	..	..
3—4 ..	*15,611*	7,936	7,675	15,562	7,920	7,642	47	15	32	2	1	1
4—5 ..	*14,442*	7,552	6,890	14,351	7,524	6,827	87	26	61	4	2	2
Total 0—5 ..	*77,450*	*39,255*	*38,195*	*77,304*	*39,208*	*38,096*	*140*	*44*	*96*	*6*	*3*	*3*
5—10 ..	*65,453*	35,769	29,684	60,529	34,376	26,153	4,831	1,337	3,494	93	56	37
10—15 ..	*61,870*	34,665	27,145	47,722	30,188	17,534	13,784	4,301	9,483	304	176	128
15—20 ..	*47,442*	25,688	21,754	14,720	12,760	1,960	31,583	12,253	19,330	1,139	675	464
20—30 ..	*86,699*	45,603	41,096	10,831	10,425	406	70,540	32,311	38,229	5,328	2,867	2,461
30—40 ..	*65,350*	36,038	29,312	3,547	3,489	58	51,278	27,614	23,664	10,525	4,935	5,590
40—50 ..	*42,525*	23,573	18,952	1,624	1,600	24	26,743	15,797	10,946	14,158	6,176	7,982
50—60 ..	*26,776*	14,833	11,943	866	854	12	12,225	8,066	4,159	13.685	5,913	7,772
60 and over ..	*19,669*	11,217	8,452	562	559	3	6,118	4,639	1,479	12,989	6,019	6,970
SIKH ..	**500**	**281**	**219**	**227**	**141**	**86**	**228**	**117**	**111**	**45**	**23**	**22**
0—1 ..	*13*	6	7	13	6	7	..	..	..	..	..	..
1—2 ..	*10*	4	6	10	4	6	..	..	..	..	..	..
2—3 ..	*14*	7	7	14	7	7	..	..	..	..	..	..
3—4 ..	*14*	7	7	14	7	7	..	..	..	..	..	..
4—5 ..	*17*	9	8	17	9	8	..	..	..	..	..	..
Total 0—5 ..	*68*	*33*	*35*	*68*	*33*	*35*	..	..	..	..	..	..
5—10 ..	*63*	34	29	59	33	26	4	*1*	3	..	..	..
10—15 ..	*56*	30	26	48	29	19	8	1	7	..	..	..
15—20 ..	*52*	32	20	26	20	6	24	11	13	2	1	1
20—30 ..	*105*	59	46	20	20	..	81	35	46	4	4	..
30—40 ..	*68*	40	28	3	3	..	60	35	25	5	2	3
40—50 ..	*43*	27	16	2	2	..	32	21	11	9	4	5
50—60 ..	*21*	11	10	..	..	..	11	7	4	10	4	6
60 and over ..	*24*	15	9	1	1	..	*8*	6	2	15	8	7
JAIN ..	**2,665**	**1,379**	**1,286**	**1,218**	**683**	**535**	**1,049**	**522**	**527**	**398**	**174**	**224**
0—1 ..	*107*	54	53	107	54	53	..	..	..	..	..	..
1—2 ..	*72*	33	39	72	33	39	..	..	..	..	..	..
2—3 ..	*87*	38	49	87	38	49	..	..	..	..	..	..
3—4 ..	*79*	37	42	79	37	42	..	..	..	..	..	..
4—5 ..	*73*	33	40	73	33	40	..	..	..	..	..	..
Total 0—5 ..	*418*	*195*	*223*	*418*	*195*	*223*	..	..	..	..	..	..
5—10 ..	*336*	174	162	331	172	159	4	2	*2*	1	..	1
10—15 ..	*307*	164	143	277	157	120	29	7	22	1	..	1
15—20 ..	*232*	120	112	88	65	23	140	53	87	4	2	2
20—30 ..	*422*	214	208	60	54	6	337	*151*	186	25	9	16
30—40 ..	*358*	187	171	24	23	1	260	134	126	74	30	44
40—50 ..	*289*	159	130	10	9	1	168	*102*	66	111	48	63
50—60 ..	*176*	92	84	6	4	2	73	46	27	97	42	55
60 and over ..	*127*	74	53	4	4	..	38	27	11	85	43	42
MUSLIM ..	**242,357**	**129,479**	**112,878**	**107,858**	**65,739**	**42,119**	**111,567**	**53,453**	**58,114**	**22,932**	**10,287**	**12,645**
0—1 ..	*9,870*	5,002	4,868	9,866	5,000	4,866	4	2	2	..	..	..
1—2 ..	*7,211*	3,556	3,655	7,202	3,552	3,650	9	4	5	..	..	..
2—3 ..	*8,003*	3,970	4,083	7,983	3,965	4,018	20	5	15	..	..	..
3—4 ..	*7,948*	4,032	3,916	7,866	4,009	3,857	80	22	58	2	1	1
4—5 ..	*7,430*	3,908	3,522	7,287	3,866	3,421	139	40	99	4	2	2
Total 0—5 ..	*40,462*	*20,468*	*19,994*	*40,204*	*20,392*	*19,812*	*252*	*73*	*179*	*6*	*3*	*3*
5—10 ..	*33,474*	18,255	15,219	29,800	17,408	12,392	3,611	814	2,797	63	33	30
10—15 ..	*31,123*	17,333	13,790	23,659	15,316	8,343	7,319	1,936	5,383	145	81	64
15—20 ..	*23,930*	12,730	11,200	8,015	6,728	1,287	15,441	5,687	9,754	474	315	159
20—30 ..	*43,932*	22,526	21,406	4,834	4,591	243	36,875	16,550	20,325	2,223	1,385	838
30—40 ..	*31,391*	16,970	14,421	853	828	25	26,305	14,181	12,124	4,233	1,961	2,272
40—50 ..	*19,244*	10,551	8,693	286	277	9	13,280	8,085	5,195	5,678	2,189	3,489
50—60 ..	*11,231*	6,230	5,001	120	116	4	5,765	3,962	1,803	5,346	2,152	3,194
60 and over ..	*7,570*	4,416	3,154	87	83	4	2,719	2,165	554	4,764	2,168	2,596
CHRISTIAN ..	**1,463**	**730**	**733**	**710**	**369**	**341**	**646**	**321**	**325**	**107**	**40**	**67**
0—1 ..	*54*	31	23	54	31	23	..	..	..	..	..	..
1—2 ..	*39*	20	19	39	20	19	..	..	..	..	..	..
2—3 ..	*48*	19	29	48	19	29	..	..	..	..	..	..
3—4 ..	*47*	19	28	47	19	28	..	..	..	..	..	..
4—5 ..	*50*	23	27	49	23	26	1	..	1	..	..	..
Total 0—5 ..	*238*	*112*	*126*	*237*	*112*	*125*	*1*	..	*1*	..	..	..
5—10 ..	*219*	112	107	196	104	92	22	7	15	1	1	..
10—15 ..	*196*	103	93	152	88	64	44	15	29	..	..	..
15—20 ..	*144*	68	76	56	31	25	84	35	49	4	2	2
20—30 ..	*241*	110	131	42	21	21	189	84	105	10	5	5
30—40 ..	*204*	96	108	16	6	10	166	84	82	22	6	16
40—50 ..	*121*	67	54	7	3	4	90	56	34	24	8	16
50—60 ..	*61*	36	25	3	3	..	37	27	10	21	6	15
60 and over ..	*39*	26	13	1	1	..	13	13	..	25	12	13

TABLE VII.—AGE, SEX

PART B.—DETAILS FOR DISTRICTS AND STATES.

KARNAL DISTRICT.

Religion and Age.	Population.			Unmarried.			Married.			Widowed.		
	Persons.	Males.	Females.	Persons.	Males.	Females.	Persons.	Males.	Females.	Persons.	Males.	Females.
1	2	3	4	5	6	7	8	9	10	11	12	13
ALL RELIGIONS ..	**852,614**	**469,870**	**382,744**	**369,668**	**231,932**	**137,736**	**382,692**	**190,974**	**191,718**	**100,254**	**46,964**	**53,290**
0—1 ..	*31,291*	15,626	15,665	31,290	15,625	15,665	1	1		..	.	.
1—2 ..	*23,973*	12,010	11,963	23,966	12,007	11,959	7	3	4	..	..	
2—3 ..	*26,969*	13,616	13,353	26,952	13,609	13,343	17	7	10	..	..	
3—4 ..	*25,613*	13,199	12,414	25,456	13,165	12,291	157	34	123	..	.	
4—5 ..	*23,222*	12,310	10,912	22,911	12,242	10,669	304	65	239	7	3	4
Total 0—5 ..	*131,068*	*66,761*	*64,307*	*130,575*	*66,648*	*63,927*	*486*	*110*	*376*	*7*		
5—10 ..	*107,311*	58,840	48,471	95,235	55,331	39,904	11,872	3,387	8,485	204	[illegible]	[illegible]
10—15 ..	*107,284*	60,274	47,010	78,917	51,074	27,843	27,797	8,864	18,933	570	[illegible]	[illegible]
15—20 ..	*92,024*	51,146	40,878	31,330	26,458	4,872	58,379	23,352	35,027	2,315	1,336	[illegible]
20—30 ..	*158,261*	86,550	71,711	22,829	21,726	1,103	124,600	59,091	65,406	10,932	5,730	5,202
30—40 ..	*112,103*	62,885	49,218	6,204	6,152	52	85,758	47,522	38,236	20,141	9,211	[illegible]
40—50 ..	*73,630*	41,516	32,114	2,692	2,667	25	45,627	28,039	17,588	25,311	10,810	[illegible]
50—60 ..	*42,239*	24,494	17,745	1,213	1,205	8	19,566	13,672	5,894	21,460	9,617	[illegible]
60 and over ..	*28,694*	17,404	11,290	673	671	2	8,707	6,934	1,773	19,314	9,799	9,515
HINDU ..	**565,286**	**313,117**	**252,169**	**245,150**	**155,795**	**89,355**	**250,724**	**124,425**	**126,299**	**69,412**	**32,897**	**36,515**
0—1 ..	*20,532*	10,249	10,283	20,532	10,249	10,283	..	..	..	.	.	
1—2 ..	*15,703*	7,868	7,835	15,700	7,867	7,833	3	1	2	.	..	.
2—3 ..	*17,866*	9,049	8,817	17,857	9,046	8,811	9	3	6	.	..	
3—4 ..	*17,044*	8,845	8,199	16,971	8,824	8,147	73	21	52	.	.	
4—5 ..	*15,300*	8,208	7,092	15,156	8,164	6,992	140	42	98	4	2	2
Total 0—5 .	*86,445*	*44,219*	*42,226*	*86,216*	*44,150*	*42,066*	*225*	*67*	*158*	*4*	*2*	*2*
5—10 ..	*71,415*	39,500	31,915	63,425	37,225	26,200	7,872	2,197	5,675	118	78	[illegible]
10—15 ..	*71,477*	40,520	30,957	52,288	34,364	17,924	18,824	5,934	12,890	365	[illegible]	[illegible]
15—20 ..	*60,622*	34,147	26,475	20,087	17,468	2,619	38,980	15,779	23,201	1,555	900	[illegible]
20—30 ..	*105,109*	57,828	47,281	15,134	14,614	520	82,394	39,255	43,139	7,581	3,959	[illegible]
30—40 ..	*75,176*	42,235	32,941	4,561	4,543	18	56,288	31,038	25,250	14,327	6,654	7,673
40—50 ..	*48,828*	27,574	21,254	2,023	2,018	5	29,070	17,806	11,264	17,735	7,750	9,985
50—60 ..	*27,721*	15,973	11,748	913	910	3	12,023	8,366	3,657	14,785	6,697	8,088
60 and over ..	*18,493*	11,121	7,372	503	503	.	5,048	3,983	1,065	12,942	[illegible]	[illegible]
SIKH ..	**16,928**	**9,692**	**7,236**	**7,561**	**4,853**	**2,708**	**7,461**	**3,835**	**3,626**	**1,906**	**1,004**	**902**
0—1 ..	*583*	301	282	583	301	282	..	..	..	..	..	.
1—2 ..	*454*	228	226	454	228	226	..	..	..	.	..	.
2—3 ..	*504*	260	244	504	260	244	..	.	..	..	..	.
3—4 .	*464*	245	219	463	245	218	1	..	1	..		
4—5 ..	*419*	230	189	415	229	186	4	1	3	..	..	
Total 0—5 .	*2,424*	*1,264*	*1,160*	*2,419*	*1,263*	*1,156*	*5*	*1*	*4*	..	.	.
5—10 .	*2,038*	1,142	896	1,888	1,101	787	149	41	108	1	..	1
10—15 ..	*2,084*	1,179	905	1,666	1,049	617	414	128	286	4	2	2
15—20 ..	*1,759*	996	763	696	571	125	1,034	406	628	29	19	[illegible]
20—30 ..	*3,043*	1,745	1,298	583	565	18	2,302	1,075	1,227	158	105	[illegible]
30—40 ..	*2,191*	1,333	858	211	209	2	1,675	942	733	305	182	123
40—50 .	*1,641*	942	699	56	53	3	1,104	658	446	481	231	250
50—60 .	*999*	627	372	28	28	..	526	372	154	445	227	218
60 and over ..	*749*	464	285	14	14	..	252	212	40	483	238	245
JAIN ..	**4,190**	**2,164**	**2,026**	**1,794**	**1,052**	**742**	**1,759**	**839**	**920**	**637**	**273**	**364**
0—1 .	*141*	76	65	141	76	65	.	..	.	..	..	..
1—2 ..	*118*	62	56	118	62	56	..	..	.	..	..	
2—3 ..	*123*	64	59	123	64	59	..	..	..	..	..	.
3—4 ..	*115*	61	54	115	61	54	..	..	..	..	..	.
4—5 ..	*112*	59	53	112	59	53	..	..	..	..	..	..
Total 0—5 ..	*609*	*322*	*287*	*609*	*322*	*287*	..	..	..	..	..	.
5—10 ..	*494*	248	246	479	247	232	15	1	14	.	..	.
10—15 ..	*480*	232	248	394	211	183	85	21	64	1	..	1
15—20 ..	*426*	209	217	130	96	34	282	109	173	14	4	10
20—30 ..	*774*	393	381	101	96	5	588	268	320	85	29	56
30—40 ..	*572*	308	264	48	48	..	396	205	191	128	55	73
40—50 ..	*416*	224	192	19	18	1	249	142	107	148	64	84
50—60 ..	*254*	133	121	10	10	..	104	68	36	140	55	85
60 and over ..	*165*	95	70	4	4	..	40	25	15	121	66	5
MUSLIM ..	**259,730**	**141,372**	**118,358**	**112,323**	**68,501**	**43,822**	**119,642**	**60,347**	**59,295**	**27,765**	**12,524**	**15,241**
0—1 ..	*9,747*	4,859	4,888	9,746	4,858	4,888	1	1	..	..	.	..
1—2 ..	*7,490*	3,754	3,736	7,486	3,752	3,734	4	2	2	..	.	..
2—3 ..	*8,237*	4,122	4,115	8,229	4,118	4,111	8	4	4	..	..	..
3—4 ..	*7,762*	3,928	3,834	7,680	3,915	3,765	82	13	69	..	..	..
4—5 ..	*7,175*	3,701	3,474	7,016	3,678	3,338	156	22	134	3		2
Total 0—5 ..	*40,411*	*20,364*	*20,047*	*40,157*	*20,321*	*19,836*	*251*	*42*	*209*	*3*	*1*	[illegible]
5—10 ..	*32,490*	17,469	15,021	28,681	16,303	12,378	3,727	1,123	2,604	82	43	[illegible]
10—15 ..	*32,423*	17,879	14,544	24,009	15,070	8,939	8,217	2,700	5,517	197	109	[illegible]
15—20 ..	*28,537*	15,433	13,104	10,230	8,165	2,065	17,603	6,865	10,738	704	403	[illegible]
20—30 ..	*48,146*	25,960	22,180	6,897	6,347	550	38,201	18,026	20,175	3,048	1,593	1,455
30—40 ..	*33,343*	18,567	14,776	1,362	1,331	31	26,707	14,956	11,751	5,274	2,280	2,994
40—50 ..	*22,252*	12,480	9,772	576	560	16	14,867	9,213	5,654	6,809	2,707	4,102
50—60 ..	*13,016*	7,607	5,409	230	254	5	6,772	4,764	2,008	5,985	2,559	3,396
60 and over ..	*9,112*	5,607	3,505	152	150	2	3,297	2,658	639	5,663	2,799	2,864
CHRISTIAN ..	**1,469**	**806**	**663**	**701**	**421**	**280**	**661**	**324**	**337**	**107**	**61**	**46**
0—1 ..	*61*	35	26	61	35	26	..	..	..	..	..	..
1—2 ..	*48*	19	29	48	19	29	..	..	..	..	.	..
2—3 ..	*60*	28	32	60	28	32	..	.	..	..	..	.
3—4 ..	*54*	26	28	53	26	27	1	..	1	..	..	..
4—5 ..	*52*	26	26	50	26	24	2	..	2	..	..	..
Total 0—5 ..	*275*	*134*	*141*	*272*	*134*	*138*	*3*	..	*3*	..	..	..
5—10 ..	*202*	112	90	185	109	76	16	3	13	1	..	1
10—15 ..	*180*	105	75	138	90	48	41	14	27	1	1	..
15—20 ..	*154*	82	72	52	41	11	100	39	61	2	2	..
20—30 ..	*274*	141	133	39	33	6	220	97	123	15	11	4
30—40 ..	*167*	91	76	8	7	1	142	79	63	17	5	12
40—50 ..	*108*	66	42	6	6	..	77	48	29	25	12	13
50—60 ..	*61*	42	19	1	1	..	39	27	12	21	14	7
60 and over ..	*48*	33	15	..	.	..	23	17	[illegible]	25		9

AND CIVIL CONDITION (BY RELIGION).

PART B.—DETAILS FOR DISTRICTS AND STATES—*continued.*

AMBALA DISTRICT.

Religion and Age.	Population.			Unmarried.			Married.			Widowed.		
	Persons.	Males.	Females.	Persons.	Males.	Females.	Persons.	Males.	Females.	Per ons.	Males.	Females.
1	2	3	4	5	6	7	8	9	10	11	12	13
ALL RELIGIONS ..	**742,902**	**416,411**	**326,491**	**328,847**	**208,416**	**120,431**	**327,940**	**165,587**	**162,353**	**86,115**	**42,408**	**43,707**
0- 1 ..	*25,291*	12,860	12,431	25,287	12,856	12,431	..	..	..	4	4	..
1- -2 ..	*19,774*	9,988	9,786	19,764	9,982	9,782	7	3	4	3	3	..
2- -3 ..	*21,439*	10,842	10,597	21,410	10,826	1 .584	18	5	13	11	11	..
3- 4 ..	*20,845*	10,695	10,150	20,701	10,650	10,051	131	35	06	13	10	3
4 -5 ..	*19,639*	10,340	9,299	19,382	10,268	9.114	244	69	175	13	3	10
Total 0- 5 ..	*106,988*	*54,725*	*52,263*	*106,544*	*54,582*	*51,962*	*400*	*112*	*288*	*44*	*31*	*13*
5- -10 .	*91,491*	49,826	41,665	83,439	47,492	35,047	7,915	2,268	5,647	137	66	71
10—15 ..	*89,359*	49,653	39,706	69,575	43,542	26,033	19,432	5,929	13,503	352	182	170
15- -20 ..	*73,834*	41,152	32,682	27,708	22,960	4,748	44,741	17,357	27,384	1,385	835	550
20- -30 ..	*131,907*	74,564	57,343	23,532	22,220	1,312	101,299	48,141	53,158	7,076	4,203	2,873
30- -40 ..	*98,058*	57,424	40,634	8,811	8,579	232	75,233	41,515	33,718	14,014	7,330	6,(84
40- -50 ..	*69,997*	40,649	29,348	4,864	4,754	110	44,692	26,433	18,259	20,41	9,46?	10,979
50- -60 ..	*44,541*	26,376	18,165	2,634	2,587	47	21,995	14,623	7,372	19,912	9,166	10,74
60 and over ..	*36,727*	22,042	14,685	1,740	1,700	40	12,233	9,209	3,024	22,754	11,133	11,621
HINDU .	**346,711**	**195,270**	**151,441**	**153,467**	**97,573**	**55,894**	**150,671**	**77,012**	**73,659**	**42,573**	**20,685**	**21,888**
0- -1 ..	*11,495*	5,852	5,643	11,495	5,852	5,643	..	.	..	.	..	..
1 -2 ..	*9,189*	4,668	4,521	9,187	4,668	4,519	2	..	2	..	..	.
2- -3 ..	*9,982*	5,101	4,881	9,975	5,098	4,877	6	2	4	1	1	.
3- -4 ..	*9,672*	4,998	4,674	9,638	4,990	4,648	32	8	24	2	..	2
4 -5 ..	*9,027*	4,758	4,269	8,963	4,744	4,219	57	13	44	7	1	6
Total 0- -5 ..	*49,365*	*25,377*	*23,988*	*49,258*	*25,352*	*23,906*	*97*	*23*	*74*	*10*	*2*	*8*
5- 10 ..	*42,000*	22,872	19,128	38,875	22,056	16,819	3,069	788	2,281	56	28	28
10- 15 ..	*41,186*	22,979	18,207	32,766	20,473	12,293	8,263	2,425	5,838	157	81	76
15- -20 ..	*34,991*	19,637	15,354	13,165	10,965	2,200	21,110	8,240	12,870	716	432	284
20- -30 ..	*64,251*	36,359	27,892	10,923	10,426	497	49,505	23,698	25,807	3,823	2,235	1,588
30- -40 ..	*47,085*	28,064	19,021	4,158	4,065	93	35,322	20,123	15,199	7,605	3,876	3,729
40- -50 ..	*32,266*	18,931	13,335	2,305	2,262	43	19,502	11,010	7 592	10,459	4,759	5,700
50- -60 ..	*20,149*	11,801	8,348	1,226	1,205	21	9,144	6,192	2,952	9,779	4,404	5,375
60 and over ..	*15,418*	9,250	6,168	791	769	22	4,659	3,613	1,046	9,968	4,868	5,100
SIKH ..	**155,555**	**88,485**	**67,070**	**68,908**	**45,347**	**23,561**	**68,724**	**33,673**	**35,051**	**17,923**	**9,465**	**8,458**
0—1 ..	*5,328*	2,741	2,587	5,328	2,741	2,587	..	..	..	.	..	..
1- -2 ..	*3,886*	2,000	1,886	3,884	1,998	1,886	2	2	..	.	..	.
2- -3 ..	*4,237*	2,171	2,066	4,233	2,169	2,064	4	2	2	..	..	..
3- -4 ..	*4,161*	2,169	1,992	4,145	2,166	1,979	15	3	12	1	..	1
4 -5 ..	*3,971*	2,138	1,833	3,938	2,130	1,808	31	8	23	2	..	2
Total 0 -5 ..	*21,583*	*11,219*	*10,364*	*21,528*	*11,204*	*10,324*	*52*	*15*	*37*	*3*	..	*3*
5- -10 ..	*19,084*	10,645	8,439	17,391	10,120	7,271	1,672	515	1,157	21	10	11
10- -15 ..	*18,957*	10,705	8,252	14,328	9,223	5,105	4,571	1,448	3,123	58	34	24
15—20 ..	*14,739*	8,231	6,508	5,054	4,394	660	9,463	3,694	5,769	222	143	79
20—30 ..	*24,543*	14,067	10,476	4,712	4,553	159	18,796	8,809	9,987	1,036	706	330
30—40 ..	*19,917*	11,662	8,255	2,648	2,622	26	14,931	7,632	7,299	2,338	1,408	930
40- -50 ..	*15,826*	9,261	6,565	1,624	1,617	7	10,288	5,619	4,669	3,914	2,025	1,889
50- -60 ..	*10,919*	6,627	4,292	958	954	4	5,562	3,503	2,059	4,399	2,170	2,229
60 and over ..	*9,987*	6,068	3,919	665	660	5	3,389	2,438	951	5,933	2,970	2,963
JAIN ..	**2,550**	**1,402**	**1,148**	**1,175**	**726**	**449**	**1,037**	**529**	**508**	**338**	**147**	**191**
0—1 ..	*72*	39	33	72	39	33	..	..	..	..	..	..
1—2 ..	*61*	28	33	61	28	33	..	..	..	..	..	..
2- -3 ..	*70*	38	32	70	38	32	..	..	..	..	..	..
3- 4 ..	*69*	39	30	69	39	30	..	..	..	..	..	..
4 -5 ..	*62*	28	34	62	28	34	..	..	..	..	..	..
Total 0- -5 ..	*334*	*172*	*162*	*334*	*172*	*162*	..	..	..	..	..	..
5- 10 ..	*311*	167	144	311	167	144	..	..	..	..	..	..
10 -15 ..	*314*	179	135	292	176	116	22	3	19	..	..	..
15- -20 ..	*248*	133	115	111	88	23	131	44	87	6	1	5
20—30 ..	*434*	228	206	71	70	1	328	146	182	35	12	23
30—40 ..	*338*	189	149	25	25	..	257	140	117	56	24	32
40—50 ..	*263*	151	112	16	15	1	160	101	59	87	35	52
50—60 ..	*180*	109	71	12	11	1	96	64	32	72	34	38
60 and over ..	*128*	74	54	3	2	1	43	31	12	82	41	41
MUSLIM ..	**230,837**	**126,913**	**103,924**	**100,963**	**61,840**	**39,123**	**104,979**	**53,124**	**51,855**	**24,895**	**11,949**	**12,946**
0—1 ..	*8,200*	4,131	4,069	8,196	4,127	4,069	..	..	..	4	4	..
1—2 ..	*6,476*	3,210	3,266	6,470	3,206	3,264	3	1	2	3	3	..
2- -3 ..	*6,975*	3,444	3,531	6,957	3,433	3,524	8	1	7	10	10	..
3- -4 ..	*6,765*	3,401	3,364	6,671	3,367	3,304	84	24	60	10	10	..
4- -5 ..	*6,400*	3,326	3,074	6,241	3,277	2,964	155	47	108	4	2	2
Total 0- -5 ..	*34,816*	*17,512*	*17,304*	*34,535*	*17,410*	*17,125*	*250*	*73*	*177*	*31*	*29*	*2*
5- -10 ..	*29,293*	15,711	13,582	26,083	14,724	11,359	3,150	959	2,191	60	28	32
10- -15 ..	*28,128*	15,361	12,767	21,484	13,263	8,221	6,507	2,031	4,476	137	67	70
15- -20 ..	*22,998*	12,583	10,415	8,738	7,023	1,715	13,820	5,302	8,518	440	258	182
20—30 ..	*40,825*	22,590	18,235	6,745	6,201	544	31,918	15,154	16,764	2,162	1,235	927
30—40 ..	*29,692*	16,939	12,753	1,798	1,719	79	23,936	13,226	10,710	3,958	1,994	1,964
40—50 ..	*21,093*	11,999	9,094	885	835	50	14,320	8,554	5,766	5,888	2,610	3,278
50—60 ..	*13,020*	7,687	5,333	428	407	21	7,013	4,756	2,257	5,579	2,524	3,055
60 and over ..	*10,972*	6,531	4,441	267	258	9	4,065	3,069	996	6,640	3,204	3,436
CHRISTIAN ..	**7,141**	**4,284**	**2,857**	**4,308**	**2,915**	**1,393**	**2,461**	**1,212**	**1,249**	**372**	**157**	**215**
0- -1 ..	*194*	97	97	194	97	97	..	..	..	..	..	..
1—2 ..	*160*	82	78	160	82	78	..	..	..	..	..	..
2—3 ..	*173*	87	86	173	87	86	..	..	..	..	..	..
3—4 ..	*177*	87	90	177	87	90	..	..	..	..	..	..
4—5 ..	*175*	87	88	175	87	88	..	..	..	..	..	..
Total 0—5 ..	*879*	*440*	*439*	*879*	*440*	*439*	..	..	..	..	..	..
5—10 ..	*788*	424	364	771	421	350	17	3	14	..	..	..
10—15 ..	*760*	422	338	702	405	297	58	17	41	..	..	..
15—20 ..	*850*	563	287	639	489	150	210	73	137	1	1	..
20- -30 ..	*1,829*	1,303	526	1,078	967	111	734	323	411	17	13	4
30- -40 ..	*1,011*	562	449	181	147	34	776	389	387	54	26	28
40—50 ..	*540*	302	238	34	25	9	416	244	172	90	33	57
50 – 60 ..	*268*	150	118	10	10	..	175	106	69	83	34	49
60 and over ..	*216*	118	98	14	11	3	75	57	18	127	50	77

TABLE VII.—AGE, SEX

PART B.—DETAILS FOR DISTRICTS AND STATES.

SIMLA DISTRICT.

Religion and Age.	Population.			Unmarried.			Married.			Widowed.		
	Persons.	Males.	Females.	Persons.	Males.	Females.	Persons.	Males.	Females.	Persons.	Males.	Females.
1	2	3	4	5	6	7	8	9	10	11	12	13
ALL RELIGIONS ..	**36,786**	**23,517**	**13,269**	**13,944**	**9,283**	**4,661**	**19,447**	**12,538**	**6,909**	**3,395**	**1,696**	**1,699**
0—1 ..	*745*	366	379	745	366	379	..	..	..	..	..	.
1—2 ..	*652*	308	344	652	308	344	..	..	..	..	..	.
2—3 .	*733*	347	386	732	346	386	1	1	..	..	..	.
3—4 ..	*734*	356	378	733	355	378	1	1	..	..	..	
4—5 ..	*706*	358	348	702	355	347	4	3	1	..		
Total 0—5 ..	*3,570*	*1,735*	*1,835*	*3,564*	*1,730*	*1,834*	*6*	*5*	*1*	..	.	.
5—10 ..	*3,197*	1,704	1,493	3,074	1,677	1,397	118	26	92	5	1	4
10—15 ..	*3,138*	1,803	1,335	2,684	1,677	1,007	434	116	318	20	10	10
15—20 ..	*3,805*	2,528	1,277	1,796	1,592	204	1,928	881	1,047	81	55	26
20—30 ..	*8,817*	6,169	2,648	2,026	1,901	125	6,397	3,984	2,413	394	284	110
30—40 ..	*6,593*	4,555	2,038	480	430	50	5,469	3,755	1,714	644	370	274
40—50 ..	*3,960*	2,708	1,252	181	159	22	3,030	2,187	843	749	362	387
50—60 ..	*2,218*	1,419	799	89	80	9	1,395	1,042	353	734	297	437
60 and over ..	*1,488*	896	592	50	37	13	670	542	128	768	317	451
HINDU ..	**28,661**	**17,839**	**10,822**	**10,795**	**7,233**	**3,562**	**14,989**	**9,220**	**5,769**	**2,877**	**1,386**	**1,491**
0—1 ..	*604*	304	300	604	304	300	..	..	..	..	..	..
1—2 ..	*519*	242	277	519	242	277	..	..	..	..	..	..
2—3 ..	*572*	265	307	572	265	307	..	..	..	..	..	..
3—4 ..	*588*	282	306	587	281	306	1	1	..	..	..	.
4—5 ..	*561*	284	277	559	282	277	2	2	..	..	.	..
Total 0—5 .	*2,844*	*1,377*	*1,467*	*2,841*	*1,374*	*1,467*	*3*	*3*	..	..	.	..
5—10 ..	*2,578*	1,379	1,199	2,471	1,359	1,112	103	19	84	4	1	3
10—15 ..	*2,553*	1,466	1,088	2,153	1,366	787	383	91	292	17	8	9
15—20 ..	*2,965*	1,923	1,042	1,368	1,245	123	1,527	631	896	70	47	23
20—30 ..	*0,644*	4,490	2,154	1,446	1,392	54	4,877	2,871	2,006	321	227	94
30—40 .	*5,008*	3,339	1,669	303	291	12	4 156	2,747	1,409	549	301	248
40—50 ..	*3,054*	2,024	1,030	123	116	7	2,291	1,611	680	640	297	343
50—60 ..	*1,798*	1,115	683	63	63	..	1,105	807	298	630	245	385
60 and over ..	*1,217*	727	490	27	27	..	544	440	104	646	260	386
SIKH ..	**760**	**532**	**228**	**250**	**156**	**94**	**461**	**344**	**117**	**49**	**82**	**17**
0—1 ..	*18*	7	11	18	7	11	..	..	..	..	..	..
1—2 ..	*16*	6	10	16	6	10	..	..	..	..	..	..
2—3 .	*21*	11	10	21	11	10	..	..	..	..	..	..
3—4 ..	*15*	10	5	15	10	5	..	..	..	..	..	..
4—5 ..	*17*	10	7	16	9	7	1	1	..	..	..	..
Total 0—5 ..	*87*	*44*	*43*	*86*	*43*	*43*	*1*	*1*	.	..	..	.
5—10 ..	*63*	35	28	60	34	26	3	1	2	..	.	..
10—15 ..	*54*	32	22	44	26	18	9	5	4	1	1	.
15—20 ..	*74*	48	26	19	16	3	53	31	22	2	1	1
20—30 ..	*205*	149	56	29	27	2	168	117	51	8	5	3
30—40 ..	*142*	110	32	9	7	2	126	98	28	7	5	2
40—50 ..	*84*	72	12	2	2	..	70	61	9	12	9	3
50—60 ..	*36*	31	5	1	1	..	26	25	1	9	5	4
60 and over ..	*15*	11	4	..	..	..	5	5	..	10	6	4
JAIN ..	**1**	**1**	..	..	..	..	**1**	**1**	..	..	..	..
40—50 ..	1	1	..	..	..	..	1	1	..	..	..	..
MUSLIM ..	**5,810**	**4,346**	**1,464**	**2,127**	**1,501**	**626**	**3,309**	**2,595**	**714**	**374**	**250**	**124**
0—1 ..	*92*	40	52	92	40	52	..	..	..	..	..	.
1—2 ..	*81*	41	40	81	41	40	..	..	..	..	..	..
2—3 ..	*94*	48	46	93	47	46	1	1	..	..	..	..
3—4 ..	*93*	45	48	93	45	48	..	..	..	..	..	.
4—5 ..	*95*	45	50	94	45	49	1	..	1	..	..	.
Total 0—5 ..	*455*	*219*	*236*	*453*	*218*	*235*	*2*	*1*	*1*	..	..	.
5—10 ..	*418*	222	196	409	218	191	8	4	4	1	..	1
10—15 ..	*407*	248	159	369	230	139	36	17	19	2	1	1
15—20 ..	*654*	509	145	323	290	33	323	213	110	8	6	2
20—30 ..	*1,701*	1,407	294	427	409	18	1,218	950	268	56	48	8
30—40 ..	*1,161*	954	207	107	100	7	977	795	182	77	59	18
40—50 ..	*591*	467	124	25	24	1	484	392	92	82	51	31
50—60 ..	*256*	198	58	9	8	1	175	148	27	72	42	30
60 and over ..	*167*	122	45	5	4	1	86	75	11	76	43	33
CHRISTIAN ..	**1,540**	**788**	**752**	**766**	**387**	**379**	**679**	**373**	**306**	**95**	**28**	**67**
0—1 ..	*30*	14	16	30	14	16	..	..	..	..	..	..
1—2 ..	*36*	19	17	36	19	17	..	..	..	..	..	..
2—3 ..	*46*	23	23	46	23	23	..	..	..	..	..	..
3—4 ..	*38*	19	19	38	19	19	..	..	..	..	..	..
4—5 ..	*32*	18	14	32	18	14	..	..	..	..	..	..
Total 0—5 ..	*182*	*93*	*89*	*182*	*93*	*89*	..	..	..	..	..	..
5—10 ..	*137*	67	70	133	65	68	4	2	2	..	..	..
10—15 ..	*122*	56	66	116	53	63	6	3	3	..	..	..
15—20 ..	*110*	46	64	85	40	45	24	5	19	1	1	..
20—30 ..	*265*	122	143	124	73	51	132	45	87	9	4	5
30—40 ..	*279*	151	128	61	32	29	207	114	93	11	5	6
40—50 ..	*230*	144	86	31	17	14	184	122	62	15	5	10
50—60 ..	*127*	74	53	16	8	8	88	61	27	23	5	18
60 and over ..	*88*	35	53	18	6	12	34	21	13	36	8	28

AND CIVIL CONDITION (BY RELIGION).

PART B.—DETAILS FOR DISTRICTS AND STATES—*continued.*

KANGRA DISTRICT.

Religion and Age.	Population.			Unmarried.			Married.			Widowed.		
	Persons.	Males.	Females.	Persons.	Males.	Females.	Persons.	Males.	Females.	Persons.	Males.	Females.
1	2	3	4	5	6	7	8	9	10	11	12	13
ALL RELIGIONS ..	801,312	415,288	386,024	353,884	216,415	137,469	346,100	165,169	180,931	101,328	33,704	67,624
0- 1 ..	27,196	13,594	13,602	27,193	13,593	13,600	3	1	2	..	..	..
1- -2 ..	20,846	10,205	10,641	20,832	10,200	10,632	14	5	9	..	..	..
2- -3 .	21,927	10,593	11,334	21,896	10,583	11,313	30	9	21	1	1	.
3- 4 .	22,990	11,233	11,757	22,826	11,211	11,615	160	20	140	4	2	2
4- -5 .	22,570	11,296	11,274	22,262	11,260	11,002	295	31	264	13	5	8
Total 0- -5 .	115,529	56,921	58,608	115,009	56,847	58,162	502	66	436	18	8	10
5- -10 ..	100,487	51,649	48,838	92,627	50,740	41,887	7,704	881	6,823	156	28	128
10- -15 ..	93,086	48,366	44,720	74,608	45,655	28,953	18,062	2,629	15,433	416	82	334
15- -20 ..	72,507	35,365	37,142	29,223	24,430	4,793	41,628	10,506	31,122	1,656	429	1,227
20- -30 .	136,416	66,432	69,984	25,668	23,576	2,092	101,819	39,951	61,868	8,929	2,905	6,024
30- 40 .	109,705	58,641	51,064	8,255	7,468	787	83,590	45,445	38,145	17,860	5,728	12,132
40- -50 ..	76,425	42,298	34,127	4,485	4,060	425	49,086	31,108	17,978	22,854	7,130	15,724
50- -60 .	52,186	30,068	22,118	2,395	2,195	200	27,064	20,203	6,861	22,727	7,670	15,057
60 and over ..	44,971	25,548	19,423	1,614	1,444	170	16,645	14,380	2,265	26,712	9,724	16,988
HINDU ..	731,215	377,050	354,165	328,374	197,706	125,668	313,840	148,587	164,753	94,501	30,757	63,744
0- -1 .	24,916	12,447	12,469	24,913	12,446	12,467	3	1	2	..	..	..
1- -2 ..	19,010	9,288	9,722	18,998	9,284	9,714	12	4	8	..	..	..
2- -3 .	19,929	9,613	10,316	19,902	9,604	10,298	26	8	18	1	1	.
3- 4 ..	20,935	10,218	10,717	20,801	10,201	10,600	130	15	115	4	2	2
4 -5 ..	20,565	10,282	10,283	20,324	10,258	10,066	232	20	212	9	4	5
Total 0- -5 ..	105,355	51,848	53,507	104,938	51,793	53,145	403	48	355	14	7	7
5—10 ..	91,393	46,883	44,510	84,836	46,265	38,571	6,421	596	5,825	136	22	114
10- 15 ..	84,431	43,760	40,671	68,445	41,702	26,743	15,619	1,993	13,626	367	65	302
15- -20 ..	65,570	31,748	33,822	26,634	22,376	4,258	37,403	9,005	28,398	1,533	367	1,166
20—30 ..	123,648	59,495	64,153	23,268	21,585	1,683	92,069	35,359	56,710	8,311	2,551	5,760
30—40 ..	100,284	53,170	47,114	7,496	6,845	651	76,148	41,175	34,973	16,640	5,150	11,490
40—50 ..	70,499	38,816	31,683	4,121	3,789	332	44,987	28,466	16,521	21,391	6,561	14,830
50- -60 ..	48,462	27,835	20,627	2,203	2,039	164	24,999	18,693	6,306	21,260	7,103	14,157
60 and over ..	41,573	23,495	18,078	1,433	1,312	121	15,291	13,252	2,039	24,849	8,931	15,918
SIKH ..	2,396	1,338	1,058	1,004	641	363	1,132	588	544	260	109	151
0 1 ..	78	42	36	78	42	36	..	..	..	..	..	.
1 -2 ..	61	32	29	61	32	29	.	..	..	..	..	..
2—3 .	59	31	28	59	31	28	.	..	..	..	..	..
3- 4 .	65	33	32	65	33	32	.	..	.	..	..	..
4- -5 ..	69	34	35	68	34	34	1	..	1	..	..	.
Total 0- -5 ..	332	172	160	331	172	159	1	.	1	..	..	..
5—10 ..	272	141	131	252	138	114	19	3	16	1	..	1
10 -15 ..	247	133	114	193	122	71	52	11	41	2	.	2
15- -20 ..	231	115	116	87	79	8	137	33	104	7	3	4
20—30 ..	461	251	210	92	88	4	345	149	196	24	14	10
30—40 ..	358	220	138	30	26	4	289	172	117	39	22	17
40—50 ..	220	131	89	8	6	2	148	103	45	64	22	42
50- -60 ..	147	89	58	7	7	..	83	65	18	57	17	40
60 and over ..	128	86	42	4	3	1	58	52	6	66	31	35
JAIN ..	94	46	48	49	27	22	31	13	18	14	6	8
0- 1 .	4	1	3	4	1	3	..	..	..	..	.	..
1 -2 ..	2	2	..	2	2	..	.	..	..	..	..	.
2- -3 ..	4	2	2	4	2	2	.	.	..	..	..	.
3- 4 ..	5	2	3	5	2	3	..	..	..	..	..	.
4- -5 ..	4	2	2	4	2	2	..	..	..	.	..	.
Total 0- -5 .	19	9	10	19	9	10	..	..	..	.	..	.
5—10 ..	15	7	8	14	7	7	1	..	1	..	..	.
10- 15 ..	13	4	9	9	4	5	4	..	4	..	..	.
15- -20 ..	8	4	4	3	3	..	5	1	4	..	..	
20- -30 ..	16	10	6	3	3	..	12	7	5	1	..	1
30- -40 .	11	5	6	1	1	..	7	3	4	3	1	2
40- -50 .	8	4	4	..	..	..	2	2	..	6	2	4
50—60 .	2	2	.	..	..	..	..	..	..	2	2	.
60 and over ..	2	1	1	.	..	..	..	..	..	2	1	1
MUSLIM ..	40,483	22,486	17,997	17,593	10,950	6,643	18,925	9,759	9,166	3,965	1,777	2,188
0 -1 ..	1,387	712	675	1,387	712	675	.	.	.	..	..	.
1 2 ..	1,090	540	550	1,089	539	550	1	1	..	..	.	.
2- 3 ..	1,171	567	604	1,170	567	603	1	.	1	..	.	.
3- 4 ..	1,207	601	606	1,187	597	590	20	4	16	..	.	.
4- -5 ..	1,192	611	581	1,150	602	548	41	9	32	1	..	1
Total 0—5 ..	6,047	3,031	3,016	5,983	3,017	2,966	63	11	49	1	..	1
5- -10 .	5,282	2,767	2,515	4,579	2,600	1,979	690	163	527	13	4	9
10- -15 ..	4,920	2,623	2,297	3,579	2,263	1,316	1,311	349	962	30	11	19
15—20 ..	3,979	2,115	1,864	1,431	1,206	225	2,483	877	1,606	65	32	33
20 -30 .	7,464	4,154	3,310	1,308	1,198	110	5,818	2,763	3,055	338	193	145
30- 40 ..	5,449	3,236	2,213	382	353	29	4,333	2,531	1,802	734	352	382
40- -50 ..	3,292	2,012	1,280	160	151	9	2,288	1,514	774	844	347	97
50- -60 ..	2,085	1,310	775	93	88	5	1,148	869	279	844	353	91
60 and over ..	1,965	1,238	727	78	74	4	791	679	112	1,096	485	11
CHRISTIAN ..	576	316	260	304	178	126	235	120	115	37	18	19
0—1 .	11	7	4	11	7	4	..	..	..	..	.	.
1 -2 .	12	7	5	12	7	5	..	..	..	..	..	.
2- -3 ..	15	7	8	15	7	8	..	..	..	.	.	
3 4 ..	12	6	6	12	6	6	..	..	..	..	.	
4—5 ..	15	10	5	15	10	5	..	..	..	.	.	
Total 0- -5 ..	65	37	28	65	37	28	..	..	..	..	.	
5- 10 ..	54	32	22	53	31	22	1	1	..	..	..	.
10- 15 ..	57	30	27	55	30	25	2	..	2	..	.	.
15- -20 ..	65	33	32	50	29	21	14	3	11	1	1	.
20- -30 ..	131	63	68	56	36	20	71	25	46	4	2	2
30- 40 ..	90	50	40	15	9	6	70	39	31	5	2	3
40- -50 ..	56	33	23	6	4	2	43	27	16	7	2	5
50—60 .	37	22	15	2	1	1	26	17	9	9		5
60 and over ..	21	16	5	2	1	1	8	8	.	11	7	4

TABLE VII.—AGE, SEX

PART B.—DETAILS FOR DISTRICTS AND STATES.

HOSHIARPUR DISTRICT.

Religion and Age.	Population.			Unmarried.			Married.			Widowed.		
	Persons.	Males.	Females.	Persons.	Males.	Females.	Persons.	Males.	Females.	Persons.	Males.	Females.
1	2	3	4	5	6	7	8	9	10	11	12	13
ALL RELIGIONS ..	**1,032,187**	**551,867**	**480,320**	**460,969**	**286,019**	**174,950**	**453,864**	**215,414**	**238,450**	**117,354**	**50,434**	**66,920**
0-1 ..	*36,565*	18,402	18,163	36,564	18,401	18,163	1	1	..	..	..	..
1-2 ..	*26,722*	13,399	13,323	26,719	13,398	13,321	3	1	2	..	..	..
2-3 ..	*28,667*	14,466	14,201	28,661	14,463	14,198	6	3	3	.	..	..
3-4 ..	*29,579*	15,198	14,381	29,331	15,151	14,180	244	47	197	4	.	4
4-5 ..	*29,198*	15,263	13,935	28,698	15,168	13,530	484	92	392	16	3	13
Total 0-5 ..	*150,731*	*76,728*	*74,003*	*149,973*	*76,581*	*73,392*	*738*	*144*	*594*	*20*	*3*	*17*
5-10 ..	*135,020*	71,521	63,499	121,116	67,796	53,320	13,733	3,659	10,074	171	66	105
10-15 ..	*125,430*	67,003	58,427	97,714	59,334	38,380	27,326	7,512	19,814	390	157	233
15-20 ..	*87,344*	45,279	42,065	34,450	27,691	6,759	51,527	16,998	34,529	1,367	590	777
20-30 ..	*162,034*	84,184	77,850	30,281	28,261	2,020	124,364	52,383	71,981	7,389	3,540	3,849
30-40 ..	*128,893*	70,333	58,560	12,470	11,950	520	101,110	51,438	49,672	15,313	6,945	8,368
40-50 ..	*98,138*	54,516	43,622	6,811	6,513	298	67,839	38,005	29,834	23,488	9,998	13,49[illegible]
50-60 ..	*70,855*	40,243	30,612	4,363	4,208	155	39,588	24,774	14,814	26,904	11,261	15,643
60 and over ..	*73,742*	42,060	31,682	3,791	3,685	106	27,639	20,501	7,138	42,312	17,874	24,438
HINDU ..	**414,353**	**219,303**	**195,050**	**183,879**	**115,551**	**68,328**	**176,316**	**82,010**	**94,306**	**54,158**	**21,742**	**32,416**
0-1 ..	*14,177*	7,099	7,078	14,177	7,099	7,078	..	..	..	..	.	.
1-2 .	*10,404*	5,194	5,210	10,403	5,194	5,209	1	..	1	..	..	.
2-3 .	*10,999*	5,501	5,498	10,996	5,500	5,496	3	1	2	..	.	..
3-4 .	*11,331*	5,798	5,533	11,262	5,781	5,481	66	17	49	3	..	3
4-5 .	*11,153*	5,822	5,331	11,016	5,788	5,228	129	34	95	8	..	8
Total 0-5 ..	*58,064*	*29,414*	*28,650*	*57,854*	*29,362*	*28,492*	*199*	*52*	*147*	*11*	..	*11*
5-10 ..	*52,269*	27,339	24,930	47,574	26,360	21,214	4,633	962	3,671	62	17	[illegible]
10-15 ..	*48,978*	25,643	23,335	39,021	23,621	15,400	9,805	1,978	7,827	152	44	[illegible]
15-20 ..	*33,992*	17,067	16,925	13,701	11,346	2,355	19,063	5,524	14,139	628	197	431
20-30 ..	*63,744*	32,212	31,532	12,577	12,066	511	47,600	18,770	28,830	3,567	1,376	[illegible]
30-40 ..	*53,178*	28,812	24,366	5,949	5,759	190	39,806	20,074	19,732	7,423	2,979	4,444
40-50 ..	*41,508*	23,236	18,272	3,185	3,102	83	27,262	15,630	11,632	11,061	4,504	6,557
50-60 ..	*31,065*	17,697	13,368	2,160	2,104	56	16,336	10,545	5,791	12,569	[illegible]	7,521
60 and over ..	*31,555*	17,883	13,672	1,858	1,831	27	11,012	8,475	2,537	18,685	7,577	11,108
SIKH ..	**173,147**	**94,652**	**78,495**	**80,425**	**51,431**	**28,994**	**73,480**	**34,227**	**39,253**	**19,242**	**8,994**	**10,248**
0-1 ..	*5,896*	2,986	2,910	5,896	2,986	2,910	..	..	..	..	..	..
1-2 ..	*4,164*	2,106	2,058	4,164	2,106	2,058	..	..	.	..	..	..
2-3 ..	*4,447*	2,271	2,176	4,447	2,271	2,176	..	..	.	..	..	..
3-4 ..	*4,617*	2,398	2,219	4,610	2,396	2,214	7	2	5	..	..	..
4-5 ..	*4,610*	2,426	2,184	4,596	2,422	2,174	14	4	10	.	.	.
Total 0-5 ..	*23,734*	*12,187*	*11,547*	*23,713*	*12,181*	*11,532*	*21*	*6*	*15*	..		.
5-10 ..	*21,430*	11,580	9,850	20,307	11,308	8,999	1,112	266	846	11	6	5
10-15 ..	*19,966*	10,949	9,017	16,869	10,165	6,704	3,070	775	2,295	27	9	18
15-20 ..	*14,329*	7,741	6,588	6,251	5,035	1,216	7,931	2,626	5,305	147	80	67
20-30 ..	*26,725*	14,265	12,460	6,235	5,892	343	19,537	7,845	11,692	953	528	425
30-40 ..	*22,010*	12,120	9,890	2,936	2,851	85	16,828	8,135	8,693	2,246	1,134	1,112
40-50 ..	*17,744*	9,848	7,896	1,820	1,766	54	12,190	6,411	5,779	3,734	1,671	2,063
50-60 ..	*13,042*	7,595	5,447	1,205	1,174	31	7,400	4,385	3,015	4,437	2,036	2,401
60 and over ..	*14,167*	8,367	5,800	1,089	1,059	30	5,391	3,778	1,613	7,687	3,530	4,157
JAIN ..	**1,016**	**579**	**437**	**545**	**349**	**196**	**326**	**162**	**164**	**145**	**68**	**77**
0-1 ..	*39*	18	21	39	18	21	..	..	..	..	..	..
1-2 ..	*26*	13	13	26	13	13	..	..	..	..	..	..
2-3 ..	*31*	14	17	31	14	17	..	..	..	..	..	..
3-4 ..	*23*	11	12	23	11	12	..	..	..	..	..	..
4-5 ..	*22*	12	10	22	12	10	..	..	..	..	..	..
Total 0-5 ..	*141*	*68*	*73*	*141*	*68*	*73*	..	..	..	..	..	..
5-10 ..	*128*	72	56	126	71	55	..	..	..	2	1	1
10-15 ..	*125*	73	52	121	72	49	4	1	3	..	..	..
15-20 ..	*95*	52	43	54	40	14	38	11	27	3	1	2
20-30 ..	*167*	98	69	53	48	5	104	46	58	10	4	6
30-40 ..	*142*	87	55	24	24	..	92	51	41	26	12	14
40-50 ..	*107*	64	43	16	16	..	48	27	21	43	21	22
50-60 ..	*59*	36	23	5	5	..	25	16	9	29	15	14
60 and over ..	*52*	29	23	5	5	..	15	10	5	32	14	18
MUSLIM ..	**328,078**	**174,351**	**153,727**	**152,178**	**91,308**	**60,870**	**143,124**	**68,987**	**74,137**	**32,776**	**14,056**	**18,720**
0-1 ..	*12,121*	6,122	5,999	12,120	6,121	5,999	1	1	..	..	..	..
1-2 ..	*8,977*	4,509	4,468	8,975	4,508	4,467	2	1	1	..	..	..
2-3 ..	*9,671*	4,868	4,803	9,669	4,866	4,803	2	2	..	..	..	..
3-4 ..	*9,951*	5,063	4,888	9,845	5,042	4,803	105	21	84	1	.	1
4-5 ..	*9,898*	5,127	4,771	9,686	5,086	4,000	207	39	168	5	2	3
Total 0-5 ..	*50,618*	*25,689*	*24,929*	*50,295*	*25,623*	*24,672*	*317*	*64*	*253*	*6*	*2*	*4*
5-10 ..	*44,928*	23,686	21,242	40,795	22,561	18,234	4,069	1,096	2,973	64	29	35
10-15 ..	*41,392*	22,143	19,249	33,268	19,749	13,519	7,984	2,329	5,655	140	65	75
15-20 ..	*28,755*	15,024	13,731	12,351	9,410	2,941	15,982	5,415	10,567	422	199	223
20-30 ..	*52,638*	27,351	25,287	9,628	8,567	1,061	40,967	17,734	23,233	2,043	1,050	993
30-40 ..	*39,814*	21,595	18,219	2,894	2,682	212	32,776	16,997	15,779	4,144	1,916	2,228
40-50 ..	*29,150*	15,930	13,220	1,433	1,301	132	21,187	11,889	9,298	6,530	2,740	3,790
50-60 ..	*20,020*	11,228	8,792	816	760	56	11,697	7,373	4,324	7,507	3,095	4,412
60 and over ..	*20,763*	11,705	9,058	698	655	43	8,145	6,090	2,055	11,920	4,960	6,960
CHRISTIAN ..	**3,764**	**2,083**	**1,681**	**2,105**	**1,245**	**860**	**1,359**	**683**	**676**	**300**	**155**	**145**
0-1 ..	*143*	72	71	143	72	71	..	..	..	..	..	..
1-2 ..	*117*	57	60	117	57	60	..	..	..	..	..	..
2-3 ..	*131*	70	61	131	70	61	..	..	..	..	..	..
3-4 ..	*126*	69	57	126	69	57	..	..	..	..	..	..
4-5 ..	*120*	60	60	120	60	60	..	..	..	..	..	..
Total 0-5 ..	*637*	*328*	*309*	*637*	*328*	*309*	..	..	..	..	..	..
5-10 ..	*583*	310	273	573	307	266	9	2	7	1	1	..
10-15 ..	*542*	297	245	498	287	211	42	8	34	2	2	..
15-20 ..	*332*	178	154	178	133	45	150	43	107	4	2	2
20-30 ..	*606*	342	264	151	132	19	434	198	236	21	12	9
30-40 ..	*432*	260	172	37	32	5	350	197	153	45	31	14
40-50 ..	*280*	158	122	19	15	4	193	110	83	68	33	35
50-60 ..	*191*	110	81	7	7	..	114	73	41	70	30	40
60 and over ..	*161*	100	61	5	4	1	67	52	15	89	44	45

AND CIVIL CONDITION (BY RELIGION).

PART B.—DETAILS FOR DISTRICTS AND STATES—*continued.*

JULLUNDUR DISTRICT.

Religion and Age.	Population.			Unmarried.			Married.			Widowed.		
	Persons.	Males.	Females.	Persons.	Males.	Females.	Persons.	Males.	Females.	Persons.	Males.	Females.
1	2	3	4	5	6	7	8	9	10	11	12	13
ALL RELIGIONS..	**943,721**	**512,667**	**431,054**	**436,141**	**265,931**	**170,210**	**410,549**	**200,048**	**210,501**	**97,031**	**46,688**	**50,343**
0—1 ..	*32,965*	17,167	15,798	32,906	17,145	15,761	54	21	33	5	1	4
1—2 ..	*24,318*	12,325	11,993	24,233	12,296	11,937	80	28	52	5	1	4
2—3 ..	*26,984*	13,572	13,412	26,676	13,506	13,170	298	63	235	10	3	7
3—4 ..	*27,759*	14,245	13,514	27,284	14 113	13,171	455	125	330	20	7	13
4—5 ..	*26,879*	14,248	12,631	26,394	14,059	12,335	448	174	274	37	15	22
Total 0—5 ..	*138,905*	*71,557*	*67,348*	*137,493*	*71,119*	*66,374*	*1,335*	*411*	*924*	*77*	*27*	*50*
5—10 ..	*123,202*	66,695	56,507	112,608	62,613	49,995	10,400	3,979	6,421	194	103	91
10—15 ..	*114,062*	62,533	51,529	91,959	54,335	37,624	21,746	7,987	13,759	357	211	146
15—20 ..	*82,774*	45,086	37,688	34,908	25,988	8,920	46,712	18,401	28,311	1,154	697	457
20—30 ..	*148,466*	81,136	67,330	31,024	26,866	4,158	111,725	50,845	60,880	5,717	3,425	2,292
30—40 ..	*115,090*	63,296	51,794	12,489	11,261	1,228	90,924	45,838	45,086	11,677	6,197	5,480
40—50 ..	*89,325*	48,261	41,064	6,744	5,838	906	63,100	32,945	30,155	19,481	9,478	10,003
50—60 ..	*63,639*	34,974	28,665	4,435	3,892	543	37,389	21,244	16,145	21,815	9,838	11,977
60 and over ..	*68,258*	39,129	29,129	4,481	4,019	462	27,218	18,398	8,820	36,559	16,712	19,847
HINDU ..	**155,242**	**85,469**	**69,773**	**75,555**	**46,602**	**28,953**	**61,628**	**31,067**	**30,561**	**18,059**	**7,800**	**10,259**
0—1 ..	*5,335*	2,812	2,523	5,319	2,803	2,516	15	9	6	1	..	1
1—2 ..	*3,795*	1,931	1,864	3,781	1,925	1,856	12	6	6	2	.	2
2—3 ..	*4,251*	2,095	2,156	4,212	2,080	2,132	37	14	23	2	1	1
3—4 ..	*4,385*	2,220	2,165	4,338	2,202	2,136	42	16	26	5	2	3
4—5 ..	*4,135*	2,225	1,910	4,090	2,204	1,886	36	17	19	9	4	5
Total 0—5 ..	*21,901*	*11,283*	*10,618*	*21,740*	*11,214*	*10,526*	*142*	*62*	*80*	*19*	*7*	*12*
5—10 ..	*19,355*	10,538	8,817	18,419	10,138	8,281	902	385	517	34	15	19
10—15 ..	*18,463*	10,179	8,284	16,149	9,397	6,752	2,260	757	1,509	48	25	23
15—20 ..	*14,150*	8,030	6,120	7,415	5,393	2,022	6,559	2,544	4,015	176	93	83
20—30 ..	*24,795*	14,038	10,757	6,294	5,365	929	17,372	8,114	9,258	1,120	550	570
30—40 ..	*19,568*	10,995	8,573	2,498	2,284	214	14,738	7,682	7,056	2,332	1,029	1,303
40—50 ..	*15,292*	8,290	7,002	1,376	1,277	99	10,040	5,473	4,567	3,876	1,540	2,336
50—60 .	*10,878*	5,942	4,936	836	770	66	5,766	3,380	2,386	4,276	1,792	2,484
60 and over ..	*10,840*	6,174	4,666	828	764	64	3,843	2,670	1,173	6,169	2,740	3,429
SIKH .	**249,571**	**139,154**	**110,417**	**115,293**	**73,910**	**41,383**	**106,464**	**51,056**	**55,408**	**27,814**	**14,188**	**13,626**
0—1 .	*8,209*	4,346	3,863	8,198	4,342	3,856	8	3	5	3	1	2
1—2 .	*5,913*	3,063	2,850	5,898	3,059	2,839	14	4	10	1	..	1
2—3 .	*6,511*	3,404	3,107	6,462	3,397	3,065	46	6	40	3	1	2
3—4 .	*6,721*	3,618	3,106	6,652	3,591	3,058	68	22	46	4	2	2
4—5	*6,589*	3,630	2,959	6,522	3,592	2,930	57	33	24	10	5	5
Total 0—5	*33,946*	*18,061*	*15,885*	*33,732*	*17,984*	*15,748*	*193*	*68*	*125*	*21*	*9*	*12*
5—10 ..	*30,784*	17,289	13,495	29,369	16,728	12,641	1,372	536	836	43	25	18
10—15 ..	*28,880*	16,388	12,501	24,445	14,848	9,597	4,358	1,483	2,875	86	57	29
15—20 ..	*21,137*	11,802	9,335	8,708	6,837	1,871	12,134	4,777	7,357	295	188	107
20—30 .	*38,177*	21,232	16,945	8,424	7,660	764	28,346	12,697	15,649	1,407	875	532
30—40 .	*31,096*	17,399	13,697	4,429	4,164	265	23,394	11,315	12,079	3,273	1,920	1,353
40—50 ..	*25,455*	13,936	11,519	2,657	2,405	252	17,477	8,794	8,683	5,321	2,737	2,584
50—60 ..	*19,088*	10,828	8,260	1,827	1,711	116	10,970	5,087	4,983	6,291	3,130	3,161
60 and over .	*20,999*	12,219	8,780	1,702	1,573	120	8,220	5,399	2,821	11,077	5,247	5,830
JAIN .	**1,379**	**727**	**652**	**721**	**445**	**276**	**515**	**227**	**288**	**143**	**55**	**88**
0—1 .	*64*	32	32	64	32	32	..	..	.	..	..	
1—2 ..	*38*	21	17	37	20	17	1	1	..	.	..	.
2—3 ..	*42*	22	20	42	22	20	..	..	..	.	..	.
3—4 ..	*47*	24	23	47	24	23	..	..	..	.	.	.
4—5 ..	*48*	28	20	48	28	20	..	..	..	.		
Total 0—5 ..	*239*	*137*	*112*	*238*	*126*	*112*	*1*	*1*	.	..	.	
5—10 ..	*202*	120	82	183	111	72	19	9	10	..	..	.
10—15 ..	*172*	100	72	137	90	47	34	10	24	1	..	1
15—20 ..	*121*	58	63	58	47	11	61	10	51	2	1	1
20—30 ..	*202*	88	114	61	43	18	135	43	92	6	2	4
30—40 ..	*172*	81	91	19	8	11	131	66	65	22	7	15
40—50 ..	*129*	73	56	15	11	4	86	56	30	28	6	22
50—60 ..	*68*	38	30	7	6	1	29	18	11	32	14	18
60 and over ..	*74*	42	32	3	3	..	19	14	5	62	25	27
MUSLIM ..	**419,556**	**223,611**	**195,945**	**196,503**	**115,841**	**80,662**	**182,198**	**88,377**	**93,821**	**40,855**	**19,398**	**21,462**
0—1 ..	*14,732*	7,503	7,229	14,704	7,495	7,209	27	8	19	1	..	1
1—2 ..	*11,213*	5,616	5,597	11,165	5,600	5,565	46	15	31	2	1	1
2—3 ..	*12,488*	6,196	6,292	12,288	6,160	6,128	196	35	161	4	1	3
3—4 ..	*12,736*	6,372	6,364	12,460	6,316	6,153	258	54	204	9	2	7
4—5 ..	*12,333*	6,367	5,966	12,123	6,299	5,824	197	64	133	13	4	9
Total 0—5 ..	*63,502*	*32,054*	*31,448*	*62,749*	*31,870*	*30,879*	*724*	*176*	*548*	*29*	*8*	*21*
5—10 ..	*55,794*	29,508	26,286	51,611	28,164	23,447	4,107	1,305	2,802	76	39	37
10—15 ..	*51,184*	27,437	23,747	42,460	24,543	17,917	8,570	2,810	5,760	154	84	70
15—20 ..	*37,030*	19,557	17,473	16,481	11,856	4,625	20,028	7,410	12,618	521	291	230
20—30 ..	*66,681*	35,506	31,175	13,341	11,190	2,151	50,827	22,820	28,007	2,513	1,496	1,017
30—40 ..	*50,899*	27,623	23,276	4,211	3,600	611	41,871	21,552	20,319	4,817	2,471	2,346
40—50 ..	*38,805*	20,767	17,838	2,300	1,821	479	27,933	14,715	13,218	8,372	4,231	4,141
50—60 ..	*27,007*	14,706	12,301	1,581	1,261	320	16,371	9,544	6,827	9,055	3,901	5,154
60 and over ..	*28,854*	16,453	12,401	1,769	1,536	233	11,767	8,045	3,722	15,318	6,872	8,446
CHRISTIAN ..	**4,323**	**2,714**	**1,609**	**2,611**	**1,837**	**774**	**1,482**	**756**	**726**	**230**	**121**	**109**
0—1 ..	*128*	65	63	128	65	63	..	..	..	..	..	..
1—2 ..	*106*	51	55	106	51	55	..	..	..	..	..	..
2—3 ..	*127*	61	66	126	60	66	1	1	..	..	..	.
3—4 ..	*122*	61	61	122	61	61	..	.	..	.	..	..
4—5 ..	*109*	60	49	108	60	48	1	..	1	.	..	..
Total 0—5 ..	*592*	*298*	*294*	*590*	*297*	*293*	*2*	*1*	*1*	.	..	.
5—10 ..	*469*	266	203	460	262	198	9	4	5	.	..	..
10—15 ..	*402*	230	172	369	218	151	32	12	20	1	..	1
15—20 ..	*492*	343	149	325	276	49	163	64	99	4	3	1
20—30 ..	*1,177*	873	304	713	653	60	448	208	240	16	12	4
30—40 ..	*523*	319	204	105	91	14	390	211	179	28	17	11
40—50 ..	*299*	161	138	24	20	4	229	120	109	40	21	25
50—60 ..	*189*	106	83	13	9	4	124	73	51	52	24	28
60 and over ..	*180*	118	62	12	11	1	85	63	22	83	44	39

TABLE VII.—AGE, SEX

PART B.—DETAILS FOR DISTRICTS AND STATES.

LUDHIANA DISTRICT.

Religion and Age.	Population.			Unmarried.			Married.			Widowed.		
	Persons.	Males.	Females.	Persons.	Males.	Females.	Persons.	Males.	Females.	Persons.	Males.	Females.
1	2	3	4	5	6	7	8	9	10	11	12	13
ALL RELIGIONS ..	**672,494**	**375,560**	**296,934**	**321,507**	**198,485**	**123,022**	**283,290**	**143,355**	**139,935**	**67,697**	**33,720**	**33,977**
0—1 ..	*23,085*	11,892	11,193	23,078	11,890	11,188	7	2	5	..	..	..
1—2 ..	*16,746*	8,500	8,246	16,702	8,493	8,209	43	7	36	1	.	1
2—3 ..	*18,496*	9,551	8,945	18,403	9,528	8,875	92	23	69	1	..	1
3—4 ..	*18,644*	9,778	8,866	18,482	9,726	8,756	100	51	109	2	1	1
4—5 .	*17,908*	9,468	8,440	17,675	9,389	8,286	226	76	150	7	3	4
Total 0—5 ..	*94,879*	*49,189*	*45,690*	*94,340*	*49,026*	*45,314*	*528*	*159*	*369*	*11*	*4*	*7*
5—10 ..	*84,875*	46,377	38,498	79,830	44,598	35,232	4,959	1,743	3,216	86	36	50
10—15 ..	*82,507*	45,930	36,577	69,306	41,166	28,140	12,981	4,657	8,324	220	107	113
15—20 .	*65,920*	37,001	28,919	29,876	22,149	7,727	35,280	14,405	20,875	764	447	317
20—30 ..	*111,723*	63,076	48,647	25,945	21,987	3,958	81,865	38,704	43,161	3,913	2,385	1,528
30—40 ..	*82,048*	46,563	35,485	10,289	8,880	1,409	62,964	33,037	29,927	8,795	4,646	4,149
40—50 ..	*63,895*	36,179	27,716	5,986	5,287	699	43,033	23,777	19,256	14,876	7,115	7,761
50—60 ..	*47,104*	27,792	19,312	3,295	2,997	298	27,179	16,839	10,340	16,630	7,956	8,674
60 and over .	*39,543*	23,453	16,090	2,640	2,395	245	14,501	10,034	4,467	22,402	11,024	11,378
HINDU ..	**102,441**	**58,174**	**44,267**	**49,738**	**31,619**	**18,119**	**40,806**	**21,051**	**19,755**	**11,897**	**5,504**	**6,393**
0—1 .	*3,398*	1,701	1,697	3,397	1,700	1,697	1	1	.	..	.	..
1—2	*2,432*	1,183	1,249	2,428	1,180	1,248	4	3	1	..	.	..
2—3 .	*2,723*	1,343	1,380	2,712	1,338	1,374	10	5	5	1	.	1
3—4 ..	*2,771*	1,400	1,371	2,754	1,395	1,359	17	5	12	.	.	.
4—5 ..	*2,628*	1,375	1,253	2,606	1,370	1,236	20	5	15	2	.	2
Total 0—5 ..	*13,952*	*7,002*	*6,950*	*13,897*	*6,983*	*6,914*	*52*	*19*	*33*	*3*	..	*3*
5—10 ..	*12,541*	6,944	5,597	11,997	6,770	5,227	523	167	356	21	7	14
10—15 ..	*12,146*	6,982	5,164	10,631	6,476	4,155	1,479	496	983	36	10	26
15—20 ..	*9,947*	5,786	4,161	4,785	3,730	1,055	5,020	2,000	3,020	142	56	86
20—30 ..	*17,591*	10,168	7,423	4,180	3,744	436	12,535	5,954	6,581	876	470	406
30—40 .	*12,301*	6,852	5,449	1,772	1,637	135	8,710	4,357	4,353	1,819	858	961
40—50 ..	*10,039*	5,878	4,161	1,090	1,010	80	6,124	3,626	2,498	2,825	1,242	1,583
50—60 ..	*7,811*	5,041	2,770	681	639	42	4,333	3,130	1,203	2,797	1,272	1,525
60 and over ..	*6,113*	3,521	2,592	705	630	75	2,030	1,302	728	3,378	1,589	1,789
SIKH ..	**312,829**	**175,676**	**137,153**	**151,412**	**94,782**	**56,630**	**129,998**	**64,541**	**65,457**	**31,419**	**16,353**	**15,066**
0—1 ..	*10,456*	5,533	4,923	10,450	5,532	4,918	6	1	5	..	..	.
1—2 ..	*7,409*	3,877	3,532	7,398	3,875	3,523	11	2	9	..	..	.
2—3 ..	*8,038*	4,326	3,712	8,022	4,321	3,701	16	5	11	..	..	..
3—4 ..	*8,292*	4,535	3,757	8,271	4,527	3,744	19	7	12	2	1	1
4—5 ..	*8,163*	4,408	3,755	8,131	4,395	3,739	25	11	14	4	2	2
Total 0—5 ..	*42,358*	*22,679*	*19,679*	*42,275*	*22,650*	*19,625*	*77*	*26*	*51*	*6*	*3*	*3*
5—10 ..	*38,500*	21,464	17,036	36,873	20,914	15,959	1,603	539	1,064	24	11	13
10—15 ..	*37,773*	21,198	16,575	32,346	19,198	13,148	5,338	1,949	3,389	89	51	38
15—20 .	*30,392*	17,085	13,307	14,304	10,255	4,049	15,789	6,635	9,154	299	195	104
20—30 .	*49,903*	28,110	21,793	13,174	10,925	2,249	35,225	16,232	18,993	1,504	953	551
30—40 ..	*38,064*	21,482	16,582	5,648	4,742	906	28,788	14,744	14,044	3,628	1,996	1,632
40—50 ..	*30,779*	17,150	13,629	3,441	3,009	432	20,791	10,793	9,998	6,547	3,348	3,199
50—60 ..	*24,445*	14,142	10,303	1,909	1,749	160	14,598	8,399	6,199	7,938	3,994	3,944
60 and over ..	*20,615*	12,366	8,249	1,442	1,340	102	7,789	5,224	2,565	11,384	5,802	5,582
JAIN ..	**1,419**	**765**	**654**	**735**	**489**	**296**	**516**	**260**	**256**	**168**	**66**	**102**
0—1 ..	*47*	24	23	47	24	23	.	..	..	..	..	..
1—2 ..	*36*	20	16	36	20	16	..	..	..	..	..	..
2—3 ..	*43*	19	24	43	19	24	..	..	..	..	..	..
3—4 ..	*41*	16	25	41	16	25	..	..	..	..	..	..
4—5 ..	*39*	20	19	39	20	19	..	..	..	..	..	..
Total 0—5 ..	*206*	*99*	*107*	*206*	*99*	*107*	..	..	..	..	..	..
5—10 ..	179	92	87	176	91	85	3	1	2	..	..	..
10—15 ..	*166*	86	80	157	84	73	9	2	7	..	..	..
15—20 ..	*125*	71	54	68	49	19	57	22	35	..	..	..
20—30 ..	*239*	138	101	58	54	4	168	79	89	13	5	8
30—40 ..	*188*	102	86	26	23	3	129	67	62	33	12	21
40—50 ..	*160*	88	72	24	20	4	92	50	42	44	18	26
50—60 ..	*90*	53	37	12	11	1	41	27	14	37	15	22
60 and over ..	*66*	36	30	8	8	..	17	12	5	41	16	25
MUSLIM ..	**235,598**	**130,149**	**105,449**	**109,923**	**66,189**	**43,734**	**103,169**	**52,991**	**50,178**	**22,506**	**10,969**	**11,537**
0—1 ..	*8,451*	4,266	4,185	8,451	4,266	4,185	..	..	.	.	..	..
1—2 ..	*6,343*	3,146	3,197	6,314	3,144	3,170	28	2	26	1	..	1
2—3 ..	*7,102*	3,569	3,533	7,037	3,557	3,480	65	12	53	.	..	..
3—4 ..	*6,937*	3,532	3,405	6,813	3,493	3,320	124	39	85	.	..	..
4—5 ..	*6,510*	3,377	3,133	6,329	3,316	3,013	180	60	120	1	1	..
Total 0—5 ..	*35,343*	*17,890*	*17,453*	*34,944*	*17,776*	*17,168*	*397*	*113*	*284*	*2*	*1*	*1*
5—10 ..	*30,905*	16,413	14,492	28,205	15,422	12,783	2,661	973	1,688	39	18	21
10—15 ..	*29,783*	16,212	13,571	24,049	14,157	9 892	5,647	2,011	3,636	87	44	43
15—20 ..	*23,376*	[illegible],984	10,392	9,892	7,586	2,306	13,191	5,219	7,972	293	170	114
20—30 ..	*40,459*	[illegible],805	17,654	7,832	6,832	1,000	31,232	15,096	16,136	1,395	877	518
30—40 ..	*29,038*	[illegible],792	12,246	2,614	2,319	295	23,348	12,810	10,538	3,076	1,663	1,413
40—50 ..	*21,212*	[illegible],144	9,068	1,310	1,159	151	14,827	8,650	6,177	5,075	2,335	2,740
50—60 ..	*13,643*	7,922	5,721	634	552	82	7,560	4,883	2,677	5,449	2,487	2,962
60 and over ..	*11,839*	[illegible],987	4,852	443	386	57	4,306	3,236	1,070	7,090	3,365	3,725
CHRISTIAN ..	**2,477**	**1,098**	**1,379**	**1,597**	**673**	**924**	**725**	**348**	**377**	**155**	**77**	**78**
0—1 ..	*73*	39	34	73	39	34	.	..	..	..	.	..
1—2 ..	*62*	37	25	62	37	25	..	..	..	..	.	..
2—3 ..	*55*	29	26	55	29	26	..	..	..	..	..	..
3—4 ..	*54*	27	27	54	27	27	..	..	..	..	..	..
4—5 ..	*59*	30	29	59	30	29	..	..	..	..	..	..
Total 0—5 .	*303*	*162*	*141*	*303*	*162*	*141*	..	..	..	..	..	..
5—10 .	*328*	162	166	314	157	157	14	5	9	..	..	..
10—15 ..	*338*	165	173	296	156	140	42	9	33	..	..	..
15—20 ..	*368*	117	251	271	87	184	95	29	66	2	1	1
20—30 ..	*510*	172	338	292	68	224	205	95	110	13	9	4
30—40 ..	*275*	131	144	77	29	48	166	87	79	32	15	17
40—50 ..	*171*	88	83	24	9	15	115	62	53	32	17	15
50—60 ..	*110*	60	50	10	2	8	65	42	23	35	16	19
60 and over ..	*74*	41	33	10	3	7	23	19	4	41	19	22

AND CIVIL CONDITION (BY RELIGION).

PART B.—DETAILS FOR DISTRICTS AND STATES—*continued.*

FEROZEPORE DISTRICT.

Religion and Age.	Population. Persons.	Population. Males.	Population. Females.	Unmarried. Persons.	Unmarried. Males.	Unmarried. Females.	Married. Persons.	Married. Males.	Married. Females.	Widowed. Persons.	Widowed. Males.	Widowed. Females.
1	2	3	4	5	6	7	8	9	10	11	12	13
ALL RELIGIONS	**1,156,732**	**636,256**	**520,476**	**591,210**	**357,318**	**233,892**	**466,135**	**235,379**	**230,756**	**99,387**	**43,559**	**55,828**
0—1	*43,642*	21,970	21,672	13,639	21,[illegible]	21,671	3	2		..	.	..
1—2	*32,313*	16,342	15,971	32,303	16,338	15,965	8	2	6	2	2	..
2—3	*35,473*	17,985	17,488	35,443	17,971	17,472	26	12	14	4	2	2
3—4	*35,284*	18,077	17,207	35,[illegible]97	18,038	17,159	81	35	46	6	4	2
[illegible]5	*33,253*	17,343	15,910	33,108	17,281	15,827	130	55	75	15	7	8
Total [illegible]5	*179,965*	*91,717*	*88,248*	*179,690*	*91,596*	*88,094*	*248*	*106*	*142*	*27*	*15*	*12*
5—10	*151,065*	80,607	70,458	146,536	79,336	67,200	4,425	1,219	3,206	104	52	52
10—15	*143,260*	78,841	64,419	128,604	74,914	53,750	14,307	3,795	10,5[illegible]2	289	132	157
15—20	*116,818*	66,420	50,398	60,663	45,432	15,231	54,776	20,228	34,548	1,379	760	619
20—30	*201,485*	13,615	87,870	49,31[illegible]	42,614	6,697	145,164	66,944	78,220	7,010	4,057	2,953
30—40	*140,215*	79,371	60,844	[illegible]38	12,190	1,448	112,409	60,372	52,037	[illegible],168	6,809	7,369
[illegible]0—50	*102,[illegible]18*	56,9[illegible]4	45,744	[illegible]	6,136	791	73,248	41,655	31,593	2[illegible],543	9,[illegible]	3,360
[illegible]0—60	*66,108*	37,052	29,056	3,[illegible]88	3,092	[illegible]96	38,805	24,[illegible]40	14,365	23,815	9,520	14,29[illegible]
60 and over	*55,098*	31,659	23,439	2,293	2,008	285	22,[illegible]53	16,620	6,[illegible]33	30,052	13,031	17,021
HINDU	**208,426**	**117,490**	**90,936**	**100,284**	**62,485**	**37,799**	**88,784**	**46,895**	**41,889**	**19,358**	**8,110**	**11,248**
[illegible]	*7,738*	3,934	3,804	7,738	3,934	3,8[illegible]4			.			
[illegible]—2	*5,566*	2,836	2,730	5,566	2,836	2,73[illegible]	.	..		.	..	..
[illegible]—3	*6,126*	3,094	3,032	6,12[illegible]	3,092	3,032	1	1	.	1		
[illegible]4	*6,078*	3,112	2,966	6,057	3,105	2,952	19	5	1[illegible]	2	2	
[illegible]	*5,652*	2,972	2,680	5,610	2,930	2,650	38	10	28	4	2	2
Total 0—5	*31,160*	*15,948*	*15,212*	*31,095*	*15,927*	*15,168*	*58*	*16*	*42*	*[illegible]*	*5*	*2*
5—10	*25,935*	13,983	11,952	24,635	13,626	11,009	1,273	343	930	27	4	13
10—15	*25,051*	13,828	11,223	21,329	12,791	8,538	3,6[illegible]5	1,010	2,645	67	27	40
15—20	*22,196*	12,775	9,421	9,822	7,839	1,983	12,0[illegible]5	4,741	7,274	359	195	164
20—30	*39,130*	23,086	16,044	8,265	7,555	710	29,082	14,570	14,512	1,783	961	822
30—40	*27,048*	15,989	11,059	2,642	2,4[illegible]9	223	21,098	12,106	8,992	3,308	1,464	1,8[illegible]4
40—50	*18,988*	11,029	7,959	1,409	1,307	102	12,[illegible]43	7,850	4,893	4,836	1,872	2,964
50—60	*11,076*	6,433	4,613	667	62[illegible]	14	5,981	4,073	1,908	4,428	1,737	2,691
60 and over	*7,842*	4,419	3,423	420	398	22	2,879	2,186	693	4,543	1,835	2,708
SIKH	**388,108**	**213,616**	**174,492**	**196,101**	**121,035**	**75,066**	**156,613**	**77,174**	**79,439**	**35,394**	**15,407**	**19,987**
0—1	*14,320*	7,249	7,071	14,318	7,248	7,070	2	1	1	.	.	
1—2	*10,026*	5,146	4,880	10,025	5,146	4,879	1	.	1	..	.	.
2—3	*11,053*	5,752	5,301	11,047	5,751	5,296	5	1	4	1	.	1
3—4	*11,100*	5,838	5,262	11,084	5,834	5,250	16	4	12	..	.	..
4—5	*10,582*	5,608	4,974	10,552	5,599	4,953	27	8	19	3	1	2
Total 0—5	*57,081*	*29,593*	*27,488*	*57,026*	*29,578*	*27,448*	*51*	*11*	*37*	*4*	*1*	*3*
5—10	*49,621*	27,127	22,494	48,431	26,826	21,605	1,174	294	880	16	7	9
10—15	*47,046*	26,196	20,850	42,982	25,076	17,906	4,004	1,091	2,913	60	29	31
15—20	*37,781*	21,330	16,451	19,866	14,670	5,196	17,556	6,449	11,107	359	211	148
20—30	*65,025*	36,214	28,811	16,412	14,422	1,990	46,810	20,782	26,028	1,803	1,010	793
30—40	*46,398*	26,074	20,324	5,391	4,973	418	36,666	19,001	17,665	4,341	2,100	2,241
40—50	*37,010*	20,162	16,848	3,168	2,920	248	26,094	13,993	12,101	7,748	3,249	4,499
50—60	*25,653*	14,196	11,457	1,730	1,579	151	15,026	9,019	6,007	8,897	3,598	5,299
60 and over	*22,493*	12,724	9,769	1,095	991	104	9,232	6,531	2,701	12,166	5,202	6,964
JAIN	**1,411**	**759**	**652**	**670**	**404**	**266**	**575**	**290**	**285**	**166**	**65**	**101**
0—1	*44*	23	21	44	23	21	..	..	.	..	.	..
1—2	*38*	21	17	38	21	17	..	.	..	.	..	..
2—3	*43*	21	22	43	21	22	..	..	..	.	..	..
3—4	*39*	19	20	39	19	20	..	..	..	..	.	..
4—5	*37*	21	16	36	20	16	1	1	..	..	..	..
Total 0—5	*201*	*105*	*96*	*200*	*104*	*96*	*1*	*1*	..	..	..	..
5—10	*164*	82	82	161	81	80	3	1	2	.	..	..
10—15	*154*	78	76	142	75	67	11	3	8	1	..	1
15—20	*136*	79	57	65	52	13	70	26	44	1	1	..
20—30	*275*	156	119	62	55	7	199	91	108	14	10	4
30—40	*192*	106	86	17	15	2	143	78	65	32	13	19
40—50	*148*	74	74	12	12	.	89	50	39	47	12	35
50—60	*93*	55	38	6	6	..	45	31	14	42	18	24
60 and over	*48*	24	24	5	4	1	14	9	5	29	11	18
MUSLIM	**515,430**	**280,323**	**235,107**	**270,835**	**159,204**	**111,631**	**203,194**	**102,620**	**100,574**	**41,401**	**18,499**	**22,902**
0—1	*19,769*	9,844	9,925	19,768	9,843	9,925	1	1	..	..	..	..
1—2	*15,368*	7,692	7,676	15,359	7,688	7,671	7	2	5	2	2	..
2—3	*16,771*	8,388	8,383	16,749	8,377	8,372	20	10	10	2	1	1
3—4	*16,624*	8,370	8,254	16,574	8,342	8,232	46	26	20	4	2	2
4—5	*15,641*	8,026	7,615	15,572	7,988	7,584	61	34	27	8	4	4
Total 0—5	*84,173*	*42,320*	*41,853*	*84,022*	*42,238*	*41,781*	*135*	*73*	*62*	*16*	*9*	*7*
5—10	*69,317*	36,149	33,168	67,394	35,362	31,832	1,866	557	1,309	57	30	27
10—15	*65,526*	35,720	29,806	59,237	34,053	25,184	6,138	1,596	4,542	151	71	80
15—20	*52,333*	29,706	22,627	28,645	21,070	7,575	23,069	8,308	14,761	619	328	291
20—30	*88,897*	49,401	39,496	22,350	18,586	3,764	63,407	28,910	34,497	3,140	1,905	1,235
30—40	*61,530*	34,411	27,119	5,193	4,449	744	50,361	26,992	23,369	5,976	2,970	3,006
40—50	*43,193*	23,840	19,353	2,209	1,803	406	31,790	18,302	13,488	9,194	3,735	5,459
50—60	*27,277*	15,208	12,069	1,039	818	191	16,494	10,506	5,988	9,744	3,854	5,890
60 and over	*23,184*	13,568	9,616	746	595	151	9,934	7,376	2,558	12,504	5,597	6,907
CHRISTIAN	**7,070**	**4,381**	**2,689**	**4,176**	**2,887**	**1,289**	**2,485**	**1,269**	**1,216**	**409**	**225**	**184**
0—1	*246*	134	112	246	134	112	..	..	..	..	..	.
1—2	*194*	93	99	194	93	99	..	..	.	..	..	..
2—3	*213*	100	113	213	100	113	..	..	..	..	..	..
3—4	*205*	108	97	205	108	97	..	..	..	..	..	..
4—5	*185*	106	79	185	106	79	..	..	..	..	..	..
Total 0—5	*1,043*	*543*	*500*	*1,043*	*543*	*500*	..	..	..	..	..	..
5—10	*815*	469	346	811	467	344	3	2	1	1	..	1
10—15	*733*	423	310	687	412	275	43	9	34	3	2	1
15—20	*772*	521	251	513	427	86	252	90	162	7	4	3
20—30	*1,817*	1,268	549	926	863	63	849	379	470	42	26	16
30—40	*976*	587	389	161	149	12	721	382	339	94	56	38
40—50	*499*	305	194	26	21	5	386	238	148	87	46	41
50—60	*247*	151	96	7	4	3	153	106	47	87	41	46
60 and over	*168*	114	54	2	1	1	78	63	15	88	50	38

TABLE VII.—AGE, SEX

PART B.—DETAILS FOR DISTRICTS AND STATES.

LAHORE DISTRICT

Religion and age.	Population.			Unmarried.			Married.			Widowed.		
	Persons.	Males.	Females.	Persons.	Males.	Females.	Persons.	Males.	Females.	Persons.	Males.	Females.
1	2	3	4	5	6	7	8	9	10	11	12	13
ALL RELIGIONS ..	**1,878,570**	**794,389**	**584,181**	**696,683**	**433,316**	**263,367**	**567,961**	**309,104**	**258,857**	**113,926**	**51,969**	**61,957**
0—1 ..	*52,816*	25,864	26,952	52,775	25,845	26,930	31	15	16	10	4	6
1—2 ..	*38,263*	19,823	18,440	38,221	19,803	18,418	30	12	18	12	8	4
2—3 ..	*41,781*	21,531	20,250	41,658	21,442	20,216	112	79	33	11	10	1
3—4 ..	*40,617*	20,921	19,696	40,454	20,827	19,627	149	86	63	14	8	6
4—5 ..	*37,905*	19,913	17,992	37,705	19,831	17,874	160	59	101	40	23	17
Total 0—5 ..	*211,382*	*108,052*	*103,330*	*210,813*	*107,748*	*103,065*	*482*	*251*	*231*	*87*	*53*	*34*
5—10 ..	*170,664*	93,269	77,395	165,497	92,107	73,390	4,962	1,093	3,869	205	69	136
10—15 ..	*159,608*	90,229	69,379	144,044	86,248	57,796	15,218	3,840	11,378	346	141	205
15—20 ..	*139,813*	83,442	56,371	75,153	58,207	16,946	62,870	24,126	38,744	1,790	1,109	681
20—30 ..	*267,391*	164,377	103,014	71,539	63,341	8,198	185,531	94,374	91,157	10,321	6,062	3,659
30—40 ..	*180,602*	111,878	68,724	18,948	16,865	2,083	143,529	84,846	58,683	18,125	10,167	7,958
40—50 ..	*117,785*	69,008	48,777	6,285	5,251	1,034	86,299	52,831	33,468	25,201	10,926	14,275
50—60 .	*69,152*	39,732	29,420	2,498	2,051	447	42,541	28,267	14,274	24,113	9,414	14,699
60 and over ..	*62,173*	34,402	27,771	1,906	1,498	408	26,529	19,476	7,053	33,738	13,428	20,310
HINDU ..	**258,719**	**159,112**	**99,607**	**129,084**	**83,845**	**45,239**	**107,875**	**65,090**	**42,785**	**21,760**	**10,177**	**11,583**
0—1 ..	*8,513*	4,356	4,157	8,504	4,352	4,152	7	2	5	2	2	
1—2 ..	*6,456*	3,428	3,028	6,451	3,424	3,027	2	1	1	3	3	..
2—3 ..	*7,304*	3,960	3,344	7,261	3,924	3,337	38	32	6	5	4	1
3—4 ..	*7,070*	3,688	3,382	7,017	3,654	3,363	51	34	17	2	..	2
4—5 ..	*6,362*	3,258	3,104	6,324	3,246	3,078	32	10	22	6	2	4
Total 0—5 ..	*35,705*	*18,690*	*17,015*	*35,557*	*18,600*	*16,957*	*130*	*79*	*51*	*18*	*11*	*7*
5—10 ..	*28,346*	15,323	13,023	27,716	15,146	12,570	547	166	381	83	11	72
10—15 ..	*27,324*	15,716	11,608	24,826	15,026	9,800	2,382	661	1,721	116	29	87
15—20 ..	*29,056*	18,983	10,072	16,536	13,420	3,116	12,140	5,330	6,810	379	233	146
20—30 ..	*57,710*	38,844	18,866	17,187	15,329	1,858	38,184	22,021	16,163	2,339	1,494	845
30—40 .	*37,493*	25,265	12,228	4,689	4,150	539	28,627	18,751	9,876	4,177	2,364	1,813
40—50 ..	*22,398*	14,315	8,083	1,609	1,388	221	15,555	10,576	4,979	5,234	2,351	2,883
50—60 ..	*11,690*	7,023	4,667	567	474	93	6,683	4,846	1,837	4,440	1,703	2,737
60 and over ..	*8,998*	4,953	4,045	397	312	85	3,627	2,660	967	4,974	1,981	2,993
SIKH ..	**244,304**	**137,580**	**106,724**	**128,348**	**77,536**	**45,812**	**98,595**	**50,285**	**48,310**	**22,361**	**9,759**	**12,602**
0—1 ..	*9,289*	4,611	4,678	9,273	4,601	4,672	10	8	2	6	2	4
1—2 ..	*6,895*	3,518	3,377	6,887	3,515	3,372	3	2	1	5	1	4
2—3 .	*7,252*	3,696	3,556	7,241	3,690	3,551	11	6	5	..	.	
3—4 ..	*7,116*	3,637	3,479	7,088	3,628	3,460	27	9	18	1	.	1
4—5 ..	*6,802*	3,594	3,208	6,755	3,579	3,176	42	11	31	5	4	1
Total 0—5 ..	*37,354*	*19,056*	*18,298*	*37,244*	*19,013*	*18,231*	*93*	*36*	*57*	*17*	*7*	*10*
5—10 ..	*30,628*	17,069	13,559	30,064	16,870	13,194	539	183	330	25	16	9
10—15 ..	*28,022*	16,172	11,850	25,661	15,495	10,166	2,310	648	1,662	51	29	22
15—20 ..	*22,784*	13,466	9,318	11,784	9,182	2,602	10,731	4,122	6,609	269	162	107
20—30 ..	*43,349*	25,373	17,976	11,506	10,360	1,146	30,323	14,001	16,232	1,520	922	598
30—40 ..	*31,719*	18,635	13,084	4,778	4,517	261	24,026	12,639	11,387	2,915	1,479	1,436
40—50 ..	*21,941*	12,060	9,881	1,231	1,103	128	16,196	9,055	7,141	4,514	1,902	2,612
50—60 ..	*14,252*	7,998	6,254	648	594	54	8,637	5,415	3,222	4,967	1,989	2,978
60 and over ..	*14,255*	7,751	6,504	432	402	30	5,740	4,096	1,644	8,083	3,253	4,830
JAIN ..	**1,450**	**777**	**673**	**808**	**486**	**322**	**507**	**249**	**258**	**135**	**42**	**93**
0—1 ..	*62*	34	28	62	34	28	..	.	.	..	..	
1—2 ..	*43*	21	22	43	21	22	..		.	..	.	.
2—3 ..	*48*	21	27	48	21	27	..	.	..	..	..	.
3—4 ..	*46*	22	24	46	22	24	..	..	.	..	..	.
4—5 ..	*46*	23	23	44	22	22	1	1	..	1		1
Total 0—5 ..	*245*	*127*	*124*	*243*	*120*	*123*	*1*	*1*	.	*1*		*1*
5—10 ..	*186*	100	86	185	100	85	1	.	1	..		
10—15 ..	*175*	96	77	165	94	71	8	2	6	.		
15—20 ..	*167*	93	74	97	72	25	67	21	46	3	.	3
20—30 ..	*295*	158	137	79	69	10	200	86	114	16	3	13
30—40 ..	*178*	104	74	19	16	3	136	79	57	23	9	14
40—50 ..	*110*	58	52	12	8	4	62	37	25	36	13	23
50—60 ..	*56*	28	28	5	4	1	22	17	5	20	7	22
60 and over ..	*40*	19	21	3	3	.	10	6	4	27	10	17
MUSLIM ..	**815,820**	**464,043**	**351,777**	**412,085**	**252,472**	**159,613**	**338,405**	**181,646**	**156,759**	**65,330**	**29,925**	**35,405**
0—1 .	*32,727*	15,741	16,986	32,711	15,736	16,975	14	5	9	2	.	2
1—2 .	*23,171*	11,970	11,201	23,142	11,957	11,185	25	9	16	4	4	..
2—3 ..	*25,334*	12,921	12,413	25,270	12,879	12,391	59	37	22	5	5	..
3—4 ..	*24,595*	12,679	11,916	24,524	12,634	11,890	63	40	23	8	5	3
4—5 ..	*23,011*	12,168	10,843	22,925	12,126	10,799	64	31	33	22	11	11
Total 0—5 ..	*128,838*	*65,479*	*63,359*	*128,572*	*65,332*	*63,240*	*225*	*122*	*103*	*41*	*25*	*16*
5—10 ..	*104,475*	56,725	47,750	100,664	55,988	44,676	3,725	703	3,022	86	34	52
10—15 ..	*97,539*	54,532	43,007	87,391	52,066	35,325	9,980	2,388	7,592	168	78	90
15—20 ..	*81,530*	47,526	34,004	42,990	33,145	9,845	37,471	13,712	23,759	1,069	669	400
20—30 ..	*154,131*	92,857	61,274	38,555	34,207	4,348	109,540	54,677	54,863	6,036	3,973	2,063
30—40 ..	*103,808*	63,485	40,323	8,627	7,530	1,097	84,922	50,124	34,798	10,259	5,831	4,428
40—50 ..	*68,598*	39,926	28,672	3,145	2,564	581	50,966	31,127	19,839	14,487	6,235	8,252
50—60 ..	*40,438*	23,093	17,345	1,154	906	248	25,415	16,793	8,622	13,869	5,394	8,475
60 and over ..	*36,463*	20,420	16,043	987	734	253	16,161	12,000	4,161	19,315	7,686	11,629
CHRISTIAN ..	**57,097**	**32,107**	**24,990**	**30,943**	**18,688**	**12,255**	**21,872**	**11,407**	**10,465**	**4,282**	**2,012**	**2,270**
0—1 ..	*2,196*	1,108	1,088	2,196	1,108	1,088	..	.	..	.	.	..
1—2 ..	*1,669*	874	795	1,669	874	795	..	..	..	..	..	.
2—3 ..	*1,815*	923	892	1,810	918	892	4	4	..	1	1	..
3—4 ..	*1,765*	886	879	1,759	880	879	3	3	..	3	3	.
4—5 ..	*1,648*	854	794	1,635	844	791	8	5	3	5	5	..
Total 0—5 ..	*9,093*	*4,645*	*4,448*	*9,069*	*4,624*	*4,445*	*15*	*12*	*3*	*9*	*9*	.
5—10 ..	*6,898*	3,979	2,919	6,784	3,940	2,844	104	32	72	10	7	3
10—15 ..	*6,419*	3,627	2,792	5,931	3,509	2,422	478	114	364	10	4	6
15—20 ..	*6,119*	3,271	2,848	3,711	2,355	1,356	2,339	872	1,467	69	44	25
20—30 ..	*11,603*	6,932	4,671	4,145	3,320	825	7,060	3,354	3,706	398	258	140
30—40 ..	*7,243*	4,267	2,976	813	635	178	5,695	3,164	2,531	735	468	267
40—50 ..	*4,639*	2,578	2,061	284	186	98	3,445	1,983	1,462	910	409	501
50—60 ..	*2,681*	1,563	1,118	120	72	48	1,758	1,175	583	803	316	487
60 and over ..	*2,402*	1,245	1,157	86	47	39	978	701	277	1,338	497	841

AND CIVIL CONDITION (BY RELIGION).

PART B.—DETAILS FOR DISTRICTS AND STATES—*continued.*

AMRITSAR DISTRICT.

Religion and Age.	Population.			Unmarried.			Married.			Widowed.		
	Persons.	Males.	Females.	Persons.	Males.	Females.	Persons.	Males.	Females.	Persons.	Males.	Females.
1	2	3	4	5	6	7	8	9	10	11	12	13
ALL RELIGIONS	**1,117,120**	**621,040**	**496,080**	**560,637**	**344,607**	**216,080**	**451,555**	**228,316**	**223,239**	**104,928**	**48,117**	**56,811**
0—1	*41,730*	21,184	20,546	41,728	21,184	20,544	2	..	2	..	..	..
1—2	*31,545*	16,001	15,544	31,532	15,997	15,535	12	4	8	1	.	1
2—3	*33,491*	17,061	16,430	33,469	17,052	16,417	20	8	12	2	1	1
3—4	*32,981*	16,880	16,101	32,952	16,865	16,087	29	15	14	..	.	..
4—5	*31,339*	16,234	15,105	31,276	16,203	15,073	54	27	27	9	4	5
Total 0—5	*171,086*	*87,360*	*83,726*	*170,957*	*87,301*	*83,656*	*117*	*54*	*63*	*12*	*5*	*7*
5—10	*145,808*	79,062	66,746	143,050	78,389	64,661	2,672	625	2,047	86	48	38
10—15	*135,346*	75,767	59,579	123,224	73,062	50,162	11,910	2,587	9,323	212	118	94
15—20	*104,058*	59,569	44,489	52,384	41,512	10,872	50,406	17,293	33,113	1,268	764	504
20—30	*192,532*	110,373	82,159	44,622	40,473	4,149	140,554	65,308	75,246	7,356	4,592	2,764
30—40	*139,097*	79,771	59,326	14,349	13,183	1,166	110,349	58,852	51,497	14,399	7,736	6,663
40—50	*100,480*	56,525	43,955	6,163	5,496	667	71,895	41,097	30,798	22,422	9,932	12,490
50—60	*65,771*	37,198	28,573	3,300	2,937	363	38,583	24,204	14,379	23,888	10,057	13,831
60 and over	*62,942*	35,415	27,527	2,588	2,254	334	25,069	18,296	6,773	35,285	14,865	20,420
HINDU	**174,392**	**101,185**	**73,207**	**89,289**	**57,325**	**31,964**	**68,106**	**36,714**	**31,392**	**16,997**	**7,146**	**9,851**
0—1	*5,460*	2,780	2,680	5,460	2,780	2,680	..	..	.	.	..	.
1—2	*4,455*	2,209	2,246	4,455	2,209	2,246	..	.	..	.	..	.
2—3	*4,904*	2,426	2,478	4,903	2,425	2,477	1	..	1	.	..	..
3—4	*4,871*	2,472	2,399	4,870	2,471	2,399	1	1	..	.	..	..
4—5	*4,641*	2,397	2,244	4,634	2,394	2,240	6	3	3	1	..	1
Total 0—5	*24,331*	*12,234*	*12,047*	*24,322*	*12,280*	*12,042*	*8*	*4*	*4*	*1*	..	*1*
5—10	*21,665*	11,724	9,941	21,359	11,640	9,719	289	78	211	17	6	11
10—15	*20,488*	11,683	8,805	18,853	11,363	7,490	1,598	303	1,295	37	17	20
15—20	*17,793*	11,140	6,653	9,766	8,226	1,540	7,801	2,792	5,009	226	122	104
20—30	*33,441*	21,094	12,347	9,456	8,772	684	22,599	11,532	11,067	1,386	790	596
30—40	*23,802*	14,467	9,335	3,641	3,390	251	17,348	9,714	7,634	2,813	1,363	1,450
40—50	*15,635*	9,108	6,527	1,006	877	129	10,582	6,684	3,898	4,047	1,547	2,500
50—60	*9,429*	5,370	4,059	494	434	60	5,141	3,499	1,642	3,794	1,437	2,357
60 and over	*7,808*	4,315	3,493	392	343	49	2,740	2,108	632	4,676	1,864	2,812
SIKH	**399,951**	**219,788**	**180,163**	**196,138**	**121,699**	**74,439**	**162,734**	**79,106**	**83,628**	**41,079**	**18,983**	**22,096**
0—1	*15,153*	7,776	7,377	15,151	7,776	7,375	2	..	2	..	..	..
1—2	*11,190*	5,772	5,418	11,180	5,770	5,410	9	2	7	1	..	1
2—3	*11,658*	6,028	5,630	11,645	6,026	5,619	12	2	10	1	..	1
3—4	*11,571*	5,988	5,583	11,561	5,984	5,577	10	4	6	..	..	..
4—5	*11,104*	5,820	5,284	11,083	5,809	5,274	17	9	8	4	2	2
Total 0—5	*60,676*	*31,384*	*29,292*	*60,620*	*31,365*	*29,255*	*50*	*17*	*33*	*6*	*2*	*4*
5—10	*51,541*	28,327	23,214	50,602	28,094	22,508	909	217	692	30	16	14
10—15	*47,525*	27,023	20,502	43,278	25,987	17,291	4,175	996	3,179	72	40	32
15—20	*35,114*	20,022	15,092	17,197	13,707	3,490	17,529	6,090	11,439	388	225	163
20—30	*64,482*	35,620	28,862	14,221	13,103	1,118	47,830	21,029	26,801	2,431	1,488	943
30—40	*48,818*	26,914	21,904	4,918	4,604	314	38,791	19,551	19,240	5,109	2,759	2,350
40—50	*38,293*	20,838	17,455	2,660	2,457	203	27,195	14,489	12,706	8,438	3,892	4,546
50—60	*26,681*	14,827	11,854	1,474	1,341	133	15,696	9,352	6,344	9,511	4,134	5,377
60 and over	*26,821*	14,833	11,988	1,168	1,041	127	10,559	7,365	3,194	15,094	6,427	8,667
JAIN	**1,272**	**691**	**581**	**735**	**429**	**306**	**402**	**202**	**200**	**135**	**60**	**75**
0—1	*47*	24	23	47	24	23	..	..	..	..	..	..
1—2	*38*	17	21	38	17	21	..	..	..	..	..	..
2—3	*45*	22	23	45	22	23	..	..	..	..	..	..
3—4	*42*	23	19	42	23	19	..	..	..	..	..	..
4—5	*37*	20	17	37	20	17	..	..	..	..	..	..
Total 0—5	*209*	*106*	*103*	*209*	*106*	*103*	..	..	..	..	..	..
5—10	*169*	86	83	169	86	83	..	..	..	..	..	..
10—15	*160*	84	76	156	82	74	4	2	2	..	..	..
15—20	*141*	81	60	84	60	24	55	21	34	2	..	2
20—30	*210*	120	90	69	56	13	133	60	73	8	4	4
30—40	*152*	80	72	21	17	4	105	51	54	26	12	14
40—50	*118*	69	49	15	12	3	65	40	25	38	17	21
50—60	*67*	41	26	7	6	1	32	23	9	28	12	16
60 and over	*46*	24	22	5	4	1	8	5	3	33	15	18
MUSLIM	**524,676**	**290,887**	**234,289**	**265,366**	**159,907**	**105,459**	**213,965**	**109,218**	**104,747**	**45,345**	**21,262**	**24,083**
0—1	*20,366*	10,261	10,105	20,366	10,261	10,105	..	..	..	..	..	..
1—2	*15,346*	7,743	7,603	15,343	7,741	7,602	3	2	1	..	..	..
2—3	*16,324*	8,301	8,023	16,317	8,295	8,022	6	5	1	1	1	..
3—4	*15,954*	8,123	7,831	15,936	8,113	7,823	18	10	8	..	..	..
4—5	*15,041*	7,734	7,307	15,009	7,720	7,289	29	13	16	3	1	2
Total 0—5	*83,031*	*42,162*	*40,869*	*82,971*	*42,130*	*40,841*	*56*	*30*	*26*	*4*	*2*	*2*
5—10	*70,074*	37,683	32,391	68,594	37,337	31,257	1,442	321	1,121	38	25	13
10—15	*64,987*	35,801	29,186	58,901	34,485	24,416	5,985	1,256	4,729	101	60	41
15—20	*49,372*	27,435	21,937	24,413	18,861	5,552	24,327	8,169	16,158	632	405	227
20—30	*91,520*	51,997	39,523	20,137	17,939	2,198	67,958	31,811	36,147	3,425	2,247	1,178
30—40	*64,313*	37,238	27,075	5,613	5,056	557	52,458	28,692	23,766	6,242	3,490	2,752
40—50	*45,104*	25,786	19,318	2,429	2,111	318	33,070	19,336	13,734	9,605	4,339	5,266
50—60	*28,757*	16,485	12,272	1,308	1,143	165	17,196	11,007	6,189	10,253	4,335	5,918
60 and over	*27,518*	15,800	11,718	1,000	845	155	11,473	8,596	2,877	15,045	6,359	8,686
CHRISTIAN	**16,619**	**8,862**	**7,757**	**9,010**	**5,188**	**3,822**	**6,247**	**3,014**	**3,233**	**1,362**	**660**	**702**
0—1	*695*	338	357	695	338	357	..	..	..	..	..	..
1—2	*510*	258	252	510	258	252	..	..	..	..	..	..
2—3	*557*	283	274	556	282	274	1	1	..	..	..	..
3—4	*541*	273	268	541	273	268	..	..	..	..	..	..
4—5	*510*	260	250	508	258	250	1	1	..	1	1	..
Total 0—5	*2,813*	*1,412*	*1,401*	*2,810*	*1,409*	*1,401*	*2*	*2*	..	*1*	*1*	..
5—10	*2,335*	1,230	1,105	2,305	1,222	1,083	30	8	22	..	..	.
10—15	*2,165*	1,165	1,000	2,018	1,135	883	145	29	116	2	1	1
15—20	*1,612*	877	735	914	651	263	679	215	464	19	1	8
20—30	*2,835*	1,513	1,322	725	592	133	2,004	858	1,146	106	63	43
30—40	*1,976*	1,046	930	148	109	39	1,620	826	794	208	111	97
40—50	*1,313*	711	602	50	36	14	970	539	431	293	[illegible]	157
50—60	*827*	468	359	17	13	4	512	318	194	298	137	161
60 and over	*743*	440	303	23	21	2	285	219	66	435	[illegible]	[illegible]

TABLE VII.—AGE, SEX

PART B.—DETAILS FOR DISTRICTS AND STATES.

GURDASPUR DISTRICT.

Religion and Age.	Population. Persons.	Population. Males.	Population. Females.	Unmarried. Persons.	Unmarried. Males.	Unmarried. Females.	Married. Persons.	Married. Males.	Married. Females.	Widowed. Persons.	Widowed. Males.	Widowed. Females.
1	2	3	4	5	6	7	8	9	10	11	12	13
ALL RELIGIONS ..	**970,898**	**531,935**	**438,963**	**490,445**	**299,825**	**190,620**	**388,173**	**190,819**	**197,354**	**92,280**	**41,291**	**50,989**
0—1 ..	*39,619*	20,075	19,544	39,614	20,074	19,540	5	1	4	..	..	..
1—2 ..	*28,079*	14,252	13,827	28,074	14,251	13,823	4	1	3	1	..	1
2—3 ..	*31,163*	15,669	15,494	31,140	15,665	15,475	23	4	19	..	..	..
3—4 ..	*30,981*	15,611	15,370	30,821	15,597	15,224	160	14	146	..	..	.
4—5 ..	*29,620*	15,323	14,297	29,325	15,297	14,028	292	26	266	3	..	3
Total 0—5 ..	*159,462*	*80,930*	*78,532*	*158,974*	*80,884*	*78,090*	*484*	*46*	*438*	*4*	..	*4*
5—10 ..	*134,576*	72,159	62,417	128,417	70,959	57,458	6,082	1,172	4,910	77	28	49
10—15 ..	*124,667*	68,266	56,401	107,987	64,766	43,221	16,426	3,389	13,037	254	111	143
15—20 ..	*89,594*	49,036	40,558	43,290	34,559	8,731	45,191	13,884	31,307	1,113	59[illegible]	[illegible]20
20—30 ..	*161,660*	89,046	72,614	35,102	32,620	2,473	119,976	52,801	67,175	6,582	3,616	2,956
30—40 ..	*117,840*	67,218	50,622	8,899	8,596	303	95,300	52,047	43,253	13,641	6,575	7,066
40—50 ..	*82,034*	46,324	35,710	4,025	3,854	171	57,296	33,859	23,437	20,71[illegible]	8,61[illegible]	12,102
50—60 ..	*52,668*	30,589	22,079	2,164	2,047	117	29,378	19,670	9,708	21,126	8,872	12,254
60 and over ..	*48,397*	28,367	20,030	1,587	1,531	56	18,040	13,951	4,089	28,770	12,885	15,885
HINDU ..	**249,404**	**136,160**	**113,244**	**121,896**	**75,743**	**46,153**	**99,035**	**49,238**	**49,797**	**28,473**	**11,179**	**17,294**
0—1 ..	*9,852*	4,933	4,919	9,851	4,933	4,918	1	.	1	.	..	
1—2 ..	*7,038*	3,560	3,478	7,035	3,559	3,476	3	1	2	..	.	
2—3 ..	*7,647*	3,880	3,767	7,642	3,878	3,764	5	2	3	..	.	
3—4 ..	*7,578*	3,843	3,735	7,538	3,841	3,697	40	2	38	..	.	.
4—5 ..	*7,253*	3,754	3,499	7,173	3,750	3,423	78	4	74	2	.	2
Total 0—5 ..	*39,368*	*19,970*	*19,398*	*39,239*	*19,961*	*19,278*	*127*	*9*	*118*	*2*	..	*2*
5—10 ..	*32,742*	17,383	15,359	30,881	17,068	13,813	1,832	307	1,525	29	8	1
10—15 ..	*30,742*	16,625	14,117	26,040	15,697	10,343	4,605	887	3,718	97	[illegible]	56
15—20 ..	*23,209*	12,718	10,491	11,191	9,188	2,003	11,654	3,371	8,283	364	159	205
20—30 ..	*42,407*	23,241	19,166	9,456	8,950	506	30,713	13,320	17,393	2,238	97	1,267
30—40 ..	*32,069*	18,322	13,747	2,654	2,542	112	24,686	13,891	10,795	4,729	1,889	2,84[illegible]
40—50 ..	*22,286*	12,496	9,790	1,245	1,181	64	14,327	8,984	5,343	6,714	2,331	4,383
50—60 ..	*14,180*	8,231	5,949	685	662	23	7,070	6,124	,946	6,425	2,445	3,98[illegible]
60 and over ..	*12,401*	7,174	5,227	*505*	494	*11*	*4,021*	*3,345*	676	*7,875*	3,[illegible]35	4,5[illegible]
SIKH ..	**178,471**	**99,724**	**78,747**	**91,705**	**57,854**	**33,851**	**69,360**	**33,165**	**36,195**	**17,406**	**8,705**	**8,701**
0—1 ..	*7,099*	3,630	3,469	7,098	3,629	3,469	1	1	..	..	.	.
1—2 ..	*4,992*	2,571	2,421	4,992	2,571	2,421	..	.	..	.	.	.
2—3 ..	*5,376*	2,744	2,632	5,375	2,744	2,631	1	..	1	..	..	..
3—4 ..	*5,335*	2,712	2,623	5,328	2,710	2,618	7	2	5	.	..	..
4—5 ..	*5,215*	2,723	2,492	5,198	2,718	2,480	17	5	12	..	..	..
Total 0—5 ..	*28,017*	*14,380*	*13,637*	*27,991*	*14,372*	*13,619*	*26*	*8*	*18*	..	..	..
5—10 ..	*23,953*	13,115	10,838	23,326	13,005	10,321	618	108	510	9	2	7
10—15 ..	*22,041*	12,455	9,586	19,926	12,063	7,863	2,088	381	1,707	27	11	16
15—20 ..	*15,356*	8,656	6,700	8,067	6,463	1,604	7,146	2,107	5,039	143	86	57
20—30 ..	*28,408*	15,801	12,607	7,121	6,705	416	20,270	8,445	11,825	1,017	651	366
30—40 ..	*22,116*	12,620	9,496	2,594	2,581	13	17,161	8,734	8,427	2,361	1,305	,056
40—50 ..	*16,397*	9,422	6,975	1,314	1,308	6	11,420	6,288	5,132	3,663	1,826	1,837
50—60 ..	*11,233*	6,733	4,500	754	745	9	6,417	4,018	2,399	4,062	1,970	2,092
60 and over ..	*10,950*	6,542	4,408	612	612	..	4,214	3,076	1,138	6,124	2,854	3,270
JAIN ..	**15**	**8**	**7**	**10**	**6**	**4**	**5**	**2**	**3**	..	..	..
0—1 ..	*1*	..	1	1	..	1	..	..	..	..	..	..
1—2 ..	*1*	1	..	1	1	..	..	.	..	..	.	..
2—3 ..	*1*	1	..	1	1	..	..	.	.	.		..
3—4 ..	*1*	1	..	1	1	..	..	..	.	..	.	.
4—5 ..	*2*	1	1	2	1	1	..	.	..	..	..	.
Total 0—5 ..	*6*	*4*	*2*	*6*	*4*	*2*	.	..	..	..	..	
5—10 ..	*1*	1	..	1	1	.	..	..	..	..	..	.
10—15 ..	..	..	..	..	..	.	..	.	..	..	..	
15—20 ..	*2*	1	1	2	1	1	..	.	..	..	..	
20—30 .	*2*	..	2	1	..	1	1	.	1	.	.	.
30—40 .	*2*	1	1	..	..	..	2	1	1	.	.	.
40—50 ..	*2*	1	1	..	..	..	2	1	1	.	.	.
50—60 ..	..	.	..	.	..	.	..	.	.	.	.	..
60 and over ..	..	..	..	.	.	.	..	..	..	..	..	..
MUSLIM .	**493,216**	**268,771**	**224,445**	**250,943**	**150,716**	**100,227**	**199,874**	**98,642**	**101,232**	**42,399**	**19,413**	**22,986**
0—1 .	*20,626*	10,496	10,130	20,623	10,496	10,127	3	..	3	..	..	..
1—2 .	*14,561*	7,365	7,196	14,559	7,365	7,194	1	..	1	1	..	1
2—3 ..	*16,408*	8,170	8,238	16,391	8,168	8,223	17	2	15	..	..	.
3—4 ..	*16,327*	8,167	8,160	16,215	8,157	8,058	112	10	102	..	..	.
4—5 ..	*15,514*	8,001	7,513	15,318	7,984	7,334	195	17	178	1		1
Total 0—5 .	*83,436*	*42,199*	*41,237*	*83,106*	*42,170*	*40,936*	*328*	*29*	*299*	*2*	..	*2*
5—10 ..	*70,594*	37,694	32,900	67,177	36,971	30,206	3,378	703	2,673	39	18	2[illegible]
10—15 .	*65,180*	35,438	29,742	56,140	33,435	22,705	8,921	1,949	6,972	119	54	65
15—20 ..	*46,253*	25,065	21,188	21,746	17,118	4,628	23,972	7,638	16,334	535	309	2[illegible]6
20—30 .	*82,318*	45,308	37,010	16,931	15,532	1,399	62,404	28,000	34,404	2,983	1,776	,207
30—40 .	*57,856*	33,028	24,828	3,357	3,206	151	48,592	26,812	21,780	5,907	3,010	2,897
40—50 ..	*39,593*	22,291	17,302	1,383	1,294	89	28,768	16,957	11,811	9,442	4,040	5,102
50—60 ..	*24,976*	14,319	10,657	668	596	72	14,535	9,647	4,888	9,773	4,076	5,697
60 and over ..	*23,010*	13,429	9,581	435	394	41	8,976	6,905	2,071	13,599	6,130	7,[illegible]9
CHRISTIAN ..	**43,243**	**23,702**	**19,541**	**23,247**	**13,863**	**9,384**	**16,581**	**8,092**	**8,489**	**3,415**	**1,747**	**1,668**
0—1 ..	*1,814*	914	900	1,814	914	900	..	..	.	..	.	.
1—2 ..	*1,318*	673	645	1,318	673	645	..	..	..	..	.	..
2—3 .	*1,539*	787	752	1,539	787	752	..	..	.	..	.	.
3—4 .	*1,530*	785	745	1,529	785	744	1	..	1	..		.
4—5 ..	*1,423*	726	697	1,421	726	695	2	..	2	..		..
Total 0—5 .	*7,624*	*3,885*	*3,739*	*7,621*	*3,885*	*3,736*	*3*	..	*3*	.	.	.
5—10 ..	*6,381*	3,467	2,914	6,275	3,455	2,820	106	12	94	.		.
10—15 ..	*5,871*	3,300	2,571	5,362	3,221	2,141	506	79	427	3	..	3
15—20 ..	*4,095*	2,236	1,859	2,110	1,630	480	1,935	578	1,357	50	[illegible]8	22
20—30 ..	*7,180*	3,939	3,241	1,457	1,306	151	5,443	2,447	2,996	280	186	94
30—40 ..	*4,902*	2,756	2,146	271	244	27	4,110	2,197	1,913	521	3[illegible]5	2[illegible]0
40—50 ..	*3,309*	1,850	1,459	70	58	12	2,486	1,433	1,053	753	359	3[illegible]4
50—60 .	*2,043*	1,166	877	60	37	13	1,232	786	446	761	343	[illegible]18
60 and over .	*1,838*	1,103	735	31	27	4	760	560	200	1,047	516	5[illegible]1

AND CIVIL CONDITION (BY RELIGION).

PART B.—DETAILS FOR DISTRICTS AND STATES—*continued.*

SIALKOT DISTRICT.

Religion and Age.	Population.			Unmarried.			Married.			Widowed.		
	Persons.	Males.	Females.	Persons.	Males.	Females.	Persons.	Males.	Females	Persons.	Males.	Females.
1	2	3	4	5	6	7	8	9	10	11	12	13
ALL RELIGIONS ..	**979,617**	**537,801**	**442,816**	**499,116**	**301,429**	**197,687**	**386,392**	**191,247**	**195,145**	**94,109**	**44,625**	**49,484**
0- 1 ..	*41,511*	20,377	21,134	41,508	20,377	21,131	2	..	2	1	..	1
1- 2 .	*30,173*	14,759	15,414	30,166	14,757	15,409	5	2	3	2	..	2
2- 3 ..	*30,012*	14,869	15,143	29,995	14,863	15,132	16	6	10	1	..	1
3- 4 ..	*29,539*	14,969	14,570	29,492	14,963	14,529	43	5	38	4	1	3
4- 5 ..	*29,090*	15,212	13,878	28,997	15,198	13,799	77	10	67	16	4	12
Total 0- 5 ..	*160,325*	*80,186*	*80,139*	*160,158*	*80,158*	*80,000*	*143*	*23*	*120*	*24*	*5*	*19*
5—10 ..	*129,672*	70,606	59,066	123,532	70,037	53,495	6,040	534	5,506	100	35	65
10- 15 ..	*117,023*	65,675	51,448	103,297	63,355	39,942	13,492	2,111	11,381	234	109	125
15- 20 ..	*87,796*	47,541	40,255	46,423	34,969	11,454	40,353	11,984	28,369	1,020	588	432
20- 30 ..	*166,697*	91,473	75,224	43,179	36,030	7,149	117,228	51,634	65,594	6,290	3,809	2,481
30- 40 ..	*120,378*	68,606	51,772	12,213	9,323	2,890	94,921	52,238	42,683	13,244	7,045	6,199
40- 50 .	*84,421*	47,258	37,163	5,586	3,801	1,785	58,807	34,539	24,268	20,028	8,918	11,110
50- 60 ..	*58,339*	33,480	24,859	2,912	2,138	774	33,250	21,509	11,741	22,177	9,833	2,3
60 and over ..	*54,966*	32,576	22,390	1,816	1,618	198	22,158	16,875	5,483	30,992	14,283	6,709
HINDU ..	**206,395**	**111,853**	**94,542**	**101,542**	**61,491**	**40,051**	**80,476**	**39,474**	**41,002**	**24,377**	**10,888**	**13,489**
0- 1 ..	*8,187*	4,045	4,142	8,187	4,045	4,142	..	..	..	.	..	.
1- 2 ..	*6,026*	2,948	3,078	6,022	2,947	3,075	2	1	1	2	..	2
2- 3 ..	*5,725*	2,575	3,150	5,717	2,572	3,145	7	3	4	1	.	1
3- 4 ..	*5,698*	2,604	3,094	5,684	2,602	3,082	14	2	12	..	..	..
4- 5 .	*5,952*	3,005	2,947	5,931	3,004	2,927	20	1	19	1	..	1
Total 0- 5 .	*31,588*	*15,177*	*16,411*	*31,541*	*15,170*	*16,371*	*43*	*7*	*36*	*4*	..	*4*
5- 10 ..	*26,857*	14,109	12,748	25,717	13,943	11,774	1,114	155	959	26	11	16
10- 15 ..	*24,522*	13,255	11,267	21,448	12,652	8,796	2,999	569	2,430	75	34	41
15- 20 ..	*17,338*	9,412	7,926	8,758	6,870	1,888	8,301	2,412	5,889	279	130	149
20- 30 ..	*34,282*	18,931	15,351	8,822	8,095	727	23,792	10,023	13,769	1,668	813	8[illegible]
30- 40 ..	*26,595*	14,922	11,673	2,554	2,329	225	20,152	10,797	9,355	3,889	1,796	2,093
40- 50 ..	*19,511*	10,940	8,571	1,246	1,111	135	12,644	7,482	5,162	5,621	2,347	3,274
50- 60 .	*13,672*	7,978	5,694	787	695	92	7,173	4,762	2,411	5,712	2,521	3,191
60 and over ..	*12,030*	7,129	4,901	669	626	43	4,258	3,267	991	7,103	3,236	3,867
SIKH ..	**94,955**	**53,996**	**40,959**	**49,642**	**31,820**	**17,822**	**35,780**	**17,546**	**18,234**	**9,533**	**4,630**	**4,903**
0- 1 ..	*3,806*	1,951	1,855	3,805	1,951	1,854	1	..	1	.	..	..
1- 2 ..	*2,645*	1,348	1,297	2,645	1,348	1,297	..	..	..	..	..	.
2- 3 ..	*2,723*	1,397	1,326	2,720	1,396	1,324	3	1	2	..	.	.
3- 4 ..	*2,733*	1,441	1,292	2,729	1,440	1,289	4	1	3	..	.	.
4- 5 ..	*2,692*	1,436	1,256	2,683	1,432	1,251	5	2	3	4	2	2
Total 0- 5 ..	*14,599*	*7,573*	*7,026*	*14,582*	*7,567*	*7,015*	*15*	*4*	*9*	*4*	*2*	*2*
5- 10 .	*12,003*	6,631	5,369	11,729	6,591	5,138	270	41	229	4	2	2
10—15 ..	*10,883*	6,169	4,714	10,048	6,023	4,025	824	140	684	11	6	5
15- 20 ..	*8,130*	4,775	3,355	4,882	3,825	1,057	3,188	912	2,276	60	38	22
20- 30 ..	*16,070*	9,324	6,746	5,077	4,671	406	10,481	4,335	6,146	512	318	194
30- 40 ..	*12,071*	7,164	4,907	1,728	1,647	81	9,113	4,804	4,309	1,230	713	517
40—50 ..	*8,710*	4,981	3,729	812	761	51	5,956	3,315	2,641	1,942	905	1,037
50—60 ..	*6,190*	3,633	2,557	444	423	21	3,531	2,215	1,316	2,215	995	1,220
60 and over ..	*6,299*	3,743	2,556	340	312	28	2,404	1,780	624	3,555	1,651	1,904
JAIN ..	**2,236**	**1,227**	**1,009**	**1,210**	**725**	**485**	**786**	**366**	**420**	**240**	**136**	**104**
0- 1 ..	*68*	38	30	68	38	30	..	..	..	..	..	..
1- 2 ..	*69*	37	32	69	37	32	..	..	..	..	..	..
2- 3 ..	*74*	37	37	73	37	36	1	..	1	..	..	.
3- 4 ..	*70*	38	32	70	38	32	..	..	..	..	..	.
4- 5 ..	*80*	43	37	77	43	34	2	.	2	1	..	1
Total 0- 5 ..	*361*	*193*	*168*	*357*	*193*	*164*	*3*	.	*3*	*1*	..	*1*
5- 10 .	*299*	161	138	287	158	129	10	2	8	2	1	1
10- 15 .	*268*	137	131	249	135	114	18	1	17	1	1	..
15- 20 ..	*231*	120	111	136	88	48	91	30	61	4	2	2
20- 30 ..	*400*	213	187	102	83	19	276	116	160	22	14	8
30- 40 ..	*271*	156	115	40	34	6	179	92	87	52	30	22
40- 50 ..	*191*	120	71	23	20	3	111	66	45	57	34	23
50- 60 ..	*122*	69	53	10	8	2	62	35	27	50	26	24
60 and over ..	*93*	58	35	6	6	.	36	24	12	51	28	23
MUSLIM ..	**609,633**	**333,637**	**275,996**	**310,170**	**185,731**	**124,439**	**244,746**	**121,604**	**123,142**	**54,717**	**26,302**	**28,415**
0- 1 ..	*26,488*	12,820	13,668	26,487	12,820	13,667	1	..	1	..	..	..
1- 2 ..	*19,331*	9,375	9,956	19,329	9,374	9,955	2	1	1	..	..	..
2- 3 ..	*19,302*	9,758	9,544	19,299	9,756	9,543	3	2	1	..	..	.
3- 4 ..	*18,845*	9,776	9,069	18,818	9,773	9,045	23	2	21	4	1	3
4- 5 .	*18,234*	9,644	8,590	18,179	9,636	8,543	46	6	40	9	2	7
Total 0- 5 ..	*102,200*	*51,373*	*50,827*	*102,112*	*51,359*	*50,753*	*75*	*11*	*64*	*13*	*3*	*10*
5- 10 .	*81,166*	44,726	36,440	76,528	44,383	32,145	4,575	323	4,252	63	20	43
10- 15 .	*73,033*	41,459	31,574	63,691	40,066	23,625	9,203	1,328	7,875	139	65	74
15- 20 ..	*56,063*	29,815	26,248	29,102	21,527	7,575	26,343	7,909	18,434	618	379	239
20- 30 ..	*104,228*	56,219	48,009	25,831	20,221	5,610	74,658	33,576	41,082	3,739	2,422	1,317
30- 40 ..	*73,838*	42,035	31,803	7,304	4,833	2,471	59,177	33,132	26,045	7,357	4,070	3,287
40- 50 ..	*50,991*	28,443	22,548	3,298	1,763	1,535	36,347	21,556	14,791	11,346	5,124	6,222
50- 60 .	*34,982*	19,943	15,039	1,367	944	623	20,410	13,251	7,159	13,005	5,748	7,257
60 and over .	*33,132*	19,624	13,508	737	635	102	13,958	10,518	3,440	18,437	8,471	9,966
CHRISTIAN ..	**66,365**	**36,579**	**29,786**	**36,533**	**21,657**	**14,876**	**24,591**	**12,254**	**12,337**	**5,241**	**2,668**	**2,573**
0- 1 ..	*2,958*	1,521	1,437	2,957	1,521	1,436	..	..	..	1	..	1
1- 2 ..	*2,101*	1,051	1,050	2,100	1,051	1,049	1	.	1	..	..	..
2- 3 ..	*2,187*	1,102	1,085	2,185	1,102	1,083	2	.	2	.	..	..
3- 4 ..	*2,192*	1,110	1,082	2,190	1,110	1,080	2	..	2	..	..	..
4- 5 ..	*2,130*	1,083	1,047	2,125	1,082	1,043	4	1	3	1	..	1
Total 0- 5 ..	*11,568*	*5,867*	*5,701*	*11,557*	*5,866*	*5,691*	*9*	*1*	*8*	*2*	..	*2*
5- 10 ..	*9,343*	4,975	4,368	9,267	4,961	4,306	71	13	58	5	1	4
10- 15 ..	*8,313*	4,554	3,759	7,857	4,478	3,379	448	73	375	8	3	5
15- 20 ..	*6,029*	3,418	2,611	3,543	2,659	884	2,427	720	1,707	59	39	20
20- 30 ..	*11,710*	6,784	4,926	3,347	2,960	387	8,014	3,582	4,432	349	242	107
30- 40 .	*7,600*	4,329	3,271	587	480	107	6,297	3,413	2,884	716	436	280
40- 50 .	*5,017*	2,773	2,244	207	146	61	3,749	2,120	1,629	1,061	507	554
50- 60 ..	*3,373*	1,857	1,516	104	68	36	2,074	1,246	828	1,195	543	652
60 and over ..	*3,412*	2,022	1,390	64	39	25	1,502	1,086	416	1,846	897	949

TABLE VII.—AGE, SEX

PART B.—DETAILS FOR DISTRICTS AND STATES.

GUJRANWALA DISTRICT.

Religion and Age.	Population.			Unmarried.			Married.			Widowed.		
	Persons.	Males.	Females.	Persons.	Males.	Females.	Persons.	Males.	Females.	Persons.	Males.	Females.
1	2	3	4	5	6	7	8	9	10	11	12	13
ALL RELIGIONS ..	**736,138**	**408,606**	**327,532**	**375,531**	**226,378**	**149,153**	**288,209**	**148,032**	**140,177**	**72,398**	**34,196**	**38,202**
0—1 ..	*28,857*	14,547	14,310	28,857	14,547	14,310	..	..	..	..	..	..
1—2 ..	*21,344*	10,843	10,501	21,342	10,841	10,501	1	1	..	1	1	..
2—3 ..	*22,828*	11,624	11,204	22,821	11,622	11,199	7	2	5	..	..	..
3—4 ..	*23,096*	11,770	11,326	23,074	11,763	11,311	22	7	15	..	..	..
4—5 ..	*22,743*	11,776	10,967	22,698	11,760	10,938	41	13	28	4	3	1
Total 0—5 ..	*118,368*	*60,560*	*58,308*	*118,792*	*60,533*	*58,259*	*71*	*23*	*48*	*5*	*4*	*1*
5—10 ..	*96,335*	51,693	44,642	94,801	51,377	43,424	1,493	305	1,188	41	11	30
10—15 ..	*83,645*	46,530	37,115	77,574	45,227	32,347	5,951	1,254	4,697	120	49	71
15—20 ..	*65,536*	37,059	28,477	35,730	26,905	8,825	28,981	9,696	19,285	825	458	367
20—30 ..	*132,412*	75,279	57.133	33,879	29,326	4,553	93,032	42,489	50,543	5,501	3,464	2,037
30—40 ..	*94,020*	54,546	39,474	8,587	7,696	891	74,652	41,013	33,639	10,781	5,837	4,944
40—50 ..	*65,443*	36,727	28,716	3,350	2,856	494	45,941	26,922	19,019	16,152	6,949	9,203
50—60 ..	*42,790*	24,414	18,376	1,793	1,561	232	23,782	15,493	8,289	17,215	7,360	9,855
60 and over ..	*37,089*	21,798	15,291	1,025	897	128	14,306	10,837	3,469	21,758	10,064	11,694
HINDU ..	**92,762**	**52,201**	**40,561**	**47,507**	**29,154**	**18,353**	**34,865**	**18,645**	**16,220**	**10,390**	**4,402**	**5,988**
0—1 ..	*3,203*	1,592	1,611	3,203	1,592	1,611	..	..	..	..	..	..
1—2 ..	*2,440*	1,233	1,207	2,440	1,233	1,207	..	.	..	..	..	..
2—3 ..	*2,676*	1,364	1,312	2,676	1,364	1,312	..	..	..	..	..	..
3—4 ..	*2,698*	1,368	1,330	2,697	1,367	1,330	1	1	..	..	..	..
4—5 ..	*2,653*	1,372	1,281	2,650	1,370	1,280	3	2	1	..	..	..
Total 0—5 ..	*13,670*	*6,929*	*6,741*	*13,666*	*6,926*	*6,740*	*4*	*3*	*1*	..	..	..
5—10 ..	*11,680*	6,257	5,423	11,543	6,229	5,314	133	27	106	4	1	3
10—15 ..	*10,620*	5,873	4,747	9,974	5,753	4,221	636	115	521	10	5	5
15—20 ..	*8,490*	4,934	3,556	5,077	3,779	1,298	3,304	1,102	2,202	109	53	56
20—30 ..	*16,477*	9,728	6,749	4,713	4,119	594	10,990	5,207	5,783	774	402	372
30—40 ..	*12,243*	7,182	5,061	1,289	1,202	87	9,306	5,291	4,015	1,648	689	959
40—50 ..	*8,887*	5,061	3,826	619	552	67	5,775	3,572	2,203	2,493	937	1,556
50—60 ..	*5,773*	3,379	2,394	348	323	25	2,971	2,032	939	2,454	1,024	1,430
60 and over ..	*4,922*	2,858	2,064	278	271	7	1,746	1,296	450	2,898	1,291	1,607
SIKH ..	**71,595**	**41,075**	**30,520**	**38,712**	**23,738**	**14,974**	**25,171**	**13,609**	**11,562**	**7,712**	**3,728**	**3,984**
0—1 ..	*2,790*	1,454	1,336	2,790	1,454	1,336	..	.	..	..	..	..
1—2 ..	*1,997*	1,053	944	1,996	1,052	944	..	..	..	1	1	..
2—3 ..	*2,126*	1,117	1,009	2,126	1,117	1,009	..	..	..	..	..	..
3—4 ..	*2,123*	1,104	1,019	2,123	1,104	1,019	..	..	..	..	..	..
4—5 ..	*2,075*	1,095	980	2,073	1,094	979	1	.	1	1	1	..
Total 0—5 ..	*11,111*	*5,823*	*5,288*	*11,108*	*5,821*	*5,287*	*1*	..	*1*	*2*	*2*	..
5—10 ..	*9,005*	4,933	4,072	8,868	4,926	3,942	131	6	125	6	1	5
10—15 ..	*7,920*	4,564	3,356	7,419	4,482	2,937	493	79	414	8	3	5
15—20 ..	*6,191*	3,733	2,458	4,400	2,918	1,482	1,734	781	953	57	34	23
20—30 ..	*12,750*	7,413	5,337	4,653	3,520	1,133	7,601	3,600	4,001	496	293	203
30—40 ..	*9,457*	5,656	3,801	1,325	1,227	98	7,019	3,845	3,174	1,113	584	529
40—50 ..	*6,620*	3,897	2,723	516	469	47	4,364	2,632	1,732	1,740	796	944
50—60 ..	*4,604*	2,714	1,890	271	244	27	2,396	1,579	817	1,937	891	1,046
60 and over ..	*3,937*	2,342	1,595	152	131	21	1,432	1,087	345	2,353	1,124	1,229
JAIN ..	**1,071**	**593**	**478**	**629**	**384**	**245**	**347**	**175**	**172**	**95**	**34**	**61**
0—1 ..	*45*	20	25	45	20	25	..	..	..	..	..	..
1—2 ..	*31*	18	13	31	18	13	..	..	..	..	..	..
2—3 ..	*33*	19	14	33	19	14	..	..	..	..	..	
3—4 ..	*33*	18	15	33	18	15	..	..	..	..	..	..
4—5 ..	*34*	20	14	34	20	14	..	.	..	..	..	..
Total 0—5 ..	*176*	*95*	*81*	*176*	*95*	*81*	..	.	..	..	..	..
5—10 ..	*156*	92	64	156	92	64	..	..	.	..	..	..
10—15 ..	*152*	89	63	148	88	60	4	1	3	..	..	..
15—20 ..	*121*	67	54	73	50	23	46	16	30	2	1	1
20—30 ..	*200*	107	93	53	43	10	139	62	77	8	2	6
30—40 ..	*109*	62	47	7	6	1	86	50	36	16	6	10
40—50 ..	*84*	39	45	10	4	6	47	28	19	27	7	20
50—60 ..	*48*	29	19	3	3	..	19	14	5	26	12	14
60 and over ..	*25*	13	12	3	3	..	6	4	2	16	6	10
MUSLIM ..	**521,343**	**287,794**	**233,549**	**263,263**	**158,388**	**104,875**	**208,234**	**105,547**	**102,687**	**49,846**	**23,859**	**25,987**
0—1 ..	*20,632*	10,380	10,252	20,632	10,380	10,252	.	..	..	..	..	..
1—2 ..	*15,239*	7,732	7,507	15,238	7,731	7,507	1	1	..	..	..	..
2—3 ..	*16,272*	8,250	8,022	16,266	8,248	8,018	6	2	4	..	..	..
3—4 ..	*16,550*	8,408	8,142	16,529	8,402	8,127	21	6	15	..	..	..
4—5 ..	*16,326*	8,428	7,898	16,289	8,416	7,873	34	10	24	3	2	1
Total 0—5 ..	*85,019*	*43,198*	*41,821*	*84,954*	*43,177*	*41,777*	*62*	*19*	*43*	*3*	*2*	*1*
5—10 ..	*68,652*	36,707	31,945	67,454	36,438	31,016	1,170	261	909	28	8	20
10—15 ..	*59,136*	32,769	26,367	54,593	31,736	22,857	4,451	995	3,456	92	38	54
15—20 ..	*46,344*	25,921	20,423	24,141	18,655	5,486	21,608	6,927	14,681	595	339	256
20—30 ..	*94,224*	53,212	41,012	22,836	20,277	2,559	67,517	30,405	37,112	3,871	2,530	1,341
30—40 ..	*66,412*	38,352	28,060	5,576	4,945	631	53,543	29,294	24,249	7,293	4,113	3,180
40—50 ..	*45,844*	25,543	20,301	2,070	1,756	314	32,814	18,978	13,836	10,960	4,809	6,151
50—60 ..	*29,799*	16,871	12,928	1,095	938	157	16,901	10,931	5,970	11,803	5,002	6,801
60 and over ..	*25,913*	15,221	10,692	544	466	78	10,168	7,737	2,431	15,201	7,018	8,183
CHRISTIAN ..	**49,364**	**26,940**	**22,424**	**25,419**	**14,713**	**10,706**	**19,590**	**10,054**	**9,536**	**4,355**	**2,173**	**2,182**
0—1 ..	*2,187*	1,101	1,086	2,187	1,101	1,086	..	..	..	..	..	..
1—2 ..	*1,637*	807	830	1,637	807	830	..	..	..	..	..	..
2—3 ..	*1,721*	874	847	1,720	874	846	1	..	1	..	..	..
3—4 ..	*1,692*	872	820	1,692	872	820	..	..	..	..	..	..
4—5 ..	*1,655*	861	794	1,652	860	792	3	1	2	..	..	..
Total 0—5 ..	*8,892*	*4,515*	*4,377*	*8,888*	*4,514*	*4,374*	*4*	*1*	*3*	..	..	..
5—10 ..	*6,842*	3,704	3,138	6,780	3,692	3,088	59	11	48	3	1	2
10—15 ..	*5,816*	3,234	2,582	5,439	3,167	2,272	367	64	303	10	3	7
15—20 ..	*4,390*	2,404	1,986	2,039	1,503	536	2,289	870	1,419	62	31	31
20—30 ..	*8,759*	4,817	3,942	1,624	1,367	257	6,783	3,213	3,570	352	237	115
30—40 ..	*5,799*	3,294	2,505	390	316	74	4,698	2,533	2,165	711	445	266
40—50 ..	*4,008*	2,187	1,821	135	75	60	2,941	1,712	1,229	932	400	532
50—60 ..	*2,566*	1,421	1,145	76	53	23	1,495	937	558	995	431	564
60 and over ..	*2,292*	1,364	928	48	26	22	954	713	241	1,290	625	665

AND CIVIL CONDITION (BY RELIGION).

PART B.—DETAILS FOR DISTRICTS AND STATES—*continued.*

SHEIKHUPURA DISTRICT.

Religion and Age.	Population.			Unmarried.			Married.			Widowed.		
	Persons.	Males.	Females.	Persons.	Males.	Females.	Persons.	Males.	Females.	Persons.	Males.	Females.
1	2	3	4	5	6	7	8	9	10	11	12	13
ALL RELIGIONS	**696,732**	**384,390**	**312,342**	**365,310**	**217,321**	**147,989**	**276,137**	**141,043**	**135,094**	**55,285**	**26,026**	**29,259**
0—1	*30,067*	15,183	14,884	30,066	15,183	14,883	1	..	1	..	..	..
1—2	*22,280*	11,167	11,113	22,273	11,166	11,107	6	1	5	1	..	1
2—3	*23,654*	11,954	11,700	23,641	11,948	11,693	12	6	6	1	..	1
3—4	*23,574*	12,150	11,424	23,541	12,137	11,404	31	12	19	2	1	1
4—5	*22,726*	11,990	10,736	22,661	11,968	10,693	56	19	37	9	3	6
Total 0—5	*122,301*	*62,444*	*59,857*	*122,182*	*62,402*	*59,780*	*106*	*38*	*68*	*13*	*4*	*9*
5—10	*96,707*	52,415	44,292	94,516	51,832	42,684	2,145	567	1,578	46	16	30
10—15	*84,574*	46,949	37,625	77,129	44,991	32,138	7,335	1,906	5,429	110	52	58
15—20	*63,059*	35,536	27,523	32,614	24,621	7,993	29,668	10,443	19,225	777	472	305
20—30	*121,261*	67,896	53,365	27,863	23,965	3,898	88,972	41,199	47,773	4,426	2,732	1,694
30—40	*82,562*	46,863	35,699	6,450	5,625	825	68,127	37,031	31,096	7,985	4,207	3,778
40—50	*56,287*	32,054	24,233	2,499	2,135	364	42,161	24,625	17,536	11,627	5,294	6,333
50—60	*35,880*	20,640	15,240	1,187	1,011	176	22,541	14,384	8,157	12,152	5,245	6,907
60 and over	*34,101*	19,593	14,508	870	739	131	15,082	10,850	4,232	18,149	8,004	10,145
HINDU	**70,146**	**40,133**	**30,013**	**35,860**	**22,154**	**13,706**	**28,030**	**15,060**	**12,970**	**6,256**	**2,919**	**3,337**
0—1	*2,739*	1,359	1,380	2,739	1,359	1,380	..	..	..	..	..	..
1—2	*2,045*	1,042	1,003	2,045	1,042	1,003	..	..	..	..	..	..
2—3	*2,177*	1,123	1,054	2,175	1,122	1,053	1	1	..	1	..	1
3—4	*2,175*	1,105	1,070	2,174	1,105	1,069	1	..	1	..	..	..
4—5	*2,082*	1,068	1,014	2,077	1,066	1,011	4	2	2	1	..	1
Total 0—5	*11,218*	*5,697*	*5,521*	*11,210*	*5,694*	*5,516*	*6*	*3*	*3*	*2*	..	*2*
5—10	*9,227*	4,975	4,252	9,029	4,923	4,106	192	50	142	6	2	4
10—15	*8,306*	4,671	3,635	7,556	4,462	3,094	739	202	537	11	7	4
15—20	*6,706*	3,983	2,723	3,368	2,714	654	3,252	1,219	2,033	86	50	36
20—30	*13,019*	7,831	5,188	3,065	2,843	222	9,413	4,678	4,735	541	310	231
30—40	*8,959*	5,377	3,582	874	818	56	7,064	4,047	3,017	1,021	512	509
40—50	*5,913*	3,512	2,371	388	356	32	4,105	2,534	1,571	1,420	652	768
50—60	*3,593*	2,184	1,409	198	181	17	2,031	1,402	629	1,364	601	763
60 and over	*3,205*	1,873	1,332	172	163	9	1,228	925	303	1,805	785	1,020
SIKH	**119,477**	**66,762**	**52,715**	**61,337**	**37,942**	**23,395**	**47,966**	**24,176**	**23,790**	**10,174**	**4,644**	**5,530**
0—1	*5,191*	2,633	2,558	5,191	2,633	2,558	..	..	..	..	..	..
1—2	*3,599*	1,857	1,742	3,599	1,857	1,742	..	..	..	..	..	..
2—3	*3,830*	2,021	1,809	3,830	2,021	1,809	..	..	..	..	..	..
3—4	*3,902*	2,078	1,824	3,900	2,077	1,823	2	1	1	..	..	..
4—5	*3,735*	2,011	1,724	3,728	2,008	1,720	7	3	4	..	..	..
Total 0—5	*20,257*	*10,600*	*9,657*	*20,248*	*10,596*	*9,652*	*9*	*4*	*5*	..	..	..
5—10	*16,167*	8,930	7,237	15,837	8,856	6,981	321	70	251	9	4	5
10—15	*14,301*	8,116	6,185	13,044	7,835	5,209	1,231	269	962	26	12	14
15—20	*10,749*	6,156	4,593	5,372	4,336	1,036	5,261	1,750	3,511	116	70	46
20—30	*20,441*	11,360	9,081	4,541	4,218	323	15,200	6,702	8,498	700	440	260
30—40	*14,302*	8,221	6,081	1,258	1,168	90	11,704	6,337	5,367	1,340	716	624
40—50	*10,122*	5,790	4,332	558	505	53	7,463	4,364	3,099	2,101	921	1,180
50—60	*6,665*	3,869	2,796	285	254	31	4,040	2,626	1,414	2,340	989	1,351
60 and over	*6,473*	3,720	2,753	194	174	20	2,737	2,054	683	3,542	1,492	2,050
JAIN	**100**	**53**	**47**	**63**	**33**	**30**	**33**	**17**	**16**	**4**	**3**	**1**
0—1	*4*	1	3	4	1	3	..	..	..	..	..	..
1—2	*2*	1	1	2	1	1	..	..	..	..	..	..
2—3	*3*	..	3	3	..	3	..	..	..	..	..	..
3—4	*2*	1	1	2	1	1	..	..	..	..	..	..
4—5	*4*	2	2	4	2	2	..	..	..	..	..	..
Total 0—5	*15*	*5*	*10*	*15*	*5*	*10*	..	..	..	..	..	..
5—10	*17*	10	7	17	10	7	..	..	..	..	..	..
10—15	*18*	9	9	18	9	9	..	..	..	..	..	..
15—20	*10*	6	4	8	5	3	2	1	1	..	..	..
20—30	*11*	5	6	5	4	1	6	1	5	..	..	..
30—40	*14*	6	8	..	..	..	14	6	8	..	..	..
40—50	*12*	10	2	..	..	..	10	8	2	2	2	..
50—60	*3*	2	1	..	..	..	1	1	..	2	1	1
60 and over	..	..	..	..	..	..	..	..	..	..	..	..
MUSLIM	**445,996**	**244,064**	**201,932**	**235,487**	**138,237**	**97,250**	**176,030**	**89,624**	**86,406**	**34,479**	**16,203**	**18,276**
0—1	*19,312*	9,796	9,516	19,311	9,796	9,515	1	..	1	..	..	..
1—2	*14,616*	7,281	7,335	14,609	7,280	7,329	6	1	5	1	..	1
2—3	*15,489*	7,733	7,756	15,478	7,728	7,750	11	5	6	..	..	..
3—4	*15,327*	7,874	7,453	15,298	7,862	7,436	27	11	16	2	1	1
4—5	*14,804*	7,840	6,964	14,755	7,823	6,932	42	14	28	7	3	4
Total 0—5	*79,548*	*40,524*	*39,024*	*79,451*	*40,489*	*38,962*	*87*	*31*	*56*	*10*	*4*	*6*
5—10	*62,245*	33,654	28,591	60,870	33,291	27,579	1,348	354	994	27	9	18
10—15	*54,060*	29,766	24,294	49,435	28,541	20,894	4,559	1,196	3,363	66	29	37
15—20	*40,149*	22,363	17,786	21,126	15,489	5,637	18,507	6,564	11,943	516	310	206
20—30	*77,590*	43,100	34,490	18,155	15,085	3,070	56,632	26,287	30,345	2,803	1,728	1,075
30—40	*52,357*	29,299	23,058	3,915	3,281	634	43,453	23,421	20,032	4,989	2,597	2,392
40—50	*35,543*	20,045	15,498	1,415	1,162	253	26,936	15,618	11,318	7,192	3,265	3,927
50—60	*22,738*	12,906	9,832	647	526	121	14,599	9,161	5,438	7,492	3,219	4,273
60 and over	*21,766*	12,407	9,359	473	373	100	9,909	6,992	2,917	11,384	5,042	6,342
CHRISTIAN	**49,266**	**26,895**	**22,371**	**27,035**	**15,635**	**11,400**	**18,627**	**9,432**	**9,195**	**3,604**	**1,828**	**1,776**
0—1	*2,221*	1,067	1,154	2,221	1,067	1,154	..	..	..	..	..	..
1—2	*1,631*	794	837	1,631	794	837	..	..	..	..	..	..
2—3	*1,752*	885	867	1,752	885	867	..	..	..	..	..	..
3—4	*1,758*	888	870	1,758	888	870	..	..	..	..	..	..
4—5	*1,703*	862	841	1,702	862	840	1	..	1	..	..	..
Total 0—5	*9,065*	*4,496*	*4,569*	*9,064*	*4,496*	*4,568*	*1*	..	*1*	..	..	..
5—10	*7,297*	3,898	3,399	7,232	3,886	3,346	63	12	51	2	..	2
10—15	*6,322*	3,510	2,812	5,958	3,441	2,517	362	68	294	2	1	1
15—20	*4,425*	2,451	1,974	2,430	1,809	621	1,950	612	1,338	45	30	15
20—30	*8,352*	4,584	3,768	1,833	1,564	269	6,204	2,819	3,385	315	201	114
30—40	*5,580*	3,186	2,394	335	290	45	4,725	2,600	2,125	520	296	224
40—50	*3,748*	2,115	1,633	117	91	26	2,881	1,665	1,216	750	359	391
50—60	*2,309*	1,345	964	41	35	6	1,465	943	522	803	367	436
60 and over	*2,168*	1,310	858	25	23	2	976	713	263	1,167	574	593

TABLE VII.—AGE, SEX

PART B.—DETAILS FOR DISTRICTS AND STATES

GUJRAT DISTRICT.

Religion and Age.	Population.			Unmarried.			Married.			Widowed.		
	Persons.	Males.	Females.	Persons.	Males.	Females.	Persons.	Males.	Females.	Persons.	Males.	Females.
1	2	3	4	5	6	7	8	9	10	11	12	13
ALL RELIGIONS ..	**922,427**	**498,336**	**424,091**	**450,379**	**271,463**	**178,916**	**384,824**	**187,821**	**197,003**	**87,224**	**39,052**	**48,172**
0—1 ..	*35,659*	18,037	17,622	35,648	18,030	17,618	9	6	3	2	1	1
1—2 ..	*26,540*	13,458	13,082	26,521	13,449	13,072	16	6	10	3	3	..
2—3 ..	*28,536*	14,661	13,875	28,489	14,641	13,848	44	17	27	3	3	..
3—4 ..	*29,559*	15,275	14,284	29,425	15,239	14,186	127	34	93	7	2	5
4—5 ..	*29,399*	15,143	14,256	29,182	15,090	14,092	200	47	153	17	6	11
Total 0—5 ..	*149,693*	*76,574*	*73,119*	*149,265*	*76,449*	*72,816*	*396*	*110*	*286*	*32*	*15*	*17*
5—10 ..	*125,099*	66,865	58,234	119,183	65,456	53,727	5,769	1,345	4,424	147	64	83
10—15 ..	*108,762*	60,009	48,753	94,738	56,457	38,281	13,756	3,430	10,326	268	122	146
15—20 ..	*76,580*	42,104	34,476	37,879	29,800	8,079	37,704	11,742	25,962	997	562	435
20—30 ..	*150,105*	80,260	69,845	33,544	29,861	3,683	110,709	47,069	63,640	5,852	3,330	2,522
30—40 ..	*115,623*	63,511	52,112	8,763	7,672	1,091	95,268	50,104	45,164	11,592	5,735	5,857
40—50 ..	*85,483*	46,646	38,837	3,841	3,205	636	63,229	35,805	27,424	18,413	7,636	10,777
50—60 ..	*58,172*	32,496	25,676	1,858	1,523	335	35,284	22,330	12,954	21,030	8,643	12,387
60 and over ..	*52,910*	29,871	23,039	1,308	1,040	268	22,709	15,886	6,823	28,893	12,945	15,948
HINDU ..	**72,346**	**39,425**	**32,921**	**36,477**	**22,312**	**14,165**	**28,711**	**14,402**	**14,309**	**7,158**	**2,711**	**4,447**
0—1 ..	*2,643*	1,368	1,275	2,643	1,368	1,275	..	..	..	..	..	..
1—2 ..	*1,994*	989	1,005	1,994	989	1,005	..	..	..	..	..	..
2—3 ..	*2,243*	1,124	1,119	2,239	1,123	1,116	4	1	3	..	..	..
3—4 ..	*2,294*	1,179	1,115	2,286	1,177	1,109	8	2	6			
4—5 ..	*2,239*	1,162	1,077	2,229	1,158	1,071	10	4	6	..	..	..
Total 0—5 ..	*11,413*	*5,822*	*5,591*	*11,391*	*5,815*	*5,576*	*22*	*7*	*15*	..	..	..
5—10 ..	*9,619*	5,076	4,543	9,278	4,998	4,280	336	77	259	5	1	4
10—15 ..	*8,617*	4,679	3,938	7,623	4,443	3,180	976	230	746	18	6	12
15—20 ..	*6,416*	3,553	2,863	3,328	2,670	658	3,007	847	2,160	81	36	45
20—30 ..	*12,253*	6,785	5,468	3,031	2,773	258	8,690	3,792	4,898	532	220	312
30—40 ..	*9,245*	5,203	4,042	965	855	110	7,201	3,974	3,227	1,079	374	705
40—50 ..	*6,649*	3,709	2,940	485	426	59	4,579	2,759	1,820	1,585	524	1,061
50—60 ..	*4,412*	2,497	1,915	228	202	26	2,423	1,605	818	1,761	690	1,071
60 and over ..	*3,722*	2,101	1,621	148	130	18	1,477	1,111	366	2,097	860	1,237
SIKH ..	**59,188**	**30,795**	**28,393**	**28,836**	**16,984**	**11,852**	**25,456**	**12,008**	**13,448**	**4,896**	**1,803**	**3,093**
0—1 ..	*2,334*	1,198	1,136	2,333	1,197	1,136	1	1	..	..	..	..
1—2 ..	*1,858*	943	915	1,855	943	912	3	..	3	..	..	..
2—3 ..	*1,966*	1,010	956	1,962	1,010	952	4	..	4	..	..	..
3—4 ..	*1,982*	1,033	949	1,972	1,031	941	10	2	8	..	..	..
4—5 ..	*1,978*	1,036	942	1,955	1,031	924	22	5	17	1	..	1
Total 0—5 ..	*10,118*	*5,220*	*4,898*	*10,077*	*5,212*	*4,865*	*40*	*8*	*32*	*1*	..	*1*
5—10 ..	*8,463*	4,512	3,951	7,989	4,414	3,575	463	94	369	11	4	7
10—15 ..	*7,486*	4,001	3,485	6,319	3,737	2,582	1,147	256	891	20	8	12
15—20 ..	*5,202*	2,619	2,583	2,172	1,673	499	2,964	921	2,043	66	25	41
20—30 ..	*9,207*	4,469	4,738	1,466	1,283	183	7,418	3,063	4,355	323	123	200
30—40 ..	*6,957*	3,515	3,442	393	317	76	5,899	2,983	2,916	665	215	450
40—50 ..	*5,268*	2,777	2,491	211	169	42	4,003	2,262	1,741	1,054	346	708
50—60 ..	*3,432*	1,939	1,493	122	103	19	2,151	1,409	742	1,159	427	732
60 and over ..	*3,055*	1,743	1,312	87	76	11	1,371	1,012	359	1,597	655	942
JAIN ..	**32**	**18**	**14**	**19**	**12**	**7**	**11**	**5**	**6**	**2**	**1**	**1**
0—1 ..	*1*	1	..	1	1	..	..	..	..	..	..	..
1—2 ..	*1*	1	..	1	1	..	..	..	..	..	..	..
2—3 ..	*2*	1	1	2	1	1	..	..	..	..	..	..
3—4 ..	..	..	..	..	..	..	..	..	..	..	..	..
4—5 ..	*2*	1	1	2	1	1	..	..	..	..	..	..
Total 0—5 ..	*6*	*4*	*2*	*6*	*4*	*2*	..	..	..	..	..	..
5—10 ..	*5*	3	2	5	3	2	..	..	..	..	..	..
10—15 ..	*3*	1	2	3	1	2	..	..	..	..	..	..
15—20 ..	*6*	3	3	3	2	1	3	1	2	..	..	..
20—30 ..	*5*	3	2	2	2	..	3	1	2	..	..	..
30—40 ..	*2*	1	1	..	..	..	2	1	1	..	..	..
40—50 ..	*2*	1	1	..	..	..	2	1	1	..	..	..
50—60 ..	*3*	2	1	..	..	..	1	1	..	2	1	1
60 and over ..	..	..	..	..	..	..	..	..	..	..	..	..
MUSLIM ..	**786,750**	**425,716**	**361,034**	**382,979**	**230,907**	**152,072**	**328,919**	**160,470**	**168,449**	**74,852**	**34,339**	**40,513**
0—1 ..	*30,504*	15,383	15,121	30,494	15,377	15,117	8	5	3	2	1	1
1—2 ..	*22,565*	11,461	11,104	22,549	11,452	11,097	13	6	7	3	3	..
2—3 ..	*24,202*	12,454	11,748	24,163	12,435	11,728	36	16	20	3	3	..
3—4 ..	*25,152*	12,992	12,160	25,036	12,960	12,076	109	30	79	7	2	5
4—5 ..	*25,044*	12,870	12,174	24,860	12,826	12,034	168	38	130	16	6	10
Total 0—5 ..	*127,467*	*65,160*	*62,307*	*127,102*	*65,050*	*62,052*	*334*	*95*	*239*	*31*	*15*	*16*
5—10 ..	*106,457*	56,969	49,488	101,375	55,741	45,634	4,952	1,170	3,782	130	58	72
10—15 ..	*92,173*	51,060	41,113	80,369	48,026	32,343	11,578	2,928	8,650	226	106	120
15—20 ..	*64,578*	35,714	28,864	32,205	25,326	6,879	31,534	9,896	21,638	839	492	347
20—30 ..	*127,851*	68,532	59,319	28,875	25,657	3,218	94,025	39,925	54,100	4,951	2,950	2,001
30—40 ..	*98,824*	54,437	44,387	7,355	6,464	891	81,685	42,869	38,816	9,784	5,104	4,680
40—50 ..	*73,217*	39,943	33,274	3,127	2,598	529	54,381	30,615	23,766	15,709	6,730	8,979
50—60 ..	*50,167*	27,954	22,213	1,502	1,214	288	30,611	19,241	11,370	18,054	7,499	10,555
60 and over ..	*46,016*	25,947	20,069	1,069	831	238	19,819	13,731	6,088	25,128	11,385	13,743
CHRISTIAN ..	**3,097**	**1,746**	**1,351**	**1,712**	**1,016**	**696**	**1,160**	**602**	**558**	**225**	**128**	**97**
0—1 ..	*132*	64	68	132	64	68	..	..	..	..	..	..
1—2 ..	*104*	57	47	104	57	47	..	..	..	..	..	..
2—3 ..	*102*	59	43	102	59	43	..	..	..	..	..	..
3—4 ..	*106*	55	51	106	55	51	..	..	..	..	..	..
4—5 ..	*109*	58	51	109	58	51	..	..	..	..	..	..
Total 0—5 ..	*553*	*293*	*260*	*553*	*293*	*260*	..	..	..	..	..	..
5—10 ..	*443*	238	205	435	237	198	8	1	7	..	..	..
10—15 ..	*377*	204	173	351	200	151	25	4	21	1	..	1
15—20 ..	*277*	159	118	155	114	41	116	40	76	6	5	1
20—30 ..	*534*	317	217	151	128	23	354	166	188	29	23	6
30—40 ..	*411*	223	188	41	27	14	330	174	156	40	22	18
40—50 ..	*263*	158	105	16	10	6	202	125	77	45	23	22
50—60 ..	*137*	87	50	6	4	2	84	61	23	47	22	25
60 and over ..	*102*	67	35	4	3	1	41	31	10	57	33	24

AND CIVIL CONDITION (BY RELIGION).

PART B.—DETAILS FOR DISTRICTS AND STATES—*continued.*

SHAHPUR DISTRICT.

Religion and Age.	Population.			Unmarried.			Married.			Widowed.		
	Persons.	Males.	Females.	Persons.	Males.	Females.	Persons.	Males.	Females.	Persons.	Males.	Females.
1	2	3	4	5	6	7	8	9	10	11	12	13
ALL RELIGIONS	**821,490**	**445,836**	**375,654**	**430,753**	**256,607**	**174,146**	**326,727**	**163,538**	**163,189**	**64,010**	**25,691**	**38,319**
0-1	*29,011*	14,494	14,517	29,003	14,492	14,511	7	2	5	1	..	1
1-2	*21,301*	10,753	10,548	21,285	10,751	10,534	16	2	14	..	..	..
2-3	*25,066*	12,547	12,519	25,028	12,536	12,492	37	11	26	1	..	1
3-4	*27,374*	13,998	13,376	27,316	13,979	13,337	53	18	35	5	1	4
4-5	*27,986*	14,683	13,303	27,902	14,657	13,246	74	24	50	10	2	8
Total 0-5	*130,738*	*66,475*	*64,263*	*130,534*	*66,415*	*64,119*	*187*	*57*	*130*	*17*	*3*	*14*
5-10	*115,791*	62,623	53,168	113,768	62,116	51,652	1,970	491	1,479	53	16	37
10-15	*98,893*	54,673	44,220	91,580	53,036	38,544	7,181	1,594	5,587	132	43	89
15-20	*73,000*	39,800	33,200	40,457	29,833	10,624	31,715	9,593	22,122	828	374	454
20-30	*141,186*	75,685	65,501	37,422	31,306	6,116	98,635	41,812	56,823	5,129	2,567	2,562
30-40	*105,195*	57,796	47,399	10,728	8,909	1,819	84,970	44,867	40,103	9,497	4,020	5,477
40-50	*72,532*	39,470	33,062	3,394	2,708	686	55,053	31,855	23,198	14,085	4,907	9,178
50-60	*46,992*	27,374	19,618	1,829	1,469	360	29,984	20,322	9,662	15,179	5,583	9,596
60 and over	*37,163*	21,940	15,223	1,041	815	226	17,032	12,947	4,085	19,090	8,178	10,912
HINDU	**88,970**	**48,641**	**40,329**	**44,007**	**26,617**	**17,390**	**36,799**	**19,142**	**17,657**	**8,164**	**2,882**	**5,282**
0-1	*3,215*	1,626	1,589	3,212	1,625	1,587	3	1	2	..	..	..
1-2	*2,206*	1,118	1,088	2,204	1,118	1,086	2	..	2	..	..	..
2-3	*2,692*	1,348	1,344	2,686	1,345	1,341	6	3	3	..	..	..
3-4	*2,799*	1,423	1,376	2,789	1,419	1,370	9	4	5	1	..	1
4-5	*2,713*	1,424	1,289	2,697	1,418	1,279	14	6	8	2	..	2
Total 0-5	*13,625*	*6,939*	*6,686*	*13,588*	*6,925*	*6,663*	*34*	*14*	*20*	*3*	..	*3*
5-10	*11,932*	6,286	5,646	11,523	6,172	5,351	399	112	287	10	2	8
10-15	*10,713*	5,824	4,889	9,499	5,525	3,974	1,190	290	900	24	9	15
15-20	*8,341*	4,751	3,590	4,012	3,276	736	4,204	1,417	2,787	125	58	67
20-30	*15,939*	8,820	7,119	3,431	3,113	318	11,757	5,393	6,364	751	314	437
30-40	*11,858*	6,651	5,207	1,033	829	204	9,428	5,309	4,119	1,397	513	884
40-50	*8,058*	4,564	3,494	469	391	78	5,621	3,555	2,066	1,968	618	1,350
50-60	*4,946*	2,809	2,137	275	239	36	2,765	1,951	814	1,906	619	1,287
60 and over	*3,558*	1,997	1,561	177	147	30	1,401	1,101	300	1,980	749	1,231
SIKH	**40,074**	**22,200**	**17,874**	**20,977**	**12,736**	**8,241**	**16,185**	**8,216**	**7,969**	**2,912**	**1,248**	**1,664**
0-1	*1,609*	820	789	1,609	820	789	..	..	..	..	..	..
1-2	*1,062*	552	510	1,061	552	509	1	..	1	..	..	..
2-3	*1,269*	674	595	1,265	673	592	4	1	3	..	..	..
3-4	*1,348*	705	643	1,344	703	641	4	2	2	..	..	..
4-5	*1,327*	678	649	1,323	676	647	4	2	2	..	..	..
Total 0-5	*6,615*	*3,429*	*3,186*	*6,602*	*3,424*	*3,178*	*13*	*5*	*8*	..	..	..
5-10	*5,723*	3,054	2,669	5,592	3,021	2,571	128	31	97	3	2	1
10-15	*5,062*	2,823	2,239	4,596	2,729	1,867	459	90	369	7	4	3
15-20	*3,784*	2,128	1,656	1,870	1,502	368	1,879	610	1,269	35	16	19
20-30	*6,936*	3,791	3,145	1,547	1,390	157	5,130	2,272	2,858	259	129	130
30-40	*4,979*	2,831	2,148	433	380	53	4,073	2,250	1,823	473	201	272
40-50	*3,272*	1,906	1,366	177	149	28	2,472	1,524	948	623	233	390
50-60	*1,989*	1,183	806	100	86	14	1,275	854	421	614	243	371
60 and over	*1,714*	1,055	659	60	55	5	756	580	176	898	420	478
JAIN	**14**	**8**	**6**	**9**	**6**	**3**	**5**	**2**	**3**	..	..	..
0-1	..	..	..	..	..	..	..	..	..	..	..	..
1-2	..	..	..	..	..	..	..	..	..	..	..	..
2-3	*1*	..	1	1	..	1	..	..	..	..	..	..
3-4	..	..	..	..	..	..	..	..	..	..	..	..
4-5	*1*	1	..	1	1	..	..	..	..	..	..	..
Total 0-5	*2*	*1*	*1*	*2*	*1*	*1*	..	..	..	..	..	..
5-10	*2*	1	1	2	1	1	..	..	..	..	..	..
10-15	*2*	1	1	2	1	1	..	..	..	..	..	..
15-20	..	..	..	..	..	..	..	..	..	..	..	..
20-30	*4*	3	1	2	2	..	2	1	1	..	..	..
30-40	*1*	1	..	1	1	..	..	..	..	..	..	..
40-50	*3*	1	2	..	..	..	3	1	2	..	..	..
50-60	..	..	..	..	..	..	..	..	..	..	..	..
60 and over	..	..	..	..	..	..	..	..	..	..	..	..
MUSLIM	**679,546**	**367,879**	**311,667**	**358,545**	**213,035**	**145,510**	**268,915**	**133,728**	**135,187**	**52,086**	**21,116**	**30,970**
0-1	*23,654*	11,778	11,876	23,649	11,777	11,872	4	1	3	1	..	1
1-2	*17,613*	8,873	8,740	17,600	8,871	8,729	13	2	11	..	..	..
2-3	*20,660*	10,307	10,353	20,632	10,300	10,332	27	7	20	1	..	1
3-4	*22,781*	11,651	11,130	22,737	11,638	11,099	40	12	28	4	1	3
4-5	*23,497*	12,347	11,150	23,434	12,330	11,104	55	15	40	8	2	6
Total 0-5	*108,205*	*54,956*	*53,249*	*108,052*	*54,916*	*53,136*	*139*	*37*	*102*	*14*	*3*	*11*
5-10	*96,212*	52,258	43,954	94,770	51,910	42,860	1,402	336	1,066	40	12	28
10-15	*81,416*	45,096	36,320	75,920	43,881	32,039	5,396	1,185	4,211	100	30	70
15-20	*59,633*	32,221	27,412	33,871	24,532	9,339	25,104	7,393	17,711	658	296	362
20-30	*116,123*	61,822	54,301	31,872	26,323	5,549	80,211	33,424	46,787	4,040	2,075	1,965
30-40	*86,842*	47,464	39,378	9,127	7,597	1,530	70,243	36,655	33,588	7,472	3,212	4,260
40-50	*60,226*	32,428	27,798	2,698	2,133	565	46,225	26,338	19,887	11,303	3,957	7,346
50-60	*39,470*	23,033	16,437	1,440	1,135	305	25,555	17,268	8,287	12,475	4,630	7,845
60 and over	*31,419*	18,601	12,818	795	608	187	14,640	11,092	3,548	15,984	6,901	9,083
CHRISTIAN	**11,294**	**6,223**	**5,071**	**6,484**	**3,787**	**2,697**	**4,088**	**2,069**	**2,019**	**722**	**367**	**355**
0-1	*478*	244	234	478	244	234	..	..	..	..	..	..
1-2	*376*	189	187	376	189	187	..	..	..	..	..	..
2-3	*405*	209	196	405	209	196	..	..	..	..	..	..
3-4	*402*	205	197	402	205	197	..	..	..	..	..	..
4-5	*393*	203	190	392	202	190	1	1	..	..	..	..
Total 0-5	*2,054*	*1,050*	*1,004*	*2,053*	*1,049*	*1,004*	*1*	*1*	..	..	..	..
5-10	*1,6,5*	892	783	1,669	892	777	6	..	6	..	..	..
10-15	*1,478*	810	668	1,403	802	601	74	8	66	1	..	1
15-20	*1,084*	611	473	652	480	172	424	128	296	8	3	5
20-30	*1,898*	1,065	833	529	440	89	1,309	590	719	60	35	25
30-40	*1,339*	750	589	115	84	31	1,095	593	502	129	73	56
40-50	*844*	498	346	43	29	14	636	384	252	165	85	80
50-60	*506*	300	206	11	6	5	337	216	121	158	78	80
60 and over	*416*	247	169	9	5	4	206	149	57	201	93	108

TABLE VII.—AGE, SEX

PART B.—DETAILS FOR DISTRICTS AND STATES.

JHELUM DISTRICT.

Religion and Age.	Population. Persons.	Population. Males.	Population. Females.	Unmarried. Persons.	Unmarried. Males.	Unmarried. Females.	Married. Persons.	Married. Males.	Married. Females.	Widowed. Persons.	Widowed. Males.	Widowed. Females.
1	2	3	4	5	6	7	8	9	10	11	12	13
ALL RELIGIONS ..	**541,076**	**282,714**	**258,362**	**256,913**	**154,809**	**102,104**	**225,464**	**106,052**	**119,412**	**58,699**	**21,853**	**36,846**
0—1 ..	*18,275*	9,292	8,983	18,268	9,280	8,979	7	3	4	..	..	..
1—2 ..	*13,921*	7,112	6,809	13,908	7,109	6,799	11	3	8	2	..	2
2—3 ..	*16,176*	8,297	7,879	16,142	8,291	7,851	32	6	26	2	..	2
3—4 ..	*17,218*	8,875	8,343	17,139	8,859	8,280	74	15	59	5	1	4
4—5 ..	*16,924*	8,803	8,121	16,801	8,774	8,027	112	27	85	11	2	9
Total 0—5 ..	*82,514*	*42,379*	*40,135*	*82,268*	*42,322*	*39,936*	*236*	*54*	*182*	*20*	*3*	*17*
5—10 ..	*70,773*	38,094	32 679	68,417	37,625	30,792	2,282	451	1,831	74	18	56
10—15 ..	*61,438*	33,711	27,727	54,748	32,453	22,295	6,538	1,218	5,320	152	40	112
15—20 ..	*45,024*	23,535	21,489	22,782	17,598	5,184	21,616	5,701	15,915	626	236	390
20—30 ..	*87,591*	42,560	45,031	19,569	17,140	2,429	64,135	23,701	40,434	3,887	1,719	2,168
30—40 ..	*70,639*	36,497	34,142	5,268	4,580	688	57,200	28,840	28,360	8,171	3,077	5,094
40—50 ..	*52,127*	27,266	24,861	2,053	1,644	409	37,514	21,375	16,139	12,560	4,247	8,313
50—60 ..	*35,878*	19,218	16,660	1,018	809	209	21,204	13,579	7,625	13,656	4,830	8,826
60 and over ..	*36,092*	19,454	15,638	800	638	162	14,739	11,133	3,606	19,553	7,683	11,870
HINDU ..	**36,068**	**19,155**	**16,913**	**17,510**	**10,663**	**6,847**	**14,266**	**7,238**	**7,028**	**4,292**	**1,254**	**3,038**
0—1 ..	*1,249*	636	613	1,247	635	612	2	1	1		..	
1—2 ..	*899*	459	440	897	459	438	2	..	2	..	..	..
2—3 ..	*1,031*	512	519	1,028	511	517	3	1	2	..		..
3—4 ..	*1,090*	548	542	1,088	547	541	2	1	1	..	..	..
4—5 ..	*1,079*	552	527	1,075	551	524	3	1	2	1	..	1
Total 0—5 ..	*5,348*	*2,707*	*2,641*	*5,335*	*2,703*	*2,632*	*12*	*4*	*8*	*1*	..	*1*
5—10 ..	*4,705*	2,468	2,237	4,575	2,444	2,131	124	23	101	6	1	5
10—15 ..	*4,192*	2,228	1,964	3,778	2,168	1,610	400	57	343	14	3	11
15—20 ..	*3,210*	1,778	1,432	1,660	1,340	320	1,492	419	1,073	58	19	39
20—30 ..	*6,016*	3,336	2,680	1,466	1,373	93	4,217	1,849	2,368	333	114	219
30—40 ..	*4,669*	2,553	2,116	362	328	34	3,645	2,044	1,601	662	181	481
40—50 ..	*3,461*	1,758	1,703	167	151	16	2,312	1,353	959	982	254	728
50—60 ..	*2,285*	1,188	1,097	95	90	5	1,234	835	399	956	263	693
60 and over ..	*2,182*	1,139	1,043	72	66	6	830	654	176	1,280	419	861
SIKH ..	**22,030**	**11,409**	**10,621**	**10,753**	**6,466**	**4,287**	**8,395**	**4,224**	**4,671**	**2,382**	**719**	**1,663**
0—1 ..	*784*	416	368	784	416	368	..	..	..	..	..	..
1—2 ..	*622*	314	308	621	314	307	..	..	..	..	..	1
2—3 ..	*681*	349	332	680	349	331	1	..	1	..	..	..
3—4 ..	*696*	359	337	695	359	336	1	..	1	..	..	..
4—5 ..	*693*	362	331	687	360	327	5	2	3	1	..	1
Total 0—5 ..	*3,476*	*1,800*	*1,676*	*3,467*	*1,798*	*1,669*	*7*	*2*	*5*	*2*	..	*2*
5—10 ..	*3,015*	1,578	1,437	2,895	1,557	1,338	117	21	96	3	..	3
10—15 ..	*2,653*	1,378	1,275	2,321	1,324	997	326	53	273	6	1	5
15—20 ..	*1,882*	983	899	897	716	181	959	260	699	26	7	19
20—30 ..	*3,460*	1,789	1,671	790	732	58	2,518	1,006	1,512	152	51	101
30—40 ..	*2,596*	1,280	1,316	199	178	21	2,058	1,026	1,032	339	76	263
40—50 ..	*2,010*	995	1,015	86	75	11	1,439	805	634	485	115	370
50—60 ..	*1,425*	757	668	57	50	7	841	562	279	527	145	382
60 and over ..	*1,513*	849	664	41	36	5	630	489	141	842	324	518
JAIN ..	**209**	**106**	**103**	**115**	**68**	**47**	**69**	**29**	**40**	**25**	**9**	**16**
0—1 ..	*8*	4	4	8	4	4	..		..	..	..	..
1—2 ..	*4*	2	2	4	2	2	..	..	..	..	..	..
2—3 ..	*6*	2	4	6	2	4	..	..	..	..	..	..
3—4 ..	*6*	3	3	6	3	3	..	..	..	..		..
4—5 ..	*7*	4	3	7	4	3	..	..	..	..	..	..
Total 0—5 ..	*31*	*15*	*16*	*31*	*15*	*16*	..	..	..	..	..	..
5—10 ..	*27*	16	11	27	16	11	..	..	..	..	..	..
10—15 ..	*26*	14	12	25	14	11	1	..	1	..	..	..
15—20 ..	*22*	7	15	12	6	6	10	1	9	..	..	..
20—30 ..	*36*	16	20	10	8	2	25	7	18	1	1	..
30—40 ..	*28*	15	13	5	5	..	19	10	9	4	..	4
40—50 ..	*16*	11	5	2	2	..	9	7	2	5	2	3
50—60 ..	*12*	8	4	..	..	..	5	4	1	7	4	3
60 and over ..	*11*	4	7	3	2	1	..	..	..	8	2	6
MUSLIM ..	**482,097**	**251,656**	**230,441**	**228,172**	**137,407**	**90,765**	**201,967**	**94,405**	**107,562**	**51,958**	**19,844**	**32,114**
0—1 ..	*16,212*	8,224	7,988	16,207	8,222	7,985	5	2	3		..	..
1—2 ..	*12,373*	6,328	6,045	12,363	6,325	6,038	9	3	6	1	..	1
2—3 ..	*14,440*	7,428	7,012	14,410	7,423	6,987	28	5	23	2	..	2
3—4 ..	*15,414*	7,960	7,454	15,338	7,945	7,393	71	14	57	5	1	4
4—5 ..	*15,128*	7,876	7,252	15,015	7,850	7,165	104	24	80	9	2	7
Total 0—5 ..	*73,567*	*37,816*	*35,751*	*73,333*	*37,765*	*35,568*	*217*	*48*	*169*	*17*	*3*	*14*
5—10 ..	*62,955*	33,993	28,962	60,851	33,571	27,280	2,040	406	1,634	64	16	48
10—15 ..	*54,503*	30,053	24,450	48,563	28,910	19,653	5,808	1,107	4,701	132	36	96
15—20 ..	*39,841*	20,732	19,109	20,164	15,506	4,658	19,136	5,016	14,120	541	210	331
20—30 ..	*77,927*	37,339	40,588	17,238	14,988	2,250	57,296	20,804	36,492	3,293	1,547	1,846
30—40 ..	*63,233*	32,573	30,660	4,685	4,056	629	51,390	25,704	25,686	7,158	2,813	4,345
40—50 ..	*46,576*	24,456	22,120	1,794	1,412	382	33,705	19,175	14,530	11,077	3,869	7,208
50—60 ..	*32,126*	17,245	14,881	862	666	196	19,106	12,164	6,942	12,158	4,415	7,743
60 and over ..	*31,369*	17,449	13,920	682	533	149	13,269	9,981	3,288	17,418	6,935	10,483
CHRISTIAN ..	**672**	**388**	**284**	**363**	**205**	**158**	**267**	**156**	**111**	**42**	**27**	**15**
0—1 ..	*22*	12	10	22	12	10	..	..	..	..	..	..
1—2 ..	*23*	9	14	23	9	14	..	..	..	..	..	..
2—3 ..	*18*	6	12	18	6	12	..	..	..	..	..	..
3—4 ..	*12*	5	7	12	5	7	..	..	..	..	..	..
4—5 ..	*17*	9	8	17	9	8	..	..	..	..	..	..
Total 0—5 ..	*92*	*41*	*51*	*92*	*41*	*51*	..	..	..	..	..	..
5—10 ..	*71*	39	32	69	37	32	1	1	..	1	1	..
10—15 ..	*64*	38	26	61	37	24	3	1	2	..	..	..
15—20 ..	*69*	35	34	49	30	19	19	5	14	1	..	1
20—30 ..	*152*	80	72	65	39	26	79	35	44	8	6	2
30—40 ..	*113*	76	37	17	13	4	88	56	32	8	7	1
40—50 ..	*64*	46	18	4	4	..	49	35	14	11	7	4
50—60 ..	*30*	20	10	4	3	1	18	14	4	8	3	5
60 and over	*17*	13	4	2	1	1	10	9	1	5	3	2

AND CIVIL CONDITION (BY RELIGION).

PART B.—DETAILS FOR DISTRICTS AND STATES—*continued.*

RAWALPINDI DISTRICT.

Religion and Age.	Population.			Unmarried.			Married.			Widowed.		
	Persons.	Males.	Females.	Persons.	Males.	Females.	Persons.	Males.	Females.	Persons.	Males.	Females.
1	2	3	4	5	6	7	8	9	10	11	12	13
ALL RELIGIONS ..	**634,357**	**342,771**	**291,586**	**303,618**	**186,955**	**116,663**	**271,228**	**134,195**	**137,033**	**59,511**	**21,621**	**37,890**
0—1 ..	*21,206*	11,044	10,162	21,195	11,036	10,159	10	7	3	1	1	..
1 -2 ..	*17,367*	9,232	8,135	17,357	9,230	8,127	9	1	8	1	1	..
2- -3 ..	*20,366*	10,839	9,527	20,330	10,830	9,500	36	9	27	..	..	..
3- -4 ..	*20,489*	10,698	9,791	20,361	10,667	9,694	126	31	95	2	..	2
4- -5 ..	*19,576*	10,024	9,552	19,357	9,972	9,385	209	49	160	10	3	7
Total 0—5 ..	*99,004*	*51,837*	*47,167*	*98,600*	*51,735*	*46,865*	*390*	*97*	*293*	*14*	*5*	*9*
5- -10 ..	*81,031*	42,501	38,530	76,818	41,548	35,270	4,134	932	3,202	79	21	58
10- -15 ..	*71,757*	38,686	33,071	61,226	36,415	24,811	10,295	2,164	8,131	236	107	129
15- -20 ..	*67,039*	30,743	26,296	27,784	22,489	5,295	28,324	7,812	20,512	931	442	489
20- -30 ..	*114,495*	60,647	53,848	27,271	24,542	2,729	82,161	33,701	48,460	5,063	2,404	2,659
30 -40 ..	*89,573*	50,177	39,396	7,468	6,511	957	72,091	39,861	32,230	10,014	3,805	6,20
40—50 ..	*55,679*	31,095	24,584	2,870	2,466	404	39,809	24,509	15,300	13,000	4,120	8,880
50—60 ..	*33,428*	18,710	14,718	966	731	235	19,893	13,959	5,934	12,569	4,020	8,549
60 and over ..	*32,351*	18,375	13,976	615	518	97	14,131	11,160	2,971	17,605	6,697	10,908
HINDU ..	**59,485**	**34,973**	**24,512**	**28,936**	**18,844**	**10,092**	**24,532**	**13,740**	**10,792**	**6,017**	**2,389**	**3,628**
0- -1 ..	*1,825*	959	866	1,825	959	866	..	..	..	..	..	..
1- -2 ..	*1,426*	739	687	1,426	739	687	..	..	..	..	..	..
2- -3 ..	*1,697*	878	819	1,696	878	818	1	..	1	..	..	..
3- -4 ..	*1,679*	861	818	1,676	860	816	3	*1*	2	..	..	..
4- -5 ..	*1,586*	806	780	1,576	802	774	8	3	5	2	1	1
Total 0- -5 ..	*8,213*	*4,243*	*3,970*	*8,199*	*4,238*	*3,961*	*12*	*4*	*8*	*2*	*1*	*1*
5- -10 ..	*6,763*	3,606	3,157	6,603	3,568	3,035	154	36	1[illegible]8	6	2	4
10- -15 ..	*6,253*	3,492	2,761	5,644	3,391	2,253	591	97	494	18	4	14
15- -20 ..	*6,147*	3,701	2,446	3,359	2,864	495	2,679	792	1,887	109	45	64
20- -30 ..	*12,675*	7,864	4,811	3,633	3,426	207	8,368	4,134	4,234	674	304	370
30- -40 ..	*8,866*	5,684	3,182	833	763	70	6,819	4,429	2,390	1,214	492	722
40 -50 ..	*5,397*	3,359	2,038	439	387	52	3,502	2,430	1,072	1,[illegible]56	542	914
50- -60 ..	*2,938*	1,770	1,168	128	121	7	1,537	1,151	386	1,273	498	775
60 and over ..	*2,233*	1,254	979	98	86	12	870	667	203	1,265	501	764
SIKH ..	**41,265**	**22,948**	**18,317**	**20,892**	**13,090**	**7,802**	**16,767**	**8,683**	**8,084**	**3,606**	**1,175**	**2,431**
0- -1 ..	*1,563*	842	721	1,562	842	720	1	..	1	..	..	..
1- -2 ..	*1,167*	589	578	1,165	588	577	1	..	1	1	1	..
2- -3 ..	*1,341*	664	677	1,336	663	673	5	1	4	..	..	..
3- 4 ..	*1,362*	683	679	1,349	681	668	13	2	11	..	..	..
4- -5 .	*1,317*	658	659	1,294	654	640	22	4	18	1	..	1
Total 0- -5 ..	*6,750*	*3,436*	*3,314*	*6,706*	*3,428*	*3,278*	*42*	*7*	*35*	*2*	*1*	*1*
5- -10 ..	*5,502*	2,869	2,633	5,252	2,838	2,414	243	30	213	7	1	6
10—15 ..	*5,070*	2,703	2,367	4,252	2,588	1,664	810	114	696	8	1	7
15—20 ..	*3,991*	2,225	1,766	2,042	1,773	269	1,909	439	1,470	40	13	27
20—30 ..	*7,322*	4,277	3,045	1,974	1,865	109	5,086	2,322	2,764	262	90	172
30- -40 ..	*5,156*	3,099	2,057	409	366	43	4,150	2,562	1,588	597	171	426
40- 50 ..	*3,463*	1,985	1,478	154	133	21	2,482	1,635	847	827	217	610
50 -60 ..	*2,133*	1,221	912	56	55	1	1,264	908	356	813	258	555
60 and over ..	*1,878*	1,133	745	47	44	3	781	666	115	1,050	423	627
JAIN ..	**1,077**	**593**	**484**	**582**	**357**	**225**	**376**	**191**	**185**	**119**	**45**	**74**
0- 1 ..	*38*	17	21	38	17	21	..	..	..	..	.	..
1- 2 ..	*32*	19	13	32	19	13	..	.	..	..	..	..
2 -3 ..	*34*	20	14	34	20	14	..	.	..	..		..
3 4 .	*31*	17	14	31	17	14	..	.	.	..		..
4- -5 ..	*29*	13	16	29	13	16	.	.	..	..	.	..
Total 0- -5 ..	*164*	*86*	*78*	*164*	*86*	*78*	..	.	..	..	..	..
5—10 ..	*139*	74	65	138	74	64	1	..	1	..	..	..
10- -15 ..	*136*	75	60	129	74	55	6	1	5	..	..	..
15- -20 ..	*102*	51	51	58	42	16	42	9	33	2	..	2
20- -30 ..	*195*	105	90	55	50	5	129	52	77	11	3	8
30- 40 ..	*147*	87	60	17	14	3	104	62	42	26	11	15
40 -50 ..	*99*	57	42	7	6	1	59	39	20	33	12	21
50 60 ..	*65*	42	23	11	8	3	28	22	6	26	12	14
60 and over ..	*31*	16	15	3	3	..	7	6	1	21	7	14
MUSLIM ..	**524,965**	**279,287**	**245,678**	**248,507**	**151,244**	**97,263**	**227,007**	**110,213**	**116,794**	**49,451**	**17,880**	**81,621**
0- -1 ..	*17,563*	9,128	8,435	17,555	9,121	8,434	7	6	1	1	1	..
1—2 ..	*14,554*	7,795	6,759	14,546	7,794	6,752	8	1	7	..	..	..
2- -3 ..	*17,099*	9,180	7,919	17,069	9,172	7,897	30	8	22	.	..	..
3- 4 ..	*17,251*	9,052	8,199	17,140	9,024	8,116	110	28	82	*1*	.	1
4- -5 ..	*16,482*	8,465	8,017	16,300	8,422	7,878	177	41	136	5	2	3
Total 0- 5 ..	*82,949*	*43,620*	*39,329*	*82,670*	*43,538*	*39,077*	*332*	*84*	*248*	*7*	*3*	*4*
5- 10 ..	*68,007*	35,629	32,378	64,215	34,749	29,466	3,728	862	2,866	64	18	46
10- 15 ..	*59,797*	32,141	27,656	50,721	30,095	20,626	8,866	1,944	6,922	210	102	108
15 -20 ..	*45,923*	24,074	21,849	21,595	17,168	4,427	23,552	6,525	17,027	776	381	395
20- -30 ..	*91,945*	46,584	45,361	20,089	17,785	2,304	67,783	26,829	40,954	4,073	1,970	2,103
30- 40 ..	*74,089*	40,462	33,627	5,882	5,102	780	60,109	32,282	27,827	8,098	3,078	5,020
40- -50 ..	*46,134*	25,357	20,777	2,192	1,891	301	33,326	20,119	13,177	10,616	3,317	7,299
50- -60 ..	*28,055*	15,530	12,525	751	540	2[illegible]1	16,901	11,763	5,138	10,403	3,227	7,[illegible]76
60 and over ..	*28,066*	15,890	12,176	452	381	71	12,410	9,775	2,635	5,204	5,734	9,470
CHRISTIAN . ..	**7,486**	**4,924**	**2,562**	**4,663**	**3,396**	**1,267**	**2,508**	**1,346**	**1,162**	**315**	**182**	**133**
0- 1 ..	*214*	97	117	212	96	116	2	1	1	..	..	..
1 -2 ..	*186*	89	97	186	89	97	..	..	..	..	.	..
2- -3 ..	*194*	97	97	194	97	97	..	.	..	.		..
3- 4 ..	*166*	85	81	165	85	80	..	.	..	1		1
4—5 ..	*158*	80	78	154	79	75	2	1	1	2	..	2
Total 0- -5 ..	*918*	*448*	*470*	*911*	*446*	*465*	*4*	*2*	*2*	*3*	.	3
5—10 ..	*611*	318	293	601	314	287	8	4	4	2	.	2
10—15 ..	*498*	272	226	476	264	212	22	8	14	..	..	..
15- -20 ..	*871*	690	181	726	640	86	141	47	94	4	3	1
20—30 ..	*2,344*	1,809	535	1,514	1,411	103	787	361	426	43	37	6
30- 40 .	*1,299*	836	463	325	264	61	895	519	376	79	53	26
40 50 ..	*572*	325	247	75	46	29	429	247	182	68	32	36
50- -60 ..	*233*	145	88	20	7	13	160	113	47	53	25	28
60 and over ..	*140*	81	59	15	4	11	62	45	17	63	32	31

TABLE VII.—AGE, SEX

PART B.—DETAILS FOR DISTRICTS AND STATES.

ATTOCK DISTRICT.

Religion and Age.	Population.			Unmarried.			Married.			Widowed.		
	Persons.	Males.	Females.	Persons.	Males.	Females.	Persons.	Males.	Females.	Persons.	Males.	Females.
1	2	3	4	5	6	7	8	9	10	11	12	13
ALL RELIGIONS ..	**583,960**	**306,949**	**277,011**	**290,851**	**171,151**	**119,700**	**237,748**	**116,410**	**121,338**	**55,361**	**19,388**	**35,973**
0- 1 .	*18,995*	9,725	9,270	18,994	9,725	9,269	1	..	1	.	..	.
1- -2 .	*15,821*	7,888	7,933	15,821	7,888	7,933	..	..	..	..	..	..
2- -3 .	*19,060*	9,736	9,324	19,058	9,735	9,323	2	1	1	.	..	
3- 4 .	*20,119*	10,528	9,591	20,097	10,524	9,573	22	4	18	.	..	.
4- -5 ..	*20,104*	10,597	9,507	20,053	10,586	9,467	48	10	38	3	1	2
Total 0- -5 ..	*94,099*	*48,474*	*45,625*	*94,023*	*48,458*	*45,565*	*73*	*15*	*58*	*3*	*1*	*2*
5- 10 ..	*81,060*	43,517	37,543	79,565	43,284	36,281	1,452	227	1,225	43	6	37
10- 15 ..	*68,516*	37,677	30,839	62,248	36,515	25,733	6,085	1,131	4,954	183	31	152
15- -20 ..	*47,305*	24,865	22,440	24,480	18,625	5,855	21,973	5,927	16,046	852	313	539
20- -30 .	*98,145*	48,580	49,565	21,398	17,552	3,846	72,014	20,043	42,971	4,733	1,985	2,7-8
30- 40 .	*77,414*	40,648	36,766	6,078	4,476	1,602	62,651	33,174	29,477	8,685	2,998	ı,687
40- -50 ..	*52,474*	27,682	24,792	1,816	1,298	518	39,080	22,899	16,181	11,578	3,485	8,093
50- -60 ..	*34,833*	18,833	16,000	714	531	183	21,503	14,176	7,327	12,616	4,126	8,490
60 and over ..	*30,114*	16,673	13,441	529	412	117	12,917	9,818	3,090	16,668	6,443	10,225
HINDU ..	**31,982**	**16,681**	**15,301**	**15,139**	**9,290**	**5,849**	**12,902**	**6,249**	**6,653**	**3,891**	**1,092**	**2,799**
0- 1 ..	*1,064*	558	506	1,063	558	505	1	..	1	.		.
1- 2 ..	*860*	451	409	860	451	409	..	.	..	..	.	.
2- -3 .	*1,017*	543	474	1,016	542	474	1	1	..	.	..	.
3- 4 .	*1,009*	530	479	1,008	530	478	1	.	1	..	..	.
4- -5 ..	*994*	521	473	989	519	470	5	2	3	..	..	.
Total 0- -5 ..	*4,944*	*2,603*	*2,341*	*4,936*	*2,600*	*2,336*	*8*	*3*	*5*	..	.	..
5- 10 ..	*4,216*	2,198	2,018	4,081	2,180	1,901	123	17	106	12	1	11
10- -15 ..	*3,685*	1,924	1,761	3,214	1,860	1,354	442	58	384	29	6	23
15- -20 ..	*2,745*	1,408	1,337	1,220	1,038	182	1,454	351	1,103	71	19	52
20- -30 ..	*5,444*	2,791	2,653	1,119	1,070	49	3,958	1,607	2,351	367	114	253
30- -40 .	*4,171*	2,223	1,948	295	280	15	3,223	1,758	1,465	653	185	468
40- -50 ..	*3,001*	1,580	1,421	142	137	5	1,997	1,238	759	862	205	657
50- -60 ..	*1,954*	999	955	78	74	4	1,049	717	332	827	208	619
60 and over .	*1,772*	905	867	54	51	3	648	500	148	1,070	364	716
SIKH ..	**19,522**	**10,279**	**9,243**	**9,161**	**5,551**	**3,610**	**8,182**	**3,949**	**4,233**	**2,179**	**779**	**1,400**
0- 1 ..	*701*	372	329	701	372	329	..	..	.	..	..	..
1- -2 ..	*555*	290	265	555	290	265	..	..	..	..	..	..
2- -3 ..	*634*	336	298	634	336	298	..	..	..	..	.	..
3- 4 ..	*654*	-348	306	652	348	304	2	..	2	.	.	..
4- -5 ..	*656*	347	309	650	346	304	5	1	4	1	.	1
Total 0- -5 .	*3,200*	*1,693*	*1,507*	*3,192*	*1,692*	*1,500*	*7*	*1*	*6*	*1*	.	*1*
5- 10 ..	*2,704*	1,428	1,276	2,581	1,406	1,175	117	20	97	6	2	4
10- 15 ..	*2,289*	1,211	1,078	1,946	1,154	792	336	54	282	7	3	4
15- 20 .	*1,509*	788	721	642	556	86	844	226	618	23	6	17
20- -30 ..	*3,092*	1,518	1,574	541	508	33	2,386	953	1,433	165	57	108
30- 40 ..	*2,468*	1,296	1,172	124	113	11	2,035	1,082	953	309	101	208
40- -50 ..	*1,794*	955	839	54	48	6	1,299	771	528	441	136	305
50—60 ..	*1,273*	726	547	42	40	2	717	498	219	514	188	326
60 and over ..	*1,193*	664	529	39	34	5	441	344	97	713	286	427
JAIN ..	**2**	**2**	..	**1**	**1**	..	**1**	**1**	..	..	..	..
20- -30 ..	*1*	1	..	1	1	..	..	.	..	..	..	..
30- 40 ..	*1*	1	..	..	..	..	1	1	..	..	..	..
MUSLIM ..	**531,793**	**279,546**	**252,247**	**266,095**	**155,963**	**110,132**	**216,427**	**106,078**	**110,349**	**49,271**	**17,505**	**31,766**
0- 1 ..	*17,220*	8,791	8,429	17,220	8,791	8,429	..	..	.	..	..	..
1 -2 ..	*14,394*	7,141	7,253	14,394	7,141	7,253	..	..	..	..	..	..
2 3 ..	*17,396*	8,850	8,546	17,395	8,850	8,545	1	..	1	.	..	..
3- 4 ..	*18,444*	9,645	8,799	18,425	9,641	8,784	19	4	15	..	..	..
4 -5 ..	*18,435*	9,719	8,716	18,395	9,711	8,684	38	7	31	2	1	1
Total 0- -5 ..	*85,889*	*44,146*	*41,743*	*85,829*	*44,134*	*41,695*	*58*	*11*	*47*	*2*	*1*	*1*
5- -10 ..	*74,078*	39,864	34,214	72,842	39,671	33,171	1,211	190	1,021	25	3	22
10—15 ..	*62,501*	34,526	27,975	57,049	33,485	23,564	5,305	1,019	4,286	147	22	125
15- -20 ..	*42,958*	22,592	20,366	22,540	16,958	5,582	19,661	5,346	14,315	757	288	469
20- -30 .	*89,352*	44,062	45,290	19,555	15,799	3,756	65,600	26,452	39,148	4,197	1,811	2,386
30- 40 .	*70,662*	37,048	33,614	5,632	4,059	1,573	57,311	30,281	27,030	7,719	2,708	5,011
40- -50 .	*47,621*	25,111	22,510	1,618	1,113	505	35,732	20,855	14,877	10,271	3,143	7,128
50- -60 ..	*31,593*	17,101	14,492	594	417	177	19,727	12,955	6,772	11,272	3,729	7,543
60 and over ..	*27,139*	15,096	12,043	436	327	109	11,822	8,969	2,853	14,881	5,800	9,081
CHRISTIAN ..	**710**	**490**	**220**	**454**	**345**	**109**	**236**	**133**	**103**	**20**	**12**	**8**
0—1 ..	*10*	4	6	10	4	6	..	..	.	..	..	..
1—2 ..	*12*	6	6	12	6	6	.	..	.	..	.	..
2- -3 ..	*13*	7	6	13	7	6	..	..	..	..		.
3- 4 ..	*12*	5	7	12	5	7	..	..	..	..	..	..
4- -5 ..	*19*	10	9	19	10	9	..	..	..	..	..	..
Total 0- -5 ..	*66*	*32*	*34*	*66*	*32*	*34*	..	..	..	..	..	..
5- 10 .	62	27	35	61	27	34	1	..	1	..	..	..
10- 15 ..	*41*	16	25	39	16	23	2	..	2	..	..	..
15- -20 ..	*92*	76	16	77	72	5	14	4	10	1	..	1
20- -30 ..	*256*	208	48	182	174	8	70	31	39	4	3	1
30- 40 ..	*112*	80	32	27	24	3	81	52	29	4	4	..
40- -50 ..	*58*	36	22	2	..	2	52	35	17	4	1	3
50- -60 ..	*13*	7	6	..	..	..	10	6	4	3	1	2
60 and over ..	*10*	8	2	..	..	..	6	5	1	4	2	1

AND CIVIL CONDITION (BY RELIGION).

PART B.—DETAILS FOR DISTRICTS AND STATES—*continued.*

MIANWALI DISTRICT.

Religion and Age.	Population.			Unmarried.			Married.			Widowed.		
	Persons.	Males.	Females.	Persons.	Males.	Females.	Persons.	Males.	Females.	Persons.	Males.	Females.
1	2	3	4	5	6	7	8	9	10	11	12	13
ALL RELIGIONS	**411,539**	**216,016**	**195,523**	**216,133**	**126,215**	**89,918**	**163,391**	**77,761**	**85,630**	**32,015**	**12,040**	**19,975**
0- 1	*14,295*	7,256	7,039	14,294	7,255	7,039	1	1	..	..		..
1- 2	*11,630*	5,868	5,762	11,625	5,864	5,761	5	4	1	..		..
2—3	*14,147*	7,077	7,070	14,140	7,073	7,067	7	4	3	..		..
3- 4	*14,725*	7,400	7,325	14,713	7,393	7,320	12	7	5	..	..	
4- 5	*14,562*	7,337	7,225	14,534	7,323	7,211	26	13	13	2	1	1
Total 0- 5	*69,359*	*34,938*	*34,421*	*69,306*	*34,908*	*34,398*	*51*	*29*	*22*	*2*	*1*	*1*
5—10	*58,968*	31,134	27,834	58,418	30,999	27,419	539	129	410	11	6	5
10- 15	*48,575*	26,375	22,200	45,946	25,885	20,061	2,583	478	2,105	46	12	34
15- 20	*34,068*	17,873	16,195	18,569	13,461	5,108	15,095	4,246	10,840	404	16[illegible]	238
20- 30	*69,963*	35,514	34,449	16,082	13,847	2,235	51,407	20,462	30,945	2,474	1,2[illegible]	1,260
30- 40	*53,151*	28,171	24,980	5,401	4,991	410	43,112	21,228	21,884	4,638	1,952	2,686
40- 50	*35,151*	18,746	16,405	1,615	1,438	177	26,594	14,995	11,599	6,942	2,313	4,629
50- 60	*24,170*	13,055	11,115	506	434	72	15,592	9,954	5,638	8,072	[illegible]	5,405
60 and over	*18,134*	10,210	7,924	290	252	38	8,418	6,240	2,178	9,426		5,708
HINDU	**49,794**	**25,656**	**24,138**	**24,813**	**14,392**	**10,421**	**20,852**	**9,859**	**10,993**	**4,12[illegible]**		**2,724**
0- 1	*1,698*	870	828	1,698	870	828	..	..	..			
1- 2	*1,298*	641	657	1,298	641	657	..	..	..			
2- 3	*1,614*	790	824	1,612	789	823	2	1	1	..		
3- 4	*1,757*	894	863	1,754	893	861	3	1	2	..		..
4- 5	*1,760*	917	843	1,751	914	837	9	3	6	..		..
Total 0- 5	*8,127*	*4,112*	*4,015*	*8,113*	*4,107*	*4,006*	*14*	*5*	*9*	..		
5- 10	*7,208*	3,770	3,438	7,032	3,735	3,297	172	34	138	4		3
10- 15	*6,065*	3,211	2,854	5,499	3,113	2,386	554	95	459	12	3	9
15- 20	*4,384*	2,247	2,137	2,037	1,578	459	2,286	647	1,639	61	22	39
20- 30	*8,462*	4,107	4,355	1,480	1,298	182	6,663	2,676	3,987	319	133	86
30- 40	*6,250*	3,281	2,969	339	294	45	5,304	2,760	2,544	607	[illegible]27	[illegible]38
40- 50	*4,357*	2,288	2,069	160	134	26	3,246	1,862	1,384	951	[illegible]92	659
50- 60	*2,831*	1,495	1,336	84	73	11	1,712	1,107	605	1,035	31[illegible]	72[illegible]
60 and over	*2,110*	1,145	965	69	60	9	901	673	228	1,140	41[illegible]	728
SIKH	**4,231**	**2,263**	**1,968**	**2,172**	**1,274**	**898**	**1,766**	**881**	**885**	**293**	**108**	**185**
0- 1	*165*	92	73	165	92	73	..	..	..	..	..	
1—2	*138*	74	64	137	73	64	1	1	..	..	..	..
2—3	*145*	74	71	145	74	71	..	..	..	..	..	..
3—4	*154*	79	75	154	79	75	..	..	..	..		..
4- 5	*166*	85	81	164	84	80	2	1	1	..	..	..
Total 0—5	*768*	*404*	*364*	*765*	*402*	*363*	*3*	*2*	*1*	..	..	
5- 10	*644*	350	294	631	344	287	12	5	7	1	1	
10- 15	*507*	282	225	467	271	196	39	11	28	1		1
15- 20	*300*	180	180	150	114	36	207	65	142	3	1	2
20—30	*748*	395	353	115	103	12	611	280	331	22	12	10
30—40	*522*	270	252	25	21	4	444	228	216	53	21	32
40- 50	*321*	176	145	9	9	..	247	146	101	65	[illegible]	44
50—60	*218*	121	97	8	8	..	137	91	46	73	22	51
60 and over	*143*	85	58	2	2	..	66	53	13	75	30	45
JAIN	**20**	**11**	**9**	**4**	**3**	**1**	**11**	**6**	**5**	**5**	**2**	**3**
4- 5	*1*	..	1	1	..	1	..	..	..	..	..	..
Total 0- 5	*1*	..	*1*	*1*	..	*1*	..	..	..	..	..	..
5- 10	*2*	1	1	1	1	..	1	..	1	..		..
10- 15	*2*	1	1	1	1	..	1	..	1	..	..	..
15- 20	*2*	1	1	..	..	..	2	1	1	..	..	
20- 30	*4*	3	*1*	1	1	..	2	1	1	1	1	..
30- 40	*4*	3	*1*	..	..	..	2	2	..	2	*1*	1
40- 50	*1*	..	*1*	..	..	..	..	..	..	1	..	1
50- 60	*2*	1	1	..	..	..	1	1	..	1		1
60 and over	*2*	1	1	..	..	..	2	1	1	..	..	..
MUSLIM	**357,109**	**187,872**	**169,237**	**188,951**	**110,435**	**78,516**	**140,592**	**66,929**	**73,663**	**27,566**	**10,508**	**17,058**
0- 1	*12,419*	6,286	6,133	12,418	6,285	6,133	1	1	..	..	..	
1- 2	*10,181*	5,147	5,034	10,177	5,144	5,033	4	3	1	..	..	
2- 3	*12,375*	6,207	6,168	12,370	6,204	6,166	5	3	2	..	..	..
3- 4	*12,803*	6,421	6,382	12,794	6,415	6,379	9	6	3	..	..	..
4- 5	*12,621*	6,329	6,292	12,604	6,319	6,285	15	9	6	2	1	1
Total 0- 5	*60,399*	*30,390*	*30,009*	*60,363*	*30,367*	*29,996*	*34*	*22*	*12*	*2*	*1*	*1*
5- 10	*51,065*	26,991	24,074	50,706	26,897	23,809	353	90	263	6		2
10- 15	*41,964*	22,862	19,102	39,944	22,481	17,463	1,987	372	1,615	33	9	24
15- 20	*29,287*	15,427	13,860	16,367	11,757	4,610	12,580	3,527	9,053	340	143	197
20—30	*60,680*	30,970	29,710	14,466	12,428	2,038	44,084	17,485	26,599	2,130	1,057	1,073
30- 40	*46,312*	24,579	21,733	5,032	4,671	361	37,310	18,210	19,100	3,970	1,698	2,272
40- 50	*30,434*	16,256	14,178	1,443	1,293	150	23,073	12,969	10,104	5,918	1,99[illegible]	[illegible]924
50- 60	*21,102*	11,426	9,676	413	352	61	13,729	8,746	4,983	6,960	2,328	4,632
60 and over	*15,866*	8,971	6,895	217	189	28	7,442	5,508	1,934	8,207	3,274	4,933
CHRISTIAN	**380**	**211**	**169**	**193**	**111**	**82**	**166**	**83**	**83**	**21**	**17**	**4**
0- 1	*13*	8	5	13	8	5	..	..	..	..		..
1—2	*13*	6	7	13	6	7	..	..	..		..	..
2—3	*13*	6	7	13	6	7	..	..	..	..	..	..
3—4	*11*	6	5	11	6	5	..	..	..	..	..	..
4—5	*14*	6	8	14	6	8	..	..	..	..	..	
Total 0- 5	*64*	*32*	*32*	*64*	*32*	*32*	..	..	..	..	..	
5- 10	*49*	22	27	48	22	26	1	..	1	..	..	..
10- 15	*37*	19	18	35	19	16	2	..	2	..	..	
15- 20	*35*	18	17	15	12	3	20	6	14	..	..	..
20- 30	*68*	38	30	20	17	3	46	19	27	2	2	..
30- 40	*62*	37	25	5	5	..	51	27	24	6	5	1
40- 50	*37*	25	12	3	2	1	27	17	10	7	6	1
50- 60	*17*	12	5	1	1	..	13	9	4	3	2	
60 and over	*11*	8	3	2	1	1	6	5	1	3	2	

AND CIVIL CONDITION (BY RELIGION).

PART B.—DETAILS FOR DISTRICTS AND STATES—*continued.*

MIANWALI DISTRICT.

Religion and Age.	Population. Persons.	Population. Males.	Population. Females.	Unmarried. Persons.	Unmarried. Males.	Unmarried. Females.	Married. Persons.	Married. Males.	Married. Females.	Widowed. Persons.	Widowed. Males.	Widowed. Females.
1	2	3	4	5	6	7	8	9	10	11	12	13
ALL RELIGIONS	**411,539**	**216,016**	**195,523**	**216,133**	**126,215**	**89,918**	**163,391**	**77,761**	**85,630**	**32,015**	**12,040**	**19,975**
0-1	*14,295*	7,256	7,039	14,294	7,255	7,039	1	1	..	..	.	..
1-2	*11,630*	5,868	5,762	11,625	5,864	5,761	5	4	1	.		.
2-3	*11,147*	7,077	7,070	14,140	7,073	7,067	7	4	3	.		
3-4	*14,725*	7,400	7,325	14,713	7,393	7,320	12	7	5	.	.	
4-5	*14,562*	7,337	7,225	14,534	7,323	7,211	26	13	13	2	1	1
Total 0-5	*69,359*	*34,938*	*34,421*	*69,306*	*34,908*	*34,398*	*51*	*29*	*22*	*2*	*1*	*1*
5-10	*58,968*	31,134	27,834	58,418	30,999	27,419	539	129	410	11	6	5
10-15	*48,575*	26,375	22,200	45,946	25,885	20,061	2,383	478	2,105	46	12	34
15-20	*34,068*	17,873	16,195	18,569	13,16[illegible]	[illegible]	15,095	4,246	10,849	404	166	238
20-30	*69,963*	35,514	34,449	16,082	13,847	2,235	51,407	20,462	30,945	2,474	1,205	1,269
30-40	*53,151*	28,171	24,980	5,401	4,991	410	43,112	21,228	21,884	4,638	1,952	2,686
40-50	*35,151*	18,746	16,405	1,615	1,438	177	26,594	14,995	11,599	6,942	2,313	4,629
50-60	*24,170*	13,055	11,115	506	434	72	15,592	9,954	5,638	8,072	[illegible]	5,405
60 and over	*18,134*	10,210	7,924	290	252	38	8,418	6,240	2,178	9,420	[illegible]	5,708
HINDU	**49,794**	**25,656**	**24,138**	**24,813**	**14,392**	**10,421**	**20,852**	**9,859**	**10,993**	**4,12[illegible]**	[illegible]	**2,724**
0-1	*1,698*	870	828	1,698	870	828	..	.	..	.		.
1-2	*1,298*	641	657	1,298	641	657	..	.	..	.		..
2-3	*1,614*	790	824	1,612	789	823	2	1	1	.		..
3-4	*1,757*	894	863	1,754	893	861	3	1	2	..		..
4-5	*1,760*	917	843	1,751	914	837	9	3	6	..		.
Total 0-5	*8,127*	*4,112*	*4,015*	*8,113*	*4,107*	*4,006*	*14*	*5*	*9*	.	..	
5-10	*7,208*	3,770	3,438	7,032	3,735	3,297	172	34	138	4		3
10-15	*6,065*	3,211	2,854	5,499	3,113	2,386	554	95	459	12	3	9
15-20	*4,384*	2,247	2,137	2,037	1,578	459	2,286	647	1,639	61	22	39
20-30	*8,462*	4,107	4,355	1,480	1,298	182	6,663	2,676	3,987	319	133	186
30-40	*6,250*	3,281	2,969	339	294	45	5,304	2,760	2,544	607	227	380
40-50	*4,357*	2,288	2,069	160	134	26	3,246	1,862	1,384	951	292	659
50-60	*2,831*	1,495	1,336	84	73	11	1,712	1,107	605	1,035	315	720
60 and over	*2,110*	1,145	965	69	60	9	901	673	228	1,140	412	728
SIKH	**4,231**	**2,263**	**1,968**	**2,172**	**1,274**	**898**	**1,766**	**881**	**885**	**293**	**108**	**185**
0-1	*165*	92	73	165	92	73	..	.	.	.	..	.
1-2	*138*	74	64	137	73	64	1	1	.	..	.	..
2-3	*145*	74	71	145	74	71	.	.	.	..	.	..
3-4	*154*	79	75	154	79	75	.	.	.	..		..
4-5	*166*	85	81	164	84	80	2	1	1	..	.	.
Total 0-5	*768*	*404*	*364*	*765*	*402*	*363*	*3*	*2*	*1*	..		.
5-10	*644*	350	294	631	344	287	12	5	7	1	1	
10-15	*507*	282	225	467	271	196	39	11	28	1	.	1
15-20	*360*	180	180	150	114	36	207	65	142	3	1	2
20-30	*748*	395	353	115	103	12	611	280	331	22	2	10
30-40	*522*	270	252	25	21	4	444	228	216	53	21	32
40-50	*321*	176	145	9	9	.	247	146	101	65	2	44
50-60	*218*	2	97	8	8		137	91	46	73	22	51
60 and over	*143*	85	58	2	2	..	66	53	13	75	30	45
JAIN	**20**	**11**	**9**	**4**	**3**	**1**	**11**	**6**	**5**	**5**	**2**	**3**
4-5	*1*	..	1	1	..	1	..	.	..	..	..	..
Total 0-5	*1*	..	*1*	*1*	..	*1*	..	.	..		..	..
5-10	*2*	1	1	1	1	..	1	..	1	..	..	.
10-15	*2*	1	1	1	1	..	1	..	1	..	.	..
15-20	*2*	1	1	..	.		2	.	1	..	.	..
20-30	*4*	3	1	1	1		2	1	1	1		..
30-40	*4*	3	1	..	..	.	2	2	.	2	1	
40-50	*1*	..	1	.	..	..	.	.	..	1	..	1
50-60	*2*	1	1	.	..	..	1	1	..	1	.	1
60 and over	*2*	1	1	.	.	.	2	1	1	.	..	..
MUSLIM	**357,109**	**187,872**	**169,237**	**188,951**	**110,435**	**78,516**	**140,592**	**66,929**	**73,663**	**27,566**	**10,508**	**17,058**
0-1	*12,419*	6,286	6,133	12,418	6,285	6,133	1	1		..	..	.
1-2	*10,181*	5,147	5,034	10,177	5,144	5,033	4	3	1	..	..	.
2-3	*12,375*	6,207	6,168	12,370	6,204	6,166	5	3	2	..	.	.
3-4	*12,803*	6,421	6,382	12,794	6,415	6,379	9	6	3	.	..	.
4-5	*12,621*	6,329	6,292	12,604	6,319	6,285	15	9	6	2	1	1
Total 0-5	*60,399*	*30,390*	*30,009*	*60,363*	*30,36[illegible]*	*29,996*	*34*	*22*	*12*	*2*	*1*	*1*
5-10	*51,065*	26,991	24,074	50,706	26,897	23,809	353	90	263	6		2
10-15	*41,964*	22,862	19,102	39,944	22,481	17,463	1,987	372	1,615	33	9	24
15-20	*29,287*	15,427	13,860	16,367	11,757	4,610	12,580	3,527	9,053	340	143	197
20-30	*60,680*	30,970	29,710	14,466	12,428	2,038	44,084	17,485	26,599	2,130	1,057	1,073
30-40	*46,319*	24,579	21,733	5,032	4,671	361	37,310	18,210	19,100	3,970	[illegible]698	[illegible]272
40-50	*30,434*	16,256	14,178	1,443	1,293	150	23,073	12,969	10,[illegible]64	5,918	1,99[illegible]	3,924
50-60	*21,102*	11,426	9,676	413	352	61	13,729	8,746	4,983	6,960	2,328	4,632
60 and over	*15,366*	8,971	6,895	217	189	28	7,442	5,508	1,934	8,207	3,274	4,933
CHRISTIAN	**380**	**211**	**169**	**193**	**111**	**82**	**166**	**83**	**83**	**21**	**17**	**4**
0-1	*13*	8	5	13	8	5	.	..	.	.	.	
1-2	*13*	6	7	13	6	7	..	..	..		..	
2-3	*13*	6	7	13	6	7	..	..	.	..	.	
3-4	*11*	6	5	11	6	5	..	..	.	..	.	.
4-5	*14*	6	8	14	6	8	..	..	..	..	.	.
Total 0-5	*64*	*32*	*32*	*64*	*32*	*32*	..	..	..	..		.
5-10	*49*	22	27	48	22	26	1	..	1	..	.	.
10-15	*37*	19	18	35	19	16	2	..	2	..	..	..
15-20	*35*	18	17	15	12	3	20	6	14	..	..	..
20-30	*68*	38	30	20	17	3	46	19	27	2	2	.
30-40	*62*	37	25	5	5	..	51	27	24	6	5	
40-50	*37*	25	12	3	2	1	27	17	10	7	6	1
50-60	*17*	12	5	1	1	.	13	9	4	3	2	1
60 and over	*11*	8	3	2	1	1	6	5	1	3		1

AND CIVIL CONDITION (BY RELIGION).

PART B.—DETAILS FOR DISTRICTS AND STATES—*continued.*

LYALLPUR DISTRICT.

Religion and Age.	Population.			Unmarried.			Married.			Widowed.		
	Persons.	Males.	Females.	Persons.	Males.	Females.	Persons.	Males.	Females.	Persons.	Males.	Females.
1	2	3	4	5	6	7	8	9	10	11	12	13
ALL RELIGIONS ..	**1,151,351**	**630,749**	**520,602**	**608,478**	**358,368**	**250,110**	**468,813**	**238,187**	**230,626**	**74,060**	**34,194**	**39,866**
0—1 ..	*48,878*	25,327	23,551	48,871	25,326	23,545	6	1	5	1	..	1
1—2 ..	*36,207*	18,435	17,772	36,153	18,427	17,726	53	8	45	1	..	1
2—3 ..	*39,633*	20,115	19,518	39,453	20,037	19,416	177	76	101	3	2	1
3—4 ..	*39,533*	20,302	19,231	39,201	20,147	19,054	329	155	174	3	.	3
4—5 ..	*37,613*	19,859	17,754	37,184	19,680	17,504	416	175	241	13	4	9
Total 0—5 ..	*201,864*	*104,038*	*97,826*	*200,862*	*103,617*	*97,245*	*981*	*415*	*566*	*21*	*6*	*15*
5—10 ..	*164,898*	87,708	77,190	156,398	84,791	71,607	8,306	2,779	5,527	194	138	56
10—15 ..	*148,918*	80,697	68,221	128,621	74,034	54,587	19,801	6,324	13,477	496	339	157
15—20 ..	*112,007*	62,097	49,910	54,433	39,825	14,608	55,930	21,150	34,780	1,644	1,122	522
20—30 ..	*194,955*	108,013	86,942	46,999	38,865	8,134	141,493	65,245	76,248	6,463	3,903	2,560
30—40 ..	*126,760*	71,758	55,002	11,311	9,512	1,799	105,571	57,039	48,532	9,878	5,207	4,671
40—50 ..	*87,478*	49,732	37,746	4,754	3,872	882	68,468	39,590	28,878	14,256	6,270	7,986
50—60 ..	*57,833*	33,162	24,671	2,537	1,978	559	39,580	24,681	14,899	15,716	6,503	9,213
60 and over ..	*56,638*	33,514	23,094	2,563	1,874	689	28,683	20,964	7,719	25,392	10,706	14,686
HINDU ..	**122,626**	**71,857**	**51,269**	**64,266**	**39,664**	**24,602**	**49,924**	**27,737**	**22,187**	**8,436**	**3,956**	**4,480**
0—1 ..	*5,412*	3,242	2,170	5,411	3,242	2,169	1	.	1	..	..	..
1—2 ..	*3,439*	1,746	1,693	3,434	1,745	1,680	5	1	4	..	..	..
2—3 ..	*4,044*	1,947	2,097	4,036	1,945	2,091	7	1	6	1	1	.
3—4 ..	*4,184*	2,054	2,130	4,172	2,048	2,124	11	6	5	1	..	1
4—5 ..	*3,928*	2,071	1,857	3,909	2,060	1,849	16	10	6	3	1	2
Total 0—5 ..	*21,007*	*11,060*	*9,947*	*20,962*	*11,040*	*9,922*	*40*	*18*	*22*	*5*	*2*	*3*
5—10 ..	*15,902*	8,424	7,478	15,495	8,288	7,207	394	132	262	13	4	9
10—15 ..	*14,275*	7,842	6,433	12,807	7,452	5,355	1,447	384	1,063	21	6	15
15—20 ..	*12,061*	7,410	4,651	6,430	5,175	1,255	5,516	2,169	3,347	115	66	49
20—30 ..	*22,855*	*14,098*	8,757	6,045	5,451	594	16,054	8,220	7,834	756	427	329
30—40 ..	*15,237*	9,431	5,806	1,454	1,316	138	12,442	7,428	5,014	1,341	687	654
40—50 ..	*10,243*	6,308	3,935	606	527	79	7,781	4,937	2,844	1,856	844	1,012
50—60 ..	*6,099*	3,772	2,327	275	234	41	3,930	2,693	1,237	1,894	845	1,049
60 and over ..	*4,947*	3,012	1,935	192	181	11	2,320	1,756	564	2,435	1,075	1,360
SIKH ..	**211,391**	**117,039**	**94,352**	**105,307**	**64,250**	**41,057**	**90,867**	**45,268**	**45,599**	**15,217**	**7,521**	**7,696**
0—1 ..	*8,837*	4,673	4,164	8,836	4,672	4,164	1	1	..	..	.	.
1—2 ..	*6,247*	3,194	3,053	6,213	3,192	3,021	34	2	32	..	.	..
2—3 ..	*6,755*	3,481	3,274	6,712	3,476	3,236	43	5	38	..	..	..
3—4 ..	*6,841*	3,626	3,215	6,820	3,618	3,202	20	8	12	1	..	1
4—5 ..	*6,542*	3,535	3,007	6,518	3,526	2,992	21	9	12	3	..	3
Total 0—5 ..	*35,222*	*18,509*	*16,713*	*35,099*	*18,484*	*16,615*	*119*	*25*	*94*	*4*	..	*4*
5—10 ..	*28,701*	15,884	12,817	27,577	15,476	12,101	1,108	401	707	16	7	9
10—15 ..	*26,324*	14,791	11,533	22,502	13,489	9,013	3,736	1,253	2,483	86	49	37
15—20 ..	*21,146*	11,847	9,299	8,745	6,723	2,022	11,864	4,686	7,178	537	438	99
20—30 ..	*36,664*	20,034	16,630	7,106	6,226	880	28,199	12,891	15,308	1,359	917	442
30—40 ..	*23,959*	13,066	10,893	2,059	1,816	243	19,933	10,241	9,692	1,967	1,009	958
40—50 ..	*17,181*	9,731	7,450	1,168	1,068	100	13,067	7,330	5,737	2,946	1,333	1,613
50—60 ..	*11,239*	6,656	4,583	580	540	40	7,638	4,726	2,912	3,021	1,390	1,631
60 and over ..	*10,955*	6,521	4,434	471	428	43	5,203	3,715	1,488	5,281	2,378	2,903
JAIN ..	**95**	**66**	**29**	**56**	**38**	**18**	**34**	**24**	**10**	**5**	**4**	**1**
0—1 ..	*4*	2	2	4	2	2	..	..	..	..	.	..
1—2 ..	*3*	2	1	3	2	1	..	..	..	..	..	.
2—3 ..	*4*	3	1	4	3	1	..	.	..	..	..	.
3—4 ..	*3*	3	..	3	3	..	..	.	..	..	..	.
4—5 ..	*5*	3	2	5	3	2	..	.	..	..	.	.
Total 0—5 ..	*19*	*13*	*6*	*19*	*13*	*6*	..	..	.	..	.	..
5—10 ..	11	8	3	11	8	3	..	..	.	..	..	..
10—15 ..	*11*	8	3	11	8	3	.	..	..	..	..	..
15—20 ..	*10*	6	4	7	4	3	3	2	1	..	..	..
20—30 ..	*17*	10	7	5	2	3	12	8	4	..	..	..
30—40 ..	*11*	9	2	2	2	..	8	6	2	1	1	..
40—50 ..	*8*	6	2	..	..	..	5	4	1	3	2	1
50—60 ..	*4*	4	..	1	1	..	2	2	..	1	1	..
60 and over ..	*4*	2	2	..	..	..	4	2	2	.	..	..
MUSLIM ..	**720,996**	**389,159**	**331,837**	**386,135**	**223,903**	**162,232**	**290,745**	**146,136**	**144,609**	**44,116**	**19,120**	**24,996**
0—1 ..	*30,591*	15,365	15,226	30,586	15,365	15,221	4	..	4	1	.	1
1—2 ..	*23,696*	12,030	11,566	23,582	12,025	11,557	13	5	8	1	..	1
2—3 ..	*25,568*	13,027	12,541	25,446	12,959	12,487	121	68	53	1	.	1
3—4 ..	*25,243*	12,919	12,321	24,958	12,784	12,174	284	135	149	1	..	1
4—5 .	*24,093*	12,623	11,470	23,732	12,474	11,258	357	148	209	4	1	3
Total 0—5 ..	*129,091*	*65,964*	*63,127*	*128,304*	*65,607*	*62,697*	*779*	*356*	*423*	*8*	*1*	*7*
5—10 ..	*106,545*	55,997	50,548	100,409	53,874	46,535	5,981	2,001	3,980	155	122	33
10—15 ..	*95,236*	50,970	44,266	82,086	46,614	35,472	12,791	4,088	8,703	359	268	91
15—20 ..	*68,922*	37,362	31,560	33,710	24,266	9,444	34,336	12,560	21,776	876	536	340
20—30 ..	*118,744*	64,669	54,075	28,834	23,572	5,262	86,095	38,935	47,160	3,815	2,162	1,653
30—40 ..	*77,051*	43,147	33,904	6,809	5,668	1,141	64,558	34,583	29,975	5,684	2,896	2,788
40—50 ..	*52,839*	29,494	23,345	2,590	1,984	606	42,084	24,169	17,915	8,165	3,341	4,824
50—60 ..	*35,987*	20,038	15,949	1,558	1,108	450	24,992	15,414	9,578	9,437	3,516	5,921
60 and over ..	*36,581*	21,518	15,063	1,835	1,210	625	19,129	14,030	5,099	15,617	6,278	9,339
CHRISTIAN ..	**45,518**	**24,899**	**20,619**	**27,170**	**15,299**	**11,871**	**15,660**	**8,110**	**7,550**	**2,688**	**1,490**	**1,198**
0—1 ..	*1,967*	985	982	1,967	985	982	..	..	..	..	..	..
1—2 ..	*1,461*	747	714	1,461	747	714	..	..	..	..	..	..
2—3 ..	*1,632*	831	801	1,631	830	801	1	1	..	..	..	.
3—4 ..	*1,660*	855	805	1,658	853	805	2	2	..	.	..	
4—5 ..	*1,575*	827	748	1,570	824	746	4	2	2	1	1	
Total 0—5 ..	*8,295*	*4,245*	*4,050*	*8,287*	*4,239*	*4,048*	*7*	*5*	*2*	*1*	*1*	
5—10 ..	*6,991*	3,699	3,292	6,924	3,681	3,243	65	17	48	2	1	
10—15 ..	*6,299*	3,364	2,935	5,952	3,301	2,651	342	59	283	5	4	1
15—20 ..	*4,498*	2,487	2,011	2,848	1,855	993	1,613	608	1,005	37	24	13
20—30 ..	*7,635*	4,185	3,450	2,544	1,803	741	4,873	2,223	2,650	218	159	59
30—40 ..	*4,715*	2,719	1,996	406	261	145	3,933	2,217	1,716	376	241	135
40—50 ..	*3,181*	1,867	1,314	121	95	26	2,508	1,488	1,020	552	284	268
50—60 ..	*2,013*	1,179	834	51	35	16	1,412	842	570	550	302	248
60 and over ..	*1,891*	1,154	737	37	29	8	907	651	256	947	474	473

TABLE VII.—AGE, SEX

PART B.—DETAILS FOR DISTRICTS AND STATES.

JHANG DISTRICT.

Religion and Age.	Population.			Unmarried.			Married.			Widowed.		
	Persons.	Males.	Females.	Persons.	Males.	Females.	Persons.	Males.	Females.	Persons.	Males.	Females.
1	2	3	4	5	6	7	8	9	10	11	12	13
ALL RELIGIONS	**664,833**	**355,671**	**309,162**	**365,811**	**212,202**	**153,609**	**252,423**	**125,533**	**126,890**	**46,599**	**17,936**	**28,663**
0—1	*24,031*	12,408	11,623	24,029	12,407	11,622	2	1	1	..	..	..
1—2	*18,099*	9,034	9,065	18,090	9,033	9,057	9	1	8	..	..	.
2—3	*22,176*	11,284	10,892	22,152	11,276	10,876	24	8	16	..	..	
3—4	*23,337*	12,001	11,336	23,304	11,987	11,317	33	14	19	..	..	.
4—5	*23,175*	12,010	11,165	23,132	11,995	11,137	42	14	28	1	1	..
Total 0—5	*110,818*	*56,737*	*54,081*	*110,707*	*56,698*	*54,009*	*110*	*38*	*72*	*1*	*1*	..
5—10	*95,151*	50,528	44,623	94,201	50,333	43,868	931	187	744	19	8	11
10—15	*81,622*	44,149	37,473	77,162	43,335	33,827	4,394	789	3,605	66	25	41
15—20	57,879	30,413	27,466	36,207	24,213	11,904	21,163	6,012	15,151	509	188	321
20—30	*110,143*	57,450	52,693	34,122	26,411	7,711	72,730	29,598	43,132	3,291	1,441	1,850
30—40	*79,979*	43,385	36,594	8,266	6,991	1,275	65,294	33,849	31,445	6,419	2,545	3,874
40—50	*56,556*	31,174	25,382	2,724	2,270	454	44,350	25,684	18,666	9,482	3,220	6,262
50—60	*38,165*	21,764	16,401	1,332	1,094	238	23,825	16,672	9,153	11,008	3,998	7,010
60 and over	*34,520*	20,071	14,449	1,090	857	233	17,626	12,704	4,922	15,804	6,510	9,294
HINDU	**102,924**	**52,999**	**49,925**	**54,906**	**30,522**	**24,384**	**40,901**	**20,006**	**20,895**	**7,117**	**2,471**	**4,646**
0—1	*3,875*	1,939	1,936	3,875	1,939	1,936	..	..	..	.	.	
1—2	*2,668*	1,369	1,299	2,668	1,369	1,299	.	..	.	..	.	
2—3	*3,256*	1,655	1,601	3,255	1,655	1,600	1	..	1	..	.	.
3—4	*3,561*	1,799	1,762	3,557	1,798	1,759	4	1	3	..	.	..
4—5	*3,478*	1,797	1,681	3,469	1,795	1,674	9	2	7	..	..	..
Total 0—5	*16,838*	*8,559*	*8,279*	*16,824*	*8,556*	*8,268*	*14*	*3*	*11*	..	..	..
5—10	*14,392*	7,317	7,075	14,183	7,278	6,905	205	37	168	4	2	2
10—15	*12,696*	6,459	6,237	11,919	6,317	5,602	765	134	631	12	8	4
15—20	*8,248*	4,234	4,014	4,868	3,241	1,627	3,308	964	2,344	72	29	43
20—30	*16,785*	8,640	8,145	4,445	3,277	1,168	11,903	5,219	6,684	437	144	[illegible]
30—40	*12,805*	6,517	6,288	1,518	992	526	10,267	5,226	5,041	1,020	299	721
40—50	*9,587*	5,024	4,563	557	414	143	7,541	4,155	3,386	1,489	455	1,034
50—60	*6,293*	3,359	2,934	344	257	87	4,191	2,500	1,691	1,758	602	1,156
60 and over	*5,280*	2,890	2,390	248	190	58	2,707	1,768	939	2,325	932	1,393
SIKH	**8,476**	**4,551**	**3,925**	**4,296**	**2,448**	**1,848**	**3,525**	**1,843**	**1,682**	**655**	**260**	**395**
0—1	*290*	154	136	290	154	136	..	..	..	..	..	..
1—2	*259*	130	129	259	130	129	..	..	..	..	.	..
2—3	*300*	153	147	299	153	146	1	.	1	..		.
3—4	*280*	144	136	280	144	136	..	..	..	..	..	..
4—5	*282*	142	140	282	142	140	..	..	..	.	.	..
Total 0—5	*1,411*	*723*	*688*	*1,410*	*723*	*687*	*1*	..	*1*	..		.
5—10	*1,213*	633	580	1,192	629	563	21	4	17	..	..	..
10—15	*1,052*	547	505	977	534	443	74	13	61	1	..	1
15—20	*714*	354	360	359	245	114	344	108	236	11	1	[illegible]
20—30	*1,379*	716	663	255	224	31	1,062	472	590	62	20	2
30—40	*1,068*	574	494	54	52	2	913	497	416	101	25	76
40—50	*702*	376	326	20	16	4	542	321	221	140	39	101
50—60	*526*	338	188	25	22	3	340	241	99	161	75	[illegible]
60 and over	*411*	290	121	4	3	1	228	187	41	179	[illegible]	[illegible]
MUSLIM	**552,853**	**297,801**	**255,052**	**306,282**	**179,048**	**127,234**	**207,768**	**103,563**	**104,205**	**38,808**	**15,190**	**23,613**
0—1	*19,844*	10,305	9,539	19,842	10,304	9,538	2	1	1	..	..	..
1—2	*15,158*	7,530	7,628	15,149	7,529	7,620	9	1	8	..		
2—3	*18,603*	9,471	9,132	18,581	9,463	9,118	22	8	14	..	.	
3—4	*19,482*	10,052	9,430	19,453	10,039	9,414	29	13	16	..	..	.
4—5	*19,396*	10,061	9,335	19,365	10,050	9,315	30	10	20	1	1	..
Total 0—5	*92,483*	*47,419*	*45,064*	*92,390*	*47,385*	*45,005*	*92*	*33*	*59*	*1*	*1*	..
5—10	*79,457*	42,529	36,928	78,744	42,380	36,364	698	143	555	15	6	[illegible]
10—15	*67,777*	37,090	30,687	64,183	36,437	27,746	3,542	636	2,906	52	17	[illegible]
15—20	*48,845*	25,784	23,061	30,942	20,701	10,241	17,477	4,925	12,552	426	158	268
20—30	*91,884*	48,037	43,847	29,392	22,885	6,507	59,704	23,878	35,826	2,788	1,274	1,514
30—40	*66,044*	36,261	29,783	6,687	5,944	743	54,066	28,101	25,965	5,291	2,216	3,075
40—50	*46,219*	25,744	20,475	2,143	1,837	306	36,229	21,184	15,045	7,847	2,723	5,124
50—60	*31,323*	18,053	13,270	963	815	148	21,274	13,919	7,355	9,086	3,319	5,767
60 and over	*28,821*	16,884	11,937	838	664	174	14,686	10,744	3,942	13,297	5,476	7,821
CHRISTIAN	**494**	**267**	**227**	**287**	**159**	**128**	**189**	**98**	**91**	**18**	**10**	**8**
0—1	*16*	8	8	16	8	8	..	..	..	..	.	.
1—2	*13*	5	8	13	5	8	..	..	..	..	..	..
2—3	*16*	5	11	16	5	11	..	..	.	..	..	..
3—4	*14*	6	8	14	6	8	..	..	.	..	..	..
4—5	*16*	10	6	14	8	6	2	2	..	..	.	..
Total 0—5	*75*	*34*	*41*	*73*	*32*	*41*	*2*	*2*	..	..	.	.
5—10	*79*	44	35	77	43	34	2	1	1	..	.	..
10—15	*81*	41	40	76	40	36	5	1	4	..	..	..
15—20	*60*	32	28	34	22	12	26	10	16	..	..	..
20—30	*74*	44	30	22	19	3	49	23	26	3	2	1
30—40	*51*	25	26	2	1	1	44	21	23	5	3	2
40—50	*46*	28	18	3	2	1	37	23	14	6	3	3
50—60	*20*	12	8	..	..	..	19	12	7	1	..	1
60 and over	*8*	7	1	..	..	..	5	5	..	3	2	1

AND CIVIL CONDITION (BY RELIGION).

PART B.—DETAILS FOR DISTRICTS AND STATES—*continued.*

MULTAN DISTRICT.

Religion and Age.	Population.			Unmarried.			Married.			Widowed.		
	Persons.	Males.	Females.	Persons.	Males.	Females	Persons.	Males.	Females.	Persons.	Males.	Females.
1	2	3	4	5	6	7	8	9	10	11	12	13
ALL RELIGIONS ..	**1,174,900**	**646,025**	**528,875**	**627,113**	**369,696**	**257,417**	**460,593**	**240,421**	**320,172**	**87,194**	**35,908**	**51,286**
0 1 ..	*42,279*	21,443	20,836	42,278	21,443	20,835	1		1	..	..	..
1 2 ..	*34,301*	17,365	16,936	34,287	17,355	16,932	12	9	3	2	.	1
2 3 .	*41,271*	21,351	19,920	41,230	21,325	19,905	36	22	14	5	4	1
3 4 ..	*42,176*	22,229	19,947	42,001	22,086	19,915	171	140	31	4	3	1
4 5 ..	*41,059*	21,741	19,318	40,752	21,479	19,273	299	258	41	8	4	4
Total 0—5 ..	*201,086*	*104,129*	*96,957*	*200,548*	*103,688*	*96,860*	*519*	*429*	*90*	*19*	*12*	*7*
5—10 ..	*163,856*	97,979	75,877	161,465	87,080	74,385	2,286	831	1,455	105	68	37
10—15 ..	*136,265*	74,734	61,531	126,887	72,786	54,101	9,120	1,800	7,320	258	148	110
15—20 ..	*104,790*	57,417	47,373	58,924	42,692	16,232	44,553	14,113	30,440	1,313	612	701
20—30 .	*217,422*	119,306	98,116	60,893	47,473	13,420	148,591	67,832	80,759	7,938	4,001	3,937
30—40 .	*151,390*	87,314	64,076	12,148	10,707	1,441	124,856	70,126	54,730	14,386	6,481	7,905
40—50 .	*94,457*	54,794	39,663	3,547	3,003	544	71,168	44,410	26,758	19,742	7,381	12,361
50—60 ..	*56,283*	32,848	23,435	1,602	1,339	263	35,369	24,183	11,186	19,312	7,326	11,986
60 and over ..	*49,351*	27,504	21,847	1,099	928	171	24,131	16,697	7,434	24,121	9,879	14,242
HINDU ..	**177,102**	**98,646**	**78,456**	**84,553**	**52,359**	**32,194**	**75,434**	**39,851**	**35,583**	**17,115**	**6,436**	**10,679**
0—1 ..	*6,068*	3,002	3,066	6,068	3,002	3,066	..	..	..	.	..	..
1—2 ..	*4,675*	2,318	2,357	4,675	2,318	2,357	..	.	..	..	.	..
2—3 ..	*5,393*	2,724	2,669	5,392	2,723	2,669	..	..	.	1	1	..
3 4 ..	*5,422*	2,791	2,631	5,419	2,790	2,629	3	1	2	..	.	.
4 5 ..	*5,322*	2,783	2,539	5,314	2,779	2,535	8	4	4	.	.	.
Total 0 5	*26,880*	*13,618*	*13,262*	*26,868*	*13,612*	*13,256*	*11*	*5*	*6*	*1*	*1*	..
5 10	*22,642*	12,110	10,532	21,993	11,949	10,044	643	160	483	6	1	5
10—15 ..	*19,999*	11,018	8,981	17,693	10,583	7,110	2,275	422	1,853	31	13	18
15—20 ..	*17,300*	9,734	7,566	7,883	6,757	1,126	9,127	2,853	6,274	290	124	166
20—30 ..	*35,060*	19,886	15,174	7,317	6,871	446	26,019	12,272	13,747	1,724	743	981
30—40 ..	*23,935*	14,137	9,798	1,647	1,485	162	19,210	11,423	7,787	3,078	1,229	1,849
40—50 ..	*15,459*	8,992	6,467	591	561	30	10,666	6,988	3,678	4,202	1,443	2,759
50 60 .	*9,178*	5,339	3,839	353	339	14	4,969	3,659	1,310	3,856	1,341	2,515
60 and over .	*6,649*	3,812	2,837	208	202	6	2,514	2,069	445	3,927	1,541	2,386
SIKH ..	**39,453**	**23,241**	**16,212**	**20,046**	**12,664**	**7,382**	**16,661**	**9,127**	**7,534**	**2,746**	**1,450**	**1,296**
0 1 ..	*1,457*	734	723	1,457	734	723	..	.	.	.	.	..
1—2 ..	*1,122*	593	529	1,121	592	529	1	1	.	..	..	..
2—3 ..	*1,278*	696	582	1,278	696	582	..	..	..	..	..	.
3 4 ..	*1,242*	657	585	1,242	657	585	..	..	..	..	..	..
4 5 ..	*1,218*	632	586	1,218	632	586	..	..	..	..	..	..
Total 0—5 ..	*6,317*	*3,312*	*3,005*	*6,316*	*3,311*	*3,005*	*1*	*1*	.	..	..	..
5—10 ..	*5,089*	2,733	2,356	5,031	2,718	2,313	57	14	43	1	1	..
10—15 ..	*4,437*	2,483	1,954	4,075	2,413	1,662	357	68	289	5	2	3
15—20 ..	*3,718*	2,216	1,502	1,891	1,597	294	1,787	600	1,187	40	19	21
20—30 ..	*7,506*	4,545	2,961	1,944	1,849	95	5,318	2,542	2,776	244	154	90
30—40 ..	*5,409*	3,449	1,960	541	529	12	4,404	2,632	1,772	464	288	176
40—50 ..	*3,380*	2,207	1,173	177	176	1	2,617	1,711	906	586	320	266
50 60 ..	*1,880*	1,224	656	43	43	..	1,266	897	369	571	284	287
60 and over .	*1,717*	1,072	645	28	28	..	854	662	192	835	382	453
JAIN ..	**440**	**220**	**220**	**194**	**100**	**94**	**196**	**102**	**94**	**50**	**18**	**32**
0—1 .	*22*	10	12	22	10	12	..	..	..	..	..	..
1—2 ..	*10*	4	6	10	4	6	.	..	..		.	..
2—3 ..	*16*	8	8	16	8	8	..	.	..	..	.	.
3—4 ..	*15*	7	8	15	7	8	..	.	..	.	..	.
4—5 ..	*13*	6	7	13	6	7	.		..	..	.	.
Total 0—5 ..	*76*	*35*	*41*	*76*	*35*	*41*	..	.	.	..	..	..
5—10 ..	*53*	26	27	53	26	27	..	.		..	..	..
10 15 ..	*48*	22	26	43	22	21	5	..	5	..	..	.
15—20	*40*	19	21	16	11	5	24	8	16	.	.	.
20—30 .	*85*	14	41	6	6	..	75	35	40	4	3	1
30—40 ..	*63*	36	27	.	.		54	34	20	9	2	7
40—50 ..	*39*	22	17	.	..	.	27	17	0	12	5	7
50—60 ..	*21*	11	10	..	..	..	11	8	3	10	3	7
60 and over ..	*15*	5	10	..	.	..	.	..	.	15	5	10
MUSLIM .	**942,937**	**515,218**	**427,719**	**514,133**	**299,452**	**214,681**	**362,513**	**188,314**	**174,199**	**66,291**	**27,452**	**38,839**
0 1 .	*34,193*	17,424	16,769	34,192	17,424	16,768	1	.	1	.	..	
1 2 ..	*28,042*	14,217	13,825	28,029	14,208	13,821	11	8	3	2	1	1
2 3 ..	*34,044*	17,644	16,400	34,005	17,620	16,385	35	21	14	4	3	1
3 4 ..	*34,933*	18,507	16,476	34,811	18,365	16,446	168	139	29	4	3	1
4 5 ..	*34,017*	18,057	15,960	33,719	17,799	15,920	290	254	36	8	4	4
Total 0 5 ..	*165,279*	*85,849*	*79,430*	*164,756*	*85,416*	*79,340*	*505*	*422*	*83*	*18*	*11*	*7*
5 10 .	*134,073*	72,030	62,043	132,445	71,328	61,117	1,530	636	894	98	66	32
10 15 ..	*110,055*	60,264	49,791	103,510	58,872	44,638	6,324	1,260	5,064	221	132	89
15 20 .	*82,240*	44,552	37,688	48,301	33,661	14,640	32,972	10,434	22,538	967	457	510
20 30 ..	*171,587*	92,822	78,765	50,528	37,727	12,801	115,191	52,065	63,126	5,868	3,030	2,838
30 40 ..	*120,153*	68,576	51,577	9,793	8,552	1,241	99,689	55,168	44,521	10,671	4,856	5,815
40 50 ..	*74,495*	42,897	31,598	2,746	2,250	496	57,030	35,158	21,872	14,719	5,489	9,230
50 60 ..	*44,584*	25,900	18,684	1,193	949	244	28,731	19,367	9,364	14,660	5,584	9,076
60 and over ..	*40,471*	22,328	18,143	861	697	164	20,541	13,804	6,737	19,069	7,827	11,242
CHRISTIAN .	**9,924**	**5,780**	**4,144**	**5,831**	**3,684**	**2,147**	**3,493**	**1,797**	**1,696**	**600**	**299**	**301**
0—1 ..	*339*	178	161	339	178	161	..	..	.	..	..	..
1 2 ..	*306*	154	152	306	154	152	..	..	..	..	..	..
2 3 ..	*364*	184	180	364	184	180	..	..	..	..	..	..
3 4 ..	*329*	171	158	329	171	158	..	..	..	..	..	..
4 5 ..	*315*	168	147	315	168	147	..	..	..	..	..	..
Total 0 5 ..	*1,653*	*855*	*798*	*1,653*	*855*	*798*	..	..	..	..	..	..
5—10 ..	*1,298*	692	606	1,295	692	603	3	..	3	..	..	..
10 15 ..	*1,140*	620	520	1,105	614	491	35	6	29	..	..	..
15 20 .	*1,051*	647	404	692	543	149	351	98	253	8	6	2
20—30 .	*2,226*	1,450	776	934	868	66	1,235	544	691	57	38	19
30—40 ..	*1,154*	692	462	123	102	21	934	532	402	97	58	39
40—50 .	*657*	402	255	20	6	14	512	335	177	125	61	64
50 60 ..	*402*	228	174	8	3	5	262	164	98	132	61	71
60 and over ..	*343*	194	149	1	1	..	161	118	43	181	75	106

TABLE VII.—AGE, SEX

PART B.— DETAILS FOR DISTRICTS AND STATES.

MUZAFFARGARH DISTRICT.

Religion and Age.	Population.			Unmarried.			Married.			Widowed.		
	Persons.	Males.	Females.	Persons.	Males.	Females.	Persons.	Males.	Females.	Persons.	Males.	Females.
1	2	3	4	5	6	7	8	9	10	11	12	13
ALL RELIGIONS ..	**591,375**	**320,674**	**270,701**	**285,117**	**172,728**	**112,389**	**256,473**	**126,937**	**129,536**	**49,785**	**21,009**	**28,777**
0 1 ..	*18,648*	9,478	9,170	18,635	9,476	9,159	13	2	11	..	..	..
1 2 ..	*14,692*	7,438	7,254	14,673	7,434	7,239	19	4	15	..	..	..
2 3 ..	*18,744*	9,563	9,181	18,694	9,549	9,145	49	14	35	1	..	1
3 4 ..	*19,576*	10,153	9,423	19,473	10,123	9,350	101	29	72	2	1	1
4 5 ..	*19,260*	10,134	9,126	19,106	10,089	9,017	148	43	105	6	2	4
Total 0 5 ..	*90,920*	*46,766*	*44,154*	*90,581*	*46,671*	*43,910*	*330*	*92*	*238*	*9*	*3*	*6*
5 10 ..	*80,700*	44,679	36,030	78,083	43,980	34,103	2,576	673	1,903	41	17	24
10 15 ..	*69,352*	39,482	29,870	61,673	37,585	24,088	7,550	1,847	5,703	129	50	79
15 20 ..	*54,020*	28,475	25,545	25,007	19,362	5,645	28,091	8,728	19,363	922	385	537
20 30 ..	*115,505*	59,459	56,046	23,013	19,532	3,481	87,369	37,351	50,018	5,123	2,576	2,547
30 40 ..	*81,781*	45,256	36,525	4,736	3,997	739	68,019	37,123	30,896	9,026	4,136	4,890
40 50 ..	*49,794*	27,983	21,811	1,234	982	252	56,631	22,439	14,192	11,929	4,562	7,367
50 60 ..	*28,749*	16,528	12,221	510	408	102	16,884	11,697	5,187	11,355	4,423	6,932
60 and over ..	*20,554*	12,055	8,499	280	211	69	9,023	6,987	2,036	11,251	4,857	6,394
HINDU ..	**72,577**	**38,284**	**34,293**	**32,073**	**19,062**	**13,011**	**32,034**	**15,979**	**16,055**	**8,470**	**3,243**	**5,227**
0 1 ..	*2,459*	1,242	1,217	2,459	1,242	1,217	.	..	..	.	..	..
1 2 ..	*1,709*	827	882	1,708	826	882	1	1	..	.	..	..
2—3 ..	*2,210*	1,097	1,113	2,202	1,093	1,109	8	4	4	..	..	..
3 4 ..	*2,328*	1,193	1,135	2,317	1,189	1,128	11	4	7	..	..	..
4—5 ..	*2,272*	1,182	1,090	2,256	1,176	1,080	16	6	10	..	..	..
Total 0 5 .	*10,978*	*5,541*	*5,437*	*10,942*	*5,526*	*5,416*	*36*	*15*	*21*	..	..	..
5 10 ..	*9,406*	5,010	4,396	8,978	4,903	4,075	422	105	317	6	2	4
10 15 ..	*8,067*	4,340	3,727	6,834	4,037	2,797	1,214	298	916	19	5	14
15 20 ..	*6,704*	3,395	3,309	2,376	1,929	447	4,193	1,417	2,776	135	49	86
20 30 ..	*14,363*	7,366	6,997	2,116	1,924	192	11,358	5,101	6,257	889	341	548
30 40 ..	*10,005*	5,445	4,560	518	468	50	7,856	4,349	3,507	1,631	628	1,003
40 50 .	*6,871*	3,775	3,096	191	170	21	4,473	2,810	1,663	2,207	795	1,412
50 60 .	*3,744*	2,102	1,642	83	73	10	1,740	1,283	457	1,921	746	1,175
60 and over ..	*2,479*	1,340	1,129	35	32	3	742	601	141	1,662	677	985
SIKH ..	**5,287**	**2,938**	**2,349**	**2.561**	**1.548**	**1,013**	**2 302**	**1,201**	**1.101**	**424**	**189**	**235**
0 1 ..	*192*	89	103	192	89	103	..	..	..	..	..	..
1 2 ..	*134*	67	67	134	67	67	.	.	..	..	..	
2 3 ..	*179*	93	86	179	93	86	..	..	..	..	..	.
3 4 .	*195*	104	91	195	104	91		..	..	..	..	.
4 5 .	*199*	104	95	197	103	94	2	1	1	..	..	.
Total 0 -5 ..	*899*	*457*	*442*	*897*	*456*	*441*	*2*	*1*	*1*	..	..	..
5 -10 .	*773*	440	333	745	427	318	27	12	15	1	1	..
10 15 .	*607*	362	245	534	336	198	73	26	47	..	..	..
15 20 .	*447*	237	210	174	148	26	266	85	181	7	4	3
20 30 .	*1,015*	530	485	158	142	16	809	365	444	48	23	25
30 40 ..	*728*	425	303	41	31	10	598	351	247	89	43	46
40 50 .	*428*	257	171	7	4	3	318	211	107	103	42	61
50 60 ..	*227*	130	97	4	3	1	135	93	42	88	34	54
60 and over .	*63*	100	63	1	1	..	74	57	17	88	42	46
MUSLIM ..	**513,265**	**279,319**	**233,946**	**250.351**	**152,053**	**98,298**	**222,041**	**109,702**	**112,339**	**40,873**	**17,564**	**23,309**
0 1 ..	*15,989*	8,144	7,845	15,976	8,142	7,834	13	2	11	..	..	..
1 2 .	*12,845*	6,541	6,304	12,827	6,538	6,289	18	3	15	..	..	..
2 3 ..	*16,347*	8,368	7,979	16,305	8,358	7,947	41	10	31	1	..	1
3 4 ..	*17,045*	8,853	8,192	16,953	8,827	8,126	90	25	65	2	1	1
4 5 ..	*16,781*	8,845	7,936	16 645	8,807	7,838	130	36	94	6	2	4
Total 0 5 ..	*79,007*	*40,751*	*38,256*	*78,706*	*40,672*	*38.034*	*292*	*76*	*216*	*9*	*3*	*6*
5 10 .	*70,487*	39.205	31,282	68,328	38.636	29,692	2.125	555	1.570	34	14	20
10 15 ..	*60,650*	34,766	25,884	54,279	33,198	21,081	6,261	1.523	4,738	110	45	65
15 20 .	*46,842*	24,829	22,013	22.439	17,277	5,162	23,623	7,220	16,403	780	332	448
20 30 .	*100,064*	51,530	48.534	20,724	17.458	3,266	75,157	31,862	43,295	4,183	2,210	1,973
30 40 .	*71,023*	30,368	31,655	4,174	3,495	679	59,546	32,410	27,136	7,303	3,463	3,840
40 50	*42,471*	23,938	18,536	1,034	807	227	31,825	19,409	12,416	9,615	3,722	5,893
50 60	*24,770*	14,290	10,480	423	332	91	15,005	10,318	4,687	9.342	3,640	5,702
60 and over ..	*17,948*	10,642	7,306	244	178	66	8,2 7	6,329	1,878	9,497	4,135	5,362
CHRISTIAN ..	**246**	**133**	**113**	**132**	**65**	**67**	**96**	**55**	**41**	**18**	**13**	**5**
0 1 .	*8*	3	5	8	3	5	..	..	..	..	..	..
1 2 ..	*4*	3	1	4	3	1	..	..	..	..	..	..
2 3 ..	*8*	5	3	8	5	3	..	..	..	..	..	..
3 4 ..	*8*	3	5	8	3	5	..	..	..	..	..	..
4 5 ..	*8*	3	5	8	3	5	..	..	..	..	..	..
Total 0 5 ..	*36*	*17*	*19*	*36*	*17*	*19*	..	..	..	..	..	..
5 10 ..	*34*	15	19	32	14	18	2	1	1	..	..	..
10—15 ..	*28*	14	14	26	14	12	2	..	2	..	..	..
15—20 ..	*27*	14	13	18	8	10	9	6	3	..	..	..
20—30 ..	*63*	33	30	15	8	7	45	23	22	3	2	1
30—40 ..	*25*	18	7	3	3	..	19	13	6	3	2	1
40—50 ..	*21*	13	8	2	1	1	15	9	6	4	3	1
50 60 ..	*8*	6	2	..	..	..	4	3	1	4	3	1
60 and over ..	*4*	3	1	..	..	..	..	..	..	4	3	1

AND CIVIL CONDITION (BY RELIGION).

PART B.—DETAILS FOR DISTRICTS AND STATES—*concluded.*

DERA GHAZI KHAN DISTRICT.

RELIGION AND AGE.	POPULATION.			UNMARRIED.			MARRIED.			WIDOWED.		
	Persons.	Males.	Females.	Persons.	Males.	Females.	Persons.	Males.	Females.	Persons.	Males.	Females.
1	2	3	4	5	6	7	8	9	10	11	12	13
ALL RELIGIONS ..	520,686	286,158	234,528	249,815	156,819	92,996	228,097	112,661	115,436	42,774	16,678	26,096
0—1 ..	17,616	8,888	8,728	17,616	8,888	8,728	..	..	..	..	..	.
1—2 ..	13,004	6,449	6,555	13,002	6,448	6,554	2	1	1	..	.	..
2—3 ..	16,672	8,439	8,233	16,662	8,434	8,228	8	4	4	2	1	1
3—4 ..	17,743	9,198	8,545	17,710	9,187	8,523	32	10	22	1	1	..
4—5 ..	17,812	9,443	8,369	17,754	9,427	8,327	54	14	40	4	2	2
Total 0—5 ..	82,847	42,417	40,430	82,744	42,384	40,360	96	29	67	7	4	3
5—10 ..	69,291	38,757	30,534	66,527	38,482	28,045	2,724	255	2,469	40	20	20
10—15 ..	56,513	32,905	23,608	49,887	31,951	17,936	6,329	907	5,622	97	47	50
15—20 ..	42,579	23,442	19,137	20,939	17,357	3,582	21,014	5,827	15,187	626	258	368
20—30 .	97,752	51,272	46,480	21,806	19,661	2,145	71,838	29,637	42,201	4,108	1,974	2,134
30—40 ..	75,701	42,249	33,452	5,505	4,950	555	62,946	34,110	28,836	7,250	3,189	4,061
40—50 ..	48,525	27,866	20,659	1,585	1,342	243	36,584	22,825	13,759	10,356	3,699	6,657
50—60 ..	28,079	15,925	12,154	435	345	90	17,331	11,968	5,363	10,313	3,612	6,701
60 and over ..	19,399	11,325	8,074	387	347	40	9,035	7,103	1,932	9,977	3,875	6,102
HINDU ..	57,390	29,812	27,578	27,647	16,133	11,514	22,942	11,355	11,587	6,801	2,824	4,477
0—1 ..	1,957	964	993	1,957	964	993	.	..	..	..	..	
1—2 ..	1,394	683	711	1,394	683	711	..	.	..	..	.	.
2—3 ..	1,750	892	858	1,748	892	856	1	.	1	1	..	1
3—4 ..	1,900	970	930	1,884	968	916	16	2	14	..	..	..
4—5 ..	1,941	992	949	1,905	987	918	34	4	30	2	1	1
Total 0—5 ..	8,942	4,501	4,441	8,888	4,494	4,394	51	6	45	3	1	2
5—10 ..	7,763	4,138	3,625	7,498	4,087	3,411	261	51	210	4		4
10—15 ..	6,620	3,596	3,024	5,837	3,447	2,390	766	144	622	17	5	12
15—20 ..	5,143	2,626	2,517	2,394	1,805	589	2,629	783	1,846	120	38	82
20—30 ..	10,635	5,222	5,413	2,197	1,651	546	7,712	3,268	4,444	726	303	423
30—40 ..	7,880	4,140	3,740	484	345	139	6,045	3,358	2,687	1,351	437	914
40—50 ..	5,369	2,903	2,466	239	211	28	3,381	2,145	1,236	1,749	547	1,202
50—60 ..	3,082	1,665	1,417	64	54	10	1,485	1,088	397	1,533	523	1,010
60 and over ..	1,956	1,021	935	46	39	7	612	512	100	1,298	470	828
SIKH ..	760	439	321	380	236	144	327	173	154	53	30	23
0—1 ..	24	12	12	24	12	12	..	.	.	..		.
1—2 ..	18	11	7	18	11	7	..	.	..	..	.	.
2—3 ..	25	14	11	25	14	11	..	..	..	..	.	
3—4 ..	31	16	15	31	16	15	..	..	..	..	..	.
4—5 ..	33	18	15	33	18	15	..	..	..	..	..	.
Total 0—5 ..	131	71	60	131	71	60	..	..	..	..	..	..
5—10 ..	109	60	49	108	60	48	1	..	1	..		..
10—15 ..	81	47	34	75	46	29	6	1	5	..	.	..
15—20 ..	65	33	32	25	20	5	38	11	27	2	2	.
20—30 ..	148	79	69	24	22	2	116	53	63	8	4	4
30—40 ..	100	65	35	11	11	.	78	46	32	11	8	3
40—50 ..	66	44	22	5	5	.	51	34	17	10	6	5
50—60 ..	36	25	11	.	..	..	25	18	7	11	7	4
60 and over ..	24	15	9	1	1	..	12	10	2	11	4	7
JAIN ..	125	71	54	69	44	25	49	26	23	7	1	6
0—1 ..	8	5	3	8	5	3	..	..	..	.	..	.
1—2 ..	2	1	1	2	1	1	..	.	..	.	..	..
2—3 ..	5	3	2	5	3	2	..	..	..	..	..	..
3—4 ..	6	3	3	6	3	3	..	..	..	..	..	..
4—5 ..	9	5	4	9	5	4	..	..	..	..	..	..
Total 0—5 ..	30	17	13	30	17	13	..	..	..	..	..	..
5—10 ..	22	14	8	22	14	8	..	..	..	..	..	.
10—15 ..	12	8	4	11	8	3	1	..	1	..	..	.
15—20 ..	6	4	2	2	2	..	4	2	2	..	..	.
20—30 ..	22	10	12	2	1	1	20	9	11	.	..	..
30—40 ..	15	9	6	1	1	..	13	8	5	1	..	1
40—50 ..	8	4	4	..	..	..	6	4	2	2	.	2
50—60 ..	8	3	5	1	1		3	1	2	4	1	3
60 and over ..	2	2	..	..	..	..	2	2	..	..	.	..
MUSLIM .	462,380	255,817	206,563	221,705	140,397	81,308	204,762	101,097	103,665	35,918	14,328	21,590
0—1 .	15,626	7,906	7,720	15,626	7,906	7,720		..	..	..	.	..
1—2 ..	11,588	5,753	5,835	11,586	5,752	5,834	2	1	1	..	.	.
2—3 ..	14,891	7,529	7,362	14,883	7,524	7,359	7	4	3	1	1	
3—4 ..	15,805	8,208	7,597	15,788	8,199	7,589	16	8	8	1	1	
4—5 ..	15,826	8,427	7,399	15,804	8,416	7,388	20	10	10	2	1	1
Total 0—5 ..	73,736	37,823	35,913	73,687	37,797	35,890	45	23	22	4	3	1
5—10 ..	61,396	34,545	26,851	58,898	34,321	24,577	2,462	204	2,258	36	20	16
10—15 ..	49,800	29,254	20,546	43,964	28,450	15,514	5,756	762	4,994	80	42	38
15—20 ..	37,362	20,777	16,585	18,517	15,529	2,988	18,341	5,030	13,311	504	218	286
20—30 ..	86,938	45,956	40,982	19,580	17,985	1,595	63,984	26,304	37,680	3,374	1,667	1,707
30—40 ..	67,700	38,031	29,669	5,008	4,592	416	56,805	30,695	26,110	5,887	2,744	3,143
40—50 ..	43,079	24,913	18,166	1,341	1,126	215	33,143	20,640	12,503	8,595	3,147	5,448
50—60 ..	24,952	14,231	10,721	370	290	80	15,817	10,860	4,957	8,765	3,081	5,684
60 and over ..	17,417	10,287	7,130	340	307	33	8,409	6,579	1,830	8,668	3,401	5,267
CHRISTIAN ..	31	19	12	14	9	5	17	10	7	..	.	.
0—1 ..	1	1	..	1	1	..	.	..	..	..	..	.
1—2 ..	2	1	1	2	1	1	..	.	.	.	.	..
2—3 .	1	1	.	1	1	..	..	.	..	..	..	
3—4 ..	1	1	..	1	1	..	..	.	..	..	..	
4—5 ..	3	1	2	3	1	2	..	..	..	..	..	
Total 0—5 ..	8	5	3	8	5	3	..	..	..	..	..	..
5—10 ..	1	..	1	1	..	1	..	..	..	..	..	..
10—15 ..	..	..	..	..	..	..	..	..	..	..	..	..
15—20 ..	3	2	1	1	1	..	2	1	1	.	.	..
20—30 ..	9	5	4	3	2	1	6	3	3	..	..	..
30—40 ..	6	4	2	1	1	..	5	3	2	..	..	.
40—50 ..	3	2	1	..	..	..	3	2	1	..	..	..
50—60 ..	1	1	..	..	.	..	1	1	..	..	..	..
60 and over ..		..	..	.			..	..	.	.	.	.

TABLE VII.—AGE, SEX

PART B.—DETAILS FOR DISTRICTS AND STATES.

DUJANA STATE.

Religion and Age.	Population.			Unmarried.			Married.			Widowed.		
	Persons.	Males.	Females.	Persons.	Males.	Females.	Persons.	Males.	Females.	Persons.	Males.	Females.
1	2	3	4	5	6	7	8	9	10	11	12	13
ALL RELIGIONS ..	**28,216**	**14,537**	**13,679**	**12,897**	**7,733**	**5,164**	**12,260**	**5,546**	**6,714**	**3,059**	**1,258**	**1,801**
0—1 ..	*1,103*	542	561	1,103	542	561	..	..	..	..	..	..
1—2 ..	*812*	412	400	812	412	400	..	..	.	..	..	..
2—3 ..	*891*	439	453	892	439	453	2	..	2	..	..	..
3—4 ..	*926*	467	459	024	467	457	2	..	2	..	..	..
4—5 ..	*864*	451	413	861	451	410	3	..	3	..	..	..
Total 0—5 ..	*4,599*	*2,311*	*2,288*	*4,592*	*2,311*	*2,281*	*7*	..	*7*	..	..	..
5—10 ..	*3,927*	2,096	1,831	3,638	2,020	1,618	285	73	212	4	3	1
10—15 ..	*3,593*	1,917	1,676	2,845	1,723	1,122	740	190	550	8	4	4
15—20 ..	*2,584*	1,269	1,315	819	692	127	1,730	564	1,166	35	13	22
20—30 ..	*4,352*	2,049	2,303	544	530	14	3,610	1,443	2,167	198	76	122
30—40 ..	*3,272*	1,683	1,589	181	180	1	2,669	1,321	1,348	422	182	240
40—50 ..	*2,492*	1,325	1,167	124	124	..	1,708	916	792	660	285	375
50—60 ..	*1,787*	987	800	81	81	..	949	610	339	757	296	461
60 and over ..	*1,610*	900	710	73	72	1	562	429	133	975	399	576
HINDU ..	**22,347**	**11,650**	**10,697**	**10,213**	**6,157**	**4,056**	**9,702**	**4,436**	**5,266**	**2,432**	**1,057**	**1,375**
0—1 ..	*868*	427	441	868	427	441	..	..	..	..	..	..
1—2 ..	*650*	331	319	650	331	319	..	..	..	..	..	..
2—3 ..	*703*	349	354	701	349	352	2	..	2	..	..	..
3—4 ..	*730*	366	364	728	366	362	2	..	2	..	..	..
4—5 ..	*689*	354	335	686	354	332	3	..	3	..	..	..
Total 0—5 ..	*3,640*	*1,827*	*1,813*	*3,633*	*1,827*	*1,806*	*7*	..	*7*	..	..	..
5—10 ..	*3,081*	1,637	1,444	2,868	1,582	1,286	210	53	157	3	2	1
10—15 ..	*2,815*	1,610	1,305	2,227	1,355	872	583	153	430	5	2	3
15—20 ..	*2,053*	1,014	1,039	627	541	86	1,397	461	936	29	12	17
20—30 ..	*3,448*	1,664	1,784	429	424	5	2,855	1,176	1,679	164	64	100
30—40 ..	*2,607*	1,372	1,235	165	165	..	2,096	1,055	1,041	346	152	194
40—50 ..	*2,010*	1,083	927	117	117	..	1,362	729	633	531	237	294
50—60 ..	*1,420*	798	622	76	76	..	746	471	275	598	251	347
60 and over ..	*1,273*	745	528	71	70	1	446	338	108	756	337	419
SIKH ..	**1**	**1**	..	**1**	**1**	..	..	..	..	..	..	..
15—20 ..	*1*	*1*	..	1	1	..	..	..	..	..	..	..
MUSLIM ..	**5,863**	**2,883**	**2,980**	**2,681**	**1,574**	**1,107**	**2,555**	**1,108**	**1,447**	**627**	**201**	**426**
0—1 ..	*235*	115	120	235	115	120	..	..	..	..	..	..
1—2 ..	*162*	81	81	162	81	81	..	..	..	..	..	..
2—3 ..	*191*	90	101	191	90	101	..	..	..	..	..	..
3—4 ..	*196*	101	95	196	101	95	..	..	..	..	..	..
4—5 ..	*174*	96	78	174	96	78	..	..	..	..	..	..
Total 0—5 ..	*958*	*483*	*475*	*958*	*483*	*475*	..	..	..	..	..	..
5—10 ..	*846*	459	387	770	438	332	75	20	55	1	1	..
10—15 ..	*778*	407	371	618	368	250	157	37	120	3	2	1
15—20 ..	*529*	254	275	190	150	40	333	103	230	6	1	5
20—30 ..	*904*	385	519	115	106	9	755	267	488	34	12	22
30—40 ..	*662*	309	353	16	15	1	570	264	306	76	30	46
40—50 ..	*482*	242	240	7	7	..	346	187	159	129	48	81
50—60 ..	*367*	189	178	5	5	..	203	139	64	159	45	114
60 and over ..	*337*	155	182	2	2	..	116	91	25	219	62	157
CHRISTIAN ..	**5**	**3**	**2**	**2**	**1**	**1**	**3**	**2**	**1**	..	..	..
4—5 ..	*1*	1	..	1	1	..	..	..	..	..	..	..
Total 0—5 ..	*1*	*1*	..	*1*	*1*	..	..	..	..	..	..	..
15—20 ..	*1*	..	1	1	.	1	.	..	..	..	..	..
30—40 ..	*3*	2	1	..	.	..	3	2	1	..	..	..

AND CIVIL CONDITION (BY RELIGION).

PART B.—DETAILS FOR DISTRICTS AND STATES—*continued.*

PATAUDI STATE.

Religion and Age.	Population.			Unmarried.			Married.			Widowed.		
	Persons.	Males.	Females.	Persons.	Males.	Females.	Persons.	Males.	Females.	Persons.	Males.	Females.
1	2	3	4	5	6	7	8	9	10	11	12	13
ALL RELIGIONS..	**18,873**	**9,922**	**8,951**	**7,936**	**4,768**	**3,168**	**8,584**	**4,175**	**4,409**	**2,358**	**979**	**1,374**
0–1 ..	*757*	347	410	757	347	410	..	..	..	..	..	..
1–2 ..	*529*	254	275	529	254	275	..	..	..	..	..	..
2–3 ..	*626*	316	310	626	316	310	..	..	..	..	..	..
3–4 ..	*570*	298	272	569	298	271	1	..	1	..	..	..
4–5 ..	*524*	280	244	516	278	238	8	2	6	..	..	..
Total 0–5 ..	*3,006*	*1,495*	*1,511*	*2,997*	*1,493*	*1,504*	*9*	*2*	*7*	..	..	..
5–10 ..	*2,418*	1,302	1,116	2,204	1,248	956	214	54	160	..	..	..
10–15 ..	*2,355*	1,289	1,066	1,761	1,112	649	587	172	415	7	5	2
15–20 ..	*1,889*	981	908	551	498	53	1,293	461	832	45	22	23
20–30 ..	*3,338*	1,681	1,657	366	361	5	2,735	1,219	1,536	217	101	116
30–40 ..	*2,478*	1,346	1,132	54	54	..	1,988	1,112	876	436	180	256
40–50 ..	*1,557*	833	724	1	1	..	1,002	625	377	554	207	347
50–60 ..	*1,032*	536	496	2	1	1	463	312	151	567	223	344
60 and over ..	*800*	459	341	..	..	..	273	218	55	527	241	286
HINDU ..	**15,596**	**8,227**	**7,369**	**6,565**	**3,958**	**2,607**	**7,035**	**3,445**	**3,590**	**1,996**	**824**	**1,172**
0–1 ..	*618*	286	332	618	286	332	..	..	..	..	..	..
1–2 ..	*435*	205	230	435	205	230	..	..	..	..	..	..
2–3 ..	*531*	267	264	531	267	264	..	..	..	..	..	..
3–4 ..	*481*	256	225	481	256	225	..	..	..	..	..	..
4–5 ..	*428*	233	195	424	231	193	4	2	2	..	..	..
Total 0–5 ..	*2,493*	*1,247*	*1,246*	*2,489*	*1,245*	*1,244*	*4*	*2*	*2*	..	..	..
5–10 ..	*1,970*	1,064	906	1,816	1,027	789	154	37	117	..	..	..
10–15 ..	*1,926*	1,059	867	1,453	921	532	467	133	334	6	5	1
15–20 ..	*1,558*	816	742	452	416	36	1,070	383	687	36	17	19
20–30 ..	*2,794*	1,412	1,382	305	300	5	2,298	1,025	1,273	191	87	104
30–40 ..	*2,084*	1,139	945	47	47	..	1,663	935	728	374	157	217
40–50 ..	*1,279*	695	584	1	1	..	808	518	290	470	176	294
50–60 ..	*836*	424	412	2	1	1	353	237	116	481	186	295
60 and over	*656*	371	285	..	..	..	218	175	43	438	196	242
SIKH .	**1**	**1**	..	..	..	.	**1**	**1**	..	..	..	..
30–40 ..	1	1	.	..	..	..	1	1	..	..	..	..
JAIN ..	**105**	**52**	**53**	**42**	**17**	**25**	**40**	**23**	**17**	**23**	**12**	**11**
0–1 ..	*3*	..	3	3	..	3	..	..	..	.	..	..
1–2 ..	*2*	1	1	2	1	1	..	..	..	..	..	..
2–3 .	*3*	1	2	3	1	2	..	..	..	..	..	..
3–4 ..	*3*	1	2	3	1	2	..	..	..	..	..	..
4–5 ..	*6*	3	3	6	3	3	..	..	..	..	..	..
Total 0–5 ..	*17*	*6*	*11*	*17*	*6*	*11*	..	..	..	..	..	..
5–10 ..	*13*	5	8	13	5	8	..	..	..	..	..	..
10–15 ..	*9*	3	6	8	3	5	1	..	1	..	..	..
15–20 ..	*10*	5	5	2	1	1	8	4	4	..	..	..
20–30 ..	*17*	10	7	1	1	..	14	8	6	2	1	1
30–40 ..	*19*	11	8	1	1	..	10	6	4	8	4	4
40–50 ..	*8*	4	4	..	..	..	4	3	1	4	1	3
50–60 ..	*6*	4	2	.	.	..	3	2	1	3	2	1
60 and over ..	*6*	4	2	.	..	..	..	..	..	6	4	2
MUSLIM ..	**3.168**	**1,640**	**1,528**	**1,329**	**793**	**536**	**1,505**	**704**	**801**	**334**	**143**	**191**
0–1 ..	*136*	61	75	136	61	75	..	..	..	..	..	..
1–2 ..	*92*	48	44	92	48	44	..	..	..	..	..	..
2–3 ..	*92*	48	44	92	48	44	..	..	..	..	..	..
3–4 ..	*86*	41	45	85	41	44	1	..	1	..	..	..
4–5 ..	*90*	44	46	86	44	42	4	..	4	..	..	..
Total 0–5 ..	*496*	*242*	*254*	*491*	*242*	*249*	*5*	..	*5*	..	..	..
5–10 ..	*434*	233	201	375	216	159	59	17	42	..	..	..
10–15 ..	*420*	227	193	300	188	112	119	39	80	1	..	1
15–20 ..	*327*	160	161	97	81	16	215	74	141	9	5	4
20–30 ..	*527*	259	268	60	60	..	443	186	257	24	13	11
30–40 ..	*373*	194	179	6	6	..	313	169	144	54	19	35
40–50 ..	*270*	134	136	..	..	..	190	104	86	80	30	50
50–60 ..	*189*	107	82	..	..	..	106	72	34	83	35	48
60 and over ..	*138*	84	54	..	..	..	55	43	12	83	41	42
CHRISTIAN ..	**3**	**2**	**1**	..	..	..	**3**	**2**	**1**	..	..	..
5–10 ..	*1*	..	1	..	..	..	1	..	1	..	..	..
30–40 ..	*1*	1	..	..	..	..	1	1	..	..	..	..
50–60 ..	*1*	1	.	.	..		1	1	..	..	..	..

TABLE VII.—AGE, SEX

PART B.—DETAILS FOR DISTRICTS AND STATES.

KALSIA STATE.

Religion and Age.	Population.			Unmarried.			Married.			Widowed.		
	Persons.	Males.	Females.	Persons.	Males.	Females.	Persons.	Males.	Females.	Persons.	Males.	Females.
1	2	3	4	5	6	7	8	9	10	11	12	13
ALL RELIGIONS ..	59,848	33,306	26,542	27,438	17,166	10,272	25,378	12,746	12,632	7,032	3,394	3,638
0—1 ..	2,172	1,119	1,053	2,170	1,119	1,051	2	..	2	..	..	..
1—2 ..	1,644	839	805	1,644	839	805	..	..	..	..	..	..
2—3 ..	1,755	899	856	1,755	899	856	..	..	..	..	..	..
3—4 ..	1,744	908	836	1,732	904	828	12	4	8	..	..	..
4—5 ..	1,698	879	819	1,665	868	797	30	9	21	3	2	1
Total 0—5 ..	9,013	4,644	4,369	8,966	4,629	4,337	44	13	31	3	2	1
5—10 ..	7,708	4,180	3,528	7,042	3,985	3,057	649	185	464	17	10	7
10—15 ..	7,361	4,104	3,257	5,839	3,621	2,218	1,485	466	1,019	37	17	20
15—20 ..	5,860	3,276	2,584	2,295	1,825	470	3,430	1,375	2,055	135	76	59
20—30 ..	10,481	5,852	4,629	1,881	1,732	149	7,971	3,765	4,206	629	355	274
30—40 ..	7,558	4,350	3,208	717	690	27	5,726	3,059	2,667	1,115	601	514
40—50 ..	5,385	3,109	2,276	373	365	8	3,436	2,018	1,418	1,576	726	850
50—60 ..	3,549	2,093	1,456	200	196	4	1,702	1,142	560	1,647	755	892
60 and over ..	2,933	1,698	1,235	125	123	2	935	723	212	1,873	852	1,021
HINDU ..	28,550	16,085	12,465	13,000	8,267	4,733	12,045	6,121	5,924	3,505	1,697	1,808
0—1 ..	1,022	534	488	1,020	534	486	2	..	2	..	..	..
1—2 ..	749	384	365	749	384	365	..	..	.	..	..	..
2—3 ..	835	429	406	835	429	406	..	..	.	..	..	..
3—4 ..	851	450	401	846	448	398	5	2	3	..	..	.
4—5 ..	812	422	390	798	416	382	12	4	8	2	2	.
Total 0—5 ..	4,269	2,219	2,050	4,248	2,211	2,037	19	6	13	2	2	.
5—10 ..	3,628	1,971	1,657	3,316	1,890	1,426	303	76	227	9	5	4
10—15 ..	3,458	1,927	1,531	2,703	1,698	1,005	739	223	516	16	6	10
15—20 ..	2,806	1,579	1,227	1,048	856	192	1,702	690	1,012	56	33	23
20—30 ..	5,190	2,960	2,230	940	883	57	3,940	1,900	2,040	310	177	133
30—40 ..	3,693	2,201	1,492	392	382	10	2,721	1,511	1,210	580	308	272
40—50 ..	2,541	1,481	1,060	193	190	3	1,541	931	610	807	360	447
50—60 ..	1,662	985	677	106	103	3	728	500	228	828	382	446
60 and over ..	1,303	762	541	54	54	..	352	284	68	897	424	473
SIKH ..	9,035	5,121	3,914	4,191	2,725	1,466	3,652	1,814	1,838	1,192	582	610
0—1 ..	287	139	148	287	139	148	..	..	..	..	..	.
1—2 ..	235	120	115	235	120	115	..	..	..	..	..	..
2—3 ..	231	123	108	231	123	108	..	..	.	..	..	..
3—4 ..	225	117	108	224	117	107	1	.	1	..	..	..
4—5 ..	235	124	111	232	124	108	3	..	3	..	..	..
Total 0—5 ..	1,213	623	590	1,209	623	586	4	..	4	..	..	..
5—10 ..	1,103	617	486	1,037	597	440	64	19	45	2	1	1
10—15 ..	1,069	616	453	891	559	332	169	54	115	9	3	6
15—20 ..	893	515	378	383	307	76	478	189	289	32	19	13
20—30 ..	1,511	883	628	340	314	26	1,071	514	557	100	55	45
30—40 ..	1,124	640	484	147	142	5	804	400	404	173	98	75
40—50 ..	903	509	394	89	88	1	561	298	263	253	123	130
50—60 ..	634	380	254	53	53	..	305	200	105	276	127	149
60 and over ..	585	338	247	42	42	..	196	140	56	347	156	191
JAIN ..	162	88	74	73	45	28	62	32	30	27	11	16
0—1 ..	2	2	..	2	2	..	..	..	..	..	..	..
1—2 ..	3	1	2	3	1	2	..	..	..	..	..	..
2—3 ..	3	1	2	3	1	2	..	..	..	..	..	..
3—4 ..	1	1	..	1	1	..	..	..	..	..	..	..
4—5 ..	4	2	2	4	2	2	..	..	..	..	..	..
Total 0—5 ..	13	7	6	13	7	6	..	..	..	.	..	..
5—10 ..	19	11	8	19	11	8	..	..	..	..	..	..
10—15 ..	23	12	11	22	12	10	1	..	1	..	..	..
15—20 ..	19	10	9	9	6	3	10	4	6	..	..	..
20—30 ..	25	12	13	3	3	..	17	8	9	5	1	4
30—40 .	20	11	9	3	3	..	14	7	7	3	1	2
40—50 .	19	11	8	2	1	1	12	8	4	5	2	3
50—60 ..	15	7	8	1	1	..	6	3	3	8	3	5
60 and over ..	9	7	2	1	1	..	2	2	..	6	4	2
MUSLIM ..	21,797	11,843	9,954	10,014	6,031	3,983	9,494	4,720	4,774	2,289	1,092	1,197
0—1 ..	852	440	412	852	440	412	..	..	..	..	..	..
1—2 ..	645	330	315	645	330	315	..	..	..	..	..	..
2—3 ..	676	341	335	676	341	335	..	..	..	..	..	..
3—4 ..	657	334	323	651	332	319	6	2	4	..	..	..
4—5 ..	633	323	310	618	318	300	14	5	9	1	..	1
Total 0—5 ..	3,463	1,768	1,695	3,442	1,761	1,681	20	7	13	1	..	1
5—10 ..	2,915	1,555	1,360	2,627	1,461	1,166	282	90	192	6	4	2
10—15 .	2,777	1,529	1,248	2,191	1,332	859	574	189	385	12	8	4
15—20 ..	2,114	1,155	959	838	644	194	1,230	488	742	46	23	23
20—30 ..	3,697	1,965	1,732	587	522	65	2,897	1,322	1,575	213	121	92
30—40 ..	2,688	1,479	1,209	174	162	12	2,158	1,125	1,033	356	192	164
40—50 ..	1,894	1,095	799	88	85	3	1,299	772	527	507	238	269
50—60 .	1,224	713	511	39	38	1	655	435	220	530	240	200
60 and over ..	1,025	584	441	28	26	2	379	292	87	618	266	352
CHRISTIAN ..	22	14	8	9	7	2	12	6	6	1	1	..
1—2 ..	2	1	1	2	1	1	..	..	..	..	..	.
4—5 ..	2	2	..	2	2	..	..	..	..	..	..	..
Total 0—5 ..	4	3	1	4	3	1	..	..	..	..	..	..
5—10 ..	3	2	1	3	2	1	..	..	..	..	..	..
10—15 ..	1	1	..	1	1	..	..	..	..	..	..	..
15—20 ..	1	..	1	..	..	..	1	..	1	..	..	..
20—30 ..	7	4	3	1	1	..	6	3	3	..	..	..
30—40 ..	2	1	1	..	..	..	2	1	1	..	..	..
40—50 ..	2	1	1	..	..	..	2	1	1	..	..	..
50—60 ..	1	1	..	..	.	..	..	..	..	1	1	..
60 and over ..	1	1	..	..	.	.	1	1	..	..	..	..

AND CIVIL CONDITION (BY RELIGION).

PART B.—DETAILS FOR DISTRICTS AND STATES—*continued.*

SIMLA HILL STATES.

Religion and Age.	Population.			Unmarried.			Married.			Widowed.		
	Persons.	Males.	Females.	Persons.	Males.	Females.	Persons.	Males.	Females.	Persons.	Males.	Females.
1	2	3	4	5	6	7	8	9	10	11	12	13
ALL RELIGIONS ..	**330,850**	**171,525**	**159,325**	**126,190**	**73,541**	**52,649**	**168,693**	**84,579**	**84,114**	**35,967**	**13,405**	**22,562**
0—1 ..	*9,360*	4,622	4,738	9,360	4,622	4,738	..	..	..	..	..	..
1—2 ..	*7,003*	3,432	3,571	7,003	3,432	3,571	..	..	..	..	..	..
2—3 ..	*7,848*	3,729	4,119	7,847	3,728	4,119	1	1	..	..	..	..
3—4 ..	*8,242*	3,940	4,302	8,208	3,929	4,279	34	11	23	..	..	..
4—5 ..	*8,201*	4,008	4,193	8,117	3,980	4,137	81	26	55	3	2	1
Total 0—5 ..	*40,654*	*19,731*	*20,923*	*40,535*	*19,691*	*20,844*	*116*	*38*	*78*	*3*	*2*	*1*
5—10 ..	*36,157*	18,397	17,760	32,882	17,563	15,319	3,207	808	2,399	68	26	42
10—15 ..	*34,157*	17,888	16,269	26,214	15,652	10,562	7,730	2,158	5,572	213	78	135
15—20 ..	*29,302*	14,910	14,392	10,764	8,211	2,553	17,816	6,339	11,477	722	360	362
20—30 ..	*58,528*	29,332	29,196	9,693	7,731	1,962	45,892	20,067	25,825	2,943	1,534	1,409
30—40 ..	*51,019*	26,680	24,339	3,257	2,578	679	42,259	21,744	20,515	5,503	2,358	3,145
40—50 ..	*36,636*	20,017	16,619	1,519	1,146	373	27,360	16,187	11,173	7,757	2,684	5,073
50—60 ..	*25,207*	13,999	11,208	797	582	215	15,793	10,586	5,207	8,617	2,831	5,786
60 and over ..	*19,190*	10,671	8,619	529	387	142	8,520	6,652	1,868	10,141	3,532	6,609
HINDU ..	**317,390**	**164,029**	**153,361**	**120,558**	**70,101**	**50,457**	**162,211**	**81,201**	**81,010**	**34,621**	**12,727**	**21,894**
0—1 ..	*8,945*	4,417	4,528	8,945	4,417	4,528	..	..	..	..	..	..
1—2 ..	*6,682*	3,268	3,414	6,682	3,268	3,414	..	..	..	..	..	..
2—3 ..	*7,489*	3,542	3,947	7,488	3,541	3,947	1	1	..	..	..	..
3—4 ..	*7,898*	3,759	4,139	7,864	3,748	4,116	34	11	23	..	..	..
4—5 ..	*7,851*	3,822	4,029	7,769	3,795	3,974	79	25	54	3	2	1
Total 0—5 ..	*38,865*	*18,808*	*20,057*	*38,748*	*18,769*	*19,979*	*114*	*37*	*77*	*3*	*2*	*1*
5—10 ..	*34,565*	17,563	17,002	31,497	16,787	14,710	3,006	753	,253	62	23	39
10—15 ..	*32,619*	17,081	15,538	25,103	14,979	10,124	7,316	2,028	,288	200	74	126
15—20 ..	*28,024*	14,230	13,794	10,274	7,844	2,430	17,055	6,042	11,013	695	344	351
20—30 ..	*56,099*	27,987	28,112	9,191	7,326	1,865	44,072	19,200	24,872	2,836	1,461	1,375
30—40 ..	*49,095*	25,557	23,538	3,054	2,407	647	40,734	20,902	19,832	5,307	2,248	3,059
40—50 ..	*35,297*	19,183	16,114	1,427	1,069	358	26,405	15,582	10,823	7,465	2,532	4,933
50—60 ..	*24,347*	13,467	10,880	755	548	207	15,281	10,233	5,048	8,311	2,686	5,625
60 and over ..	*18,479*	10,153	8,326	509	372	137	8,228	6,424	1,804	9,742	3,357	6,385
SIKH ..	**1,817**	**1,001**	**816**	**667**	**416**	**251**	**950**	**494**	**456**	**200**	**91**	**109**
0—1 ..	*69*	28	41	69	28	41	..	..	..	..	..	..
1—2 ..	*46*	24	22	46	24	22	..	..	..	..	..	..
2—3 ..	*44*	24	20	44	24	20	..	..	..	..	..	..
3—4 ..	*44*	26	18	44	26	18	..	..	..	..	..	..
4—5 ..	*50*	30	20	50	30	20	..	..	..	..	..	..
Total 0—5 ..	*253*	*132*	*121*	*253*	*132*	*121*	..	..	..	..	..	..
5—10 ..	*208*	111	97	181	107	74	27	4	23	..	..	..
10—15 ..	*205*	105	100	134	83	51	70	22	48	1	..	1
15—20 ..	*178*	93	85	36	34	2	139	57	82	3	2	1
20—30 ..	*324*	165	159	29	28	1	279	128	131	16	9	7
30—40 ..	*268*	154	114	21	20	1	217	120	97	30	14	16
40—50 ..	*187*	124	63	7	7	..	133	95	38	47	22	25
50—60 ..	*108*	67	41	5	4	1	57	43	14	46	20	26
60 and over ..	*86*	50	36	1	1	..	28	25	3	57	24	33
JAIN ..	**141**	**78**	**63**	**80**	**50**	**30**	**30**	**15**	**15**	**31**	**13**	**18**
0—1 ..	*5*	2	3	5	2	3	..	..	..	..	..	..
1—2 ..	*5*	3	2	5	3	2	..	..	..	..	..	..
2—3 ..	*3*	1	2	3	1	2	..	..	..	..	..	..
3—4 ..	*2*	1	1	2	1	1	..	..	..	..	..	..
4—5 ..	*4*	2	2	4	2	2	..	..	..	..	..	..
Total 0—5 ..	*19*	*9*	*10*	*19*	*9*	*10*	..	..	..	..	..	..
5—10 ..	*17*	8	9	17	8	9	..	..	..	..	..	..
10—15 ..	*17*	7	10	16	7	9	1	..	1	..	..	..
15—20 ..	*12*	7	5	8	6	2	3	..	3	1	1	..
20—30 ..	*27*	18	9	10	10	..	13	5	8	4	3	1
30—40 ..	*16*	13	3	4	4	..	8	7	1	4	2	2
40—50 ..	*12*	4	8	3	3	..	..	..	..	9	1	8
50—60 ..	*11*	6	5	1	1	..	1	1	..	9	4	5
60 and over ..	*10*	6	4	2	2	..	4	2	2	4	2	2
MUSLIM ..	**10,017**	**5,705**	**4,312**	**4,149**	**2,650**	**1,499**	**4,848**	**2,513**	**2,335**	**1,020**	**542**	**478**
0—1 ..	*316*	160	156	316	160	156	..	..	..	..	..	..
1—2 ..	*252*	129	123	252	129	123	..	..	..	..	..	..
2—3 ..	*286*	146	140	286	146	140	..	..	..	..	..	..
3—4 ..	*274*	140	134	274	140	134	..	..	..	..	..	..
4—5 ..	*262*	136	126	260	135	125	2	1	1	..	..	..
Total 0—5 ..	*1,390*	*711*	*679*	*1,388*	*710*	*678*	*2*	*1*	*1*	..	..	..
5—10 ..	*1,214*	638	576	1,036	586	450	172	49	123	6	3	3
10—15 ..	*1,165*	625	540	814	517	297	339	104	235	12	4	8
15—20 ..	*945*	525	420	335	288	47	588	224	364	22	13	9
20—30 ..	*1,808*	1,047	761	340	324	16	1,384	663	721	84	60	24
30—40 ..	*1,417*	848	569	134	128	6	1,134	629	505	149	91	58
40—50 ..	*958*	605	353	64	60	4	674	423	251	220	122	98
50—60 ..	*605*	388	217	27	27	..	347	245	102	231	116	115
60 and over ..	*515*	318	197	11	10	1	208	175	33	296	133	163
CHRISTIAN ..	**176**	**81**	**95**	**107**	**48**	**59**	**58**	**30**	**28**	**11**	**3**	**8**
0—1 ..	*4*	4	..	4	4	..	..	..	..	..	..	..
1—2 ..	*4*	2	2	4	2	2	..	..	..	..	..	..
2—3 ..	*6*	4	2	6	4	2	..	..	..	..	..	..
4—5 ..	*6*	4	2	6	4	2	..	..	..	..	..	..
Total 0—5 ..	*20*	*11*	*6*	*20*	*14*	*6*	..	..	..	..	..	..
5—10 ..	*19*	9	10	19	9	10	..	..	..	..	..	..
10—15 ..	*16*	8	8	16	8	8	..	..	..	..	..	..
15—20 ..	*16*	5	11	9	4	5	6	1	5	1	..	1
20—30 ..	*34*	14	20	19	7	12	14	7	7	1	..	1
30—40 ..	*28*	12	16	8	3	5	16	8	8	4	1	3
40—50 ..	*22*	10	12	7	1	6	13	8	5	2	1	1
50—60 ..	*14*	6	8	5	1	4	8	5	3	1	..	1
60 and over ..	*7*	3	4	4	1	3	1	1	..	2	1	1

TABLE VII.—AGE, SEX

PART B.—DETAILS FOR DISTRICTS AND STATES.

LOHARU STATE.

Religion and Age.	Population.			Unmarried.			Married.			Widowed.		
	Persons.	Males.	Females.	Persons.	Males.	Females.	Persons.	Males.	Females.	Persons.	Males.	Females.
1	2	3	4	5	6	7	8	9	10	11	12	13
ALL RELIGIONS ..	**23,338**	**12,326**	**11,012**	**10,864**	**6,884**	**3,980**	**10,403**	**4,612**	**5,791**	**2,071**	**830**	**1,241**
0—1 ..	*847*	400	447	847	400	447	..	..	..	..	..	..
1—2 ..	*665*	326	339	665	326	339	..	..	..	..	..	.
2—3 ..	*808*	406	402	805	405	400	3	1	2	..	..	..
3—4 ..	*766*	401	365	755	399	356	11	2	9	..	..	..
4—5 ..	*716*	384	332	689	379	310	24	4	20	3	1	2
Total 0—5 ..	*3,802*	*1,917*	*1,885*	*3,761*	*1,909*	*1,852*	*38*	*7*	*31*	*3*	*1*	*2*
5—10 ..	*3,305*	1,740	1,565	2,858	1,661	1,197	441	77	364	6	2	4
10—15 ..	*3,107*	1,632	1,475	2,256	1,458	798	838	170	668	13	4	9
15—20 ..	*2,315*	1,224	1,091	819	735	84	1,465	476	989	31	13	18
20—30 ..	*3,491*	1,778	1,713	635	601	34	2,750	1,134	1,616	106	43	63
30—40 ..	*2,424*	1,283	1,141	211	203	8	1,985	982	1,003	228	98	130
40—50 ..	*2,094*	1,137	957	157	153	4	1,492	815	677	445	160	276
50—60 ..	*1,461*	844	617	95	92	*3*	846	*534*	*312*	520	*218*	302
60 and over ..	*1,339*	771	568	72	72	..	548	417	131	719	282	437
HINDU ..	**20,198**	**10,717**	**9,481**	**9,362**	**6,006**	**3,356**	**8,984**	**3,956**	**5,028**	**1,852**	**755**	**1,097**
0—1 ..	*724*	342	382	724	342	382	..	..	..	..	..	..
1—2 ..	*566*	281	285	566	281	285	..	..	..	..	..	..
2—3 ..	*693*	349	344	692	349	343	1	..	1	..	..	..
3—4 ..	*655*	343	312	645	342	303	10	1	9	..	..	..
4—5 ..	*612*	332	280	589	329	260	20	2	18	3	1	2
Total 0—5 ..	*3,250*	*1,647*	*1,603*	*3,216*	*1,643*	*1,573*	*31*	*3*	*28*	*3*	*1*	*2*
5—10 ..	*2,834*	1,491	1,343	2,440	1,425	1,015	390	65	325	4	1	3
10—15 ..	*2,676*	1,408	1,268	1,933	1,260	673	734	145	589	9	3	6
15—20 ..	*2,008*	1,070	938	710	649	61	1,272	411	861	26	10	16
20—30 ..	*3,002*	1,545	1,457	558	535	23	2,355	973	1,382	89	37	52
30—40 ..	*2,070*	1,099	971	196	191	5	1,676	824	852	198	84	114
40—50 ..	*1,834*	996	838	148	145	3	1,297	703	594	389	148	241
50—60 ..	*1,311*	760	551	92	89	3	750	469	281	469	202	267
60 and over ..	*1,213*	701	512	69	69	..	479	368	116	665	269	396
SIKH ..	**2**	**2**	..	**1**	**1**	..	**1**	**1**	..	..	..	..
5—10 ..	*1*	1	..	1	1	..	..	..	..	..	..	..
40—50 ..	*1*	1	..	..	..	..	1	1	..	..	..	..
JAIN ..	**18**	**7**	**11**	**9**	**3**	**6**	**9**	**4**	**5**	..	..	..
0—1 ..	*3*	..	3	3	..	3	..	..	..	..	..	..
2—3 ..	*1*	1	..	1	1	..	..	..	..	..	..	..
4—5 ..	*2*	..	2	2	..	2	..	..	..	..	..	..
Total 0—5 ..	*6*	*1*	*5*	*6*	*1*	*5*	..	..	..	..	..	..
5—10 ..	*2*	1	1	2	1	1	..	..	..	..	..	..
10—15 ..	*1*	..	1	..	..	..	1	..	1	..	..	..
15—20 ..	*2*	1	1	1	1	..	1	..	1	..	..	..
20—30 ..	*5*	2	3	..	..	..	5	2	3	..	..	..
30—40 ..	*1*	1	..	..	..	..	1	1	..	..	..	..
40—50 ..	*1*	1	..	..	..	..	1	1	..	..	..	..
MUSLIM ..	**3,119**	**1,600**	**1,519**	**1,491**	**874**	**617**	**1,409**	**651**	**758**	***219***	***75***	***144***
0—1 ..	*120*	58	62	120	58	62	..	..	..	..	..	..
1—2 ..	*99*	45	54	99	45	54	..	..	..	..	..	..
2—3 ..	*114*	56	58	112	55	57	2	1	1	..	..	..
3—4 ..	*111*	58	53	110	57	53	1	1	..	..	..	..
4—5 ..	*102*	52	50	98	50	48	4	2	2	..	..	..
Total 0—5 ..	*546*	*269*	*277*	*539*	*265*	*274*	*7*	*4*	*3*	..	..	..
5—10 ..	*468*	247	221	415	234	181	51	12	39	2	1	1
10—15 ..	*430*	224	206	323	198	125	103	25	78	4	1	3
15—20 ..	*304*	153	151	107	85	22	192	65	127	5	3	2
20—30 ..	*484*	231	253	77	66	11	390	159	231	17	6	11
30—40 ..	*353*	183	170	15	12	3	308	157	151	30	14	16
40—50 ..	*258*	139	119	9	8	1	193	110	83	56	21	35
50—60 ..	*150*	84	66	3	3	..	96	65	31	51	16	35
60 and over ..	*126*	70	56	3	3	..	69	54	15	54	13	41
CHRISTIAN ..	**1**	..	**1**	**1**	..	**1**	..	..	..	..	..	..
15—20 ..	*1*	..	1	1	..	1	..	..	..	..	..	..

AND CIVIL CONDITION (BY RELIGION).

PART B.—DETAILS FOR DISTRICTS AND STATES—*continued.*

SIRMOOR STATE.

Religion and Age.	Population.			Unmarried.			Married.			Widowed.		
	Persons.	Males.	Females.	Persons.	Males.	Females.	Persons.	Males.	Females.	Persons.	Males.	Females.
1	2	3	4	5	6	7	8	9	10	11	12	13
ALL RELIGIONS ..	**148,568**	**82,384**	**66,184**	**47,047**	**28,970**	**18,077**	**87,846**	**47,932**	**39,914**	**13,675**	**5,482**	**8,193**
0—1 ..	3,551	1,830	1,721	3,507	1,789	1,718	44	41	3	..	..	..
1—2 ..	3,439	1,770	1,669	3,333	1,681	1,652	106	89	17	..	..	..
2—3 ..	3,817	1,907	1,910	3,627	1,771	1,856	190	136	54	..	..	..
3—4 ..	3,883	1,911	1,972	3,534	1,701	1,833	347	209	138	2	1	1
4—5 ..	3,839	1,942	1,897	3,362	1,672	1,690	470	267	203	7	3	4
Total 0—5 ..	18,529	9,360	9,169	17,363	8,614	8,749	1,157	742	415	9	4	5
5—10 ..	16,674	8,926	7,748	12,358	6,844	5,514	4,273	2,059	2,214	43	23	20
10—15 .	15,774	8,698	7,076	9,017	5,738	3,279	6,667	2,913	3,754	90	47	43
15—20 ..	13,900	7,542	6,358	3,270	2,915	355	10,375	4,463	5,912	255	164	91
20—30 ..	28,083	15,275	12,808	2,986	2,868	118	24,016	11,772	12,244	1,081	635	446
30—40 ..	23,197	13,365	9,832	1,108	1,068	40	20,007	11,369	8,638	2,082	928	1,154
40—50 ..	15,223	9,122	6,101	500	486	14	11,752	7,520	4,232	2,971	1,116	1,855
50—60 ..	9,610	5,683	3,927	255	248	7	6,080	4,268	1,812	3,275	1,167	2,108
60 and over ..	7,578	4,413	3,165	190	189	1	3,519	2,826	693	3,869	1,398	2,471
HINDU ..	**139,031**	**76,922**	**62,109**	**42,766**	**26,239**	**16,527**	**83,471**	**45,650**	**37,821**	**12,794**	**5,033**	**7,761**
0—1 ..	3,230	1,658	1,572	3,186	1,617	1,569	44	41	3	..	.	.
1—2 ..	3,179	1,631	1,548	3,073	1,542	1,531	106	89	17	..	..	..
2—3 ..	3,541	1,761	1,780	3,353	1,625	1,728	188	136	52	..	..	..
3—4 ..	3,611	1,771	1,840	3,267	1,562	1,705	342	208	134	2	1	1
4—5 ..	3,566	1,804	1,762	3,102	1,540	1,562	457	261	196	7	3	4
Total 0—5 ..	17,127	8,625	8,502	15,981	7,886	8,095	1,137	735	402	9	4	5
5—10 .	15,394	8,246	7,148	11,257	6,224	5,033	4,097	2,001	2,096	40	21	19
10—15 ..	14,550	8,021	6,529	8,115	5,169	2,946	6,353	2,809	3,544	82	43	39
15—20 ..	12,928	6,984	5,944	2,909	2,609	300	9,784	4,221	5,563	235	154	81
20—30 ..	26,308	14,235	12,073	2,650	2,551	99	22,667	11,103	11,564	991	581	410
30—40 ..	21,992	12,630	9,362	990	955	35	19,061	10,826	8,235	1,941	849	1,092
40—50 ..	14,448	8,636	5,812	460	447	13	11,206	7,173	4,033	2,782	1,016	1,766
50—60 ..	9,128	5,386	3,742	234	229	5	5,804	4,082	1,722	3,090	1,075	2,015
60 and over ..	7,156	4,159	2,997	170	169	1	3,362	2,700	662	3,624	1,290	2,334
SIKH ..	**2,418**	**1,353**	**1,060**	**1,162**	**734**	**428**	**1,028**	**514**	**514**	**223**	**105**	**118**
0—1 ..	97	49	48	97	49	48	..	..	.	..	..	..
1—2 ..	63	37	26	63	37	26	..	..	..	..	..	..
2—3 ..	73	39	34	73	39	34	..	..	..	..	..	..
3—4 ..	77	38	39	77	38	39	..	..	..	..	..	.
4—5 ..	76	36	40	73	34	39	3	2	1	..	..	..
Total 0—5 ..	386	199	187	383	197	186	3	2	1	..	..	..
5—10 ..	336	176	160	301	162	139	34	13	21	1	1	..
10—15 ..	315	171	144	242	152	90	71	17	54	2	2	..
15—20 ..	236	135	101	88	78	10	144	54	90	4	3	1
20—30 ..	431	253	178	84	82	2	330	161	169	17	10	7
30—40 ..	290	171	119	39	38	1	217	117	100	34	16	18
40—50 ..	182	110	72	14	14	..	124	77	47	44	19	25
50—60 ..	115	69	46	4	4	..	65	41	24	46	24	22
60 and over ..	122	69	53	7	7	..	40	32	8	75	30	45
JAIN ..	**52**	**38**	**14**	**27**	**20**	**7**	**19**	**13**	**6**	**6**	**5**	**1**
0—1 ..	2	2	..	2	2	..	..	..	..	..	..	..
2—3 ..	1	1	..	1	1	..	..	..	..	..	..	..
3—4 ..	1	1	..	1	1	..	..	..	..	..	..	..
4—5 ..	3	2	1	3	2	1	..	..	..	..	..	..
Total 0—5 ..	7	6	1	7	6	1	..	..	..	..	..	
5—10 ..	10	7	3	10	7	3	..	..	..	..	..	..
10—15 ..	9	7	2	8	6	2	1	1	..	..	..	..
15—20 ..	4	2	2	2	1	1	2	1	1	..	..	..
20—30 ..	8	6	2	..	..	..	7	5	2	1	1	..
30—40 ..	5	3	2	..	..	..	5	3	2	..	..	..
40—50 ..	4	3	1	..	..	..	3	2	1	1	1	..
50—60 ..	4	3	1	..	..	..	1	1	..	3	2	1
60 and over ..	1	1	..	..	..	..	..	..	..	1	1	..
MUSLIM ..	**7,020**	**4,047**	**2,973**	**3,064**	**1,964**	**1,100**	**3,308**	**1,744**	**1,564**	**648**	**339**	**309**
0—1 ..	220	120	100	220	120	100	..	..	..	..	..	..
1—2 ..	195	101	94	195	101	94	..	..	..	..	..	..
2—3 ..	200	105	95	198	105	93	2	..	2	..	..	..
3—4 ..	192	101	91	187	100	87	5	1	4	..	..	..
4—5 ..	192	100	92	182	96	86	10	4	6	..	..	.
Total 0—5 ..	999	527	472	982	522	460	17	5	12	..	..	..
5—10 ..	927	493	434	784	448	336	141	44	97	2	1	1
10—15 ..	894	495	399	646	407	239	242	86	156	6	2	4
15—20 ..	726	418	308	268	225	43	442	186	256	16	7	9
20—30 ..	1,330	778	552	251	234	17	1,007	501	506	72	43	29
30—40 ..	902	559	343	78	75	3	719	421	298	105	63	42
40—50 ..	586	372	214	26	25	1	417	267	150	143	80	63
50—60 ..	358	222	136	16	15	1	207	141	66	135	66	69
60 and over ..	298	183	115	13	13	..	116	93	23	169	77	92
CHRISTIAN ..	**52**	**24**	**28**	**28**	**13**	**15**	**20**	**11**	**9**	**4**	..	**4**
0—1 ..	2	1	1	2	1	1	..	..	..	..	..	..
1—2 ..	2	1	1	2	1	1	..	..	..	..	..	..
2—3 ..	2	1	1	2	1	1	..	..	..	..	..	..
3—4 ..	2	..	2	2	..	2	..	..	..	..	..	..
4—5 ..	2	..	2	2	..	2	..	..	..	..	..	..
Total 0—5 ..	10	3	7	10	3	7	..	..	..	..	..	..
5—10 ..	7	4	3	6	3	3	1	1	..	..	..	..
10—15 ..	6	4	2	6	4	2	..	..	..	..	..	..
15—20 ..	6	3	3	3	2	1	3	1	2	..	..	..
20—30 ..	6	3	3	1	1	..	5	2	3	..	..	..
30—40 ..	8	2	6	1	..	1	5	2	3	2	..	2
40—50 ..	3	1	2	..	..	..	2	1	1	1	..	1
50—60 ..	5	3	2	1	..	1	3	3	..	1	..	1
60 and over ..	1	1	..	..	..	..	1	1	..	..	..	..

TABLE VII.—AGE, SEX

PART B.—DETAILS FOR DISTRICTS AND STATES.

BILASPUR STATE.

Religion and Age.	Population.			Unmarried.			Married.			Widowed.		
	Persons.	Males.	Females.	Persons.	Males.	Females.	Persons.	Males.	Females.	Persons.	Males.	Females.
1	2	3	4	5	6	7	8	9	10	11	12	13
ALL RELIGIONS ..	**100,994**	**53,154**	**47,840**	**39,093**	**25,801**	**13,292**	**48,399**	**23,376**	**25,023**	**13,502**	**3,977**	**9,525**
0—1 ..	*3,144*	1,571	1,573	3,144	1,571	1,573	..	..	..	..	..	..
1—2 ..	*2,294*	1,173	1,121	2,294	1,173	1,121	..	..	..	..	..	..
2—3 ..	*2,485*	1,234	1,251	2,485	1,234	1,251	..	..	..	..	..	..
3—4 ..	*2,588*	1,283	1,305	2,558	1,278	1,280	30	5	25	..	..	..
4—5 ..	*2,615*	1,343	1,272	2,551	1,332	1,219	64	11	53	..	..	..
Total 0—5 ..	*13,126*	*6,604*	*6,522*	*13,032*	*6,588*	*6,444*	*94*	*16*	*78*	..	..	..
5—10 ..	*11,823*	6,226	5,597	10,138	5,989	4,149	1,655	228	1,427	30	9	21
10—15 ..	*11,055*	5,898	5,157	7,793	5,323	2,470	3,180	550	2,630	82	25	57
15—20 .	*9,159*	4,573	4,586	3,023	2,835	188	5,893	1,682	4,211	243	56	187
20—30 ..	*17,703*	8,826	8,877	2,902	2,861	41	13,669	5,686	7,983	1,132	279	853
30—40 ..	*14,246*	7,584	6,662	1,025	1,025	..	10,881	5,055	4,926	2,340	604	1,736
40—50 ..	*9,907*	5,452	4,455	541	541	..	6,512	4,109	2,403	2,854	802	2,052
50—60 ..	*7,349*	4,250	3,099	369	369	..	3,958	2,938	1,020	3,022	943	2,079
60 and over ..	*6,626*	3,741	2,885	270	270	..	2,557	2,212	345	3,799	1,259	2,540
HINDU ..	**99,023**	**52,068**	**46,955**	**38,300**	**25,284**	**13,016**	**47,438**	**22,916**	**24,522**	**13,285**	**3,868**	**9,417**
0—1 ..	*3,073*	1,534	1,539	3,073	1,534	1,539	..	.	..	..	..	..
1—2 ..	*2,245*	1,146	1,099	2,245	1,146	1,099	..	..	..	..	..	..
2—3 ..	*2,443*	1,212	1,231	2,443	1,212	1,231	..	..	..	..	..	..
3—4 ..	*2,542*	1,259	1,283	2,512	1,254	1,258	30	5	25	..	..	..
4—5 ..	*2,555*	1,309	1,246	2,492	1,298	1,194	63	11	52	..	..	..
Total 0—5 ..	*12,858*	*6,460*	*6,398*	*12,765*	*6,444*	*6,321*	*93*	*16*	*77*	..	..	..
5—10 ..	*11,572*	6,090	5,482	9,922	5,863	4,059	1,621	219	1,402	29	8	21
10—15 ..	*10,818*	5,777	5,041	7,634	5,222	2,412	3,103	530	2,573	81	25	56
15—20 ..	*8,986*	4,489	4,497	2,975	2,791	184	5,769	1,643	4,126	242	55	187
20—30 ..	*17,364*	8,662	8,702	2,849	2,809	40	13,398	5,580	7,818	1,117	273	844
30—40 ..	*13,979*	7,430	6,549	1,010	1,010	..	10,668	5,837	4,831	2,301	583	1,718
40—50 ..	*9,733*	5,353	4,380	531	531	..	6,393	4,039	2,354	2,809	783	2,026
50—60 ..	*7,215*	4,163	3,052	358	358	..	3,883	2,883	1,000	2,974	922	2,052
60 and over ..	*6,498*	3,644	2,854	256	256	..	2,510	2,169	341	3,732	1,219	2,513
SIKH ..	**507**	**280**	**227**	**219**	**147**	**72**	**237**	**106**	**131**	**51**	**27**	**24**
0—1 ..	*18*	9	9	18	9	9	.	..	..	..	.	.
1—2 ..	*11*	5	6	11	5	6	..	..	..	..	..	..
2—3 ..	*11*	6	5	11	6	5	..	..	..	..	..	..
3—4 ..	*14*	8	6	14	8	6	..	..	..	..	..	..
4—5 ..	*17*	10	7	16	10	6	1	..	1	..	..	..
Total 0—5 ..	*71*	*38*	*33*	*70*	*38*	*32*	*1*	..	*1*	..	..	..
5—10 ..	*65*	34	31	57	33	24	8	1	7	..	..	..
10—15 ..	*60*	29	31	41	25	16	19	4	15	..	..	..
15—20 ..	*47*	25	22	15	15	..	32	10	22	..	..	..
20—30 ..	*78*	40	38	16	16	..	60	24	36	2	..	2
30—40 ..	*59*	32	27	6	6	..	48	23	25	5	3	2
40—50 ..	*48*	24	24	2	2	..	35	16	19	11	6	5
50—60 ..	*40*	26	14	4	4	..	22	16	6	14	6	8
60 and over ..	*39*	32	7	8	8	..	12	12	..	19	12	7
MUSLIM ..	**1,458**	**804**	**654**	**571**	**369**	**202**	**721**	**353**	**368**	**166**	**82**	**84**
0—1 ..	*53*	28	25	53	28	25	..	..	..	..	..	..
1—2 ..	*38*	22	16	38	22	16	..	..	..	..	..	..
2—3 ..	*31*	16	15	31	16	15	..	..	..	..	..	..
3—4 ..	*32*	16	16	32	16	16	..	..	..	..	..	..
4—5 ..	*42*	24	18	42	24	18	..	..	..	..	..	..
Total 0—5 ..	*196*	*106*	*90*	*196*	*106*	*90*	..	..	..	..	..	..
5—10 ..	*184*	102	82	158	93	65	25	8	17	1	1	..
10—15 ..	*176*	91	85	117	75	42	58	16	42	1	..	1
15—20 ..	*126*	59	67	33	29	4	92	29	63	1	1	..
20—30 ..	*261*	124	137	37	36	1	211	82	129	13	6	7
30—40 ..	*208*	122	86	9	9	..	165	95	70	34	18	16
40—50 ..	*125*	75	50	8	8	..	83	54	29	34	13	21
50—60 ..	*93*	60	33	7	7	..	52	38	14	34	15	19
60 and over ..	*89*	65	24	6	6	..	35	31	4	48	28	20
CHRISTIAN ..	**6**	**2**	**6**	**3**	**1**	**2**	**3**	**1**	**2**	..	..	..
4—5 ..	*1*	..	1	1	..	1	..	..	..	..	..	..
Total 0—5 ..	*1*	..	*1*	*1*	..	*1*	..	..	..	..	..	..
5—10 ..	*2*	..	2	1	..	1	1	..	1	..	..	..
10—15 ..	*1*	1	..	1	1	..	..	..	..	..	..	..
40—50 ..	*1*	..	1	..	..	..	1	..	1	..	..	..
50—60 ..	*1*	1	..	..	..	..	1	1	..	..	..	..

AND CIVIL CONDITION (BY RELIGION).

PART B. DETAILS FOR DISTRICTS AND STATES—*continued.*

MANDI STATE.

Religion and Age.	Population.			Unmarried.			Married.			Widowed.		
	Persons.	Males.	Females.	Persons.	Males.	Females.	Persons.	Males.	Females.	Persons.	Males.	Females.
1	2	3	4	5	6	7	8	9	10	11	12	13
ALL RELIGIONS ..	**207,465**	**107,876**	**99,589**	**88,859**	**54,185**	**34,674**	**95,154**	**46,627**	**48,527**	**23,452**	**7,064**	**16,388**
0—1 ..	6,500	3,209	3,291	6,499	3,209	3,290	1	..	1	..	..	.
1—2 ..	5,807	2,864	2,943	5,803	2,864	2,939	3	..	3	1	..	1
2—3 ..	5,879	2,873	3,006	5,872	2,872	3,000	7	1	6	..	..	..
3—4 ..	5,720	2,817	2,903	5,690	2,816	2,874	30	1	29	..	..	..
4—5 ..	5,431	2,723	2,708	5,367	2,718	2,649	61	4	57	3	1	2
Total 0—5 ..	*29,337*	*14,486*	*14,851*	*29,231*	*14,479*	*14,752*	*102*	*6*	*96*	*4*	*1*	*3*
5—10 ..	24,130	12,384	11,746	22,736	12,185	10,551	1,354	189	1,165	40	10	30
10—15 ..	22,447	11,636	10,811	18,550	11,026	7,524	3,789	582	3,207	108	28	80
15—20 ..	20,235	10,296	9,939	7,921	6,735	1,186	11,903	3,421	8,482	411	140	271
20—30 ..	38,071	19,755	18,316	7,174	6,774	400	29,043	12,251	16,792	1,854	730	1,124
30—40 ..	27,720	14,708	13,012	1,808	1,659	149	22,437	11,904	10,533	3,475	1,145	2,330
40—50 ..	18,961	10,203	8,758	699	648	51	13,551	8,319	5,232	4,711	1,236	3,475
50—60 ..	13,647	7,556	6,091	424	388	36	7,847	5,643	2,204	5,376	1,525	3,851
60 and over ..	12,917	6,852	6,065	316	291	25	5,128	4,312	816	7,473	2,249	5,224
HINDU ..	**199,935**	**102,614**	**97,321**	**85,727**	**51,939**	**33,788**	**91,248**	**43,875**	**47,368**	**22,965**	**6,800**	**16,165**
0—1 .	6,316	3,109	3,207	6,315	3,109	3,206	1	..	1	..	..	..
1—2 .	5,641	2,775	2,866	5,637	2,775	2,862	3	..	3	1	..	1
2—3 ..	5,719	2,790	2,929	5,713	2,790	2,923	6	.	6	..	..	..
3—4 .	5,583	2,745	2,838	5,553	2,744	2,809	30	1	29	..	..	..
4—5 ..	5,290	2,651	2,639	5,229	2,646	2,583	58	4	54	3	1	2
Total 0—5 ..	*28,549*	*14,070*	*14,479*	*28,447*	*14,064*	*14,383*	*98*	*5*	*93*	*4*	*1*	*3*
5—10 ..	23,511	12,053	11,458	22,155	11,865	10,290	1,319	179	1,140	37	9	28
10—15 ..	21,825	11,294	10,531	18,050	10,719	7,331	3,672	549	3,123	103	26	77
15—20 ..	19,327	9,654	9,673	7,491	6,343	1,148	11,433	3,175	8,258	403	136	267
20—30 ..	35,899	18,051	17,848	6,521	6,138	383	27,587	11,232	16,355	1,791	681	1,110
30—40 ..	26,429	13,701	12,728	1,670	1,525	145	21,383	11,095	10,288	3,376	1,081	2,295
40—50 ..	18,392	9,771	8,621	669	621	48	13,098	7,961	5,137	4,625	1,189	3,436
50—60 ..	13,351	7,341	6,010	415	380	35	7,647	5,475	2,172	5,289	1,486	3,803
60 and over ..	12,652	6,679	5,973	309	284	25	5,006	4,204	802	7,337	2,191	5,146
SIKH ..	**899**	**612**	**287**	**326**	**217**	**109**	**523**	**363**	**160**	**50**	**32**	**18**
0—1 ..	25	12	13	25	12	13	..	..	..	..	..	..
1—2 ..	21	11	10	21	11	10	..	..	..	..	.	..
2—3 ..	22	11	11	22	11	11	..	..	.	..	..	..
3—4 .	17	8	9	17	8	9	..	..	.	..	..	..
4—5 ..	17	8	9	16	8	8	1	..	1	..	..	..
Total 0—5 ..	*102*	*50*	*52*	*101*	*50*	*51*	*1*	..	*1*	..	..	..
5—10 ..	67	36	31	66	36	30	1	.	1	..	..	..
10—15 ..	63	34	29	56	33	23	6	.	6	1	1	..
15—20 ..	111	69	42	37	33	4	73	36	37	1	.	1
20—30 ..	280	201	79	47	46	1	226	149	77	7	6	1
30—40 ..	172	140	32	15	15	..	144	116	28	13	9	4
40—50 ..	61	51	10	4	4	..	46	40	6	11	7	4
50—60 ..	25	19	6	..	..	..	17	14	3	8	5	3
60 and over .	18	12	6	..	..	..	9	8	1	9	4	5
MUSLIM ..	**6,351**	**4,464**	**1,887**	**2,680**	**1,948**	**732**	**3,250**	**2,295**	**955**	**421**	**221**	**200**
0—1 ..	146	80	66	146	80	66	..	..	..	..	..	..
1—2 ..	133	73	60	133	73	60	..	..	..	..	..	..
2—3 ..	128	67	61	127	66	61	1	1	..	..	..	..
3—4 .	117	62	55	117	62	55	..	..	..	..	..	..
4—5 .	118	62	56	116	62	54	2	..	2	..	..	.
Total 0—5 ..	*642*	*344*	*298*	*639*	*343*	*296*	*3*	*1*	*2*	..	..	
5—10 ..	536	288	248	499	277	222	34	10	24	3	1	2
10—15 ..	540	299	241	430	267	163	107	32	75	3	..	3
15—20 ..	773	561	212	382	351	31	385	206	179	6	4	2
20—30 ..	1,821	1,449	372	380	566	14	1,186	841	345	55	42	13
30—40 ..	1,066	827	239	115	112	3	871	665	206	80	50	30
40—50 ..	487	366	121	24	22	2	390	305	85	73	39	34
50—60 ..	251	180	71	6	5	1	168	142	26	77	33	44
60 and over ..	235	150	85	5	5	..	106	93	13	124	52	72
CHRISTIAN .	**141**	**92**	**49**	**53**	**33**	**20**	**84**	**56**	**28**	**4**	**3**	**1**
0—1 ..	4	2	2	4	2	2	..	..	..	..	..	..
1—2 ..	5	2	3	5	2	3	..	..	..	..	..	..
2—3 ..	6	3	3	6	3	3	..	..	..	..	..	..
3—4 ..	1	1	..	1	1	..	..	..	..	..	.	..
4—5 .	2	..	2	2	..	2	.	..	..	.	..	..
Total 0—5 ..	*18*	*8*	*10*	*18*	*8*	*10*	..	..	..	..	..	..
5—10 ..	7	3	4	7	3	4	..	..	..	..	..	..
10—15 ..	6	3	3	6	3	3	..	.	..	..	.	..
15—20 ..	8	5	3	4	4	..	4	1	3	..	..	..
20—30 ..	38	26	12	13	12	1	25	14	11	..	..	..
30—40 ..	39	30	9	4	3	1	32	24	8	3	3	..
40—50 .	14	9	5	1	..	1	13	9	4	..	..	.
50—60 .	8	6	2	..	..	..	8	6	2	..	.	..
60 and over ..	3	2	1	..	..	..	2	2	..	1	.	1

TABLE VII.—AGE, SEX

PART B.—DETAILS FOR DISTRICTS AND STATES.

SUKET STATE.

Religion and Age.	Population.			Unmarried.			Married.			Widowed.		
	Persons.	Males.	Females.	Persons.	Males.	Females.	Persons.	Males.	Females.	Persons.	Males.	Females.
1	2	3	4	5	6	7	8	9	10	11	12	13
ALL RELIGIONS ..	**58,408**	**30,851**	**27,557**	**23,931**	**14,699**	**9,232**	**27,445**	**13,691**	**13,754**	**7,032**	**2,461**	**4,571**
0—1 ..	*1,512*	757	755	1,512	757	755	..	..	..	..	..	..
1—2 ..	*1,293*	627	666	1,292	627	665	1	..	1	..	..	..
2—3 ..	*1,402*	661	741	1,399	659	740	3	2	1	..	..	..
3—4 ..	*1,473*	706	767	1,462	701	761	10	5	5	1	..	1
4—5 ..	*1,503*	732	771	1,478	720	758	22	11	11	3	1	2
Total 0—5 ..	*7,183*	*3,483*	*3,700*	*7,143*	*3,464*	*3,679*	*36*	*18*	*18*	*4*	*1*	*3*
5—10 ..	*6,492*	3,369	3,123	6,195	3,300	2,895	281	66	215	16	3	13
10—15 ..	*6,129*	3,291	2,838	5,027	3,041	1,986	1,074	242	832	28	8	20
15—20 ..	*5,509*	2,859	2,650	2,112	1,800	312	3,275	1,004	2,271	122	55	67
20—30 ..	*10,836*	5,504	5,332	2,043	1,871	172	8,140	3,368	4,772	653	265	388
30—40 ..	*8,958*	4,814	4,144	770	669	101	6,918	3,675	3,243	1,270	470	800
40—50 ..	*6,180*	3,450	2,730	340	295	45	4,196	2,618	1,578	1,644	537	1,107
50—60 .	*3,977*	2,302	1,675	186	166	20	2,212	1,618	594	1,579	518	1,061
60 and over ..	*3,144*	1,779	1,365	115	93	22	1,313	1,082	231	1,716	604	1,112
HINDU ..	**57,616**	**30,427**	**27,189**	**23,570**	**14,499**	**9,071**	**27,081**	**13,494**	**13,587**	**6,965**	**2,434**	**4,531**
0—1 ..	*1,474*	740	734	1,474	740	734	..	..	..	..	..	..
1—2 ..	*1,278*	621	657	1,277	621	656	1	..	1	..	..	..
2—3 ..	*1,382*	653	729	1,379	651	728	3	2	1	..	..	..
3—4 ..	*1,448*	692	756	1,437	687	750	10	5	5	1	..	1
4—5 ..	*1,469*	712	757	1,445	701	744	21	10	11	3	1	2
Total 0—5 ..	*7,051*	*3,418*	*3,633*	*7,012*	*3,400*	*3,612*	*35*	*17*	*18*	*4*	*1*	*3*
5—10 ..	*6,378*	3,311	3,067	6,095	3,246	2,849	267	62	205	16	3	13
10—15 ..	*6,037*	3,245	2,792	4,961	3,004	1,957	1,048	233	815	28	8	20
15—20 ..	*5,434*	2,818	2,616	2,083	1,777	306	3,230	986	2,244	121	55	66
20—30 ..	*10,694*	5,430	5,264	2,019	1,855	164	8,030	3,312	4,718	645	263	382
30—40 ..	*8,848*	4,757	4,091	762	665	97	6,826	3,624	3,202	1,260	468	792
40—50 ..	*6,116*	3,409	2,707	338	294	44	4,150	2,585	1,565	1,628	530	1,098
50—60 ..	*3,941*	2,278	1,663	186	166	20	2,191	1,601	590	1,564	511	1,053
60 and over ..	*3,117*	1,761	1,356	114	92	22	1,304	1,074	230	1,699	595	1,104
SIKH ..	**44**	**33**	**11**	**19**	**17**	**2**	**22**	**15**	**7**	**3**	**1**	**2**
1—2 ..	*1*	..	1	1	..	1	..	..	..	..	..	..
3—4 ..	*1*	1	..	1	1	..	..	..	..	..	..	..
4—5 ..	*2*	2	..	2	2	..	..	..	..	..	..	..
Total 0—5 ..	*4*	*3*	*1*	*4*	*3*	1	..	..	..	..	..	..
5—10 ..	*7*	6	1	7	6	1	..	..	..	..	..	..
10—15 ..	*3*	3	..	3	3	..	..	..	..	..	..	..
15—20 ..	*4*	3	1	2	2	..	2	1	1	..	..	..
20—30 ..	*8*	5	3	2	2	..	4	2	2	2	1	1
30—40 ..	*8*	5	3	1	1	..	7	4	3	..	..	..
40—50 ..	*5*	4	1	..	..	..	5	4	1	..	..	..
50—60 ..	*3*	3	..	..	..	..	3	3	..	..	..	..
60 and over ..	*2*	1	1	..	..	..	1	1	..	1	..	1
MUSLIM ..	**733**	**382**	**351**	**331**	**177**	**154**	**338**	**179**	**159**	**64**	**26**	**38**
0—1 ..	*38*	17	21	38	17	21	..	..	..	..	..	..
1—2 ..	*14*	6	8	14	6	8	..	..	..	..	..	..
2—3 ..	*19*	7	12	19	7	12	..	..	..	..	..	..
3—4 ..	*24*	13	11	24	13	11	..	..	..	..	..	..
4—5 ..	*32*	18	14	31	17	14	1	1	..	..	..	..
Total 0—5 ..	*127*	*61*	*66*	*126*	*60*	*66*	*1*	*1*	..	..	..	..
5—10 ..	*107*	52	55	93	48	45	14	4	10	..	..	..
10—15 ..	*89*	43	46	63	34	29	26	9	17	..	..	..
15—20 ..	*68*	36	32	24	19	5	43	17	26	1	..	1
20—30 ..	*128*	67	61	18	13	5	104	53	51	6	1	5
30—40 ..	*98*	49	49	4	1	3	84	46	38	10	2	8
40—50 ..	*58*	36	22	2	1	1	40	28	12	16	7	9
50—60 ..	*33*	21	12	..	..	..	18	14	4	15	7	8
60 and over ..	*25*	17	8	1	1	..	8	7	1	16	9	7
CHRISTIAN ..	**1**	**1**	..	**1**	**1**	..	..	..	..	..	..	..
15—20 ..	*1*	1	..	1	1	..	..	..	..	..	..	..

AND CIVIL CONDITION (BY RELIGION).

PART B.—DETAILS FOR DISTRICTS AND STATES—*continued.*

KAPURTHALA STATE.

Religion and Age.	Population.			Unmarried.			Married.			Widowed.		
	Persons.	Males.	Females.	Persons.	Males.	Females.	Persons.	Males.	Females.	Persons.	Males.	Females.
1	2	3	4	5	6	7	8	9	10	11	12	13
ALL RELIGIONS ..	**316,757**	**171,529**	**145,228**	**154,778**	**91,725**	**63,053**	**130,657**	**64,912**	**65,745**	**31,322**	**14,892**	**16,430**
0—1 ..	*10,716*	5,415	5,301	10,709	5,414	5,295	7	1	6	..	..	..
1—2 ..	*8,779*	4,375	4,404	8,776	4,375	4,401	3	..	3	..	..	..
2—3 ..	*9,346*	4,743	4,603	9,326	4,735	4,591	20	8	12	..	..	..
3—4 ..	*9,174*	4,734	4,440	9,142	4,718	4,424	28	15	13	4	1	3
4—5 ..	*8,990*	4,693	4,297	8,941	4,667	4,274	39	23	16	10	3	7
Tatal 0—5 ..	*47,005*	*23,960*	*23,045*	*46,894*	*23,909*	*22,985*	*97*	*47*	*50*	*14*	*4*	*10*
5—10 ..	*40,867*	21,978	18,889	39,948	21,648	18,300	874	317	557	45	13	32
10—15 ..	*38,514*	20,970	17,544	34,626	19,808	14,818	3,816	1,137	2,679	72	25	47
15—20 ..	*28,881*	15,407	13,474	14,463	10,292	4,171	14,049	4,936	9,113	369	179	190
20—30 ..	*52,775*	28,247	24,528	11,800	9,848	1,952	39,019	17,271	21,748	1,956	1,128	828
30—40 ..	*40,254*	22,299	17,955	3,487	3,099	388	32,601	17,050	15,551	4,166	2,150	2,016
40—50 ..	*29,480*	16,552	12,928	1,847	1,621	226	21,162	11,972	9,190	6,471	2,959	3,512
50—60 ..	*19,368*	10,920	8,448	962	820	142	11,249	6,833	4,416	7,157	3,267	3,890
60 and over ..	*19,613*	11,196	8,417	751	680	71	7,790	5,349	2,441	11,072	5,167	5,905
HINDU ..	**54,145**	**29,590**	**24,555**	**27,074**	**16,512**	**10,562**	**21,438**	**10,609**	**10,824**	**5,638**	**2,469**	**3,169**
0—1 ..	*1,783*	897	886	1,781	896	885	2	1	1	.	..	.
1—2 ..	*1,462*	733	729	1,461	733	728	1	..	1	.	..	.
2—3 ..	*1,550*	807	743	1,545	805	740	5	2	3	.	..	..
3—4 ..	*1,558*	822	736	1,552	819	733	6	3	3	..	..	..
4—5 ..	*1,571*	828	743	1,562	822	740	7	5	2	2	1	1
Total 0—5 ..	*7,924*	*4,087*	*3,837*	*7,901*	*4,075*	*3,826*	*21*	*11*	*10*	2	*1*	*1*
5—10 ..	*7,048*	3,820	3,228	6,924	3,769	3,155	115	48	67	9	3	6
10—15 ..	*6,647*	3,687	2,960	6,039	3,507	2,532	598	176	422	10	4	6
15—20 ..	*4,990*	2,759	2,231	2,609	1,946	663	2,312	785	1,527	69	28	41
20—30 ..	*8,824*	4,796	4,028	2,080	1,815	265	6,376	2,794	3,582	368	187	181
30—40 ..	*6,817*	3,734	3,083	694	640	54	5,339	2,753	2,586	784	341	443
40—50 ..	*5,319*	2,960	2,359	395	366	29	3,630	2,047	1,583	1,294	547	747
50—60 .	*3,428*	1,945	1,483	237	209	28	1,873	1,168	705	1,318	568	750
60 and over ..	*3,148*	1,802	1,346	195	185	10	1,169	827	342	1,784	790	994
SIKH ..	**72,177**	**39,729**	**32,448**	**33,742**	**20,498**	**13,244**	**31,185**	**15,624**	**15,561**	**7,250**	**3,607**	**8,648**
0—1 ..	*2,312*	1,228	1,084	2,312	1,228	1,084	..	..	..	..	..	..
1—2 ..	*1,927*	955	972	1,927	955	972	..	..	..	..	..	..
2—3 ..	*2,011*	1,023	988	2,008	1,023	985	3	..	3	..	..	..
3—4 ..	*1,935*	999	936	1,932	999	933	3	..	3	..	..	..
4—5 ..	*1,875*	967	908	1,870	965	905	5	2	3	..	..	..
Total 0—5 ..	*10,060*	*5,172*	*4,888*	*10,049*	*5,170*	*4,879*	*11*	*2*	*9*	.	..	.
5—10 ..	*8,792*	4,776	4,016	8,637	4,727	3,910	152	48	104	3	1	2
10—15 ..	*8,438*	4,682	3,756	7,588	4,416	3,172	842	262	580	8	4	4
15—20 ..	*6,450*	3,519	2,931	3,057	2,230	827	3,331	1,256	2,075	62	33	29
20—30 ..	*11,686*	6,410	5,276	2,469	2,175	294	8,824	4,000	4,824	393	235	158
30—40 ..	*9,310*	5,173	4,137	879	804	75	7,509	3,868	3,641	922	501	421
40—50 ..	*7,074*	3,992	3,082	511	465	46	5,149	2,833	2,316	1,414	694	720
50—60 ..	*4,963*	2,877	2,086	266	244	22	3,078	1,849	1,229	1,619	784	835
60 and over ..	*5,404*	3,128	2,276	286	267	19	2,289	1,506	783	2,829	1,355	1,474
JAIN ..	**27**	**15**	**12**	**15**	**10**	**5**	**10**	**4**	**6**	**2**	**1**	**1**
0—1 ..	*1*	1	..	1	1	..	..	..	..	..	..	..
1—2 .	*2*	1	1	2	1	1	..	..	..	..	..	..
2—3 ..	*2*	2	..	2	2	..	..	..	..	..	..	..
4—5 ..	*2*	2	..	2	2	.	..	..	..	..	..	..
Total 0—5 ..	*7*	*6*	*1*	7	*6*	*1*	..	..	..	..	..	..
5—10 ..	*3*	1	2	3	1	2	..	..	.	.	..	..
10—15 ..	*3*	1	2	3	1	2	..	..	..	..	..	..
15—20 ..	*2*	..	2	..	..	..	2	..	2	..	..	..
20—30 ..	*5*	3	2	2	2	..	3	1	2	..	..	..
30—40 ..	*1*	..	1	..	..	..	1	..	1	..	..	..
40—50 ..	*1*	..	1	..	..	..	..	..	..	1	..	1
50—60 .	*3*	2	1	..	.	..	3	2	1	.	..	..
60 and over ..	*2*	2	.	..	..	..	1	1	..	1	1	..
MUSLIM ..	**179,251**	**96,240**	**83,011**	**89,316**	**52,073**	**37,243**	**72,487**	**35,849**	**36,638**	**17,448**	**8,318**	**9,130**
0—1 ..	*6,229*	3,082	3,147	6,224	3,082	3,142	5	..	5	..	.	..
1—2 ..	*5,082*	2,526	2,556	5,080	2,526	2,554	2	..	2	..	.	..
2—3 ..	*5,460*	2,746	2,714	5,449	2,740	2,709	11	6	5.	..	..	..
3—4 ..	*5,350*	2,744	2,606	5,328	2,732	2,596	18	11	7	4	1	3
4—5 ..	*5,218*	2,730	2,488	5,186	2,714	2,472	24	14	10	8	2	6
Total 0—5 ..	*27,339*	*13,823*	*13,511*	*27,267*	*13,794*	*13,473*	*60*	*31*	*29*	*12*	*3*	*9*
5—10 ..	*23,574*	12,597	10,977	23,031	12,419	10,612	515	170	345	28	8	20
10—15 ..	*22,005*	11,820	10,185	19,965	11,285	8,080	1,994	519	1,475	46	16	30
15—20 ..	*16,368*	8,566	7,802	8,541	5,928	2,613	7,599	2,525	5,074	228	113	115
20—30 ..	*30,417*	16,089	14,328	7,050	5,706	1,344	22,220	9,708	12,512	1,147	675	472
30—40 .	*22,712*	12,605	10,107	1,826	1,585	241	18,561	9,797	8,764	2,325	1,223	1,102
40—50 ..	*16,067*	9,046	7,021	920	773	147	11,595	6,662	4,933	3,552	1,611	1,941
50—60 ..	*10,330*	5,767	4,563	456	365	91	5,894	3,598	2,296	3,980	1,804	2,176
60 and over ..	*10,439*	5,922	4,517	260	218	42	4,049	2,839	1,210	6,130	2,865	3,265
CHRISTIAN ..	**983**	**511**	**472**	**460**	**248**	**212**	**448**	**227**	**221**	**75**	**86**	**39**
0—1 ..	*29*	13	16	29	13	16	..	..	..	..	..	.
1—2 ..	*29*	14	15	29	14	15	..	..	..	..	..	..
2—3 ..	*32*	14	18	31	14	17	1	..	1	..	..	..
3—4 .	*32*	14	18	32	14	18	..	..	..	..	..	..
4—5 .	*37*	18	19	37	18	19	..	..	..	..	..	..
Total 0—5 ..	*159*	*73*	*86*	*158*	*73*	*85*	*1*	..	*1*	..	..	..
5—10 ..	*143*	74	69	149	73	67	3	1	2	..	.	..
10—15 .	*112*	60	52	101	57	44	11	3	8	..	.	..
15—20 ..	*78*	42	36	37	27	10	39	13	26	2	2	..
20—30 ..	*157*	83	74	19	15	4	133	66	67	5	2	3
30—40 ..	*142*	74	68	2	1	1	128	66	62	12	7	5
40—50 .	*88*	50	38	1	1	..	71	40	31	16	9	7
50—60 .	*54*	32	22	2	1	1	33	22	11	19	9	10
60 and over ..	*50*	23	27	..	..	..	29	16	13	21	7	14

TABLE VII.—AGE, SEX

PART B.—DETAILS FOR DISTRICTS AND STATES.

MALER KOTLA STATE.

Religion and Age.	Population.			Unmarried.			Married.			Widowed.		
	Persons.	Males.	Females.	Persons.	Males.	Females.	Persons.	Males.	Females.	Persons.	Males.	Females.
1	2	3	4	5	6	7	8	9	10	11	12	13
ALL RELIGIONS ..	**83,072**	**45,883**	**37,189**	**39,267**	**23,960**	**15,307**	**35,183**	**17,849**	**17,334**	**8,622**	**4,074**	**4,548**
0- -1 ..	*3,309*	1,630	1,679	3,303	1,626	1,677	6	4	2	..	.	.
1- -2 ..	*2,211*	1,109	1,102	2,201	1,102	1,099	9	6	3	1	1	.
2- -3 ..	*2,380*	1,193	1,187	2,365	1,186	1,179	14	7	7	1	.	1
3- -4 ..	2,305	1,182	1,123	2,292	1,177	1,115	13	5	8	..	..	..
4—5 ..	*2,169*	1,151	1,018	2,144	1,141	1,003	22	8	14	3	2	1
Total 0—5 ..	*12,374*	*6,265*	*6,109*	*12,305*	*6,232*	*6,073*	*64*	*30*	*34*	*5*	*3*	*2*
5—10 ..	*10,329*	5,406	4,923	9,694	5,234	4,460	619	162	457	16	10	6
10—15 ..	*9,949*	5,234	4,715	8,221	4,758	3,463	1,700	462	1,238	28	14	14
15- -20 ..	*7,936*	4,363	3,573	3,306	2,610	696	4,531	1,696	2,835	99	57	42
20- -30 ..	*13,637*	7,755	5,882	2,988	2,657	331	10,146	4,787	5,359	503	311	192
30- -40 ..	*10,073*	5,926	4,147	1,233	1,114	119	7,840	4,279	3,561	1,000	533	467
40- -50 ..	*8,087*	4,694	3,393	772	684	88	5,495	3,170	2,319	1,820	834	986
50- -60 ..	*5,635*	3,264	2,371	455	415	40	3,012	1,896	1,116	2,168	953	1,215
60 and over ..	*5,052*	2,976	2,076	293	256	37	1,776	1,361	415	2,983	1,359	1,624
HINDU ..	**21,252**	**11,713**	**9,539**	**10,296**	**6,281**	**4,015**	**8,643**	**4,376**	**4,267**	**2,313**	**1,056**	**1,257**
0- -1 ..	*843*	410	433	841	408	433	2	2	..	..	..	.
1—2 ..	*547*	273	274	544	271	273	3	2	1	..	..	..
2—3 ..	*594*	291	303	591	289	302	3	2	1	..	..	.
3—4 ..	*611*	306	305	607	303	304	4	3	1	..	..	..
4- -5 ..	*574*	303	271	569	300	269	4	2	2	1	1	..
Total 0- -5 ..	*3,169*	*1,583*	*1,586*	*3,152*	*1,571*	*1,581*	*16*	*11*	*5*	*1*	*1*	.
5- 10 ..	*2,636*	1,379	1,257	2,515	1,340	1,175	114	36	78	7	3	4
10- -15 ..	*2,523*	1,323	1,200	2,118	1,200	918	398	121	277	7	2	5
15- -20 ..	*2,103*	1,165	938	876	688	188	1,201	462	739	26	15	11
20—30 ..	*3,715*	2,145	1,570	827	746	81	2,745	1,323	1,422	143	76	67
30—40 ..	*2,604*	1,544	1,060	350	327	23	1,947	1,069	878	307	148	159
40—50 ..	*1,946*	1,120	826	227	206	21	1,219	684	535	500	230	270
50—60 ..	*1,353*	773	580	150	136	14	619	385	234	584	252	332
60 and over ..	*1,203*	681	522	81	67	14	384	285	99	738	329	409
SIKH ..	**28,982**	**16,114**	**12,868**	**14,023**	**8,882**	**5,141**	**11,684**	**5,617**	**6,067**	**3,275**	**1,615**	**1,660**
0- 1 ..	*1,126*	565	561	1,123	564	559	3	1	2	.	.	.
1- -2 ..	*752*	375	377	749	373	376	2	1	1	1	1	.
2- -3 ..	*820*	425	395	814	424	390	5	1	4	1	..	1
3- 4 ..	*787*	412	375	783	412	371	4	..	4	..	..	..
4- -5 ..	*739*	374	365	752	372	360	5	1	4	2	1	1
Total 0—5 .	*4,224*	*2,151*	*2,073*	*4,201*	*2,145*	*2,056*	*19*	*4*	*15*	*4*	*2*	*2*
5—10 ..	*3,503*	1,821	1,682	3,320	1,779	1,541	178	38	140	5	4	1
10—15 ..	*3,397*	1,825	1,572	2,834	1,692	1,142	551	127	424	12	6	6
15- -20 ..	*2,680*	1,492	1,188	1,170	974	196	1,478	498	980	32	20	12
20- -30 ..	*4,583*	2,605	1,978	1,103	1,065	98	3,261	1,427	1,834	159	113	46
30- -40 ..	*3,475*	2,054	1,421	582	537	45	2,548	1,307	1,241	345	210	135
40—50 ..	*2,939*	1,689	1,250	382	350	32	1,874	1,026	848	683	313	370
50- -60 ..	*2,160*	1,276	884	223	208	15	1,098	668	430	839	400	439
60 and over ..	*2,021*	1,201	820	148	132	16	677	522	155	1,196	547	649
JAIN ..	**1,286**	**699**	**587**	**571**	**332**	**239**	**578**	**310**	**268**	**137**	**57**	**80**
0—1 ..	*42*	27	15	42	27	15	..	..	..	..	..	..
1—2 ..	*37*	16	21	37	16	21	..	..	..	..	..	..
2—3 ..	*39*	17	22	39	17	22	..	..	..	..	..	..
3—4 ..	*30*	14	16	30	14	16	..	..	.	..	..	..
4—5 ..	*32*	15	17	30	14	16	2	1	1	..	..	..
Total 0—5 ..	*180*	*89*	*91*	*178*	*88*	*90*	*2*	*1*	*1*	..	..	..
5- 10 .	*144*	75	69	141	74	67	3	1	2	..	..	..
10- 15 ..	*147*	80	67	131	73	58	16	7	9	..	.	..
15- 20 ..	*133*	66	67	53	36	17	78	30	48	2		2
20—30 ..	*211*	112	99	32	30	2	168	77	91	11	5	6
30- -40 .	*161*	94	67	15	13	2	123	72	51	23	9	14
40—50 ..	*144*	82	62	13	11	2	95	56	39	36	15	21
50—60 ..	*99*	59	40	5	5	..	62	41	21	32	13	19
60 and over ..	*67*	42	25	3	2	1	31	25	6	33	15	18
MUSLIM ..	**31,417**	**17,280**	**14,137**	**14,318**	**8,434**	**5,884**	**14,208**	**7,504**	**6,704**	**2,891**	**1,342**	**1,549**
0- -1 ..	*1,290*	626	664	1,289	625	664	1	1	..	.	..	.
1- -2 ..	*874*	444	430	870	441	429	4	3	1	..	..	..
2- -3 ..	*924*	458	466	918	454	464	6	4	2	..	..	.
3- -4 ..	*873*	448	425	868	446	422	5	2	3	..		..
4- -5 ..	*819*	456	363	808	452	356	11	4	7	..	..	.
Total 0—5 ..	*4,780*	*2,432*	*2,348*	*4,753*	*2,418*	*2,335*	*27*	*14*	*13*	..	..	.
5—10 ..	*4,032*	2,125	1,907	3,704	2,035	1,669	324	87	237	4	3	1
10—15 ..	*3,870*	2,002	1,868	3,129	1,790	1,339	732	206	526	9	6	3
15—20 ..	*3,010*	1,634	1,376	1,203	909	294	1,768	703	1,065	39	22	17
20—30 ..	*5,109*	2,883	2,226	960	812	148	3,959	1,954	2,005	190	117	73
30- -40 ..	*3,811*	2,218	1,593	283	234	49	3,205	1,819	1,386	323	165	158
40- -50 ..	*3,035*	1,787	1,248	148	115	33	2,288	1,398	890	599	274	325
50- -60 ..	*2,015*	1,151	864	77	66	11	1,226	798	428	712	287	425
60 and over ..	*1,755*	1,048	707	61	55	6	679	525	154	1,015	468	5-7
CHRISTIAN ..	**135**	**77**	**58**	**59**	**31**	**28**	**70**	**42**	**28**	**6**	**4**	**2**
0—1 ..	*8*	2	6	8	2	6	..	..	..	..	..	..
1—2 ..	*1*	1	..	1	1	..	..	..	..	..	..	..
2—3 ..	*3*	2	*1*	3	2	*1*	..	..	..	..	..	..
3—4 ..	*4*	2	2	4	2	2	..	..	..	..	..	...
4—5 ..	*5*	3	2	5	3	2	..	..	..	..	..	..
Total 0—5 ..	*21*	*10*	*11*	*21*	*10*	*11*	..	..	..	..	..	..
5—10 ..	*14*	6	8	14	6	8	..	..	..	..	..	..
10—15 ..	*12*	4	8	9	3	6	3	1	2	..	..	..
15—20 ..	*10*	6	4	4	3	1	6	3	3	..	..	.
20—30 ..	*19*	10	9	6	4	2	13	6	7	..	..	.
30- -40 ..	*22*	16	6	3	3	..	17	12	5	2	1	1
40- -50 ..	*23*	16	7	2	2	..	19	12	7	2	2	..
50—60 ..	*8*	5	3	..	..	..	7	4	3	*1*	1	.
60 and over ..	*6*	4	2	..	..	..	5	4	1	1	..	1

AND CIVIL CONDITION (BY RELIGION).

PART B.—DETAILS FOR DISTRICTS AND STATES—*continued.*

FARIDKOT STATE.

Religion and Age.	Population.			Unmarried.			Married.			Widowed.		
	Persons.	Males.	Females.	Persons.	Males.	Females.	Persons.	Males.	Females.	Persons.	Males.	Females.
1	2	3		5	6	7	8	9	10	11	12	13
ALL RELIGIONS ..	164,364	91,163	73,201	81,496	49,883	31,613	68,562	35,034	33,528	14,306	6,246	8,060
0-1 .	6,262	3,223	3,039	6,262	3,223	3,039	.	.	.	.	..	..
1-2 ..	4,459	2,237	2,222	4,459	2,237	2,222	..	..	.	..	..	..
2-3 ..	4,798	2,439	2,359	4,798	2,439	2,359	.	..		..	.	..
3-4 ..	4,694	2,425	2,269	4,694	2,425	2,269	.	..	..	..		..
4-5 .	4,473	2,362	2,111	4,472	2,361	2,111	1	1	..	.	..	..
Total 0-5	24,686	12,686	12,000	24,685	12,685	12,000	1	1	..	.	.	.
5-10 ..	21,214	11,501	9,713	20,736	11,397	9,339	476	102	374	2	2	..
10-15 ..	20,250	11,112	9,138	18,385	10,628	7,757	1,850	474	1,376	15	10	5
15-20 ..	16,366	9,324	7,042	8,136	6,113	2,023	8,034	3,088	4,946	196	123	73
20-30 ..	28,116	16,159	11,957	6,181	5,696	485	21,018	9,917	11,101	917	546	371
30-40 .	19,596	11,236	8,360	1,690	1,681	9	16,158	8,672	7,486	1,748	883	865
40-50 ..	15,254	8,579	6,675	955	955	..	11,097	6,261	4,836	3,202	1,363	1,839
50-60	10,384	5,828	4,556	490	490	..	6,259	3,878	2,381	3,635	1,460	2,175
60 and over	8,498	4,738	3,760	238	238	..	3,069	2,641	1,028	4,591	1,859	2,732
HINDU ..	19,271	11,231	8,040	9,207	5,957	3,250	8,146	4,441	3,705	1,918	833	1,085
0-1 ..	689	361	328	689	361	328	.	..		..	..	..
1-2 ..	492	252	240	492	252	240	..	..	..	..	..	..
2-3 ..	540	283	257	540	283	257	..	..	.	.	.	.
3-4 ..	526	273	253	526	273	253	..	.	..	.	..	..
4-5 .	484	255	229	483	254	229	.. 1	1	..	.	..	..
Total 0-5 .	2,731	1,424	1,307	2,730	1,423	1,307	1	1	.	.	..	..
5-10 ..	2,299	1,259	1,040	2,232	1,249	983	66	9	57	1	1	..
10-15 ..	2,211	1,231	980	1,942	1,171	771	266	59	207	3	1	2
15-20 ..	1,955	1,143	812	869	709	160	1,055	421	634	31	13	18
20-30 ..	3,628	2,243	1,385	825	796	29	2,641	1,356	1,285	162	91	71
30-40 ..	2,611	1,618	993	279	279	.	2,019	1,189	830	313	150	163
40-50 ..	1,875	1,149	726	174	174	.	1,246	785	461	455	190	265
50-60 ..	1,124	688	436	109	109	.	572	396	176	443	183	260
60 and over ..	837	476	361	47	47	..	280	225	55	510	204	306
SIKH ..	92,880	51,414	41,466	46,325	28,552	17,773	38,311	19,313	18,998	8,244	3,549	4,695
0-1 ..	3,481	1,818	1,663	3,481	1,818	1,663	.	..	..	..	..	..
1-2 .	2,486	1,247	1,239	2,486	1,247	1,239	..	..	..	..	..	..
2-3 ..	2,660	1,341	1,319	2,660	1,341	1,319	..	.	.	..	..	..
3-4 ..	2,613	1,353	1,260	2,613	1,353	1,260	..	.	..	..	..	..
4-5 ..	2,491	1,325	1,166	2,491	1,325	1,166	..	.	..	..	..	..
Total 0-5 ..	13,731	7,084	6,647	13,731	7,084	6,647	.	..	..	..	..	..
5-10 ..	11,790	6,458	5,332	11,530	6,398	5,132	260	60	200	..	..	.
10-15 .	11,338	6,263	5,075	10,366	5,992	4,374	965	260	699	7	5	2
15-20 ..	9,236	5,325	3,911	4,827	3,538	1,289	4,311	1,722	2,589	98	65	33
20-30 ..	15,729	9,030	6,699	3,683	3,357	326	11,587	5,402	6,185	459	271	188
30-40 ..	10,861	6,234	4,627	1,086	1,081	5	8,875	4,682	4,193	900	471	429
40-50 ..	8,703	4,781	3,922	635	635	..	6,257	3,379	2,878	1,811	767	1,044
50-60 .	6,293	3,409	2,884	312	312	..	3,770	2,222	1,548	2,211	875	1,336
60 and over .	5,199	2,830	2,369	155	155	..	2,286	1,580	706	2,758	1,095	1,663
JAIN .	550	292	258	272	151	121	225	120	105	53	21	82
0-1 .	16	6	10	16	6	10	..	..	..	.	..	..
1-2 ..	15	8	7	15	8	7	..	..	.	..	.	..
2-3 ..	15	9	6	15	9	6	..	..	..	..	..	..
3-4 ..	11	5	6	11	5	6	..	..	..	..	..	..
4-5 ..	17	8	9	17	8	9	..	..	..	..	..	..
Total 0-5 ..	74	36	38	74	36	38	..	..	..	..	..	..
5-10 ..	79	38	41	79	38	41	..	..	..	..	..	..
10-15 ..	77	37	40	71	36	35	6	1	5	..	..	..
15-20 ..	59	29	30	27	21	6	31	8	23	1	..	1
20-30 ..	96	55	41	11	11	..	84	44	40	1	..	1
30-40 ..	61	37	24	5	4	1	49	27	22	7	6	1
40-50 ..	43	26	17	3	3	..	30	19	11	10	4	6
50-60 ..	34	22	12	1	1	..	21	17	4	12	4	8
60 and over ..	27	12	15	1	1	.	4	4	..	22	7	15
MUSLIM ..	49,912	27,236	22,676	24,843	14,695	10,148	21,096	10,751	10,245	3,973	1,790	2,183
0-1 ..	2,048	1,024	1,024	2,048	1,024	1,024	..	..	..	..	.	..
1-2 ..	1,437	712	725	1,437	712	725	..	..	..	..	..	..
2-3 .	1,548	783	765	1,548	783	765	..	.	..	..	..	..
3-4 .	1,506	769	737	1,506	769	737	.	.	.	..	.	..
4-5 ..	1,435	745	690	1,435	745	690	.	..	..	..	..	..
Total 0-5 ..	7,974	4,033	3,941	7,974	4,033	3,941	..	..	.	..	.	..
5-10 .	6,769	3,593	3,176	6,624	3,560	3,064	144	32	112	1	1	..
10-15 .	6,343	3,433	2,910	5,752	3,291	2,461	586	138	448	5	4	1
15-20 ..	4,932	2,720	2,212	2,331	1,782	549	2,538	896	1,642	63	42	21
20-30 ..	8,353	4,653	3,700	1,605	1,475	130	6,465	3,004	3,461	283	174	109
30-40 ..	5,837	3,225	2,612	313	310	3	5,012	2,664	2,348	512	251	261
40-50 ..	4,475	2,535	1,940	143	143	..	3,437	2,003	1,434	895	389	506
50-60 .	2,852	1,663	1,189	68	68	..	1,844	1,207	637	940	388	552
60 and over ..	2,377	1,381	906	33	33	..	1,070	807	263	1,274	541	733
CHRISTIAN ..	167	100	67	84	54	30	71	37	34	12	9	3
0-1 ..	3	2	1	3	2	1	..	..	..	..	..	..
1-2 ..	3	2	1	3	2	1	..	..	..	..	..	..
2-3 ..	6	5	1	6	5	1	..	..	.	..	..	..
3-4 ..	4	4	..	4	4	..	..	..	.	..	..	..
4-5 ..	6	4	2	6	4	2	..	..	..	..	..	.
Total 0-5 ..	22	17	5	22	17	5	..	..	..	..	..	.
5-10 ..	28	13	15	26	13	13	2	..	2	..	..	.
10-15 ..	31	13	18	24	12	12	7	1	6	..	..	..
15-20 ..	20	12	8	6	6	..	13	5	8	1	1	..
20-30 ..	23	16	7	5	5	..	16	9	7	2	2	..
30-40 ..	16	10	6	1	1	..	15	9	6	.	.	.
40-50 ..	16	11	5	..	..	.	11	8	3	5	3	2
50-60 ..	6	4	2	..	.	.	4	3	1	2	1	1
60 and over ..	5	4	1	..	.	..	3	2	1	2	2	..

TABLE VII.—AGE, SEX

PART B.—DETAILS FOR DISTRICTS AND STATES.

CHAMBA STATE.

Religion and Age.	Population.			Unmarried.			Married.			Widowed.		
	Persons.	Males.	Females.	Persons.	Males.	Females.	Persons.	Males.	Females.	Persons.	Males.	Females.
1	2	3	4	5	6	7	8	9	10	11	12	13
ALL RELIGIONS ..	**146,870**	**76,059**	**70,811**	**64,160**	**38,610**	**25,550**	**65,788**	**31,288**	**34,500**	**16,922**	**6,161**	**10,761**
0—1 ..	*4,042*	2,016	2,026	4,042	2,016	2,026	..	..	..	..	..	..
1—2 ..	*3,574*	1,792	1,782	3,572	1,790	1,782	2	2	..	..	..	..
2—3 ..	*4,201*	2,022	2,179	4,192	2,017	2,175	9	5	4	..	..	..
3—4 ..	*4,100*	1,956	2,144	4,077	1,950	2,127	22	6	16	1	..	1
4—5 ..	*3,946*	1,923	2,023	3,906	1,914	1,992	36	8	28	4	1	3
Total 0—5 ..	*19,863*	*9,709*	*10,154*	*19,789*	*9,687*	*10,102*	*69*	*21*	*48*	*5*	*1*	*4*
5—10 ..	*17,818*	9,018	8,800	16,787	8,838	7,949	1,000	166	834	31	14	17
10—15 ..	*16,274*	8,367	7,907	13,592	7,905	5,687	2,620	439	2,181	62	23	39
15—20 ..	*13,422*	6,501	6,921	5,505	4,484	1,021	7,626	1,897	5,729	291	120	171
20—30 ..	*26,965*	13,272	13,693	5,484	4,980	504	19,969	7,622	12,347	1,512	670	842
30—40 ..	*20,411*	10,917	9,494	1,703	1,555	148	15,976	8,246	7,730	2,732	1,116	1,616
40—50 ..	*13,717*	7,676	6,041	674	602	72	9,545	5,840	3,705	3,498	1,234	2,264
50—60 ..	*9,499*	5,628	3,871	357	318	39	5,483	4,061	1,422	3,659	1,249	2,410
60 and over ..	*8,901*	4,971	3,930	269	241	28	3,500	2,996	504	5,132	1,734	3,398
HINDU ..	**134,717**	**69,673**	**65,044**	**58,668**	**35,402**	**23,266**	**60,189**	**28,572**	**31,617**	**15,860**	**5,699**	**10,161**
0—1 ..	*3,663*	1,817	1,846	3,663	1,817	1,846	..	..	..	..	..	..
1—2 ..	*3,215*	1,608	1,607	3,214	1,607	1,607	1	1	..	..	..	..
2—3 ..	*3,793*	1,829	1,964	3,787	1,825	1,962	6	4	2	..	..	..
3—4 ..	*3,730*	1,782	1,948	3,712	1,778	1,934	17	4	13	1	..	1
4—5 ..	*3,567*	1,736	1,831	3,535	1,730	1,805	29	5	24	3	1	2
Total 0—5 ..	*17,963*	*8,772*	*9,196*	*17,911*	*8,757*	*9,154*	*53*	*14*	*39*	*4*	*1*	*3*
5—10 ..	*16,198*	8,192	8,006	15,287	8,041	7,246	882	137	745	29	14	15
10—15 ..	*14,842*	7,622	7,220	12,431	7,226	5,205	2,352	373	1,979	59	23	36
15—20 ..	*12,268*	5,956	6,312	5,088	4,153	935	6,915	1,693	5,222	265	110	155
20—30 ..	*24,780*	12,213	12,567	5,125	4,666	459	18,239	6,927	11,312	1,416	620	796
30—40 ..	*18,862*	10,064	8,798	1,608	1,472	136	14,679	7,552	7,127	2,575	1,040	1,535
40—50 ..	*12,730*	7,084	5,646	636	567	69	8,808	5,378	3,430	3,286	1,139	2,147
50—60 ..	*8,848*	5,211	3,637	333	297	36	5,064	3,749	1,315	3,451	1,165	2,286
60 and over ..	*8,221*	4,559	3,662	249	223	26	3,197	2,749	448	4,775	1,587	3,188
SIKH ..	**112**	**63**	**49**	**59**	**37**	**22**	**42**	**21**	**21**	**11**	**5**	**6**
0—1 ..	*2*	..	2	2	..	2	..	..	..	..	..	..
1—2 ..	*3*	1	2	3	1	2	..	..	..	..	..	..
2—3 ..	*4*	1	3	4	1	3	..	..	..	..	..	..
3—4 ..	*2*	1	1	2	1	1	..	..	..	..	..	..
4—5 ..	*3*	2	1	3	2	1	..	..	..	..	..	.
Total 0—5 ..	*14*	*5*	*9*	*14*	*5*	*9*	..	..	..	..	.	.
5—10 ..	*13*	8	5	12	8	4	1	..	1	..	..	..
10—15 ..	*15*	9	6	14	9	5	1	..	1	..	..	..
15—20 ..	*13*	8	5	10	7	3	3	1	2	..	..	..
20—30 ..	*20*	10	10	7	6	1	11	3	8	2	1	1
30—40 ..	*13*	6	7	..	..	..	12	5	7	1	1	..
40—50 ..	*11*	8	3	2	2	.	6	5	1	3	1	2
50—60 ..	*6*	6	..	..	..	..	5	5	..	1	1	..
60 and over ..	*7*	3	4	..	..	..	3	2	1	4	1	3
JAIN ..	**3**	**1**	**2**	**1**	**1**	..	**1**	..	**1**	**1**	..	**1**
5—10 ..	*1*	1	..	1	1	..	..	..	..	..	..	..
15—20 ..	*1*	..	1	..	..	..	1	..	1	..	..	..
60 and over ..	*1*	..	1	..	..	..	..	..	..	1	..	1
MUSLIM ..	**10,839**	**5,706**	**5,133**	**4,924**	**2,898**	**2,026**	**4,974**	**2,407**	**2,567**	**941**	**401**	**540**
0—1 ..	*340*	179	161	340	179	161	..	..	..	..	..	..
1—2 ..	*329*	171	158	328	170	158	1	1	..	..	..	..
2—3 ..	*360*	173	187	357	172	185	3	1	2	..	..	..
3—4 ..	*331*	157	174	326	155	171	5	2	3	..	..	.
4—5 ..	*335*	165	170	329	163	166	5	2	3	1	..	1
Total 0—5 ..	*1,695*	*845*	*850*	*1,680*	*839*	*841*	*14*	*6*	*8*	*1*	..	*1*
5—10 ..	*1,460*	743	717	1,352	718	634	108	25	83	..	..	..
10—15 ..	*1,296*	675	621	1,047	616	431	246	59	187	3	..	3
15—20 ..	*1,034*	494	540	369	298	71	641	186	455	24	10	14
20—30 ..	*1,952*	958	994	321	285	36	1,545	626	919	86	47	39
30—40 ..	*1,376*	760	616	87	78	9	1,149	617	532	140	65	75
40—50 ..	*867*	518	349	33	31	2	645	405	240	189	82	107
50—60 ..	*560*	354	206	18	17	1	357	264	93	185	73	112
60 and over ..	*599*	359	240	17	16	1	269	219	50	313	124	189
CHRISTIAN ..	**94**	**57**	**37**	**47**	**30**	**17**	**37**	**19**	**18**	**10**	**8**	**2**
0—1 ..	*4*	3	1	4	3	1	.	..	..	..	..	..
1—2 ..	*2*	1	1	2	1	1	.	..	..	..	..	..
2—3 ..	*4*	3	1	4	3	1	..	..	..	..	..	..
3—4 ..	*4*	2	2	4	2	2	..	..	..	..	..	..
4—5 ..	*5*	2	3	5	2	3		..	.	..	..	..
Total 0—5 ..	*19*	*11*	*8*	*19*	*11*	*8*	..	.	..	..	..	..
5—10 ..	*14*	8	6	12	8	4	1	..	1	1	..	1
10—15 ..	*5*	4	1	5	4	1	..	..	..	..	..	..
15—20 ..	*5*	3	2	3	3	..	2	..	2	..	..	..
20—30 ..	*22*	9	13	4	3	1	18	6	12	..	..	..
30—40 ..	*16*	12	4	1	..	1	14	11	3	1	1	..
40—50 ..	*4*	3	1	1	..	1	2	2	..	1	1	..
50—60 ..	*5*	4	1	2	1	1	..	.	.	3	3	..
60 and over ..	*4*	3	1	..	..	..	..	..	..	4	3	1

AND CIVIL CONDITION (BY RELIGION).

PART B.—DETAILS FOR DISTRICTS AND STATES—*continued*.

PATIALA STATE.

Religion and Age.	Population.			Unmarried.			Married.			Widowed.		
	Persons.	Males.	Females.	Persons.	Males.	Females.	Persons.	Males.	Females.	Persons.	Males.	Females.
1	2	3	4	5	6	7	8	9	10	11	12	13
ALL RELIGIONS ..	**1,625,520**	**900,597**	**724,923**	**761,750**	**482,109**	**279,641**	**692,033**	**338,910**	**353,123**	**171,737**	**79,578**	**92,159**
0- -1 ..	60,698	30,577	30,121	60,696	30,576	30,120	2	1	1	..	..	..
1- -2 ..	43,666	22,082	21,584	43,655	22,079	21,576	11	3	8	..	..	..
2- -3 ..	48,802	24,725	24,077	48,757	24,716	24,041	43	7	36	2	2	.
3- -4 ..	48,061	24,613	23,448	47,826	24,551	23,275	229	59	170	6	3	.
4- -5 ..	44,710	23,275	21,435	44,311	23,172	21,139	391	100	291	8	3	3
Total 0- -5 ..	245,937	125,272	120,665	245,245	125,094	120,151	676	170	506	16	8	8
5- -10 ..	205,724	110,702	95,022	190,587	106,950	83,637	14,866	3,613	11,253	271	139	132
10- -15 ..	198,766	109,765	89,001	160,186	98,799	61,387	37,926	10,616	27,310	654	350	304
15- -20 ..	164,215	92,052	72,163	66,657	54,919	11,738	94,898	35,577	59,321	2,660	1,556	1,104
20- -30 ..	282,053	157,825	124,228	55,893	53,292	2,601	213,965	97,597	116,368	12,193	6,936	5,259
30- -40 .	200,315	114,659	85,656	20,562	20,484	78	154,489	81,879	72,610	25,264	12,296	12,968
40- -50 ..	149,894	85,366	64,528	11,844	11,813	31	97,632	55,851	41,781	40,418	17,702	22,716
50- -60 ..	99,820	58,211	41,609	6,501	6,490	11	50,693	33,066	17,627	42,626	18,655	23,971
60 and over ..	78,796	46,745	32,051	4,275	4,268	7	26,888	20,541	6,347	47,633	21,936	25,697
HINDU ..	**621,145**	**340,466**	**280,679**	**285,304**	**180,132**	**105,172**	**265,118**	**129,044**	**136,074**	**70,723**	**31,290**	**39,433**
0- -1 ..	23,267	11,645	11,622	23,267	11,645	11,622	..	..	..	..	..	.
1- -2 ..	16,589	8,282	8,307	16,585	8,280	8,305	4	2	2	..	..	..
2- -3 ..	19,026	9,548	9,478	19,016	9,545	9,471	10	3	7	..	..	..
3- -4 ..	18,900	9,623	9,277	18,824	9,605	9,219	75	18	57	1	.	1
4- -5 ..	17,627	9,146	8,481	17,476	9,111	8,365	148	35	113	3	..	3
Total 0- -5 ..	95,409	48,244	47,165	95,168	48,186	46,982	237	58	179	4	..	4
5- -10 ..	79,010	42,364	36,646	73,071	40,982	32,089	5,842	1,336	4,506	97	46	51
10- -15 ..	75,269	41,507	33,762	59,488	37,106	22,382	15,526	4,265	11,261	255	136	119
15- -20 ..	61,855	34,281	27,574	22,645	19,414	3,231	38,001	14,230	23,771	1,209	637	572
20- -30 .	108,188	59,213	48,975	18,788	18,313	475	83,707	38,041	45,666	5,693	2,859	2,834
30- -40 ..	77,981	43,875	34,106	7,479	7,468	11	59,016	31,389	27,627	11,486	5,018	6,468
40- -50 ..	57,070	32,289	24,781	4,390	4,388	2	35,450	20,639	14,811	17,230	7,262	9,968
50- -60 ..	37,415	21,724	15,751	2,569	2,369	..	17,914	11,846	6,068	16,992	7,309	9,683
60 and over ..	28,888	16,969	11,919	1,706	1,706	..	9,425	7,240	2,185	17,757	8,023	9,734
SIKH ..	**632,972**	**357,193**	**275,779**	**303,451**	**196,693**	**106,758**	**264,681**	**129,420**	**135,261**	**64,840**	**31,080**	**33,760**
0- 1 ..	23,110	11,724	11,386	23,110	11,724	11,386	..	..	..	..	..	..
1- -2 ..	16,391	8,462	7,929	16,390	8,461	7,929	1	1	..	..	..	..
2- -3 ..	18,096	9,392	8,704	18,083	9,387	8,696	11	3	8	2	2	..
3- -4 ..	17,746	9,224	8,522	17,682	9,207	8,475	60	14	46	4	3	1
4- -5 ..	16,381	8,584	7,797	16,277	8,562	7,715	102	20	82	2	2	.
Total 0- -5 ..	91,724	47,386	44,338	91,542	47,341	44,201	174	38	136	8	7	1
5- -10 ..	77,732	42,219	35,513	72,675	41,040	31,635	4,966	1,127	3,839	91	52	39
10- -15 ..	76,513	42,697	33,816	63,243	39,019	24,224	13,062	3,559	9,503	208	119	89
15- -20 ..	64,245	36,896	27,349	28,727	23,364	5,363	34,723	13,016	21,707	795	516	279
20- -30 ..	109,827	63,372	46,455	25,808	24,496	1,312	80,298	36,496	43,802	3,721	2,380	1,341
30- -40 ..	77,883	45,769	32,114	10,198	10,177	21	59,273	31,055	28,218	8,412	4,537	3,875
40- -50 ..	60,103	34,601	25,502	5,952	5,950	2	39,346	21,850	17,496	14,805	6,801	8,004
50- -60 ..	41,381	24,269	17,112	3,203	3,203	..	21,293	13,574	7,719	16,885	7,492	9,393
60 and over ..	33,564	19,984	13,580	2,103	2,103	..	11,546	8,705	2,841	19,915	9,176	10,739
JAIN ..	**3,578**	**1,875**	**1,703**	**1,707**	**996**	**711**	**1,420**	**679**	**741**	**451**	**200**	**251**
0- -1 ..	147	69	78	147	69	78	..	..	..	..	..	..
1- -2 ..	105	49	56	105	49	56	..	..	..	..	..	..
2- -3 ..	129	63	66	129	63	66	..	..	..	..	..	..
3- -4 ..	122	64	58	122	64	58	..	..	.	..	..	..
4- -5 ..	109	55	54	109	55	54	..	..	..	..	..	..
Total 0- -5 ..	612	300	312	612	300	312	..	..	..	..	..	..
5- -10 ..	457	232	225	435	223	212	20	8	12	2	1	1
10- -15 ..	419	214	205	348	194	154	68	18	50	3	2	1
15- -20 ..	365	184	181	122	92	30	231	86	145	12	6	6
20- -30 ..	585	312	273	90	87	3	456	212	244	39	13	26
30- -40 ..	437	234	203	51	51	.	305	150	155	81	33	48
40- -50 ..	344	194	150	28	28	..	202	113	89	114	53	61
50- -60 ..	216	127	89	16	16	..	103	64	39	97	47	50
60 and over ..	143	78	65	5	5	..	35	28	7	103	45	58
MUSLIM ..	**363,920**	**198,945**	**164,975**	**169,367**	**103,135**	**66,232**	**159,149**	**78,950**	**80,199**	**35,404**	**16,860**	**18,544**
0- -1 ..	14,006	7,047	6,959	14,004	7,046	6,958	2	1	1	..	..	.
1- -2 ..	10,460	5,227	5,233	10,454	5,227	5,227	6	.	6	..	..	.
2- -3 ..	11,418	5,655	5,763	11,396	5,654	5,742	22	1	21	..	..	.
3- -4 .	11,162	5,631	5,531	11,067	5,604	5,463	94	27	67	1	..	1
4- -5 .	10,476	5,425	5,051	10,332	5,379	4,953	141	45	96	3	1	2
Total 0- -5 ..	57,522	28,985	28,537	57,253	28,910	28,343	265	74	191	4	1	3
5- -10 ..	48,010	25,618	22,392	43,913	24,441	19,472	4,017	1,138	2,879	80	39	41
10- -15 ..	46,091	25,095	20,996	36,697	22,244	14,453	9,206	2,758	6,448	188	93	95
15- -20 ..	37,328	20,463	16,865	14,995	11,918	3,077	21,696	8,151	13,545	637	394	243
20- -30 ..	62,751	34,552	28,199	11,084	10,285	799	48,951	22,602	26,349	2,716	1,665	1,051
30- -40 ..	43,563	24,533	19,030	2,802	2,758	44	35,532	19,093	16,439	5,229	2,682	2,547
40- -50 ..	32,045	18,103	13,942	1,461	1,435	26	22,389	13,108	9,281	8,195	3,560	4,635
50- -60 ..	20,548	11,969	8,579	703	692	11	11,267	7,502	3,765	8,578	3,775	4,803
60 and over ..	16,062	9,627	6,435	459	452	7	5,826	4,524	1,302	9,777	4,651	5,126
CHRISTIAN ..	**1,449**	**806**	**643**	**708**	**434**	**274**	**636**	**322**	**314**	**105**	**50**	**55**
0- -1 ..	53	26	27	53	26	27	..	..	..	..	..	.
1- -2 ..	49	26	23	49	26	23	..	..	..	..	..	.
2- -3 ..	49	26	23	49	26	23	..	..	..	..	..	.
3- -4 ..	41	24	17	41	24	17	..	..	..	..	..	.
4- -5 ..	44	26	18	44	26	18	..	..	..	..	..	
Total 0- -5 ..	236	128	108	236	128	108	..	..	..	..	.	..
5- -10 ..	199	104	95	183	100	83	15	3	12	1	1	.
10- -15 ..	181	95	86	148	86	62	33	9	24	..	..	.
15- -20 ..	144	76	68	58	45	13	83	31	52	3	..	3
20- -30 ..	238	134	104	49	44	5	182	85	97	7	5	2
30- -40 ..	183	100	83	16	14	2	149	77	72	18	9	9
40- -50 ..	151	86	65	9	8	1	109	67	42	33	11	22
50- -60 ..	77	54	23	7	7	..	49	38	11	21	9	12
60 and over	40	29	11	2	2	..	16	12	4	22	15	7

TABLE VII.—AGE, SEX

PART B.—DETAILS FOR DISTRICTS AND STATES.

JIND STATE.

Religion and Age.		Population.			Unmarried.			Married.			Widowed.		
		Persons.	Males.	Females.	Persons.	Males.	Females.	Persons.	Males.	Females.	Persons.	Males.	Females.
1		2	3	4	5	6	7	8	9	10	11	12	13
ALL RELIGIONS	..	**324,676**	**176,383**	**148,298**	**145,340**	**90,666**	**54,674**	**145,805**	**70,823**	**74,982**	**33,531**	**14,894**	**18,637**
0- 1	..	*11,852*	5,800	5,962	11,850	5,889	5,961	2	1	1	..	..	..
1- -2	..	*8,941*	4,371	4,570	8,925	4,365	4,560	16	6	10	..	..	..
2- -3	..	*10,458*	5,131	5,327	10,409	5,116	5,293	49	15	34	..	.	..
3- -4	..	*10,130*	5,086	5,044	9,968	5,050	4,918	159	36	123	3	..	3
4 -5	..	*9,456*	4,920	4,536	9,190	4,857	4,333	256	60	196	10	3	7
Total 0- -5	..	*50,837*	*25,398*	*25,439*	*50,342*	*25,277*	*25,065*	*482*	*118*	*364*	*13*	*3*	*10*
5- 10	..	*43,937*	23,481	20,456	38,227	21,792	16,435	5,593	1,624	3,969	117	65	52
10- -15	.	*42,367*	23,257	19,110	30,459	19,274	11,185	11,692	3,850	7,842	210	133	83
15- -20	..	*33,070*	18,222	14,848	10,703	9,121	1,582	21,705	8,733	12,972	662	368	294
20- -30	..	*54,840*	29,698	25,142	8,600	8,221	379	43,313	19,984	23,329	2,927	1,493	1,434
30- 40	..	*39,042*	21,708	17,334	3,154	3,138	16	30,269	16,040	14,229	5,619	2,530	3,089
40- -50	..	*28,472*	15,951	12,521	1,892	1,885	7	18,631	10,700	7,922	7,949	3,357	4,592
50- -60	..	*18,174*	10,544	7,630	1,137	1,132	5	9,250	6,093	3,157	7,787	3,310	4,468
60 and over	..	*13,937*	8,124	5,813	826	826	..	4,870	3,672	1,198	8,241	3,626	4,615
HINDU	..	**243,561**	**131,270**	**112,291**	**107,802**	**66,873**	**40,929**	**110,046**	**53,055**	**56,991**	**25,713**	**11,342**	**14,371**
0- 1	..	*8,877*	4,399	4,478	8,876	4,390	4,477	1	.	1	..	..	..
1- -2	..	*6,701*	3,252	3,449	6,690	3,248	3,442	11	4	7	..	..	..
2- -3	..	*7,908*	3,852	4,056	7,874	3,844	4,030	34	8	26	..	..	..
3- 4	..	*7,702*	3,844	3,858	7,576	3,819	3,757	123	25	98	3	..	*3*
4- -5	..	*7,165*	3,723	3,442	6,958	3,678	3,280	198	43	155	9	2	7
Total 0- -5	..	*38,353*	*19,070*	*19,283*	*37,974*	*18,988*	*18,986*	*367*	*80*	*287*	*12*	*2*	*10*
5- 10	..	*33,457*	17,810	15,647	28,856	16,436	12,420	4,518	1,332	3,186	83	42	41
10- 15	..	*32,237*	17,598	14,639	22,664	14,340	8,324	9,410	3,160	6,250	163	98	65
15- -20	..	*24,659*	13,463	11,196	7,402	6,402	1,000	16,738	6,781	9,957	519	280	230
20- -30	..	*40,374*	21,493	18,881	5,745	5,553	192	32,338	14,819	17,519	2,291	1,121	1,170
30- -40	..	*29,097*	15,992	13,105	2,231	2,225	6	22,397	11,791	10,606	4,469	1,976	2,493
40- -50	..	*21,390*	11,885	9,505	1,397	1,396	1	13,820	7,889	5,931	6,173	2,600	3,573
50- -60	..	*13,601*	7,857	5,744	877	877	..	6,856	4,474	2,382	5,868	2,506	3,362
60 and over	..	*10,393*	6,102	4,291	656	656	..	3,602	2,729	873	6,135	2,717	3,418
SIKH	..	**33,290**	**19,183**	**14,107**	**16,145**	**10,629**	**5,516**	**13,876**	**7,033**	**6,843**	**3,269**	**1,521**	**1,748**
0- 1	..	*1,119*	563	556	1,119	563	556	..	..	..	..	..	..
1- -2	..	*901*	455	446	901	455	446	..	..	..	..	..	..
2 -3	..	*930*	460	461	928	468	460	2	1	1	..	..	..
3- 4	..	*891*	460	431	887	458	420	4	2	2	.	..	..
4 -5	..	*865*	463	402	859	462	397	6	1	5	..	..	..
Total 0- -5	..	*4,706*	*2,410*	*2,296*	*4,694*	*2,406*	*2,288*	*12*	*4*	*8*	..	.	.
5- -10	..	*3,995*	2,183	1,812	3,736	2,120	1,616	252	58	194	7	5	2
10- 15	..	*3,967*	2,239	1,728	3,287	2,044	1,243	669	188	481	11	7	4
15- 20	..	*3,530*	2,086	1,444	1,625	1,338	287	1,867	723	1,144	38	25	13
20- -30	..	*6,036*	3,659	2,377	1,623	1,442	81	4,306	2,084	2,222	207	133	74
30—40	.	*4,114*	2,477	1,637	621	620	1	3,061	1,629	1,432	432	228	204
40- -50	..	*3,188*	1,894	1,294	368	368	..	2,060	1,195	865	760	331	429
50- -60	.	*2,145*	1,277	868	182	182	..	1,088	727	361	875	308	507
60 and over	..	*1,609*	958	651	109	109	..	561	425	136	939	424	515
JAIN	..	**1,613**	**896**	**717**	**733**	**439**	**294**	**671**	**352**	**319**	**209**	**105**	**104**
0- 1	..	*54*	22	32	54	22	32	..	..	.	..	..	..
1 -2	..	*42*	20	22	42	20	22	.	..	..	..	..	..
2 -3	..	*53*	25	28	53	25	28	..	..	..	..	..	.
3- 4	..	*49*	25	24	49	25	24	..	..	..	.	..	..
4 -5	..	*48*	26	22	48	26	22	..	..	..	..	..	..
Total 0- -5	..	*246*	*118*	*128*	*246*	*118*	*128*	..	..	..	..	..	..
5- -10	..	*207*	111	96	194	105	89	12	5	7	1	1	..
10—15	..	*192*	112	80	153	94	59	36	16	20	3	2	1
15- -20	..	*163*	93	70	52	41	11	103	48	55	8	4	4
20- -30	.	*295*	163	132	44	39	5	224	111	113	27	13	14
30- 40	.	*212*	131	81	27	26	1	149	85	64	36	20	16
40- -50	..	*144*	81	63	9	8	1	89	48	41	46	25	21
50 -60	..	*90*	53	37	3	3	..	42	28	14	45	22	23
60 and over	..	*64*	34	30	5	5	..	16	11	5	43	18	25
MUSLIM	..	**46,002**	**24,915**	**21,087**	**20,547**	**12,656**	**7,891**	**21,121**	**10,335**	**10,786**	**4,334**	**1,924**	**2,410**
0—1	..	*1,792*	898	894	1,791	897	894	1	1	..	..	..	..
1- —2	..	*1,289*	639	650	1,284	637	647	5	2	3	..	..	.
2—3	..	*1,560*	780	780	1,547	774	773	13	6	7	..	..	..
3- 4	.	*1,482*	754	728	1,450	745	705	32	9	23	..	..	..
4- —5	..	*1,370*	703	667	1,317	686	631	52	16	36	1	1	..
Total 0- -5	..	*7,493*	*3,774*	*3,719*	*7,389*	*3,739*	*3,650*	*103*	*34*	*69*	*1*	*1*	..
5- -10	..	*6,253*	3,364	2,889	5,416	3,118	2,298	811	229	582	26	17	9
10- 15	..	*5,951*	3,297	2,654	4,336	2,785	1,551	1,576	486	1,090	39	26	13
15- -20	..	*4,697*	2,570	2,127	1,611	1,332	279	2,989	1,179	1,810	97	59	38
20- —30	..	*8,099*	4,365	3,734	1,277	1,180	97	6,421	2,960	3,461	401	225	176
30—40	..	*5,591*	3,091	2,500	274	266	8	4,637	2,520	2,117	680	305	375
40- -50	..	*3,725*	2,076	1,649	116	111	5	2,640	1,564	1,076	969	401	568
50- -60	..	*2,326*	1,350	976	72	69	3	1,255	858	397	999	423	576
60 and over	..	*1,867*	1,028	839	56	56	..	689	505	184	1,122	467	655
CHRISTIAN	..	**210**	**119**	**91**	**113**	**69**	**44**	**91**	**48**	**43**	**6**	**2**	**4**
0- -1	..	10	8	2	10	8	2	..	..	..	..	..	..
1—2	..	8	5	3	8	5	3	..	..	..	..	..	..
2- -3	..	*7*	5	2	7	5	2	..	..	..	..	..	..
3- -4	..	*6*	3	3	6	3	3	..	..	..	..	..	..
4- -5	..	*8*	5	3	8	5	3	..	..	..	..	..	..
Total 0- -5	..	*39*	*26*	*13*	*39*	*26*	*13*	..	..	..	.	..	..
5—10	..	*25*	13	12	25	13	12	..	..	.	..	..	..
10—15	..	*20*	11	9	19	11	8	1	..	1	..	..	..
15—20	..	*21*	10	11	13	8	5	8	2	6	..	..	..
20- -30	..	*36*	18	18	11	7	4	24	10	14	1	1	..
30- 40	..	*28*	17	11	1	1	..	25	15	10	2	1	1
40- —50	..	*25*	15	10	2	2	..	22	13	9	1	..	1
50—60	..	*12*	7	5	3	1	2	9	6	3	..	..	..
60 and over	..	*4*	2	2	..	..	..	2	2	..	2	..	2

AND CIVIL CONDITION (BY RELIGION).

PART B.—DETAILS FOR DISTRICTS AND STATES—*continued.*

NABHA STATE.

Religion and Age.	Population.			Unmarried.			Married.			Widowed.		
	Persons.	Males.	Females.	Persons.	Males.	Females.	Persons.	Males.	Females.	Persons.	Males.	Females.
1	2	3	4	5	6	7	8	9	10	11	12	13
ALL RELIGIONS ..	**287,574**	**158,086**	**129,488**	**136,459**	**85,992**	**50,467**	**120,786**	**58,532**	**62,254**	**30,829**	**13,562**	**16,767**
0—1 ..	11,007	5,510	5,497	11,004	3,508	5,496	3	2	1	..	..	..
1—2 ..	7,576	3,808	3,768	7,571	3,806	3,765	5	2	3	..	..	..
2—3 ..	8,420	4,272	4,148	8,411	4,270	4,141	9	2	7	..	..	..
3—4 .	8,319	4,288	4,031	8,294	4,283	4,011	25	5	20	..	..	.
4—5 .	7,969	4,185	3,784	7,876	4,154	3,722	87	30	57	6	1	5
Total 0—5 ..	43,291	22,063	21,228	43,156	22,021	21,135	129	41	88	6	1	5
5—10 ..	36,659	19,668	16,991	34,518	19,185	15,333	2,106	469	1,037	35	4	21
10—15 ..	34,772	19,024	15,748	28,914	17,509	11,405	5,776	1,476	4,300	82	39	43
15—20 ..	27,342	15,084	12,258	11,377	9,296	2,081	15,616	5,607	10,009	349	181	168
20—30 ..	48,341	26,041	21,700	9,714	9,222	492	36,813	16,474	20,339	1,814	945	869
30—40 ..	35,320	19,856	15,464	3,948	3,941	7	27,223	14,008	13,215	4,149	1,907	2,242
40—50 ..	27,109	15,367	11,742	2,375	2,370	5	17,806	9,982	7,824	6,928	3,015	3,913
50—60 ..	18,839	10,976	7,863	1,422	1,416	6	9,749	6,244	3,505	7,668	3,316	4,352
60 and over ..	15,901	9,407	6,494	1,035	1,032	3	5,568	4,231	1,337	9,298	4,144	5,154
HINDU ..	**132,348**	**71,592**	**60,756**	**62,246**	**38,765**	**23,481**	**55,295**	**26,410**	**28,885**	**14,807**	**6,417**	**8,390**
0—1 ..	5,227	2,590	2,637	5,227	2,590	2,637	..	.	..	..	..	..
1—2 ..	3,497	1,754	1,743	3,496	1,754	1,742	1	.	1	..	..	..
2—3 ..	4,064	2,080	1,984	4,061	2,080	1,981	3	..	3	..	..	.
3—4 ..	4,042	2,087	1,955	4,030	2,083	1,947	12	4	8	..	..	..
4—5 ..	3,831	1,981	1,850	3,795	1,968	1,827	32	13	19	4	..	4
Total 0—5 ..	20,661	10,492	10,169	20,609	10,475	10,134	48	17	31	4	..	4
5—10 ..	17,358	9,237	8,121	16,372	9,039	7,333	969	193	776	17	5	12
10—15 ..	16,170	8,800	7,370	13,291	8,103	5,188	2,834	683	2,151	45	14	31
15—20 ..	12,302	6,675	5,627	4,599	3,909	690	7,514	2,679	4,835	189	87	102
20—30 ..	21,893	11,696	10,197	3,815	3,686	129	17,066	7,542	9,524	1,012	468	544
30—40 ..	16,279	8,882	7,397	1,603	1,599	4	12,459	6,358	6,101	2,217	925	1,292
40—50 ..	12,257	6,896	5,361	933	931	2	7,880	4,496	3,384	3,444	1,469	1,975
50—60 ..	8,452	4,828	3,624	589	588	1	4,204	2,675	1,529	3,659	1,565	2,094
60 and over ..	6,976	4,086	2,890	435	435	..	2,321	1,767	554	4,220	1,884	2,336
SIKH ..	**97,452**	**55,262**	**42,190**	**47,361**	**30,986**	**16,375**	**40,012**	**19,606**	**20,406**	**10,079**	**4,670**	**5,409**
0—1 ..	3,469	1,780	1,689	3,468	1,779	1,689	1	1	..	..	..	..
1—2 ..	2,435	1,246	1,189	2,433	1,244	1,189	2	2	..	..	..	..
2—3 ..	2,586	1,316	1,270	2,583	1,314	1,269	3	2	1	..	..	..
3—4 ..	2,565	1,333	1,232	2,561	1,332	1,229	4	1	3	..	..	..
4—5 ..	2,455	1,318	1,137	2,436	1,310	1,126	19	8	11	..	..	..
Total 0—5 ..	13,510	6,993	6,517	13,481	6,979	6,502	29	14	15	..	..	..
5—10 ..	11,624	6,350	5,274	11,067	6,229	4,838	550	116	434	7	5	2
10—15 ..	11,352	6,329	5,023	9,773	5,920	3,853	1,562	395	1,167	17	14	3
15—20 ..	9,406	5,391	4,015	4,573	3,639	934	4,748	1,703	3,045	85	49	36
20—30 ..	16,725	9,697	7,028	4,265	4,020	245	11,991	5,392	6,599	469	285	184
30—40 ..	12,226	7,220	5,006	1,866	1,865	1	9,134	4,703	4,431	1,226	652	574
40—50 ..	9,704	5,592	4,112	1,173	1,172	1	6,263	3,385	2,878	2,268	1,035	1,233
50—60 ..	6,892	4,110	2,782	676	675	1	3,577	2,271	1,306	2,639	1,164	1,475
60 and over ..	6,013	3,580	2,433	487	487	..	2,158	1,627	531	3,368	1,466	1,902
JAIN ..	**309**	**163**	**146**	**158**	**90**	**68**	**104**	**54**	**50**	**47**	**19**	**28**
0—1 ..	13	6	7	13	6	7	..	..	..	..	..	..
1—2 ..	4	2	2	4	2	2	..	..	..	..	..	..
2—3 ..	11	4	7	11	4	7	..	..	..	..	..	..
3—4 ..	7	2	5	7	2	5	..	..	..	..	..	..
4—5 ..	14	8	6	14	8	6	..	..	..	..	..	..
Total 0—5 ..	49	22	27	49	22	27	..	..	.	..	..	..
5—10 ..	39	19	20	39	19	20	..	..	..	..	..	..
10—15 ..	37	16	21	34	16	18	3	..	3	..	..	..
15—20 ..	26	17	9	12	10	2	13	6	7	1	1	.
20—30 .	55	29	26	9	8	1	41	19	22	5	2	3
30—40 .	34	18	16	5	5	.	21	12	9	8	1	7
40—50 .	37	22	15	6	6	..	19	13	6	12	3	9
50—60 ..	20	13	7	4	4	..	5	3	2	11	6	5
60 and over ..	12	7	5	..	..	..	2	1	1	10	6	4
MUSLIM ..	**57,393**	**31,027**	**26,366**	**26,672**	**16,129**	**10,543**	**25,334**	**12,447**	**12,887**	**5,887**	**2,451**	**2,936**
0—1 ..	2,298	1,134	1,164	2,296	1,133	1,163	2	1	1	..	..	..
1—2 ..	1,640	806	834	1,638	806	832	2	..	2	..	..	.
2—3 ..	1,759	872	887	1,756	872	884	3	..	3	..	..	.
3—4 .	1,705	866	839	1,696	866	830	9	..	9	..	..	..
4—5 .	1,669	878	791	1,631	868	763	36	9	27	2	1	1
Total 0—5 ..	9,071	4,556	4,515	9,017	4,545	4,472	52	10	42	2	1	1
5—10 ..	7,637	4,061	3,576	7,039	3,897	3,142	587	160	427	11	4	7
10—15 ..	7,213	3,879	3,334	5,816	3,470	2,346	1,377	398	979	20	11	9
15—20 ..	5,608	3,001	2,607	2,193	1,738	455	3,341	1,219	2,122	74	44	30
20—30 ..	9,623	5,197	4,426	1,609	1,492	117	7,686	3,515	4,171	328	190	138
30—40 ..	6,770	3,728	3,042	471	469	2	5,603	2,931	2,672	696	328	308
40—50 ..	5,103	2,851	2,252	261	259	2	3,641	2,086	1,555	1,201	506	695
50—60 ..	3,469	2,020	1,449	153	149	4	1,960	1,292	668	1,356	579	777
60 and over ..	2,899	1,734	1,165	113	110	3	1,087	836	251	1,699	788	911
CHRISTIAN ..	**66**	**36**	**30**	**21**	**21**	..	**38**	**12**	**26**	**7**	**3**	**4**
20—30 ..	45	22	23	16	16	..	29	6	23	..	..	.
30—40 ..	11	8	3	3	3	..	6	4	2	2	1	1
40—50 ..	5	3	2	2	2	..	2	1	1	1	..	1
50—60 ..	4	3	1	..	..	.	1	1	..	3	2	1
60 and over ..	1	..	1	..	..	..	.	..	..	1	..	1

TABLE VII.—AGE, SEX AND CIVIL CONDITION (BY RELIGION).

PART B. DETAILS FOR DISTRICTS AND STATES—*concluded.*

BAHAWALPUR STATE.

Religion and Age.	Population.			Unmarried.			Married.			Widowed.		
	Persons.	Males.	Females.	Persons	Males.	Females.	Persons.	Males.	Females.	Persons.	Males.	Females.
1	2	3	4	5	6	7	8	9	10	11	12	13
ALL RELIGIONS ..	**984,612**	**545,103**	**439,509**	**495,943**	**304,394**	**191,549**	**408,541**	**206,638**	**201,903**	**80,128**	**34,071**	**46,057**
0—1 ..	*36,380*	18,468	•17,912	36,371	18,464	17,907	9	4	5	..	..	..
1—2 ..	*29,531*	15,010	14,521	29,513	15,007	14,506	18	3	15	..	..	..
2—3 ..	*33,674*	17,181	16,493	33,619	17,164	16,455	54	16	38	1	1	.
3—4 ..	*33,887*	17,616	16,271	33,782	17,573	16,209	98	39	59	7	4	3
4—5 ..	*32,897*	17,391	15,506	32,766	17,332	15,434	121	54	67	10	5	5
Total 0—5 ..	*166,369*	*85,666*	*80,703*	*166,051*	*85,540*	*80,511*	*300*	*116*	*184*	*18*	*10*	*8*
5—10 ..	*132,308*	73,359	58,949	129,273	72,537	56,736	2,950	786	2,164	85	36	49
10—15 ..	*110,187*	63,066	47,121	98,936	60,418	38,518	10,995	2,546	8,449	256	102	154
15—20 ..	*84,684*	45,556	39,128	39,432	31,686	7,746	43,945	13,272	30,673	1,307	598	70[illegible]
20—30 ..	*190,380*	102,319	88,061	44,039	38,918	5,121	138,698	59,352	79,346	7,643	4,049	3,59[illegible]
30—40 ..	*133,243*	76,386	56,857	11,654	10,015	1,639	107,358	59,695	47,663	14,231	6,676	7,555
40—50 ..	*82,672*	48,363	34,209	3,843	3,126	717	59,709	37,855	21,854	19,020	7,382	11,638
50—60 ..	*47,392*	28,278	19,114	1,656	1,311	345	28,260	20,176	8,084	17,476	6,791	10,685
60 and over ..	*37,47[illegible]*	22,110	15,367	1,059	843	216	16,326	12,840	3,486	20,092	8,427	11,66[illegible]
HINDU ..	**145,007**	**81,897**	**63,110**	**69,178**	**43,425**	**25,753**	**60,968**	**32,423**	**28,545**	**14,861**	**6,049**	**8,812**
0—1 ..	*5,289*	2,617	2,672	5,282	2,614	2,668	7	3	4	..	.	..
1—2 ..	*3,874*	1,948	1,920	3,869	1,948	1,921	5	.	5	..	.	..
2—3 ..	*4,382*	2,225	2,157	4,368	2,221	2,147	14	4	10	.	..	..
3—4 ..	*4,509*	2,330	2,173	4,481	2,325	2,156	25	10	15	3	1	2
4—5 ..	*4,431*	2,367	2,064	4,405	2,357	2,048	24	9	15	2	1	1
Total 0—5 ..	*22,485*	*11,493*	*10,992*	*22,405*	*11,465*	*10,940*	*75*	*26*	*49*	*5*	*2*	*3*
5—10 ..	*18,179*	9,894	8,285	17,310	9,660	7,650	846	225	621	23	9	14
10—15 ..	*16,019*	8,956	7,063	13,478	8,293	5,185	2,473	632	1,841	68	31	37
15—20 ..	*14,159*	8,007	6,152	6,054	5,122	932	7,798	2,744	5,054	307	141	166
20—30 ..	*29,176*	16,696	12,480	6,611	5,967	644	21,004	9,999	11,005	1,561	730	831
30—40 ..	*20,087*	12,054	8,033	2,026	1,780	246	15,162	9,051	6,111	2,899	1,223	1,676
40—50 ..	*13,133*	7,930	5,203	783	690	93	8,448	5,772	2,676	3,902	1,468	2,434
50—60 ..	*7,060*	4,262	2,798	333	295	38	3,619	2,710	909	3,108	1,257	1,851
60 and over ..	*4,709*	2,605	2,104	178	153	25	1,543	1,264	279	2,988	1,188	1,800
SIKH ..	**34,896**	**20,000**	**14,896**	**17,908**	**11,105**	**6,803**	**14,751**	**7,773**	**6,978**	**2,237**	**1,122**	**1,115**
0—1 ..	*1,398*	687	711	1,397	686	711	1	1	..	..	..	..
1—2 ..	*1,079*	550	529	1,079	550	529	..	..	.	..	..	..
2—3 ..	*1,147*	601	546	1,146	600	546	.	..	..	1	1	..
3—4 ..	*1,157*	622	535	1,155	622	533	2	..	2	..	..	..
4—5 ..	*1,146*	628	518	1,140	627	513	5	1	4	1	..	1
Total 0—5 ..	*5,927*	*3,088*	*2,839*	*5,917*	*3,085*	*2,832*	*8*	*2*	*6*	2	*1*	*1*
5—10 ..	*4,693*	2,629	2,064	4,587	2,592	1,995	104	36	68	2	1	1
10—15 ..	*4,046*	2,333	1,713	3,653	2,204	1,449	385	125	260	8	4	4
15—20 ..	*3,302*	1,907	1,395	1,567	1,256	311	1,695	629	1,066	40	22	18
20—30 ..	*6,665*	3,779	2,886	1,510	1,361	149	4,967	2,306	2,661	188	112	76
30—40 ..	*4,372*	2,607	1,765	412	372	40	3,641	2,054	1,587	319	181	138
40—50 ..	*2,890*	1,769	1,121	162	144	18	2,217	1,379	838	511	246	265
50—60 ..	*1,728*	1,106	622	66	60	6	1,136	795	341	526	251	275
60 and over ..	*1,273*	782	491	34	31	3	598	447	151	641	304	337
JAIN ..	**12**	**7**	**5**	**6**	**3**	**3**	**5**	**3**	**2**	**1**	**1**	..
0—1 ..	2	1	1	2	1	1	..	..	..	..	..	..
2—3 ..	*1*	1	..	1	1	.	..	..	..	..	..	..
Total 0—5 ..	*3*	*2*	*1*	*3*	*2*	*1*	..	..	..	..	..	..
5—10 ..	*1*	..	1	1	..	1	..	..	..	..	..	..
10—15 ..	*2*	1	1	2	1	1	.	..	..	..	.	.
15—20 ..	*1*	..	1		.	..	1	..	1	..	..	..
20—30 ..	*4*	3	1	..	..	..	3	2	1	1	1	..
40—50 ..	*1*	1	..	.	..	..	1	1	..	..	..	..
MUSLIM ..	**799,176**	**440,054**	**359,122**	**405,967**	**248,137**	**157,830**	**330,574**	**165,249**	**165,325**	**62,635**	**26,668**	**35,967**
0—1 ..	*29,327*	14,977	14,350	29,326	14,977	14,349	1	..	1	..	..	..
1—2 ..	*24,348*	12,394	11,954	24,335	12,391	11,944	13	3	10	..	..	..
2—3 ..	*27,909*	14,227	13,682	27,869	14,215	13,654	40	12	28	.	..	..
3—4 ..	*28,047*	14,563	13,484	27,972	14,531	13,441	71	29	42	4	3	1
4—5 ..	*27,227*	14,348	12,879	27,128	14,300	12,828	92	44	48	7	4	3
Total 0—5 ..	*136,858*	*70,509*	*66,349*	*136,630*	*70,414*	*66,216*	*217*	*88*	*129*	*11*	*7*	*4*
5—10 ..	*108,801*	60,481	48,320	106,754	59,936	46,818	1,987	519	1,468	60	26	34
10—15 ..	*89,460*	51,397	38,063	81,200	49,562	31,638	8,081	1,768	6,313	179	67	112
15—20 ..	*66,720*	35,362	31,358	31,567	25,128	6,439	34,200	9,804	24,396	953	430	523
20—30 ..	*153,588*	81,306	72,282	35,713	31,423	4,290	112,045	46,723	65,322	5,830	3,160	2,670
30—40 ..	*107,949*	61,223	46,726	9,130	7,799	1,340	87,861	48,192	39,669	10,949	5,232	5,717
40—50 ..	*66,200*	38,450	27,750	2,874	2,272	602	48,789	30,563	18,226	14,587	5,615	8,922
50—60 ..	*38,424*	22,804	15,620	1,252	953	299	23,413	16,611	6,802	13,759	5,240	8,519
60 and over ..	*31,176*	18,522	12,654	838	650	188	13,981	10,981	3,000	16,357	6,891	9,466
CHRISTIAN ..	**1,054**	**618**	**441**	**548**	**340**	**208**	**452**	**247**	**205**	**54**	**26**	**28**
0—1 ..	*41*	23	18	41	23	18	..	..	..	..	..	..
1—2 ..	*32*	18	14	32	18	14	..	..	..	..	..	..
2—3 ..	*36*	21	15	36	21	15	..	..	..	..	..	..
3—4 ..	*33*	20	13	33	20	13	..	..	..	..	..	..
4—5 ..	*26*	15	11	26	15	11	..	..	..	..	..	..
Total 0—5 ..	*168*	*97*	*71*	*168*	*97*	*71*	..	..	..	..	..	..
5—10 ..	*127*	70	57	127	70	57	..	..	..	..	..	..
10—15 ..	*115*	64	51	108	61	47	7	3	4	..	..	..
15—20 ..	*95*	50	45	51	37	14	43	13	20	1	..	1
20—30 ..	*219*	130	89	67	55	12	141	67	74	11	8	3
30—40 ..	*151*	91	60	16	12	4	125	72	53	10	7	3
40—50 ..	*92*	58	34	5	4	1	76	49	27	11	5	6
50—60 ..	*57*	32	25	5	3	2	40	26	14	12	3	9
60 and over ..	*30*	21	9	1	1	..	20	17	3	9	3	6

TABLE VII.—AGE, SEX AND CIVIL CONDITION (BY RELIGION).

PART. C.—DETAILS FOR CITIES AND SELECTED TOWNS—*continued.*

LAHORE CITY.

Religion and Age.	Population.			Unmarried.			Married.			Widowed.		
	Persons.	Males.	Females.	Persons.	Males.	Females.	Persons.	Males.	Females.	Persons.	Males.	Females.
1	2	3	4	5	6	7	8	9	10	11	12	13
ALL RELIGIONS ..	**429,747**	**274,587**	**155,160**	**212,318**	**145,490**	**66,828**	**188,349**	**114,444**	**73,905**	**29,080**	**14,653**	**14,427**
0—1 ..	*12,531*	6,661	5,870	12,526	6,656	5,870	3	3	..	2	2	..
1—2 ..	*10,006*	5,491	4,515	10,001	5,487	4,514	2	1	1	3	3	..
2—3 ..	*11,487*	6,190	5,297	11,464	6,174	5,290	17	10	7	6	6	
3—4 ..	*10,838*	5,665	5,173	10,812	5,653	5,159	24	11	13	2	1	1
4—5 ..	*9,875*	5,183	4,692	9,836	5,172	4,664	32	9	23	7	2	5
Total 0—5 ..	*54,737*	*29,190*	*25,547*	*54,639*	*29,142*	*25,497*	*78*	*34*	*44*	*20*	*14*	*6*
5—10 ..	*43,583*	23,707	19,876	41,430	23,465	17,965	2,127	231	1,896	26	11	15
10—15 ..	*42,660*	24,618	18,042	37,954	23,745	14,209	4,639	837	3,802	67	36	31
15—20 ..	*52,093*	34,748	17,345	30,599	25,493	5,106	20,897	8,860	12,037	597	395	202
20—30 ..	*104,633*	72,388	32,245	34,393	31,604	2,789	66,664	38,229	28,435	3,576	2,555	1,021
30—40 ..	*66,883*	47,551	19,332	9,449	8,742	707	51,639	35,189	16,450	5,795	3,620	2,175
40—50 ..	*35,913*	24,059	11,854	2,518	2,190	328	26,261	18,626	7,635	7,134	3,243	3,891
50—60 ..	*17,115*	10,940	6,175	773	639	134	10,558	8,013	2,545	5,784	2,288	3,496
60 and over ..	*12,130*	7,386	4,744	563	470	93	5,486	4,425	1,061	6,081	2,491	3,590
HINDU ..	**139,125**	**91,667**	**47,458**	**67,363**	**47,282**	**20,081**	**61,723**	**39,332**	**22,391**	**10,039**	**5,053**	**4,986**
0—1 ..	*3,666*	1,874	1,792	3,664	1,872	1,792	..	..	..	2	2	..
1—2 ..	*3,095*	1,744	1,351	3,091	1,740	1,351	1	1	..	3	3	..
2—3 ..	*3,578*	2,024	1,554	3,566	2,017	1,549	8	3	5	4	4	
3—4 ..	*3,350*	1,787	1,563	3,334	1,783	1,551	15	4	11	1	..	1
4—5 ..	*2,978*	1,564	1,414	2,956	1,560	1,396	20	4	16	2	..	2
Total 0—5 ..	*16,667*	*8,993*	*7,674*	*16,611*	*8,972*	*7,639*	*44*	*12*	*32*	*12*	*9*	*3*
5—10 ..	*13,052*	7,178	5,874	12,772	7,079	5,693	265	93	172	15	6	9
10—15 ..	*13,246*	7,853	5,393	12,074	7,488	4,586	1,146	353	793	26	12	14
15—20 ..	*17,874*	12,417	5,457	10,312	8,982	1,330	7,355	3,300	4,055	207	135	72
20—30 ..	*36,043*	25,895	10,148	11,348	10,795	553	23,374	14,182	9,192	1,321	918	403
30—40 ..	*21,805*	15,843	5,962	2,898	2,749	149	16,749	11,776	4,973	2,158	1,318	840
40—50 ..	*11,716*	8,124	3,592	917	842	75	8,295	6,115	2,180	2,504	1,167	1,337
50—60 ..	*5,381*	3,444	1,937	275	241	34	3,146	2,437	709	1,960	766	1,194
60 and over ..	*3,341*	1,920	1,421	156	134	22	1,349	1,064	285	1,836	722	1,114
SIKH ..	**23,477**	**15,526**	**7,951**	**13,275**	**9,442**	**3,833**	**9,295**	**5,724**	**3,571**	**907**	**360**	**547**
0—1 ..	*642*	327	315	639	324	315	3	3	..	..	..	..
1—2 ..	*495*	247	248	495	247	248	..	..	..	..	..	..
2—3 ..	*586*	305	281	586	305	281	..	..	..	..	..	..
3—4 ..	*533*	278	255	533	278	255	..	..	..	..		..
4—5 ..	*489*	252	237	489	252	237	..	..	..	..		..
Total 0—5 ..	*2,745*	*1,409*	*1,336*	*2,742*	*1,406*	*1,336*	*3*	*3*	..	..	..	..
5—10 ..	*2,115*	1,147	968	2,103	1,141	962	12	6	6	..	..	..
10—15 ..	*2,040*	1,179	861	1,895	1,141	754	141	35	106	4	3	1
15—20 ..	*2,969*	2,029	940	1,775	1,367	408	1,162	638	524	32	24	8
20—30 ..	*6,089*	4,271	1,818	2,598	2,288	310	3,410	1,943	1,467	81	40	41
30—40 ..	*4,642*	3,612	1,030	1,996	1,955	41	2,527	1,619	908	119	38	81
40—50 ..	*1,550*	999	551	88	77	11	1,246	865	381	216	57	159
50—60 ..	*796*	521	275	40	32	8	528	400	128	228	89	139
60 and over ..	*531*	359	172	38	35	3	266	215	51	227	109	118
JAIN ..	**791**	**442**	**349**	**446**	**281**	**165**	**285**	**144**	**141**	**60**	**17**	**43**
0—1 ..	*28*	16	12	28	16	12	..	..	..	..	..	..
1—2 ..	*24*	12	12	24	12	12	..	..	..	..	..	..
2—3 ..	*29*	15	14	29	15	14	..	..	..	..	..	..
3—4 ..	*25*	13	12	25	13	12	..	..	..	..	..	..
4—5 ..	*23*	11	12	22	11	11	..	..	..	1	..	1
Total 0—5 ..	*129*	*67*	*62*	*128*	*67*	*61*	..	..	..	*1*	..	*1*
5—10 ..	*98*	51	47	98	51	47	..	..	..	..	..	..
10—15 ..	*95*	53	42	91	52	39	4	1	3	..	..	..
15—20 ..	*106*	66	40	64	53	11	39	13	26	3	..	3
20—30 ..	*182*	104	78	54	49	5	120	54	66	8	1	7
30—40 ..	*97*	58	39	6	6	..	82	48	34	9	4	5
40—50 ..	*45*	22	23	2	1	1	26	16	10	17	5	12
50—60 ..	*27*	14	13	3	2	1	11	9	2	13	3	10
60 and over ..	*12*	7	5	..	..	..	3	3	..	9	4	5

TABLE VII.—AGE, SEX

PART C.—DETAILS FOR CITIES AND SELECTED TOWNS.

LAHORE CITY.—(concld).

Religion and Age.		Population.			Unmarried.			Married.			Widowed.		
		Persons.	Males.	Females.	Persons.	Males.	Females.	Persons.	Males.	Females.	Persons.	Males.	Females.
1		2	3	4	5	6	7	8	9	10	11	12	13
MUSLIM	.	**249,315**	**156,486**	**92,829**	**121,329**	**82,046,**	**39,283**	**110,832**	**65,699**	**45,133**	**17,154**	**8,741**	**8,413**
0—1	..	*7,762*	4,210	3,552	7,762	4,210	3,552	..	..	..	..	..	..
1—2	..	*6,039*	3,296	2,743	6,038	3,296	2,742	1	..	1	..	..	..
2—3	..	*6,892*	3,651	3,241	6,885	3,646	3,239	6	4	2	1	1	.
3—4	..	*6,549*	3,398	3,151	6,543	3,394	3,149	6	4	2	..	..	..
4—5	..	*6,030*	3,167	2,863	6,018	3,163	2,855	9	3	6	3	1	2
Total 0—5	..	*33,272*	*17,722*	*15,550*	*33,246*	*17,709*	*15,537*	*22*	*11*	*11*	*4*	*2*	*2*
5—10	..	*26,681*	14,488	12,193	24,840	14,358	10,482	1,832	126	1,706	9	4	5
10—15	..	*25,739*	14,755	10,984	22,438	14,302	8,136	3,270	435	2,835	31	18	13
15—20	..	*29,197*	18,986	10,211	17,075	14,094	2,981	11,781	4,665	7,116	341	227	114
20—30	..	*57,704*	38,363	18,841	17,808	16,286	1,522	37,844	21,058	16,786	2,052	1,519	533
30—40	..	*37,727*	26,373	11,354	3,954	3,579	375	30,447	20,651	9,796	3,326	2,143	1,183
40—50	..	*21,083*	13,969	7,114	1,302	1,136	166	15,598	10,933	4,665	4,183	1,900	2,283
50—60	.	*10,167*	6,504	3,663	360	311	49	6,398	4,836	1,562	3,409	1,357	2,052
60 and over	..	*7,745*	4,826	2,919	306	271	35	3,640	2,984	656	3,799	1,571	2,228
CHRISTIAN	..	**16,875**	**10,368**	**6,507**	**9,816**	**6,386**	**3,430**	**6,147**	**3,506**	**2,641**	**912**	**476**	**436**
0—1	..	*431*	234	197	431	234	197	..	..	..	..	..	..
1—2	.	*350*	192	158	350	192	158	..	..	..	..	..	..
2—3	..	*398*	194	204	394	190	204	3	3	..	1	1	.
3—4	..	*380*	188	192	376	184	192	3	3	..	1	1	.
4—5	..	*351*	186	165	347	183	164	3	2	1	1	1	.
Total 0—5	..	*1,910*	*994*	*916*	*1,898*	*983*	*915*	*9*	*8*	*1*	*3*	*3*	..
5—10	.	*1,624*	835	789	1,604	828	776	18	6	12	2	1	1
10—15	.	*1,528*	771	757	1,445	756	689	78	13	65	5	2	3
15—20	..	*1,936*	1,243	693	1,364	990	374	558	244	314	14	9	5
20—30	..	*4,579*	3,232	1,347	2,564	2,170	394	1,902	986	916	113	76	37
30—40	.	*2,578*	1,642	936	583	445	138	1,814	1,082	732	181	115	66
40—50	..	*1,494*	932	562	205	132	73	1,078	687	391	211	113	98
50—60	..	*729*	448	281	91	52	39	464	323	141	174	73	101
60 and over	..	*497*	271	226	62	30	32	226	157	69	209	84	125
OTHERS	..	**164**	**98**	**66**	**89**	**53**	**36**	**67**	**39**	**28**	**6**	**6**	**2**
0—1	..	*2*	..	2	2	..	2	..	..	..	..	..	..
1—2	..	*3*	..	3	3	..	3	..	..	..	..	..	..
2—3	..	*4*	1	3	4	1	3	..	..	..	..	..	..
3—4	..	*1*	1	..	1	1	..	..	..	..	..	..	..
4—5	.	*4*	3	1	4	3	1	..	..	..	..	..	..
Total 0—5	..	*14*	*5*	*9*	*14*	*5*	*9*	..	..	..	..	..	..
5—10	..	*13*	8	5	13	8	5	..	..	..	..	..	..
10—15	..	*12*	7	5	11	6	5	..	..	..	1	1	..
15—20	..	*11*	7	4	9	7	2	2	..	2	..	..	..
20—30	..	*36*	23	13	21	16	5	14	6	8	1	1	..
30—40	..	*34*	23	11	12	8	4	20	13	7	2	2	..
40—50	.	*25*	13	12	4	2	2	18	10	8	3	1	2
50—60	..	*15*	9	6	4	1	3	11	8	3	..	..	..
60 and over	..	*4*	3	1	1	..	1	2	2	..	1	1	.

AND CIVIL CONDITION (BY RELIGION).

PART C.—DETAILS FOR CITIES AND SELECTED TOWNS—*continued.*

AMRITSAR CITY.

Religion and Age.	Population.			Unmarried.			Married.			Widowed.		
	Persons.	Males.	Females.	Persons.	Males.	Females.	Persons.	Males.	Females.	Persons.	Males.	Females.
1	2	3	4	5	6	7	8	9	10	11	12	13
ALL RELIGIONS ..	**264,840**	**158,985**	**105,855**	**133,564**	**86,492**	**47,072**	**110,097**	**62,712**	**47,385**	**21,179**	**9,781**	**11,898**
0—1 ..	*7,567*	3,819	3,748	7,567	3,819	3,748	..	..	..	..	..	..
1—2 ..	*6,314*	3,169	3,145	6,314	3,169	3,145	..	..	..	..	..	..
2—3 ..	*7,318*	3,660	3,658	7,318	3,660	3,658	..	..	..	..	..	..
3—4 ..	*7,050*	3,590	3,460	7,047	3,587	3,460	3	3	..	..	..	..
4—5 ..	*6,590*	3,416	3,174	6,578	3,408	3,170	11	8	3	1	..	1
Total 0—5 ..	*34,839*	*17,654*	*17,185*	*34,824*	*17,643*	*17,181*	*14*	*11*	*3*	*1*	..	*1*
5—10 ..	*30,983*	16,916	14,067	30,509	16,748	13,761	437	145	292	37	23	14
10—15 ..	*29,729*	17,122	12,607	27,348	16,599	10,749	2,314	482	1,832	67	41	26
15—20 ..	*27,850*	17,546	10,304	15,390	12,700	2,690	12,076	4,623	7,453	384	223	161
20—30 ..	*54,683*	35,266	19,417	16,074	14,500	1,574	36,414	19,329	17,085	2,195	1,437	758
30—40 ..	*38,716*	24,761	13,955	5,821	5,255	566	29,031	17,299	11,732	3,864	2,207	1,657
40—50 ..	*24,238*	15,211	9,027	1,898	1,605	293	17,332	11,483	5,849	5,008	2,123	2,885
50—60 ..	*13,335*	8,143	5,192	992	853	139	7,759	5,520	2,239	4,584	1,770	2,814
60 and over ..	*10,467*	6,366	4,101	708	589	119	4,720	3,820	900	5,039	1,957	3,082
HINDU ..	**97,837**	**59,544**	**38,293**	**50,472**	**33,765**	**16,707**	**38,894**	**22,155**	**16,739**	**8,471**	**3,624**	**4,847**
0—1 ..	*2,630*	1,338	1,292	2,630	1,338	1,292	..	..	..	..	..	..
1—2 ..	*2,284*	1,115	1,169	2,284	1,115	1,169	..	..	..	..	..	..
2—3 ..	*2,614*	1,289	1,325	2,614	1,289	1,325	..	..	..	..	..	..
3—4 ..	*2,561*	1,309	1,252	2,560	1,308	1,252	1	1	..	..	..	..
4—5 ..	*2,437*	1,261	1,176	2,432	1,258	1,174	4	3	1	1	..	1
Total 0—5 ..	*12,526*	*6,312*	*6,214*	*12,520*	*6,308*	*6,212*	*5*	*4*	*1*	*1*	..	*1*
5—10 ..	*11,521*	6,328	5,193	11,370	6,269	5,101	140	56	84	11	3	8
10—15 ..	*11,164*	6,608	4,556	10,233	6,422	3,811	907	175	732	24	11	13
15—20 ..	*10,948*	7,311	3,637	6,182	5,455	727	4,623	1,771	2,852	143	85	58
20—30 ..	*20,951*	14,153	6,798	6,609	6,144	465	13,500	7,487	6,013	842	522	320
30—40 ..	*14,478*	9,304	5,174	2,543	2,342	201	10,329	6,134	4,195	1,606	828	778
40—50 ..	*8,509*	5,171	3,338	579	474	105	5,793	3,907	1,886	2,137	790	1,347
50—60 ..	*4,609*	2,635	1,974	256	211	45	2,449	1,741	708	1,904	683	1,221
60 and over ..	*3,131*	1,722	1,409	180	140	40	1,148	880	268	1,803	702	1,101
SIKH ..	**32,009**	**18,721**	**13,288**	**15,267**	**9,984**	**5,283**	**13,634**	**7,395**	**6,239**	**3,108**	**1,342**	**1.766**
0—1 ..	*983*	517	466	983	517	466	..	..	..	..	..	..
1—2 ..	*720*	370	350	720	370	350	..	..	..	..	..	..
2—3 ..	*851*	433	418	851	433	418	..	..	..	..	..	..
3—4 ..	*818*	429	389	817	428	389	1	1	..	..	..	..
4—5 ..	*770*	415	355	767	412	355	3	3	..	..	..	..
Total 0—5 ..	*4,142*	*2,164*	*1,978*	*4,138*	*2,160*	*1,978*	*4*	*4*	..	..	..	..
5—10 ..	*3,679*	2,075	1,604	3,615	2,054	1,561	57	17	40	7	4	3
10—15 ..	*3,498*	2,077	1,421	3,233	2,023	1,210	253	47	206	12	7	5
15—20 ..	*3,179*	2,003	1,176	1,708	1,437	271	1,420	540	880	51	26	25
20—30 ..	*6,299*	3,807	2,492	1,646	1,495	151	4,327	2,134	2,193	326	178	148
30—40 ..	*4,729*	2,856	1,873	509	455	54	3,697	2,151	1,546	523	250	273
40—50 ..	*3,241*	1,880	1,361	222	192	30	2,308	1,400	908	711	288	423
50—60 ..	*1,853*	1,094	759	103	89	14	1,043	725	318	707	280	427
60 and over ..	*1,389*	765	624	93	79	14	525	377	148	771	309	462
JAIN ..	**604**	**329**	**275**	**341**	**206**	**135**	**209**	**104**	**105**	**54**	**19**	**35**
0—1 ..	*20*	10	10	20	10	10	..	..	..	..	..	..
1—2 ..	*20*	10	10	20	10	10	..	..	..	..	..	..
2—3 ..	*25*	12	13	25	12	13	..	..	..	..	..	..
3—4 ..	*20*	10	10	20	10	10	..	..	..	..	..	..
4—5 ..	*20*	10	10	20	10	10	..	..	..	..	..	..
Total 0—5 ..	*105*	*52*	*53*	*105*	*52*	*53*	..	..	..	..	..	..
5—10 ..	*79*	40	39	79	40	39	..	..	..	..	..	..
10—15 ..	*76*	42	34	72	40	32	4	2	2	..	..	..
15—20 ..	*71*	44	27	38	32	6	31	12	19	2	..	2
20—30 ..	*99*	56	43	26	24	2	68	30	38	5	2	3
30—40 ..	*70*	35	35	8	7	1	53	24	29	9	4	5
40—50 ..	*52*	31	21	7	6	1	34	22	12	11	3	8
50—60 ..	*30*	18	12	3	3	..	16	12	4	11	3	8
60 and over ..	*22*	11	11	3	2	1	3	2	1	16	7	9

TABLE VII.—AGE, SEX

PART C.—DETAILS FOR CITIES AND SELECTED TOWNS.

AMRITSAR CITY.—(*concld*).

Religion and Age.	Population.			Unmarried.			Married.			Widowed.		
	Persons.	Males.	Females.	Persons.	Males.	Females.	Persons.	Males.	Females.	Persons.	Males.	Females.
1	2	3	4	5	6	7	8	9	10	11	12	13
MUSLIM ..	**132,362**	**79,324**	**53,038**	**66,295**	**41,919**	**24,376**	**56,676**	**32,677**	**23,999**	**9,391**	**4,728**	**4,663**
0—1 ..	*3,879*	1,927	1,952	3,879	1,927	1,952	..	..	..	..	..	..
1—2 ..	*3,245*	1,658	1,587	3,245	1,658	1,587	..	.	..	..	.	..
2—3 ..	*3,778*	1,903	1,875	3,778	1,903	1,875	..	..	..	..	..	..
3—4 ..	*3,601*	1,816	1,785	3,600	1,815	1,785	1	1	..	..	..	..
4—5 ..	*3,309*	1,704	1,605	3,306	1,703	1,603	3	1	2	..	..	..
Total 0—5 ..	*17,812*	*9,008*	*8,804*	*17,808*	*9,006*	*8,802*	*4*	*2*	*2*	..	..	..
5—10 ..	*15,460*	8,366	7,094	15,206	8,279	6,927	235	71	164	19	16	3
10—15 ..	*14,749*	8,289	6,460	13,584	8,014	5,570	1,135	253	882	30	22	8
15—20 ..	*13,391*	8,056	5,335	7,287	5,676	1,611	5,920	2,271	3,649	184	109	75
20—30 ..	*26,895*	16,979	9,916	7,580	6,684	896	18,309	0,571	8,738	1,006	724	282
30—40 ..	*19,146*	12,398	6,748	2,707	2,422	285	14,754	8,874	5,880	1,685	1,102	58:
40—50 ..	*12,279*	8,039	4,240	1,069	924	145	9,089	6,084	3,005	2,121	1,031	1,090
50—60 ..	*6,767*	4,351	2,416	623	547	76	4,205	3,008	1,197	1,939	796	1,14:
60 and over ..	*5,863*	3,838	2,025	431	367	64	3,025	2,543	482	2,407	928	1,479
CHRISTIAN ..	**1,819**	**941**	**878**	**1,091**	**560**	**531**	**583**	**319**	**264**	**145**	**62**	**83**
0—1 ..	*45*	21	24	45	21	24	..	..	..	..	..	.
1—2 ..	*40*	15	25	40	15	25	..	..	..	..	..	..
2—3 ..	*47*	22	25	47	22	25	..	..	..	..	..	..
3—4 ..	*48*	25	23	48	25	23	..	..	.	..	..	..
4—5 ..	*47*	22	25	47	22	25	..	..	..	..	..	.
Total 0—5 ..	*227*	*105*	*122*	*227*	*105*	*122*	..	..	..	..	..	..
5—10 ..	*220*	96	124	218	96	122	2	..	2	..	..	..
10—15 ..	*222*	94	128	209	89	120	12	4	8	1	1	.
15—20 ..	*234*	119	115	164	93	71	67	24	43	3	2	1
20—30 ..	*393*	241	152	198	143	55	180	88	92	15	10	5
30—40 ..	*260*	144	116	40	24	25	171	98	73	40	22	18
40—50 ..	*141*	77	64	18	6	12	96	61	35	27	10	17
50—60 ..	*66*	38	28	7	3	4	40	29	11	19	6	13
60 and over ..	*56*	27	29	1	1	..	15	15	..	40	11	29
OTHERS ..	**209**	**126**	**83**	**98**	**58**	**40**	**101**	**62**	**39**	**10**	**6**	**4**
0—1 ..	*10*	6	4	10	6	4	..	..	..	..	..	..
1—2 ..	*5*	1	4	5	1	4	..	..	..	..	..	..
2—3 ..	*3*	1	2	3	1	2	..	..	..	..	..	..
3—4 ..	*2*	1	1	2	1	1	..	.	..	..	..	.
4—5 ..	*7*	4	3	6	3	3	1	1	..	..	..	.
Total 0—5 ..	*27*	*13*	*14*	*26*	*12*	*14*	*1*	*1*	..	..	..	..
5—10 .	*24*	11	13	21	10	11	3	1	2	..	..	..
10—15 ..	*20*	12	8	17	11	6	3	1	2	..	..	..
15—20 ..	*27*	13	14	11	7	4	15	5	10	1	1	.
20—30 ..	*46*	30	16	15	10	5	30	19	11	1	1	..
30—40 ..	*33*	24	9	5	5	..	27	18	9	1	1	..
40—50 ..	*16*	13	3	3	3	..	12	9	3	1	1	..
50—60 ..	*10*	7	3	..	..	..	6	5	1	4	2	2
60 and over ..	*6*	3	3	..	..	..	4	3	1	2	..	2

AND CIVIL CONDITION (BY RELIGION).

PART C.—DETAILS FOR CITIES AND SELECTED TOWNS—*continued.*

MULTAN CITY.

Religion and Age.	Population.			Unmarried.			Married.			Widowed.		
	Persons.	Males.	Females.	Persons.	Males.	Females.	Persons.	Males.	Females.	Persons.	Males.	Females.
1	2	3	4	5	6	7	8	9	10	11	12	13
ALL RELIGIONS ..	**119,457**	**68,119**	**51,338**	**61,352**	**36,449**	**24,903**	**47,099**	**27,229**	**19,870**	**11,006**	**4,441**	**6,565**
0—1 ..	*3,630*	1,797	1,833	3,629	1,797	1,832	1	..	1	..	..	..
1—2 ..	*2,594*	1,278	1,316	2,593	1,278	1,315	1	..	1	..	..	..
2—3 ..	*3,207*	1,589	1,618	3,198	1,588	1,610	7	..	7	2	1	1
3—4 ..	*3,151*	1,592	1,559	3,139	1,590	1,549	11	2	9	1	..	1
4—5 ..	*2,927*	1,514	1,413	2,913	1,508	1,405	11	5	6	3	1	2
Total 0—5 ..	*15,509*	*7,770*	*7,739*	*15,472*	*7,761*	*7,711*	*31*	*7*	*24*	*6*	*2*	*4*
5—10 ..	*13,820*	7,554	6,266	13,562	7,457	6,105	251	96	155	7	1	6
10—15 ..	*13,200*	7,436	5,764	12,162	7,227	4,935	1,021	203	818	17	6	11
15—20 ..	*12,748*	7,340	5,408	7,890	5,563	2,327	4,697	1,695	3,002	161	82	7[illegible]
20—30 ..	*25,304*	14,977	10,327	9,712	6,328	3,384	14,473	8,039	6,434	1,119	610	509
30—40 ..	*17,125*	10,397	6,728	1,620	1,357	263	13,623	8,168	5,455	1,882	872	1,010
40—50 ..	*10,990*	6,482	4,508	553	456	97	7,675	4,982	2,693	2,762	1,044	1,718
50—60 ..	*6,125*	3,598	2,527	226	184	42	3,521	2,545	976	2,378	869	1,509
60 and over ..	*4,636*	2,565	2,071	155	116	39	1,807	1,494	313	2,674	955	1,719
HINDU ..	**40,424**	**22,585**	**17,839**	**19,147**	**12,047**	**7,100**	**16,673**	**9,002**	**7,671**	**4,604**	**1,536**	**3,068**
0—1 ..	*1,260*	633	627	1,260	633	627	..	..	..	..	..	..
1—2 ..	*882*	437	445	882	437	445	..	..	..	..	..	..
2—3 ..	*1,040*	513	527	1,039	512	527	..	..	..	1	1	..
3—4 ..	*1,063*	543	520	1,063	543	520	..	..	..	..	..	..
4—5 ..	*1,074*	572	502	1,072	571	501	2	1	1	..	..	..
Total 0—5 ..	*5,319*	*2,698*	*2,621*	*5,316*	*2,696*	*2,620*	*2*	*1*	*1*	*1*	*1*	..
5—10 ..	*4,750*	2,565	2,185	4,621	2,497	2,124	129	68	61	..	..	..
10—15 ..	*4,587*	*2,536*	*2,051*	*4,120*	2,425	1,695	404	109	355	3	2	1
15—20 ..	*4,394*	2,568	1,826	2,319	1,930	389	2,004	607	1,397	71	31	4[illegible]
20—30 ..	*8,100*	4,789	3,311	1,985	1,833	152	5,633	2,737	2,896	482	219	263
30—40 ..	*5,634*	3,266	2,368	510	404	106	4,270	2,548	1,722	854	314	540
40—50 ..	*3,936*	2,199	1,737	157	148	9	2,588	1,690	898	1,191	361	830
50—60 ..	*2,204*	1,218	986	75	71	4	1,111	830	281	1,018	317	701
60 and over ..	*1,500*	746	754	44	43	1	472	412	60	984	291	69[illegible]
SIKH ..	**2,960**	**1,828**	**1,132**	**1,500**	**995**	**505**	**1,249**	**741**	**508**	**211**	**92**	**119**
0—1 ..	*79*	36	43	79	36	43	..	..	..	..	..	..
1—2 ..	*70*	35	35	70	35	35	..	..	..	..	..	..
2—3 ..	*88*	49	39	88	49	39	..	..	..	..	..	..
3—4 ..	*80*	47	33	80	47	33	..	..	..	..	..	..
4—5 ..	*80*	45	35	80	45	35	..	..	..	..	..	..
Total 0—5 ..	*397*	*212*	*185*	*397*	*212*	*185*	..	..	..	..	..	..
5—10 ..	*320*	172	148	320	172	148	..	..	..	..	..	..
10—15 ..	*295*	156	139	269	151	118	25	5	20	1	..	1
15—20 ..	*400*	259	141	221	187	34	177	71	106	2	1	1
20—30 ..	*730*	494	236	231	214	17	481	271	210	18	9	9
30—40 ..	*332*	260	122	41	39	2	296	200	96	45	21	2[illegible]
40—50 ..	*246*	156	90	17	16	1	177	119	58	52	21	3[illegible]
50—60 ..	*112*	72	40	1	4	..	70	54	16	38	14	2[illegible]
60 and over ..	*78*	47	31	.	.	..	23	21	2	55	26	2
JAIN ..	**424**	**211**	**213**	**188**	**98**	**90**	**186**	**95**	**91**	**50**	**18**	**32**
0—1 ..	*22*	10	12	22	10	12	..	..	..	..	..	..
1—2 ..	*10*	4	6	10	4	6	..	..	..	..	..	..
2—3 ..	*15*	8	7	15	8	7	..	..	..	..	..	..
3—4 ..	*14*	7	7	14	7	7	..	..	..	..	..	..
4—5 ..	*12*	6	6	12	6	6	..	..	..	..	..	..
Total 0—5 ..	*73*	*35*	*38*	*73*	*35*	*38*	..	..	..	..	..	..
5—10 ..	*51*	25	26	51	25	26	..	..	..	..	..	..
10—15 ..	*48*	22	26	43	22	21	5	..	5	..	..	..
15—20 ..	*38*	18	20	15	10	5	23	8	15	..	..	..
20—30 ..	*82*	42	40	6	6	..	72	33	39	4	3	1
30—40 ..	*61*	34	27	..	..	..	52	32	20	9	2	7
40—50 ..	*36*	20	16	..	..	..	24	15	9	12	5	7
50—60 ..	*20*	10	10	..	..	..	10	7	3	10	3	7
60 and over ..	*15*	5	10	..	..	..	..	..	..	15	5	10

TABLE VII.—AGE, SEX

PART C.—DETAILS FOR CITIES AND SELECTED TOWNS.

MULTAN CITY.—*(concld.)*

Religion and Age.	Population.			Unmarried.			Married.			Widowed.		
	Persons.	Males.	Females.	Persons.	Males.	Females.	Persons.	Males.	Females.	Persons.	Males.	Females.
1	2	3	4	5	6	7	8	9	10	11	12	13
MUSLIM ..	**72,134**	**41,221**	**30,913**	**38,471**	**21,852**	**16,619**	**27,773**	**16,710**	**11,063**	**5,890**	**2,659**	**3,231**
0—1 ..	*2,173*	1,068	1,105	2,172	1,068	1,104	1	..	1	..	..	..
1—2 .	*1,554*	763	791	1,553	763	790	1	..	1	..	..	.
2—3 ..	*1,972*	972	1,000	1,964	972	992	7	..	7	1	.	1
3—4 ..	*1,912*	951	961	1,900	949	951	11	2	9	1	.	1
4—5 ..	*1,676*	849	827	1,665	844	821	8	4	4	3	1	2
Total 0—5 ..	*9,287*	*4,603*	*4,684*	*9,254*	*4,596*	*4,658*	*28*	*6*	*22*	*5*	*1*	*4*
5—10 ..	*8,370*	4,616	3,754	8,245	4,588	3,657	118	27	91	7	1	6
10—15 ..	*7,988*	4,575	3,413	7,477	4,486	2,991	498	85	413	13	4	9
15—20 ..	*7,491*	4,203	3,288	5,058	3,200	1,858	2,349	956	1,393	84	47	37
20—30 ..	*15,270*	8,800	6,470	6,853	3,680	3,173	7,835	4,767	3,068	582	353	229
30—40 ..	*10,560*	6,510	4,041	980	842	138	8,656	5,174	3,482	924	503	421
40—50 ..	*6,531*	3,948	2,583	357	283	74	4,725	3,036	1,689	1,449	629	820
50—60 ..	*3,659*	2,222	1,437	138	105	33	2,269	1,610	659	1,252	507	745
60 and over ..	*2,978*	1,735	1,243	109	72	37	1,295	1,049	246	1,574	614	960
CHRISTIAN ..	**1,823**	**1,278**	**545**	**1,298**	**994**	**304**	**448**	**250**	**198**	**77**	**34**	**43**
0—1 ..	*36*	20	16	36	20	16	..	..	..	..	.	
1—2 ..	*36*	19	17	36	19	17	..	..	..	.	..	
2—3 ..	*38*	16	22	38	16	22	..	.	..	..	..	..
3—4 ..	*29*	15	14	29	15	14	..	.	..	..	..	..
4—5	*32*	18	14	32	18	14	..	..	..	..	..	..
Total 0—5 ..	*171*	*88*	*83*	*171*	*88*	*83*	..	..	..	..	.	..
5—10 ..	*131*	66	65	131	66	65	..	..	..	.	..	..
10—15 ..	*118*	54	64	113	53	60	5	1	4	..	.	..
15—20 ..	*258*	200	58	222	188	34	36	12	24	..	..	..
20—30 ..	*719*	606	113	565	530	35	144	69	75	10	7	3
30—40 ..	*234*	150	84	74	62	12	145	79	66	15	9	6
40—50 ..	*106*	71	35	15	5	10	75	59	16	16	7	9
50—60 ..	*56*	29	27	6	1	5	33	22	11	17	6	11
60 and over ..	*30*	14	16	1	1	..	10	8	2	19	5	14
OTHERS ..	**1,692**	**996**	**696**	**748**	**463**	**285**	**770**	**431**	**339**	**174**	**102**	**72**
0—1 ..	*60*	30	30	60	30	30	..	..	..	..	..	..
1—2 ..	*42*	20	22	42	20	22	..	..	..	..	.	..
2—3 ..	*54*	31	23	54	31	23	..	..	..	..	.	..
3—4 ..	*53*	29	24	53	29	24	..	..	..	.	..	..
4—5 ..	*53*	24	29	52	24	28	1	..	1	..	.	..
Total 0—5 ..	*262*	*134*	*128*	*261*	*134*	*127*	*1*	..	*1*	..		..
5—10 ..	*198*	110	88	194	109	85	4	1	3	..		
10—15 ..	*164*	93	71	140	90	50	24	3	21	..	.	..
15—20 ..	*167*	92	75	55	48	7	108	41	67	4	3	1
20—30 ..	*403*	246	157	72	65	7	308	162	146	23	19	4
30—40 ..	*254*	168	86	15	10	5	204	135	69	35	23	12
40—50 ..	*135*	88	47	7	4	3	86	63	23	42	21	21
50—60 ..	*74*	47	27	3	3	..	28	22	6	43	22	21
60 and over ..	*35*	18	17	1	..	1	7	4	8	27	14	13

AND CIVIL CONDITION (BY RELIGION).

PART C.—DETAILS FOR CITIES AND SELECTED TOWNS—*continued.*

RAWALPINDI TOWN.

Religion and Age.	Population.			Unmarried.			Married.			Widowed.		
	Persons.	Males.	Females.	Persons.	Males.	Females.	Persons.	Males.	Females.	Persons.	Males.	Females.
1	2	3	4	5	6	7	8	9	10	11	12	13
ALL RELIGIONS ..	**119,284**	**75,971**	**43,313**	**57,838**	**39,581**	**18,257**	**52,524**	**32,349**	**20,175**	**8,922**	**4,041**	**4,881**
0—1 ..	*3,500*	1,840	1,660	3,497	1,839	1,658	3	1	2	..	.	.
1—2 ..	*2,691*	1,395	1,296	2,689	1,394	1,295	1	..	1	1	1	..
2—3 ..	*3,084*	1,605	1,470	3,075	1,602	1,473	9	3	6	..	.	..
3—4 ..	*3,011*	1,554	1,457	2,991	1,550	1,441	19	4	15	1		1
4—5 ..	*2,884*	1,478	1,406	2,847	1,469	1,378	32	7	25	5	2	3
Total 0—5 ..	*15,170*	*7,872*	*7,298*	*15,099*	*7,854*	*7,245*	*64*	*15*	*49*	*7*	*3*	*4*
5—10 ..	*12,217*	6,634	5,583	11,859	6,562	5,297	346	69	277	12	3	9
10—15 ..	*11,673*	6,659	5,014	10,318	6,445	3,873	1,332	207	1,125	23	7	16
15—20 ..	*13,453*	8,728	4,725	7,660	6,709	951	5,628	1,936	3,692	165	83	82
20—30 ..	*29,579*	20,608	8,971	9,803	9,270	533	18,606	10,007	7,999	1,170	731	439
30—40 ..	*19,447*	13,775	5,672	2,018	1,830	188	15,308	10,902	4,406	2,121	1,043	1,078
40—50 ..	*10,031*	6,838	3,193	685	576	109	7,227	5,380	1,847	2,119	882	1,237
50—60 ..	*4,679*	2,995	1,684	265	229	36	2,680	2,119	561	1,734	647	1,087
60 and over ..	*3,035*	1,862	1,173	131	106	25	1,333	1,114	219	1,571	642	929
HINDU ..	**40,161**	**24,669**	**15,492**	**19,513**	**13,054**	**6,459**	**17,198**	**10,103**	**7,095**	**3,450**	**1,512**	**1,938**
0—1 ..	*1,165*	623	542	1,165	623	542	..	..	..			..
1—2 ..	*942*	498	444	942	498	444	..	..	..	..	..	.
2—3 ..	*1,118*	596	522	1,118	596	522	..	..	.	..	..	.
3—4 ..	*1,068*	553	515	1,067	553	514	1	..	1	.	.	.
4—5 ..	*1,001*	511	490	995	508	487	5	2	3	1	1	..
Total 0—5 ..	*5,294*	*2,781*	*2,513*	*5,287*	*2,778*	*2,509*	*6*	*2*	*4*	*1*	*1*	..
5—10 ..	*4,262*	2,306	1,956	4,167	2,278	1,889	90	26	64	5	2	3
10—15 ..	*4,047*	2,300	1,747	3,646	2,223	1,423	390	73	317	11	4	7
15—20 ..	*4,554*	2,818	1,736	2,497	2,145	352	1,981	636	1,345	76	37	39
20—30 ..	*9,403*	6,182	3,221	2,822	2,664	158	6,146	3,284	2,862	435	234	201
30—40 ..	*6,263*	4,292	1,971	617	555	62	4,863	3,368	1,495	783	369	414
40—50 ..	*3,637*	2,407	1,230	340	292	48	2,427	1,757	670	870	358	512
50—60 ..	*1,647*	983	664	75	69	6	882	641	241	690	273	417
60 and over ..	*1,054*	600	454	62	50	12	413	316	97	579	234	345
SIKH .	**15,532**	**9,399**	**6,133**	**7,675**	**5,130**	**2,545**	**6,746**	**3,852**	**2,894**	**1,111**	**417**	**694**
0—1 ..	*591*	335	256	590	335	255	1	..	1	.	.	
1—2 ..	*407*	198	209	405	197	208	1	..	1	1	1	.
2—3 ..	*459*	222	237	454	221	233	5	1	4		.	.
3—4 ..	*449*	227	222	437	225	212	12	2	10	.	.	..
4—5 .	*433*	218	215	415	216	199	18	2	16	..	.	..
Total 0—5 ..	*2,339*	*1,200*	*1,139*	*2,301*	*1,194*	*1,107*	*37*	*5*	*32*	*1*	*1*	.
5—10 ..	*1,782*	936	846	1,679	926	753	100	10	90	3	..	3
10—15 ..	*1,798*	930	868	1,403	901	502	390	28	362	5	1	4
15—20 ..	*1,809*	1,066	743	949	866	83	844	193	651	16	7	9
20—30 ..	*3,424*	2,309	1,115	1,058	993	65	2,250	1,257	993	116	59	57
30—40 ..	*2,158*	1,536	622	174	152	22	1,751	1,293	458	233	91	142
40—50	*1,221*	807	414	75	63	12	864	651	213	282	93	189
50—60 ..	*605*	368	237	24	23	1	336	265	71	245	80	165
60 and over ..	*396*	247	149	12	12	..	174	150	24	210	85	125
JAIN ..	**1,025**	**563**	**462**	**554**	**339**	**215**	**357**	**183**	**174**	**114**	**41**	**73**
0—1 ..	*34*	14	20	34	14	20	..	..	.	..	..	.
1—2 ..	*32*	19	13	32	19	13	..	..	.	..	.	..
2—3 ..	*32*	19	13	32	19	13	..	..	.	..	..	..
3—4 ..	*29*	16	13	29	16	13	..	..	..	..	..	..
4—5 ..	*26*	12	14	26	12	14	..	..	..	..	..	.
Total 0—5 ..	*153*	*80*	*73*	*153*	*80*	*73*	..	..	..	..	..	..
5—10 ..	*132*	71	61	131	71	60	1	..	1	..	..	..
10—15 ..	*132*	73	59	126	72	54	6	1	5	..	.	..
15—20 .	*97*	50	47	57	41	16	38	9	29	2	.	2
20—30 ..	*187*	101	86	53	48	5	123	50	73	11	3	8
30—40 ..	*140*	82	58	17	14	3	98	58	40	25	10	15
40—50 ..	*94*	53	41	7	6	1	56	37	19	31	10	21
50—60 ..	*62*	39	23	9	6	3	28	22	6	25	11	14
60 and over ..	*28*	14	14	1	1	..	7	6	1	20	7	13

TABLE VII.—AGE, SEX

PART C.—DETAILS FOR CITIES AND SELECTED TOWNS.

RAWALPINDI TOWN.—(*concld*).

Religion and Age.		Population.			Unmarried.			Married.			Widowed.	
	Persons.	Males.	Females.	Persons.	Males.	Females.	Persons.	Males.	Females.	Persons.	Males.	Females.
1	2	3		5	6	7	8	9	10	11	12	13
MUSLIM ..	**55,637**	**36,732**	**18,905**	**25,721**	**17,823**	**7,898**	**25,939**	**16,987**	**8,952**	**3,977**	**1,922**	**2,055**
0- 1 .	*1,510*	780	730	1,510	780	730	..	.	..	..	..	..
1 -2 ..	*1,140*	598	542	1,140	598	542	.	..	..	..	..	.
2- -3 ..	*1,299*	680	619	1,295	678	617	4	2	2	..	..	..
3- 4	*1,317*	681	636	1,311	679	632	6	2	4	..	..	..
4 -5 .	*1,284*	664	620	1,274	661	613	8	2	6	2	1	1
Total 0- -5 ..	*6,550*	*3,403*	*3,147*	*6,530*	*3,396*	*3,134*	*18*	*6*	*12*	*2*	*1*	*1*
5- 10 ..	*5,504*	3,039	2,465	5,355	3,009	2,346	147	29	118	2	1	1
10- 15 .	*5,256*	3,115	2,141	4,723	3,015	1,708	526	98	428	7	2	5
15- -20 .	*6,165*	4,131	2,034	3,458	3,038	420	2,640	1,057	1,583	67	36	31
20- -30 .	*14,326*	10,274	4,052	4,389	4,184	205	9,367	5,688	3,679	570	402	168
30- -40 .	*9,675*	7,087	2,588	895	851	44	7,770	5,709	2,061	1,010	527	483
40- -50 ..	*4,561*	3,271	1,290	191	167	24	3,489	2,706	783	881	398	483
50- -60	*2,164*	1,481	683	137	124	13	1,296	1,092	204	731	265	466
60 and over .	*1,436*	931	505	43	39	4	686	602	84	707	290	417
CHRISTIAN .	**6,850**	**4,562**	**2,288**	**4,337**	**3,211**	**1,126**	**2,246**	**1,202**	**1,044**	**267**	**149**	**118**
0- 1 .	*197*	87	110	195	86	109	2	1	1	.	..	..
1- 2	*168*	81	87	168	81	87	..	..	..	.	..	..
2 -3 ..	*175*	88	87	175	88	87	..	..	..	..	..	
3- 4 ..	*148*	77	71	147	77	70	.	..	.	1	..	1
4- -5 ..	*136*	71	65	133	70	63	1	1	..	2	.	2
Total 0- -5	*824*	*404*	*420*	*818*	*402*	*416*	*3*	*2*	*1*	*3*	..	*3*
5 – 10 ..	*528*	277	251	518	273	245	8	4	4	2	..	2
10- 15 ..	*435*	238	197	416	231	185	19	7	12	..	.	..
15- -20 ..	*824*	661	163	695	617	78	125	41	84	4	3	1
20- 30 ..	*2,225*	1,734	491	1,475	1,376	99	712	325	387	38	33	5
30- 40 ..	*1,195*	769	426	313	256	57	812	467	345	70	46	24
40- -50 ..	*504*	288	216	69	45	24	380	220	160	55	23	32
50- -60 ..	*197*	122	75	20	7	13	135	97	38	42	18	24
60 and over ..	*118*	69	49	13	4	9	52	39	13	53	26	27
OTHERS ..	**79**	**46**	**33**	**38**	**24**	**14**	**38**	**22**	**16**	**3**	..	**3**
0- 1 ..	*3*	1	2	3	1	2	..	..	..	..	..	..
1- -2 .	*2*	1	1	2	1	1	..	..	..	..	..	..
2- -3 ..	*1*	..	1	1	..	1	..	..	..	..	..	..
3—4 .	..	..	..	..	..	..	..	..	..	.	..	..
4—5 .	*4*	2	2	4	2	2		.	..	..	..	..
Total 0- 5 .	*10*	*4*	*6*	*10*	*4*	*6*	..	..	..	..	..	..
5— 10 .	*9*	5	4	9	5	4	..	..	.	.	..	..
10— 15 .	*5*	3	2	4	3	1	1	..	1	..	..	..
15—20 .	*4*	2	2	4	2	2	..	..	..	.	.	..
20- -30 .	*14*	8	6	6	5	1	8	3	5	..	..	..
30- 40 .	*16*	9	7	2	2	..	14	7	7	..	..	..
40 -50 ..	*14*	12	2	3	3	..	11	9	2	..	..	..
50- -60 .	*4*	2	2	..	..	..	3	2	1	1	..	1
60 and over ..	*3*	1	2	..	..	.	1	1	..	2	..	2

AND CIVIL CONDITION (BY RELIGION).

PART C.—DETAILS FOR CITIES AND SELECTED TOWNS—*continued.*

SIALKOT TOWN.

Religion and Age.	Population.			Unmarried.			Married.			Widowed.		
	Persons.	Males.	Females.	Persons.	Males.	Females.	Persons.	Males.	Females.	Persons.	Males.	Females.
1	2	3	4	5	6	7	8	9	10	11	12	13
ALL RELIGIONS ..	**100,973**	**59,894**	**41,079**	**51,918**	**32,928**	**18,990**	**41,648**	**23,600**	**18,048**	**7,407**	**3,366**	**4,041**
0- 1 ..	*3,613*	1,856	1,757	3,613	1,856	1,757	..	..	..	..	..	..
1- -2 ..	*2,695*	1,361	1,334	2,691	1,360	1,331	2	1	1	2	.	2
2 -3 ..	*3,028*	1,519	1,509	3,017	1,515	1,502	10	4	6	1	..	1
3- 4 ..	*2,896*	1,494	1,402	2,889	1,492	1,397	6	2	4	1	..	1
4 -5 .	*2,738*	1,449	1,289	2,716	1,443	1,273	16	5	11	6	1	5
Total 0- -5 ..	*14,970*	*7,679*	*7,291*	*14,926*	*7,666*	*7,260*	*34*	*12*	*22*	*10*	*1*	*9*
5 10 ..	*11,992*	6,577	5,415	11,779	6,518	5,261	200	57	143	13	2	11
10 -15 ..	*11,213*	6,387	4,826	10,360	6,194	4,166	834	186	648	19	7	12
15- -20 ..	*11,213*	6,910	4,303	6,222	5,021	1,201	4,844	1,803	3,041	147	86	61
20- -30 .	*21,846*	13,948	7,898	6,448	5,797	651	14,626	7,673	6,953	772	478	294
30- -40 .	*13,658*	8,706	4,952	1,390	1,154	236	10,982	6,873	4,109	1,286	679	607
40- -50 ..	*7,930*	4,822	3,108	452	342	110	5,792	3,806	1,986	1,686	674	1,012
50- -60 ..	*4,426*	2,654	1,772	195	143	52	2,685	1,904	781	1,546	607	939
60 and over ..	*3,725*	2,211	1,514	146	93	53	1,651	1,286	365	1,928	832	1,096
HINDU ..	**18,644**	**11,098**	**7,546**	**9,498**	**6,084**	**3,414**	**7,487**	**4,277**	**3,210**	**1,659**	**737**	**922**
0—1 ..	*641*	348	293	641	348	293	..	..	..	.	..	..
1- -2 .	*472*	229	243	468	228	240	2	1	1	2	.	2
2- -3 ..	*539*	276	263	532	273	259	6	3	3.	1	..	1
3- 4 ..	*532*	291	241	529	289	240	3	2	1	..	..	
4- -5 ..	*508*	277	231	505	276	229	2	1	1	1	..	1
Total 0- -5 ..	*2,692*	*1,421*	*1,271*	*2,675*	*1,414*	*1,261*	*13*	*7*	*6*	*4*	..	*4*
5 -10 .	*2,158*	1,175	983	2,124	1,163	961	32	11	21	2	1	1
10- -15 .	*2,055*	1,160	895	1,898	1,126	772	152	33	119	5	1	4
15- -20 ..	*2,082*	1,299	783	1,191	970	221	857	310	547	34	19	15
20- -30 ..	*3,949*	2,485	1,464	1,150	1,032	118	2,624	1,347	1,277	175	106	69
30- -40 ..	*2,534*	1,625	909	279	238	41	1,954	1,236	718	301	151	150
40- -50 .	*1,633*	1,014	619	105	85	20	1,126	775	351	402	154	248
50- -60 ..	*906*	568	338	52	41	11	493	373	120	361	154	207
60 and over ..	*635*	351	284	24	15	9	236	185	51	375	151	224
SIKH ..	**4,931**	**3,338**	**1,593**	**2,381**	**1,662**	**719**	**2,206**	**1,493**	**713**	**344**	**183**	**161**
0- 1 ..	*129*	50	79	129	50	79	..	..	..	..	..	..
1 -2 .	*100*	52	48	100	52	48	..	..	..	.	.	..
2- -3 .	*122*	65	57	120	64	56	2	1	1	..	..	..
3- -4 ..	*113*	60	53	112	60	52	1	..	1	..	..	..
4- 5 ..	*106*	55	51	104	54	50	2	1	1	..	..	.
Total 0- -5 ..	*570*	*282*	*288*	*565*	*280*	*285*	*5*	*2*	*3*	..	..	..
5 -10 .	*449*	251	198	445	249	196	2	1	1	2	1	1
10- -15 ..	*428*	259	169	407	252	155	21	7	14	..	..	..
15- -20 ..	*641*	477	164	381	333	48	256	142	114	4	2	2
20- -30 ..	*1,342*	1,016	326	426	406	20	869	577	292	47	33	14
30- 40 .	*765*	578	187	101	94	7	596	440	156	68	44	24
40- -50 ..	*348*	228	120	32	30	2	243	164	79	73	34	39
50 -60 ..	*211*	131	80	13	11	2	130	94	36	68	26	42
60 and over ..	*177*	116	61	11	7	4	84	66	18	82	43	39
JAIN ..	**1,570**	**858**	**712**	**857**	**515**	**342**	**566**	**266**	**300**	**147**	**77**	**70**
0- 1 ..	*46*	26	20	46	26	20	..	..	..	..	..	..
1- -2 .	*51*	26	25	51	26	25	..	..	..	..	.	..
2- -3 ..	*56*	26	30	55	26	29	1	..	1	..	.	..
3—4 ..	*49*	26	23	49	26	23	..	..	..	..	..	..
4- -5 ..	*59*	32	27	56	32	24	2	..	2	1	..	1
Total 0- -5 ..	*261*	*136*	*125*	*257*	*136*	*121*	*3*	..	*3*	*1*	..	*1*
5- 10 ..	*217*	121	96	210	119	91	6	2	4	1	..	1
10- -15 .	*189*	104	85	179	102	77	9	1	8	1	1	..
15- -20 ..	*169*	93	76	98	67	31	69	25	44	2	1	1
20- 30 ..	*291*	152	139	69	55	14	211	90	121	11	7	4
30- 40 .	*179*	96	83	20	16	4	124	62	62	35	18	17
40- -50 ..	*132*	81	51	16	13	3	77	46	31	39	22	17
50- -60 ..	*84*	47	37	5	4	1	45	27	18	34	16	18
60 and over ..	*48*	28	20	3	3	..	22	13	9	23	12	11

TABLE VII.—AGE, SEX

PART C.—DETAILS FOR CITIES AND SELECTED TOWNS.

SIALKOT TOWN—(concld).

Religion and Age.	Population.			Unmarried.			Married.			Widowed.		
	Persons.	Males.	Females.	Persons.	Males.	Females.	Persons.	Males.	Females.	Persons.	Males.	Females.
1	2	3	4	5	6	7	8	9	10	11	12	13
MUSLIM ..	**69,700**	**40,605**	**29,095**	**35,288**	**21,827**	**13,461**	**29,540**	**16,602**	**12,938**	**4,872**	**2,176**	**2,696**
0–1 ..	*2,579*	1,307	1,272	2,579	1,307	1,272	..	..	..	..	..	..
1–2 ..	*1,929*	987	942	1,929	987	942	..	..	..	..	..	..
2–3 ..	*2,155*	1,078	1,077	2,155	1,078	1,077	..	..	..	..	..	..
3–4 ..	*2,052*	1,044	1,008	2,049	1,044	1,005	2	..	2	1	..	1
4–5 ..	*1,915*	1,007	908	1,904	1,004	900	8	2	6	3	1	2
Total 0–5 ..	*10,630*	*5,423*	*5,207*	*10,616*	*5,420*	*5,196*	*10*	*2*	*8*	*4*	*1*	*3*
5–10 ..	*8,569*	4,711	3,858	8,407	4,669	3,738	155	42	113	7	..	7
10–15 ..	*8,041*	4,598	3,443	7,410	4,452	2,958	619	142	477	12	4	8
15–20 ..	*7,609*	4,534	3,075	4,032	3,193	839	3,475	1,280	2,195	102	61	41
20–30 ..	*14,325*	8,779	5,546	3,572	3,133	439	10,260	5,345	4,915	493	301	192
30–40 ..	*9,356*	5,872	3,484	780	626	154	7,767	4,817	2,950	809	429	380
40–50 ..	*5,441*	3,262	2,179	262	189	73	4,093	2,635	1,438	1,086	418	668
50–60 ..	*3,037*	1,804	1,233	111	80	31	1,920	1,347	573	1,006	377	629
60 and over ..	*2,692*	1,622	1,070	98	65	33	1,241	972	269	1,353	585	768
CHRISTIAN ..	**6,095**	**3,986**	**2,109**	**3,875**	**2,835**	**1,040**	**1,836**	**959**	**877**	**384**	**192**	**192**
0–1 ..	*214*	123	91	214	123	91	..	..	..	..	..	..
1–2 ..	*142*	67	75	142	67	75	..	..	..	..	..	..
2–3 ..	*155*	74	81	154	74	80	1	..	1	..	..	..
3–4 ..	*149*	73	76	149	73	76	..	..	..	..	..	..
4–5 ..	*148*	77	71	145	76	69	2	1	1	1	..	1
Total 0–5 ..	*808*	*414*	*394*	*804*	*413*	*391*	*3*	*1*	*2*	*1*	..	*1*
5–10 ..	*595*	318	277	589	317	272	5	1	4	1	..	1
10–15 ..	*496*	265	231	462	261	201	33	3	30	1	1	..
15–20 ..	*707*	506	201	518	458	60	184	45	139	5	3	2
20–30 ..	*1,933*	1,515	418	1,231	1,171	60	656	313	343	46	31	15
30–40 ..	*820*	534	286	210	180	30	537	317	220	73	37	36
40–50 ..	*375*	236	139	37	25	12	253	166	87	85	45	40
50–60 ..	*188*	104	84	14	7	7	97	63	34	77	34	43
60 and over ..	*173*	94	79	10	3	7	68	50	18	95	41	54
OTHERS ..	**33**	**9**	**24**	**19**	**5**	**14**	**13**	**3**	**10**	**1**	**1**	..
0–1 ..	*4*	2	2	4	2	2	..	..	..	..	..	..
1–2 ..	*1*	..	1	1	..	1	..	..	..	..	..	..
2–3 ..	*1*	..	1	1	..	1	..	..	..	..	..	..
3–4 ..	*1*	..	1	1	..	1	..	..	..	..	..	..
4–5 ..	*2*	1	1	2	1	1	..	..	..	..	..	..
Total 0–5 ..	*9*	*3*	*6*	*9*	*3*	*6*	..	..	..	..	..	..
5–10 ..	*4*	*1*	3	4	1	3	..	..	..	..	..	..
10–15 ..	*4*	1	3	4	1	3	..	..	..	..	..	..
15–20 ..	*5*	1	4	2	..	2	3	1	2	..	..	..
20–30 ..	*6*	1	5	..	..	..	6	1	5	..	..	..
30–40 ..	*4*	1	3	..	..	..	4	1	3	..	..	..
40–50 ..	*1*	1	..	..	..	..	..	..	..	1	1	..
50–60 ..	..	..	..	..	..	..	..	..	..	..	..	..
60 and over ..	..	..	..	..	..	..	..	..	..	..	..	..

AND CIVIL CONDITION (BY RELIGION).

PART C.—DETAILS FOR CITIES AND SELECTED TOWNS—*continued.*

AMBALA TOWN

Religion and Age.	Population. Persons.	Males.	Females.	Unmarried. Persons.	Males.	Females.	Married. Persons.	Males.	Females.	Widowed. Persons.	Males.	Females.
1	2	3	4	5	6	7	8	9	10	11	12	13
ALL RELIGIONS ..	**86,592**	**51,523**	**35,069**	**38,295**	**24,604**	**13,691**	**39,647**	**22,292**	**17,355**	**8,650**	**4,627**	**4,023**
0—1 ..	*2,601*	1,285	1,316	2,601	1,285	1,316	..	..	..	..	..	..
1—2 ..	*1,953*	967	986	1,953	967	986	..	..	..	..	..	..
2—3 ..	*2,184*	1,087	1,097	2,184	1,087	1,097	..	..	..	..	..	..
3—4 ..	*2,184*	1,096	1,088	2,174	1,093	1,081	10	3	7	..	..	..
4—5 ..	*2,069*	1,063	1,006	2,043	1,055	988	22	7	15	4	1	3
Total 0—5 ..	*10,991*	*5,498*	*5,493*	*10,955*	*5,487*	*5,468*	*32*	*10*	*22*	*4*	*1*	*3*
5—10 ..	*9,458*	5,083	4,375	8,933	4,916	4,017	505	158	347	20	9	11
10—15 ..	*9,195*	5,135	4,060	7,714	4,690	3,015	1,444	415	1,029	37	21	16
15—20 ..	*9,558*	5,816	3,742	4,314	3,632	682	5,046	2,049	2,997	198	135	63
20—30 ..	*18,901*	11,957	6,944	4,604	4,271	333	13,327	7,009	6,318	970	677	293
30—40 ..	*12,638*	8,120	4,518	1,089	988	101	10,002	6,204	3,798	1,547	928	619
40—50 ..	*7,888*	4,943	2,945	399	359	40	5,437	3,580	1,857	2,052	1,004	1,048
50—60 ..	*4,498*	2,814	1,684	174	155	19	2,479	1,775	704	1,845	884	961
60 and over ..	*3,465*	2,157	1,308	113	97	16	1,375	1,092	283	1,977	968	1,009
HINDU ..	**39,945**	**23,894**	**16,051**	**16,874**	**10,966**	**5,908**	**18,632**	**10,572**	**8,060**	**4,439**	**2,356**	**2,083**
0—1 ..	*1,202*	598	604	1,202	598	604	..	..	..	..	..	..
1—2 ..	*863*	431	432	863	431	432	..	..	..	..	..	..
2—3 ..	*971*	493	478	971	493	478	..	..	..	..	..	..
3—4 ..	*993*	510	483	989	508	481	4	2	2	..	..	..
4—5 ..	*930*	494	436	919	490	429	9	4	5	2	..	2
Total 0—5 ..	*4,959*	*2,526*	*2,433*	*4,944*	*2,520*	*2,424*	*13*	*6*	*7*	*2*	..	*2*
5—10 ..	*4,269*	2,358	1,911	4,074	2,298	1,776	182	53	129	13	7	6
10—15 ..	*4,222*	2,426	1,796	3,545	2,238	1,307	657	174	483	20	14	6
15—20 ..	*4,334*	2,600	1,734	1,743	1,516	227	2,488	1,012	1,476	103	72	31
20—30 ..	*8,680*	5,406	3,274	1,693	1,597	96	6,460	3,449	3,011	527	360	167
30—40 ..	*6,176*	4,022	2,154	515	474	41	4,804	3,048	1,756	857	500	357
40—50 ..	*3,744*	2,366	1,378	208	190	18	2,460	1,652	808	1,076	524	552
50—60 ..	*2,069*	1,280	789	91	82	9	1,039	755	284	939	443	496
60 and over ..	*1,492*	910	582	61	51	10	529	423	106	902	436	466
SIKH ..	**4,143**	**2,845**	**1,298**	**1,816**	**1,317**	**499**	**1,993**	**1,303**	**690**	**334**	**225**	**109**
0—1 ..	*95*	44	51	95	44	51	..	..	..	..	..	..
1—2 ..	*77*	38	39	77	38	39	..	..	..	..	..	..
2—3 ..	*80*	38	42	80	38	42	..	..	..	..	..	..
3—4 ..	*79*	39	40	79	39	40	..	..	..	..	..	..
4—5 ..	*72*	40	32	72	40	32	..	..	..	..	..	..
Total 0—5 ..	*403*	*199*	*204*	*403*	*199*	*204*	..	..	..	..	..	..
5—10 ..	*327*	180	147	310	174	136	17	6	11	..	..	..
10—15 ..	*336*	195	141	283	176	107	53	19	34	..	..	..
15—20 ..	*613*	447	166	327	292	35	276	146	130	10	9	1
20—30 ..	*1,123*	832	291	378	361	17	690	426	264	55	45	10
30—40 ..	*643*	478	165	87	87	..	496	348	148	60	43	17
40—50 ..	*354*	256	98	15	15	..	263	196	67	76	45	31
50—60 ..	*198*	150	48	8	8	..	128	99	29	62	43	19
60 and over ..	*146*	108	38	5	5	..	70	63	7	71	40	31
JAIN ..	**1,269**	**694**	**575**	**583**	**356**	**227**	**523**	**265**	**258**	**163**	**73**	**90**
0—1 ..	*35*	16	19	35	16	19	..	..	..	..	..	..
1—2 ..	*28*	12	16	28	12	16	..	..	..	..	..	..
2—3 ..	*38*	24	14	38	24	14	..	..	..	..	..	..
3—4 ..	*37*	22	15	37	22	15	..	..	..	..	..	..
4—5 ..	*31*	11	20	31	11	20	..	..	..	..	..	..
Total 0—5 ..	*169*	*85*	*84*	*169*	*85*	*84*	..	..	..	..	..	..
5—10 ..	*145*	*72*	73	145	72	73	..	..	..	..	..	..
10—15 ..	*149*	84	65	137	82	55	12	2	10	..	..	..
15—20 ..	*127*	69	58	59	47	12	64	21	43	4	1	3
20—30 ..	*226*	122	104	42	41	1	166	73	93	18	8	10
30—40 ..	*170*	95	75	13	13	..	129	67	62	28	15	13
40—50 ..	*138*	76	62	8	7	1	85	53	32	45	16	29
50—60 ..	*87*	56	31	8	7	1	44	31	13	35	18	17
60 and over ..	*58*	35	23	2	2	..	23	18	5	33	15	18

TABLE VII.—AGE, SEX

PART C.—DETAILS FOR CITIES AND SELECTED TOWNS.

AMBALA TOWN.—(concld).

Religion and Age.	Population.			Unmarried.			Married.			Widowed.		
	Persons.	Males.	Females.	Persons.	Males.	Females.	Persons.	Males.	Females.	Persons.	Males.	Females.
1	2	3	4	5	6	7	8	9	10	11	12	13
MUSLIM ..	**38,089**	**21,981**	**16,108**	**16,861**	**10,346**	**6,515**	**17,643**	**9,711**	**7,932**	**3,585**	**1,924**	**1,661**
0—1 ..	*1,213*	602	611	1,213	602	611	..	..	..	..	..	..
1—2 ..	*929*	462	467	929	462	467	..	..	..	..	..	..
2—3 ..	*1,037*	503	534	1,037	503	534	..	..	..	..	..	..
3—4 ..	*1,017*	497	520	1,011	496	515	6	1	5	..	..	..
4—5 ..	*976*	490	486	961	486	475	13	3	10	2	1	1
Total 0—5 ..	*5,172*	*2,554*	*2,618*	*5,151*	*2,549*	*2,602*	*19*	*4*	*15*	*2*	*1*	*1*
5—10 ..	*4,495*	2,370	2,125	4,182	2,269	1,913	306	99	207	7	2	5
10—15 ..	*4,307*	2,350	1,957	3,569	2,124	1,445	721	219	502	17	7	10
15—20 ..	*4,063*	2,374	1,689	1,801	1,461	340	2,181	860	1,321	81	53	28
20—30 ..	*7,708*	4,646	3,062	1,584	1,436	148	5,759	2,950	2,809	365	260	105
30—40 ..	*5,181*	3,228	1,953	336	300	36	4,261	2,568	1,693	584	360	224
40—50 ..	*3,451*	2,128	1,323	145	127	18	2,483	1,594	889	823	407	416
50—60 ..	*2,043*	1,280	763	60	51	9	1,198	856	342	785	373	412
60 and over ..	*1,669*	1,051	618	33	29	4	715	561	154	921	461	460
CHRISTIAN ..	**3,138**	**2,103**	**1,035**	**2,158**	**1,617**	**541**	**851**	**437**	**414**	**129**	**49**	**80**
0—1 ..	*56*	25	31	56	25	31	..	..	..	..	..	..
1—2 ..	*55*	24	31	55	24	31	..	..	..	..	..	..
2—3 ..	*58*	29	29	58	29	29	..	..	..	..	..	..
3—4 ..	*58*	28	30	58	28	30	..	..	..	..	..	..
4—5 ..	*60*	28	32	60	28	32	..	..	..	..	..	..
Total 0—5 ..	*287*	*134*	*153*	*287*	*134*	*153*	..	..	..	..	..	..
5—10 ..	*222*	103	119	222	103	119	..	..	..	..	..	..
10—15 ..	*181*	80	101	180	79	101	1	1	..	..	..	..
15—20 ..	*420*	325	95	384	316	68	36	9	27	..	..	..
20—30 ..	*1,159*	947	212	906	835	71	248	108	140	5	4	1
30—40 ..	*467*	296	171	137	113	24	312	173	139	18	10	8
40—50 ..	*201*	117	84	23	20	3	146	85	61	32	12	20
50—60 ..	*101*	48	53	7	7	..	70	34	36	24	7	17
60 and over ..	*100*	53	47	12	10	2	38	27	11	50	16	34
OTHERS ..	**8**	**6**	**2**	**3**	**2**	**1**	**5**	**4**	**1**	..	..	..
0—1 ..	..	..	..	..	..	..	..	..	..	..	..	..
1—2 ..	*1*	..	1	1	..	1	..	..	..	..	..	..
2—3 ..	..	..	..	..	..	..	..	..	..	..	..	..
3—4 ..	..	..	..	..	..	..	..	..	..	..	..	..
4—5 ..	..	..	..	..	..	..	..	..	..	..	..	..
Total 0—5 ..	*1*	..	*1*	*1*	..	*1*	..	..	..	..	..	..
5—10 ..	..	..	..	..	..	..	..	..	..	..	..	..
10—15 ..	..	..	..	..	..	..	..	..	..	..	..	..
15—20 ..	*1*	1	..	..	..	..	1	1	..	..	..	..
20—30 ..	*5*	4	1	1	1	..	4	3	1	..	..	..
30—40 ..	*1*	1	..	1	1		..	..	..	..	..	..
40—50 ..	..	..	..	..	..	..	..	..	..	..	..	..
50—60 ..	..	..	..	..	..	..	..	..	..	..	..	..
60 and over ..	..	..	..	..	..	..	..	..	..	..	..	..

AND CIVIL CONDITION (BY RELIGION).

PART C.—DETAILS FOR CITIES AND SELECTED TOWNS.—*continued.*

JULLUNDUR TOWN.

Religion and Age.	Population.			Unmarried.			Married.			Widowed.		
	Persons.	Males.	Females.	Persons.	Males.	Females.	Persons.	Males.	Females.	Persons.	Males.	Females.
1	2	3	4	5	6	7	8	9	10	11	12	13
ALL RELIGIONS ..	**89,030**	**51,119**	**37,911**	**44,626**	**27,137**	**17,489**	**35,691**	**19,606**	**16,085**	**8,713**	**4,376**	**4,337**
0—1 ..	2,938	1,535	1,403	2,922	1,530	1,392	16	5	11	..	..	..
1—2 ..	2,175	1,060	1,115	2,164	1,056	1,108	10	4	6	1	..	1
2—3 ..	2,490	1,189	1,301	2,460	1,172	1,288	27	16	11	3	1	2
3—4 ..	2,495	1,230	1,265	2,469	1,216	1,253	25	14	11	1	..	1
4—5 ..	2,318	1,209	1,109	2,286	1,193	1,093	23	11	12	9	5	4
Total 0—5 ..	12,416	6,223	6,193	12,301	6,167	6,134	101	50	51	14	6	8
5—10 ..	10,563	5,682	4,881	10,123	5,472	4,651	424	202	222	16	8	8
10—15 ..	10,033	5,600	4,433	8,950	5,214	3,736	1,063	376	687	20	10	10
15—20 ..	9,430	5,765	3,665	5,404	4,001	1,403	3,887	1,678	2,209	139	86	[illegible]
20—30 ..	17,261	10,549	6,712	5,333	4,391	942	11,202	5,702	5,500	726	456	270
30—40 ..	12,091	7,341	4,750	1,371	1,148	223	9,533	5,566	3,967	1,187	627	560
40—50 ..	7,966	4,673	3,293	617	409	208	4,956	2,878	2,078	2,393	1,386	1,007
50—60 ..	4,782	2,613	2,169	327	183	144	2,651	1,752	899	1,804	678	[illegible]
60 and over ..	4,488	2,673	1,815	200	152	48	1,874	1,402	472	2,414	1,119	[illegible]
HINDU ..	**27,940**	**16,734**	**11,206**	**14,865**	**8,982**	**5,383**	**10,657**	**6,579**	**4,078**	**2,918**	**1,173**	**1,745**
0—1 ..	807	451	356	799	446	353	8	5	3	..	..	..
1—2 ..	648	327	321	644	325	319	4	2	2	..	..	..
2—3 ..	768	351	417	756	345	411	10	5	5	2	1	..
3—4 ..	745	356	389	737	351	386	8	5	3	..	..	..
4—5 ..	606	329	277	598	324	274	5	3	2	3	2	1
Total 0—5 ..	3,574	1,814	1,760	3,534	1,791	1,743	35	20	15	5	3	2
5—10 ..	3,050	1,683	1,367	2,918	1,585	1,333	125	95	30	7	3	4
10—15 ..	3,073	1,776	1,297	2,776	1,642	1,134	288	130	158	9	4	5
15—20 ..	3,190	2,136	1,054	2,129	1,522	607	1,015	586	429	46	28	18
20—30 ..	5,771	3,835	1,936	2,077	1,619	458	3,427	2,054	1,373	267	162	105
30—40 ..	3,965	2,570	1,395	596	540	56	2,956	1,840	1,116	413	190	223
40—50 ..	2,465	1,398	1,067	186	156	30	1,598	1,006	592	681	236	445
50—60 ..	1,560	805	755	90	77	13	737	481	256	733	247	486
60 and over ..	1,292	717	575	59	50	9	476	367	109	757	300	457
SIKH ..	**3,003**	**2,148**	**855**	**1,390**	**1,045**	**345**	**1,436**	**978**	**458**	**177**	**125**	**52**
0—1 ..	88	47	41	87	47	40	1	..	1	..	..	..
1—2 ..	60	29	31	59	29	30	1	..	1	..	..	..
2—3 ..	63	35	28	62	34	28	1	1	..	..	..	..
3—4 ..	59	36	23	59	36	23	..	..	..	..	..	..
4—5 ..	53	30	23	52	30	22	1	..	1	..	..	..
Total 0—5 ..	323	177	146	319	176	143	4	1	3	..	..	..
5—10 ..	251	153	98	246	151	95	5	2	3	..	..	..
10—15 ..	302	216	86	267	192	75	35	24	11	..	..	..
15—20 ..	447	352	95	233	215	18	210	134	76	4	3	1
20—30 ..	789	587	202	231	223	8	532	343	189	26	21	5
30—40 ..	448	335	113	64	58	6	348	248	100	36	29	7
40—50 ..	227	163	64	21	21	..	173	122	51	33	20	13
50—60 ..	125	93	32	7	7	..	83	65	18	35	21	14
60 and over ..	91	72	19	2	2	..	46	39	7	43	31	12
JAIN ..	**1,014**	**515**	**499**	**513**	**317**	**196**	**398**	**162**	**236**	**103**	**86**	**67**
0—1 ..	45	23	22	45	23	22	..	..	..	..	..	..
1—2 ..	31	17	14	30	16	14	1	1	..	..	..	
2—3 ..	34	17	17	34	17	17	..	..	..	..	..	
3—4 ..	36	17	19	36	17	19	..	..	..	..	..	
4—5 ..	36	20	16	36	20	16	..	..	..	..	..	..
Total 0—5 ..	182	94	88	181	93	88	1	1	..	..	..	..
5—10 ..	158	95	63	139	86	53	19	9	10	..	..	..
10—15 ..	134	79	55	105	71	34	29	8	21	..		..
15—20 ..	90	39	5	38	32	6	50	6	44	2	1	1
20—30 ..	137	55	82	34	29	5	99	25	74	4	1	3
30—40 ..	125	56	69	9	3	6	102	50	52	14	3	1
40—50 ..	91	46	45	6	2	4	64	40	24	21	4	17
50—60 ..	46	23	23	1	1	..	19	12	7	26	10	[illegible]
60 and over ..	51	28	23	..	..	..	15	11	4	36	17	[illegible]

TABLE VII.—AGE, SEX

PART C.—DETAILS FOR CITIES AND SELECTED TOWNS.

JULLUNDUR TOWN—(concld).

Religion and Age.	Population.			Unmarried.			Married.			Widowed.		
	Persons.	Males.	Females.	Persons.	Males.	Females.	Persons.	Males.	Females.	Persons.	Males.	Females.
1	2	3	4	5	6	7	8	9	10	11	12	13
MUSLIM ..	**52,577**	**28,878**	**23,699**	**25,939**	**15,051**	**10,888**	**21,388**	**10,935**	**10,453**	**5,250**	**2,892**	**2,358**
0—1 ..	*1,847*	930	917	1,840	930	9 0	7	..	7	..	.	..
1—2 ..	*1,331*	634	697	1,327	633	694	3	1	2	1	.	1
2—3 .	*1,495*	719	776	1,481	712	769	13	7	6	1	..	1
3—4 .	*1,536*	759	777	1,520	751	769	15	8	7	1	..	1
4—5 .	*1,514*	771	743	1,496	763	733	13	6	7	5	2	3
Total 0—5	*7,723*	*3,813*	*3,910*	*[illegible],661*	*3,[illegible]89*	*3,875*	*[illegible]1*	*22*	*29*	*8*	*2*	*6*
5—10 ..	*6,653*	3,507	3,[illegible]46	6,431	3,435	2,996	215	69	146	7	3	4
10—15 ..	*6,110*	3,306	2,804	5,507	3,137	2,370	593	164	429	10	5	5
15—20	*5,149*	2,859	2,290	2,700	1,957	743	2,368	852	1,516	81	50	31
20—30 .	*9,298*	5,125	4,173	2,302	1,871	431	6,392	3,000	3,592	404	254	150
30—40 ..	*6,958*	4,0[illegible]5	2,943	603	462	141	5,687	3,185	2,502	668	368	300
40—50 ..	*4,487*	2,890	[illegible],997	383	214	169	2,906	1,583	1,323	1,598	[illegible],093	505
50—60 ..	*2,916*	1,618	1,298	219	90	129	1,720	1,136	584	977	392	585
60 and over .	*2,883*	1,745	1,138	130	96	34	1,256	924	332	1,497	725	772
CHRISTIAN ..	**1,533**	**1,187**	**346**	**1,159**	**980**	**179**	**332**	**182**	**150**	**42**	**25**	**17**
0—1 ..	*29*	14	15	29	14	15	.	..	.	.	..	.
1—2 .	*25*	13	12	25	13	12	.	.	..	..	.	.
2—3 .	*26*	11	15	26	11	15	..	..	..	.	.	..
3—4 ..	*21*	8	13	21	8	13		.		.	..	..
4—5 ..	*20*	10	10	20	10	10	..		..	.	..	..
Total 0—5 .	*121*	*56*	*65*	*121*	*56*	*65*	..	..	.	..	.	.
5—10 .	*70*	34	36	69	34	35	1	..	1	..	..	..
10—15 .	*54*	25	29	53	25	28	1	.	1	..	..	..
15—20 ..	*237*	206	31	212	199	13	24	6	18	1	1	..
20—30 ..	*722*	643	79	609	584	25	109	56	53	4	3	1
30—40 .	*204*	142	62	77	68	9	120	72	48	7	2	5
40—50 ..	*70*	44	26	10	8	2	51	31	20	9	5	4
50—60 ..	*28*	18	10	4	3	1	17	12	5	7	3	4
60 and over ..	*27*	19	8	4	3	1	9	5	4	14	11	3
OTHERS .	**2,963**	**1,657**	**1,306**	**1,260**	**762**	**498**	**1,480**	**770**	**710**	**223**	**125**	**98**
0—1 ..	*122*	70	52	122	70	52	..	.	..	..	..	..
1—2 ..	*80*	40	40	79	40	39	1	..	1	..	..	..
2—3 .	*104*	56	48	101	53	48	3	3	..	..	.	..
3—4 ..	*98*	54	44	96	53	43	2	1	1	..	..	..
4—5 .	*89*	49	40	84	46	38	4	2	2	1	1	..
Total 0—5 .	*493*	*269*	*224*	*482*	*262*	*220*	*10*	*6*	*4*	*1*	*1*	..
5—10 ..	*381*	210	171	320	181	139	59	27	32	2	2	..
10—15 .	*360*	198	162	242	147	95	117	50	67	1	1	..
15—20 ..	*317*	173	144	92	76	16	220	94	126	5	3	2
20—30 ..	*544*	304	240	80	65	15	443	224	219	21	15	6
30—40 .	*381*	213	168	22	17	5	320	171	149	39	25	14
40—50 .	*226*	132	94	11	8	3	164	96	68	51	28	23
50—60 ..	*117*	66	51	6	5	1	75	46	29	36	15	21
60 and over ..	*141*	92	52	5	1	4	72	56	16	67	35	32

AND CIVIL CONDITION (BY RELIGION).

PART C.—DETAILS FOR CITIES AND SELECTED TOWNS.—*continued.*

FEROZEPORE TOWN.

Religion and Age.	Population.			Unmarried.			Married.			Widowed.		
	Persons.	Males.	Females.	Persons.	Males.	Females.	Persons.	Males.	Females.	Persons.	Males.	Females.
1	2	3	4	5	6	7	8	9	10	11	12	13
ALL RELIGIONS ..	**64,634**	**38,884**	**25,750**	**30,314**	**19,690**	**10,624**	**28,409**	**16,352**	**12,057**	**5,911**	**2,842**	**3,069**
0—1 ..	*1,968*	1,010	958	1,968	1,010	958	..	..	.	..	..	..
1—2 ..	*1,493*	779	714	1,493	779	714		..	..	..	..	..
2—3 ..	*1,655*	831	824	1,655	831	824	..	.	..	..	..	.
3—4 ..	*1,611*	814	797	1,611	814	797	..	..	..	..	..	..
4—5 ..	*1,506*	793	713	1,504	791	713	2	2	..	..	..	..
Total 0—5 ..	*8,233*	*4,227*	*4,006*	*8,231*	*4,225*	*4,006*	*2*	*2*	..	..	..	..
5—10 ..	*6,944*	3,704	3,240	6,758	3,646	3,112	184	56	128	2	2	.
10—15 ..	*6,739*	3,723	3,016	6,013	3,539	2,474	712	172	540	14	12	2
15—20 ..	*7,320*	4,586	2,734	3,718	3,096	622	3,471	1,399	2,072	131	91	40
20—30 ..	*14,721*	9,680	5,041	4,096	3,797	299	9,939	5,406	4,533	686	477	209
30—40 ..	*9,578*	6,239	3,339	963	898	65	7,421	4,674	2,747	1,194	667	527
40—50 ..	*5,761*	3,548	2,213	352	328	24	3,991	2,646	1,345	1,418	574	844
50—60 ..	*3,069*	1,844	1,225	121	105	16	1,727	1,252	475	1,221	487	734
60 and over ..	*2,269*	1,333	936	62	56	6	962	745	217	1,245	532	713
HINDU ..	**26,936**	**16,119**	**10,817**	**12,175**	**7,944**	**4,231**	**11,880**	**6,865**	**5,015**	**2,881**	**1,310**	**1,571**
0—1 ..	*803*	412	391	803	412	391	..	..	..	..	..	..
1—2 ..	*595*	319	276	595	319	276	..	..	..	..	..	..
2—3 ..	*668*	355	313	668	355	313	..	..	..	..	..	..
3—4 ..	*651*	343	308	651	343	308	..	..	..	..	.	..
4—5 ..	*626*	341	285	624	339	285	2	2	..	..	.	.
Total 0—5 ..	*3,343*	*1,770*	*1,573*	*3,341*	*1,768*	*1,573*	*2*	*2*	..	..	..	..
5—10 ..	*2,917*	1,588	1,329	2,846	1,565	1,281	70	22	48	1	1	..
10—15 ..	*2,857*	1,604	1,253	2,567	1,535	1,032	289	68	221	1	1	.
15—20 ..	*2,961*	1,825	1,136	1,446	1,202	244	1,456	584	872	59	39	20
20—30 ..	*5,963*	3,847	2,116	1,392	1,302	90	4,220	2,319	1,901	351	226	125
30—40 ..	*4,068*	2,637	1,431	364	354	10	3,109	1,985	1,124	595	298	297
40—50 ..	*2,540*	1,540	1,000	141	140	1	1,674	1,115	559	725	285	440
50—60 ..	*1,353*	786	567	46	46	..	700	501	199	607	239	368
60 and over ..	*934*	522	412	32	32	..	360	269	91	542	221	321
SIKH ..	**4,439**	**2,899**	**1,540**	**2,089**	**1,412**	**677**	**2,045**	**1,335**	**710**	**805**	**152**	**153**
0—1 ..	*120*	71	49	120	71	49	..	..	..	..	..	..
1—2 ..	*81*	46	35	81	46	35	..	..	..	..	..	..
2—3 ..	*93*	53	40	93	53	40	..	.	.	..	..	..
3—4 ..	*90*	51	39	90	51	39	..	..	.	..	.	..
4—5 ..	*82*	46	36	82	46	36	..	..	..	..	.	.
Total 0—5 ..	*466*	*267*	*199*	*466*	*267*	*199*	..	.	..	..	..	..
5—10 ..	*432*	221	211	422	217	205	10	4	6	..	..	..
10—15 ..	*449*	237	212	418	226	192	31	11	20		.	..
15—20 ..	*565*	394	171	305	249	56	255	141	114	5	4	1
20—30 ..	*1,118*	806	312	342	321	21	747	464	283	29	21	8
30—40 ..	*706*	514	192	95	91	4	550	383	167	61	40	21
40—50 ..	*366*	246	120	26	26	..	269	186	83	71	34	37
50—60 ..	*106*	132	64	10	10	..	122	98	24	64	24	40
60 and over ..	*141*	82	59	5	5	..	61	48	13	75	29	46
JAIN ..	**511**	**263**	**248**	**214**	**121**	**93**	**240**	**127**	**113**	**57**	**15**	**42**
0—1 ..	*17*	8	9	17	8	9	..	..	..	..	..	..
1—2 ..	*12*	7	5	12	7	5	..	.	..	..	..	..
2—3 ..	*17*	8	9	17	8	9	..	..	..	..	..	..
3—4 ..	*15*	8	7	15	8	7	..	..	..	.	..	..
4—5 ..	*12*	6	6	12	6	6	..	..	..	..	..	..
Total 0—5 ..	*73*	*37*	*36*	*73*	*37*	*36*	..	..	..	..	..	..
5—10 ..	*57*	27	30	56	27	29	1	..	1	..	..	..
10—15 ..	*55*	28	27	49	26	23	6	2	4	..	..	..
15—20 ..	*51*	30	21	20	17	3	31	13	18	..	..	..
20—30 ..	*112*	61	51	14	12	2	90	44	46	8	5	3
30—40 ..	*68*	35	33	2	2	..	57	32	25	9	1	8
40—50 ..	*55*	26	29	..	..	..	34	20	14	21	6	15
50—60 ..	*28*	15	13	..	..	..	16	12	4	12	3	9
60 and over ..	*12*	4	8	..	..	..	5	4	1	7	..	

PART C.—DETAILS FOR CITIES AND SELECTED TOWNS.

FEROZEPORE TOWN—(concld).

Religion and Age.	Population.			Unmarried.			Married.			Widowed.		
	Persons.	Males.	Females.	Persons.	Males.	Females.	Persons.	Males.	Females.	Persons.	Males.	Females.
1	2	3	4	5	6	7	8	9	10	11	12	13
MUSLIM ..	**28,464**	**16,760**	**11,704**	**13,384**	**8,374**	**5,010**	**12,649**	**7,158**	**5,491**	**2,431**	**1,228**	**1,203**
0—1 ..	906	458	448	906	458	448	..	..	..	..	..	..
1—2 ..	711	361	350	711	361	350	..	..	..	..	..	..
2—3 ..	777	370	407	777	370	407	..	..	..	..	..	..
3—4 ..	756	360	396	756	360	396	..	..	..	..	..	..
4—5 ..	701	350	351	701	350	351	..	..	..	..	..	..
Total 0—5 ..	*3,851*	*1,899*	*1,952*	*3,851*	*1,899*	*1,952*	..	..	..	..	..	..
5—10 ..	3,162	1,669	1,493	3,072	1,642	1,430	89	26	63	1	1	..
10—15 ..	3,028	1,669	1,359	2,674	1,580	1,094	341	78	263	13	11	2
15—20 ..	3,240	1,963	1,277	1,602	1,313	289	1,575	605	970	63	45	18
20—30 ..	6.172	3,910	2,262	1,550	1,394	156	4,351	2,313	2,038	271	203	68
30—40 ..	4,073	2,624	1,449	376	332	44	3,234	2,010	1,224	463	282	181
40—50 ..	2,489	1,531	958	171	148	23	1,768	1,161	607	550	222	328
50—60 ..	1,359	835	524	63	47	16	805	584	221	491	204	287
60 and over ..	1,090	660	430	25	19	6	486	381	105	579	260	319
CHRISTIAN ..	**2,942**	**2,040**	**902**	**1,925**	**1,505**	**420**	**920**	**477**	**443**	**97**	**58**	**39**
0—1 ..	73	37	36	73	37	36	..	..	..	..	..	..
1—2 ..	64	30	34	64	30	34	..	..	..	..	..	..
2—3 ..	68	31	37	68	31	37	..	..	..	..	..	..
3—4 ..	65	37	28	65	37	28	..	..	..	..	..	..
4—5 ..	53	33	20	53	33	20	..	..	..	..	..	..
Total 0—5 ..	*323*	*168*	*155*	*323*	*168*	*155*	..	..	..	..	..	..
5—10 ..	235	122	113	235	122	113	..	..	..	..	..	..
10—15 ..	201	99	102	196	99	97	5	..	5	..	..	..
15—20 ..	344	279	65	291	266	25	53	13	40	..	..	..
20—30 ..	1,062	861	201	745	720	25	309	135	174	8	6	2
30—40 ..	476	312	164	119	114	5	325	174	151	32	24	8
40—50 ..	183	122	61	14	14	..	152	99	53	17	9	8
50—60 ..	69	38	31	2	2	..	46	29	17	21	7	14
60 and over ..	49	39	10	..	..	..	30	27	3	19	12	7
OTHERS ..	**1,342**	**803**	**539**	**527**	**334**	**193**	**675**	**390**	**285**	**140**	**79**	**61**
0—1 ..	49	24	25	49	24	25	..	..	..	..	..	..
1—2 ..	30	16	14	30	16	14	..	..	..	..	..	..
2—3 ..	32	14	18	32	14	18	..	..	..	..	..	..
3—4 ..	34	15	19	34	15	19	..	..	..	..	..	..
4—5 ..	32	17	15	32	17	15	..	..	..	..	..	..
Total 0—5 ..	*177*	*86*	*91*	*177*	*86*	*91*	..	..	..	..	..	..
5—10 ..	141	77	64	127	73	54	14	4	10	..	..	..
10—15 ..	149	86	63	109	73	36	40	13	27	..	..	..
15—20 ..	159	95	64	54	49	5	101	43	58	4	3	1
20—30 ..	294	195	99	53	48	5	222	131	91	19	16	3
30—40 ..	187	117	70	7	5	2	146	90	56	34	22	12
40—50 ..	128	83	45	..	..	..	94	65	29	34	18	16
50—60 ..	64	38	26	..	..	..	38	28	10	26	10	16
60 and over ..	43	26	17	..	..	..	20	16	4	23	10	13

AND CIVIL CONDITION (BY RELIGION).

PART C.—DETAILS FOR CITIES AND SELECTED TOWNS.—*continued.*

LUDHIANA TOWN.

Religion and Age.	Population.			Unmarried.			Married.			Widowed.		
	Persons.	Males.	Females.	Persons.	Males.	Females.	Persons.	Males.	Females.	Persons.	Males.	Females.
1	2	3	4	5	6	7	8	9	10	11	12	13
ALL RELIGIONS ..	**68,586**	**40,032**	**28,554**	**33,584**	**20,889**	**12,695**	**28,612**	**15,812**	**12,800**	**6,390**	**3,331**	**3,059**
0—1 ..	*2,122*	1,125	997	2,120	1,123	997	2	2	..	..	..	..
1—2 ..	*1,701*	860	841	1,696	836	840	5	4	1	..	..	..
2—3 ..	*1,768*	889	879	1,757	883	874	10	6	4	1	..	1
3—4 ..	*1,723*	883	840	1,706	877	829	16	6	10	1	..	1
4—5 ..	*1,678*	889	789	1,645	877	768	32	12	20	1	..	1
Total 0—5 ..	*8,992*	*4,646*	*4,346*	*8,924*	*4,616*	*4,308*	*65*	*30*	*35*	*3*	..	*3*
5—10 ..	*8,049*	4,376	3,673	7,687	4,245	3,442	353	127	226	9	4	5
10—15 ..	*7,970*	4,516	3,454	7,062	4,200	2,862	892	304	588	16	12	4
15—20 ..	*7,572*	4,511	3,061	4,053	3,039	1,014	3,455	1,426	2,029	64	46	18
20—30 ..	*13,556*	8,153	5,403	3,777	3,107	670	9,289	4,666	4,623	490	380	110
30—40 ..	*9,504*	5,890	3,614	1,120	921	199	7,238	4,302	2,936	1,146	667	479
40—50 ..	*6,211*	3,918	2,293	463	377	86	4,153	2,768	1,385	1,595	773	822
50—60 ..	*3,567*	2,172	1,395	173	132	41	1,971	1,379	592	1,423	661	762
60 and over ..	*3,165*	1,830	1,315	325	252	73	1,196	810	386	1,644	788	856
HINDU ..	**20,364**	**12,200**	**8,164**	**10,043**	**6,668**	**3,375**	**8,219**	**4,592**	**3,627**	**2,102**	**940**	**1,162**
0—1 ..	*572*	301	271	571	300	271	1	1	..	..	..	..
1—2 ..	*464*	236	228	462	235	227	2	1	1	..	..	..
2—3 ..	*468*	232	236	463	231	232	4	1	3	1	..	1
3—4 ..	*474*	245	229	467	245	222	6	..	6	1	..	1
4—5 ..	*479*	257	222	468	256	212	10	1	9	1	..	1
Total 0—5 ..	*2,457*	*1,271*	*1,186*	*2,431*	*1,267*	*1,164*	*23*	*4*	*19*	*3*	.	*3*
5—10 ..	*2,385*	1,397	988	2,293	1,362	931	87	35	52	5	..	5
10—15 ..	*2,386*	1,493	893	2,187	1,410	777	194	82	112	5	1	4
15—20 ..	*2,228*	1,449	779	1,273	1,022	251	936	424	512	19	3	16
20—30 ..	*4,051*	2,470	1,581	1,132	994	138	2,713	1,362	1,351	206	114	92
30—40 ..	*2,875*	1,732	1,143	315	271	44	2,142	1,263	879	418	198	220
40—50 ..	*1,814*	1,157	657	123	105	18	1,136	815	321	555	237	318
50—60 ..	*1,086*	665	421	70	60	10	573	413	160	443	192	251
60 and over ..	*1,082*	566	516	219	177	42	415	194	221	448	195	253
SIKH ..	**3,445**	**2,321**	**1,124**	**1,544**	**1,055**	**489**	**1,611**	**1,084**	**527**	**290**	**182**	**108**
0—1 ..	*86*	47	39	85	46	39	1	1	..	..	..	..
1—2 ..	*65*	33	32	64	32	32	1	1	..	..	..	..
2—3 ..	*64*	36	28	62	35	27	2	1	1	..	..	..
3—4 ..	*59*	35	24	59	35	24	..	..	..	..	..	..
4—5 ..	*57*	32	25	56	31	25	1	1	..	..	..	..
Total 0—5 ..	*331*	*183*	*148*	*326*	*179*	*147*	*5*	*4*	*1*	..	..	..
5—10 ..	*282*	158	124	261	149	112	20	8	12	1	1	..
10—15 ..	*351*	220	131	289	185	104	59	32	27	3	3	..
15—20 ..	*501*	359	142	260	203	57	235	151	84	6	5	1
20—30 ..	*795*	557	238	236	200	36	524	332	192	35	25	10
30—40 ..	*496*	350	146	76	62	14	364	253	111	56	35	21
40—50 ..	*348*	262	86	49	40	9	235	183	52	64	39	25
50—60 ..	*193*	137	56	18	14	4	117	86	31	58	37	21
60 and over ..	*148*	95	53	29	23	6	52	35	17	67	37	30
JAIN ..	**344**	**172**	**172**	**165**	**91**	**74**	**134**	**69**	**65**	**45**	**12**	**33**
0—1 ..	*12*	7	5	12	7	5	..	..	..	..	..	..
1—2 ..	*11*	6	5	11	6	5	..	..	..	..	..	..
2—3 ..	*10*	4	6	10	4	6	..	..	..	..	..	..
3—4 ..	*7*	3	4	7	3	4	..	..	..	..	..	..
4—5 ..	*8*	5	3	8	5	3	..	..	..	..	..	..
Total 0—5 ..	*48*	*25*	*23*	*48*	*25*	*23*	..	..	..	..	..	..
5—10 ..	*40*	19	21	39	19	20	1	..	1	..	..	..
10—15 ..	*41*	16	25	37	15	22	4	1	3	..	..	..
15—20 ..	*35*	18	17	17	10	7	18	8	10	..	..	..
20—30 ..	*59*	34	25	11	11	..	44	22	22	4	1	3
30—40 ..	*44*	21	23	7	6	1	29	13	16	8	2	6
40—50 ..	*44*	21	23	3	2	1	27	16	11	14	3	11
50—60 ..	*21*	11	10	2	2	..	9	7	2	10	2	8
60 and over ..	*12*	7	5	1	1	..	2	2	..	9	4	5

TABLE VII.—AGE, SEX

PART C.—DETAILS FOR CITIES AND SELECTED TOWNS

LUDHIANA TOWN—(concld).

Religion and Age.	Population.			Unmarried.			Married.			Widowed.		
	Persons.	Males.	Females.	Persons.	Males.	Females.	Persons.	Males.	Females.	Persons.	Males.	Females.
1	2	3	4	5	6	7	8	9	10	11	12	13
MUSLIM ..	**42,981**	**24,704**	**18,277**	**20,883**	**12,696**	**8,187**	**18,272**	**9,881**	**8,391**	**3,826**	**2,127**	**1,699**
0—1 ..	*1,419*	752	667	1,419	752	667	..	..	..	..	..	.
1—2 ..	*1,131*	568	563	1,129	566	563	2	2	..	..	..	.
2—3 ..	*1,195*	600	595	1,192	597	595	3	3	..	..	.	
3—4 ..	*1,159*	589	570	1,149	583	566	10	6	4	.	..	.
4—5 ..	*1,105*	579	526	1,085	569	516	20	10	10	..	..	..
Total 0—5 ..	*6,009*	*3,088*	*2,921*	*5,974*	*3,067*	*2,907*	*35*	*21*	*14*	..	..	.
5—10 ..	*5,209*	2,716	2,493	4,971	2,633	2,338	235	80	155	3	3	.
10—15 ..	*5,050*	2,699	2,351	4,432	2,507	1,925	611	185	426	7	7	.
15—20 ..	*4,558*	2,626	1,932	2,302	1,755	547	2,220	835	1,385	36	36	.
20—30 ..	*8,275*	4,982	3,293	2,138	1,850	288	5,905	2,900	3,005	232	232	.
30—40 ..	*5,908*	3,698	2,210	655	557	98	4,010	2,719	1,291	643	422	221
40—50 ..	*3,898*	2,420	1,478	268	223	45	2,695	1,717	978	935	480	45[illegible]
50—60 ..	*2,196*	1,320	876	76	56	20	1,242	853	389	878	41	467
60 and over ..	*1,878*	1,155	723	67	48	19	719	571	148	1,092	536	556
CHRISTIAN ..	**1,049**	**386**	**663**	**795**	**273**	**522**	**195**	**93**	**102**	**59**	**20**	**39**
0—1 ..	*24*	12	12	24	12	12	..	..	..	..	..	.
1—2 ..	*23*	13	10	23	13	10	..	..	..	..	.	.
2—3 ..	*17*	9	8	17	9	8	.	..	..	..	.	.
3—4 ..	*14*	7	7	14	7	7	.	..	.	..	.	..
4—5 ..	*18*	10	8	18	10	8	..	..	.	..	..	.
Total 0—5 ..	*96*	*51*	*45*	*96*	*51*	*45*	..	..	..	..	..	..
5—10 ..	*86*	57	29	84	56	28	2	1	1	..	..	..
10—15 ..	*96*	61	35	84	60	24	12	1	11	..	..	
15—20 ..	*219*	46	173	189	40	149	28	5	23	2	1	1
20—30 ..	*307*	68	239	246	38	208	53	26	27	8	4	4
30—40 ..	*116*	48	68	64	22	42	38	21	17	14	5	9
40—50 ..	*65*	28	37	17	4	13	35	18	17	13	6	7
50—60 ..	*41*	19	22	7	..	7	21	15	6	13	4	9
60 and over ..	*23*	8	15	8	2	6	6	6	..	9	..	9
OTHERS ..	**403**	**249**	**154**	**154**	**106**	**48**	**181**	**93**	**88**	**68**	**50**	**18**
0—1 ..	*9*	6	3	9	6	3	..	..	..	..	..	..
1—2 ..	*7*	4	3	7	4	3	..	..	.	..	..	..
2—3 ..	*14*	8	6	13	7	6	1	1	..	..	..	..
3—4 ..	*10*	4	6	10	4	6	..	..	..	..	.	..
4—5 ..	*11*	6	5	10	6	4	1	..	1	..	..	..
Total 0—5 ..	*51*	*28*	*23*	*49*	*27*	*22*	*2*	*1*	*1*	..	..	..
5—10 ..	*47*	29	18	39	26	13	8	3	5	..	..	..
10—15 ..	*46*	27	19	33	23	10	12	3	9	1	1	..
15—20 ..	*31*	13	18	12	9	3	18	3	15	1	1	..
20—30 ..	*69*	42	27	14	14	..	50	24	26	5	4	1
30—40 ..	*65*	41	24	3	3	..	55	33	22	7	5	2
40—50 ..	*42*	30	12	3	3	..	25	19	6	14	8	6
50—60 ..	*30*	20	10	..	..	..	9	5	4	21	15	6
60 and over ..	*22*	19	3	1	1	..	2	2	..	19	16	3

AND CIVIL CONDITION (BY RELIGION).

PART C.—DETAILS FOR CITIES AND SELECTED TOWNS.—*continued.*

LYALLPUR TOWN.

Religion and Age.	Population.			Unmarried			Married.			Widowed.		
	Persons.	Males.	Females.	Persons.	Males.	Females.	Persons.	Males.	Females.	Persons.	Males.	Females.
1	2	3	4	5	6	7	8	9	10	11	12	13
ALL RELIGIONS ..	**42,922**	**27,489**	**15,433**	**20,643**	**13,611**	**7,032**	**20,051**	**12,797**	**7,254**	**2,228**	**1,081**	**1,147**
0—1 ..	*1,249*	616	633	1,249	616	633	..	..	..	..	..	..
1—2 ..	*996*	497	499	996	497	499	..	..	..	..	..	..
2—3 ..	*1,169*	592	577	1,167	590	577	2	2	..	..	..	
3—4 ..	*1,115*	571	544	1,115	571	544	..	..	..	..	..	
4—5 ..	*1,016*	530	486	1,009	526	483	7	4	3	..		
Total 0—5 ..	*5,545*	*2,806*	*2,739*	*5,536*	*2,800*	*2,736*	*9*	*6*	*3*	..	..	..
5—10 ..	*4,586*	2,508	2,078	4,521	2,483	2,038	63	23	40	2	2	
10—15 ..	*4,524*	2,659	1,865	4,175	2,561	1,614	344	94	250	5	4	1
15—20 ..	*5,300*	3,583	1,717	2,974	2,551	423	2,280	1,005	1,275	46	27	19
20—30 ..	*10,554*	7,392	3,162	2,840	2,662	178	7,384	4,497	2,887	330	233	97
30—40 ..	*6,301*	4,431	1,870	420	391	29	5,434	3,778	1,656	447	262	185
40—50 ..	*3,548*	2,445	1,103	106	97	9	2,947	2,155	792	495	193	302
50—60 ..	*1,635*	1,099	536	45	43	2	1,139	878	261	451	178	273
60 and over ..	*929*	566	363	26	23	3	451	361	90	452	182	270
HINDU ..	**19,992**	**12,880**	**7,112**	**10,016**	**6,778**	**3,238**	**8,862**	**5,582**	**3,280**	**1,114**	**520**	**594**
0—1 ..	*543*	267	276	543	267	276		..	..	..	..	
1—2 ..	*434*	225	209	434	225	209	..	..	..	..	..	..
2—3 ..	*531*	274	257	530	273	257	1	1	..	..		
3—4 ..	*517*	264	253	517	264	253	..	..	..	..	..	..
4—5 ..	*474*	242	232	470	240	230	4	2	2	..	..	..
Total 0—5 ..	*2,499*	*1,272*	*1,227*	*2,494*	*1,269*	*1,225*	*5*	*3*	*2*	..	..	..
5—10 ..	*2,140*	1,151	989	2,112	1,140	972	28	11	17	..	..	..
10—15 ..	*2,129*	1,244	885	1,979	1,202	777	149	41	108	1	1	..
15—20 ..	*2,488*	1,712	776	1,441	1,250	191	1,029	452	577	18	10	8
20—30 ..	*5,081*	3,642	1,439	1,559	1,494	65	3,379	2,063	1,316	143	85	58
30—40 ..	*2,952*	2,087	865	305	297	8	2,412	1,662	750	235	128	107
40—50 ..	*1,533*	1,020	513	78	78	..	1,175	825	350	280	117	163
50—60 ..	*758*	499	259	31	31	..	479	359	120	248	109	139
60 and over ..	*412*	253	159	17	17	..	206	166	40	189	70	119
SIKH ..	**5,181**	**3,243**	**1,938**	**2,561**	**1,672**	**889**	**2,363**	**1,451**	**912**	**257**	**120**	**187**
0—1 ..	*176*	85	91	176	85	91	..	..	..	..	..	..
1—2 ..	*121*	58	63	121	58	63	..	..	..	..	..	..
2—3 ..	*141*	73	68	141	73	68	..	..	..	..	..	..
3—4 ..	*136*	69	67	136	69	67	..		..	..	..	
4—5 ..	*122*	63	59	120	62	58	2	1	1		..	..
Total 0—5 ..	*696*	*348*	*348*	*694*	*347*	*347*	*2*	*1*	*1*	..	..	..
5—10 ..	*562*	299	263	559	299	260	3	..	3	..	..	..
10—15 ..	*552*	311	241	517	303	214	35	8	27	..	..	..
15—20 ..	*654*	437	217	356	302	54	291	131	160	7	4	3
20—30 ..	*1,282*	873	409	346	332	14	903	523	380	33	18	15
30—40 ..	*717*	496	221	61	61	..	613	413	200	43	22	21
40—50 ..	*391*	263	128	14	14	..	324	226	98	53	23	30
50—60 ..	*205*	137	68	9	9		137	106	31	59	22	37
60 and over ..	*122*	79	43	5	5	..	35	43	12	62	31	31
JAIN ..	**65**	**47**	**18**	**42**	**30**	**12**	**19**	**14**	**5**	**4**	**3**	**1**
0—1 ..	*4*	2	2	4	2	2	..	..	..	..	..	..
1—2 ..	*2*	1	1	2	1	1	..	..	..	..	..	..
2—3 ..	*2*	2	..	2	2	..	..	..	..	..	..	..
3—4 ..	*3*	3	..	3	3	..		..	..	..	..	..
4—5 ..	*4*	3	1	4	3	1	..	..	..	..		..
Total 0—5 ..	*15*	*11*	*4*	*15*	*11*	*4*	..	..	..	..	..	..
5—10 ..	*9*	8	1	9	8	1	..	..	..	..	..	..
10—15 ..	*6*	5	1	6	5	1	..	..	..	..	..	..
15—20 ..	*6*	3	3	5	2	3	1	1	..	..	..	..
20—30 ..	*11*	6	5	5	2	3	6	4	2	..	..	..
30—40 ..	*8*	6	2	1	1	..	6	4	2	1	1	..
40—50 ..	*7*	5	2	..	..	..	5	4	1	2	1	1
50—60 ..	*3*	3	..	1	1	..	1	1	..	1	1	..
60 and over ..	..	..	..	..	..	..	..	..	..	..	..	..

TABLE VII.—AGE, SEX

PART C.—DETAILS FOR CITIES AND SELECTED TOWNS.

LYALLPUR TOWN—(*concld*).

Religion and Age.	Population.			Unmarried.			Married.			Widowed.		
	Persons.	Males.	Females.	Persons.	Males.	Females.	Persons.	Males.	Females.	Persons.	Males.	Females.
1	2	3	4	5	6	7	8	9	10	11	12	13
MUSLIM ..	**15,534**	**10,115**	**5,419**	**6,910**	**4,481**	**2,429**	**7,906**	**5,273**	**2,633**	**718**	**361**	**357**
0—1 ..	*433*	209	224	433	209	224	..	..	..	..	..	..
1—2 ..	*378*	182	196	378	182	196	..	..	..	..	..	..
2—3 ..	*427*	209	218	426	208	218	1	1	..	..	..	..
3—4 ..	*395*	202	193	395	202	193	..	..	..	..	..	..
4—5 ..	*351*	189	162	350	188	162	1	1	..	..	..	..
Total 0—5 ..	*1,984*	*991*	*993*	*1,982*	*980*	*993*	*2*	*2*	..	..	..	..
5—10 ..	*1,598*	912	686	1,568	898	670	28	12	16	2	2	..
10—15 ..	*1,588*	972	616	1,444	928	516	141	42	99	3	2	1
15—20 ..	*1,929*	1,308	621	1,057	911	146	855	386	469	17	11	6
20—30 ..	*3,703*	2,599	1,104	816	740	76	2,750	1,741	1,009	137	118	19
30—40 ..	*2,335*	1,658	677	28	11	17	2,160	1,551	609	147	96	51
40—50 ..	*1,466*	1,065	401	8	2	6	1,326	1,025	301	132	38	94
50—60 ..	*595*	411	184	3	1	2	473	376	97	119	34	85
60 and over ..	*336*	199	137	4	1	3	171	138	33	161	60	101
CHRISTIAN ..	**1,988**	**1,102**	**886**	**1,056**	**618**	**438**	**812**	**418**	**394**	**120**	**66**	**54**
0—1 ..	*84*	48	36	84	48	36	..	..	..	..	..	..
1—2 ..	*53*	29	24	53	29	24	..	..	..	..	..	..
2—3 ..	*63*	33	30	63	33	30	..	..	..	..	..	..
3—4 ..	*63*	32	31	63	32	31	..	..	..	..	..	..
4—5 ..	*61*	30	31	61	30	31	..	..	..	..	..	..
Total 0—5 ..	*324*	*172*	*152*	*324*	*172*	*152*	..	..	..	..	..	..
5—10 ..	*266*	132	134	262	132	130	4	..	4	..	..	..
10—15 ..	*237*	121	116	221	120	101	16	1	15	..	..	..
15—20 ..	*208*	112	96	111	82	29	93	28	65	4	2	2
20—30 ..	*433*	244	189	107	88	19	312	146	166	14	10	4
30—40 ..	*265*	167	98	24	20	4	223	134	89	18	13	5
40—50 ..	*137*	83	54	6	3	3	106	68	38	25	12	13
50—60 ..	*66*	42	24	1	1	..	42	30	12	23	11	12
60 and over ..	*52*	29	23	..	..	..	16	11	5	36	18	18
OTHERS ..	**162**	**102**	**60**	**58**	**32**	**26**	**89**	**59**	**30**	**15**	**11**	**4**
0—1 ..	*9*	5	4	9	5	4	..	..	..	..	..	..
1—2 ..	*8*	2	6	8	2	6	..	..	..	..	..	..
2—3 ..	*5*	1	4	5	1	4	..	..	..	..	..	..
3—4 ..	*1*	1	..	1	1	..	..	..	..	..	..	..
4—5 ..	*4*	3	1	4	3	1	..	..	..	..	..	..
Total 0—5 ..	*27*	*12*	*15*	*27*	*12*	*15*	..	..	..	..	..	..
5—10 ..	*11*	6	5	11	6	5	..	..	..	..	..	..
10—15 ..	*12*	6	6	8	3	5	3	2	1	1	1	..
15—20 ..	*15*	11	4	4	4	..	11	7	4	..	..	..
20—30 ..	*44*	28	16	7	6	1	34	20	14	3	2	1
30—40 ..	*24*	17	7	1	1	..	20	14	6	3	2	1
40—50 ..	*14*	9	5	..	..	..	11	7	4	3	2	1
50—60 ..	*8*	7	1	..	..	..	7	6	1	1	1	..
60 and over ..	*7*	6	1	..	..	..	3	3	..	4	3	1

AND CIVIL CONDITION (BY RELIGION).

PART C.—DETAILS FOR CITIES AND SELECTED TOWNS.—*continued.*

SARGODHA TOWN.

Religion and Age.	Population.			Unmarried.			Married.			Widowed.		
	Persons.	Males.	Females.	Persons.	Males.	Females.	Persons.	Males.	Females.	Persons.	Males.	Females.
1	2	3	4	5	6	7	8	9	10	11	12	13
ALL RELIGIONS ..	**26,761**	**16,498**	**10,263**	**13,358**	**8,625**	**4,733**	**11,726**	**7,065**	**4,661**	**1,677**	**808**	**869**
0—1 ..	*906*	464	442	905	463	442	1	1	..	..	..	..
1—2 ..	*610*	320	290	609	320	289	1	..	1	..	..	..
2—3 ..	*759*	394	365	754	392	362	5	2	3	..	..	..
3—4 ..	*772*	402	370	769	401	368	3	1	2	..	..	
4—5 ..	*749*	392	357	744	391	353	4	1	3	1	..	1
Total 0—5 ..	*3,796*	*1,972*	*1,824*	*3,781*	*1,967*	*1,814*	*14*	*5*	*9*	*1*	..	*1*
5—10 ..	*3,167*	1,720	1,447	3,082	1,695	1,387	80	24	56	5	1	4
10—15 ..	*2,996*	1,750	1,246	2,725	1,670	1,055	263	77	186	8	3	5
15—20 ..	*2,943*	1,891	1,052	1,620	1,356	264	1,283	512	771	40	23	17
20—30 ..	*5,946*	3,880	2,066	1,584	1,458	126	4,146	2,279	1,867	216	143	73
30—40 ..	*4,034*	2,710	1,324	352	303	49	3,311	2,203	1,108	371	204	167
40—50 ..	*2,277*	1,525	752	135	100	26	1,700	1,224	476	442	192	250
50—60 ..	*1,060*	719	341	51	45	6	672	531	141	337	143	194
60 and over ..	*542*	331	211	28	22	6	257	210	47	257	99	158
HINDU ..	**11,674**	**7,021**	**4,653**	**5,742**	**3,659**	**2,083**	**5,102**	**2,983**	**2,119**	**830**	**379**	**451**
0—1 ..	*393*	202	191	392	201	191	1	1	..	..	..	..
1—2 ..	*279*	141	138	279	141	138	..	..	..	..	..	..
2—3 ..	*332*	161	171	330	159	171	2	2	..	..	..	..
3—4 ..	*326*	162	164	325	161	164	1	1	..	..	..	..
4—5 ..	*303*	158	145	300	158	142	2	..	2	1	..	1
Total 0—5 ..	*1,633*	*824*	*809*	*1,626*	*820*	*806*	*6*	*4*	*2*	*1*	..	*1*
5—10 ..	*1,404*	762	642	1,345	743	6 2	35	18	37	4	1	3
10—15 ..	*1,375*	790	585	1,220	741	479	150	47	103	5	2	3
15—20 ..	*1,294*	811	483	678	562	116	594	236	358	22	13	9
20—30 ..	*2,543*	1,621	922	642	597	45	1,797	958	839	104	66	38
30—40 ..	*1,719*	1,120	599	133	117	16	1,396	908	488	190	95	95
40—50 ..	*1,003*	649	354	61	48	13	724	510	214	218	91	127
50—60 ..	*471*	309	162	20	18	2	281	224	57	170	67	103
60 and over ..	*232*	135	97	17	13	4	99	78	21	116	44	72
SIKH ..	**5,201**	**3,333**	**1,868**	**2,669**	**1,804**	**865**	**2,231**	**1,398**	**833**	**301**	**131**	**170**
0—1 ..	*176*	92	84	176	92	84	..	..	..	..	..	..
1—2 ..	*106*	62	44	105	62	43	1	..	1	..	..	..
2—3 ..	*138*	75	63	135	75	60	3	..	3	..	..	..
3—4 ..	*148*	82	66	146	82	64	2	..	2	..	..	..
4—5 ..	*153*	87	66	152	86	66	1	1	..	..	..	..
Total 0—5 ..	*721*	*398*	*323*	*714*	*397*	*317*	*7*	*1*	*6*	..	..	..
5—10 ..	*630*	367	263	621	363	258	9	4	5	..	..	..
10—15 ..	*618*	396	222	576	382	194	41	14	27	1	..	1
15—20 ..	*596*	414	182	348	303	45	242	108	134	6	3	3
20—30 ..	*1,124*	756	368	290	260	30	791	469	322	43	27	16
30—40 ..	*740*	484	256	75	61	14	605	395	210	60	28	32
40—50 ..	*435*	298	137	26	20	6	336	250	86	73	28	45
50—60 ..	*212*	147	65	14	13	1	142	110	32	56	24	32
60 and over ..	*125*	73	52	5	5	..	58	47	11	62	21	41
JAIN ..	**1**	**1**	..	..	..	..	**1**	**1**	..	..	..	..
0—1 ..	..	..	..	..	..	..	..	..	..	..	..	..
1—2 ..	..	..	..	..	..	..	..	..	..	..	..	..
2—3 ..	..	..	..	..	..	..	..	..	..	..	..	..
3—4 ..	..	..	..	..	..	..	..	..	..	..	..	..
4—5 ..	..	..	..	..	..	..	..	..	..	..	..	..
Total 0—5 ..	..	..	..	..	..	..	..	..	..	..	..	..
5—10 ..	..	..	..	..	..	..	..	..	..	..	..	..
10—15 ..	..	..	..	..	..	..	..	..	..	..	..	..
15—20 ..	..	..	..	..	..	..	..	..	..	..	..	..
20—30 ..	..	..	..	..	..	..	..	..	..	..	..	..
30—40 ..	..	..	..	..	..	..	..	..	..	..	..	..
40—50 ..	*1*	1	..	..	..	..	1	1	..	..	..	..
50—60 ..	..	..	..	..	..	..	..	..	..	..	..	..
60 and over ..	..	..	..	..	..	..	..	..	..	..	..	..

TABLE VII.—AGE, SEX AND CIVIL CONDITION (BY RELIGION).

PART C.—DETAILS FOR CITIES AND SELECTED TOWNS.—*concluded.*

SARGODHA TOWN—(*concld*).

Religion and Age.	Population.			Unmarried.			Married.			Widowed.		
	Persons.	Males.	Females.	Persons.	Males.	Females.	Persons.	Males.	Females.	Persons.	Males.	Females.
1	2	3	4	5	6	7	8	9	10	11	12	13
MUSLIM ..	**9,146**	**5,786**	**3,360**	**4,512**	**2,962**	**1,550**	**4,125**	**2,547**	**1,578**	**509**	**277**	**232**
0—1 ..	*307*	154	153	307	154	153	..	..	..	..	.	..
1—2 .	*202*	105	97	202	105	97	..	..	..	..	..	..
2—3 ..	*261*	145	116	261	145	116	..	..	..	.	..	..
3—4 ..	*278*	150	128	278	150	128	..	..	..	..	..	..
4—5 ..	*270*	138	132	269	138	131	1	..	1	..	..	..
Total 0—5 ..	*1,318*	*692*	*626*	*1,317*	*692*	*625*	*1*	..	*1*	..	..	..
5—10 .	*1,021*	550	71	1,005	548	457	15	2	13	1	..	1
10—15 ..	*895*	523	372	827	507	320	66	15	51	2	1	1
15—20 ..	*974*	628	346	550	465	85	412	156	256	12	7	5
20—30 ..	*2,138*	1,426	712	614	574	10	1,458	804	654	66	48	18
30—40 ..	*1,482*	1,051	431	133	120	13	1,239	859	380	110	72	38
40—50 ..	*798*	556	242	44	38	6	609	448	161	145	70	75
50—60 ..	*351*	245	106	17	14	3	231	183	48	103	48	55
60 and over ..	*169*	115	54	5	4	1	94	80	14	70	31	39
CHRISTIAN ..	**704**	**341**	**363**	**407**	**185**	**222**	**260**	**135**	**125**	**37**	**21**	**16**
0—1 ..	*27*	14	13	27	14	13	..	..	..	..	..	..
1—2 ..	*22*	11	11	22	11	11	..	..	..	..	..	..
2—3 ..	*26*	12	14	26	12	14	..	..	..	..	..	..
3—4 ..	*18*	8	10	18	8	10	..	.	..	..	..	..
4—5 .	*19*	7	12	19	7	12	.	..	..	..	..	..
Total 0—5 ..	*112*	*52*	*60*	*112*	*52*	*60*	..	..	..	..	..	..
5—10 ..	*102*	37	65	102	37	65	..	..	..	..	..	..
10—15 ..	*100*	37	63	96	36	60	4	1	3	..	..	..
15—20 ..	*75*	36	39	43	25	18	32	11	21	..	..	..
20—30 ..	*140*	77	63	38	27	11	99	48	51	3	2	1
30—40 ..	*93*	55	38	11	5	6	71	41	30	11	9	2
40—50 ..	*40*	21	19	4	3	1	30	15	15	6	3	3
50—60 ..	*26*	18	8	..	..	..	18	14	4	8	4	4
60 and over ..	*16*	8	8	1	..	1	6	5	1	9	3	6
OTHERS ..	**35**	**16**	**19**	**28**	**15**	**13**	**7**	**1**	**6**	..	..	..
0—1 ..	*3*	2	1	3	2	1	..	..	..	..	..	..
1—2 ..	*1*	1	..	1	1	..	..	..	..	..	..	..
2—3 ..	*2*	1	1	2	1	1	..	..	..	..	..	..
3—4 ..	*2*	..	2	2	..	2	..	..	..	..	..	..
4—5 ..	*4*	2	2	4	2	2	..	..	..	..	..	..
Total 0—5 ..	*12*	*6*	*6*	*12*	*6*	*6*	..	..	..	..	..	..
5—10 ..	*10*	4	6	9	4	5	1	..	1	..	..	..
10—15 ..	*8*	4	4	6	4	2	2	..	2	..	..	..
15—20 ..	*4*	2	2	1	1	..	3	1	2	..	..	..
20—30 ..	*1*	..	1	..	..	..	1	..	1	..	..	..
30—40 ..	..	..	..	..	..	.	..	..	..	..	..	..
40—50 ..	..	..	..	..	..	..	.	..	..	..	..	..
50—60 ..	..	..	..	..	..	..	..	..	..	..	..	..
60 and over ..	..	..	..	..	..	..	..	..	..	..	..	..

TABLE VIII.

CIVIL CONDITION BY AGE FOR SELECTED CASTES AND TRIBES.

1. The castes selected for this Table are those which contributed at least 8 *per mille* to the total population of the Punjab in 1921, the criminal tribes, Bawaria, Harni, Pakhiwara and Sansi, being also included.

2. For the purposes of this Table, the Punjab has been split up into four main divisions, *viz* :—

A.—Eastern Punjab, including the Ambala Division except Simla District and the States of Loharu, Dujana, Pataudi, Kalsia and Sirmoor.

B.—Central Punjab, Hills, including the Simla and Kangra Districts, the Simla Hill States and the States of Bilaspur, Mandi, Suket and Chamba.

C.—Central Punjab, Plains, including the Jullundur Division except Kangra District, Lahore Division, the Gujrat, Lyallpur and Jhang Districts, the Phulkian States, and the States of Kapurthala, Faridkot and Maler Kotla.

D.—Western Punjab, including the remaining Districts in the Rawalpindi and Multan Divisions and the State of Bahawalpur ;

and these are referred to as A, B, C and D in column 2 of the Table.

3. The figures for some localities and religions, not shown in 1921 (Table IX), are now shown when so warranted by the numerical strength.

4. In this Table, figures for Arya (Vedic Dharm), Brahmo and Dev-Dharm, are included in those for Hindus, but to illustrate the civil condition of those classes, separate figures have been printed as Table VIII-A in Part III of the Report.

TABLE VIII.—CIVIL CONDITION

Serial No.	Caste or Tribe. 1	Locality. 2	Sex. 3	Population dealt with. 4	Unmarried. Total. 5	0—6 6	7—13 7	14—16 8	17—23 9	24—43 10	44 and over. 11
1	AGGARWAL (Hindu)	A. C.	Males	187,699	101,377	33,551	30,186	10,521	11,153	11,848	4,118
2			Females	159,421	63,533	32,449	25,171	4,475	1,030	303	1[illegible]5
3	AGGARWAL (Jain)	A. C.	Males	12,683	6,386	2,322	2,065	747	583	524	14
4			Females	11,538	4,679	2,311	1,887	371	68	33	9
5	AHIR (Hindu)	A. C.	Males	120,103	62,512	22,787	20,632	6,917	5,970	4,770	1,436
6			Females	97,409	38,356	21,493	14,962	1,619	213	54	15
7	AHIR (Muslim)	D.	Males	1,248	685	236	202	59	111	68	9
8			Females	1,060	510	219	171	53	28	32	7
9	ARAIN (Muslim)	A. C. D.	Males	725,840	398,778	147,894	127,663	42,485	43,475	30,251	7,010
10			Females	602,254	271,505	139,746	100,541	18,091	8,191	3,521	1,415
11	ARORA (Hindu)	C. D.	Males	352,791	192,349	67,577	58,662	21,032	24,902	16,871	3,305
12			Females	306,057	132,819	66,454	51,062	9,010	3,339	2,477	477
13	ARORA (Sikh)	C. D.	Males	59,934	33,435	12,270	10,625	3,625	3,880	2,261	77[illegible]
14			Females	50,779	23,031	11,594	8,835	1,703	546	272	81
15	AWAN (Muslim)	C. D.	Males	287,897	160,638	59,544	49,754	17,592	18,863	13,241	1,644
16			Females	250,858	110,369	55,267	40,680	7,727	3,666	2,462	567
17	BAWARIA (Hindu)	A. C. D.	Males	8,420	4,619	1,989	1,497	460	434	203	36
18			Females	[illegible],625	3,540	1,887	1,328	225	62	29	9
19	BAWARIA (Sikh)	C. D.	Males	8,192	4,329	1,675	1,441	406	422	335	50
20			Females	7,066	3,854	1,853	1,420	432	95	37	17
21	BILOCH (Muslim)	A. C. D.	Males	341,543	190,470	70,303	59,055	19,263	23,201	17,126	1,432
22			Females	283,148	120,407	64,951	42,926	6,765	3,593	1,798	37[illegible]
23	BRAHMAN (Hindu)	A.B.C.D.	Males	576,735	310,015	93,450	87,744	35,329	40,728	38,739	14,026
24			Females	474,647	173,153	89,491	67,284	11,460	3,212	1,275	431
25	BRAHMAN (Sikh)	C. D.	Males	3,911	2,122	600	504	222	314	348	134
26			Females	2,053	1,054	493	373	101	42	29	16
27	CHAMAR (Hindu)	A.B.C.D.	Males	366,739	174,821	70,309	60,953	18,415	14,362	8,508	2,274
28			Females	318,224	115,226	68,798	40,671	3,958	1,053	592	154
29	CHAMAR (Ad-Dharmi)	A.B.C.D.	Males	139,641	61,376	27,126	20,848	4,093	4,082	4,196	1,031
30			Females	116,708	39,182	24,751	10,965	845	1,316	977	328
31	CHAMAR (Sikh)	A. C.	Males	85,446	43,152	16,102	13,990	4,909	4,297	2,957	897
32			Females	70,271	27,993	15,491	10,266	1,690	398	91	57
33	CHHIMBA (Hindu)	A. C.	Males	11,338	5,670	1,883	1,686	635	670	578	218
34			Females	9,623	3,662	2,025	1,291	284	38	16	8
35	CHHIMBA (Sikh)	C.	Males	9,182	4,840	1,531	1,316	613	551	582	247
36			Females	7,559	2,892	1,468	1,035	238	64	69	18
37	CHHIMBA (Muslim)	A. C. D.	Males	28,696	14,962	5,908	4,782	1,560	1,581	899	232
38			Females	24,710	10,636	5,595	3,676	777	387	167	34
39	CHUHRA (Hindu)	A.B.C.D.	Males	200,293	104,530	41,040	35,144	11,192	10,159	5,827	1,168
40			Females	167,931	72,543	39,160	26,497	4,328	1,544	782	232
41	CHUHRA (Ad-Dharmi)	A. C. D.	Males	47,315	26,984	10,033	8,680	2,945	2,862	2,135	329
42			Females	39,233	18,303	9,413	6,897	1,202	439	284	68
43	CHUHRA (Sikh)	C.	Males	85,481	48,465	17,792	15,722	5,579	5,907	2,782	683
44			Females	71,860	32,010	16,240	11,576	2,908	937	206	83
45	CHUHRA (Muslim)	C. D.	Males	11,886	6,734	2,737	2,053	781	642	444	77
46			Females	10,264	5,054	2,525	1,721	524	190	82	12
47	CHUHRA (Christian)	A. C. D.	Males	19,024	10,271	4,035	3,387	1,039	1,144	567	99
48			Females	15,891	7,384	4,091	2,162	616	275	209	31
49	DAGI AND KOLI (Hindu)	A. B. C.	Males	94,043	40,205	15,507	13,207	4,099	3,963	2,752	6[illegible]
50			Females	87,327	28,653	16,192	9,748	1,424	627	520	142
51	DHOBI (Hindu)	A. C.	Males	5,824	2,699	1,123	860	261	247	173	36
52			Females	4,608	1,832	1,049	651	91	19	17	5
53	DHOBI (Muslim)	A. C. D.	Males	87,947	47,378	18,197	14,804	4,920	5,357	3,320	780
54			Females	74,097	32,235	16,817	11,333	2,287	1,065	500	233
55	FAQIR (Hindu)	C. D.	Males	15,297	9,403	2,063	1,820	862	1,022	1,961	1,67[illegible]
56			Females	7,864	3,181	1,583	1,169	225	98	76	3[illegible]
57	FAQIR (Sikh)	C.	Males	3,174	2,055	233	291	165	191	585	600
58			Females	1,310	497	221	175	46	23	18	1[illegible]
59	FAQIR (Muslim)	A. C. D.	Males	138,503	73,247	27,937	22,917	7,592	7,134	5,781	1,88[illegible]
60			Females	115,466	48,982	26,015	17,532	3,093	1,435	622	[illegible]85
61	GUJJAR (Hindu)	A.B.C.D.	Males	96,208	48,866	16,372	15,225	5,488	5,689	4,926	1,16[illegible]
62			Females	74,231	24,903	14,679	8,730	1,195	224	68	[illegible]
63	GUJJAR (Sikh)	C.	Males	1,253	588	215	171	45	59	74	2[illegible]
64			Females	1,068	331	203	97	11	5	13	2
65	GUJJAR (Muslim)	A.B.C.D.	Males	283,585	144,958	53,047	47,592	15,200	14,665	11,982	2,472
66			Females	237,762	95,065	53,067	33,076	5,369	2,335	968	25[illegible]
67	HARNI (Muslim)	C.	Males	2,004	1,191	386	537	105	85	63	15
68			Females	1,383	694	363	304	18	2	6	1
69	JAT (Hindu)	A.B.C.D.	Males	547,351	270,044	95,995	85,673	27,619	27,257	24,370	9,121
70			Females	444,958	159,077	90,827	59,006	6,853	1,52[illegible]	691	178
71	JAT (Sikh)	A. C. D.	Males	1,213,819	673,526	201,878	195,121	70,889	84,607	88,712	32,319
72			Females	919,333	366,736	178,399	138,758	30,923	12,786	4,506	1,364
73	JAT (Muslim)	A. C. D.	Males	1,604,250	918,823	329,085	289,175	88,455	112,272	89,173	10,663
74			Females	1,336,569	607,773	310,991	218,100	40,790	24,462	11,099	2,331
75	JHIWAR (Hindu)	A. B. C.	Males	68,171	34,592	12,776	11,098	3,842	3,507	2,591	778
76			Females	56,911	22,417	12,058	8,247	1,461	418	179	54
77	JHIWAR (Sikh)	C.	Males	29,365	16,065	5,906	5,301	1,637	1,571	1,199	451
78			Females	25,846	10,853	5,646	4,111	710	267	89	30
79	JHIWAR (Muslim)	C. D.	Males	50,952	27,523	10,680	9,106	2,874	2,888	1,558	417
80			Females	43,776	19,595	10,006	7,261	1,445	574	249	60
81	JULAHA (Hindu)	A. B. C.	Males	27,560	12,870	4,580	3,993	1,599	1,464	997	237
82			Females	23,593	7,779	4,405	2,801	296	207	59	11
83	JULAHA (Sikh)	C.	Males	1,978	861	319	284	86	75	73	24
84			Females	1,662	522	285	198	23	9	5	2

BY AGE FOR SELECTED CASTES—*continued.*

Married. Total. 12	0—6 13	7—13 14	14—16 15	17—23 16	24—43 17	44 and over 18	Widowed. Total. 19	0—6 20	7—13 21	14—16 22	17—23 23	24—43 24	44 and over 25	Serial No.
67,685	27	603	2,607	13,557	35,ƽ32	15,359	18,637	4	21	59	494	5,888	12,17	1
68,410	253	1,875	6,396	19,310	31,970	8,606	27,478	10	32	112	951	9,853	16,52	2
4,905	2	39	180	1,008	2,563	1,113	1,392	..	3	2	34	475	878	3
4,957	2	93	420	1,392	2,378	672	1,902	..	3	4	65	731	1,009	4
46,127	19	724	2,167	7,854	24,663	10,700	11,464	1	18	60	305	3,321	7,759	5
46,925	69	2,192	4,742	11,311	22,220	6,391	12,128	3	14	29	217	3,255	8.610	6
445	..	2	10	84	214	135	118	..	..	..	3	35	8	7
450	2	4	10	93	247	94	100	..	..	1	5	25	69	8
276,034	680	4,340	7,221	35,868	150,283	77,642	51,028	13	337	210	1,505	15,450	33,51	9
273,77	803	11,046	19,007	63,632	134,613	44,670	56,978	30	100	205	92.	12,013	43,709	10
137,189	59	703	1,717	15,984	77,958	40,768	23,253	5	19	51	548	7,059	15,571	11
132,314	161	2,944	8,852	32,379	69,832	18,146	40,924	10	63	97	925	12,757	27.07	12
22,513	14	202	424	3,266	11,646	6,961	3,986	2	5	15	105	1,051	2,808	13
22,105	25	435	1,297	5,359	11,347	3,642	5,643	3	7	18	152	1,490	3,973	14
110,420	121	761	1,311	8,791	63,015	36,421	16,839	2	35	28	409	4,656	11,709	15
111,597	122	2,359	6,048	21,168	62,911	18,989	28,892	6	43	101	508	7,390	20,844	16
3,341	6	73	106	515	1,807	834	460	..	1	1	28	148	282	17
3,407	15	159	303	865	1,599	466	678	..	2	11	28	223	414	18
3,334	..	18	80	593	1,711	932	529	..	..	3	12	130	384	19
3,211	1	44	161	736	1,679	590	601	..	..	2	35	151	41	20
131,752	73	630	1,518	12,759	75,123	41,649	19,321	4	27	186	420	7,042	11,642	21
137,271	164	4,061	7,248	28,000	77,802	19,996	25,470	5	30	69	577	6,487	18,302	22
209,773	108	1,752	4,767	28,520	113,028	61,589	56,947	8	69	169	1,348	16,758	38,595	23
207,642	447	9,283	18,087	51,804	99,870	28,151	93,852	23	193	555	3,220	30,735	59,120	24
1,419	1	3	23	192	758	442	370	..	..	..	4	105	261	25
1,220	4	30	81	264	608	233	379	..	..	..	4	114	261	26
162,536	191	5,830	9,885	29,361	82,890	34,379	29,382	3	160	372	1,386	9,923	17,538	27
166, 42	626	15,303	19,928	39,596	74,716	15,973	36,856	10	145	232	728	11,469	24,272	28
66,416	239	5,976	5,500	10,342	28,370	15,989	11,849	3	61	116	396	3,642	7,631	29
66,033	622	9,690	7,560	13,412	24,968	9,781	11,493	8	57	156	457	2,328	8,487	30
34,465	30	838	1,877	6,032	16,810	8,878	7,829	4	27	59	248	2,363	5,128	31
35,070	52	1,915	3,561	8,269	16,21	5,059	7,208	2	13	29	90	1,519	5,555	32
4,221	3	110	180	759	2,040	1,129	1,447	..	9	11	63	399	96	33
4,661	15	335	489	1,156	1,985	681	1,300	1	3	4	25	302	965	34
3,393	6	90	132	502	1,600	1,063	949	..	1	3	57	209	679	35
3,754	8	178	33?	844	1,606	785	913	..	1	1	12	173	726	36
11,438	6	175	357	1,816	5,754	3,330	2,296	2	9	14	88	653	1 30	37
11,420	15	494	935	2,430	5,686	1,86	2,654	..	2	8	67	675	1,902	38
80,199	144	2,403	4,06	13,610	42,050	17.932	15,564	5	89	171	741	5,492	9,066	39
80,057	321	5,027	7,566	19,279	38,620	9,244	15,331	5	47	70	324	4,719	10,166	40
17,121	11	323	532	2,750	8,912	4,593	3,210	..	6	22	115	932	2, 5	41
17,785	32	494	1,509	4,124	8,645	2,981	3,145	1	3	15	48	719	2, 9	42
31,454	7	271	870	4,933	17, 04	8,269	5,562	4	11	22	251	1,671	3,60	43
32,774	30	903	2,364	8,631	16,294	4,552	7,070	..	15	10	100	1,661	5,237	44
4,375	1	28	130	584	2,545	1,087	777	..	..	3	38	278	458	45
4,288	1	88	319	835	2,239	806	922	..	3	3	30	242	644	46
7,393	2	163	233	1,206	3,999	1,790	1,360	..	7	9	60	560	724	47
7,183	19	305	570	1,754	3,336	1,199	1 324	..	4	3	46	343	928	48
47,048	311	1,186	1,519	5,136	25,096	14,40	6,190	4	32	59	294	2.123	3,67	49
47,401	266	2,485	3,828	9,165	24,735	6,922	11,273	4	34	70	267	2,853	8, 6	50
2,614	1	41	135	478	1,474	485	511	..	1	5	34	100	281	51
2,26	5	113	227	587	1,134	198	512	..	4	6	15	169	318	52
33,491	26	446	974	4,638	17,620	9,787	7,078	2	16	33	283	2,383	4,361	53
34,160	58	1,073	2,427	7,661	17,275	5,666	7 702	5	10	34	133	2,014	5 456	54
4,488	2	86	142	639	2,103	1,516	1,406	..	..	4	42	404	956	55
3,536	6	131	255	808	1,579	737	1,147	1	..	6	39	277	824	56
762	1	2	27	96	310	326	357	..	..	3	10	79	26	57
645	..	20	48	134	287	156	168	..	..	1	3	21	143	58
52,985	85	1,504	2,298	8,244	26,726	14,128	12,271	..	45	85	483	3,750	7,89	59
54,281	282	3,494	4,925	12,494	24,892	8,194	12,203	3	32	84	259	2,912	8,88	60
38,517	79	1,409	1,845	6,000	19,675	9,509	8,825	1	36	54	305	2,750	5,679	61
39,049	147	3,829	3,825	8,222	18,178	4,848	10,279	1	42	65	203	2,820	7,118	62
538	1	32	31	62	221	191	127	..	..	..	1	34	92	63
601	2	74	47	99	258	121	136	..	1	..	2	25	108	64
115,138	161	3,168	4,298	14,908	60,357	32,246	23,489	2	89	17	564	6,892	15,82	65
116,497	604	9,214	9,65	23,945	54,553	18,527	26,200	12	94	113	474	6,246	19,261	66
689	1	16	16	77	337	242	124	..	1	1	5	27	[illegible]	67
562	1	31	54	98	250	128	127	..	..	..	1	24	102	68
225,087	270	9 809	15,613	41,007	107,133	51,255	52,220	14	272	407	2,003	16,720	32,8	69
230,474	857	20,330	25,829	52,825	102,530	28,103	55,407	15	123	180	838	15,216	39,03	70
436,231	151	4,739	11,471	59,529	214,965	145,376	104,062	21	138	302	1,988	25,032	76,581	71
438,345	476	13,825	28,458	93,302	213,735	88,529	114,252	25	109	269	1,195	21,219	91,435	72
588,540	565	5,262	8,993	60,073	327,567	185,180	96,387	22	126	237	2,095	28,889	65,518	73
598,152	1,228	17,221	30,872	127,429	323,863	97,539	130,644	35	177	360	2,216	31,008	96,848	74
26,582	22	556	1,001	4,231	13,947	6,825	6,997	1	13	37	256	2,244	4,446	75
27,479	52	1,831	2,710	6,422	12,803	3,661	7,015	..	13	31	148	1,920	4,903	76
10,707	9	113	377	1,773	5,211	3,224	2,593	..	13	9	120	739	1,712	77
12,136	5	388	939	2,841	5,808	2,155	2,857	..	4	20	33	505	2,2	78
19,007	27	396	623	2,848	9,643	5,470	4,422	..	11	19	159	1,220	3,01	79
20,208	88	877	1,546	4,794	9,458	3,445	3,973	..	7	15	79	895	2,977	80
12,477	23	180	391	1,727	6,496	3,660	2,213	1	4	6	82	695	1 425	81
12,191	33	871	1,348	2,927	5,639	1,373	3,023	1	13	22	95	1,103	2,389	82
896	..	31	45	136	412	272	221	..	1	..	10	64	146	83
931	2	75	75	223	383	173	209	..	..	..	4	29	176	84

TABLE VIII.—CIVIL CONDITION

Serial No.	Caste or Tribe.	Locality.	Sex.	Population dealt with.	Unmarried.						
					Total.	0—6	7—13	14—16	17—23	24—43	44 and over.
	1	2	3	4	5	6	7	8	9	10	11
85	JULAHA (Muslim)	.. A.B.C.D.	Males ..	*331,748*	179,225	67,052	56,444	19,774	20,241	13,105	2,609
86			Females ..	*280,831*	124,974	64,002	45,079	9,265	4,152	1,945	531
87	KAMBOH (Hindu)	.. A. C. D.	Males ..	*20,593*	10,936	3,939	3,380	1,244	1,336	831	206
88			Females ..	*16,872*	7,158	3,566	2,709	593	216	66	8
89	KAMBOH (Sikh)	.. C. D.	Males ..	*52,610*	27,661	10,934	9,201	2,741	2,651	1,678	456
90			Females ..	*46,127*	19,866	10,219	7,546	1,446	432	164	59
91	KAMBOH (Muslim)	.. C. D.	Males ..	*52,670*	28,173	10,678	9,261	3,149	3,018	1,649	418
92			Females ..	*44,083*	19,772	10,134	7,497	1,414	496	181	50
93	KASHMIRI (Muslim)	.. C. D.	Males ..	*111,920*	60,734	19,954	17,724	6,472	9,605	6,014	965
94			Females ..	*87,120*	37,586	18,509	13 454	3,160	1,639	573	251
95	KHATRI (Hindu)	.. A.B.C.D.	Males ..	*254,289*	144,374	45,145	40,039	16,146	22,690	16,236	4 118
96			Females ..	*206,562*	89,287	42,482	34,487	7,753	2,802	1,339	424
97	KHATRI (Sikh)	.. C. D.	Males ..	*28,715*	15,786	5,580	4,644	1,554	2,000	1,546	462
98			Females ..	*25,281*	10,880	5,337	4,044	984	341	139	35
99	KUMHAR (Hindu)	.. A. B. C.	Males ..	*84,616*	41,235	15,877	14,101	4,611	3,745	2,225	676
100			Females ..	*72,297*	26,532	15,322	9,431	1,215	347	173	44
101	KUMHAR (Sikh)	.. C.	Males ..	*17,206*	9,518	3,415	3,136	1,029	1,042	649	227
102			Females ..	*14,032*	5,799	2,844	2,255	469	149	56	26
103	KUMHAR (Muslim)	.. A. C. D.	Males ..	*228,843*	125,537	48,206	40,862	12,813	13,421	8,516	1,719
104			Females ..	*194,587*	86,677	45,582	30,360	6,190	2,899	1,387	259
105	LOHAR (Hindu)	.. A. B. C.	Males ..	*30,002*	19,746	6,865	6,324	2,195	2,230	1,702	430
106			Females ..	*34,561*	12,325	6,787	4,435	681	228	148	46
107	LOHAR (Sikh)	.. A. C.	Males .	*8,805*	4,670	1,597	1,472	589	434	418	160
108			Females .	*7,665*	3,007	1,516	1,103	267	70	31	20
109	LOHAR (Muslim)	. A. C. D.	Males ..	*130,333*	70,395	26,711	22,752	7,646	7,732	4,413	1,141
110			Females ..	*111,243*	48,907	25,666	17,299	3,520	1,455	699	268
111	MACHHI (Muslim)	.. A. C. D.	Males ..	*171,458*	94,808	36,086	30,444	9,471	10,543	7,202	1,062
112			Females ..	*143,333*	63,957	33,804	22,184	4,465	2,114	1,150	240
113	MEO (Muslim)	.. A.	Males ..	*67,129*	34,814	13,549	12,540	4,119	3,193	1,308	105
114			Females .	*57,666*	23,076	12,805	8,798	1,233	216	20	4
115	MIRASI (Muslim)	.. A. C. D.	Males ..	*129,147*	71,560	25,791	22,052	7,688	8,951	5,833	1,245
116			Females ..	*112,513*	49,920	24,964	17,660	4,020	2,094	850	332
117	MOCHI (Hindu)	.. C.	Males ..	*3,081*	1,201	421	315	158	200	94	13
118			Females ..	*1,519*	613	336	210	31	27	7	2
119	MOCHI (Muslim)	.. C. D.	Males ..	*251,102*	135,597	51,801	43,470	14,038	15,238	9,379	1,671
120			Females ..	*209,914*	93,643	47,893	34,226	6,855	3,054	1,204	411
121	MUSSALI (Muslim)	.. C. D.	Males ..	*221,321*	128,271	51,543	39,748	12,154	14,335	9,206	1,285
122			Females ..	*190,974*	95,123	49,264	33,198	6,542	4,180	1,648	29
123	NAI (Hindu)	.. A. B. C.	Males ..	*55,634*	27,541	9,582	8,762	3,077	2,991	2,315	814
124			Females ..	*45,506*	16,581	9,033	6,210	917	254	98	69
125	NAI (Sikh)	.. C.	Males .	*21,741*	11,832	3,718	3,448	1,262	1,394	1,478	532
126			Females ..	*17,416*	7,097	3,464	2,680	632	191	92	38
127	NAI (Muslim)	.. A. C. D.	Males ..	*127,164*	67,388	25,096	21,170	7,149	7,838	5,158	977
128			Females ..	*108,691*	48,103	24,829	16,611	3,708	1,877	830	248
129	PAKHIWARA (Muslim)	.. C.	Males ..	*1,748*	945	380	291	97	96	64	11
130			Females ..	*1,352*	623	314	225	51	21	10	2
131	PATHAN (Muslim)	.. A. C. D.	Males ..	*190,923*	106,340	34,686	31,326	11,339	10,219	11,245	1,525
132			Females ..	*154,479*	67,962	33,753	23,770	5,802	2,978	1,360	299
133	KANET (Hindu)	.. A. B. C.	Males ..	*154,909*	68,953	24,062	21,771	7,279	7,978	6,305	1,558
134			Females ..	*145,520*	46,190	25,256	16,712	2,594	878	600	150
135	KANET (Buddhist)	.. B.	Males ..	*2,403*	1,305	209	416	146	253	217	64
136			Females ..	*2,439*	1,247	272	295	173	276	172	59
137	RAJPUT (Hindu)	.. A.B.C.D.	Males ..	*322,692*	168,673	50,262	47,687	19,390	25,153	20,171	6,010
138			Females ..	*254,682*	90,899	46,524	33,414	5,946	2,805	1,692	518
139	RAJPUT (Sikh)	.. C. D.	Males ..	*27,933*	15,228	6,083	4,068	2,285	1,536	986	270
140			Females ..	*21,661*	9,498	5,313	3,173	623	261	109	19
141	RAJPUT (Muslim)	.. A. C. D.	Males ..	*917,462*	519,215	182,430	159,666	57,825	68,947	43,449	6,898
142			Females ..	*801,070*	360,548	179,245	128,286	29,929	14,526	7,208	1,354
143	RATHI (Hindu)	.. B.	Males ..	*67,255*	36,266	12,511	11,517	3,504	4,363	3,565	806
144			Females ..	*66,820*	23,741	12,765	9,308	1,132	319	160	57
145	SAINI (Hindu)	. A. C.	Males ..	*40,809*	20,779	7,022	6,526	2,396	2,271	1,878	686
146			Females ..	*33,429*	12,509	6,830	4,653	785	153	63	25
147	SAINI (Sikh)	.. A. C.	Males ..	*44,696*	23,856	8,764	7,772	2,329	2,007	2,010	974
148			Females ..	*38,269*	15,609	7,965	6,104	1,249	188	78	25
149	SANSI (Hindu)	.. A. C.	Males ..	*14,628*	7,789	3,110	2,532	735	781	521	110
150			Females ..	*12,037*	5,619	2,918	2,068	364	140	113	16
151	SAYAD (Muslim)	.. A. C. D.	Males ..	*157,818*	86,947	29,769	26,305	9,346	12,528	7,699	1,300
152			Females ..	*135,484*	59,523	28,033	20,872	5,517	3,179	1,443	479
153	SHEIKH (Muslim)	.. A. C. D.	Males ..	*227,172*	117,989	40,267	36,158	13,199	16,869	9,922	1,574
154			Females ..	*180,382*	76,611	38,132	27,750	6,042	2,788	1,223	676
155	SUNAR (Hindu)	.. A.B.C.D.	Males ..	*53,763*	28,682	10,127	9,053	3,090	3,351	2,333	728
156			Females ..	*46,263*	18,365	9,378	7,076	1,262	391	203	55
157	SUNAR (Sikh)	.. C. D.	Males ..	*13,683*	7,656	2,751	2,388	740	807	723	247
158			Females ..	*11,683*	5,003	2,471	1,925	378	118	85	26
159	SUNAR (Muslim)	.. C. D.	Males ..	*17,440*	9,699	3,711	2,919	1,014	1,180	681	194
160			Females ..	*14,954*	6,914	3,514	2,326	578	311	136	49
161	TARKHAN (Hindu)	.. A. B. C.	Males ..	*78,979*	39,552	14,287	12,940	4,376	3,828	3,130	991
162			Females ..	*67,748*	24,355	13,898	8,992	1,001	272	144	48
163	TARKHAN (Sikh)	.. A. C. D.	Males ..	*87,891*	46,833	16,005	14,427	4,798	5,324	4,820	1,459
164			Females ..	*70,555*	28,357	14,345	10,793	2,124	662	288	145
165	TARKHAN (Muslim)	.. A. C. D.	Males ..	*188,299*	102,389	38,789	32,463	10,926	11,715	7,255	1,241
166			Females ..	*158,530*	71,022	36,497	25,211	4,918	2,855	1,220	321
167	TELI (Muslim)	.. A. C. D.	Males ..	*184,552*	99,077	37,036	31,894	11,089	10,910	6,859	1,289
168			Females ..	*158,743*	67,404	35,185	24,475	4,441	2,214	784	305

BY AGE FOR SELECTED CASTES—*concluded*.

Married.							Widowed.							
Total. 12	0—6 13	7—13 14	14—16 15	17—23 16	24—43 17	44 and over 18	Total. 19	0—6 20	7—13 21	14—16 22	17—23 23	24—43 24	44 and over. 25	Serial No.
124,479	76	1,491	3,075	16,386	65,826	37,625	28,044	2	37	108	1,212	8,399	18,286	85
126,587	244	4,564	8,800	28,883	63,675	20,421	29,270	10	53	101	627	7,070	21,409	86
7,890	5	107	268	1,208	4,217	2,085	1,767	1	..	12	43	518	1,193	87
7,778	9	370	554	1,936	3,783	1,126	1,936	..	4	6	49	567	1,310	88
21,282	14	294	658	3,272	10,635	6,400	3,667	..	4	20	106	1,022	2,515	89
22,383	32	825	1,698	5,081	10,568	4,179	3,878	4	14	11	65	836	2,948	90
20,940	18	344	637	3,224	10,694	6,023	3,557	..	10	17	128	1,028	2,374	91
20,276	55	897	1,475	4,874	9,594	3,381	4,035	..	8	18	83	923	3,003	92
43,290	24	302	655	5,097	25,404	11,814	7,890	..	12	19	272	2,602	4,985	93
38,776	34	1,221	2,462	8,847	20,425	5,767	10,758	2	14	29	160	2,397	8,147	94
92,748	43	423	951	9,827	53,334	28,170	17,167	5	11	35	356	5,066	11,694	95
86,083	60	1,304	5,005	20,872	45,993	12,840	31,192	6	40	74	627	9,176	21,269	96
10,829	5	54	197	1,205	5,504	3,864	2,100	..	3	18	72	514	1,493	97
11,123	16	255	671	2,403	5,729	2,051	3,276	1	3	5	53	911	2,303	98
36,357	23	857	1,953	6,559	18,487	8,478	7,024	3	18	50	286	2,170	4,497	99
36,580	94	2,765	3,983	9,167	16,109	4,462	9,185	6	21	41	195	2,483	6,439	100
6,314	10	74	241	980	3,126	1,883	1,374	..	3	12	55	381	923	101
6,482	2	195	488	1,395	3,094	,308	1,751	1	2	5	74	322	1,347	102
87,145	134	1,034	2,314	11,669	46,247	25,747	16,161	8	22	139	531	4,956	10,505	103
88,572	158	3,213	6,145	19,901	44,779	14,286	19,338	3	25	58	414	4,675	14,163	104
16,676	26	345	681	2,401	8,639	4,474	3,480	1	12	20	147	1,138	2,162	105
17,424	55	1,361	1,736	3,817	8,398	2,057	4,812	1	17	24	97	1,317	3,356	106
3,266	..	71	182	553	1,427	1,033	869	..	3	4	19	219	624	107
3,818	4	138	328	831	1,776	741	830	..	2	2	16	170	64	108
50,478	38	815	1,614	7,492	26,375	14,144	9,460	4	35	43	387	2,839	6,152	109
51,170	125	2,158	3,789	11,929	24,926	8,243	11,166	5	18	53	253	2,667	8,170	110
64,214	53	816	,603	7,887	35,498	18,357	12,436	..	20	48	437	3,082	7,949	111
65,234	104	2,146	4,415	14,497	33,827	10,245	14,142	3	24	55	300	3,628	10,132	112
27,208	23	427	1,073	4,481	16,010	5,284	5,017	2	14	42	245	1,867	2,847	113
28,243	62	1,353	2,482	6,829	15,074	2,443	6,347	1	24	32	112	2,195	3,083	114
47,824	37	514	1,155	6,072	25,302	14,744	9,763	2	23	61	465	3,060	6,152	115
50,128	134	1,259	2,981	11,308	25,763	8,688	12,465	1	22	54	312	3,071	9,032	116
1,622	..	64	74	290	978	216	258	..	..	..	18	132	108	117
775	..	36	76	199	377	87	131	..	..	..	5	48	77	118
93,816	121	925	2,041	12,043	52,017	28,669	19,689	2	23	54	532	6,332	12,746	119
94,618	120	3,545	6,026	21,057	48,923	15,947	21,653	4	38	97	426	5,500	15,588	120
79,353	56	481	1,290	8,758	44,657	24,111	13,697	1	19	59	436	4,939	8,243	121
81,169	89	1,665	4,345	8,810	43,388	12,863	14,682	5	24	60	406	3,618	10,569	122
22,209	14	432	1,078	3,829	10,997	5,859	3,884	1	13	27	203	1,834	3,806	123
22,538	60	1,497	2,237	5,497	10,360	2,887	6,387	1	28	15	138	1,821	4,384	124
7,773	3	69	260	1,245	3,680	2,507	2,136	..	2	18	92	552	1,472	125
8,195	5	227	608	1,794	3,898	1,663	2,124	..	..	6	39	457	1,022	126
49,522	39	712	1,313	6,840	26,066	14,352	10,254	2	31	64	377	3,205	6,525	127
49,501	126	1,773	3,423	11,144	24,858	8,177	11,087	..	21	52	282	2,553	8,179	128
649	..	4	10	88	354	193	154	..	1	1	7	42	103	129
616	..	20	49	44	299	104	113	..	..	..	6	34	73	130
72,639	42	359	930	7,379	40,530	23,399	11,944	1	13	47	425	4,032	7,426	131
68,589	71	1,317	3,493	15,416	37,128	11,164	17,928	..	24	60	415	4,711	12,718	132
75,134	464	1,930	2,243	9,410	36,670	24,417	10,822	3	33	61	416	3,359	6,950	133
77,088	374	4,051	5,659	17,170	38,822	11,012	22,242	8	51	112	380	5,563	16,128	134
1,010	..	6	14	67	506	417	88	..	..	1	..	20	67	135
978	1	..	13	88	375	301	214	3	..	..	2	41	168	136
127,903	58	1,008	2,574	15,572	69,310	39,381	26,116	..	23	97	714	8,289	16,993	137
117,736	198	6,089	10,631	29,268	56,404	15,146	46,047	2	102	266	1,460	14,619	29,598	138
11,040	6	45	238	2,384	4,935	3,432	1,665	2	5	5	39	545	1,069	139
10,110	6	181	607	2,120	5,752	1,444	2,053	..	2	7	50	441	1,653	140
341,330	309	3,143	6,389	36,248	188,735	106,506	56,917	8	137	236	1,772	16,040	38,724	141
346,145	707	13,630	21,963	78,355	180,491	50,999	94,377	22	140	298	1,936	25,654	66,327	142
25,919	12	174	403	2,298	13,597	9,435	5,070	..	3	10	122	1,471	3,464	143
31,112	127	1,894	2,873	7,772	15,319	3,127	11,967	2	27	39	302	3,155	8,442	144
15,843	8	277	663	2,420	7,968	4,507	4,187	..	7	14	121	1,193	2,852	145
16,156	11	995	1,504	3,629	7,556	2,461	4,764	..	7	23	90	1,211	3,433	146
16,656	6	256	699	2,003	7,681	5,411	4,184	..	5	9	85	1,240	2,845	147
17,888	15	631	1,509	3,685	8,621	3,427	4,772	..	5	9	63	1,222	3,473	148
5,568	13	108	224	861	2,853	1,509	1,271	..	5	8	36	434	788	149
5,237	8	188	417	1,256	2,587	781	1,181	..	4	2	19	286	870	150
59,925	44	385	1,129	6,698	32,227	19,442	10,946	3	13	24	317	3,519	7,070	151
58,294	42	1,216	3,303	13,303	31,233	9,197	17,667	3	14	64	374	4,632	12,580	152
92,065	115	1,443	2,392	12,922	50,938	24,225	17,118	5	56	106	765	6,067	10,119	153
85,204	290	3,804	6,184	21,006	42,504	11,326	18,567	5	53	91	488	4,857	13,073	154
20,767	25	349	693	3,193	10,600	3,007	4,314	..	10	22	138	1,342	2,802	155
20,554	27	940	1,773	5,214	9,469	3,131	6,344	..	14	30	173	1,829	4,298	156
5,073	2	66	166	837	2,514	1,488	954	..	1	2	46	234	671	157
5,331	7	184	392	1,330	2,537	881	1,349	..	5	6	18	333	987	158
6,587	5	75	255	932	3,511	1,809	1,134	..	1	6	65	382	700	159
6,586	13	190	487	1,614	3,187	1,095	1,454	..	4	6	42	387	1,015	160
31,064	37	786	1,548	5,302	15,692	8,299	7,763	..	24	48	298	2,301	5,092	161
34,792	120	2,654	3,767	8,129	15,086	4,436	8,601	..	15	42	175	2,318	6,051	162
33,184	16	355	1,246	5,448	15,892	10,227	7,874	1	8	36	217	2,118	5,494	163
34,734	43	1,006	2,639	8,051	16,082	6,913	7,464	2	1	18	148	1,602	5,693	164
71,145	55	733	1,583	9,363	37,520	21,891	14,765	..	10	61	401	5,154	9,139	165
71,381	96	2,376	4,527	16,995	35,340	12,047	16,127	2	43	68	426	3,960	11,628	166
70,783	82	1,308	2,590	11,521	36,286	18,996	14,692	6	40	74	485	4,702	9,385	167
70,655	181	3,753	5,603	16,506	33,631	10,981	15,684	7	43	57	294	3,826	11,457	168

TABLE IX.

INFIRMITIES.

1. This Table corresponds with Table XII of 1921 and is divided into two parts. Part I shows the distribution of the persons afflicted according to age, and Part II their distribution according to locality.

2. Dual infirmities were recorded. Persons afflicted with two or more infirmities have been shown under each of the infirmities in question in columns 5 to 16. The total under infirmities, therefore, exceeds the total number of persons afflicted as given in columns 2 to 4. The statement below shows the number of persons suffering from more than one infirmity :—

INFIRMITY. 1	Persons. 2	Males. 3	Females. 4
Insane and Deaf-mutes	192	116	76
Insane and Blind	66	28	38
Insane and Lepers	29	17	12
Deaf-mutes and Blind	135	85	50
Deaf-mutes and Lepers	24	17	7
Blind and Lepers	13	7	6
Insane, Deaf-mutes and Blind ..	26	16	10
Insane, Blind and Lepers ..	2	2	..
Blind, Deaf-mutes and Lepers ..	1	..	1
Insane, Deaf-mutes and Lepers ..	3	2	1
Insane, Deaf-mutes, Blind and Lepers ..	3	1	2

TABLE IX.—INFIRMITIES.

PART I.—DISTRIBUTION BY AGE—*continued.*

Age.		Population Afflicted.			Insane.			Deaf-mutes.			Blind.			Lepers.	
		Persons.	Males.	Females.	Persons.	Males.	Females.	Persons.	Males.	Females.	Persons.	Males.	Females.	Persons.	Males.	Females.
1		2	3	4	5	6	7	8	9	10	11	12	13	14	15	16
PUNJAB	..	**99,779**	**56,773**	**43,006**	**8,339**	**5,619**	**2,720**	**19,532**	**12,347**	**7,185**	**69,673**	**37,141**	**32,532**	**2,767**	**1,979**	**788**
0—1	..	*130*	76	54	3	2	1	25	16	9	97	55	42	6	4	2
1—2	.	*214*	114	100	12	5	7	53	27	26	147	81	66	6	3	3
2—3	..	*417*	228	189	30	24	6	148	70	78	238	135	103	11	5	6
3—4	..	*598*	344	254	25	20	5	291	166	125	280	159	121	5	2	3
4—5	..	*1,049*	601	448	125	68	57	492	286	206	422	241	181	28	14	14
Total 0—5	..	*2,408*	*1,363*	*1,045*	*195*	*119*	*76*	*1,009*	*565*	*444*	*1,184*	*671*	*513*	*56*	*28*	*28*
5—10	..	*5,743*	3,426	2,317	732	476	256	2,657	1,622	1,035	2,334	1,315	1,019	90	50	40
10—15	..	*6,277*	3,813	2,464	884	597	287	2,780	1,721	1,059	2,567	1,461	1,106	102	67	35
15—20	..	*5,509*	3,470	2,039	921	626	295	2,169	1,377	792	2,315	1,400	915	157	105	52
20—25	..	*5,586*	3,551	2,035	904	616	288	2,060	1,335	725	2,467	1,499	968	185	120	65
25—30	..	*5,332*	3,325	2,007	857	604	253	1,724	1,119	605	2,555	1,464	1,091	239	164	75
30—35	..	*5,090*	3,151	1,939	803	569	234	1,485	966	519	2,548	1,435	1,113	266	189	77
35—40	.	*5,206*	3,092	2,114	746	514	232	1,168	766	402	3,001	1,587	1,414	324	244	80
40—45	..	*5,312*	3,065	2,247	649	441	208	975	635	340	3,432	1,794	1,638	280	206	74
45—50	..	*6,471*	3,513	2,958	509	337	172	819	532	287	4,850	2,411	2,439	331	258	73
50—55	..	*6,447*	3,424	3,023	369	241	128	643	425	218	5,163	2,541	2,622	293	233	60
55—60	..	*7,921*	4,231	3,690	262	157	105	558	373	185	6,963	3,601	3,362	162	113	49
60—65	..	*8,237*	4,419	3,818	197	127	70	483	316	167	7,444	3,896	3,548	129	89	40
65—70	.	*7,099*	3,854	3,245	118	70	48	315	193	122	6,616	3,554	3,062	73	48	25
70 and over	..	*17,141*	9,076	8,065	193	125	68	687	402	285	16,234	8,512	7,722	80	65	15
BRITISH TERRITORY	..	**82,091**	**46,616**	**35,475**	**7,220**	**4,853**	**2,367**	**16,161**	**10,258**	**5,903**	**57,254**	**30,405**	**26,849**	**1,853**	**1,326**	**527**
0—1	..	*111*	66	45	2	2	..	21	14	7	83	47	36	6	4	2
1—2	..	*186*	97	89	12	5	7	47	25	22	125	66	59	6	3	3
2—3	..	*355*	193	162	23	17	6	126	60	66	201	114	87	11	5	6
3—4	..	*518*	295	223	17	13	4	257	145	112	241	137	104	4	1	3
4—5	..	*876*	501	375	106	56	50	420	243	177	336	194	142	27	14	13
Total 0—5	..	*2,046*	*1,152*	*894*	*160*	*93*	*67*	*871*	*487*	*384*	*986*	*558*	*428*	*54*	*27*	*27*
5—10	.	*4,870*	2,802	1,978	619	400	219	2,272	1,379	893	1,965	1,101	864	76	44	32
10—15	..	*5,302*	3,213	2,089	762	515	247	2,359	1,460	899	2,147	1,213	934	78	52	26
15—20	..	*4,575*	2,892	1,683	798	539	259	1,813	1,173	640	1,888	1,138	750	115	72	43
20—25	..	*4,632*	2,954	1,678	783	528	255	1,718	1,129	589	2,022	1,233	789	131	76	[illegible]
25—30	.	*4,400*	2,752	1,648	755	530	225	1,418	930	488	2,104	1,212	892	156	100	56
30—35	.	*4,226*	2,623	1,603	718	505	213	1,234	810	424	2,108	1,191	917	177	124	53
35—40	..	*4,220*	2,498	1,722	645	449	196	944	625	319	2,449	1,279	1,170	206	157	49
40—45	..	*4,355*	2,502	1,853	578	398	180	795	527	268	2,820	1,452	1,368	183	135	48
45—50	..	*5,240*	2,832	2,408	432	289	143	642	419	223	3,978	1,964	2,014	212	174	38
50—55	..	*5,244*	2,748	2,496	321	205	116	505	329	176	4,253	2,073	2,180	178	151	27
55—60	.	*6,377*	3,393	2,984	224	131	93	439	292	147	5,631	2,908	2,723	99	70	29
60—65	..	*6,666*	3,583	3,083	168	106	62	386	252	134	6,035	3,168	2,867	86	62	24
65—70	.	*5,801*	3,142	2,659	94	57	37	242	142	100	5,433	2,914	2,519	51	37	14
70 and over	..	*14,137*	7,440	6,697	163	108	55	523	304	219	13,435	7,001	6,434	51	45	6
PUNJAB STATES	.	**17,688**	**10,157**	**7,531**	**1,119**	**766**	**353**	**3,371**	**2,089**	**1,282**	**12,419**	**6,736**	**5,683**	**914**	**653**	**261**
A.—Having Political Relations with the Punjab Government.		**2,140**	**1,221**	**919**	**131**	**97**	**34**	**835**	**465**	**370**	**955**	**503**	**452**	**227**	**162**	**65**
0—1	.	..	..	..	.	..	..	..	..	..	..	..	..	..	..	..
1—2	..	*1*	1	..	..	..	..	..	.	..	1	1	..	..	..	..
2—3	..	*11*	5	6	3	3	..	4	..	4	5	3	2	..	..	..
3—4	..	*6*	3	3	..	..	.	6	3	3	..	..	..	.	..	..
4—5	..	*27*	16	11	1	.	1	16	8	8	10	8	2	..	..	..
Total 0—5	..	*45*	*25*	*20*	*4*	*3*	*1*	*26*	*11*	*15*	*16*	*12*	*4*	..	.	..
5—10	..	*124*	78	46	8	8	..	93	56	37	20	13	7	4	2	2
10—15	..	*171*	98	73	11	8	3	125	69	56	30	17	13	6	4	2
15—20	..	*160*	81	79	15	11	4	104	43	61	30	20	10	11	7	4
20—25	..	*146*	79	67	15	12	3	85	37	48	30	[illegible]	13	17	14	3
25—30	.	*154*	96	58	14	11	3	87	51	36	35	19	16	19	16	3
30—35		*133*	79	34	10	9	1	73	39	34	30	17	13	20	14	6
35—40	..	*137*	83	54	12	8	4	55	34	21	38	20	18	32	21	11
40—45	..	*113*	73	40	6	3	3	44	31	13	38	21	17	25	18	7
45—50	..	*149*	83	66	11	6	5	49	30	19	61	29	32	30	20	10
50—55	..	*116*	70	46	7	6	1	23	17	6	61	30	31	25	17	8
55—60	..	*137*	77	60	5	4	1	21	13	8	95	47	48	16	13	
60—65	..	*149*	83	66	6	5	1	20	13	7	111	55	56	12	10	2
65—70	..	*122*	69	53	4	3	1	12	8	4	101	55	46	5	3	2
70 and over	..	*284*	147	137	3	..	3	18	13	5	259	131	128	5	3	2

TABLE IX.—INFIRMITIES.

PART I.—DISTRIBUTION BY AGE—*concluded*.

Age.	Population Afflicted.			Insane.			Deaf-mutes.			Blind.			Lepers.		
	Persons.	Males.	Females.	Persons.	Males.	Females.	Persons.	Males.	Females.	Persons.	Males.	Females.	Persons.	Males.	Females.
1	2	3	4	5	6	7	8	9	10	11	12	13	14	15	16
B.—Having Political relations with the Government of India.	15,548	8,936	6,612	988	669	319	2,536	1,624	912	11,464	6,233	5,231	687	491	196
0—1 ..	*19*	10	9	1	..	1	4	2	2	14	8	6	..	..	..
1—2 ..	*27*	16	11	..	..	..	6	2	4	21	14	7	..	..	..
2—3 ..	*51*	30	21	4	4	..	18	10	8	32	18	14	..	..	..
3—4 ..	*74*	46	28	8	7	1	28	18	10	39	22	17	1	1	..
4—5 ..	*146*	84	62	18	12	6	56	35	21	76	39	37	1	..	1
Total 0—5 ..	*317*	*186*	*131*	*31*	*23*	*8*	*112*	*67*	*45*	*182*	*101*	*81*	*2*	*1*	*1*
5—10 ..	*749*	456	293	105	68	37	292	187	105	349	201	148	10	4	6
10—15 ..	*804*	502	302	111	74	37	296	192	104	390	231	159	18	11	7
15—20 ..	*774*	497	277	108	76	32	252	161	91	397	242	155	31	26	5
20—25 ..	*808*	518	290	106	76	30	257	169	88	415	249	166	37	30	7
25—30 ..	*778*	477	301	88	63	25	219	138	81	416	233	183	64	48	16
30—35 ..	*731*	449	282	75	55	20	178	117	61	410	227	183	69	51	18
35—40 ..	*849*	511	338	89	57	32	169	107	62	514	288	226	86	66	20
40—45 ..	*844*	490	354	65	40	25	136	77	59	574	321	253	72	53	19
45—50 ..	*1,082*	598	484	66	42	24	128	83	45	811	418	393	89	64	25
50—55 ..	*1,087*	606	481	41	30	11	115	79	36	849	438	411	90	65	25
55—60 ..	*1,407*	761	646	33	22	11	98	68	30	1,237	646	591	47	30	17
60—65 ..	*1,422*	753	669	23	16	7	77	51	26	1,298	673	625	31	17	14
65—70 ..	*1,176*	643	533	20	10	10	61	43	18	1,082	585	497	17	8	9
70 and over ..	*2,720*	1,489	1,231	27	17	10	146	85	61	2,540	1,380	1,160	24	17	7

TABLE IX.—INFIRMITIES.

PART II.—DISTRIBUTION BY DISTRICTS.

Serial No.	District or State.	Population Afflicted.			Insane.			Deaf-mutes.			Blind.			Lepers.		
		Persons.	Males.	Females.	Persons.	Males.	Females.	Persons.	Males.	Females.	Persons.	Males.	Females.	Persons.	Males.	Females.
	1	2	3	4	5	6	7	8	9	10	11	12	13	14	15	16
	PUNJAB ..	**99,779**	**56,778**	**43,006**	**8,339**	**5,619**	**2,720**	**19,532**	**12,347**	**7,185**	**69,673**	**37,141**	**32,532**	**2,767**	**1,979**	**788**
	BRITISH TERRITORY ..	**82,091**	**46,616**	**35,475**	**7,220**	**4,853**	**2,367**	**16,161**	**10,258**	**5,903**	**57,254**	**30,405**	**26,849**	**1,853**	**1,326**	**527**
	AMBALA DIVISION ..	**15,187**	**8,399**	**6,788**	**900**	**620**	**280**	**1,817**	**1,120**	**697**	**12,165**	**6,402**	**5,763**	**366**	**294**	**72**
1	Hissar ..	*3,940*	2,135	1,805	278	196	82	404	267	137	3,215	1,626	1,589	65	57	8
2	Rohtak ..	*2,009*	1,139	870	105	76	29	269	176	93	1,622	875	747	18	16	2
3	Gurgaon ..	*2,826*	1,514	1,312	107	77	30	277	172	105	2,421	1,246	1,175	23	19	4
4	Karnal ..	*2,841*	1,634	1,207	193	126	67	291	193	98	2,345	1,303	1,042	24	20	4
5	Ambala ..	*3,285*	1,785	1,500	204	133	71	539	290	249	2,478	1,316	1,162	79	55	24
6	Simla ..	*286*	192	94	13	12	1	37	22	15	84	36	48	157	127	30
	JULLUNDUR DIVISION ..	**20,689**	**11,655**	**9,034**	**1,118**	**745**	**373**	**4,735**	**2,959**	**1,776**	**14,504**	**7,699**	**6,805**	**441**	**312**	**129**
7	Kangra ..	*4,029*	2,343	1,686	93	60	33	2,324	1,392	932	1,301	665	636	311	226	85
8	Hoshiarpur ..	*5,474*	2,934	2,540	348	230	118	1,025	652	373	4,165	2,079	2,086	19	17	2
9	Jullundur ..	*4,259*	2,265	1,994	247	172	75	531	341	190	3,480	1,750	1,730	5	5	..
10	Ludhiana ..	*2,880*	1,683	1,197	192	120	72	287	188	99	2,351	1,350	1,001	72	38	34
11	Ferozepore ..	*4,047*	2,430	1,617	238	163	75	568	386	182	3,207	1,855	1,352	34	26	8
	LAHORE DIVISION ..	**17,095**	**10,009**	**7,086**	**1,969**	**1,431**	**538**	**2,972**	**1,925**	**1,047**	**11,740**	**6,346**	**5,394**	**466**	**337**	**129**
12	Lahore ..	*4,255*	2,656	1,599	1,159	906	253	628	421	207	2,454	1,319	1,135	19	14	5
13	Amritsar ..	*3,502*	1,969	1,533	152	101	51	402	254	148	2,626	1,372	1,254	324	242	82
14	Gurdaspur ..	*2,827*	1,658	1,169	162	105	57	663	410	253	1,980	1,128	852	28	18	10
15	Sialkot ..	*2,475*	1,403	1,012	149	100	49	474	314	160	1,755	967	788	41	25	16
16	Gujranwala ..	*1,901*	1,054	847	165	95	70	378	238	140	1,347	708	639	29	22	7
17	Sheikhupura ..	*2,195*	1,269	926	182	124	58	427	288	139	1,578	852	726	25	16	9
	RAWALPINDI DIVISION ..	**11,685**	**6,587**	**5,098**	**1,204**	**771**	**433**	**3,029**	**1,887**	**1,142**	**7,157**	**3,733**	**3,424**	**354**	**230**	**124**
18	Gujrat ..	*2,497*	1,436	1,061	195	143	52	543	354	189	1,719	915	804	44	28	16
19	Shahpur ..	*2,677*	1,513	1,164	316	207	109	687	440	247	1,089	876	813	24	16	8
20	Jhelum ..	*2,010*	1,093	917	189	97	92	553	340	213	1,184	608	576	84	48	36
21	Rawalpindi ..	*1,436*	858	578	151	95	56	440	260	180	690	388	302	163	115	48
22	Attock ..	*1,729*	938	791	209	137	72	505	305	200	996	486	510	23	12	11
23	Mianwali ..	*1,336*	749	587	144	92	52	301	188	113	879	460	419	16	11	5
	MULTAN DIVISION ..	**17,435**	**9,966**	**7,469**	**2,029**	**1,286**	**743**	**3,608**	**2,367**	**1,241**	**11,688**	**6,225**	**5,463**	**226**	**153**	**73**
24	Montgomery ..	*3,151*	1,854	1,297	292	189	103	688	443	245	2,163	1,209	954	30	23	7
25	Lyallpur ..	*3,513*	1,992	1,521	341	214	127	663	435	228	2,502	1,339	1,163	26	18	8
26	Jhang ..	*2,275*	1,344	931	378	256	122	593	365	228	1,298	715	583	33	21	12
27	Multan ..	*3,652*	2,151	1,501	435	260	175	826	552	274	2,323	1,292	1,031	93	63	30
28	Muzaffargarh ..	*2,561*	1,368	1,193	334	197	137	438	294	144	1,784	874	910	15	8	7
29	Dera Ghazi Khan ..	*2,283*	1,257	1,026	249	170	79	400	278	122	1,618	796	822	29	20	9
	PUNJAB STATES ..	**17,688**	**10,157**	**7,531**	**1,119**	**766**	**353**	**3,371**	**2,089**	**1,282**	**12,419**	**6,736**	**5,683**	**914**	**653**	**261**
	A.—HAVING POLITICAL RELATIONS WITH THE PUNJAB GOVERNMENT. ..	**2,140**	**1,221**	**919**	**131**	**97**	**34**	**835**	**465**	**370**	**955**	**503**	**452**	**227**	**162**	**65**
1	Dujana ..	*125*	88	37	8	7	1	27	21	6	88	58	30	2	2	..
2	Pataudi ..	*61*	30	31	2	2	..	5	2	3	53	26	27	1	..	1
3	Kalsia ..	*336*	191	145	31	21	10	104	55	49	205	118	87	1	1	..
4	SIMLA HILL STATES ..	**1,618**	**912**	**706**	**90**	**67**	**23**	**699**	**387**	**312**	**609**	**301**	**308**	**223**	**159**	**64**
	Bashahr ..	*570*	305	265	12	9	3	382	208	174	120	53	67	57	36	21
	Nalagarh ..	*175*	98	77	11	8	3	46	28	18	118	62	56	..	..	..
	Keonthal ..	*242*	148	94	8	7	1	83	47	36	99	55	44	54	40	14
	Baghal ..	*72*	50	22	12	10	2	23	15	8	36	25	11	1	..	1
	Jubbal ..	*253*	137	116	17	9	8	68	34	34	104	41	63	64	53	11
	Other Simla Hill States ..	*306*	174	132	30	24	6	97	55	42	132	65	67	47	30	17
	B.—HAVING POLITICAL RELATIONS WITH THE GOVERNMENT OF INDIA. ..	**15,548**	**8,936**	**6,612**	**988**	**669**	**319**	**2,536**	**1,624**	**912**	**11,464**	**6,233**	**5,231**	**687**	**491**	**196**
5	Loharu ..	*81*	43	38	5	3	2	14	9	5	59	28	31	3	3	..
6	Sirmoor ..	*834*	488	346	50	31	19	293	170	123	347	168	179	145	119	26
7	Bilaspur ..	*133*	82	51	6	4	2	57	30	27	57	38	19	13	10	3
8	Mandi ..	*957*	532	425	32	21	11	249	141	108	380	167	213	298	205	93
9	Suket ..	*121*	66	55	..	..	..	52	25	27	46	24	22	23	17	6
10	Kapurthala ..	*865*	469	396	55	38	17	156	91	65	654	337	317	3	3	..
11	Maler Kotla ..	*182*	111	71	9	7	2	22	13	9	153	93	60	1	1	..
12	Faridkot ..	*557*	325	232	30	21	9	44	28	16	480	274	206	3	2	1
13	Chamba ..	*83*	49	34	5	3	2	14	9	5	53	27	26	12	10	2
14	Patiala (Phulkian States) ..	*6,306*	3,644	2,662	309	222	87	642	447	195	5,295	2,925	2,370	78	59	19
15	Jind (Phulkian States) ..	*896*	497	399	48	29	19	130	90	40	721	381	340	7	5	2
16	Nabha (Phulkian States) ..	*1,386*	817	569	70	52	18	137	98	39	1,185	673	512	2	1	1
17	Bahawalpur ..	*3,147*	1,813	1,334	369	238	131	726	473	253	2,034	1,098	936	99	56	43

TABLE X.

OCCUPATION OR MEANS OF LIVELIHOOD.

1. All occupations are divided into four classes, twelve sub-classes, fifty-five orders and one hundred and ninety-five groups. The scheme is the same as in 1921, except that there were then fifty-six orders and one hundred and ninety-one groups. All the columns for certain groups, the headings of which appear below, were blank for the whole Province and have therefore been omitted from the Table.

(8) Cultivators of Jhum, taungya and shifting areas. Cultivation of (9) Cinchona, (10) Coconut. (11) Coffee, (12) Ganja, (13) Pan Vine, (14) Rubber. (25) Raising of Silkworms. (26) Lac-cultivation. Exploitation of (30) Iron, (31) Lead, Silver and Zinc, (32) Manganese, (33) Coal, (38) Mica, (39) Precious and semi-precious stones. (48) Industry in hair (horse hair), etc. Manufacturers of (79) Opium, (80) Ganja. (155) Navy.

2. The Table deals with the entire population without regard to religion; the figures for Lahore, Amritsar and Multan cities, have been given separately. All non-working dependants have been thrown together, while earners have been divided into those following each occupation as principal means of livelihood and those following it as an occupation subsidiary to some other. Working dependants engaged in each occupation, who were included in actual workers at the last Census have been shown separately.

3. In group 192, only prisoners undergoing rigorous imprisonment are shown as working-dependants. All other kinds of prisoners as well as inmates of asylums, poor houses etc., were not separately sorted and have been included in the total of non-working dependants.

TABLE X—OCCUPATION OR MEANS OF

DETAILS FOR DISTRICTS,

Serial No.	District or State.	Total all classes: Total Population.	Total all classes: Population: Total earners principal occupation: Males.	Total all classes: Population: Total earners principal occupation: Females.	Total all classes: Population: Total working dependants: Males.	Total all classes: Population: Total working dependants: Females.	Total all classes: Population: Total non-working dependants: Males.	Total all classes: Population: Total non-working dependants: Females.	Total all classes: Total earners with subsidiary occupation: Males.	Total all classes: Total earners with subsidiary occupation: Females.	Class / Sub-Class / Order / Group. / Total: Total earners principal occupation: Males.	Class / Sub-Class / Order / Group. / Total: Total earners principal occupation: Females.
	1	2	3	4	5	6	7	8	9	10	11	12
	PUNJAB ..	28,490,857	7,979,157	536,593	1,028,792	948,658	6,553,245	11,444,412	788,137	36,343	4,750,984	236,842
	BRITISH TERRITORY ..	23,580,852	6,487,009	441,538	789,776	607,935	5,603,725	9,650,869	602,300	29,856	3,718,644	178,185
	AMBALA DIVISION ..	4,077,565	1,083,919	90,016	223,272	297,341	919,665	1,463,352	135,168	6,265	680,099	37,619
1	Hissar ..	899,479	223,472	13,311	82,623	106,464	179,595	294,014	30,491	1,103	158,801	6,142
2	Rohtak ..	805,621	201,565	14,815	47,439	82,482	183,851	275,469	31,261	1,924	126,441	7,100
3	Gurgaon ..	740,163	189,992	18,108	43,667	71,695	164,854	251,847	20,949	1,147	126,106	10,585
4	Karnal ..	852,614	218,944	22,723	23,694	17,729	227,232	342,290	21,939	1,357	139,926	7,788
5	Ambala ..	742,902	233,162	19,983	24,283	14,343	158,966	292,165	27,464	666	123,881	5,661
6	Simla ..	36,786	16,784	1,074	1,566	4,628	5,167	7,567	3,064	68	4,944	343
	JULLUNDUR DIVISION	4,606,446	1,296,695	90,459	178,779	178,175	1,016,164	1,846,174	150,772	6,007	818,225	47,919
7	Kangra ..	801,312	234,549	29,713	33,734	113,980	147,005	242,331	39,411	2,221	179,302	24,558
8	Hoshiarpur ..	1,032,187	291,694	16,965	37,656	46,476	222,517	416,879	37,927	1,123	185,196	7,467
9	Jullundur ..	943,721	248,191	16,893	54,241	8,950	210,235	405,211	29,584	721	136,886	5,641
10	Ludhiana ..	672,494	209,746	11,383	18,577	4,689	147,237	280,862	19,194	865	122,251	4,560
11	Ferozepore .	1,156,732	312,515	15,505	34,571	4,080	289,170	500,891	24,656	1,077	194,590	5,693
	LAHORE DIVISION ..	5,879,075	1,686,243	94,659	158,308	51,848	1,433,110	2,454,907	119,178	4,097	794,745	20,577
12	Lahore ..	1,378,570	441,645	24,352	19,291	4,542	333,453	555,287	14,433	877	166,041	4,308
13	Amritsar .	1,117,120	315,470	20,599	43,808	31,408	261,762	444,073	24,754	1,532	125,366	4,096
14	Gurdaspur ..	970,898	271,147	13,849	31,734	4,489	229,054	420,625	27,848	538	157,037	3,624
15	Sialkot ..	979,617	265,478	11,513	27,116	4,968	244,707	425,835	24,414	273	135,833	2,589
16	Gujranwala ..	736,138	210,791	13,859	19,122	2,597	178,693	311,076	15,509	607	101,432	1,543
17	Sheikhupura ..	696,732	181,712	10,487	17,237	3,844	185,441	298,011	12,215	270	109,036	4,415
	RAWALPINDI DIVISION	3,914,849	1,031,160	98,527	126,208	53,838	935,254	1,669,862	90,604	4,319	599,077	53,891
18	Gujrat ..	922,427	255,261	15,209	38,041	12,996	205,034	395,886	15,830	483	144,722	5,376
19	Shahpur ..	821,490	241,385	14,195	14,142	4,129	190,309	357,330	18,262	327	135,732	3,683
20	Jhelum ..	511,076	136,444	30,127	21,137	22,340	125,133	205,895	14,578	1,235	70,034	21,719
21	Rawalpindi ..	634,357	151,171	14,172	15,292	4,547	176,308	272,867	11,137	968	92,322	8,190
22	Attock ..	583,960	144,720	15,337	26,197	7,252	138,032	254,422	16,480	962	88,767	8,722
23	Mianwali ..	411,539	102,179	9,487	11,399	2,574	102,438	183,462	14,317	344	67,500	6,191
	MULTAN DIVISION ..	5,102,917	1,388,992	67,877	103,209	26,733	1,299,532	2,216,574	106,583	9,166	826,466	18,189
24	Montgomery ..	999,772	269,015	13,606	14,111	4,058	269,330	429,652	18,231	270	170,346	3,948
25	Lyallpur ..	1,151,351	294,596	24,402	40,052	14,193	296,101	482,007	18,177	6,574	169,066	7,320
26	Jhang ..	664,833	184,323	7,056	11,478	961	159,870	301,145	14,148	492	95,589	1,091
27	Multan ..	1,174,900	308,428	9,098	18,000	1,294	319,597	518,483	19,996	577	165,070	1,724
28	Muzaffargarh ..	591,375	162,553	6,542	9,693	2,247	148,428	261,912	18,559	779	106,757	1,919
29	Dera Ghazi Khan ..	520,681	170,077	7,173	9,875	3,980	106,206	223,375	17,472	476	119,670	2,187
	PUNJAB STATES ..	4,910,005	1,492,148	95,055	239,016	340,782	949,520	1,793,543	185,837	6,487	1,032,340	58,657
	A.—Having Political relations with the Punjab Government. ..	437,787	124,161	9,152	36,204	97,607	68,925	101,738	16,199	426	99,525	6,363
1	Dujana ..	28,216	8,170	291	297	2,628	6,070	10,760	1,818	26	5,557	136
2	Pataudi ..	18,873	5,443	895	403	33	4,076	8,023	851	38	3,545	430
3	Kalsia ..	59,848	18,591	1,538	2,516	769	12,199	24,235	2,358	60	11,391	406
4	SIMLA HILL STATES ..	330,850	91,957	6,428	32,988	94,177	46,560	58,720	11,172	302	79,032	5,391
	Bashahr ..	101,389	22,975	2,530	14,711	35,237	13,907	15,029	1,144	10	22,156	2,510
	Nalagarh ..	50,015	14,707	1,102	3,287	8,638	8,641	13,640	2,487	90	11,159	783
	Keonthal ..	48,093	14,389	968	5,344	13,769	6,001	7,622	1,150	36	11,422	771
	Baghal ..	26,352	9,345	496	373	7,806	3,739	4,593	1,694	58	8,003	407
	Jubbal ..	27,172	7,831	216	2,952	8,346	3,724	4,103	1,143	2	7,492	200
	Other Simla Hill States ..	71,829	22,710	1,116	6,321	20,381	10,568	13,733	3,554	106	18,800	721
	B.—Having Political relations with the Government of India. ..	4,472,218	1,367,987	85,903	202,812	243,116	880,595	1,691,805	169,638	6,061	932,815	52,294
5	Loharu ..	23,338	6,071	245	1,544	2,492	4,711	8,275	538	36	4,848	104
6	Sirmoor ..	148,568	46,118	1,409	12,902	26,086	23,364	38,689	4,720	148	36,939	879
7	Bilaspur ..	100,994	30,652	2,729	7,122	19,071	15,380	26,040	4,162	331	25,210	2,012
8	Mandi ..	207,465	53,409	6,089	17,712	50,307	36,755	43,193	28,855	1,847	40,968	5,035
9	Suket ..	58,408	18,206	812	7,211	14,543	5,344	12,202	1,109	290	16,172	575
10	Kapurthala ..	316,757	97,849	5,321	1,595	1,073	72,085	138,834	13,869	474	60,398	2,150
11	Maler Kotla ..	83,072	24,251	1,358	3,008	521	18,624	35,310	3,195	66	10,425	377
12	Faridkot ..	161,364	51,258	2,015	9,409	178	30,496	71,008	4,790	185	32,556	771
13	Chamba ..	146,870	33,612	1,974	19,645	39,093	22,802	29,744	5,340	181	26,872	1,325
14	Patiala (Phulkian States)	1,625,520	537,074	46,284	77,482	70,046	286,041	608,593	67,808	1,667	367,683	28,974
15	Jind (Phulkian States)	324,676	77,716	4,227	21,036	14,913	77,631	129,153	9,954	258	50,706	2,080
16	Nabha (Phulkian States)	287,574	77,412	3,828	14,661	2,866	66,013	122,794	9,764	280	48,532	1,887
17	Bahawalpur ..	984,612	314,269	9,612	9,485	1,927	221,349	427,970	15,534	298	211,506	6,125
18	*Cities.* Lahore ..	429,747	170,295	5,933	4,339	445	99,953	148,782	3,019	64	16,860	296
19	*Cities.* Amritsar ..	264,840	93,845	3,215	1,617	72	63,523	102,568	785	19	7,694	87
20	*Cities.* Multan ..	119,457	31,604	1,061	145	47	36,370	50,230	958	23	3,555	56

LIVELIHOOD.—GENERAL TABLE.

STATES AND CITIES.—*continued.*

A.—PRODUCTION OF RAW MATERIALS.

I.—EXPLOITATION OF ANIMALS AND VEGETATION.

Order I.—Pasture and Agriculture.

SUB-ORDER (*a*).—CULTIVATION.

of Class A.				Total Sub-Class I.						*Total of Order I.*						
Total working dependants.		Total earners with subsidiary occupation.		Total earners principal occupation.		Total working dependants.		Total earners with subsidiary occupation.		Total earners principal occupation.		Total working dependants.		Total earners with subsidiary occupation.		
Males.	Females.	Males.	Females.	Males.	Females.	Males.	Females.	Males.	Females.	Males.	Females.	Males.	Females.	Males.	Females.	Serial No.
13	14	15	16	17	18	19	20	21	22	23	24	25	26	27	28	
867,080	819,539	486,982	20,009	4,746,048	236,226	866,820	819,466	486,789	20,008	4,741,058	236,151	866,558	819,405	485,645	20,007	
650,305	497,951	369,598	15,377	3,714,085	177,579	650,077	497,920	369,457	15,376	3,710,182	177,535	649,848	497,887	368,459	15,375	
203,230	268,971	77,412	3,724	679,333	37,579	203,214	268,969	77,350	3,723	678,901	37,576	203,194	268,940	77,296	3,723	
76,871	99,203	15,888	590	158,665	6,140	76,858	99,202	15,881	590	158,605	6,139	76,852	99,173	15,870	50	1
43,248	74,658	20,286	1,275	126,216	7,096	43,248	74,657	20,265	1,275	126,197	7,096	43,248	74,657	20,265	1,?75	2
40,900	66,941	13,891	798	125,811	10,581	40,900	66,941	13,879	797	125,794	10,581	40,900	66,941	13,874	797	3
19,096	13,516	11,966	610	139,829	7,758	19,093	13,515	11,944	610	139,637	7,756	19,082	13,515	11,908	610	4
22,109	10,080	14,136	405	123,868	5,661	22,109	10,080	14,136	405	123,731	5,661	22,106	10,080	14,134	40?	5
1,006	4,574	1,245	46	4,944	343	1,006	4,574	1,245	46	4,937	343	1,006	4,574	1,245	46	6
150,589	155,066	86,837	3,552	817,707	47,870	150,565	155,058	86,780	3,552	816,788	47,864	150,503	155,054	86,143	3,551	
31,360	108,353	22,411	1,371	178,898	24,509	31,360	108,345	22,364	1,371	178,396	24,506	31,314	108,341	2?,843	1,370	7
33,862	37,292	21,576	829	185,172	7,467	33,862	37,292	21,573	829	185,055	7,467	33,861	37,292	21,54?	82?	8
40,784	3,894	17,827	280	136,882	5,641	40,761	3,894	17,827	280	136,809	5,640	40,756	3,894	17,80?	2?0	9
14,605	3,071	8,916	369	122,198	4,560	14,604	3,071	8,914	369	122,131	4,560	14,598	3,071	8,851	360	10
29,978	2,456	16,107	703	104,557	5,693	29,978	2,456	16,102	703	194,307	5,691	29,974	2,456	16,099	?3	11
118,729	19,192	69,645	1,294	794,590	20,567	118,725	19,190	69,641	1,294	793,478	20,555	118,694	19,170	69,457	1,294	
11,450	390	7,842	415	165,916	4,306	11,450	388	7,838	415	165,553	4,304	11,450	388	7,825	415	12
32,319	16,186	13,955	383	125,360	4,098	32,319	16,186	13,955	383	125,310	4,098	32,314	16,186	13,943	383	13
25,202	498	13,590	141	157,037	3,624	25,202	498	13,590	141	156,733	3,624	25,196	478	13,465	141	14
21,830	344	16,781	65	135,832	2,589	21,830	344	16,781	65	135,570	2,589	21,814	344	16,754	65	15
14,941	482	9,323	160	101,429	1,535	14,941	482	0,323	160	101,325	1,535	14,937	482	9,316	16?	16
12,987	1,292	8,154	130	109,016	4,415	12,983	1,202	8,154	130	108,987	4,405	12,983	1,292	8,154	13?	17
99,738	89,424	59,078	2,332	595,984	53,382	99,554	39,405	59,060	2,332	595,791	53,382	99,548	39,405	59,033	2,382	
29,347	10,381	9,132	176	144,641	5,376	29,342	10,381	9,129	176	144,602	5,376	29,342	10,381	9,126	176	18
11,794	1,567	13,677	146	135,423	3,653	11,774	1,548	13,677	146	135,403	3,653	11,774	1,548	13,677	146	19
16,581	16,160	7,576	617	68,823	21,255	16,563	16,160	7,571	617	68,820	21,255	16,563	16,160	7,571	617	20
11,313	3,663	5,636	487	92,322	8,190	11,313	3,663	5,636	487	92,286	8,190	11,305	3,663	5,631	487	21
21,533	5,932	11,401	621	87,697	8,718	21,516	5,932	11,391	621	87,676	8,718	21,516	5,932	11,385	621	22
9,170	1,721	11,656	285	67,078	6,190	9,046	1,721	11,656	285	67,004	6,190	9,043	1,721	11,643	285	23
78,019	15,298	76,626	4,475	826,471	18,181	78,019	15,298	76,626	4,475	825,224	18,158	77,914	15,298	76,530	4,475	
10,566	1,905	12,941	72	170,332	3,940	10,566	1,905	12,941	72	170,117	3,922	10,559	1,905	12,918	72	24
32,378	10,600	10,459	3,415	169,066	7,320	32,378	10,600	10,459	3,415	168,997	7,320	32,374	10,600	10,456	3,415	25
6,881	63	10,570	83	95,587	1,091	6,881	63	10,570	83	95,499	1,091	6,878	63	10,566	83	26
13,500	301	15,060	187	165,059	1,724	13,500	301	15,060	187	164,743	1,720	13,418	301	15,037	187	27
7,596	638	15,025	430	106,757	1,919	7,596	638	15,025	430	106,480	1,918	7,592	638	14,904	43?	28
7,098	1,791	12,571	288	119,670	2,187	7,098	1,791	12,571	288	119,388	2,187	7,093	1,791	12,559	288	20
216,775	321,588	117,384	4,632	1,031,963	58,647	216,743	321,546	117,332	4,632	1,030,876	58,616	216,710	321,538	117,186	4,632	
34,965	95,968	6,064	269	99,449	6,362	34,961	95,967	6,054	269	99,403	6,361	34,958	95,967	6,036	269	
267	2,356	947	18	5,557	136	267	2,355	947	18	5,557	136	267	2,355	947	18	1
395	3	574	23	3,544	430	395	3	574	23	3,544	430	395	3	574	2?	2
2,138	84	1,196	29	11,390	406	2,138	84	1,195	29	11,380	406	2,138	84	1,195	2?	3
32,165	93,525	3,347	199	78,958	5,390	32,161	93,525	3,338	199	78,922	5,389	32,158	93,525	3,320	199	4
14,553	35,191	196	4	22,145	2,510	14,550	35,191	196	4	22,141	2,510	14,547	35,191	190	4	
3,230	8,605	827	57	11,159	782	3,230	8,605	827	57	11,141	781	3,230	8,605	827	57	
5,166	13,657	237	29	11,361	770	5,165	13,657	229	29	11,358	770	5,165	13,657	226	29	
351	7,613	705	52	8,003	407	351	7,613	705	52	8,001	407	351	7,613	705	52	
2,871	8,282	210	1	7,491	200	2,871	8,282	210	1	7,487	200	2,871	8,282	207	1	
5,994	20,177	1,172	56	18,799	721	5,994	20,177	1,171	56	18,794	721	5,994	20,177	1,165	56	
181,810	225.620	111,320	4,363	932,514	52,285	181,782	225,579	111,278	4,363	931,473	52,255	181,752	225,571	111,150	4,363	
1,518	2,426	359	14	4,848	104	1,518	2,426	359	14	4,846	104	1,518	2,426	359	14	5
12,674	25,693	2,828	123	36,934	879	12,674	25,693	2,828	123	36,930	879	12,674	25,693	2,827	123	6
6,861	18,836	2,062	300	25,210	2,012	6,861	18,836	2,051	300	25,205	2,012	6,861	18,836	2,011	300	7
17,526	50,183	21,270	1,762	40,958	5,035	17,526	50,183	21,264	1,762	40,929	5,035	17,526	50,183	21,257	1,762	8
7,056	13,886	327	271	16,172	569	7,056	13,885	321	271	16,172	569	7,056	13,885	312	271	9
1,248	345	10,099	320	60,398	2,150	1,248	345	10,099	320	60,226	2,147	1,248	345	10,066	320	10
2,176	176	1,134	5	10,425	377	2,176	176	1,134	5	10,422	377	2,176	176	1,134	5	11
8,969	92	3,328	145	32,555	771	8,969	92	3,328	145	32,529	771	8,969	92	3,328	145	12
19,280	38,621	1,844	100	26,872	1,325	19,280	38,621	1,844	100	26,842	1,325	19,277	38,621	1,818	100	13
65,422	59,356	43,551	823	367,535	28,974	65,407	59,322	43,551	823	367,462	28,974	65,398	59,317	43,551	823	14
18,746	13,214	5,186	147	50,632	2,077	18,733	13,208	5,167	147	50,613	2,077	18,733	13,208	5,155	147	15
13,130	1,968	4,658	166	48,532	1,887	13,136	1,968	4,658	166	48,522	1,887	13,136	1,968	4,658	166	16
7,198	824	14,674	187	211,443	6,125	7,198	824	14,674	187	210,775	6,098	7,180	821	14,674	187	17
297	40	1,435	12	16,769	296	297	40	1,435	12	16,648	296	297	40	1,431	12	18
414	9	204	..	7,688	87	414	9	201	..	7,677	87	414	9	204	..	19
94	..	338	2	3,549	56	94	..	338	2	3,549	56	94	..	338	2	20

TABLE X—OCCUPATION OR MEANS OF

DETAILS FOR DISTRICTS,

Class — A.—PRODUCTION OF RAW MATERIALS.

Sub-class — I.—EXPLOITATION OF ANIMALS AND VEGITATION.

Order — Order I.—Pasture and agriculture.

SUB-ORDER (a).—CULTIVATION.

Serial No.	Group .. / DISTRICT OR STATE.	Total of Sub-Order (a). Total earners principal occupation. Males.	Females.	Total working dependants. Males.	Females.	Total earners with subsidiary occupation. Males.	Females.	1.—Non-cultivating proprietors taking rent i. money or kind. Total earners principal occupation. Males.	Females.	Total working dependants. Males.	Females.	Total earners with subsidiary occupation. Males.	Females.	2 -Es... Total earn. principal occupation. Males.	Females.
1	2	29	30	31	32	33	34	35	36	37	38	39	40	41	42
	PUNJAB ..	**4,537,644**	**229,878**	**802,842**	**810,350**	**466,995**	**19,486**	**228,373**	**66,395**	**18,854**	**7,051**	**136,381**	**7,235**	**2,175**	**5**
	BRITISH TERRITORY ..	**3,541,523**	**172,409**	**602,027**	**494,839**	**352,760**	**15,127**	**192,531**	**54,301**	**17,583**	**6,639**	**114,483**	**5,264**	**1,782**	**5**
	AMBALA DIVISION ..	**647,127**	**36,271**	**180,699**	**267,566**	**74,138**	**3,667**	**14,489**	**8,575**	**291**	**381**	**18,533**	**1,279**	**69**	.
1	Hissar ..	154,202	6,008	68,620	98,764	15,167	579	1,558	833	25	26	4,605	180	44	..
2	Rohtak ..	123,118	7,030	39,648	74,563	19,884	1,269	2,786	1,905	97	152	3,368	368	3	..
3	Gurgaon ..	122,448	10,384	36,258	66,804	13,348	788	1,056	824	24	11	2,224	219	13	.
4	Karnal ..	128,236	7,443	15,721	13,348	11,302	603	3,118	2,238	68	115	3,457	202	[illegible]	.
5	Ambala ..	114,688	5,161	19,478	9,535	13,355	383	5,879	2,770	76	77	4,795	214	2	..
6	Simla ..	4,435	245	974	4,552	1,082	45	92	5	1	..	84	6	..	..
	JULLUNDUR DIVISION	**793,611**	**46,422**	**145,544**	**154,552**	**83,461**	**3,472**	**52,276**	**14,913**	**4,151**	**2,601**	**30,351**	**1,800**	**308**	.
7	Kangra ..	170,765	23,361	30,051	107,936	20,715	1,300	5,417	3,128	198	311	6,075	618	3	..
8	Hoshiarpur ..	181,888	7,326	32,846	37,273	21,183	828	8,616	3,244	340	370	8,093	464	..	.
9	Jullundur ..	133,900	5,588	40,118	3,885	17,395	280	20,299	3,637	1,822	1,332	7,353	191	304	.
10	Ludhiana ..	118,211	4,512	14,169	3,064	8,533	365	9,786	2,266	499	289	3,887	223	..	..
11	Ferozepore ..	188,847	5,635	28,360	2,304	15,635	699	8,158	2,638	1,292	299	4,943	304	1	.
	LAHORE DIVISION ..	**757,959**	**20,122**	**108,845**	**19,117**	**66,497**	**1,282**	**43,634**	**9,752**	**3,017**	**947**	**18,636**	**519**	**98**	..
12	Lahore ..	154,715	3,989	9,352	378	7,353	414	11,180	1,938	384	90	2,267	87	35	.
13	Amritsar ..	117,913	4,075	30,349	16,169	13,407	377	9,144	2,554	608	276	3,510	143	1	.
14	Gurdaspur ..	150,810	3,604	23,236	477	12,559	140	7,677	2,456	728	134	4,608	92	55	.
15	Sialkot ..	131,619	2,556	21,086	335	16,380	65	8,978	1,477	704	143	3,288	32	..	..
16	Gujranwala ..	97,573	1,524	13,068	480	9,113	158	3,515	650	196	50	2,073	121	..	..
17	Sheikhupura ..	105,329	4,374	11,754	1,278	7,685	128	3,140	677	397	245	2,890	44	7	..
	RAWALPINDI DIVISION	**570,488**	**52,153**	**94,014**	**38,670**	**55,435**	**2,309**	**35,904**	**16,949**	**5,738**	**2,068**	**19,017**	**927**	**110**	..
18	Gujrat ..	140,081	5,344	28,227	10,379	8,875	176	7,497	2,524	1,202	103	2,999	73	36	..
19	Shahpur ..	125,420	3,581	10,757	1,519	12,499	146	5,819	1,839	258	137	6,832	73	64	.
20	Jhelum ..	66,277	20,712	15,301	15,622	7,280	613	6,296	4,260	933	286	1,673	147	..	.
21	Rawalpindi ..	90,336	8,169	10,840	3,663	5,508	487	8,913	4,096	1,396	646	2,025	327	..	.
22	Attock ..	85,143	8,383	20,303	5,816	11,075	614	2,903	1,812	382	288	3,042	137	9	.
23	Mianwali ..	63,231	5,964	8,586	1,671	10,198	273	4,476	2,418	1,567	608	2,446	170	1	.
	MULTAN DIVISION ..	**772,338**	**17,441**	**72,925**	**14,934**	**73,229**	**4,397**	**46,228**	**4,112**	**4,886**	**642**	**27,946**	**739**	**1,197**	
24	Montgomery ..	161,449	3,747	9,813	1,874	12,376	67	13,858	691	829	71	5,487	32	163	.
25	Lyallpur ..	158,174	7,138	31,189	10,431	9,570	3,395	7,396	1,000	1,900	155	1,422	157	127	.
26	Jhang ..	90,627	1,087	6,561	63	10,403	83	5,072	577	247	22	4,004	48	170	.
27	Multan ..	151,554	1,567	12,648	293	14,610	186	10,866	712	826	144	5,848	114	727	
28	Muzaffargarh ..	98,045	1,820	6,393	620	14,605	397	5,070	582	323	137	4,592	192	9	.
29	Dera Ghazi Khan ..	112,489	2,082	6,321	1,653	11,665	269	3,966	550	261	113	6,593	196	1	.
	PUNJAB STATES ..	**996,121**	**57,469**	**200,815**	**315,511**	**114,225**	**4,359**	**35,842**	**12,094**	**1,271**	**412**	**21,898**	**1,971**	**393**	.
	A.—HAVING POLITICAL RELATIONS WITH THE PUNJAB GOVERNMENT. ..	**96,652**	**6,220**	**33,345**	**95,208**	**5,415**	**251**	**1,027**	**835**	**14**	**16**	**1,705**	**151**	**2**	.
1	Dujana ..	5,446	136	232	2,355	941	18	30	52	5	4	408	15	.	.
2	Pataudi ..	3,364	426	392	3	550	22	126	48	..	..	301	17	..	.
3	Kalsia ..	10,407	393	1,769	83	1,127	29	603	316	1	1	410	15	1	
4	**SIMLA HILL STATES** ..	**77,435**	**5,265**	**30,952**	**92,767**	**2,797**	**182**	**268**	**419**	**8**	**11**	**586**	**104**	**1**	.
	Bashahr ..	21,682	2,472	14,406	35,138	93	4	1	..	..	..	..	.	..	.
	Nalagarh ..	10,923	768	3,177	8,605	779	56	171	327	1	.	171	33	..	.
	Koonthal ..	11,082	750	5,112	13,596	168	15	16	6	1	.	68	8	.	
	Baghal ..	7,874	397	163	7,509	678	52	20	19	6	11	102	40	.	
	Jubbal ..	7,413	192	2,648	8,166	119	1	8	2	..	..	21	..	..	
	Other Simla Hill States ..	18,461	686	5,446	19,753	960	54	52	65	..	..	164	23	1	
	B.—HAVING POLITICAL RELATIONS WITH THE GOVERNMENT OF INDIA. ..	**899,469**	**51,249**	**167,470**	**220,303**	**108,820**	**4,108**	**34,815**	**11,259**	**1,257**	**396**	**20,193**	**1,820**	**391**	..
5	Loharu ..	4,667	99	842	2,060	352	12	52	.	..	..	16	..	..	..
6	Sirmoor ..	35,591	849	12,131	25,495	2,528	121	129	52	1	2	1,455	79	..	.
7	Bilaspur ..	23,952	1,900	6,642	18,786	1,943	300	222	276	10	75	664	197	..	.
8	Mandi ..	39,549	4,942	14,193	47,281	20,474	1,757	2,447	1,037	1	1	2,063	758	2	..
9	Suket ..	15,631	524	6,492	13,865	220	45	70	31	15	4	198	23	..	..
10	Kapurthala ..	59,145	2,141	1,167	344	9,932	319	3,167	884	142	43	3,056	133	..	..
11	Maler Kotla ..	9,953	372	2,090	169	1,044	5	1,213	274	71	18	542	4	12	..
12	Faridkot ..	31,464	762	7,881	84	3,248	144	2,337	509	22	17	1,509	125	..	..
13	Chamba ..	25,922	1,232	18,946	38,385	1,345	91	415	744	1	1	299	7	2	..
14	Patiala (Phulkian States)	358,616	28,739	63,561	58,082	43,541	818	13,268	5,219	321	129	3,816	288	275	..
15	Jind (Phulkian States)	49,244	2,046	14,929	13,116	5,013	146	840	671	23	19	1,101	90	..	..
16	Nabha (Phulkian States)	46,561	1,861	12,348	1,950	4,507	164	2,353	935	..	..	2,675	112	12	.
17	Bahawalpur	199,174	5,782	6,248	686	14,673	186	8,302	627	650	87	2,799	4	88	.
18	*Cities.* Lahore ..	14,262	163	249	40	1,283	12	4,655	66	38	0	328	8	35	..
19	*Cities.* Amritsar ..	5,668	87	349	9	204	..	378	67	68	9	1	..	..	..
20	*Cities.* Multan ..	3,079	48	94	..	333	1	986	17	72	.	277	1	87	..

LIVELIHOOD.—GENERAL TABLE.

STATES AND CITIES.—*continued.*

A.—PRODUCTION OF RAW MATERIALS.—*continued.*

I.—EXPLOITATION OF ANIMALS AND VEGETATION.—*continued.*

1. Pasture and Agriculture.—*continued.*

(a) CULTIVATION,—*continued.*

agents and managers of owners.				*3.—Estate agents and managers of Government.*						*4.—Rent collectors, clerks, etc.*						*5.—Cultivating owners.*						*6.—Tenant Cultivators.*		
Total working dependants.		Total earners with subsidiary occupation.		Total earners principal occupation.		Total working dependants.		Total earners with subsidiary occupation.		Total earners principal occupation.		Total working dependants.		Total earners with subsidiary occupation.		Total earners principal occupation.		Total working dependants.		Total earners with subsidiary occupation.		Total earner principal occupation.		
Males.	Females.	Males.	Females.	Males.	Females.	Males.	Females.	Males.	Females.	Males.	Females.	Males.	Females.	Males	Females.	Males.	Females.	Males.	Females.	Males.	Females.	Males.	Females.	Serial No.
43	44	45	46	47	48	49	50	51	52	53	54	55	56	57	58	59	60	61	62	63	64	65	66	
194	**9**	**128**	..	**163**	..	**1**	..	**19**	..	**1,106**	..	**40**	**17**	**31**	..	**2,314,804**	**84,478**	**228,867**	**196,080**	**113,218**	**3,831**	**1,363,751**	**33,682**	
182	..	**108**	..	**97**	..	..	..	**4**	..	**468**	..	**18**	.	**19**	..	**1,707,744**	**54,454**	**103,850**	**45,995**	**58,522**	**2,382**	**1,128,014**	**29,449**	
..	..	**4**	..	**81**	..	..	..	**4**	..	**234**	..	**2**	..	**13**	..	**373,754**	**8,851**	**2,609**	**80**	**6,865**	**137**	**161,930**	**3,236**	
..	..	1	..	46	..	..	..	..	..	196	..	1	..	11	..	69,831	1,637	64	39	2,066	20	68,713	1,471	
..	..	1	..	14	..	..	..	..	..	2	..	1	..	1	..	90,347	2,209	31	6	1,100	23	14,230	32[illegible]	2
..	..	2	..	14	..	..	..	3	..	8	..	..	..	..	..	72,224	2,164	2,453	1	1,070	28	28,193	838	3
..	..	..	..	3	..	..	..	..	..	14	..	..	..	..	..	72,673	1,497	31	16	592	7	27,020	210	4
..	..	..	..	3	..	..	..	1	..	15	..	..	..	..	..	65,136	1,207	18	..	1,397	34	23,235	352	5
..	..	..	..	1	..	..	..	..	..	5	..	..	..	1	..	3,543	137	12	18	640	25	537	49	6
35	..	**15**	..	**1**	..	..	..	..	..	**44**	..	..	..	..	..	**457,443**	**14,725**	**15,870**	**22,721**	**14,087**	**905**	**164,974**	**12,637**	
..	..	..	..	1	..	..	..	..	..	..	..	..	..	..	..	131,801	9,082	5,091	21,711	7,180	398	27,217	9,523	7
..	..	..	..	..	..	..	..	..	..	1	..	..	..	..	..	93,386	1,839	48	116	1,392	97	59,591	1,720	8
35	..	14	..	..	..	..	..	..	..	40	..	..	..	..	..	72,018	873	5,322	383	2,355	41	15,543	78	9
..	..	..	..	..	..	..	..	..	..	3	..	..	..	..	..	81,689	1,540	488	63	636	13	5,779	520	10
..	..	1	..	..	..	..	..	..	..	..	..	..	..	..	..	77,649	1,385	4,921	448	2,524	356	56,844	796	11
..	..	..	..	..	..	..	..	..	..	**24**	..	..	..	..	..	**357,871**	**4,268**	**29,009**	**6,024**	**9,830**	**156**	**220,915**	**1,357**	
..	..	..	..	..	..	..	..	..	..	1	..	..	..	..	..	62,744	777	3,207	101	1,238	43	45,914	478	12
..	..	..	..	..	..	..	..	..	..	17	..	..	..	..	..	59,849	844	6,669	5,216	2,573	33	25,129	177	13
..	..	..	..	..	..	..	..	..	..	4	..	..	..	..	..	85,986	805	8,079	97	1,995	37	38,237	182	14
..	..	..	..	..	..	..	..	..	..	..	..	..	..	..	..	75,177	582	6,677	37	1,814	9	25,323	211	15
..	..	..	..	..	..	..	..	..	..	2	..	..	..	..	..	35,204	262	1,283	34	1,014	16	45,811	206	16
..	..	..	..	..	..	..	..	..	..	..	..	..	..	..	..	38,821	993	2,194	539	1,176	19	40,501	103	17
3	..	**14**	..	**6**	..	..	..	..	..	**19**	..	**16**	..	**4**	..	**290,033**	**23,199**	**31,950**	**16,423**	**13,708**	**648**	**203,910**	**9,327**	
2	..	..	..	..	..	..	..	..	..	1	..	..	..	..	..	80,977	1,961	15,499	9,953	2,036	23	45,731	555	8
1	..	11	..	6	..	..	..	..	..	18	..	16	..	4	..	46,353	349	1,319	718	849	16	56,048	414	19
..	..	..	..	..	..	..	..	..	..	..	..	..	..	..	..	48,401	12,679	4,690	3,557	3,101	366	9,592	3,517	20
..	..	..	..	..	..	..	..	..	..	..	..	..	..	..	..	43,030	2,329	4,069	313	1,356	132	32,625	863	21
..	..	3	..	..	..	..	..	..	..	..	..	..	..	..	..	35,194	4,140	6,238	1,571	3,862	54	41,255	2,236	22
..	..	..	..	..	..	..	..	..	..	..	..	..	..	..	..	35,818	1,741	135	311	2,499	57	18,659	1,742	23
144	..	**75**	..	**9**	..	..	..	..	..	**142**	..	..	..	**2**	..	**228,643**	**8,416**	**24,412**	**747**	**14,087**	**536**	**376,285**	**2,892**	
1	..	4	..	..	..	..	..	..	..	2	..	..	..	..	..	20,630	445	1,009	13	2,158	8	110,134	936	24
..	..	11	..	..	..	..	..	..	..	125	..	..	..	2	..	70,042	1,449	15,141	300	2,867	346	41,644	348	25
..	..	7	..	..	..	..	..	..	..	..	..	..	..	..	..	31,979	60	2,972	8	1,040	3	43,374	85	26
143	..	52	..	9	..	..	..	..	..	8	..	..	..	..	..	31,239	277	2,661	54	1,779	29	91,708	166	27
..	..	..	..	..	..	..	..	..	..	..	..	..	..	..	..	40,864	752	1,994	86	4,708	111	32,428	335	28
..	..	1	..	..	..	..	..	..	..	7	..	..	..	..	..	33,869	433	635	86	1,485	39	56,497	722	29
12	**9**	**20**	..	**66**	..	**1**	..	**15**	..	**643**	..	**22**	**17**	**12**	..	**607,060**	**30,024**	**125,017**	**150,085**	**54,696**	**1,449**	**285,787**	**4,233**	
..	..	**1**	..	..	..	..	..	..	..	**1**	..	..	..	..	..	**74,311**	**3,047**	**5,607**	**14,952**	**589**	**9**	**14,924**	**561**	
..	..	..	..	..	..	..	..	..	..	..	..	..	..	..	..	4,647	77	4	..	54	..	338	2	1
..	..	..	..	..	..	..	..	..	..	1	..	..	..	..	..	1,696	36	..	..	29	..	698	9	2
..	..	..	..	..	..	..	..	..	..	..	..	..	..	..	..	6,373	46	.	.	43	1	1,587	10	3
..	..	**1**	..	..	..	..	..	..	..	..	..	..	..	..	..	**61,595**	**2,868**	**5,603**	**14,952**	**463**	**8**	**12,301**	**540**	4
..	..	..	..	..	..	..	..	..	..	..	..	..	..	..	..	20,184	1,204	5,603	14,952	.	..	98	2	
..	..	..	..	..	..	..	..	..	..	..	..	..	..	..	..	9,340	362	..	..	215	7	1,277	72	
..	..	1	..	..	..	..	..	..	..	..	..	..	..	..	..	7,156	513	..	..	1	1	3,301	171	
..	..	..	..	..	..	..	..	..	..	..	..	..	..	..	..	5,135	234	..	..	.	..	2,582	133	
..	..	..	..	..	..	..	..	..	..	..	..	..	..	..	..	5,654	121	..	..	..	..	1,640	66	
..	..	..	..	..	..	..	..	..	..	..	..	..	..	..	..	14,126	434	..	..	247	..	3,403	96	
12	**9**	**19**	..	**66**	..	**1**	..	**15**	..	**642**	..	**22**	**17**	**12**	..	**532,749**	**26,977**	**119,410**	**135,083**	**54,107**	**1,440**	**220,813**	**3,672**	
..	..	..	..	..	..	..	..	..	..	..	..	..	..	..	..	3,735	65	9	..	32	1	457	16	5
..	..	..	..	..	..	..	..	..	..	20	..	..	..	..	..	20,505	454	12	..	139	3	12,234	292	6
..	..	..	..	..	..	..	..	..	..	6	..	..	..	..	..	12,541	1,042	42	3	376	..	10,430	510	7
..	..	3	..	..	..	..	..	..	..	..	..	..	..	..	..	25,851	1,763	14,187	47,278	11,964	875	9,677	619	8
..	..	..	..	..	..	..	..	..	..	..	..	..	..	..	..	15,263	433	6,463	13,848	..	22	44	4	9
..	..	..	..	..	..	..	..	..	..	..	..	..	..	..	..	37,285	665	830	248	4,168	121	7,996	158	10
..	..	1	..	..	..	..	..	..	..	..	..	..	..	..	..	6,259	65	1,716	138	80	1	588	1	11
..	..	..	..	..	..	..	..	..	..	..	..	..	..	..	..	17,319	146	7,416	51	722	18	3,345	8	12
..	..	..	..	..	..	..	..	..	..	..	..	..	..	..	..	22,925	364	18,940	38,117	866	75	1,894	18	13
12	9	..	..	25	..	..	..	..	..	512	..	22	17	..	..	236,336	19,697	52,663	33,445	26,511	256	62,127	908	14
..	..	..	..	18	..	1	..	..	..	1	..	..	..	..	..	38,409	834	4,850	3	612	5	5,877	196	15
..	..	3	..	..	..	..	..	..	..	..	..	..	..	..	..	30,554	528	11,266	1,903	363	8	5,878	113	16
..	..	12	..	23	..	..	..	15	..	103	..	..	..	12	..	65,767	921	1,016	49	8,274	55	100,266	829	17
..	..	..	..	..	..	..	..	..	..	..	..	..	..	..	..	3,770	24	89	15	183	3	3,347	53	18
..	..	..	..	..	..	..	..	..	..	9	..	..	..	..	..	1,190	10	2	..	6	..	3,134	4	19
15	..	4	..	3	..	..	..	..	..	5	..	..	..	..	..	433	16	7	..	52	..	899	1	20

TABLE X.—OCCUPATION OR MEANS OF

DETAILS FOR DISTRICTS,

Class — A.—PRODUCTION OF RAW MATERIALS.

Sub-class — I.—EXPLOITATION OF ANIMALS AND VEGITATION.

Order — I. —Pasture and Agriculture.

SUB-ORDER (a).—CULTIVATION.—*concluded.* | Sub-order (b).—Cultivation of special crops, fruit, etc. (planters, managers, clerks and labourers).

Group — *Tenant Cultivators—concluded.* | 7.—*Agricultural labourers.* | *Total Sub-order* (b).

Serial No.	District or State.	Total working dependants. Males.	Total working dependants. Females.	Total earners with subsidiary occupation. Males.	Total earners with subsidiary occupation. Females.	Total earners principal occupation. Males.	Total earners principal occupation. Females.	Total working dependants. Males.	Total working dependants. Females.	Total earners with subsidiary occupation. Males.	Total earners with subsidiary occupation. Females.	Total earners principal occupation. Males.	Total earners principal occupation. Females.	Total working dependants. Males.	Total working dependants. Females.	Total earners with subsidiary occupation. Males.	Total earners with subsidiary occupation. Females.
1	2	67	68	69	70	71	72	73	74	75	76	77	78	79	80	81	82
	PUNJAB	520,866	577,825	153,907	3,507	627,272	45,318	34,020	29,418	63,311	4,913	6,945	839	155	96	648	15
	BRITISH TERRITORY	452,268	417,461	126,682	2,940	510,892	34,200	28,126	24,744	52,942	4,541	6,250	838	142	65	567	10
	AMBALA DIVISION	173,047	256,050	30,133	597	96,570	15,609	4,750	11,055	18,586	1,654	1,338	7	24	26	211	9
1	Hissar	68,027	97,841	7,341	209	13,820	2,067	503	858	1,143	170	202	1	2	1	..	..
2	Rohtak	37,000	67,572	7,713	100	15,736	2,593	2,519	6,833	7,701	778	80	1	3	.	14	..
3	Gurgaon	32,842	64,132	4,686	142	20,938	6,558	939	2,660	5,363	399	285	..	6	.	25	1
4	Karnal	15,171	12,669	4,245	46	25,401	3,498	451	548	3,008	258	157	..	12	3	13	..
5	Ambala	19,046	9,312	5,897	88	20,418	832	338	146	1,265	47	310	5	1	22	40	8
6	Simla	961	4,524	251	12	257	61	..	10	106	2	304	..	..	..	119	.
	JULLUNDUR DIVISION	119,908	127,187	26,737	591	118,565	4,147	5,580	2,043	12,271	176	1,452	684	44	33	235	1
7	Kangra	24,390	85,624	6,724	228	6,326	1,628	372	290	736	56	1,025	677	37	33	210	1
8	Hoshiarpur	32,010	35,643	6,150	237	20,294	523	448	1,144	5,548	30	188	6	1	..	17	..
9	Jullundur	30,054	1,988	5,753	15	24,796	1,000	1,985	182	1,920	33	11	..	..	..	..	..
10	Ludhiana	12,465	2,691	2,622	90	20,954	180	717	21	1,388	39	58	..	..	..	..	
11	Ferozepore	20,089	1,241	5,488	21	46,195	816	2,058	406	2,679	18	170	1	6	..	8	..
	LAHORE DIVISION	68,102	11,199	29,084	260	135,417	4,750	8,717	947	8,947	347	1,825	118	51	..	47	.
12	Lahore	3,291	150	3,434	12	34,841	796	470	28	394	272	1,149	116	36	..	6	..
13	Amritsar	18,663	10,380	5,695	193	23,773	500	4,509	297	1,629	8	248	1	..	..	..	..
14	Gurdaspur	13,598	143	4,427	9	18,851	161	831	103	1,529	2	239	..	14	..	18	..
15	Sialkot	13,895	78	9,155	13	22,141	286	810	77	2,123	11	101	..	1	..	21	..
16	Gujranwala	10,601	293	4,015	18	12,951	406	988	103	2,011	4	65	1	..	..	2	..
17	Sheikhupura	8,054	155	2,338	15	22,860	2,601	1,109	339	1,261	50	23	..	..	..		..
	RAWALPINDI DIVISION	53,521	18,760	20,178	597	40,506	2,678	2,786	1,419	2,519	137	740	22	9	2	43	..
18	Gujrat	11,042	110	3,147	20	5,839	304	482	213	693	60	377	20	1	..	4	..
19	Shahpur	8,675	387	4,002	12	16,912	979	488	277	801	45	254	2	2	..	..	..
20	Jhelum	9,611	11,710	2,327	89	1,928	256	67	63	179	11	32	..	1	2	39	..
21	Rawalpindi	5,225	2,702	1,863	27	5,768	881	150	2	264	1	8	..	2	..	..	..
22	Attock	12,272	3,121	3,847	417	5,782	195	1,411	836	321	6	60	..	3	..	..	..
23	Mianwali	6,696	724	4,992	32	4,277	63	188	28	261	14	9	..	..	..	2	..
	MULTAN DIVISION	37,690	4,265	20,550	895	119,834	7,016	6,293	9,280	10,619	2,227	895	7	14	4	81	..
24	Montgomery	7,601	1,334	3,968	18	16,642	1,675	373	456	759	9	71	..	..	..	..	..
25	Lyallpur	11,971	1,185	2,032	777	38,840	4,341	2,177	8,591	3,236	2,115	339	..	3	..	26	..
26	Jhang	2,766	23	2,888	2	9,532	365	576	10	2,464	30	8	..	..	..	..	..
27	Multan	8,466	53	6,158	18	16,997	107	552	42	773	25	438	6	11	4	2	..
28	Muzaffargarh	3,412	284	3,240	55	19,674	151	664	113	2,065	39	12	1	..	..	2	..
29	Dera Ghazi Khan	3,474	1,386	2,264	25	18,149	377	1,951	68	1,322	9	27	..	..	..	1	..
	PUNJAB STATES	68,598	160,364	27,225	567	116,380	11,118	5,894	4,674	10,369	372	695	1	18	31	81	5
	A.—HAVING POLITICAL RELATIONS WITH THE PUNJAB GOVERNMENT.	27,407	79,729	2,397	73	6,387	1,777	317	511	723	18	190	..	4	..	32	..
1	Dujana	217	2,312	207	1	431	5	6	39	272	2	3	..	..	..	..	..
2	Pataudi	383	..	132	1	843	313	9	3	88	4	31	..	..	..	..	..
3	Kalsia	1,644	57	535	13	1,843	21	124	25	139	..	32	..	..	..	..	..
4	SIMLA HILL STATES	25,163	77,360	1,523	58	3,270	1,438	178	444	224	12	124	..	4	..	32	..
	Bashahr	8,649	19,825	68	3	1,399	1,266	154	361	25	1	6	..	..	..	..	
	Nalagarh	3,175	8,604	376	15	135	7	1	1	17	1	22	..	..	..	1	..
	Keonthal	5,099	13,568	91	4	609	60	12	28	8	2	70	..	2	..	4	.
	Baghal	157	7,497	506	12	137	11	..	1	9	..	8	..	..	..	0	.
	Jubbal	2,648	8,164	93	1	111	3	..	2	5	..	..	..	..	..	3	..
	Other Simla Hill States	5,435	19,702	389	23	879	91	11	51	160	8	18	..	2	..	18	..
	B.—HAVING POLITICAL RELATIONS WITH THE GOVERNMENT OF INDIA.	41,191	80,635	24,828	494	109,993	9,341	5,577	4,163	9,646	354	505	1	9	31	49	5
5	Loharu	819	2,048	266	9	423	18	14	12	38	2	..	..	..	..	..	..
6	Sirmoor	12,096	25,490	876	18	2,703	51	22	3	58	21	92	1	..	1	11	..
7	Bilaspur	6,582	18,701	861	100	753	72	8	7	42	3	5	..	..	..	..	..
8	Mandi	1	..	6,239	108	1,572	1,523	4	2	205	16	7	..	..	..	1	..
9	Suket	2	1	11	..	254	56	12	12	11	..	..	..	..	..	..	..
10	Kapurthala	129	10	1,081	15	10,697	434	66	43	1,627	50	4	..	..	..	..	..
11	Maler Kotla	73	1	221	..	1,881	32	230	12	200	..	9	..	..	..	1	..
12	Faridkot	354	..	853	1	8,463	99	89	16	164	..	17	..	..	..	1	..
13	Chamba	1	201	124	1	686	106	4	66	56	8	..	..	2	..	23	..
14	Patiala (Phulkian States)	7,115	21,409	8,404	78	46,073	2,915	3,428	3,073	4,810	196	142	..	4	30	10	5
15	Jind (Phulkian States)	9,361	12,622	1,904	24	4,099	345	694	472	1,396	27	101	..	1	..	3	..
16	Nabha (Phulkian States)	880	16	939	15	7,764	285	202	31	527	29	50	..	2	..	..	..
17	Bahawalpur	3,778	136	3,049	125	24,625	3,405	804	414	512	2	78	..	..	..	..	..
18	*Cities.* Lahore	99	15	753	1	2,455	20	23	4	19	..	722	41	27	..	..	..
19	*Cities.* Amritsar	279	..	190	..	957	6	..	..	7	..	228	..	..	..	..	..
20	*Cities.* Multan	..	..	..	..	666	14	..	..	..	..	151	1	..	..	2	..

LIVELIHOOD.—GENERAL TABLE.

STATES AND CITIES.—*continued.*

A.—PRODUCTION OF RAW MATERIALS.—*continued.*

I.—EXPLOITATION OF ANIMALS AND VEGETATION.—*continued.*

1.—Pasture and Agriculture.—*continued.*

Sub-order (*b*). Cultivation of special crops, fruit, etc. | Sub-order (*c*).—Forestry.

15.—*Tea.*						16.—*Market gardeners, flower and fruit growers.*						*Total Sub-order (c).*						17.—*Forest Officers, Rangers, Guards, etc.*						18.—*Wood-cutters and charcoal burners.*				
Total earners principal occupation.		Total working dependants.		Total earners with subsidiary occupation.		Total earners principal occupation.		Total working dependants.		Total earners with subsidiary occupation.		Total earners principal occupation.		Total working dependants.		Total earners with subsidiary occupation		Total earners principal occupation.		Total working dependants.		Total earners with subsidiary occupation		Total earners principal occupation.		Total working dependants		
Males.	Females.	Males.	Females.	Males.	Females.	Males.	Females.	Males.	Females.	Males.	Females.	Males.	Females.	Males.	Females.	Males.	Females.	Males.	Females.	Males.	Females.	Males.	Females.	Males.	Females.	Males.	Females.	Serial No.
83	84	85	86	87	88	89	90	91	92	93	94	95	96	97	98	99	100	101	102	103	104	105	106	107	108	109	110	
951	**473**	**28**	**20**	**126**	.	**5,994**	**866**	**127**	**76**	**522**	**15**	**14,814**	**1,192**	**981**	**815**	**1,845**	**22**	**3,676**	**10**	**90**	**2**	**613**	**1**	**9,917**	**669**	**751**	**205**	
948	**473**	**28**	**20**	**125**	..	**5,302**	**365**	**114**	**45**	**442**	**10**	**13,384**	**1,116**	**884**	**738**	**1,190**	**20**	**2,885**	**10**	**71**	**2**	**245**	**1**	**9,452**	**611**	**721**	**179**	
..	..	..	..	..	..	**1,888**	**7**	**24**	**26**	**211**	**9**	**2,236**	**760**	**152**	**647**	**370**	**12**	**276**	**1**	**42**	..	**16**	..	**1,335**	**330**	**68**	**98**	
..	..	..	..	..	..	202	1	2	1	..	..	100	27	44	2	10	..	53	..	41	..	3	..	43	10	3	1	1
..	..	..	..	..	..	80	1	3	..	14	..	163	24	22	44	4	1	14	1	1	..	1	..	98	14	14	1	2
..	..	..	..	..	..	285	..	6	..	25	1	217	175	19	74	41	2	19	..	..	..	9	..	159	..	19	3	3
..	..	..	..	..	..	157	..	12	3	13	..	533	143	16	31	87	1	9	..	..	..	..	..	443	136	13	31	4
..	..	..	..	..	..	310	5	1	22	40	8	1,181	391	51	496	227	8	139	..	..	..	2	..	592	170	19	32	5
..	..	..	..	..	..	304	..	..	..	119	..	42	..	..	..	1	..	42	..	..	..	1	..	..	..	..	..	6
948	**473**	**28**	**20**	**125**	..	**504**	**211**	**16**	**13**	**110**	**1**	**1,202**	**57**	**29**	**50**	**277**	**7**	**670**	**2**	**3**	..	**163**	**1**	**366**	**25**	**25**	**44**	
948	473	28	20	125	..	77	204	9	13	85	1	843	22	15	43	190	7	577	2	3	..	130	1	117	20	12	43	7
..	..	..	..	..	..	188	6	1	..	17	..	108	..	..	..	67	..	38	..	..	..	30	..	70	..	..	..	8
..	..	..	..	..	..	11	..	..	..	..	..	98	25	3	4	11	..	34	..	..	..	3	..	48	..	2	.	9
..	..	..	..	..	..	58	..	..	..	..	..	83	8	3	3	7	..	4	..	..	..	..	..	79	5	3	1	10
..	..	..	..	..	..	170	1	6	..	8	..	70	2	8	..	2	..	17	..	..	..	..	..	52	..	8	.	11
..	..	..	..	..	..	**1,825**	**118**	**51**	..	**47**	..	**3,183**	**129**	**154**	..	**134**	..	**880**	..	**1**	..	..	..	**2,183**	**106**	**181**	..	
..	..	..	..	..	..	1,149	116	36	..	5	..	720	125	3	..	3	..	381	..	..	..	..	..	338	105	3	.	12
..	..	..	..	..	..	248	1	..	..	..	..	915	..	26	..	5	..	186	..	..	..	..	..	685	..	7	..	13
..	..	..	..	..	..	239	..	14	..	18	..	614	3	108	..	77	..	160	..	1	..	..	..	384	..	101	..	14
..	..	..	..	..	..	101	..	1	..	21	..	265	..	14	..	18	..	27	..	..	..	..	..	238	..	14	..	15
..	..	..	..	..	..	65	1	..	..	2	..	380	..	2	..	29	..	88	..	..	..	..	..	492	..	2	..	16
..	.	..	..	..	..	23	..	..	..	1	..	89	1	1	..	2	..	38	..	..	..	..	..	46	1	1	..	17
..	..	..	..	..	..	**740**	**32**	**9**	**2**	**43**	..	**5,049**	**142**	**516**	**36**	**253**	**1**	**620**	**7**	**15**	**2**	**32**	..	**4,360**	**127**	**474**	**32**	
..	..	..	..	..	..	377	20	1	..	2	..	2,103	3	279	..	67	..	75	..	1	..	3	..	2,028	3	278	..	18
..	..	..	..	..	..	254	2	2	..	..	..	2,154	12	81	27	133	..	79	..	2	..	18	..	2,043	12	63	27	19
..	..	..	..	..	..	32	..	1	2	39	..	322	4	27	..	37	..	211	..	5	..	6	..	74	..	11	..	20
..	..	..	..	..	..	8	..	2	..	..	..	221	..	7	..	4	..	218	..	7	..	4	..	3	..	..	..	21
..	..	..	..	..	..	60	.	3	..	..	..	209	116	122	7	11	1	31	..	..	..	..	..	178	112	122	5	22
..	..	..	..	..	..	9	..	..	..	2	..	40	7	..	2	1	..	6	7	..	2	1	..	34	..	..	.	23
..	..	..	..	..	..	**895**	**7**	**14**	**4**	**31**	..	**1,714**	**28**	**33**	**5**	**156**	..	**439**	..	**10**	..	**34**	..	**1,208**	**23**	**28**	**5**	
..	..	..	..	..	..	71	..	..	..	..	..	275	23	7	5	31	..	35	..	..	..	2	..	240	23	7	5	24
..	..	..	..	..	..	339	..	3	..	26	..	171	..	4	..	46	..	115	..	4	..	3	..	39	..	.	..	25
..	..	..	..	..	..	8	..	..	..	..	..	699	..	1	..	41	..	19	..	..	..	..	..	645	..	1	..	26
..	..	..	..	..	..	438	6	11	4	2	..	342	5	7	..	31	..	226	..	6	..	29	..	108	..	1	..	27
..	..	..	..	..	..	12	1	..	..	2	..	60	..	..	..	2	..	27	..	..	..	..	..	26	..	..	..	28
..	..	..	..	..	..	27	..	..	..	1	..	167	..	14	..	5	..	17	..	..	..	..	..	150	..	14	..	29
3	..	.	..	**1**	..	**692**	**1**	**13**	**31**	**80**	**5**	**1,430**	**76**	**97**	**77**	**655**	**2**	**791**	..	**19**	.	**368**	..	**465**	**58**	**30**	**26**	
..	..	..	..	..	..	**190**	..	**4**	..	**32**	..	**348**	**12**	**19**	**8**	**250**	..	**164**	..	**12**	..	**206**	..	**188**	**12**	**3**	**3**	
..	..	..	..	..	..	3	..	..	..	..	..	..	..	..	..	..	..	..	..	..	..	..	..	..	.	..	..	1
..	..	..	..	..	..	31	..	..	..	..	..	1	..	..	..	..	..	..	..	..	..	..	..	..	.	..	.	2
..	..	..	..	..	..	32	..	..	..	..	..	82	..	5	..	17	..	26	..	..	..	5	..	39	..	1	..	3
..	..	..	..	..	..	**124**	..	**4**	..	**32**	..	**265**	**12**	**14**	**3**	**233**	..	**188**	..	**12**	..	**201**	..	**99**	**12**	**2**	**3**	4
..	..	..	..	..	..	6	..	..	..	..	..	97	..	7	..	47	..	42	..	7	..	45	..	55	..	..	..	
..	..	..	..	..	..	22	..	..	..	1	..	78	10	1	..	27	..	28	..	1	..	5	..	22	10	.	..	
.	..	.	..	..	..	70	..	2	..	4	..	44	2	..	..	24	..	43	..	..	..	24	..	1	2	..	..	
..	..	..	..	..	..	8	..	..	..	6	..	2	..	2	1	4	..	1	..	..	..	4	..	1	..	2	1	
..	..	..	..	..	..	..	..	..	..	3	..	3	..	1	..	63	..	3	..	1	..	63	..	..	..	..	..	
..	..	..	..	..	..	18	..	2	..	18	..	41	..	3	2	68	..	21	..	3	..	60	..	20	..	..	2	
3	..	..	..	**1**	.	**502**	**1**	**9**	**31**	**48**	**5**	**1,082**	**64**	**78**	**74**	**405**	**2**	**627**	..	**7**	..	**162**	..	**327**	**46**	**27**	**23**	
..	..	..	..	..	..	..	..	..	..	..	..	..	..	..	1	..	..	..	..	..	..	..	..	..	..	..	1	5
1	..	..	..	..	..	91	1	..	1	11	..	201	8	1	..	52	1	142	..	1	..	21	..	53	6	.	..	6
..	..	..	..	..	..	5	..	..	..	..	..	9	..	..	..	18	..	6	..	..	..	8	..	3	..	.	..	7
2	..	..	..	1	..	5	..	..	..	..	..	160	7	7	..	103	..	156	..		..	100	..	4	7	.	..	8
..	..	..	..	..	..	..	..	..	..	..	..	11	2	3	..	7	..	11	..	2	..	6	..	..	2	1	..	9
..	..	..	..	..	..	4	..	..	..	..	..	12	..	..	..	..	..	12	..	2	..	..	..	..	..	..	..	10
..	..	..	..	..	..	9	..	..	..	1	..	17	1	3	5	2	..	..	..	..	..	..	..	17	1	3	5	11
..	..	..	..	..	..	17	..	..	..	..	..	5	..	..	..	..	..	..	..	..	..	..	..	5	..	..	..	12
..	..	..	..	..	..	..	..	2	..	23	..	218	9	29	39	211	1	120	..	..	..	27	..	89	6	5	1	13
..	..	..	..	..	..	142	..	4	30	10	5	172	..	31	22	..	..	91	..	1	..	..	..	29	..	18	13	14
..	..	..	..	..	..	101	..	1	..	3	..	68	23	2	6	6	..	7	..	..	..	..	..	54	20	..	3	15
..	..	..	..	..	..	50	..	2	..	..	..	145	14	2	1	6	..	39	..	1	..	..	..	52	4	..	..	16
..	..	..	..	..	..	78	..	..	..	..	..	64	..	..	..	..	..	43	..	..	..	..	..	21	..	..	..	17
..	..	..	..	..	..	722	41	27	..	..	..	230	60	..	..	..	..	218	..	..	..	..	..	12	40	..	..	18
..	..	..	..	..	..	228	..	..	..	..	..	625	..	22	..	..	..	132	..	..	..	..	..	458	..	3	..	19
..	..	..	..	..	..	151	1	..	..	2	..	18	5	..	..	..	..	10	..	..	..	..	..	8	..	.	..	20

TABLE X.—OCCUPATION OR MEANS OF LIVELIHOOD.
DETAILS FOR DISTRICTS.

Class .. A.—PRODUCTION OF RAW MATERIALS.

Sub-class .. I.—EXPLOITATION OF ANIMALS AND VEGETATION.

Order .. 1.—Pasture and Agriculture.

Sub-Order (c). Forestry—*concluded.* | Sub-Order (d). Stock Raising.

Group: 18.—*Wood cutters and charcoal burners.* | 19.—*Collectors of Forest produce.* | 20.—*Collectors of lac.* | *Total Sub-Order* (d).

Serial No.	District or State.	18.—Total earners with subsidiary occupation. Males.	Females.	19.—Total earners principal occupation. Males.	Females.	19.—Total working dependants. Males.	Females.	19.—Total earners with subsidiary occupation. Males.	Females.	20.—Total earners principal occupation. Males.	Females.	20.—Total earners with subsidiary occupation. Males.	Females.	Total Sub-Order (d). Total earners principal occupation. Males.	Females.	Total working dependants. Males.	Females.	Total earners with subsidiary occupation. Males.	Females.
1	2	111	112	113	114	115	116	117	118	119	120	121	122	123	124	125	126	127	128
	PUNJAB	1,071	9	1,211	518	140	608	158	12	10	..	3	..	181,607	4,238	62,577	8,142	16,132	484
	BRITISH TERRITORY	800	8	1,037	495	92	557	142	11	10	..	3	..	148,977	3,168	46,792	2,223	13,917	218
	AMBALA DIVISION	223	2	625	429	42	549	130	10	..	..	1	..	28,183	535	22,317	699	2,553	85
1	Hissar	7	..	4	17	..	1	..	..	..	..	..	..	4,101	103	8,186	406	693	11
2	Rohtak	1	1	51	9	..	15	2	..	..	..	..	..	2,836	41	3,575	50	363	5
3	Gurgaon	21	..	39	175	..	71	10	2	..	..	1	..	2,844	22	4,617	63	460	6
4	Karnal	86	1	81	7	3	..	1	..	..	..	..	..	10,711	170	3,333	133	506	6
5	Ambala	108	..	450	221	32	464	117	8	..	..	..	..	7,535	101	2,574	25	488	6
6	Simla	..	..	..	..	..	..	..	..	..	..	..	..	156	98	32	22	43	1
	JULLUNDUR DIVISION	109	6	166	30	1	6	3	..	..	..	2	..	20,518	700	4,886	419	2,169	71
7	Kangra	60	6	149	..	..	..	..	..	..	..	..	..	5,763	446	1,211	329	728	62
8	Hoshiarpur	35	..	..	..	..	..	..	..	..	..	2	..	2,868	135	1,014	19	276	1
9	Jullundur	5	..	16	25	1	4	3	..	..	..	..	..	2,800	27	635	5	400	..
10	Ludhiana	7	..	..	3	..	2	..	..	..	..	..	..	3,779	40	426	4	311	4
11	Ferozepore	2	..	1	2	..	..	..	..	..	..	..	..	5,308	52	1,600	62	454	4
	LAHORE DIVISION	126	..	110	28	22	..	8	..	10	..	..	..	30,487	186	9,643	53	2,779	12
12	Lahore	3	..	1	20	..	..	..	..	..	..	..	..	8,948	74	2,059	10	464	1
13	Amritsar	5	..	34	..	19	..	..	..	10	..	..	..	6,231	22	1,938	17	531	6
14	Gurdaspur	69	..	70	3	3	..	8	..	..	..	..	..	5,070	17	1,838	1	811	1
15	Sialkot	18	..	..	..	..	..	..	..	..	..	..	..	3,585	33	713	9	335	..
16	Gujranwala	29	..	..	..	..	..	..	..	..	..	..	..	3,107	10	1,867	2	172	2
17	Sheikhupura	2	..	5	..	..	..	..	..	..	..	..	..	3,546	30	1,228	14	466	2
	RAWALPINDI DIVISION	220	..	69	8	27	2	1	1	..	..	..	..	19,513	1,065	5,004	697	3,302	22
18	Gujrat	64	..	..	..	..	..	..	..	..	..	..	..	2,041	9	835	2	182	..
19	Shahpur	114	..	32	..	16	..	1	..	..	..	..	..	7,574	58	934	2	1,045	..
20	Jhelum	31	..	37	4	11	..	..	..	..	..	..	..	2,189	539	1,234	536	215	4
21	Rawalpindi	..	..	..	..	..	..	..	..	..	..	..	..	1,721	21	456	..	119	..
22	Attock	11	..	..	4	..	2	..	1	..	..	..	..	2,264	219	1,088	109	299	6
23	Mianwali	..	..	..	..	..	..	..	..	..	..	..	..	3,724	219	457	48	1,442	12
	MULTAN DIVISION	122	..	67	5	..	..	..	..	..	..	..	..	50,276	682	4,942	355	3,114	78
24	Montgomery	29	..	..	..	..	..	..	..	..	..	..	..	8,321	152	739	26	511	5
25	Lyallpur	43	..	17	..	..	..	..	..	..	..	..	..	10,313	182	1,178	169	814	20
26	Jhang	41	..	35	..	..	..	..	..	..	..	..	..	4,165	4	316	..	122	..
27	Multan	2	..	8	5	..	..	..	..	..	..	..	..	12,409	142	752	4	394	1
28	Muzaffargarh	2	..	7	..	..	..	..	..	..	..	..	..	8,363	97	1,190	18	385	33
29	Dera Ghazi Khan	5	..	..	..	..	..	..	..	..	..	..	..	6,705	105	758	138	888	19
	PUNJAB STATES	271	1	174	18	48	51	16	1	..	..	..	..	32,630	1,070	15,785	5,919	2,215	266
	A.—HAVING POLITICAL RELATIONS WITH THE PUNJAB GOVERNMENT.	40	..	46	..	4	..	4	..	..	..	..	..	2,218	129	1,590	756	339	18
1	Dujana	..	..	..	..	..	..	..	..	..	..	..	..	108	..	35	..	6	..
2	Pataudi	..	..	1	..	..	..	..	..	..	..	..	..	148	4	3	..	24	1
3	Kalsia	11	..	17	..	4	..	1	..	..	..	..	..	859	13	364	1	51	..
4	SIMLA HILL STATES	29	..	28	..	..	..	3	..	..	..	..	..	1,098	112	1,188	755	258	17
	Bashahr	2	..	..	..	..	..	..	..	..	..	..	..	356	38	134	53	56	..
	Nalagarh	19	..	28	..	..	..	3	..	..	..	..	..	116	3	52	..	20	1
	Keonthal	..	..	..	..	..	..	..	..	..	..	..	..	162	18	51	61	30	14
	Baghal	..	..	..	..	..	..	..	..	..	..	..	..	117	10	186	103	17	..
	Jubbal	..	..	..	..	..	..	..	..	..	..	..	..	71	8	222	116	22	..
	Other Simla Hill States	8	..	..	..	..	..	..	..	..	..	..	..	274	35	543	422	119	2
	B.—HAVING POLITICAL RELATIONS WITH THE GOVERNMENT OF INDIA.	231	1	128	18	44	51	12	1	..	..	..	..	30,417	941	14,195	5,163	1,876	248
5	Loharu	..	..	..	..	..	..	..	..	..	..	..	..	179	5	676	365	7	2
6	Sirmoor	31	..	6	2	..	..	..	1	..	..	..	..	1,046	21	512	197	236	1
7	Bilaspur	10	..	..	..	..	..	..	..	..	..	..	..	1,239	112	219	50	50	..
8	Mandi	3	..	..	..	5	..	..	..	..	..	..	..	1,213	86	3,326	2,902	679	5
9	Suket	1	..	..	..	..	..	..	..	..	..	..	..	530	43	561	20	85	226
10	Kapurthala	..	..	..	..	..	..	..	..	..	..	..	..	1,065	6	81	1	134	1
11	Maler Kotla	2	..	..	..	..	..	..	..	..	..	..	..	443	4	83	2	87	..
12	Faridkot	..	..	..	..	..	..	..	..	..	..	..	..	1,043	9	1,088	8	80	1
13	Chamba	178	1	9	3	23	38	6	..	..	..	..	..	702	84	300	197	239	8
14	Patiala } Phulkian States	..	..	52	..	13	9	..	..	..	..	..	..	8,532	235	1,802	1,183		
15	Jind } Phulkian States	2	..	7	3	1	3	4	..	..	..	..	..	1,200	8	3,801	86	133	1
16	Nabha } Phulkian States	4	..	54	10	2	1	2	..	..	..	..	..	1,766	12	784	17	145	[illegible]
17	Bahawalpur	..	..	..	..	..	..	..	..	..	..	..	..	11,459	316	932	135	1	1
18	Cities. Lahore	..	..	..	20	..	..	..	..	..	..	..	..	1,422	32	21	..	148	..
19	Cities. Amritsar	..	..	25	..	19	..	..	..	10	..	..	..	1,156	..	43	..	..	..
20	Cities. Multan	..	..	..	5	..	..	..	..	..	..	..	..	301	2	..	..	3	1

LIVELIHOOD.—GENERAL TABLE.

STATES AND CITIES.—*continued.*

A.—PRODUCTION OF RAW MATERIALS.—*continued.*

I.—EXPLOITATION OF ANIMALS AND VEGETATION.—*continued.*

1.—Pasture and Agriculture.—*concluded.*

Sub-Order (*d*). Stock Raising.—*concluded.*

Sub-Order (*e*).—Raising of small animals and insects.

21.—*Cattle and buffalo breeders and keepers.*						22.—*Breeders of transport animals.*						23.—*Herdsmen, shepherds and breeders of other animals.*						*Total Sub-Order (e).* 24.—*Birds, bees, etc.*						
Total earners principal occupation.		Total working dependants.		Total earners with subsidiary occupation.		Total earners principal occupation.		Total working dependants.		Total earners with subsidiary occupation.		Total earners principal occupation.		Total working dependants.		Total earners with subsidiary occupation.		Total earners principal occupation.		Total working dependants.		Total earners with subsidiary occupation.		
Males.	Females.	Males.	Females.	Males.	Females.	Males.	Females.	Males.	Females.	Males.	Females.	Males.	Females.	Males.	Females.	Males.	Females.	Males.	Females.	Males.	Females.	Males.	Females.	Serial No.
129	130	131	132	133	134	135	136	137	138	139	140	141	142	143	144	145	146	147	148	149	150	151	152	
30,803	**1,285**	**5,540**	**2,014**	**2,265**	**76**	**17,894**	**341**	**1,265**	**111**	**1,458**	**8**	**132,910**	**2,612**	**55,772**	**6,017**	**12,409**	**400**	**48**	**4**	**3**	**2**	**25**	.	
19,505	**923**	**3,447**	**523**	**1,765**	**59**	**14,328**	**213**	**630**	**20**	**1,087**	**8**	**115,144**	**2,032**	**42,715**	**1,680**	**11,065**	**151**	**48**	**4**	**3**	**2**	**25**	.	
2,935	**82**	**373**	**76**	**633**	**8**	**62**	..	**42**	**1**	..	..	**25,186**	**453**	**21,902**	**622**	**1,920**	**27**	**17**	**3**	**2**	**2**	**24**	.	
622	18	159	65	212	..	.	..	.	..	..	..	3,479	85	8,027	341	481	11	..	..	..	..	.	..	1
88	5	50	3	20	2	2	..	4	..	..	..	2,746	36	3,521	47	343	3	..	..	..	..	..	..	2
181	2	6	3	72	1	..	..	..	..	..	..	2,663	20	4,611	60	388	5	..	..	..	..	..	..	3
992	23	61	3	75	4	58	..	33	1	..	..	9,661	147	3,239	129	431	2	..	..	..	..	..	.	4
1,033	34	97	2	252	1	2	..	5	..	..	..	6,500	67	2,472	23	236	5	17	3	2	2	24	..	5
19	..	..	..	2	..	..	..	..	..	..	..	137	98	32	22	41	1	..	..	..	..	..	..	6
2,227	**203**	**350**	**53**	**187**	**40**	**391**	..	**43**	..	**94**	..	**17,900**	**497**	**4,493**	**366**	**1,888**	**31**	**5**	**1**	..	..	**1**	..	
1,056	62	128	47	49	39	144	..	14	..	67	..	4,563	384	1,069	282	612	23	..	..	..	..	..	..	7
182	110	93	1	63	..	46	..	2	..	2	..	2,640	25	919	18	211	1	3	..	..	.	1	..	8
81	11	26	3	9	..	10	..	..	..	..	..	2,709	16	609	2	391	..	..	..	..	.	..	.	9
833	19	102	2	58	1	67	.	..	..	9	..	2,879	21	324	2	244	3	..	..	..	.	..	.	10
75	1	1	..	8	.	124	..	27	..	16	..	5,109	51	1,572	62	430	4	2	1	..	..	..	..	11
2,236	**88**	**687**	**2**	**174**	..	**1,197**	..	**138**	.	**131**	..	**27,054**	**148**	**8,818**	**51**	**2,474**	**12**	**24**	..	**1**	..	.	..	
694	27	38	1	6	..	745	..	6	..	18	..	7,509	47	2,015	9	440	1	21	..	..	..	.	..	12
385	2	17	1	10	..	112	..	2	..	11	..	5,734	20	1,919	16	510	6	3	..	1	..	..	..	13
1,034	4	610	..	150	..	319	..	44	..	89	..	3,717	13	1,184	1	572	1	..	..	..	..	..	..	14
121	..	22	..	8	..	21	..	86	..	13	..	3,443	33	605	9	314	..	..	..	..	.	..	..	15
..	1	..	..	..	..	..	..	..	..	..	..	3,107	9	1,867	2	172	2	..	..	..	..	..	..	16
2	4	..	..	..	..	..	..	..	..	..	..	3,544	26	1,228	14	466	2	..	..	..	..	..	..	17
5,173	**454**	**1,297**	**361**	**172**	..	**2,730**	**80**	**168**	**15**	**412**	**4**	**11,610**	**531**	**3,544**	**321**	**2,718**	**18**	**1**	..	..	..	..	..	
1,334	..	322	..	61	..	25	..	..	..	5	..	682	9	513	2	116	..	..	..	..	..	..	..	18
2,019	23	411	1	53	..	1,994	3	100	..	327	..	3,561	32	423	1	665	..	1	..	..	..	..	..	19
161	310	5	301	1	..	248	77	31	15	7	4	1,780	152	1,198	220	207	..	..	..	..	..	..	.	20
491	..	85	..	35	..	3	..	..	..	..	..	1,227	21	371	..	84	..	..	..	..	..	..	..	21
939	107	413	59	22	..	126	..	13	..	72	..	1,199	112	662	50	205	6	..	..	..	..	..	.	22
229	14	61	..	..	..	334	..	19	..	1	..	3,161	205	377	48	1,441	12	..	..	..	..	..	..	23
6,934	**146**	**740**	**31**	**599**	**11**	**9,948**	**133**	**244**	**4**	**450**	**4**	**33,394**	**403**	**3,958**	**320**	**2,065**	**63**	**1**	..	..	.	..	.	
1,329	6	47	..	147	..	1,055	5	49	..	48	..	5,937	141	643	26	316	5	1	..	..	..	..	..	24
3,156	90	410	31	340	11	850	..	52	..	62	..	6,307	92	716	138	412	9	..	..	..	..	.	..	25
520	..	25	..	40	..	704	1	18	..	2	..	2,941	3	273	..	80	..	..	..	..	..	..	.	26
1,087	4	124	.	46	..	4,153	107	67	2	144	..	7,169	31	561	2	204	1	..	..	..	..	..	.	27
105	..	100	..	..	..	1,139	13	31	2	31	4	7,119	84	1,068	16	354	29	..	..	..	.	..	..	28
737	46	34	..	26	..	2,047	7	27	..	163	..	3,921	52	697	138	699	19	..	..	..	.	..	..	29
11,298	**362**	**2,093**	**1,491**	**500**	**17**	**3,566**	**128**	**685**	**91**	**371**	..	**17,766**	**580**	**13,057**	**4,337**	**1,344**	**249**	..	..	..	..	..	..	
22	**3**	..	**1**	**5**	**14**	..	..	..	..	..	..	**2,191**	**126**	**1,590**	**755**	**334**	**4**	..	..	..	..	..	.	
..	..	..	..	..	..	..	..	..	..	..	..	108	..	35	..	6	..	..	..	..	..	..	..	1
..	..	..	..	..	..	..	..	..	..	..	..	148	4	3	..	24	1	..	..	..	..	..	.	2
..	..	..	..	..	..	..	..	..	..	..	..	859	13	364	1	51	..	..	..	..	..	..	..	3
22	**8**	..	**1**	**5**	**14**	..	..	..	..	..	..	**1,076**	**109**	**1,188**	**754**	**253**	**3**	..	..	..	..	..	..	4
2	..	..	..	..	..	..	..	..	..	..	..	354	38	134	53	50	..	..	..	..	..	..	..	
..	..	..	..	.	..	..	..	..	..	..	..	118	3	52	..	20	1	..	..	..	..	..		
9	3	..	..	.	14	..	..	..	..	..	..	153	15	51	61	30	..	..		..	..	..		
..	..	..	..	..	..	..	..	..	..	..	..	117	10	186	103	17	..	..	..	..	..	..		
11	..	..	1	..	..	..	..	..	..	..	..	60	8	222	115	22	..	..	..	..	..	..	..	
..	..	..	.	5	..	..	..	..	..	..	..	274	35	543	422	114	2	..	..	..	..	..	..	
11,276	**359**	**2,093**	**1,490**	**495**	**3**	**3,566**	**128**	**635**	**91**	**371**	.	**15,575**	**454**	**11,467**	**3,582**	**1,010**	**245**	..	.	.	.	.	..	
..	..	..	..	..	..	..	..	.	..	..	..	179	5	676	365	7	2	..	..	.	.	.	.	5
255	..	5	5	76	..	..	.	.	..	..	..	791	21	537	192	160	1	..	..	.	..	..	.	6
..	..	..	..	..	..	..	.	.	..	..	..	1,239	112	219	50	50	..	..	..	.	..	..	.	7
126	41	5	915	251	2	100	.	.	..	238	..	987	45	3,321	1,987	190	3	..	.	..	..	..	.	8
10	4	5	..	1	..	84	2	..	..	31	..	486	37	556	20	53	226	..	.	..	..	.	.	9
24	..	..	..	..	..	20	.	..	..	24	..	1,021	6	81	1	110	1	..	..	.	.	..	.	10
23	.	..	..	3	.	46	2	7	1	38	..	374	2	76	1	46	..	..	.	.	.	.	.	11
88	8	478	6	19	.	21	.	..	..	8	..	934	1	610	2	53	1	..	.	.	.	.	..	12
138	15	40	61	89	1	113	30	23	2	32	..	451	39	237	134	118	7	..	.	.	..	.	.	13
2,912	75	507	487	..	..	2,709	72	584	83	..	.	2,911	88	711	613	..	..	..	.	.	.	.	.	14
..	..	..	.	..	..	..	..	..	..	..	..	1,200	8	3,801	86	133	1	..	..	.	.	.	.	15
1,187	3	656	3	56	..	6	..	3	..	..	..	573	9	125	14	89	2	.	.	.	.	.	.	16
6,513	213	397	13	..	..	517	22	18	5	..	..	4,429	81	517	117	1	1	..	.	.	.	.	.	17
332	26	2	..	3	..	489	..	5	..	13	..	601	6	14	..	132	.	12		.			..	18
293	..	..	..	..	..	..	..	..	..	..	..	863	..	43	.	.	.	.	.	.	.	.	.	19
39	..	..	..	..	..	107	.	..	..	3	.	155	2	..	..	..	1	..	.	..	..	.	..	20

TABLE X—OCCUPATION OR MEANS OF
DETAILS FOR DISTRICTS,

Class .. A.—PRODUCTION OF RAW MATERIALS.

Sub-class .. I.—EXPLOITATION OF ANIMALS AND VEGETATION—*concluded.*

Order .. 2.—Fishing and Hunting—*concluded.*

Group .. *Total Order 2.* | 27.—*Fishing and pearling.* | 28.—*Hunting.* | Total Sub-class II.

Serial No.	District or State.	Total Order 2. Total earners principal occupation. Males.	Females.	Total working dependants. Males.	Females.	Total earners with subsidiary occupation. Males.	Females.	27. Total earners principal occupation. Males.	Females.	Total working dependants. Males.	Females.	Total earners with subsidiary occupation. Males.	Females.	28. Total earners principal occupation. Males.	Females.	Total working dependants. Males.	Females.	Total earners with subsidiary occupation. Males.	Females.	Total Sub-class II. Total earners principal occupation. Males.	Females.	Total working dependants. Males.	Females.
1	2	153	154	155	156	157	158	159	160	161	162	163	164	165	166	167	168	169	170	171	172	173	174
	PUNJAB	**4,990**	**75**	**262**	**61**	**1,144**	**1**	**4,811**	**42**	**239**	**61**	**989**	**1**	**679**	**33**	**23**	..	**155**	..	**4,936**	**616**	**260**	**73**
	BRITISH TERRITORY	**3,903**	**44**	**229**	**53**	**998**	**1**	**3,296**	**12**	**206**	**53**	**843**	**1**	**607**	**32**	**23**	..	**155**	..	**4,559**	**606**	**228**	**31**
	AMBALA DIVISION	432	8	20	29	54	..	382	1	19	29	44	..	50	2	1	..	10	..	766	40	16	2
1	Hissar	60	1	6	29	11	..	54	1	6	29	6	..	6	..	..	..	5	..	136	2	13	1
2	Rohtak	19	..	..	..	..	..	19	..	..	..	..	..	..	..	..	..	..	..	225	4	..	1
3	Gurgaon	17	..	..	..	5	..	15	..	..	..	1	..	2	..	..	..	4	..	295	4	..	..
4	Karnal	192	2	11	..	36	..	161	..	10	..	35	..	31	2	1	..	1	..	97	30	3	..
5	Ambala	137	..	3	..	2	..	128	..	3	..	2	..	9	..	..	..	..	..	13	..	..	..
6	Simla	7	..	..	..	..	..	5	..	..	..	..	..	2	..	..	..	..	..	..	..	..	..
	JULLUNDUR DIVISION	919	6	62	4	637	1	845	6	62	4	612	1	74	..	..	..	25	..	518	49	24	8
7	Kangra	502	3	46	4	521	1	496	3	46	4	519	1	6	..	..	..	2	..	404	49	..	8
8	Hoshiarpur	117	..	1	..	29	..	59	..	1	..	9	..	58	..	..	..	20	..	24	..	..	..
9	Jullundur	73	1	5	..	21	..	71	1	5	..	21	..	2	..	..	..	..	..	4	..	23	..
10	Ludhiana	67	..	6	..	63	..	62	..	6	..	63	..	5	..	..	..	..	..	53	..	1	.
11	Ferozepore	160	2	4	..	3	..	157	2	4	..	..	..	3	..	..	..	3	..	33	..	..	..
	LAHORE DIVISION	1,112	12	81	20	184	..	816	..	20	20	71	..	296	12	11	..	113	..	155	10	4	2
12	Lahore	363	2	..	..	13	..	345	..	..	..	8	..	18	2	..	..	5	..	125	2	..	2
13	Amritsar	50	..	5	..	12	..	40	..	5	..	11	..	10	..	..	..	1	..	6	..	..	..
14	Gurdaspur	304	..	6	20	125	..	152	..	2	20	33	..	152	..	4	..	92	..	..	..	..	..
15	Sialkot	262	..	16	..	27	..	195	..	9	..	15	..	67	..	7	..	12	..	1	..	..	..
16	Gujranwala	104	..	4	..	7	..	55	..	4	..	4	..	49	..	..	..	3	..	3	8	..	..
17	Sheikhupura	29	10	..	..	..	..	29	..	..	..	..	..	..	10	..	..	..	..	20	..	4	..
	RAWALPINDI DIVISION	193	.	11	..	27	..	154	..	11	..	24	..	39	..	..	..	8	..	3,093	499	184	19
18	Gujrat	39	..	..	..	3	..	14	..	..	..	3	..	25	..	..	..	..	..	81	..	5	..
19	Shahpur	20	..	..	..	..	..	16	..	..	..	..	..	4	..	..	..	..	..	300	30	20	19
20	Jhelum	3	..	..	..	..	..	3	..	..	..	..	..	..	..	..	..	..	..	1,211	464	18	..
21	Rawalpindi	36	..	8	..	5	..	36	..	8	..	5	..	..	..	..	..	..	..	..	..	..	..
22	Attock	21	..	..	..	6	..	21	..	..	..	6	..	..	..	..	..	..	..	1,070	4	17	..
23	Mianwali	74	..	3	..	13	..	64	..	3	..	10	..	10	..	..	..	3	..	422	1	124	..
	MULTAN DIVISION	1,247	23	105	..	96	..	1,099	5	94	..	92	..	148	18	11	..	4	..	27	8	.	..
24	Montgomery	215	18	7	..	23	..	132	..	5	..	21	..	83	18	2	..	2	..	14	8	..	.
25	Lyallpur	69	..	4	..	3	..	56	..	..	..	2	..	13	..	4	..	1	..	.	..	..	.
26	Jhang	88	..	3	..	4	..	61	..	..	..	4	..	27	..	3	..	..	..	2	..	..	..
27	Multan	316	4	82	..	23	..	297	4	80	..	22	..	19	..	2	..	1	..	11	..	..	..
28	Muzaffargarh	277	1	4	..	31	..	277	1	4	..	31	..	..	..	..	..	..	..	..	..	..	..
29	Dera Ghazi Khan	282	..	5	..	12	..	276	..	5	..	12	..	6	..	..	..	..	..	..	..	..	..
	PUNJAB STATES	**1,087**	**31**	**33**	**8**	**146**	..	**1,015**	**30**	**33**	**8**	**146**	..	**72**	**1**	..	..	..	..	**377**	**10**	**32**	**42**
	A.—Having Political Relations with the Punjab Government.	46	1	8	..	18	..	25	..	8	..	18	..	21	1	..	..	..	..	76	1	4	1
1	Dujana	..	..	..	..	..	..	..	..	..	..	..	..	..	..	..	..	..	..	..	..	..	1
2	Pataudi	..	..	..	..	..	..	..	..	..	..	..	..	..	..	..	..	..	..	1	..	..	..
3	Kalsia	10	..	..	..	..	..	5	..	..	..	..	..	5	..	..	..	..	..	1	..	.	..
4	SIMLA HILL STATES	36	1	8	..	18	..	20	..	8	..	18	..	16	1	..	..	..	..	74	1	4	..
	Bashahr	4	..	3	..	6	..	4	..	3	..	6	..	..	..	..	..	..	..	11	..	3	..
	Nalagarh	18	1	..	..	..	..	2	..	..	..	..	..	16	1	..	..	..	..	..	..	..	..
	Keonthal	3	..	..	..	3	..	3	..	..	..	3	..	..	..	..	..	..	..	61	1	1	..
	Baghal	2	..	..	..	..	..	2	..	..	..	..	..	..	..	..	..	..	..	..	..	..	..
	Jubbal	4	..	..	..	3	..	4	..	..	..	3	..	..	..	..	..	..	..	1	..	..	..
	Other Simla Hill States	5	..	..	..	6	..	5	..	..	..	6	..	..	..	..	..	..	..	1	..	..	..
	B.—Having Political Relations with the Government of India.	1,041	30	30	8	128	..	990	30	30	8	128	..	51	..	..	..	..	..	301	9	28	41
5	Loharu	2	..	..	..	..	..	..	..	..	..	..	..	2	..	..	..	..	..	..	..	.	..
6	Sirmoor	4	..	..	..	1	..	4	..	..	..	1	..	..	..	..	..	..	..	5	..	..	..
7	Bilaspur	5	..	..	..	40	..	5	..	..	..	40	..	..	..	..	..	..	..	..	..	..	..
8	Mandi	29	..	..	..	7	..	29	..	..	..	7	..	..	..	..	..	..	..	10	..	..	..
9	Suket	..	..	..	..	9	..	..	..	..	..	9	..	..	..	..	..	..	..	..	6	..	1
10	Kapurthala	172	3	..	..	33	..	166	3	..	..	33	..	6	..	..	..	..	..	..	..	..	..
11	Maler Kotla	3	..	..	..	..	..	..	..	..	..	..	..	3	..	..	..	..	..	..	..	..	..
12	Faridkot	26	..	..	..	..	..	26	..	..	..	..	..	..	..	..	..	..	..	1	.	..	.
13	Chamba	30	..	3	..	26	..	30	..	3	..	26	..	..	..	..	..	..	..	.	..	..	..
14	Patiala (Phulkian States)	73	..	9	5	..	..	52	..	9	5	..	..	21	..	..	..	..	..	148	..	15	34
15	Jind (Phulkian States)	19	..	..	..	12	..	3	..	..	..	12	..	16	..	..	..	..	..	74	3	13	6
16	Nabha (Phulkian States)	10	..	..	..	..	..	7	..	..	..	..	..	3	..	..	..	..	..	..	..	.	..
17	Bahawalpur	668	27	18	3	..	..	668	27	18	3	..	..	..	..	..	..	..	..	63	..	..	..
18	*Cities.* Lahore	121	..	..	..	4	..	108	..	..	..	..	..	13	..	..	..	4	..	91	..	..	..
19	*Cities.* Amritsar	11	..	..	..	..	..	11	..	..	..	..	..	..	..	..	..	..	..	6	..	..	..
20	*Cities.* Multan	..	..	..	..	..	..	..	..	..	..	..	..	..	..	..	..	..	..	6	..	..	..

LIVELIHOOD—GENERAL TABLE.

STATES AND CITIES. *continued.*

A. PRODUCTION OF RAW MATERIALS. *continued.*

II.—EXPLOITATION OF MINERALS.—*continued.*

3. Metallic Minerals.—*concluded.* **4. Non-Metallic Minerals.**

Total Sub-class II concld.: Total earners with subsidiary occupation, Males 175	Females 176	Total Order 3: Total earners principal occupation, Males 177	Females 178	Total working dependants, Males 179	Females 180	Total earners with subsidiary occupation, Males 181	Females 182	29. Gold: Total earners principal occupation, Males 183	Females 184	Total earners with subsidiary occupation, Males 185	Females 186	34.—Other Metallic Minerals: Total earners principal occupation, Males 187	Females 188	Total working dependants, Males 189	Females 190	Total Order 4: Total earners principal occupation, Males 191	Females 192	Total working dependants, Males 193	Females 194	Total earners with subsidiary occupation, Males 195	Females 196	35. Coal: Total earners principal occupation, Males 197	Females 198	Total working dependants, Males 199	Females 200	Total earners with subsidiary occupation, Males 201	Females 202	Serial No.
193	1	11	4	3	..	12	..	3	.	12	.	8	4	3	..	4,925	612	257	73	181	1	107	1	4	.	36	.	
141	1	10	4	3	..	1	..	2	..	1	..	8	4	3	..	4,549	602	225	31	140	1	92	.	3	.	28		
62	1	2	.	..	.	1	.	2	..	1	..	..	..	..	..	764	40	16	2	61	1	4	.	.	..	.		
..	..			..	..	..				..	..	..	..		..	136	2	13		7	..	..	.					1
2	.	2	..	..	..	1	.	2	.	1	..	..	..	.	..	22	.	..		29	..	..	.		.	.	.	2
12	1	..	..	.	..	..	..	..	..	.	..	..	..	..	..	29		..	..	..		.	..	..			..	3
22	..	..	..	.	..	..	..	..	..	.		..	..	.	..	97	30	3	..	22	.	1	..			.	.	4
.	..	..	..	..	..	.	.	..	..	..	..	..	..	..	..	3	..	..	.	..	..	.		..	.			5
..	..	.	..	..	..	.	.									..	.	..	.	..	..	.			.	.		6
57	..	..	.	..	..	.	..	..	..	..	..	.	.	..	..	518	49	24	8	57	..	29	..	..		25	..	
47	..	.	.	..	..	..	.	..	..	.	..	..	..	..	..	404	49	.	8	47	.	90	..	..	.	25		7
3	..	..	..	..	..	..	.	..	..	.	..	..	..	..	..	24	..	.	..	5	..	.		.		.		8
..	..	..	..	..	.	.	..	..	..	.	..	..	..	..	..	4	.	23	.	.	..	.		.	..	.	.	9
2	..	..	..	..	..	..	..	..	..	..	..	..	..	..	..	73	.	1	..	2	..	..	.	.	.	.		10
5	..	..	..	..	..	..	..	..	..	..	..	..	..	.	..	23	.	.	..	5	..	..	.	..	.	.		11
4	..	..	..	.	..	.	..	..	..	..	..	..	.	..	.	155	10	4	2	4	.	..	.	..	.	1	.	
4	..	..	..	..	.	..	..	..	..	..	..	..	..	..	..	125	2	..	2	1	..	.		.	.		.	12
..	..	..	.	.	.	..	..	..	..	.	..	..	..	..	..	6	..	..	.	..	..	.		..	.		.	13
.	..	..	.	..	..	..	..	..	..	..	..	..	..	..	..	.	..	..	..	..	..	.		..	..	..	.	14
..	..	..	..	..	.	..	..	..	..	..	..	..	..	..	..	1	..	..	..	..	..	.	..	..	.	.		15
..	..	..	..	..	..	..	..	.	..	..	..	..	..	..	.		8	..	..	..	..	.	..	.	.			16
	.	..	..	..	..	..	..	..	..	..	..	..	.	..	..	20	..	1	..	..		..	..		..			17
18	.	8	4	3	..	..	..	..	..	.	..	8	4	3	..	3,085	495	181	19	18	..	59	.	3		2	..	
3	..	..	..	..	.	..	..	..	..	.	..	..	..	..	..	[illegible]	..	5	..	.	.	48	..	3		2	..	18
..	..	..	..	..	..	..	..	..	..	.	..	..	..	.	.	369	50	20	19	.		..	..		.	.		19
5	..	8	.	..	..	..	..	..	.	..	..	8	..		.	1,203	464	18	..	5		..	.		..	.		20
..	..	..	..	..	..	.	.	..	..	..	.	..	..	..	..	..	..	..	..	..	..	.	..	..	..	.	.	21
10	.	.	4	.	..	.	.	..	..	..	..	..	4	..	..	1,070	..	17	.	3	..	11	..	..		.	..	22
..	..	..	..	3	..	..	.	..	..	..	..	..	..	3	..	122	1	12	..	..	..	..		..	.	.	..	23
.	.	..	..	..	..	..	..	..	..	..	..	..	..	..	..	27	8	..	..	..	..	..	..	..	..	.	..	
..	..	..	..	.	..	..	..	..	..	..	..	..	..	.	.	14	8	..	..	.	.	..	..	.	..	.		24
..	.	..	..	.	..	..	..	..	..	..	.	..	..	..	..	..	..	..	..	..	..	..	.	..	..	.		25
..	..	..	..	.	..	..	..	..	..	.	..	..	..	..	..	2	..	..	..	..	..	..	.	..	.	.		26
.	..	..	..	..	..	..	..	..	..	.	..	..	..	..	..	1	.	..	..	..	..	..	.	..	..	.	.	27
..	..	..	..	..	..	..	..	..	.	..	..	..	.	..	..	..	..	.	..	..	..	..	..	.		.	..	28
..	..	.	..	..	..	..	.	..	..	..	..	..	..	..	..	..	..	..	..	..	..	..	..		..	..	.	29
52	..	1	..	..	..	11	..	1	..	11	..	.	..	..	..	376	10	32	42	41	..	15	1	1	.	8		
10	..	1	.	..	..	..	.	1	.	..	..	..	.	.	..	75	1	4	1	10	..	15	1	1	.	8		
..	.	.	..	..	..	..	.	..	..	..	..	..	..	.	..	..	..	..	1	..	..	.	.	..	..	.		1
..	.	.	..	..	..	..	..	..	..	..	..	..	..	..	..	1	..	.	..	..	.	..		..		.		2
1	..	.	..	.	..	..	..	..	..	..	..	.	..	..	..	1	.	.	..	.	..	..	.	..		.		3
9	..	1	..	..	..	..	..	1	..	.	..	..	..	..	..	73	1	4	..	9	..	15	1	1		8		4
..	..	..	..	..	..	..	..	..	..	..	.	..	..	..	..	11	..	3	..	..	..	2	..	.	..		..	
..	..	..	.	.	..	..	..	..	..	..	..	..	.	.	.	..	..	..	.	..	.	.	..		..			
8	..	..	.	..	.	..	..	.	.	..	..	..	..	.	..	6	1	1	.	5	.	15	1	1	..	-		
..	.	..	..	..	..	..	.	..	..	..	..	..	..	.	..	..	..	..	..	..	..	..	.	..	.	.	.	
..	..	..	..	..	..	..	.	..	.	..	..	..	..	.	..	1	.	..	..	..	..	..		..	.	.	.	
1	..		..	..	..	..	..	.	..	..	..	..	..	..	..	..	.	..	..	1	..	..	.				.	
42	..	..	..	..	..	11	..	.	..	11	..	..	..	.	..	301	9	28	41	31	..	..	.	.	..	.	.	
..	..	..	..	..	.	..	..	..	.	..	..	..	..	..	..	..	..	..	.	.	..	..		..	.	.	.	5
..	..	..	.	..	..	..	.	..	..	.	..	..	..	..	..	5	.	..	.	..	.	..	..	.	.			6
11	.	..	..	..	..	11	.	..	..	11	..	..	..	..	..	..	..	.	..	..	.		..	..	.			7
6	..	..	..	..	..	.	..	..	..	..	..	..	..	..	..	10	..	.	..	6	..	..	.	..	.	.	.	8
6	..	..	..	..	..	..	..	..	..	.	..	..	.	..	..	..	6	..	1	6	..	.		..	.	.		9
..	..	..	..	..	..	..	..	..	.	..	..	..	..	..	..	..	..	..	..	..	..	..	.	..	.	..	.	10
..	..	..	..	..	..	..	..	..	..	..	..	..	..	..	..	..	..	..	..	..	..	..	.	..	.	.	.	11
..	..	..	..	..	..	..	..	..	..	..	..	..	..	..	..	1	..	..	..	..	..	..	.	.	.	.	.	12
.	..	..	..	..	..	..	..	..	..	..	..	..	..	..	..	..	..	..	..	..	..	..	..	.	.	.	.	13
..	..	..	..	..	.	..	..	..	..	..	..	..	..	..	..	148	..	15	34	..	..	..	..	.	.	..		14
19	.	..	..	..	..	..	.	.	..	..	..	..	..	..	..	74	3	13	6	19	..	..	..	..	..	.	.	15
..	..	..	..	..	..	..	.	..	..	..	..	..	..	..	.	..	..	..	..	..	..	..	.	..	..	.	.	16
..	..	..	..	..	..	..	..	..	..	.	..	..	..	..	..	63	.	..	..	.	..	..	..	.		.		17
..	..	..	..	..	..	..	..	..	..	..	..	..	..	..	..	91	.	..	..	..	..	..	..	.	..	.		18
..	.	..	..	..	..	..	..	.	..	..	..	..	..	..	..	6	..	.	..	..	..	..		..			.	19
..	..	..	..	..	..	..	.	..	..	..	..	..	..	..	..	6	.	..	..	..	..	..	.		.	.	..	20

TABLE X.—OCCUPATION OR MEANS OF
DETAILS FOR DISTRICTS,

Class .. A.—PRODUCTION OF RAW MATERIALS.—*concluded.*
Sub-class .. II.—EXPLOITATION OF MINERALS.—*concluded.*
Order .. 4.—Non-Metallic Minerals.—*concluded.*

Serial No.	District or State.	36.—*Petroleum.* Total earners principal occupation. Males.	Females.	Total working dependants. Males.	Females.	Total earners with subsidiary occupation. Males.	Females.	37.—*Building materials including stone, etc.* Total earners principal occupation. Males.	Females.	40.—*Salt, saltpetre and other saline substances.* Total earners principal occupation. Males.	Females.	Total working dependants. Males.	Females.	Total earners with subsidiary occupation. Males.	Females.	41.—*Other Non-metallic Minerals.* Total earners principal occupation. Males.	Females.	Total working dependants. Males.	Females.	Total earners with subsidiary occupation. Males.	Females.
1	2	203	204	205	206	207	208	209	210	211	212	213	214	215	216	217	218	219	220	221	222
	PUNJAB	1,059	..	17	..	10	..	1	..	2,326	546	66	62	56	1	1,432	65	170	11	79	..
	BRITISH TERRITORY	1,059	..	17	..	10	..	..	..	2,043	543	38	22	38	1	1,355	59	167	9	64	..
	AMBALA DIVISION	..	..	..	..	..	..	..	..	346	30	14	1	25	1	414	10	2	1	36	..
1	Hissar	..	..	..	..	..	..	..	..	125	1	13	..	2	..	11	1	..	1	5	..
2	Rohtak	..	..	..	..	..	..	..	..	66	..	..	1	1	..	157	4	..	..	19	..
3	Gurgaon	..	..	..	..	..	..	..	..	62	..	..	..	..	1	233	4	..	..	12	..
4	Karnal	..	..	..	..	..	..	..	..	83	29	1	..	22	..	13	1	2	..	..	..
5	Ambala	..	..	..	..	..	..	..	..	10	..	..	..	..	..	..	..	..	..	..	..
6	Simla	..	..	..	..	..	..	..	..	..	..	..	..	..	..	..	..	..	..	..	..
	JULLUNDUR DIVISION	..	..	..	..	..	..	..	..	36	..	..	..	8	..	453	49	24	8	24	..
7	Kangra	..	..	..	..	..	..	..	..	..	..	..	..	..	..	375	49	..	8	22	..
8	Hoshiarpur	..	..	..	..	..	..	..	..	24	..	..	..	3	..	..	..	..	..	..	..
9	Jullundur	..	..	..	..	..	..	..	..	..	..	..	..	..	..	4	..	23	..	..	..
10	Ludhiaua	..	..	..	..	..	..	..	..	..	..	..	..	..	..	53	..	1	..	2	..
11	Ferozepore	..	..	..	..	..	..	..	..	12	..	..	..	5	..	21	..	..	..	..	..
	LAHORE DIVISION	..	..	..	..	..	..	..	..	155	10	4	2	3	..	..	..	..	..	..	..
12	Lahore	..	..	..	..	..	..	..	..	125	2	..	2	3	..	..	..	..	..	..	..
13	Amritsar	..	..	..	..	..	..	..	..	6	..	..	..	..	..	..	..	..	..	..	..
14	Gurdaspur	..	..	..	..	..	..	..	..	..	..	..	..	..	..	..	..	..	..	..	..
15	Sialkot	..	..	..	..	..	..	..	..	1	..	..	..	..	..	..	..	..	..	..	..
16	Gujranwala	..	..	..	..	..	..	..	..	3	8	..	..	..	..	..	..	..	..	..	..
17	Sheikhupura	..	..	..	..	..	..	..	..	20	..	4	..	..	..	..	..	..	..	..	..
	RAWALPINDI DIVISION	1,059	..	17	..	10	..	..	..	1,479	495	20	19	2	..	488	..	141	..	4	..
18	Gujrat	..	..	..	..	..	..	..	..	22	..	..	..	..	..	11	..	2	..	1	..
19	Shahpur	..	..	..	..	..	..	..	..	305	30	20	19	..	..	4	..	..	..	..	..
20	Jhelum	..	..	..	..	..	..	..	..	1,146	464	..	..	2	..	57	..	18	..	3	..
21	Rawalpindi	..	..	..	..	..	..	..	..	..	..	..	..	..	..	..	..	..	..	..	..
22	Attock	1,059	..	17	..	10	..	..	..	..	..	..	..	..	..	..	..	..	..	..	..
23	Mianwali	..	..	..	..	..	..	..	..	6	1	..	..	..	..	416	..	121	..	..	..
	MULTAN DIVISION	..	..	..	..	..	..	..	..	27	8	..	..	..	..	..	..	..	..	..	..
24	Montgomery	..	..	..	..	..	..	..	..	14	8	..	..	..	..	..	..	..	..	..	..
25	Lyallpur	..	..	..	..	..	..	..	..	..	..	..	..	..	..	..	..	..	..	..	..
26	Jhang	..	..	..	..	..	..	..	..	2	..	..	..	..	..	..	..	..	..	..	..
27	Multan	..	..	..	..	..	..	..	..	11	..	..	..	..	..	..	..	..	..	..	..
28	Muzaffargarh	..	..	..	..	..	..	..	..	..	..	..	..	..	..	..	..	..	..	..	..
29	Dera Ghazi Khan	..	..	..	..	..	..	..	..	..	..	..	..	..	..	..	..	..	..	..	..
	PUNJAB STATES	..	..	..	..	..	..	1	..	283	3	28	40	18	..	77	6	3	2	15	..
	A.—Having Political relations with the Punjab Government.	..	..	..	..	..	..	1	..	..	..	..	..	..	..	59	..	3	1	2	..
1	Dujana	..	..	..	..	..	..	..	..	..	..	..	..	..	..	..	..	..	1	..	..
2	Pataudi	..	..	..	..	..	..	..	..	..	..	..	..	..	..	1	..	..	..	..	..
3	Kalsia	..	..	..	..	..	..	..	..	..	..	..	..	..	..	1	..	..	..	1	..
4	SIMLA HILL STATES	..	..	..	..	..	..	1	..	..	..	..	..	..	..	57	..	3	..	1	..
	Bashahr	..	..	..	..	..	..	..	..	..	..	..	..	..	..	9	..	3	..	..	..
	Nalagarh	..	..	..	..	..	..	..	..	..	..	..	..	..	..	..	..	..	..	..	..
	Keonthal	..	..	..	..	..	..	1	..	..	..	..	..	..	..	47	..	..	..	1	..
	Baghal	..	..	..	..	..	..	..	..	..	..	..	..	..	..	..	..	..	..	..	..
	Jubbal	..	..	..	..	..	..	..	..	..	..	..	..	..	..	1	..	..	..	..	..
	Other Simla Hill States	..	..	..	..	..	..	..	..	..	..	..	..	..	..	..	..	..	..	..	..
	B.—Having Political relations with the Government of India.	..	..	..	..	..	..	..	..	283	3	28	40	18	..	18	6	..	1	13	..
5	Loharu	..	..	..	..	..	..	..	..	..	..	..	..	..	..	..	..	..	..	..	..
6	Sirmoor	..	..	..	..	..	..	..	..	..	..	..	..	..	..	5	..	..	..	..	..
7	Bilaspur	..	..	..	..	..	..	..	..	..	..	..	..	..	..	..	..	..	..	..	..
8	Mandi	..	..	..	..	..	..	..	..	3	..	..	..	2	..	7	..	..	..	4	..
9	Suket	..	..	..	..	..	..	..	..	..	..	..	..	..	..	..	6	..	1	6	..
10	Kapurthala	..	..	..	..	..	..	..	..	..	..	..	..	..	..	..	..	..	..	..	..
11	Maler Kotla	..	..	..	..	..	..	..	..	..	..	..	..	..	..	..	..	..	..	..	..
12	Faridkot	..	..	..	..	..	..	..	..	..	..	..	..	..	..	1	..	..	..	..	..
13	Chamba	..	..	..	..	..	..	..	..	..	..	..	..	..	..	..	..	..	..	..	..
14	Patiala (Phulkian States)	..	..	..	..	..	..	..	..	148	..	15	34	..	..	..	..	..	..	..	..
15	Jind (Phulkian States)	..	..	..	..	..	..	..	..	69	3	13	6	16	..	5	..	..	..	3	..
16	Nabha (Phulkian States)	..	..	..	..	..	..	..	..	..	..	..	..	..	..	..	..	..	..	..	..
17	Bahawalpur	..	..	..	..	..	..	..	..	63	..	..	..	..	..	..	..	..	..	..	..
18	*Cities.* Lahore	..	..	..	..	..	..	..	..	91	..	..	..	..	..	..	..	..	..	..	..
19	*Cities.* Amritsar	..	..	..	..	..	..	..	..	6	..	..	..	..	..	..	..	..	..	..	..
20	*Cities.* Multan	..	..	..	..	..	..	..	..	6	..	..	..	..	..	..	..	..	..	..	..

B.—PREPARATION AND SUPPLY OF MATERIAL SUBSTANCES.—*continued.*

III.—INDUSTRY.—*continued.*

5.—Textiles.—*continued.*

Total Class B.						Total Sub-class III.						Total Order 5.						
Total earners principal occupation.		Total working dependants.		Total earners with subsidiary occupation.		Total earners principal occupation.		Total working dependants.		Total earners with subsidiary occupation.		Total earners principal occupation.		Total working dependants.		Total earners with subsidiary occupation.		
Males.	Females.	Males.	Females.	Males.	Females.	Males.	Females.	Males.	Females.	Males.	Females.	Males.	Females.	Males.	Females.	Males.	Females.	Ser. No.
223	224	225	226	227	228	229	230	231	232	233	234	235	236	237	238	239	240	
2,208,731	205,858	114,772	105,727	191,780	11,908	1,428,740	184,470	79,811	98,588	117,970	10,697	304,038	47,516	16,733	32,341	25,951	4,365	
1,916,531	181,567	99,878	92,028	147,403	10,739	1,247,594	163,666	69,638	85,858	87,584	9,794	270,687	43,749	15,117	28,621	20,497	4,128	
301,323	40,592	16,246	25,446	37,240	1,917	191,057	34,784	8,529	23,134	20,481	1,537	34,225	6,801	1,380	5,448	4,932	643	
48,082	5,579	4,639	6,398	11,487	380	26,922	4,654	2,566	5,871	7,612	311	5,310	1,556	439	1,336	[illegible]	186	1
60,186	[illegible]	3,442	7,396	6,819	372	40,545	5,971	2,329	[illegible]	4,006	176	7,307	853	362	992	932	203	2
48,775	6,269	2,121	4,383	[illegible]	268	30,463	5,307	1,432	4,028	1,818	[illegible]	[illegible]	[illegible]	[illegible]	363	602	54	3
61,251	[illegible]	4,286	3,765	6,927	577	41,694	10,687	1,083	3,386	3,453	393	6,354	[illegible]	198	1,323	742	48	
75,960	9,574	1,247	3,465	6,861	[illegible]	48,222	[illegible]	[illegible]	2,973	2,931	[illegible]	[illegible]	2,176	289	1,423	754	52	5
7,069	302	[illegible]	39	1,042	8	3,211	[illegible]	6	37	662	1	57	4	1	1	34	..	6
320,149	27,937	19,451	19,697	36,013	1,689	230,262	25,786	12,654	18,903	24,928	1,597	60,782	8,783	2,790	9,366	5,585	305	
39,636	3,324	1,656	4,855	10,776	[illegible]	28,795	2,961	[illegible]	4,691	[illegible]	656	3,805	1,081	153	1,213	898	97	7
78,276	6,327	2,945	8,290	9,342	160	62,776	7,073	2,742	8,129	[illegible]	39	21,237	[illegible]	817	6,063	2,396	35	8
72,499	7,829	9,533	4,173	7,859	295	[illegible]	7,206	4,656	3,901	4,696	273	13,580	2,264	891	1,493	1,238	55	9
57,191	4,075	2,479	1,069	[illegible]	307	[illegible]	3,820	2,006	923	[illegible]	302	[illegible]	[illegible]	590	253	616	83	10
72,547	6,382	2,838	1,380	3,692	[illegible]	41,153	5,733	1,884	1,259	2,349	233	9,138	1,400	330	344	437	35	11
611,975	51,035	27,592	26,976	34,084	2,052	377,363	46,826	21,199	25,820	18,149	1,948	86,954	10,972	5,638	7,575	4,219	762	
181,073	13,545	3,409	3,203	[illegible]	339	[illegible]	12,739	2,856	[illegible]	2,531	326	17,923	3,082	467	729	348	172	12
134,134	[illegible]	8,727	13,212	7,765	890	80,085	10,679	6,437	12,942	3,651	854	[illegible]	[illegible]	1,717	4,728	1,166	286	13
78,936	[illegible]	5,433	2,089	9,483	320	55,373	6,604	4,307	2,927	4,703	307	5,775	1,633	1,770	505	1,172	148	14
91,495	6,025	3,810	3,974	[illegible]	130	64,449	5,255	3,032	[illegible]	2,550	96	[illegible]	[illegible]	465	634	788	27	15
77,731	8,592	[illegible]	1,606	4,926	304	49,061	7,865	[illegible]	[illegible]	3,159	276	6,678	[illegible]	921	589	496	101	16
48,007	4,052	2,912	1,992	2,827	69	31,788	3,684	1,867	[illegible]	[illegible]	59	6,805	858	298	390	249	28	17
299,678	28,576	19,611	10,862	19,795	1,266	208,446	25,251	14,729	9,809	13,208	1,116	40,506	6,794	2,837	2,927	3,101	489	
84,997	7,593	7,096	2,178	4,589	207	62,937	6,808	[illegible]	2,114	2,958	168	11,149	1,418	984	416	585	19	18
72,706	5,803	1,697	1,736	2,689	74	47,952	4,990	[illegible]	1,535	1,512	69	9,509	778	260	477	372	9	19
45,181	6,088	3,388	5,002	4,634	467	33,297	3,326	2,646	4,438	[illegible]	117	[illegible]	1,747	568	1,434	1,242	254	20
33,720	3,053	3,029	545	3,989	274	20,975	2,863	1,736	430	[illegible]	247	3,974	1,545	[illegible]	277	310	106	21
38,634	4,079	3,079	969	2,976	265	27,854	3,725	2,460	860	2,268	169	5,818	862	387	174	332	60	22
24,540	1,060	1,322	432	1,818	39	15,431	1,630	925	382	965	26	3,897	444	215	149	260	11	23
383,406	38,427	16,978	9,047	20,271	3,815	240,466	31,019	12,527	8,192	10,818	3,596	48,220	10,399	2,472	3,305	2,660	1,929	
61,782	6,077	1,705	1,523	2,659	66	38,349	5,093	1,200	1,387	1,912	59	6,014	1,541	154	751	635	27	24
85,238	12,795	5,573	3,023	5,759	2,918	56,791	12,123	4,765	2,929	4,074	2,879	11,474	2,971	1,306	779	863	1,655	25
66,574	3,921	[illegible]	639	2,787	292	43,649	3,476	2,890	663	1,229	236	9,188	1,237	588	229	383	68	26
94,484	[illegible]	[illegible]	760	2,037	173	62,752	4,148	2,168	702	1,449	159	13,280	1,725	122	428	283	81	27
30,571	2,679	1,499	[illegible]	2,466	220	23,355	[illegible]	972	1,129	[illegible]	171	5,652	1,246	87	860	304	75	28
35,751	3,343	2,029	1,940	3,963	146	15,570	3,262	532	1,442	959	92	2,672	1,676	116	256	192	43	29
292,200	24,291	14,894	13,699	44,377	1,169	181,146	20,804	10,173	12,730	30,386	903	33,351	3,767	1,616	3,720	5,454	287	
17,126	1,844	830	1,843	6,030	110	11,436	1,378	592	1,163	4,108	87	2,042	388	117	491	893	34	
12,014	166	20	257	480	4	1,374	95	11	223	191	4	261	2	..	50	48	1	1
1,332	403	5	27	103	14	783	322	2	27	47	12	113	18	1	1	11	8	2
5,345	879	257	562	718	21	3,719	624	206	450	411	13	1,119	257	83	263	127	7	3
8,485	456	548	497	4,720	71	5,560	837	373	463	3,459	58	549	111	33	177	707	18	4
572	14	111	33	673	6	419	12	86	18	535	1	66	2	21	4	239	..	
2,718	203	40	24	1,053	16	2,032	177	22	22	810	15	300	83	1	10	219	11	
1,610	100	118	75	506	5	774	35	49	68	330	3	23	.	3	1	27	1	
1,038	30	16	166	596	2	724	24	10	164	441	1	52	13	1	139	[illegible]	.	
224	2	48	43	595	1	772	1	46	43	474	..	5	..	1	..	43	..	
2,273	107	215	158	1,298	41	[illegible]	98	160	148	869	38	63	13	6	23	65	6	
275,074	22,447	14,064	12,856	38,347	1,059	169,710	19,426	9,581	11,567	26,278	816	31,309	3,379	1,499	3,229	4,561	203	
726	89	20	36	154	18	533	33	13	28	75	8	123	6	5	8	31	2	5
6,018	230	161	328	1,305	16	4,465	[illegible]	124	317	835	10	355	27	17	77	50	1	6
4,321	682	180	175	1,163	21	3,471	556	144	170	859	21	630	281	25	54	200	14	7
7,187	636	102	94	5,067	42	3,222	520	64	90	3,593	20	319	33	3	64	131	5	8
1,290	142	104	632	611	19	761	120	49	600	465	19	86	5	2	75	10	..	9
24,007	2,089	264	642	2,450	89	19,006	1,930	231	636	1,724	78	4,177	530	60	128	517	24	10
8,943	460	597	198	936	30	4,883	382	408	159	386	25	683	163	54	117	84	15	11
10,470	932	272	65	926	17	5,717	757	167	47	591	15	1,393	134	13	..	30	2	12
3,889	361	262	437	2,336	58	2,727	276	208	394	1,960	50	194	81	[illegible]	99	374	34	13
109,363	12,518	8,765	7,460	18,000	613	69,738	10,967	5,983	6,995	13,120	472	12,867	906	861	1,432	2,599	54	14
18,869	1,614	1,701	1,433	2,836	70	12,647	1,449	1,301	1,371	1,672	59	2,358	436	253	503	349	39	15
20,008	1,220	981	736	2,446	58	12,203	1,012	624	666	971	39	2,309	399	128	291	179	13	16
59,953	1,574	655	130	117	8	28,334	1,227	260	104	7	..	5,815	378	47	81	7	..	17
96,713	2,860	501	244	1,009	24	37,839	2,582	387	200	355	22	3,392	303	30	33	69	1	18
59,099	2,190	874	42	552	18	28,847	1,407	472	29	219	18	6,490	292	158	22	75	18	19
17,196	500	43	21	413	5	9,274	443	30	14	46	5	2,859	97	15	2	2	1	20

TABLE X.—OCCUPATION OR MEANS OF
DETAILS FOR DISTRICTS,

Class ..	B. PREPARATION AND SUPPLY OF MATERIAL SUBSTANCES.
Sub-class ..	III. INDUSTRY.
Order ..	5. Textiles.

Group ..	42.—Cotton ginning, cleaning and pressing.	43.—Cotton spinning, sizing and weaving.	44. Jute pressing, spinning and weaving.

Serial No.	DISTRICT OR STATE.	Total earners principal occupation. Males.	Females.	Total working dependants. Males	Females	Total earners with subsidiary occupation. Males.	Females.	Total earners principal occupation. Males.	Females.	Total working dependants. Males.	Females.	Total earners with subsidiary occupation. Males.	Females.	Total earners principal occupation. Males.	Females.	Total working dependants. Males.	Females.	Total earners with subsidiary occupation. Males.	Females.
1		241	242	243	244	245	246	247	248	249	250	251	252	253	254	255	256	257	258
	PUNJAB ..	31,567	2,777	1,523	1,240	5,299	126	240,250	39,498	13,[illegible]03	28,348	16,218	3,891	940	223	77	107	164	1
	BRITISH TERRITORY ..	27,901	2,691	1,338	1,226	4,566	121	214,381	36,671	12,346	24,991	12,514	3,674	932	223	73	106	158	1
	AMBALA DIVISION ..	4,858	256	120	89	1,276	18	24,346	5,582	994	4,523	2,791	608	52	28	2	7	34	..
1	Hissar ..	[illegible]	[illegible]	1	[illegible]	358	6	3,[illegible]77	1,367	[illegible]	[illegible]	1,3[illegible]	178	18	.	.	2	4	.
2	Rohtak ..	[illegible]	7	[illegible]	7	332		[illegible]	772	261	860	[illegible]	103	..	.	..	..	.	
3	Gurgaon ..	[illegible]	20	[illegible]	1	[illegible]	1	[illegible]	[illegible]	[illegible]	298	358	[illegible]	16	.	.	3	9	.
4	Karnal ..	1,257	82	[illegible]	16	[illegible]	7	[illegible]	1,170	170	1,[illegible]	[illegible]	[illegible]	10	28	.	2	[illegible]	.
5	Ambala ..	[illegible],262	53	6	5	173	..	[illegible]	[illegible]	172	[illegible]	397	48	8	.			.	..
6	Simla ..	20	..	..	.		..	28	1	..	..	7	..	..	.	..		.	..
	JULLUNDUR DIVISION ..	4,794	554	217	386	1,065	12	51,011	7,423	2,279	8,386	3,697	278	776	148	48	96	114	..
7	Kangra ..	[illegible]	27	..	[illegible]	31	6	3,[illegible]87	[illegible]	148	[illegible],11	868	[illegible]	.	..	..	.	2	
8	Hoshiarpur ..	1,[illegible]	[illegible]	[illegible]	[illegible]	148	5	20,7[illegible]	2,103	608	[illegible]	[illegible]	[illegible]	731	[illegible]	31	[illegible]	71	..
9	Jullundur ..	1,[illegible]	[illegible]	104		217	..	1[illegible],518	1,[illegible]	721	[illegible],410	806	55	[illegible]	22	7	1	34	.
10	Ludhiana ..	1,132	15	[illegible]	.	235	.	8,1[illegible]7	1,[illegible]79	[illegible]42	92	293	79		..		..		.
11	Ferozepur ..	[illegible]75	73	33	1	52	1	7,16[illegible]	1,[illegible]37	200	268	134	[illegible]	[illegible]4	18		1	7	.
	LAHORE DIVISION ..	10,011	589	592	427	1,177	18	67,501	9,461	4,638	6,767	2,327	486	48		.	..	1	..
12	Lahore ..	[illegible]	[illegible]	35	3	73	.	[illegible]	2,[illegible]7	281	[illegible]	21	171	31	.	.			..
13	Amritsar ..	[illegible]	78	[illegible]	228	184	1	[illegible]	2,[illegible]	1,3[illegible]2	[illegible],250	270	[illegible]	..	..	.	.	.	
14	Gurdaspur ..	2,[illegible]	[illegible]	16	15	[illegible]98	[illegible]	[illegible]2,381	1,484	1,5[illegible]7	[illegible]78	787	140	1	..	.	.	1	.
15	Sialkot ..	[illegible]	[illegible]	[illegible]	.	170	2	3,172	1,262	36[illegible]	621	586	25	.	.	.	.	.	
16	Gujranwala ..	1,101	16	22	7	[illegible]	1	[illegible],891	[illegible]	863	578	399	58	.			.		.
17	Shekhupura ..	[illegible]	[illegible]	48	15	[illegible]	6	[illegible]	596	218	232	144	[illegible]	..	.	.			..
	RAWALPINDI DIVISION	3,554	593	256	93	824	45	33,833	5,458	2,312	2,845	2,092	429	49	5	21	1	7	..
18	Gujrat ..	[illegible]	[illegible]	13	[illegible]	[illegible]	5	[illegible]	[illegible],221	[illegible]	3,[illegible]	[illegible]	[illegible]	.	..	.	..	2	.
19	Shahpur ..	[illegible]	37	39	6	133	1	7,589	64[illegible]	225	465	[illegible]	7	3	1		..	3	..
20	Jhelum ..	[illegible]	6	62	3	[illegible]12	.	4,[illegible]	1,390	[illegible]	1,313	685	244	..	.	..	..	..	
21	Rawalpindi ..	[illegible]	[illegible]	2	[illegible]	29	32	3,[illegible]	1,[illegible]65	398	[illegible]	268	72	..	.	.		.	..
22	Attock ..	[illegible]	26	[illegible]	[illegible]	49	6	[illegible]	744	318	118	2[illegible]7	72	1	4	2	1	2	..
23	Mianwali ..	11[illegible]	..	..	..	6	..	2,991	2[illegible]8	1[illegible]1	129	2[illegible]8	11	..	..	..	.		.
	MULTAN DIVISION ..	4,686	699	153	231	224	28	37,660	8,747	2,128	2,670	1,607	1,873	7	42	2	2	2	1
24	Montgomery ..	[illegible]	281	1	[illegible]	1	5	[illegible]	1,935	132	560	218	[illegible]	..	..	..	..	.	..
25	Lyallpur ..	1,[illegible]	182	21	[illegible]	1[illegible]8	18	8,62[illegible]	2,778	1,153	768	638	1,[illegible]7	.		.	..	..	..
26	Jhang ..	[illegible]	29	1	[illegible]	35	2	7,63[illegible]	1,144	57	[illegible]	307	58	.	..		..		.
27	Multan ..	[illegible]	85	15	[illegible]	36	2	10,900	[illegible]	49	3,[illegible]	[illegible]	67	7	.	.	..	.	
28	Muzaffargarh ..	271	2	2	7	4	.	3,530	[illegible]	110	585	100	71	..	..	.	.	.	
29	Dera Ghazi Khan ..	[illegible]	[illegible]	3	10	[illegible]	1	1,886	1,[illegible]	83	235	142	[illegible]	..	42	..	-	.	1
	PUNJAB STATES ..	3,666	8[illegible]	184	14	783	5	25,869	2,827	1,257	3,357	3,704	217	8		4	1	6	..
	A. HAVING POLITICAL RELATIONS WITH THE PUNJAB GOVERNMENT. ..	266	7	..	1	82	..	1,440	343	62	420	377	33	6		.	1	5	
1	Dujana ..	36	..	..	..	16	..	[illegible]84	1	.	18	30	.	[illegible]		.	1		..
2	Pataudi ..	17	.	..	..	[illegible]	.	80	10	.	3	4	8	..	..	..	..	.	
3	Kalsia ..	156	2	..	.	14	.	858	229	5	200	[illegible]	7	..	..	.			
4	SIMLA HILL STATES ..	57	5	..	.	52	..	318	103	5	171	263	17	..					
	Bashahr ..	..	.	..	..	.	.	..	2	..	4	2	.	..	..	.	.	.	
	Nalagarh ..	48		.	..	45	..	24[illegible]	79	[illegible]	10	170	1[illegible]	..		..	..	..	.
	Keonthal ..	[illegible]	..	.	..	..	..		..	.	..	.	..	..	.	.			.
	Baghal ..	..	..	..	..	[illegible]	..	29	12	.	134	4	.	..	..	.			
	Jubbal ..	.	..	..	..	..	..	5	..	1	..	13	.	.	.	..	.		.
	Other Simla Hill States ..	8	1	..	..	1	..	42	10	3	23	41	[illegible]	.		..	.	.	..
	B. HAVING POLITICAL RELATIONS WITH THE GOVERNMENT OF INDIA...	3,400	79	184	13	651	5	24,429	2,484	1,195	2,937	3,327	184	2	.	4	..	1	.
5	Loharu ..	27	.	..	..	17	1	74	5	5	7	12	1	..		..	.		..
6	Sirmoor ..	[illegible]1	.	1	..	4	..	296	[illegible]	16	77	38	1	..	..	.		..	.
7	Bilaspur ..	25	19	..	1	8	1	770	261	21	38	158	13	1	..	4	..	..	
8	Mandi ..	32	.	..	.	20	..	258	2[illegible]	.	61	107	4	..	..		..	.	
9	Suket ..	.	..	..	.	..	..	86	5	2	75	8	..	.	.	.			
10	Kapurthala ..	200	20	4	.	22	..	3,497	375	5[illegible]	428	419	24	.	.	..	.		..
11	Maler Kotla ..	70	.	4	.	18	..	527	157	47	112	30	15	..		..		.	.
12	Faridkot ..	132	.	..	..	1	..	1,213	133	11	..	28	2		.	..	.	1	..
13	Chamba ..	20	.	1	.	48	.	163	66	22	92	46	22	..	.	..		.	.
14	Patiala (Phulkian States)	1,918	27	131	5	363	3	9,798	479	697	1,293	2,118	50	..	..	..	..	..	.
15	Jind (Phulkian States)	320	1	26	4	89	..	1,734	401	189	486	227	39	..	..	..	..	.	.
16	Nabha (Phulkian States)	412	8	17	..	81	..	1,603	362	104	268	[illegible]97	13	.	.	.		.	.
17	Bahawalpur ..	153	4	.	.	..	..	4,607	185	25	..	..	.	..	..	..	.		
18	*Cities.* Lahore ..	375	15	1	3	27	..	2,011	218	16	20	35	1	25	.	..	..	.	.
19	*Cities.* Amritsar ..	46	1	..	..	2	..	4,365	139	102	..	13	.	..	..		.		..
20	*Cities.* Multan ..	35	..	.	..	..	..	2,508	93	.	..	2	1	7	..	..			..

LIVELIHOOD—GENERAL TABLE.

STATES AND CITIES.—*continued.*

B.—PREPARATION AND SUPPLY OF MATERIAL SUBSTANCES.—*continued.*

III.—INDUSTRY—*continued.*

5.—Textiles—*continued.*

45.—*Rope, twine, string and other fibres.* Total earners principal occupation. Males.	Females.	Total working dependants. Males.	Females.	Total earners with subsidiary occupation. Males.	Females.	46.—*Wool carding, spinning and weaving.* Total earners principal occupation. Males.	Females.	Total working dependants. Males.	Females.	Total earners with subsidiary occupation. Males.	Females.	47.—*Silk spinning and weaving.* Total earners principal occupation. Males.	Females.	Total working dependants. Males.	Females.	Total earners with subsidiary occupation. Males.	Females.	49.—*Dyeing, bleaching, printing, preparation and sponging of textile.* Total earners principal occupation. Males.	Females.	Total working dependants. Males.	Females.	Total earners with subsidiary occupation. Males.	Females.	Serial No.
259	260	261	262	263	264	265	266	267	268	269	270	271	272	273	274	275	276	277	278	279	280	281	282	
11,011	**2,184**	**614**	**1,507**	**2,299**	**261**	**1,987**	**806**	**90**	**245**	**712**	**29**	**967**	**224**	**18**	**23**	**8**	**2**	**16,678**	**1,425**	**791**	**765**	**1,240**	**52**	
9,785	**1,760**	**563**	**1,344**	**2,164**	**260**	**1,756**	**711**	**48**	**210**	**124**	**15**	**939**	**222**	**12**	**22**	**8**	**2**	**14,624**	**1,251**	**736**	**676**	**952**	**52**	
842	**470**	**71**	**308**	**457**	**5**	**410**	**110**	**14**	**51**	**59**	**2**	..	..	..	..	..	..	**3,649**	**358**	**179**	**470**	**814**	**10**	
10	..	4	.	128	..	7	..	3	.	..	..	.	..	..	..	..	..	940	103	91	169	156		1
120	7	12	9	27	..	8	1	5	1	9	..	.	..	..	..	..	..	881	58	43	106	69	6	2
17	11	2	7	6	1	24	5	4	19	5	..	..	..	..	..	..	..	581	52	30	37	21	1	3
240	178	7	63	139	1	348	99	1	30	2	2	..	..	..	..	..	..	855	135	11	158	56		4
455	274	46	229	157	3	9	2	..	..	15	..	..	..	..	..	..	..	387	5	2	..	12		5
..		.	.	.	..	14	3	1	1	28	..	..	..	..	..	..	..	5	..	..	..	.	..	6
2,826	**853**	**203**	**351**	**583**	**6**	**260**	**81**	**3**	**52**	**53**	**7**	..	**40**	..	..	..	..	**1,020**	**87**	**39**	**77**	**121**	**2**	
7	1	..	10	3	1	147	81	1	52	36	7	..	..	..	..	..	..	88	10	3	26	18	..	7
1,332	20	63	188	189	1	62	..	..	..	5	..	..	..	..	..	..	..	183	3	1	2	27	.	8
277	62	27	23	33	.	..	..	..	..	..	..	.	40	..	..	..	..	203	26	20	46	48	..	9
298	132	32	56	70	3	17	.	..	..	..	..	..	..	..	..	..	..	118	14	1	1	16	1	10
912	138	81	74	218	1	34	..	2	..	12	..	..	..	..	..	..	..	428	34	14	2	12		11
1,901	**475**	**104**	**316**	**450**	**242**	**914**	**70**	**21**	**1**	**6**	..	**704**	**51**	..	**1**	**1**	..	**5,681**	**217**	**288**	**35**	**249**	**13**	
698	174	22	94	28	1	73	19	1	.	1	.	393	3	.	..	..	..	1,153	111	25	13	35	.	12
869	260	56	218	359	241	623	33	1	..	..	.	311	48	..	1	1	..	2,206	63	152	22	47	.	13
141	..	7	..	14	..	215	18	19	1	5	..	..	..	..	..	..	..	481	5	31	..	109	..	14
56	19	13	..	37	..	..	..	.	..	..	..	..	..	..	..	..	..	700	15	18	..	15	..	15
101	13	..	4	12	..	..	.	.	..	..	..	..	..	..	..	..	..	570	12	36	..	28	1	16
36	..	6	..	..	..	3	..	.	..	..	..	..	..	..	..	..	..	569	11	26	..	15	1	17
628	**3**	**44**	**1**	**22**	**1**	**131**	**268**	**10**	**101**	**2**	**6**	**225**	**69**	**8**	**20**	**2**	**2**	**2,056**	**398**	**186**	**66**	**152**	**6**	
27	..	1	..	4	..	3	5	1	..	1	..	..	2	.	..	..	..	666	30	50	6	55	1	18
91	3	10	1	..	1	..	74	..	..	.	..	3	5	..	..	..	..	187	18	3	4	..	.	19
3	..	..	.	..	..	120	165	3	52	1	4	200	60	4	20	2	2	332	126	74	46	12	3	20
34	.	1	.	..	..	..	3	.	..	.	..	21	2	1	..	..	..	153	11	18	..	3	2	21
..	..	..	.	..		7	21	6	49	.	2	..	..	..	..	..	..	106	67	12	..	24	.	22
473	..	32	.	18	..	1	..	..	.	.	..	1	..	..	..	..	.	312	46	29	10	18	..	23
3,588	**459**	**141**	**368**	**702**	**6**	**41**	**182**	..	**5**	**4**	..	**10**	**62**	**4**	**1**	**5**	..	**2,218**	**196**	**44**	**28**	**116**	**21**	
281	..	7	..	396	.	..	.	..	..	..	..	10	..	4	..	5	..	147	28	..	12	3	2	24
231	..	14	..	46	..	..	..	..	..	..	..	..	..	..	..	..	..	944	11	28	..	66	.	25
350	2	2	..	11	..	10	.	..	..	3	..	..	..	..	..	.	..	273	62	2	6	25	5	26
727	20	31	95	36	1	..	..	..	..	..	..	..	1	..	..	..	..	328	70	7	10	9	11	27
1,460	323	39	268	196	4	1	..	..	..	1	..	..	..	..	..	..	..	282	1	6	..	3	..	28
539	114	28	5	17	1	..	182	.	5	..	..	..	61	..	1	..	..	44	24	1	..	8	..	29
1,226	**424**	**51**	**163**	**135**	**1**	**231**	**95**	**42**	**35**	**588**	**14**	**28**	**2**	**1**	**1**	..	..	**2,054**	**174**	**55**	**89**	**288**	.	
80	**3**	**25**	**61**	**24**	..	**175**	**24**	**30**	**6**	**289**	**1**	..	.	..	..	..	..	**74**	**9**	.	**2**	**116**	..	
..	..	..	..	..	..	..	..	.	..	..	..	..	..	..	..	..	..	35	1	.	1	3	..	1
6	1	1	..	1	..	..	..	..	.	..	..	..	..	..	..	..	..	10	7	.	..	..	..	2
70	2	22	61	19	..	16	21	4	1	7	..	..	..	..	..	..	.	18	1	..	..	7		3
4	..	**2**	..	**4**	..	**159**	**8**	**26**	**5**	**282**	**1**	..	..	..	..	.	..	**11**	..	..	**1**	**106**	.	4
..	.	..	..	..	..	106	..	21	..	237	..	..	..	..	..	..	..	..	..	..	..	.		
2	..	..	..	2	..	..	..	..	..	.	..	..	..	..	..	..	..	9	..	..	..	2	..	
..	..	..	..	..	..	20	..	3	1	26	1	..	..	..	..	..	..	1	..	..	..	1		
..	..	.	..	..	..	22	1	1	4	1	..	..	..	..	..	..	..	1	..	..	1	103	..	
..	..	..	..	.	..	..	..	..	..	..	..	..	..	..	..	..	..	..	..	..	..	..	.	
2	..	2	..	2	..	11	2	1	..	18	..	..	..	..	..	..	..	..	.	..	..	..	.	
1,146	**421**	**26**	**102**	**111**	**1**	**56**	**71**	**12**	**29**	**299**	**13**	**28**	**2**	**1**	**1**	..	..	**1,980**	**165**	**55**	**87**	**172**	.	
9	1	..	.	2	..	.	..	..	..	..	..	..	.	..	.	..	..	13	.	..	1	.		5
4	1		..	..	..	13	..	..	..	8	..		.	..	..	..	..	11	..	..	..	..		6
5	..	.	..	2	..	19	..	..	12	2	..	..	..	..	..	..	..	1	1	..	..	.		7
1	..	.	..	.	..	12	4	..	1	4	1	..	..	..	..	..	..	16	3	3	2	.		8
..	.	.	..	..	..	..	..	..	.	2	..	.	..	..	..	..	..	..	..	..	..	..	.	9
145	119	..	..	39	..	..	..	..	..	..	..	2	..	.	..	..	.	273	7	..	..	37	..	10
35	3	2	4	21	..	..	..	..	..	..	..	..	..	.	..	..	.	57	3	1	1	6	..	11
38	.	.	..	..	.	..	.	..	..	..	..	1	..	..	:	..	..	8	1	2	..	..	..	12
..	..	..	..	..	.	5	15	7	6	278	12	..	..	..	..	..	..	6	..	1	..	2	.	13
355	162	19	45	22	1	..	51	.	6	..	..	..	.	..	..	..	..	702	96	8	68	96	.	14
33	6	2	..	7	..	6	..	5	..	4	..	..	..	..	..	..	..	257	25	31	13	22	.	15
78	..	2	1	11	..	1	1	..	4	1	..	25	2	1	1	..	.	149	4	3	..	9	.	16
443	129	1	52	7	..	..	..	..	..	..	..	..	..	..	..	..	..	487	25	6	2	..	.	17
36	..	..	..	..	..	63	9	1	..	1	..	393	3	.	..	..	..	355	56	12	10	6	..	18
11	.	34	22	57	18	605	33	.	..	.	..	301	45	..	..	1	..	1,149	4	22	.	2	..	19
152	1	13	2	..	..	..	..	..	..	..	..	..	1	..	..	..	..	157	2	2	..	..	.	20

TABLE X—OCCUPATION OR MEANS OF
DETAILS FOR DISTRICTS,

Class .. B.—PREPARATION AND SUPPLY OF MATERIAL SUBSTANCES.

Sub-class .. III.—INDUSTRY.

Order .. 5.—Textiles—concluded. | 6.—Hides, Skins and hard Materials from the

Group .. 50—*Lace, crepe, embroideries, fringes, etc., and insufficiently described textile industries.* | *Total Order 6.* | 51.—*Working in leather.* | 52.—*Furriers and persons occupied with feathers and bristles; brush makers.*

Serial No.	District or State.	50 Total earners principal occupation. Males.	Females.	Total working dependants. Males.	Females.	Total earners with subsidiary occupation. Males.	Females.	Total Order 6. Total earners principal occupation. Males.	Females.	Total working dependants. Males.	Females.	Total earners with subsidiary occupation. Males.	Females.	51. Total earners principal occupation. Males.	Females.	Total working dependants. Males.	Females.	Total earners with subsidiary occupation. Males.	Females.	52. Total earners principal occupation. Males.	Females.
1	2	283	284	285	286	287	288	289	290	291	292	293	294	295	296	297	298	299	300	301	302
	PUNJAB	633	379	23	106	11	3	13,927	1,155	1,228	682	1,162	31	13,860	1,155	1,226	676	1,156	31	1	..
	BRITISH TERRITORY	369	220	1	46	11	3	11,134	232	799	163	1,029	28	11,080	232	799	160	1,023	28	1	..
	AMBALA DIVISION	70	2	..	..	1	..	2,447	43	129	111	496	9	2,422	43	129	108	490	9	1	..
1	Hissar	7	..	..	..	..	..	584	17	84	67	282	9	584	17	84	67	282	9	..	..
2	Rohtak	8	..	..	..	..	..	593	7	25	38	42	..	575	7	25	35	36	..	..	..
3	Gurgaon	15	2	..	..	1	..	293	5	4	4	25	..	293	5	4	4	25	..	..	..
4	Karnal	25	..	..	..	..	..	343	4	4	2	28	..	343	4	4	2	28	..	..	..
5	Ambala	15	..	..	..	..	..	634	10	12	..	119	..	627	10	12	..	119	..	1	..
6	Simla	..	..	..	..	..	..	..	..	..	..	..	..	..	..	..	..	..	..	..	..
	JULLUNDUR DIVISION	95	97	1	18	2	..	2,041	68	305	21	280	19	2,041	68	305	21	280	19	..	..
7	Kangra	24	..	1	..	..	..	..	1	..	1	..	..	..	1	..	1	..	..	..	..
8	Hoshiarpur	..	2	..	7	..	..	624	3	3	10	56	1	624	3	3	10	56	1	..	..
9	Jullundur	71	94	..	11	..	..	843	57	266	10	149	18	843	57	266	10	149	18	..	..
10	Ludhiana	..	1	..	..	..	..	175	2	16	..	40	..	175	2	16	..	40	..	..	..
11	Ferozepore	..	..	..	..	2	..	399	5	20	..	35	..	399	5	20	..	35	..	..	..
	LAHORE DIVISION	194	109	..	28	8	3	3,561	39	129	31	87	..	3,536	39	129	31	87	..	..	..
12	Lahore	134	2	..	..	..	..	1,361	33	5	6	14	..	1,348	33	5	6	14	..	..	..
13	Amritsar	13	70	..	..	..	..	474	1	20	..	28	..	462	1	20	..	28	..	..	..
14	Gurdaspur	31	31	..	28	8	3	289	..	19	25	15	..	289	..	19	25	15	..	..	..
15	Sialkot	..	..	..	..	..	..	1,283	5	80	..	9	..	1,283	5	80	..	9	..	..	..
16	Gujranwala	16	6	..	..	..	..	134	..	5	..	14	..	134	..	5	..	14	..	..	..
17	Sheikhupura	..	..	..	..	..	..	20	..	..	..	7	..	20	..	..	..	7	..	..	..
	RAWALPINDI DIVISION	..	..	..	..	..	..	745	64	90	..	8	..	745	64	90	..	8	..	..	..
18	Gujrat	..	..	..	..	..	..	211	10	3	..	4	..	211	10	3	..	4	..	..	..
19	Shahpur	..	..	..	..	..	..	57	4	2	..	..	..	57	4	2	..	..	..	..	..
20	Jhelum	..	..	..	..	..	..	423	50	75	..	1	..	423	50	75	..	1	..	..	..
21	Rawalpindi	..	..	..	..	..	..	34	..	3	..	1	..	34	..	3	..	1	..	..	..
22	Attock	..	..	..	..	..	..	20	..	7	..	1	..	20	..	7	..	1	..	..	..
23	Mianwali	..	..	..	..	..	..	..	..	..	..	1	..	..	..	..	..	1	..	..	..
	MULTAN DIVISION	10	12	..	..	..	..	2,340	18	146	..	158	..	2,336	18	146	..	158	..	..	..
24	Montgomery	2	..	..	..	..	..	1,297	2	37	..	93	..	1,297	2	37	..	93	..	..	..
25	Lyallpur	..	..	..	..	..	..	556	1	92	..	44	..	556	1	92	..	44	..	..	..
26	Jhang	..	..	..	..	..	..	35	4	..	..	..	..	35	4	..	..	..	..	..	..
27	Multan	..	..	..	..	..	..	1	..	..	..	..	..	1	..	..	..	..	..	..	..
28	Muzaffargarh	8	11	..	..	..	..	233	..	15	..	17	..	232	..	15	..	17	..	..	..
29	Dera Ghazi Khan	..	1	..	..	..	..	218	11	2	..	4	..	215	11	2	..	4	..	..	..
	PUNJAB STATES	269	159	22	60	..	..	2,793	923	429	519	133	3	2,780	923	427	516	133	3	..	..
	A.—HAVING POLITICAL RELATIONS WITH THE PUNJAB GOVERNMENT.	1	2	..	..	..	..	110	1	..	..	4	..	110	1	..	..	4	..	..	..
1	Dujana	..	..	..	..	..	..	9	..	..	..	..	..	9	..	..	..	..	..	..	..
2	Pataudi	..	..	..	..	..	..	19	..	..	..	3	..	19	..	..	..	3	..	..	..
3	Kalsia	1	2	..	..	..	..	75	1	..	..	1	..	75	1	..	..	1	..	..	..
4	SIMLA HILL STATES	..	..	..	..	..	..	7	..	..	..	..	..	7	..	..	..	..	..	..	..
	Bashahr	..	..	..	..	..	..	7	..	..	..	..	..	7	..	..	..	..	..	..	..
	Nalagarh	..	..	..	..	..	..	..	..	..	..	..	..	..	..	..	..	..	..	..	..
	Keonthal	..	..	..	..	..	..	..	..	..	..	..	..	..	..	..	..	..	..	..	..
	Baghal	..	..	..	..	..	..	..	..	..	..	..	..	..	..	..	..	..	..	..	..
	Jubbal	..	..	..	..	..	..	..	..	..	..	..	..	..	..	..	..	..	..	..	..
	Other Simla Hill States	..	..	..	..	..	..	..	..	..	..	..	..	..	..	..	..	..	..	..	..
	B.—HAVING POLITICAL RELATIONS WITH THE GOVERNMENT OF INDIA.	268	157	22	60	..	..	2,683	922	429	519	129	3	2,670	922	427	516	129	3	..	..
5	Loharu	..	..	..	..	..	..	17	..	..	1	..	..	17	..	..	1	..	..	..	..
6	Sirmoor	..	..	..	..	..	..	..	..	..	..	1	..	..	..	..	..	1	..	..	..
7	Bilaspur	..	..	..	..	..	..	22	2	9	4	34	1	22	2	9	4	34	1	..	..
8	Mandi	..	..	..	..	..	..	..	..	..	..	..	..	..	..	..	..	..	..	..	..
9	Suket	..	..	..	..	..	..	..	..	..	..	..	..	..	..	..	..	..	..	..	..
10	Kapurthala	..	9	..	..	..	..	226	1	1	..	86	2	226	1	1	..	86	2	..	..
11	Maler Kotla	..	..	..	..	..	..	7	2	..	..	..	..	7	2	..	..	..	..	..	..
12	Faridkot	..	..	..	..	..	..	20	..	..	..	1	..	20	..	..	..	1	..	..	..
13	Chamba	..	..	..	1	..	..	1	..	..	..	..	..	1	..	..	..	..	..	..	..
14	Patiala (Phulkian States)	94	91	6	15	..	..	2,226	912	419	514	..	..	2,213	912	417	511	..	..	..	..
15	Jind (Phulkian States)	8	..	..	..	..	..	17	..	..	..	..	..	17	..	..	..	..	..	..	..
16	Nabha (Phulkian States)	41	22	1	17	..	..	120	5	..	..	7	..	120	5	..	..	7	..	..	..
17	Bahawalpur	125	35	15	27	..	..	27	..	..	..	..	..	27	..	..	..	..	..	..	..
18	Cities. Lahore	134	2	..	..	..	..	686	16	..	..	9	..	673	16	..	..	9	..	..	..
19	Cities. Amritsar	13	70	..	..	..	..	195	..	5	..	4	..	183	..	5	..	4	..	..	..
20	Cities. Multan	..	..	..	..	..	..	1	..	..	..	..	..	1	..	..	..	..	..	..	..

LIVELIHOOD.—GENERAL TABLE.

STATES AND CITIES.—*continued.*

B.—PREPARATION AND SUPPLY OF MATERIAL SUBSTANCES—*continued.*

III.—INDUSTRY—*continued.*

Animal kingdom—*concluded.* | **7. Wood.**

53.—*Bone, ivory, horn, shell, etc., workers (except buttons).* Total earners principal occupation		Total working dependants		Total earners with subsidiary occupation		*Total Order 7.* Total earners principal occupation		Total working dependants		Total earners with subsidiary occupation		54.—*Sawyers.* Total earners principal occupation		Total working dependants		Total earners with subsidiary occupation		55.—*Carpenters, turners and joiners, etc.* Total earners principal occupation		Total working dependants		Total earners with subsidiary occupation		Serial No.
Males.	Females.	Males.	Females.	Males.	Females.	Males.	Females.	Males.	Females.	Males.	Females.	Males.	Females.	Males.	Females.	Males.	Females.	Males.	Females.	Males.	Females.	Males.	Females.	
303	304	305	306	307	308	309	310	311	312	313	314	315	316	317	318	319	320	321	322	323	324	325	326	
66	..	**2**	**6**	**6**	..	**177,715**	**5,893**	**9,534**	**3,549**	**17,720**	**252**	**4,953**	**33**	**390**	**68**	**282**	**1**	**149,571**	**1,974**	**7,997**	**884**	**14,553**	**49**	
53	..	..	**3**	**6**	..	**153,667**	**5,204**	**7,714**	**3,055**	**12,486**	**191**	**1,998**	**17**	**66**	**6**	**105**	**1**	**132,797**	**1,732**	**6,802**	**655**	**10,117**	**38**	
24	..	..	**3**	**6**	..	**19,429**	**382**	**860**	**147**	**3,316**	**33**	**243**	**4**	**1**	**1**	**17**	..	**16,461**	**63**	**727**	**36**	**2,211**	**9**	
..	..	..	..	..	..	2,489	29	229	21	1,274	4	12	..	..	..	1	..	2,237	5	199	8	1,144	3	1
18	..	..	3	6	..	3,941	42	255	35	538	1	1	..	..	..	..	..	3,354	16	210	20	350	1	2
..	..	..	..	..	..	2,898	34	120	27	310	2	19	..	..	..	3	..	2,583	16	104	1	84	1	3
..	..	..	..	..	..	4,279	102	126	12	577	24	109	1	..	..	9	..	3,459	14	115	1	218	3	4
6	..	..	..	..	..	5,411	168	129	49	547	2	78	..	1	..	2	..	4,451	10	98	6	378	1	5
..	..	..	..	..	..	411	7	1	3	70	..	24	3	..	1	2	..	377	2	1	..	57	..	6
..	..	..	..	..	..	**29,492**	**928**	**1,286**	**580**	**3,562**	**47**	**174**	**5**	..	**5**	**25**	**1**	**24,469**	**205**	**1,087**	**31**	**3,067**	**2**	
..	..	..	..	..	..	6,177	446	132	373	1,346	44	174	5	..	5	25	1	3,579	55	36	17	1,086	2	7
..	..	..	..	..	..	6,708	223	193	77	781	2	..	..	..	..	..	..	5,869	45	174	5	676	..	8
..	..	..	..	..	..	5,863	117	505	89	328	1	..	..	..	..	..	..	5,439	59	467	6	310	..	9
..	..	..	..	..	..	5,216	62	189	5	461	..	..	..	..	..	..	..	4,778	19	164	1	393	..	10
..	..	..	..	..	..	5,528	80	267	36	646	..	..	..	..	..	..	..	4,804	27	246	2	602	..	11
25	..	..	..	..	..	**45,715**	**860**	**2,457**	**236**	**2,164**	**18**	**1,081**	**2**	**49**	..	**38**	..	**42,021**	**522**	**2,284**	**145**	**1,783**	**11**	
13	..	..	..	..	..	12,251	279	413	46	458	7	55	2	1	..	4	..	11,297	144	395	17	430	4	12
12	..	..	..	..	..	8,545	118	599	93	416	8	417	..	..	..	..	..	7,502	87	561	60	293	7	13
..	..	..	..	..	..	6,889	78	512	3	664	1	3	..	..	..	..	..	6,476	19	499	1	584	..	14
..	..	..	..	..	..	8,128	35	313	5	202	..	531	..	48	..	32	..	7,236	35	233	5	124	..	15
..	..	..	..	..	..	6,027	142	345	18	239	2	68	..	..	..	2	..	5,790	33	339	2	175	..	16
..	..	..	..	..	..	3,875	208	275	71	185	..	7	..	..	..	..	..	3,720	204	257	60	177	..	17
..	..	..	..	..	..	**27,077**	**1,717**	**1,995**	**1,008**	**2,169**	**15**	**376**	**6**	**9**	..	**23**	..	**23,862**	**726**	**1,815**	**421**	**1,909**	**3**	
..	..	..	..	..	..	8,610	140	637	80	627	5	66	..	1	..	3	..	7,591	139	576	78	541	2	18
..	..	..	..	..	..	5,829	446	131	40	196	2	..	..	..	..	..	..	5,443	433	121	29	159	..	19
..	..	..	..	..	..	4,835	144	603	717	527	1	27	3	..	..	..	..	4,216	44	552	283	450	..	20
..	..	..	..	..	..	2,358	51	219	8	280	6	183	..	3	..	17	..	2,086	35	214	8	256	1	21
..	..	..	..	..	..	3,458	666	326	142	363	1	84	3	5	..	3	..	2,822	31	282	7	349	..	22
..	..	..	..	..	..	1,987	270	79	16	176	..	16	..	..	..	..	..	1,704	44	70	16	154	..	23
4	..	..	..	..	..	**31,954**	**1,317**	**1,116**	**1,089**	**1,275**	**78**	**124**	..	**7**	..	**2**	..	**25,984**	**216**	**889**	**22**	**1,147**	**13**	
..	..	..	..	..	..	5,379	73	100	6	167	..	15	..	..	..	..	..	4,480	36	79	6	165	..	24
..	..	..	..	..	..	6,291	146	273	22	345	9	..	..	..	..	..	..	5,047	78	263	12	319	9	25
..	..	..	..	..	..	5,187	39	169	2	139	45	7	..	..	..	..	..	4,414	12	78	1	130	..	26
..	..	..	..	..	..	9,489	657	277	33	259	10	..	..	..	..	..	..	6,371	52	192	3	206	2	27
1	..	..	..	..	..	3,131	77	259	21	112	4	..	..	..	..	..	..	2,532	12	248	..	81	2	28
3	..	..	..	..	..	2,477	325	38	1,005	253	10	102	..	7	..	2	..	2,240	26	29	..	243	..	29
13	..	**2**	**3**	..	..	**24,048**	**689**	**1,820**	**494**	**5,234**	**61**	**2,955**	**16**	**824**	**57**	**177**	..	**16,774**	**242**	**1,195**	**229**	**4,436**	**11**	
..	..	..	..	..	..	**1,605**	**63**	**88**	**73**	**744**	**33**	**146**	**16**	**17**	**57**	**97**	..	**1,121**	**2**	**48**	**1**	**426**	..	1
..	..	..	..	..	..	99	..	..	1	13	..	..	..	..	..	..	..	87	..	..	..	8	..	
..	..	..	..	..	..	96	..	..	..	14	..	..	..	..	..	..	..	90	..	..	..	..	..	2
..	..	..	..	..	..	477	2	24	..	116	2	1	..	..	..	..	..	381	1	18	..	53	..	3
..	..	..	..	..	..	**933**	**61**	**64**	**72**	**601**	**31**	**145**	**16**	**17**	**57**	**97**	..	**563**	**1**	**30**	**1**	**365**	..	4
..	..	..	..	..	..	124	5	25	4	106	1	23	..	3	..	3	..	64	..	18	..	86	..	
..	..	..	..	..	..	299	19	4	4	73	1	..	..	..	..	..	..	212	..	..	..	46	..	
..	..	..	..	..	..	182	11	11	33	55	..	100	11	9	33	17	..	77	..	2	..	32	..	
..	..	..	..	..	..	37	..	1	..	36	..	..	..	..	..	..	..	34	..	1	..	36	..	
..	..	..	..	..	..	43	1	3	11	167	..	4	..	..	10	72	..	37	1	3	1	82	..	
..	..	..	..	..	..	248	25	20	20	164	29	18	5	5	14	5	..	139	..	6	..	83	..	
13	..	**2**	**3**	..	..	**22,443**	**626**	**1,732**	**421**	**4,490**	**28**	**2,809**	..	**307**	..	**80**	..	**15,653**	**240**	**1,147**	**228**	**4,010**	**11**	
..	..	..	..	..	..	56	..	2	7	2	1	1	..	..	..	..	..	38	..	..	..	2	..	
..	..	..	..	..	..	699	7	29	32	121	6	8	..	..	..	..	..	533	..	16	..	89	..	6
..	..	..	..	..	..	332	16	17	8	36	..	..	..	..	..	..	..	182	1	9	2	29	..	7
..	..	..	..	..	..	966	164	41	2	857	6	135	..	..	..	72	..	680	123	39	2	664	..	8
..	..	..	..	..	..	47	26	5	203	56	..	..	..	..	..	..	..	47	26	5	200	54	..	
..	..	..	..	..	..	1,944	84	18	..	115	7	..	..	..	..	..	..	1,816	13	18	..	95	..	
..	..	..	..	..	..	613	12	82	3	31	..	..	..	..	..	..	..	598	10	82	3	19	..	1
..	..	..	..	..	..	954	..	15	..	267	..	..	..	..	..	..	..	894	..	15	..	267	..	12
..	..	..	..	..	..	365	13	16	15	226	1	10	..	..	..	8	..	343	8	11	7	158	..	1
13	..	2	3	..	..	10,949	151	1,246	121	2,190	5	2,512	..	307	..	..	..	7,119	..	730	4	2,190	5	4
..	..	..	..	..	..	1,250	13	152	8	375	2	..	..	..	..	..	..	1,106	3	120	3	292	1	
..	..	..	..	..	..	1,841	29	95	6	214	..	104	..	..	..	..	..	1,589	15	95	3	151	..	
..	..	..	..	..	..	2,427	111	14	16	..	..	39	..	..	..	..	..	708	41	7	4	..	..	7
13	..	..	..	..	..	5,034	61	41	16	91	..	25	..	..	..	..	..	4,548	25	40	10	90	..	8
12	..	..	..	..	..	2,859	4	70	..	8	..	417	..	..	..	..	..	2,140	4	70	..	7	..	9
..	..	..	..	..	..	365	16	..	..	8	2	..	..	..	..	..	..	352	14	..	..	8	..	

TABLE X.—OCCUPATION OR MEANS OF
DETAILS FOR DISTRICTS,

Class .. B. -PREPARATION AND SUPPLY OF MATERIAL SUBSTANCES.

Sub-class .. III.--INDUSTRY.

Order .. 7. Wood--*concluded.* | 8. Metals.

Group .. 56.--*Basket-makers, and other industries of woody materials, including leaves and thatchers and builders working with bamboo, reeds or similar materials.* | *Total Order 8.* | 57.--*Smelting, forging and rolling of iron and other Metals.*

Serial No.	District or State.	56. Total earners principal occupation. Males.	Females.	56. Total working dependants. Males.	Females.	56. Total earners with subsidiary occupation. Males.	Females.	Total Order 8. Total earners principal occupation. Males.	Females.	Total Order 8. Total working dependants. Males.	Females.	Total Order 8. Total earners with subsidiary occupation. Males.	Females.	57. Total earners principal occupation. Males.	Females.	57. Total working dependants. Males.	Females.	57. Total earners with subsidiary occupation. Males.	Females.
1	2	327	328	329	330	331	332	333	334	335	336	337	338	339	340	341	342	343	344
	PUNJAB ..	**23,191**	**3,886**	**1,147**	**2,602**	**2,885**	**202**	**87,127**	**1,084**	**4,904**	**732**	**7,084**	**41**	**357**	**2**	**11**	**15**	**9**	..
	BRITISH TERRITORY ..	**18,872**	**3,455**	**846**	**2,394**	**2,264**	**152**	**75,517**	**1,028**	**4,102**	**622**	**4,665**	**85**	**47**	..	..	..	..	..
	AMBALA DIVISION ..	**2,725**	**315**	**132**	**110**	**1,088**	**24**	**12,843**	**96**	**474**	**109**	**887**	**1**	**4**	..	..	..	..	..
1	Hissar ..	240	24	30	13	129	1	1,854	12	163	45	396	..	..	..	..	..	..	..
2	Rohtak ..	586	26	45	15	188	..	2,664	32	108	44	94	..	..	..	..	..	..	..
3	Gurgaon ..	296	18	16	26	243	1	1,456	11	51	1	46	..	..	..	..	..	..	..
4	Karnal ..	711	87	11	11	350	21	3,230	30	63	15	141	..	..	..	..	..	..	..
5	Ambala ..	882	158	30	43	167	1	3,543	10	89	4	183	1	4	..	..	..	..	..
6	Simla ..	10	2	..	2	11	..	96	1	..	..	27	..	..	..	..	..	..	..
	JULLUNDUR DIVISION	**4,849**	**718**	**199**	**544**	**470**	**44**	**11,869**	**154**	**503**	**13**	**1,328**	**14**	..	..	..	..	..	..
7	Kangra ..	2,424	386	96	351	235	41	2,299	14	51	2	714	4	..	..	..	..	..	..
8	Hoshiarpur ..	839	178	19	72	105	2	2,967	20	21	6	200	..	..	..	..	..	..	..
9	Jullundur ..	424	58	38	83	18	1	2,882	50	222	1	187	6	..	..	..	..	..	..
10	Ludhiana ..	438	43	25	4	68	..	1,874	17	119	2	129	..	..	..	..	..	..	..
11	Ferozepore ..	724	53	21	34	44	..	1,847	53	90	2	98	4	..	..	..	..	..	..
	LAHORE DIVISION ..	**2,613**	**336**	**124**	**91**	**343**	**7**	**25,557**	**283**	**1,438**	**78**	**815**	**9**	**35**	..	..	..	..	..
12	Lahore ..	899	133	17	29	24	3	6,947	87	236	10	93	4	35	..	..	..	..	..
13	Amritsar ..	626	31	38	33	123	1	5,654	25	479	6	156	3	..	..	..	..	..	..
14	Gurdaspur ..	410	59	13	2	80	1	4,682	15	294	..	237	2	..	..	..	..	..	..
15	Sialkot ..	361	..	32	..	46	..	2,978	37	114	..	81	..	..	..	..	..	..	..
16	Gujranwala ..	169	109	6	16	62	2	3,181	5	225	3	96	..	..	..	..	..	..	..
17	Sheikhupura ..	148	4	18	11	8	..	2,115	113	90	39	152	..	..	..	..	..	..	..
	RAWALPINDI DIVISION	**2,839**	**985**	**171**	**582**	**237**	**12**	**13,963**	**380**	**1,336**	**411**	**1,072**	**10**	..	..	..	..	..	..
18	Gujrat ..	953	1	60	2	83	3	3,280	63	450	91	219	4	..	..	..	..	..	..
19	Shahpur ..	386	13	10	11	37	2	2,624	35	16	73	69	..	..	..	..	..	..	..
20	Jhelum ..	592	97	51	434	77	1	2,499	73	135	148	282	1	..	..	..	..	..	..
21	Rawalpindi ..	89	16	2	..	7	5	1,437	23	152	4	109	3	..	..	..	..	..	..
22	Attock ..	552	632	39	135	11	1	2,890	69	478	38	315	2	..	..	..	..	..	..
23	Mianwali ..	267	226	9	..	22	..	1,233	117	105	57	78	..	..	..	..	..	..	..
	MULTAN DIVISION ..	**5,846**	**1,101**	**220**	**1,067**	**126**	**65**	**11,285**	**115**	**351**	**11**	**563**	**1**	**8**	..	..	..	..	..
24	Montgomery ..	884	37	21	..	2	..	1,852	13	70	..	82	..	..	..	..	..	..	..
25	Lyallpur ..	344	68	10	10	26	..	3,132	13	154	2	267	1	..	..	..	..	..	..
26	Jhang ..	766	27	91	1	9	45	1,949	9	29	..	35	..	8	..	..	..	..	..
27	Multan ..	3,118	605	85	30	53	8	2,774	59	70	8	93	..	..	..	..	..	..	..
28	Muzaffargarh ..	599	65	11	21	28	2	746	19	14	1	53	..	..	..	..	..	..	..
29	Dera Ghazi Khan ..	135	299	2	1,005	8	10	832	2	14	..	33	..	..	..	..	..	..	..
	PUNJAB STATES ..	**4,319**	**431**	**301**	**208**	**621**	**50**	**11,610**	**56**	**802**	**110**	**2,419**	**6**	**310**	**2**	**11**	**15**	**9**	..
	A.--HAVING POLITICAL RELATIONS WITH THE PUNJAB GOVERNMENT. ..	**338**	**45**	**23**	**15**	**221**	**33**	**891**	**6**	**78**	**21**	**442**	..	..	..	..	..	..	..
1	Dujana ..	12	..	..	1	5	..	34	..	1	..	4	..	..	..	..	..	..	..
2	Pataudi ..	6	..	..	..	14	..	22	..	1	..	..	..	..	..	..	..	..	..
3	Kalsia ..	95	1	6	..	63	2	199	..	13	..	17	..	..	..	..	..	..	..
4	SIMLA HILL STATES ..	**225**	**44**	**17**	**14**	**139**	**31**	**636**	**6**	**63**	**21**	**421**	..	..	..	..	..	..	..
	Bashahr ..	37	5	4	4	17	1	50	..	21	..	91	..	..	..	..	..	..	..
	Nalagarh ..	87	19	4	4	27	1	190	2	5	..	62	..	..	..	..	..	..	..
	Keonthal ..	5	..	..	..	6	..	88	1	11	2	51	..	..	..	..	..	..	..
	Baghal ..	3	..	..	..	..	..	109	2	1	16	26	..	..	..	..	..	..	..
	Jubbal ..	2	..	..	..	13	..	27	..	9	2	35	..	..	..	..	..	..	..
	Other Simla Hill States ..	91	20	9	6	76	29	172	1	16	1	156	..	..	..	..	..	..	..
	B.--HAVING POLITICAL RELATIONS WITH THE GOVERNMENT OF INDIA. ..	**3,981**	**386**	**278**	**193**	**400**	**17**	**10,719**	**50**	**724**	**89**	**1,977**	**6**	**310**	**2**	**11**	**15**	**9**	..
5	Loharu ..	17	..	2	7	..	1	42	2	5	1	..	..	..	..	..	..	..	..
6	Sirmoor ..	158	7	13	32	32	6	637	5	12	..	82	1	225	2	..	..	9	..
7	Bilaspur ..	150	15	8	6	7	..	386	9	19	7	145	2	..	..	..	..	..	..
8	Mandi ..	151	41	2	..	121	1	735	9	2	2	337	..	..	..	..	..	..	..
9	Suket ..	..	..	..	3	2	..	127	1	10	1	51	..	..	..	..	..	..	..
10	Kapurthala ..	128	71	..	..	20	7	982	1	4	..	53	..	..	..	..	..	..	..
11	Maler Kotla ..	15	2	..	..	12	..	552	5	69	..	16	..	..	..	..	..	..	..
12	Faridkot ..	60	..	..	..	..	..	375	..	28	..	56	..	..	..	..	..	..	..
13	Chamba ..	12	5	5	8	60	1	187	..	18	..	174	..	..	..	..	..	..	..
14	Patiala } Phulkian States.	1,318	151	209	117	..	..	3,491	..	420	15	897	2	85	..	11	15	..	..
15	Jind } Phulkian States.	144	10	32	5	83	1	771	1	84	..	109	..	..	..	..	..	..	..
16	Nabha } Phulkian States.	148	14	..	3	63	..	695	14	46	63	57	1	..	..	..	..	..	..
17	Bahawalpur ..	1,680	70	7	12	..	..	1,739	3	7	..	..	..	..	..	..	..	..	..
18	*Cities.* Lahore ..	461	36	1	..	1	..	3,742	22	20	10	14	..	35	..	..	..	..	..
19	*Cities.* Amritsar ..	302	..	..	..	1	..	2,857	1	12	..	22	..	..	..	..	..	..	..
20	*Cities.* Multan ..	13	2	..	..	..	..	615	20	1	..	5	..	..	..	..	..	..	..

B.—PREPARATION AND SUPPLY OF MATERIAL SUBSTANCES—*continued.*

III.—INDUSTRY—*continued.*

8. Metals—*continued.*

58.—*Makers of arms, guns, etc.*						59.—*Blacksmiths, other workers in iron, makers of implements.*						60.—*Workers in brass, copper and bell-metal.*						61.—*Workers in other Metals (except precious metals).*						
Total earners principal occupation.		Total working dependants.		Total earners with subsidiary occupation.		Total earners principal occupation.		Total working dependants.		Total earners with subsidiary occupation.		Total earners principal occupation.		Total working dependants.		Total earners with subsidiary occupation.		Total earners principal occupation.		Total, working dependants.		Total earners with subsidiary occupation.		
Males.	Females.	Males.	Females.	Males.	Females.	Males.	Females.	Males.	Females.	Males.	Females.	Males.	Females.	Males.	Females.	Males.	Females.	Males.	Females.	Males.	Females.	Males.	Females.	Serial No.
345	346	347	348	349	350	351	352	353	354	355	356	357	358	359	360	361	362	363	364	365	366	367	368	
78	6	2	..	17	..	79,744	1,031	4,714	710	6,856	34	4,719	38	122	5	107	7	2,223	7	55	2	95	.	
75	6	2	..	12	.	70,245	980	3,950	620	4,501	29	3,486	35	101	..	76	6	1,658	7	49	2	76	..	
9	1	..	..	..	..	11,132	88	444	109	857	1	1,400	3	17	..	13	..	297	4	13	..	17	..	
..	..	..	..	..	..	1,698	12	157	45	393	..	107	..	4	..	..	..	49	..	2	..	3	..	1
1	..	..	..	..	..	2,579	32	102	44	90	..	62	..	3	..	3	..	22	..	3	..	1	..	2
2	1	..	..	..	..	1,042	8	50	1	45	..	388	2	1	..	..	..	23	..	..	..	1	..	3
5	..	..	..	..	..	2,832	26	57	15	135	..	326	1	..	..	4	..	67	3	6	..	2	..	4
..	..	..	..	..	..	2,905	9	78	4	167	1	514	..	9	..	6	..	120	1	2	..	10	..	5
1	..	..	..	..	..	76	1	..	..	27	..	3	..	..	..	..	..	16	..	..	..	..	..	6
..	..	..	..	..	..	11,075	125	444	18	1,291	8	460	28	44	..	30	6	334	1	15	..	7	..	
..	..	..	..	..	..	2,202	13	33	2	707	4	94	1	18	..	7	..	3	..	..	..	..	..	7
.	..	..	..	..	..	2,666	9	19	6	193	..	186	11	..	..	2	..	115	..	2	..	5	..	8
..	..	..	..	..	..	2,716	34	196	1	167	..	121	16	23	..	20	6	45	..	3	..	..	..	9
..	..	..	..	..	..	1,747	16	106	2	127	..	28	..	3	..	1	..	99	1	10	..	1	..	10
..	..	..	..	..	..	1,744	53	90	2	97	4	31	..	..	..	..	..	72	..	..	..	1	..	11
15	..	..	..	4	..	23,645	279	1,387	78	761	9	1,158	4	36	..	25	..	704	..	15	..	25	.	
..	..	..	..	..	..	6,448	87	231	10	85	4	274	..	5	..	2	..	190	..	..	..	6	..	12
..	..	..	..	..	..	5,122	24	462	6	146	3	293	2	9	..	5	..	239	..	8	..	5	..	13
..	..	..	..	..	..	4,128	15	290	..	217	2	453	..	1	..	18	..	101	..	3	..	2	..	14
..	..	..	..	..	..	2,738	35	99	..	69	..	94	2	15	..	..	..	141	..	..	..	12	..	15
14	..	..	..	4	..	3,108	5	219	3	92	..	39	..	6	..	..	..	20	..	..	..	..	..	16
1	..	..	..	..	..	2,101	113	86	59	152	..	..	..	..	..	..	..	13	..	4	..	..	..	17
22	..	2	..	8	..	13,614	380	1,325	409	1,051	10	192	..	4	..	2	..	135	..	5	2	11	..	
..	..	..	..	..	..	3,182	63	450	91	207	4	24	..	..	..	1	..	74	..	..	..	11	..	18
8	..	..	..	8	..	2,548	35	11	71	61	..	27	..	..	..	..	..	41	..	5	2	..	.	19
..	..	..	..	..	..	2,369	73	135	149	281	1	124	..	..	..	1	..	6	..	..	..	..	..	20
14	..	2	..	..	..	1,422	23	150	4	109	3	..	..	..	..	..	..	1	..	..	..	..	..	21
..	..	..	..	..	..	2,864	69	474	38	315	2	17	..	4	..	..	..	9	..	..	..	..	..	22
..	..	..	..	..	..	1,229	117	105	57	78	..	..	..	..	..	..	..	4	..	..	..	..	..	23
29	5	..	..	..	..	10,779	108	350	11	541	1	281	..	..	..	6	..	188	2	1	..	16	..	
26	5	..	..	..	..	1,810	8	70	..	82	..	5	..	..	..	..	..	11	..	..	..	..	..	24
..	..	..	..	..	..	3,098	13	154	2	264	1	24	..	..	..	3	..	10	..	..	..	..	.	25
1	..	..	..	..	..	1,827	9	29	..	32	..	103	..	..	..	3	..	10	..	..	..	..	.	26
..	..	..	..	..	..	2,540	59	70	8	79	..	137	..	..	..	..	..	97	..	..	..	14	.	27
..	..	..	..	..	..	724	19	14	1	53	..	1	..	..	..	..	..	21	..	..	..	..	..	28
2	..	..	..	..	..	780	..	13	..	31	..	11	..	..	..	..	..	39	2	1	..	2	..	29
3	..	..	..	5	..	9,499	51	764	90	2,355	5	1,233	3	21	5	31	1	565	..	6	..	19	.	
..	..	..	..	4	..	856	6	78	21	433	..	18	..	..	.	5	..	17	..	..	..	..	..	
..	..	..	..	..	..	31	..	1	..	4	..	..	..	..	..	..	..	3	..	.	..	..	..	1
..	..	..	..	..	..	18	..	1	..	..	..	1	..	..	..	..	..	3	..	.	..	..	..	2
..	..	..	..	.	..	187	..	13	..	17	..	6	..	..	..	..	..	0	..	.	..	..	..	3
..	.	..	..	4	..	620	6	63	21	412	..	11	..	..	..	5	..	5	..	..	..	.		4
..	..	..	..	..	..	48	.	21	..	91	..	1	..	..	..	..	..	1	.	..	..	..	.	
..	..	..	..	1	..	190	2	5	..	61	..	..	..	..	..	..	..	..	.	..	..	..	.	
..	..	..	..	1	..	85	1	11	2	45	..	3	..	..	..	5	..	..	..	..	..	..	..	
..	..	..	..	..	..	109	2	1	16	26	..	..	..	..	..	..	..	..	..	..	..	..	..	
..	..	.	..	..	.	27	..	9	2	35	..	.	..	..	..	..	..	..	..	..	..	.	..	
..	..	..	..	2	..	161	1	16	1	154	..	7	..	..	..	..	..	4	..	.	..	.	..	
3	..	.	..	1	..	8,643	45	686	69	1,922	5	1,215	3	21	5	26	1	548	..	6	..	19	..	
..	..	..	.	..	..	42	2	5	1	..	..	..	..	..	..	..	..	..	..	..	..	..	..	5
2	..	..	..	1	.	394	2	11	..	49	..	10	1	1	..	22	1	6	..	.	..	1	..	6
1	..	..	..	..	.	377	7	19	2	145	2	1	2	..	5	..	..	7	..	..	..	..	..	7
..	..	..	..	..	.	735	9	2	2	337	..	..	..	..	..	..	..	..	..	..	..	..	.	8
..	..	..	..	..	..	125	1	10	1	49	.	2	..	..	..	2	..	..	.	..	.	..	.	9
..	..	..	..	..	..	903	1	4	..	53	.	64	..	..	.	..	.	15	..	..	.	..	.	10
..	..	..	..	..	.	441	5	62	..	14	..	82	..	7	..	2	..	29	..	..	.	.	.	11
..	..	..	..	..	..	328	..	28	.	56	..	2	..	..	..	..	..	45	..	..	..	..	.	12
..	..	..	..	..	..	180	..	15	.	173	..	..	..	..	..	..	..	7	..	3	.	1	.	13
..	..	..	..	..	..	3,176	..	393	..	883	2	109	..	13	..	..	..	121	..	3	.	14	.	14
..	..	..	.	.	..	715	1	84	..	107	..	13	..	..	..	..	.	43	.	.	..	2	.	15
..	..	..	..	..	..	646	14	46	63	56	1	29	..	..	..	..	..	20	.	..	..	1	.	16
..	..	..	..	..	..	581	3	7	..	..	..	903	..	..	..	..	..	255	..	..	..	..	.	17
..	..	..	..	..	..	3,334	22	15	10	6	..	265	.	5	..	2	..	108	..	..	..	6	.	18
..	..	..	..	..	..	2,473	..	12	..	22	..	225	1	..	..	..	..	159	..	..	.	..	.	19
..	..	..	..	..	..	494	20	1	..	5	..	101	..	..	..	..	..	20	..	.	.	..	..	20

TABLE X.—OCCUPATION OR MEANS OF
DETAILS FOR DISTRICTS,

Class .. B.—PREPARATION AND SUPPLY OF METARIAL SUBSTANCES.

Sub-class .. III.—INDUSTRY.

Order .. 9. Ceramics.

Serial No.	District or State.	Group 62.—*Workers in mints, die-sinkers, etc.* Total earners principal occupation. Males.	Females.	*Total Order 9.* Total earners principal occupation. Males.	Females.	Total working dependants. Males.	Females.	Total earners with subsidiary occupation. Males.	Females.	63.—*Potters and makers of earthen-ware.* Total earners principal occupation. Males.	Females.	Total working dependants. Males.	Females.	Total earners with subsidiary occupation. Males.	Females.	64.—*Brick, and tile-makers.* Total earners principal occupation. Males.	Females.
1	2	369	370	371	372	373	374	375	376	377	378	379	380	381	382	383	384
	PUNJAB ..	6	..	119,466	4,780	7,072	3,057	7,414	129	96,845	3,055	6,079	2,731	5,517	95	21,138	1,605
	BRITISH TERRITORY ..	6	..	106,698	4,457	6,393	2,574	6,113	115	85,466	2,793	5,473	2,370	4,328	83	19,973	1,556
	AMBALA DIVISION ..	1	..	14,161	589	707	1,002	1,071	22	11,391	402	545	889	641	9	2,215	148
1	Hissar ..	..	..	2,471	91	305	348	462	4	1,727	48	210	317	303	4	669	34
2	Rohtak ..	..	..	3,138	148	126	163	165	1	2,740	106	107	132	104	1	288	27
3	Gurgaon ..	1	..	2,909	107	139	236	52	6	2,582	91	137	225	24	2	119	4
4	Karnal ..	..	..	3,332	181	96	183	274	11	2,611	104	54	152	153	2	678	76
5	Ambala ..	..	..	2,309	62	41	72	110	..	1,730	53	37	63	49	..	460	7
6	Simla ..	..	..	2	..	..	..	8	..	1	..	..	..	8	..	1	..
	JULLUNDUR DIVISION	..	..	13,464	608	686	581	1,311	14	11,658	449	610	573	1,078	14	1,669	158
7	Kangra ..	..	..	1,531	49	55	359	382	9	1,472	49	54	359	375	9	34	..
8	Hoshiarpur ..	..	..	1,966	50	55	70	123	..	1,792	47	54	66	52	..	133	2
9	Jullundur ..	..	..	3,215	170	221	94	294	3	2,663	170	194	94	204	3	552	..
10	Ludhiana ..	..	..	2,542	93	179	24	365	1	2,209	72	154	24	334	1	290	21
11	Ferozepore ..	..	..	4,210	246	176	34	147	1	3,522	111	154	30	113	1	660	135
	LAHORE DIVISION ..	5	..	28,449	1,156	1,606	160	1,191	22	22,125	359	1,505	133	871	22	6,078	771
12	Lahore ..	..	..	9,309	802	324	39	348	6	5,818	123	307	13	189	6	3,336	660
13	Amritsar ..	..	..	3,392	88	357	74	154	10	2,644	45	322	73	118	10	731	43
14	Gurdaspur ..	..	..	3,642	60	239	20	278	2	2,853	48	210	20	232	2	728	5
15	Sialkot ..	5	..	4,761	21	155	6	119	..	4,341	21	150	6	80	..	414	..
16	Gujranwala ..	..	..	4,525	101	339	3	171	..	3,905	38	329	3	145	..	620	63
17	Sheikhupura ..	..	..	2,820	84	192	18	126	4	2,564	84	187	18	107	4	249	..
	RAWALPINDI DIVISION	..	..	20,911	1,305	1,282	648	1,182	25	17,380	1,067	1,130	608	872	18	3,460	199
18	Gujrat ..	..	..	6,043	299	422	186	278	5	4,569	237	311	184	146	5	1,408	24
19	Shahpur ..	..	..	5,547	224	105	45	204	8	4,428	71	85	29	115	2	1,118	153
20	Jhelum ..	..	..	2,628	612	323	364	363	9	2,270	593	320	362	346	9	358	19
21	Rawalpindi ..	..	..	2,693	39	137	26	160	2	2,347	36	127	8	95	1	342	2
22	Attock ..	..	..	2,472	87	177	22	133	1	2,368	87	169	22	128	1	104	..
23	Mianwali ..	..	..	1,528	44	118	5	44	..	1,398	43	118	3	42	..	130	1
	MULTAN DIVISION ..	..	..	29,713	799	2,112	183	1,358	32	22,912	516	1,683	167	866	20	6,551	280
24	Montgomery ..	..	..	5,178	111	250	9	128	..	4,281	71	247	7	114	..	895	40
25	Lyallpur ..	..	..	5,303	252	252	35	621	20	3,841	173	224	21	317	17	1,460	76
26	Jhang ..	..	..	7,331	43	856	3	196	8	6,198	5	856	3	195	..	1,133	38
27	Multan ..	..	..	8,120	180	591	6	202	2	5,610	89	221	6	68	1	2,500	91
28	Muzaffargarh ..	..	..	2,217	85	72	65	81	2	1,692	50	49	65	46	2	324	35
29	Dera Ghazi Khan ..	..	..	1,564	128	91	65	130	..	1,290	128	86	65	126	..	239	..
	PUNJAB STATES ..	..	..	12,768	323	679	483	1,301	14	11,379	262	606	361	1,189	12	1,165	49
	A.—HAVING POLITICAL RELATIONS WITH THE PUNJAB GOVERNMENT. ..	..	..	523	24	16	33	101	..	484	24	16	33	99	..	38	..
1	Dujana ..	..	..	139	2	..	23	..	..	135	2	..	23	..	..	4	..
2	Pataudi ..	..	..	72	7	..	..	3	..	70	7	..	..	3	..	2	..
3	Kalsia ..	..	..	192	12	12	9	3	..	162	12	12	9	1	..	30	..
4	SIMLA HILL STATES ..	..	..	120	3	4	1	95	..	117	3	4	1	95	..	2	..
	Bashahr ..	..	..	..	1	..	..	10	..	..	1	..	..	10	..	..	..
	Nalagarh ..	..	..	55	..	..	..	9	..	55	..	..	..	9	..	..	..
	Keonthal ..	..	..	8	1	..	..	3	..	5	1	..	..	3	..	2	..
	Baghal ..	..	..	30	..	..	..	15	..	30	..	..	..	15	..	..	..
	Jubbal ..	..	..	4	..	3	1	22	..	4	..	3	1	22	..	..	..
	Other Simla Hill States ..	..	..	23	1	1	..	36	..	23	1	1	..	36	..	..	..
	B.—HAVING POLITICAL RELATIONS WITH THE GOVERNMENT OF INDIA. ..	..	..	12,245	299	663	450	1,200	14	10,895	238	590	328	1,090	12	1,127	49
5	Loharu ..	..	..	48	2	..	2	..	..	24	..	..	..	..	..	3	..
6	Sirmoor ..	..	..	84	1	..	..	22	..	81	1	..	..	20	..	2	..
7	Bilaspur ..	..	..	192	18	7	16	36	..	189	18	7	16	36	..	..	..
8	Mandi ..	..	..	195	7	5	2	204	..	194	7	5	2	203	..	1	..
9	Suket ..	..	..	9	1	..	..	..	..	2	1	..	..	..	..	4	..
10	Kapurthala ..	..	..	1,341	40	7	7	106	4	1,203	31	6	7	101	4	122	8
11	Maler Kotla ..	..	..	296	7	13	7	17	..	240	7	12	1	10	..	56	..
12	Faridkot ..	..	..	498	5	8	..	32	..	388	..	8	..	32	..	110	5
13	Chamba ..	..	..	91	7	16	1	225	1	91	7	16	1	225	1	..	..
14	Patiala (Phulkian States)	..	..	3,125	104	428	383	413	8	2,670	90	369	282	380	6	305	14
15	Jind (Phulkian States)	..	..	1,225	44	90	25	120	1	1,000	24	78	12	60	1	225	20
16	Nabha (Phulkian States)	..	..	1,014	23	71	7	25	..	908	20	71	7	23	..	105	2
17	Bahawalpur ..	..	..	4,127	40	18	..	..	..	3,905	32	18	..	..	..	194	..
18	*Cities.* Lahore ..	..	..	1,951	97	43	..	34	..	1,100	10	31	..	7	..	740	87
19	*Cities.* Amritsar ..	..	..	460	13	5	..	5	..	387	8	2	..	3	..	64	5
20	*Cities.* Multan ..	..	..	96	26	..	..	1	..	62	26	..	..	1	..	25	..

LIVELIHOOD.—GENERAL TABLE.

STATES AND CITIES.—*continued.*

B.—PREPARATION AND SUPPLY OF MATERIAL SUBSTANCES—*continued.*

III.—INDUSTRY—*continued.*

9. Ceramics—*concluded.* | 10. Chemical products properly so-called and analogous.

64.—*Brick and tile makers, concld.* Total working dependants. Males.	Females.	64.—Total earners with subsidiary occupation. Males.	Females.	65.—*Other workers in ceramics.* Total earners principal occupation. Males.	Females.	Total working dependants. Males.	Females.	Total earners with subsidiary occupation. Males.	Females.	*Total Order 10.* Total earners principal occupation. Males.	Females.	Total working dependants. Males.	Females.	Total earners with subsidiary occupation. Males.	Females.	66.—*Manufacture of matches, fire-works and other explosives.* Total earners principal occupation. Males.	Females.	Total working dependants. Males.	Females.	Total earners with subsidiary occupation. Males.	Females.	67.—*Manufacture of aerated and mineral waters and ice.* Total earners principal occupation. Males.	Females.	Total working dependants. Males.	Females.	Total earners with subsidiary occupation. Males.	Females.	Serial No.
385	386	387	388	389	390	391	392	393	394	395	396	397	398	399	400	401	402	403	404	405	406	407	408	409	410	411	412	
955	**231**	**1,770**	**33**	**1,483**	**120**	**38**	**95**	**127**	**1**	**42,301**	**1,701**	**2,574**	**1,230**	**4,595**	**62**	**1,048**	**4**	**44**	**15**	**92**	..	**923**	**6**	**35**	..	**24**	..	
896	**138**	**1,660**	**31**	**1,259**	**108**	**24**	**66**	**125**	**1**	**37,847**	**1,452**	**2,383**	**1,022**	**3,700**	**53**	**905**	**3**	**33**	**2**	**71**	..	**769**	**6**	**23**	..	**24**	..	
156	**76**	**389**	**13**	**555**	**39**	**6**	**37**	**41**	..	**5,131**	**417**	**200**	**298**	**666**	**3**	**31**	**1**	**1**	**1**	**3**	..	**91**	**6**	..	..	**3**	..	
91	31	130	..	75	9	4	..	29	..	450	19	47	40	158	2	9	..	1	..	1	..	9	..	..	..	.	.	1
18	6	60	..	110	15	1	25	1	..	984	67	39	34	116	1	2	..	..	..	2	..	7	6	..	..	..	..	2
11	..	19	4	208	12	1	11	9	..	1,070	27	69	39	41	..	12	1	..	1	..	..	4	..	..	..	..	..	3
42	31	121	9	43	1	..	..	..	..	952	203	20	157	183	..	5	..	..	..	..	..	6	..	..	..	..	..	4
4	8	59	..	119	2	..	1	2	..	1,667	101	25	28	106	..	3	..	..	..	..	..	59	..	..	..	3	.	5
..	..	..	..	..	..	..	..	..	..	8	..	..	..	2	..	..	..	..	..	..	..	6	..	..	..	..	..	6
72	**8**	**226**	..	**137**	**1**	**4**	..	**7**	..	**7,743**	**212**	**354**	**241**	**781**	**19**	**303**	..	**8**	**1**	**32**	..	..	..	..	..	..	..	
..	..	5	..	25	..	1	..	2	..	809	86	48	107	313	19	19	..	..	..	..	..	..	..	..	..	..	..	7
1	4	69	..	41	1	..	..	2	..	2,259	30	93	35	129	..	118	..	4	..	19	..	..	..	..	..	..	..	8
27	..	90	..	..	..	..	..	..	..	1,269	40	77	90	136	..	96	..	4	1	13	..	..	..	..	..	..	..	9
25	..	29	..	43	..	..	..	2	..	2,333	39	108	..	53	..	33	..	..	..	..	..	..	..	..	..	..	..	10
19	4	33	..	28	..	3	..	1	..	1,073	17	28	9	30	..	37	..	..	..	..	..	..	..	..	..	..	..	11
100	**16**	**291**	..	**246**	**26**	**1**	**11**	**29**	..	**15,028**	**386**	**954**	**194**	**1,319**	**11**	**398**	**1**	**23**	..	**18**	..	**457**	..	**5**	..	**9**	..	
16	15	131	..	155	19	1	11	28	..	3,761	93	236	5	420	.	17	1	..	..	1	..	355	..	5	..	7	..	12
35	1	36	..	17	..	..	..	..	..	2,981	71	362	37	264	10	180	..	10	..	4	..	27	..	..	..	..	..	13
20	..	40	..	61	7	..	..	1	..	3,234	21	170	6	396	..	112	..	8	..	10	..	29	..	..	..	..	..	14
5	..	39	..	8	..	..	..	..	..	2,772	68	90	4	89	..	58	..	..	..	..	..	43	..	..	..	2	..	15
10	..	26	..	..	..	..	..	..	..	997	15	54	[illegible]	[illegible]	..	20	..	5	..	3	..	..	..	..	..	..	..	16
5	..	19	..	7	..	..	..	..	..	1,283	118	42	40	80	1	11	..	..	..	..	..	3	..	..	..	..	..	17
141	**22**	**263**	**6**	**71**	**39**	**11**	**18**	**47**	**1**	**5,663**	**385**	**496**	**285**	**710**	**20**	**92**	**1**	**1**	..	**5**	..	**87**	..	**1**	..	**2**	.	
106	2	126	..	66	38	5	..	6	..	2,197	100	170	17	169	1	64	1	1	..	4	..	19	..	1	..	1	..	18
14	16	53	6	1	..	6	..	36	..	738	43	38	20	84	..	23	..	..	..	1	..	59	..	..	..	.	..	19
3	2	17	..	..	..	.	..	..	..	981	92	63	105	111	11	5	..	..	..	..	..	4	..	..	..	.	..	20
10	..	60	..	4	1	..	18	5	1	359	17	88	..	100	1	..	..	..	..	..	..	2	..	..	..	..	..	21
8	..	5	..	..	..	..	..	..	..	1,093	123	134	48	222	7	..	..	..	..	..	..	3	..	..	..	1	..	22
..	2	2	..	..	..	..	..	..	..	95	10	3	5	24	..	..	..	..	..	..	..	..	..	..	..	..	..	23
427	**16**	**491**	**12**	**250**	**3**	**2**	..	**1**	..	**4,282**	**52**	**379**	**4**	**224**	..	**81**	..	..	..	**13**	..	**134**	..	**17**	..	**10**	..	
3	2	14	..	2	..	..	..	..	..	336	9	7	2	23	..	4	..	..	..	..	..	2	..	..	..	..	..	24
28	14	304	3	2	3	..	..	..	..	2,177	18	295	2	106	..	2	..	..	..	..	..	1	..	..	..	..	..	25
..	..	1	8	..	..	..	..	..	..	987	1	44	..	30	..	7	..	..	..	..	..	3	..	..	..	2	..	26
370	..	134	1	10	..	..	..	..	..	297	4	14	..	18	..	15	..	..	..	..	..	..	..	..	..	..	..	27
21	..	34	..	201	..	2	..	1	..	238	4	17	..	32	..	5	..	..	..	13	..	128	..	17	..	8	..	28
5	..	4	..	35	..	..	..	..	..	247	16	2	..	15	..	48	..	..	..	..	..	..	..	..	..	..	..	29
59	**93**	**110**	**2**	**224**	**12**	**14**	**29**	**2**	.	**4,454**	**249**	**191**	**208**	**895**	**9**	**143**	**1**	**11**	**13**	**21**	..	**154**	..	**12**	..	..	..	
..	..	**2**	..	**1**	..	..	..	..	..	**287**	**24**	**11**	**14**	**64**	..	**21**	..	**1**	..	**6**	..	**10**	..	**2**	..	..	..	
..	..	..	..	..	..	..	..	..	..	21	..	..	..	6	..	5	..	..	..	..	..	..	..	..	..	..	..	1
..	..	..	..	..	..	..	..	..	..	17	..	..	..	..	..	..	..	..	..	..	..	..	..	..	..	..	..	2
..	..	2	..	..	..	..	..	..	..	132	24	7	13	28	..	..	..	..	..	1	..	10	..	1	..	..	..	3
..	..	..	..	**1**	..	..	..	..	..	**117**	..	**4**	**1**	**30**	.	**16**	..	**1**	..	**5**	..	..	..	**1**	..	..	..	4
..	..	..	..	..	..	..	..	..	..	..	..	..	..	..	..	..	..	..	..	..	..	..	..	..	..	..	..	
..	..	..	..	1	..	..	..	..	..	78	..	..	..	22	..	11	..	..	..	..	..	..	..	..	..	..	..	
..	..	..	..	..	..	..	..	..	..	1	..	..	..	..	..	..	..	..	..	..	..	..	..	..	..	..	..	
..	..	..	..	..	..	..	..	..	..	9	..	..	..	2	..	..	..	..	..	..	..	..	..	..	..	..	..	
..	..	..	..	..	..	..	..	..	..	..	..	..	..	..	..	..	..	..	..	..	..	..	..	..	..	..	..	
..	..	..	..	..	..	..	..	..	..	29	..	4	1	6	..	5	..	1	..	5	..	..	..	1	..	..	..	
59	**93**	**108**	**2**	**223**	**12**	**14**	**29**	**2**	..	**4,167**	**225**	**180**	**194**	**831**	**9**	**122**	**1**	**10**	**13**	**15**	..	**144**	..	**10**	..	..	..	
..	..	..	..	21	2	..	2	.	..	..	..	..	..	..	..	..	..	..	..	..	..	..	..	..	..	..	..	5
..	..	2	..	1	..	..	..	..	..	138	10	5	18	26	..	12	..	1	2	..	..	1	..	..	..	..	..	6
..	..	..	..	3	..	..	..	..	..	108	4	2	4	16	..	4	1	..	..	..	..	..	..	..	..	..	..	7
..	..	1	..	..	..	..	..	..	..	51	2	2	4	50	..	1	..	..	..	1	..	..	..	..	..	..	..	8
..	..	..	..	3	..	..	..	..	..	25	3	..	..	8	..	..	..	..	..	..	..	..	..	..	..	..	..	9
..	..	3	..	16	1	1	..	2	..	626	13	7	..	69	..	26	..	..	..	11	..	..	..	..	..	..	..	10
1	6	7	..	..	..	..	..	..	..	162	1	21	1	2	..	..	..	..	..	..	..	..	..	..	..	..	..	11
..	..	..	..	..	..	..	..	..	..	173	5	1	..	10	.	4	..	..	..	..	..	..	..	..	..	..	..	12
..	..	..	..	..	..	..	..	..	..	95	6	13	24	135	.	1	..	..	..	..	..	..	..	..	..	..	..	13
46	74	33	2	150	..	13	27	..	..	1,924	161	110	135	474	8	65	..	9	11	..	..	75	..	5	..	..	..	14
12	13	60	..	..	..	..	..	..	..	83	8	2	1	23	1	1	..	..	..	3	..	7	..	1	..	..	..	15
..	..	2	..	1	1	..	..	..	..	263	8	8	7	18	..	4	..	..	..	..	..	..	..	..	..	..	..	16
..	..	..	..	28	8	..	..	..	..	519	4	9	..	..	.	4	..	..	..	..	..	61	..	4	..	..	..	17
11	..	16	..	111	..	1	..	11	..	807	..	12	..	7	.	3	..	..	..	..	..	343	..	5	..	7	..	18
3	..	2	..	9	..	..	..	..	..	743	2	8	..	9	..	44	..	..	..	..	..	11	..	..	..	..	..	19
..	..	..	..	9	..	..	..	..	..	26	1	..	..	..	.	7	..	..	..	..	..	..	..	..	..	..	..	20

TABLE X.—OCCUPATION OR MEANS OF

DETAILS FOR DISTRICTS

Class .. B.—PREPARATION AND SUPPLY OF MATERIAL SUBSTANCES.

Sub-class .. III.—INDUSTRY.

Order .. 10.—Chemical products properly so called and analogous.—*concluded.* | 11.—Food Industries.

District or State.	68.—*Manufacture and refining of vegetable oils.* Total earners principal occupation.		Total working dependants.		Total earners with subsidiary occupation.		69. *Manufacture & refining of mineral oils.* Total earners principal occupation.		70.—*Others.* Total earners principal occupation.		Total working dependants.		Total earners with subsidiary occupation.		*Total Order 11.* Total earners principal occupation.		Total working dependants.		Total earners with subsidiary occupation.	
	Males.	Females.	Males.	Females.	Males.	Females.	Males.	Females.	Males.	Females.	Males.	Females.	Males.	Females.	Males.	Females.	Males.	Females.	Males.	Females.
2	413	414	415	416	417	418	419	420	421	422	423	424	425	426	427	428	429	430	431	432
PUNJAB ..	39,337	1,680	2,486	1,201	4,420	62	5	..	988	11	9	14	59	..	57,296	21,976	2,002	5,932	5,840	2,220
BRITISH TERRITORY ..	35,211	1,432	2,318	1,006	3,548	53	2	..	960	11	9	14	57	..	48,503	20,228	1,792	5,555	4,434	2,098
AMBALA DIVISION ..	4,981	410	199	297	660	3	2	..	20	..	..	..	..	..	5,993	3,987	202	606	748	517
1 Hissar ..	431	19	46	40	157	2	..	..	1	..	..	..	..	..	1,028	621	81	301	96	65
2 Rohtak ..	975	61	39	34	114	1	..	..	..	..	..	..	..	..	852	479	29	65	133	189
3 Gurgaon ..	1,054	26	69	38	41	..	..	..	..	..	..	..	..	..	1,049	717	45	94	124	84
4 Karnal ..	938	203	20	157	183	..	..	..	3	..	..	..	..	..	1,237	1,295	29	81	210	123
5 Ambala ..	1,581	101	25	28	163	..	2	..	22	..	..	..	..	..	1,568	873	17	65	157	56
6 Simla ..	2	..	..	..	2	..	..	..	..	..	..	..	..	..	259	2	1	..	28	..
JULLUNDUR DIVISION	7,422	204	346	226	789	19	..	..	18	8	..	14	10	..	9,629	3,593	321	1,493	1,812	592
7 Kangra ..	790	86	48	107	313	19	..	..	..	..	..	..	..	..	3,074	735	125	416	1,176	236
8 Hoshiarpur ..	2,136	30	89	35	107	..	..	..	5	..	..	..	3	..	2,037	436	29	211	320	60
9 Jullundur ..	1,173	32	73	75	116	..	..	..	..	8	..	14	7	..	1,423	559	106	306	148	114
10 Ludhiana ..	2,288	39	108	..	153	..	..	..	12	..	..	..	..	..	1,207	631	6	253	73	107
11 Ferozepore ..	1,035	17	28	9	50	..	..	..	1	..	..	..	..	..	1,888	1,332	55	307	95	75
LAHORE DIVISION ..	13,514	384	922	194	1,251	11	..	..	659	1	4	..	41	..	13,508	2,198	573	1,178	882	547
12 Lahore ..	3,284	91	231	5	410	..	..	..	105	1	..	..	2	..	4,824	655	157	201	117	54
13 Amritsar ..	2,546	71	352	37	260	10	..	..	228	..	..	..	..	..	3,364	528	258	399	275	281
14 Gurdaspur ..	3,058	21	162	6	366	..	..	..	35	..	..	..	20	..	1,165	292	46	140	175	114
15 Sialkot ..	2,474	68	88	4	76	..	..	..	197	..	2	..	11	..	2,207	360	63	172	178	80
16 Gujranwala ..	900	15	49	2	59	..	..	..	77	..	..	..	8	..	1,159	86	23	111	74	15
17 Sheikhupura ..	1,252	118	40	140	80	1	..	..	17	..	2	..	..	..	789	277	26	155	63	3
RAWALPINDI DIVISION	5,406	382	494	285	701	20	..	..	78	2	..	..	2	..	8,684	5,213	437	1,169	488	200
18 Gujrat ..	2,077	99	168	17	162	1	..	..	37	..	..	..	2	..	2,825	1,943	84	311	159	55
19 Shahpur ..	645	41	38	20	83	..	..	..	11	2	..	..	..	..	1,956	1,365	36	360	48	19
20 Jhelum ..	972	92	63	195	111	11	..	..	..	..	..	..	..	..	1,312	376	51	225	118	37
21 Rawalpindi ..	556	17	88	..	100	1	..	..	1	..	..	..	..	..	596	137	65	26	45	28
22 Attock ..	1,090	123	134	48	221	7	..	..	..	..	..	..	..	..	1,499	1,166	187	143	84	60
23 Mianwali ..	66	10	3	5	24	..	..	..	29	..	..	..	..	..	496	226	14	104	34	1
MULTAN DIVISION ..	3,888	52	357	4	197	..	..	..	179	..	5	..	4	..	10,689	5,237	259	1,109	504	242
24 Montgomery ..	330	9	7	2	23	..	..	..	..	..	..	..	..	..	2,167	1,537	36	393	36	22
25 Lyallpur ..	2,174	18	295	2	106	..	..	..	..	..	..	..	..	..	4,889	1,811	143	319	364	149
26 Jhang ..	818	1	44	..	24	..	..	..	159	..	..	..	4	..	607	692	14	249	32	8
27 Multan ..	271	4	9	..	18	..	..	..	11	..	5	..	..	..	2,085	506	41	93	40	[illegible]
28 Muzaffargarh ..	105	4	..	..	11	..	..	..	..	..	..	..	..	..	463	202	17	34	27	10
29 Dera Ghazi Khan ..	190	16	2	..	15	..	..	..	9	..	..	..	..	..	478	489	8	21	5	[illegible]
PUNJAB STATES ..	4,126	248	168	195	872	9	3	..	28	..	..	..	2	..	8,793	1,748	210	377	1,406	122
A.- HAVING POLITICAL RELATIONS WITH THE PUNJAB GOVERNMENT. ..	254	24	8	14	57	..	..	..	2	..	..	..	1	..	623	136	12	27	340	13
1 Dujana ..	16	..	..	..	6	..	..	..	..	..	..	..	..	..	4	..	..	2	..	3
2 Patandi ..	17	..	..	..	..	..	..	..	..	..	..	..	..	..	15	53	..	1	2	3
3 Kalsia ..	122	24	6	13	27	..	..	..	..	..	..	..	..	..	137	52	2	16	14	4
4 SIMLA HILL STATES ..	99	..	2	1	24	..	..	..	2	..	..	..	1	..	467	31	10	8	324	3
Bashahr ..	..	..	..	..	..	..	..	..	..	..	..	..	..	..	2	..	1	..	..	..
Nalagarh ..	65	..	..	..	21	..	..	..	2	..	..	..	1	..	251	21	1	1	80	2
Keonthal ..	1	..	..	..	..	..	..	..	..	..	..	..	..	..	15	..	1	..	7	..
Baghal ..	9	..	..	..	2	..	..	..	..	..	..	..	..	..	69	..	1	..	82	..
Jubbal ..	..	..	..	..	..	..	..	..	..	..	..	..	..	..	5	..	1	1	65	..
Other Simla Hill States ..	24	..	2	1	1	..	..	..	..	..	..	..	..	..	125	10	5	6	90	1
B.- HAVING POLITICAL RELATIONS WITH THE GOVERNMENT OF INDIA. ..	3,872	224	160	181	815	9	3	..	26	..	..	..	1	..	8,170	1,612	198	350	1,066	109
5 Loharu ..	..	..	..	..	..	..	..	..	..	..	..	..	..	..	3	1	..	..	..	3
6 Sirmoor ..	123	10	4	16	26	..	..	..	2	..	..	..	..	..	282	9	2	1	101	1
7 Bilaspur ..	104	3	2	4	16	..	..	..	..	..	..	..	..	..	554	71	15	27	112	4
8 Mandi ..	50	2	2	4	49	..	..	..	..	..	..	..	..	..	216	46	1	7	187	2
9 Suket ..	25	3	..	..	8	..	..	..	..	..	..	..	..	..	107	19	5	8	60	..
10 Kapurthala ..	599	13	7	..	58	..	..	..	1	..	..	..	..	..	1,105	135	10	38	130	9
11 Maler Kotla ..	148	1	21	1	1	..	..	..	14	..	..	..	1	..	65	27	3	17	22	7
12 Faridkot ..	165	5	1	..	10	..	3	..	1	..	..	..	..	..	246	176	1	7	2	
13 Chamba ..	94	6	13	24	135	..	..	..	..	..	..	..	..	..	153	12	10	8	111	
14 Patiala } Phulkian States	1,784	161	96	124	474	8	..	..	..	..	..	..	..	..	3,871	758	129	201	290	
15 Jind } Phulkian States	73	8	1	1	20	1	..	..	2	..	..	..	..	..	564	101	5	9	32	
16 Nabha } Phulkian States	259	8	8	7	18	..	..	..	..	..	..	..	..	..	291	127	3	27	19	
17 Bahawalpur ..	448	4	5	..	..	..	..	..	6	..	..	..	..	..	713	130	14	..	..	..
18 *Cities.* Lahore ..	383	..	7	..	..	..	..	..	78	..	..	..	..	..	2,320	70	10	..	13	..
19 *Cities.* Amritsar ..	460	2	8	..	9	..	..	..	228	..	..	..	..	..	2,414	28	37	..	7	..
20 *Cities.* Multan ..	19	1	..	..	..	..	..	..	..	..	..	..	..	..	353	10	6	3	..	1

LIVELIHOOD--GENERAL TABLE.

STATES AND CITIES.—*continued.*

PREPARATION AND SUPPLY OF MATERIAL SUBSTANCES—*continued.*

III.—INDUSTRY—*continued.*

11.—Food Industries—*continued.*

71.—*Rice pounders and huskers and flour grinders.*						72.—*Grain parchers, etc.*						73.—*Butchers.*						74.—*Makers of sugar molasses and gur.*						
Total earners principal occupation.		Total working dependants.		Total earners with subsidiary occupation.		Total earners principal occupation.		Total working dependants.		Total earners with subsidiary occupation.		Total earners principal occupation.		Total working dependants.		Total earners with subsidiary occupation.		Total earners principal occupation.		Total working dependants.		Total earners with subsidiary occupation.		
Males.	Females.	Males.	Females.	Males.	Females.	Males.	Females.	Males.	Females.	Males.	Females.	Males.	Females.	Males.	Females.	Males.	Females.	Males.	Females.	Males.	Females.	Males.	Females.	Serial No.
433	434	435	436	437	438	439	440	441	442	443	444	445	446	447	448	449	450	451	452	453	454	455	456	
8,585	**11,041**	**178**	**1,713**	**2,285**	**1,070**	**6,575**	**5,452**	**507**	**2,654**	**1,178**	**972**	**15,053**	**93**	**500**	**38**	**662**	..	**1,156**	..	**37**	..	**236**	.	
5,826	**10,087**	**144**	**1,611**	**1,428**	**1,011**	**5,609**	**4,791**	**443**	**2,389**	**935**	**917**	**13,543**	**89**	**474**	**38**	**586**	.	**764**	..	**20**	..	**216**	..	
881	**3,346**	**18**	**282**	**84**	**455**	**1,137**	**502**	**35**	**300**	**136**	**61**	**2,038**	**35**	**85**	**15**	**133**	..	**316**	.	**17**	.	**201**	.	
137	366	5	68	15	52	125	227	8	179	39	13	327	18	37	10	26	.	13	..	2	.	4	.	1
77	417	2	15	4	189	246	56	9	20	7	..	16	..	2	..	3	.	256	..	14	.	100	.	2
55	663	1	56	5	84	259	28	10	20	34	..	541	11	33	5	79	.	22	..	1	..	2	.	3
105	1,132	1	25	3	108	320	128	5	55	28	14	393	1	12	.	21	..	3	..	.	..	36	..	4
478	768	8	38	31	22	184	63	3	26	28	34	487	4	1	..	4	.	22	..	.		59	..	5
29	..	1	..	26	..	3	..	.	..	..	..	123	1	..		..	..	..	..	..	..	..	..	6
3,337	**1,730**	**109**	**625**	**1,145**	**364**	**808**	**1,538**	**20**	**829**	**209**	**196**	**1,596**	**16**	**31**	..	**49**		**307**	..	**2**	..	**10**	..	
2,348	724	71	415	910	236	..	1	..	1	..	..	78	2	1	..	3	.	..	.	.	.	.	.	7
716	332	24	61	217	7	46	84	..	148	53	53	396	3	2	..	24	.		.	.	..		.	8
99	131	10	18	101	8	69	369	3	275	43	102	574	9	25	..	12	..	12	..	..	..	6	..	9
98	171	1	98	5	78	282	326	2	154	39	29	377	2	..	..	8	..	21	..	..		..	..	10
76	372	3	33	3	35	461	738	15	251	74	12	171	..	3	.	2	..	274	..	2	.	4	..	11
788	**538**	**15**	**81**	**136**	**33**	**859**	**1,236**	**210**	**911**	**364**	**485**	**3,934**	**9**	**118**	**2**	**82**	.	**137**	..	**1**	..	**5**		
116	75	1	4	3	3	355	514	81	196	31	42	1,300	..	14	..	21	.	136	..	1	..	5	..	12
122	77	7	2	28	20	130	421	117	396	133	26	92	5	47	1	11	..	1	..	..	..	..	..	13
178	191	1	18	47	9	59	89	..	115	41	103	309	1	9	..	6	..	..	..	..	..	..	..	14
190	167	5	7	33	1	266	116	5	141	108	78	642	..	31	.	6	..	..	..	..	..	..	..	15
113	21	1	..	2	..	5	7	..	16	31	..	465	1	10	..	23	..	..	..	..	.	..	.	16
69	7	..	..	3	..	44	89	7	47	..	1	297	2	7	1	15	..	..	..	..	..	..		17
430	**1,707**	**2**	**411**	**33**	**66**	**719**	**533**	**67**	**213**	**56**	**64**	**2,938**	**18**	**176**	**19**	**195**	..	**3**	..	..		.		
163	238	1	206	5	5	163	159	1	19	18	13	675	12	9	..	29	..	..	..	..	.	.	..	18
125	307	1	8	10	10	12	17	..	3	..	..	837	2	21	..	22	..	..	..	..	.	.	.	19
40	196	..	122	1	13	144	47	8	37	7	3	558	4	42	1	85	..	.	..	.	.	..	..	2
29	92	..	6	1	9	29	33	6	12	11	19	55	.	..	..	5	..	..	.	.	.	..	.	21
58	728	..	58	9	29	335	208	52	49	18	29	404	..	90	18	29	..	..	.	..	.	..	.	22
15	146	..	11	7	..	36	69	..	93	2	..	409	..	14	..	25	..	3	.	.	.	.		23
390	**2,766**	..	**312**	**30**	**93**	**2,086**	**982**	**111**	**136**	**170**	**111**	**3,037**	**11**	**64**	**2**	**127**	.	**1**	.	..	..	.		
21	757	..	81	2	3	449	243	19	11	15	12	572	1	5	..	11	..	..	..	..	.	.	.	24
141	903	..	141	12	35	1,568	681	88	103	150	91	928	..	28	..	81	..	.	..	.	.	..	.	25
122	154	..	8	15	5	4	14	..	16	..	2	405	..	14	..	13	..	.	..	.	.	..	..	26
74	379	..	31	..	26	2	5	..	4	..	3	837	10	13	2	9	..	1	..	..	..	..	..	27
..	146	..	32	..	10	60	35	4	2	5	..	139	..	3	..	11	..	..	..	..	..	.	.	28
32	427	..	19	1	14	3	1	..	..	..	3	156	..	1	..	2	..	..	..	.	..	.	.	20
2,759	**954**	**34**	**102**	**857**	**59**	**966**	**661**	**64**	**265**	**243**	**55**	**1,510**	**4**	**26**	.	**76**	..	**392**	..	**17**	.	**20**	.	
467	**123**	**5**	**10**	**295**	**11**	**39**	**12**	..	**17**	**10**	**2**	**43**	**1**	..	..	**1**	..	**1**	..	..	..	**4**	..	
..	..	..	1	..	3	4	..	..	1	..	..	..	..	..	..	..	..	..	..	..	..	.	..	1
4	52	..	1	..	3	8	1	..	..	..	..	3	..	..	..	..	..	..	..	..	..	..	..	2
63	41	..	..	4	3	24	10	.	16	6	1	20	1	..	..	..	..	1	..	..	..	4	..	3
400	**30**	**5**	**8**	**291**	**2**	**8**	**1**	..	..	**4**	**1**	**20**	..	..	..	**1**	..	..	..	..	..	..	..	4
..	..	.	..	..	..	..	..	..	..	..	..	..	..	..	..	..	..	..	..	..	..	..	..	
243	20	1	1	71	1	..	1	..	..	1	1	6	..	..	..	..	..	..	..	..	..	..	..	
7	..	..	..	6	..	.	..	..	..	..	..	2	..	..	..	..	..	..	..	..	..	..	..	
64	..	1	.	80	..	..	..	..	..	..	..	..	..	..	..	..	..	..	..	..	..	..	..	
4	..	1	1	65	..	..	..	..	..	..	..	..	..	..	..	..	..	..	..	..	..	..	..	
82	10	2	6	69	1	3	..	..	..	3	..	12	..	..	..	1	..	..	..	..	..	..	..	
2,292	**881**	**29**	**92**	**562**	**48**	**927**	**649**	**64**	**248**	**233**	**53**	**1,467**	**3**	**26**	..	**75**	..	**391**	..	**17**	..	**16**	.	
..	1	..	..	..	3	.	.	..	..	..	..	..	..	..	..	..	..	..	..	..	..	..	.	5
266	8	2	..	101	1	4	1	..	1	..	.	9	..	..	..	..	..	..	..	..	..	..	.	6
548	69	15	27	112	4	..	..	..	..	..	.	1	..	..	..	..	..	..	..	..	..	..	..	7
138	45	1	7	163	2	..	..	..	..	..	.	28	..	..	4	4	..	..	..	..	..	..	.	8
71	19	5	8	60	..	15	..	..	..	..	..	1	..	..	..	..	..	..	..	..	..	..	..	9
16	50	..	12	7	..	204	81	..	26	70	9	443	2	10	..	50	..	..	..	..	..	..	..	10
6	17	..	6	1	1	4	9	..	11	19	6	43	1	2	..	..	..	..	..	..	..	..	..	11
63	2	..	..	..	..	14	171	..	7	1	..	46	..	1	..	..	..	..	..	..	..	..	..	12
31	8	6	6	110	1	..	..	..	..	..	..	11	..	..	..	..	..	..	..	..	..	..	..	13
809	316	..	19	..	26	458	340	50	175	126	32	351	..	11	..	20	..	382	..	17	..	..	..	14
51	82	..	6	3	6	22	7	2	2	8	..	52	..	..	..	..	..	5	..	..	..	13	..	15
78	84	..	1	5	4	77	37	..	26	9	6	6	..	..	.	1	..	4	..	..	..	3	.	16
215	130	..	..	.	..	39	..	12	..	..	..	444	..	2	..	..	.	..	..	..	..	..	..	17
75	..	..	..	.	..	57	12	..	..	1	..	749	..	2	..	5	..	136	..	1	..	5	..	18
26	..	..	..	..	..	14	3	..	..	.	..	647	3	..	..	..	..	1	..	..	..	..	..	19
..	9	..	..	..	1	2	..	..	..	..	..	176	..	..	..	..	..	..	..	..	..	..	..	20

TABLE X.—OCCUPATION OR MEANS OF
DETAILS FOR DISTRICTS

Class .. B.—PREPARATION AND SUPPLY OF MATERIAL SUBSTANCES.

Sub-class .. III.—INDUSTRY.

Order .. 11.—Food Industries.

Group .. 75.—*Sweetmeat and condiment-makers.* | 76.—*Toddy drawers.* | 77.—*Brewers and distillers.* | 78.—*Manufacturers of tobacco.*

Serial No.	District or State.	75. Total earners principal occupation. Males.	Females.	75. Total working dependants. Males.	Females.	75. Total earners with subsidiary occupation. Males.	Females.	76. Total earners principal occupation. Males.	Females.	77. Total earners principal occupation. Males.	Females.	77. Total working dependants. Males.	Females.	77. Total earners with subsidiary occupation. Males.	Females.	78. Total earners principal occupation. Males.	Females.	78. Total working dependants. Males.	Females.
1	2	457	458	459	460	461	462	463	464	465	466	467	468	469	470	471	472	473	474
	PUNJAB ..	13,643	52	366	1	804	..	77	..	246	..	10	..	8	..	518	172	24	5
	BRITISH TERRITORY ..	11,724	44	333	1	643	..	..	..	148	..	9	..	8	..	515	172	24	5
	AMBALA DIVISION ..	729	8	30	..	152	..	..	..	3	..	..	..	8	..	16	..	..	..
1	Hissar ..	273	..	23	..	6	..	..	..	..	..	..	..	..	..	3	..	..	..
2	Rohtak ..	42	..	1	..	19	..	..	..	..	..	..	..	..	..	1	..	..	..
3	Gurgaon ..	52	..	..	..	..	..	..	..	..	..	..	..	..	..	..	..	..	..
4	Karnal ..	244	..	3	..	121	..	..	..	1	..	..	..	..	..	1	..	..	..
5	Ambala ..	92	7	3	..	4	..	..	..	2	..	..	..	8	..	10	..	..	..
6	Simla ..	26	1	..	..	2	..	..	..	..	..	..	..	..	..	1	..	..	..
	JULLUNDUR DIVISION	2,815	22	187	1	145	..	..	..	18	..	..	..	..	..	..	..	..	..
7	Kangra ..	458	8	34	..	26	..	..	..	..	..	..	..	..	..	..	..	..	..
8	Hoshiarpur ..	824	2	3	1	24	..	..	..	..	..	..	..	..	..	..	..	..	..
9	Jullundur ..	651	1	68	..	76	..	..	..	..	..	..	..	..	..	..	..	..	..
10	Ludhiana ..	331	10	3	..	10	..	..	..	18	..	..	..	..	..	..	..	..	..
11	Ferozepore ..	551	1	29	..	9	..	..	..	..	..	..	..	..	..	..	..	..	..
	LAHORE DIVISION ..	4,435	8	120	..	199	..	..	..	56	..	4	..	..	..	..	..	..	..
12	Lahore ..	1,666	..	5	..	11	..	..	..	..	..	..	..	..	..	..	..	..	..
13	Amritsar ..	1,098	1	58	..	94	..	..	..	52	..	4	..	..	..	..	..	..	..
14	Gurdaspur ..	469	..	31	..	78	..	..	..	4	..	..	..	..	..	..	..	..	..
15	Sialkot ..	634	1	16	..	5	..	..	..	..	..	..	..	..	..	..	..	..	..
16	Gujranwala ..	349	..	8	..	5	..	..	..	..	..	..	..	..	..	..	..	..	..
17	Sheikhupura ..	219	6	2	..	6	..	..	..	..	..	..	..	..	..	..	..	..	..
	RAWALPINDI DIVISION	779	2	14	..	32	..	..	..	71	..	5	..	..	..	480	172	24	5
18	Gujrat ..	500	..	4	..	29	..	..	..	..	..	..	..	..	..	33	..	..	..
19	Shahpur ..	72	1	1	..	..	..	..	..	..	..	..	..	..	..	..	..	..	..
20	Jhelum ..	17	..	..	..	..	..	..	..	..	..	..	..	..	..	..	..	..	..
21	Rawalpindi ..	23	..	2	..	..	..	..	..	71	..	5	..	..	..	80	..	11	..
22	Attock ..	136	1	7	..	3	..	..	..	..	..	..	..	..	..	367	172	13	5
23	Mianwali ..	31	..	..	..	..	..	..	..	..	..	..	..	..	..	..	..	..	..
	MULTAN DIVISION ..	2,966	4	32	..	115	..	..	..	..	..	..	..	..	..	19	..	..	..
24	Montgomery ..	436	4	..	..	4	..	..	..	..	..	..	..	..	..	..	..	..	..
25	Lyallpur ..	1,547	..	25	..	88	..	..	..	..	..	..	..	..	..	..	..	..	..
26	Jhang ..	3	..	..	..	..	..	..	..	..	..	..	..	..	..	13	..	..	..
27	Multan ..	653	..	1	..	14	..	..	..	..	..	..	..	..	..	6	..	..	..
28	Muzaffargarh ..	168	..	4	..	8	..	..	..	..	..	..	..	..	..	..	..	..	..
29	Dera Ghazi Khan ..	159	..	2	..	1	..	..	..	..	..	..	..	..	..	..	..	..	..
	PUNJAB STATES ..	1,919	8	33	..	161	..	77	..	98	..	1	..	..	..	3	..	..	..
	A.—HAVING POLITICAL RELATIONS WITH THE PUNJAB GOVERNMENT. ..	33	..	3	..	9	..	..	..	4	..	1	..	..	..	1	..	..	..
1	Dujana ..	..	..	..	..	..	..	..	..	..	..	..	..	..	..	..	..	..	..
2	Pataudi ..	..	..	..	..	..	..	..	..	..	..	..	..	..	..	..	..	..	..
3	Kalsia ..	28	..	2	..	..	..	..	..	..	..	..	..	..	..	1	..	..	..
4	SIMLA HILL STATES ..	5	..	1	..	9	..	..	..	4	..	1	..	..	..	..	..	..	..
	Bashahr ..	..	..	..	..	..	..	..	..	2	..	1	..	..	..	..	..	..	..
	Nalagarh ..	1	..	..	..	8	..	..	..	..	..	..	..	..	..	..	..	..	..
	Keonthal ..	3	..	1	..	..	..	..	..	..	..	..	..	..	..	..	..	..	..
	Baghal ..	..	..	..	..	1	..	..	..	..	..	..	..	..	..	..	..	..	..
	Jubbal ..	1	..	..	..	..	..	..	..	..	..	..	..	..	..	..	..	..	..
	Other Simla Hill States ..	..	..	..	..	..	..	..	..	2	..	..	..	..	..	..	..	..	..
	B.—HAVING POLITICAL RELATIONS WITH THE GOVERNMENT OF INDIA. ..	1,886	8	30	..	152	..	77	..	94	..	..	..	..	..	2	..	..	..
5	Loharu ..	..	..	..	..	..	..	..	..	..	..	..	..	..	..	..	..	..	..
6	Sirmoor ..	..	..	..	..	..	..	..	..	..	..	..	..	..	..	1	..	..	..
7	Bilaspur ..	..	..	..	..	..	..	..	..	..	..	..	..	..	..	..	..	..	..
8	Mandi ..	50	1	..	..	20	..	..	..	..	..	..	..	..	..	..	..	..	..
9	Suket ..	20	..	..	..	..	..	..	..	..	..	..	..	..	..	..	..	..	..
10	Kapurthala ..	254	2	..	..	3	..	..	..	78	..	..	..	..	..	..	..	..	..
11	Maler Kotla ..	10	..	1	..	2	..	..	..	..	..	..	..	..	..	..	..	..	..
12	Faridkot ..	75	..	..	..	1	..	..	..	..	..	..	..	..	..	..	..	..	..
13	Chamba ..	41	..	..	..	1	..	..	..	..	..	..	..	..	..	..	..	..	..
14	Patiala (Phulkian States)	1,105	3	29	..	119	..	77	..	..	..	..	..	..	..	..	..	..	..
15	Jind (Phulkian States)	297	2	..	..	6	..	..	..	1	..	..	..	..	..	1	..	..	..
16	Nabha (Phulkian States)	34	..	..	..	..	..	..	..	..	..	..	..	..	..	..	..	..	..
17	Bahawalpur ..	.	..	..	..	..	..	..	..	15	..	..	..	..	..	..	..	..	..
18	C'nes. Lahore ..	895	..	..	..	..	..	..	..	..	..	..	..	..	..	..	..	..	..
19	C'nes. Amritsar ..	647	1	6	..	..	..	..	..	52	..	4	..	..	..	..	..	..	..
20	C'nes. Multan ..	85	..	..	..	..	..	..	..	..	..	..	..	..	..	..	..	..	..

LIVELIHOOD—GENERAL TABLE.

STATES AND CITIES.—*continued*.

B.—PREPARATION AND SUPPLY OF MATERIAL SUBSTANCES—*continued*.

III.—INDUSTRY—*continued*.

11.—Food Industries—*concluded*.								12.—Industries of Dress and the Toilet.												
78.—*Manufacturers of tobacco.—concluded.*		81.—*Others.*						*Total Order* 12.						82.—*Boot, shoe, sandal and clog-makers*						
Total earners with subsidiary occupation.		Total earners principal occupation.		Total working dependants.		Total earners with subsidiary occupation.		Total earners principal occupation.		Total working dependants.		Total earners with subsidiary occupation.		Total earners principal occupation.		Total working dependants.		Total earners with subsidiary occupation.		
Males.	Females.	Males.	Females.	Males.	Females.	Males.	Females.	Males.	Females.	Males.	Females.	Males.	Females.	Males.	Females.	Males.	Females.	Males.	Females.	Serial No.
475	476	477	478	479	480	481	482	483	484	485	486	487	488	489	490	491	492	493	494	
25	2	11,443	5,166	380	1,521	642	176	394,947	22,303	21,095	16,514	32,878	1,424	197,048	6,132	11,722	9,577	19,082	600	
23	2	10,374	5,045	345	1,511	595	168	341,400	20,034	18,422	13,972	23,404	1,212	167,845	5,198	10,201	7,722	12,239	428	
2	..	873	96	17	59	32	1	52,486	2,686	2,049	4,584	5,884	175	26,678	713	729	1,957	2,962	58	
..	..	150	10	6	44	6	..	7,563	442	654	1,270	2,334	22	3,750	156	249	538	1,364	11	1
..	..	63	6	1	..	..	..	12,212	711	655	1,015	1,611	48	6,823	141	216	227	643	1	2
1	..	120	15	..	13	3	..	9,013	696	345	1,549	512	49	3,952	202	126	789	232	4	3
..	..	170	34	8	1	1	1	11,962	434	239	430	768	48	6,697	106	66	174	389	37	4
1	..	293	31	2	1	22	..	11,237	355	154	307	498	7	5,284	98	71	228	245	4	5
..	..	77	..	..	..	..	..	499	48	2	13	161	1	172	10	1	1	89	1	6
..	..	748	287	22	38	254	32	67,674	2,981	4,466	3,471	8,248	320	33,870	1,095	2,959	2,784	5,528	197	
..	..	190	..	19	..	237	..	8,980	418	749	2,194	2,978	234	5,439	185	625	2,003	2,134	174	7
..	..	55	15	..	1	2	..	15,789	542	1,272	461	1,921	29	8,116	234	1,097	338	1,419	14	8
..	..	18	49	..	13	1	4	15,492	889	1,250	504	1,627	31	6,495	342	545	343	1,042	1	9
..	..	130	22	..	1	11	..	13,627	521	588	189	1,007	15	7,250	147	424	52	727	6	10
..	..	355	201	3	23	3	28	13,786	611	607	123	715	11	6,570	187	268	48	206	2	11
..	..	3,299	407	105	234	96	29	88,115	5,939	4,631	3,466	3,544	247	37,029	1,430	2,825	1,755	1,273	39	
..	..	1,199	66	51	1	26	9	19,208	1,465	562	328	364	40	8,055	414	301	213	107	20	12
..	..	1,092	24	29	..	9	..	18,844	1,306	1,265	1,811	491	59	7,203	528	605	1,270	184	2	13
..	..	146	11	5	7	3	2	12,528	639	993	202	1,229	27	4,888	104	558	53	322	4	14
..	..	475	76	6	24	6	1	14,108	857	639	625	502	10	5,432	173	248	99	237	2	15
..	..	227	57	4	95	13	15	13,673	1,157	499	197	438	93	6,349	82	216	49	151	3	16
..	..	160	173	10	107	39	2	9,754	515	673	303	520	18	5,102	129	397	71	272	8	17
17	2	3,264	2,781	149	521	155	68	62,070	4,850	4,169	1,800	3,012	222	35,171	1,256	2,360	1,107	1,157	92	
..	..	1,291	1,534	69	86	78	37	18,166	888	1,660	142	596	26	10,626	135	964	75	229	3	18
..	..	910	1,038	13	349	16	9	14,807	451	328	88	372	13	8,777	65	185	28	178	..	19
..	..	553	129	1	65	25	21	9,795	1,728	666	1,220	648	120	5,608	781	351	938	271	78	20
..	..	309	12	41	8	28	..	6,737	417	543	68	561	24	3,584	77	213	10	187	6	21
17	2	199	57	25	13	8	..	8,504	560	653	251	579	32	4,365	135	400	55	218	5	22
..	..	2	11	..	..	..	1	4,061	306	319	31	256	7	2,211	63	247	1	74	..	23
4	..	2,190	1,474	52	659	58	38	71,055	4,078	3,107	651	2,716	248	34,597	704	1,828	119	1,319	42	
..	..	689	532	12	301	4	7	10,733	462	368	78	606	3	5,235	72	210	9	363		24
..	..	705	224	2	75	33	23	13,712	1,140	1,182	188	778	81	6,798	312	690	77	396	10	25
4	..	60	524	..	225	..	1	13,473	953	594	79	346	76	7,169	18	398	5	178	..	26
..	..	512	112	27	56	17	4	21,654	616	557	106	448	22	9,610	116	280	18	145	3	27
..	..	96	21	6	..	3	..	6,673	409	299	121	356	50	3,440	57	189	10	140	16	28
..	..	128	61	5	2	1	3	4,810	498	107	79	182	16	2,345	129	61	..	97	12	29
2	..	1,069	121	35	10	47	8	53,547	2,269	2,678	2,542	9,474	212	29,708	934	1,521	1,855	6,843	172	
2	..	35	..	3	..	19	..	3,054	157	199	257	1,109	4	1,744	42	132	121	658	4	
..	..	..	..	..	..	..	..	523	22	7	79	108	..	363	4	2	..	27	.	1
2	..	..	..	..	..	..	..	207	63	..	10	11	..	61	17	..	1	9	.	2
..	..	..	..	..	..	..	..	648	24	33	26	29	..	258	9	18	12	5	.	3
..	..	35	..	3	..	19	..	1,676	48	159	142	961	4	1,082	12	112	108	617	4	4
..	..	..	..	..	..	..	..	48	2	10	4	55	..	13	..	3	2	9	..	
..	.	1	..	..	..	..	..	560	10	11	2	298	..	275	2	5	1	197	..	
..	..	3	..	..	..	1	..	173	10	19	20	147	1	82	2	12	15	92	1	
..	..	5	..	..	..	1	..	347	9	5	9	159	1	290	1	2	4	126	1	
..	..	..	..	..	..	..	..	56	..	22	27	66	..	49	..	15	18	28	..	
..	..	26	..	3	..	17	..	492	17	92	80	236	2	353	7	75	68	165	9	
..	..	1,034	121	32	10	28	8	50,493	2,112	2,474	2,285	8,365	208	27,959	892	1,389	1,734	6,185	168	
..	..	3	..	..	..	..	..	191	14	4	7	42	..	107	7	2	2	6	.	5
..	..	2	..	..	..	..	..	1,587	45	49	147	330	1	954	26	29	102	113	.	6
..	..	5	2	..	..	..	..	1,027	143	43	37	254	..	705	119	16	27	153	.	7
..	..	..	..	..	..	..	..	1,376	167	5	9	717	6	808	44	4	5	487	1	8
..	..	..	..	..	..	..	..	289	55	25	312	252	19	187	40	21	300	222	19	9
..	..	20	..	..	..	..	..	5,764	156	87	23	357	4	2,466	58	35	3	144	..	10
..	..	..	..	..	..	..	..	1,517	44	106	8	193	2	919	4	79	..	170	1	11
..	..	48	..	..	..	..	..	1,551	67	34	8	125	8	766	13	16	..	30	..	12
..	..	40	4	4	2	..	..	1,310	138	90	226	637	12	777	118	75	211	513	10	13
..	..	689	99	22	7	25	5	18,075	719	1,296	1,223	4,626	147	11,005	368	740	969	3,935	135	14
..	..	135	10	3	1	2	3	4,111	139	446	151	469	4	2,466	39	242	86	233	2	15
..	..	92	6	3	..	1	..	3,899	116	103	131	363	5	2,075	16	85	29	179	..	16
..	..	..	..	..	..	..	..	9,796	309	96	3	..	..	4,724	40	45	..	..	..	17
..	..	408	58	7	..	2	..	8,179	620	124	59	54	7	2,658	52	43	27	2	4	18
..	..	1,027	21	27	..	7	..	7,135	510	148	..	33	..	1,827	215	24	.	12	..	19
..	..	90	1	6	3	..	..	3,362	13	..	..	17	..	1,170	3	..	..	12	..	20

TABLE X.—OCCUPATION OR MEANS OF
DETAILS FOR DISTRICTS,

Class .. B.—PREPARATION AND SUPPLY OF MATERIAL SUBSTANCES.

Sub-class .. III.—INDUSTRY.

Order .. 12. Industries of Dress and the Toilet.

Group .. 83.—*Tailors, milliners, dress-makers and darners.* 84.—*Embroiderers, hat-makers and makers of other articles of wear.* 85.—*Washing and Cleaning.*

Serial No.	District or State.	83. Total earners principal occupation. Males.	Females.	Total working dependants. Males.	Females.	Total earners with subsidiary occupation. Males.	Females.	84. Total earners principal occupation. Males.	Females.	Total working dependants. Males.	Females.	Total earners with subsidiary occupation. Males.	Females.	85. Total earners principal occupation. Males.	Females.	Total working dependants. Males.	Females.	Total earners with subsidiary occupation. Males.	Females.
1	2	495	496	497	498	499	500	501	502	503	504	505	506	507	508	509	510	511	512
	PUNJAB ..	**60,930**	**9,867**	**2,703**	**2,731**	**4,801**	**460**	**1,102**	**282**	**36**	**104**	**44**	**42**	**46,274**	**3,190**	**1,663**	**1,141**	**2,002**	**132**
	BRITISH TERRITORY ..	**51,240**	**9,282**	**2,202**	**2,479**	**3,852**	**444**	**1,058**	**267**	**25**	**81**	**43**	**42**	**41,697**	**2,720**	**1,558**	**975**	**1,746**	**124**
	AMBALA DIVISION ..	**7,873**	**705**	**264**	**546**	**738**	**21**	**56**	**12**	**6**	**54**	**4**	**37**	**3,773**	**455**	**153**	**391**	**216**	**4**
1	Hissar ..	1,322	128	87	75	191	1	5	2	3	10	..	..	293	16	21	67	26	2
2	Rohtak ..	1,290	116	70	78	179	2	2	..	..	1	..	..	639	58	34	73	55	..
3	Gurgaon ..	1,146	166	30	237	114	7	4	1	..	39	..	37	657	151	25	131	17	..
4	Karnal ..	1,382	171	39	117	55	8	2	3	..	2	2	..	1,157	111	63	88	106	2
5	Ambala ..	2,327	121	37	35	127	3	17	3	3	2	2	..	950	84	10	24	12	..
6	Simla ..	206	3	1	4	67	..	7	..	..	..	..	..	77	35	..	8	..	..
	JULLUNDUR DIVISION	**12,751**	**1,172**	**579**	**457**	**948**	**84**	**644**	**51**	**11**	**17**	**38**	..	**6,167**	**218**	**218**	**90**	**429**	**16**
7	Kangra ..	1,188	197	29	147	171	53	..	..	..	..	..	..	758	31	27	42	212	5
8	Hoshiarpur ..	2,606	227	62	90	235	7	22	1	..	3	..	..	1,618	38	34	18	46	..
9	Jullundur ..	3,876	303	291	102	282	17	115	38	6	4	33	..	1,719	40	121	21	80	10
10	Ludhiana ..	2,484	191	70	81	117	4	497	12	5	10	1	..	611	17	10	2	21	..
11	Ferozepore ..	2,597	254	127	37	143	3	10	..	..	..	4	..	1,461	92	26	7	70	1
	LAHORE DIVISION ..	**14,911**	**3,279**	**531**	**1,004**	**1,027**	**128**	**270**	**36**	**6**	..	**1**	..	**12, 05**	**630**	**549**	**140**	**437**	**11**
12	Lahore ..	3,106	781	64	78	141	19	19	..	..	..	..	..	3,181	185	78	8	72	1
13	Amritsar ..	5,127	323	160	213	108	7	128	34	1	..	..	..	3,051	102	203	77	65	2
14	Gurdaspur ..	2,117	436	91	128	480	19	9	1	..	..	..	..	2,070	54	91	6	172	3
15	Sialkot ..	1,682	468	66	396	104	4	96	1	..	..	1	..	2,549	87	95	12	62	1
16	Gujranwala ..	1,622	773	84	86	90	73	..	..	..	..	..	..	1,283	158	44	17	38	3
17	Sheikhupura ..	1,257	298	60	103	104	6	18	..	5	..	..	..	771	44	38	20	28	1
	RAWALPINDI DIVISION	**7,741**	**1,895**	**603**	**232**	**695**	**50**	**80**	**36**	**2**	**5**	..	**2**	**6,079**	**744**	**279**	**149**	**329**	**55**
18	Gujrat ..	2,000	405	125	26	131	17	13	..	..	..	..	..	1,551	168	137	39	112	6
19	Shahpur ..	1,537	261	33	47	85	8	13	7	..	2	..	2	1,542	61	35	5	74	2
20	Jhelum ..	1,082	636	119	92	99	22	..	..	..	..	..	..	884	202	30	30	21	9
21	Rawalpindi ..	1,323	179	193	21	194	6	52	3	2	..	..	..	832	124	40	37	64	12
22	Attock ..	1,306	207	108	37	157	3	2	26	..	3	..	..	848	178	34	30	38	23
23	Mianwali ..	493	187	25	9	29	4	..	..	..	..	..	..	422	11	3	8	20	3
	MULTAN DIVISION ..	**7,964**	**2,231**	**225**	**240**	**449**	**151**	**8**	**132**	..	**5**	..	**3**	**12,773**	**673**	**359**	**205**	**335**	**38**
24	Montgomery ..	1,423	343	49	50	94	2	..	3	..	..	..	..	1,421	41	58	16	64	..
25	Lyallpur ..	1,628	600	50	63	134	51	..	8	..	..	..	..	1,631	90	140	8	82	11
26	Jhang ..	1,302	808	28	48	85	70	..	2	..	..	..	..	2,250	16	26	7	31	1
27	Multan ..	2,871	114	68	15	66	2	..	14	..	..	..	3	5,161	371	73	73	51	14
28	Muzaffargarh ..	481	191	21	37	52	22	8	40	..	3	..	..	1,504	99	50	70	74	12
29	Dera Ghazi Khan ..	259	175	9	27	18	4	..	65	..	2	..	..	806	56	12	31	33	..
	PUNJAB STATES ..	**9,690**	**585**	**501**	**252**	**949**	**16**	**44**	**15**	**11**	**28**	**1**	..	**4,577**	**470**	**105**	**166**	**256**	**8**
	A.—HAVING POLITICAL RELATIONS WITH THE PUNJAB GOVERNMENT. ..	**499**	**27**	**39**	**33**	**206**	..	**4**	**9**	**2**	**21**	**1**	..	**222**	**39**	**9**	**15**	**47**	..
1	Dujana ..	45	1	..	1	1	..	3	9	2	21	..	..	24	8	..	..	..	..
2	Pataudi ..	42	..	..	..	..	..	1	..	..	..	..	..	18	13	..	..	..	..
3	Kalsia ..	104	4	8	7	8	..	..	..	..	..	..	..	80	4	2	6	..	..
4	**SIMLA HILL STATES** ..	**308**	**22**	**31**	**25**	**197**	..	..	..	..	..	**1**	..	**100**	**14**	**7**	**9**	**47**	..
	Bashahr ..	32	..	7	2	46	..	..	..	..	..	..	..	1	2	..	..	..	..
	Nalagarh ..	119	6	1	1	13	..	..	..	..	..	..	..	39	2	..	..	19	..
	Keonthal ..	46	6	7	5	52	..	..	..	..	..	..	..	25	2	..	..	2	..
	Baghal ..	24	4	1	5	6	..	..	..	..	..	..	..	11	4	2	..	14	..
	Jubbal ..	7	..	7	9	36	..	..	..	..	..	..	..	..	..	..	..	..	..
	Other Simla Hill States ..	80	6	8	3	44	..	..	..	..	..	1	..	24	4	5	9	12	..
	B.—HAVING POLITICAL RELATIONS WITH THE GOVERNMENT OF INDIA. ..	**9,191**	**558**	**462**	**219**	**743**	**16**	**40**	**6**	**9**	**2**	..	..	**4,355**	**431**	**96**	**151**	**209**	**8**
5	Loharu ..	23	2	..	..	..	..	..	..	..	..	..	..	6	2	..	2	..	..
6	Sirmoor ..	348	15	11	33	100	1	..	..	..	..	..	..	39	..	..	11	3	..
7	Bilaspur ..	85	16	4	5	6	..	..	..	..	..	..	..	79	8	4	5	20	..
8	Mandi ..	391	101	1	2	111	2	..	..	..	..	..	..	30	22	..	2	37	3
9	Suket ..	59	5	2	4	18	..	..	..	..	1	..	..	14	10	1	7	7	..
10	Kapurthala ..	1,225	69	40	8	31	2	1	..	..	..	..	..	672	14	2	12	88	2
11	Maler Kotla ..	253	18	15	7	14	..	..	1	..	..	..	..	67	4	2	1	..	..
12	Faridkot ..	426	27	4	4	20	..	..	..	..	..	..	..	104	14	7	4	3	1
13	Chamba ..	420	9	7	3	78	1	..	3	..	..	..	..	42	6	1	12	4	1
14	Patiala (Phulkian States)	4,003	195	292	125	270	8	..	..	..	..	..	..	590	134	33	64	41	..
15	Jind (Phulkian States)	522	21	37	13	66	2	..	..	..	..	..	..	131	9	17	8	6	..
16	Nabha (Phulkian States)	736	21	34	15	29	..	4	2	..	1	..	..	92	23	15	20	..	1
17	Bahawalpur ..	700	59	15	..	..	..	35	..	9	..	..	..	2,469	185	14	3	..	..
18	*Cities.* Lahore ..	1,491	423	27	4	36	3	19	..	..	..	..	..	1,731	117	26	6	14	..
19	*Cities.* Amritsar ..	3,161	197	66	..	..	..	127	32	..	..	..	..	1,294	65	43	..	21	..
20	*Cities.* Multan ..	769	5	..	..	5	..	..	1	..	..	..	..	1,062	4	..	..	..	..

LIVELIHOOD.—GENRAL TABLE.

STATES AND CITIES.—*continued.*

B.—PREPARATION AND SUPPLY OF MATERIAL SUBSTANCES—*continued*

III. INDUSTRY—*continued.*

12. Industries of Dress and the Toilet—*concluded*																		13. Furniture Industries.								
86.—*Barbers, hair-dressers and wig-makers.*						87. *Other industries connected with the toilet.*						*Total Order 13.*						88.—*Cabinet makers, carriage painters, etc.*						89. *Upholsterers, tent makers, etc.*		
Total earners principal occupation.		Total working dependants.		Total earners with subsidiary occupation.		Total earners principal occupation.		Total working dependants		Total earners with subsidiary occupation.		Total earners principal occupation.		Total working dependants.		Total earners with subsidiary occupation.		Total earners principal occupation.		Total working dependants.		Total earners with subsidiary occupation.		Total earners principal occupation.		
Males.	Females.	Males.	Females.	Males.	Females.	Males.	Females.	Males.	Females.	Males.	Females.	Males.	Females.	Males.	Females.	Males.	Females.	Males.	Females.	Males.	Females.	Males.	Females.	Males.	Females.	Serial No.
513	514	515	516	517	518	519	520	521	522	523	524	525	526	527	528	529	530	531	532	533	534	535	536	537	538	
89,316	**2,816**	**4,967**	**2,960**	**6,938**	**190**	**277**	**16**	**4**	**1**	**11**	..	**1,028**	**45**	**17**	**9**	**8**	..	**440**	**33**	**17**	**9**	**8**	..	**588**	**12**	
79,789	**2,551**	**4,432**	**2,715**	**5,513**	**174**	**271**	**16**	**4**	..	**11**	..	**1,008**	**45**	**17**	**9**	**8**	..	**420**	**33**	**17**	**9**	**8**	..	**588**	**12**	
14,026	**794**	**896**	**1,636**	**1,965**	**55**	**80**	**7**	**1**	..	**4**	..	**101**	**1**	..	..	**7**	..	**99**	**1**	..	..	**7**	..	**2**	..	
1,991	140	293	580	753	8	2	..	1	..	..	..	14	..	..	..	..	..	13	..	..	..	..	..	..	..	1
3,453	396	335	636	734	45	5	..	..	..	..	..	10	..	..	..	2	..	10	..	..	..	2	..	..	..	2
3,233	127	164	353	149	1	21	6	..	..	..	..	10	1	..	..	4	..	10	1	..	..	4	..	..	..	3
2,701	43	71	49	213	..	1	..	..	..	3	..	13	..	..	..	..	..	13	..	..	..	..	..	..	..	4
2,608	48	33	18	111	..	51	1	..	..	1	..	39	..	..	..	1	..	38	..	..	..	1	..	1	..	5
37	..	..	..	5	..	..	..	..	..	..	..	15	..	..	..	..	..	15	..	..	..	..	..	..	..	6
14,179	**486**	**697**	**123**	**1,305**	**23**	**63**	**9**	**2**	..	..	..	..	..	..	..	..	..	..	..	..	..	..	..	..	..	
1,594	5	68	2	461	2	1	..	..	..	..	..	..	..	..	..	..	..	..	..	..	..	..	..	..	..	7
3,386	40	77	12	221	8	41	2	2	..	..	..	..	..	..	..	..	..	..	..	..	..	..	..	..	..	8
3,278	159	287	34	190	3	9	7	..	..	..	..	..	..	..	..	..	..	..	..	..	..	..	..	..	..	9
2,777	154	79	43	141	5	8	..	..	..	..	..	..	..	..	..	..	..	..	..	..	..	..	..	..	..	10
3,144	78	186	31	292	5	4	..	..	..	..	..	..	..	..	..	..	..	..	..	..	..	..	..	..	..	11
22,982	**564**	**1,220**	**567**	**806**	**69**	**18**	..	..	..	..	..	**647**	**23**	..	..	**1**	..	**62**	**11**	..	..	**1**	..	**585**	**12**	
4,847	85	119	29	44	..	..	..	..	..	..	..	40	11	..	..	..	..	40	11	..	..	..	..	..	..	12
3,320	119	296	251	134	48	15	..	..	..	..	..	585	12	..	..	..	..	..	..	..	..	..	..	585	12	13
3,444	44	253	15	255	1	..	..	..	..	..	..	17	..	..	..	..	..	17	..	..	..	..	..	..	..	14
4,349	128	230	118	98	3	..	..	..	..	..	..	..	..	..	..	..	..	..	..	..	..	..	..	..	..	15
4,416	144	155	45	159	14	3	..	..	..	..	..	3	..	..	..	1	..	3	..	..	..	1	..	..	..	16
2,606	44	167*	109	116	3	..	..	..	..	..	..	2	..	..	..	..	..	2	..	..	..	..	..	..	..	17
12,934	**419**	**925**	**307**	**827**	**13**	**65**	..	..	..	**4**	..	**107**	..	..	..	..	..	**107**	..	..	..	..	..	..	..	
3,976	180	434	2	121	..	..	..	..	..	..	..	86	..	..	..	..	..	86	..	..	..	..	..	..	..	18
2,913	37	73	6	35	1	25	..	..	..	..	..	..	..	..	..	..	..	..	..	..	..	..	..	..	..	19
2,181	109	166	160	263	11	40	..	..	..	4	..	..	..	..	..	..	..	..	..	..	..	..	..	..	..	20
946	34	95	..	116	..	..	..	..	..	..	..	..	..	..	..	..	..	..	..	..	..	..	..	..	..	21
1,983	14	111	126	166	1	..	..	..	..	..	..	..	..	..	..	..	..	..	..	..	..	..	..	..	..	22
935	45	44	13	133	..	..	..	..	..	..	..	21	..	..	..	..	..	21	..	..	..	..	..	..	..	23
15,668	**338**	**694**	**82**	**610**	**14**	**45**	..	**1**	..	**3**	..	**153**	**21**	**17**	**9**	..	..	**152**	**21**	**17**	**9**	..	..	**1**	..	
2,054	3	51	3	85	..	..	..	..	..	..	..	5	..	..	..	..	..	[illegible]	..	..	..	..	..	..	..	24
3,655	130	302	40	166	9	..	..	..	..	..	..	9	4	..	..	..	..	9	4	..	..	..	..	..	..	25
2,752	109	142	19	52	5	..	..	..	..	..	..	..	..	..	..	..	..	..	..	..	..	..	..	..	..	26
4,012	1	136	..	180	..	..	..	..	..	..	..	..	..	..	..	..	..	..	..	..	..	..	..	..	..	27
1,239	22	39	1	90	..	1	..	..	..	..	..	..	..	..	..	..	..	..	..	..	..	..	..	..	..	28
1,356	73	24	19	31	..	44	..	1	..	3	..	139	17	17	9	..	..	139	17	17	9	..	..	..	..	29
8,527	**265**	**535**	**245**	**1,425**	**16**	**6**	..	..	**1**	..	..	**20**	..	..	..	..	..	**20**	..	..	..	..	..	..	..	
585	**40**	**17**	**67**	**197**	..	..	..	..	..	..	..	**1**	..	..	..	..	..	**1**	..	..	..	..	..	..	..	
88	..	3	57	80	..	..	..	..	..	..	..	..	..	..	..	..	..	..	..	..	..	..	..	..	..	1
85	33	..	9	2	..	..	..	..	..	..	..	..	..	..	..	..	..	..	..	..	..	..	..	..	..	2
206	7	5	1	16	..	..	..	..	..	..	..	..	..	..	..	..	..	..	..	..	..	..	..	..	..	3
206	..	**9**	..	**99**	..	..	..	..	..	..	..	**1**	..	..	..	..	..	**1**	..	..	..	..	..	..	..	4
2	..	..	..	..	..	..	..	..	..	..	..	..	..	..	..	..	..	..	..	..	..	..	..	..	..	
127	..	5	..	69	..	..	..	..	..	..	..	..	..	..	..	..	..	..	..	..	..	..	..	..	..	
20	..	..	..	1	..	..	..	..	..	..	..	1	..	..	..	..	..	1	..	..	..	..	..	..	..	
22	..	..	..	13	..	..	..	..	..	..	..	..	..	..	..	..	..	..	..	..	..	..	..	..	..	
..	..	..	..	2	..	..	..	..	..	..	..	..	..	..	..	..	..	..	..	..	..	..	..	..	..	
35	..	4	..	14	..	..	..	..	..	..	..	..	..	..	..	..	..	..	..	..	..	..	..	..	..	
8,942	**225**	**518**	**178**	**1,228**	**16**	**6**	..	..	**1**	..	..	**19**	..	..	..	..	..	**19**	..	..	..	..	..	..	..	
55	3	2	3	36	..	..	..	..	..	..	..	..	..	..	..	..	..	..	..	..	..	..	..	..	..	5
241	4	9	..	114	..	5	..	..	1	..	..	1	..	..	..	..	..	1	..	..	..	..	..	..	..	6
158	..	19	..	75	..	..	..	..	..	..	..	..	..	..	..	..	..	..	..	..	..	..	..	..	..	7
127	..	..	..	82	..	..	..	..	..	..	..	..	..	..	..	..	..	..	..	..	..	..	..	..	..	8
29	..	1	..	5	..	..	..	..	..	..	..	..	..	..	..	..	..	..	..	..	..	..	..	..	..	9
1,400	15	10	..	94	..	..	..	..	..	..	..	..	..	..	..	..	..	..	..	..	..	..	..	..	..	10
278	17	10	..	9	1	..	..	..	..	..	..	..	..	..	..	..	..	..	..	..	..	..	..	..	..	11
255	13	7	..	72	7	..	..	..	..	..	..	..	..	..	..	..	..	..	..	..	..	..	..	..	..	12
70	2	7	..	42	..	1	..	..	..	..	..	..	..	..	..	..	..	..	..	..	..	..	..	..	..	13
2,477	22	231	65	380	4	..	..	..	..	..	..	..	..	..	..	..	..	..	..	..	..	..	..	..	..	14
992	70	150	44	164	..	..	..	..	..	..	..	1	..	..	..	..	..	1	..	..	..	..	..	..	..	15
992	54	59	66	155	4	..	..	..	..	..	..	5	..	..	..	..	..	5	..	..	..	..	..	..	..	16
1,868	25	13	..	..	..	..	..	..	..	..	..	12	..	..	..	..	..	12	..	..	..	..	..	..	..	17
2,280	28	28	22	2	..	..	..	..	..	..	..	40	11	..	..	..	..	40	11	..	..	..	..	..	..	18
711	1	15	..	..	..	15	..	..	..	..	..	585	12	..	..	..	..	..	..	..	..	..	..	585	12	19
361	..	..	..	..	..	..	..	..	..	..	..	..	..	..	..	..	..	..	..	..	..	..	..	..	..	20

TABLE X.—OCCUPATION OR MEANS OF
DETAILS FOR DISTRICTS,

Class	..	B.—PREPARATION AND SUPPLY OF MATERIAL SUBSTANCES.
Sub-class	..	III.—INDUSTRY.
Order	..	14.—Building Industries. / 15.—Construction of Means of Transport—*continued.*
Group	..	Total Order 14. / 90.—*Lime-burners, cement workers, excavators and well sinkers, stone cutters and dressers, brick layers and masons. Builders (other than buildings made of bamboo or similar materials), painters, etc.* / Total Order 15. / 91.—*Persons engaged in making, assembling or repairing motor vehicles or cycles.*

Serial No.	District or State.	Total earners principal occupation. Males.	Total earners principal occupation. Females.	Total working dependants. Males.	Total working dependants. Females.	Total earners with subsidiary occupation. Males.	Total earners with subsidiary occupation. Females.	Total Order 15. Total earners principal occupation. Males.	Females.	Total working dependants. Males.	Females.	Total earners with subsidiary occupation. Males.	Females.	91. Total earners principal occupation. Males.	Females.	Total working dependants. Males.	Females.	Total earners with subsidiary occupation. Males.	Females.
1	2	539	540	541	542	543	544	545	546	547	548	549	550	551	552	553	554	555	556
	PUNJAB ..	**40,281**	**683**	**1,003**	**164**	**3,256**	**21**	**1,328**	..	**33**	**1**	**19**	..	**1,026**	..	**18**	..	**15**	..
	BRITISH TERRITORY ..	**33,459**	**591**	**789**	**150**	**2,503**	**20**	**965**	..	**18**	**1**	**15**	..	**927**	..	**16**	..	**13**	..
	AMBALA DIVISION ..	**9,619**	**394**	**117**	**120**	**841**	**7**	**74**	..	**2**	**1**	**5**	..	**58**	..	..	..	**3**	..
1	Hissar ..	1,699	107	36	45	151	1	11	..	2	..	1	..	8	..	..	..	1	..
2	Rohtak ..	983	9	26	18	79	..	3	..	..	..	2	..	3	..	..	..	..	..
3	Gurgaon ..	1,159	74	9	9	79	2	11	..	..	..	1	..	..	..	..	..	..	..
4	Karnal ..	2,473	121	22	33	214	4	14	..	..	..	1	..	14	..	..	..	1	..
5	Ambala ..	2,701	81	13	15	173	..	33	..	..	1	..	..	32	..	..	..	1	..
6	Simla ..	604	2	11	..	145	..	2	..	..	..	..	..	1	..	..	..	..	..
	JULLUNDUR DIVISION ..	**5,395**	**78**	**224**	**9**	**609**	**5**	**110**	..	**1**	..	**2**	..	**107**	..	**1**	..	**2**	..
7	Kangra ..	396	37	5	4	113	4	10	..	..	..	..	..	10	..	..	..	..	..
8	Hoshiarpur ..	953	10	18	4	177	..	9	..	1	..	2	..	9	..	1	..	2	..
9	Jullundur ..	2,120	19	154	1	223	..	28	..	..	..	..	..	28	..	..	..	..	..
10	Ludhiana ..	925	5	6	..	71	..	20	..	..	..	..	..	20	..	..	..	..	..
11	Ferozepore ..	1,001	2	41	..	25	1	43	..	..	..	..	..	40	..	..	..	..	..
	LAHORE DIVISION ..	**8,958**	**29**	**185**	**7**	**366**	..	**530**	..	..	..	**7**	..	**525**	..	..	..	**7**	..
12	Lahore ..	2,738	10	21	1	24	..	299	..	..	..	3	..	296	..	..	..	3	..
13	Amritsar ..	2,037	..	78	..	103	..	99	..	..	..	..	..	98	..	..	..	..	..
14	Gurdaspur ..	983	..	30	..	57	..	23	..	..	..	1	..	23	..	..	..	1	..
15	Sialkot ..	1,840	4	25	..	122	..	30	..	..	..	..	..	30	..	..	..	..	..
16	Gujranwala ..	950	7	19	1	45	..	66	..	..	..	3	..	66	..	..	..	3	..
17	Sheikhupura ..	410	8	12	5	15	..	13	..	..	..	..	..	12	..	..	..	..	..
	RAWALPINDI DIVISION	**3,898**	**60**	**168**	**12**	**455**	**6**	**188**	..	**13**	..	**1**		**188**	..	**18**	..	**1**	..
18	Gujrat ..	1,004	1	66	..	45	..	31	..	..	..	..	..	31	..	..	..	..	..
19	Shahpur ..	755	1	34	..	17	..	15	..	..	..	1	..	15	..	..	..	1	..
20	Jhelum ..	1,213	38	56	8	322	6	6	..	..	..	..	..	6	..	..	..	..	..
21	Rawalpindi ..	247	13	9	..	40	..	135	..	13	..	..	..	135	..	13	..	..	..
22	Attock ..	57	3	..	..	7	..	1	..	..	..	..	..	1	..	..	..	..	..
23	Mianwali ..	122	4	3	4	24	..	..	..	..	..	..	..	..	..	..	..	..	..
	MULTAN DIVISION ..	**6,089**	**35**	**95**	**2**	**232**	**2**	**68**	..	**2**	..	..	..	**49**	..	**2**	..	..	..
24	Montgomery ..	713	1	10	1	23	..	..	..	..	..	..	..	..	..	..	..	..	..
25	Lyallpur ..	543	11	2	..	29	..	49	..	2	..	..	..	44	..	2	..	..	..
26	Jhang ..	635	9	..	..	10	..	9	..	..	..	..	..	..	..	..	..	..	..
27	Multan ..	1,567	1	15	..	14	..	3	..	..	..	..	..	3	..	..	..	..	..
28	Muzaffargarh ..	2,100	10	51	1	86	2	..	..	..	..	..	..	..	..	..	..	..	..
29	Dera Ghazi Khan ..	531	3	17	..	70	..	2	..	..	..	..	..	2	..	..	..	..	..
	PUNJAB STATES ..	**6,822**	**92**	**214**	**14**	**753**	**1**	**363**	..	**15**	..	**4**	..	**99**	..	**2**	..	**2**	..
	A.—HAVING POLITICAL RELATIONS WITH THE PUNJAB GOVERNMENT. ..	**653**	**19**	**15**	**11**	**216**	**1**	**1**	..	..	..	..	..	**1**	..	..	..	..	..
1	Dujana ..	10	..	..	11	..	..	..	..	..	..	..	..	..	..	..	..	..	..
2	Pataudi ..	33	3	..	..	3	..	1	..	..	..	..	..	1	..	..	..	..	..
3	Kalsia ..	133	3	3	..	25	..	..	..	..	..	..	..	..	..	..	..	..	..
4	SIMLA HILL STATES ..	**477**	**13**	**12**	..	**188**	**1**	..	..	..	..	..	..	..	..	..	..	..	..
	Bashahr ..	73	..	4	..	18	..	..	..	..	..	..	..	..	..	..	..	..	..
	Nalagarh ..	145	5	..	..	40	1	..	..	..	..	..	..	..	..	..	..	..	..
	Keonthal ..	149	8	1	..	16	..	..	..	..	..	..	..	..	..	..	..	..	..
	Baghal ..	7	..	1	..	3	..	..	..	..	..	..	..	..	..	..	..	..	..
	Jubbal ..	14	..	3	..	43	..	..	..	..	..	..	..	..	..	..	..	..	..
	Other Simla Hill States ..	89	..	3	..	68	..	..	..	..	..	..	..	..	..	..	..	..	..
	B.—HAVING POLITICAL RELATIONS WITH THE GOVERNMENT OF INDIA. ..	**6,169**	**73**	**199**	**3**	**537**	..	**362**	..	**15**	..	**4**	..	**98**	..	**2**	..	**2**	..
5	Loharu ..	10	1	..	..	..	..	..	..	..	..	..	..	..	..	..	..	..	..
6	Sirmoor ..	315	1	2	..	72	..	..	..	..	..	..	..	..	..	..	..	..	..
7	Bilaspur ..	32	..	..	..	15	..	..	..	..	..	..	..	..	..	..	..	..	..
8	Mandi ..	422	31	1	..	193	..	..	..	..	..	..	..	..	..	..	..	..	..
9	Suket ..	11	..	1	..	3	..	..	..	..	..	..	..	..	..	..	..	..	..
10	Kapurthala ..	417	1	4	..	37	..	2	..	..	..	..	..	2	..	..	..	..	..
11	Maler Kotla ..	449	9	23	..	3	..	..	..	..	..	..	..	..	..	..	..	..	..
12	Faridkot ..	154	..	..	..	9	..	15	..	..	..	..	..	15	..	..	..	..	..
13	Chamba ..	94	..	3	..	30	..	..	..	..	..	..	..	..	..	..	..	..	..
14	Patiala (Phulkian States) ..	1,661	18	91	3	91	..	294	..	13	..	2	..	42	..	2	..	2	..
15	Jind (Phulkian States) ..	390	5	23	..	57	..	2	..	..	..	..	..	2	..	..	..	..	..
16	Nabha (Phulkian States) ..	624	7	15	..	27	..	19	..	2	..	2	..	7	..	..	..	..	..
17	Bahawalpur ..	1,590	..	36	..	..	..	30	..	..	..	..	..	30	..	..	..	..	..
18	*Cities.* Lahore ..	1,724	3	11	..	1	..	292	..	..	..	3	..	289	..	..	..	3	..
19	*Cities.* Amritsar ..	1,015	..	13	..	..	..	87	..	..	..	..	..	87	..	..	..	..	..
20	*Cities.* Multan ..	517	..	2	..	..	..	3	..	..	..	..	..	3	..	..	..	..	..

LIVELIHOOD.—GENERAL TABLE.

STATES AND CITIES.—*continued.*

B.—PREPARATION AND SUPPLY OF MATERIAL SUBSTANCES—*continued.*

III.—INDUSTRY—*continued.*

15.—Construction of Means of Transport—*concluded.* 92.—*Carriage, cart, palki, etc., makers and wheel wrights.* Total earners principal occupation.		Total working dependants.		Total earners with subsidiary occupation.		93.—*Ship, boat, aeroplane builders.* Total earners principal occupation.		16.—Production and Transmission of Physical Force. *Total Order 16.* Total earners principal occupation.		Total working dependants.		94.—*Heat, light, electricity, motive power, etc. Gas-works and electric light and power.* Total earners with subsidiary occupation.		17. Miscellaneous and undefined industries—*continued.* *Total Order 17.* Total earners principal occupation.		Total working dependants.		Total earners with subsidiary occupation.		95.—*Printers, engravers, book binders, etc.* Total earners principal occupation.		Total working dependants.		Total earners with subsidiary occupation.		
Males.	Females.	Males.	Females.	Males.	Females.	Males.	Females.	Males.	Females.	Males.	Females.	Males.	Females.	Males.	Females.	Males.	Females.	Males.	Females.	Males.	Females.	Males.	Females.	Males.	Females.	Serial No.
557	558	559	560	561	562	563	564	565	566	567	568	569	570	571	572	573	574	575	576	577	578	579	580	581	582	
288	..	15	1	4	..	14	..	2,895	6	20	1	868	..	188,391	77,328	13,596	34,376	11,175	2,152	3,508	9	20	..	63	..	
24	..	2	1	2	..	14	..	1,959	6	19	1	37	..	164,750	66,640	12,073	30,113	8,693	1,914	3,328	9	6	..	56	..	
16	..	2	1	2	..	..	..	164	1	..	..	5	..	34,384	19,387	2,409	10,708	1,623	127	313	1	..	..	7	..	
3	..	2	..	..	..	..	..	3	..	..	..	..	..	3,446	1,760	526	2,398	490	18	14	..	..	..	1	..	1
..	..	..	..	2	..	..	..	4	..	..	..	..	..	7,854	3,628	904	4,441	291	33	13	..	..	..	..	..	2
11	..	..	..	..	..	..	..	2	..	..	..	..	..	5,959	3,115	506	1,706	122	38	10	..	..	..	1	..	3
..	..	..	..	..	..	..	..	16	..	..	..	..	..	7,489	6,625	280	1,144	315	35	19	..	..	..	1	..	4
1	..	..	1	..	..	..	..	65	1	..	..	3	..	8,452	4,154	187	999	220	3	70	1	..	..	3	..	5
1	..	..	..	..	..	..	..	74	..	..	..	2	..	1,184	107	..	20	185	..	187	..	..	..	1	..	6
3	..	..	..	..	..	..	..	81	..	..	..	..	..	21,982	8,386	1,718	3,128	1,410	262	155	..	..	..	1	..	
..	..	..	..	..	..	..	..	55	..	..	..	..	..	1,659	94	48	22	133	3	17	..	..	..	..	..	7
..	..	..	..	..	..	..	..	1	..	..	..	..	..	6,226	2,043	240	1,192	360	12	6	..	..	..	1	..	8
..	..	..	..	..	..	..	..	11	..	..	..	..	..	5,893	3,131	964	1,313	366	45	46	..	..	..	..	..	9
..	..	..	..	..	..	..	..	5	..	..	..	..	..	5,973	1,129	196	197	450	96	63	..	..	..	..	..	10
3	..	..	..	..	..	..	..	9	..	..	..	..	..	5,231	1,987	270	404	101	106	23	..	..	..	..	..	11
..	..	..	..	..	..	5	..	1,543	3	19	..	27	..	58,798	24,938	3,569	12,895	3,527	332	2,616	6	2	..	39	..	
..	..	..	..	..	..	3	..	884	3	11	..	9	..	16,514	6,219	428	1,751	333	43	1,817	6	..	..	29	..	12
..	..	..	..	..	..	1	..	327	..	1	..	3	..	13,536	5,932	1,317	5,794	595	197	479	..	..	..	4	..	13
..	..	..	..	..	..	..	..	116	..	2	..	9	..	6,030	3,866	322	2,026	475	13	33	..	1	..	1	..	14
..	..	..	..	..	..	..	..	91	..	..	..	..	..	11,274	2,523	1,088	2,136	460	9	162	..	..	..	..	..	15
..	..	..	..	..	..	..	..	75	..	..	..	6	..	7,392	4,895	160	405	1,506	65	93	..	1	..	4	..	16
..	..	..	..	..	..	1	..	50	..	5	..	..	..	3,852	1,503	254	763	158	5	32	..	..	..	1	..	17
..	..	..	..	..	..	..	..	68	2	..	1	..	..	25,066	4,981	1,906	1,553	1,010	129	119	..	2	..	1	..	
..	..	..	..	..	..	..	..	2	..	..	..	..	..	9,333	1,946	1,334	871	276	23	30	..	..	..	..	..	18
..	..	..	..	..	..	..	..	..	..	..	..	..	..	6,115	1,652	202	432	149	8	41	..	..	..	1	..	19
..	..	..	..	..	..	..	..	6	..	..	..	..	..	3,440	466	106	127	180	8	..	..	..	..	..	..	20
..	..	..	..	..	..	..	..	31	1	..	..	..	..	2,174	620	84	71	105	77	35	..	2	..	..	..	21
..	..	..	..	..	..	..	..	18	1	..	1	..	..	2,024	188	111	41	232	6	7	..	..	..	..	..	22
..	..	..	..	..	..	..	..	11	..	..	..	..	..	1,980	109	69	11	68	7	6	..	..	..	..	..	23
5	..	..	..	..	..	9	..	103	..	..	..	5	..	24,520	8,948	2,471	1,829	1,123	1,064	125	2	2	..	8	..	
..	..	..	..	..	..	..	..	73	..	..	..	5	..	4,602	1,941	168	147	115	7	..	..	..	..	..	..	24
5	..	..	..	..	..	..	..	29	..	..	..	..	..	8,687	5,736	1,064	1,582	657	984	60	..	2	..	..	..	25
..	..	..	..	..	..	9	..	..	..	..	..	..	..	4,248	489	596	41	38	31	8	..	..	..	..	..	26
..	..	..	..	..	..	..	..	..	..	..	..	..	..	3,482	400	481	23	92	11	19	..	..	..	..	..	27
..	..	..	..	..	..	..	..	..	..	..	..	..	..	1,902	265	41	26	126	28	17	..	..	..	7	..	28
..	..	..	..	..	..	..	..	1	..	..	..	..	..	1,599	97	121	5	75	3	21	2	..	..	1	..	29
264	..	13	..	2	..	..	..	936	..	1	..	831	..	21,641	10,688	1,523	4,263	2,482	238	180	..	14	..	7	..	
..	..	..	..	..	..	..	..	24	..	..	..	4	..	1,622	560	56	236	191	2	21	..	..	..	2	..	
..	..	..	..	..	..	..	..	..	..	..	..	..	..	274	69	3	57	12	..	..	..	..	..	..	..	1
..	..	..	..	..	..	..	..	..	..	..	..	..	..	188	178	..	15	..	1	..	..	..	..	..	..	2
..	..	..	..	..	..	..	..	1	..	..	..	..	..	606	249	29	123	51	..	3	..	..	..	..	..	3
..	..	..	..	..	..	..	..	23	..	..	..	4	..	554	64	24	41	128	1	18	..	..	..	2	..	4
..	..	..	..	..	..	..	..	..	..	..	..	..	..	16	2	4	6	16	..	..	..	..	..	1	..	
..	..	..	..	..	..	..	..	..	..	..	..	..	..	167	37	..	5	7	..	1	..	..	..	1	..	
..	..	..	..	..	..	..	..	9	..	..	..	..	..	123	4	3	12	24	1	14	..	..	..	..	..	
..	..	..	..	..	..	..	..	..	..	..	..	..	..	64	..	..	..	4	..	..	..	..	..	..	..	
..	..	..	..	..	..	..	..	..	..	..	..	3	..	18	..	4	1	30	..	1	..	..	..	..	..	
..	..	..	..	..	..	..	..	14	..	..	..	1	..	164	21	13	17	47	..	2	..	..	..	..	..	
264	..	13	..	2	..	..	..	912	..	1	..	827	..	20,019	10,128	1,467	4,027	2,291	236	159	..	14	..	5	..	
..	..	..	..	..	..	..	..	..	..	..	..	..	..	43	27	2	2	..	2	..	..	..	..	..	..	5
..	..	..	..	..	..	..	..	..	..	..	..	..	..	367	72	8	42	50	..	2	..	..	..	2	..	6
..	..	..	..	..	..	..	..	..	..	..	..	..	..	191	12	7	13	11	..	1	..	..	..	..	..	7
..	..	..	..	..	..	..	..	694	..	..	..	826	..	248	61	4	..	91	1	1	..	..	..	1	..	8
..	..	..	..	..	..	..	..	..	..	..	..	..	..	60	10	1	1	23	..	..	..	..	..	..	..	9
..	..	..	..	..	..	..	..	..	..	..	..	..	..	2,422	969	33	140	254	28	12	..	..	..	..	..	10
..	..	..	..	..	..	..	..	6	..	1	..	..	..	333	112	36	6	18	1	17	..	..	..	..	..	11
..	..	..	..	..	..	..	..	..	..	..	..	..	..	338	370	67	32	59	5	5	..	..	..	..	..	12
..	..	..	..	..	..	..	..	15	..	..	..	..	..	222	19	11	11	48	1	1	..	..	..	..	..	13
252	..	11	..	..	..	..	..	127	..	..	..	..	..	11,128	7,238	970	2,968	1,538	185	85	..	14	..	..	..	14
..	..	..	..	..	..	..	..	31	..	..	..	1	..	1,844	702	246	674	137	3	3	..	..	..	..	..	15
12	..	2	..	2	..	..	..	23	..	..	..	..	..	1,100	284	63	134	60	10	7	..	..	..	2	..	16
..	..	..	..	..	..	..	..	16	..	..	..	..	..	1,523	252	19	4	..	..	25	..	..	..	..	..	17
..	..	..	..	..	..	3	..	842	1	11	..	9	..	8,830	1,378	85	82	51	14	1,596	6	..	..	29	..	18
..	..	..	..	..	..	..	..	129	..	..	..	..	..	3,878	605	16	7	56	..	416	..	..	..	..	..	19
..	..	..	..	..	..	..	..	..	..	..	..	..	..	1,077	260	6	9	13	1	15	..	..	..	..	..	20

TABLE X.—OCCUPATION OR MEANS OF

DETAILS FOR DISTRICTS,

Class .. B.—PREPARATION AND SUPPLY OF MATERIAL SUBSTANCES—*continued.*

Sub-class .. III.—INDUSTRY.

Order .. 17.—Miscellaneous and undefined Industries.

Serial No.	District or State	96.—*Makers of musical instruments.* Total earners principal occupation. Males.	Females.	Total working dependants. Males.	Females.	97.—*Makers of clocks and surgical or scientific instruments, etc.* Total earners principal occupation. Males.	Females.	Total working dependants. Males.	Females.	Total earners with subsidiary occupation. Males.	Females.	98.—*Makers of jewellery and ornaments.* Total earners principal occupation. Males.	Females.	Total working dependants. Males.	Females.	Total earners with subsidiary occupation. Males.	Females.	99.—*Other miscellaneous and undefined industries (toy-making taxidermy, etc.).* Total earners principal occupation. Males.	Females.	Total working dependants. Males.	Females.	Total earners with subsidiary occupation. Males.	Females.
1	2	583	584	585	586	587	588	589	590	591	592	593	594	595	596	597	898	599	600	601	602	603	604
	PUNJAB	175	..	1	..	1,685	..	14	..	45	..	53,465	591	2,298	109	2,423	28	5,269	584	155	192	294	26
	BRITISH TERRITORY	150	..	1	..	1,494	..	12	..	30	..	46,162	512	1,780	91	1,756	24	5,094	572	148	183	283	26
	AMBALA DIVISION	14	..	..	..	150	..	..	..	4	..	7,485	29	856	7	810	2	310	81	2	47	21	4
1	Hissar	2	..	..	..	17	..	..	..	1	..	1,522	6	143	3	196	..	29	..	..	..	1	..
2	Rohtak	2	..	..	..	12	..	..	..	..	..	1,629	6	99	3	15	..	27	..	1	16	..	..
3	Gurgaon	4	..	..	..	7	..	..	..	..	..	868	1	30	1	4	1	74	1	1	20	1	..
4	Karnal	..	..	..	..	22	..	..	..	1	..	1,593	6	54	..	32	..	40	72	..	10	1	4
5	Ambala	4	..	..	..	79	..	..	..	2	..	1,815	9	30	..	9	1	136	8	..	1	18	..
6	Simla	2	..	..	..	13	..	..	..	..	..	58	1	..	..	54	..	4	..	..	..	..	..
	JULLUNDUR DIVISION	8	..	..	..	130	..	1	..	2	..	8,995	55	370	13	522	19	554	84	20	61	8	..
7	Kangra	7	..	..	..	2	..	..	..	1	..	1,214	19	19	7	119	2	8	..	4	..	1	..
8	Hoshiarpur	..	..	..	..	4	..	..	..	1	..	1,959	11	39	3	46	2	8	4	..	..	..	..
9	Jullundur	..	..	..	..	44	..	1	..	..	..	2,222	8	175	2	141	15	437	25	8	61	2	..
10	Ludhiana	1	..	..	..	41	..	..	..	..	..	1,410	4	55	..	155	..	50	1	2	..	1	..
11	Ferozepore	..	..	..	..	39	..	..	..	..	..	2,190	13	82	1	61	..	51	4	16	..	4	..
	LAHORE DIVISION	102	..	..	..	907	..	10	..	9	..	13,441	59	509	4	428	..	3,355	124	73	30	174	..
12	Lahore	30	..	..	..	702	..	9	..	4	..	2,957	21	80	4	55	..	345	8	5	2	7	..
13	Amritsar	19	..	..	..	91	..	..	..	..	..	3,144	15	160	..	79	..	245	28	39	20	10	..
14	Gurdaspur	2	..	..	..	24	..	..	..	1	..	2,361	4	81	..	168	..	93	12	..	3	6	..
15	Sialkot	3	..	..	..	25	..	..	..	4	..	2,125	10	65	..	18	..	2,448	57	14	..	148	..
16	Gujranwala	48	..	..	..	61	..	..	..	..	..	1,710	7	47	..	94	..	74	19	..	5	2	..
17	Sheikhupura	..	..	..	..	4	..	1	..	..	..	1,144	2	76	..	14	..	160	..	15	..	1	..
	RAWALPINDI DIVISION	16	..	1	..	45	..	..	..	2	..	8,331	266	294	40	248	..	569	229	42	29	59	21
18	Gujrat	..	..	..	..	12	..	..	..	..	..	1,767	10	59	2	25	..	125	1	2	..	8	..
19	Shahpur	..	..	..	..	10	..	..	..	2	..	2,095	145	43	1	22	..	..	..	..	..	..	..
20	Jhelum	..	..	..	..	5	..	..	..	..	..	1,354	53	48	13	47	..	147	71	5	4	3	..
21	Rawalpindi	..	..	..	..	4	..	..	..	..	..	577	5	36	1	44	..	117	157	7	25	8	21
22	Attock	16	..	1	..	14	..	..	..	..	..	1,097	19	76	22	85	..	161	..	..	..	39	..
23	Mianwali	..	..	..	..	..	..	..	..	..	..	1,441	34	32	1	25	..	19	..	28	..	1	..
	MULTAN DIVISION	10	..	..	..	262	..	1	..	13	..	7,910	103	251	27	248	3	306	104	1	16	21	1
24	Montgomery	..	..	..	..	4	..	..	..	..	..	1,178	15	78	..	23	..	138	77	..	16	..	1
25	Lyallpur	10	..	..	..	174	..	..	..	4	..	1,539	15	47	7	57	2	23	17	1	..	2	..
26	Jhang	..	..	..	..	20	..	..	..	1	..	1,379	34	58	18	53	..	2	..	..	..	..	..
27	Multan	..	..	..	..	38	..	..	..	3	..	2,208	33	46	2	47	1	142	8	..	..	19	..
28	Muzaffargarh	..	..	..	..	18	..	..	..	5	..	836	3	3	..	45	..	1	..	..	..	..	..
29	Dera Ghazi Khan	..	..	..	..	8	..	1	..	..	..	770	3	19	..	23	..	..	2	..	..	..	..
	PUNJAB STATES	25	..	..	..	191	..	2	..	15	..	7,303	79	518	18	667	4	175	12	7	9	11	..
	A.—HAVING POLITICAL RELATIONS WITH THE PUNJAB GOVERNMENT.	..	..	..	..	5	..	1	..	..	..	520	..	30	3	119	1	8	1	..	..	3	..
1	Dujana	..	..	..	..	..	..	..	..	..	..	54	..	..	..	1	..	..	..	..	..	..	..
2	Pataudi	..	..	..	..	..	..	..	..	..	..	38	..	..	..	..	..	..	1	..	..	..	..
3	Kalsia	..	..	..	..	1	..	..	..	..	..	126	..	11	1	7	..	2	..	..	..	1	..
4	SIMLA HILL STATES	..	..	..	..	4	..	1	..	..	..	302	..	19	2	111	1	6	..	..	..	2	..
	Bashahr	..	..	..	..	..	..	1	..	..	..	10	..	3	1	15	..	..	..	..	..	..	..
	Nalagarh	..	..	..	..	..	..	..	..	..	..	113	..	..	..	1	..	4	..	..	..	2	..
	Keonthal	..	..	..	..	2	..	..	..	..	..	36	..	2	..	24	1	..	..	..	..	..	..
	Baghal	..	..	..	..	1	..	..	..	..	..	58	..	..	..	3	..	2	..	..	..	..	..
	Jubbal	..	..	..	..	..	..	..	..	..	..	15	..	4	1	30	..	..	..	..	..	..	..
	Other Simla Hill States	..	..	..	..	1	..	..	..	..	..	70	..	10	..	38	..	..	..	..	..	..	..
	B.—HAVING POLITICAL RELATIONS WITH THE GOVERNMENT OF INDIA.	25	..	..	..	186	..	1	..	15	..	6,783	79	488	15	548	3	167	11	7	9	8	..
5	Loharu	..	..	..	..	..	..	..	..	..	..	14	..	2	..	..	..	..	..	..	..	..	..
6	Sirmoor	..	..	..	..	1	..	..	..	..	..	178	..	7	1	42	..	..	..	..	..	..	..
7	Bilaspur	..	..	..	..	..	..	..	..	..	..	170	7	6	12	11	..	1	..	..	..	..	..
8	Mandi	..	..	..	..	8	..	..	..	..	..	168	2	3	..	74	..	1	..	..	..	..	..
9	Suket	..	..	..	..	..	..	..	..	..	..	51	2	1	..	23	..	1	..	..	..	1	..
10	Kapurthala	..	..	..	..	56	..	..	..	10	..	546	11	5	..	16	2	39	1	..	..	4	..
11	Maler Kotla	..	..	..	..	16	..	..	..	1	..	302	9	34	..	11	..	49	..	..	..	..	..
12	Faridkot	..	..	..	..	5	..	..	..	..	..	274	1	14	..	9	..	3	1	..	..	..	..
13	Chamba	..	..	..	..	2	..	..	..	1	..	178	..	6	2	44	1	1	..	..	..	2	..
14	Patiala (Phulkian States)	25	..	..	..	56	..	..	..	..	..	2,915	13	317	..	294	..	45	5	7	5	..	..
15	Jind (Phulkian States)	..	..	..	..	6	..	1	..	..	..	495	2	45	..	15	..	2	..	..	..	..	..
16	Nabha (Phulkian States)	..	..	..	..	9	..	..	..	3	..	589	6	33	..	9	..	5	4	..	4	1	..
17	Bahawalpur	..	..	..	..	27	..	..	..	..	..	903	26	15	..	..	..	20	..	..	..	..	..
18	*Cities.* Lahore	30	..	..	..	690	..	9	..	1	..	971	2	12	..	11	..	323	8	5	..	7	..
19	*Cities.* Amritsar	19	..	..	..	91	..	..	..	..	..	1,692	2	10	..	56	..	133	22	4	7	..	..
20	*Cities.* Multan	..	..	..	..	29	..	..	..	3	..	410	30	5	..	7	1	74	..	..	..	..	..

LIVELIHOOD.—GENERAL TABLE.

STATES AND CITIES.—*continued.*

B.—PREPARATION AND SUPPLY OF MATERIAL SUBSTANCES—*continued.*

III.—INDUSTRY—*concluded.*						IV.—TRANSPORT.														
17.—Miscellaneous and undefined Industries—*concluded.*						18.—Transport by air.								19.—Transport by water—*continued.*						
100.—*Scavenging.*						Total Sub-class IV.						*Total order* 18. 101.—*Persons concerned with aerodromes and aeroplanes.*		*Total Order* 19.						
Total earners principal occupation.		Total working dependants.		Total earners with subsidiary occupation.		Total earners principal occupation.		Total working dependants.		Total earners with subsidiary occupation.		Total earners principal occupation.		Total earners principal occupation.		Total working dependants.		Total earners with subsidiary occupation.		
Males.	Females.	Males.	Females.	Males.	Females.	Males.	Females.	Males.	Females.	Males.	Females.	Males.	Females.	Males.	Females.	Males.	Females.	Males.	Females.	Serial No.
605	606	607	608	609	610	611	612	613	614	615	616	617	618	619	620	621	622	623	624	
122,289	**76,144**	**11,108**	**34,075**	**8,350**	**2,098**	**216,860**	**2,740**	**5,743**	**1,018**	**17,726**	**168**	**7**	..	**16 094**	**227**	**436**	**58**	**1,155**	**8**	
108,522	**65,547**	**10,126**	**29,839**	**6,568**	**1,864**	**190,574**	**2,354**	**5,232**	**888**	**14,752**	**139**	**7**	..	**12,526**	**193**	**421**	**58**	**670**	**5**	
26,112	**19,276**	**2,051**	**10,654**	**1,281**	**121**	**29,744**	**804**	**1,092**	**292**	**6,039**	**64**	**5**	..	**1,975**	**82**	**17**	**89**	**169**	**3**	
1,862	1,754	383	2,395	291	18	5,196	60	236	92	1,671	17	..	..	414	4	3	..	85	1	1
6,171	3,620	804	4,422	276	33	3,308	33	102	59	921	5	..	..	406	7	5	22	21	2	2
4,996	3,113	475	1,685	116	37	4,227	38	99	11	782	3	..	..	126	8	3	..	9	..	3
5,815	6,547	232	1,134	280	31	5,053	276	125	122	1,364	37	..	..	650	63	3	17	40	..	4
6,348	4,136	157	998	188	2	9,768	314	105	8	1,156	1	5	..	373	..	3	..	14	..	5
920	106	..	20	130	..	2,192	83	425	..	145	1	..	..	6	..	..	..	..	..	6
12,140	**8,297**	**1,317**	**3,054**	**877**	**243**	**21,231**	**212**	**550**	**66**	**2,263**	**9**	..	..	**991**	**46**	**53**	..	**119**	..	
411	75	25	15	12	1	3,150	58	110	65	518	9	..	..	164	4	2	..	70	..	7
3,249	2,030	201	1,189	312	10	2,966	4	36	..	769	..	..	..	114	2	2	..	18	..	8
3,144	3,098	780	1,250	223	30	4,140	15	158	1	269	..	..	..	63	2	2	..	..	..	9
2,408	1,124	139	197	294	96	3,791	19	129	..	424	..	..	..	105	1	44	..	5	..	10
2,928	1,970	172	403	36	106	7,184	116	117	..	283	..	..	..	545	37	3	..	26	..	11
38,377	**24,749**	**2,975**	**12,861**	**2,877**	**332**	**77,252**	**406**	**1,802**	**7**	**3,131**	..	..	..	**4,606**	**14**	**256**	..	**152**	..	
10,663	6,184	334	1,745	238	43	39,574	311	144	..	633	..	..	..	1,248	13	..	..	3	..	12
9,558	5,889	1,118	5,774	502	197	13,521	44	736	1	498	..	..	..	685	1	4	..	16	..	13
3,517	3,850	240	2,023	299	13	5,605	17	398	..	558	..	..	..	598	..	218	..	106	..	14
6,511	2,456	1,009	2,156	290	9	5,010	2	157	..	703	..	..	..	386	..	1	..	5	..	15
5,606	4,869	112	400	1,406	65	8,283	14	155	1	264	..	..	..	994	..	7	..	14	..	16
2,522	1,501	162	763	142	5	5,259	18	212	5	475	..	..	..	695	..	26	..	8	..	17
15,986	**4,486**	**1,567**	**1,484**	**700**	**108**	**26,779**	**488**	**958**	**28**	**1,637**	**7**	**2**	..	**2,009**	**50**	**58**	**19**	**78**	**2**	
7,399	1,935	1,273	869	243	23	6,955	186	298	6	495	3	..	..	486	..	8	..	13	..	18
3,969	1,507	159	431	124	8	5,662	71	42	21	219	3	..	..	886	48	9	19	24	2	19
1,934	342	53	110	130	8	3,687	99	155	1	269	..	..	..	121	1	2	..	8	..	20
1,441	458	39	45	53	56	4,059	11	152	..	287	..	2	..	77	..	2	..	1	..	21
729	169	34	19	108	6	2,663	33	52	..	233	..	..	..	95	..	..	..	18	..	22
514	75	9	10	42	7	3,753	33	259	..	134	1	..	..	344	1	37	..	14	..	23
15,907	**8,739**	**2,216**	**1,786**	**833**	**1,060**	**35,568**	**499**	**880**	**445**	**1,682**	**59**	..	..	**2,945**	**1**	**37**	..	**152**	..	
3,282	1,849	90	131	92	6	6,308	67	110	29	245	..	..	..	50	..	4	..	6	..	24
6,881	5,724	1,014	1,575	594	982	5,920	37	218	4	376	1	..	..	761	..	2	..	14	..	25
2,839	455	538	23	4	31	4,504	9	27	..	228	..	..	..	637	..	..	..	19	..	26
1,075	359	435	26	23	10	6,984	236	83	8	152	6	..	..	328	1	24	..	25	..	27
1,030	262	38	26	69	28	6,930	133	114	14	423	2	..	..	441	..	3	..	29	..	28
800	90	101	5	51	3	4,922	17	278	390	258	50	..	..	728	..	4	..	59	..	29
13,767	**10,597**	**982**	**4,236**	**1,782**	**234**	**26,286**	**386**	**511**	**180**	**2,974**	**29**	..	..	**3,568**	**34**	**15**	..	**485**	**3**	
1,068	**559**	**25**	**233**	**67**	**1**	**1,308**	**22**	**37**	**86**	**576**	**4**	..	..	**42**	..	**3**	..	**5**	..	
220	69	3	57	11	..	27	..	..	..	8	..	..	..	1	..	..	..	..	..	1
150	177	..	15	..	1	137	3	1	..	17	..	..	..	..	..	..	..	..	..	2
474	249	18	122	43	..	431	8	16	80	135	4	..	..	14	..	..	..	..	..	3
224	**64**	**4**	**39**	**13**	..	**708**	**11**	**20**	**6**	**416**	..	..	..	**27**	..	**3**	..	**5**	..	4
6	2	..	5	..	..	30	..	1	..	17	..	..	..	6	..	..	..	..	..	
49	37	..	5	3	..	150	..	3	..	81	..	..	..	1	..	..	..	..	..	
73	4	1	12	..	..	248	8	2	1	34	..	..	..	1	..	..	..	..	..	
3	..	..	..	1	..	25	..	..	..	10	..	..	..	8	..	..	..	..	..	
2	..	..	..	..	..	14	..	..	..	63	..	..	..	..	..	..	..	4	..	
91	21	3	17	9	..	241	3	14	5	211	..	..	..	11	..	3	..	1	..	
12,699	**10,038**	**957**	**4,003**	**1,715**	**233**	**24,983**	**364**	**474**	**94**	**2,398**	**25**	..	..	**3,526**	**34**	**12**	..	**480**	**3**	
29	27	..	2	..	2	19	1	..	..	7	8	..	..	..	..	..	..	..	..	5
186	72	1	41	6	..	439	2	..	..	68	..	..	..	77	..	..	..	8	..	6
19	5	1	1	..	..	138	..	8	..	71	..	..	..	34	..	..	..	16	..	7
70	59	1	..	16	1	643	4	1	..	735	3	..	..	89	..	..	..	380	3	8
8	8	..	1	1	..	58	..	..	..	11	..	..	..	..	..	..	..	8	..	9
1,769	957	28	140	224	26	787	3	..	..	61	..	..	..	56	1	..	..	2	..	10
149	103	2	6	6	1	970	..	43	..	75	..	..	..	1	..	..	..	..	..	11
51	368	53	32	50	5	1,142	..	8	..	17	..	..	..	2	..	..	..	1	..	12
40	19	5	9	1	..	139	13	10	..	38	..	..	..	..	..	3	..	9	..	13
8,002	7,220	632	2,963	1,244	185	7,428	17	126	31	154	..	..	..	689	..	6	..	39	..	14
1,338	700	200	674	122	3	1,838	21	112	22	461	..	..	..	264	..	..	..	11	..	15
490	274	30	130	45	10	2,562	82	101	41	695	14	..	..	184	..	..	..	6	..	16
548	226	4	4	..	..	8,820	221	65	..	5	..	..	..	2,130	33	3	..	..	..	17
5,220	1,362	59	82	3	14	31,096	89	6	..	247	..	..	..	707	..	..	..	..	..	18
1,527	581	2	..	..	..	5,461	10	1	..	11	..	..	..	342	..	..	..	3	..	19
549	230	1	9	3	..	1,768	..	9	1	..	..	..	..	61	..	2	..	..	..	20

TABLE X.—OCCUPATION OR MEANS OF
DETAILS FOR DISTRICTS,

Serial No.	Class .. / Sub-class .. / Order .. / Group ..	B.—PREPARATION AND SUPPLY OF MATERIAL SUBSTANCES. IV.—TRANSPORT. 19.—Transport by water.—*concluded.*																	
		102.—*Ship-owners, boat-owners and their employees, officers, mariners, etc., ships-brokers, boatmen and tow-men.*						103.—*Persons (other than labourers) employed in harbours, docks, rivers and canals, including pilots.*						104.—*Labourers employed on harbours, docks, rivers and canals.*					
	District or State.	Total earners principal occupation.		Total working dependants.		Total earners with subsidiary occupation.		Total earners principal occupation.		Total working dependants.		Total earners with subsidiary occupation.		Total earners principal occupation.		Total working dependants.		Total earners with subsidiary occupation.	
		Males.	Females.	Males.	Females.	Males.	Females.	Males.	Females.	Males.	Females.	Males.	Females.	Males.	Females.	Males.	Females.	Males.	Females.
1	2	625	626	627	628	629	630	631	632	633	634	635	636	637	638	639	640	641	642
	PUNJAB ..	3,350	24	302	..	424	..	10,356	4	67	..	193	..	2,388	199	67	58	538	8
	BRITISH TERRITORY ..	3,008	15	293	..	381	..	7,492	4	61	..	112	..	2,031	174	67	58	177	5
	AMBALA DIVISION ..	88	..	5	..	7	..	1,400	..	7	..	33	..	487	82	5	39	129	3
1	Hissar ..	5	..	1	..	1	..	342	..	1	..	5	..	67	4	1	..	79	1
2	Rohtak ..	2	..	..	..	..	..	291	..	3	..	6	..	113	7	2	22	15	2
3	Gurgaon ..	6	..	3	..	6	..	110	..	..	..	3	..	10	8	..	..	..	..
4	Karnal ..	41	..	..	..	..	..	367	..	1	..	5	..	242	63	2	17	35	..
5	Ambala ..	30	..	1	..	..	..	288	..	2	..	14	..	55	..	..	..	..	..
6	Simla ..	4	..	..	..	..	..	2	..	..	..	..	..	..	..	..	..	..	..
	JULLUNDUR DIVISION	501	9	7	..	108	..	253	1	2	..	11	..	237	36	44	..	..	..
7	Kangra ..	163	4	2	..	70	..	1	..	..	..	..	..	..	..	..	..	..	..
8	Hoshiarpur ..	108	2	2	..	17	..	6	..	..	..	1	..	..	..	..	..	..	..
9	Jullundur ..	50	2	1	..	..	..	12	..	1	..	..	..	1	..	..	..	..	..
10	Ludhiana ..	18	1	..	..	4	..	26	..	..	..	1	..	61	..	44	..	..	..
11	Ferozepore ..	162	..	2	..	17	..	208	1	1	..	9	..	175	36	..	..	..	..
	LAHORE DIVISION ..	420	2	222	..	120	..	3,854	2	27	..	28	..	332	10	7	..	4	..
12	Lahore ..	70	1	..	..	1	..	1,085	2	..	..	2	..	93	10	..	..	..	..
13	Amritsar ..	56	1	2	..	10	..	625	..	2	..	5	..	4	..	..	..	1	..
14	Gurdaspur ..	181	..	217	..	103	..	354	..	1	..	2	..	63	..	..	..	1	..
15	Sialkot ..	59	..	..	..	..	..	264	..	..	..	3	..	63	..	1	..	2	..
16	Gujranwala ..	15	..	2	..	3	..	919	..	5	..	11	..	60	..	..	..	..	..
17	Sheikhupura ..	39	..	1	..	3	..	607	..	19	..	5	..	49	..	6	..	..	..
	RAWALPINDI DIVISION	770	4	45	..	53	..	584	1	6	..	18	..	655	45	7	19	7	2
18	Gujrat ..	59	..	6	..	6	..	153	..	2	..	7	..	274	..	..	..	..	..
19	Shahpur ..	191	2	..	..	8	..	321	1	2	..	9	..	374	45	7	19	7	2
20	Jhelum ..	83	1	2	..	7	..	38	..	..	..	1	..	..	..	..	..	..	..
21	Rawalpindi ..	16	..	..	..	..	..	54	..	2	..	1	..	7	..	..	..	..	..
22	Attock ..	89	..	..	..	18	..	6	..	..	..	..	..	..	..	..	..	..	..
23	Mianwali ..	332	1	37	..	14	..	12	..	..	..	..	..	..	..	..	..	..	..
	MULTAN DIVISION ..	1,224	..	14	..	93	..	1,401	..	19	..	22	..	320	1	4	..	37	..
24	Montgomery ..	45	..	4	..	5	..	5	..	..	..	1	..	..	..	..	..	..	..
25	Lyallpur ..	25	..	2	..	8	..	583	..	..	..	6	..	153	..	..	..	..	..
26	Jhang ..	460	..	..	..	18	..	161	..	..	..	..	..	16	..	..	..	1	..
27	Multan ..	157	..	6	..	22	..	171	..	18	..	3	..	..	1	..	..	..	..
28	Muzaffargarh ..	177	..	2	..	20	..	264	..	1	..	9	..	..	..	..	..	..	..
29	Dera Ghazi Khan ..	360	..	..	..	20	..	217	..	..	..	3	..	151	..	4	..	36	..
	PUNJAB STATES ..	347	9	9	..	43	..	2,864	..	6	..	81	..	357	25	..	..	361	3
	A.—Having Political relations with the Punjab Government. ..	7	..	3	..	1	..	23	..	..	..	4	..	12	..	..	..	..	..
1	Dujana ..	..	..	..	..	..	..	1	..	..	..	..	..	..	..	..	..	..	..
2	Pataudi ..	..	..	..	..	..	..	..	..	..	..	..	..	..	..	..	..	..	..
3	Kalsia ..	1	..	..	..	..	..	13	..	..	..	..	..	..	..	..	..	..	..
4	SIMLA HILL STATES ..	6	..	3	..	1	..	9	..	..	..	4	..	12	..	..	..	..	..
	Bashahr ..	6	..	..	..	..	..	..	..	..	..	..	..	..	..	..	..	..	..
	Nalagarh ..	..	..	..	..	..	..	1	..	..	..	..	..	..	..	..	..	..	..
	Keonthal ..	..	..	..	..	..	..	..	..	..	..	..	..	1	..	..	..	..	..
	Baghal ..	..	..	..	..	..	..	8	..	..	..	..	..	..	..	..	..	..	..
	Jubbal ..	..	..	..	..	..	..	..	..	..	..	4	..	..	..	..	..	..	..
	Other Simla Hill States ..	..	..	3	..	1	..	..	..	..	..	..	..	11	..	..	..	..	..
	B.—Having Political relations with the Government of India. ..	340	9	6	..	42	..	2,841	..	6	..	77	..	345	25	..	..	361	3
5	Loharu ..	..	..	..	..	..	..	..	..	..	..	..	..	..	..	..	..	..	..
6	Sirmoor ..	39	..	..	..	3	..	5	..	..	..	5	..	33	..	..	..	..	..
7	Bilaspur ..	30	..	..	..	11	..	1	..	..	..	..	..	3	..	..	..	5	..
8	Mandi ..	31	..	..	..	5	..	16	..	..	..	19	..	42	..	..	..	356	3
9	Suket ..	..	..	..	..	8	..	..	..	..	..	..	..	..	..	..	..	..	..
10	Kapurthala ..	56	1	..	..	2	..	..	..	..	..	..	..	..	..	..	..	..	..
11	Maler Kotla ..	..	..	..	..	..	..	1	..	..	..	..	..	..	..	..	..	..	..
12	Faridkot ..	..	..	..	..	..	..	2	..	..	..	1	..	..	..	..	..	..	..
13	Chamba ..	..	..	3	..	9	..	..	..	..	..	..	..	..	..	..	..	..	..
14	Patiala (Phulkian States)	14	..	..	..	3	..	675	..	6	..	36	..	..	..	..	..	..	..
15	Jind (Phulkian States)	14	..	..	..	1	..	246	..	..	..	10	..	4	..	..	..	..	..
16	Nabha (Phulkian States)	..	..	..	..	..	..	184	..	..	..	6	..	..	..	..	..	..	..
17	Bahawalpur ..	156	8	3	..	..	..	1,711	..	..	..	..	..	263	25	..	..	..	..
18	*Cities.* Lahore ..	4	..	..	..	..	..	641	..	..	..	..	..	62	..	..	..	..	..
19	*Cities.* Amritsar ..	..	..	..	..	..	..	342	..	..	..	3	..	..	..	..	..	..	..
20	*Cities.* Multan ..	..	..	..	..	..	..	61	..	2	..	..	..	..	..	..	..	..	..

LIVELIHOOD—GENERAL TABLE.

STATES AND CITIES.—*continued.*

B.—PREPARATION AND SUPPLY OF MATERIAL SUBSTANCES—*continued.*

IV. TRANSPORT—*continued.*

20—Transport by Road.

Total Order 20.						105.—*Persons (other than labourers) employed on the construction and maintenance of roads and bridges.*						106.—*Labourers employed on roads and bridges.*						107.—*Owners, managers, and employees (excluding personal servants) connected with mechanically driven vehicles (including trams).*						
Total earners principal occupation.		Total working dependants.		Total earners with subsidiary occupation.		Total earners principal occupation.		Total working dependants.		Total earners with subsidiary occupation.		Total earners principal occupation.		Total working dependants.		Total earners with subsidiary occupation.		Total earners principal occupation.		Total working dependants.		Total earners with subsidiary occupation.		
Males.	Females.	Males.	Females.	Males.	Females.	Males.	Females.	Males.	Females.	Males.	Females.	Males.	Females.	Males.	Females.	Males.	Females.	Males.	Females.	Males.	Females.	Males.	Females.	Serial No.
643	644	645	646	647	648	649	650	651	652	653	654	655	656	657	658	659	660	661	662	663	664	665	666	
107,788	**1,962**	**4,288**	**917**	**14,177**	**159**	**2,586**	**26**	**65**	**17**	**192**	..	**7,491**	**630**	**72**	**99**	**624**	**8**	**7,580**	**3**	**101**	..	**478**	..	
96,761	**1,628**	**3,931**	**737**	**12,314**	**133**	**1,942**	**26**	**56**	**4**	**176**	..	**6,600**	**605**	**44**	**73**	**449**	**8**	**6,748**	**3**	**98**	..	**459**	..	
17,541	**670**	**1,034**	**247**	**5,615**	**61**	**219**	..	**4**	**3**	**42**	..	**2,882**	**387**	**27**	**1**	**298**	**2**	**902**	..	**8**	..	**57**	..	
2,780	48	208	87	1,434	16	24	..	..	..	1	..	63	25	4	..	33	..	148	..	3	..	7	..	1
2,041	25	97	36	873	3	20	..	..	3	2	..	127	5	3	..	14	..	322	..	4	..	34	..	2
2,436	28	90	11	756	3	87	..	1	..	25	..	162	..	1	..	15	..	140	..	..	..	4	..	3
2,772	182	114	105	1,308	37	27	..	3	..	..	..	277	67	..	1	12	1	175	..	1	..	7	..	4
5,801	308	100	8	1,124	1	58	..	..	..	12	..	2,229	214	18	..	214	..	117	..	..	..	5	..	5
1,711	79	425	..	120	1	3	..	..	..	2	..	24	76	1	..	10	1	..	..	..	..	..	..	6
9,232	**82**	**269**	**65**	**1,698**	**9**	**259**	..	**15**	..	**13**	..	**971**	**38**	**6**	**65**	**72**	**3**	**1,211**	..	**26**	..	**132**	..	
1,946	52	62	65	351	9	246	..	15	..	6	..	667	36	4	65	69	3	136	..	6	..	21	..	7
1,924	1	28	..	700	..	13	..	..	..	7	..	15	..	..	..	..	..	171	..	2	..	18	..	8
1,687	9	79	..	186	..	..	..	..	..	..	..	31	..	1	..	..	..	301	..	6	..	21	..	9
1,115	9	55	..	230	..	..	..	..	..	..	..	80	1	1	..	3	..	230	..	5	..	36	..	10
2,560	11	45	..	231	..	..	..	..	..	..	..	178	1	..	..	..	..	373	..	7	..	36	..	11
37,357	**332**	**1,463**	**7**	**2,561**	..	**819**	..	**17**	**1**	**109**	..	**1,551**	**19**	**6**	..	**12**	..	**2,821**	**2**	**19**	..	**65**	..	
12,097	257	124	..	382	..	265	..	..	..	3	..	943	19	2	..	1	..	624	..	..	..	..	..	12
8,967	30	716	1	421	..	43	..	1	..	5	..	270	..	3	..	5	..	820	2	12	..	21	..	13
3,617	16	165	..	431	..	..	..	..	..	..	..	56	..	..	..	1	..	412	..	..	..	15	..	14
3,579	1	147	..	661	..	50	..	..	..	..	..	94	..	..	..	3	..	27	..	..	..	..	..	15
5,562	11	145	1	224	..	45	..	..	..	..	..	174	..	1	..	2	..	12	..	..	..	..	..	16
3,535	17	166	5	442	..	416	..	16	1	101	..	14	..	..	..	..	..	426	..	7	..	29	..	17
13,106	**362**	**492**	**6**	**1,254**	**4**	**613**	**26**	**20**	..	**7**	..	**992**	**156**	**5**	**3**	**66**	**2**	**1,442**	..	**26**	..	**43**	..	
3,587	181	178	5	381	2	141	..	2	..	..	..	161	154	..	3	3	2	247	..	14	..	22	..	18
2,833	19	33	1	192	1	59	1	..	..	2	..	528	2	..	..	11	..	476	..	1	..	8	..	19
1,463	90	64	..	155	..	16	..	..	..	..	..	126	..	..	..	42	..	207	..	5	..	4	..	20
2,212	7	129	..	252	..	388	..	18	..	5	..	64	..	5	..	5	..	212	..	5	..	6	..	21
1,115	33	47	..	171	..	1	4	..	..	..	..	1	..	..	..	..	..	208	..	1	..	3	..	22
1,896	32	41	..	103	1	8	21	..	..	..	..	112	..	..	..	5	..	92	..	..	..	..	..	23
19,525	**182**	**673**	**412**	**1,186**	**59**	**32**	..	..	..	**5**	..	**204**	**5**	..	**4**	**1**	**1**	**72**	**1**	**19**	..	**162**	..	
1,993	..	57	..	187	..	6	..	..	..	..	..	60	..	..	..	..	..	07	..	2	..	101	..	24
3,116	29	174	4	210	1	..	..	..	..	..	..	34	5	..	4	..	..	5	..	..	..	..	..	25
2,892	9	27	..	191	..	17	..	..	..	5	..	3	..	..	..	..	..	36	..	..	..	10	..	26
3,541	43	46	4	116	6	..	..	..	..	..	..	64	..	..	..	1	..	56	1	..	..	..	..	27
3,963	84	95	14	293	2	..	..	..	..	..	..	..	..	..	..	..	..	26	..	15	..	42	..	28
4,020	17	274	390	189	50	9	..	..	..	..	..	43	..	..	..	..	..	42	..	2	..	9	..	29
11,027	**334**	**357**	**180**	**1,863**	**26**	**644**	..	**9**	**13**	**16**	..	**891**	**25**	**28**	**26**	**175**	..	**832**	..	**8**	..	**19**	..	
926	**21**	**25**	**86**	**386**	**4**	**4**	..	..	..	**11**	..	**283**	**4**	**10**	**8**	**75**	..	**23**	..	**1**	..	**4**	..	
13	..	..	..	6	..	..	..	..	..	..	..	..	..	..	..	1	..	1	..	..	..	..	..	1
93	3	1	..	17	..	..	..	..	..	..	..	..	..	..	..	..	..	..	..	..	..	..	..	2
382	8	13	80	131	4	..	..	..	..	..	..	214	2	4	2	16	..	..	..	..	..	..	..	3
438	**10**	**11**	**6**	**232**	..	**4**	..	..	..	**11**	..	**69**	**2**	**6**	**6**	**58**	..	**22**	..	**1**	..	**4**	..	4
20	..	..	..	2	..	..	..	..	..	1	..	8	..	..	..	..	..	..	..	..	..	..	..	
136	..	3	..	80	..	..	..	..	..	..	..	29	..	..	..	18	..	11	..	..	..	1	..	
152	8	2	1	16	..	3	..	..	..	..	..	20	..	1	1	6	..	2	..	1	..	..	..	
13	..	..	..	6	..	..	..	..	..	..	..	2	..	..	..	..	..	..	..	..	..	..	..	
14	..	..	..	51	..	..	..	..	..	2	..	..	..	..	..	24	..	..	..	..	..	..	..	
103	2	6	5	77	..	1	..	..	..	8	..	10	2	5	5	10	..	9	..	..	..	3	..	
10,101	**313**	**332**	**94**	**1,477**	**22**	**640**	..	**9**	**13**	**5**	..	**608**	**21**	**18**	**18**	**100**	..	**809**	..	**2**	..	**15**	..	
15	1	..	..	7	8	..	..	..	..	..	..	..	..	..	..	..	..	2	..	..	..	..	..	5
322	2	..	..	48	..	3	..	..	..	3	..	142	2	..	..	22	..	12	..	..	..	..	..	6
93	..	8	..	54	..	..	..	..	..	..	..	2	..	..	..	3	..	..	..	..	..	..	..	7
225	4	..	..	123	..	1	..	..	..	2	..	97	..	..	..	56	..	44	..	..	..	13	..	8
57	..	..	..	..	..	..	..	..	..	..	..	..	..	..	..	..	..	..	..	..	..	..	..	9
182	2	..	..	25	..	1	..	..	..	..	..	10	..	..	..	..	..	16	..	..	..	..	..	10
462	..	12	..	35	..	..	..	..	..	..	..	18	..	..	..	1	..	52	..	1	..	2	..	11
695	..	7	..	15	..	2	..	..	..	..	..	48	..	..	..	..	..	39	..	1	..	..	..	12
42	13	..	..	14	..	..	..	..	..	..	..	24	13	..	..	10	..	5	..	..	..	..	..	13
2,412	2	81	31	31	..	612	..	9	13	..	..	95	..	15	18	..	..	598	..	..	..	..	..	14
498	21	110	22	445	..	..	..	..	..	..	..	30	6	..	..	..	..	24	..	..	..	..	..	15
1,944	80	100	41	680	14	16	..	..	..	..	..	111	..	3	..	8	..	11	..	..	..	..	..	16
3,154	188	14	..	..	..	5	..	..	..	..	..	31	..	..	..	..	..	6	..	..	..	..	..	17
6,891	52	1	..	11	..	237	..	..	..	3	..	593	..	..	..	1	..	450	..	..	..	..	..	18
2,594	3	1	..	2	..	15	..	1	..	..	..	106	..	..	..	..	..	595	..	..	..	2	..	19
515	..	7	1	..	..	..	..	..	..	..	..	12	..	..	..	..	..	123	..	..	..	..	..	20

TABLE X.—OCCUPATION OR MEANS OF
DETAILS FOR DISTRICTS,

Class .. B.—PREPARATION AND SUPPLY OF MATERIAL SUBSTANCES.

Sub-class .. IV.—TRANSPORT.

Order .. 20.—Transport by Road.

Group	108.—Owners, managers and employees (excluding personal servants) connected with other vehicles.						109.—Palki, etc., bearers and owners.						110.—Pack elephant, camel, mule, ass, and bullock owners and drivers.						111—Porters and messengers.	
District or State.	Total earners principal occupation.		Total working dependants.		Total earners with subsidiary occupation.		Total earners principal occupation.		Total working dependants.		Total earners with subsidiary occupation.		Total earners principal occupation.		Total working dependants.		Total earners with subsidiary occupation.		Total earners principal occupation.	
	Males.	Females.	Males.	Females.	Males.	Females.	Males.	Females.	Males.	Females.	Males.	Females.	Males.	Females.	Males.	Females.	Males.	Females.	Males.	Females.
2	667	668	669	670	671	672	673	674	675	676	677	678	679	680	681	682	683	684	685	686
PUNJAB ..	**24,641**	**87**	**897**	..	**2,806**	**1**	**1,270**	**22**	**49**	..	**105**	..	**42,358**	**758**	**2,074**	**524**	**6,596**	**75**	**21,862**	**436**
BRITISH TERRITORY ..	**21,732**	**53**	**766**	..	**2,379**	**1**	**1,226**	**22**	**49**	..	**71**	..	**39,400**	**584**	**2,003**	**507**	**6,216**	**75**	**19,113**	**335**
AMBALA DIVISION ..	**2,453**	**5**	**90**	..	**982**	**1**	**64**	..	..	..	**5**	..	**3,754**	**77**	**329**	**91**	**2,497**	**15**	**7,267**	**201**
1 Hissar ..	414	..	26	..	300	..	..	..	..	..	..	..	688	5	96	46	429	4	1,145	18
2 Rohtak ..	365	..	27	..	265	..	4	..	..	..	..	..	669	18	62	32	518	3	534	2
3 Gurgaon ..	264	..	3	..	59	1	..	..	..	..	..	..	846	26	80	7	601	2	937	2
4 Karnal ..	673	3	24	..	202	..	15	..	..	..	2	..	882	26	41	4	550	6	723	86
5 Ambala ..	734	2	10	..	156	..	10	..	..	..	2	..	646	2	50	2	393	..	2,001	90
6 Simla ..	3	..	..	..	..	..	29	..	..	..	1	..	25	..	..	..	6	..	1,627	3
JULLUNDUR DIVISION ..	**1,934**	**4**	**49**	..	**263**	..	**158**	..	**14**	..	..	..	**3,019**	**17**	**119**	.	**1,009**	..	**1,680**	**28**
7 Kangra ..	1	..	..	..	..	..	158	..	14	..	..	..	619	4	16	.	191	..	119	12
8 Hoshiarpur ..	206	..	..	..	26	..	..	..	..	..	..	..	1,315	1	26	..	649	..	4	..
9 Jullundur ..	731	..	26	..	49	..	..	..	..	..	..	..	458	8	31	..	66	..	163	1
10 Ludhiana ..	370	1	11	..	125	..	..	..	..	..	..	..	98	1	31	..	25	..	337	6
11 Ferozepore ..	623	3	13	..	63	..	..	..	..	..	..	..	329	3	15	..	78	..	1,057	4
LAHORE DIVISION ..	**12,195**	**42**	**425**	..	**730**	..	**217**	..	..	..	**1**	..	**15,123**	**233**	**813**	**6**	**1,371**	..	**5,131**	**36**
12 Lahore ..	4,326	36	67	..	50	..	217	..	..	..	..	..	3,626	100	30	..	310	..	2,096	12
13 Amritsar ..	3,612	3	243	..	86	..	..	..	..	..	1	..	2,428	16	382	1	200	..	1,704	9
14 Gurdaspur ..	768	2	29	..	117	..	..	..	..	..	..	..	2,067	6	134	..	260	..	314	8
15 Sialkot ..	1,281	1	33	..	417	..	..	..	..	..	..	..	1,511	..	69	..	189	..	616	..
16 Gujranwala ..	1,573	..	11	..	16	..	..	..	..	..	..	..	3,667	11	127	1	191	..	91	..
17 Sheikhupura ..	605	..	42	..	44	..	..	..	..	..	..	..	1,824	10	71	4	221	..	250	7
RAWALPINDI DIVISION	**2,286**	**2**	**63**	..	**261**	..	**162**	**22**	**6**	..	**4**	..	**5,075**	**142**	**304**	**2**	**603**	**2**	**2,536**	**14**
18 Gujrat ..	469	..	15	..	47	..	58	22	..	..	1	..	1,702	5	98	2	155	..	809	..
19 Shahpur ..	938	1	22	..	104	..	..	..	..	..	..	..	173	8	2	..	29	1	659	7
20 Jhelum ..	173	..	18	..	5	..	25	..	3	..	1	..	916	87	38	..	103	..	..	3
21 Rawalpindi ..	494	..	6	..	15	..	71	..	3	..	2	..	864	5	81	..	200	..	119	2
22 Attock ..	181	1	2	..	90	..	..	..	..	..	..	..	479	26	44	..	71	..	245	2
23 Mianwali ..	31	..	..	..	..	..	8	..	..	..	..	..	941	11	41	..	36	1	704	..
MULTAN DIVISION ..	**2,864**	..	**139**	..	**143**	..	**625**	..	**29**	..	**61**	..	**12,429**	**115**	**438**	**408**	**736**	**58**	**2,499**	**61**
24 Montgomery ..	613	..	38	..	25	..	23	..	..	..	..	..	461	..	8	..	41	..	623	..
25 Lyallpur ..	1,368	..	73	..	81	..	600	..	29	..	61	..	657	4	72	.	37	..	452	20
26 Jhang ..	117	..	..	..	3	..	..	..	..	..	..	..	1,834	9	17	..	171	..	785	..
27 Multan ..	187	..	..	..	4	..	..	..	..	..	..	..	2,990	42	44	4	92	6	44	..
28 Muzaffargarh ..	496	..	11	..	27	..	2	..	..	..	..	..	2,671	43	42	14	218	2	668	41
29 Dera Ghazi Khan ..	83	..	17	..	3	..	..	..	..	..	..	..	3,816	17	235	390	177	30	27	..
PUNJAB STATES ..	**2,909**	**34**	**131**	..	**427**	..	**44**	..	..	..	**34**	..	**2,958**	**174**	**71**	**17**	**380**	..	**2,749**	**101**
A.—HAVING POLITICAL RELATIONS WITH THE PUNJAB GOVERNMENT. ..	**112**	..	**3**	..	**24**	..	**9**	..	..	..	**3**	..	**372**	**3**	**5**	..	**161**	..	**123**	**14**
1 Dujana ..	8	..	..	..	1	..	..	..	..	..	..	..	1	..	..	..	4	..	3	..
2 Pataudi ..	17	..	..	..	5	..	..	..	..	..	..	..	67	3	1	..	12	..	9	..
3 Kalsia ..	57	..	3	..	11	..	..	..	..	..	..	..	58	..	..	..	11	..	53	6
4 SIMLA HILL STATES ..	**30**	..	..	..	**7**	..	**9**	..	..	..	**3**	..	**246**	..	**4**	..	**134**	..	**58**	**8**
Bashahr ..	..	..	..	..	..	..	..	..	..											
Nalagarh ..	8	..	..	..	2	..	9	..	..	..	..	..	12	..	..	..	1	..	..	..
Keonthal ..	19	..	..	..	..	..	..	..	..	..	2	..	78	..	3	..	37	..	1	..
Baghal ..	..	..	..	..	..	..	..	..	..	..	1	..	52	..	..	..	9	..	36	8
Jubbal ..	..	..	..	..	..	..	..	..	..	..	..	..	11	..	..	..	8	..	..	..
Other Simla Hill States ..	3	..	..	..	5	..	..	..	..	..	..	..	14	..	..	..	10	..	..	..
										..	..	..	79	..	1	..	51	..	1	..
B.—HAVING POLITICAL RELATIONS WITH THE GOVERNMENT OF INDIA. ..	**2,797**	**34**	**128**	..	**403**	..	**35**	..	..	..	**31**	..	**2,586**	**171**	**66**	**17**	**219**	..	**2,626**	**87**
5 Loharu ..	3	..	..	..	..	..	..	..	..	..	..	..	..	..	..	..	6	..	10	1
6 Sirmoor ..	9	..	..	..	9	..	..	..	..	..	..	..	151	..	..	..	8	..	5	..
7 Bilaspur ..	..	..	..	..	..	..	9	..	..	..	27	..	32	..	1	..	11	..	30	..
8 Mandi ..	1	..	..	..	..	..	..	..	..	..	..	..	81	..	..	..	48	..	1	4
9 Suket ..	..	..	..	..	..	..	..	..	..	..	..	..	17	..	..	..	..	..	40	..
10 Kapurthala ..	89	..	..	..	8	..	18	..	..	..	4	..	48	2	..	..	13	..	..	..
11 Maler Kotla ..	167	..	4	..	9	..	..	..	..	..	..	..	50	..	2	..	13	..	175	..
12 Faridkot ..	36	..	1	..	10	..	..	..	..	..	..	..	104	..	5	..	5	..	378	..
13 Chamba ..	..	..	..	..	..	..	..	..	..	..	..	..	13	..	..	..	4	..	..	..
14 Patiala (Phulkian States)	447	2	29	..	31	..	8	..	..	..	..	..	652	..	28	..	..	..	..	..
15 Jind (Phulkian States)	277	1	80	..	334	..	..	..	..	..	..	..	137	12	30	17	108	..	30	2
16 Nabha (Phulkian States)	18	..	..	..	2	..	..	..	..	..	..	..	..	..	..	..	..	..	1,788	80
17 Bahawalpur ..	1,750	31	14	..	..	..	..	..	..	..	..	..	1,211	157	..	..	..	..	151	..
18 *Cities.* Lahore ..	3,821	35	..	..	..	..	217	..	..	..	..	..	645	6	..	..	7	..	928	11
19 *Cities.* Amritsar ..	1,613	3	..	..	..	..	..	..	..	..	..	..	105	..	..	..	..	..	160	..
20 *Cities.* Multan ..	155	..	..	..	..	..	..	..	..	..	..	..	225	..	7	1	..	..	..	..

LIVELIHOOD.—GENERAL TABLE.

STATES AND CITIES.—*continued.*

B.—PREPARATION AND SUPPLY OF MATERIAL SUBSTANCES—*continued.*

IV.—TRANSPORT—*concluded.*

Transport by Road—*concluded.* III.—*Porters and messengers—concld.*				21.—Transport by Rail. *Total Order 21.*						112.—*Railway employees of all kinds other than coolies.*						113.—*Labourers employed on railway construction and maintenance and coolies, and porters employed on railway-premises.*						22.—Post Office, Telegraph and Telephone Services. *Total Order 22.* 114.—*Post Office, Telegraph and Telephone Services.*						
Total working dependants.		Total earners with subsidiary occupation.		Total earners principal occupation.		Total working dependants.		Total earners with subsidiary occupation		Total earners principal occupation.		Total working dependants.		Total earners with subsidiary occupation.		Total earners principal occupation.		Total working dependants.		Total earners with subsidiary occupation.		Total earners principal occupation.		Total working dependants.		Total earners with subsidiary occupation.		Serial No.
Males. 687	Females. 688	Males. 689	Females. 690	Males. 691	Females. 692	Males. 693	Females. 694	Males. 695	Females. 696	Males. 697	Females. 698	Males. 699	Females. 700	Males. 701	Females. 702	Males. 703	Females. 704	Males. 705	Females. 706	Males. 707	Females. 708	Males. 709	Females. 710	Males. 711	Females. 712	Males. 713	Females. 714	
1,030	277	3,376	75	81,948	527	815	38	1,697	1	52,077	269	316	28	966	1	29,871	258	499	10	731	..	11,023	24	204	5	697	..	
915	153	2,564	49	71,235	509	685	38	1,223	1	44,345	267	244	28	790	1	26,890	242	441	10	433	..	10,045	24	195	5	545	..	
576	152	1,734	48	8,679	47	30	1	78	..	5,751	13	17	..	34	..	2,928	34	13	1	44	..	1,544	5	11	5	177	..	
79	41	664	12	1,779	8	15	..	15	..	1,269	1	10	..	4	..	510	7	5	..	11	..	223	..	10	5	137	..	1
1	1	40	..	710	1	..	1	20	..	443	1	..	..	8	..	262	..	..	1	12	..	151	..	..	..	7	..	2
5	4	52	..	1,490	2	6	..	14	..	844	2	5	..	8	..	646	..	1	..	6	..	175	..	..	..	3	..	3
45	100	535	30	1,480	31	7	..	10	..	639	5	2	..	7	..	841	26	5	..	3	..	151	..	1	..	6	..	4
22	6	342	1	3,048	5	2	..	12	..	2,417	4	..	..	..	..	631	1	2	..	12	..	541	1	..	..	6	..	5
424	..	101	..	172	..	..	..	7	..	134	..	..	..	7	..	38	..	..	..	..	..	303	4	..	..	18	..	6
40	..	209	6	8,848	84	152	1	300	..	5,937	29	58	..	213	..	2,921	55	94	1	87	..	2,160	..	76	..	146	..	
7	..	64	6	738	2	4	..	33	..	387	1	3	..	29	..	351	1	1	..	4	..	302	..	42	..	64	..	7
..	..	..	..	640	1	5	..	24	..	325	..	1	..	13	..	315	1	4	..	11	..	288	..	1	..	27	..	8
16	..	50	..	2,011	4	52	1	71	..	1,213	2	23	..	27	..	798	2	29	1	44	..	379	..	25	..	12	..	9
7	..	41	..	1,665	9	24	..	151	..	1,415	9	24	..	139	..	250	..	..	..	12	..	906	..	6	..	38	..	10
10	..	54	..	3,794	68	67	..	21	..	2,587	17	7	..	5	..	1,207	51	60	..	16	..	285	..	2	..	5	..	11
183	..	278	..	31,896	44	67	..	353	..	21,606	34	33	..	295	..	10,290	10	84	..	58	..	3,898	16	16	..	65	..	
25	..	18	..	24,743	26	9	..	230	..	16,632	25	7	..	229	..	8,111	1	2	..	1	..	1,486	15	11	..	18	..	12
75	..	103	..	3,131	12	15	..	27	..	2,114	6	2	..	8	..	1,017	6	13	..	19	..	738	1	1	..	34	..	13
2	..	38	..	980	1	13	..	19	..	651	..	11	..	13	..	329	1	2	..	6	..	410	..	2	..	2	..	14
45	..	52	..	718	1	8	..	31	..	457	1	2	..	23	..	261	..	6	..	8	..	327	..	1	..	6	..	15
6	..	15	..	1,504	3	3	..	24	..	1,189	1	..	..	..	..	315	2	3	..	24	..	223	..	..	..	2	..	16
30	..	47	..	820	1	19	..	22	..	563	1	11	..	22	..	257	..	8	..	..	..	209	..	1	..	3	..	17
68	1	270	..	10,093	18	332	3	242	1	6,018	15	117	1	151	1	4,075	8	215	2	91	..	1,569	3	76	..	63	..	
49	..	153	..	2,310	4	55	1	86	1	1,570	4	53	1	82	1	740	..	2	..	4	..	572	1	57	..	15	..	18
8	1	38	..	1,699	4	..	1	1	..	859	1	..	..	..	..	840	3	..	1	1	..	244	..	..	..	2	..	19
..	..	..	..	1,943	6	77	1	85	..	583	6	40	..	16	..	1,360	..	37	1	69	..	160	2	12	..	21	..	20
11	..	10	..	1,363	4	16	..	19	..	950	4	7	..	9	..	413	..	8	..	10	..	405	..	6	..	15	..	21
..	..	7	..	1,332	..	4	..	37	..	1,103	..	4	..	30	..	229	..	..	..	7	..	121	..	1	..	7	..	22
..	..	62	..	1,446	..	181	..	14	..	953	..	13	..	14	..	493	..	168	..	..	..	67	..	..	..	3	..	23
48	..	78	..	11,719	316	104	33	250	..	5,043	176	19	27	97	..	6,676	140	85	6	153	..	1,379	..	16	..	94	..	
9	..	20	..	3,996	67	48	29	48	..	1,341	66	11	27	15	..	2,655	1	37	2	33	..	269	..	1	..	4	..	24
..	..	31	..	1,672	8	29	..	103	..	864	8	1	..	28	..	808	..	28	..	75	..	371	..	13	..	49	..	25
10	..	2	..	854	..	..	..	14	..	363	..	..	..	1	..	491	..	..	..	13	..	121	..	..	..	4	..	26
2	..	19	..	2,922	192	13	4	8	..	1,283	53	1	..	..	..	1,639	139	12	4	8	..	193	..	..	..	3	..	27
27	..	6	..	2,229	49	14	..	69	..	1,157	49	6	..	49	..	1,072	..	8	..	20	..	297	..	2	..	32	..	28
..	..	..	..	46	..	..	..	8	..	135	..	..	..	4	..	11	..	..	..	4	..	128	..	..	..	2	..	29
115	124	812	26	10,713	18	130	..	474	..	7,732	2	72	..	176	..	2,981	16	58	..	298	..	978	..	9	..	152	..	
6	78	108	4	235	1	3	..	118	..	170	1	..	..	91	..	65	..	8	..	22	..	100	..	6	..	72	..	
..	..	..	..	9	..	..	..	2	..	8	..	..	..	2	..	1	..	..	..	..	..	4	..	..	..	..	..	1
..	..	..	..	29	..	..	..	..	..	19	..	..	..	..	..	10	..	..	..	..	..	15	..	..	..	..	..	2
6	78	93	4	27	..	3	..	3	..	15	..	..	..	..	..	12	..	3	..	3	..	8	..	..	..	1	..	3
..	..	15	..	170	1	..	..	108	..	128	1	..	..	89	..	42	..	..	..	19	..	73	..	6	..	71	..	4
..	..	..	..	3	..	..	..	1	..	..	..	..	..	1	..	3	..	..	..	..	..	1	..	1	..	14	..	
..	..	..	..	8	..	..	..	..	..	4	..	..	..	..	..	4	..	..	..	..	..	5	..	..	..	1	..	
..	..	..	..	47	..	..	..	1	..	45	..	..	..	1	..	2	..	..	..	..	..	48	..	..	..	17	..	
..	..	..	..	..	..	..	..	..	..	..	..	..	..	..	..	..	..	..	..	..	..	4	..	..	..	4	..	
..	..	15	..	..	..	..	..	..	..	..	..	..	..	..	..	..	..	..	..	..	..	..	..	..	..	8	..	
..	..	..	..	112	1	..	..	106	..	79	1	..	..	87	..	33	..	..	..	19	..	15	..	5	..	27	..	
109	46	704	22	10,478	17	127	..	361	..	7,562	1	72	..	85	..	2,916	16	55	..	276	..	878	..	8	..	80	..	
..	..	1	8	..	..	..	..	..	..	..	..	..	..	..	..	..	..	..	..	..	..	4	..	..	..	..	..	5
..	..	6	..	1	..	..	..	..	..	1	..	..	..	..	..	..	..	..	..	..	..	39	..	..	..	12	..	6
7	..	10	..	6	..	..	..	1	..	2	..	..	..	..	..	4	..	..	..	1	..	5	..	..	..	..	..	7
..	..	4	..	306	..	1	..	214	..	98	..	..	..	7	..	208	..	1	..	207	..	23	..	..	..	18	..	8
..	..	..	..	..	..	..	..	..	..	..	..	..	..	..	..	..	..	..	..	..	..	1	..	..	..	3	..	9
..	..	..	..	506	..	..	..	31	..	189	..	..	..	21	..	317	..	..	..	10	..	43	..	..	..	3	..	10
5	..	10	..	487	..	31	..	39	..	59	..	2	..	2	..	428	..	29	..	37	..	20	..	..	..	1	..	11
..	..	..	..	430	..	1	..	1	..	57	..	1	..	1	..	373	..	..	..	..	..	15	..	..	..	..	..	12
..	..	..	..	81	..	7	..	9	..	..	..	..	..	..	..	81	..	7	..	9	..	16	..	..	..	6	..	13
..	..	..	..	3,965	15	36	..	61	..	3,000	..	18	..	49	..	965	15	18	..	12	..	362	..	3	..	23	..	14
..	5	3	..	968	..	2	..	2	..	830	..	2	..	2	..	138	..	..	..	..	..	108	..	..	..	3	..	15
97	41	670	14	339	2	1	..	2	..	194	1	1	..	2	..	145	1	..	..	..	..	95	..	..	..	7	..	16
..	..	..	..	3,389	..	48	..	1	..	3,132	..	48	..	1	..	257	..	..	..	..	..	147	..	..	..	4	..	17
1	..	..	..	22,495	22	1	..	225	..	14,607	21	1	..	224	..	7,888	1	..	..	1	..	1,003	15	4	..	11	..	18
..	..	..	..	2,070	6	..	..	..	..	1,546	6	..	..	..	..	524	..	..	..	..	..	455	1	..	..	6	..	19
..	..	..	..	1,143	..	..	..	..	..	252	..	..	..	..	..	891	..	..	..	..	..	49	..	..	..	..	..	20

TABLE X.—OCCUPATION OR MEANS OF
DETAILS FOR DISTRICTS,

Serial No.	Class / Sub-class / Order / Group	B.—Preparation and supply of material substances. V.—Trade. 23.—Banks, establishments of credit, exchange and insurance. Total Sub-class V. Total earners principal occupation. Males.	Females.	Total working dependants. Males.	Females.	Total earners with subsidiary occupation. Males.	Females.	Total Order 23. 115.—Bank managers, money-lenders, exchange and insurance agents, money-changers and brokers and their employees. Total earners principal occupation. Males.	Females.	Total working dependants. Males.	Females.	Total earners with subsidiary occupation. Males.	Females.	24.—Brokerage, commission and export. Total order 24. 116.—Brokers, commission agents, commercial travellers, warehouse owners and employees. Total earners principal occupation. Males.	Females.	Total working dependants. Males.	Females.	Total earners with subsidiary occupation. Males.	Females.
1	District or State. 2	715	716	717	718	719	720	721	722	723	724	725	726	727	728	729	730	731	732
	PUNJAB ..	**563,131**	**18,648**	**29,218**	**6,121**	**56,084**	**1,043**	**36,662**	**1,460**	**5,249**	**108**	**14,272**	**121**	**9,927**	**24**	**342**	**6**	**346**	..
	BRITISH TERRITORY ..	**478,363**	**15,547**	**25,008**	**5,332**	**45,067**	**806**	**30,923**	**1,191**	**4,661**	**88**	**11,513**	**86**	**8,193**	**21**	**293**	**6**	**288**	..
	AMBALA DIVISION ..	**80,522**	**5,004**	**6,625**	**2,020**	**10,720**	**316**	**9,828**	**367**	**2,852**	**26**	**8,775**	**28**	**1,711**	**1**	**86**	..	**67**	..
1	Hissar ..	15,964	865	1,837	435	2,204	52	1,403	76	105	19	573	8	627	1	68	..	33	..
2	Rohtak ..	16,333	700	811	492	1,893	42	2,379	64	78	3	802	9	166	..	..	..	4	..
3	Gurgaon ..	14,085	924	590	344	1,501	30	1,616	48	24	2	812	4	198	..	5	..	3	..
4	Karnal ..	14,504	1,198	3,078	263	2,110	147	2,669	123	2,627	2	737	3	276	..	12	..	12	..
5	Ambala ..	17,970	1,269	239	484	2,777	39	1,626	56	18	..	844	4	377	..	1	..	9	..
6	Simla ..	1,666	48	70	2	235	6	135	..	..	..	7	..	67	..	..	..	6	..
	JULLUNDUR DIVISION	**68,656**	**1,939**	**6,247**	**728**	**8,822**	**83**	**5,647**	**149**	**576**	**10**	**1,584**	**13**	**786**	**3**	**69**	**1**	**88**	..
7	Kangra ..	7,691	302	180	99	1,605	18	370	12	12	2	188	2	25	1	..	..	5	..
8	Hoshiarpur ..	12,534	350	167	161	2,108	21	1,458	59	27	3	550	5	14	..	..	..	..	..
9	Jullundur ..	15,740	518	4,719	211	2,887	22	1,553	20	450	1	381	3	188	..	64	..	12	..
10	Ludhiana ..	11,781	236	344	136	1,162	5	853	25	10	4	204	..	112	..	..	..	..	..
11	Ferozepore ..	20,910	533	837	121	1,060	17	1,413	33	77	..	261	3	447	2	5	1	21	..
	LAHORE DIVISION ..	**157,360**	**3,803**	**4,591**	**1,149**	**12,804**	**104**	**8,810**	**521**	**158**	**37**	**2,431**	**26**	**4,324**	**11**	**119**	**1**	**115**	..
12	Lahore ..	45,792	495	409	87	1,252	13	2,042	56	12	21	192	3	1,207	3	3	..	17	..
13	Amritsar ..	39,628	960	1,534	269	3,616	36	1,719	300	70	8	866	17	2,442	7	109	..	43	..
14	Gurdaspur ..	17,957	517	638	62	4,222	13	1,529	53	12	5	619	2	106	..	5	..	11	..
15	Sialkot ..	22,036	768	621	372	1,414	4	1,483	45	44	1	252	1	121	..	..	..	3	..
16	Gujranwala ..	20,387	713	556	276	1,503	28	1,623	64	14	2	363	3	223	..	..	..	17	..
17	Sheikhupura ..	11,560	350	833	83	797	10	414	3	6	..	139	..	225	1	2	1	24	..
	RAWALPINDI DIVISION	**64,453**	**2,892**	**3,924**	**1,025**	**4,950**	**143**	**2,824**	**129**	**169**	**15**	**987**	**15**	**225**	**5**	**14**	..	**26**	..
18	Gujrat ..	15,105	599	988	58	1,136	36	970	46	87	1	169	3	23	..	..	..	1	..
19	Shahpur ..	19,092	733	503	180	958	12	747	33	35	4	407	5	108	..	..	..	16	..
20	Jhelum ..	8,197	663	587	563	571	20	419	35	24	8	63	6	..	..	..	..	..	..
21	Rawalpindi ..	8,686	179	1,141	65	1,091	27	273	1	5	..	27	..	53	5	14	..	9	..
22	Attock ..	8,017	321	567	109	475	36	316	10	17	2	133	1	41	..	..	..	..	..
23	Mianwali ..	5,356	397	138	50	719	12	99	4	1	..	138	..	..	..	..	..	..	..
	MULTAN DIVISION ..	**107,372**	**1,909**	**3,621**	**410**	**7,771**	**160**	**3,814**	**25**	**906**	..	**2,786**	**4**	**1,147**	**1**	**5**	**4**	**42**	..
24	Montgomery ..	17,125	317	395	107	501	7	395	12	17	..	54	4	252	..	..	4	4	..
25	Lyallpur ..	22,527	635	590	90	1,309	38	118	..	..	..	169	..	373	..	..	..	11	..
26	Jhang ..	18,421	436	734	36	1,330	56	118	5	..	..	207	..	39	..	..	..	4	..
27	Multan ..	24,748	228	270	40	1,036	8	263	..	1	..	49	..	252	1	5	..	16	..
28	Muzaffargarh ..	9,289	229	413	29	849	47	316	4	..	..	57	..	56	..	..	..	3	..
29	Dera Ghazi Khan ..	15,262	64	1,219	108	2,746	4	2,604	4	888	..	2,250	..	175	..	..	..	4	..
	PUNJAB STATES ..	**84,768**	**3,101**	**4,210**	**789**	**11,017**	**237**	**5,739**	**269**	**588**	**20**	**2,759**	**35**	**1,734**	**3**	**49**	..	**58**	..
	A.—HAVING POLITICAL RELATIONS WITH THE PUNJAB GOVERNMENT. ..	**4,387**	**444**	**201**	**94**	**1,346**	**19**	**347**	**26**	**13**	..	**291**	**2**	**117**	..	**1**	..	**6**	..
1	Dujana ..	613	11	9	34	290	..	12	..	..	..	57	..	1	..	..	..	1	..
2	Pataudi ..	412	78	2	..	39	2	73	2	2	..	20	..	53	..	..	..	..	..
3	Kalsia ..	1,195	247	35	32	172	4	143	8	1	..	24	1	24	..	..	..	..	..
4	SIMLA HILL STATES ..	**2,167**	**108**	**155**	**28**	**845**	**13**	**119**	**16**	**10**	..	**190**	**1**	**39**	..	**1**	..	**5**	..
	Bashahr ..	123	2	24	15	121	5	1	..	..	..	..	..	1	..	..	..	1	..
	Nalagarh ..	516	26	15	2	162	1	83	12	8	..	98	..	9	..	..	..	..	..
	Keonthal ..	588	57	67	6	142	2	2	..	..	..	..	..	5	..	..	..	..	..
	Baghal ..	289	6	6	2	144	1	24	2	1	..	71	1	3	..	..	..	1	..
	Jubbal ..	38	1	2	..	58	1	..	..	..	..	..	..	4	..	..	..	3	..
	Other Simla Hill States ..	613	16	41	3	218	3	9	2	1	..	21	..	17	..	1	..	..	..
	B.—HAVING POLITICAL RELATIONS WITH THE GOVERNMENT OF INDIA. ..	**80,381**	**2,657**	**4,009**	**695**	**9,671**	**218**	**5,392**	**243**	**575**	**20**	**2,468**	**33**	**1,617**	**3**	**48**	..	**52**	..
5	Loharu ..	174	35	2	8	72	2	1	..	..	1	1	..	9	..	2	..	..	..
6	Sirmoor ..	1,144	51	37	11	382	6	104	1	..	..	162	..	12	..	..	..	..	..
7	Bilaspur ..	709	26	28	5	233	..	131	15	11	..	77	..	..	..	..	..	..	..
8	Mandi ..	1,322	112	37	4	739	19	42	4	..	..	126	3	2	..	..	..	1	..
9	Suket ..	471	22	55	32	135	..	..	..	..	..	..	..	..	..	..	..	..	..
10	Kapurthala ..	4,214	156	33	6	663	11	371	27	1	..	138	1	1	..	..	..	..	..
11	Maler Kotla ..	3,090	78	146	39	475	5	127	6	7	1	218	2	2	..	..	..	..	..
12	Faridkot ..	3,611	175	97	18	318	2	64	3	1	..	9	..	392	..	7	..	17	..
13	Chamba ..	1,023	72	44	53	338	8	19	5	..	..	23	..	1	..	..	..	..	..
14	Patiala (Phulkian States)	32,197	1,534	2,656	424	4,726	141	3,535	151	521	17	1,190	18	239	..	..	..	..	..
15	Jind (Phulkian States)	4,384	144	288	40	703	11	579	31	29	1	457	9	253	1	4	..	8	..
16	Nabha (Phulkian States)	5,243	126	256	29	780	5	67	..	5	..	2	..	385	2	6	..	26	..
17	Bahawalpur ..	22,799	126	330	26	105	8	352	..	..	..	65	..	321	..	29	..	..	..
18	Cities. Lahore ..	27,778	189	108	44	407	2	1,383	13	..	19	15	..	880	..	1	..	13	..
19	Cities. Amritsar ..	24,791	713	401	13	322	..	775	255	..	..	2	..	2,096	7	109	..	41	..
20	Cities. Multan ..	6,154	57	4	6	367	..	6	..	..	..	..	..	75	..	..	..	..	..

B.—PREPARATION AND SUPPLY OF MATERIAL SUBSTANCES—*continued.*

V.—TRADE—*continued.*

25.—Trade in textiles. Total Order 25. 117.—*Trade in piece-goods, wool, cotton, silk, hair and other textiles.*						26.—Trade in skins, leather and furs. Total Order 26. 118.—*Trade in skins, leather, furs, feathers, horn, etc., and the articles made from these.*						27.—Trade in wood. Total Order 27.						119. *Trade in wood (not fire-wood.)*						
Total earners principal occupation.		Total working dependants.		Total earners with subsidiary occupation.		Total earners principal occupation.		Total working dependants.		Total earners with subsidiary occupation.		Total earners principal occupation.		Total working dependants.		Total earners with subsidiary occupation.		Total earners principal occupation.		Total working dependants.		Total earners with subsidiary occupation.		
Males.	Females.	Males.	Females.	Males.	Females.	Males.	Females.	Males.	Females.	Males.	Females.	Males.	Females.	Males.	Females.	Males.	Females.	Males.	Females.	Males.	Females.	Males.	Females.	Serial No.
733	734	735	736	737	738	739	740	741	742	743	744	745	746	747	748	749	750	751	752	753	754	755	756	
50,293	**635**	**2,383**	**167**	**3,610**	**80**	**10,559**	**106**	**534**	**23**	**574**	..	**10,305**	**548**	**262**	**219**	**1,027**	**66**	**7,835**	**447**	**220**	**139**	**690**	**64**	
44,955	**610**	**2,118**	**162**	**2,923**	**75**	**9,176**	**66**	**486**	**23**	**492**	..	**9,154**	**337**	**204**	**111**	**714**	**41**	**7,017**	**259**	**171**	**70**	**572**	**41**	
5,500	**118**	**228**	**35**	**585**	**53**	**943**	**29**	**58**	**23**	**54**	..	**1,058**	**200**	**18**	**52**	**243**	**37**	**891**	**198**	**18**	**48**	**182**	**37**	
1,495	5	109	2	71	3	372	3	46	11	13	..	116	61	2	2	33	..	106	61	2	2	22	..	1
1,303	6	54	2	94	..	166	..	9	..	6	..	64	..	..	..	4	..	53	..	..	..	4	..	2
599	4	16	..	36	..	102	1	..	1	8	..	86	6	1	1	15	..	72	6	1	1	15	..	3
992	81	31	17	204	46	133	25	1	11	19	..	335	133	11	49	81	37	314	131	11	45	80	37	4
958	21	18	14	168	4	168	..	2	..	8	..	454	..	4	..	110	..	343	..	4	..	61	..	5
153	1	..	..	12	..	2	..	..	..	..	..	3	..	..	..	..	..	3	..	..	..	..	..	6
6,209	**43**	**698**	**9**	**687**	**1**	**1,099**	**8**	**118**	..	**72**	..	**1,192**	**72**	**39**	**51**	**132**	..	**619**	**9**	**29**	**16**	**100**	..	
1,464	24	30	..	236	..	68	3	12	..	5	..	57	57	..	35	1	..	56	..	..	..	1	..	7
889	..	17	..	53	..	170	3	..	..	46	..	291	6	3	..	90	..	233	6	..	..	81	..	8
1,730	7	605	4	271	1	403	..	97	..	16	..	201	1	19	..	13	..	192	1	17	..	12	..	9
1,075	3	21	5	101	..	152	1	2	..	3	..	322	..	..	..	1	..	4	..	..	..	1	..	10
1,051	9	25	..	26	..	306	1	7	..	2	..	321	8	17	16	27	..	134	2	12	16	5	..	11
14,559	**89**	**408**	**12**	**687**	**4**	**4,401**	**2**	**101**	..	**174**	..	**2,000**	**27**	**78**	**5**	**86**	**4**	**1,764**	**27**	**75**	**5**	**84**	**4**	
2,248	19	12	..	26	..	995	1	5	..	6	..	614	..	..	..	5	2	426	..	..	..	3	2	12
5,775	25	100	9	233	..	1,058	..	35	..	23	..	571	..	14	..	27	..	543	..	14	..	27	..	13
1,550	8	147	..	78	..	533	..	20	..	45	..	161	1	9	..	26	1	145	1	7	..	26	1	14
2,247	31	43	3	57	1	632	..	20	..	67	..	343	..	40	..	3	..	343	..	40	..	3	..	15
1,708	4	14	..	134	..	770	1	6	..	17	..	66	..	..	..	4	..	66	..	..	..	4	..	16
1,031	2	92	..	109	3	413	..	15	..	16	..	245	26	15	5	21	1	241	26	14	5	21	1	17
9,640	**199**	**622**	**15**	**618**	**2**	**677**	**3**	**144**	..	**52**	..	**357**	**9**	**2**	..	**10**	..	**349**	**9**	**2**	..	**10**	..	
3,936	10	288	2	308	2	330	3	13	..	20	..	117	..	..	..	1	..	117	..	..	..	1	..	18
1,397	94	7	..	51	..	116	..	4	..	6	..	34	4	..	..	1	..	26	4	..	..	1	..	19
960	80	78	8	55	..	58	..	2	..	4	..	108	3	..	..	..	..	108	3	..	..	..	..	20
1,811	..	195	..	136	..	32	..	..	..	..	..	42	..	1	..	..	..	42	..	1	..	..	..	21
1,023	15	54	5	16	..	60	..	125	..	11	..	18	1	..	..	1	..	18	1	..	..	1	..	22
513	..	..	..	52	..	81	..	..	..	11	..	38	1	1	..	7	..	38	1	1	..	7	..	23
9,047	**161**	**162**	**91**	**396**	**15**	**2,056**	**24**	**65**	..	**140**	..	**4,547**	**29**	**67**	**3**	**243**	..	**3,394**	**16**	**47**	**1**	**196**	..	
807	5	6	..	26	..	237	9	7	..	6	..	435	4	7	..	11	..	284	4	5	..	10	..	24
3,397	18	24	..	136	..	665	..	33	..	37	..	3,245	..	13	..	119	..	2,308	..	11	..	114	..	25
1,055	11	23	..	34	1	272	..	1	..	3	..	104	..	..	..	5	..	104	..	..	..	5	..	26
1,630	72	21	17	35	2	457	..	10	..	25	..	341	19	17	3	5	..	312	6	8	1	4	..	27
1,103	51	34	5	105	9	239	14	6	..	58	..	103	..	16	..	45	..	67	..	9	..	5	..	28
1,055	4	54	69	60	3	186	1	8	..	11	..	319	6	14	..	58	..	319	6	14	..	58	..	29
5,338	**25**	**265**	**5**	**687**	**5**	**1,383**	**40**	**48**	..	**82**	..	**1,151**	**211**	**58**	**108**	**318**	**25**	**818**	**188**	**49**	**69**	**118**	**23**	
275	..	**17**	..	**129**	..	**37**	..	..	..	**1**	..	**51**	**2**	**12**	**15**	**25**	..	**50**	**2**	**12**	**15**	**25**	..	
61	..	..	..	..	..	15	..	..	..	..	..	..	..	7	15	..	..	..	..	7	15	..	..	1
17	..	..	..	..	..	1	..	..	..	..	..	..	1	..	..	..	..	..	1	..	..	..	..	2
56	..	3	..	17	..	18	..	..	..	1	..	30	..	3	..	4	..	30	..	3	..	4	..	3
141	..	**12**	..	**112**	..	**3**	..	..	..	..	..	**21**	**1**	**2**	..	**21**	..	**20**	**1**	**2**	..	**21**	..	4
12	..	4	..	81	..	1	..	..	..	..	..	..	..	..	..	..	..	..	..	..	..	..	..	
15	..	..	..	3	..	..	..	..	..	..	..	12	..	..	..	7	..	12	..	..	..	7	..	
26	..	2	..	3	..	2	..	..	..	..	..	3	..	2	..	6	..	3	..	2	..	6	..	
6	..	..	..	1	..	..	..	..	..	..	..	..	1	..	..	3	..	..	1	..	..	3	..	
1	..	..	..	5	..	..	..	..	..	..	..	1	..	..	..	3	..	1	..	..	..	3	..	
81	..	6	..	19	..	..	..	..	..	..	..	5	..	..	..	2	..	4	..	..	..	2	..	
5,063	**25**	**248**	**5**	**558**	**5**	**1,346**	**40**	**48**	..	**81**	..	**1,100**	**209**	**46**	**93**	**288**	**25**	**768**	**186**	**37**	**54**	**93**	**23**	
8	..	..	..	..	..	..	..	..	..	2	..	2	..	..	..	..	..	2	..	..	..	..	..	5
91	1	19	3	4	..	..	..	..	..	1	..	90	10	..	2	9	1	90	10	..	2	9	1	6
124	2	3	1	21	..	..	..	..	..	..	..	..	..	..	..	..	..	..	..	..	..	..	..	7
302	7	2	..	89	2	10	..	..	..	2	..	90	10	..	..	98	..	13	..	..	..	14	..	8
64	..	7	..	14	..	1	..	..	..	..	..	24	4	2	30	17	..	..	..	..	..	..	..	9
386	8	..	..	44	..	238	..	..	..	56	..	95	..	1	..	14	..	54	..	1	..	8	..	10
214	1	24	..	19	..	79	..	1	..	7	..	69	..	..	2	7	2	69	..	..	2	7	2	11
286	..	3	..	21	..	17	28	..	..	..	..	77	5	5	6	9	..	66	5	5	6	9	..	12
147	5	3	1	80	3	2	..	..	..	..	..	124	8	7	9	93	2	11	..	..	..	5	..	13
1,186	..	89	..	229	..	211	..	13	..	..	..	418	169	28	44	15	20	353	169	28	44	15	20	14
253	..	13	..	10	..	6	..	1	..	..	..	1	2	..	..	..	..	1	2	..	..	..	..	15
271	1	9	..	20	..	25	2	..	..	..	..	42	1	1	..	26	..	41	..	1	..	26	..	16
1,731	..	76	..	7	..	757	..	33	..	13	..	68	..	2	..	..	..	68	..	2	..	..	..	17
1,684	12	..	..	..	..	469	..	..	..	..	..	487	..	..	..	2	..	311	..	..	..	..	..	18
4,632	23	34	..	41	..	826	..	22	..	..	..	425	..	..	..	2	..	403	..	..	..	2	..	19
194	1	..	..	2	..	204	..	..	..	7	..	31	1	..	..	..	..	26	1	..	..	..	..	20

TABLE X.—OCCUPATION OR MEANS OF
DETAILS FOR DISTRICTS,

Serial No.	Class / Sub-class / Order / Group — District or State	B.—PREPARATION AND SUPPLY OF MATERIAL SUBSTANCES. V.—TRADE. 27.—Trade in wood—concluded. 120.—Trade in barks. Total earners principal occupation. Males.	Females.	120. Total earners with subsidiary occupation. Males.	Females.	121.—Trade in bamboos and canes. Total earners principal occupation. Males.	Females.	121. Total working dependants. Males.	Females.	121. Total earners with subsidiary occupation. Males.	Females.	122.—Trade in thatches and other forest produce. Total earners principal occupation. Males.	Females.	122. Total working dependants. Males.	Females.	122. Total earners with subsidiary occupation. Males.	Females.	28.—Trade in Metals. Total Order 28. 123.—Trade in metals, machinery, knives, tools, etc. Total earners principal occupation. Males.	Females.	123. Total working dependants. Males.	Females.	123. Total earners with subsidiary occupation. Males.	Females.
1	2	757	758	759	760	761	762	763	764	765	766	767	768	769	770	771	772	773	774	775	776	777	778
	PUNJAB	37	3	..	1	2,412	91	33	76	336	1	21	7	9	4	1	..	3,190	628	121	221	292	36
	BRITISH TERRITORY	37	..	..	..	2,080	76	24	37	141	..	20	2	9	4	1	..	2,853	601	104	210	211	33
	AMBALA DIVISION	23	..	..	..	138	..	..	..	61	..	6	2	..	4	..	..	260	169	23	98	8	18
1	Hissar	7	..	..	..	2	..	..	..	11	..	1	..	..	..	..	..	36	23	3	17	2	13
2	Rohtak	..	..	..	..	11	..	..	..	..	..	..	..	..	..	..	..	55	16	5	26	1	..
3	Gurgaon	3	..	..	..	11	..	..	..	..	..	..	..	..	..	..	..	38	1	..	4	1	1
4	Karnal	3	..	..	..	14	..	..	..	1	..	4	2	..	4	..	..	41	15	6	13	1	2
5	Ambala	10	..	..	..	100	..	..	..	49	..	1	..	..	..	..	..	72	114	9	38	2	2
6	Simla	..	..	..	..	..	..	..	..	..	..	..	..	..	..	..	..	18	..	..	..	1	..
	JULLUNDUR DIVISION	6	..	..	..	566	63	10	35	32	..	1	..	..	..	..	..	463	183	16	78	20	6
7	Kangra	..	..	..	..	..	57	..	35	..	..	1	..	..	..	..	..	208	6	10	..	15	..
8	Hoshiarpur	4	..	..	..	54	..	3	..	9	..	..	..	..	..	..	..	43	94	..	27	..	..
9	Jullundur	..	..	..	..	9	..	2	..	1	..	..	..	..	..	..	..	59	37	1	19	2	6
10	Ludhiana	2	..	..	..	316	..	..	..	..	..	..	..	..	..	..	..	73	10	..	12	..	..
11	Ferozepore	..	..	..	..	187	6	5	..	22	..	..	..	..	..	..	..	80	36	5	20	3	..
	LAHORE DIVISION	..	..	..	..	231	..	3	..	2	..	5	..	..	..	..	..	1,473	114	32	34	27	1
12	Lahore	..	..	..	..	183	..	..	..	2	..	5	..	..	..	..	..	188	12	3	16	..	..
13	Amritsar	..	..	..	..	28	..	..	..	..	..	..	..	..	..	..	..	636	3	1	1	..	..
14	Gurdaspur	..	..	..	..	16	..	2	..	..	..	..	..	..	..	..	..	83	6	2	..	3	..
15	Sialkot	..	..	..	..	..	..	..	..	..	..	..	..	..	..	..	..	265	..	3	..	18	..
16	Gujranwala	..	..	..	..	..	..	..	..	..	..	..	..	..	..	..	..	180	29	..	..	6	..
17	Sheikhupura	..	..	..	..	4	..	1	..	..	..	..	..	..	..	..	..	121	64	23	17	..	1
	RAWALPINDI DIVISION	7	..	..	..	1	..	..	..	..	..	..	..	..	..	..	..	121	38	22	..	15	8
18	Gujrat	..	..	..	..	..	..	..	..	..	..	..	..	..	..	..	..	12	38	..	..	..	8
19	Shahpur	7	..	..	..	1	..	..	..	..	..	..	..	..	..	..	..	..	..	..	..	..	..
20	Jhelum	..	..	..	..	..	..	..	..	..	..	..	..	..	..	..	..	2	..	..	..	..	..
21	Rawalpindi	..	..	..	..	..	..	..	..	..	..	..	..	..	..	..	..	87	..	22	..	15	..
22	Attock	..	..	..	..	..	..	..	..	..	..	..	..	..	..	..	..	15	..	..	..	..	..
23	Mianwali	..	..	..	..	..	..	..	..	..	..	..	..	..	..	..	..	5	..	..	..	..	..
	MULTAN DIVISION	1	..	..	..	1,144	13	11	2	46	..	8	..	9	..	1	..	536	97	11	..	141	..
24	Montgomery	..	..	..	..	151	..	2	..	1	..	..	..	..	..	..	..	17	39	..	..	..	..
25	Lyallpur	..	..	..	..	937	..	2	..	5	..	..	..	..	..	..	..	285	57	..	..	102	..
26	Jhang	..	..	..	..	..	..	..	..	..	..	..	..	..	..	..	..	19	..	..	..	10	..
27	Multan	1	..	..	..	20	13	..	2	..	..	8	..	9	..	1	..	63	..	..	..	..	..
28	Muzaffargarh	..	..	..	..	36	..	7	..	40	..	..	..	..	..	..	..	120	1	11	..	29	..
29	Dera Ghazi Khan	..	..	..	..	..	..	..	..	..	..	..	..	..	..	..	..	32	..	..	..	..	..
	PUNJAB STATES	..	3	..	1	332	15	9	39	195	1	1	5	..	..	..	..	337	27	17	11	81	3
	A.—HAVING POLITICAL RELATIONS WITH THE PUNJAB GOVERNMENT.	..	..	..	..	1	..	..	..	..	..	..	..	..	..	..	..	14	2	..	3	2	..
1	Dujana	..	..	..	..	..	..	..	..	..	..	..	..	..	..	..	..	..	..	..	..	..	..
2	Pataudi	..	..	..	..	..	..	..	..	..	..	..	..	..	..	..	..	5	2	..	..	..	..
3	Kalsia	..	..	..	..	..	..	..	..	..	..	..	..	..	..	..	..	..	..	..	3	..	..
4	SIMLA HILL STATES	..	..	..	..	1	..	..	..	..	..	..	..	..	..	..	..	9	..	..	..	2	..
	Bashahr	..	..	..	..	..	..	..	..	..	..	..	..	..	..	..	..	..	..	..	..	..	..
	Nalagarh	..	..	..	..	..	..	..	..	..	..	..	..	..	..	..	..	5	..	..	..	..	..
	Keonthal	..	..	..	..	..	..	..	..	..	..	..	..	..	..	..	..	1	..	..	..	..	..
	Baghal	..	..	..	..	..	..	..	..	..	..	..	..	..	..	..	..	2	..	..	..	..	..
	Jubbal	..	..	..	..	..	..	..	..	..	..	..	..	..	..	..	..	..	..	..	..	2	..
	Other Simla Hill States	..	..	..	..	1	..	..	..	..	..	..	..	..	..	..	..	1	..	..	..	..	..
	B.—HAVING POLITICAL RELATIONS WITH THE GOVERNMENT OF INDIA.	..	3	..	1	331	15	9	39	195	1	1	5	..	..	..	..	323	25	17	8	79	3
5	Loharu	..	..	..	..	..	..	..	..	..	..	..	..	..	..	..	..	..	..	..	..	..	..
6	Sirmoor	..	..	..	..	..	..	..	..	..	..	..	..	..	..	..	..	3	..	..	..	..	..
7	Bilaspur	..	..	..	..	..	..	..	..	..	..	..	..	..	..	..	..	..	..	..	..	..	..
8	Mandi	..	..	..	..	76	5	..	..	84	..	1	5	..	..	..	..	7	..	..	..	3	..
9	Suket	..	..	..	..	24	4	2	30	17	..	..	..	..	..	..	..	1	..	..	..	..	..
10	Kapurthala	..	..	..	..	41	..	..	..	6	..	..	..	..	..	..	..	17	16	..	..	5	3
11	Maler Kotla	..	..	..	..	..	..	..	..	..	..	..	..	..	..	..	..	89	3	16	4	65	..
12	Faridkot	..	..	..	..	11	..	..	..	..	..	..	..	..	..	..	..	23	..	..	..	5	..
13	Chamba	..	3	..	1	113	5	7	9	88	1	..	..	..	..	..	..	14	..	..	..	1	..
14	Patiala } Phulkian States	..	..	..	..	65	..	..	..	..	..	..	..	..	..	..	..	115	..	..	..	..	..
15	Jind } Phulkian States	..	..	..	..	..	..	..	..	..	..	..	..	..	..	..	..	10	..	..	..	..	..
16	Nabha } Phulkian States	..	..	..	..	1	1	..	..	..	..	..	..	..	..	..	..	40	6	1	4	..	..
17	Bahawalpur	..	..	..	..	..	..	..	..	..	..	..	..	..	..	..	..	4	..	..	..	..	..
18	*Cities* { Lahore	..	..	..	..	171	..	..	..	2	..	5	..	..	..	..	..	178	..	1	..	..	..
19	*Cities* { Amritsar	..	..	..	..	22	..	..	..	..	..	..	..	..	..	..	..	422	..	1	..	..	..
20	*Cities* { Multan	..	..	..	..	5	..	..	..	..	..	..	..	..	..	..	..	24	..	..	..	..	..

B.—PREPARATION AND SUPPLY OF MATERIAL SUBSTANCES—*continued*.

V.—TRADE—*continued*.

29.—Trade in pottery, bricks and tiles. Total Order 29. 124.—*Trade in pottery, bricks, and tiles.*						30.—Trade in chemical products. Total order 30. 125.—*Drugs, dyes, paints, petroleum, explosives, etc.*						31.—Hotels, Cafes, restaurants, etc. Total Order 31.						126.—*Vendors of wine, liquors, aerated waters and ice.*						
Total earners principal occupation.		Total working dependants.		Total earners with subsidiary occupation.		Total earners principal occupation.		Total working dependants.		Total earners with subsidiary occupation.		Total earners principal occupation.		Total working dependants.		Total earners with subsidiary occupation.		Total earners principal occupation.		Total working dependants.		Total earners with subsidiary occupation.		
Males.	Females.	Males.	Females.	Males.	Females.	Males.	Females.	Males.	Females.	Males.	Females.	Males.	Females.	Males.	Females.	Males.	Females.	Males.	Females.	Males.	Females.	Males.	Females.	Serial No.
779	780	781	782	783	784	785	786	787	788	789	790	791	792	793	794	795	796	797	798	799	800	801	802	
2,414	**259**	**238**	**123**	**422**	**4**	**5,672**	**42**	**103**	**2**	**206**	..	**12,625**	**112**	**117**	**1**	**609**	**3**	**4,152**	**14**	**65**	..	**218**	**3**	
2,201	**252**	**223**	**106**	**361**	**4**	**5,142**	**40**	**100**	**2**	**191**	..	**11,176**	**106**	**100**	**1**	**509**	**1**	**3,275**	**11**	**50**	..	**139**	**1**	
80	**35**	**3**	**3**	**4**	..	**594**	**19**	**8**	..	**23**	..	**1,006**	**14**	**5**	**1**	**38**	..	**255**	**1**	..	..	**17**	..	
5	23	2	3	..	..	38	1	1	..	2	..	156	1	3	..	7	..	61	..	..	..	1	..	1
14	2	..	..	1	..	38	1	2	..	2	..	79	1	1	1	5	..	18	1	..	..	4	..	2
11	..	..	..	..	..	79	10	1	..	1	..	235	4	..	..	8	..	36	..	..	..	1	..	3
20	10	1	..	3	..	156	7	2	..	10	..	134	1	..	..	2	..	56	..	..	..	..	..	4
24	..	..	..	..	..	275	..	2	..	6	..	314	5	1	..	14	..	68	..	..	..	11	..	5
6	..	..	..	..	..	8	..	..	..	2	..	88	2	..	..	2	..	13	..	..	..	..	..	6
139	**48**	**31**	**44**	**11**	..	**799**	**2**	**9**	..	**46**	..	**1,120**	**11**	**16**	..	**51**	..	**660**	**2**	**10**	..	**39**	..	
..	..	..	..	..	..	3	..	..	..	1	..	32	4	..	..	1	..	5	1	..	..	..	..	7
56	14	20	5	3	..	375	2	1	..	30	..	145	..	3	..	12	..	124	..	3	..	11	..	8
19	9	1	37	1	..	230	..	6	..	10	..	286	1	10	..	22	..	212	1	4	..	17	..	9
26	23	..	..	3	..	91	..	..	..	..	..	310	2	..	..	7	..	138	..	..	..	7	..	10
38	3	10	2	4	..	91	..	2	..	5	..	347	4	3	..	9	..	181	..	3	..	4	..	11
660	**14**	**49**	**31**	**177**	..	**1,582**	**8**	**17**	..	**56**	..	**6,571**	**47**	**52**	..	**274**	**1**	**1,351**	**6**	**24**	..	**37**	**1**	
111	..	3	..	..	..	748	6	..	..	7	..	2,724	6	19	..	108	1	698	3	13	..	9	1	12
93	11	21	18	165	..	551	..	13	..	11	..	2,538	31	18	..	96	..	99	..	2	..	5	..	13
63	..	8	..	3	..	121	2	2	..	15	..	86	8	1	..	6	..	60	1	1	..	2	..	14
141	2	2	..	5	..	37	..	..	..	23	..	615	..	5	..	37	..	168	..	1	..	..	..	15
182	..	..	..	4	..	57	..	..	..	..	..	480	2	7	..	27	..	244	2	7	..	21	..	16
70	1	15	13	..	..	18	..	2	..	..	..	128	..	2	..	..	..	82	..	..	..	..	..	17
33	..	..	**4**	**5**	..	**321**	**11**	**22**	**2**	**13**	..	**928**	**16**	**11**	..	**39**	..	**266**	**1**	**8**	..	**14**	..	
20	..	..	..	3	..	35	8	..	1	..	..	160	..	..	..	11	..	102	..	..	..	7	..	18
5	..	..	4	..	..	137	3	4	1	10	..	207	..	..	..	12	..	19	..	..	..	..	..	19
..	..	..	..	..	..	37	..	..	..	..	..	158	2	..	..	..	..	42	..	..	..	..	..	20
1	..	..	..	..	..	19	..	..	..	..	..	193	7	11	..	15	..	73	..	8	..	7	..	21
..	..	..	..	..	..	86	..	18	..	3	..	90	..	..	..	..	..	20	..	..	..	..	..	22
7	..	..	..	2	..	7	..	..	..	..	..	30	7	..	..	1	..	10	1	..	..	..	..	23
1,289	**154**	**140**	**24**	**164**	**4**	**1,896**	..	**44**	..	**53**	..	**1,551**	**18**	**16**	..	**107**	..	**743**	**1**	**8**	..	**32**	..	
350	2	6	..	27	..	160	..	2	..	..	..	331	1	..	..	37	..	107	..	..	..	..	..	24
586	120	122	21	115	4	162	..	14	..	..	..	471	7	3	..	14	..	208	1	3	..	11	..	25
..	..	..	..	..	..	6	..	..	..	..	..	158	..	..	..	8	..	70	..	..	..	2	..	26
161	3	..	2	..	..	1,324	..	14	..	27	..	144	10	..	..	..	..	125	..	..	..	..	..	27
150	29	12	1	22	..	65	..	13	..	25	..	147	..	13	..	47	..	80	..	5	..	19	..	28
42	..	..	..	..	..	179	..	1	..	1	..	300	..	..	..	1	..	144	..	..	..	..	..	29
213	**7**	**15**	**17**	**61**	..	**530**	**2**	**3**	..	**15**	..	**1,449**	**6**	**17**	..	**100**	**2**	**877**	**3**	**15**	..	**79**	**2**	
1	..	..	..	..	..	**21**	..	..	..	**5**	..	**94**	**1**	..	..	**21**	**1**	**62**	**1**	..	..	**11**	**1**	
..	..	..	..	..	..	2	..	..	..	..	..	..	..	..	..	..	..	..	..	..	..	..	..	1
..	..	..	..	..	..	..	..	..	..	..	..	2	..	..	..	..	..	..	..	..	..	..	..	2
..	..	..	..	..	..	6	..	..	..	1	..	7	..	..	..	..	..	3	..	..	..	..	..	3
1	..	..	..	..	..	**13**	..	..	..	**4**	..	**85**	**1**	..	..	**21**	**1**	**59**	**1**	..	..	**11**	**1**	4
..	..	..	..	..	..	1	..	..	..	..	..	7	..	..	..	..	..	4	..	..	..	..	..	
..	..	..	..	..	..	7	..	..	..	..	..	12	..	..	..	..	..	10	..	..	..	..	..	
..	..	..	..	..	..	..	..	..	..	..	..	17	1	..	..	1	1	14	1	..	..	1	1	
..	..	..	..	..	..	..	..	..	..	..	..	..	..	..	..	..	..	..	..	..	..	..	..	
..	..	..	..	..	..	..	..	..	..	..	..	3	..	..	..	5	..	3	..	..	..	2	..	
1	..	..	..	..	..	5	..	..	..	4	..	46	..	..	..	15	..	28	..	..	..	8	..	
212	**7**	**15**	**17**	**61**	..	**509**	**2**	**3**	..	**10**	..	**1,355**	**5**	**17**	..	**79**	**1**	**815**	**2**	**15**	..	**68**	**1**	
..	..	..	..	..	..	..	1	..	..	..	..	10	..	..	..	..	..	10	..	..	..	..	..	5
..	..	..	..	..	..	3	..	..	..	..	..	14	..	..	..	1	..	11	..	..	..	1	..	6
..	..	..	..	..	..	1	..	..	..	..	..	1	..	..	..	..	..	1	..	..	..	..	..	7
..	..	..	..	..	..	8	..	..	..	1	..	46	1	..	..	36	1	38	1	..	..	28	1	8
38	4	4	..	13	..	..	..	..	..	..	..	8	..	..	..	1	..	8	..	..	..	1	..	9
3	..	..	..	..	..	61	..	..	..	8	..	84	..	..	..	10	..	79	..	..	..	10	..	10
2	3	..	..	..	..	68	..	3	..	1	..	74	4	4	..	7	..	34	1	3	..	6	..	11
..	..	..	..	..	..	7	..	..	..	..	..	77	..	2	..	3	..	34	..	1	..	3	..	12
..	..	..	..	..	..	12	..	..	..	..	..	22	..	..	..	6	..	13	..	..	..	5	..	13
112	..	11	17	..	..	285	..	..	..	..	..	588	..	8	..	6	..	259	..	8	..	6	..	14
..	..	..	..	..	..	5	..	..	..	..	..	29	..	2	..	3	..	28	..	2	..	3	..	15
4	..	..	..	48	..	16	1	..	..	..	..	79	..	1	..	6	..	52	..	1	..	5	..	16
33	..	..	..	..	..	43	..	..	..	..	..	323	..	..	..	..	..	228	..	..	..	..	..	17
81	..	3	..	..	..	663	..	..	..	2	..	2,401	5	11	..	96	1	581	2	8	..	5	1	18
3	..	..	..	..	..	261	..	..	..	2	..	2,164	31	15	..	92	..	66	..	..	..	3	..	19
2	..	..	..	..	..	123	..	..	..	..	..	26	10	..	..	..	..	21	..	..	..	..	..	20

TABLE X.—OCCUPATION OR MEANS OF
DETAILS FOR DISTRICTS,

Serial No.	District or State.	803	804	805	806	807	808	809	810	811	812	813	814	815	816	817	818	819	820
	Class ..	B.—PREPARATION AND SUPPLY OF MATERIAL SUBSTANCES.																	
	Sub-class ..	V.—TRADE.																	
	Order ..	31. Hotels, cafes, restaurants etc.—*concluded.*												32. Other trade in foodstuffs.					
	Group ..	127.—*Owners and Managers of hotels, cook-shops, sarais, etc., (and employees).*						128.—*Hawkers of drink and foodstuffs.*						*Total Order 32.*					
		Total earners principal occupation.		Total working dependants.		Total earners with subsidiary occupation.		Total earners principal occupation.		Total working dependants.		Total earners with subsidiary occupation.		Total earners principal occupation.		Total working dependants.		Total earners with subsidiary occupation.	
		Males.	Females.	Males.	Females.	Males.	Females.	Males.	Females.	Males.	Females.	Males.	Females.	Males.	Females.	Males.	Females.	Males.	Females.
1	2	803	804	805	806	807	808	809	810	811	812	813	814	815	816	817	818	819	820
	PUNJAB ..	2,631	78	14	..	248	..	5,842	20	38	1	148	..	149,599	9,434	5,226	3,529	12,902	443
	BRITISH TERRITORY ..	2,205	75	13	..	227	..	5,696	20	37	1	143	..	130,885	7,652	4,432	3,189	11,048	326
	AMBALA DIVISION ..	241	7	1	..	17	..	510	6	4	1	4	..	16,949	2,649	559	1,146	1,812	102
1	Hissar ..	25	..	1	..	6	..	67	1	2	..	..	..	3,409	258	222	172	318	9
2	Rohtak ..	15	..	..	..	1	..	46	..	1	1	..	..	3,061	334	125	313	269	24
3	Gurgaon ..	83	4	..	..	4	..	116	..	..	..	3	..	2,536	459	79	205	154	9
4	Karnal ..	5	..	..	..	1	..	73	1	..	..	1	..	2,981	571	92	134	459	32
5	Ambala ..	38	1	..	..	3	..	208	4	1	..	..	..	4,650	988	41	321	577	22
6	Simla ..	75	2	..	..	2	..	..	..	..	..	..	..	312	39	..	1	35	6
	JULLUNDUR DIVISION	184	9	..	..	7	..	276	..	6	..	5	..	14,537	907	751	470	1,893	45
7	Kangra ..	17	3	..	..	1	..	10	..	..	..	..	..	1,554	121	52	59	498	13
8	Hoshiarpur ..	15	..	..	..	1	..	6	..	..	..	..	..	2,797	116	23	98	631	15
9	Jullundur ..	17	..	..	..	..	..	57	..	6	..	5	..	3,492	285	453	139	357	8
10	Ludhiana ..	84	2	..	..	..	..	88	..	..	..	..	..	2,483	102	92	104	208	4
11	Ferozepore ..	51	4	..	..	5	..	115	..	..	..	..	..	4,211	283	131	70	199	5
	LAHORE DIVISION ..	1,284	35	4	..	132	..	3,936	6	24	..	105	..	41,558	1,750	1,117	767	4,485	31
12	Lahore ..	874	..	..	..	91	..	1,152	3	6	..	8	..	12,791	152	73	20	319	2
13	Amritsar ..	36	30	..	..	..	..	2,403	1	16	..	91	..	11,685	214	446	204	578	13
14	Gurdaspur ..	26	5	..	..	4	..	..	2	..	..	..	..	5,216	365	172	31	2,548	8
15	Sialkot ..	236	..	4	..	37	..	211	..	..	..	..	..	5,317	592	185	289	581	2
16	Gujranwala ..	86	..	..	..	..	..	150	..	..	..	6	..	4,232	400	139	203	177	5
17	Sheikhupura ..	26	..	..	..	..	..	20	..	2	..	..	..	2,312	27	102	20	232	1
	RAWALPINDI DIVISION	45	13	..	..	1	..	617	2	3	..	24	..	10,751	1,390	918	602	984	51
18	Gujrat ..	13	..	..	..	..	..	45	..	..	..	4	..	2,902	357	213	44	97	15
19	Shahpur ..	5	..	..	..	..	..	273	..	..	..	12	..	1,890	380	36	146	163	4
20	Jhelum ..	..	..	..	..	..	..	116	2	..	..	..	..	2,236	317	245	324	165	8
21	Rawalpindi ..	5	7	..	..		..	115		3	..	8	..	1,992	37	345	26	334	12
22	Attock ..	2	..	..	..	..	..	68	..	..	..	..	..	1,093	78	56	29	97	3
23	Mianwali ..	20	6	..	..	1	..	..	..	..	..	..	..	638	221	23	33	128	9
	MULTAN DIVISION ..	451	11	8	..	70	..	357	6	..	..	5	..	47,095	956	1,087	204	1,924	97
24	Montgomery ..	194	1	..	..	37	..	30	..	..	..	..	..	10,776	239	115	98	297	3
25	Lyallpur ..	136	..	..	..	3	..	127	6	..	..	..	..	4,303	163	269	43	283	15
26	Jhang ..	12	..	..	..	1	..	76	..	..	..	5	..	7,536	346	249	35	444	49
27	Multan ..	16	10	..	..	..	..	3	..	..	..	..	..	12,568	70	66	8	365	6
28	Muzaffargarh ..	58	..	8	..	28	..	..	..	..	..	..	..	5,136	99	170	18	285	23
29	Dera Ghazi Khan ..	35	..	..	..	1	..	121	..	..	..	..	..	6,776	39	218	2	250	1
	PUNJAB STATES ..	426	3	1	..	16	..	146	..	1	..	5	..	18,714	1,782	794	340	1,854	117
	A.—Having Political relations with the Punjab Government. ..	24	..	..	..	8	..	8	..	..	..	2	..	780	369	34	61	216	11
1	Dujana ..	..	..	..	..	..	..	..	..	..	..	..	..	66	8	2	18	22	..
2	Pataudi ..	..	..	..	..	..	..	2	..	..	..	..	..	48	61	..	..	1	..
3	Kalsia ..	2	..	..	..	..	..	2	..	..	..	..	..	391	232	6	22	47	3
4	SIMLA HILL STATES ..	22	..	..	..	8	..	4	..	..	..	2	..	275	68	26	21	146	8
	Bashahr ..	3	..	..	..	..	..	..	..	..	..	..	..	1	..	11	14	2	4
	Nalagarh ..	2	..	..	..	..	..	..	..	..	..	..	..	69	10	1	..	5	1
	Keonthal ..	3	..	..	..	..	..	..	..	..	..	..	..	145	47	11	4	59	1
	Baghal ..	..	..	..	..	..	..	..	..	..	..	..	..	1	2	..	2	17	..
	Jubbal ..	..	..	..	..	3	..	..	..	..	..	..	..	2	1	..	..	20	..
	Other Simla Hill States ..	14	..	..	..	5	..	4	..	..	..	2	..	57	8	3	1	43	2
	B.—Having Political relations with the Government of India. ..	402	3	1	..	8	..	138	..	1	..	3	..	17,934	1,413	760	279	1,638	106
5	Loharu ..	..	..	..	..	..	..	..	..	..	..	..	..	15	30	..	3	..	..
6	Sirmoor ..	3	..	..	..	..	..	..	..	..	..	..	..	277	29	..	6	123	5
7	Bilaspur ..	..	..	..	..	..	..	..	..	..	..	..	..	53	..	1	1	57	..
8	Mandi ..	8	..	..	..	6	..	..	..	..	..	2	..	487	38	30	4	316	4
9	Suket ..	..	..	..	..	..	..	..	..	..	..	..	..	18	14	..	2	16	..
10	Kapurthala ..	5	..	..	..	..	..	..	..	..	..	..	..	1,140	68	14	6	182	7
11	Maler Kotla ..	20	3	1	..	1	..	..	..	..	..	..	..	1,362	49	64	18	85	1
12	*Faridkot* ..	..	..	..	..	..	..	*43*	..	*1*	..	..	..	*596*	72	20	7	*206*	*1*
13	Chamba ..	9	..	..	..	1	..	..	..	..	..	..	..	109	16	12	27	26	2
14	Patiala (Phulkian States)	252	..	..	..	..	..	77	..	..	..	..	..	6,239	955	363	169	356	84
15	Jind (Phulkian States)	1	..	..	..	..	..	..	..	..	..	..	..	2,911	90	227	28	201	2
16	Nabha (Phulkian States)	9	..	..	..	..	..	18	..	..	..	1	..	666	50	22	8	70	..
17	Bahawalpur ..	95	..	..	..	..	..	..	..	..	..	..	..	4,061	2	7	..	..	..
18	*Cities.* Lahore ..	827	..	..	..	91	..	993	3	3	..	..	..	8,673	95	30	15	51	..
19	*Cities.* Amritsar ..	14	30	..	..	..	..	2,084	1	15	..	89	..	8,221	120	115	..	28	..
20	*Cities.* Multan ..	3	10	..	..	..	..	2	..	..	..	..	..	2,056	18	..	..	7	..

B.—PREPARATION AND SUPPLY OF MATERIAL SUBSTANCES—*continued.*

V. TRADE—*continued.*

32.—Other trade in foodstuffs.—*continued.*

129.—*Grain and pulse dealers.*						130.—*Dealers in sweet-meats, sugar and spices.*						131.—*Dealers in dairy products, eggs and poultry.*						132.—*Dealers in animals for food.*						
Total earners principal occupation.		Total working dependants.		Total earners with subsidiary occupation.		Total earners principal occupation.		Total working dependants.		Total earners with subsidiary occupation.		Total earners principal occupation.		Total working dependants.		Total earners with subsidiary occupation.		Total earners principal occupation.		Total working dependants.		Total earners with subsidiary occupation.		
Males.	Females.	Males.	Females.	Males.	Females.	Males.	Females.	Males.	Females.	Males.	Females.	Males.	Females.	Males.	Females.	Males.	Females.	Males.	Females.	Males.	Females.	Males.	Females.	Serial No.
821	822	823	824	825	826	827	828	829	830	831	832	833	834	835	836	837	838	839	840	841	842	843	844	
36,530	**282**	**1,746**	**79**	**1,984**	**10**	**13,559**	**80**	**880**	**6**	**743**	**7**	**18,790**	**1,095**	**540**	**585**	**4,560**	**118**	**2,723**	**21**	**130**	**2**	**602**	**4**	
27,917	**204**	**1,297**	**76**	**1,732**	**8**	**11,455**	**27**	**337**	**5**	**542**	**1**	**17,150**	**964**	**476**	**546**	**4,127**	**94**	**2,429**	**21**	**120**	**2**	**405**	**4**	
3,956	**28**	**192**	**86**	**210**	**1**	**3,119**	**10**	**80**	**3**	**152**	..	**1,669**	**112**	**26**	**17**	**354**	**17**	**85**	**2**	**5**	..	**28**	**2**	
1,313	12	106	25	36	1	484	2	28	..	42	..	246	8	11	12	28	1	19	1	1	..	2	..	1
799	9	28	..	21	..	543	1	9	2	11	..	126	3	3	..	25	1	5	..	3	..	1	..	2
743	3	15	11	16	..	587	1	18	..	7	..	179	9	1	..	22	3	3	..	..	..	..	..	3
655	1	38	..	102	..	508	2	20	..	17	..	290	10	6	..	75	3	42	..	..	..	..	2	4
410	3	5	..	35	..	925	4	5	1	48	..	789	45	5	4	203	3	16	..	1	..	25	..	5
36	..	..	..	..	..	72	..	..	..	27	..	39	37	..	1	1	6	..	1	..	..	..	..	6
2,917	**26**	**85**	**2**	**190**	..	**1,491**	**2**	**122**	..	**179**	**1**	**2,367**	**210**	**103**	**80**	**793**	**26**	**467**	**5**	**38**	**1**	**91**	**1**	
318	8	..	..	42	..	411	1	8	..	36	..	515	80	30	51	371	8	35	2	..	..	20	..	7
820	4	3	..	61	..	347	..	4	..	30	..	459	29	6	2	175	9	79	..	1	..	15	..	8
685	8	77	2	33	..	239	1	103	..	81	1	513	58	44	13	114	6	57	2	17	..	7	..	9
267	2	5	..	29	..	222	..	..	..	11	..	444	15	6	12	72	2	51	1	..	1	22	..	10
827	4	..	..	25	..	272	..	7	..	21	..	436	28	17	2	61	1	245	..	20	..	27	1	11
9,192	**40**	**320**	**18**	**491**	**2**	**4,804**	**5**	**51**	**1**	**78**	..	**8,223**	**341**	**211**	**193**	**2,697**	**14**	**1,482**	**13**	**76**	..	**232**	**1**	
2,192	7	3	..	61	..	2,445	4	22	1	39	..	2,671	40	6	2	156	..	356	5	1	..	5	1	12
3,557	8	159	14	139	..	624	1	8	..	6	..	2,587	108	126	118	163	9	361	1	52	..	91	..	13
759	14	34	2	59	..	595	..	4	..	7	..	928	105	32	19	2,194	4	68	..	2	..	17	..	14
727	1	15	..	95	..	559	..	3	..	4	..	1,264	55	21	37	116	..	101	..	5	..	30	..	15
1,502	8	89	2	45	2	490	..	13	..	22	..	620	26	22	..	54	..	323	7	3	..	24	..	16
455	2	20	..	92	..	91	..	1	..	..	..	153	7	4	17	14	1	273	..	13	..	65	..	17
3,048	**49**	**388**	**6**	**406**	..	**1,286**	**8**	**29**	**1**	**64**	..	**1,571**	**152**	**95**	**175**	**82**	**12**	**109**	..	..	..	**39**	..	
738	9	15	..	24	..	184	2	..	1	..	..	836	48	82	4	21	7	19	..	..	..	..	..	18
158	1	2	..	73	..	412	4	6	..	1	..	310	17	4	2	24	2	38	..	..	..	13	..	19
429	36	36	6	5	..	222	1	1	..	8	..	261	52	8	169	29	..	2	..	..	..	..	..	20
1,363	..	308	..	253	..	306	..	15	..	48	..	45	1	1	..	4	1	..	..	..	..	..	..	21
355	3	27	..	51	..	100	1	7	..	..	..	62	27	..	..	4	2	50	..	..	..	26	..	22
5	..	..	..	..	..	62	..	..	..	7	..	57	7	..	..	..	..	..	..	..	..	..	..	23
8,804	**61**	**312**	**14**	**435**	**5**	**755**	**2**	**55**	..	**69**	..	**3,320**	**149**	**41**	**81**	**201**	**25**	**286**	**1**	**1**	**1**	**15**	..	
3,714	40	7	14	169	..	338	2	1	..	27	..	622	29	3	57	27	2	114	1	..	..	6	..	24
2,167	17	165	..	112	4	36	..	..	..	..	..	567	29	7	3	64	3	136	..	1	..	6	..	25
77	..	..	..	..	..	83	..	3	..	16	..	220	5	1	..	18	..	1	..	..	..	..	..	26
293	1	28	..	22	..	8	..	..	..	..	..	940	27	5	3	15	6	20	..	..	..	3	..	27
332	..	34	..	22	..	130	..	36	..	25	..	438	43	18	17	34	14	14	..	..	..	..	..	28
2,221	3	78	..	110	1	160	..	15	..	1	..	533	16	7	1	43	..	1	..	..	1	..	..	29
8,613	**78**	**449**	**3**	**252**	**2**	**2,104**	**58**	**43**	**1**	**201**	**6**	**1,640**	**131**	**64**	**39**	**433**	**24**	**294**	..	**10**	..	**197**	..	
70	..	**2**	..	**7**	..	**129**	..	**2**	..	**26**	..	**145**	**61**	**22**	**21**	**118**	**9**	**8**	..	..	..	..	..	
18	..	..	..	..	..	15	..	..	..	..	..	..	..	..	..	..	..	..	..	..	..	..	..	1
7	..	..	..	..	..	12	..	..	..	..	..	3	..	..	..	..	..	..	..	..	..	..	..	2
31	..	1	..	4	..	37	..	..	..	3	..	12	3	2	..	12	2	..	..	..	..	..	..	3
14	..	**1**	..	**3**	..	**65**	..	**2**	..	**23**	..	**130**	**58**	**20**	**21**	**106**	**7**	**8**	..	..	..	..	..	4
..	..	..	..	..	..	..	..	..	..	..	..	1	..	10	14	2	4	..	..	..	..	..	..	
13	..	1	..	1	..	25	..	..	..	1	..	2	..	..	..	1	..	3	..	..	..	..	..	
..	..	..	..	1	..	22	..	1	..	2	..	114	47	9	4	53	1	..	..	..	..	..	..	
..	..	..	..	..	..	..	..	..	..	..	..	..	2	..	2	17	..	..	..	..	..	..	..	
..	..	..	..	..	..	..	..	..	..	..	..	2	1	..	..	20	..	..	..	..	..	..	..	
1	..	..	..	1	..	18	..	1	..	20	..	11	8	1	1	13	2	..	..	..	..	..	..	
8,543	**78**	**447**	**3**	**245**	**2**	**1,975**	**58**	**41**	**1**	**175**	**6**	**1,495**	**70**	**42**	**18**	**315**	**15**	**291**	..	**10**	..	**197**	..	
..	..	..	..	..	..	10	..	..	..	..	..	1	..	..	..	..	..	..	..	..	..	..	..	5
31	..	..	..	3	..	45	..	..	..	1	..	122	6	..	..	90	5	2	..	..	..	..	..	6
5	..	..	..	..	..	19	..	..	..	3	..	..	..	..	1	47	..	..	..	..	..	..	..	7
11	..	..	..	8	..	..	..	..	..	..	..	15	4	..	..	18	3	..	..	..	..	..	..	8
7	..	..	..	3	..	..	..	..	..	..	..	4	3	..	..	11	..	..	..	..	..	..	..	9
213	4	2	..	25	..	87	..	3	..	5	..	232	12	..	1	62	1	14	..	..	..	9	..	10
195	2	18	..	..	..	12	..	1	..	..	..	308	10	17	..	24	..	..	..	..	..	..	..	11
50	23	2	..	1	1	2	..	..	..	..	..	51	..	..	..	1	..	206	..	10	..	188	..	12
14	..	..	..	2	..	..	..	..	..	..	..	50	2	10	15	17	2	..	..	..	..	..	..	13
2,115	..	217	..	..	..	1,309	51	26	..	162	6	561	24	15	1	31	4	65	..	..	..	..	..	14
2,389	46	198	3	169	1	..	..	..	..	..	..	91	3	..	..	4	..	4	..	..	..	..	..	15
96	3	3	..	34	..	269	2	11	1	4	..	23	6	..	..	10	..	..	..	..	..	..	..	16
3,417	..	7	..	..	..	132	..	..	..	..	..	37	..	..	..	..	..	..	..	..	..	..	..	17
1,262	6	..	..	..	..	2,136	..	19	..	36	..	1,848	24	..	..	6	..	89	..	..	..	..	..	18
2,726	5	110	..	15	..	381	..	..	..	..	..	1,701	52	1	..	3	..	83	..	..	..	..	..	19
43	1	..	..	..	..	3	..	..	..	..	..	431	2	..	..	7	..	..	..	..	..	..	..	20

TABLE X.—OCCUPATION OR MEANS OF DETAILS FOR DISTRICTS,

Serial No.	Class / Sub-class / Order / Group	B.—PREPARATION AND SUPPLY OF MATERIAL SUBSTANCES. V.—TRADE. 32. Other trade in foodstuffs. 133.—Dealers in fodder for animals. Total earners principal occupation.		Total working dependants.		Total earners with subsidiary occupation.		134.—Dealers in other foodstuffs. Total earners principal occupation.		Total working dependants.		Total earners with subsidiary occupation.		135.—Dealers in tobacco. Total earners principal occupation.		Total working dependants.		Total earners with subsidiary occupation.		136.— Total earners principal occupation.	
	District or State.	Males.	Females.	Males.	Females.	Males.	Females.	Males.	Females.	Males.	Females.	Males.	Females.	Males.	Females.	Males.	Females.	Males.	Females.	Males.	Females.
1	2	845	846	847	848	849	850	851	852	853	854	855	856	857	858	859	860	861	862	863	864
	PUNJAB	**5,387**	**1,849**	**245**	**552**	**648**	**45**	**70,008**	**6,094**	**2,172**	**2,305**	**4,269**	**258**	**1,952**	**13**	**12**	..	**49**	**1**	**611**	..
	BRITISH TERRITORY	**4,869**	**1,567**	**223**	**523**	**585**	**38**	**65,062**	**4,859**	**1,967**	**2,037**	**3,588**	**180**	**1,631**	**10**	**11**	..	**42**	**1**	**334**	..
	AMBALA DIVISION	**1,059**	**1,153**	**25**	**351**	**137**	**32**	**6,591**	**1,340**	**223**	**739**	**918**	**49**	**401**	**4**	**7**	..	**8**	**1**	**40**	..
1	Hissar	71	5	5	..	1	..	1,204	230	69	135	208	6	57	..	2	..	..	1	13	..
2	Rohtak	53	34	1	15	7	4	1,456	286	77	296	204	19	67	1	4	..	..	..	3	..
3	Gurgaon	70	21	8	..	10	4	909	425	36	194	94	2	40	..	1	..	5	..	2	..
4	Karnal	241	223	4	55	63	8	1,153	334	24	79	198	19	80	1	..	..	1	..	10	..
5	Ambala	622	870	7	281	56	16	1,729	64	17	35	206	3	134	2	..	..	..	..	12	..
6	Simla	2	..	..	..	..	..	140	1	..	..	3	..	23	..	..	..	2	..	..	..
	JULLUNDUR DIVISION	**868**	**224**	**106**	**147**	**128**	**4**	**6,181**	**439**	**295**	**240**	**508**	**13**	**102**	**1**	**2**	..	..	..	**144**	..
7	Kangra	117	15	1	4	16	..	152	15	13	4	13	5	6	..	..	..	..	..	..	..
8	Hoshiarpur	91	24	1	10	27	2	954	59	8	86	322	4	14	..	..	..	..	..	33	..
9	Jullundur	356	134	96	73	28	1	1,594	82	114	51	94	..	9	..	2	..	..	..	39	..
10	Ludhiana	115	22	8	59	48	1	1,307	62	73	32	25	1	43	..	..	..	..	..	34	..
11	Ferozepore	189	29	..	1	9	..	2,174	221	87	67	54	3	30	1	..	..	..	..	38	..
	LAHORE DIVISION	**1,848**	**24**	**65**	..	**149**	..	**15,308**	**1,324**	**394**	**555**	**780**	**14**	**611**	**3**	..	..	**8**	..	**84**	..
12	Lahore	638	20	..	..	4	..	4,016	73	41	17	52	1	410	3	..	..	2	..	62	..
13	Amritsar	501	1	22	..	62	..	3,950	95	79	72	113	4	92	..	..	..	..	..	13	..
14	Gurdaspur	235	2	9	..	24	..	2,586	244	91	10	247	4	44	..	..	..	..	..	1	..
15	Sialkot	451	1	34	..	55	..	2,171	535	107	252	280	2	43	..	..	..	..	..	1	..
16	Gujranwala	13	..	..	..	4	..	1,284	359	12	201	28	3	..	..	..	..	..	..	..	..
17	Sheikhupura	10	..	..	..	..	..	1,301	18	64	3	60	..	22	..	..	..	1	..	7	..
	RAWALPINDI DIVISION	**525**	**124**	**8**	**25**	**131**	**2**	**3,825**	**1,055**	**396**	**395**	**247**	**37**	**375**	**2**	**2**	..	**14**	..	**7**	..
18	Gujrat	71	..	..	..	1	..	981	298	116	39	48	8	73	..	..	..	3	..	..	..
19	Shahpur	168	3	4	3	10	..	731	355	20	141	34	2	67	..	..	..	7	..	1	..
20	Jhelum	25	..	..	..	..	..	1,291	227	200	149	123	8	6	1	..	..	..	..	..	..
21	Rawalpindi	..	..	..	12	..	..	267	36	21	14	29	11	5	..	..	..	..	..	6	..
22	Attock	57	1	..	..	6	..	274	45	20	29	6	1	195	1	2	..	4	..	..	..
23	Mianwali	204	120	4	10	114	2	281	94	19	23	7	7	29	..	..	..	..	..	..	..
	MULTAN DIVISION	**569**	**42**	**19**	..	**40**	..	**33,157**	**701**	**659**	**108**	**1,140**	**67**	**142**	..	..	..	**17**	..	**59**	..
24	Montgomery	..	19	..	..	..	..	5,973	148	104	27	68	1	15	..	..	..	..	..	..	..
25	Lyallpur	136	2	5	..	40	..	1,261	115	91	40	61	8	..	..	..	..	..	..	..	..
26	Jhang	13	..	..	..	..	..	7,138	341	245	35	409	49	..	..	..	..	..	..	4	..
27	Multan	..	8	..	..	..	..	11,276	34	33	5	325	..	10	..	..	..	..	..	20	..
28	Muzaffargarh	159	10	14	..	..	..	4,007	46	68	1	183	9	32	..	..	..	17	..	23	..
29	Dera Ghazi Khan	261	3	..	..	..	..	3,502	17	118	..	94	..	85	..	..	..	..	..	12	..
	PUNJAB STATES	**518**	**282**	**22**	**29**	**63**	**7**	**4,946**	**1,235**	**205**	**268**	**681**	**78**	**321**	**3**	**1**	..	**7**	..	**277**	..
	A.—HAVING POLITICAL RELATIONS WITH THE PUNJAB GOVERNMENT.	**223**	**233**	**3**	..	**12**	**2**	**193**	**75**	**5**	**40**	**51**	..	**7**	..	..	..	..	..	**9**	..
1	Dujana	1	..	1	..	..	..	32	8	1	18	22	..	..	..	..	..	..	..	..	..
2	Pataudi	..	4	..	..	..	..	25	57	..	..	1	..	..	..	..	..	..	..	1	..
3	Kalsia	218	220	..	..	6	1	91	9	3	22	22	..	..	..	..	..	..	..	2	..
4	SIMLA HILL STATES	**4**	**9**	**2**	..	**6**	**1**	**45**	**1**	**1**	..	**6**	..	**7**	..	..	..	..	..	**6**	..
	Bashahr	..	..	1	..	..	..	..	..	..	..	..	..	..	..	..	..	..	..	..	..
	Nalagarh	2	9	..	..	..	1	21	1	..	..	2	..	..	..	..	..	..	..	3	..
	Keonthal	2	..	..	..	1	..	5	..	1	..	1	..	1	..	..	..	..	..	1	..
	Baghal	..	..	..	..	..	..	..	..	..	..	..	..	..	..	..	..	..	..	..	..
	Jubbal	..	..	..	..	..	..	..	..	..	..	..	..	..	..	..	..	..	..	..	..
	Other Simla Hill States	..	..	1	..	5	..	19	..	..	..	3	..	6	..	..	..	..	..	2	..
	B.—HAVING POLITICAL RELATIONS WITH THE GOVERNMENT OF INDIA.	**295**	**49**	**19**	**29**	**51**	**5**	**4,753**	**1,160**	**200**	**228**	**630**	**78**	**314**	**3**	**1**	..	**7**	..	**268**	..
5	Loharu	..	..	..	..	..	..	3	30	..	3	..	..	..	..	..	..	..	..	1	..
6	Sirmoor	31	12	..	..	25	..	42	11	..	6	4	..	2	..	..	..	..	..	2	..
7	Bilaspur	4	..	..	..	..	..	25	..	1	..	7	..	..	..	..	..	..	..	..	..
8	Mandi	1	11	..	1	..	1	459	23	30	3	288	..	1	..	..	..	2	..	..	..
9	Suket	3	7	..	..	2	..	4	4	..	2	..	..	..	..	..	..	..	..	..	..
10	Kapurthala	95	13	..	..	17	4	483	39	9	5	60	2	9	..	..	..	..	..	7	..
11	Maler Kotla	40	..	1	1	3	..	773	37	27	17	54	1	20	..	..	..	3	..	14	..
12	Faridkot	6	1	..	..	2	..	253	48	7	7	13	..	4	..	1	..	..	..	24	..
13	Chamba	3	5	..	2	2	..	42	9	2	10	5	..	..	..	..	..	..	..	..	..
14	Patiala (Phulkian States)	112	..	18	25	..	..	1,687	880	87	143	163	74	175	..	..	..	..	..	125	..
15	Jind (Phulkian States)	..	..	..	..	..	..	394	40	29	25	28	1	22	1	..	..	..	..	11	..
16	Nabha (Phulkian States)	..	..	..	..	..	..	177	39	8	7	8	..	24	..	..	..	2	..	77	..
17	Bahawalpur	..	..	..	..	..	..	411	..	..	..	..	..	57	2	..	..	..	..	7	..
18	Cities. Lahore	613	20	..	..	..	..	2,366	42	11	15	7	..	306	3	..	..	2	..	52	..
19	Cities. Amritsar	145	..	..	..	..	..	3,146	63	4	..	10	..	58	..	..	..	..	..	1	..
20	Cities. Multan	..	1	..	..	..	..	1,558	14	..	..	..	..	8	..	..	..	..	..	12	..

B.—PREPARATION AND SUPPLY OF MATERIAL SUBSTANCES—*continued.*																												
V.—TRADE—*continued.*																												
32. Other trade in foodstuffs—*concluded.*										33.—Trade in clothing and toilet articles.						34. Trade in furniture.												
Dealers in opium.				137.—*Dealers in Ganja.*						*Total Order 33.* 138.—*Trade in ready-made clothing and other articles of dress and the toilet (hats, umbrellas, socks, ready-made shoes, perfumes, etc.).*						*Total Order 34.*						139.—*Trade in furniture, carpets, curtains and bedding.*						
Total working dependants.		Total earners with subsidiary occupation.		Total earners principal occupation.		Total working dependants.		Total earners with subsidiary occupation.		Total earners principal occupation.		Total working dependants.		Total earners with subsidiary occupation.		Total earners principal occupation.		Total working dependants.		Total earners with subsidiary occupation.		Total earners principal occupation.		Total working dependants.		Total earners with subsidiary occupation.		
Males.	Females.	Males.	Females.	Males.	Females.	Males.	Females.	Males.	Females.	Males.	Females.	Males.	Females.	Males.	Females.	Males.	Females.	Males.	Females.	Males.	Females.	Males.	Females.	Males.	Females.	Males.	Females.	Serial No.
865	866	867	868	869	870	871	872	873	874	875	876	877	878	879	880	881	882	883	884	885	886	887	888	889	890	891	892	
..	..	45	..	39	..	1	..	2	..	8,960	103	358	24	624	6	2,746	72	57	23	127	..	960	47	25	18	39	..	
..	..	25	..	38	..	1	..	2	..	7,523	82	325	24	497	4	2,401	51	57	13	31	..	849	27	25	8	12	..	
..	..	8	..	29	..	1	..	2	..	2,658	46	78	24	199	3	474	11	18	3	14	..	221	9	9	3	4	..	
..	..	1	..	2	..	..	..	..	..	589	5	22	..	19	..	138	3	12	3	5	..	13	1	7	3	..	..	1
..	..	..	..	9	..	..	..	..	..	651	20	5	6	14	..	20	..	..	..	1	..	10	..	..	..	..	..	2
..	..	..	..	3	..	..	..	..	..	402	14	27	16	4	..	97	..	..	..	1	..	12	..	..	..	1	..	3
..	..	3	..	2	..	..	..	..	..	370	2	18	1	5	..	53	8	6	..	4	..	42	8	2	..	2	..	4
..	..	2	..	13	..	1	..	2	..	510	2	6	..	141	3	143	..	..	..	3	..	121	..	..	..	1	..	5
..	..	2	..	..	..	..	..	..	..	131	3	..	1	16	..	23	..	..	..	..	..	23	..	..	..	..	..	6
..	..	4	..	..	..	..	..	..	..	725	8	11	..	47	..	251	13	15	5	6	..	117	13	15	5	2	..	
..	..	..	..	..	..	..	..	..	..	57	1	..	..	1	..	37	..	..	..	4	..	..	..	..	..	..	..	7
..	..	1	..	..	..	..	..	..	..	123	2	4	..	5	..	13	..	..	..	..	..	..	..	..	..	..	..	8
..	..	..	..	..	..	..	..	..	..	71	1	2	..	3	..	34	3	..	2	2	..	..	3	..	2	2	..	9
..	..	1	..	..	..	..	..	..	..	266	3	3	..	23	..	127	10	15	3	..	..	105	10	15	3	..	..	10
..	..	2	..	..	..	..	..	..	..	208	1	2	..	15	..	40	..	..	..	..	..	12	..	..	..	..	..	11
..	..	5	..	1	..	..	..	..	..	1,480	24	44	..	57	..	1,329	17	2	3	1	..	477	..	1	..	..	..	
..	..	..	..	1	..	..	..	..	..	467	3	17	..	19	..	1,049	..	..	..	..	..	350	..	..	..	..	..	12
..	..	4	..	..	..	..	..	..	..	575	3	3	..	..	..	106	..	1	..	..	..	48	..	..	..	..	..	13
..	..	..	..	..	..	..	..	..	..	237	..	11	..	12	..	57	17	1	3	1	..	14	..	1	..	..	..	14
..	..	1	..	..	..	..	..	..	..	93	..	5	..	9	..	63	..	..	..	..	..	51	..	..	..	..	..	15
..	..	..	..	..	..	..	..	..	..	69	18	..	..	14	..	14	..	..	..	..	..	14	..	..	..	..	..	16
..	..	..	..	..	..	..	..	..	..	39	..	8	..	3	..	40	..	..	..	..	..	..	..	..	..	..	..	17
..	..	1	..	5	..	..	..	..	..	2,482	4	187	..	193	1	281	8	22	2	8	..	27	3	..	..	6	..	
..	..	..	..	..	..	..	..	..	..	33	..	..	..	2	..	54	..	..	2	2	..	..	..	..	..	..	..	18
..	..	1	..	5	..	..	..	..	..	1,938	4	21	..	26	1	72	2	..	..	4	..	23	2	..	..	4	..	19
..	..	..	..	..	..	..	..	..	..	90	..	17	..	58	..	13	2	..	..	..	..	..	..	..	..	..	..	20
..	..	..	..	..	..	..	..	..	..	264	..	142	..	104	..	112	..	21	..	..	..	..	..	..	..	..	..	21
..	..	..	..	..	..	..	..	..	..	142	..	..	..	..	..	22	4	1	..	1	..	4	1	..	..	1	..	22
..	..	..	..	..	..	..	..	..	..	15	..	7	..	3	..	8	..	..	..	1	..	..	..	..	..	1	..	23
..	..	7	..	8	..	..	..	..	..	183	..	5	..	1	..	66	2	..	..	2	..	7	2	..	..	..	..	
..	..	..	..	..	..	..	..	..	..	35	..	..	..	..	..	9	..	..	..	2	..	..	..	..	..	..	..	24
..	..	..	..	..	..	..	..	..	..	17	..	..	..	..	..	..	..	..	..	..	..	..	..	..	..	..	..	25
..	..	1	..	..	..	..	..	..	..	28	..	..	..	..	..	2	..	..	..	..	..	..	..	..	..	..	..	26
..	..	..	..	1	..	..	..	..	..	3	..	..	..	..	..	4	..	..	..	..	..	..	..	..	..	..	..	27
..	..	4	..	1	..	..	..	..	..	27	..	..	..	..	..	21	..	..	..	..	..	3	..	..	..	..	..	28
..	..	2	..	1	..	..	..	..	..	73	..	5	..	1	..	30	2	..	..	..	..	4	2	..	..	..	..	29
..	..	20	..	1	..	..	..	..	..	1,487	21	33	..	127	2	345	21	..	10	96	..	111	20	..	10	27	..	
..	..	2	..	1	..	..	..	..	..	150	5	2	..	68	2	45	1	..	..	42	..	15	..	..	..	..	..	
..	..	..	..	..	..	..	..	..	..	13	1	..	..	2	..	25	..	..	..	41	..	..	..	..	..	..	..	1
..	..	..	..	..	..	..	..	..	..	10	2	..	..	..	2	..	..	..	..	..	..	..	..	..	..	..	..	2
..	..	..	..	..	..	..	..	..	..	52	1	..	..	28	..	16	..	..	..	1	..	14	..	..	..	..	..	3
..	..	2	..	1	..	..	..	..	..	75	1	2	..	38	..	4	1	..	..	..	..	1	..	..	..	..	..	4
..	..	..	..	..	..	..	..	..	..	..	..	..	..	..	..	..	..	..	..	..	..	..	..	..	..	..	..	
..	..	..	..	..	..	..	..	..	..	22	..	..	..	5	..	3	1	..	..	..	..	..	..	..	..	..	..	
..	..	1	..	..	..	..	..	..	..	30	1	1	..	26	..	..	..	..	..	..	..	..	..	..	..	..	..	
..	..	..	..	1	..	..	..	..	..	1	..	..	..	..	..	..	..	..	..	..	..	..	..	..	..	..	..	
..	..	..	..	..	..	..	..	..	..	4	..	..	..	1	..	..	..	..	..	..	..	..	..	..	..	..	..	
..	..	1	..	..	..	..	..	..	..	18	..	1	..	6	..	1	..	..	..	..	..	1	..	..	..	..	..	
..	..	18	..	..	..	..	..	..	..	1,287	16	31	..	59	..	300	20	..	10	54	..	96	20	..	10	27	..	
..	..	..	..	..	..	..	..	..	..	4	..	..	..	..	..	..	..	..	..	..	..	..	..	..	..	..	..	5
..	..	..	..	..	..	..	..	..	..	37	3	..	..	5	..	1	..	..	..	..	..	1	..	..	..	..	..	6
..	..	..	..	..	..	..	..	..	..	2	..	..	..	..	..	1	..	..	..	..	..	..	..	..	..	..	..	7
..	..	..	..	..	..	..	..	..	..	50	2	..	..	..	..	..	1	..	..	..	..	..	1	..	..	..	..	8
..	..	..	..	..	..	..	..	..	..	..	..	..	..	..	..	2	..	..	..	..	..	2	..	..	..	..	..	9
..	..	4	..	..	..	..	..	..	..	51	..	..	..	5	..	..	..	..	..	..	..	..	..	..	..	..	..	10
..	..	1	..	..	..	..	..	..	..	81	3	3	..	..	..	5	..	..	..	..	..	4	..	..	..	..	..	11
..	..	1	..	..	..	..	..	..	..	163	..	3	..	3	..	..	..	..	..	..	..	..	..	..	..	..	..	12
..	..	..	..	..	..	..	..	..	..	13	..	..	..	2	..	..	..	..	..	..	..	..	..	..	..	..	..	13
..	..	..	..	..	..	..	..	..	..	649	8	24	..	39	..	217	..	..	..	..	..	62	..	..	..	..	..	14
..	..	..	..	..	..	..	..	..	..	88	..	..	..	3	..	29	7	..	2	..	..	12	7	..	2	..	..	15
..	..	12	..	..	..	..	..	..	..	95	..	1	..	2	..	30	12	..	8	54	..	15	12	..	8	27	..	16
..	..	..	..	..	..	..	..	..	..	54	..	..	..	..	..	15	..	..	..	..	..	..	..	..	..	..	..	17
..	..	..	..	1	..	..	..	..	..	463	..	17	..	19	..	999	..	..	..	..	..	330	..	..	..	..	..	18
..	..	..	..	..	..	..	..	..	..	461	3	1	..	..	..	91	..	..	..	..	..	44	..	..	..	..	..	19
..	..	..	..	1	..	..	..	..	..	2	..	..	..	..	..	2	..	..	..	..	..	..	..	..	..	..	..	20

TABLE X.—OCCUPATION OR MEANS OF
DETAILS FOR DISTRICTS,

Class: B.—PREPARATION AND SUPPLY OF MATERIAL SUBSTANCES.
Sub-class: V.—TRADE.

Serial No.	District or State.	84. Trade in furniture—concld. 140.—Hardware, cooking utensils, porcelain, crockery, glassware, bottles, articles for gardening, etc. Total earners principal occupation. Males.	Females.	Total working dependants. Males.	Females.	Total earners with subsidiary occupation. Males.	Females.	35. Trade in building materials. Total Order 35. 141.—Trade in building materials (other than bricks, tiles and woody materials). Total earners principal occupation. Males.	Females.	Total working dependants. Males.	Females.	Total earners with subsidiary occupation. Males.	Females.	36. Trade in means of Transport. Total Order 36. Total earners principal occupation. Males.	Females.	Total working dependants. Males.	Females.	Total earners with subsidiary occupation. Males.	Females.	142.—Dealers and hirers, in mechanical transport motors, cycles, etc. Total earners principal occupation. Males.	Females.	Total working dependants. Males.	Females.	Total earners with subsidiary occupation. Males.	Females.
1	2	893	894	895	896	897	898	899	900	901	902	903	904	905	906	907	908	909	910	911	912	913	914	915	916
	PUNJAB	1,786	25	32	5	88	..	884	18	28	34	20	..	13,396	35	358	75	1,923	15	657	3	8	..	10	..
	BRITISH TERRITORY	1,552	24	32	5	19	..	640	11	16	32	12	..	10,290	26	314	74	1,475	14	479	3	8	..	5	..
	AMBALA DIVISION	253	2	9	..	10	..	164	10	12	32	12	..	5,428	15	106	72	638	12	70	2	1	..	5	..
1	Hissar	125	2	5	..	5	..	30	..	1	..	1	..	721	..	11	..	128	..	8	..	..	..	..	..
2	Rohtak	10	..	..	..	1	..	45	5	4	32	9	..	1,036	5	31	1	65	..	10	2	1	..	4	..
3	Gurgaon	85	..	..	..	..	..	57	..	..	..	..	..	2,239	6	60	2	142	..	8	..	..	..	1	..
4	Karnal	11	..	4	..	2	..	20	3	7	..	..	..	792	1	2	..	54	12	7	..	..	..	..	..
5	Ambala	22	..	..	..	2	..	12	2	..	..	2	..	618	3	2	69	248	..	32	..	..	..	..	..
6	Simla	..	..	..	..	..	..	..	..	..	..	..	..	22	..	..	..	1	..	5	..	..	..	..	..
	JULLUNDUR DIVISION	134	..	..	..	4	..	18	..	..	..	..	..	742	2	10	2	178	..	14	..	..	..	..	..
7	Kangra	37	..	..	..	4	..	1	..	..	..	..	..	40	..	..	..	4	..	..	..	..	..	..	..
8	Hoshiarpur	13	..	..	..	..	..	..	..	..	..	..	..	165	..	2	..	68	..	..	..	..	..	..	..
9	Jullundur	34	..	..	..	..	..	..	..	..	..	..	..	261	2	3	2	52	..	6	..	..	..	..	..
10	Ludhiana	22	..	..	..	..	..	9	..	..	..	..	..	148	..	..	..	34	..	..	..	..	..	..	..
11	Ferozepore	28	..	..	..	..	..	8	..	..	..	..	..	128	..	5	..	20	..	8	..	..	..	..	..
	LAHORE DIVISION	852	17	1	3	1	..	402	1	4	..	..	..	2,104	6	89	..	270	1	315	1	7	..	..	..
12	Lahore	699	..	..	..	..	..	385	..	..	..	..	..	562	3	..	..	31	1	160	1	..	..	..	..
13	Amritsar	58	..	1	..	..	..	15	..	4	..	..	..	466	3	28	..	37	..	14	..	..	..	..	..
14	Gurdaspur	43	17	..	3	1	..	1	..	..	..	..	..	247	..	23	..	90	..	108	..	..	..	..	..
15	Sialkot	12	..	..	..	..	..	1	..	..	..	..	..	295	..	17	..	38	..	12	..	..	..	..	..
16	Gujranwala	..	..	..	..	..	..	..	..	..	..	..	..	282	..	13	..	50	..	15	..	..	..	..	..
17	Sheikhupura	40	..	..	..	..	..	..	1	..	..	..	..	252	..	8	..	24	..	6	..	7	..	..	..
	RAWALPINDI DIVISION	254	5	22	2	2	..	14	..	..	..	..	..	973	3	28	..	192	1	38	..	..	..	..	..
18	Gujrat	54	..	..	2	2	..	3	..	..	..	..	..	370	..	18	..	40	..	6	..	..	..	..	..
19	Shahpur	49	..	..	..	..	..	6	..	..	..	..	..	62	..	..	..	8	..	13	..	..	..	..	..
20	Jhelum	13	2	..	..	..	..	..	..	..	..	..	..	80	..	4	..	41	..	3	..	..	..	..	..
21	Rawalpindi	112	..	21	..	..	..	..	..	..	..	..	..	51	..	1	..	9	..	14	..	..	..	..	..
22	Attock	18	3	1	..	..	..	5	..	..	..	..	..	101	3	5	..	82	1	2	..	..	..	..	..
23	Mianwali	8	..	..	..	..	..	..	..	..	..	..	..	309	..	..	..	12	..	..	..	..	..	..	..
	MULTAN DIVISION	59	..	..	..	2	..	42	..	..	..	..	..	1,043	..	81	..	197	..	42	..	..	..	..	..
24	Montgomery	9	..	..	..	2	..	..	..	..	..	..	..	159	..	..	..	..	..	3	..	..	..	..	..
25	Lyallpur	..	..	..	..	..	..	1	..	..	..	..	..	293	..	55	..	64	..	8	..	..	..	..	..
26	Jhang	2	..	..	..	..	..	..	..	..	..	..	..	194	..	3	..	23	..	8	..	..	..	..	..
27	Multan	4	..	..	..	..	..	5	..	..	..	..	..	235	..	17	..	62	..	10	..	..	..	..	..
28	Muzaffargarh	18	..	..	..	..	..	..	..	..	..	..	..	56	..	5	..	9	..	..	..	..	..	..	..
29	Dera Ghazi Khan	26	..	..	..	..	..	36	..	..	..	..	..	106	..	1	..	39	..	13	..	..	..	..	..
	PUNJAB STATES	234	1	..	..	69	..	244	7	12	2	8	..	3,106	9	44	1	448	1	178	..	..	..	5	..
	A.—Having Political relations with the Punjab Government.	30	1	..	..	42	..	14	..	..	..	2	..	213	..	..	1	78	..	1	..	..	..	1	..
1	Dujana	25	..	..	..	41	..	13	..	..	..	..	..	104	..	..	..	49	..	..	..	..	..	..	..
2	Pataudi	..	..	..	..	..	..	..	..	..	..	..	..	60	..	..	..	..	..	..	..	..	..	..	..
3	Kalsia	2	..	..	..	1	..	..	..	..	..	..	..	38	..	..	..	3	..	..	..	..	..	..	..
4	SIMLA HILL STATES	3	1	..	..	..	..	1	..	..	..	2	..	11	..	..	1	21	..	1	..	..	..	1	..
	Bashahr	..	..	..	..	..	..	..	..	..	..	..	..	1	..	..	..	..	..	..	..	..	..	..	..
	Nalagarh	3	1	..	..	..	..	..	..	..	..	1	..	6	..	..	1	10	..	1	..	..	..	..	..
	Keonthal	..	..	..	..	..	..	..	..	..	..	..	..	1	..	..	..	1	..	..	..	..	..	1	..
	Baghal	..	..	..	..	..	..	..	..	..	..	..	..	1	..	..	..	..	..	..	..	..	..	..	..
	Jubbal	..	..	..	..	..	..	..	..	..	..	..	..	..	..	..	..	..	..	..	..	..	..	..	..
	Other Simla Hill States	..	..	..	..	..	..	1	..	..	..	1	..	2	..	..	..	10	..	..	..	..	..	..	..
	B.—Having Political relations with the Government of India.	204	..	..	..	27	..	230	7	12	2	6	..	2,893	9	44	..	375	1	177	..	..	..	4	..
5	Loharu	..	..	..	..	..	..	2	..	..	..	..	..	51	..	..	..	59	1	..	..	..	..	..	..
6	Sirmoor	..	..	..	..	..	..	..	..	1	..	3	..	36	..	..	..	20	..	..	..	..	..	..	..
7	Bilaspur	1	..	..	..	..	..	..	..	..	..	..	..	3	..	4	..	4	..	..	..	..	..	..	..
8	Mandi	..	..	..	..	..	..	..	3	..	..	..	..	..	..	..	..	..	..	..	..	..	..	..	..
9	Suket	..	..	..	..	..	..	..	..	..	..	..	..	1	..	..	..	..	..	..	..	..	..	..	..
10	Kapurthala	..	..	..	..	..	..	..	..	..	..	..	..	78	3	2	..	12	..	7	..	..	..	1	..
11	Maler Kotla	1	..	..	..	..	..	4	..	..	..	..	..	222	..	4	..	40	..	2	..	..	..	1	..
12	Faridkot	..	..	..	..	..	..	..	..	..	..	..	..	115	..	6	..	16	..	..	..	..	..	..	..
13	Chamba	..	..	..	..	..	..	..	..	..	..	..	..	..	..	..	..	..	..	..	..	..	..	..	..
14	Patiala (Phulkian States)	155	..	..	..	..	..	91	..	2	..	2	..	1,679	..	..	..	..	..	125	..	..	..	..	..
15	Jind (Phulkian States)	17	..	..	..	..	..	45	4	9	2	1	..	54	3	..	..	1	..	..	..	..	..	..	..
16	Nabha (Phulkian States)	15	..	..	..	27	..	1	..	..	..	..	..	597	3	28	..	208	..	14	..	..	..	3	..
17	Bahawalpur	15	..	..	..	..	..	87	..	..	..	..	..	62	..	..	..	15	..	29	..	..	..	..	..
18	Cities.—Lahore	669	..	..	..	..	..	363	..	..	..	..	..	185	1	..	..	..	..	150	1	..	..	..	..
19	Cities.—Amritsar	47	..	..	..	..	..	15	..	4	..	..	..	56	..	..	..	..	..	14	..	..	..	..	..
20	Cities.—Multan	2	..	..	..	..	..	3	..	..	..	..	..	74	..	2	..	..	..	7	..	..	..	..	..

LIVELIHOOD—GENERAL TABLE.

STATES AND CITIES.—*continued*.

B.—PREPARATION AND SUPPLY OF MATERIAL SUBSTANCES—*continued*.

V. TRADE—*continued*.

36. Trade in means of Transport—*concluded*.												37. Trade in fuel.						38. Trade in articles of luxury.						
143.—*Dealers and hirers in other carriages, carts, boats, etc.*						144.—*Dealers and hirers of elephants, camels, horses, cattle, asses, mules, etc.*						*Total Order 37.* 145.—*Dealers in fire-wood, charcoal, coal, cowdung, etc.*						*Total Order 38.*						
Total earners principal occupation.		Total working dependants.		Total earners with subsidiary occupation.		Total earners principal occupation.		Total working dependants.		Total earners with subsidiary occupation.		Total earners principal occupation.		Total working dependants.		Total earners with subsidiary occupation.		Total earners principal occupation.		Total working dependants.		Total earners with subsidiary occupation.		Serial No.
Males.	Females.	Males.	Females.	Males.	Females.	Males.	Females.	Males.	Females.	Males.	Females.	Males.	Females.	Males.	Females.	Males.	Females.	Males.	Females.	Males.	Females.	Males.	Females.	
917	918	919	920	921	922	923	924	925	926	927	928	929	930	931	932	933	934	935	936	937	938	939	940	
806	..	14	..	83	..	11,933	32	336	75	1,880	15	6,024	1,187	242	332	685	52	5,154	410	110	299	308	12	
214	..	5	..	34	..	9,597	23	301	74	1,436	14	5,559	1,101	208	242	647	44	4,132	307	86	236	190	10	
124	..	3	..	7	..	5,234	13	102	72	626	12	759	461	37	163	174	30	1,126	223	38	125	31	9	
..	..	..	..	..	..	713	..	11	..	128	..	183	262	20	77	38	8	171	31	9	40	16	5	1
66	..	..	..	..	..	960	3	30	1	61	..	39	20	3	17	58	7	190	36	13	22	2	..	2
57	..	3	..	7	..	2,174	6	57	2	134	..	128	152	12	65	8	10	183	69	4	31	1	3	3
..	..	..	..	..	..	785	1	2	..	54	12	27	22	..	..	16	3	209	65	7	30	8	1	4
1	..	..	..	..	..	585	3	2	69	248	..	343	5	2	4	51	2	366	21	5	2	3	..	5
..	..	..	..	..	..	17	..	..	..	1	..	39	..	..	..	3	..	7	1	..	..	1	..	6
29	..	2	..	24	..	639	2	8	2	154	..	401	50	15	34	58	2	507	22	4	1	44	1	
..	..	..	..	..	..	40	..	..	..	4	..	17	2	..	..	..	..	10	1	2	..	..	..	7
25	..	2	..	24	..	140	..	..	..	44	..	107	6	..	26	48	..	105	15	..	1	13	1	8
..	..	..	..	..	..	255	2	3	2	52	..	77	15	2	3	8	..	236	1	2	..	28	..	9
4	..	..	..	..	..	144	..	..	..	34	..	131	12	13	2	..	..	108	1	..	..	3	..	10
..	..	..	..	..	..	120	..	5	..	20	..	69	15	..	3	..	2	48	4	..	..	..	..	11
35	..	..	..	..	..	1,754	5	82	..	270	1	1,129	337	12	19	58	..	1,966	44	23	80	82	..	
..	..	..	..	..	..	402	2	..	..	31	1	526	12	3	..	6	..	858	2	10	..	21	..	12
..	..	..	..	..	..	452	3	28	..	37	..	208	250	4	13	16	..	295	10	3	1	3	..	13
..	..	..	..	..	..	139	..	23	..	90	..	60	14	..	5	2	..	84	10	..	1	6	..	14
..	..	..	..	..	..	283	..	17	..	38	..	222	..	5	1	29	..	612	15	9	75	51	..	15
..	..	..	..	..	..	267	..	13	..	50	..	111	61	..	..	5	..	74	4	1	3	..	..	16
35	..	..	..	..	..	211	..	1	..	24	..	1	..	..	..	..	..	43	3	..	..	1	..	17
22	..	..	..	..	..	913	3	28	..	192	1	1,102	189	127	25	267	7	214	13	2	20	6	..	
..	..	..	..	..	..	364	..	18	..	40	..	643	30	43	3	19	5	28	..	..	..	..	..	18
22	..	..	..	..	..	27	..	..	..	8	..	45	33	2	12	17	..	102	11	..	2	1	..	19
..	..	..	..	..	..	77	..	4	..	41	..	176	1	72	..	10	..	27	1	..	..	..	..	20
..	..	..	..	..	..	37	..	1	..	9	..	86	..	7	..	19	..	31	1	1	18	3	..	21
..	..	..	..	..	..	99	3	5	..	82	1	5	2	..	..	2	..	10	..	1	..	..	..	22
..	..	..	..	..	..	309	..	..	..	12	..	141	123	3	10	200	2	16	..	..	..	2	..	23
4	..	..	..	3	..	997	..	81	..	194	..	2,168	64	17	1	92	5	319	5	19	10	27	..	
..	..	..	..	..	..	156	..	..	..	..	..	516	..	..	..	19	..	18	..	..	..	1	..	24
..	..	..	..	..	..	285	..	55	..	64	..	881	1	..	1	7	..	58	..	6	..	..	..	25
4	..	..	..	3	..	182	..	3	..	20	..	374	63	3	..	11	5	53	..	..	..	..	..	26
..	..	..	..	..	..	225	..	17	..	62	..	152	..	14	..	..	..	41	3	..	10	4	..	27
..	..	..	..	..	..	56	..	5	..	9	..	75	..	..	..	53	..	110	2	13	..	22	..	28
..	..	..	..	..	..	93	..	1	..	39	..	170	..	..	..	2	..	39	..	..	..	..	..	29
592	..	9	..	49	..	2,336	9	35	1	394	1	465	86	34	90	38	8	1,022	103	24	63	118	2	
..	..	..	..	1	..	212	..	..	1	71	..	9	6	..	3	3	..	67	12	1	7	4	..	
..	..	..	..	1	..	104	..	..	..	48	..	1	..	..	..	1	..	10	..	..	1	..	..	1
..	..	..	..	..	..	60	..	..	..	..	..	3	..	..	..	..	..	5	7	..	..	..	..	2
..	..	..	..	..	..	38	..	..	..	3	..	2	1	..	1	2	..	44	4	..	6	..	..	3
..	..	..	..	..	..	10	..	..	1	20	..	3	5	..	2	..	..	8	1	1	..	4	..	4
..	..	..	..	..	..	1	..	..	..	..	..	..	..	..	..	..	..	..	..	..	..	..	..	
..	..	..	..	..	..	5	..	..	1	10	..	..	..	..	..	..	..	3	1	..	..	1	..	
..	..	..	..	..	..	1	..	..	..	..	..	..	5	..	2	..	..	1	..	..	..	..	..	
..	..	..	..	..	..	1	..	..	..	..	..	..	..	..	..	..	..	1	..	..	..	2	..	
..	..	..	..	..	..	..	..	..	..	..	..	..	..	..	..	..	..	..	..	..	..	..	..	
..	..	..	..	..	..	2	..	..	..	10	..	3	..	..	..	..	..	3	..	1	..	1	..	
592	..	9	..	48	..	2,124	9	35	..	823	1	456	80	34	87	85	8	955	91	28	56	114	2	
..	..	..	..	..	..	51	..	..	..	59	1	..	2	..	4	..	1	1	..	..	..	..	..	5
..	..	..	..	..	..	36	..	..	..	20	..	1	..	..	..	..	..	24	..	..	..	..	..	6
..	..	..	..	..	..	3	..	4	..	4	..	3	..	..	..	1	..	9	..	..	..	..	..	7
..	..	..	..	..	..	..	..	..	..	..	..	..	25	..	..	..	5	4	..	..	..	1	..	8
..	..	..	..	..	..	1	..	..	..	..	..	..	..	..	..	2	..	..	..	..	..	..	..	9
..	..	..	..	..	..	66	3	2	..	11	..	1	..	..	..	..	..	16	..	..	..	..	..	10
..	..	..	..	..	..	220	..	4	..	39	..	5	3	4	14	3	..	25	..	..	..	..	..	11
..	..	..	..	..	..	116	..	6	..	16	..	3	..	..	..	..	..	6	..	..	..	..	..	12
..	..	..	..	..	..	..	..	..	..	..	..	47	33	3	16	10	..	5	..	..	..	..	..	13
421	..	..	..	..	..	1,133	..	..	..	..	..	272	..	27	48	..	..	522	73	19	47	105	2	14
..	..	..	..	..	..	54	3	..	..	1	..	25	..	..	..	9	..	82	6	1	7	7	..	15
171	..	9	..	48	..	412	3	19	..	158	..	16	17	..	5	10	2	66	12	3	2	1	..	16
..	..	..	..	..	..	33	..	..	..	15	..	83	..	..	..	..	..	195	..	..	..	..	..	17
..	..	..	..	..	..	35	..	..	..	..	..	355	4	..	..	..	..	815	..	10	..	7	..	18
..	..	..	..	..	..	42	..	..	..	..	..	111	241	..	13	1	..	173	7	3	..	..	..	19
..	..	..	..	..	..	67	..	2	..	..	..	59	..	..	..	..	..	21	1	..	6	..	..	20

TABLE X.—OCCUPATION OR MEANS OF
DETAILS FOR DISTRICTS,

Serial No.	Class / Sub-class / Order / Group / District or State																				
	Class ..	B.—PREPARATION AND SUPPLY OF MATERIAL SUBSTANCES.																			
	Sub-class ..	V.—TRADE.																			
	Order ..	and those pertaining to letters and the arts and sciences—*concluded*.																		39. Trade of other sorts.	
	Group ..	146.—*Dealers in precious stones, jewellery (real and imitation), clocks, optical instruments, etc.*						147.—*Dealers in common bangles, bead necklaces, fans, small articles, toys, hunting and fishing tackle, flowers, etc.*						148.—*Publishers, book-sellers, stationers, dealers in music, pictures, musical instruments and curiosities.*						*Total Order* 39.	
		Total earners principal occupation		Total working dependants.		Total earners with subsidiary occupation.		Total earners principal occupation.		Total working dependants.		Total earners with subsidiary occupation.		Total earners principal occupation.		Total working dependants.		Total earners with subsidiary occupation.		Total earners principal occupation.	
	District or State.	Males.	Females.	Males.	Females.	Males.	Females.	Males.	Females.	Males.	Females.	Males.	Females.	Males.	Females.	Males.	Females.	Males.	Females.	Males.	Females.
1	2	941	942	943	944	945	946	947	948	949	950	951	952	953	954	955	956	957	958	959	960
	PUNJAB ..	280	..	3	..	8	..	3,049	408	75	299	202	12	1,825	2	32	..	98	..	234,721	3,575
	BRITISH TERRITORY ..	152	..	3	..	8	..	2,284	305	51	236	86	10	1,696	2	32	..	96	..	193,160	3,093
	AMBALA DIVISION ..	47	..	3	..	1	..	968	222	34	125	26	9	111	1	1	..	4	..	31,989	637
1	Hissar ..	4	..	..	..	1	..	144	31	8	40	13	5	23	..	1	..	2	..	6,475	112
2	Rohtak ..	1	..	..	..	..	..	172	36	13	22	2	..	17	..	..	..	..	..	7,027	190
3	Gurgaon ..	5	..	2	..	..	..	173	69	2	31	1	3	5	..	..	..	..	..	5,479	150
4	Karnal ..	..	..	..	..	..	..	197	65	7	30	8	1	12	..	..	..	..	..	5,296	131
5	Ambala ..	37	..	1	..	..	..	281	21	4	2	1	..	48	..	..	..	2	..	7,060	52
6	Simla ..	..	..	..	..	..	..	1	..	..	..	1	..	6	1	..	..	..	..	652	2
	JULLUNDUR DIVISION	13	..	..	..	..	..	152	22	2	1	11	1	342	..	2	..	33	..	34,021	417
7	Kangra ..	..	..	..	..	..	..	..	1	..	..	..	..	10	..	2	..	..	..	3,748	70
8	Hoshiarpur ..	2	..	..	..	..	..	96	15	..	1	10	1	7	..	..	..	3	..	5,783	33
9	Jullundur ..	..	..	..	..	..	..	13	1	2	..	..	..	223	..	..	..	28	..	6,891	136
10	Ludhiana ..	11	..	..	..	..	..	41	1	..	..	1	..	56	..	..	..	2	..	5,495	44
11	Ferozepore ..	..	..	..	..	..	..	2	4	..	..	..	..	46	..	..	..	..	..	12,104	134
	LAHORE DIVISION ..	70	..	..	..	..	..	991	44	13	80	38	..	905	..	10	..	44	..	63,067	791
12	Lahore ..	70	..	..	..	..	..	231	2	3	..	8	..	557	..	7	..	13	..	18,277	220
13	Amritsar ..	..	..	..	..	..	..	187	10	3	1	..	..	108	..	..	..	3	..	10,897	103
14	Gurdaspur ..	..	..	..	..	..	..	56	10	..	1	6	..	28	..	..	..	..	..	7,823	33
15	Sialkot ..	..	..	..	..	..	..	509	15	7	75	24	..	103	..	2	..	27	..	9,549	83
16	Gujranwala ..	..	..	..	..	..	..	..	4	..	3	..	..	74	..	1	..	..	..	10,313	130
17	Sheikhupura ..	..	..	..	..	..	..	8	3	..	..	..	..	35	..	..	..	1	..	6,208	222
	RAWALPINDI DIVISION	12	..	..	..	..	..	31	12	1	20	6	..	171	1	1	..	..	..	33,510	875
18	Gujrat ..	..	..	..	..	..	..	..	..	..	..	..	..	28	..	..	..	..	..	5,463	107
19	Shahpur ..	..	..	..	..	..	..	..	11	..	2	1	..	102	..	..	..	..	..	12,136	169
20	Jhelum ..	6	..	..	..	..	..	..	1	..	..	..	..	21	..	..	..	..	..	3,833	222
21	Rawalpindi ..	..	..	..	..	..	..	20	..	1	18	3	..	11	1	..	..	..	..	3,639	128
22	Attock ..	..	..	..	..	..	..	1	..	..	..	..	..	9	..	1	..	..	..	4,990	208
23	Mianwali ..	6	..	..	..	..	..	10	..	..	..	2	..	..	..	..	..	..	..	3,449	41
	MULTAN DIVISION ..	10	..	..	..	7	..	142	5	1	10	5	..	167	..	18	..	15	..	30,578	873
24	Montgomery ..	3	..	..	..	1	..	5	..	..	..	..	..	10	..	..	..	..	..	2,628	6
25	Lyallpur ..	..	..	..	..	..	..	15	..	1	..	..	..	43	..	5	..	..	..	7,672	269
26	Jhang ..	..	..	..	..	..	..	34	..	..	..	..	..	19	..	..	..	..	..	8,463	11
27	Multan ..	1	..	..	..	..	..	26	3	..	10	4	..	14	..	..	..	..	..	7,105	50
28	Muzaffargarh ..	3	..	..	..	6	..	49	2	..	..	1	..	58	..	13	..	15	..	1,565	29
29	Dera Ghazi Khan ..	3	..	..	..	..	..	13	..	..	..	..	..	23	..	..	..	..	..	3,140	8
	PUNJAB STATES ..	128	..	..	..	..	..	765	103	24	63	116	2	129	..	..	..	2	..	41,561	482
	A.—Having Political relations with the Punjab Government. ..	1	..	..	..	..	..	65	12	1	7	3	..	1	..	..	..	1	..	2,152	20
1	Dujana ..	..	..	..	..	..	..	10	..	..	1	..	..	..	..	..	..	..	..	290	2
2	Pataudi ..	..	..	..	..	..	..	5	7	..	..	..	..	..	..	..	..	..	..	136	3
3	Kalsia ..	..	..	..	..	..	..	44	4	..	6	..	..	..	..	..	..	..	..	368	1
4	SIMLA HILL STATES ..	1	..	..	..	..	..	6	1	1	..	8	..	1	..	..	..	1	..	1,359	14
	Bashahr ..	..	..	..	..	..	..	..	..	..	..	..	..	..	..	..	..	..	..	98	2
	Nalagarh ..	..	..	..	..	..	..	3	1	..	..	1	..	..	..	..	..	..	..	270	2
	Keonthal ..	..	..	..	..	..	..	..	..	..	..	..	..	1	..	..	..	..	..	355	3
	Baghal ..	1	..	..	..	..	..	..	..	..	..	2	..	..	..	..	..	..	..	250	1
	Jubbal ..	..	..	..	..	..	..	..	..	..	..	..	..	..	..	..	..	..	..	23	..
	Other Simla Hill States ..	..	..	..	..	..	..	3	..	1	..	..	..	..	..	..	..	1	..	363	6
	B.—Having Political relations with the Government of India. ..	127	..	..	..	..	..	700	91	23	56	113	2	128	..	..	..	1	..	39,409	462
5	Loharu ..	..	..	..	..	..	..	1	..	..	..	..	..	..	..	..	..	..	..	71	2
6	Sirmoor ..	..	..	..	..	..	..	24	..	..	..	..	..	..	..	..	..	..	..	451	7
7	Bilaspur ..	..	..	..	..	..	..	9	..	..	..	..	..	..	..	..	..	..	..	381	9
8	Mandi ..	..	..	..	..	..	..	4	..	..	..	1	..	..	..	..	..	..	..	274	21
9	Suket ..	..	..	..	..	..	..	..	..	..	..	..	..	..	..	..	..	..	..	294	..
10	Kapurthala ..	..	..	..	..	..	..	..	..	..	..	..	..	16	..	..	..	..	..	1,677	34
11	Maler Kotla ..	..	..	..	..	..	..	15	..	..	..	..	..	10	..	..	..	..	..	662	6
12	Faridkot ..	..	..	..	..	..	..	..	..	..	..	..	..	6	..	..	..	..	..	1,785	57
13	Chamba ..	..	..	..	..	..	..	1	..	..	..	..	..	4	..	..	..	..	..	508	5
14	Patiala } Phulkian States.	125	..	..	..	..	..	332	73	19	47	105	2	65	..	..	..	..	..	15,839	178
15	Jind } Phulkian States.	1	..	..	..	..	..	76	6	1	7	6	..	5	..	..	..	1	..	14	..
16	Nabha } Phulkian States.	1	..	..	..	..	..	56	12	3	2	1	..	9	..	..	..	..	..	2,843	19
17	Bahawalpur ..	..	..	..	..	..	..	182	..	..	..	..	..	13	..	..	..	..	..	14,610	124
18	*Cities.* Lahore ..	70	..	..	..	..	..	205	..	3	..	4	..	540	..	7	..	3	..	7,099	59
19	*Cities.* Amritsar ..	..	..	..	..	..	..	80	7	3	..	..	..	93	..	..	..	..	..	4,059	26
20	*Cities.* Multan ..	1	..	..	..	..	..	13	1	..	6	..	..	7	..	..	..	..	..	3,252	26

LIVELIHOOD.—GENERAL TABLE.

STATES AND CITIES—*continued.*

B.—PREPARATION AND SUPPLY OF MATERIAL SUBSTANCES—*concluded.*

V. TRADE—*concluded.*

39. Trade of other sorts—*concluded.*

Total Order 39.—concld.				*149.—Dealers in rags, stable refuse, etc.*						*150.—General store-keepers and shop-keepers otherwise unspecified.*						*151.—Itinerant traders, pedlars and hawkers (of other than food, etc.).*						*152.—Other trades (including farmers of pounds, tolls and markets).*						
Total working dependants		Total earners with subsidiary occupation.		Total earners principal occupation.		Total working dependants.		Total earners with subsidiary occupation.		Total earners principal occupation.		Total working dependants.		Total earners with subsidiary occupation.		Total earners principal occupation.		Total working dependants.		Total earners with subsidiary occupation.		Total earners principal occupation.		Total working dependants		Total earners with subsidiary occupation.		
Males.	Females.	Males.	Females.	Males.	Females.	Males.	Females.	Males.	Females.	Males.	Females.	Males.	Females.	Males.	Females.	Males.	Females.	Males.	Females.	Males.	Females.	Males.	Females.	Males.	Females.	Males.	Females.	Serial No.
961	962	963	964	965	966	967	968	969	970	971	972	973	974	975	976	977	978	979	980	981	982	983	984	985	986	987	988	
13,490	985	18,137	205	328	1	10	..	18	1	230,057	3,522	11,222	923	16,745	203	3,006	49	110	12	142	1	1,330	3	2,148	..	1,232	..	
11,281	813	13,965	168	319	1	10	..	18	1	188,763	3,053	9,015	801	12,599	167	2,834	31	110	12	122	..	1,244	3	2,146	..	1,226	..	
2,496	217	3,043	24	205	..	10	..	8	..	31,714	634	2,484	217	3,026	24	26	..	..	..	..	..	44	3	2	..	9	..	
1,201	89	945	6	4	..	..	..	..	..	6,461	112	1,201	89	944	6	6	..	..	..	..	..	4	..	..	..	1	..	1
481	69	556	2	1	..	..	..	..	..	7,024	190	479	69	556	2	..	..	..	..	..	..	2	..	2	..	..	..	2
361	17	307	3	..	..	..	..	..	..	5,461	150	361	17	306	3	3	..	..	..	..	..	15	..	..	..	1	..	3
255	6	495	11	200	..	10	..	1	..	5,086	128	245	6	492	11	2	..	..	..	..	..	8	3	..	..	2	..	4
128	36	591	2	..	..	..	..	7	..	7,031	52	128	36	579	2	15	..	..	..	..	..	14	..	..	..	5	..	5
70	..	149	..	..	..	..	..	..	..	651	2	70	..	149	..	..	..	..	..	..	..	1	..	..	..	..	..	6
3,869	23	3,957	15	21	1	..	..	..	1	32,711	415	1,722	23	2,730	14	159	1	4	..	22	..	1,130	..	2,143	..	1,205	..	
62	3	646	3	21	..	..	..	..	..	3,710	70	61	3	642	3	15	..	1	..	3	..	2	..	..	..	1	..	7
67	1	559	..	..	..	..	..	..	..	5,705	32	66	1	550	..	78	1	1	..	9	..	..	..	..	..	..	..	8
3,004	4	1,709	4	..	1	..	..	..	1	5,724	135	859	4	511	3	60	..	2	..	10	..	1,107	..	2,143	..	1,188	..	9
188	6	575	1	..	..	..	..	..	..	5,487	44	188	6	575	1	..	..	..	..	..	..	8	..	..	..	..	..	10
548	9	468	7	..	..	..	..	..	..	12,035	134	548	9	452	7	6	..	..	..	..	..	13	..	..	..	16	..	11
2,286	160	3,924	36	78	..	..	..	6	..	61,324	769	2,231	153	3,869	36	1,638	22	55	7	47	..	27	..	..	..	2	..	
249	30	495	4	18	..	..	..	..	..	18,186	220	246	30	494	4	73	..	3	..	..	..	..	..	..	..	1	..	12
664	15	1,518	6	37	..	..	..	..	..	10,259	85	653	9	1,505	6	599	18	11	6	13	..	2	..	..	..	..	..	13
225	17	757	2	..	..	..	..	..	..	7,584	33	223	17	746	2	235	..	2	..	11	..	4	..	..	..	..	..	14
243	3	241	..	23	..	..	..	6	..	9,388	82	241	3	234	..	138	1	2	..	..	..	..	..	..	..	1	..	15
362	68	685	20	..	..	..	..	..	..	9,977	130	357	68	674	20	336	..	5	..	11	..	..	..	..	..	..	..	16
543	27	228	4	..	..	..	..	..	..	5,930	219	511	26	216	4	257	3	32	1	12	..	21	..	..	..	..	..	17
1,634	340	1,585	58	15	..	..	..	4	..	32,831	868	1,590	335	1,558	58	643	7	43	5	23	..	21	..	1	..	..	..	
326	5	463	3	6	..	..	..	..	..	5,362	107	312	5	462	3	78	..	13	..	1	..	17	..	1	..	..	..	18
394	11	236	2	..	..	..	..	..	..	12,125	162	394	6	236	2	10	7	..	5	..	..	1	..	..	..	..	..	19
145	223	175	6	..	..	..	..	..	..	3,745	222	145	223	175	6	88	..	..	..	..	..	..	..	..	..	..	..	20
376	21	420	15	..	..	..	..	..	..	3,226	128	348	21	398	15	410	..	28	..	22	..	3	..	..	..	..	..	21
290	73	129	31	9	..	..	..	4	..	4,926	208	288	73	125	31	55	..	2	..	..	..	..	..	..	..	..	..	22
103	7	162	1	..	..	..	..	..	..	3,447	41	103	7	162	1	2	..	..	..	..	..	..	..	..	..	..	..	23
996	73	1,456	35	..	..	..	..	..	..	30,183	372	988	73	1,416	35	368	1	8	..	30	..	22	..	..	..	10	..	
235	5	17	..	..	..	..	..	..	..	2,627	6	235	5	15	..	1	..	..	..	2	..	..	..	..	..	..	..	24
51	25	252	19	..	..	..	..	..	..	7,581	269	47	25	250	19	81	..	4	..	..	..	7	..	..	..	2	..	25
455	1	581	1	..	..	..	..	..	..	8,306	11	455	1	557	1	152	..	..	..	21	..	5	..	..	..	3	..	26
105	..	448	..	..	..	..	..	..	..	7,035	50	102	..	440	..	68	..	3	..	6	..	2	..	..	..	2	..	27
120	5	89	15	..	..	..	..	..	..	1,559	29	120	5	86	15	..	..	..	..	..	..	6	..	..	..	3	..	28
30	37	69	..	..	..	..	..	..	..	3,072	7	29	37	68	..	66	1	1	..	1	..	2	..	..	..	..	..	29
2,209	122	4,172	37	9	..	..	..	..	..	41,294	464	2,207	122	4,146	36	172	18	..	..	20	1	86	..	2	..	6	..	
121	4	458	3	..	..	..	..	..	..	2,141	19	121	4	450	3	5	1	..	..	6	..	6	..	..	..	2	..	
..	..	117	..	..	..	..	..	..	..	290	2	..	..	117	..	..	..	..	..	..	..	..	..	..	..	..	..	1
..	..	18	..	..	..	..	..	..	..	134	3	..	..	13	..	1	..	..	..	5	..	..	..	..	..	..	..	2
20	..	44	..	..	..	..	..	..	..	362	1	20	..	42	..	1	..	..	..	..	..	5	..	..	..	2	..	3
101	4	279	3	..	..	..	..	..	..	1,355	13	101	4	278	3	3	1	..	..	1	..	1	..	..	..	..	..	4
9	1	37	1	..	..	..	..	..	..	98	2	9	1	37	1	..	..	..	..	..	..	..	..	..	..	..	..	
6	1	32	..	..	..	..	..	..	..	267	2	6	1	32	..	2	..	..	..	..	..	1	..	..	..	..	..	
51	..	46	..	..	..	..	..	..	..	354	2	51	..	46	..	1	1	..	..	..	..	..	..	..	..	..	..	
5	..	49	..	..	..	..	..	..	..	250	1	5	..	48	..	..	..	..	..	1	..	..	..	..	..	..	..	
2	..	19	1	..	..	..	..	..	..	23	..	2	..	19	1	..	..	..	..	..	..	..	..	..	..	..	..	
28	2	96	1	..	..	..	..	..	..	363	6	28	2	96	1	..	..	..	..	..	..	..	..	..	..	..	..	
2,088	118	3,714	34	9	..	..	..	..	..	39,153	445	2,086	118	3,696	38	167	17	..	..	14	1	80	..	2	..	4	..	
..	..	10	..	..	..	..	..	..	..	71	2	..	..	10	..	..	..	..	..	..	..	..	..	..	..	..	..	5
17	..	54	..	..	..	..	..	..	..	451	7	17	..	54	..	..	..	..	..	..	..	..	..	..	..	..	..	6
9	3	73	..	..	..	..	..	..	..	380	9	9	3	73	..	..	..	..	..	..	..	1	..	..	..	..	..	7
5	..	66	4	..	..	..	..	..	..	212	10	5	..	56	3	32	11	..	..	10	1	..	..	..	..	..	..	8
42	..	72	..	..	..	..	..	..	..	294	..	42	..	72	..	..	..	..	..	..	..	..	..	..	..	..	..	9
15	..	191	..	..	..	..	..	..	..	1,650	30	15	..	191	..	27	4	..	..	..	..	..	..	..	..	..	..	10
16	..	23	..	..	..	..	..	..	..	656	6	16	..	23	..	..	..	..	..	..	..	6	..	..	..	..	..	11
50	5	29	1	..	..	..	..	..	..	1,785	57	50	5	29	1	..	..	..	..	..	..	..	..	..	..	..	..	12
19	..	97	1	1	..	..	..	..	..	474	3	19	..	93	1	33	2	..	..	4	..	..	..	..	..	..	..	13
1,551	82	2,784	17	6	..	..	..	..	..	15,720	178	1,551	82	2,784	17	75	..	..	..	..	..	38	..	..	..	..	..	14
2	..	3	..	2	..	..	..	..	..	..	..	..	..	..	..	..	..	..	..	..	..	12	..	2	..	3	..	15
179	2	307	3	..	..	..	..	..	..	2,835	19	179	2	306	3	..	..	..	..	..	..	8	..	..	..	1	..	16
183	26	5	8	..	..	..	..	..	..	14,595	124	183	26	5	8	..	..	..	..	..	..	15	..	..	..	..	..	17
35	10	202	1	18	..	..	..	..	..	7,662	59	35	10	202	1	19	..	..	..	..	..	..	..	..	..	..	..	18
97	..	113	..	27	..	..	..	..	..	3,672	23	97	..	113	..	358	3	..	..	..	..	2	..	..	..	..	..	19
2	..	351	..	..	..	..	..	..	..	3,219	26	1	..	350	..	31	..	1	..	..	..	2	..	..	..	1	..	20

TABLE X.—OCCUPATION OR MEANS OF
DETAILS FOR DISTRICTS,

Class .. C. PUBLIC ADMINISTRATION AND LIBERAL ARTS.
Sub-class .. VI. PUBLIC FORCE.
Order .. 40 Army.

Serial No.	Group / District or State.	Total Class C. — Total earners principal occupation. Males.	Females.	Total working dependants. Males.	Females.	Total earners with subsidiary occupation. Males.	Females.	Total Sub-class VI. — Total earners principal occupation. Males.	Females.	Total working dependants. Males.	Females.	Total earners with subsidiary occupation. Males.	Females.	Total Order 40. — Total earners principal occupation. Males.	Females.	Total working dependants. Males.	Females.	Total earners with subsidiary occupation. Males.	Females.
1	2	989	990	991	992	993	994	995	996	997	998	999	1000	1001	1002	1003	1004	1005	1006
	PUNJAB ..	381,106	20,598	8,117	3,942	50,985	1,205	102,680	38	899	3	8,947	5	49,975	9	225	..	2,534	..
	BRITISH TERRITORY ..	313,711	17,353	6,603	2,497	37,395	982	81,824	37	776	3	6,380	4	40,727	9	159	..	1,682	..
	AMBALA DIVISION ..	45,398	3,231	464	538	11,455	331	13,832	11	72	..	2,099	..	5,539	9	28	..	680	.
1	Hissar ..	8,001	428	179	149	1,742	67	2,024	..	18	..	296	..	228	..	3	..	55	.
2	Rohtak ..	6,063	332	90	102	2,004	69	1,661	1	33	..	320	..	273	..	19	..	71	.
3	Gurgaon ..	6,389	448	67	77	1,780	41	1,595	..	10	..	453	..	211	..	4	..	22	.
4	Karnal ..	7,726	777	49	97	2,086	100	1,428	1	4	..	143	..	44	..	..	..	9	.
5	Ambala ..	14,712	1,056	62	108	3,687	53	6,041	..	7	..	872	..	4,150	..	2	..	517	.
6	Simla ..	2,507	190	17	5	156	1	1,083	9	..	..	15	..	633	9	..	..	6	.
	JULLUNDUR DIVISION	55,707	3,580	2,282	410	11,024	163	18,194	1	134	..	1,695	..	10,875	..	46	..	411	..
7	Kangra ..	7,550	312	338	58	2,456	15	2,648	..	13	..	491	..	1,566	..	8	..	177	..
8	Hoshiarpur ..	10,619	797	237	75	2,812	29	1,995	..	16	..	492	..	501	..	9	..	89	..
9	Jullundur ..	13,735	1,020	1,384	128	2,271	42	4,633	..	73	..	186	..	3,255	..	17	..	30	..
10	Ludhiana ..	9,601	781	152	116	2,305	25	2,013	1	20	..	350	..	397	..	10	..	86	.
11	Ferozepore ..	14,202	620	171	33	1,180	52	6,905	..	12	..	176	..	5,156	..	2	..	29	..
	LAHORE DIVISION ..	99,712	4,528	1,012	435	6,100	160	24,679	9	182	1	1,155	2	12,128	..	13	..	225	..
12	Lahore ..	39,094	1,285	196	93	603	30	9,884	3	25	..	28	..	5,772	..	2	..	5	..
13	Amritsar ..	16,459	864	214	90	1,242	10	3,129	..	32	1	202	..	543	..	1	..	12	..
14	Gurdaspur ..	12,468	731	159	79	2,091	33	2,219	5	20	..	492	2	774	..	5	..	201	..
15	Sialkot ..	15,543	835	131	62	1,125	46	6,887	1	44	..	232	..	4,988	..	4	..	7	..
16	Gujranwala ..	9,042	553	75	56	509	24	1,332	..	14	..	107	..	33	..	1	..	..	..
17	Sheikhupura ..	7,106	260	237	55	530	17	1,228	..	47	..	94	..	18	..	..	..	..	..
	RAWALPINDI DIVISION	51,715	3,192	1,794	779	4,877	120	15,020	16	213	2	1,015	..	8,936	..	58	..	345	..
18	Gujrat ..	11,137	719	579	236	1,183	19	1,675	14	87	2	214	..	466	..	29	..	33	..
19	Shahpur ..	9,774	631	66	43	671	18	793	..	7	..	101	..	6	..	..	..	..	..
20	Jhelum ..	10,146	572	567	364	985	38	5,043	1	52	..	238	..	4,155	..	2	..	163	..
21	Rawalpindi ..	10,286	565	366	49	613	7	4,857	..	41	..	162	..	3,441	..	22	..	53	..
22	Attock ..	7,088	517	186	58	1,160	34	1,714	1	21	..	267	..	684	..	1	..	94	..
23	Mianwali ..	3,284	188	30	29	265	4	938	..	5	..	33	..	184	..	4	..	2	..
	MULTAN DIVISION ..	61,179	2,872	1,051	335	3,939	208	10,099	..	175	..	416	2	3,249	..	14	..	21	..
24	Montgomery ..	10,597	378	160	26	760	12	1,396	..	18	..	69	..	193	..	6	..	3	.
25	Lyallpur ..	11,643	889	471	77	811	76	1,621	..	49	..	95	..	603	..	6	..	2	..
26	Jhang ..	8,130	375	60	34	398	16	842	..	..	..	12	..	2	..	..	..	..	..
27	Multan ..	18,526	472	166	44	922	46	4,287	..	54	..	45	..	2,315	..	..	..	..	..
28	Muzaffargarh ..	6,941	467	145	77	665	55	1,018	..	50	..	173	2	43	..	2	..	7	..
29	Dera Ghazi Khan ..	5,342	291	49	77	383	3	935	..	4	..	22	..	93	..	..	..	9	..
	PUNJAB STATES ..	67,395	3,245	1,514	1,445	13,590	223	20,856	1	123	..	2,567	1	9,248	..	66	..	852	..
	A.—HAVING POLITICAL RELATIONS WITH THE PUNJAB GOVERNMENT. ..	3,223	196	134	58	2,727	15	736	..	8	..	380	..	214	..	3	..	83	..
1	Dujana ..	262	10	2	4	236	..	90	..	..	..	68	..	58	..	..	..	33	..
2	Pataudi ..	285	30	3	2	114	..	108	..	3	..	16	..	40	..	3	..	2	..
3	Kalsia ..	850	53	20	6	253	1	220	..	..	..	63	..	90	..	..	..	29	..
4	SIMLA HILL STATES ..	1,826	103	109	46	2,124	14	318	..	5	..	233	..	26	..	..	..	19	..
	Bashahr ..	156	2	17	5	180	..	18	..	1	..	15	..	1	..	..	..	1	..
	Nalagarh ..	534	41	8	6	522	9	127	..	..	..	56	..	15	..	..	..	4	..
	Keonthal ..	390	12	12	11	321	1	75	..	..	..	37	..	6	..	..	..	14	..
	Baghal ..	128	16	6	7	267	..	17	..	..	..	21	..	..	..	..	..	..	..
	Jubbal ..	71	1	14	4	247	..	..	..	..	..	29	..	..	..	..	..	..	..
	Other Simla Hill States ..	547	31	52	13	587	4	81	..	4	..	75	..	4	..	..	..	..	..
	B.—HAVING POLITICAL RELATIONS WITH THE GOVERNMENT OF INDIA.	64,172	3,049	1,380	1,387	10,863	208	20,120	1	115	..	2,127	1	9,034	..	63	..	769	..
5	Loharu ..	186	4	2	2	8	2	71	..	..	..	..	..	21	..	..	..	..	..
6	Sirmoor ..	1,564	40	41	6	357	2	604	..	11	..	17	..	376	..	..	..	..	..
7	Bilaspur ..	588	23	31	2	612	..	154	..	4	..	86	..	67	..	3	..	37	..
8	Mandi ..	1,717	109	47	20	1,582	16	209	..	..	..	439	..	104	..	..	..	164	..
9	Suket ..	594	46	24	5	148	..	69	..	6	..	34	..	34	..	..	..	1	..
10	Kapurthala ..	5,978	308	20	15	619	24	2,009	..	..	..	109	..	889	..	..	..	39	..
11	Maler Kotla ..	2,302	131	50	16	504	19	1,154	..	11	..	99	..	916	..	11	..	35	..
12	Faridkot ..	3,541	103	32	2	346	22	824	..	4	..	29	..	362	..	..	..	13	..
13	Chamba ..	1,346	73	31	4	677	5	295	1	1	..	22	1	208	..	1	..	5	..
14	Patiala (Phulkian States)	24,971	1,633	845	1,259	2,645	42	8,187	..	58	..	1,108	..	3,330	..	44	..	412	..
15	Jind (Phulkian States)	3,343	121	50	18	1,145	13	1,579	..	12	..	107	..	990	..	1	..	35	..
16	Nabha (Phulkian States)	4,339	260	66	20	1,489	28	1,204	..	..	..	125	..	494	..	..	..	28	..
17	Bahawalpur ..	13,703	198	141	18	731	35	3,761	..	8	..	12	..	1,243	..	3	..	..	..
18	*Cities.* Lahore ..	30,903	763	45	37	61	..	8,415	..	5	..	3	..	5,570	..	..	..	1	..
19	*Cities.* Amritsar ..	7,663	200	1	..	23	..	1,547	..	..	..	12	..	423	..	..	..	..	..
20	*Cities.* Multan ..	6,693	120	8	12	33	..	3,215	..	..	..	..	..	2,315	..	..	..	..	..

LIVELIHOOD—GENERAL TABLE.

STATES AND CITIES.—*continued.*

C.—PUBLIC ADMINISTRATION AND LIBERAL ARTS.—*continued.*																												
VI.—PUBLIC FORCE.—*continued.*																												
40. Army—*concluded.*												42. Air Force.				43. Police.												
153.—*Army (Imperial).*						154.—*Army (Indian States).*						*Total Order 42.* 156. *Air Force.*				*Total Order 43.*						157.—*Police.*						
Total earners principal occupation.		Total working dependants.		Total earners with subsidiary occupation.		Total earners principal occupation.		Total working dependants.		Total earners with subsidiary occupation.		Total earners principal occupation.		Total earners with subsidiary occupation.		Total earners principal occupation.		Total working dependants.		Total earners with subsidiary occupation.		Total earners principal occupation.		Total working dependants.		Total earners with subsidiary occupation.		Serial No.
Males.	Females.	Males.	Females.	Males.	Females.	Males.	Females.	Males.	Females.	Males.	Females.	Males.	Females.	Males.	Females.	Males.	Females.	Males.	Females.	Males.	Females.	Males.	Females.	Males.	Females.	Males.	Females.	
1007	1008	1009	1010	1011	1012	1013	1014	1015	1016	1017	1018	1019	1020	1021	1022	1023	1024	1025	1026	1027	1028	1029	1030	1031	1032	1033	1034	
40,172	**9**	**165**	..	**1,682**	..	**9,803**	..	**60**	..	**852**	..	**187**	..	**4**	..	**52,568**	**29**	**674**	**3**	**6,409**	**5**	**29,014**	**12**	**183**	..	**1,166**	..	
39,816	**9**	**157**	..	**1,682**	..	**911**	..	**2**	..	..	..	**136**	..	**4**	..	**40,961**	**28**	**617**	**3**	**4,694**	**4**	**22,095**	**12**	**157**	..	**716**	..	
5,537	**9**	**28**	..	**680**	..	**2**	..	..	..	..	..	**118**	..	**4**	..	**8,175**	**2**	**44**	..	**1,415**	..	**4,068**	**2**	**2**	..	**84**	..	
227	..	3	..	55	..	1	..	..	..	..	..	..	..	..	..	1,796	..	15	..	241	..	695	..	..	..	21	..	1
273	..	19	..	71	..	..	..	..	..	..	..	..	..	..	..	1,388	1	14	..	249	..	720	1	..	..	26	..	2
211	..	4	..	22	..	..	..	..	..	..	..	..	..	..	..	1,384	..	6	..	431	..	624	..	1	..	7	..	3
44	..	..	..	9	..	..	..	..	..	..	..	..	..	..	..	1,381	1	4	..	134	..	664	1	..	..	6	..	4
4,150	..	2	..	517	..	..	..	..	..	..	..	118	..	4	..	1,773	..	5	..	351	..	1,068	..	1	..	19	..	5
632	9	..	..	6	..	1	..	..	..	..	..	..	..	..	..	450	..	..	..	9	..	297	..	..	..	5	..	6
10,865	..	**46**	..	**411**	..	**10**	..	..	..	..	..	..	..	..	..	**7,319**	**1**	**88**	..	**1,284**	..	**3,494**	..	**24**	..	**175**	..	
1,566	..	8	..	177	..	..	..	..	..	..	..	..	..	..	..	1,082	..	5	..	314	..	477	..	2	..	72	..	7
501	..	9	..	89	..	..	..	..	..	..	..	..	..	..	..	1,494	..	7	..	403	..	538	..	..	..	25	..	8
3,255	..	17	..	30	..	..	..	..	..	..	..	..	..	..	..	1,378	..	56	..	156	..	542	..	17	..	8	..	9
397	..	10	..	86	..	..	..	..	..	..	..	..	..	..	..	1,616	1	10	..	264	..	956	..	3	..	47	..	10
5,146	..	2	..	29	..	10	..	..	..	..	..	..	..	..	..	1,749	..	10	..	147	..	981	..	2	..	23	..	11
11,275	..	**13**	..	**225**	..	**853**	..	..	..	..	..	**18**	..	..	..	**12,533**	**9**	**169**	**1**	**930**	**2**	**7,441**	**9**	**37**	..	**74**	..	
4,919	..	2	..	5	..	853	..	..	..	..	..	18	..	..	..	4,094	3	23	..	23	..	3,711	3	21	..	5	..	12
543	..	1	..	12	..	..	..	..	..	..	..	..	..	..	..	2,586	..	31	1	190	..	1,629	..	6	..	17	..	13
774	..	5	..	201	..	..	..	..	..	..	..	..	..	..	..	1,445	5	15	..	291	2	401	5	1	..	17	..	14
4,988	..	4	..	7	..	..	..	..	..	..	..	..	..	..	..	1,899	1	40	..	225	..	672	1	5	..	31	..	15
33	..	1	..	..	..	..	..	..	..	..	..	..	..	..	..	1,299	..	13	..	107	..	543	..	1	..	..	..	16
18	..	..	..	..	..	..	..	..	..	..	..	..	..	..	..	1,210	..	47	..	94	..	485	..	3	..	4	..	17
8,936	..	**58**	..	**345**	..	..	..	..	..	..	..	..	..	..	..	**6,084**	**16**	**155**	**2**	**670**	..	**3,481**	**1**	**53**	..	**247**	..	
466	..	29	..	33	..	..	..	..	..	..	..	..	..	..	..	1,209	14	58	2	181	..	579	..	24	..	30	..	18
6	..	..	..	..	..	..	..	..	..	..	..	..	..	..	..	787	..	7	..	101	..	52	..	..	..	..	..	19
4,155	..	2	..	163	..	..	..	..	..	..	..	..	..	..	..	888	1	50	..	75	..	743	1	10	..	28	..	20
3,441	..	22	..	53	..	..	..	..	..	..	..	..	..	..	..	1,416	..	19	..	109	..	1,122	..	18	..	85	..	21
684	..	1	..	94	..	..	..	..	..	..	..	..	..	..	..	1,030	1	20	..	173	..	708	..	..	..	98	..	22
184	..	4	..	2	..	..	..	..	..	..	..	..	..	..	..	754	..	1	..	31	..	277	..	1	..	6	..	23
3,203	..	**12**	..	**21**	..	**46**	..	**2**	..	..	..	..	..	..	..	**6,850**	..	**161**	..	**395**	**2**	**3,611**	..	**41**	..	**136**	..	
178	..	6	..	3	..	15	..	..	..	..	..	..	..	..	..	1,203	..	12	..	66	..	586	..	1	..	9	..	24
603	..	6	..	2	..	..	..	..	..	..	..	..	..	..	..	1,015	..	43	..	93	..	327	..	2	..	22	..	25
2	..	..	..	..	..	..	..	..	..	..	..	..	..	..	..	840	..	..	..	12	..	553	..	..	..	2	..	26
2,315	..	..	..	..	..	..	..	..	..	..	..	..	..	..	..	1,972	..	54	..	45	..	1,002	..	..	..	..	..	27
12	..	..	..	7	..	31	..	2	..	..	..	..	..	..	..	975	..	48	..	166	2	542	..	38	..	102	..	28
93	..	..	..	9	..	..	..	..	..	..	..	..	..	..	..	842	..	4	..	13	..	601	..	..	..	1	..	29
356	..	**8**	..	..	..	**8,892**	..	**58**	..	**852**	..	**1**	..	..	..	**11,607**	**1**	**57**	..	**1,715**	**1**	**6,919**	..	**26**	..	**450**	..	
..	..	..	..	..	..	**214**	..	**3**	..	**83**	..	..	..	..	..	**522**	..	**5**	..	**297**	..	**376**	..	**2**	..	**189**	..	
..	..	..	..	..	..	58	..	..	..	33	..	..	..	..	..	32	..	..	..	35	..	15	..	..	..	8	..	1
..	..	..	..	..	..	40	..	3	..	2	..	..	..	..	..	68	..	..	..	14	..	32	..	..	..	2	..	2
..	..	..	..	..	..	90	..	..	..	29	..	..	..	..	..	130	..	..	..	34	..	75	..	..	..	3	..	3
..	..	..	..	..	..	**26**	..	..	..	**19**	..	..	..	..	..	**292**	..	**5**	..	**214**	..	**254**	..	**2**	..	**126**	..	4
..	..	..	..	..	..	1	..	..	..	1	..	..	..	..	..	17	..	1	..	14	..	17	..	1	..	13	..	
..	..	..	..	..	..	15	..	..	..	4	..	..	..	..	..	112	..	..	..	52	..	74	..	..	..	5	..	
..	..	..	..	..	..	6	..	..	..	14	..	..	..	..	..	69	..	..	..	23	..	69	..	..	..	17	..	
..	..	..	..	..	..	..	..	..	..	..	..	..	..	..	..	17	..	..	..	21	..	17	..	..	..	10	..	
..	..	..	..	..	..	..	..	..	..	..	..	..	..	..	..	..	..	..	..	29	..	..	..	..	..	27	..	
..	..	..	..	..	..	4	..	..	..	..	..	..	..	..	..	77	..	4	..	75	..	77	..	1	..	54	..	
356	..	**8**	..	..	..	**8,678**	..	**55**	..	**769**	..	**1**	..	..	..	**11,085**	**1**	**52**	..	**1,418**	**1**	**6,543**	..	**24**	..	**311**	..	
..	..	..	..	..	..	21	..	..	..	..	..	..	..	..	..	50	..	..	..	..	..	40	..	..	..	..	..	5
..	..	..	..	..	..	376	..	..	..	..	..	..	..	..	..	228	..	11	..	17	..	209	..	..	..	4	..	6
..	..	..	..	..	..	67	..	3	..	37	..	..	..	..	..	87	..	1	..	49	..	75	..	..	..	21	..	7
..	..	..	..	..	..	104	..	..	..	164	..	..	..	..	..	105	..	..	..	275	..	86	..	..	..	82	..	8
..	..	..	..	..	..	34	..	..	..	1	..	..	..	..	..	35	..	6	..	33	..	28	..	..	..	3	..	9
..	..	..	..	..	..	889	..	..	..	39	..	1	..	..	..	1,119	..	..	..	70	..	982	..	..	..	50	..	10
..	..	..	..	..	..	916	..	11	..	35	..	..	..	..	..	238	..	..	..	64	..	221	..	..	..	22	..	11
2	..	..	..	..	..	360	..	..	..	13	..	..	..	..	..	462	..	4	..	16	..	246	..	4	..	11	..	12
..	..	..	..	..	..	208	..	1	..	5	..	..	..	..	..	87	1	..	..	17	1	72	..	..	..	4	..	13
354	..	8	..	..	..	2,976	..	36	..	412	..	..	..	..	..	4,857	..	14	..	696	..	2,939	..	14	..	104	..	14
..	..	..	..	..	..	990	..	1	..	35	..	..	..	..	..	589	..	11	..	72	..	318	..	1	..	1	..	15
..	..	..	..	..	..	494	..	..	..	28	..	..	..	..	..	710	..	..	..	97	..	405	..	..	..	9	..	16
..	..	..	..	..	..	1,243	..	3	..	..	..	..	..	..	..	2,518	..	5	..	12	..	922	..	5	..	..	..	17
4,717	..	..	..	1	..	853	..	..	..	..	..	18	..	..	..	2,827	..	5	..	2	..	2,827	..	5	..	2	..	18
423	..	..	..	..	..	..	..	..	..	..	..	..	..	..	..	1,124	..	..	..	12	..	1,124	..	..	..	12	..	19
2,315	..	..	..	..	..	..	..	..	..	..	..	..	..	..	..	900	..	..	..	..	..	900	..	..	..	..	..	20

TABLE X.—OCCUPATION OR MEANS OF
DETAILS FOR DISTRICTS,

Serial No.	Class / Sub-class / Order / Group / District or State	C.—PUBLIC ADMINISTRATION AND LIBERAL ARTS.																			
	Sub-class	VI.—PUBLIC FORCE—*concld.*						VII.—PUBLIC ADMINISTRATION.													
	Order	43. Police—*concluded.*						44. Public Administration.													
	Group	158.—*Village watchmen.*						Total Sub-Class. VII. *Total Order 44.*						159.—*Service of the State.*						160.—	
		Total earners principal occupation.		Total working dependants.		Total earners with subsidiary occupation.		Total earners principal occupation.		Total working dependants.		Total earners with subsidiary occupation.		Total earners principal occupation.		Total working dependants.		Total earners with subsidiary occupation.		Total earners principal occupation.	
	District or State.	Males.	Females.	Males.	Females.	Males.	Females.	Males.	Females.	Males.	Females.	Males.	Females.	Males.	Females.	Males.	Females.	Males.	Females.	Males.	Females.
1	2	1035	1036	1037	1038	1039	1040	1041	1042	1043	1044	1045	1046	1047	1048	1049	1050	1051	1052	1053	1054
	PUNJAB	23,554	17	491	3	5,243	5	94,543	959	1,148	66	20,406	112	5 0009	286	563	6	1,307	3	13,884	280
	BRITISH TERRITORY	18,866	16	460	3	3,978	4	76,912	531	969	56	14,535	44	49,986	286	563	6	1,302	3	252	..
	AMBALA DIVISION	4,107	..	42	..	1,331	..	7,830	24	45	1	5,874	12	3,501	8	24	..	174	..	67	..
1	Hissar	1,101	..	15	..	220	..	1,323	8	4	..	714	..	688	3	2	..	13	..	1	..
2	Rohtak	668	..	14	..	223	..	1,154	7	6	..	1,050	..	418	3	1	..	41	..	..	..
3	Gurgaon	760	..	5	..	424	..	1,362	3	7	..	954	..	475	..	3	..	7	..	7	..
4	Karnal	720	..	4	..	128	..	1,185	1	10	..	1,276	4	474	1	3	..	52	..	29	..
5	Ambala	705	..	4	..	332	..	2,027	5	3	1	1,808	8	1,057	1	..	..	32	..	28	..
6	Simla	153	..	..	..	4	..	779	..	15	..	72	..	389	..	15	..	29	..	2	..
	JULLUNDUR DIVISION	3,825	1	64	..	1,109	..	9,217	91	199	15	4,118	12	5,619	42	138	1	460	..	..	..
7	Kangra	605	..	3	..	242	..	885	4	8	1	572	..	523	4	6	1	128	..	..	..
8	Hoshiarpur	956	..	7	..	378	..	1,950	7	46	1	1,076	..	1,336	4	43	..	108	..	..	..
9	Jullundur	836	..	39	..	148	..	2,333	19	69	11	805	12	1,528	4	61	..	53	..	..	..
10	Ludhiana	660	1	7	..	217	..	1,624	25	26	1	1,201	..	794	3	21	..	156	..	..	..
11	Ferozepore	768	..	8	..	124	..	2,425	36	50	1	464	..	1,438	27	7	..	15	..	..	..
	LAHORE DIVISION	5,092	..	132	1	856	2	27,094	233	106	7	2,355	14	19,603	179	66	5	225	1	162	..
12	Lahore	383	..	2	..	18	..	16,155	107	20	1	287	1	13,492	68	12	..	47	..	162	..
13	Amritsar	957	..	25	1	173	..	3,178	81	16	5	574	1	1,730	81	6	5	12	1	..	..
14	Gurdaspur	1,044	..	14	..	274	2	2,695	18	10	1	778	12	1,583	4	5	..	64	..	..	..
15	Sialkot	1,227	..	35	..	194	..	1,433	16	3	..	496	..	562	16	..	..	75	..	..	..
16	Gujranwala	756	..	12	..	107	..	1,696	7	2	..	20	..	615	6	..	..	..	..	..	..
17	Sheikhupura	725	..	44	..	90	..	1,037	4	55	..	200	..	1,621	4	43	..	27	..	..	..
	RAWALPINDI DIVISION	2,603	15	102	2	428	..	9,793	62	208	14	1,030	1	5,915	32	61	..	140	..	23	..
18	Gujrat	630	14	34	2	151	..	1,662	2	87	..	397	..	837	1	6	..	19	..	5	..
19	Shahpur	735	..	7	..	101	..	3,9[illegible]6	16	7	..	259	1	2,959	7	6	..	56	..	15	..
20	Jhelum	145	..	40	..	47	..	1,154	16	50	..	103	..	475	5	7	..	4	..	3	..
21	Rawalpindi	294	..	1	..	24	..	1,088	20	20	..	42	..	774	17	9	..	23	..	..	..
22	Attock	322	1	20	..	75	..	1,315	7	35	13	117	..	540	2	25	..	24	..	..	..
23	Mianwali	477	..	..	..	25	..	668	1	9	1	112	..	330	..	8	..	14	..	..	..
	MULTAN DIVISION	3,239	..	120	..	259	2	22,978	121	411	19	1,158	5	15,348	25	274	..	303	2	..	..
24	Montgomery	617	..	11	..	57	..	4,577	33	23	..	329	..	2,603	5	..	..	35	..	..	..
25	Lyallpur	691	..	41	..	71	..	3,957	17	311	19	234	..	2,431	..	236	..	38	..	..	..
26	Jhang	287	..	..	..	10	..	1,999	11	8	..	183	1	1,282	7	4	..	21	..	..	..
27	Multan	970	..	54	..	45	..	8,175	46	41	..	144	3	6,703	8	18	..	102	2	..	..
28	Muzaffargarh	433	..	10	..	64	2	2,834	13	25	..	165	1	1,868	4	16	..	72	..	..	..
29	Dera Ghazi Khan	241	..	4	..	12	..	1,436	1	3	..	103	..	461	1	..	..	35	..	..	..
	PUNJAB STATES	4,688	1	31	..	1,265	1	17,631	428	179	10	5,871	68	23	..	..	..	5	..	13,632	280
	A.—Having Political relations with the Punjab Government.	146	..	3	..	158	..	910	4	28	6	1,181	2	6	..	..	..	..	..	698	4
1	Dujana	17	..	..	..	27	..	54	..	1	..	82	..	..	..	..	..	..	..	48	..
2	Pataudi	36	..	..	..	12	..	43	..	..	..	79	..	..	..	..	..	..	..	29	..
3	Kalsia	55	..	..	..	31	..	149	..	..	..	102	..	2	..	..	..	..	..	108	..
4	SIMLA HILL STATES	38	..	3	..	88	..	664	4	27	6	918	2	4	..	..	..	..	..	513	4
	Bashahr	..	..	..	..	1	..	98	..	7	..	91	..	..	..	..	..	..	..	91	..
	Nalagarh	38	..	..	..	47	..	134	..	..	..	307	2	..	..	..	..	..	..	96	..
	Keonthal	..	..	..	..	6	..	192	..	1	4	179	..	4	..	..	..	..	..	126	..
	Baghal	..	..	..	..	11	..	20	4	1	..	93	..	..	..	..	..	..	..	11	4
	Jubbal	..	..	..	..	2	..	32	..	8	..	99	..	..	..	..	..	..	..	32	..
	Other Simla Hill States	..	..	3	..	21	..	188	..	10	2	149	..	..	..	..	..	..	..	157	..
	B.—Having Political relations with the Government of India.	4,542	1	28	..	1,107	1	16,721	424	151	4	4,690	66	17	..	..	..	5	..	12,934	276
5	Loharu	10	..	..	..	..	..	56	..	1	..	4	..	..	..	..	..	..	..	42	..
6	Sirmoor	19	..	11	..	13	..	454	8	4	..	189	..	..	..	..	..	..	..	249	8
7	Bilaspur	12	..	1	..	28	..	154	..	4	..	370	..	..	..	..	..	..	..	110	..
8	Mandi	19	..	..	..	193	..	624	11	..	1	559	1	2	..	..	..	5	..	527	11
9	Suket	7	..	6	..	30	..	173	2	8	..	32	..	..	..	..	..	..	..	122	2
10	Kapurthala	137	..	..	..	20	..	1,941	57	..	..	282	8	..	..	..	..	..	..	1,782	54
11	Maler Kotla	17	..	..	..	42	..	460	24	13	..	328	15	..	..	..	..	..	..	282	12
12	Faridkot	216	..	..	..	5	..	1,465	42	1	..	224	1	..	..	..	..	..	..	1,172	42
13	Chamba	15	1	..	..	13	1	691	41	9	..	297	..	..	..	..	..	..	..	601	39
14	Patiala (Phulkian States)	1,918	..	..	..	592	..	3,216	125	7	1	289	..	..	..	..	..	..	..	1,980	..
15	Jind (Phulkian States)	271	..	10	..	71	..	756	13	3	2	712	..	..	..	..	..	..	..	634	13
16	Nabha (Phulkian States)	305	..	..	..	88	..	916	18	..	..	687	6	3	..	..	..	..	..	720	12
17	Bahawalpur	1,596	..	..	..	12	..	5,815	83	101	..	717	35	12	..	..	..	..	..	4,713	83
18	*Cities.* Lahore	..	..	..	..	..	..	14,364	75	7	1	8	..	12,411	50	..	..	6	..	159	..
19	*Cities.* Amritsar	..	..	..	..	..	..	1,901	9	..	..	..	..	1,288	9	..	..	..	..	..	..
20	*Cities.* Multan	..	..	..	..	..	..	2,059	4	6	..	2	..	1,865	4	..	..	2	..	..	..

C.—PUBLIC ADMINISTRATION AND LIBERAL ARTS.—*continued.*

VII.—PUBLIC ADMINISTRATION.—*concluded.* 44. Public Administration—*concluded.* Service of Indian and Foreign States. Total working dependants. Males.	Females.	Service of Indian and Foreign States. Total earners with subsidiary occupation. Males.	Females.	161.—*Municipal and other local (not village) service.* Total earners principal occupation. Males.	Females.	161. Total working dependants. Males.	Females.	161. Total earners with subsidiary occupation. Males.	Females.	162.—*Village-officials and servants other than watchmen.* Total earners principal occupation. Males.	Females.	162. Total working dependants. Males.	Females.	162. Total earners with subsidiary occupation. Males.	Females.	VIII.—PROFESSIONS & LIBERAL ARTS. Total Sub-Class VIII. Total earners principal occupation. Males.	Females.	Total Sub-Class VIII. Total working dependants. Males.	Females.	Total Sub-Class VIII. Total earners with subsidiary occupation. Males.	Females.	Serial No.
1055	1056	1057	1058	1059	1060	1061	1062	1063	1064	1065	1066	1067	1068	1069	1070	1071	1072	1073	1074	1075	1076	
152	9	1,176	22	16,067	356	166	35	468	43	14,588	87	267	16	17,455	44	183,883	19,601	6,070	3,878	21,682	1,088	
1	..	37	..	14,803	217	164	35	380	37	11,871	28	241	15	12,816	4	154,975	16,785	4,858	2,438	16,480	934	
1	..	37	..	2,204	16	9	..	120	10	2,058	..	11	1	5,543	2	23,736	3,196	847	537	3,482	319	
..	..	..	..	305	5	2	..	2	..	329	..	..	..	699	..	4,654	420	157	149	732	67	1
..	..	..	..	344	4	1	..	19	..	392	..	4	..	990	..	3,248	324	51	102	634	69	2
..	..	16	..	323	3	2	..	9	..	557	..	2	..	922	..	3,432	445	50	77	373	41	3
1	..	17	..	307	..	4	..	8	2	375	..	2	..	1,199	2	5,113	775	35	97	667	96	4
..	..	3	..	543	4	..	..	62	8	399	..	3	1	1,711	..	6,644	1,051	52	107	1,007	45	5
..	..	1	..	382	..	..	..	20	..	6	..	..	..	22	..	645	181	2	5	69	1	6
..	..	..	..	1,638	49	7	13	92	12	1,960	..	54	1	3,566	..	28,296	3,438	1,949	895	5,211	151	
..	..	..	..	4	..	..	..	1	..	358	..	2	..	44	..	4,017	308	317	57	1,393	15	7
..	..	..	..	415	3	1	1	29	..	199	..	2	..	939	..	6,674	790	175	74	1,244	29	8
..	..	..	..	347	15	1	11	29	12	458	..	7	..	723	..	6,769	1,001	1,242	117	1,280	30	9
..	..	..	..	321	22	1	1	11	..	509	..	4	..	1,034	..	5,964	755	106	115	754	25	10
..	..	..	..	551	9	4	..	22	..	436	..	39	1	427	..	4,872	584	109	32	540	52	11
..	..	..	..	4,497	54	26	2	48	12	2,882	..	14	..	2,082	1	47,939	4,286	724	427	2,590	144	
..	..	..	..	1,989	39	5	1	6	..	512	..	3	..	234	1	13,055	1,175	151	92	288	29	12
..	..	..	..	797	..	6	..	4	..	651	..	4	..	558	..	10,152	783	166	84	466	9	13
..	..	..	..	535	14	3	1	35	12	577	..	2	..	679	..	7,554	708	129	78	821	19	14
..	..	..	..	744	..	3	..	..	..	127	..	..	..	421	..	7,223	818	84	62	397	46	15
..	..	..	..	341	1	..	..	3	..	740	..	2	..	17	..	6,014	546	59	56	382	24	16
..	..	..	..	91	..	9	..	..	..	225	..	3	..	173	..	3,941	256	135	55	236	17	17
..	..	..	..	1,912	27	20	1	44	..	1,943	3	127	13	846	1	26,902	3,114	1,373	763	2,832	119	
..	..	..	..	228	1	..	..	10	..	592	..	81	..	368	..	7,800	703	405	234	572	19	18
..	..	..	..	489	9	..	..	..	..	443	..	1	..	203	1	5,075	615	52	43	311	17	19
..	..	..	..	537	11	10	..	15	..	139	..	33	..	84	..	3,949	555	465	364	644	38	20
..	..	..	..	150	3	6	..	3	..	164	..	5	..	16	..	4,341	545	305	49	409	7	21
..	..	..	..	276	2	4	..	15	..	499	3	6	13	78	..	4,059	509	130	45	776	34	22
..	..	..	..	232	1	..	1	1	..	106	..	1	..	97	..	1,678	187	16	28	120	4	23
..	..	..	..	4,552	71	102	19	76	3	3,078	25	35	..	779	..	28,102	2,751	465	316	2,365	201	
..	..	..	..	1,393	27	4	..	19	..	581	1	19	..	275	..	4,624	345	119	26	362	12	24
..	..	..	..	1,102	17	75	19	7	..	424	..	..	..	189	..	6,065	872	111	58	482	76	25
..	..	..	..	491	4	..	..	9	1	226	..	4	..	153	..	5,289	364	52	34	208	15	26
..	..	..	..	880	14	22	..	12	1	592	24	1	..	30	..	6,064	426	71	44	733	43	27
..	..	..	..	384	9	1	..	21	1	582	..	8	..	72	..	3,089	454	70	77	327	52	28
..	..	..	..	302	..	..	..	8	..	673	..	3	..	60	..	2,971	290	42	77	258	3	29
151	9	1,139	22	1,264	139	2	..	88	6	2,712	9	26	1	4,639	40	28,908	2,816	1,212	1,435	5,152	154	
20	6	327	..	88	..	..	..	10	..	118	..	8	..	844	2	1,577	192	98	52	1,166	13	
1	..	8	..	..	..	..	..	..	..	6	..	..	..	74	..	118	10	1	4	86	..	1
..	..	2	..	7	..	..	..	..	..	7	..	..	..	77	..	134	30	..	2	19	..	2
..	..	2	..	5	..	..	..	..	..	34	..	..	..	100	..	481	53	20	6	88	1	3
19	6	315	..	76	..	..	..	10	..	71	..	8	..	593	2	844	99	77	40	978	12	4
5	..	44	..	..	..	..	..	1	..	7	..	2	..	46	..	40	2	9	5	74	..	
..	..	2	..	8	..	..	..	..	..	30	..	..	..	305	2	273	41	8	6	159	7	
1	4	101	..	54	..	..	..	4	..	8	..	..	..	74	..	123	12	11	7	105	1	
..	..	37	..	..	..	..	..	..	..	9	..	1	..	56	..	91	12	5	7	153	..	
6	..	32	..	..	..	..	..	..	..	..	..	2	..	67	..	39	1	6	4	119	..	
7	2	99	..	14	..	..	..	5	..	17	..	3	..	45	..	278	31	38	11	363	4	
181	3	812	22	1,176	139	2	..	78	6	2,594	9	18	1	3,795	38	27,331	2,624	1,114	1,383	3,986	141	
..	..	2	..	2	..	..	..	..	..	12	..	1	..	2	..	59	4	1	2	4	2	5
3	..	19	..	23	..	..	..	4	..	182	..	1	..	166	..	506	32	26	6	151	2	6
2	..	32	..	..	..	..	..	..	..	44	..	2	..	338	..	280	23	23	2	156	..	7
..	1	270	..	25	..	..	..	4	..	70	..	..	..	280	1	884	98	47	19	584	15	8
5	..	21	..	..	..	..	..	..	..	51	..	3	..	11	..	352	44	10	5	82	..	9
..	..	119	7	42	..	..	..	3	..	117	3	..	..	160	1	2,028	251	20	15	228	16	10
12	..	34	14	69	8	..	..	40	1	109	4	1	..	254	..	688	107	26	16	77	4	11
1	..	23	1	47	..	..	..	..	..	246	..	..	..	201	..	1,252	61	27	2	93	21	12
7	..	137	..	2	..	..	..	..	..	88	2	2	..	160	..	360	31	21	4	358	4	13
..	..	137	..	305	125	2	..	7	..	931	..	5	1	145	..	15,568	1,508	780	1,258	1,248	42	14
..	2	4	..	33	..	..	..	..	..	89	..	3	..	708	..	1,008	108	35	16	326	13	15
..	..	12	..	155	6	..	..	20	5	38	..	..	..	655	1	2,219	242	66	20	677	22	16
101	..	2	..	473	..	..	..	..	..	617	..	..	..	715	35	4,127	115	32	18	2	..	17
..	..	..	..	1,765	25	5	1	..	..	29	..	2	..	2	..	8,124	688	33	36	50	..	18
..	..	..	..	590	..	..	..	..	..	23	..	..	..	..	..	4,215	191	1	..	11	..	19
..	..	..	..	182	..	6	..	..	..	12	..	..	..	..	..	1,419	116	2	12	31	..	20

TABLE X.—OCCUPATION OR MEANS OF
DETAILS FOR DISTRICTS,

Class ..	C.—PUBLIC ADMINISTRATION AND LIBERAL ARTS.																		
Sub-class ..	VIII.—PROFESSIONS AND LIBERAL ARTS.																		
Order ..	45. Religion.																		
Group ..	*Total Order 45.*						163.—*Priests, ministers, etc.*						164.—*Monks, nuns, religious mendicants.*						
	Total earners principal occupation.		Total working dependants.		Total earners with subsidiary occupation.		Total earners principal occupation.		Total working dependants.		Total earners with subsidiary occupation.		Total earners principal occupation.		Total working dependants.		Total earners with subsidiary occupation.		
Serial No.	District or State.	Males.	Females.	Males.	Females.	Males.	Females.	Males.	Females.	Males.	Females.	Males.	Females.	Males.	Females.	Males.	Females.	Males.	Females.
1	2	1077	1078	1079	1080	1081	1082	1083	1084	1085	1086	1087	1088	1089	1090	1091	1092	1093	1094
	PUNJAB ..	**89,495**	**5,922**	**4,429**	**2,406**	**14,986**	**463**	**63,873**	**4,396**	**2,802**	**1,985**	**10,641**	**340**	**3,520**	**149**	**54**	**56**	**245**	**6**
	BRITISH TERRITORY ..	**71,199**	**4,267**	**3,445**	**1,126**	**11,215**	**387**	**49,954**	**2,895**	**1,942**	**730**	**8,180**	**270**	**2,283**	**127**	**29**	**53**	**169**	**4**
	AMBALA DIVISION ..	**9,445**	**903**	**193**	**178**	**2,440**	**136**	**7,694**	**792**	**165**	**162**	**2,174**	**126**	**92**	**17**	..	**1**	**8**	**2**
1	Hissar ..	1,654	121	67	65	540	30	1,342	104	57	60	508	30	14	1	..	..	..	..
2	Rohtak ..	1,003	97	34	32	456	35	821	95	32	32	442	35	41	1	..	..	1	..
3	Gurgaon ..	1,240	99	38	12	253	18	954	83	30	7	203	15	19	..	..	..	2	..
4	Karnal ..	2,392	333	23	31	518	38	2,120	289	20	28	485	33	16	11	..	..	5	2
5	Ambala ..	3,088	250	31	38	657	15	2,439	221	26	35	529	13	1	4	..	1	..	..
6	Simla ..	68	3	..	..	16	..	18	..	..	..	7	..	1	..	..	..	..	..
	JULLUNDUR DIVISION	**12,856**	**923**	**1,593**	**194**	**3,705**	**56**	**6,972**	**532**	**510**	**165**	**2,034**	**88**	**137**	**12**	**6**	..	..	**1**
7	Kangra ..	1,841	85	300	41	1,075	7	1,681	77	297	41	1,073	7	126	..	..	..	..	..
8	Hoshiarpur ..	3,107	245	131	25	757	13	587	52	10	..	89	1	..	..	..	..	..	..
9	Jullundur ..	2,457	259	1,005	50	944	11	1,449	111	101	47	223	11	..	..	..	..	..	..
10	Ludhiana ..	3,330	274	85	69	581	11	2,100	249	68	68	425	8	9	12	6	..	..	1
11	Ferozepore ..	2,121	60	72	9	348	14	1,155	43	34	9	224	11	2	..	..	..	..	..
	LAHORE DIVISION ..	**19,262**	**753**	**336**	**81**	**1,523**	**54**	**14,444**	**540**	**270**	**50**	**1,237**	**46**	**701**	**6**	**3**	**3**	**42**	..
12	Lahore ..	3,342	152	39	16	128	6	2,325	96	28	14	106	5	53	..	..	..	6	..
13	Amritsar ..	3,184	72	87	14	204	4	1,905	2	56	1	126	..	..	..	..	..	..	..
14	Gurdaspur ..	4,104	223	66	17	515	4	3,090	177	57	7	430	1	239	..	..	..	1	..
15	Sialkot ..	3,685	178	49	5	298	39	3,352	167	45	5	287	39	2	..	..	..	..	..
16	Gujranwala ..	3,331	80	42	10	252	..	2,619	59	37	7	212	..	360	4	..	3	35	..
17	Sheikhupura ..	1,616	48	53	19	126	1	1,153	39	47	16	76	1	47	2	3	..	..	..
	RAWALPINDI DIVISION	**15,072**	**1,141**	**1,032**	**555**	**2,217**	**70**	**12,677**	**721**	**842**	**312**	**1,876**	**29**	**420**	**75**	**12**	**4**	**72**	..
18	Gujrat ..	5,408	333	365	212	414	9	5,079	320	336	211	371	9	..	..	..	..	..	..
19	Shahpur ..	2,433	201	37	15	266	5	2,196	182	32	12	236	5	4	..	..	1	1	..
20	Jhelum ..	1,960	271	377	282	559	35	1,594	100	364	57	527	9	..	13	..	1	..	..
21	Rawalpindi ..	2,290	145	190	12	332	3	1,489	38	72	4	186	2	..	1	..	..	..	..
22	Attock ..	2,347	149	52	29	572	18	1,721	59	34	23	485	4	416	61	12	2	71	..
23	Mianwali ..	634	42	11	5	74	..	598	22	4	5	71	..	..	..	..	..	..	..
	MULTAN DIVISION ..	**14,564**	**547**	**291**	**118**	**1,330**	**51**	**8,167**	**310**	**155**	**41**	**859**	**31**	**988**	**17**	**8**	**45**	**47**	**1**
24	Montgomery ..	2,798	63	103	14	264	3	1,276	8	30	..	133	2	..	..	..	..	..	..
25	Lyallpur ..	2,500	103	56	22	235	18	1,285	73	27	21	196	18	150	..	..	..	..	..
26	Jhang ..	3,602	198	51	17	156	9	2,921	196	51	17	144	9	170	2	..	..	4	..
27	Multan ..	3,354	49	34	..	438	6	1,073	9	16	..	197	..	351	6	..	..	17	1
28	Muzaffargarh ..	1,278	106	30	18	139	15	1,133	14	23	1	120	2	..	..	..	..	..	..
29	Dera Ghazi Khan ..	1,032	28	17	47	98	..	479	10	8	2	69	..	262	9	8	45	26	..
	PUNJAB STATES ..	**18,296**	**1,655**	**984**	**1,280**	**3,771**	**96**	**13,919**	**1,501**	**860**	**1,255**	**2,461**	**70**	**1,237**	**22**	**25**	**3**	**76**	**2**
	A.—Having Political relations with the Punjab Government. ..	**758**	**53**	**50**	**15**	**689**	**9**	**540**	**40**	**25**	**9**	**411**	**5**	**26**	**7**	**2**	**2**	**6**	**2**
1	Dujana ..	71	2	1	1	55	..	68	1	1	..	46	..	..	1	..	1	..	..
2	Pataudi ..	65	7	..	..	18	..	50	7	..	..	18	..	7	..	..	..	..	..
3	Kalsia ..	245	6	17	1	56	..	185	6	7	1	37	..	1	..	..	..	..	..
4	SIMLA HILL STATES ..	**377**	**38**	**32**	**18**	**560**	**9**	**237**	**26**	**17**	**8**	**310**	**5**	**18**	**6**	**2**	**1**	**6**	**2**
	Bashahr ..	8	..	2	3	16	..	6	..	..	2	10	..	..	..	..	..	1	..
	Nalagarh ..	144	26	7	2	121	6	126	17	7	..	106	3	..	5	..	1	1	2
	Keonthal ..	42	..	6	..	69	1	14	..	1	..	27	..	..	..	2	..	..	..
	Baghal ..	61	6	5	4	106	..	..	5	..	4	..	..	16	1	..	..	2	..
	Jubbal ..	8	1	2	2	64	..	..	..	..	..	..	..	..	..	..	..	..	..
	Other Simla Hill States ..	114	5	10	2	184	2	91	4	9	2	167	2	2	..	..	..	2	..
	B.—Having Political relations with the Government of India. ..	**17,538**	**1,602**	**934**	**1,265**	**3,082**	**87**	**13,379**	**1,461**	**835**	**1,246**	**2,050**	**65**	**1,211**	**15**	**23**	**1**	**70**	..
5	Loharu ..	35	2	1	..	3	2	29	1	1	..	2	2	1	..	..	..	..	..
6	Sirmoor ..	279	14	13	2	116	..	131	6	12	..	80	..	15	2	..	1	..	..
7	Bilaspur ..	219	20	21	..	124	..	148	20	20	..	104	..	2	..	..	..	6	..
8	Mandi ..	585	28	47	13	538	12	100	2	30	..	79	..	8	..	..	..	..	..
9	Suket ..	308	17	10	1	62	..	9	2	..	1	..	..	..	..	..	..	..	..
10	Kapurthala ..	824	82	17	1	92	11	281	47	1	1	19	8	..	..	..	..	..	..
11	Maler Kotla ..	337	30	16	2	56	4	..	1	..	..	..	..	..	..	..	..	..	..
12	Faridkot ..	899	13	25	..	57	2	15	12	..	..	..	2	689	1	22	..	55	..
13	Chamba ..	246	9	16	2	232	3	2	..	..	..	1	..	..	1	..	..	..	..
14	Patiala } Phulkian States.	9,821	1,133	695	1,226	909	21	9,018	1,123	695	1,226	909	21	413	10	..	..	..	..
15	Jind } Phulkian States.	483	51	14	2	296	13	418	49	14	2	289	13	..	..	..	..	..	..
16	Nabha } Phulkian States.	1,417	166	56	11	595	19	1,201	161	53	11	565	19	64	1	1	..	9	..
17	Bahawalpur ..	2,085	37	9	5	2	..	2,027	37	9	5	2	..	19	..	..	..	..	..
18	*Cities.* Lahore ..	1,604	62	7	5	5	..	916	33	3	5	5	..	10	..	..	..	..	..
19	*Cities.* Amritsar ..	974	10	..	..	..	..	709	..	..	..	..	..	..	..	..	..	..	..
20	*Cities.* Multan ..	718	16	..	..	..	..	196	1	..	..	..	..	39	..	..	..	..	..

LIVELIHOOD.—GENERAL TABLE.

STATES AND CITIES.—*continued.*

C.—PUBLIC ADMINISTRATION AND LIBERAL ARTS—*continued.*

VIII.—PROFESSIONS AND LIBERAL ARTS—*continued.*

45.—Religion.—*concluded.* 165.—*Other religious workers.* Total earners principal occupation. Males. 1095	Females. 1096	Total working dependants. Males. 1097	Females. 1098	Total earners with subsidiary occupation. Males. 1099	Females. 1100	166.—*Servants in religious edifices, burial and burning grounds, pilgrim conductors, circumcisers, etc.* Total earners principal occupation. Males. 1101	Females. 1102	Total working dependants. Males. 1103	Females. 1104	Total earners with subsidiary occupation. Males. 1105	Females. 1106	46. Law. *Total Order 46.* Total earners principal occupation. Males. 1107	Females. 1108	Total working dependants. Males. 1109	Females. 1110	Total earners with subsidiary occupation. Males. 1111	Females. 1112	167.—*Lawyers of all kinds including (Qazis, Law-agents, and Mukhtars).* Total earners principal occupation. Males. 1113	Females. 1114	Total working dependants. Males. 1115	Females. 1116	Total earners with subsidiary occupation. Males. 1117	Females. 1118	Serial No.
5,055	552	222	264	415	43	17,047	825	1,851	101	3,685	74	10,129	..	108	..	422	..	5,228	..	51	..	206	..	
4,728	541	215	263	387	42	14,234	704	1,259	80	2,479	51	8,941	..	98	..	311	..	4,735	..	48	..	178	..	
452	23	9	6	50	2	1,207	71	19	9	208	6	1,168	..	5	..	8	..	506	..	1	..	3	..	
25	3	1	1	1	..	273	13	9	4	31	..	276	..	1	..	..	..	109	..	..	..	..	..	1
37	..	..	..	5	..	104	1	2	..	8	..	218	..	..	..	3	..	88	..	..	..	1	..	2
152	8	7	4	22	2	115	8	1	1	26	1	101	..	1	..	..	..	49	..	..	..	..	..	3
17	..	..	..	2	..	239	33	3	3	26	3	221	..	1	..	3	..	77	..	..	..	1	..	4
201	10	1	1	20	..	447	15	4	1	108	2	327	..	2	..	1	..	155	..	1	..	1	..	5
20	2	..	..	..	..	29	1	..	..	9	..	45	..	..	..	1	..	28	..	..	..	..	..	6
251	101	22	1	34	1	5,496	278	1,055	28	1,637	16	1,599	..	38	..	65	..	745	..	14	..	25	..	
11	7	..	..	..	..	23	1	3	..	2	..	374	..	..	..	16	..	67	..	..	..	2	..	7
..	..	..	..	..	..	2,520	193	121	25	668	12	283	..	2	..	14	..	129	..	2	..	9	..	8
117	91	7	..	21	..	891	57	897	3	700	..	384	..	36	..	22	..	246	..	12	..	14	..	9
15	3	..	1	2	1	1,206	10	11	..	154	1	307	..	..	..	5	..	180	..	..	..	..	..	10
108	..	15	..	11	..	856	17	23	..	113	3	251	..	..	..	8	..	123	..	..	..	..	..	11
2,300	106	43	9	99	3	1,817	101	20	19	145	5	3,755	..	18	..	76	..	2,135	..	8	..	19	..	
464	31	8	..	12	..	500	25	3	2	4	1	1,613	..	13	..	17	..	991	..	8	..	8	..	12
976	21	23	..	16	..	303	49	8	13	62	4	685	..	3	..	23	..	473	..	..	..	7	..	13
555	40	8	9	68	3	220	6	1	1	16	..	487	..	..	..	30	..	223	..	..	..	2	..	14
116	3	2	..	..	..	215	8	2	..	11	..	374	..	1	..	3	..	203	..	..	..	2	..	15
70	8	..	..	1	..	282	9	5	..	4	..	464	..	1	..	3	..	163	..	..	..	..	..	16
119	3	2	..	2	..	297	4	1	3	48	..	132	..	..	..	..	..	82	..	..	..	..	..	17
1,200	227	114	230	169	29	775	118	64	9	100	12	1,308	..	28	..	33	..	692	..	21	..	24	..	
328	9	29	1	43	..	1	4	..	..	..	..	373	..	3	..	5	..	153	..	1	..	..	..	18
103	11	..	1	..	..	130	8	5	1	22	..	324	..	3	..	1	..	177	..	3	..	1	..	19
273	102	13	223	39	26	93	56	..	1	..	..	154	..	7	..	3	..	115	..	7	..	3	..	20
317	66	65	4	84	1	484	40	53	4	62	..	247	..	5	..	3	..	119	..	..	..	..	..	21
143	19	..	1	..	2	67	10	6	3	16	12	165	..	10	..	21	..	89	..	10	..	20	..	22
36	20	7	..	3	..	..	..	..	..	..	..	45	..	..	..	..	..	39	..	..	..	..	..	23
525	84	27	17	85	7	4,939	136	101	15	389	12	1,091	..	9	..	129	..	657	..	4	..	107	..	
..	7	..	..	..	..	1,522	48	73	14	131	1	158	..	4	..	3	..	49	..	..	..	1	..	24
464	12	27	..	32	..	601	18	2	1	7	..	395	..	4	..	18	..	216	..	4	..	18	..	25
8	..	..	..	..	..	503	..	..	..	8	..	86	..	..	..	1	..	81	..	..	..	1	..	26
22	2	..	..	1	..	1,908	32	18	..	223	5	184	..	..	..	70	..	106	..	..	..	70	..	27
19	56	..	17	2	7	126	36	7	..	17	6	162	..	..	..	24	..	154	..	..	..	10	..	28
12	7	..	..	..	..	279	2	1	..	3	..	106	..	1	..	13	..	51	..	..	..	7	..	29
327	11	7	1	28	1	2,813	121	92	21	1,206	23	1,188	..	10	..	111	..	493	..	3	..	28	..	
32	2	3	1	1	..	160	4	20	3	271	2	67	..	2	..	33	..	23	..	..	..	15	..	
..	..	..	..	..	..	3	..	..	..	9	..	..	..	..	..	2	..	..	..	..	..	1	..	1
6	..	..	..	..	..	2	..	..	..	..	..	1	..	..	..	..	..	..	..	..	..	..	..	2
25	..	3	..	1	..	34	..	7	..	18	..	23	..	..	..	1	..	7	..	..	..	..	..	3
1	2	..	1	..	..	121	4	13	3	244	2	43	..	2	..	30	..	16	..	..	..	14	..	4
..	..	..	..	..	..	2	..	2	1	5	..	2	..	2	..	6	..	..	..	..	..	1	..	
..	2	..	1	..	..	18	2	..	..	14	1	18	..	..	..	1	..	8	..	..	..	1	..	
..	..	..	..	..	..	28	..	3	..	42	1	6	..	..	..	4	..	1	..	..	..	2	..	
..	..	..	..	..	..	45	..	5	..	104	..	1	..	..	..	1	..	1	..	..	..	1	..	
..	..	..	..	..	..	8	1	2	2	64	..	2	..	..	..	..	..	..	..	..	..	..	..	
1	..	..	..	..	..	20	1	1	..	15	..	14	..	..	..	18	..	6	..	..	..	9	..	
295	9	4	..	27	1	2,653	117	72	18	935	21	1,121	..	8	..	78	..	470	..	3	..	13	..	
..	..	..	..	..	..	5	1	..	..	1	..	2	..	..	..	..	..	..	..	..	..	..	..	5
3	..	..	..	..	..	130	6	1	1	36	..	25	..	..	..	..	..	9	..	..	..	..	..	6
1	..	..	..	..	..	68	..	1	..	14	..	9	..	..	..	1	..	..	..	..	..	..	..	7
1	..	..	..	..	..	476	26	17	13	459	12	11	..	..	..	4	..	9	..	..	..	3	..	8
..	..	..	..	..	..	299	15	10	..	62	..	4	..	..	..	2	..	..	..	..	..	1	..	9
130	6	3	..	20	1	413	29	13	..	53	2	137	..	..	..	10	..	80	..	..	..	1	..	10
..	..	..	..	..	..	337	29	10	2	56	4	58	..	..	..	..	..	12	..	..	..	..	..	11
..	..	..	..	..	..	195	..	3	..	2	..	3	..	..	..	..	..	2	..	..	..	..	..	12
..	..	..	..	..	..	244	8	16	2	231	3	..	..	..	..	..	..	..	..	..	..	..	..	13
65	..	..	..	..	..	325	..	..	..	..	..	477	..	8	..	36	..	221	..	3	..	..	..	14
19	..	..	..	..	..	46	2	..	..	7	..	18	..	..	..	1	..	3	..	..	..	..	..	15
61	3	1	..	7	..	91	1	1	..	14	..	184	..	..	..	24	..	101	..	..	..	8	..	16
15	..	..	..	..	..	24	..	..	..	..	..	193	..	..	..	..	..	33	..	..	..	..	..	17
282	29	4	..	..	..	396	..	..	..	..	..	1,454	..	11	..	15	..	905	..	8	..	8	..	18
263	10	..	..	..	..	2	..	..	..	..	..	519	..	..	..	5	..	399	..	..	..	5	..	19
..	..	..	..	..	..	483	15	..	..	..	..	145	..	..	..	15	..	78	..	..	..	15	..	20

TABLE X.—OCCUPATION OR MEANS OF

DETAILS FOR DISTRICTS.

Class .. C.—PUBLIC ADMINISTRATION AND LIBERAL ARTS.

Sub-class .. VIII. PROFESSIONS AND LIBERAL ARTS.

Order .. 46. *Law—concluded.* | 47. Medicine.

Serial No.	District or State.	Group 168.—*Lawyers' clerks, Petition-writers, etc.* Total earners principal occupation. Males.	Females.	Total working dependants. Males.	Females.	Total earners with subsidiary occupation. Males.	Females.	*Total Order 47.* Total earners principal occupation. Males.	Females.	Total working dependants. Males.	Females.	Total earners with subsidiary occupation. Males.	Females.	169.—*Registered medical practitioners including oculists.* Total earners principal occupation. Males.	Females.	Total working dependants. Males.	Females.	Total earners with subsidiary occupation. Males.	Females.	170.—*Other the healing-* Total earners principal occupation. Males.	Females.
1	2	1119	1120	1121	1122	1123	1124	1125	1126	1127	1128	1129	1130	1131	1132	1133	1134	1135	1136	1137	1138
	PUNJAB	**4,901**	..	**57**	..	**216**	..	**20,858**	**7,627**	**268**	**932**	**2,137**	**478**	**9,660**	**418**	**119**	**43**	**940**	**6**	**6,323**	**118**
	BRITISH TERRITORY	**4,206**	..	**50**	..	**133**	..	**18,342**	**7,002**	**235**	**860**	**1,703**	**429**	**9,050**	**387**	**109**	**43**	**820**	**6**	**5,001**	**116**
	AMBALA DIVISION	**682**	..	**4**	..	**5**	..	**2,253**	**1,415**	**26**	**211**	**271**	**155**	**434**	**28**	..	..	**15**	..	**843**	**6**
1	Hissar	167	..	1	..	..	..	437	152	20	28	40	35	82	5	..	..	1	..	161	..
2	Rohtak	130	..	..	..	2	..	319	110	..	41	35	33	64	2	..	..	7	..	114	..
3	Gurgaon	52	..	1	..	..	..	321	225	..	47	33	22	58	4	..	..	..	..	65	..
4	Karnal	144	..	1	..	2	..	381	300	3	40	34	39	66	..	..	..	1	..	160	1
5	Ambala	172	..	1	..	..	..	680	518	3	52	117	25	120	12	..	..	5	..	332	5
6	Simla	17	..	..	..	1	..	115	110	..	3	12	1	44	5	..	..	1	..	11	..
	JULLUNDUR DIVISION	**854**	..	**24**	..	**40**	..	**2,839**	**1,662**	**48**	**151**	**503**	**81**	**1,161**	**31**	**19**	..	**209**	**1**	**1,290**	**8**
7	Kangra	307	..	..	..	11	..	259	151	..	14	150	5	111	9	..	..	39	..	117	3
8	Hoshiarpur	154	..	..	..	5	..	774	385	9	29	180	16	298	2	7	..	87	..	368	1
9	Jullundur	138	..	24	..	8	..	824	539	25	56	81	19	317	4	5	..	38	..	437	..
10	Ludhiana	127	..	..	..	5	..	513	313	..	35	42	6	164	..	..	..	4	..	233	2
11	Ferozepore	128	..	..	..	8	..	469	254	9	17	50	35	271	16	7	..	41	1	135	2
	LAHORE DIVISION	**1,620**	..	**10**	..	**57**	..	**6,906**	**1,880**	**61**	**258**	**459**	**71**	**4,132**	**186**	**37**	**30**	**315**	**4**	**1,229**	**76**
12	Lahore	622	..	5	..	9	..	2,163	466	18	44	79	19	1,125	87	8	6	61	..	248	3
13	Amritsar	212	..	3	..	16	..	2,069	435	10	64	55	4	1,440	29	5	4	22	..	433	28
14	Gurdaspur	264	..	..	..	28	..	885	343	9	58	167	14	571	18	4	9	149	..	93	5
15	Sialkot	171	..	1	..	1	..	590	284	9	35	31	7	381	13	9	2	26	..	110	3
16	Gujranwala	301	..	1	..	3	..	608	222	3	34	60	16	296	18	3	..	27	..	121	1
17	Sheikhupura	50	..	..	..	..	..	591	130	12	23	58	11	319	21	8	9	30	4	224	36
	RAWALPINDI DIVISION	**616**	..	**7**	..	**9**	..	**2,505**	**955**	**60**	**105**	**136**	**31**	**1,784**	**127**	**36**	**13**	**100**	**1**	**413**	**20**
18	Gujrat	220	..	2	..	5	..	528	238	9	21	43	7	357	11	6	..	22	..	92	5
19	Shahpur	147	..	..	..	..	..	629	160	6	8	13	9	575	90	4	..	12	1	22	4
20	Jhelum	39	..	..	..	..	..	413	137	12	22	12	..	176	16	4	13	9	..	159	8
21	Rawalpindi	128	..	5	..	3	..	452	224	26	30	20	4	303	4	15	..	17	..	83	..
22	Attock	76	..	..	..	1	..	258	127	7	4	38	8	202	4	7	..	29	..	33	3
23	Mianwali	6	..	..	..	..	..	225	69	..	20	11	3	171	2	..	..	11	..	24	..
	MULTAN DIVISION	**434**	..	**5**	..	**22**	..	**3,839**	**1,090**	**45**	**135**	**334**	**91**	**1,539**	**15**	**17**	..	**181**	..	**1,226**	**6**
24	Montgomery	109	..	4	..	2	..	282	170	4	12	18	1	183	4	4	..	15	..	33	1
25	Lyallpur	179	..	..	..	..	..	1,136	409	13	20	82	38	540	8	12	..	41	..	340	2
26	Jhang	5	..	..	..	..	..	373	63	..	5	20	3	245	2	..	..	18	..	117	1
27	Multan	78	..	..	..	..	..	1,108	201	14	41	135	35	188	1	1	..	104	..	323	1
28	Muzaffargarh	8	..	..	..	14	..	614	104	10	37	49	14	260	..	..	..	..	..	311	..
29	Dera Ghazi Khan	55	..	1	..	6	..	326	143	4	20	30	..	123	..	..	..	3	..	102	1
	PUNJAB STATES	**695**	..	**7**	..	**83**	..	**2,516**	**625**	**33**	**72**	**434**	**49**	**610**	**31**	**10**	..	**120**	..	**1,322**	**2**
	A.—HAVING POLITICAL RELATIONS WITH THE PUNJAB GOVERNMENT.	**44**	..	**2**	..	**18**	..	**154**	**69**	**4**	**10**	**126**	**4**	**24**	..	**1**	..	**6**	..	**79**	..
1	Dujana	..	..	..	..	1	..	10	1	..	..	1	..	1	..	..	..	..	..	1	..
2	Pataudi	1	..	..	..	..	..	14	18	..	2	..	..	1	..	..	..	..	..	8	..
3	Kalsia	16	..	..	..	1	..	37	22	..	4	10	1	7	..	..	..	..	..	18	..
4	SIMLA HILL STATES	**27**	..	**2**	..	**16**	..	**93**	**28**	**4**	**4**	**115**	**3**	**15**	..	**1**	..	**6**	..	**52**	..
	Bashahr	2	..	2	..	5	..	3	..	..	..	9	..	2	..	..	..	..	..	..	..
	Nalagarh	10	..	..	..	..	..	30	10	..	..	25	1	2	..	..	..	..	..	23	..
	Keonthal	5	..	..	..	2	..	15	6	1	..	4	..	5	..	..	..	..	..	5	..
	Baghal	..	..	..	..	..	..	5	3	..	1	29	..	1	..	..	..	..	..	3	..
	Jubbal	2	..	..	..	..	..	3	..	1	..	2	..	..	..	..	..	1	..	1	..
	Other Simla Hill States	8	..	..	..	9	..	37	9	2	3	46	2	5	..	1	..	5	..	20	..
	B.—HAVING POLITICAL RELATIONS WITH THE GOVERNMENT OF INDIA.	**651**	..	**5**	..	**65**	..	**2,362**	**556**	**29**	**62**	**308**	**45**	**586**	**31**	**9**	..	**114**	..	**1,243**	**2**
5	Loharu	2	..	..	..	..	..	5	2	..	1	1	..	1	..	..	..	..	..	1	..
6	Sirmoor	16	..	..	..	..	..	43	12	..	1	5	2	15	1	..	..	1	..	13	..
7	Bilaspur	9	..	..	..	1	..	5	2	..	1	17	..	1	..	..	..	..	..	2	..
8	Mandi	2	..	..	..	1	..	83	19	..	..	19	2	19	2	..	..	1	..	63	..
9	Suket	4	..	..	..	1	..	15	4	..	..	4	..	..	..	..	..	..	..	11	..
10	Kapurthala	57	..	..	..	9	..	272	88	1	13	33	..	101	6	..	..	16	..	66	1
11	Maler Kotla	46	..	..	..	..	..	62	35	2	8	9	..	40	11	1	..	1	..	17	..
12	Faridkot	1	..	..	..	..	..	84	42	1	2	18	19	19	..	..	..	1	..	64	..
13	Chamba	..	..	..	..	..	..	42	10	1	2	48	1	31	..	1	..	30	..	11	..
14	Patiala (Phulkian States)	256	..	5	..	36	..	940	265	10	29	124	21	304	5	6	..	64	..	453	..
15	Jind (Phulkian States)	15	..	..	..	1	..	108	10	2	2	5	..	19	2	1	..	..	..	46	1
16	Nabha (Phulkian States)	83	..	..	..	16	..	143	61	7	3	25	..	16	2	..	..	..	..	83	..
17	Bahawalpur	160	..	..	..	..	..	560	6	5	..	..	..	21	2	..	..	..	..	413	..
18	*Cities.* Lahore	549	..	3	..	7	..	1,582	219	8	15	11	..	755	78	8	5	..	..	88	..
19	*Cities.* Amritsar	120	..	..	..	..	..	903	59	..	..	1	..	505	1	..	..	..	..	267	..
20	*Cities.* Multan	67	..	..	..	..	..	202	31	1	12	6	..	37	..	..	..	2	..	55	..

C.—PUBLIC ADMINISTRATION AND LIBERAL ARTS—*continued*.

VIII.—PROFESSIONS AND LIBERAL ARTS—*continued*.

47. Medicine—*concluded*.

48. Instruction.

persons practising arts without being registered. Total working dependants.		Total earners with subsidiary occupation.		*171.—Dentists.* Total earners principal occupation.		Total earners with subsidiary occupation.		*172.—Midwives, Vaccinators, compounders, nurses, masseurs, etc.* Total earners principal occupation.		Total working dependants.		Total earners with subsidiary occupation.		*173.—Veterinary Surgeons.* Total earners principal occupation.		Total working dependants.		Total earners with subsidiary occupation.		*Total Order 48.* Total earners principal occupation.		Total working dependants.		Total earners with subsidiary occupation.		Serial No.
Males.	Females.	Males.	Females.	Males.	Females.	Males.	Females.	Males.	Females.	Males.	Females.	Males.	Females.	Males.	Females.	Males.	Females.	Males.	Females.	Males.	Females.	Males.	Females.	Males.	Females.	
1139	1140	1141	1142	1143	1144	1145	1146	1147	1148	1149	1150	1151	1152	1153	1154	1155	1156	1157	1158	1159	1160	1161	1162	1163	1164	
99	13	983	5	401	9	24	..	4,241	7,082	46	876	183	467	233	..	4	..	7	..	34,425	3,968	459	171	1,527	37	
81	13	709	4	363	9	12	..	3,716	6,490	41	804	156	419	212	..	4	..	6	..	31,474	3,755	429	169	1,230	36	
15	1	201	1	15	..	..	..	894	1,381	11	210	50	154	67	..	..	..	5	..	5,926	448	12	15	181	2	
11	..	30	..	2	..	..	..	181	147	9	28	9	35	11	..	..	..	..	..	1,055	69	1	12	9	..	1
..	..	21	..	..	..	..	..	121	108	..	41	4	33	20	..	..	..	3	..	1,251	43	6	1	72	..	2
..	..	25	..	..	..	..	..	188	221	..	47	8	22	10	..	..	..	..	..	1,005	59	1	..	34	1	3
2	..	27	..	5	..	..	..	136	299	1	40	6	39	14	..	..	..	..	..	1,154	60	1	2	7	..	4
2	1	98	1	7	..	..	..	212	501	1	51	12	24	9	..	..	..	2	..	1,356	169	2	..	33	1	5
..	..	..	..	1	..	..	..	56	105	..	3	11	1	3	..	..	..	..	..	105	43	1	..	26	..	6
19	1	260	1	..	..	..	..	386	1,623	5	150	33	79	2	..	..	..	1	..	6,437	601	97	18	333	7	
..	1	110	1	..	..	..	..	31	139	..	13	1	4	..	..	..	..	..	..	1,302	70	16	2	108	1	7
..	..	74	..	..	..	..	..	107	382	2	29	18	16	1	..	..	..	1	..	1,419	98	..	1	69	..	8
17	..	38	..	..	..	..	..	70	555	3	56	5	19	..	..	..	..	..	..	1,609	109	71	6	54	..	9
..	..	30	..	..	..	..	..	115	311	..	35	8	6	1	..	..	..	..	..	973	131	6	6	45	6	10
2	..	8	..	..	..	..	..	63	236	..	17	1	34	..	..	..	..	..	..	1,134	193	4	3	57	..	11
8	6	93	1	313	..	11	..	1,117	1,618	12	222	40	66	115	..	4	..	..	..	9,333	1,298	91	44	181	5	
1	..	7	1	272	..	11	..	491	376	9	38	..	18	27	..	..	..	..	..	2,369	466	15	23	26	3	12
3	6	30	..	41	..	..	..	151	378	2	54	3	4	4	..	..	..	..	..	2,513	180	34	3	72	..	13
1	..	7	..	..	..	..	..	138	320	..	49	11	14	83	..	4	..	..	..	1,341	133	7	3	38	..	14
..	..	..	..	..	..	..	..	99	268	..	33	5	7	..	..	..	..	..	..	1,417	270	10	6	19	..	15
..	..	22	..	..	..	..	..	191	203	..	34	20	16	..	..	..	..	..	..	932	194	3	1	7	..	16
3	..	27	..	..	..	..	..	47	73	1	14	1	7	1	..	..	..	..	..	758	53	22	8	19	2	17
17	5	26	1	18	9	..	..	271	799	7	87	10	29	19	..	..	..	..	..	5,857	794	185	78	360	14	
1	..	13	..	2	..	..	..	77	222	2	21	7	7	..	..	..	..	..	..	1,127	105	8	1	71	1	18
2	..	..	1	7	..	..	..	11	66	..	8	1	7	14	..	..	..	..	..	1,268	219	2	11	23	3	19
6	5	3	..	6	9	..	..	72	104	2	4	..	..	..	..	..	..	..	..	969	127	56	56	68	2	20
8	..	2	..	..	..	..	..	66	220	3	30	1	4	..	..	..	..	..	..	1,155	165	76	6	52	..	21
..	..	8	..	..	..	..	..	22	120	..	4	1	8	1	..	..	..	..	..	732	114	40	3	111	7	22
..	..	..	..	3	..	..	..	23	67	..	20	..	3	4	..	..	..	..	..	606	64	3	1	35	1	23
22	..	129	..	17	..	1	..	1,048	1,069	6	185	23	91	9	..	..	..	..	..	8,921	619	44	14	175	8	
..	..	..	..	1	..	..	..	65	165	..	12	3	1	..	..	..	..	..	..	429	62	2	..	10	..	24
1	..	40	..	13	..	..	..	243	399	..	20	1	38	..	..	..	..	..	..	942	144	12	2	45	3	25
..	..	2	..	..	..	..	..	10	60	..	5	..	3	1	..	..	..	..	..	763	101	1	12	15	3	26
10	..	28	..	..	..	1	..	597	199	3	41	2	35	..	..	..	..	..	..	296	73	6	..	16	..	27
7	..	40	..	..	..	..	..	43	104	3	37	9	14	..	..	..	..	..	..	818	168	12	..	61	..	28
4	..	19	..	3	..	..	..	90	142	..	20	8	..	8	..	..	..	..	..	873	71	11	..	28	2	29
18	..	274	1	38	..	12	..	525	592	5	72	27	48	21	..	..	..	1	..	2,951	213	80	2	297	1	
2	..	106	1	..	..	..	..	48	69	1	10	13	3	3	..	..	..	1	..	219	16	18	1	107	..	
..	..	..	..	..	..	..	..	8	1	..	..	1	..	..	..	..	..	..	..	19	2	..	..	4	..	1
..	..	..	..	..	..	..	..	5	18	..	2	..	..	..	..	..	..	..	..	27	1	..	..	1	..	2
..	..	9	..	..	..	..	..	11	22	..	4	1	1	1	..	..	..	..	..	61	6	..	..	5	..	3
2	..	97	1	..	..	..	..	24	28	1	4	11	2	2	..	..	..	1	..	109	7	18	1	97	..	4
..	..	5	..	..	..	..	..	1	..	..	..	4	..	..	..	..	..	..	..	10	..	2	..	19	..	
..	..	24	..	..	..	..	..	4	10	..	..	..	1	1	..	..	..	1	..	31	1	1	..	1	..	
1	..	4	..	..	..	..	..	4	6	..	..	..	..	1	..	..	..	..	..	22	2	..	..	6	..	
..	..	28	..	..	..	..	..	1	3	..	1	1	..	..	..	..	..	..	..	8	1	..	1	6	..	
..	..	1	..	..	..	..	..	2	..	1	..	..	..	..	..	..	..	..	..	1	..	..	..	12	..	
1	..	35	1	..	..	..	..	12	9	..	3	6	1	..	..	..	..	..	..	37	3	15	..	53	..	
16	..	168	..	38	..	12	..	477	523	4	62	14	45	18	..	..	..	..	..	2,782	197	12	1	190	1	
..	..	1	..	..	..	..	..	1	2	..	1	..	..	2	..	..	..	..	..	7	..	..	..	..	..	5
..	..	3	..	1	..	..	..	12	11	..	1	1	2	2	..	..	..	..	..	130	4	..	..	18	..	6
..	..	15	..	..	..	..	..	2	2	..	1	2	..	..	..	..	..	..	..	22	..	..	..	4	..	7
..	..	18	..	..	..	..	..	1	17	..	..	..	2	..	..	..	..	..	..	17	14	..	..	1	..	8
..	..	4	..	..	..	..	..	4	4	..	..	..	..	..	..	..	..	..	..	11	..	..	..	..	..	9
1	..	15	..	..	..	..	..	105	81	..	13	2	..	..	..	..	..	..	..	405	45	..	..	55	1	10
1	..	8	..	..	..	..	..	5	24	..	8	..	..	..	..	..	..	..	..	101	7	1	..	1	..	11
1	..	17	..	..	..	..	..	..	42	..	2	..	19	1	..	..	..	..	..	129	4	..	..	18	..	12
..	..	18	..	..	..	..	..	..	10	..	2	..	1	..	..	..	..	..	..	39	10	..	..	..	..	13
..	..	39	..	25	..	12	..	153	260	4	29	9	21	5	..	..	..	..	..	810	57	9	..	79	..	14
1	..	5	..	..	..	..	..	41	7	..	2	..	..	2	..	..	..	..	..	195	23	2	1	6	..	15
7	..	25	..	..	..	..	..	42	59	..	3	..	..	3	..	..	..	..	..	182	8	..	..	3	..	16
5	..	..	..	12	..	..	..	111	4	..	..	..	..	3	..	..	..	..	..	684	25	..	..	..	..	17
..	..	..	..	270	..	11	..	444	141	..	10	..	..	25	..	..	..	..	..	1,416	373	7	14	7	..	18
..	..	..	..	41	..	..	..	87	58	..	..	1	..	3	..	..	..	..	..	1,131	78	1	..	4	..	19
..	..	3	..	..	..	1	..	110	31	1	12	..	..	..	..	..	..	..	..	102	56	..	..	..	..	20

TABLE X.—OCCUPATION OR MEANS OF
DETAILS FOR DISTRICTS,

Class: C.—PUBLIC ADMINISTRATION AND LIBERAL ARTS.

Sub-class: VIII.—PROFESSIONS AND LIBERAL ARTS.

Order: 48. Instruction—*concluded.* / 49. Letters, Arts and Sciences (other than 44).

Group: 174.—*Professors and teachers of all kinds.* / 175.—*Clerks and servants connected with education.* / *Total Order* 49.

Serial No.	District or State.	174. Total earners principal occupation. Males.	Females.	Total working dependants. Males.	Females.	Total earners with subsidiary occupation. Males.	Females.	175. Total earners principal occupation. Males.	Females.	Total working dependants. Males.	Females.	Total earners with subsidiary occupation. Males.	Females.	Total Order 49. Total earners principal occupation. Males.	Females.	Total working dependants. Males.	Females.	Total earners with subsidiary occupation. Males.	Females.
1	2	1165	1166	1167	1168	1169	1170	1171	1172	1173	1174	1175	1176	1177	1178	1179	1180	1181	1182
	PUNJAB	32,252	3,633	452	168	1,470	35	2,173	335	7	3	57	2	28,976	2,084	806	364	2,560	110
	BRITISH TERRITORY	29,592	3,488	422	166	1,198	34	1,8 82	317	7	3	32	2	25,019	1,761	651	283	2,021	102
	AMBALA DIVISION	5,669	381	11	14	167	1	257	62	1	1	14	1	4,924	485	111	133	582	26
1	Hissar	1,010	55	1	12	9	..	45	14	..	..	..	..	1,232	78	68	44	143	2
2	Rohtak	1,222	41	6	1	69	..	29	2	..	..	3	..	457	74	11	28	68	1
3	Gurgaon	937	51	1	..	33	..	68	8	..	..	1	1	765	62	10	18	53	..
4	Karnal	1,118	52	1	1	6	..	36	8	..	1	1	..	965	82	7	24	105	19
5	Ambala	1,302	148	1	..	32	1	54	21	1	..	1	..	1,193	114	14	17	199	4
6	Simla	80	34	1	..	18	..	25	9	..	..	5	..	312	25	1	2	14	..
	JULLUNDUR DIVISION	6,214	571	97	18	329	7	223	30	..	..	4	..	4,565	252	178	32	605	7
7	Kangra	1,301	65	16	2	107	1	1	5	..	..	1	..	241	2	1	..	44	2
8	Hoshiarpur	1,351	86	..	1	67	..	68	12	..	..	2	..	1,091	62	33	19	224	..
9	Jullundur	1,545	108	71	6	54	..	64	1	..	..	..	..	1,495	74	105	5	179	..
10	Ludhiana	944	120	6	6	45	6	29	11	..	..	..	..	841	37	15	5	81	2
11	Ferozepore	1,073	192	4	3	56	..	61	1	..	..	1	..	897	77	24	3	77	3
	LAHORE DIVISION	8,523	1,163	89	48	180	5	810	135	2	1	1	..	8,683	355	218	44	351	14
12	Lahore	1,888	381	14	23	26	3	481	85	1	..	..	..	3,242	91	66	9	38	1
13	Amritsar	2,251	158	33	2	71	..	262	22	1	1	1	..	2,027	96	32	3	112	1
14	Gurdaspur	1,309	120	7	3	38	..	35	13	..	..	..	..	734	9	47	..	71	1
15	Sialkot	1,402	260	10	6	19	..	15	10	..	..	..	..	1,157	86	15	16	46	..
16	Gujranwala	917	191	3	1	7	..	15	3	..	..	..	..	679	50	10	11	51	8
17	Sheikhupura	756	53	22	8	19	2	2	2	..	..	..	..	844	23	48	5	33	3
	RAWALPINDI DIVISION	5,555	778	181	77	351	13	302	16	4	1	9	1	2,160	224	68	25	86	4
18	Gujrat	998	102	8	1	69	1	129	3	..	..	2	..	364	27	20	..	40	2
19	Shahpur	1,235	217	2	11	23	3	33	2	..	..	..	..	421	35	4	9	8	..
20	Jhelum	962	123	56	55	68	1	7	4	..	1	..	1	453	20	13	4	2	1
21	Rawalpindi	1,052	158	72	6	52	..	103	7	4	..	..	..	197	11	8	1	2	..
22	Attock	702	114	40	3	104	7	30	..	..	..	7	..	557	119	21	9	34	1
23	Mianwali	606	64	3	1	35	1	..	..	..	..	..	..	168	12	2	2	..	..
	MULTAN DIVISION	3,631	545	44	14	171	8	290	74	..	..	4	..	4,687	495	76	49	397	51
24	Montgomery	380	59	2	..	10	..	49	3	..	..	..	..	957	50	6	..	67	8
25	Lyallpur	893	113	12	2	45	3	49	31	..	..	..	..	1,092	216	26	14	102	17
26	Jhang	759	101	1	12	15	3	4	..	..	..	..	..	465	2	..	..	11	..
27	Multan	272	64	6	..	16	..	24	9	..	..	..	..	1,122	103	17	3	74	2
28	Muzaffargarh	607	161	12	..	57	..	11	7	..	..	4	..	417	76	18	22	54	23
29	Dera Ghazi Khan	720	47	11	..	28	2	153	24	..	..	..	..	634	48	9	10	89	1
	PUNJAB STATES	2,660	195	30	2	272	1	291	18	..	..	25	..	3,957	323	155	81	539	8
	A.—HAVING POLITICAL RELATIONS WITH THE PUNJAB GOVERNMENT.	195	15	18	1	96	..	24	1	..	..	11	..	379	54	24	26	211	..
1	Dujana	17	2	..	..	4	..	2	..	..	..	..	..	18	5	..	3	24	..
2	Pataudi	26	1	..	..	1	..	1	..	..	..	..	..	27	4	..	..	..	..
3	Kalsia	58	5	..	..	5	..	6	1	..	..	..	..	112	19	3	1	16	..
4	SIMLA HILL STATES	94	7	18	1	86	..	15	..	..	..	11	..	222	26	21	22	171	..
	Bashahr	10	..	2	..	19	..	..	..	..	..	..	..	17	2	3	2	24	..
	Nalagarh	27	1	1	..	..	..	4	..	..	..	1	..	50	4	..	4	11	..
	Keonthal	17	2	..	..	6	..	5	..	..	..	..	..	38	4	4	7	22	..
	Baghal	7	1	..	1	6	..	1	..	..	..	..	..	16	2	..	1	11	..
	Jubbal	1	..	..	..	12	..	..	..	..	..	..	..	25	..	3	2	41	..
	Other Simla Hill States	32	3	15	..	43	..	5	..	..	..	10	..	76	14	11	6	62	..
	B.—HAVING POLITICAL RELATIONS WITH THE GOVERNMENT OF INDIA.	2,465	180	12	1	176	1	267	17	..	..	14	..	3.578	269	131	55	328	8
5	Loharu	7	..	..	..	..	..	..	..	..	..	..	..	10	..	..	1	..	..
6	Sirmoor	71	3	..	..	6	..	59	1	..	..	12	..	29	2	13	3	12	..
7	Bilaspur	20	..	..	..	3	..	2	..	..	..	1	..	25	1	2	1	10	..
8	Mandi	16	14	..	..	1	..	1	..	..	..	..	..	188	37	..	6	22	1
9	Suket	11	..	..	..	..	..	..	..	..	..	..	..	14	23	..	4	14	..
10	Kapurthala	405	45	..	..	55	1	..	..	..	..	..	..	390	36	2	1	38	4
11	Maler Kotla	99	7	1	..	1	..	2	..	..	..	..	..	130	35	13	6	11	..
12	Faridkot	123	4	..	..	18	..	6	..	..	..	..	..	137	2	1	..	..	..
13	Chamba	39	10	..	..	..	..	..	..	..	..	..	..	33	2	4	..	78	..
14	Patiala (Phulkian States)	764	57	9	..	79	..	46	..	..	..	..	..	1,520	53	58	3	100	..
15	Jhind (Phulkian States)	183	19	2	1	5	..	12	4	..	..	1	..	204	24	17	11	18	..
16	Nabha (Phulkian States)	145	4	..	..	8	..	37	4	..	..	..	..	293	7	3	6	25	3
17	Bahawalpur	582	17	..	..	..	..	102	8	..	..	..	..	605	47	18	13	..	..
18	*Cities.* Lahore	989	292	6	14	7	..	427	81	1	..	..	..	2,068	34	..	2	12	..
19	*Cities.* Amritsar	974	78	..	..	4	..	157	..	1	..	..	..	688	44	..	..	1	..
20	*Cities.* Multan	102	48	..	..	..	..	..	8	..	..	..	..	252	13	1	..	10	..

C.—PUBLIC ADMINISTRATION AND LIBERAL ARTS.—*continued*.

VIII.—PROFESSIONS AND LIBERAL ARTS.—*continued*.

49. Letters, Arts and Sciences (other than 44).—*continued*.

176.—*Public scribes, stenographers, etc.*						177.—*Architects, surveyors, engineers and their employees (not being States servants).*						178.—*Authors, editors, journalists and photographers.*						179.—*Artists, sculptors, and image-makers.*						180.—*Scientists, (astronomers, botanists, etc).*				
Total earners principal occupation.		Total working dependants.		Total earners with subsidiary occupation.		Total earners principal occupation.		Total working dependants.		Total earners with subsidiary occupation.		Total earners principal occupation.		Total working dependants.		Total earners with subsidiary occupation.		Total earners principal occupation.		Total working dependants.		Total earners with subsidiary occupation.		Total earners principal occupation.		Total earners with subsidiary occupation.		
Males.	Females.	Males.	Females.	Males.	Females.	Males.	Females.	Males.	Females.	Males.	Females.	Males.	Females.	Males.	Females.	Males.	Females.	Males.	Females.	Males.	Females.	Males.	Females.	Males.	Females.	Males.	Females.	Serial No.
1183	1184	1185	1186	1187	1188	1189	1190	1191	1192	1193	1194	1195	1196	1197	1198	1199	1200	1201	1202	1203	1204	1205	1206	1207	1208	1209	1210	
438	10	12	..	59	..	647	..	2	..	29	..	684	..	7	..	6	..	2,401	22	29	30	126	..	123	2	5	..	
408	10	12	..	59	..	530	..	1	..	11	..	663	..	6	..	4	..	2,034	22	27	30	124	..	94	..	5	..	
55	6	..	..	8	..	28	..	..	..	1	..	50	..	..	..	1	..	522	5	2	12	7	..	1	..	..	..	
11	..	..	..	..	..	2	..	..	..	..	..	4	..	..	..	..	..	84	..	..	..	1	..	1	..	..	..	1
1	..	..	..	..	..	1	..	..	..	..	..	4	..	..	..	..	..	15	..	..	..	4	..	..	..	..	..	2
12	..	..	..	2	..	..	..	..	..	..	..	1	..	..	..	..	..	21	..	1	6	1	..	..	..	..	..	3
8	..	..	..	2	..	..	..	..	..	..	..	6	..	..	..	1	..	37	4	..	2	..	..	..	..	..	..	4
17	..	..	..	4	..	18	..	..	..	..	..	23	..	..	..	..	..	124	..	..	4	1	..	..	..	..	..	5
6	6	..	..	..	..	7	..	..	..	1	..	12	..	..	..	..	..	241	1	1	..	..	..	..	..	..	..	6
81	..	10	..	14	..	43	..	..	..	..	..	94	..	..	..	2	..	58	3	1	..	6	..	4	..	1	..	
..	..	..	..	1	..	3	..	..	..	..	..	1	..	..	..	..	..	2	..	1	..	..	..	3	..	1	..	7
11	..	..	..	2	..	16	..	..	..	..	..	5	..	..	..	1	..	11	..	..	..	1	..	..	..	..	..	8
58	..	10	..	8	..	17	..	..	..	..	..	21	..	..	..	..	..	15	3	..	..	4	..	..	..	..	..	9
8	..	..	..	..	..	..	..	..	..	..	..	36	..	..	..	..	..	25	..	..	..	1	..	..	..	..	..	10
4	..	..	..	3	..	7	..	..	..	..	..	31	..	..	..	1	..	5	..	..	..	..	..	1	..	..	..	11
232	..	2	..	33	..	367	..	..	..	..	..	463	..	6	..	1	..	778	1	3	..	30	..	81	..	1	..	
117	..	..	..	..	..	326	..	..	..	..	..	351	..	..	..	..	..	572	..	2	..	14	..	81	..	..	..	12
77	..	..	..	26	..	41	..	..	..	..	..	32	..	1	..	..	..	84	1	..	..	..	..	..	..	1	..	13
15	..	2	..	7	..	..	..	..	..	..	..	41	..	..	..	1	..	58	..	1	..	9	..	..	..	..	..	14
19	..	..	..	..	..	..	..	..	..	..	..	26	..	..	..	..	..	26	..	..	..	..	..	..	..	..	..	15
2	..	..	..	..	..	..	..	..	..	..	..	7	..	..	..	..	..	29	..	..	..	7	..	..	..	..	..	16
2	..	..	..	..	..	..	..	..	..	..	..	6	..	5	..	..	..	9	..	..	..	..	..	..	..	..	..	17
3	3	..	..	..	..	10	..	..	..	1	..	21	..	..	..	..	..	346	7	21	8	11	..	3	..	3	..	
..	..	..	..	..	..	..	..	..	..	..	..	5	..	..	..	..	..	4	1	..	..	..	..	..	..	..	..	18
..	..	..	..	..	..	..	..	..	..	..	..	5	..	..	..	..	..	81	1	2	6	2	..	3	..	3	..	19
..	..	..	..	..	..	..	..	..	..	..	..	..	..	..	..	..	..	88	2	2	2	1	..	..	..	..	..	20
2	3	..	..	..	..	9	..	..	..	..	..	4	..	..	..	..	..	24	..	..	..	1	..	..	..	..	..	21
..	..	..	..	..	..	1	..	..	..	1	..	7	..	..	..	..	..	101	3	15	..	7	..	..	..	..	..	22
1	..	..	..	..	..	..	..	..	..	..	..	..	..	..	..	..	..	48	..	2	..	..	..	..	..	..	..	23
37	1	..	..	4	..	82	..	1	..	9	..	35	..	..	..	..	..	330	6	..	10	70	..	5	..	..	..	
..	..	..	..	..	..	2	..	..	..	..	..	17	..	..	..	..	..	..	..	..	..	..	..	..	..	..	..	24
13	..	..	..	1	..	20	..	..	..	..	..	7	..	..	..	..	..	18	..	..	..	..	..	..	..	..	..	25
2	..	..	..	1	..	..	..	..	..	..	..	5	..	..	..	..	..	..	..	..	..	..	..	..	..	..	..	26
3	1	..	..	..	..	54	..	1	..	9	..	1	..	..	..	..	..	18	3	..	..	2	..	5	..	..	..	27
2	..	..	..	..	..	6	..	..	..	..	..	..	..	..	..	..	..	8	3	..	10	..	..	..	..	..	..	28
17	..	..	..	2	..	..	..	..	..	..	..	5	..	..	..	..	..	286	..	..	..	68	..	..	..	..	..	29
30	..	..	..	..	..	117	..	1	..	18	..	21	..	1	..	2	..	367	..	2	..	2	..	29	2	..	..	
5	..	..	..	..	..	3	..	..	..	..	..	2	..	1	..	1	..	34	..	1	..	1	..	..	..	..	..	
..	..	..	..	..	..	..	..	..	..	..	..	..	..	..	..	..	..	..	..	..	..	..	..	..	..	..	..	1
5	..	..	..	..	..	..	..	..	..	..	..	..	..	..	..	..	..	1	..	..	..	..	..	..	..	..	..	2
..	..	..	..	..	..	..	..	..	..	..	..	..	..	..	..	..	..	23	..	..	..	1	..	..	..	..	..	3
..	..	..	..	..	..	3	..	..	..	..	..	2	..	1	..	1	..	10	..	1	..	..	..	..	..	..	..	4
..	..	..	..	..	..	..	..	..	..	..	..	..	..	..	..	1	..	2	..	1	..	..	..	..	..	..	..	
..	..	..	..	..	..	..	..	..	..	..	..	..	..	..	..	..	..	..	..	..	..	..	..	..	..	..	..	
..	..	..	..	..	..	..	..	..	..	..	..	1	..	..	..	..	..	..	..	..	..	..	..	..	..	..	..	
..	..	..	..	..	..	..	..	..	..	..	..	..	..	..	..	..	..	..	..	..	..	..	..	..	..	..	..	
..	..	..	..	..	..	1	..	..	..	..	..	1	..	1	..	..	..	..	..	..	..	..	..	..	..	..	..	
..	..	..	..	..	..	2	..	..	..	..	..	..	..	..	..	..	..	8	..	..	..	..	..	..	..	..	..	
25	..	..	..	..	..	114	..	1	..	18	..	19	..	..	..	1	..	338	..	1	..	1	..	29	2	..	..	
..	..	..	..	..	..	..	..	..	..	..	..	..	..	..	..	..	..	..	..	..	..	..	..	..	..	..	..	5
..	..	..	..	..	..	1	..	..	..	4	..	..	..	..	..	1	..	..	..	..	..	..	..	..	..	..	..	6
1	..	..	..	..	..	..	..	..	..	1	..	..	..	..	..	..	..	1	..	..	..	..	..	..	..	..	..	7
..	..	..	..	..	..	..	..	..	..	..	..	1	..	..	..	..	..	2	..	..	..	..	..	..	..	..	..	8
..	..	..	..	..	..	..	..	..	..	..	..	..	..	..	..	..	..	..	..	..	..	..	..	2	..	..	..	9
..	..	..	..	..	..	27	..	..	..	1	..	..	..	..	..	..	..	..	..	..	..	..	..	..	..	..	..	10
..	..	..	..	..	..	..	..	..	..	..	..	..	..	..	..	..	..	..	..	..	..	..	..	..	..	..	..	11
..	..	..	..	..	..	..	..	..	..	..	..	..	..	..	..	..	..	1	..	..	..	..	..	2	..	..	..	12
..	..	..	..	..	..	..	..	..	..	..	..	..	..	..	..	..	..	..	..	..	..	..	..	..	..	..	..	13
24	..	..	..	..	..	86	..	1	..	12	..	6	..	..	..	..	..	306	..	..	..	..	..	25	2	..	..	14
..	..	..	..	..	..	..	..	..	..	..	..	4	..	..	..	..	..	6	..	..	..	..	..	..	..	..	..	15
..	..	..	..	..	..	..	..	..	..	..	..	1	..	..	..	..	..	8	..	1	..	1	..	..	..	..	..	16
..	..	..	..	..	..	..	..	..	..	..	..	7	..	..	..	..	..	9	..	..	..	..	..	..	..	..	..	17
117	..	..	..	..	..	326	..	..	..	..	..	347	..	..	..	..	..	307	..	..	..	2	..	80	..	..	..	18
34	..	..	..	1	..	40	..	..	..	..	..	29	..	..	..	..	..	76	1	..	..	..	..	..	..	..	..	19
..	1	..	..	..	..	32	..	..	..	..	..	1	..	..	..	..	..	5	3	..	..	..	..	4	..	..	..	20

TABLE X.—OCCUPATION OR MEANS OF
DETAILS FOR DISTRICTS,

Class .. C.—PUBLIC ADMINISTRATION AND LIBERAL-

Sub-class .. VIII. -PROFESSIONS AND LIBERAL-

Order .. 49. Letters, arts and sciences (other-

Serial No.	District or State.	181.—Horoscope casters, astrologers, fortune-tellers, wizards, witches and mediums. Total earners principal occupation. Males.	Females.	Total working dependants. Males.	Females.	Total earners with subsidiary occupation. Males.	Females.	182.—Musicians (composers and performers other than military), actors, dancers, etc. Total earners principal occupation. Males.	Females.	Total working dependants. Males.	Females.	Total earners with subsidiary occupation. Males.	Females.	183. Managers and employees of places of public entertainments, race courses, societies, clubs. Total earners principal occupation. Males.	Females.	Total working dependants. Males.	Females.	Total earners with subsidiary occupation. Males.	Females.	184.—Conrecitors, ex- and … Total earners principal occupation. Males.	Females.
1	2	1211	1212	1213	1214	1215	1216	1217	1218	1219	1220	1221	1222	1223	1224	1225	1226	1227	1228	1229	1230
	PUNJAB ..	1,198	3	3	1	78	..	19,054	1,758	620	305	2,049	88	175	21	..	4	3	..	4,256	268
	BRITISH TERRITORY ..	879	3	1	..	27	..	16,455	1,461	486	225	1,599	84	153	19	..	4	3	..	3,803	246
	AMBALA DIVISION ..	155	..	..	..	17	..	3,362	416	88	114	504	25	46	3	..	..	3	..	705	5
1	Hissar ..	14	..	..	..	5	..	909	74	53	42	126	2	9	..	..	..	..	..	198	4
2	Rohtak ..	18	..	..	..	1	..	394	74	9	28	61	1	3	..	..	..	..	..	21	..
3	Gurgaon ..	4	..	..	..	2	..	669	61	9	12	42	..	1	..	..	..	2	..	57	1
4	Karnal ..	46	..	..	..	1	..	597	78	6	22	88	19	5	..	..	..	1	..	266	..
5	Ambala ..	63	..	..	..	8	..	770	114	11	8	174	3	15	..	..	..	..	..	163	..
6	Simla ..	10	..	..	..	..	..	23	15	..	2	13	..	13	3	..	..	..	..	..	..
	JULLUNDUR DIVISION	175	1	1	..	7	..	3,052	245	137	32	538	7	10	1	..	..	..	..	1,048	2
7	Kangra ..	1	..	..	..	..	..	212	2	..	..	41	2	4	..	..	..	..	..	15	..
8	Hoshiarpur ..	93	..	1	..	5	..	758	62	28	19	209	..	..	..	..	..	..	..	197	..
9	Jullundur ..	23	..	..	..	..	..	1,086	71	87	5	162	..	2	..	..	..	..	..	273	..
10	Ludhiana ..	23	..	..	..	2	..	531	35	14	5	57	2	..	..	..	..	..	..	218	2
11	Ferozepore ..	35	1	..	..	..	..	465	75	8	3	69	3	4	1	..	..	..	..	345	..
	LAHORE DIVISION ..	479	2	..	..	3	..	5,286	309	167	39	254	14	56	11	..	1	..	..	941	32
12	Lahore ..	211	..	..	..	..	..	1,692	82	64	5	17	1	56	..	..	..	..	..	162	9
13	Amritsar ..	229	2	..	..	..	..	1,011	72	15	2	69	1	..	11	..	1	..	..	227	10
14	Gurdaspur ..	39	..	..	..	2	..	534	9	42	..	51	1	..	..	..	..	..	..	47	..
15	Sialkot ..	..	..	..	..	1	..	965	75	15	16	45	..	..	..	..	..	..	..	121	11
16	Gujranwala ..	..	..	..	..	..	..	567	48	10	11	42	8	..	..	..	..	..	..	74	2
17	Sheikhupura ..	..	..	..	..	..	..	517	23	21	5	30	3	..	..	..	..	..	..	310	..
	RAWALPINDI DIVISION	33	..	..	..	..	..	1,684	210	47	15	70	4	13	4	..	2	..	..	47	..
18	Gujrat ..	9	..	..	..	..	..	321	26	20	..	39	2	1	..	..	..	..	..	24	..
19	Shahpur ..	1	..	..	..	..	..	331	34	2	3	3	..	..	..	..	..	..	..	..	..
20	Jhelum ..	..	..	..	..	..	..	362	18	11	2	1	1	3	..	..	..	..	..	..	..
21	Rawalpindi ..	7	..	..	..	..	..	129	7	8	1	1	..	9	1	..	..	..	..	13	..
22	Attock ..	16	..	..	..	..	..	432	116	6	9	26	1	..	..	..	..	..	..	..	..
23	Mianwali ..	..	..	..	..	..	..	109	9	..	..	..	..	..	3	..	2	..	..	10	..
	MULTAN DIVISION ..	37	..	..	..	..	..	3,071	281	47	25	233	34	28	..	..	1	..	..	1,062	207
24	Montgomery ..	6	..	..	..	..	..	755	50	6	..	53	8	..	..	..	..	..	..	177	..
25	Lyallpur ..	11	..	..	..	..	..	249	22	5	1	59	..	28	..	..	..	..	..	746	194
26	Jhang ..	5	..	..	..	..	..	450	2	..	..	10	..	..	..	..	..	..	..	3	..
27	Multan ..	1	..	..	..	..	..	940	90	14	3	53	2	..	..	..	..	..	..	100	9
28	Muzaffargarh ..	..	..	..	..	..	..	370	69	13	12	40	23	..	..	..	..	..	..	31	4
29	Dera Ghazi Khan ..	14	..	..	..	..	..	307	48	9	9	18	1	..	..	..	1	..	..	5	..
	PUNJAB STATES ..	319	..	2	1	51	..	2,599	297	134	80	450	4	22	2	..	..	..	..	453	22
	A.—Having Political relations with the Punjab Government. ..	17	..	2	1	38	..	272	51	19	25	170	..	4	1	..	..	..	..	42	2
1	Dujana ..	..	..	..	..	1	..	18	5	..	3	23	..	..	..	..	..	..	..	..	..
2	Pataudi ..	..	..	..	..	..	..	21	4	..	..	..	..	..	..	..	..	..	..	..	..
3	Kalsia ..	3	..	..	..	1	..	61	17	2	1	14	..	..	..	..	..	..	..	25	2
4	SIMLA HILL STATES ..	14	..	2	1	36	..	172	25	17	21	133	..	4	1	..	..	..	..	17	..
	Bashahr ..	1	..	..	..	..	..	14	2	2	2	23	..	..	..	..	..	..	..	..	..
	Nalagarh ..	1	..	..	..	..	..	36	4	..	4	11	..	..	..	..	..	..	..	13	.
	Keonthal ..	4	..	..	..	2	..	29	3	4	7	20	..	4	1	..	..	..	..	..	..
	Baghal ..	1	..	..	..	2	..	12	2	..	1	9	..	..	..	..	..	..	..	3	..
	Jubbal ..	4	..	2	..	27	..	19	..	..	2	14	..	..	..	..	..	..	..	..	..
	Other Simla Hill States ..	3	..	..	1	5	..	62	14	11	5	36	..	..	..	..	..	..	..	1	..
	B.—Having Political relations with the Government of India ..	302	..	..	..	18	..	2,327	246	115	55	280	4	18	1	..	..	..	..	411	20
5	Loharu ..	2	..	..	..	..	..	7	..	..	1	..	..	1	..	..	..	..	..	..	..
6	Sirmoor ..	1	..	..	..	1	..	14	2	12	3	6	..	1	..	..	..	..	..	12	..
7	Bilaspur ..	1	..	..	..	3	..	16	1	2	1	6	..	..	..	..	..	..	..	6	..
8	Mandi ..	..	..	..	..	..	..	185	37	..	6	22	1	..	..	..	..	..	..	..	..
9	Suket ..	..	..	..	..	..	..	12	23	..	4	13	..	..	..	..	..	..	..	..	..
10	Kapurthala ..	18	..	..	..	..	..	196	20	..	1	32	..	..	..	..	..	..	..	149	16
11	Maler Kotla ..	8	..	..	..	2	..	100	35	12	6	6	..	..	..	..	..	..	..	22	..
12	Faridkot ..	..	..	..	..	..	..	115	2	1	..	..	..	..	..	..	..	..	..	19	..
13	Chamba ..	2	..	..	..	3	..	31	2	4	..	75	..	..	..	..	..	..	..	..	..
14	Patiala (Phulkian States) ..	255	..	..	..	..	..	741	51	54	3	88	..	..	..	..	..	..	..	77	..
15	Jind (Phulkian States) ..	4	..	..	..	2	..	154	23	10	11	16	..	6	1	..	..	..	..	30	..
16	Nabha (Phulkian States) ..	10	..	..	..	2	..	203	3	2	6	16	3	5	..	..	..	..	..	66	4
17	Bahawalpur ..	1	..	..	..	..	..	553	47	18	13	..	..	5	..	..	..	..	..	30	..
18	*Cities.* Lahore ..	202	..	..	..	..	..	648	34	..	2	3	..	9	..	..	..	..	..	32	..
19	*Cities.* Amritsar ..	97	..	..	..	..	..	401	43	..	..	..	..	..	..	..	..	..	..	11	..
20	*Cities.* Multan ..	..	..	..	..	..	..	140	3	..	..	4	..	..	..	..	..	..	..	70	6

LIVELIHOOD—GENERAL TABLE.

STATES AND CITIES.—*continued.*

ARTS—*concluded.* ARTS—*concluded.* (than 44)—*concluded.* Jugglers, acrobats, exhibitors of curiosities, wild animals, etc. Total working dependants.		Total earners with subsidiary occupation.		D.—MISCELLANEOUS. Total Class D. Total earners principal occupation.		Total working dependants.		Total earners with subsidiary occupation.		IX.—PERSONS LIVING ON THEIR INCOME. 50. Persons living principally on their Income. Total Sub-class IX. Total Order 50. 185. —Proprietors (other than of agricultural land), fund and scholarship holders and pensioners. Total earners principal occupation.		Total working dependants		Total earners with subsidiary occupation.		X.—DOMESTIC SERVICE.—*continued.* 51. Domestic Service—*continued.* Total Sub-class X. Total Order 51. Total earners principal occupation.		Total working dependants.		Total earners with subsidiary occupation.		
Males.	Females.	Males.	Females.	Males.	Females.	Males.	Females.	Males.	Females.	Males.	Females.	Males.	Females.	Males.	Females.	Males.	Females.	Males.	Females.	Males.	Females.	Serial No.
1231	1232	1233	1234	1235	1236	1237	1238	1239	1240	1241	1242	1243	1244	1245	1246	1247	1248	1249	1250	1251	1252	
133	**24**	**205**	**22**	**638,336**	**73,295**	**38,823**	**19,450**	**58,390**	**3,221**	**26,866**	**3,676**	**1,977**	**896**	**27,654**	**574**	**220,797**	**30,208**	**7,298**	**10,231**	**9,783**	**1,340**	
118	**24**	**189**	**18**	**538,123**	**64,433**	**32,990**	**15,459**	**47,904**	**2,758**	**21,618**	**3,008**	**1,718**	**775**	**23,999**	**481**	**191,889**	**27,237**	**6,298**	**8,507**	**7,056**	**1,207**	
21	**7**	**41**	**1**	**57,099**	**8,574**	**3,332**	**2,386**	**9,061**	**293**	**2,573**	**587**	**273**	**206**	**5,595**	**107**	**27,671**	**4,836**	**677**	**1,427**	**1,549**	**83**	
15	2	11	..	8,588	1,162	934	714	1,374	66	298	74	16	5	676	18	3,740	457	173	252	205	16	1
2	..	2	..	8,875	676	659	326	2,152	57	530	103	100	92	1,692	27	3,076	276	117	136	154	11	2
..	..	4	..	8,722	806	579	294	1,177	40	497	111	129	62	590	19	3,175	304	152	134	139	10	3
1	..	12	..	10,041	1,999	263	352	960	70	372	55	7	9	403	11	5,113	1,376	101	309	233	33	4
3	5	12	1	18,609	3,692	865	690	2,777	47	769	171	21	32	2,006	26	11,041	2,335	134	594	431	9	5
..	..	..	..	2,264	239	32	10	621	13	107	23	..	6	219	6	1,526	88	..	2	387	4	6
29	..	**37**	..	**102,614**	**11,073**	**6,457**	**3,002**	**16,898**	**608**	**6,082**	**1,035**	**808**	**276**	**10,314**	**189**	**37,527**	**5,525**	**1,868**	**2,040**	**1,886**	**295**	
..	..	1	..	8,061	1,519	380	714	4,368	138	929	345	26	82	3,053	80	3,869	634	248	412	759	12	7
4	..	6	..	17,603	2,374	612	819	4,197	105	1,345	306	59	57	2,278	44	6,485	1,369	124	637	233	34	8
8	..	5	..	25,071	2,405	2,510	815	1,634	104	2,105	121	43	29	566	4	8,753	1,555	993	636	357	76	9
1	..	21	..	20,703	1,967	1,341	443	3,022	164	1,171	165	520	65	1,475	32	7,376	981	109	244	211	109	10
16	..	4	..	31,176	2,810	1,584	211	3,677	72	532	98	160	43	2,942	20	11,044	986	394	81	326	31	11
40	**4**	**29**	..	**179,811**	**18,519**	**10,975**	**5,245**	**9,344**	**591**	**5,880**	**658**	**201**	**157**	**3,538**	**42**	**70,014**	**8,140**	**2,103**	**3,433**	**1,772**	**357**	
..	4	7	..	55,437	5,214	4,236	856	1,572	93	2,289	200	72	80	784	13	22,635	1,689	275	595	197	29	12
16	..	16	..	39,511	3,954	2,548	1,020	1,702	249	1,337	256	58	35	966	14	15,772	2,300	908	1,334	326	174	13
2	..	1	..	22,707	2,356	940	923	2,684	44	628	68	14	20	980	9	9,639	1,209	276	638	630	24	14
..	..	..	..	22,607	2,054	1,345	388	1,841	32	908	63	35	19	593	6	8,502	1,128	267	481	178	24	15
..	..	2	..	22,586	3,171	805	453	751	119	489	53	5	1	89	..	7,811	1,264	194	200	245	83	16
22	..	3	..	16,963	1,760	1,101	505	704	54	229	18	17	2	124	..	5,655	490	183	185	196	23	17
..	..	**1**	..	**80,690**	**12,878**	**5,065**	**2,778**	**6,854**	**601**	**5,535**	**664**	**395**	**119**	**3,107**	**119**	**22,698**	**3,918**	**835**	**916**	**728**	**205**	
..	..	1	..	11,405	1,521	1,019	201	926	81	1,053	114	146	15	351	18	4,354	394	307	124	144	30	18
..	..	..	..	23,173	4,078	585	783	1,225	89	810	96	25	25	585	24	5,801	1,297	187	227	109	46	19
..	..	..	..	11,083	1,748	601	814	1,383	113	2,130	222	72	27	460	47	2,554	709	61	385	175	37	20
..	..	..	..	14,843	2,364	584	290	1,709	200	470	105	27	31	1,191	21	5,823	727	58	77	133	31	21
..	..	..	..	10,331	2,019	1,399	293	943	102	613	89	107	12	285	7	3,097	530	52	96	119	39	22
..	..	..	..	6,855	1,148	877	392	578	16	459	38	18	9	235	2	1,069	261	167	7	48	2	23
28	**18**	**81**	**17**	**117,909**	**13,389**	**7,161**	**2,053**	**5,747**	**670**	**1,548**	**114**	**41**	**17**	**1,445**	**24**	**33,979**	**4,818**	**815**	**691**	**1,121**	**267**	
..	..	14	..	26,290	3,203	1,680	604	1,871	120	388	17	28	1	1,208	8	8,774	1,112	112	198	290	88	24
21	13	42	17	28,649	3,398	1,630	493	1,148	165	388	45	7	10	68	2	8,357	1,717	271	369	380	117	25
..	..	..	..	11,030	1,669	886	225	393	101	183	1	3	..	5	..	3,673	506	204	34	101	20	26
2	..	10	..	30,348	2,290	1,813	199	1,377	171	255	20	..	..	120	3	9,441	598	141	37	139	7	27
5	..	14	..	9,281	1,177	453	360	403	74	207	5	2	4	29	9	1,352	461	27	39	60	33	28
..	..	1	..	9,311	1,352	699	172	565	39	127	26	1	2	15	2	2,182	421	60	14	142	2	29
15	..	**16**	**4**	**100,213**	**8,862**	**5,833**	**3,991**	**10,486**	**463**	**5,248**	**668**	**259**	**121**	**3,655**	**93**	**28,908**	**2,971**	**1,000**	**1,724**	**2,727**	**133**	
1	..	**1**	..	**4,287**	**749**	**275**	**238**	**1,378**	**32**	**183**	**40**	**8**	**14**	**422**	**23**	**1,833**	**362**	**62**	**135**	**484**	**5**	
..	..	..	..	337	39	8	11	146	4	48	8	1	4	114	3	119	28	1	5	11	1	1
..	..	..	..	281	32	..	1	60	1	48	11	..	1	54	1	117	18	..	..	2	..	2
1	..	..	..	1,005	200	101	117	191	9	46	9	6	..	133	6	472	153	23	107	36	2	3
..	..	**1**	..	**2,664**	**478**	**166**	**109**	**981**	**18**	**41**	**12**	**1**	**9**	**121**	**13**	**1,125**	**163**	**38**	**23**	**435**	**2**	4
..	..	..	..	91	4	30	8	95	..	..	..	..	..	..	..	46	1	11	1	85	..	
..	..	..	..	296	76	9	3	85	8	21	6	1	1	40	8	123	48	..	1	14	..	
..	..	..	..	967	85	48	26	86	1	16	..	..	..	20	1	546	16	11		47	..	
..	..	..	..	176	13	..	20	127	4	..	..	..	8	37	3	73	16	..	..	78	1	
..	..	..	..	44	13	19	17	91	..	1	..	..	..	2	..	33	5	2	15	69	..	
..	..	1	..	1,090	257	60	35	497	5	3	6	..	..	22	1	304	77	14	6	142	1	
14	..	**15**	**4**	**95,926**	**8,113**	**5,558**	**3,753**	**9,108**	**431**	**5,065**	**628**	**251**	**107**	**3,283**	**70**	**27,075**	**2,609**	**938**	**1,589**	**2,243**	**128**	
..	..	..	..	311	48	1	28	17	2	31	4	1	4	1	..	56	12	..	..	7	..	5
1	..	..	..	1,567	260	26	59	230	7	50	11	..	1	84	1	734	99	6	33	43	1	6
..	..	..	..	533	112	50	58	325	10	32	17	5	13	224	8	195	28	23	16	48	1	7
..	..	..	..	3,537	309	37	10	936	27	141	14	1	3	144	7	699	34	..	3	344	7	8
..	..	1	..	240	49	27	20	23	..	..	4	..	..	2	..	52	29	4	16	16	..	9
2	..	5	4	7,466	771	63	71	701	41	367	66	13	29	208	6	2,745	412	15	23	100	23	10
1	..	3	..	2,581	390	185	131	621	12	144	44	13	6	248	5	720	148	20	28	38	1	11
..	..	..	..	4,691	209	136	19	190	1	148	12	..	2	91	1	1,723	49	69	4	39	..	12
..	..	..	..	1,505	215	72	31	483	18	238	34	..	3	109	4	360	56	2	14	57	7	13
3	..	..	..	35,057	3,159	2,450	1,981	3,612	189	2,603	287	172	36	742	14	10,725	1,058	600	1,217	1,420	70	14
7	..	..	..	4,798	412	339	248	787	28	376	27	22	8	469	2	1,642	106	76	116	75	3	15
..	..	6	..	4,533	461	478	142	1,171	28	607	33	19	2	911	22	1,253	161	52	119	56	1	16
..	..	..	..	29,107	1,715	1,491	955	12	68	148	25	5	..	..	..	6,102	417	71	..	..	14	17
..	..	7	..	25,819	2,014	3,496	124	514	28	1,767	142	24	53	435	4	13,023	660	33	7	4	3	18
..	..	..	..	19,389	738	328	21	6	1	355	128	1	..	..	1	7,534	268	4	1	..	..	19
1	..	6	..	4,160	385	..	14	174	16	131	19	..	..	100	3	3,068	161	..	..	16	2	20

TABLE X.—OCCUPATION OR MEANS OF

DETAILS FOR DISTRICTS,

Class .. D.—MISCELLANEOUS.

Sub-class .. X.—DOMESTIC SERVICE—*concluded.* | XI.—INSUFFICIENTLY DESCRIBED

Order .. 51. Domestic Service—*concluded.* | 52.—General terms which do not indicate a definite occupation.

Group .. 186.—*Private motor-drivers and cleaners.* | 187.—*Other domestic service.* | Total Order 52. | Total Sub-Class XI.

Serial No.	District or State.	186.—Total earners principal occupation. Males.	Females.	Total working dependants. Males.	Females.	Total earners with subsidiary occupation. Males.	Females.	187.—Total earners principal occupation. Males.	Females.	Total working dependants. Males.	Females.	Total earners with subsidiary occupation. Males.	Females.	Total Order 52.—Total earners principal occupation. Males.	Females.	Total working dependants. Males.	Females.	Total Sub-Class XI.—Total earners with subsidiary occupation. Males.	Females.
1	2	1253	1254	1255	1256	1257	1258	1259	1260	1261	1262	1263	1264	1265	1266	1267	1268	1269	1270
	PUNJAB ..	3,672	1	35	..	140	..	217,125	30,207	7,263	10,231	9,643	1,840	216,371	16,991	5,495	3,232	10,718	600
	BRITISH TERRITORY ..	3,372	1	34	..	128	..	188,517	27,236	6,264	8,507	6,928	1,207	180,731	15,259	4,754	1,981	8,670	444
	AMBALA DIVISION ..	502	..	1	..	15	..	27,169	4,836	676	1,427	1,534	83	7,500	1,116	123	226	288	22
1	Hissar ..	11	..	..	..	..	..	3,729	457	178	252	205	16	1,409	126	71	148	97	10
2	Rohtak ..	25	..	1	..	1	..	3,051	276	116	136	153	11	1,504	63	24	43	48	1
3	Gurgaon ..	37	..	..	..	1	..	3,138	304	152	134	135	10	634	21	17	27	12	..
4	Karnal ..	74	..	..	..	1	..	5,039	1,376	101	309	232	33	494	25	7	3	16	..
5	Ambala ..	347	..	..	..	11	..	10,694	2,335	134	594	420	9	2,849	772	3	5	102	8
6	Simla ..	8	..	..	..	1	..	1,518	88	..	2	386	4	610	109	1	..	13	3
	JULLUNDUR DIVISION	666	1	22	..	80	..	36,861	5,524	1,846	2,040	1,806	295	32,617	2,193	1,281	322	3,116	64
7	Kangra ..	33	..	..	..	6	..	3,836	634	248	442	753	42	1,238	177	23	93	340	21
8	Hoshiarpur ..	134	..	..	..	17	..	6,351	1,369	124	637	216	34	3,455	286	114	50	1,140	17
9	Jullundur ..	349	..	22	..	21	..	8,404	1,555	971	636	336	76	8,851	275	758	52	423	16
10	Ludhiana ..	53	1	..	..	16	..	7,323	980	109	244	195	109	6,962	478	105	75	1,000	9
11	Ferozepore ..	97	..	..	..	20	..	10,947	986	394	81	306	34	12,111	979	281	52	213	1
	LAHORE DIVISION ..	1,630	..	8	..	11	..	68,384	8,140	2,095	3,433	1,761	357	59,432	4,166	996	322	1,762	94
12	Lahore ..	991	..	6	..	3	..	21,644	1,689	269	595	194	20	21,468	1,929	129	71	326	39
13	Amritsar ..	74	..	..	..	3	..	15,698	2,300	908	1,334	323	174	13,137	461	78	49	88	20
14	Gurdaspur ..	14	..	..	..	..	..	9,625	1,269	276	638	630	24	4,660	140	247	7	515	4
15	Sialkot ..	349	..	2	..	3	..	8,153	1,128	265	481	175	24	6,205	315	170	51	449	1
16	Gujranwala ..	191	..	..	..	2	..	7,620	1,264	194	200	243	83	7,952	1,005	51	40	135	22
17	Sheikhupura ..	11	..	..	..	..	..	5,644	490	183	185	106	23	6,015	316	321	104	249	8
	RAWALPINDI DIVISION	101	..	1	..	2	..	22,597	3,918	834	916	726	205	31,794	3,410	989	385	1,859	122
18	Gujrat ..	50	..	..	..	2	..	4,304	394	307	124	142	30	4,566	363	278	8	258	6
19	Shahpur ..	..	..	..	..	..	..	5,801	1,207	187	227	109	46	10,543	1,191	106	62	291	4
20	Jhelum ..	11	..	1	..	..	..	2,543	709	63	385	175	37	3,751	137	113	6	513	..
21	Rawalpindi ..	29	..	..	..	..	..	5,794	727	58	77	133	51	6,300	763	275	137	338	82
22	Attock ..	8	..	..	..	..	..	3,089	530	52	96	119	39	3,698	617	114	34	319	24
23	Mianwali ..	3	..	..	..	..	..	1,066	261	167	7	48	2	2,936	309	103	138	140	6
	MULTAN DIVISION ..	473	..	2	..	20	..	33,506	4,818	813	691	1,101	267	49,888	4,374	1,365	726	1,645	142
24	Montgomery ..	..	..	..	..	..	..	8,774	1,112	112	198	290	88	11,541	1,494	204	360	275	17
25	Lyallpur ..	415	..	2	..	19	..	7,942	1,717	269	369	370	117	12,996	610	707	21	474	16
26	Jhang ..	..	..	..	..	..	..	3,673	506	204	34	101	20	4,381	446	29	14	134	60
27	Multan ..	..	..	..	..	..	..	9,441	598	141	37	139	7	12,893	834	241	118	496	16
28	Muzaffargarh ..	38	..	..	..	1	..	1,514	461	27	39	59	33	3,764	541	50	163	80	17
29	Dera Ghazi Khan ..	20	..	..	..	..	..	2,162	424	60	14	142	2	3,813	449	134	50	186	16
	PUNJAB STATES ..	300	..	1	..	12	..	28,608	2,971	999	1,724	2,715	133	35,640	1,732	741	1,251	2,048	156
	A.—HAVING POLITICAL RELATIONS WITH THE PUNJAB GOVERNMENT ..	28	..	..	..	..	..	1,805	382	62	135	484	5	1,034	98	45	15	378	2
1	Dujana ..	..	..	..	..	..	..	119	28	1	5	11	1	25	..	1	..	4	..
2	Pataudi ..	4	..	..	..	..	..	113	18	..	..	2	..	3	..	..	..	..	..
3	Kalsia ..	19	..	..	..	..	..	453	153	23	107	36	2	44	2	2	1	2	..
4	SIMLA HILL STATES ..	5	..	..	..	..	..	1,120	163	38	23	435	2	962	96	42	14	372	2
	Bashahr ..	..	..	..	..	..	..	46	1	11	1	85	..	36	2	4	..	7	..
	Nalagarh ..	..	..	..	..	..	..	123	48	..	1	14	..	47	2	..	..	16	..
	Keonthal ..	2	..	..	..	..	..	544	16	11	..	47	..	304	46	17	12	18	..
	Baghal ..	..	..	..	..	..	..	73	16	..	..	78	1	12	..	..	..	12	..
	Jubbal ..	..	..	..	..	..	..	33	5	2	15	69	..	..	..	..	..	18	..
	Other Simla Hill States ..	3	..	..	..	..	..	301	77	14	6	142	1	563	46	21	2	301	2
	B.—HAVING POLITICAL RELATIONS WITH THE GOVERNMENT OF INDIA ..	272	..	1	..	12	..	26,803	2,609	937	1,589	2,231	128	34,606	1,634	696	1,236	1,670	154
5	Loharu ..	7	..	..	..	..	..	49	12	..	..	7	..	38	1	..	..	1	..
6	Sirmoor ..	6	..	..	..	1	..	728	99	6	33	42	1	459	74	8	2	54	1
7	Bilaspur ..	2	..	..	..	3	..	193	28	23	16	45	1	21	2	4	3	12	..
8	Mandi ..	12	..	..	..	4	..	687	31	..	3	340	7	2,333	137	1	..	327	7
9	Suket ..	..	..	..	..	..	..	52	29	4	16	16	..	105	..	5	..	5	..
10	Kapurthala ..	11	..	..	..	1	..	2,734	412	15	23	99	23	1,757	111	8	7	262	1
11	Maler Kotla ..	..	..	..	..	..	..	729	148	20	28	38	1	945	106	59	71	285	2
12	Faridkot ..	..	..	..	..	..	..	1,723	49	69	4	39	..	1,586	39	9	..	22	..
13	Chamba ..	..	..	..	..	..	..	360	56	2	14	57	7	678	82	9	1	270	6
14	Patiala (Phulkian States)	51	..	..	..	..	..	10,674	1,058	000	1,217	1,420	70	10,500	777	158	390	252	75
15	Jind (Phulkian States)	18	..	1	..	..	..	1,624	106	75	116	75	3	1,188	144	114	60	136	14
16	Nabha (Phulkian States)	70	..	..	..	3	..	1,183	161	52	119	53	1	394	53	9	2	32	..
17	Bahawalpur ..	95	..	..	..	..	..	6,067	417	71	..	..	14	14,602	108	312	700	12	48
18	Cities. Lahore ..	749	..	4	..	..	..	12,274	660	29	7	4	3	9,296	881	18	51	73	16
19	Cities. Amritsar ..	48	..	..	..	..	..	7,486	268	4	1	..	..	9,806	251	..	20	3	..
20	Cities. Multan ..	..	..	..	..	..	..	3,068	161	..	..	16	2	188	70	..	..	53	8

LIVELIHOOD.—GENERAL TABLE.

STATES AND CITIES—continued.

OCCUPATIONS.

D.—MISCELLANEOUS.—*continued.*

52.—General terms which do not indicate a definite occupation

188.—*Manufacturers, business-men and contractors otherwise unspecified.*						189.—*Cashiers, accountants, book-keepers, clerks and other employes in unspecified offices and ware-houses and shops.*						190.—*Mechanics, otherwise unspecified.*						191.—*Labourers and workmen otherwise unspecified.*						
Total earners principal occupation.		Total working dependants.		Total earners with subsidiary occupation.		Total earners principal occupation.		Total working dependants.		Total earners with subsidiary occupation.		Total earners principal occupation.		Total working dependants.		Total earners with subsidiary occupation.		Total earners principal occupation.		Total working dependants.		Total earners with subsidiary occupation.		
Males.	Females.	Males.	Females.	Males.	Females.	Males.	Females.	Males.	Females.	Males.	Females.	Males.	Females.	Males.	Females.	Males.	Females.	Males.	Females.	Males.	Females.	Males.	Females.	Serial No.
1271	1272	1273	1274	1275	1276	1277	1278	1279	1280	1281	1282	1283	1284	1285	1286	1287	1288	1289	1290	1291	1292	1293	1294	
10,995	**66**	**191**	**4**	**627**	..	**9,468**	**100**	**120**	**3**	**256**	**1**	**1,378**	**18**	**9**	..	**58**	..	**194,530**	**16,807**	**5,175**	**3,225**	**9,777**	**599**	
9,297	**33**	**158**	**1**	**455**	..	**8,511**	**96**	**109**	**3**	**135**	**1**	**751**	**16**	**2**	..	**4**	..	**162,172**	**15,114**	**4,485**	**1,977**	**8,076**	**443**	
454	..	**3**	**1**	**20**	..	**2,058**	**27**	**33**	..	**48**	..	**201**	..	**1**	..	**2**	..	**4,787**	**1,089**	**86**	**225**	**218**	**22**	
50	..	..	..	2	..	462	1	23	..	24	..	12	..	..	..	..	..	885	125	48	148	71	10	1
50	..	1	..	4	..	668	6	..	..	8	..	5	..	..	..	..	..	775	57	23	43	36	1	2
59	..	..	..	3	..	207	..	3	..	..	..	30	..	1	..	1	..	338	21	13	27	8	..	3
43	..	..	1	1	..	113	2	6	..	..	..	37	..	..	..	..	..	301	23	1	2	15	..	4
182	..	1	..	9	..	477	1	1	..	14	..	112	..	..	..	1	..	2,078	771	1	5	78	8	5
64	..	1	..	1	..	131	17	..	..	2	..	5	..	..	..	..	..	410	92	..	..	10	3	6
1,610	**5**	**75**	..	**172**	..	**1,040**	**3**	**5**	**3**	**44**	..	**10**	..	..	..	..	..	**29,957**	**2,185**	**1,201**	**319**	**2,900**	**64**	
83	..	..	..	22	..	6	..	..	..	4	..	..	..	..	..	..	..	1,149	177	23	93	314	21	7
170	..	1	..	22	..	216	..	..	..	9	..	..	..	..	..	..	..	3,069	286	113	50	1,109	17	8
441	2	68	..	76	..	281	..	3	..	18	..	..	..	..	..	..	..	8,129	273	687	52	329	16	9
552	2	2	..	22	..	358	..	2	..	13	..	..	..	..	..	..	..	6,052	474	101	75	965	9	10
364	1	4	..	30	..	179	3	..	3	..	..	10	..	..	..	..	..	11,558	975	277	49	183	1	11
3,601	**6**	**16**	..	**102**	..	**4,074**	**7**	**18**	..	**10**	**1**	**340**	**1**	**1**	..	**2**	..	**51,417**	**4,152**	**961**	**322**	**1,648**	**93**	
1,753	3	5	..	20	..	2,745	6	2	..	1	..	218	1	..	..	2	..	16,717	1,910	122	71	303	39	12
432	..	1	..	12	..	825	..	11	..	5	..	37	..	..	..	..	..	11,843	461	66	49	71	20	13
412	1	5	..	22	..	156	1	..	..	2	1	21	..	..	..	..	..	4,071	138	242	7	491	3	14
540	1	2	..	5	..	223	..	4	..	2	..	64	..	1	..	..	..	5,378	314	163	51	442	1	15
322	1	2	..	4	..	115	..	..	..	..	..	..	..	..	..	..	..	7,515	1,004	49	40	131	22	16
142	..	1	..	39	..	10	..	1	..	..	..	..	..	..	..	..	..	5,863	316	319	104	210	8	17
2,056	**1**	**60**	..	**61**	..	**622**	**37**	**41**	..	**30**	..	**87**	..	..	..	..	..	**29,079**	**3,372**	**888**	**385**	**1,768**	**122**	
245	..	12	..	5	..	11	..	..	..	..	..	..	..	..	..	..	..	4,310	363	266	8	253	6	18
1,012	..	16	..	33	..	197	33	..	..	..	..	..	..	..	..	..	..	9,334	1,158	90	62	258	4	19
531	1	24	..	6	..	37	..	9	..	2	..	36	..	..	..	..	..	3,147	136	80	6	505	..	20
110	..	5	..	2	..	294	3	32	..	26	..	1	..	..	..	..	..	5,895	760	238	137	310	82	21
116	..	3	..	11	..	14	1	..	..	..	..	..	..	..	..	..	..	3,508	646	111	34	308	24	22
42	..	..	..	4	..	69	..	..	..	2	..	..	..	..	..	..	..	2,825	309	103	138	134	6	23
1,576	**21**	**4**	..	**100**	..	**717**	**22**	**12**	..	**3**	..	**163**	**15**	..	..	..	..	**46,932**	**4,316**	**1,349**	**726**	**1,542**	**142**	
199	2	4	..	5	..	16	..	..	..	..	..	..	..	..	..	..	..	11,326	1,492	200	360	270	17	24
225	..	..	..	10	..	349	10	9	..	..	..	148	15	..	..	..	..	12,274	585	698	21	464	16	25
701	..	..	..	21	..	281	9	..	..	..	..	6	..	..	..	..	..	3,393	437	29	14	113	60	26
279	19	..	..	43	..	15	3	..	..	..	..	9	..	..	..	..	..	12,590	812	241	118	453	16	27
140	..	..	..	9	..	47	..	3	..	3	..	..	..	..	..	..	..	3,577	541	47	163	68	17	28
32	..	..	..	12	..	9	..	..	..	..	..	..	..	..	..	..	..	3,772	449	134	50	174	16	29
1,698	**33**	**83**	**3**	**172**	..	**957**	**4**	**11**	..	**121**	..	**627**	**2**	**7**	..	**54**	..	**32,358**	**1,693**	**690**	**1,248**	**1,701**	**156**	
28	..	**1**	..	**18**	..	**212**	**4**	**4**	..	**57**	..	**2**	..	..	..	**11**	..	**792**	**94**	**40**	**15**	**292**	**2**	
..	..	..	..	..	..	..	..	..	..	3	..	..	..	..	..	..	..	25	..	1	..	1	..	1
1	..	..	..	..	..	..	..	..	..	..	..	..	..	..	..	..	..	2	..	..	..	..	..	2
2	..	..	..	..	..	33	1	2	..	2	..	2	..	..	..	..	..	7	1	..	1	..	..	3
25	..	**1**	..	**18**	..	**179**	**3**	**2**	..	**52**	..	..	..	..	..	**11**	..	**758**	**98**	**39**	**14**	**291**	**2**	4
6	..	..	..	..	..	24	..	1	..	7	..	..	..	..	..	..	..	6	2	3	..	..	..	
1	..	..	..	1	..	5	..	..	..	1	..	..	..	..	..	..	..	41	2	..	..	14	..	
11	..	1	..	4	..	36	..	1	..	13	..	..	..	..	..	..	..	257	46	15	12	1	..	
..	..	..	..	..	..	1	..	..	..	..	..	..	..	..	..	..	..	11	..	..	..	12	..	
..	..	..	..	..	..	..	..	..	..	7	..	..	..	..	..	11	..	..	..	..	..	..	..	
7	..	..	..	13	..	113	3	..	..	24	..	..	..	..	..	..	..	443	43	21	2	264	2	
1,670	**33**	**32**	**3**	**154**	..	**745**	..	**7**	..	**64**	..	**625**	**2**	**7**	..	**43**	..	**31,566**	**1,599**	**650**	**1,233**	**1,409**	**154**	
..	..	..	..	..	..	13	..	..	..	1	..	..	..	..	..	..	..	25	1	..	..	..	..	5
2	..	..	..	..	..	14	..	1	..	3	..	..	1	..	..	..	..	443	73	7	2	51	1	6
1	..	..	..	..	..	..	..	..	..	7	..	..	..	..	..	..	..	20	2	4	3	5	..	7
10	..	..	..	13	..	16	..	..	..	3	..	..	..	..	..	..	..	2,307	137	1	..	311	7	8
..	..	..	..	..	..	90	..	2	..	..	..	..	..	..	..	..	..	15	..	3	..	5	..	9
431	6	..	3	58	..	71	..	..	..	25	..	5	1	1	..	..	..	1,250	104	7	4	179	1	10
9	..	..	..	..	..	44	..	..	..	4	..	2	..	..	..	..	..	890	106	59	71	281	2	11
52	..	..	..	3	..	..	..	..	..	..	..	4	..	..	..	..	..	1,530	39	9	..	19	..	12
24	..	..	..	19	..	21	..	..	..	7	..	1	..	..	..	..	..	632	82	9	1	244	6	13
519	..	18	..	53	..	129	..	1	..	13	..	581	..	6	..	42	..	9,271	777	133	390	144	75	14
4	..	..	..	..	..	5	..	..	..	..	..	..	..	..	..	..	..	1,179	144	114	60	136	14	15
39	9	2	..	8	..	136	..	3	..	1	..	32	..	..	..	1	..	187	44	4	2	22	..	16
579	18	12	..	..	..	206	..	..	..	..	..	..	..	..	..	..	..	13,817	90	300	700	12	48	17
1,541	3	4	..	15	..	1,956	4	..	..	..	..	204	1	..	..	..	..	5,595	873	14	51	58	16	18
835	..	..	..	3	..	740	..	..	..	..	..	27	..	..	..	..	..	8,704	251	..	20	..	..	19
34	..	..	..	38	..	..	3	..	..	..	..	4	..	..	..	..	..	150	67	..	..	15	8	20

TABLE X.—OCCUPATION OR MEANS OF
DETAILS FOR DISTRICTS,

Class ..	D.—MISCELLANEOUS.																			
Sub-class ..	XII.—UNPRODUCTIVE.																			
Order ..						53. Inmates of Jails, Asylums and Alms houses.								54. Beggars, vagrants, prostitutes.						
Group ..	Total Sub-Class XII.						Total Order 53.							Total Order 54.						
							192.—Inmates of Jails, asylums and alms houses.													
	Total earners principal occupation.		Total working dependants.		Total earners with subsidiary occupation.		Total earners principal occupation.		Total working dependants.		Total earners with subsidiary occupation.		Total earners Principal occupation.		Total working dependants.		Total earners with subsidiary occupation.			
Serial No. / District or State.	Males.	Females.	Males.	Females.	Males.	Females.	Males.	Females.	Males.	Females.	Males.	Females.	Males.	Females.	Males.	Females.	Males.	Females.		

Serial No.	District or State.	1295 Males	1296 Females	1297 Males	1298 Females	1299 Males	1300 Females	1301 Males	1302 Females	1303 Males	1304 Females	1305 Males	1306 Females	1307 Males	1308 Females	1309 Males	1310 Females	1311 Males	1312 Females
1	2	1295	1296	1297	1298	1299	1300	1301	1302	1303	1304	1305	1306	1307	1308	1309	1310	1311	1312
	PUNJAB ..	**174,302**	**22,420**	**24,053**	**5,091**	**10,235**	**707**	..	..	**15,525**	**169**	..	..	**174,134**	**22,409**	**8,520**	**4,922**	**10,197**	**707**
	BRITISH TERRITORY ..	**143,885**	**18,929**	**20,220**	**4,196**	**8,179**	**626**	..	..	**12,950**	**84**	..	..	**143,726**	**18,918**	**7,264**	**4,112**	**8,170**	**626**
	AMBALA DIVISION ..	**19,355**	**2,085**	**2,259**	**527**	**1,629**	**81**	..	..	**1,336**	**8**	..	..	**19,346**	**2,085**	**923**	**519**	**1,625**	**81**
1	Hissar ..	3,141	505	674	309	396	22	..	..	257	2	..	..	3,139	505	417	307	396	22
2	Rohtak ..	3,705	234	418	55	258	18	..	..	255	1	..	..	3,765	234	163	54	258	18
3	Gurgaon ..	4,416	370	281	71	427	11	..	..	105	1	..	..	4,416	370	176	70	427	11
4	Karnal ..	4,062	543	148	31	308	26	..	..	49	..	..	..	4,056	543	99	31	305	26
5	Ambala ..	3,950	414	707	59	238	4	..	..	639	4	..	..	3,949	414	68	55	237	4
6	Simla ..	21	19	31	2	2	..	..	..	31	..	..	..	21	19	..	2	2	..
	JULLUNDUR DIVISION	**26,388**	**2,320**	**2,500**	**364**	**1,582**	**55**	..	..	**1,260**	**14**	..	..	**26,387**	**2,320**	**1,240**	**350**	**1,582**	**55**
7	Kangra ..	2,025	363	83	97	216	15	..	..	27	..	..	..	2,025	363	56	97	216	15
8	Hoshiarpur ..	6,318	413	315	75	546	10	..	..	77	14	..	..	6,318	413	238	61	546	10
9	Jullundur ..	5,362	452	746	98	288	8	..	..	361	..	..	..	5,362	452	385	98	288	8
10	Ludhiana ..	5,194	345	607	59	336	14	..	..	253	..	..	..	5,194	345	354	59	336	14
11	Ferozepore ..	7,489	747	749	35	196	8	..	..	542	..	..	..	7,488	747	207	35	196	8
	LAHORE DIVISION ..	**44,485**	**5,555**	**7,675**	**1,333**	**2,272**	**98**	..	..	**5,172**	**1**	..	..	**44,462**	**5,545**	**2,502**	**1,332**	**2,272**	**98**
12	Lahore ..	9,050	1,396	3,760	110	265	12	..	..	3,532	1	..	..	9,029	1,391	227	109	265	12
13	Amritsar ..	9,265	937	1,504	502	412	41	..	..	318	..	..	..	9,263	937	1,186	502	412	41
14	Gurdaspur ..	7,780	879	403	258	559	7	..	..	165	..	..	..	7,780	879	238	258	559	7
15	Sialkot ..	6,992	558	873	37	619	1	..	..	589	..	..	..	6,902	558	284	37	619	1
16	Gujranwala ..	6,334	849	555	212	282	14	..	..	348	..	..	..	6,334	849	207	212	282	14
17	Sheikhupura ..	5,064	936	580	214	135	23	..	..	220	..	..	..	5,064	931	360	214	135	23
	RAWALPINDI DIVISION	**20,663**	**4,886**	**2,846**	**1,353**	**1,160**	**155**	..	..	**1,730**	**14**	..	..	**20,642**	**4,886**	**1,116**	**1,339**	**1,160**	**155**
18	Gujrat ..	4,432	650	288	54	173	27	..	..	77	..	..	..	4,432	650	211	54	173	27
19	Shahpur ..	6,019	1,494	267	469	240	15	..	..	72	1	..	..	6,019	1,494	195	468	240	15
20	Jhelum ..	2,648	680	352	396	235	29	..	..	156	8	..	..	2,648	680	196	388	235	29
21	Rawalpindi ..	2,250	769	224	45	137	46	..	..	84	..	..	..	2,247	769	140	45	137	46
22	Attock ..	2,923	753	1,126	151	220	32	..	..	896	5	..	..	2,923	753	230	146	220	32
23	Mianwali ..	2,391	540	589	238	155	6	..	..	445	..	..	..	2,373	540	144	238	155	6
	MULTAN DIVISION ..	**32,994**	**4,083**	**4,940**	**619**	**1,536**	**237**	..	..	**3,452**	**47**	..	..	**32,889**	**4,082**	**1,483**	**572**	**1,531**	**237**
24	Montgomery ..	5,587	580	1,336	45	98	7	..	..	1,200	..	..	..	5,587	580	136	45	98	7
25	Lyallpur ..	6,908	1,026	645	93	217	30	..	..	151	..	..	..	6,897	1,026	494	93	217	30
26	Jhang ..	5,793	716	650	177	153	21	..	..	422	..	..	..	5,772	716	228	177	153	21
27	Multan ..	7,759	838	1,431	44	622	145	..	..	1,215	..	..	..	7,693	837	212	44	618	145
28	Muzaffargarh ..	3,758	470	374	154	234	15	..	..	23	..	..	..	3,758	470	351	154	234	15
29	Dera Ghazi Khan ..	3,189	453	504	106	212	19	..	..	441	47	..	..	3,182	453	62	59	211	19
	PUNJAB STATES ..	**30,417**	**3,491**	**3,833**	**895**	**2,056**	**81**	..	..	**2,575**	**85**	..	..	**30,408**	**3,491**	**1,256**	**810**	**2,027**	**81**
	A.—HAVING POLITICAL RELATIONS WITH THE PUNJAB GOVERNMENT ..	**1,237**	**249**	**160**	**74**	**94**	**2**	..	..	**82**	**3**	..	..	**1,237**	**249**	**76**	**71**	**88**	**2**
1	Dujana ..	145	3	5	2	17	..	..	..	..	..	..	..	145	3	5	2	17	..
2	Pataudi ..	113	3	..	..	4	..	..	..	..	..	..	..	113	3	..	..	4	..
3	Kalsia ..	443	36	70	9	20	1	..	..	42	2	..	..	443	36	28	7	20	1
4	SIMLA HILL STATES ..	**536**	**207**	**85**	**63**	**53**	**1**	..	..	**40**	**1**	..	..	**536**	**207**	**43**	**62**	**47**	**1**
	Bashahr ..	9	1	15	7	3	..	..	..	..	..	..	..	9	1	15	7	3	..
	Nalagarh ..	105	20	8	1	15	..	..	..	7	..	..	..	105	20	1	1	11	..
	Keonthal ..	101	23	20	14	1	..	..	..	6	1	..	..	101	23	14	13	1	..
	Baghal ..	91	27	..	12	..	..	..	..	..	..	..	..	91	27	..	12	..	..
	Jubbal ..	10	8	17	2	2	..	..	..	15	..	..	..	10	8	2	2	2	..
	Other Simla Hill States ..	220	128	25	27	32	1	..	..	12	..	..	..	220	128	11	27	30	1
	B.—HAVING POLITICAL RELATIONS WITH THE GOVERNMENT OF INDIA ..	**29,180**	**3,242**	**3,673**	**821**	**1,962**	**79**	..	..	**2,493**	**82**	..	..	**29,171**	**3,242**	**1,180**	**739**	**1,939**	**79**
5	Loharu ..	186	31	3	24	8	2	..	..	..	..	..	..	186	31	3	24	8	2
6	Sirmoor ..	324	76	12	23	49	4	..	..	..	..	..	..	324	76	12	23	49	4
7	Bilaspur ..	285	65	18	26	41	1	..	..	..	..	..	..	285	65	18	26	41	1
8	Mandi ..	364	124	35	4	121	6	..	..	33	4	..	..	364	124	2	..	121	6
9	Suket ..	83	16	18	4	..	..	..	..	16	1	..	..	83	16	2	3	..	..
10	Kapurthala ..	2,597	185	27	12	131	11	..	..	..	..	..	..	2,597	185	27	12	131	11
11	Maler Kotla ..	763	92	93	26	50	4	..	..	58	..	..	..	763	92	35	26	50	4
12	Faridkot ..	1,234	109	58	13	38	..	..	..	..	..	..	..	1,234	109	58	13	38	..
13	Chamba ..	229	43	61	13	47	1	..	..	56	1	..	..	221	43	5	12	24	1
14	Patiala } Phulkian States.	11,139	1,037	1,520	338	1,198	30	..	..	867	48	..	..	11,139	1,037	653	290	1,198	30
15	Jind } Phulkian States.	1,592	135	327	64	107	9	..	..	203	3	..	..	1,592	135	124	61	107	9
16	Nabha } Phulkian States.	2,189	164	398	19	172	5	..	..	337	3	..	..	2,188	164	61	16	172	5
17	Bahawalpur ..	8,195	1,165	1,103	255	..	6	..	..	923	22	..	..	8,195	1,165	180	233	..	6
18	Cities. { Lahore ..	1,733	331	3,421	13	2	5	..	..	3,407	1	..	..	1,733	331	14	12	2	5
19	Cities. { Amritsar ..	1,694	91	323	..	3	..	..	..	318	..	..	..	1,692	91	5	..	3	..
20	Cities. { Multan ..	773	135	..	14	5	3	..	..	..	..	..	..	773	135	..	14	5	3

LIVELIHOOD.—GENERAL TABLE.

STATES AND CITIES.—*concluded.*

D. MISCELLANEOUS.—*concluded.*

XII. UNPRODUCTIVE.—*concluded.*

54. Beggars, Vagrants, Prostitutes.—*concluded.*												55. Other unclassified non-productive Industries. Total Order 55.						
193.—*Beggars and vagrants.*						194.—*Procurers and prostitutes.*						195.—*Other unclassified non-productive industries.*						
Total earners principal occupation.		Total working dependants.		Total earners with subsidiary occupation.		Total earners principal occupation.		Total working dependants.		Total earners with subsidiary occupation.		Total earners principal occupation.		Total working dependants.		Total earners with subsidiary occupation.		
Males.	Females.	Males.	Females.	Males.	Females.	Males.	Females.	Males.	Females.	Males.	Females.	Males.	Females.	Males.	Females.	Males.	Females.	Serial No.
1313	1314	1315	1316	1317	1318	1319	1320	1321	1322	1323	1324	1325	1326	1327	1328	1329	1330	
173,910	21,281	8,517	4,908	10,189	677	224	1,128	3	14	8	30	168	11	8	..	38	..	
143,531	17,999	7,261	4,101	8,168	604	195	919	3	11	2	22	159	11	6	..	9	..	
19,846	1,912	923	512	1,625	72	..	173	..	7	..	9	9	..	..	..	4	..	
3,139	487	417	307	396	22	..	18	..	..	..	..	2	..	..	..	..	..	1
3,765	229	163	54	258	18	..	5	..	..	..	..	..	..	..	..	..	..	2
4,416	360	176	70	427	7	..	10	..	..	..	4	..	..	..	..	..	..	3
4,056	485	99	25	305	21	..	58	..	6	..	5	6	..	..	..	3	..	4
3,949	345	68	55	237	4	..	69	..	..	..	..	1	..	..	..	1	..	5
21	6	..	1	2	..	..	13	..	1	..	..	..	..	..	..	..	..	6
26,855	2,092	1,240	350	1,582	55	32	228	..	..	..	..	1	..	..	..	..	..	
2,025	363	56	97	216	15	..	..	..	..	..	..	..	..	..	..	..	..	7
6,318	406	238	61	546	10	..	7	..	..	..	..	..	..	..	..	..	..	8
5,361	385	385	98	288	8	1	67	..	..	..	..	..	..	..	..	..	..	9
5,175	232	354	59	336	14	19	113	..	..	..	..	..	..	..	..	..	..	10
7,476	706	207	35	196	8	12	41	..	..	..	..	1	..	..	..	..	..	11
44,323	5,878	2,502	1,329	2,272	93	139	172	..	3	..	5	23	10	1	..	..	..	
8,894	1,260	227	108	265	7	135	131	..	1	..	5	21	5	1	..	..	..	12
9,263	925	1,186	502	412	41	..	12	..	..	..	..	2	..	..	..	..	..	13
7,780	879	238	258	559	7	..	..	..	..	..	..	..	..	..	..	..	..	14
6,988	529	284	35	619	1	4	29	..	2	..	..	..	..	..	..	..	..	15
6,334	849	207	212	282	14	..	..	..	..	..	..	..	..	..	..	..	..	16
5,064	931	360	214	135	23	..	..	..	..	..	..	..	5	..	..	..	..	17
20,642	4,797	1,113	1,338	1,158	154	..	89	3	1	2	1	21	..	..	..	..	..	
4,432	641	211	54	173	27	..	9	..	..	..	..	..	..	..	..	..	..	18
6,019	1,470	195	468	239	15	..	21	..	..	1	..	..	..	..	..	..	..	19
2,648	650	196	388	235	29	..	30	..	..	..	..	..	..	..	..	..	..	20
2,247	763	140	45	137	46	..	6	..	..	..	..	3	..	..	..	..	..	21
2,923	735	227	145	219	31	..	18	3	1	1	1	..	..	..	..	..	..	22
2,373	538	144	238	155	6	..	2	..	..	..	..	18	..	..	..	..	..	23
32,865	3,825	4,483	572	1,531	230	24	257	..	..	..	7	105	1	5	..	5	..	
5,587	501	136	45	98	3	..	76	..	..	..	4	..	..	..	..	..	..	24
6,894	935	494	93	217	30	3	91	..	..	..	..	11	..	..	..	..	..	25
5,764	707	228	177	153	21	8	9	..	..	..	..	21	..	..	..	..	..	26
7,693	786	212	44	618	142	..	51	..	..	..	3	66	1	4	..	4	..	27
3,758	469	351	154	234	15	..	1	..	..	..	..	8	..	..	..	..	..	28
3,169	424	62	59	211	19	13	29	..	..	..	..	7	..	1	..	1	..	29
30,379	3,282	1,256	807	2,021	73	29	209	..	3	6	8	9	..	2	..	29	..	
1,237	249	76	70	88	2	..	..	..	1	5	..	..	..	2	..	6	..	
145	3	5	2	17	..	..	..	..	..	..	..	..	..	..	..	..	..	1
113	3	..	..	4	..	..	..	..	..	..	..	..	..	..	..	..	..	2
443	36	28	7	20	1	..	..	..	..	..	..	..	..	..	..	..	..	3
536	207	43	61	42	1	..	..	..	1	5	..	..	..	2	..	6	..	4
9	1	15	6	3	..	..	..	..	1	..	..	..	..	..	..	..	..	
105	20	1	1	11	..	..	..	..	..	..	..	..	..	..	..	4	..	
101	23	14	13	1	..	..	..	..	..	..	..	..	..	..	..	..	..	
91	27	..	12	..	..	..	..	..	..	..	..	..	..	..	..	..	..	
10	8	2	2	2	..	..	..	..	..	..	..	..	..	..	..	..	..	
220	128	11	27	25	1	..	..	..	..	5	..	..	..	2	..	2	..	
29,142	3,033	1,180	737	1,938	71	29	209	..	2	1	8	9	..	..	..	23	..	
186	30	3	23	8	2	..	1	..	1	..	..	..	..	..	..	..	..	5
324	76	12	23	49	4	..	..	..	..	..	..	..	..	..	..	..	..	6
285	65	18	26	41	1	..	..	..	..	..	..	..	..	..	..	..	..	7
364	124	2	..	121	6	..	..	..	..	..	..	..	..	..	..	..	..	8
83	16	2	3	..	..	..	..	..	..	..	..	..	..	..	..	..	..	9
2,593	184	27	12	130	11	4	1	..	..	1	..	..	..	..	..	..	..	10
763	92	35	26	50	4	..	..	..	..	..	..	..	..	..	..	..	..	11
1,234	98	58	13	38	..	..	11	..	..	..	..	..	..	..	..	..	..	12
221	43	5	12	24	1	..	..	..	..	..	..	8	..	..	..	23	..	13
11,139	921	653	289	1,198	22	..	116	..	1	..	8	..	..	..	..	..	..	14
1,591	135	124	61	107	9	1	..	..	..	..	..	..	..	..	..	..	..	15
2,188	148	61	16	172	5	..	16	..	..	..	..	1	..	..	..	..	..	16
8,171	1,101	180	233	..	6	24	64	..	..	..	..	..	..	..	..	..	..	17
1,599	259	14	11	2	..	134	72	..	1	..	5	..	..	..	..	..	..	18
1,692	79	5	..	3	..	..	12	..	..	..	..	2	..	..	..	..	..	19
773	87	..	14	5	..	..	48	..	..	..	3	..	..	..	..	..	..	20

TABLE XI.

OCCUPATION OF SELECTED CASTES, TRIBES OR RACES.

1. This Table shows the occupations followed by certain castes, as well as Europeans, Armenians and Anglo-Indians.

2. The number of earners, following the traditional occupation of the caste as their principal means of livelihood, is shown in columns 10 and 11, and as a subsidiary means of livelihood in columns 12 and 13. The number of earners, who have some other occupation as their principal means of livelihood, is shown in column 18 and onwards.

3. The figures of all working dependants appear in columns 7 and 8, and of those following their traditional occupations in columns 14 and 15.

4. In the case of Europeans and Anglo-Indians, no occupation has been assumed to be traditional.

5. The castes and the localities for this Table are the same as in Tables VIII and XIV, with the exception that Europeans and Anglo-Indians have been shown for the whole of the Province with details of the Districts which returned fifty or more persons of each nationality. The number of Armenians being very small, their figures have been given for the whole Province.

TABLE XI.—OCCUPATION OF

Serial No.	Caste, Tribe or Race.	Traditional Occupation.	Religion.	Locality.	Population dealt with.					Number of earners whose traditional caste occupation was returned as their			
					Earners.		Working Dependants.		Non-Working Dependants.	Principal means of Livelihood.		Subsidiary means of Livelihood.	
					Males.	Females.	Males.	Females.	Both Sexes.	Males.	Females.	Males.	Females.
	1	2	3	4	5	6	7	8	9	10	11	12	13
1	Aggarwal ..	*Trade* ..	Hindu ..	A. C. ..	93,071	3,626	9,301	2,166	238,956	74,577	1,282	3,825	69
2	" ..	" ..	Jain ..	A. C. ..	6,265	246	457	57	17,196	5,066	88	154	2
3	Ahir ..	*Agriculture* ..	Hindu ..	A. C. ..	54,044	2,075	19,316	29,577	112,500	44,929	1,436	4,546	55
4	" ..	" ..	Muslim ..	D. ..	660	43	117	24	1,464	529	28	9	..
5	Arain ..	" ..	Muslim ..	A. C. D. ..	348,903	13,693	51,516	15,034	898,949	270,288	6,735	7,759	499
6	Arora ..	*Trade* ..	Hindu ..	C. D. ..	188,796	6,036	6,939	931	456,146	128,043	1,060	2,612	45
7	" ..	" ..	Sikh ..	C. D. ..	30,084	1,440	1,636	386	77,167	20,798	645	437	9
8	Awan ..	*Agriculture* ..	Muslim ..	C. D. ..	133,819	8,975	25,206	13,331	357,374	101,698	5,372	3,133	350
9	Bawaria ..	*Crime and Hunting.* ..	Hindu ..	A.C.D. ..	3,910	633	450	663	10,389	155	59	7	..
10	" ..	" ..	Sikh ..	C. D. ..	4,164	275	437	163	10,819	587	21	32	3
11	Biloch ..	*Camel Driving* ..	Muslim ..	A. C. D. ..	186,416	4,958	14,197	4,000	415,120	23,625	942	1,783	84
12	Brahman ..	*Priests* ..	Hindu ..	A. B. C. D. ..	309,288	20,909	47,252	73,553	600,380	43,687	4,521	10,176	923
13	" ..	" ..	Sikh ..	C. D. ..	2,215	129	170	30	4,020	615	55	27	1
14	Chamar ..	*Shoe-making* ..	Hindu ..	A. B. C. D. ..	197,830	22,338	26,555	55,845	382,395	48,791	1,755	7,442	1,547
15	" ..	" ..	Ad-dharmi	A. B. C. D. ..	74,257	4,543	5,029	8,249	164,271	18,065	766	2,476	7
16	" ..	" ..	Sikh ..	A. C. ..	45,745	1,811	4,500	3,197	100,464	13,840	147	853	235
17	Chhimba ..	*Dyeing* ..	Hindu ..	A. C. ..	6,232	378	953	1,207	12,191	1,401	133	159	51
18	" ..	" ..	Sikh ..	C. ..	5,036	282	632	142	10,649	1,126	102	90	33
19	" ..	" ..	Muslim ..	A. C. D. ..	14,759	923	1,168	1,299	35,257	6,105	391	277	35
20	Chuhra ..	*Sweeping* ..	Hindu ..	A. B. C. D. ..	108,686	35,526	8,861	19,782	195,369	52,306	32,205	1,889	341
21	" ..	" ..	Ad-Dharmi	A. C. D. ..	25,870	6,032	1,123	1,895	51,619	10,062	6,102	259	38
22	" ..	" ..	Sikh ..	C. ..	46,160	5,839	2,855	2,340	100,147	5,407	4,316	253	14
23	" ..	" ..	Muslim ..	C. D. ..	6,203	862	306	201	14,578	1,849	645	75	4
24	" ..	" ..	Christian ..	A. C. D. ..	10,235	2,544	746	1,285	20,105	4,621	2,334	59	11
25	Dagi and Koli. ..	*Agriculture* ..	Hindu ..	A. B. C. ..	47,660	3,720	17,594	48,437	63,959	38,123	2,192	548	98
26	Dhobi ..	*Washing* ..	Hindu ..	A. C. ..	3,387	327	218	354	6,146	2,683	260	36	15
27	" ..	" ..	Muslim ..	A. C. D. ..	46,053	3,459	3,025	2,206	107,301	29,450	1,929	746	89
28	Faqir ..	*Begging* ..	Hindu ..	C. D. ..	9,132	556	701	124	12,648	5,551	353	258	8
29	" ..	" ..	Sikh ..	C. ..	2,044	108	122	30	2,180	1,237	80	43	..
30	" ..	" ..	Muslim ..	A. C. D. ..	72,112	4,765	6,470	3,827	166,795	35,642	2,163	2,287	133
31	Gujjar ..	*Agriculture and Cattle breeding.* ..	Hindu ..	A. B. C. D. ..	49,103	1,885	14,163	19,141	86,147	41,175	1,077	2,341	111
32	" ..	" ..	Sikh ..	C. ..	662	22	106	317	1,214	566	18	66	7
33	" ..	" ..	Muslim ..	A. B. C. D. ..	139,532	5,232	27,104	15,620	333,859	117,945	3,381	3,396	67
34	Harni ..	*Crime* ..	Muslim ..	C. ..	912	46	98	..	2,331	47	2	..	2
35	Jat ..	*Agriculture* ..	Hindu ..	A. B. C. D. ..	258,712	9,823	90,467	137,602	495,705	232,210	6,264	13,092	693
36	" ..	" ..	Sikh ..	A. C. D. ..	595,333	20,472	154,848	19,790	1,342,709	536,677	15,590	39,039	2,688
37	" ..	" ..	Muslim ..	A. C. D. ..	816,559	30,830	97,828	24,909	1,970,693	626,604	19,333	12,434	1,063
38	Jhiwar ..	*Baking and water carrying.*	Hindu ..	A. B. C. ..	36,685	6,351	3,268	5,699	73,079	16,015	4,642	937	697
39	" ..	" ..	Sikh ..	C. ..	15,239	3,803	1,612	1,876	32,681	10,403	3,383	481	303
40	" ..	" ..	Muslim ..	C. D. ..	26,209	3,621	2,347	2,187	60,364	16,978	2,236	398	124
41	Julaha ..	*Weaving* ..	Hindu ..	A. B. C. ..	16,566	2,272	1,987	6,713	23,615	4,347	782	1,071	50
42	" ..	" ..	Sikh ..	C. ..	1,175	98	172	341	1,854	892	63	68	1
43	" ..	" ..	Muslim ..	A. B. C. D. ..	177,146	12,541	12,045	14,228	396,619	127,877	8,744	3,279	500
44	Kamboh ..	*Agriculture* ..	Hindu ..	A. C. D. ..	11,043	473	1,989	197	23,763	9,254	135	306	3
45	" ..	" ..	Sikh ..	C. D. ..	26,121	876	3,582	310	67,848	23,262	477	784	17
46	" ..	" ..	Muslim ..	C. D. ..	26,580	1,047	3,240	1,742	64,144	18,791	446	1,174	47
47	Kashmiri ..	*Weaving* ..	Muslim ..	C. D. ..	59,570	3,102	3,227	1,338	131,803	15,010	1,047	573	18
48	Khatri ..	*Trade* ..	Hindu ..	A. B. C. D. ..	129,709	5,101	5,853	1,062	319,126	75,083	1,227	1,971	120
49	" ..	" ..	Sikh ..	C. D. ..	14,502	812	788	146	37,748	6,906	255	239	12
50	Kumhar ..	*Pot-making* ..	Hindu ..	A. B. C. ..	43,515	2,343	6,818	10,183	94,054	19,991	782	1,680	244
51	" ..	" ..	Sikh ..	C. ..	8,625	301	1,212	309	20,791	2,454	99	121	15
52	" ..	" ..	Muslim ..	A. C. D. ..	115,943	5,035	10,042	3,436	288,974	67,662	2,241	2,431	244
53	Lohar ..	*Blacksmith* ..	Hindu ..	A. B. C. ..	21,239	1,179	3,878	8,161	40,006	10,974	262	2,031	39
54	" ..	" ..	Sikh ..	A. C. ..	4,493	203	503	107	11,154	2,908	52	231	3
55	" ..	" ..	Muslim ..	A. C. D. ..	64,224	1,973	7,024	3,093	165,262	44,464	810	2,176	14
56	Machhi ..	*Baking and Water-carrying.*	Muslim ..	A. C. D. ..	90,243	13,352	6,349	5,521	199,326	48,201	10,692	1,532	203
57	Meo ..	*Agriculture* ..	Muslim ..	A. ..	31,460	1,501	10,309	25,718	55,807	27,897	873	158	19
58	Mirasi ..	*Begging* ..	Muslim ..	A. C. D. ..	68,431	6,453	4,808	2,595	159,373	45,414	4,490	1,328	201
59	Mochi ..	*Shoe-making* ..	Hindu ..	C. ..	2,178	92	59	16	2,255	1,358	42	18	..
60	" ..	" ..	Muslim ..	C. D. ..	130,462	6,043	8,619	5,673	310,219	94,728	2,725	1,917	39
61	Mussalli ..	*Sweeping* ..	Muslim ..	C. D. ..	114,598	11,555	8,469	6,265	271,408	37,755	6,127	1,444	57

SELECTED CASTES, TRIBES OR RACES.—*continued.*

Number of Working Dependants following the traditional Occupation of their Caste.		Number of earners returning their traditional occupation as their Principal means of livelihood who had some subsidiary occupation.		RECORDED PRINCIPAL OCCUPATION OF EARNERS, OTHER THAN TRADITIONAL OCCUPATION OF CASTE (BY ORDERS). I.—Exploitation of Animals and Vegetation. Income from rent of land.		Cultivators of all kinds.		Agents and managers of landed Estates, planters, Forest Officers and their clerks, Rent Collectors, etc.		Field-labourers, wood-cutters etc.		Raisers of livestocks, milkmen and herdsmen.		Fishing and Hunting.		II.—Exploitation of Minerals. Owners, Managers Clerks, etc.		Labourers.		Serial No.
Males.	Females.	Males.	Females.	Males.	Females.	Males.	Females.	Males.	Females.	Males.	Females.	Males.	Females.	Males.	Females.	Males.	Females.	Males	Females.	
14	15	16	17	18	19	20	21	22	23	24	25	26	27	28	29	30	31	32	33	
4,459	238	8,673	85	1,356	453	6,021	167	74	..	312	22	76	2	..	..	22	..	5	2	1
207	5	489	4	127	22	164	9	9	1	8	6	..	..	..	..	3	..	..	..	2
13,231	10,032	4,140	132	182	173	..	..	114	3	1,465	138	645	11	5	..	3	..	44	2	3
49	1	24	3	7	1	..	..	5	..	9	1	19	1	..	..	..	..	..	..	4
43,913	8,448	23,177	799	2,180	709	..	..	2,210	19	17,651	908	5,063	110	111	..	17	..	546	63	5
3,367	238	9,725	90	6,738	656	15,217	142	507	9	2,484	56	312	20	10	..	40	..	675	7	6
724	11	1,317	110	689	146	2,808	39	307	..	368	22	146	1	1	..	32	..	98		7
20,333	8,559	13,050	1,115	1,263	809	..	..	248	30	2,841	136	2,606	93	45	..	23	1	1,076	136	8
10	58	29	..	9	3	1,423	15	7	1	831	81	331	18	..	..	..	..	28	..	9
139	43	131	2	54	29	1,886	11	35	..	1,178	46	78	8	..	..	..	..	45	2	10
2,334	907	6,074	76	5,680	588	109,249	763	303	18	13,806	314	10,184	148	143	1	1	..	292	60	11
4,751	654	6,693	346	9,322	4,358	138,644	6,543	775	21	5,139	369	2,620	142	35	1	47	..	222	9	12
57	12	72	1	99	18	483	2	4	..	55	2	10	..	..	..	4	..	6	..	13
2,946	2,541	14,901	300	356	124	49,131	1,388	134	8	59,243	11,957	7,260	299	8	22	16	..	351	27	14
366	244	3,482	131	243	45	7,606	156	1,602	..	21,793	866	898	18	..	..	..	..	3	6	15
1,148	100	2,987	22	172	31	7,996	68	5	8	11,649	267	1,808	4	..	..	..	..	18	7	16
79	40	162	10	23	7	1,392	25	2	..	244	11	44	2	..	..	..	..	4	..	17
62	49	100	1	73	21	1,271	5	..	..	312	5	56	..	..	..	..	..	..	..	18
282	222	582	52	79	13	2,442	36	122	..	1,086	42	283	3	5	..	4	..	24	1	19
3,248	11,687	8,217	1,391	55	9	8,296	47	977	11	30,167	705	3,875	86	3	1	4	..	276	60	20
318	1,068	1,917	582	8	2	714	1	17	..	12,288	419	348	6	..	..	2	..	26	2	21
512	879	832	253	109	19	7,148	57	7	..	22,786	456	2,687	17	4	..	..	..	58	3	22
109	131	146	45	..	1	528	5	8	4	2,352	42	96	..	1	..	..	..	92	9	23
392	1,112	281	93	2	..	506	5	3	..	2,696	77	205	8	5	..	..	..	25	3	24
15,624	39,686	7,369	101	29	33	..	..	80	2	4,061	915	831	145	7	..	1	..	46	28	25
55	135	133	11	..	1	182	6	8	1	130	27	24	2	2	..	..	..	9	..	26
1,170	711	2,545	106	308	36	5,230	60	66	4	1,622	92	633	4	18	..	1	..	109	23	27
181	35	309	5	342	28	1,392	18	16	..	241	7	37	..	1	..	..	..	3	..	28
84	3	78	3	94	6	207	7	1	..	44	1	5	..	..	..	..	..	1	..	29
1,976	319	4,252	111	819	152	13,307	184	83	7	5,707	434	2,720	50	44	..	1	..	74	9	30
10,434	13,408	2,809	98	344	390	..	..	157	..	1,223	115	..	..	8	..	3	..	101	60	31
44	213	51	2	..	2	..	..	1	..	14	..	..	..	..	..	..	..	..	..	32
20,777	13,718	11,569	202	2,320	821	..	..	158	5	4,548	84	..	..	38	..	..	1	275	15	33
23	..	6	..	78	8	527	2	3	..	68	..	28	..	..	..	..	..	..	..	34
64,086	108,190	16,651	674	2,876	2,254	..	..	231	1	4,825	244	3,127	43	11	2	12	..	113	10	35
99,557	14,821	59,675	1,281	10,432	2,572	..	..	386	2	8,523	147	4,706	27	15	1	11	..	372	42	36
74,088	13,538	65,971	1,985	5,909	1,523	..	..	920	28	39,355	1,428	31,545	419	710	15	93	..	622	73	37
.986	1,754	2,492	426	164	37	5,401	124	29	40	3,642	259	521	5	144	4	..	..	42	4	38
014	1,123	1,261	552	72	12	1,337	9	6	..	502	35	172	5	24	..	3	..	10	5	39
1,136	987	1,374	229	125	23	2,218	13	47	1	1,202	29	558	8	189	4	..	..	40	8	40
159	964	935	98	77	35	6,636	348	89	59	1,491	412	449	51	7	..	1	..	94	44	41
62	282	166	9	..	1	102	4	1	..	47	5	5	..	..	..	..	..	..	..	42
5,829	8,871	9,463	507	950	138	14,585	182	402	18	6,785	272	3,794	26	60	1	1	..	333	45	43
943	156	351	13	128	97	..	..	2	..	136	124	248	..	..	..	..	..	4	..	44
2,691	153	1,997	9	14	16	..	..	31	1	597	224	277	1	5	1	..	..	133	2	45
1,695	815	1,409	25	121	38	..	..	66	1	1,006	69	542	8	47	..	7	..	16	6	46
1,104	880	1,778	110	546	117	5,673	122	132	3	1,562	31	822	13	32	..	..	..	258	23	47
2,775	39	8,314	211	4,029	583	5,911	144	372	8	1,060	17	1,071	47	9	..	82	1	156	22	48
310	39	668	5	722	141	1,630	43	97	..	137	6	45	2	9	..	21	..	132	2	49
960	1,052	4,724	54	121	81	9,777	296	355	4	1,976	273	425	12	12	..	14	1	336	15	50
162	118	312	8	105	24	2,297	19	2	..	581	8	153	..	2	..	..	..	53	2	51
3,681	1,312	7,843	292	587	91	13,288	176	116	4	7,668	250	1,537	19	27	3	4	2	230	32	52
526	131	2,580	16	208	69	6,342	251	20	39	1,707	209	209	53	2	6	4	..	40	27	53
157	31	359	3	135	24	548	26	17	..	426	3	25	..	..	..	..	..	11	..	54
2,852	419	4,888	162	514	132	7,341	117	126	6	4,961	92	477	20	20	1	37	2	127	16	55
2,656	2,722	4,493	995	497	58	18,706	158	161	5	5,884	290	1,966	27	427	3	..	..	321	18	56
8,603	16,575	1,236	82	207	151	..	..	4	.	1,763	361	637	1	70	..	..	..	5	..	57
1,931	1,111	3,135	390	291	32	3,600	60	108	5	2,778	182	593	8	36	4	53	3	156	3	58
36	13	55	..	1	1	22	..	..	..	37	..	4	..	..	..	..	..	5	..	59
4,584	2,369	7,445	219	540	105	10,551	149	332	..	6,823	241	1,729	16	79	3	18	..	122	58	60
3,681	1,689	4,860	520	189	28	16,205	181	121	14	26,428	1,379	2,677	62	162	..	142	..	285	29	61

TABLE XI.—OCCUPATION OF

Serial No.	Caste, Tribe or Race.	Traditional Occupation.	Religion.	Locality.	Population dealt with. Earners. Males.	Population dealt with. Earners. Females.	Population dealt with. Working Dependants. Males.	Population dealt with. Working Dependants. Females.	Population dealt with. Non-Working Dependants. Both Sexes.	Number of earners whose traditional caste occupation was returned as their Principal means of livelihood. Males.	Principal means of livelihood. Females.	Subsidiary means of livelihood. Males.	Subsidiary means of livelihood. Females.
	1	2	3	4	5	6	7	8	9	10	11	12	13
62	Nai	*Shaving*	Hindu	A. B. C.	30,160	1,753	3,383	5,530	60,314	22.538	1,266	2,525	604
63	„	„	Sikh	C.	11,506	633	1,331	306	25,381	6,842	389	640	87
64	„	„	Muslim	A. C. D.	67,421	2,767	5,298	2,635	157,734	53,483	1,497	2,044	54
65	Pakhiwara	*Crime, Fowling and Hunting.*	Muslim	C.	302	84	69	28	2,117	71	41	..	..
66	Pathan	*Agriculture*	Muslim	A. C. D.	101,206	5,779	12,444	2,763	223.210	43,671	2,000	2,030	84
67	Kanet	*Agriculture*	Hindu	A. B. C.	82,031	5,441	26,860	75,483	110,614	74,870	4,196	1,050	70
68	„	„	Buddhist	B.	1,158	235	740	1,664	1,045	977	149	1	..
69	Rajput	*Agriculture*	Hindu	A. B. C. D.	177,658	11,756	35,255	51,539	301,166	126,169	7.803	6,016	117
70	„	„	Sikh	C. D.	14,514	946	2,127	415	31,592	8,485	332	355	86
71	„	„	Muslim	A. C. D.	459,782	18,652	64,953	20,135	1,155,010	339,500	9,040	9,771	529
72	Rathi	*Agriculture*	Hindu	B.	31,178	2,139	12,953	32,989	54,816	28,813	1,840	467	34
73	Saini	„	Hindu	A. C.	21,752	1,039	3,921	3,424	44,102	17,397	562	471	6
74	„	„	Sikh	A. C.	20,752	907	5,141	3,004	53,161	18,097	728	426	47
75	Sansi	*Crime*	Hindu	A. C.	7,154	1,553	566	825	16,567	267	135	3	14
76	Sayad	*Priests*	Muslim	A. C. D.	80,952	3,695	6,301	1,940	200,414	21,234	1,064	1,864	94
77	Sheikh	*Trade*	Muslim	A. C. D.	121,980	5,085	6,536	2,882	271,071	43,933	1,325	884	89
78	Sunar	*Goldsmith*	Hindu	A. B. C. D.	28,247	907	2,302	1,315	66,255	23,939	252	849	71
79	„	„	Sikh	C. D.	6,832	210	444	144	17,736	5,531	63	128	..
80	„	„	Muslim	C. D.	8,882	342	678	174	22,318	7,226	128	99	13
81	Tarkhan	*Carpentry*	Hindu	A. B. C.	40,815	1,550	6,309	10,343	87,710	24,332	239	3,981	42
82	„	„	Sikh	A. C. D.	46,258	1,169	5,257	463	105,299	27,554	225	2,312	11
83	„	„	Muslim	A. C. D.	96,791	3,007	7,179	2,349	237,503	69,445	1,100	2,360	129
84	Teli	*Oil Pressing*	Muslim	A. C. D.	92,899	4,307	9,317	6,253	225,519	36,916	1,666	2,772	229
85	European	..	Christian	**PUNJAB**	12,281	798	46	7	6,963	..	..	..	..
86	„	..	„	Gurgaon	29	10	..	..	40	..	..	..	..
87	„	..	„	Ambala	1,571	85	..	..	1,260	..	..	..	..
88	„	..	„	Simla	285	83	..	..	378	..	..	..	..
89	„	..	„	Kangra	34	16	..	1	36	..	..	..	..
90	„	..	„	Jullundur	922	5	12	..	232	..	..	..	..
91	„	..	„	Ferozepore	636	19	..	..	1,098	..	..	..	..
92	„	..	„	Lahore	3,169	314	9	2	1,557	..	..	..	..
93	„	..	„	Amritsar	100	7	..	..	85	..	..	..	..
94	„	..	„	Gurdaspur	57	11	..	..	139	..	..	..	..
95	„	..	„	Sialkot	1,671	33	1	..	518	..	..	..	..
96	„	..	„	Jhelum	91	13	..	..	91	..	..	..	..
97	„	..	„	Rawalpindi	2,325	56	24	..	862	..	..	..	..
98	„	..	„	Attock	248	18	..	..	63	..	..	..	..
99	„	..	„	Mianwali	26	6	..	..	32	..	..	..	..
100	„	..	„	Montgomery	38	10	..	..	61	..	..	..	..
101	„	..	„	Lyallpur	21	13	..	..	22	..	..	..	..
102	„	..	„	Jhang	22	..	..	..	28	..	..	..	..
103	„	..	„	Multan	760	19	..	..	111	..	..	..	..
104	„	..	„	Mandi	74	4	..	..	63	..	..	..	..
105	„	..	„	Patiala	30	6	..	..	75	..	..	..	..
106	„	..	„	Jind	19	5	..	1	56	..	..	..	..
107	„	..	„	Bahawalpur	30	..	..	..	33	..	..	..	..
108	Armenian	..	„	**Punjab**	2	2	..	..	..	..	..	..	..
109	Anglo-Indians	..	„	**PUNJAB**	1,351	212	52	2	2,008	..	..	..	..
110	„	..	„	Gurgaon	18	1	..	..	73	..	..	..	..
111	„	..	„	Ambala	81	17	..	..	307	..	..	..	..
112	„	..	„	Simla	46	34	..	..	155	..	..	..	..
113	„	..	„	Ferozepore	25	2	..	..	44	..	..	..	..
114	„	..	„	Lahore	639	59	8	..	335	..	..	..	..
115	„	..	„	Rawalpindi	189	40	13	..	357	..	..	..	..
116	„	..	„	Mianwali	21	10	..	..	26	..	..	..	..
117	„	..	„	Multan	47	8	..	..	38	..	..	..	..
118	„	..	„	Patiala	24	8	..	..	99	..	..	..	..
119	„	..	„	Bahawalpur	118	3	23	..	303	..	..	..	..

SELECTED CASTES, TRIBES OR RACES.—*continued.*

Number of Working Dependants following the traditional occupation of their caste.		Number of earners returning their traditional occupation as their principal means of livelihood who had some subsidiary occupation.		RECORDED PRINCIPAL OCCUPATION OF EARNERS, OTHER THAN TRADITIONAL OCCUPATION OF CASTE (BY ORDERS).																
				I.—Exploitation of Animals and Vegetation.												II.—Exploitation of Minerals.				
				Income from rent of land.		Cultivators of all kinds.		Agents and managers of landed estates, planters, Forest Officers and their clerks, Rent Collectors, etc.		Field labourers, wood-cutters, etc.		Raisers of livestock, milkmen and herdsmen.		Fishing and hunting.		Owners, Managers, Clerks, etc.		Labourers.		
Males.	Females.	Males.	Females.	Males.	Females.	Males.	Females.	Males.	Females.	Males.	Females.	Males.	Females.	Males.	Females.	Males.	Females.	Males.	Females.	Serial No.
14	15	16	17	18	19	20	21	22	23	24	25	26	27	28	29	30	31	32	33	
1,305	1,660	3,758	63	147	46	4,430	137	52	..	696	55	158	5	..	..	..	..	3	..	62
740	115	846	25	219	40	2,082	15	84	..	609	10	121	1	1	..	..	..	22	1	63
2,728	879	4,986	272	415	89	5,671	120	47	..	2,186	147	470	12	5	..	..	..	143	15	64
11	7	9	2	10	2	151	1	10	..	60	..	9	..	80	..	..	..	..	..	65
6,690	1,495	7,505	422	3,746	537	..	..	226	15	2,797	97	1,463	56	52	..	42	..	412	21	66
22,727	67,670	8,208	314	122	244	..	..	248	2	1,673	500	1,837	108	5	..	7	..	52	10	67
734	1,662	14	1	..	..	..	..	..	..	66	78	4	1	..	..	..	..	..	..	68
26,942	43,832	21,993	947	1,122	625	..	..	769	7	4,169	1,015	2,582	121	23	..	45	15	562	39	69
1,066	66	875	62	88	20	..	..	17	1	302	8	131	..	14	..	3	..	130	7	70
49,577	16,524	37,611	1,385	7,138	3,745	..	..	835	1	17,651	435	9,750	115	342	1	160	1	1,066	224	71
12,313	31,724	4,089	165	25	25	..	..	82	..	494	43	512	38	16	..	4	..	28	2	72
3,184	2,854	1,125	98	295	195	..	..	65	1	710	44	429	4	61	..	..	..	4	..	73
4,117	2,612	1,841	29	323	58	..	..	8	..	255	10	150	4	..	..	..	..	7	..	74
24	28	15	80	9	5	1,147	5	14	..	1,063	169	1,275	41	41	8	..	..	32	9	75
1,548	752	3,133	157	4,156	982	23,769	386	257	8	2,093	24	957	5	63	..	79	1	134	3	76
1,750	438	2,963	159	1,655	391	12,736	179	374	..	5,458	216	1,706	35	59	2	161	..	308	30	77
885	41	1,724	9	180	36	1,516	89	10	..	160	21	62	..	..	..	3	2	8	2	78
268	5	448	8	84	11	308	3	6	1	78	..	23	..	1	..	..	..	10	..	79
280	34	496	19	76	17	451	6	5	2	111	25	75	2	9	..	3	..	32	..	80
1,359	372	5,356	42	249	177	10,612	507	6	5	2,659	150	305	5	6	..	..	1	12	6	81
1,857	41	2,678	19	1,207	285	8,549	109	193	12	3,127	17	271	1	4	..	6	..	148	12	82
3,469	651	6,747	229	1,042	213	11,415	297	384	3	6,702	206	599	22	35	..	56	..	98	18	83
2,378	1,117	6,299	219	1,218	131	18,824	192	644	4	7,294	243	3,031	22	169	..	9	..	201	35	84
..	..	..	..	3	4	2	..	20	2	..	..	4	..	..	..	27	6	2	..	85
..	..	..	..	..	1	..	..	..	..	..	..	..	..	..	..	..	..	..	..	86
..	..	..	..	1	3	..	..	1	..	..	..	..	..	..	..	..	..	..	..	87
..	..	..	..	..	..	..	..	..	..	..	..	4	..	..	..	25	5	2	..	88
..	..	..	..	2	..	..	..	..	2	..	..	..	..	..	..	..	..	..	..	89
..	..	..	..	..	..	..	..	..	..	..	..	..	..	..	..	..	..	..	..	90
..	..	..	..	..	..	..	..	..	..	..	..	..	..	..	..	..	..	..	..	91
..	..	..	..	..	..	2	..	2	..	..	..	..	..	..	..	..	..	..	..	92
..	..	..	..	..	..	..	..	..	..	..	..	..	..	..	..	..	..	..	..	93
..	..	..	..	..	..	..	..	3	..	..	..	..	..	..	..	..	1	..	..	94
..	..	..	..	..	..	..	..	..	..	..	..	..	..	..	..	..	..	..	..	95
..	..	..	..	..	..	..	..	..	..	..	..	..	..	..	..	2	..	..	..	96
..	..	..	..	..	..	..	..	2	..	..	..	..	..	..	..	..	..	..	..	97
..	..	..	..	..	..	..	..	..	..	..	..	..	..	..	..	..	..	..	..	98
..	..	..	..	..	..	..	..	2	..	..	..	..	..	..	..	..	..	..	..	99
..	..	..	..	..	..	..	..	2	..	..	..	..	..	..	..	..	..	..	..	100
..	..	..	..	..	..	..	..	7	..	..	..	..	..	..	..	..	..	..	..	101
..	..	..	..	..	..	..	..	..	..	..	..	..	..	..	..	..	..	..	..	102
..	..	..	..	..	..	..	..	..	..	..	..	..	..	..	..	..	..	..	..	103
..	..	..	..	..	..	..	..	..	..	..	..	..	..	..	..	..	..	..	..	104
..	..	..	..	..	..	..	..	1	..	..	..	..	..	..	..	..	..	..	..	105
..	..	..	..	..	..	..	..	..	..	..	..	..	..	..	..	..	..	..	..	106
..	..	..	..	..	..	..	..	..	..	..	..	..	..	..	..	..	..	..	..	107
..	..	..	..	..	..	..	..	..	..	..	..	..	..	..	..	..	..	..	..	108
..	..	..	..	1	..	3	..	6	..	..	..	1	..	..	..	9	1	..	..	109
..	..	..	..	..	..	..	..	..	..	..	..	..	..	..	..	..	..	..	..	110
..	..	..	..	1	..	..	..	..	..	..	..	..	..	..	..	..	..	..	..	111
..	..	..	..	..	..	..	..	..	..	..	..	..	..	..	..	2	..	..	..	112
..	..	..	..	..	..	..	..	..	..	..	..	..	..	..	..	..	..	..	..	113
..	..	..	..	..	..	2	..	1	..	..	..	..	..	..	..	..	..	..	..	114
..	..	..	..	..	..	..	..	1	..	..	..	..	..	..	..	5	..	..	..	115
..	..	..	..	..	..	..	..	..	..	..	..	..	..	..	..	..	..	..	..	116
..	..	..	..	..	..	..	..	..	..	..	..	..	..	..	..	..	..	..	..	117
..	..	..	..	..	..	..	..	..	..	..	..	..	..	..	..	..	..	..	..	118
..	..	..	..	..	..	1	..	..	..	..	..	1	..	..	..	..	..	..	..	119

TABLE XI.—OCCUPATION OF

Serial No.	Caste, Tribe or Race.	Traditional Occupation.	Religion.	Locality.	RECORDED PRINCIPAL OCCUPATION OF EARNERS OTHER									
					III.—Industries.				IV.—Transport.				V.—Trade.	
					Owners, Managers, Clerks, etc.		Artizans and other Workmen.		Owners, Managers, Ships' Officers, etc.		Labourers, Boatmen, Carter's Palki-bearers etc.			
					Males.	Females.	Males.	Females.	Males.	Females.	Males.	Females.	Males.	Females.
	1	2	3	4	34	35	36	37	38	39	40	41	42	43
1	Aggarwal	Trade	Hindu	A. C.	147	..	1,086	1,305	430	1	678	8	..	..
2	,,	,,	Jain	A. C.	2	..	185	83	32	1	39	1	..	.
3	Ahir	Agriculture	Hindu	A. C.	27	3	657	116	138	..	1,759	24	453	51
4	,,	,,	Muslim	D.	..	..	5	3	2	..	34	1	2	..
5	Arain	Agriculture	Muslim	A. C. D.	126	..	7,117	1,372	1,264	2	7,403	26	10,535	1,619
6	Arora	Trade	Hindu	C. D.	419	6	4,454	1,447	1,302	79	2,900	30	..	..
7	,,	,,	Sikh	C. D.	44	..	638	261	146	..	376	..	..	..
8	Awan	Agriculture	Muslim	C. D.	70	2	3,225	650	285	..	3,500	30	1,867	106
9	Bawaria	Crime and Hunting	Hindu	A. C. D	..	..	190	52	..	..	53	7	66	3
10	,,	,, ,,	Sikh	C. D.	1	..	145	70	..	..	11	..	13	35
11	Biloch	Camel Driving	Muslim	A. C. D.	142	..	3,484	678	242	..	2,471	5	1,219	63
12	Brahman	Priests	Hindu	A. B. C. D.	350	19	7,062	1,640	3,475	..	6,993	61	38,962	381
13	,,	,,	Sikh	C. D.	9	..	74	12	16	..	57	..	238	4
14	Chamar	Shoe-making	Hindu	A. B. C. D.	18	1	14,311	3,013	193	17	5,694	572	1,465	1,131
15	,,	,,	Ad-dharmi	A. B. C. D.	16	..	18,084	1,470	59	..	713	101	442	54
16	,,	,,	Sikh	A. C.	5	..	4,223	576	1	..	3,276	181	177	2
17	Chhimba	Dyeing	Hindu	A. C.	10	8	2,458	147	9	..	97	1	263	5
18	,,	,,	Sikh	C.	31	..	1,741	116	5	..	37	..	134	1
19	,,	,,	Muslim	A. C. D.	30	..	2,835	263	56	15	201	3	348	4
20	Chuhra	Sweeping	Hindu	A. B. C. D.	33	5	2,265	207	118	..	1,750	95	624	74
21	,,	,,	Ad-dharmi	A. C. D.	2	..	352	54	51	..	133	16	160	2
22	,,	,,	Sikh	C.	3	..	2,106	190	6	.	1,261	220	255	43
23	,,	,,	Muslim	C. D.	8	..	324	31	2	..	125	..	62	..
24	,,	,,	Christian	A. C. D.	..	..	287	36	24	..	105	1	142	2
25	Dagi and Koli.	Agriculture	Hindu	A. B. C.	56	7	2,688	207	24	..	521	24	153	11
26	Dhobi	Washing	Hindu	A. C.	3	..	50	11	2	..	96	3	37	1
27	,,	,,	Muslim	A. C. D.	12	4	4,475	883	81	5	403	8	615	14
28	Faqir	Begging	Hindu	C. D.	6	..	142	10	19	..	67	1	267	8
29	,,	,,	Sikh	C.	..	..	31	4	1	..	12	..	24	1
30	,,	,,	Muslim	A. C. D.	28	..	2,916	524	104	2	1,289	38	1,748	42
31	Gujjar	Agriculture and Cattle breeding.	Hindu	A. B. C. D.	6	..	507	88	40	..	1,810	30	275	14
32	,,	,,	Sikh	C.	..	..	4	..	1	..	2	..	5	..
33	,,	,,	Muslim	A. B. C. D.	24	..	1,176	302	171	4	2,478	14	2,369	62
34	Harni	Crime	Muslim	C.	..	..	16	1	..	..	26	..	86	25
35	Jat	Agriculture	Hindu	A. B. C. D.	35	..	1,285	365	225	..	2,357	13	1,473	88
36	,,	,,	Sikh	A. C. D.	174	..	2,639	504	524	3	2,881	10	2,953	67
37	,,	,,	Muslim	A. C. D.	312	11	23,289	2,373	1,833	11	16,430	70	8,864	268
38	Jhiwar	Baking and Water carrying.	Hindu	A. B. C.	40	31	2,931	398	126	13	1,139	28	1,786	322
39	,,	,,	Sikh	C.	5	..	420	143	22	..	269	1	605	20
40	,,	,,	Muslim	C. D.	6	24	1,423	368	14	..	476	17	927	25
41	Julaha	Weaving	Hindu	A. B. C.	28	..	1,104	232	28	..	502	48	162	7
42	,,	,,	Sikh	C.	..	..	28	8	1	..	6	..	22	..
43	,,	,,	Muslim	A. B. C. D.	30	1	3,929	998	205	3	2,300	22	3,577	67
44	Kamboh	Agriculture	Hindu	A. C. D.	2	..	176	56	9	..	133	14	501	3
45	,,	,,	Sikh	C. D.	4	..	289	66	45	..	66	1	403	8
46	,,	,,	Muslim	C. D.	33	..	799	191	67	..	985	27	1,380	116
47	Kashmiri	Weaving	Muslim	C. D.	164	..	9,890	680	549	..	2,352	7	7,802	116
48	Khatri	Trade	Hindu	A. B. C. D.	447	16	7,265	1,332	3,226	18	3,957	8	..	..
49	,,	,,	Sikh	C. D.	41	..	1,029	151	228	..	339	3	..	..
50	Kumhar	Pot-making	Hindu	A. B. C.	11	..	2,892	380	181	..	3,330	150	1,335	55
51	,,	,,	Sikh	C.	..	..	335	62	5	..	1,269	3	763	8
52	,,	,,	Muslim	A. C. D.	34	6	2,771	752	98	5	10,629	82	3,769	145
53	Lohar	Blacksmith	Hindu	A. B. C.	7	4	*849	*140	33	..	165	15	201	9
54	,,	,,	Sikh	A. C.	9	..	*181	*57	8	..	45	..	44	1
55	,,	,,	Muslim	A. C. D.	83	..	*1,598	*336	108	1	734	13	827	28
56	Machhi	Baking and Water-carrying.	Muslim	A. C. D.	28	..	2,728	684	120	4	1,943	29	1,980	60
57	Meo	Agriculture	Muslim	A.	..	..	85	63	3	..	211	3	234	19
58	Mirasi	Begging	Muslim	A. C. D.	33	1	3,183	303	57	1	752	10	1,025	34
59	Mochi	Shoe-making	Hindu	C.	2	..	194	28	2	..	158	5	44	1
60	,,	,,	Muslim	C. D.	84	3	8,281	1,190	119	..	891	15	1,485	46
61	Mussalli	Sweeping	Muslim	C. D.	219	..	7,249	603	133	1	2,459	77	1,029	65

* *Exclusive of the numbers shown in columns 10 and 11 as following the traditional Occupation of the Caste.*

SELECTED CASTES, TRIBES OR RACES.—*continued.*

THAN TRADITIONAL OCCUPATION OF CASTE (BY ORDERS).

Serial No.	VI.—Public Force. Commissioned and Gazetted Officers. Males. 44	Females. 45	Others. Males. 46	Females. 47	VII.—Public Administration. Gazetted Officers. Males. 48	Females. 49	Others. Males. 50	Females. 51
1	16	..	180	..	102	..	1,552	3
2	2	..	9	..	35	..	152	..
3	13	..	346	..	5	..	343	1
4	..	..	2	..	..	..	5	..
5	99	..	1,400	..	119	..	3,499	32
6	41	.	665	..	210	..	3,689	41
7	8	..	85	..	41	..	352	4
8	85	..	2,513	.	71	1	1,555	3
9	..	..	45	..	..	..	227	..
10	..	..	1	..	..	..	12	..
11	22	..	1,221	..	44	1	1,700	5
12	146	..	2,897	..	372	2	7,754	28
13	8	..	91	..	1	..	59	..
14	..	..	173	..	..	..	433	5
15	..	..	40	..	..	..	526	..
16	..	..	40	..	..	..	106	..
17	..	..	15	..	..	..	19	..
18	1	..	41	..	..	..	25	..
19	..	..	66	..	..	..	71	..
20	..	..	304	..	..	..	1,023	40
21	..	..	6	..	..	..	181	10
22	..	..	53	..	..	..	355	17
23	..	..	8	..	..	..	58	6
24	1	..	13	..	..	..	33	1
25	..	..	64	..	..	..	158	5
26	..	..	11	..	..	..	6	..
27	..	..	70	..	2	..	206	1
28	1	..	6	..	..	..	34	..
29	..	..	4	..	..	..	11	..
30	1	..	267	..	3	..	645	6
31	2	..	207	..	3	..	244	2
32	1	..	11	..	..	..	11	..
33	39	..	1,073	..	39	..	860	2
34	.	..	..	..	..	..	4	..
35	87	..	1,341	..	46	..	746	..
36	349	..	6,967	..	178	..	2,328	5
37	162	..	3,745	..	167	1	6,748	30
38	1	..	95	..	..	..	337	1
39	2	..	98	..	..	..	175	10
40	3	..	70	..	..	..	270	6
41	..	..	72	..	..	..	178	23
42	..	..	1	..	..	..	4	..
43	3	..	355	..	1	..	1,084	16
44	5	..	8	..	..	..	56	..
45	3	..	235	..	..	..	151	2
46	2	..	473	..	7	..	181	..
47	79	..	1,597	..	126	..	1,161	5
48	118	..	1,124	..	420	1	5,462	40
49	27	..	197	..	43	1	581	1
50	14	..	32	..	..	..	81	2
51	14	..	31	..	..	..	23	..
52	..	..	119	..	..	..	317	5
53	..	..	56	..	..	..	41	..
54	..	..	11	.	..	..	17	..
55	..	..	211	..	..	..	205	2
56	..	..	143	..	6	..	644	29
57	..	..	41	..	..	..	113	..
58	1	..	236	..	4	..	463	12
59	..	..	..	..	..	..	15	..
60	..	..	219	..	..	..	596	3
61	..	..	166	..	..	..	501	2

Serial No.	VIII.—Arts and Professions. Religious. Males. 52	Females. 53	Lawyers, Doctors and Teachers. Males. 54	Females. 55	Others. Males. 56	Females. 57	IX.—Persons living on their Income. Males. 58	Females. 59
1	50	1	1,565	26	205	18	335	152
2	3	..	186	2	10	2	39	14
3	14	..	93	..	25	12	74	20
4	2	..	9	1	2	..	1	..
5	1,091	15	1,976	87	407	168	343	85
6	652	16	2,855	190	361	52	1,303	153
7	567	13	536	48	102	7	310	58
8	1,649	58	998	56	284	60	714	129
9	8	..	..	..	3	2	8	..
10	4	..	..	..	13	6	..	3
11	604	9	778	35	218	52	312	12
12	*165	*6	8,901	373	2,339	84	1,814	328
13	*7	..	63	10	16	..	60	3
14	31	9	78	20	411	277	24	9
15	41	1	21	14	41	193	57	6
16	68	11	9	2	68	63	58	6
17	1	1	11	2	20	..	6	..
18	28	..	17	..	6	2	32	4
19	140	3	63	2	53	31	29	1
20	91	3	43	10	360	199	40	13
21	14	..	19	2	54	36	14	..
22	47	..	14	..	173	36	137	15
23	14	..	5	2	15	1	1	..
24	12	2	29	10	33	12	36	..
25	4	..	14	..	22	14	9	5
26	..	..	6	..	11	1	..	1
27	308	8	125	21	70	22	65	4
28	339	12	211	..	54	13	36	6
29	265	1	39	2	2	1	10	..
30	1,756	51	392	59	575	354	102	17
31	9	1	34	2	22	1	39	15
32	..	..	..	..	1	..	2	..
33	404	7	527	21	196	118	331	45
34	..	..	7	1	..	4	1	..
35	67	..	501	15	241	6	432	95
36	1,656	28	1,888	107	561	63	2,813	496
37	3,941	95	3,968	182	1,113	264	1,397	143
38	17	3	276	7	945	85	49	30
39	44	2	55	6	42	30	74	3
40	45	10	42	23	06	241	56	8
41	4	1	16	5	36	22	32	1
42	2	..	3	..	8	..	2	..
43	1,739	51	657	69	302	299	218	44
44	3	..	16	1	10	3	10	1
45	65	..	52	8	50	..	87	13
46	105	1	127	7	45	14	25	6
47	509	32	674	145	369	191	458	58
48	257	22	4,119	280	751	70	2,246	324
49	337	9	479	43	96	9	374	41
50	4	1	48	6	58	19	33	11
51	56	..	27	5	31	6	26	10
52	553	15	230	33	181	88	134	17
53	13	1	24	1	18	11	6	1
54	4	..	3	4	5	3	11	10
55	183	10	130	20	145	16	120	26
56	194	8	144	62	342	445	96	21
57	16	..	69	9	5	10	9	5
58	327	25	326	20	4,955	491	118	28
59	1	..	1	..	4	1	..	..
60	420	16	206	40	151	271	98	23
61	341	15	45	8	275	43	85	38

Serial No.	X.—Domestic Service. Males. 60	Females. 61	XI.—Contractors, Clerks, Cashiers, etc., otherwise unspecified. Males. 62	Females. 63	XII.—Labourers unspecified. Males. 64	Females. 65	XIII.—Beggars, Prostitutes, Criminals and Inmates of Jails and Asylums. Males. 66	Females. 67
1	2,155	59	463	3	344	110	145	12
2	106	[illegible]	67	..	10	..	11	11
3	985	30	44	7	1,35[illegible]	46	81	2
4	9	1	..	..	12	5	6	1
5	4,508	394	583	23	8,798	1,019	1,069	307
6	6,273	362	1,096	49	7,406	1,528	1,135	133
7	670	50	189	8	558	116	215	21
8	2,440	255	202	1	2,880	788	1,681	259
9	72	6	..	..	353	120	101	266
10	9	32	12	..	52	8	28	4
11	2,062	211	119	..	6,776	820	1,719	233
12	14,853	696	1,814	11	4,535	335	6,365	981
13	131	10	18	..	26	5	66	8
14	1,443	93	148	9	6,848	1,367	1,270	235
15	398	66	10	1	2,322	700	377	78
16	369	8	24	..	1,491	383	342	47
17	92	10	8	..	82	20	31	6
18	55	3	6	..	19	20	2[illegible]	3
19	238	36	28	1	348	59	103	19
20	1,529	161	44	..	3,558	1,164	945	431
21	159	51	37	3	986	266	246	60
22	642	71	6	2	2,298	318	598	59
23	88	7	10	..	373	88	184	21
24	288	25	6	..	1,071	17	92	11
25	415	36	31	..	273	56	50	40
26	41	4	19	1	48	7	19	1
27	389	70	38	1	1,218	181	339	89
28	123	2	4	3	171	26	69	69
29	19	..	1	1	33	4	3	..
30	1,632	71	82	15	1,504	222	571	365
31	758	36	20	1	2,048	38	68	15
32	19	1	..	..	21	..	3	1
33	1,708	87	157	5	1,954	181	742	77
34	1	..	1	..	11	1	8	2
35	2,196	102	161	3	3,221	258	893	60
36	3,296	184	439	15	1,792	477	2,773	132
37	8,844	857	717	59	21,728	2,712	7,403	935
38	1,438	115	57	7	1,084	172	106	24
39	602	43	12	1	215	82	70	13
40	428	98	21	98	698	327	157	54
41	328	35	34	1	758	119	93	47
42	22	2	..	..	21	13	8	2
43	2,837	264	81	11	3,562	885	1,410	385
44	180	10	7	..	120	25	15	4
45	110	7	13	1	178	47	42	1
46	349	19	123	..	1,017	83	176	17
47	2,381	167	609	9	6,202	191	613	145
48	6,973	369	2,027	9	2,851	408	693	95
49	502	32	227	1	189	59	114	10
50	606	71	80	2	1,232	143	71	49
51	126	10	22	1	202	40	48	4
52	959	135	153	17	4,221	668	656	249
53	153	27	18	..	119	33	30	21
54	26	8	3	..	44	15	12	..
55	577	56	100	8	853	186	274	75
56	1,904	230	109	2	3,068	358	631	149
57	51	1	2	..	8	..	30	5
58	1,794	260	71	..	1,520	273	537	213
59	53	1	54	..	222	10	1	3
60	1,232	181	57	7	1,870	741	831	210
61	2,708	306	57	12	12,268	1,704	3,099	861

* *Exclusive of the numbers shown in columns 10 and 11 as following the traditional Occupation of the Caste.*

Serial No.	Caste, Tribe or Race.	Traditional Occupation.	Religion.	Locality.	RECORDED PRINCIPAL OCCUPATION OF EARNERS OTHER: III.—Industries. Owners, Managers, Clerks, etc.		III.—Industries. Artizans and other Workmen.		IV.—Transport. Owners, Managers, Ships' Officers, etc.		IV.—Transport. Labourers, Boatmen, Carters, Palki-bearers, etc.		V.—Trade.	
					Males.	Females.	Males.	Females.	Males.	Females.	Males.	Females.	Males.	Females.
	1	2	3	4	34	35	36	37	38	39	40	41	42	43
62	Nai ..	*Shaving* ..	Hindu ..	A. B. C. ..	3	..	340	85	44	..	233	9	362	23
63	,, ..	,, ..	Sikh ..	C. ..	3	..	272	74	27	..	102	2	245	5
64	,, ..	,, ..	Muslim ..	A. C. D. ..	3	1	998	307	74	1	370	7	623	13
65	Pakhiwara ..	*Crime, Fowling and Hunting.*	Muslim ..	C. ..	..	..	58	10	..	..	..	1	214	11
66	Pathan ..	*Agriculture* ..	Muslim ..	A. C. D. ..	67	36	8,559	1,133	1,182	2	5,502	96	7,905	344
67	Kanet ..	*Agriculture* ..	Hindu ..	A. B. C. ..	1	..	582	118	10	..	402	33	409	44
68	,, ..	,, ..	Buddhist ..	B. ..	..	..	2	..	..	..	10	3	6	1
69	Rajput ..	*Agriculture* ..	Hindu ..	A. B. C. D. ..	355	6	7,199	569	807	1	5,183	64	5,152	162
70	,, ..	,, ..	Sikh ..	C. D. ..	17	..	2,045	313	51	9	317	3	833	23
71	,, ..	,, ..	Muslim ..	A. C. D. ..	334	..	20,160	1,735	1,230	14	9,173	134	10,154	329
72	Rathi ..	*Agriculture* ..	Hindu ..	B. ..	11	..	126	47	3	2	117	..	107	6
73	Saini ..	*Agriculture* ..	Hindu ..	A. C. ..	40	..	259	60	53	1	452	9	494	41
74	,, ..	*Agriculture* ..	Sikh ..	A. C. ..	3	..	108	31	16	..	263	1	216	4
75	Sansi ..	*Crime* ..	Hindu ..	A. C. ..	..	..	210	30	2	..	47	16	246	105
76	Sayad ..	*Priests* ..	Muslim ..	A. C. D. ..	101	1	3,719	353	769	3	2,774	11	2,969	36
77	Sheikh ..	*Trade* ..	Muslim ..	A. C. D. ..	261	20	19,009	1,262	1,103	10	6,094	39	..	..
78	Sunar ..	*Goldsmith* ..	Hindu ..	A. B. C. D. ..	7	5	*475	*241	39	2	146	5	806	48
79	,, ..	,, ..	Sikh ..	C. D. ..	5	..	*47	*65	4	..	31	..	431	11
80	,, ..	,, ..	Muslim ..	C. D. ..	27	..	*148	*69	18	..	70	1	243	7
81	Tarkhan ..	*Carpentery* ..	Hindu ..	A. B. C. ..	4	..	*1,459	*288	45	3	151	17	212	11
82	,, ..	,, ..	Sikh ..	A. C. D. ..	21	1	*1,267	*280	124	..	950	6	493	17
83	,, ..	,, ..	Muslim ..	A. C. D. ..	224	..	*1,713	*409	206	2	489	24	1,019	40
84	Teli ..	*Oil Pressing* ..	Muslim ..	A. C. D. ..	108	4	10,326	908	155	4	2,688	33	3,967	87
85	European ..	..	Christian ..	**PUNJAB** ..	**50**	**6**	**40**	**44**	**518**	**25**	**48**	**2**	**166**	**26**
86	,, ..	..	,, ..	Gurgaon ..	..	..	5	4	17	..	1	..	2	..
87	,, ..	..	,, ..	Ambala ..	8	..	7	12	23	..	15	2	16	..
88	,, ..	..	,, ..	Simla ..	32	6	7	..	25	4	17	..	25	3
89	,, ..	..	,, ..	Kangra ..	..	..	1	1	8	..	..	..	..	3
90	,, ..	..	,, ..	Jullundur ..	..	..	..	..	1	..	..	..	3	..
91	,, ..	..	,, ..	Ferozepore	..	..	..	..	..	..	..	..	42	..
92	,, ..	..	,, ..	Lahore ..	..	..	8	19	298	15	1	..	33	12
93	,, ..	..	,, ..	Amritsar ..	..	..	..	..	39	4	..	..	..	..
94	,, ..	..	,, ..	Gurdaspur	2	..	11	..	3	..	..	..	..	..
95	,, ..	..	,, ..	Sialkot ..	..	..	..	..	25	..	..	..	..	..
96	,, ..	..	,, ..	Jhelum ..	..	..	..	..	..	..	..	..	..	..
97	,, ..	..	,, ..	Rawalpindi	..	..	..	..	..	..	..	..	24	..
98	,, ..	..	,, ..	Attock ..	..	..	..	..	..	..	..	..	4	..
99	,, ..	..	,, ..	Mianwali ..	3	..	..	..	..	..	..	..	3	..
100	,, ..	..	,, ..	Montgomery	..	..	..	..	..	..	..	..	2	3
101	,, ..	..	,, ..	Lyallpur ..	..	..	..	..	..	..	..	..	..	..
102	,, ..	..	,, ..	Jhang ..	..	..	..	..	..	..	..	..	..	..
103	,, ..	..	,, ..	Multan ..	4	..	..	..	..	..	..	..	6	3
104	,, ..	..	,, ..	Mandi ..	1	..	..	..	55	..	..	..	..	..
105	,, ..	..	,, ..	Patiala ..	..	..	..	..	3	..	..	..	1	..
106	,, ..	..	,, ..	Jind ..	..	..	..	..	..	..	9	..	..	..
107	,, ..	..	,, ..	Bahawalpur	..	..	..	..	9	..	..	..	..	..
108	Armenian ..	..	,,	Punjab ..	..	..	..	..	..	..	..	..	1	..
109	Anglo-Indians	..	Christian ..	**PUNJAB** ..	**35**	**4**	**17**	**3**	**337**	**4**	**50**	..	**78**	**16**
110	,, ..	..	,, ..	Gurgaon ..	..	..	..	..	10	..	8	..	..	..
111	,, ..	..	,, ..	Ambala ..	..	..	2	..	16	1	27	..	1	1
112	,, ..	..	,, ..	Simla ..	5	4	..	..	..	..	..	..	7	2
113	,, ..	..	,, ..	Ferozepore	..	..	..	..	11	..	3	..	6	..
114	,, ..	..	,, ..	Lahore ..	..	..	6	2	256	2	1	..	36	2
115	,, ..	..	,, ..	Rawalpindi	21	..	..	..	..	..	..	..	15	10
116	,, ..	..	,, ..	Mianwali ..	4	..	..	..	..	..	..	..	4	..
117	,, ..	..	,, ..	Multan ..	..	..	..	..	..	..	..	..	2	1
118	,, ..	..	,, ..	Patiala ..	..	..	..	..	2	..	..	..	..	..
119	,, ..	..	,, ..	Bahawalpur	..	..	5	..	11	..	..	..	..	..

* *Exclusive of the numbers shown in columns 10 and 11 as following the traditional Occupation of the Caste.*

SELECTED CASTES, TRIBES OR RACES.—*concluded.*

THAN TRADITIONAL OCCUPATION OF CASTE (BY ORDERS).

VI.—Public Force.				VII.—Public Administration.				VIII.—Arts and Professions.						IX.—Persons living on thier income.		X.—Domestic Service.		XI.—Contractors, Clerks, Cashiers, etc. Otherwise unspecified.		XIII.—Labourers unspecified.		XIII.—Beggars, Prostitutes, Criminals and Inmates of Jails and Asylums.		
Commissioned and Gazetted Officers.		Others.		Gazetted Officers.		Others.		Religious.		Lawyers, Doctors and Teachers.		Others.												
Males.	Females.	Males.	Females.	Males.	Females.	Males.	Females.	Males.	Females.	Males.	Females.	Males.	Females.	Males.	Females.	Males.	Females.	Males.	Females.	Males.	Females.	Males.	Females.	Serial No.
44	45	46	47	48	49	50	51	52	53	54	55	56	57	58	59	60	61	62	63	64	65	66	67	
..	..	41	..	..	..	110	5	55	7	165	6	173	18	15	9	334	47	15	2	179	20	67	13	62
2	..	89	..	..	..	48	..	56	..	71	2	228	24	57	5	182	31	5	..	105	28	34	6	63
..	..	115	..	..	..	185	3	168	10	323	18	118	82	78	8	805	130	29	1	758	190	354	116	64
..	..	..	..	..	..	3	..	3	..	..	2	2	2	1	..	42	6	..	1	42	4	46	3	65
154	..	4,738	..	215	..	3,411	7	766	13	1,267	82	391	88	1,068	146	4,283	350	646	5	7,063	378	1,580	373	66
1	..	212	..	2	..	277	2	38	1	114	11	24	1	20	29	768	57	27	7	270	38	60	40	67
..	..	..	..	..	..	..	..	1	..	2	..	..	1	1	..	..	..	..	..	..	..	89	2	68
190	..	3,135	..	133	1	2,850	17	94	6	1,011	35	428	58	1,343	372	7,877	372	372	8	5,361	361	727	99	69
33	..	156	..	10	2	226	..	73	2	114	14	69	18	67	3	541	30	61	1	651	148	80	12	70
267	..	6,166	..	258	..	5,895	19	2,386	40	3,108	173	1,026	344	2,547	362	7,411	463	878	12	9,358	1,037	2,989	428	71
32	..	180	..	..	..	150	..	5	..	52	..	2	..	77	60	247	53	3	2	78	20	14	1	72
5	..	93	..	1	..	224	3	15	..	119	3	26	2	29	4	557	35	57	..	206	39	161	36	73
7	..	280	..	2	..	188	2	71	3	246	5	16	11	117	25	193	4	30	3	47	13	109	5	74
..	..	1	..	..	..	27	..	48	3	13	1	9	6	2	1	147	1	8	..	327	67	2,219	951	75
240	..	2,604	..	276	..	3,421	23	*93	*4	2,490	155	425	37	820	55	2,135	91	393	2	1,647	142	3,334	309	76
396	..	2,314	..	380	1	4,395	17	1,240	31	2,505	162	1,555	236	1,042	115	6,698	316	1,071	18	4,558	279	2,969	401	77
8	..	60	..	4	..	98	1	10	4	121	13	32	22	45	15	194	33	44	..	177	103	103	13	78
4	..	22	..	1	..	23	..	29	1	41	3	6	4	39	4	47	11	5	..	17	29	39	4	79
4	..	15	..	..	..	33	..	20	..	34	..	2	7	27	..	62	18	34	..	93	36	64	24	80
..	..	20	..	..	..	30	..	14	..	34	3	26	13	39	6	171	12	37	2	324	81	68	24	81
4	..	110	..	11	..	229	3	149	4	123	16	212	28	163	26	484	23	136	..	558	96	165	8	82
2	..	147	..	9	..	146	1	338	11	207	23	118	56	148	21	394	94	138	15	1,291	338	426	115	83
..	..	502	..	3	..	675	10	273	12	199	40	245	230	156	14	1,460	128	101	3	3,250	392	485	149	84
1,194	1	9,061	8	221	5	298	67	179	121	222	264	72	117	62	27	34	65	63	8	..	..	..	..	85
..	..	..	..	..	..	..	..	..	..	4	3	..	2	..	..	..	..	..	..	..	..	..	..	86
165	..	1,242	1	17	..	12	2	9	..	19	46	17	14	19	5	..	..	..	..	..	..	..	..	87
22	1	15	4	20	1	17	7	12	5	25	28	11	7	16	2	..	4	10	6	..	..	..	..	88
13	..	..	..	..	..	..	..	5	3	2	1	..	3	1	1	2	2	..	..	..	..	..	..	89
55	..	857	..	2	..	..	..	1	..	2	1	..	3	..	1	..	..	1	..	..	..	..	..	90
21	..	505	..	5	..	55	7	8	5	..	7	..	..	..	..	..	..	..	..	..	..	..	..	91
272	..	2,201	..	43	4	152	39	17	27	45	83	7	68	25	13	22	32	41	2	..	..	..	..	92
5	..	18	3	8	..	27	..	1	..	2	..	..	..	..	..	..	..	..	..	..	..	..	..	93
9	..	7	..	5	..	2	..	3	1	7	6	2	2	1	1	..	..	2	..	..	..	..	..	94
411	..	1,108	..	40	..	..	..	28	11	27	11	32	8	..	3	..	..	..	..	..	..	..	..	95
4	..	73	..	4	..	..	..	4	8	4	5	..	..	..	..	..	..	..	..	..	..	..	..	96
146	..	2,099	..	9	..	..	..	15	12	21	18	..	..	..	..	4	26	5	..	..	..	..	..	97
10	..	198	..	8	..	1	8	16	10	11	..	..	..	..	..	..	..	..	..	..	..	..	..	98
2	..	..	..	4	..	..	..	7	2	5	4	..	..	..	..	..	..	..	..	..	..	..	..	99
6	..	5	..	3	..	..	..	7	4	13	3	..	..	..	..	..	..	..	..	..	..	..	..	100
2	..	..	..	1	..	..	..	..	1	11	12	..	..	..	..	..	..	..	..	..	..	..	..	101
..	..	..	..	6	..	15	..	1	..	..	..	..	..	..	..	..	..	..	..	..	..	..	..	102
25	..	706	..	10	..	..	2	5	6	4	8	..	..	..	..	..	..	..	..	..	..	..	..	103
1	..	..	..	12	..	..	..	3	..	2	2	..	2	..	..	..	..	..	..	..	..	..	..	104
2	..	6	..	2	..	8	..	1	..	5	4	1	1	..	..	..	1	..	..	..	..	..	..	105
..	..	..	..	2	..	1	..	2	..	2	2	1	2	..	1	2	..	..	..	..	..	..	..	106
..	..	14	..	..	..	4	..	..	..	2	..	..	..	..	..	1	..	..	..	..	..	..	..	107
..	..	1	..	..	..	..	..	..	..	..	2	..	..	..	..	..	..	..	..	..	..	..	..	108
31	..	290	6	60	2	180	18	52	30	92	72	18	27	31	7	25	25	40	1	..	1	..	..	109
..	..	..	..	..	..	..	..	..	..	..	1	..	..	..	..	..	..	..	..	..	..	..	..	110
1	..	..	..	4	..	6	3	..	..	13	5	..	3	10	4	..	..	..	..	..	..	..	..	111
12	..	1	6	3	1	..	2	3	3	8	11	4	5	1	..	..	..	..	..	..	..	..	..	112
..	..	1	..	..	..	4	2	..	..	..	..	..	..	..	..	..	..	..	..	..	..	..	..	113
..	..	43	..	38	1	128	6	16	6	31	17	5	12	19	3	19	7	38	1	..	..	..	..	114
5	..	130	..	..	..	..	..	4	7	8	9	..	..	..	..	..	14	..	..	..	..	..	..	115
..	..	..	..	..	..	1	..	7	3	5	7	..	..	..	..	..	..	..	..	..	..	..	..	116
4	..	27	..	2	..	4	..	5	3	3	4	..	..	..	..	..	..	..	..	..	..	..	..	117
2	..	4	..	3	..	6	..	3	..	4	3	..	2	..	..	..	3	..	..	..	..	..	..	118
..	..	75	..	4	..	12	..	2	1	1	..	..	..	..	..	6	1	..	..	..	1	..	..	119

* *Exclusive of the numbers shown in columns 10 and 11 as following the traditional Occupation of the Caste.*

TABLE XII.

EDUCATED UNEMPLOYMENT.

The figures of educated unemployment are given in a marginal Table in Chapter VIII of the Report.

TABLE XIII.

LITERACY BY RELIGION AND AGE.

1. This Table is divided into three parts. Part A shows the literacy by religion and age for the Province as a whole and detail for the British Territory and Punjab States by main religions (Hindu, Jain, Sikh, Muslim and Christian). Part B gives the figures for Districts and States by main religions, and Part C details similar to B for cities and selected towns.

2. Christians in the main Table include all races. The figures for Indian Christians for the whole Province are given below, as also the detail by main sects.

Number of Indian Christians who are Literate:—

Age.	Total Population.		Literate.		Literate in English.	
	Males.	Females.	Males.	Females.	Males.	Females.
1	2	3	4	5	6	7
PUNJAB	215,527	180,102	12,864	8,749	6,569	5,067
0—10	..	..	801	722	305	313
10—15	..	..	1,385	1,223	525	519
15—20	..	..	1,967	1,556	976	771
20 and over	..	..	8,711	5,248	4,763	3,464
British Territory	213,607	178,537	12,664	8,635	6,456	5,005
0—10	..	..	794	720	303	313
10—15	..	..	1,372	1,216	516	515
15—20	..	..	1,957	1,542	971	763
20 and over	..	..	8,541	5,157	4,666	3,414
Punjab States	1,920	1,565	200	114	113	62
(*a*) :- Having Political relations with the Punjab Government	*75*	*77*	*41*	*29*	*22*	*11*
0—10	..	..	4	1	..	..
10—15	..	..	4	2	3	..
15—20	..	..	4	5	2	3
20 and over	..	..	29	21	17	8
(*b*) :—Having Political relations with the Government of India	*1,845*	*1,488*	*159*	*85*	*91*	*51*
0—10	..	..	3	1	2	..
10—15	..	..	9	5	6	4
15—20	..	..	6	9	3	5
20 and over	..	..	141	70	80	42

Literacy among Indian Christians by Main Sects:—

Province.	Sect.	Total Strength of Sect.		Literate.		Illiterate.	
		Males.	Females.	Males.	Females.	Males.	Females.
1	2	3	4	5	6	7	8
PUNJAB ..	Roman Catholics ..	27,173	18,622	2,231	975	24,942	17,647
	*Syrians ..	125	50	102	17	23	33
	Others ..	188,229	161,450	10,531	7,757	177,698	153,673

*Other than Romo-Syrian.

TABLE XIII.—LITERACY BY RELIGION AND AGE.

PART A.—PROVINCIAL SUMMARY.

Serial No.	Religion and Age.	POPULATION.											
		TOTAL.			LITERATE.			ILLITERATE.			LITERATE IN ENGLISH.		
		Persons.	Males.	Females.	Persons.	Males.	Females.	Persons.	Males.	Females.	Persons.	Males.	Females.
	1	2	3	4	5	6	7	8	9	10	11	12	13
	PUNJAB.												
1	**ALL RELIGIONS**	**28,490,857**	**15,561,194**	**12,929,663**	**1,421,942**	**1,258,742**	**163,200**	**27,068,915**	**14,302,452**	**12,766,463**	**269,098**	**249,003**	**20,095**
2	0—5 ..	*4,480,160*	2,284,228	2,195,932	..	..	..	4,480,160	2,284,228	2,195,932	..	..	..
3	5—10 ..	*3,765,322*	2,025,061	1,740,261	69,620	55,416	14,204	3,695,702	1,969,645	1,726,057	7,449	6,076	1,373
4	10—15 ..	*3,428,151*	1,888,698	1,539,453	143,560	118,555	25,005	3,284,591	1,770,143	1,514,448	22,333	19,756	2,577
5	15—20 ..	*2,656,926*	1,456,871	1,200,055	221,358	190,307	31,051	2,435,568	1,266,564	1,169,004	53,938	50,078	3,860
6	20 and over..	*14,160,298*	7,906,336	6,253,962	987,404	894,464	92,940	13,172,894	7,011,872	6,161,022	185,378	173,093	12,285
7	**HINDU** ..	**8,599,720**	**4,685,705**	**3,914,015**	**662,547**	**594,803**	**68,244**	**7,937,173**	**4,091,402**	**3,845,771**	**112,818**	**107,947**	**4,871**
8	0—5 ..	*1,277,077*	645,446	631,631	..	..	..	1,277,077	645,446	631,631	..	..	..
9	5—10 ..	*1,085,926*	578,259	507,667	29,093	22,901	6,192	1,056,833	555,358	501,475	2,398	2,099	299
10	10—15 ..	*1,028,197*	561,173	467,024	61,116	50,263	10,853	967,081	510,910	456,171	8,691	8,017	674
11	15—20 ..	*835,009*	456,924	378,085	98,340	85,188	13,152	736,669	371,736	364,933	22,182	21,097	1,085
12	20 and over ..	*4,373,511*	2,443,903	1,929,608	473,998	435,951	38,047	3,899,513	2,007,952	1,891,561	79,547	76,734	2,813
13	**AD-DHARMI** ..	**418,789**	**228,509**	**190,280**	**5,745**	**5,191**	**554**	**413,044**	**223,318**	**189,726**	**487**	**475**	**12**
14	0—5 ..	*68,639*	35,111	33,528	..	..	..	68,639	35,111	33,528	..	..	..
15	5—10 ..	*58,910*	31,996	26,914	315	272	43	58,595	31,724	26,871	10	10	..
16	10—15 ..	*54,337*	30,028	24,309	649	575	74	53,688	29,453	24,235	33	33	..
17	15—20 ..	*38,908*	21,060	17,848	916	813	103	37,992	20,247	17,745	79	75	4
18	20 and over ..	*197,995*	110,314	87,681	3,865	3,531	334	194,130	106,783	87,347	365	357	8
19	**SIKH** ..	**4,071,624**	**2,270,946**	**1,800,678**	**285,266**	**246,208**	**39,063**	**3,786,358**	**2,024,743**	**1,761,615**	**45,898**	**42,880**	**2,518**
20	0—5 ..	*608,864*	315,981	292,883	..	..	..	608,864	315,981	292,883	..	..	..
21	5—10 ..	*519,294*	284,604	234,690	13,505	10,328	3,177	505,789	274,276	231,513	1,309	1,126	183
22	10—15 ..	*487,357*	273,106	214,251	28,516	22,676	5,840	458,841	250,430	208,411	4,597	4,185	412
23	15—20 ..	*381,145*	215,989	165,156	42,786	35,320	7,466	338,359	180,669	157,690	10,548	9,896	652
24	20 and over ..	*2,074,964*	1,181,266	893,698	200,459	177,879	22,580	1,874,505	1,003,387	871,118	28,944	27,673	1,271
25	**JAIN** ..	**43,140**	**22,962**	**20,178**	**11,024**	**9,701**	**1,323**	**32,116**	**13,261**	**18,855**	**1,702**	**1,608**	**94**
26	0—5 ..	*6,607*	3,310	3,297	..	..	..	6,607	3,310	3,297	..	..	..
27	5—10 ..	*5,465*	2,861	2,604	549	409	140	4,916	2,452	2,464	62	56	6
28	10—15 ..	*5,203*	2,755	2,448	1,044	820	224	4,159	1,935	2,224	176	160	16
29	15—20 ..	*4,303*	2,274	2,029	1,602	1,324	278	2,701	950	1,751	336	314	22
30	20 and over ..	*21,562*	11,762	9,800	7,829	7,148	681	13,733	4,614	9,119	1,128	1,078	50
31	**BUDDHIST** ..	**7,753**	**3,770**	**3,983**	**450**	**405**	**45**	**7,303**	**3,365**	**3,938**	**21**	**19**	**2**
32	0—5 ..	*802*	412	390	..	..	..	802	412	390	..	..	..
33	5—10 ..	*789*	393	396	7	5	2	782	388	394	..	..	..
34	10—15 ..	*810*	412	398	10	9	1	800	403	397	..	..	..
35	15—20 ..	*774*	364	410	43	37	6	731	327	404	3	2	1
36	20 and over ..	*4,578*	2,189	2,389	390	354	36	4,188	1,835	2,353	18	17	1
37	**ZOROASTRIAN**	**569**	**358**	**211**	**268**	**178**	**90**	**301**	**180**	**121**	**208**	**143**	**60**
38	0—5 ..	*62*	37	25	..	..	..	62	37	25	..	..	..
39	5—10 ..	*54*	34	20	15	9	6	39	25	14	13	7	6
40	10—15 ..	*47*	30	17	19	12	7	28	18	10	13	7	6
41	15—20 ..	*47*	31	16	20	14	6	27	17	10	17	12	5
42	20 and over ..	*359*	226	133	214	143	71	145	83	62	160	117	43
43	**MUSLIM** ..	**14,929,896**	**8,116,383**	**6,813,513**	**421,209**	**378,742**	**42,467**	**14,508,687**	**7,737,641**	**6,771,046**	**85,894**	**80,740**	**5,154**
44	0—5 ..	*2,446,037*	1,247,352	1,198,685	..	..	..	2,446,037	1,247,352	1,198,685	..	..	..
45	5—10 ..	*2,036,821*	1,095,547	941,274	24,125	20,436	3,689	2,012,696	1,075,111	937,585	2,577	2,242	335
46	10—15 ..	*1,800,325*	992,593	807,732	49,032	42,518	6,514	1,751,293	950,075	801,218	7,218	6,554	664
47	15—20 ..	*1,356,081*	737,411	618,670	71,993	63,743	8,250	1,284,088	673,668	610,420	17,250	16,150	1,100
48	20 and over ..	*7,290,632*	4,043,480	3,247,152	276,059	252,045	24,014	7,014,573	3,791,435	3,223,138	58,849	55,794	3,055
49	**CHRISTIAN** ..	**419,853**	**232,556**	**186,797**	**35,430**	**24,017**	**11,413**	**383,923**	**208,539**	**175,384**	**22,574**	**15,191**	**7,383**
50	0—5 ..	*72,071*	36,579	35,492	..	..	..	72,071	36,579	35,492	..	..	..
51	5—10 ..	*58,062*	31,367	26,695	2,010	1,056	954	56,052	30,311	25,741	1,079	536	543
52	10—15 ..	*51,873*	28,601	23,272	3,174	1,682	1,492	48,699	26,919	21,780	1,605	800	805
53	15—20 ..	*40,656*	22,817	17,839	5,658	3,868	1,790	34,998	18,949	16,049	3,523	2,532	991
54	20 and over ..	*196,691*	113,192	83,499	24,588	17,411	7,177	172,103	95,781	76,322	16,367	11,323	5,044
55	**JEW** ..	**13**	**5**	**8**	**3**	**2**	**1**	**10**	**3**	**7**	**1**	..	**1**
56	0—5 ..	*1*	..	1	..	..	..	1	..	1	..	..	..
57	5—10 ..	*1*	..	1	1	..	1	..	..	..	1	..	1
58	10—15 ..	*2*	..	2	..	..	..	2	..	2	..	..	..
59	15—20 ..	*3*	1	2	..	..	..	3	1	2	..	..	..
60	20 and over ..	*6*	4	2	2	2	..	4	2	2	..	..	..
	BRITISH TERRITORY.												
1	**ALL RELIGIONS**	**23,580,852**	**12,880,510**	**10,700,342**	**1,247,757**	**1,097,044**	**150,713**	**22,333,095**	**11,783,466**	**10,549,629**	**249,607**	**230,390**	**19,217**
2	0—5 ..	*3,740,549*	1,909,178	1,831,371	..	..	..	3,740,549	1,909,178	1,831,371	..	..	..
3	5—10 ..	*3,143,832*	1,691,328	1,452,504	64,051	50,810	13,241	3,079,781	1,640,518	1,439,263	7,089	5,759	1,330
4	10—15 ..	*2,851,094*	1,571,550	1,279,544	131,389	108,112	23,277	2,719,705	1,463,438	1,256,267	20,996	18,522	2,474
5	15—20 ..	*2,190,257*	1,203,432	986,825	198,402	160,647	28,755	1,991,855	1,033,785	958,070	50,197	46,499	3,698
6	20 and over ..	*11,655,120*	6,505,022	5,150,098	853,915	768,475	85,440	10,801,205	5,736,547	5,064,658	171,325	159,610	11,715

TABLE XIII.—LITERACY BY RELIGION AND AGE.
PART A.—PROVINCIAL SUMMARY.—*continued.*

Serial No.	Religion and Age.	POPULATION.											
		TOTAL.			LITERATE.			ILLITERATE.			LITERATE IN ENGLISH.		
		Persons.	Males.	Females.	Persons.	Males.	Females.	Persons.	Males.	Females.	Persons	Males.	Females.
	1	2	3	4	5	6	7	8	9	10	11	12	13
	BRITISH TERRITORY.												
7	HINDU ..	**6,328,588**	**3,465,534**	**2,863,054**	**556,636**	**494,710**	**61,926**	**5,771,952**	**2,970,824**	**2,801,128**	**101,905**	**97,311**	**4,594**
8	0—5 ..	*950,275*	481,960	468,315	..	..	..	950,275	481,960	468,315	..	..	..
9	5—10 ..	*806,808*	430,878	375,930	26,022	20,342	5,680	780,786	410,536	370,250	2,188	1,902	286
10	10—15 ..	*765,555*	419,127	346,428	54,146	44,199	9,947	711,409	374,928	336,481	7,916	7,275	641
11	15—20 ..	*617,594*	340,821	276,773	84,720	72,697	12,023	532,874	268,124	264,750	20,169	19,139	1,030
12	20 and over ..	*3,188,356*	1,792,748	1,395,608	391,748	357,472	34,276	2,796,608	1,435,276	1,361,332	71,632	68,995	2,637
13	SIKH ..	**3,064,144**	**1,703,584**	**1,360,560**	**247,313**	**211,828**	**35,485**	**2,816,831**	**1,491,756**	**1,325,075**	**42,180**	**39,833**	**2,347**
14	0—5 ..	*462,939*	240,647	222,292	..	..	..	462,939	240,647	222,292	..	..	..
15	5—10 ..	*395,365*	217,179	178,186	12,270	9,346	2,924	383,095	207,833	175,262	1,253	1,079	174
16	10—15 ..	*366,576*	205,771	160,805	25,886	20,527	5,359	340,690	185,244	155,446	4,348	3,964	384
17	15—20 ..	*280,813*	158,524	122,289	38,030	31,260	6,770	242,783	127,264	115,519	9,852	9,246	606
18	20 and over ..	*1,558,451*	881,463	676,988	171,127	150,695	20,432	1,387,324	730,768	656,556	26,727	25,544	1,183
19	JAIN ..	**35,284**	**18,751**	**16,533**	**9,265**	**8,060**	**1,205**	**26,019**	**10,691**	**15,328**	**1,539**	**1,449**	**90**
20	0—5 ..	*5,374*	2,708	2,666	..	..	..	5,374	2,708	2,666	..	..	..
21	5—10 ..	*4,473*	2,352	2,121	494	365	129	3,979	1,987	1,992	58	52	6
22	10—15 ..	*4,267*	2,265	2,002	930	724	206	3,337	1,541	1,796	164	148	16
23	15—20 ..	*3,506*	1,860	1,646	1,373	1,120	253	2,133	740	1,393	301	281	20
24	20 and over ..	*17,664*	9,566	8,098	6,468	5,851	617	11,196	3,715	7,481	1,016	968	48
25	MUSLIM ..	**13,332,460**	**7,241,612**	**6,090,848**	**393,659**	**353,305**	**40,354**	**12,938,801**	**6,888,307**	**6,050,494**	**81,341**	**76,334**	**5,007**
26	0—5 ..	*2,184,488*	1,113,879	1,070,609	..	..	..	2,184,488	1,113,879	1,070,609	..	..	..
27	5—10 ..	*1,822,654*	978,898	843,756	22,965	19,444	3,521	1,799,689	959,454	840,235	2,511	2,184	327
28	10—15 ..	*1,610,827*	887,055	723,772	46,645	40,424	6,221	1,564,182	846,631	717,551	6,964	6,318	647
29	15—20 ..	*1,210,478*	659,280	551,198	67,746	59,896	7,850	1,142,732	599,384	543,348	16,312	15,238	1,074
30	20 and over ..	*6,504,013*	3,602,500	2,901,513	256,303	233,541	22,762	6,247,710	3,368,959	2,878,751	55,554	52,595	2,959
31	CHRISTIAN ..	**414,788**	**230,018**	**184,770**	**34,593**	**23,528**	**11,065**	**380,195**	**206,490**	**173,705**	**21,945**	**14,840**	**7,105**
32	0—5 ..	*71,353*	36,188	35,165	..	..	..	71,353	36,188	35,165	..	..	..
33	5—10 ..	*57,473*	31,061	26,412	1,969	1,032	937	55,504	30,029	25,475	1,055	525	530
34	10—15 ..	*51,367*	28,333	23,034	3,110	1,647	1,463	48,257	26,686	21,571	1,558	778	780
35	15—20 ..	*40,249*	22,604	17,645	5,579	3,832	1,747	34,670	18,772	15,898	3,466	2,508	958
36	20 and over ..	*194,346*	111,832	82,514	23,935	17,017	6,918	170,411	94,815	75,596	15,866	11,029	4,837
	PUNJAB STATES.												
1	ALL RELIGIONS	**4,910,005**	**2,680,684**	**2,229,321**	**174,185**	**161,698**	**12,487**	**4,735,820**	**2,518,986**	**2,216,834**	**19,491**	**18,613**	**878**
2	0—5 ..	*739,611*	375,050	364,561	..	..	..	739,611	375,050	364,561	..	..	..
3	5—10 ..	*621,490*	333,733	287,757	5,569	4,606	963	615,921	329,127	286,794	360	317	43
5	10—15 ..	*577,057*	317,148	259,909	12,171	10,443	1,728	564,886	306,705	258,181	1,337	1,234	103
4	15—20 ..	*466,669*	253,439	213,230	22,956	20,660	2,296	443,713	232,779	210,934	3,741	3,579	162
6	20 and over ..	*2,505,178*	1,401,314	1,103,864	133,489	125,989	7,500	2,371,689	1,275,325	1,096,364	14,053	13,483	570
7	HINDU	**2,271,132**	**1,220,171**	**1,050,961**	**105,911**	**99,593**	**6,318**	**2,165,221**	**1,120,578**	**1,044,643**	**10,913**	**10,636**	**277**
8	0—5 ..	*326,802*	163,486	163,316	..	..	..	326,802	163,486	163,216	..	..	..
9	5—10 ..	*279,118*	147,381	131,737	3,071	2,559	512	276,047	144,822	131,225	210	197	13
10	10—15 ..	*262,642*	142,046	120,596	6,970	6,064	906	255,672	135,982	119,690	775	742	33
11	15—20 ..	*217,415*	116,103	101,312	13,620	12,491	1,129	203,795	103,612	100,183	2,013	1,958	55
12	20 and over ..	*1,185,155*	651,155	534,000	82,250	78,479	3,771	1,102,905	572,676	530,229	7,915	7,739	176
13	SIKH ..	**1,007,480**	**567,362**	**440,118**	**37,953**	**34,375**	**3,578**	**969,527**	**532,987**	**436,540**	**3,218**	**3,047**	**171**
14	0—5 ..	*145,925*	75,334	70,591	..	..	..	145,925	75,334	70,591	..	..	..
15	5—10 ..	*123,929*	67,425	56,504	1,235	982	253	122,694	66,443	56,251	56	47	9
16	10—15 ..	*120,781*	67,335	53,446	2,630	2,149	481	118,151	65,186	52,965	249	221	28
17	15—20 ..	*100,332*	57,465	42,867	4,756	4,060	696	95,576	53,405	42,171	696	650	46
18	20 and over ..	*516,513*	299,803	216,710	29,332	27,184	2,148	487,181	272,619	214,562	2,217	2,129	88
19	JAIN ..	**7,856**	**4,211**	**3,645**	**1,759**	**1,641**	**118**	**6,097**	**2,570**	**3,527**	**163**	**159**	**4**
20	0—5 ..	*1,233*	602	631	..	..	..	1,233	602	631	..	..	..
21	5—10 ..	*992*	509	483	55	44	11	937	465	472	4	4	..
22	10—15 ..	*936*	490	446	114	96	18	822	394	428	12	12	..
23	15—20 ..	*797*	414	383	229	204	25	568	210	358	35	33	2
24	20 and over ..	*3,898*	2,196	1,702	1,361	1,297	64	2,537	899	1,638	112	110	2
25	MUSLIM ..	**1,597,436**	**874,771**	**722,665**	**27,550**	**25,437**	**2,113**	**1,569,886**	**849,334**	**720,552**	**4,553**	**4,406**	**147**
26	0—5 ..	*261,549*	133,473	128,076	..	..	..	261,549	133,473	128,076	..	..	..
27	5—10 ..	*214,167*	116,649	97,518	1,160	992	168	213,007	115,657	97,350	66	58	8
28	10—15 ..	*189,498*	105,538	83,960	2,387	2,094	293	187,111	103,444	83,667	254	237	17
29	15—20 ..	*145,603*	78,131	67,472	4,247	3,847	400	141,356	74,284	67,072	938	912	26
30	20 and over ..	*786,619*	440,980	345,639	19,756	18,504	1,252	766,863	422,476	344,387	3,295	3,199	96
31	CHRISTIAN ..	**4,565**	**2,538**	**2,027**	**837**	**489**	**348**	**3,728**	**2,049**	**1,679**	**629**	**351**	**278**
32	0—5 ..	*718*	391	327	..	..	..	718	391	327	..	..	..
33	5—10 ..	*589*	306	283	41	24	17	548	282	266	24	11	13
34	10—15 ..	*506*	268	238	64	35	29	442	233	209	47	22	25
35	15—20 ..	*407*	213	194	79	36	43	328	177	151	57	24	33
36	20 and over ..	*2,345*	1,360	985	653	394	259	1,692	966	726	501	294	207

TABLE XIII.—LITERACY BY RELIGION AND AGE.

PART A.—PROVINCIAL SUMMARY.—*concluded.*

Serial No.	Religion and Age.	POPULATION. Total. Persons.	Total. Males.	Total. Females.	Literate. Persons.	Literate. Males.	Literate. Females.	Illiterate. Persons.	Illiterate. Males.	Illiterate. Females.	Literate in English. Persons.	Literate in English. Males.	Literate in English. Females.
	1	2	3	4	5	6	7	8	9	10	11	12	13
	PUNJAB STATES.												
	A.—Having Political Relations with the Punjab Government.												
1	ALL RELIGIONS.	**437,787**	**229,290**	**208,497**	**15,870**	**14,791**	**1,079**	**421,917**	**214,499**	**207,418**	**1,881**	**1,564**	**117**
2	0—5 ..	*57,272*	28,181	29,091	..	..	..	57,272	28,181	29,091	..	..	..
3	5—10 ..	*50,210*	25,975	24,235	514	440	74	49,696	25,535	24,161	31	26	5
4	10—15 ..	*47,466*	25,198	22,268	1,100	979	121	46,366	24,219	22,147	118	111	7
5	15—20 ..	*39,635*	20,436	19,199	1,901	1,727	174	37,734	18,709	19,025	310	294	16
6	20 and over ..	*243,204*	129,500	113,704	12,355	11,645	710	230,849	117,855	112,994	1,222	1,133	89
7	HINDU ..	**383,883**	**199,991**	**183,892**	**13,811**	**12,972**	**839**	**370,072**	**187,019**	**183,058**	**1,340**	**1,275**	**65**
8	0—5 ..	*49,267*	24,101	25,166	..	..	..	49,267	24,101	25,166	..	..	..
9	5—10 ..	*43,244*	22,235	21,009	430	372	58	42,814	21,863	20,951	27	23	4
10	10—15 ..	*40,818*	21,577	19,241	936	834	102	39,882	20,743	19,139	98	93	5
11	15—20 ..	*34,441*	17,639	16,802	1,624	1,491	133	32,817	16,148	16,669	255	245	10
12	20 and over ..	*216,113*	114,439	101,674	10,821	10,275	546	205,292	104,164	101,128	960	914	46
13	SIKH ..	**10,854**	**6,124**	**4,730**	**662**	**576**	**86**	**10,192**	**5,548**	**4,644**	**85**	**85**	..
14	0—5 ..	*1,166*	755	711	..	..	..	1,166	755	711	..	..	..
15	5—10 ..	*1,311*	728	583	25	18	7	1,286	710	576	2	2	..
16	10—15 ..	*1,274*	721	553	43	35	8	1,231	686	545	7	7	..
17	15—20 ..	*1,072*	609	463	80	66	14	992	543	449	16	16	..
18	20 and over ..	*5,731*	3,311	2,420	514	457	57	5,217	2,854	2,363	60	60	..
19	JAIN ..	**408**	**218**	**190**	**140**	**129**	**11**	**268**	**89**	**179**	**11**	**11**	..
20	0—5 ..	*49*	22	27	..	..	..	49	22	27	..	..	..
21	5—10 ..	*49*	24	25	6	4	2	43	20	23	..	..	..
22	10—15 ..	*49*	22	27	9	7	2	40	15	25	..	..	..
23	15—20 ..	*41*	22	19	18	16	2	23	6	17	4	4	..
24	20 and over ..	*220*	128	92	107	102	5	113	26	87	7	7	..
25	MUSLIM ..	**40,845**	**22,071**	**18,774**	**1,136**	**1,056**	**80**	**39,709**	**21,015**	**18,694**	**181**	**168**	**13**
26	0—5 ..	*6,307*	3,204	3,103	..	..	..	6,307	3,204	3,103	..	..	..
27	5—10 ..	*5,409*	2,885	2,524	46	42	4	5,363	2,843	2,520	2	1	1
28	10—15 ..	*5,140*	2,788	2,352	105	99	6	5,035	2,689	2,346	9	8	1
29	15—20 ..	*3,909*	2,094	1,815	168	150	18	3,741	1,944	1,797	28	27	1
30	20 and over ..	*20,080*	11,100	8,980	817	765	52	19,263	10,335	8,928	142	132	10
31	CHRISTIAN ..	**206**	**100**	**106**	**114**	**51**	**63**	**92**	**49**	**43**	**64**	**25**	**39**
32	0—5 ..	*25*	18	7	..	..	..	25	18	7	..	..	..
33	5—10 ..	*23*	11	12	7	4	3	16	7	9	..	..	..
34	10—15 ..	*17*	9	8	7	4	3	10	5	5	4	3	1
35	15—20 ..	*18*	5	13	11	4	7	7	1	6	7	2	5
36	20 and over ..	*123*	57	66	89	39	50	34	18	16	53	20	33
	B.—Having Political Relations with the Government of India.												
1	ALL RELIGIONS.	**4,472,218**	**2,451,394**	**2,020,824**	**158,815**	**146,907**	**11,408**	**4,313,903**	**2,304,487**	**2,009,416**	**17,810**	**17,049**	**761**
2	0—5 ..	*682,339*	346,869	335,470	..	..	..	682,339	346,869	335,470	..	..	..
3	5—10 ..	*571,280*	307,758	263,522	5,055	4,166	889	566,225	303,592	262,633	329	291	38
4	10—15 ..	*529,591*	291,950	237,641	11,071	9,464	1,607	518,520	282,486	236,034	1,219	1,123	96
5	15—20 ..	*427,034*	233,003	194,031	21,055	18,933	2,122	405,979	214,070	191,909	3,431	3,285	146
6	20 and over ..	*2,261,974*	1,271,814	990,160	121,134	114,344	6,790	2,140,840	1,157,470	983,370	12,831	12,350	481
7	HINDU ..	**1,887,249**	**1,020,180**	**867,069**	**92,100**	**86,621**	**5,479**	**1,795,149**	**933,559**	**861,590**	**9,573**	**9,361**	**212**
8	0—5 ..	*277,535*	139,385	138,150	..	..	..	277,535	139,385	138,150	..	..	..
9	5—10 ..	*235,874*	125,146	110,728	2,641	2,187	454	233,233	122,959	110,274	183	174	9
10	10—15 ..	*221,824*	120,469	101,355	6,034	5,230	804	215,790	115,239	100,551	677	649	28
11	15—20 ..	*182,974*	98,464	84,510	11,996	11,000	996	170,978	87,464	83,514	1,758	1,713	45
12	20 and over ..	*969,042*	536,716	432,326	71,429	68,204	3,225	897,613	468,512	429,101	6,955	6,825	130
13	SIKH ..	**996,626**	**561,238**	**435,388**	**37,291**	**33,799**	**3,492**	**959,335**	**527,439**	**431,896**	**3,133**	**2,962**	**171**
14	0—5 ..	*144,459*	74,579	69,880	..	..	..	144,459	74,579	69,880	..	..	..
15	5—10 ..	*122,618*	66,697	55,921	1,210	964	246	121,408	65,733	55,675	54	45	9
16	10—15 ..	*119,507*	66,614	52,893	2,587	2,114	473	116,920	64,500	52,420	242	214	28
17	15—20 ..	*99,260*	56,856	42,404	4,676	3,994	682	94,584	52,862	41,722	680	634	46
18	20 and over ..	*510,782*	296,492	214,290	28,818	26,727	2,091	481,964	269,765	212,199	2,157	2,069	88
19	JAIN ..	**7,448**	**3,993**	**3,455**	**1,619**	**1,512**	**107**	**5,829**	**2,481**	**3,348**	**152**	**148**	**4**
20	0—5 ..	*1,184*	580	604	..	..	..	1,184	580	604	..	..	..
21	5—10 ..	*943*	485	458	49	40	9	894	445	449	4	4	..
22	10—15 ..	*887*	468	419	105	89	16	782	370	403	12	12	..
23	15—20 ..	*756*	392	364	211	188	23	545	204	341	31	29	2
24	20 and over ..	*3,078*	2,068	1,010	1,254	1,195	59	2,424	873	1,551	105	103	2
25	MUSLIM ..	**1,556,591**	**852,700**	**703,891**	**26,414**	**24,381**	**2,033**	**1,530,177**	**828,319**	**701,858**	**4,372**	**4,238**	**134**
26	0—5 ..	*255,242*	130,269	124,973	..	..	..	255,242	130,269	124,973	..	..	..
27	5—10 ..	*208,758*	113,764	94,994	1,114	950	164	207,644	112,814	94,830	64	57	7
28	10—15 ..	*184,358*	102,750	81,608	2,282	1,995	287	182,076	100,755	81,321	245	229	16
29	15—20 ..	*141,694*	76,037	65,657	4,079	3,697	382	137,615	72,340	65,275	910	885	25
30	20 and over ..	*766,539*	429,880	336,659	18,939	17,739	1,200	747,600	412,141	335,459	3,153	3,067	86
31	CHRISTIAN ..	**4,359**	**2,438**	**1,921**	**723**	**438**	**285**	**3,636**	**2,000**	**1,636**	**565**	**326**	**239**
32	0—5 ..	*693*	373	320	..	..	..	693	373	320	..	..	..
33	5—10 ..	*566*	295	271	34	20	14	532	275	257	24	11	13
34	10—15 ..	*489*	259	230	57	31	26	432	228	204	43	19	24
35	15—20 ..	*389*	208	181	68	32	36	321	176	145	50	22	28
36	20 and over ..	*2,222*	1,303	919	564	355	209	1,658	948	710	448	274	174

TABLE XIII.—LITERACY BY RELIGION AND AGE.

PART B.—DETAILS OF DISTRICTS AND STATES.

POPULATION.

District or State	Religion and Age.	Total. Persons.	Total. Males.	Total. Females.	Literate. Persons.	Literate. Males.	Literate. Females.	Illiterate. Persons.	Illiterate. Males.	Illiterate. Females.	Literate in English. Persons.	Literate in English. Males.	Literate in English. Females.
1	2	3	4	5	6	7	8	9	10	11	12	13	14
HISSAR.	ALL RELIGIONS ..	899,479	485,690	413,789	30,091	28,348	1,743	869,388	457,342	412,046	3,291	3,166	125
	0—5 ..	141,901	71,724	70,177	..	..	..	141,901	71,724	70,177	..	..	..
	5—10 ..	120,440	63,570	56,870	1,294	1,112	182	119,146	62,458	56,688	62	59	3
	10—15 ..	116,873	62,723	54,150	2,867	2,596	271	114,006	60,127	53,879	226	219	7
	15—20 ..	93,746	51,323	42,423	4,725	4,404	321	89,021	46,919	42,102	622	587	35
	20 and over ..	426,519	236,350	190,169	21,205	20,236	969	405,314	216,114	189,200	2,381	2,301	80
	HINDU ..	583,420	315,578	267,842	21,998	20,834	1,164	561,422	294,744	266,678	2,061	2,027	34
	0—5 ..	90,456	45,725	44,731	..	..	..	90,456	45,725	44,731	..	..	..
	5—10 ..	77,166	40,608	36,558	974	842	132	76,192	39,766	36,426	42	41	1
	10—15 ..	75,325	40,368	34,957	2,136	1,942	194	73,189	38,426	34,763	161	160	1
	15—20 ..	61,135	33,594	27,541	3,515	3,306	209	57,620	30,288	27,332	417	401	16
	20 and over ..	279,338	155,283	124,055	15,373	14,744	629	263,965	140,539	123,426	1,441	1,425	16
	SIKH ..	55,169	30,542	24,627	2,094	1,985	109	53,075	28,557	24,518	183	176	7
	0—5 ..	8,196	4,299	3,897	..	..	..	8,196	4,299	3,897	..	..	..
	5—10 ..	7,187	3,841	3,346	74	70	4	7,113	3,771	3,342	4	4	..
	10—15 ..	7,011	3,805	3,206	191	181	10	6,820	3,624	3,196	9	9	..
	15—20 ..	5,600	3,197	2,403	286	261	25	5,314	2,936	2,378	31	29	2
	20 and over ..	27,175	15,400	11,775	1,543	1,473	70	25,632	13,927	11,705	139	134	5
	JAIN ..	5,988	3,137	2,851	1,658	1,548	110	4,330	1,589	2,741	183	180	3
	0—5 ..	945	463	482	..	..	..	945	463	482	..	..	..
	5—10 ..	789	404	385	62	47	15	727	357	370	3	3	..
	10—15 ..	767	411	356	139	121	18	628	290	338	16	15	1
	15—20 ..	615	342	273	263	240	23	352	102	250	32	31	1
	20 and over ..	2,872	1,517	1,355	1,194	1,140	54	1,678	377	1,301	132	131	1
	MUSLIM ..	253,784	135,840	117,944	4,137	3,877	260	249,647	131,963	117,684	731	712	19
	0—5 ..	42,112	21,132	20,980	..	..	..	42,112	21,132	20,980	..	..	..
	5—10 ..	35,131	18,628	16,503	168	147	21	34,963	18,481	16,482	7	7	..
	10—15 ..	33,619	18,055	15,564	382	343	39	33,237	17,712	15,525	35	31	4
	15—20 ..	26,294	14,141	12,153	631	585	46	25,663	13,556	12,107	125	120	5
	20 and over ..	116,628	63,884	52,744	2,956	2,802	154	113,672	61,082	52,590	564	554	10
	CHRISTIAN ..	1,107	583	524	203	103	100	904	480	424	132	70	62
	0—5 ..	191	104	87	..	..	..	191	104	87	..	..	..
	5—10 ..	165	87	78	16	6	10	149	81	68	6	4	2
	10—15 ..	149	82	67	19	9	10	130	73	57	5	4	1
	15—20 ..	101	48	53	29	11	18	72	37	35	16	5	11
	20 and over ..	501	262	239	139	77	62	362	185	177	105	57	48
ROHTAK.	ALL RELIGIONS ..	805,621	432,855	372,766	27,890	26,585	1,305	777,731	406,270	371,461	3,615	3,501	114
	0—5 ..	126,331	64,361	61,970	..	..	..	126,331	64,361	61,970	..	..	..
	5—10 ..	106,225	57,298	48,927	1,263	1,156	107	104,962	56,142	48,820	83	77	6
	10—15 ..	104,902	57,690	47,212	3,009	2,823	186	101,893	54,867	47,026	354	338	16
	15—20 ..	83,996	44,685	39,311	4,662	4,418	244	79,334	40,267	39,067	837	813	24
	20 and over ..	384,167	208,821	175,346	18,956	18,188	768	365,211	190,633	174,578	2,341	2,273	68
	HINDU ..	655,963	353,935	302,028	21,721	20,980	741	634,242	332,955	301,287	2,536	2,491	45
	0—5 ..	101,309	51,767	49,542	..	..	..	101,309	51,767	49,542	..	..	..
	5—10 ..	86,002	46,591	39,411	1,005	937	68	84,997	45,654	39,343	57	55	2
	10—15 ..	85,597	47,352	38,245	2,446	2,332	114	83,151	45,020	38,131	262	255	7
	15—20 ..	68,614	36,694	31,920	3,742	3,599	143	64,872	33,095	31,777	628	618	10
	20 and over ..	314,441	171,531	142,910	14,528	14,112	416	299,913	157,419	142,494	1,589	1,563	26
	SIKH ..	596	328	268	107	90	17	489	238	251	47	45	2
	0—5 ..	109	40	69	..	..	..	109	40	69	..	..	..
	5—10 ..	76	40	36	6	4	2	70	36	34	1	1	..
	10—15 ..	62	34	28	6	4	2	56	30	26	2	1	1
	15—20 ..	62	33	29	12	9	3	50	24	26	4	4	..
	20 and over ..	287	181	106	83	73	10	204	108	96	40	39	1
	JAIN ..	6,375	3,320	3,055	1,507	1,364	143	4,868	1,956	2,912	163	158	5
	0—5 ..	912	447	465	..	..	..	912	447	465	..	..	..
	5—10 ..	763	390	373	61	44	17	702	346	356	2	1	1
	10—15 ..	754	390	364	127	101	26	627	289	338	16	14	2
	15—20 ..	635	329	306	198	173	25	437	168	281	33	32	1
	20 and over ..	3,311	1,764	1,547	1,121	1,046	75	2,190	718	1,472	112	111	1
	MUSLIM ..	137,880	72,820	65,060	4,387	4,040	347	133,493	68,780	64,713	785	756	29
	0—5 ..	23,119	11,661	11,458	..	..	..	23,119	11,661	11,458	..	..	..
	5—10 ..	18,673	9,902	8,771	176	157	19	18,497	9,745	8,752	18	16	2
	10—15 ..	17,816	9,547	8,269	406	364	42	17,410	9,183	8,227	67	63	4
	15—20 ..	14,203	7,395	6,808	686	621	65	13,517	6,774	6,743	163	155	8
	20 and over ..	64,069	34,315	29,754	3,119	2,898	221	60,950	31,417	29,533	537	522	15
	CHRISTIAN ..	4,807	2,452	2,355	168	111	57	4,639	2,341	2,298	84	51	33
	0—5 ..	882	446	436	..	..	..	882	446	436	..	..	..
	5—10 ..	711	375	336	15	14	1	696	361	335	5	4	1
	10—15 ..	673	367	306	24	22	2	649	345	304	7	5	2
	15—20 ..	482	234	248	24	16	8	458	218	240	9	4	5
	20 and over ..	2,059	1,030	1,029	105	59	46	1,954	971	983	63	38	25

TABLE XIII.—LITERACY

PART B.—DETAILS OF DISTRICTS AND STATES.

District or State.	Religion and Age.	Population. Total. Persons.	Total. Males.	Total. Females.	Literate. Persons.	Literate. Males.	Literate. Females.	Illiterate. Persons.	Illiterate. Males.	Illiterate. Females.	Literate in English. Persons.	Literate in English. Males.	Literate in English. Females.
1	2	3	4	5	6	7	8	9	10	11	12	13	14
GURGAON.	ALL RELIGIONS ..	740,163	398,513	341,650	24,601	22,924	1,677	715,562	375,589	339,973	2,986	2,867	119
	0—5 ..	*118,636*	60,063	58,573	..	..	..	118,636	60,063	58,573	..	..	..
	5—10 ..	*99,545*	54,344	45,201	1,246	1,105	141	98,299	53,239	45,060	69	61	8
	10—15 ..	*93,492*	52,295	41,197	2,680	2,431	249	90,812	49,864	40,948	246	241	5
	15—20 ..	*71,800*	38,638	33,162	3,829	3,520	309	67,971	35,118	32,853	645	627	18
	20 and over ..	*356,690*	193,173	163,517	16,846	15,868	978	339,844	177,305	162,539	2,026	1,938	88
	HINDU ..	493,174	266,641	226,533	18,296	17,172	1,124	474,878	249,469	225,409	1,999	1,979	20
	0—5 ..	*77,450*	39,255	38,195	..	..	..	77,450	39,255	38,195	..	..	..
	5—10 ..	*65,453*	35,769	29,684	888	785	103	64,565	34,984	29,581	48	47	1
	10—15 ..	*61,810*	34,665	27,145	1,956	1,772	184	59,854	32,893	26,961	192	192	..
	15—20 ..	*47,442*	25,688	21,754	2,832	2,625	207	44,610	23,063	21,547	457	451	6
	20 and over ..	*241,019*	131,264	109,755	12,620	11,990	630	228,399	119,274	109,125	1,302	1,289	13
	SIKH ..	500	281	219	70	56	14	430	225	205	29	29	..
	0—5 ..	*68*	33	35	..	..	..	68	33	35	..	..	..
	5—10 ..	*63*	34	29	7	4	3	56	30	26	..	..	..
	10—15 ..	*56*	30	26	6	3	3	50	27	23	1	1	..
	15—20 ..	*52*	32	20	9	7	2	43	25	18	7	7	..
	20 and over ..	*261*	152	109	48	42	6	213	110	103	21	21	..
	JAIN ..	2,665	1,379	1,286	803	720	83	1,862	659	1,203	91	90	1
	0—5 ..	*418*	195	223	..	..	..	418	195	223	..	..	..
	5—10 ..	*336*	174	162	32	25	7	304	149	155	2	2	..
	10—15 ..	*307*	164	143	65	52	13	242	112	130	5	5	..
	15—20 ..	*232*	120	*112*	108	89	19	124	31	93	22	22	..
	20 and over ..	*1,372*	726	646	598	554	44	774	172	602	62	61	1
	MUSLIM ..	242,357	129,479	112,878	5,066	4,765	301	237,291	124,714	112,577	689	683	6
	0—5 ..	*40,462*	20,468	19,994	..	..	..	40,462	20,468	19,994	..	..	..
	5—10 ..	*33,474*	18,255	15,219	282	262	20	33,192	17,993	15,199	11	10	1
	10—15 ..	*31,123*	17,333	13,790	605	569	36	30,518	16,764	13,754	41	41	..
	15—20 ..	*23,930*	12,730	11,200	837	780	57	23,093	11,950	11,143	139	137	2
	20 and over ..	*113,368*	60,693	52,675	3,342	3,154	188	110,026	57,539	52,487	498	495	3
	CHRISTIAN ..	1,463	730	733	363	208	155	1,100	522	578	175	83	92
	0—5 ..	*238*	112	126	..	..	..	238	112	126	..	..	..
	5—10 ..	*219*	112	107	37	29	8	182	83	99	8	2	6
	10—15 ..	*196*	103	93	48	35	13	148	68	80	7	2	5
	15—20 ..	*144*	68	76	43	19	24	101	49	52	20	10	10
	20 and over ..	*666*	335	331	235	125	110	431	210	221	140	69	71
KARNAL.	ALL RELIGIONS ..	852,614	469,870	382,744	27,938	25,942	1,996	824,676	443,928	380,748	4,041	3,935	106
	0—5 ..	*131,068*	66,761	64,307	..	..	..	131,068	66,761	64,307	..	..	..
	5—10 ..	*107,311*	58,840	48,471	1,160	1,019	141	106,151	57,821	48,330	84	76	8
	10—15 ..	*107,284*	60,274	47,010	2,706	2,442	264	104,578	57,832	46,746	325	313	12
	15—20 ..	*92,024*	51,146	40,878	4,390	4,003	387	87,634	47,143	40,491	805	787	18
	20 and over ..	*414,927*	232,849	182,078	19,682	18,478	1,204	395,245	214,371	180,874	2,827	2,759	68
	HINDU ..	565,286	313,117	252,169	18,680	17,720	960	546,606	295,397	251,209	2,426	2,392	34
	0—5 ..	*86,445*	44,219	42,226	..	..	..	86,445	44,219	42,226	..	..	..
	5—10 ..	*71,415*	39,500	31,915	809	728	81	70,606	38,772	31,834	60	57	3
	10—15 ..	*71,477*	40,520	30,957	1,838	1,700	138	69,639	38,820	30,819	231	229	2
	15—20 ..	*60,622*	34,147	26,475	2,938	2,755	183	57,684	31,392	26,292	524	520	4
	20 and over ..	*275,327*	154,731	120,596	13,095	12,537	558	262,232	142,194	120,038	1,611	1,586	25
	SIKH ..	16,928	9,692	7,236	765	686	79	16,163	9,006	7,157	142	141	1
	0—5 ..	*2,424*	1,264	1,160	..	..	..	2,424	1,264	1,160	..	..	..
	5—10 ..	*2,038*	1,142	896	31	26	5	2,007	1,116	891	3	3	..
	10—15 ..	*2,084*	1,179	905	56	47	9	2,028	1,132	896	6	6	..
	15—20 ..	*1,759*	996	763	98	83	15	1,661	913	748	24	23	1
	20 and over ..	*8,623*	5,111	3,512	580	530	50	8,043	4,581	3,462	109	109	..
	JAIN ..	4,190	2,164	2,026	1,062	1,001	61	3,128	1,163	1,965	106	105	1
	0—5 ..	*609*	322	287	..	..	..	609	322	287	..	..	..
	5—10 ..	*494*	248	246	27	21	6	467	227	240	1	1	..
	10—15 ..	*480*	232	248	74	64	10	406	168	238	7	7	..
	15—20 ..	*426*	209	217	150	137	13	276	72	204	21	20	1
	20 and over ..	*2,181*	1,153	1,028	811	779	32	1,370	374	996	77	77	..
	MUSLIM ..	259,730	141,372	118,358	7,252	6,426	826	252,478	134,946	117,532	1,255	1,228	27
	0—5 ..	*40,411*	20,364	20,047	..	..	..	40,411	20,364	20,047	..	..	..
	5—10 ..	*32,490*	17,469	15,021	288	242	46	32,202	17,227	14,975	18	15	3
	10—15 ..	*32,423*	17,879	14,544	725	625	100	31,698	17,254	14,444	74	68	6
	15—20 ..	*28,537*	15,433	13,104	1,176	1,013	163	27,361	14,420	12,941	225	218	7
	20 and over ..	*125,869*	70,227	55,642	5,063	4,546	517	120,806	65,681	55,125	938	927	11
	CHRISTIAN ..	1,469	806	663	173	103	70	1,296	703	593	112	69	43
	0—5 ..	*275*	134	141	..	..	..	275	134	141	..	..	..
	5—10 ..	*202*	112	90	5	2	3	197	110	87	2	..	2
	10—15 ..	*180*	105	75	12	5	7	168	100	68	7	3	4
	15—20 ..	*154*	82	72	26	13	13	128	69	59	11	6	5
	20 and over ..	*658*	373	285	130	83	47	528	290	238	92	60	32

BY RELIGION AND AGE.

PART B.—DETAILS OF DISTRICTS AND STATES.—*continued.*

District or State.	Religion and Age.	Population. Total. Persons.	Total. Males.	Total. Females.	Literate. Persons.	Literate. Males.	Literate. Females.	Illiterate. Persons.	Illiterate. Males.	Illiterate. Females.	Literate in English. Persons.	Literate in English. Males.	Literate in English. Females.
1	2	3	4	5	6	7	8	9	10	11	12	13	14
AMBALA.	ALL RELIGIONS ..	742,902	416,411	326,491	49,504	43,314	6,190	693,398	373,097	320,301	11,519	10,743	776
	0—5 ..	106,988	54,725	52,263	..	..	..	106,988	54,725	52,263	..	..	..
	5—10 ..	91,491	49,826	41,665	2,213	1,663	550	89,278	48,163	41,115	388	305	83
	10—15 ..	89,359	49,653	39,706	4,719	3,798	921	84,640	45,855	38,785	998	869	129
	15—20 ..	73,834	41,152	32,682	7,671	6,568	1,103	66,163	34,584	31,579	2,296	2,170	126
	20 and over ..	381,230	221,055	160,175	34,901	31,285	3,616	346,329	189,770	156,559	7,837	7,399	438
	HINDU ..	346,711	195,270	151,441	24,111	21,605	2,506	322,600	173,665	148,935	4,862	4,746	116
	0—5 ..	49,365	25,377	23,988	..	..	..	49,365	25,377	23,988	..	..	..
	5—10 ..	42,000	22,872	19,128	979	747	232	41,021	22,125	18,896	95	85	10
	10—15 ..	41,186	22,979	18,207	2,171	1,786	385	39,015	21,193	17,822	368	352	16
	15—20 ..	34,991	19,637	15,354	3,606	3,110	496	31,385	16,527	14,858	943	918	25
	20 and over ..	179,169	104,405	74,764	17,355	15,962	1,393	161,814	88,443	73,371	3,456	3,391	65
	SIKH ..	155,555	88,485	67,070	9,699	8,874	825	145,856	79,611	66,245	1,376	1,333	43
	0—5 ..	21,583	11,219	10,364	..	..	..	21,583	11,219	10,364	..	..	..
	5—10 ..	19,084	10,645	8,439	318	279	39	18,766	10,366	8,400	20	17	3
	10—15 ..	18,957	10,705	8,252	876	794	82	18,081	9,911	8,170	131	123	8
	15—20 ..	14,739	8,231	6,508	1,558	1,409	149	13,181	6,822	6,359	372	357	15
	20 and over ..	81,192	47,685	33,507	6,947	6,392	555	74,245	41,293	32,952	853	836	17
	JAIN ..	2,550	1,402	1,148	876	731	145	1,674	671	1,003	182	176	6
	0—5 ..	334	172	162	..	..	..	334	172	162	..	..	..
	5—10 ..	311	167	144	53	42	11	258	125	133	4	4	..
	10—15 ..	314	179	135	104	80	24	210	99	111	19	18	1
	15—20 ..	248	133	115	120	95	25	128	38	90	33	33	..
	20 and over ..	1,343	751	592	599	514	85	744	237	507	126	121	5
	MUSLIM ..	230,837	126,913	103,924	11,311	9,706	1,605	219,526	117,207	102,319	2,428	2,378	50
	0—5 ..	34,816	17,512	17,304	..	..	..	34,816	17,512	17,304	..	..	..
	5—10 ..	29,293	15,711	13,582	600	442	158	28,693	15,269	13,424	72	69	3
	10—15 ..	28,128	15,361	12,767	1,202	928	274	26,926	14,433	12,493	209	203	6
	15—20 ..	22,998	12,583	10,415	1,819	1,535	284	21,179	11,048	10,131	474	465	9
	20 and over ..	115,602	65,746	49,856	7,690	6,801	889	107,912	58,945	48,967	1,673	1,641	32
	CHRISTIAN ..	7,141	4,284	2,857	3,497	2,389	1,108	3,644	1,895	1,749	2,668	2,108	560
	0—5 ..	879	440	439	..	..	..	879	440	439	..	..	..
	5—10 ..	788	424	364	262	153	109	526	271	255	196	130	66
	10—15 ..	760	422	338	366	210	156	394	212	182	271	173	98
	15—20 ..	850	563	287	566	417	149	284	146	138	474	397	77
	20 and over ..	3,864	2,435	1,429	2,303	1,609	694	1,561	826	735	1,727	1,408	319
SIMLA.	ALL RELIGIONS ..	36,786	23,517	13,269	7,518	6,297	1,221	29,268	17,220	12,048	2,813	2,411	402
	0—5 ..	3,570	1,735	1,835	..	..	..	3,570	1,735	1,835	..	..	..
	5—10 ..	3,197	1,704	1,493	338	233	105	2,859	1,471	1,388	67	39	28
	10—15 ..	3,138	1,803	1,335	555	416	139	2,583	1,387	1,196	130	87	43
	15—20 ..	3,805	2,528	1,277	933	764	169	2,872	1,764	1,108	308	265	43
	20 and over ..	23,076	15,747	7,329	5,692	4,884	808	17,384	10,863	6,521	2,308	2,020	288
	HINDU ..	28,661	17,839	10,822	5,013	4,495	518	23,648	13,344	10,304	1,489	1,465	24
	0—5 ..	2,844	1,377	1,467	..	..	..	2,844	1,377	1,467	..	..	..
	5—10 ..	2,578	1,379	1,199	215	164	51	2,363	1,215	1,148	22	20	2
	10—15 ..	2,553	1,465	1,088	385	315	70	2,168	1,150	1,018	57	52	5
	15—20 ..	2,965	1,923	1,042	663	573	90	2,302	1,350	952	181	175	6
	20 and over ..	17,721	11,695	6,026	3,750	3,443	307	13,971	8,252	5,719	1,229	1,218	11
	SIKH ..	760	532	228	341	281	60	419	251	168	115	107	8
	0—5 ..	87	44	43	..	..	..	87	44	43	..	..	..
	5—10 ..	63	35	28	12	9	3	51	26	25	2	2	..
	10—15 ..	54	32	22	16	11	5	38	21	17	5	2	3
	15—20 ..	74	48	26	36	27	9	38	21	17	10	8	2
	20 and over ..	482	373	109	277	234	43	205	139	66	98	95	3
	JAIN ..	1	1	..	1	1	..	..	..	..	1	1	..
	0—5 ..	..	..	..	..	..	..	..	..	..	..	..	..
	5—10 ..	..	..	..	..	..	..	..	..	..	..	..	..
	10—15 ..	..	..	..	..	..	..	..	..	..	..	..	..
	15—20 ..	..	..	..	..	..	..	..	..	..	..	..	..
	20 and over ..	1	1	..	1	1	..	..	..	..	1	1	..
	MUSLIM ..	5,810	4,346	1,464	1,135	1,010	125	4,675	3,336	1,339	498	490	8
	0—5 ..	455	219	236	..	..	..	455	219	236	..	..	..
	5—10 ..	418	222	196	52	37	15	366	185	181	6	6	..
	10—15 ..	407	248	159	80	59	21	327	189	138	17	16	1
	15—20 ..	654	509	145	157	134	23	497	375	122	66	63	3
	20 and over ..	3,876	3,148	728	846	780	66	3,030	2,368	662	409	405	4
	CHRISTIAN ..	1,540	788	752	1,028	510	518	512	278	234	710	348	362
	0—5 ..	182	93	89	..	..	..	182	93	89	..	..	..
	5—10 ..	137	67	70	59	23	36	78	44	34	37	11	26
	10—15 ..	122	56	66	74	31	43	48	25	23	51	17	34
	15—20 ..	110	46	64	77	30	47	33	16	17	51	19	32
	20 and over ..	989	526	463	818	426	392	171	100	71	571	301	270

TABLE XIII.—LITERACY

PART B.—DETAILS OF DISTRICTS AND STATES.

District or State.	Religion and Age.	Population. Total. Persons.	Population. Total. Males.	Population. Total. Females.	Population. Literate. Persons.	Population. Literate. Males.	Population. Literate. Females.	Population. Illiterate. Persons.	Population. Illiterate. Males.	Population. Illiterate. Females.	Literate in English. Persons.	Literate in English. Males.	Literate in English. Females.
1	2	3	4	5	6	7	8	9	10	11	12	13	14
KANGRA.	**ALL RELIGIONS** ..	**801,312**	**415,288**	**386,024**	**39,899**	**37,077**	**2,822**	**761,418**	**378,211**	**383,202**	**3,881**	**3,723**	**108**
	0—5 ..	*115,529*	56,921	58,608	..	..	..	115,529	56,921	58,608	..	..	..
	5—10 ..	*100,487*	51,649	48,838	1,629	1,408	221	98,858	50,241	48,617	100	92	8
	10—15 ..	*93,086*	48,366	44,720	3,441	3,032	409	89,645	45,334	44,311	330	321	9
	15—20 ..	*72,507*	35,365	37,142	5,232	4,659	573	67,275	30,706	36,569	836	821	15
	20 and over ..	*419,703*	222,987	196,716	29,597	27,978	1,619	390,106	195,009	195,097	2,565	2,489	76
	HINDU ..	**731,215**	**377,050**	**354,165**	**37,419**	**34,947**	**2,472**	**693,796**	**342,103**	**351,693**	**3,334**	**3,305**	**29**
	0—5 ..	*105,355*	51,848	53,507	..	..	..	105,355	51,848	53,507	..	..	..
	5—10 ..	*91,393*	46,883	44,510	1,529	1,328	201	89,864	45,555	44,309	87	83	4
	10—15 ..	*84,431*	43,760	40,671	3,253	2,877	376	81,178	40,883	40,295	295	291	4
	15—20 ..	*65,570*	31,748	33,822	4,921	4,400	521	60,649	27,348	33,301	758	752	6
	20 and over ..	*384,466*	202,811	181,655	27,716	26,342	1,374	356,750	176,469	180,281	2,194	2,179	15
	SIKH ..	**2,396**	**1,338**	**1,058**	**417**	**371**	**46**	**1,979**	**967**	**1,012**	**92**	**86**	**6**
	0—5 ..	*332*	172	160	..	..	..	332	172	160	..	..	..
	5—10 ..	*272*	141	131	14	10	4	258	131	127	1	1	..
	10—15 ..	*247*	133	114	28	23	5	219	110	109	5	5	..
	15—20 ..	*231*	115	116	48	40	8	183	75	108	10	8	2
	20 and over ..	*1,314*	777	537	327	298	29	987	479	508	76	72	4
	JAIN ..	**94**	**46**	**48**	**19**	**19**	..	**75**	**27**	**48**	**1**	**1**	..
	0—5 ..	*19*	9	10	..	..	..	19	9	10	..	..	..
	5—10 ..	*15*	7	8	1	1	..	14	6	8	..	..	..
	10—15 ..	*13*	4	9	2	2	..	11	2	9	..	..	..
	15—20 ..	*8*	4	4	3	3	..	5	1	4	..	..	..
	20 and over ..	*39*	22	17	13	13	..	26	9	17	1	1	..
	MUSLIM ..	**40,483**	**22,486**	**17,997**	**1,272**	**1,132**	**140**	**39,211**	**21,354**	**17,857**	**243**	**238**	**5**
	0—5 ..	*6,047*	3,031	3,016	..	..	..	6,047	3,031	3,016	..	..	..
	5—10 ..	*5,282*	2,767	2,515	67	58	9	5,215	2,709	2,506	6	5	1
	10—15 ..	*4,920*	2,623	2,297	123	108	15	4,797	2,515	2,282	22	21	1
	15—20 ..	*3,979*	2,115	1,864	184	157	27	3,795	1,958	1,837	53	53	..
	20 and over ..	*20,255*	11,950	8,305	898	809	89	19,357	11,141	8,216	162	159	3
	CHRISTIAN ..	**576**	**316**	**260**	**263**	**138**	**125**	**313**	**178**	**135**	**153**	**86**	**67**
	0—5 ..	*65*	37	28	..	..	..	65	37	28	..	..	..
	5—10 ..	*54*	32	22	12	6	6	42	26	16	6	3	3
	10—15 ..	*57*	30	27	23	10	13	34	20	14	8	4	4
	15—20 ..	*65*	33	32	29	16	13	36	17	19	13	7	6
	20 and over ..	*335*	184	151	199	106	93	136	78	58	126	72	54
HOSHIARPUR.	**ALL RELIGIONS** ..	**1,032,187**	**551,867**	**480,320**	**59,016**	**53,991**	**5,025**	**973,171**	**497,876**	**475,295**	**8,601**	**8,478**	**123**
	0—5 ..	*150,731*	76,728	74,003	..	..	..	150,731	76,728	74,003	..	..	..
	5—10 ..	*135,020*	71,521	63,499	3,259	2,826	433	131,761	68,695	63,066	167	159	8
	10—15 ..	*125,430*	67,003	58,427	7,231	6,433	798	118,199	60,570	57,629	881	863	18
	15—20 ..	*87,344*	45,279	42,065	9,839	8,858	981	77,505	36,421	41,084	2,308	2,275	33
	20 and over ..	*533,662*	291,336	242,326	38,687	35,874	2,813	494,975	255,462	239,513	5,245	5,181	64
	HINDU ..	**414,353**	**219,303**	**195,050**	**30,796**	**27,909**	**2,887**	**383,557**	**191,394**	**192,163**	**4,729**	**4,695**	**34**
	0—5 ..	*58,064*	29,414	28,650	..	..	..	58,064	29,414	28,650	..	..	..
	5—10 ..	*52,269*	27,339	24,930	1,625	1,348	277	50,644	25,991	24,653	93	92	1
	10—15 ..	*48,978*	25,643	23,335	3,565	3,077	488	45,413	22,566	22,847	465	459	6
	15—20 ..	*33,992*	17,067	16,925	4,921	4,355	566	29,071	12,712	16,359	1,209	1,198	11
	20 and over ..	*221,050*	119,840	101,210	20,685	19,129	1,556	200,365	100,711	99,654	2,962	2,946	16
	SIKH ..	**173,147**	**94,652**	**78,495**	**14,855**	**13,443**	**1,412**	**158,292**	**81,209**	**77,083**	**1,970**	**1,953**	**17**
	0—5 ..	*23,734*	12,187	11,547	..	..	..	23,734	12,187	11,547	..	..	..
	5—10 ..	*21,430*	11,580	9,850	706	615	91	20,724	10,965	9,759	24	23	1
	10—15 ..	*19,966*	10,949	9,017	1,663	1,475	188	18,303	9,474	8,829	221	218	3
	15—20 ..	*14,329*	7,741	6,588	2,377	2,113	264	11,952	5,628	6,324	588	584	4
	20 and over ..	*93,688*	52,195	41,493	10,109	9,240	869	83,579	42,955	40,624	1,137	1,128	9
	JAIN ..	**1,016**	**579**	**437**	**336**	**280**	**56**	**680**	**299**	**381**	**47**	**46**	**1**
	0—5 ..	*141*	68	73	..	..	..	141	68	73	..	..	..
	5—10 ..	*128*	72	56	19	12	7	109	60	49	..	..	..
	10—15 ..	*125*	73	52	34	25	9	91	48	43	5	4	1
	15—20 ..	*95*	52	43	52	38	14	43	14	29	11	11	..
	20 and over ..	*527*	314	213	231	205	26	296	109	187	31	31	..
	MUSLIM ..	**328,078**	**174,351**	**153,727**	**11,013**	**10,461**	**552**	**317,065**	**163,890**	**153,175**	**1,650**	**1,605**	**45**
	0—5 ..	*50,618*	25,689	24,929	..	..	..	50,618	25,689	24,929	..	..	..
	5—10 ..	*44,928*	23,686	21,242	790	747	43	44,138	22,939	21,199	46	41	5
	10—15 ..	*41,392*	22,143	19,249	1,740	1,650	90	39,652	20,493	19,159	182	175	7
	15—20 ..	*28,755*	15,024	13,731	2,192	2,077	115	26,563	12,947	13,616	482	470	12
	20 and over ..	*162,385*	87,809	74,576	6,291	5,987	304	156,094	81,822	74,272	940	919	21
	CHRISTIAN ..	**3,764**	**2,083**	**1,681**	**110**	**52**	**58**	**3,654**	**2,031**	**1,623**	**47**	**21**	**26**
	0—5 ..	*637*	328	309	..	..	..	637	328	309	..	..	..
	5—10 ..	*583*	310	273	6	1	5	577	309	268	1	..	1
	10—15 ..	*542*	297	245	12	3	9	530	294	236	2	1	1
	15—20 ..	*332*	178	154	22	9	13	310	169	141	11	5	6
	20 and over ..	*1,670*	970	700	70	39	31	1,600	931	669	33	15	18

BY RELIGION AND AGE.

PART B.—DETAILS OF DISTRICTS AND STATES.—*continued.*

District or State.	Religion and Age.	Population. Total. Persons.	Total. Males.	Total. Females.	Literate. Persons.	Literate. Males.	Literate. Females.	Illiterate. Persons.	Illiterate. Males.	Illiterate. Females.	Literate in English. Persons.	Literate in English. Males.	Literate in English. Females.
1	2	3	4	5	6	7	8	9	10	11	12	13	14
JULLUNDUR.	**ALL RELIGIONS** ..	**943,721**	**512,667**	**431,054**	**52,263**	**45,963**	**6,300**	**891,458**	**466,704**	**424,754**	**10,666**	**10,074**	**592**
	0–5 ..	*138,905*	71,557	67,348	..	..	..	138,905	71,557	67,348	..	..	..
	5–10 ..	*123,202*	66,695	56,507	2,847	2,434	413	120,355	64,261	56,094	253	222	31
	10–15 ..	*114,062*	62,533	51,529	6,190	5,286	904	107,872	57,247	50,625	1,072	960	112
	15–20 ..	*82,774*	45,086	37,688	8,833	7,539	1,294	73,941	37,547	36,394	2,494	2,339	155
	20 and over ..	*484,778*	266,796	217,982	34,393	30,704	3,689	450,385	236,092	214,293	6,847	6,553	294
	HINDU ..	**155,242**	**85,469**	**69,773**	**20,916**	**17,902**	**3,014**	**134,326**	**67,567**	**66,759**	**4,375**	**4,007**	**368**
	0–5 ..	*21,901*	11,283	10,618	..	..	..	21,901	11,283	10,618	..	..	.
	5–10 ..	*19,355*	10,538	8,817	1,063	850	213	18,292	9,688	8,604	99	86	13
	10–15 ..	*18,463*	10,179	8,284	2,286	1,798	488	16,177	8,381	7,796	483	409	74
	15–20 ..	*14,150*	8,030	6,120	3,350	2,706	644	10,800	5,324	5,476	1,064	970	94
	20 and over ..	*81,373*	45,439	36,934	14,217	12,548	1,669	67,156	32,891	34,265	2,729	2,542	187
	SIKH ..	**249,571**	**139,154**	**110,417**	**11,574**	**10,321**	**1,253**	**237,997**	**128,833**	**109,164**	**2,138**	**2,112**	**26**
	0–5 ..	*33,946*	18,061	15,885	..	..	..	33,946	18,061	15,885	..	..	..
	5–10 ..	*30,784*	17,289	13,495	586	523	63	30,198	16,766	13,432	46	46	..
	10–15 ..	*28,889*	16,388	12,501	1,330	1,203	127	27,559	15,185	12,374	245	244	1
	15–20 ..	*21,137*	11,802	9,335	1,896	1,682	214	19,241	10,120	9,121	508	505	3
	20 and over ..	*134,815*	75,614	59,201	7,762	6,913	849	127,053	68,701	58,352	1,339	1,317	2
	JAIN ..	**1,379**	**727**	**652**	**243**	**200**	**43**	**1,136**	**527**	**609**	**52**	**48**	
	0–5 ..	*239*	127	112	..	..	..	239	127	112	..	..	..
	5–10 ..	*202*	120	82	25	21	4	177	99	78	13	13	..
	10–15 ..	*172*	100	72	36	29	7	136	71	65	16	15	
	15–20 ..	*121*	58	63	34	25	9	87	33	54	7	6	
	20 and over ..	*645*	322	323	148	125	23	497	197	300	16	14	
	MUSLIM ..	**419,556**	**223,611**	**195,945**	**17,092**	**15,497**	**1,595**	**402,464**	**208,114**	**194,350**	**3,581**	**3,481**	**10**
	0–5 ..	*63,502*	32,054	31,448	..	..	..	63,502	32,054	31,448	..	..	..
	5–10 ..	*55,794*	29,508	26,286	1,039	932	107	54,755	28,576	26,179	65	59	
	10–15 ..	*51,184*	27,437	23,747	2,207	1,980	227	48,977	25,457	23,520	254	237	1
	15–20 ..	*37,030*	19,557	17,473	3,057	2,720	337	33,973	16,837	17,136	786	755	3
	20 and over ..	*212,046*	115,056	96,991	10,789	9,865	924	201,257	105,190	96,067	2,476	2,430	4
	CHRISTIAN ..	**4,323**	**2,714**	**1,609**	**1,214**	**994**	**220**	**3,109**	**1,720**	**1,389**	**433**	**340**	**9**
	0–5 ..	*592*	298	294	..	..	..	592	208	294	..	..	..
	5–10 ..	*469*	266	203	64	43	21	405	223	182	27	15	1
	10–15 ..	*402*	230	172	184	147	37	218	83	135	66	47	1
	15–20 ..	*492*	343	149	294	241	53	198	102	96	113	87	2
	20 and over ..	*2,368*	1,677	791	672	563	109	1,696	1,014	682	227	191	3
LUDHIANA.	**ALL RELIGIONS** ..	**672,494**	**375,560**	**296,934**	**66,554**	**58,749**	**7,805**	**605,940**	**316,811**	**289,129**	**11,999**	**11,291**	**70**
	0–5 ..	*94,879*	49,189	45,690	..	..	..	94,879	49,189	45,690	..	..	..
	5–10 ..	*84,875*	46,377	38,498	3,690	2,893	797	81,185	43,484	37,701	295	269	2
	10–15 ..	*82,507*	45,930	36,577	7,810	6,448	1,362	74,697	39,482	35,215	1,338	1,255	8
	15–20 ..	*65,920*	37,001	28,919	10,817	9,237	1,580	55,103	27,764	27,339	3,095	2,919	17
	20 and over ..	*344,313*	197,063	147,250	44,237	40,171	4,066	300,076	156,892	143,184	7,271	6,848	42
	HINDU ..	**102,441**	**58,174**	**44,267**	**16,674**	**14,511**	**2,163**	**85,767**	**43,663**	**42,104**	**3,762**	**3,597**	**16**
	0–5 ..	*13,952*	7,002	6,950	..	..	..	13,952	7,002	6,950	..	..	..
	5–10 ..	*12,541*	6,944	5,597	866	659	207	11,675	6,285	5,390	103	93	6
	10–15 ..	*12,146*	6,982	5,164	1,761	1,419	342	10,385	5,563	4,822	377	353	2
	15–20 ..	*9,947*	5,786	4,161	2,671	2,237	434	7,276	3,549	3,727	893	842	5
	20 and over ..	*53,855*	31,400	22,305	11,376	10,196	1,180	42,479	21,264	21,215	2,389	2,309	8
	SIKH ..	**312,829**	**175,676**	**137,153**	**37,585**	**34,572**	**3,013**	**275,244**	**141,104**	**134,140**	**5,179**	**5,054**	**12**
	0–5 ..	*42,358*	22,679	19,679	..	..	..	42,358	22,679	19,679	..	..	..
	5–10 ..	*38,500*	21,464	17,036	1,973	1,609	364	36,527	19,855	16,672	123	116	
	10–15 ..	*37,773*	21,198	16,575	4,380	3,771	609	33,393	17,427	15,966	722	705	1
	15–20 ..	*30,392*	17,085	13,307	5,793	5,167	626	24,599	11,918	12,681	1,580	1,542	3
	20 and over ..	*163,806*	93,250	70,556	25,430	24,025	1,414	138,367	69,225	69,142	2,754	2,691	6
	JAIN ..	**1,419**	**765**	**654**	**355**	**297**	**58**	**1,064**	**468**	**596**	**64**	**63**	..
	0–5 ..	*206*	99	107	..	..	..	206	99	107	..	..	..
	5–10 ..	*179*	92	87	18	13	5	161	79	82	2	2	..
	10–15 ..	*166*	86	80	38	28	10	128	58	70	7	6	..
	15–20 ..	*125*	71	54	55	43	12	70	28	42	13	13	..
	20 and over ..	*743*	417	326	244	213	31	499	204	295	42	42	..
	MUSLIM ..	**235,598**	**130,149**	**105,449**	**10,875**	**8,813**	**2,062**	**224,723**	**121,336**	**103,387**	**2,552**	**2,401**	**151**
	0–5 ..	*35,343*	17,890	17,453	..	..	..	35,343	17,890	17,453	..	..	..
	5–10 ..	*30,905*	16,413	14,492	740	569	171	30,165	15,844	14,321	59	51	8
	10–15 ..	*29,783*	16,212	13,571	1,462	1,152	310	28,321	15,060	13,261	194	171	23
	15–20 ..	*23,376*	12,984	10,392	2,093	1,679	414	21,283	11,305	9,978	525	478	47
	20 and over ..	*116,191*	66,650	49,541	6,580	5,413	1,167	109,611	61,237	48,374	1,774	1,701	73
	CHRISTIAN ..	**2,477**	**1,098**	**1,379**	**751**	**254**	**497**	**1,726**	**844**	**882**	**393**	**128**	**265**
	0–5 ..	*303*	162	141	..	..	..	303	162	141	..	..	..
	5–10 ..	*328*	162	166	76	27	49	252	135	117	7	6	1
	10–15 ..	*338*	165	173	136	46	90	202	119	83	34	16	18
	15–20 ..	*368*	117	251	150	59	91	218	58	160	73	33	40
	20 and over ..	*1,140*	492	648	389	122	267	751	370	381	279	73	206

TABLE XIII.—LITERACY

PART B.—DETAILS OF DISTRICTS AND STATES.

District or State.	Religion and Age.	Population. Total. Persons.	Total. Males.	Total. Females.	Literate. Persons.	Literate. Males.	Literate. Females.	Illiterate. Persons.	Illiterate. Males.	Illiterate. Females.	Literate in English. Persons.	Literate in English. Males.	Literate in English. Females.
1	2	3	4	5	6	7	8	9	10	11	12	13	14
FEROZEPORE.	**ALL RELIGIONS** ..	**1,156,732**	**636,256**	**520,476**	**56,822**	**50,278**	**6,544**	**1,099,910**	**585,978**	**513,932**	**10,405**	**9,708**	**697**
	0—5 ..	*179,965*	91,717	88,248	..	..	..	179,965	91,717	88,248	..	..	..
	5—10 ..	*151,065*	80,607	70,458	3,037	2,316	721	148,028	78,291	69,737	386	295	91
	10—15 ..	*143,260*	78,841	64,419	5,629	4,476	1,153	137,631	74,365	63,266	884	743	141
	15—20 ..	*116,818*	66,420	50,398	8,726	7,465	1,261	108,092	58,955	49,137	2,129	1,963	166
	20 and over ..	*565,624*	318,671	246,953	39,430	36,021	3,409	526,194	282,650	243,544	7,006	6,707	299
	HINDU ..	**208,426**	**117,490**	**90,936**	**25,804**	**22,965**	**2,839**	**182,622**	**94,525**	**88,097**	**4,720**	**4,506**	**214**
	0—5 ..	*31,160*	15,948	15,212	..	..	..	31,160	15,948	15,212	..	..	..
	5—10 ..	*25,935*	13,983	11,952	1,413	1,099	314	24,522	12,884	11,638	170	147	23
	10—15 ..	*25,051*	13,828	11,223	2,546	2,052	494	22,505	11,776	10,729	428	386	42
	15—20 ..	*22,196*	12,775	9,421	3,880	3,341	539	18,316	9,434	8,882	958	904	54
	20 and over ..	*104,084*	60,956	43,128	17,965	16,473	1,492	86,119	44,483	41,636	3,164	3,069	95
	SIKH ..	**388,108**	**213,616**	**174,492**	**17,565**	**15,466**	**2,099**	**370,543**	**198,150**	**172,393**	**2,023**	**1,924**	**99**
	0—5 ..	*57,081*	29,593	27,488	..	..	..	57,081	29,593	27,488	..	..	..
	5—10 ..	*49,621*	27,127	22,494	863	627	236	48,758	26,500	22,258	76	66	10
	10—15 ..	*47,046*	26,196	20,850	1,740	1,339	401	45,306	24,857	20,449	240	213	27
	15—20 ..	*37,781*	21,330	16,451	2,588	2,158	430	35,193	19,172	16,021	520	488	32
	20 and over ..	*196,579*	109,370	87,209	12,374	11,342	1,032	184,205	98,028	86,177	1,187	1,157	30
	JAIN ..	**1,411**	**759**	**652**	**471**	**383**	**88**	**940**	**376**	**564**	**75**	**74**	**1**
	0—5 ..	*201*	105	96	..	..	..	201	105	96	..	..	..
	5—10 ..	*164*	82	82	26	17	9	138	65	73	5	5	..
	10—15 ..	*151*	78	76	41	29	12	113	49	64	8	8	..
	15—20 ..	*136*	79	57	64	49	15	72	30	42	16	16	..
	20 and over ..	*756*	415	341	340	288	52	416	127	289	46	45	1
	MUSLIM ..	**515,430**	**280,323**	**235,107**	**10,726**	**9,601**	**1,125**	**504,704**	**270,722**	**233,982**	**1,943**	**1,856**	**87**
	0—5 ..	*84,173*	42,320	41,853	..	..	..	84,173	42,320	41,853	..	..	..
	5—10 ..	*69,317*	36,149	33,168	615	513	102	68,702	35,636	33,066	64	53	11
	10—15 ..	*65,526*	35,720	29,806	1,144	971	173	64,382	34,749	29,633	125	107	18
	15—20 ..	*52,333*	29,706	22,627	1,803	1,603	200	50,530	28,103	22,427	344	323	21
	20 and over ..	*244,081*	136,428	107,653	7,164	6,514	650	236,917	129,914	107,003	1,410	1,373	37
	CHRISTIAN ..	**7,070**	**4,381**	**2,689**	**1,989**	**1,609**	**380**	**5,081**	**2,772**	**2,309**	**1,609**	**1,313**	**296**
	0—5 ..	*1,043*	543	500	..	..	..	1,043	543	500	..	..	..
	5—10 ..	*815*	469	346	105	48	57	710	421	289	69	22	47
	10—15 ..	*733*	423	310	134	63	71	599	360	239	81	27	54
	15—20 ..	*772*	521	251	354	277	77	418	244	174	286	227	59
	20 and over ..	*3,707*	2,425	1,282	1,396	1,221	175	2,311	1,204	1,107	1,173	1,037	136
LAHORE.	**ALL RELIGIONS** ..	**1,378,570**	**794,389**	**584,181**	**132,883**	**109,951**	**22,932**	**1,245,687**	**684,438**	**561,249**	**48,692**	**42,777**	**5,915**
	0—5 ..	*211,382*	108,052	103,330	..	..	..	211,382	108,052	103,330	..	..	..
	5—10 ..	*170,664*	93,269	77,395	6,803	4,540	2,263	163,861	88,729	75,132	1,215	808	407
	10—15 ..	*159,608*	90,229	69,379	12,661	9,099	3,562	146,947	81,130	65,817	3,198	2,443	755
	15—20 ..	*139,813*	83,442	56,371	21,379	17,468	3,911	118,434	65,974	52,460	0,003	7,927	1,076
	20 and over ..	*697,103*	419,397	277,706	92,040	78,844	13,196	605,063	340,553	264,510	35,276	31,599	3,677
	HINDU ..	**258,719**	**159,112**	**99,607**	**48,699**	**41,703**	**6,996**	**210,020**	**117,409**	**92,611**	**17,639**	**16,461**	**1,178**
	0—5 ..	*35,705*	18,690	17,015	..	..	..	35,705	18,690	17,015	..	..	..
	5—10 ..	*28,346*	15,323	13,023	1,960	1,271	689	26,386	14,052	12,334	186	100	86
	10—15 ..	*27,324*	15,716	11,608	4,121	3,056	1,065	23,203	12,660	10,543	974	792	182
	15—20 ..	*29,055*	18,983	10,072	7,815	6,561	1,254	21,240	12,422	8,818	3,221	2,962	259
	20 and over ..	*138,289*	90,400	47,889	34,803	30,815	3,988	103,486	59,585	43,901	13,258	12,607	651
	SIKH ..	**244,304**	**137,580**	**106,724**	**14,117**	**12,389**	**1,728**	**230,187**	**125,191**	**104,996**	**3,461**	**2,977**	**484**
	0—5 ..	*37,354*	19,056	18,298	..	..	..	37,354	19,056	18,298	..	..	..
	5—10 ..	*30,628*	17,069	13,559	629	480	149	29,999	16,589	13,410	71	42	29
	10—15 ..	*28,022*	16,172	11,850	1,228	989	239	26,794	15,183	11,611	210	156	54
	15—20 ..	*22,784*	13,466	9,318	2,141	1,900	241	20,643	11,566	9,077	924	769	155
	20 and over ..	*125,516*	71,817	53,699	10,119	9,020	1,099	115,397	62,797	52,600	2,256	2,010	246
	JAIN ..	**1,450**	**777**	**673**	**475**	**370**	**105**	**975**	**407**	**568**	**169**	**158**	**11**
	0—5 ..	*243*	121	124	..	..	..	243	121	124	..	..	..
	5—10 ..	*136*	100	86	31	24	7	155	76	79	7	6	1
	10—15 ..	*173*	96	77	57	41	16	116	55	61	16	14	2
	15—20 ..	*167*	93	74	93	69	24	74	24	50	37	35	2
	20 and over ..	*679*	367	312	294	236	58	385	131	254	109	103	6
	MUSLIM ..	**815,820**	**464,043**	**351,777**	**60,121**	**49,361**	**10,760**	**755,699**	**414,682**	**341,017**	**20,532**	**18,822**	**1,710**
	0—5 ..	*128,838*	65,479	63,359	..	..	..	128,838	65,479	63,359	..	..	..
	5—10 ..	*104,475*	56,725	47,750	3,641	2,523	1,118	100,834	54,202	46,632	677	555	122
	10—15 ..	*97,539*	54,532	43,007	6,503	4,700	1,803	91,036	49,832	41,204	1,573	1,328	245
	15—20 ..	*81,530*	47,526	34,004	9,952	8,056	1,896	71,578	39,470	32,108	3,775	3,460	315
	20 and over ..	*403,438*	239,781	163,657	40,025	34,082	5,943	363,413	205,699	157,714	14,507	13,479	1,028
	CHRISTIAN ..	**57,097**	**32,107**	**24,990**	**9,342**	**6,043**	**3,299**	**47,755**	**26,064**	**21,691**	**6,796**	**4,294**	**2,502**
	0—5 ..	*9,093*	4,645	4,448	..	..	..	9,093	4,645	4,448	..	..	..
	5—10 ..	*6,898*	3,979	2,919	536	239	297	6,362	3,740	2,622	268	102	166
	10—15 ..	*6,419*	3,627	2,792	742	·06	436	5,677	3,321	2,356	419	150	269
	15—20 ..	*6,119*	3,271	2,848	1,366	874	492	4,753	2,397	2,356	1,038	696	342
	20 and over ..	*28,568*	16,585	11,983	6,698	4,624	2,074	21,870	11,961	9,909	5,071	3,346	1,725

BY RELIGION AND AGE.

PART B.—DETAILS OF DISTRICTS AND STATES.—*continued.*

District or State.	Religion and Age.	Population. Total. Persons.	Population. Total. Males.	Population. Total. Females.	Population. Literate. Persons.	Population. Literate. Males.	Population. Literate. Females.	Population. Illiterate. Persons.	Population. Illiterate. Males.	Population. Illiterate. Females.	Literate in English. Persons.	Literate in English. Males.	Literate in English. Females.
1	2	3	4	5	6	7	8	9	10	11	12	13	14
AMRITSAR.	ALL RELIGIONS ..	1,117,120	621,040	496,080	75,026	64,027	10,999	1,042,094	557,013	485,081	17,422	15,499	1,923
	0—5 ..	*171,086*	87,360	83,726	..	..	..	171,086	87,360	83,726	..	..	..
	5—10 ..	*145,808*	79,062	66,746	3,901	2,998	903	141,907	76,064	65,843	451	352	99
	10—15 ..	*135,346*	75,767	59,579	7,935	6,366	1,569	127,411	69,401	58,010	1,324	1,156	168
	15—20 ..	*104,058*	59,569	44,489	11,898	9,857	2,041	92,160	49,712	42,448	3,469	3,096	373
	20 and over ..	*560,822*	319,282	241,540	51,292	44,806	6,486	509,530	274,476	235,054	12,178	10,895	1,283
	HINDU ..	174,392	101,185	73,207	26,896	23,760	3,136	147,496	77,425	70,071	5,450	5,278	172
	0—5 ..	*24,331*	12,284	12,047	..	..	..	24,331	12,284	12,047	..	..	..
	5—10 ..	*21,665*	11,724	9,941	1,091	874	217	20,574	10,850	9,724	79	73	6
	10—15 ..	*20,488*	11,683	8,805	2,356	1,900	456	18,132	9,783	8,349	311	301	10
	15—20 ..	*17,793*	11,140	6,653	4,124	3,488	636	13,669	7,652	6,017	975	941	34
	20 and over ..	*90,115*	54,354	35,761	19,325	17,498	1,827	70,790	36,856	33,934	4,085	3,963	122
	SIKH ..	399,951	219,788	180,163	23,219	19,922	3,297	376,732	199,866	176,866	5,443	5,360	83
	0—5 ..	*60,676*	31,384	29,292	..	..	..	60,676	31,384	29,292	..	..	..
	5—10 ..	*51,541*	28,327	23,214	1,195	893	302	50,346	27,434	22,912	162	159	3
	10—15 ..	*47,525*	27,023	20,502	2,406	1,912	494	45,119	25,111	20,008	484	470	14
	15—20 ..	*35,114*	20,022	15,092	3,570	3,093	477	31,544	16,929	14,615	1,283	1,264	19
	20 and over ..	*205,095*	113,032	92,063	16,048	14,024	2,024	189,047	99,008	90,039	3,514	3,467	47
	JAIN ..	1,272	691	581	257	166	91	1,015	525	490	30	29	1
	0—5 ..	*209*	106	103	..	..	..	209	106	103	..	..	..
	5—10 ..	*169*	86	83	29	17	12	140	09	71	..	..	..
	10—15 ..	*160*	84	76	48	29	19	112	55	57	2	2	..
	15—20 ..	*141*	81	60	53	31	22	88	50	38	5	5	..
	20 and over ..	*593*	334	259	127	89	38	466	245	221	23	22	1
	MUSLIM ..	524,676	290,387	234,289	23,723	19,711	4,012	500,953	270,676	230,277	6,073	4,532	1,541
	0—5 ..	*83,031*	42,162	40,869	..	..	..	83,031	42,162	40,869	..	..	..
	5—10 ..	*70,074*	37,683	32,391	1,527	1,182	345	68,547	36,501	32,046	190	106	84
	10—15 ..	*64,987*	35,801	29,186	3,006	2,470	536	61,981	33,331	28,650	486	356	130
	15—20 ..	*49,372*	27,435	21,937	3,973	3,166	807	45,399	24,269	21,130	1,125	831	294
	20 and over ..	*257,212*	147,306	109,906	15,217	12,893	2,324	241,995	134,413	107,582	4,272	3,239	1,033
	CHRISTIAN ..	16,619	8,862	7,757	905	450	455	15,714	8,412	7,302	415	289	126
	0—5 ..	*2,813*	1,412	1,401	..	..	..	2,813	1,412	1,401	..	..	..
	5—10 ..	*2,335*	1,230	1,105	59	32	27	2,276	1,198	1,078	20	14	6
	10—15 ..	*2,165*	1,165	1,000	118	54	64	2,047	1,111	936	41	27	14
	15—20 ..	*1,612*	877	735	176	77	99	1,436	800	636	79	53	26
	20 and over ..	*7,694*	4,178	3,516	552	287	265	7,142	3,891	3,251	275	195	80
GURDASPUR.	ALL RELIGIONS ..	970,898	531,935	438,963	41,443	36,877	4,566	929,455	495,058	434,397	7,500	7,072	428
	0—5 ..	*159,462*	80,930	78,532	..	..	..	159,462	80,930	78,532	..	..	..
	5—10 ..	*134,576*	72,159	62,417	2,359	1,970	389	132,217	70,189	62,028	230	201	29
	10—15 ..	*124,667*	68,266	56,401	5,061	4,310	751	119,606	63,956	55,650	776	714	62
	15—20 ..	*89,594*	49,036	40,558	6,905	5,950	955	82,689	43,086	39,603	1,709	1,621	88
	20 and over ..	*462,599*	261,544	201,055	27,118	24,647	2,471	435,481	236,897	198,584	4,785	4,536	249
	HINDU ..	249,404	136,160	113,244	17,499	15,282	2,217	231,905	120,878	111,027	2,997	2,909	88
	0—5 ..	*39,368*	19,970	19,398	..	..	..	39,368	19,970	19,398	..	..	..
	5—10 ..	*32,742*	17,383	15,359	907	688	219	31,835	16,605	15,140	73	67	6
	10—15 ..	*30,742*	16,625	14,117	2,006	1,604	402	28,736	15,021	13,715	266	250	16
	15—20 ..	*23,209*	12,718	10,491	2,873	2,403	470	20,336	10,315	10,021	659	633	26
	20 and over ..	*123,343*	69,464	53,879	11,713	10,587	1,126	111,630	58,877	52,753	1,999	1,959	40
	SIKH ..	178,471	99,724	78,747	7,754	7,026	728	170,717	92,698	78,019	1,201	1,179	22
	0—5 ..	*28,017*	14,380	13,637	..	..	..	28,017	14,380	13,637	..	..	..
	5—10 ..	*23,953*	13,115	10,838	423	375	48	23,530	12,740	10,790	34	32	2
	10—15 ..	*22,041*	12,455	9,586	890	791	99	21,151	11,664	9,487	137	132	5
	15—20 ..	*15,356*	8,656	6,700	1,181	1,034	147	14,175	7,622	6,553	282	276	6
	20 and over ..	*89,104*	51,118	37,986	5,260	4,826	434	83,844	46,292	37,552	748	739	9
	JAIN ..	15	8	7	8	3	5	7	5	2	3	3	..
	0—5 ..	*6*	4	2	..	..	..	6	4	2	..	..	..
	5—10 ..	*1*	1	..	..	..	..	1	1	..	..	..	..
	10—15 ..	..	..	..	..	..	..	..	..	..	..	..	..
	15—20 ..	*2*	1	1	2	1	1	..	..	..	1	1	..
	20 and over ..	*6*	2	4	6	2	4	..	..	..	2	2	..
	MUSLIM ..	493,216	268,771	224,445	15,169	13,892	1,277	478,047	254,879	223,168	2,790	2,645	145
	0—5 ..	*83,436*	42,199	41,237	..	..	..	83,436	42,199	41,237	..	..	..
	5—10 ..	*70,594*	37,694	32,900	959	858	101	69,635	36,836	32,799	85	77	8
	10—15 ..	*65,180*	35,438	29,742	2,046	1,829	217	63,134	33,609	29,525	309	285	24
	15—20 ..	*46,253*	25,065	21,188	2,669	2,387	282	43,584	22,678	20,906	675	633	42
	20 and over ..	*227,753*	128,375	99,378	9,495	8,818	677	218,258	119,557	98,701	1,721	1,650	71
	CHRISTIAN ..	43,243	23,702	19,541	946	635	311	42,297	23,067	19,230	505	332	173
	0—5 ..	*7,624*	3,885	3,739	..	..	..	7,624	3,885	3,739	..	..	..
	5—10 ..	*6,381*	3,467	2,914	66	47	19	6,315	3,420	2,895	38	25	13
	10—15 ..	*5,871*	3,300	2,571	111	82	29	5,760	3,218	2,542	64	47	17
	15—20 ..	*4,095*	2,236	1,859	168	116	52	3,927	2,120	1,807	90	76	14
	20 and over ..	*19,272*	10,814	8,458	601	390	211	18,671	10,424	8,247	313	184	129

TABLE XIII.—LITERACY

PART B.—DETAILS OF DISTRICTS AND STATES.

District or State.	Religion and Age.	Population. Total. Persons.	Population. Total. Males.	Population. Total. Females.	Literate. Persons.	Literate. Males.	Literate. Females.	Illiterate. Persons.	Illiterate. Males.	Illiterate. Females.	Literate in English. Persons.	Literate in English. Males.	Literate in English. Females.
1	2	3	4	5	6	7	8	9	10	11	12	13	14
SIALKOT.	**ALL RELIGIONS** ..	**979,617**	**537,301**	**442,316**	**39,419**	**34,441**	**4,978**	**940,198**	**502,860**	**437,338**	**9,220**	**8,333**	**887**
	0—5 ..	*160,325*	80,186	80,139	..	..	..	160,325	80,186	80,139	..	..	..
	5—10 ..	*129,672*	70,606	59,066	2,271	1,786	485	127,401	68,820	58,581	395	321	74
	10—15 ..	*117,023*	65,575	51,448	4,726	3,862	864	112,297	61,713	50,584	937	820	117
	15—20 ..	*87,796*	47,541	40,255	6,818	5,808	1,010	80,978	41,733	39,245	1,801	1,623	178
	20 and over ..	*484,801*	273,393	211,408	25,604	22,985	2,619	459,197	250,408	208,789	6,087	5,569	518
	HINDU ..	**206,395**	**111,853**	**94,542**	**10,601**	**9,178**	**1,423**	**195,794**	**102,675**	**93,119**	**3,259**	**3,045**	**214**
	0—5 ..	*31,588*	15,177	16,411	..	..	..	31,588	15,177	16,411	..	..	..
	5—10 ..	*26,857*	14,109	12,748	745	580	165	26,112	13,529	12,583	173	147	26
	10—15 ..	*24,522*	13,255	11,267	1,411	1,151	260	23,111	12,104	11,007	330	300	30
	15—20 ..	*17,338*	9,412	7,926	1,744	1,489	255	15,594	7,923	7,671	537	496	41
	20 and over ..	*106,090*	59,900	46,190	6,701	5,958	743	99,389	53,942	45,447	2,219	2,102	117
	SIKH ..	**94,955**	**53,996**	**40,959**	**5,174**	**4,407**	**767**	**89,781**	**49,589**	**40,192**	**989**	**907**	**82**
	0—5 ..	*14,599*	7,573	7,026	..	..	..	14,599	7,573	7,026	..	..	..
	5—10 ..	*12,003*	6,634	5,369	260	193	67	11,743	6,441	5,302	48	37	11
	10—15 ..	*10,883*	6,169	4,714	524	407	117	10,359	5,762	4,597	111	92	19
	15—20 ..	*8,130*	4,775	3,355	795	650	145	7,335	4,125	3,210	212	197	15
	20 and over ..	*49,340*	28,845	20,495	3,595	3,157	438	45,745	25,688	20,057	618	581	37
	JAIN ..	**2,236**	**1,227**	**1,009**	**324**	**212**	**112**	**1,912**	**1,015**	**897**	**153**	**105**	**48**
	0—5 ..	*361*	193	168	..	..	..	361	193	168	..	..	..
	5—10 ..	*299*	161	138	34	22	12	265	139	126	13	9	4
	10—15 ..	*268*	137	131	53	33	20	215	104	111	27	20	7
	15—20 ..	*231*	120	111	64	36	28	167	84	83	31	20	11
	20 and over ..	*1,077*	616	461	173	121	52	904	495	409	82	56	26
	MUSLIM ..	**609,633**	**333,637**	**275,996**	**19,419**	**17,657**	**1,762**	**590,214**	**315,980**	**274,234**	**3,839**	**3,691**	**148**
	0—5 ..	*102,200*	51,373	50,827	..	..	..	102,200	51,373	50,827	..	..	..
	5—10 ..	*81,166*	44,726	36,440	1,073	911	162	80,093	43,815	36,278	109	99	10
	10—15 ..	*73,033*	41,459	31,574	2,376	2,090	286	70,657	39,369	31,288	375	355	20
	15—20 ..	*56,063*	29,815	26,248	3,433	3,066	367	52,630	26,749	25,881	848	809	39
	20 and over ..	*297,171*	166,264	130,907	12,537	11,590	947	284,634	154,674	129,960	2,507	2,428	79
	CHRISTIAN ..	**66,365**	**36,579**	**29,786**	**3,895**	**2,984**	**911**	**62,470**	**33,595**	**28,875**	**975**	**582**	**393**
	0—5 ..	*11,568*	5,867	5,701	..	..	..	11,568	5,867	5,701	..	..	..
	5—10 ..	*9,343*	4,975	4,368	157	79	78	9,186	4,896	4,290	51	28	23
	10—15 ..	*8,313*	4,554	3,759	359	179	180	7,954	4,375	3,579	92	52	40
	15—20 ..	*6,029*	3,418	2,611	782	567	215	5,247	2,851	2,396	172	101	71
	20 and over ..	*31,112*	17,765	13,347	2,597	2,159	438	28,515	15,606	12,909	660	401	259
GUJRANWALA	**ALL RELIGIONS** ..	**736,138**	**408,606**	**327,532**	**39,503**	**32,802**	**6,701**	**696,635**	**375,804**	**320,831**	**7,033**	**6,376**	**657**
	0—5 ..	*118,868*	60,560	58,308	..	..	..	118,868	60,560	58,308	..	..	..
	5—10 ..	*96,335*	51,693	44,642	2,401	1,797	604	93,934	49,896	44,038	148	133	15
	10—15 ..	*83,645*	46,530	37,115	4,482	3,433	1,049	79,163	43,097	36,066	596	526	70
	15—20 ..	*65,536*	37,059	28,477	6,103	4,864	1,239	59,433	32,195	27,238	1,421	1,263	158
	20 and over ..	*371,754*	212,764	158,990	26,517	22,708	3,809	345,237	190,056	155,181	4,868	4,454	414
	HINDU ..	**92,762**	**52,201**	**40,561**	**16,748**	**13,767**	**2,981**	**76,014**	**38,434**	**37,580**	**3,791**	**3,406**	**385**
	0—5 ..	*13,670*	6,929	6,741	..	..	..	13,670	6,929	6,741	..	..	..
	5—10 ..	*11,680*	6,257	5,423	1,013	725	288	10,667	5,532	5,135	71	67	4
	10—15 ..	*10,620*	5,873	4,747	1,899	1,389	510	8,721	4,484	4,237	320	282	38
	15—20 ..	*8,490*	4,934	3,556	2,460	1,892	568	6,030	3,042	2,988	752	661	91
	20 and over ..	*48,302*	28,208	20,094	11,376	9,761	1,615	36,926	18,447	18,479	2,648	2,396	252
	SIKH ..	**71,595**	**41,075**	**30,520**	**6,060**	**4,806**	**1,254**	**65,535**	**36,269**	**29,266**	**1,264**	**1,178**	**86**
	0—5 ..	*11,111*	5,823	5,288	..	..	..	11,111	5,823	5,288	..	..	..
	5—10 ..	*9,005*	4,933	4,072	373	250	123	8,632	4,683	3,949	39	34	5
	10—15 ..	*7,920*	4,564	3,356	682	487	195	7,238	4,077	3,161	127	111	16
	15—20 ..	*6,191*	3,733	2,458	890	671	219	5,301	3,062	2,239	268	240	28
	20 and over ..	*37,368*	22,022	15,346	4,115	3,398	717	33,253	18,624	14,629	830	793	37
	JAIN ..	**1,071**	**593**	**478**	**331**	**275**	**56**	**740**	**318**	**422**	**89**	**86**	**3**
	0—5 ..	*176*	95	81	..	..	..	176	95	81	..	..	..
	5—10 ..	*156*	92	64	35	29	6	121	63	58	2	2	..
	10—15 ..	*152*	89	63	58	48	10	94	41	53	7	7	..
	15—20 ..	*121*	67	54	56	43	13	65	24	41	16	15	1
	20 and over ..	*466*	250	216	182	155	27	284	95	189	64	62	2
	MUSLIM ..	**521,343**	**287,794**	**233,549**	**15,790**	**13,564**	**2,226**	**505,553**	**274,230**	**231,323**	**1,638**	**1,558**	**80**
	0—5 ..	*85,019*	43,198	41,821	..	..	..	85,019	43,198	41,821	..	..	..
	5—10 ..	*68,652*	36,707	31,945	953	769	184	67,699	35,938	31,761	31	27	4
	10—15 ..	*59,136*	32,769	26,367	1,781	1,457	324	57,355	31,312	26,043	121	111	10
	15—20 ..	*46,344*	25,921	20,423	2,600	2,187	413	43,744	23,734	20,010	339	315	24
	20 and over ..	*262,192*	149,199	112,993	10,456	9,151	1,305	251,736	140,048	111,688	1,147	1,105	42
	CHRISTIAN ..	**49,364**	**26,940**	**22,424**	**574**	**390**	**184**	**48,790**	**26,550**	**22,240**	**251**	**148**	**103**
	0—5 ..	*8,892*	4,515	4,377	..	..	..	8,892	4,515	4,377	..	..	..
	5—10 ..	*6,842*	3,704	3,138	27	24	3	6,815	3,680	3,135	5	3	2
	10—15 ..	*5,816*	3,234	2,582	62	52	10	5,754	3,182	2,572	21	15	6
	15—20 ..	*4,390*	2,404	1,986	97	71	26	4,293	2,333	1,960	46	32	14
	20 and over ..	*23,424*	13,083	10,341	388	243	145	23,036	12,840	10,196	179	98	81

BY RELIGION AND AGE.

PART B.—DETAILS OF DISTRICTS AND STATES.—*continued.*

District or State.	Religion and Age.	Population. Total. Persons.	Total. Males.	Total. Females.	Literate. Persons.	Literate. Males.	Literate. Females.	Illiterate. Persons.	Illiterate. Males.	Illiterate. Females.	Literate in English. Persons.	Literate in English. Males.	Literate in English. Females.
1	2	3	4	5	6	7	8	9	10	11	12	13	14
SHEIKHUPURA.	ALL RELIGIONS ..	696,732	384,890	312,342	26,868	24,063	2,805	669,864	360,327	309,537	3,535	3,381	154
	0—5 ..	*122,301*	62,444	59,857	..	..	..	122,301	62,444	59,857	..	..	..
	5—10 ..	*96,707*	52,415	44,292	1,359	1,122	237	95,348	51,293	44,053	90	86	4
	10—15 ..	*84,574*	46,949	37,625	2,814	2,376	438	81,760	44,573	37,187	310	293	17
	15—20 ..	*63,059*	35,536	27,523	4,239	3,691	548	58,820	31,845	26,975	723	685	38
	20 and over ..	*330,091*	187,046	143,045	18,456	16,874	1,582	311,635	170,172	141,463	2,412	2,317	95
	HINDU ..	70,146	40,138	30,018	10,065	8,638	1,427	60,081	31,495	28,586	1,487	1,395	92
	0—5 ..	*11,218*	5,697	5,521	..	..	..	11,218	5,697	5,521	..	..	..
	5—10 ..	*9,227*	4,975	4,252	475	333	142	8,752	4,642	4,110	30	28	2
	10—15 ..	*8,306*	4,671	3,635	964	709	255	7,342	3,962	3,380	102	90	12
	15—20 ..	*6,706*	3,983	2,723	1,506	1,219	287	5,200	2,764	2,436	243	217	26
	20 and over ..	*34,689*	20,807	13,882	7,120	6,377	743	27,569	14,430	13,139	1,112	1,060	52
	SIKH ..	119,477	66,762	52,715	8,076	7,111	965	111,401	59,651	51,750	898	878	20
	0—5 ..	*20,257*	10,600	9,657	..	..	..	20,257	10,600	9,657	..	..	..
	5—10 ..	*16,167*	8,930	7,237	365	295	70	15,802	8,635	7,167	23	21	2
	10—15 ..	*14,301*	8,116	6,185	780	655	125	13,521	7,461	6,060	101	96	5
	15—20 ..	*10,749*	6,156	4,593	1,251	1,077	174	9,498	5,079	4,419	232	227	5
	20 and over ..	*58,003*	32,960	25,043	5,680	5,084	596	52,323	27,876	24,447	542	534	8
	JAIN ..	100	53	47	33	28	5	67	25	42	5	4	1
	0—5 ..	*15*	5	10	..	..	..	15	5	10	..	..	..
	5—10 ..	*17*	10	7	6	5	1	11	5	6	..	..	..
	10—15 ..	*18*	9	9	3	2	1	15	7	8	1	1	..
	15—20 ..	*10*	6	4	5	4	1	5	2	3	3	2	1
	20 and over ..	*40*	23	17	19	17	2	21	6	15	1	1	..
	MUSLIM ..	445,996	244,064	201,932	8,308	8,008	300	437,688	236,056	201,632	1,040	1,040	..
	0—5 ..	*79,548*	40,524	39,024	..	..	..	79,548	40,524	39,024	..	..	..
	5—10 ..	*62,245*	33,654	28,591	491	471	20	61,754	33,183	28,571	35	35	..
	10—15 ..	*54,060*	29,766	24,294	1,024	979	45	53,036	28,787	24,249	104	104	..
	15—20 ..	*40,149*	22,363	17,786	1,417	1,354	63	38,732	21,009	17,723	231	231	..
	20 and over ..	*209,994*	117,757	92,237	5,376	5,204	172	204,618	112,553	92,065	670	670	..
	CHRISTIAN ..	49,266	26,895	22,371	270	165	105	48,996	26,730	22,266	101	60	41
	0—5 ..	*9,065*	4,496	4,569	..	..	..	9,065	4,496	4,569	..	..	..
	5—10 ..	*7,297*	3,898	3,399	16	12	4	7,281	3,886	3,395	2	2	..
	10—15 ..	*6,322*	3,510	2,812	25	13	12	6,297	3,497	2,800	1	1	..
	15—20 ..	*4,425*	2,451	1,974	43	21	22	4,382	2,430	1,952	13	7	6
	20 and over ..	*22,157*	12,540	9,617	186	119	67	21,971	12,421	9,550	85	50	35
GUJRAT.	ALL RELIGIONS ..	922,427	498,336	424,091	44,620	39,402	5,218	877,807	458,934	418,873	7,468	7,297	171
	0—5 ..	*149,693*	76,574	73,119	..	..	..	140,693	76,574	73,119	..	..	..
	5—10 ..	*125,099*	66,865	58,234	2,127	1,674	453	122,972	65,191	57,781	210	197	13
	10—15 ..	*108,762*	60,009	48,753	4,504	3,650	854	104,258	56,359	47,899	637	617	20
	15—20 ..	*76,580*	42,104	34,476	6,518	5,480	1,038	70,062	36,624	33,438	1,388	1,359	29
	20 and over ..	*462,293*	252,784	209,509	31,471	28,598	2,873	430,822	224,186	206,636	5,233	5,124	109
	HINDU ..	72,346	39,425	32,921	13,269	11,447	1,822	59,077	27,978	31,099	2,766	2,690	76
	0—5 ..	*11,413*	5,822	5,591	..	..	..	11,413	5,822	5,591	..	..	..
	5—10 ..	*9,619*	5,076	4,543	621	455	166	8,998	4,621	4,377	52	43	9
	10—15 ..	*8,617*	4,679	3,938	1,302	989	313	7,315	3,690	3,625	191	179	12
	15—20 ..	*6,416*	3,553	2,863	1,969	1,600	369	4,447	1,953	2,494	500	486	14
	20 and over ..	*36,281*	20,295	15,986	9,377	8,403	974	26,904	11,892	15,012	2,023	1,982	41
	SIKH ..	59,188	30,795	28,393	13,233	10,938	2,295	45,955	19,857	26,098	1,996	1,990	6
	0—5 ..	*10,118*	5,220	4,898	..	..	..	10,118	5,220	4,898	..	..	..
	5—10 ..	*8,463*	4,512	3,951	553	361	192	7,910	4,151	3,759	94	94	..
	10—15 ..	*7,486*	4,001	3,485	1,125	764	361	6,361	3,237	3,124	215	215	..
	15—20 ..	*5,202*	2,619	2,583	1,647	1,194	453	3,555	1,425	2,130	310	309	1
	20 and over ..	*27,919*	14,443	13,476	9,908	8,619	1,289	18,011	5,824	12,187	1,377	1,372	5
	JAIN ..	32	18	14	1	..	1	31	18	13	..	..	..
	0—5 ..	*6*	4	2	..	..	..	6	4	2	..	..	..
	5—10 ..	*5*	3	2	1	..	1	4	3	1	..	..	..
	10—15 ..	*3*	1	2	..	..	..	3	1	2	..	..	..
	15—20 ..	*6*	3	3	..	..	..	6	3	3	..	..	..
	20 and over ..	*12*	7	5	..	..	..	12	7	5	..	..	..
	MUSLIM ..	786,750	425,716	361,034	17,870	16,855	1,015	768,880	408,861	360,019	2,584	2,544	40
	0—5 ..	*127,467*	65,160	62,307	..	..	..	127,467	65,160	62,307	..	..	..
	5—10 ..	*106,457*	56,969	49,488	939	849	90	105,518	56,120	49,398	60	58	2
	10—15 ..	*92,173*	51,060	41,113	2,059	1,883	176	90,114	49,177	40,937	226	220	6
	15—20 ..	*64,578*	35,714	28,864	2,875	2,667	208	61,703	33,047	28,656	568	558	10
	20 and over ..	*396,075*	216,813	179,262	11,997	11,456	541	384,078	205,357	178,721	1,730	1,708	22
	CHRISTIAN ..	3,097	1,746	1,351	209	124	85	2,888	1,622	1,266	122	73	49
	0—5 ..	*553*	293	260	..	..	..	353	293	260	..	..	..
	5—10 ..	*443*	238	205	11	7	4	432	231	201	4	2	2
	10—15 ..	*377*	204	173	15	11	4	362	193	169	5	3	2
	15—20 ..	*277*	159	118	21	13	8	256	146	110	10	6	4
	20 and over ..	*1,447*	852	595	162	93	69	1,285	759	526	103	62	41

TABLE XIII.—LITERACY

PART B.—DETAILS OF DISTRICTS AND STATES.

District or State.	Religion and Age.	Population. Total. Persons.	Total. Males.	Total. Females.	Literate. Persons.	Literate. Males.	Literate. Females.	Illiterate. Persons.	Illiterate. Males.	Illiterate. Females.	Literate in English. Persons.	Literate in English. Males.	Literate in English. Females.
1	2	3	4	5	6	7	8	9	10	11	12	13	14
SHAHPUR.	ALL RELIGIONS ..	821,490	445,836	375,654	45,284	37,121	8,163	776,206	408,715	367,491	7,113	6,694	419
	0—5 ..	*130,738*	66,475	64,263	..	..	..	130,738	66,475	64,263	..	..	..
	5—10 ..	*115,791*	62,623	53,168	2,711	1,995	716	113,080	60,628	52,452	248	220	28
	10—15 ..	*98,893*	54,673	44,220	5,309	3,934	1,375	93,584	50,739	42,845	826	740	86
	15—20 ..	*73,000*	39,800	33,200	7,327	5,570	1,757	65,673	34,230	31,443	1,500	1,367	133
	20 and over ..	*403,068*	222,265	180,803	29,937	25,622	4,315	373,131	196,643	176,488	4,539	4,367	172
	HINDU ..	88,970	48,641	40,329	17,856	14,737	3,119	71,114	33,904	37,210	3,175	3,090	85
	0—5 ..	*13,625*	6,939	6,686	..	..	..	13,625	6,939	6,686	..	..	..
	5—10 ..	*11,932*	6,286	5,646	1,014	711	303	10,918	5,575	5,343	112	103	9
	10—15 ..	*10,713*	5,824	4,889	1,928	1,418	510	8,785	4,406	4,379	347	329	18
	15—20 ..	*8,341*	4,751	3,590	2,596	2,017	579	5,745	2,734	3,011	583	562	21
	20 and over ..	*44,359*	24,841	19,518	12,318	10,591	1,727	32,041	14,250	17,791	2,133	2,096	37
	SIKH ..	40,074	22,200	17,874	10,808	7,185	3,623	29,266	15,015	14,251	1,330	1,164	166
	0—5 ..	*6,615*	3,429	3,186	..	..	..	6,615	3,429	3,186	..	..	..
	5—10 ..	*5,723*	3,054	2,669	697	408	289	5,026	2,646	2,380	57	43	14
	10—15 ..	*5,062*	2,823	2,239	1,387	757	630	3,675	2,066	1,609	209	164	45
	15—20 ..	*3,784*	2,128	1,656	1,836	974	862	1,948	1,154	794	328	264	64
	20 and over ..	*18,890*	10,766	8,124	6,888	5,046	1,842	12,002	5,720	6,282	736	693	43
	JAIN ..	14	8	6	6	5	1	8	3	5	1	1	..
	0—5 ..	*2*	1	1	..	..	..	2	1	1	..	..	..
	5—10 ..	*2*	1	1	..	..	..	2	1	1	..	..	..
	10—15 ..	*2*	1	1	..	..	..	2	1	1	..	..	..
	15—20 ..	..	..	..	..	..	..	..	..	..	..	..	..
	20 and over ..	*8*	5	3	6	5	1	2	..	2	1	1	..
	MUSLIM ..	679,546	367,879	311,667	16,216	14,933	1,283	663,330	352,946	310,384	2,421	2,311	110
	0—5 ..	*108,205*	54,956	53,249	..	..	..	108,205	54,956	53,249	..	..	..
	5—10 ..	*96,212*	52,258	43,954	977	862	115	95,235	51,396	43,839	76	71	5
	10—15 ..	*81,416*	45,096	36,320	1,947	1,728	219	79,469	43,368	36,101	259	237	22
	15—20 ..	*59,633*	32,221	27,412	2,832	2,541	291	56,801	29,680	27,121	567	528	39
	20 and over ..	*334,080*	183,348	150,732	10,460	9,802	658	323,620	173,546	150,074	1,519	1,475	44
	CHRISTIAN ..	11,294	6,223	5,071	356	222	134	10,938	6,001	4,937	181	123	58
	0—5 ..	*2,054*	1,050	1,004	..	..	..	2,054	1,050	1,004	..	..	..
	5—10 ..	*1,675*	892	783	20	12	8	1,655	880	775	3	3	..
	10—15 ..	*1,478*	810	668	42	27	15	1,436	783	653	10	9	1
	15—20 ..	*1,084*	611	473	55	31	24	1,029	580	449	22	13	9
	20 and over ..	*5,003*	2,860	2,143	239	152	87	4,764	2,708	2,056	146	98	48
JHELUM.	ALL RELIGIONS ..	541,076	282,714	258,362	34,062	29,607	4,455	507,014	253,107	253,907	4,693	4,387	306
	0—5 ..	*82,514*	42,379	40,135	..	..	..	82,514	42,379	40,135	..	..	..
	5—10 ..	*70,773*	38,094	32,679	2,054	1,702	352	68,719	36,392	32,327	172	153	19
	10—15 ..	*61,438*	33,711	27,727	4,173	3,476	697	57,265	30,235	27,030	462	412	50
	15—20 ..	*45,024*	23,535	21,489	5,691	4,784	907	39,333	18,751	20,582	920	847	73
	20 and over ..	*281,327*	144,995	136,332	22,144	19,645	2,499	259,183	125,350	133,833	3,139	2,975	164
	HINDU ..	36,068	19,155	16,913	8,924	7,350	1,574	27,144	11,805	15,339	1,640	1,574	66
	0—5 ..	*5,348*	2,707	2,641	..	..	..	5,348	2,707	2,641	..	..	..
	5—10 ..	*4,705*	2,468	2,237	488	348	140	4,217	2,120	2,097	35	32	3
	10—15 ..	*4,192*	2,228	1,964	951	697	254	3,241	1,531	1,710	122	109	13
	15—20 ..	*3,210*	1,778	1,432	1,315	1,011	304	1,895	767	1,128	289	270	19
	20 and over ..	*18,613*	9,974	8,639	6,170	5,294	876	12,443	4,680	7,763	1,194	1,163	31
	SIKH ..	22,030	11,409	10,621	6,605	5,024	1,581	15,425	6,385	9,040	794	718	76
	0—5 ..	*3,476*	1,800	1,676	..	..	..	3,476	1,800	1,676	..	..	..
	5—10 ..	*3,015*	1,578	1,437	356	237	119	2,659	1,341	1,318	17	14	3
	10—15 ..	*2,653*	1,378	1,275	715	479	236	1,938	899	1,039	85	72	13
	15—20 ..	*1,382*	983	899	991	693	298	891	290	601	178	157	21
	20 and over ..	*11,004*	5,670	5,334	4,543	3,615	928	6,461	2,055	4,406	514	475	39
	JAIN ..	209	106	103	59	52	7	150	54	96	17	17	..
	0—5 ..	*31*	15	16	..	..	..	31	15	16	..	..	..
	5—10 ..	*27*	16	11	5	4	1	22	12	10	..	..	..
	10—15 ..	*26*	14	12	7	5	2	19	9	10	1	1	..
	15—20 ..	*22*	7	15	7	5	2	15	2	13	3	3	..
	20 and over ..	*103*	54	49	40	38	2	63	16	47	13	13	..
	MUSLIM ..	482,097	251,656	230,441	18,200	17,005	1,195	463,897	234,651	229,246	2,024	1,944	80
	0—5 ..	*73,567*	37,816	35,751	..	..	..	73,567	37,816	35,751	..	..	..
	5—10 ..	*62,955*	33,993	28,962	1,194	1,107	87	61,761	32,886	28,875	109	101	8
	10—15 ..	*54,503*	30,053	24,450	2,486	2,286	200	52,017	27,767	24,250	241	222	19
	15—20 ..	*39,841*	20,732	19,109	3,342	3,055	287	36,499	17,677	18,822	428	406	22
	20 and over ..	*251,231*	129,062	122,169	11,178	10,557	621	240,053	118,505	121,548	1,246	1,215	31
	CHRISTIAN ..	672	388	284	274	176	98	398	212	186	218	134	84
	0—5 ..	*92*	41	51	..	..	..	92	41	51	..	..	..
	5—10 ..	*71*	39	32	11	6	5	60	33	27	11	6	5
	10—15 ..	*64*	38	26	14	9	5	50	29	21	13	8	5
	15—20 ..	*69*	35	34	36	20	16	33	15	18	22	11	11
	20 and over ..	*376*	235	141	213	141	72	163	94	69	172	109	63

BY RELIGION AND AGE.

PART B.—DETAILS OF DISTRICTS AND STATES.—*continued.*

District or State.	Religion and age.	Population. Total. Persons.	Total. Males.	Total. Females.	Literate. Persons.	Literate. Males.	Literate. Females.	Illiterate. Persons.	Illiterate. Males.	Illiterate. Females.	Literate in English. Persons.	Literate in English. Males.	Literate in English. Females.
1	2	3	4	5	6	7	8	9	10	11	12	13	14
RAWALPINDI.	**ALL RELIGIONS** ..	**634,357**	**342,771**	**291,586**	**61,008**	**52,087**	**8,921**	**573,349**	**290,684**	**282,665**	**24,968**	**22,629**	**2,389**
	0—5 ..	*99,004*	51,837	47,167	..	..	..	99,004	51,837	47,167	..	..	..
	5—10 ..	*81,031*	42,501	38,530	3,563	2,777	786	77,468	39,724	37,744	1,156	946	210
	10—15 ..	*71,757*	38,686	33,071	6,436	5,181	1,255	65,321	33,505	31,816	2,408	2,094	314
	15—20 ..	*57,039*	30,743	26,296	9,479	7,978	1,501	47,560	22,765	24,795	4,154	3,810	344
	20 and over ..	*325,526*	179,004	146,522	41,530	36,151	5,379	283,996	142,853	141,143	17,250	15,779	1,471
	HINDU ..	**59,485**	**34,973**	**24,512**	**17,256**	**14,915**	**2,441**	**42,129**	**20,058**	**22,071**	**6,311**	**6,115**	**196**
	0—5 ..	*8,213*	4,243	3,970	..	..	..	8,213	4,243	3,970	..	..	..
	5—10 ..	*6,763*	3,606	3,157	902	651	251	5,861	2,955	2,906	181	173	8
	10—15 ..	*6,253*	3,492	2,761	1,544	1,172	372	4,709	2,320	2,389	443	422	21
	15—20 ..	*6,147*	3,701	2,446	2,560	2,165	395	3,587	1,536	2,051	1,025	979	46
	20 and over ..	*32,109*	19,931	12,178	12,350	10,927	1,423	19,759	9,004	10,755	4,662	4,541	121
	SIKH ..	**41,265**	**22,948**	**18,317**	**13,556**	**9,603**	**3,953**	**27,709**	**13,345**	**14,364**	**5,890**	**4,659**	**731**
	0—5 ..	*6,750*	3,436	3,314	..	..	..	6,750	3,436	3,314	..	..	..
	5—10 ..	*5,502*	2,869	2,633	801	512	289	4,701	2,357	2,344	266	196	70
	10—15 ..	*5,070*	2,703	2,367	1,599	1,057	542	3,471	1,646	1,825	626	504	122
	15—20 ..	*3,991*	2,225	1,766	2,193	1,460	733	1,798	765	1,033	949	819	130
	20 and over ..	*19,952*	11,715	8,237	8,963	6,574	2,389	10,989	5,141	5,818	3,549	3,140	409
	JAIN ..	**1,077**	**593**	**484**	**257**	**242**	**15**	**820**	**351**	**469**	**61**	**58**	**3**
	0—5 ..	*164*	86	78	..	..	..	164	86	78	..	..	..
	5—10 ..	*739*	74	65	19	14	5	120	60	60	2	2	..
	10—15 ..	*135*	75	60	27	23	4	108	52	56	6	6	..
	15—20 ..	*102*	51	51	26	24	2	76	27	49	12	11	1
	20 and over ..	*537*	307	230	185	181	4	352	126	226	41	39	2
	MUSLIM ..	**524,965**	**279,287**	**245,678**	**25,267**	**24,013**	**1,254**	**499,698**	**255,274**	**244,424**	**8,885**	**8,661**	**224**
	0—5 ..	*82,949*	43,620	39,329	..	..	..	82,949	43,620	39,329	..	..	..
	5—10 ..	*68,007*	35,629	32,378	1,621	1,492	129	66,386	34,137	32,249	504	478	26
	10—15 ..	*59,797*	32,141	27,656	3,006	2,809	197	56,791	29,332	27,459	1,098	1,059	39
	15—20 ..	*45,923*	24,074	21,849	3,995	3,761	234	41,928	20,313	21,615	1,501	1,456	45
	20 and over ..	*268,289*	143,823	124,466	16,645	15,951	694	251,644	127,872	123,772	5,782	5,668	114
	CHRISTIAN ..	**7,486**	**4,924**	**2,562**	**4,532**	**3,287**	**1,245**	**2,954**	**1,637**	**1,317**	**4,292**	**3,119**	**1,173**
	0—5 ..	*918*	448	470	..	..	..	918	448	470	..	..	..
	5—10 ..	*611*	318	293	219	108	111	392	210	182	202	97	105
	10—15 ..	*498*	272	226	259	120	139	239	152	87	234	103	131
	15--20 ..	*871*	690	181	703	567	136	168	123	45	666	545	121
	20 and over ..	*4,588*	3,196	1,392	3,351	2,492	859	1,237	704	533	3,190	2,374	816
ATTOCK.	**ALL RELIGIONS** ..	**583,960**	**306,949**	**277,011**	**23,036**	**19,610**	**3,426**	**560,924**	**287,339**	**273,585**	**3,030**	**2,879**	**151**
	0—5 ..	*94,099*	48,474	45,625	..	..	..	94,099	48,474	45,625	..	..	..
	5—10 ..	*81,060*	43,517	37,543	1,160	885	275	79,900	42,632	37,268	52	38	14
	10—15 ..	*68,516*	37,677	30,839	2,348	1,855	493	66,168	35,822	30,346	186	164	22
	15—20 ..	*47,305*	24,865	22,440	3,323	2,734	589	43,982	22,131	21,851	600	572	28
	20 and over ..	*292,980*	152,416	140,564	16,205	14,136	2,069	276,775	138,280	138,495	2,192	2,105	87
	HINDU ..	**31,932**	**16,631**	**15,301**	**6,355**	**5,284**	**1,071**	**25,577**	**11,347**	**14,230**	**863**	**840**	**23**
	0—5 ..	*4,944*	2,603	2,341	..	..	..	4,944	2,603	2,341	..	..	..
	5—10 ..	*4,216*	2,198	2,018	291	200	91	3,925	1,998	1,927	5	3	2
	10—15 ..	*3,685*	1,924	1,761	586	423	163	3,099	1,501	1,598	41	35	6
	15—20 ..	*2,745*	1,408	1,337	835	646	189	1,910	762	1,148	151	144	7
	20 and over ..	*16,342*	8,498	7,844	4,643	4,015	628	11,699	4,483	7,216	666	658	8
	SIKH ..	**19,522**	**10,279**	**9,243**	**5,336**	**4,288**	**1,098**	**14,136**	**5,991**	**8,145**	**391**	**386**	**5**
	0—5 ..	*3,200*	1,693	1,507	..	..	..	3,200	1,693	1,507	..	..	..
	5—10 ..	*2,704*	1,428	1,276	242	155	87	2,462	1,273	1,189	9	9	..
	10—15 ..	*2,289*	1,211	1,078	472	326	146	1,817	885	932	32	32	..
	15—20 ..	*1,509*	788	721	677	497	180	832	291	541	86	84	2
	20 and over ..	*9,820*	5,159	4,661	3,995	3,310	685	5,825	1,849	3,976	264	261	3
	JAIN ..	**2**	**2**	..	**2**	**2**	..	..	..	..	**2**	**2**	..
	0—5 ..	..	..	..	..	..	..	..	..	..	..	..	..
	5—10 ..	..	..	..	..	..	..	..	..	..	..	..	..
	10—15 ..	..	..	..	..	..	..	..	..	..	..	..	..
	15—20 ..	..	..	..	..	..	..	..	..	..	..	..	..
	20 and over ..	*2*	2	..	2	2	..	..	..	..	2	2	..
	MUSLIM ..	**531,793**	**279,546**	**252,247**	**10,824**	**9,672**	**1,152**	**520,969**	**269,874**	**251,095**	**1,358**	**1,324**	**34**
	0—5 ..	*85,889*	44,146	41,743	..	..	..	85,889	44,146	41,743	..	..	..
	5—10 ..	*74,078*	39,864	34,214	611	523	88	73,467	39,341	34,126	23	20	3
	10—15 ..	*62,501*	34,526	27,975	1,272	1,097	175	61,229	33,429	27,800	98	89	9
	15—20 ..	*42,958*	22,592	20,366	1,736	1,525	211	41,222	21,067	20,155	292	281	11
	20 and over ..	*266,367*	138,418	127,949	7,205	6,527	678	259,162	131,891	127,271	945	934	11
	CHRISTIAN ..	**710**	**490**	**220**	**469**	**364**	**105**	**241**	**126**	**115**	**416**	**327**	**89**
	0—5 ..	*66*	32	34	..	..	..	66	32	34	..	..	..
	5—10 ..	*62*	27	35	16	7	9	46	20	26	15	6	9
	10—15 ..	*41*	16	25	18	9	9	23	7	16	15	8	7
	15—20 ..	*92*	76	16	75	66	9	17	10	7	71	63	8
	20 and over ..	*449*	339	110	360	282	78	89	57	32	315	250	65

TABLE XIII.—LITERACY

PART B.—DETAILS OF DISTRICTS AND STATES.

District or State	Religion and age.	Population. Total. Persons.	Total. Males.	Total. Females.	Literate. Persons.	Literate. Males.	Literate. Females.	Illiterate. Persons.	Illiterate. Males.	Illiterate. Females.	Literate in English. Persons.	Literate in English. Males.	Literate in English. Females.
1	2	3	4	5	6	7	8	9	10	11	12	13	14
MIANWALI.	ALL RELIGIONS ..	**411,539**	**216,016**	**195,523**	**15,450**	**14,295**	**1,155**	**396,089**	**201,721**	**194,368**	**2,172**	**2,126**	**46**
	0—5 ..	*69,359*	34,938	34,421	..	..	..	69,359	34,938	34,421	..	.	.
	5—10 ..	*58,968*	31,134	27,834	634	526	108	58,334	30,608	27,726	62	58	4
	10—15 ..	*48,575*	26,375	22,200	1,433	1,255	178	47,142	25,120	22,022	204	200	4
	15—20 ..	*34,068*	17,873	16,195	2,387	2,166	221	31,681	15,707	15,974	454	446	8
	20 and over ..	*200,569*	105,696	94,873	10,996	10,348	648	189,573	95,348	94,225	1,452	1,422	30
	HINDU ..	**49,794**	**25,656**	**24,138**	**9,532**	**8,692**	**840**	**40,262**	**16,964**	**23,298**	**1,177**	**1,165**	**12**
	0—5 ..	*8,127*	4,112	4,015	..	..	..	8,127	4,112	4,015	..	..	..
	5—10 ..	*7,208*	3,770	3,438	374	294	80	6,834	3,476	3,358	29	29	..
	10—15 ..	*6,065*	3,211	2,854	833	697	136	5,232	2,514	2,718	107	106	1
	15—20 ..	*4,384*	2,247	2,137	1,435	1,254	181	2,949	993	1,956	248	245	3
	20 and over ..	*24,010*	12,316	11,694	6,890	6,447	413	17,120	5,869	11,251	793	785	8
	SIKH ..	**4,231**	**2,263**	**1,968**	**984**	**835**	**149**	**3,247**	**1,428**	**1,819**	**177**	**174**	**3**
	0—5 ..	*768*	404	364	..	..	..	768	404	364	..	..	
	5—10 ..	*644*	350	294	43	26	17	601	324	277	7	6	1
	10—15 ..	*507*	282	225	78	56	22	429	226	203	17	17	.
	15—20 ..	*360*	180	180	131	114	17	229	66	163	36	35	1
	20 and over ..	*1,952*	1,047	905	732	639	93	1,220	408	812	117	116	1
	JAIN ..	**20**	**11**	**9**	**9**	**8**	**1**	**11**	**3**	**8**	**3**	**3**	..
	0—5 ..	*1*	..	1	..	..	..	1	..	1	..	..	..
	5—10 ..	*2*	1	1	..	..	..	2	1	1	..	..	..
	10—15 ..	*2*	1	1	1	1	..	1	..	1	1	1	..
	15—20 ..	*2*	1	1	2	1	1	..	..	..	1	1	..
	20 and over ..	*13*	8	5	6	6	..	7	2	5	1	1	..
	MUSLIM ..	**357,109**	**187,872**	**169,237**	**4,835**	**4,702**	**133**	**352,274**	**183,170**	**169,104**	**747**	**740**	**7**
	0—5 ..	*60,399*	30,390	20,009	..	..	..	60,399	30,390	30,009	..	..	..
	5—10 ..	*51,065*	26,991	24,074	210	201	9	50,855	26,790	24,065	19	18	1
	10—15 ..	*41,964*	22,862	19,102	509	493	16	41,455	22,369	19,086	71	70	1
	15—20 ..	*29,287*	15,427	13,860	808	791	17	28,479	14,636	13,843	165	164	1
	20 and over ..	*174,394*	92,202	82,192	3,308	3,217	91	171,086	88,985	82,101	492	488	4
	CHRISTIAN ..	**380**	**211**	**169**	**88**	**56**	**32**	**292**	**155**	**137**	**66**	**42**	**24**
	0—5 ..	*64*	32	32	..	..	..	64	32	32	..	..	..
	5—10 ..	*49*	22	27	7	5	2	42	17	25	7	5	2
	10—15 ..	*37*	19	18	12	8	4	25	11	14	8	6	2
	15—20 ..	*35*	18	17	11	6	5	24	12	12	4	1	3
	20 and over ..	*195*	120	75	58	37	21	137	83	54	47	30	17
MONTGOMERY.	ALL RELIGIONS ..	**999,772**	**552,456**	**447,316**	**40,407**	**36,017**	**4,390**	**959,365**	**516,439**	**442,926**	**6,466**	**6,223**	**243**
	0—5 ..	*175,680*	89,401	86,279	..	..	..	175,680	89,401	86,279	..	..	..
	5—10 ..	*140,594*	75,317	65,277	1,707	1,366	341	138,887	73,951	64,936	118	104	14
	10—15 ..	*122,227*	68,025	54,202	3,756	3,172	584	118,471	64,853	53,618	438	408	30
	15—20 ..	*91,542*	51,862	39,680	6,334	5,460	874	85,208	46,402	38,806	1,225	1,168	57
	20 and over ..	*469,729*	267,851	201,878	28,610	26,019	2,591	441,119	241,832	199,287	4,685	4,543	142
	HINDU ..	**120,664**	**69,445**	**51,219**	**16,562**	**14,760**	**1,802**	**104,102**	**54,685**	**49,417**	**2,510**	**2,447**	**63**
	0—5 ..	*19,779*	10,293	9,486	..	..	..	19,779	10,293	9,486	..	..	..
	5—10 ..	*15,636*	8,298	7,338	619	466	153	15,017	7,832	7,185	49	44	5
	10—15 ..	*15,354*	8,950	6,404	1,400	1,143	257	13,954	7,807	6,147	178	168	10
	15—20 ..	*12,680*	7,725	4,955	2,462	2,081	381	10,218	5,644	4,574	485	469	16
	20 and over ..	*57,215*	34,179	23,036	12,081	11,070	1,011	45,134	23,109	22,025	1,798	1,766	32
	SIKH ..	**148,155**	**82,261**	**65,894**	**11,747**	**10,071**	**1,676**	**136,408**	**72,190**	**64,218**	**2,057**	**1,989**	**68**
	0—5 ..	*26,100*	13,186	12,914	..	..	..	26,100	13,186	12,914	..	..	..
	5—10 ..	*21,014*	11,292	9,722	482	358	124	20,532	10,934	9,598	40	34	6
	10—15 ..	*18,171*	9,995	8,176	973	761	212	17,198	9,234	7,964	115	103	12
	15—20 ..	*13,515*	7,496	6,019	1,691	1,364	327	11,824	6,132	5,692	365	345	20
	20 and over ..	*69,355*	40,292	29,063	8,601	7,588	1,013	60,754	32,704	28,050	1,337	1,307	30
	JAIN ..	**38**	**28**	**10**	**19**	**19**	..	**19**	**9**	**10**	**6**	**6**	..
	0—5 ..	*9*	6	3	..	..	..	9	6	3	..	.	..
	5—10 ..	*3*	3	..	1	1	..	2	2	..	..	.	..
	10—15 ..	*5*	3	2	2	2	..	3	1	2	1	1	..
	15—20 ..	*5*	4	1	4	4	..	1	..	1	1	1	..
	20 and over ..	*16*	12	4	12	12	..	4	..	4	4	4	..
	MUSLIM ..	**697,542**	**381,956**	**315,586**	**11,299**	**10,563**	**736**	**686,243**	**371,393**	**314,850**	**1,681**	**1,632**	**49**
	0—5 ..	*123,286*	62,710	60,576	..	..	..	123,286	62,710	60,576	.	..	..
	5—10 ..	*99,011*	52,989	16,022	573	517	56	98,438	52,472	15,966	27	25	2
	10—15 ..	*84,699*	46,650	38,049	1,308	1,209	99	83,391	45,441	37,950	138	133	5
	15—20 ..	*62,247*	34,914	27,333	2,041	1,905	136	60,206	33,009	27,197	347	333	14
	20 and over ..	*328,299*	184,693	143,606	7,377	6,932	445	320,922	177,761	143,161	1,169	1,141	28
	CHRISTIAN ..	**17,245**	**9,618**	**7,627**	**599**	**427**	**172**	**16,646**	**9,191**	**7,455**	**207**	**144**	**63**
	0—5 ..	*3,197*	1,619	1,578	..	..	..	3,197	1,619	1,578	..	..	..
	5—10 ..	*2,592*	1,406	1,186	23	16	7	2,569	1,390	1,179	2	1	1
	10—15 ..	*2,266*	1,265	1,001	54	38	16	2,212	1,227	985	5	2	3
	15—20 ..	*1,642*	943	699	104	74	30	1,538	869	669	26	19	7
	20 and over ..	*7,548*	4,385	3,163	418	299	119	7,130	4,086	3,044	174	122	52

BY RELIGION AND AGE.

PART B.—DETAILS OF DISTRICTS AND STATES,—*continued.*

District or State.	Religion and age.	POPULATION. Total. Persons.	Total. Males.	Total. Females.	Literate. Persons.	Literate. Males.	Literate. Females.	Illiterate. Persons.	Illiterate. Males.	Illiterate. Females.	Literate in English. Persons.	Literate in English. Males.	Literate in English. Females.
1	2	3	4	5	6	7	8	9	10	11	12	13	14
LYALLPUR.	ALL RELIGIONS ..	1,151,351	630,749	520,602	64,421	56,241	8,080	1,086,930	574,408	512,522	10,888	10,187	701
	0—5 ..	*201,864*	104,038	97,826	..	..	..	201,864	104,038	97,826	..	..	..
	5—10 ..	*164,898*	87,708	77,190	3,813	3,248	565	161,085	84,460	76,625	238	217	21
	10—15 ..	*148,918*	80,697	68,221	8,128	6,920	1,208	140,790	73,777	67,013	881	833	48
	15—20 ..	*112,007*	62,097	49,910	12,085	10,262	1,823	99,922	51,835	48,087	2,466	2,334	132
	20 and over ..	*523,664*	296,209	227,455	40,395	35,911	4,484	483,269	260,298	222,971	7,303	6,803	500
	HINDU ..	122,626	71,357	51,269	23,124	19,558	3,566	99,502	51,799	47,703	4,289	3,929	360
	0—5 ..	*21,007*	11,060	9,947	..	..	..	21,007	11,060	9,947	..	..	..
	5—10 ..	*15,902*	8,424	7,478	1,292	1,017	275	14,610	7,407	7,203	71	62	9
	10—15 ..	*14,275*	7,842	6,433	2,568	1,969	599	11,707	5,873	5,834	280	258	22
	15—20 ..	*12,061*	7,410	4,651	3,905	3,123	782	8,156	4,287	3,869	858	805	53
	20 and over ..	*59,381*	36,621	22,760	15,359	13,449	1,910	44,022	23,172	20,850	3,080	2,804	276
	SIKH ..	211,391	117,039	94,352	18,236	16,104	2,132	193,155	100,935	92,220	2,485	2,422	63
	0—5 ..	*35,222*	18,509	16,713	..	..	..	35,222	18,509	16,713	..	..	..
	5—10 ..	*28,701*	15,884	12,817	989	824	165	27,712	15,060	12,652	60	59	1
	10—15 ..	*26,324*	14,791	11,533	2,165	1,809	356	24,159	12,982	11,177	217	214	3
	15—20 ..	*21,146*	11,847	9,299	3,306	2,795	511	17,840	9,052	8,788	573	559	14
	20 and over ..	*99,998*	56,008	43,990	11,776	10,676	1,100	88,222	45,332	42,890	1,635	1,590	45
	JAIN ..	95	66	29	31	29	2	64	37	27	14	14	..
	0—5 ..	*19*	13	6	..	..	..	19	13	6	..	..	..
	5—10 ..	*11*	8	3	3	3	..	8	5	3	1	1	..
	10—15 ..	*11*	8	3	5	5	..	6	3	3	3	3	..
	15—20 ..	*10*	6	4	6	5	1	4	1	3	2	2	..
	20 and over ..	*44*	31	13	17	16	1	27	15	12	8	8	..
	MUSLIM ..	720,996	389,159	331,837	20,998	19,063	1,935	699,998	370,096	329,902	3,776	3,567	209
	0—5 ..	*129,091*	65,964	63,127	..	..	..	129,091	65,964	63,127	..	..	..
	5—10 ..	*106,545*	55,997	50,548	1,393	1,305	88	105,152	54,692	50,460	85	78	7
	10—15 ..	*95,236*	50,970	44,266	3,104	2,916	188	92,132	48,054	44,078	340	321	19
	15—20 ..	*68,922*	37,362	31,560	4,508	4,061	447	64,414	33,301	31,113	969	918	51
	20 and over ..	*321,202*	178,866	142,336	11,993	10,781	1,212	309,209	168,085	141,124	2,382	2,250	132
	CHRISTIAN ..	45,518	24,899	20,619	806	584	222	44,712	24,315	20,397	213	154	59
	0—5 ..	*8,295*	4,245	4,050	..	..	..	8,295	4,245	4,050	..	..	..
	5—10 ..	*6,991*	3,699	3,292	76	53	23	6,915	3,646	3,269	23	19	4
	10—15 ..	*6,299*	3,364	2,935	136	99	37	6,163	3,265	2,898	31	27	4
	15—20 ..	*4,495*	2,487	2,011	150	110	40	4,348	2,377	1,971	38	28	10
	20 and over ..	*19,435*	11,104	8,331	444	322	122	18,991	10,782	8,200	121	80	41
JHANG.	ALL RELIGIONS ..	664,833	355,671	309,162	30,499	25,383	5,116	634,334	330,288	304,046	3,265	2,807	458
	0—5 ..	*110,818*	56,737	54,081	..	..	..	110,818	56,737	54,081	..	..	..
	5—10 ..	*95,151*	50,528	44,623	1,791	1,350	441	93,360	49,178	44,182	99	73	26
	10—15 ..	*81,622*	44,149	37,473	3,606	2,770	836	78,016	41,379	36,637	300	242	58
	15—20 ..	*57,879*	30,413	27,466	4,809	3,890	919	53,070	26,523	26,547	727	639	88
	20 and over ..	*319,363*	173,844	145,519	20,293	17,373	2,920	299,070	156,471	142,590	2,139	1,853	286
	HINDU ..	102,924	52,999	49,925	17,912	14,679	3,233	85,012	38,320	46,692	1,820	1,489	331
	0—5 ..	*16,838*	8,559	8,279	..	..	..	16,838	8,559	8,279	..	..	..
	5—10 ..	*14,392*	7,317	7,075	890	627	263	13,502	6,690	6,812	57	37	20
	10—15 ..	*12,696*	6,459	6,237	1,791	1,315	476	10,905	5,144	5,761	179	138	41
	15—20 ..	*8,248*	4,234	4,014	2,569	2,003	566	5,679	2,231	3,448	395	332	63
	20 and over ..	*50,750*	26,430	24,320	12,662	10,734	1,928	38,088	15,696	22,392	1,189	982	207
	SIKH ..	8,476	4,551	3,925	1,658	1,022	636	6,818	3,529	3,289	206	116	90
	0—5 ..	*1,411*	723	688	..	..	..	1,411	723	688	..	..	..
	5—10 ..	*1,213*	633	580	72	44	28	1,141	589	552	7	4	3
	10—15 ..	*1,052*	547	505	180	101	79	872	446	426	20	8	12
	15—20 ..	*714*	354	360	259	142	117	455	212	243	36	16	20
	20 and over ..	*4,086*	2,294	1,792	1,147	735	412	2,939	1,559	1,380	143	88	55
	JAIN ..	..	..	..	..	..	..	..	..	..	..	..	..
	0—5 ..	..	..	..	..	..	..	..	..	..	..	..	..
	5—10 ..	..	..	..	..	..	..	..	..	..	..	..	..
	10—15 ..	..	..	..	..	..	..	..	..	..	..	..	..
	15—20 ..	..	..	..	..	..	..	..	..	..	..	..	..
	20 and over ..	..	..	..	..	..	..	..	..	..	..	..	..
	MUSLIM ..	552,853	297,801	255,052	10,908	9,667	1,241	541,945	288,134	253,811	1,236	1,199	37
	0—5 ..	*92,483*	47,419	45,064	..	..	..	92,483	47,419	45,064	..	..	..
	5—10 ..	*79,457*	42,529	36,928	826	676	150	78,631	41,853	36,778	35	32	3
	10—15 ..	*67,777*	37,090	30,687	1,629	1,349	280	66,148	35,741	30,407	100	95	5
	15—20 ..	*48,845*	25,784	23,061	1,977	1,743	234	46,868	24,041	22,827	296	291	5
	20 and over ..	*264,291*	144,979	119,312	6,476	5,899	577	257,815	139,080	118,735	805	781	24
	CHRISTIAN ..	494	267	227	21	15	6	473	252	221	3	3	..
	0—5 ..	*75*	34	41	..	..	..	75	34	41	..	..	..
	5—10 ..	*79*	44	35	3	3	..	76	41	35	..	..	..
	10—15 ..	*81*	41	40	6	5	1	75	36	39	1	1	..
	15—20 ..	*60*	32	28	4	2	2	56	30	26	..	..	..
	20 and over ..	*199*	116	83	8	5	3	191	111	80	2	2	..

TABLE XIII.—LITERACY

PART B.—DETAILS OF DISTRICTS AND STATES.

District or State.	Religion and Age.	POPULATION. Total. Persons.	Total. Males.	Total. Females.	Literate. Persons.	Literate. Males.	Literate. Females.	Illiterate. Persons.	Illiterate. Males.	Illiterate. Females.	Literate in English. Persons.	Literate in English. Males.	Literate in English. Females.
1	2	3	4	5	6	7	8	9	10	11	12	13	14
MULTAN.	ALL RELIGIONS ..	1,174,900	646,025	528,875	57,321	53,131	4,190	1,117,579	592,894	524,685	9,268	8,765	503
	0—5 ..	*201,086*	104,129	96,957	..	..	..	201,086	104,129	96,957	..	..	..
	5—10 ..	*163,856*	87,979	75,877	2,266	1,926	340	161,590	86,053	75,537	203	152	51
	10—15 ..	*136,265*	74,734	61,531	4,653	4,062	591	131,612	70,672	60,940	569	495	74
	15—20 ..	*104,790*	57,417	47,373	8,449	7,651	798	96,341	49,766	46,575	1,754	1,675	79
	20 and over ..	*568,903*	321,766	247,137	41,953	39,492	2,461	526,950	282,274	244,676	6,742	6,443	299
	HINDU ..	177,102	98,646	78,456	32,116	29,650	2,466	144,986	68,996	75,990	4,567	4,419	148
	0—5 ..	*26,880*	13,618	13,262	..	..	..	26,880	13,618	13,262	..	..	..
	5—10 ..	*22,642*	12,110	10,532	1,270	1,037	233	21,372	11,073	10,299	77	57	20
	10—15 ..	*19,999*	11,018	8,981	2,635	2,235	400	17,364	8,783	8,581	300	272	28
	15—20 ..	*17,300*	9,734	7,566	4,797	4,299	498	12,503	5,435	7,068	946	921	25
	20 and over ..	*90,281*	52,166	38,115	23,414	22,079	1,335	66,867	30,087	36,780	3,244	3,169	75
	SIKH ..	39,453	23,241	16,212	5,074	4,502	572	34,379	18,739	15,640	755	728	27
	0—5 ..	*6,317*	3,312	3,005	..	..	..	6,317	3,312	3,005	..	..	..
	5—10 ..	*5,089*	2,733	2,356	169	142	27	4,920	2,591	2,329	19	16	3
	10—15 ..	*4,437*	2,483	1,954	341	292	49	4,096	2,191	1,905	55	51	4
	15—20 ..	*3,718*	2,216	1,502	703	596	107	3,015	1,620	1,395	133	127	6
	20 and over ..	*19,892*	12,497	7,395	3,861	3,472	389	16,031	9,025	7,006	548	534	14
	JAIN ..	440	220	220	97	84	13	343	136	207	16	16	..
	0—5 ..	*76*	35	41	..	..	..	76	35	41	..	..	..
	5—10 ..	*53*	26	27	5	2	3	48	24	24	1	1	..
	10—15 ..	*48*	22	26	6	2	4	42	20	22	..	..	..
	15—20 ..	*40*	19	21	4	2	2	36	17	19	..	..	..
	20 and over ..	*223*	118	105	82	78	4	141	40	101	15	15	..
	MUSLIM ..	942,937	515,218	427,719	18,357	17,662	695	924,580	497,556	427,024	3,214	3,158	56
	0—5 ..	*165,279*	85,849	79,430	..	..	..	165,270	85,849	79,430	..	..	..
	5—10 ..	*134,073*	72,030	62,043	743	707	36	133,330	71,323	62,007	62	60	2
	10—15 ..	*110,055*	60,264	49,791	1,550	1,470	80	108,505	58,794	49,711	151	148	3
	15—20 ..	*82,240*	44,552	37,688	2,746	2,624	122	79,494	41,928	37,566	573	559	14
	20 and over ..	*451,290*	252,523	198,767	13,318	12,861	457	437,972	239,662	198,310	2,428	2,391	37
	CHRISTIAN ..	9,924	5,780	4,144	1,499	1,104	395	8,425	4,876	3,749	634	378	256
	0—5 ..	*1,653*	855	798	..	..	..	1,653	855	798	..	..	..
	5—10 ..	*1,298*	692	606	63	28	35	1,235	664	571	40	15	25
	10—15 ..	*1,140*	620	520	101	51	50	1,039	569	470	58	20	38
	15—20 ..	*1,051*	647	404	167	105	62	884	542	342	88	55	33
	20 and over ..	*4,782*	2,966	1,816	1,168	920	248	3,614	2,046	1,568	448	288	160
MUZAFFARGARH.	ALL RELIGIONS ..	591,375	320,674	270,701	18,267	17,330	937	573,108	303,344	269,764	1,159	1,141	18
	0—5 ..	*90,920*	46,766	44,154	..	..	..	90,920	46,766	44,154	..	..	..
	5—10 ..	*80,700*	44,670	36,030	598	521	77	80,102	44,149	35,953	12	12	..
	10—15 ..	*69,352*	39,482	29,870	1,302	1,172	130	68,050	38,310	20,740	50	46	4
	15—20 ..	*54,020*	28,475	25,545	2,451	2,275	176	51,569	26,200	25,369	183	178	5
	20 and over ..	*296,333*	161,281	135,102	13,916	13,362	554	282,467	147,919	134,548	914	905	9
	HINDU ..	72,577	38,284	34,293	12,073	11,452	621	60,504	26,832	33,672	631	631	..
	0—5 ..	*10,978*	5,541	5,437	..	..	..	10,978	5,541	5,437	..	..	..
	5—10 ..	*9,406*	5,010	4,396	345	294	51	9,061	4,716	4,345	8	8	..
	10—15 ..	*8,067*	4,340	3,727	724	637	87	7,343	3,703	3,640	30	30	..
	15—20 ..	*6,704*	3,395	3,309	1,447	1,332	115	5,257	2,063	3,194	89	89	..
	20 and over ..	*37,422*	19,998	17,424	9,557	9,189	368	27,865	10,809	17,056	504	504	..
	SIKH ..	5,287	2,938	2,349	467	384	83	4,820	2,554	2,266	29	28	1
	0—5 ..	*899*	457	442	..	..	..	899	457	442	..	..	..
	5—10 ..	*773*	440	333	24	15	9	749	425	324	..	..	..
	10—15 ..	*607*	362	245	41	30	11	566	332	234	..	..	..
	15—20 ..	*447*	237	210	57	45	12	390	192	198	3	3	..
	20 and over ..	*2,561*	1,442	1,119	345	294	51	2,216	1,148	1,068	26	25	1
	JAIN ..	..	..	..	..	..	..	..	..	..	..	..	..
	0—5 ..	..	..	..	..	..	..	..	..	..	..	..	..
	5—10 ..	..	..	..	..	..	..	..	..	..	..	..	..
	10—15 ..	..	..	..	..	..	..	..	..	..	..	..	..
	15—20 ..	..	..	..	..	..	..	..	..	..	..	..	..
	20 and over ..	..	..	..	..	..	..	..	..	..	..	..	..
	MUSLIM ..	513,265	279,319	233,946	5,688	5,470	218	507,577	273,849	233,728	474	467	7
	0—5 ..	*79,007*	40,751	38,256	..	..	..	79,007	40,751	38,256	..	..	..
	5—10 ..	*70,487*	39,205	31,282	227	210	17	70,260	38,995	31,265	4	4	..
	10—15 ..	*60,650*	34,766	25,884	533	502	31	60,117	34,264	25,853	19	16	3
	15—20 ..	*46,842*	24,829	22,013	941	895	46	45,901	23,934	21,967	88	85	3
	20 and over ..	*256,279*	139,768	116,511	3,987	3,863	124	252,292	135,905	116,387	363	362	1
	CHRISTIAN ..	246	133	113	39	24	15	207	109	98	25	15	10
	0—5 ..	*36*	17	19	..	..	..	36	17	19	..	..	..
	5—10 ..	*34*	15	19	2	2	..	32	13	19	..	..	..
	10—15 ..	*28*	14	14	4	3	1	24	11	13	1	..	1
	15—20 ..	*27*	14	13	6	3	3	21	11	10	3	1	2
	20 and over ..	*121*	73	48	27	16	11	94	57	37	21	14	7

BY RELIGION AND AGE.

PART B.—DETAILS OF DISTRICTS AND STATES.—*continued.*

District or State.	Religion and age.	POPULATION.									Literate in English.		
		Total.			Literate.			Illiterate.					
		Persons.	Males.	Females.	Persons.	Males.	Females.	Persons.	Males.	Females.	Persons.	Males.	Females.
1	2	3	4	5	6	7	8	9	10	11	12	13	14
DERA GHAZI KHAN.	ALL RELIGIONS ..	520,686	286,158	234,528	16,144	15,091	1,053	504,542	271,067	233,475	1,948	1,920	28
	0—5 ..	*82,847*	42,417	40,430	..	..	..	82,847	42,417	40,430	..	..	..
	5—10 ..	*69,291*	38,757	30,534	557	462	95	68,734	38,295	30,439	32	31	1
	10—15 ..	*56,513*	32,905	23,608	1,225	1,038	187	55,288	31,867	23,421	111	111	..
	15—20 ..	*42,579*	23,442	19,137	2,550	2,324	226	40,029	21,118	18,911	326	323	3
	20 and over ..	*269,456*	148,637	120,819	11,812	11,267	545	257,644	137,370	120,274	1,479	1,455	24
	HINDU ..	57,390	29,812	27,578	9,621	8,818	803	47,769	20,994	26,775	1,240	1,218	22
	0—5 ..	*8,942*	4,501	4,441	..	..	..	8,942	4,501	4,441	..	..	..
	5—10 ..	*7,763*	4,138	3,625	359	284	75	7,404	3,854	3,550	24	23	1
	10—15 ..	*6,620*	3,596	3,024	784	625	159	5,836	2,971	2,865	76	76	..
	15—20 ..	*5,143*	2,626	2,517	1,269	1,107	162	3,874	1,519	2,355	181	178	3
	20 and over ..	*28,922*	14,951	13,971	7,209	6,802	407	21,713	8,149	13,564	959	941	18
	SIKH ..	760	439	321	87	66	21	673	373	300	20	20	..
	0—5 ..	*131*	71	60	..	..	..	131	71	60	..	..	..
	5—10 ..	*109*	60	49	7	2	5	102	58	44	..	..	..
	10—15 ..	*81*	47	34	8	3	5	73	44	29	..	..	..
	15—20 ..	*65*	33	32	10	5	5	55	28	27	..	..	..
	20 and over ..	*374*	228	146	62	56	6	312	172	140	20	20	..
	JAIN ..	125	71	54	25	21	4	100	50	50	5	5	..
	0—5 ..	*30*	17	13	..	..	..	30	17	13	..	..	..
	5—10 ..	*22*	14	8	1	1	..	21	13	8	..	..	..
	10—15 ..	*12*	8	4	3	2	1	9	6	3	..	..	..
	15—20 ..	*6*	4	2	4	3	1	2	1	1	1	1	..
	20 and over ..	*55*	28	27	17	15	2	38	13	25	4	4	..
	MUSLIM ..	462,380	255,817	206,563	6,401	6,179	222	455,979	249,638	206,341	674	671	3
	0—5 ..	*73,736*	37,823	35,913	..	..	..	73,736	37,823	35,913	..	..	..
	5—10 ..	*61,396*	34,545	26,851	190	175	15	61,206	34,370	26,836	8	8	..
	10—15 ..	*49,800*	29,254	20,546	430	408	22	49,370	28,846	20,524	35	35	..
	15—20 ..	*37,362*	20,777	16,585	1,266	1,208	58	36,096	19,569	16,527	143	143	..
	20 and over ..	*240,086*	133,418	106,668	4,515	4,388	127	235,571	129,030	106,541	488	485	3
	CHRISTIAN ..	31	19	12	10	7	3	21	12	9	9	6	3
	0—5 ..	*8*	5	3	..	..	..	8	5	3	..	..	..
	5—10 ..	*1*	..	1	..	..	..	1	..	1	..	..	..
	10—15 ..	..	..	..	..	..	..	..	..	..	..	..	..
	15—20 ..	*3*	2	1	1	1	..	2	1	1	1	1	..
	20 and over ..	*19*	12	7	9	6	3	10	6	4	8	5	3
DUJANA.	ALL RELIGIONS ..	28,216	14,537	13,679	574	554	20	27,642	13,983	13,659	28	26	2
	0—5 ..	*4,599*	2,311	2,288	..	..	..	4,599	2,311	2,288	..	..	..
	5—10 ..	*3,927*	2,096	1,831	19	18	1	3,908	2,078	1,830	..	..	..
	10—15 ..	*3,593*	1,917	1,676	48	46	2	3,545	1,871	1,674	2	2	..
	15—20 ..	*2,584*	1,269	1,315	85	80	5	2,499	1,189	1,310	7	6	1
	20 and over ..	*13,513*	6,944	6,569	422	410	12	13,091	6,534	6,557	19	18	1
	HINDU ..	22,347	11,650	10,697	414	405	9	21,933	11,245	10,688	7	7	..
	0—5 ..	*3,640*	1,827	1,813	..	..	..	3,640	1,827	1,813	..	..	..
	5—10 ..	*3,081*	1,637	1,444	16	15	1	3,065	1,622	1,443	..	..	..
	10—15 ..	*2,815*	1,510	1,305	36	35	1	2,779	1,475	1,304	..	..	..
	15—20 ..	*2,053*	1,014	1,039	59	56	3	1,994	958	1,036	2	2	..
	20 and over ..	*10,758*	5,662	5,096	303	299	4	10,455	5,363	5,092	5	5	..
	SIKH ..	1	1	..	1	1	..	..	..	..	..	..	..
	0—5 ..	..	..	..	..	..	..	..	..	..	..	..	..
	5—10 ..	..	..	..	..	..	..	..	..	..	..	..	..
	10—15 ..	..	..	..	..	..	..	..	..	..	..	..	..
	15—20 ..	*1*	1	..	1	1	..	..	..	..	..	..	..
	20 and over ..	..	..	..	..	..	..	..	..	..	..	..	..
	JAIN ..	..	..	..	..	..	..	..	..	..	..	..	..
	0—5 ..	..	..	..	..	..	..	..	..	..	..	..	..
	5—10 ..	..	..	..	..	..	..	..	..	..	..	..	..
	10—15 ..	..	..	..	..	..	..	..	..	..	..	..	..
	15—20 ..	..	..	..	..	..	..	..	..	..	..	..	..
	20 and over ..	..	..	..	..	..	..	..	..	..	..	..	..
	MUSLIM ..	5,863	2,883	2,980	155	146	9	5,708	2,737	2,971	17	17	..
	0—5 ..	*958*	483	475	..	..	..	958	483	475	..	..	..
	5—10 ..	*846*	459	387	3	3	..	843	456	387	..	..	..
	10—15 ..	*778*	407	371	12	11	1	766	396	370	2	2	..
	15—20 ..	*529*	254	275	24	23	1	505	231	274	4	4	..
	20 and over ..	*2,752*	1,280	1,472	116	109	7	2,636	1,171	1,465	11	11	..
	CHRISTIAN ..	5	3	2	4	2	2	1	1	..	4	2	[illegible]
	0—5 ..	*1*	1	..	..	..	..	1	1	..	..	..	..
	5—10 ..	..	..	..	..	..	..	..	..	..	..	..	..
	10—15 ..	..	..	..	..	..	..	..	..	..	..	..	..
	15—20 ..	*1*	..	1	1	..	1	..	..	..	1	..	..
	20 and over ..	*3*	2	1	3	2	1	..	..	..	3	2	

TABLE XIII.—LITERACY

PART B.—DETAILS OF DISTRICTS AND STATES.

District or State.	Religion and Age.	Population. Total. Persons.	Total. Males.	Total. Females.	Literate. Persons.	Literate. Males.	Literate. Females.	Illiterate. Persons.	Illiterate. Males.	Illiterate. Females.	Literate in English. Persons.	Literate in English. Males.	Literate in English. Females.
1	2	3	4	5	6	7	8	9	10	11	12	13	14
PATAUDI.	ALL RELIGIONS ..	18,873	9,922	8,951	916	859	57	17,957	9,063	8,894	80	80	..
	0—5 ..	*3,006*	1,495	1,511	..	..	..	3,006	1,495	1,511	..	..	..
	5—10 ..	*2,418*	1,302	1,116	38	33	5	2,380	1,269	1,111	1	1	..
	10—15 ..	*2,355*	1,289	1,066	91	84	7	2,264	1,205	1,059	8	8	..
	15—20 ..	*1,889*	981	908	143	131	12	1,746	850	896	21	21	..
	20 and over ..	*9,205*	4,855	4,350	644	611	33	8,561	4,244	4,317	50	50	..
	HINDU ..	15,596	8,227	7,369	704	668	36	14,892	7,559	7,338	59	59	..
	0—5 ..	*2,493*	1,247	1,246	..	..	..	2,493	1,247	1,246	..	..	..
	5—10 ..	*1,970*	1,064	906	26	24	2	1,944	1,040	904	..	..	..
	10—15 ..	*1,926*	1,059	867	73	68	5	1,853	991	862	7	7	..
	15—20 ..	*1,558*	816	742	115	108	7	1,443	708	735	17	17	..
	20 and over ..	*7,649*	4,041	3,608	490	468	22	7,159	3,573	3,586	35	35	..
	SIKH ..	1	1	..	..	..	..	1	1	..	..	..	..
	0—5 ..	..	..	..	..	..	..	..	..	..	..	..	..
	5—10 ..	..	..	..	..	..	..	..	..	..	..	..	..
	10—15 ..	..	..	..	..	..	..	..	..	..	..	..	..
	15—20 ..	..	..	..	..	..	..	..	..	..	..	..	..
	20 and over ..	*1*	1	..	..	..	..	1	1	..	..	..	..
	JAIN ..	105	52	53	45	41	4	60	11	49	2	2	..
	0—5 ..	*17*	6	11	..	..	..	17	6	11	..	..	..
	5—10 ..	*13*	5	8	3	2	1	10	3	7	..	..	..
	10—15 ..	*9*	3	6	4	3	1	5	..	5	..	..	..
	15—20 ..	*10*	5	5	5	4	1	5	1	4	1	1	..
	20 and over ..	*56*	33	23	33	32	1	23	1	22	1	1	..
	MUSLIM ..	3,168	1,640	1,528	164	148	16	3,004	1,492	1,512	19	19	..
	0—5 ..	496	242	254	..	..	..	496	242	254	..	..	..
	5—10 ..	*434*	233	201	8	7	1	426	226	200	1	1	..
	10—15 ..	*420*	227	193	14	13	1	406	214	192	1	1	..
	15—20 ..	*321*	160	161	23	19	4	298	141	157	3	3	..
	20 and over ..	*1,497*	778	719	119	109	10	1,378	669	709	14	14	..
	CHRISTIAN ..	3	2	1	3	2	1	..	..	..	..	..	..
	0—5 ..	..	..	..	..	..	..	..	..	..	..	..	..
	5—10 ..	*1*	..	1	1	..	1	..	..	..	..	..	..
	10—15 ..	..	..	..	..	..	..	..	..	..	..	..	..
	15—20 ..	..	..	..	..	..	..	..	..	..	..	..	..
	20 and over ..	*2*	2	..	2	2	..	..	..	..	..	..	..
KALSIA.	ALL RELIGIONS ..	59,848	33,306	26,542	2,305	2,048	257	57,543	31,258	26,285	212	210	2
	0—5 ..	*9,013*	4,644	4,369	..	..	..	9,013	4,644	4,369	..	..	..
	5—10 ..	*7,708*	4,180	3,528	88	71	17	7,620	4,109	3,511	2	2	..
	10—15 ..	*7,361*	4,104	3,257	199	161	38	7,162	3,943	3,219	12	12	..
	15—20 ..	*5,860*	3,276	2,584	326	270	56	5,534	3,006	2,528	46	46	..
	20 and over ..	*29,906*	17,102	12,804	1,692	1,546	146	28,214	15,556	12,658	152	150	2
	HINDU ..	28,550	16,085	12,465	1,326	1,161	165	27,224	14,924	12,300	122	121	1
	0—5 ..	*4,269*	2,219	2,050	..	..	..	4,269	2,219	2,050	..	..	..
	5—10 ..	*3,628*	1,971	1,657	52	39	13	3,576	1,932	1,644	..	..	..
	10—15 ..	*3,458*	1,927	1,531	116	86	30	3,342	1,841	1,501	5	5	..
	15—20 ..	*2,806*	1,579	1,227	190	151	39	2,616	1,428	1,188	27	27	..
	20 and over ..	*14,389*	8,389	6,000	968	885	83	13,421	7,504	5,917	90	89	1
	SIKH ..	9,035	5,121	3,914	508	443	65	8,527	4,678	8,849	56	56	..
	0—5 ..	*1,213*	623	590	..	..	..	1,213	623	590	..	..	..
	5—10 ..	*1,103*	617	486	18	14	4	1,085	603	482	2	2	..
	10—15 ..	[illegible]	616	453	33	27	6	1,036	589	447	4	4	..
	15—20 ..	[illegible]	515	378	57	47	10	836	468	368	10	10	..
	20 and over ..	*4,757*	2,750	2,007	400	355	45	4,357	2,395	1,962	40	40	..
	JAIN ..	162	88	74	42	40	2	120	48	72	3	3	..
	0—5 ..	*13*	7	6	..	..	..	13	7	6	..	..	..
	5—10 ..	*19*	11	8	1	1	..	18	10	8	..	..	..
	10—15 ..	*23*	12	11	3	3	..	20	9	11	..	..	..
	15—20 ..	*19*	10	9	7	6	1	12	4	8	1	1	..
	20 and over ..	*88*	48	40	31	30	1	57	18	39	2	2	..
	MUSLIM ..	21,797	11,848	9,954	425	402	23	21,372	11,441	9,931	29	29	..
	0—5 ..	*3,463*	1,768	1,695	..	..	..	3,463	1,768	1,695	..	..	..
	5—10 ..	*2,915*	1,555	1,360	17	17	..	2,898	1,538	1,360	..	..	..
	10—15 ..	*2,777*	1,529	1,248	47	45	2	2,730	1,484	1,246	3	3	..
	15—20 ..	*2,114*	1,155	959	72	66	6	2,042	1,089	953	8	8	..
	20 and over ..	*10,528*	5,836	4,692	289	274	15	10,239	5,562	4,677	18	18	..
	CHRISTIAN ..	22	14	8	4	2	2	18	12	6	2	1	1
	0—5 ..	*4*	3	1	..	..	..	4	3	1	..	..	..
	5—10 ..	*3*	2	1	..	..	..	3	2	1	..	..	..
	10—15 ..	*1*	1	..	..	..	..	1	1	..	..	..	..
	15—20 ..	*1*	..	1	..	..	..	1	..	1	..	..	..
	20 and over ..	*13*	8	5	4	2	2	9	6	3	2	1	1

BY RELIGION AND AGE.

PART B.—DETAILS OF DISTRICTS AND STATES.—*continued.*

District or State.	Religion and Age.	Population. Total. Persons.	Total. Males.	Total. Females.	Literate. Persons.	Literate. Males.	Literate. Females.	Illiterate. Persons.	Illiterate. Males.	Illiterate. Females.	Literate in English. Persons.	Literate in English. Males.	Literate in English. Females.
1	2	3	4	5	6	7	8	9	10	11	12	13	14
BASHAHR.	ALL RELIGIONS	104,389	51,593	52,796	2,330	2,268	62	102,059	49,325	52,734	216	216	..
	0—5	14,381	6,858	7,523	..	..	..	14,381	6,858	7,523	..	..	..
	5—10	12,188	6,030	6,158	70	69	1	12,118	5,961	6,157	7	7	..
	10—15	11,150	5,657	5,493	159	157	2	10,991	5,500	5,491	15	15	..
	15—20	8,770	4,357	4,413	262	258	4	8,508	4,099	4,400	40	40	..
	20 and over	57,900	28,691	29,209	1,839	1,784	55	56,061	26,907	29,154	154	154	..
	HINDU	102,388	50,610	51,778	2,317	2,256	61	100,071	48,354	51,717	216	216	..
	0—5	14,172	6,754	7,418	..	..	..	14,172	6,754	7,418	..	..	..
	5—10	11,961	5,917	6,044	70	69	1	11,891	5,848	6,043	7	7	..
	10—15	10,941	5,558	5,383	159	157	2	10,782	5,401	5,381	15	15	..
	15—20	8,550	4,279	4,311	262	258	4	8,328	4,021	4,307	40	40	..
	20 and over	56,724	28,102	28,622	1,826	1,772	54	54,898	26,330	28,568	154	154	..
	SIKH	10	5	5	1	1	..	9	4	5	..	..	..
	0—5	..	..	..	..	..	..	..	..	..	..	..	..
	5—10	2	1	1	..	..	..	2	1	1	..	..	..
	10—15	2	..	2	..	..	..	2	..	2	..	..	..
	15—20	..	..	..	..	..	..	..	..	..	..	..	..
	20 and over	6	4	2	1	1	..	5	3	2	..	..	..
	JAIN	..	..	..	..	..	..	..	..	..	..	..	..
	0—5	..	..	..	..	..	..	..	..	..	..	..	..
	5—10	..	..	..	..	..	..	..	..	..	..	..	..
	10—15	..	..	..	..	..	..	..	..	..	..	..	..
	15—20	..	..	..	..	..	..	..	..	..	..	..	..
	20 and over	..	..	..	..	..	..	..	..	..	..	..	..
	MUSLIM	674	345	329	5	4	1	669	341	328	..	..	..
	0—5	98	43	55	..	..	..	98	43	55	..	..	..
	5—10	88	43	45	..	..	..	88	43	45	..	..	..
	10—15	70	36	34	..	..	..	70	36	34	..	..	..
	15—20	52	28	24	..	..	..	52	28	24	..	..	..
	20 and over	366	195	171	5	4	1	361	191	170	..	..	..
	CHRISTIAN	16	10	6	1	1	..	15	9	6	..	..	..
	0—5	4	4	..	..	..	..	4	4	..	..	..	..
	5—10	4	2	2	..	..	..	4	2	2	..	..	..
	10—15	2	1	1	..	..	..	2	1	1	..	..	..
	15—20	1	..	1	..	..	..	1	..	1	..	..	..
	20 and over	5	3	2	1	1	..	4	2	2	..	..	..
NALAGARH.	ALL RELIGIONS	50,015	26,635	23,380	1,493	1,429	64	48,522	25,206	23,316	203	150	53
	0—5	6,321	3,150	3,171	..	..	..	6,321	3,150	3,171	..	..	..
	5—10	5,605	2,916	2,689	36	31	5	5,569	2,885	2,684	5	2	3
	10—15	5,706	3,028	2,678	88	83	5	5,618	2,945	2,673	20	16	4
	15—20	4,869	2,561	2,308	182	173	9	4,687	2,388	2,299	50	43	7
	20 and over	27,514	14,980	12,534	1,187	1,142	45	26,327	13,838	12,489	128	89	39
	HINDU	42,150	22,333	19,817	1,278	1,227	51	40,872	21,106	19,766	171	120	51
	0—5	5,164	2,546	2,618	..	..	..	5,164	2,546	2,618	..	..	..
	5—10	4,615	2,393	2,222	29	26	3	4,586	2,367	2,219	5	2	3
	10—15	4,738	2,518	2,220	76	72	4	4,662	2,446	2,216	18	14	4
	15—20	4,101	2,153	1,948	150	144	6	3,951	2,009	1,942	40	34	6
	20 and over	23,532	12,723	10,809	1,023	985	38	22,509	11,738	10,771	108	70	38
	SIKH	1,396	752	644	59	57	2	1,337	695	642	8	8	..
	0—5	197	106	91	..	..	..	197	106	91	..	..	..
	5—10	168	85	83	3	2	1	165	83	82	..	..	..
	10—15	167	84	83	4	4	..	163	80	83	1	1	..
	15—20	138	74	64	8	8	..	130	66	64	3	3	..
	20 and over	726	403	323	44	43	1	682	360	322	4	4	..
	JAIN	141	78	63	53	48	5	88	30	58	6	6	..
	0—5	19	9	10	..	..	..	19	9	10	..	..	..
	5—10	17	8	9	2	1	1	15	7	8	..	..	..
	10—15	17	7	10	2	1	1	15	6	9	2	2	..
	15—20	12	7	5	6	6	..	6	1	5	4	4	..
	20 and over	76	47	29	43	40	3	33	7	26			
	MUSLIM	6,815	3,464	2,851	97	93	4	6,218	3,371	2,847	14	14	..
	0—5	939	488	451	..	..	..	939	488	451	..	..	..
	5—10	803	429	374	1	1	..	802	428	374	..	..	..
	10—15	783	418	365	6	6	..	777	412	365	1	1	..
	15—20	617	327	290	17	15	2	600	312	288	4	4	..
	20 and over	3,173	1,802	1,371	73	71	2	3,100	1,731	1,369	9	9	..
	CHRISTIAN	13	8	5	6	4	2	7	4	3	4	2	2
	0—5	2	1	1	..	..	..	2	1	1	..	..	..
	5—10	2	1	1	1	1	..	1	..	1	..	..	..
	10—15	1	1	..	..	..	..	1	1	..	1	..	1
	15—20	1	..	1	1	..	1	..	..	..	3	2	1
	20 and over	7	5	2	4	3	1	3	2	1			

TABLE XIII.—LITERACY

PART B.—DETAILS OF DISTRICTS AND STATES.

District or State.	Religion and age.	Population. Total. Persons.	Total. Males.	Total. Females.	Literate. Persons.	Literate. Males.	Literate. Females.	Illiterate. Persons.	Illiterate. Males.	Illiterate. Females.	Literate in English. Persons.	Literate in English. Males.	Literate in English. Females.
1	2	3	4	5	6	7	8	9	10	11	12	13	14
KEONTHAL.	**ALL RELIGIONS**	**48,093**	**25,784**	**22,359**	**2,431**	**2,248**	**183**	**45,662**	**23,486**	**22,176**	**365**	**335**	**30**
	0—5	*4,905*	2,367	2,538	..	..	..	4,905	2,367	2,538	..	..	..
	5—10	*4,694*	2,390	2,304	78	69	9	4,616	2,321	2,295	3	3	..
	10—15	*4,436*	2,324	2,112	142	132	10	4,294	2,192	2,102	15	14	1
	15—20	*4,189*	2,147	2,042	274	250	24	3,915	1,897	2,018	50	47	3
	20 and over	*29,869*	16,506	13,363	1,937	1,797	140	27,932	14,709	13,223	297	271	26
	HINDU	**46,805**	**24,885**	**21,920**	**2,200**	**2,075**	**125**	**44,605**	**22,810**	**21,795**	**259**	**259**	..
	0—5	*4,796*	2,305	2,491	..	..	..	4,796	2,305	2,491	..	..	..
	5—10	*4,584*	2,334	2,250	66	60	6	4,518	2,274	2,244	3	3	..
	10—15	*4,323*	2,264	2,059	125	117	8	4,198	2,147	2,051	11	11	..
	15—20	*4,064*	2,068	1,996	244	229	15	3,820	1,839	1,981	41	41	..
	20 and over	*29,038*	15,914	13,124	1,765	1,669	96	27,273	14,245	13,028	204	204	..
	SIKH	**93**	**60**	**33**	**36**	**27**	**9**	**57**	**33**	**24**	**10**	**10**	..
	0—5	*15*	8	7	..	..	..	15	8	7	..	..	..
	5—10	*8*	5	3	2	1	1	6	4	2	..	..	..
	10—15	*7*	4	3	2	2	..	5	2	3	1	1	..
	15—20	*10*	6	4	7	5	2	3	1	2	2	2	..
	20 and over	*53*	37	16	25	19	6	28	18	10	7	7	..
	JAIN	..	..	..	..	..	..	..	..	..	..	..	..
	0—5	..	..	..	..	..	..	..	..	..	..	..	..
	5—10	..	..	..	..	..	..	..	..	..	..	..	..
	10—15	..	..	..	..	..	..	..	..	..	..	..	..
	15—20	..	..	..	..	..	..	..	..	..	..	..	..
	20 and over	..	..	..	..	..	..	..	..	..	..	..	..
	MUSLIM	**1,125**	**765**	**360**	**140**	**127**	**13**	**985**	**638**	**347**	**55**	**55**	..
	0—5	*92*	53	39	..	..	..	92	53	39	..	..	..
	5—10	*98*	49	49	8	7	1	90	42	48	..	..	..
	10—15	*102*	54	48	13	12	1	89	42	47	1	1	..
	15—20	*107*	71	36	18	14	4	89	57	32	4	4	..
	20 and over	*726*	538	188	101	94	7	625	444	181	50	50	..
	CHRISTIAN	**70**	**24**	**46**	**55**	**19**	**36**	**15**	**5**	**10**	**41**	**11**	**30**
	0—5	*2*	1	1	..	..	..	2	1	1	..	..	..
	5—10	*4*	2	2	2	1	1	2	1	1	..	..	..
	10—15	*4*	2	2	2	1	1	2	1	1	2	1	1
	15—20	*8*	2	6	5	2	3	3	..	3	3	..	3
	20 and over	*52*	17	35	46	15	31	6	2	4	36	10	26
BAGHAL.	**ALL RELIGIONS**	**26,352**	**13,457**	**12,895**	**1,158**	**1,111**	**47**	**25,194**	**12,346**	**12,848**	**25**	**25**	..
	0—5	*3,144*	1,571	1,573	..	..	..	3,144	1,571	1,573	..	..	..
	5—10	*2,815*	1,468	1,347	26	21	5	2,789	1,447	1,342	..	..	..
	10—15	*2,679*	1,393	1,286	47	42	5	2,632	1,351	1,281	1	1	..
	15—20	*2,462*	1,158	1,304	103	99	4	2,359	1,059	1,300	3	3	..
	20 and over	*15,252*	7,867	7,385	982	949	33	14,270	6,918	7,352	21	21	..
	HINDU	**26,013**	**13,241**	**12,772**	**1,134**	**1,088**	**46**	**24,879**	**12,153**	**12,726**	**25**	**25**	..
	0—5	*3,107*	1,547	1,560	..	..	..	3,107	1,547	1,560	..	..	..
	5—10	*2,778*	1,447	1,331	23	19	4	2,755	1,428	1,327	..	..	..
	10—15	*2,640*	1,370	1,270	44	39	5	2,596	1,331	1,265	1	1	..
	15—20	*2,430*	1,139	1,291	101	97	4	2,329	1,042	1,287	3	3	..
	20 and over	*15,058*	7,738	7,320	966	933	33	14,092	6,805	7,287	21	21	..
	SIKH	**8**	**6**	**2**	**2**	**2**	..	**6**	**4**	**2**	..	..	..
	0—5	..	..	..	..	..	..	..	..	..	..	..	..
	5—10	..	..	..	..	..	..	..	..	..	..	..	..
	10—15	*1*	1	..	..	..	..	1	1	..	..	..	..
	15—20	..	..	..	..	..	..	..	..	..	..	..	..
	20 and over	*7*	5	2	2	2	..	5	3	2	..	..	..
	JAIN	..	..	..	..	..	..	..	..	..	..	..	..
	0—5	..	..	..	..	..	..	..	..	..	..	..	..
	5—10	..	..	..	..	..	..	..	..	..	..	..	..
	10—15	..	..	..	..	..	..	..	..	..	..	..	..
	15—20	..	..	..	..	..	..	..	..	..	..	..	..
	20 and over	..	..	..	..	..	..	..	..	..	..	..	..
	MUSLIM	**324**	**203**	**121**	**22**	**21**	**1**	**302**	**182**	**120**	..	..	..
	0—5	*37*	24	13	..	..	..	37	24	13	..	..	..
	5—10	*36*	20	16	3	2	1	33	18	15	..	..	..
	10—15	*38*	22	16	3	3	..	35	19	16	..	..	..
	15—20	*32*	19	13	2	2	..	30	17	13	..	..	..
	20 and over	*181*	118	63	14	14	..	167	104	63	..	..	..
	CHRISTIAN	..	..	..	..	..	..	..	..	..	..	..	..
	0—5	..	..	..	..	..	..	..	..	..	..	..	..
	5—10	..	..	..	..	..	..	..	..	..	..	..	..
	10—15	..	..	..	..	..	..	..	..	..	..	..	..
	15—20	..	..	..	..	..	..	..	..	..	..	..	..
	20 and over	..	..	..	..	..	..	..	..	..	..	..	..

BY RELIGION AND AGE.

PART B.—DETAILS OF DISTRICTS AND STATES.—*continued.*

District or State.	Religion and Age.	POPULATION.									Literate in English.		
		Total.			Literate.			Illiterate.					
		Persons.	Males.	Females.	Persons.	Males.	Females.	Persons.	Males.	Females.	Persons.	Males.	Females.
1	2	3	4	5	6	7	8	9	10	11	12	13	14
JUBBAL.	ALL RELIGIONS ..	27,172	14,507	12,665	735	694	41	26,437	13,813	12,624	82	80	2
	0—5 ..	*3,296*	1,617	1,679	..	..	..	3,296	1,617	1,679	..	..	..
	5—10 ..	*2,887*	1,512	1,375	13	12	1	2,874	1,500	1,374	..	..	..
	10—15 ..	*2,639*	1,447	1,192	33	29	4	2,606	1,418	1,188	2	1	1
	15—20 ..	*2,232*	1,202	1,030	74	68	6	2,158	1,134	1,024	11	10	1
	20 and over ..	*16,118*	8,729	7,389	615	585	30	15,503	8,144	7,359	69	69	..
	HINDU ..	26,813	14,311	12,502	726	687	39	26,087	13,624	12,463	82	80	2
	0—5 ..	*3,225*	1,584	1,641	..	..	..	3,225	1,584	1,641	..	..	..
	5—10 ..	*2,836*	1,487	1,349	12	11	1	2,824	1,476	1,348	..	..	..
	10—15 ..	*2,599*	1,424	1,175	32	28	4	2,567	1,396	1,171	2	1	1
	15—20 ..	*2,203*	1,185	1,018	73	68	5	2,130	1,117	1,013	11	10	1
	20 and over ..	*15,960*	8,631	7,319	609	580	29	15,341	8,051	7,290	69	69	..
	SIKH ..	9	5	4	2	..	2	7	5	2	..	..	..
	0—5 ..	*1*	..	1	..	..	..	1	..	1	..	..	..
	5—10 ..	*1*	1	..	..	..	..	1	1	..	..	..	..
	10—15 ..	..	..	..	..	..	..	..	..	..	..	..	..
	15—20 ..	*2*	1	1	1	..	1	1	1	..	..	..	..
	20 and over ..	*6*	3	2	1	..	1	4	3	1	..	..	..
	JAIN ..	..	..	..	..	..	..	..	..	..	..	..	..
	0—5 ..	..	..	..	..	..	..	..	..	..	..	..	..
	5—10 ..	..	..	..	..	..	..	..	..	..	..	..	..
	10—15 ..	..	..	..	..	..	..	..	..	..	..	..	..
	15—20 ..	..	..	..	..	..	..	..	..	..	..	..	..
	20 and over ..	..	..	..	..	..	..	..	..	..	..	..	..
	MUSLIM ..	350	191	159	7	7	..	343	184	159	..	..	..
	0—5 ..	*70*	33	37	..	..	..	70	33	37	..	..	..
	5—10 ..	*50*	24	26	1	1	..	49	23	26	..	..	..
	10—15 ..	*40*	23	17	1	1	..	39	22	17	..	..	..
	15—20 ..	*27*	16	11	..	..	..	27	16	11	..	..	..
	20 and over ..	*163*	95	68	5	5	..	158	90	68	..	..	..
	CHRISTIAN ..	..	..	..	..	..	..	..	..	..	..	..	..
	0—5 ..	..	..	..	..	..	..	..	..	..	..	..	..
	5—10 ..	..	..	..	..	..	..	..	..	..	..	..	..
	10—15 ..	..	..	..	..	..	..	..	..	..	..	..	..
	15—20 ..	..	..	..	..	..	..	..	..	..	..	..	..
	20 and over ..	..	..	..	..	..	..	..	..	..	..	..	..
OTHER SIMLA HILL STATES.	ALL RELIGIONS ..	74,829	39,599	35,230	3,928	3,580	348	70,901	36,019	34,882	470	442	28
	0—5 ..	*8,607*	4,168	4,439	..	..	..	8,607	4,168	4,439	..	..	..
	5—10 ..	*7,968*	4,081	3,887	146	116	30	7,822	3,965	3,857	13	11	2
	10—15 ..	*7,547*	4,039	3,508	293	245	48	7,254	3,794	3,460	43	42	1
	15—20 ..	*6,780*	3,485	3,295	452	398	54	6,328	3,087	3,241	82	78	4
	20 and over ..	*43,927*	23,826	20,101	3,037	2,821	216	40,890	21,005	19,885	332	311	21
	HINDU ..	73,221	38,649	34,572	3,712	3,405	307	69,509	35,244	34,265	399	388	11
	0—5 ..	*8,401*	4,072	4,329	..	..	..	8,401	4,072	4,329	..	..	..
	5—10 ..	*7,791*	3,985	3,806	136	109	27	7,655	3,876	3,779	12	11	1
	10—15 ..	*7,378*	3,947	3,431	275	232	43	7,103	3,715	3,388	39	39	..
	15—20 ..	*6,636*	3,406	3,230	430	380	50	6,206	3,026	3,180	74	71	3
	20 and over ..	*43,015*	23,239	19,776	2,871	2,684	187	40,144	20,555	19,589	274	267	7
	SIKH ..	301	173	128	53	45	8	248	128	120	11	11	..
	0—5 ..	*40*	18	22	..	..	..	40	18	22	..	..	..
	5—10 ..	*29*	19	10	2	1	1	27	18	9	..	..	..
	10—15 ..	*28*	16	12	4	2	2	24	14	10	1	1	..
	15—20 ..	*28*	12	16	6	5	1	22	7	15	1	1	..
	20 and over ..	*176*	108	68	41	37	4	135	71	64	9	9	..
	JAIN ..	..	..	..	..	..	..	..	..	..		..	..
	0—5 ..	..	..	..	..	..	..	..	..	..		..	..
	5—10 ..	..	..	..	..	..	..	..	..	..		..	..
	10—15 ..	..	..	..	..	..	..	..	..		..	..	..
	15—20 ..	..	..	..	..	..	..	..	..		..	..	..
	20 and over ..	..	..	..	..	..	..	..	..		..	..	..
	MUSLIM ..	1,229	737	492	121	108	13	1,108	629	479	47	34	13
	0—5 ..	*154*	70	84	..	..	..	154	70	84	..	..	..
	5—10 ..	*139*	73	66	5	4	1	134	69	65	1	..	1
	10—15 ..	*132*	72	60	9	8	1	123	64	59	1	..	1
	15—20 ..	*110*	64	46	12	11	1	98	53	45	5	4	1
	20 and over ..	*694*	458	236	95	85	10	599	373	226	40	30	10
	CHRISTIAN ..	77	39	38	41	21	20	36	18	18	13	9	4
	0—5 ..	*12*	8	4	..	..	..	12	8	4	..	..	..
	5—10 ..	*9*	4	5	3	2	1	6	2	4	..	..	..
	10—15 ..	*9*	4	5	5	3	2	4	1	3	2	2	..
	15—20 ..	*6*	3	3	4	2	2	2	1	1	2	2	..
	20 and over ..	*41*	20	21	29	14	15	12	6	6	9	5	4

TABLE XIII.—LITERACY

PART B.—DETAILS OF DISTRICTS AND STATES.

District or State.	Religion and age.	POPULATION. Total. Persons.	Total. Males.	Total. Females.	Literate. Persons.	Literate. Males.	Literate. Females.	Illiterate. Persons.	Illiterate. Males.	Illiterate. Females.	Literate in English. Persons.	Literate in English. Males.	Literate in English. Females.
1	2	3	4	5	6	7	8	9	10	11	12	13	14
LOHARU.	ALL RELIGIONS ..	23,338	12,326	11,012	358	332	26	22,980	11,994	10,986	25	22	3
	0—5 ..	3,802	1,917	1,885	..	..	..	3,802	1,917	1,885	..	..	..
	5—10 ..	3,305	1,740	1,565	14	13	1	3,291	1,727	1,564	..	..	..
	10—15 ..	3,107	1,632	1,475	23	21	2	3,084	1,611	1,473	3	2	1
	15—20 ..	2,315	1,224	1,091	52	43	9	2,263	1,181	1,082	3	3	..
	20 and over ..	10,809	5,813	4,996	269	255	14	10.540	5,558	4,982	19	17	2
	HINDU ..	20,198	10,717	9,481	282	266	16	19,916	10,451	9,465	6	6	..
	0—5 ..	3,250	1,647	1,603	..	..	..	3,250	1,647	1,603	..	..	..
	5—10 ..	2,834	1,491	1,343	10	10	..	2,824	1,481	1,343	..	..	..
	10—15 ..	2,676	1,408	1,268	17	17	..	2,659	1,391	1,268	2	2	..
	15—20 ..	2,008	1,070	938	37	31	6	1,971	1,039	932	1	1	..
	20 and over ..	9,430	5,101	4,329	218	208	10	9,212	4,893	4,319	3	3	..
	SIKH ..	2	2	..	2	2	..	..	..	..	..	..	..
	0—5 ..	..	..	..	..	..	..	..	..	..	..	..	..
	5—10 ..	1	1	..	1	1	..	..	..	..	..	..	..
	10—15 ..	..	..	..	..	..	..	..	..	..	..	..	..
	15—20 ..	..	..	..	..	..	..	..	..	..	..	..	..
	20 and over ..	1	1	..	1	1	..	..	..	..	..	..	..
	JAIN ..	18	7	11	9	5	4	9	2	7	1	1	..
	0—5 ..	6	1	5	..	..	..	6	1	5	..	..	..
	5—10 ..	2	1	1	..	..	..	2	1	1	..	..	..
	10—15 ..	1	..	1	1	..	1	..	..	..	..	..	..
	15—20 ..	2	1	1	2	1	1	..	..	..	..	..	..
	20 and over ..	7	4	3	6	4	2	1	..	1	1	1	..
	MUSLIM ..	3,119	1,600	1,519	64	59	5	3,055	1,541	1,514	17	15	2
	0—5 ..	546	269	277	..	..	..	546	269	277	..	..	..
	5—10 ..	468	247	221	3	2	1	465	245	220	..	..	..
	10—15 ..	430	224	206	5	4	1	425	220	205	1	..	1
	15—20 ..	304	153	151	12	11	1	292	142	150	2	2	..
	20 and over ..	1,371	707	664	44	42	2	1,327	665	662	14	13	1
	CHRISTIAN ..	1	..	1	1	..	1	..	..	..	1	..	1
	0—5 ..	..	..	..	..	..	..	..	..	..	..	..	..
	5—10 ..	..	..	..	..	..	..	..	..	..	..	..	..
	10—15 ..	..	..	..	..	..	..	..	..	..	..	..	..
	15—20 ..	1	..	1	1	..	1	..	..	..	1	..	1
	20 and over ..	..	..	..	..	..	..	..	..	..	..	..	..
SIRMOOR	ALL RELIGIONS ..	148,568	82,384	66,184	4,798	4,370	423	143,775	78,014	65,761	499	486	13
	0—5 ..	18,529	9,360	9,169	..	..	..	18,529	9,360	9,169	..	..	..
	5—10 ..	16,674	8,926	7,748	160	110	50	16,514	8,816	7,698	10	10	..
	10—15 ..	15,774	8,698	7,076	294	216	78	15,480	8,482	6,998	31	29	2
	15—20 ..	13,900	7,542	6,358	535	456	79	13,365	7,086	6,279	85	82	3
	20 and over ..	83,691	47,858	35,833	3,804	3,588	216	79,887	44,270	35,617	373	365	8
	HINDU ..	139,031	76,922	62,109	4,277	3,909	368	134,754	73,013	61,741	418	413	5
	0—5 ..	17,127	8,625	8,502	..	..	..	17,127	8,625	8,502	..	..	..
	5—10 ..	15,394	8,246	7,148	135	93	42	15,259	8,153	7,106	6	6	..
	10—15 ..	14,550	8,021	6,529	248	181	67	14,302	7,840	6,462	22	20	2
	15—20 ..	12,928	6,984	5,944	465	395	70	12,463	6,589	5,874	67	66	1
	20 and over ..	79,032	45,046	33,986	3,429	3,240	189	75,603	41,806	33,797	323	321	2
	SIKH ..	2,413	1,353	1,060	196	179	17	2,217	1,174	1,043	9	7	2
	0—5 ..	386	199	187	..	..	..	386	199	187	..	..	..
	5—10 ..	336	176	160	7	4	3	329	172	157	..	..	..
	10—15 ..	315	171	144	14	10	4	301	161	140	1	1	..
	15—20 ..	236	135	101	24	22	2	212	113	99	2	1	1
	20 and over ..	1,140	672	468	151	143	8	989	529	460	6	5	1
	JAIN ..	52	38	14	36	28	8	16	10	6	12	12	..
	0—5 ..	7	6	1	..	..	..	7	6	1	..	..	..
	[illegible] ..	10	7	3	7	5	2	3	2	1	2	2	..
	10— ..	9	7	2	7	5	2	2	2	..	3	3	..
	15— ..	4	2	2	4	2	2	..	..	..	2	2	..
	20 and ..	22	16	6	18	16	2	4	..	4	5	5	..
	MUSLIM ..	,020	4,047	2,973	265	243	22	6,755	3,804	2,951	45	45	..
	0—5 ..	999	527	472	..	..	..	999	527	472	..	..	..
	5—10 ..	927	493	434	10	7	3	917	486	431	1	1	..
	10—15 ..	894	495	399	22	17	5	872	478	394	3	3	..
	15—20 ..	726	418	308	41	37	4	685	381	304	13	13	..
	20 and over ..	,474	2,114	1,360	192	182	10	3,282	1,932	1,350	28	28	..
	CHRISTIAN ..	52	24	28	19	11	8	33	13	20	15	9	6
	0—5 ..	10	3	7	..	..	..	10	3	7	..	..	..
	5—10 ..	7	4	3	1	1	..	6	3	3	1	1	..
	10—15 ..	6	4	2	3	3	..	3	1	2	2	2	..
	15—20 ..	6	3	3	1	..	1	5	3	2	1	..	1
	20 and over ..	23	10	13	14	7	7	9	3	6	11	6	5

BY RELIGION AND AGE.

PART B.—DETAILS OF DISTRICTS AND STATES.—*continued.*

District or State.	Religion and Age.	POPULATION. Total. Persons.	Total. Males.	Total. Females.	Literate. Persons.	Literate. Males.	Literate. Females.	Illiterate. Persons.	Illiterate. Males.	Illiterate. Females.	Literate in English. Persons.	Literate in English. Males.	Literate in English. Females.
1	2	3	4	5	6	7	8	9	10	11	12	13	14
BILASPUR.	ALL RELIGIONS ..	100,994	53,154	47,840	2,520	2,420	100	98,474	50,734	47,740	161	161	..
	0—5 ..	*13,126*	6,604	6,522	..	..	..	13,126	6,604	6,522	..	..	..
	5—10 ..	*11,823*	6,226	5,597	55	53	2	11,768	6,173	5,595	3	3	..
	10—15 ..	*11,055*	5,898	5,157	118	111	7	10,937	5,787	5,150	11	11	..
	15—20 ..	*9,159*	4,573	4,586	239	225	14	8,920	4,348	4,572	33	33	..
	20 and over ..	*55,831*	29,853	25,978	2,108	2,031	77	53,723	27,822	25,901	114	114	..
	HINDU ..	99,028	52,068	46,955	2,445	2,347	98	96,578	49,721	46,857	156	156	..
	0—5 ..	*12,858*	6,460	6,398	..	..	..	12,858	6,460	6,398	..	..	..
	5—10 ..	*11,572*	6,090	5,482	53	51	2	11,519	6,039	5,480	2	2	..
	10—15 ..	*10,818*	5,777	5,041	113	106	7	10,705	5,671	5,034	11	11	..
	15—20 ..	*8,986*	4,489	4,497	230	217	13	8,756	4,272	4,484	31	31	..
	20 and over ..	*54,789*	29,252	25,537	2,049	1,973	76	52,740	27,279	25,461	112	112	..
	SIKH ..	507	280	227	53	51	2	454	229	225	3	3	..
	0—5 ..	*71*	38	33	..	..	..	71	38	33	..	..	..
	5—10 ..	*65*	34	31	1	1	..	64	33	31	..	..	..
	10—15 ..	*60*	29	31	2	2	..	58	27	31	..	..	..
	15—20 ..	*47*	25	22	7	7	..	40	18	22	1	1	..
	20 and over ..	*264*	154	110	43	41	2	221	113	108	2	2	..
	JAIN ..	..	..	..	..	..	..	..	..	..	..	..	..
	0—5 ..	..	..	..	..	..	..	..	..	..	..	..	..
	5—10 ..	..	..	..	..	..	..	..	..	..	..	..	..
	10—15 ..	..	..	..	..	..	..	..	..	..	..	..	..
	15—20 ..	..	..	..	..	..	..	..	..	..	..	..	..
	20 and over ..	..	..	..	..	..	..	..	..	..	..	..	..
	MUSLIM ..	1,458	804	654	20	20	..	1,438	784	654	..	..	..
	0—5 ..	*196*	106	90	..	..	..	196	106	90	..	..	..
	5—10 ..	*184*	102	82	..	..	..	184	102	82	..	..	..
	10—15 ..	*176*	91	85	1	1	..	175	90	85	..	..	..
	15—20 ..	*126*	59	67	1	1	..	125	58	67	..	..	..
	20 and over ..	*776*	446	330	18	18	..	758	428	330	..	..	..
	CHRISTIAN ..	6	2	4	2	2	..	4	..	4	2	2	..
	0—5 ..	*1*	..	1	..	..	..	1	..	1	..	..	..
	5—10 ..	*2*	..	2	..	..	..	2	..	2	..	..	..
	10—15 ..	*1*	1	..	1	1	..	..	..	..	1	1	..
	15—20 ..	..	..	..	..	..	..	..	..	..	..	..	..
	20 and over ..	*2*	1	1	1	1	..	1	..	1	1	1	..
MANDI.	ALL RELIGIONS ..	207,465	107,876	99,589	9,766	9,144	622	197,699	98,732	98,967	843	793	50
	0—5 ..	*29,337*	14,486	14,851	..	..	..	29,337	14,486	14,851	..	..	..
	5—10 ..	*24,130*	12,384	11,746	239	186	53	23,891	12,198	11,693	11	8	3
	10—15 ..	*22,447*	11,636	10,811	501	419	82	21,946	11,217	10,729	44	41	3
	15—20 ..	*20,235*	10,296	9,939	1,198	1,075	123	19,037	9,221	9,816	159	151	8
	20 and over ..	*111,316*	59,074	52,242	7,828	7,464	364	103,488	51,610	51,878	629	593	36
	HINDU ..	199,935	102,614	97,321	8,957	8,423	534	190,978	94,191	96,787	593	578	15
	0—5 ..	*28,549*	14,070	14,479	..	..	..	28,549	14,070	14,479	..	..	..
	5—10 ..	*23,511*	12,053	11,458	211	166	45	23,300	11,887	11,413	6	6	..
	10—15 ..	*21,825*	11,294	10,531	464	391	73	21,361	10,903	10,458	37	36	1
	15—20 ..	*19,327*	9,654	9,673	1,095	986	109	18,232	8,668	9,564	129	125	4
	20 and over ..	*106,723*	55,543	51,180	7,187	6,880	307	99,536	48,663	50,873	421	411	10
	SIKH ..	899	612	287	296	262	34	603	350	253	51	48	3
	0—5 ..	*102*	50	52	..	..	..	102	50	52	..	..	..
	5—10 ..	*67*	36	31	11	7	4	56	29	27	2	1	1
	10—15 ..	*63*	34	29	11	7	4	52	27	25	3	3	..
	15—20 ..	*111*	69	42	36	31	5	75	38	37	4	3	1
	20 and over ..	*556*	423	133	238	217	21	318	206	112	42	41	1
	JAIN ..	..	..	..	..	..	..	..	..	..	..	..	..
	0—5 ..	..	..	..	..	..	..	..	..	..	..	..	..
	5—10 ..	..	..	..	..	..	..	..	..	..	..	..	..
	10—15 ..	..	..	..	..	..	..	..	..	..	..	..	..
	15—20 ..	..	..	..	..	..	..	..	..	..	..	..	..
	20 and over ..	..	..	..	..	..	..	..	..	..	..	..	..
	MUSLIM ..	6,351	4,464	1,887	392	373	19	5,959	4,091	1,868	117	114	3
	0—5 ..	*642*	344	298	..	..	..	642	344	298	..	..	..
	5—10 ..	*536*	288	248	12	11	1	524	277	247	..	..	..
	10—15 ..	*540*	299	241	21	19	2	519	280	239	2	2	..
	15—20 ..	*773*	561	212	57	52	5	716	509	207	22	21	1
	20 and over ..	*3,860*	2,972	888	302	291	11	3,558	2,681	877	93	91	2
	CHRISTIAN ..	141	92	49	93	64	29	48	28	20	73	45	28
	0—5 ..	*18*	8	10	..	..	..	18	8	10	..	..	..
	5—10 ..	*7*	3	4	3	1	2	4	2	2	3	1	2
	10—15 ..	*6*	3	3	2	..	2	4	3	1	2	..	2
	15—20 ..	*8*	5	3	5	3	2	3	2	1	4	2	2
	20 and over ..	*102*	73	29	83	60	23	19	13	6	64	42	22

TABLE XIII.—LITERACY

PART B.—DETAILS OF DISTRICTS AND STATES.

District or State.	Religion and Age.	Population. Total. Persons.	Total. Males.	Total. Females.	Literate. Persons.	Literate. Males.	Literate. Females.	Illiterate. Persons.	Illiterate. Males.	Illiterate. Females.	Literate in English. Persons.	Literate in English. Males.	Literate in English. Females.
1	2	3	4	5	6	7	8	9	10	11	12	13	14
SUKET.	ALL RELIGIONS ..	58,408	30,851	27,557	1,181	1,126	55	57,227	29,725	27,502	65	64	1
	0—5 ..	*7,183*	3,483	3,700	..	..	..	7,183	3,483	3,700	..	..	..
	5—10 ..	*6,492*	3,369	3,123	44	38	6	6,448	3,331	3,117	2	2	..
	10—15 ..	*6,129*	3,291	2,838	76	68	8	6,053	3,223	2,830	3	3	..
	15—20 ..	*5,509*	2,859	2,650	121	110	11	5,388	2,749	2,639	12	12	..
	20 and over ..	*33,095*	17,849	15,246	940	910	30	32,155	16,939	15,216	48	47	1
	HINDU ..	57,616	30,427	27,189	1,132	1,077	55	56,484	29,350	27,134	62	61	1
	0—5 ..	*7,051*	3,418	3,633	..	..	..	7,051	3,418	3,633	..	..	..
	5—10 ..	*6,378*	3,311	3,067	39	33	6	6,339	3,278	3,061	2	2	..
	10—15 ..	*6,037*	3,245	2,792	71	63	8	5,966	3,182	2,784	3	3	..
	15—20 ..	*5,434*	2,818	2,616	117	106	11	5,317	2,712	2,605	11	11	..
	20 and over ..	*32,716*	17,635	15,081	905	875	30	31,811	16,760	15,051	46	45	1
	SIKH ..	44	33	11	10	10	..	34	23	11	1	1	..
	0—5 ..	*4*	3	1	..	..	..	4	3	1	..	..	..
	5—10 ..	*7*	6	1	1	1	..	6	5	1	..	..	..
	10—15 ..	*3*	3	..	..	..	..	3	3	..	..	..	..
	15—20 ..	*4*	3	1	1	1	..	3	2	1	1	1	..
	20 and over ..	*26*	18	8	8	8	..	18	10	8	..	..	..
	JAIN ..	..	..	..	..	..	..	..	..	..	..	..	..
	0—5 ..	..	..	..	..	..	..	..	..	..	..	..	..
	5—10 ..	..	..	..	..	..	..	..	..	..	..	..	..
	10—15 ..	..	..	..	..	..	..	..	..	..	..	..	..
	15—20 ..	..	..	..	..	..	..	..	..	..	..	..	..
	20 and over ..	..	..	..	..	..	..	..	..	..	..	..	..
	MUSLIM ..	733	382	351	39	39	..	694	343	351	2	2	..
	0—5 ..	*127*	61	66	..	..	..	127	61	66	..	..	..
	5—10 ..	*107*	52	55	4	4	..	103	48	55	..	..	..
	10—15 ..	*89*	43	46	5	5	..	84	38	46	..	..	..
	15—20 ..	*68*	36	32	3	3	..	65	33	32	..	..	..
	20 and over ..	*342*	190	152	27	27	..	315	163	152	2	2	..
	CHRISTIAN ..	1	1	..	..	..	..	1	1	..	..	..	..
	0—5 ..	..	..	..	..	..	..	..	..	..	..	..	..
	5—10 ..	..	..	..	..	..	..	..	..	..	..	..	..
	10—15 ..	..	..	..	..	..	..	..	..	..	..	..	..
	15—20 ..	1	1	..	..	..	..	1	1	..	..	..	..
	20 and over ..	..	..	..	..	..	..	..	..	..	..	..	..
KAPURTHALA.	ALL RELIGIONS ..	316,757	171,529	145,228	11,219	9,703	1,516	305,538	161,826	143,712	2,345	2,221	124
	0—5 ..	*47,005*	23,960	23,045	..	..	..	47,005	23,960	23,045	..	..	..
	5—10 ..	*40,867*	21,978	18,889	602	465	137	40,265	21,513	18,752	98	90	8
	10—15 ..	*38,514*	20,970	17,544	1,283	1,031	252	37,231	19,939	17,292	310	290	20
	15—20 ..	*28,881*	15,407	13,474	1,846	1,556	290	27,035	13,851	13,184	511	485	26
	20 and over ..	*161,490*	89,214	72,276	7,488	6,651	837	154,002	82,563	71,439	1,426	1,356	70
	HINDU ..	54,145	29,590	24,555	5,034	4,194	840	49,111	25,396	23,715	1,264	1,220	44
	0—5 ..	*7,924*	4,087	3,837	..	..	..	7,924	4,087	3,837	..	..	..
	5—10 ..	*7,048*	3,820	3,228	287	211	76	6,761	3,609	3,152	62	57	5
	10—15 ..	*6,647*	3,687	2,960	610	470	140	6,037	3,217	2,820	182	174	8
	15—20 ..	*4,990*	2,759	2,231	804	648	156	4,186	2,111	2,075	253	245	8
	20 and over ..	*27,536*	15,237	12,299	3,333	2,865	468	24,203	12,372	11,831	767	744	23
	SIKH ..	72,177	39,729	32,448	2,767	2,443	324	69,410	37,286	32,124	409	388	21
	0—5 ..	*10,060*	5,172	4,888	..	..	..	10,060	5,172	4,888	..	..	..
	5—10 ..	*8,792*	4,776	4,016	119	90	29	8,673	4,686	3,987	13	13	..
	10—15 ..	*8,438*	4,682	3,756	261	203	58	8,177	4,479	3,698	50	45	5
	15—20 ..	*6,450*	3,519	2,931	440	373	67	6,010	3,146	2,864	104	97	7
	20 and over ..	*38,437*	21,580	16,857	1,947	1,777	170	36,490	19,803	16,687	242	233	9
	JAIN ..	27	15	12	4	4	..	23	11	12	2	2	..
	0—5 ..	*7*	6	1	..	..	..	7	6	1	..	..	..
	5—10 ..	*3*	1	2	..	..	..	3	1	2	..	..	..
	10—15 ..	*3*	1	2	..	..	..	3	1	2	..	..	..
	15—20 ..	*2*	..	2	..	..	..	2	..	2	..	..	..
	20 and over ..	*12*	7	5	4	4	..	8	3	5	2	2	..
	MUSLIM ..	179,251	96,240	83,011	3,293	2,962	331	175,958	93,278	82,680	642	597	45
	0—5 ..	*27,339*	13,828	13,511	..	..	..	27,339	13,828	13,511	..	..	..
	5—10 ..	*23,574*	12,597	10,977	193	162	31	23,381	12,435	10,946	23	20	3
	10—15 ..	*22,005*	11,820	10,185	409	355	54	21,596	11,465	10,131	78	71	7
	15—20 ..	*16,368*	8,566	7,802	585	522	63	15,783	8,044	7,739	149	141	8
	20 and over ..	*89,965*	49,429	40,536	2,106	1,923	183	87,859	47,506	40,353	392	365	27
	CHRISTIAN ..	983	511	472	33	16	17	950	495	455	24	10	14
	0—5 ..	*159*	73	86	..	..	..	159	73	86	..	..	..
	5—10 ..	*143*	74	69	..	..	..	143	74	69	..	..	..
	10—15 ..	*112*	60	52	..	..	..	112	60	52	..	..	..
	15—20 ..	*78*	42	36	3	..	3	75	42	33	3	..	3
	20 and over ..	*491*	262	229	30	16	14	461	246	215	21	10	11

BY RELIGION AND AGE.

PART B.—DETAILS OF DISTRICTS AND STATES.—*continued.*

District or State.	Religion and Age.	Population. Total. Persons.	Total. Males.	Total. Females.	Literate. Persons.	Literate. Males.	Literate. Females.	Illiterate. Persons.	Illiterate. Males.	Illiterate. Females.	Literate in English. Persons.	Literate in English. Males.	Literate in English. Females.
1	2	3	4	5	6	7	8	9	10	11	12	13	14
MALERKOTLA.	**ALL RELIGIONS**	**83,072**	**45,883**	**37,189**	**4,625**	**4,297**	**328**	**78,447**	**41,586**	**86,861**	**605**	**576**	**29**
	0—5	*12,374*	6,265	6,109	..	..	..	12,374	6,265	6,109	..	..	..
	5—10	*10,329*	5,406	4,923	170	140	30	10,159	5,266	4,893	17	14	3
	10—15	*9,949*	5,234	4,715	350	299	51	9,599	4,935	4,664	49	43	6
	15—20	*7,936*	4,363	3,573	606	553	53	7,330	3,810	3,520	111	106	5
	20 and over	*42,484*	24,615	17,869	3,499	3,305	194	38,985	21,310	17,675	428	413	15
	HINDU	**21,252**	**11,713**	**9,539**	**1,838**	**1,728**	**110**	**19,414**	**9,985**	**9,429**	**222**	**219**	**3**
	0—5	*3,169*	1,583	1,586	..	..	..	3,169	1,583	1,586	..	..	..
	5—10	*2,636*	1,379	1,257	62	56	6	2,574	1,323	1,251	6	6	..
	10—15	*2,523*	1,323	1,200	129	118	11	2,394	1,205	1,189	22	22	..
	15—20	*2,103*	1,165	938	254	233	21	1,849	932	917	46	46	..
	20 and over	*10,821*	6,263	4,558	1,393	1,321	72	9,428	4,942	4,486	148	145	3
	SIKH	**28,982**	**16,114**	**12,868**	**1,163**	**1,073**	**90**	**27,819**	**15,041**	**12,778**	**60**	**52**	**8**
	0—5	*4,224*	2,151	2,073	..	..	..	4,224	2,151	2,073	..	..	..
	5—10	*3,503*	1,821	1,682	56	44	12	3,447	1,777	1,670	3	2	1
	10—15	*3,397*	1,825	1,572	104	84	20	3,293	1,741	1,552	10	7	3
	15—20	*2,680*	1,492	1,188	140	127	13	2,540	1,365	1,175	17	15	2
	20 and over	*15,178*	8,825	6,353	863	818	45	14,315	8,007	6,308	30	28	2
	JAIN	**1,286**	**699**	**587**	**368**	**353**	**15**	**918**	**346**	**572**	**26**	**24**	**2**
	0—5	*180*	89	91	..	..		180	89	91	..	..	..
	5—10	*144*	75	69	12	10	2	132	65	67	1	1	..
	10—15	*147*	80	67	27	24	3	120	56	64	4	4	..
	15—20	*133*	66	67	44	41	3	89	25	64	7	6	1
	20 and over	*682*	389	293	285	278	7	397	111	286	14	13	1
	MUSLIM	**31,417**	**17,280**	**14,137**	**1,238**	**1,128**	**110**	**30,179**	**16,152**	**14,027**	**290**	**276**	**14**
	0—5	*4,780*	2,432	2,348	..	..	..	4,780	2,432	2,348	..	..	..
	5—10	*4,032*	2,125	1,907	40	30	10	3,992	2,095	1,897	7	5	2
	10—15	*3,870*	2,002	1,868	90	73	17	3,780	1,929	1,851	13	10	3
	15—20	*3,010*	1,634	1,376	168	152	16	2,842	1,482	1,360	41	39	2
	20 and over	*15,725*	9,087	6,638	940	873	67	14,785	8,214	6,571	229	222	7
	CHRISTIAN	**135**	**77**	**58**	**18**	**15**	**3**	**117**	**62**	**55**	**7**	**5**	**2**
	0—5	*21*	10	11	..	..	..	21	10	11	..	..	..
	5—10	*14*	6	8	..	..	..	14	6	8	..	..	..
	10—15	*12*	4	8	..	..	..	12	4	8	..	..	..
	15—20	*10*	6	4	..	..	..	10	6	4	..	..	..
	20 and over	*78*	51	27	18	15	3	60	36	24	7	5	2
FARIDKOT.	**ALL RELIGIONS**	**164,364**	**91,163**	**73,201**	**7,977**	**7,490**	**487**	**156,387**	**83,673**	**72,714**	**993**	**980**	**13**
	0—5	*24,686*	12,686	12,000	..	..	..	24,686	12,686	12,000	..	..	..
	5—10	*21,214*	11,501	9,713	233	208	25	20,981	11,293	9,688	11	10	1
	10—15	*20,250*	11,112	9,138	555	492	63	19,695	10,620	9,075	45	43	2
	15—20	*16,366*	9,324	7,042	1,143	1,044	99	15,223	8,280	6,943	188	185	3
	20 and over	*81,848*	46,540	35,308	6,046	5,746	300	75,802	40,794	35,008	749	742	7
	HINDU	**19,271**	**11,231**	**8,040**	**3,160**	**2,976**	**184**	**16,111**	**8,255**	**7,856**	**352**	**350**	**2**
	0—5	*2,731*	1,424	1,307	..	..	..	2,731	1,424	1,307	..	..	..
	5—10	*2,299*	1,259	1,040	71	58	13	2,228	1,201	1,027	6	6	..
	10—15	*2,211*	1,231	980	178	152	26	2,033	1,079	954	18	18	..
	15—20	*1,955*	1,143	812	432	395	37	1,523	748	775	51	51	..
	20 and over	*10,075*	6,174	3,901	2,479	2,371	108	7,596	3,803	3,793	277	275	2
	SIKH	**92,880**	**51,414**	**41,466**	**3,775**	**3,529**	**246**	**89,105**	**47,885**	**41,220**	**270**	**261**	**9**
	0—5	*13,731*	7,084	6,647	..	..	..	13,731	7,084	6,647	..	..	..
	5—10	*11,790*	6,458	5,332	130	119	11	11,660	6,339	5,321	5	4	1
	10—15	*11,338*	6,263	5,075	295	265	30	11,043	5,998	5,045	19	17	2
	15—20	*9,236*	5,325	3,911	523	475	48	8,713	4,850	3,863	59	57	2
	20 and over	*46,785*	26,284	20,501	2,827	2,670	157	43,958	23,614	20,344	187	183	4
	JAIN	**550**	**292**	**258**	**166**	**151**	**15**	**384**	**141**	**243**	**18**	**18**	..
	0—5	*74*	36	38	..	..	..	74	36	38	..	..	..
	5—10	*79*	38	41	6	6	..	73	32	41	..	..	..
	10—15	*77*	37	40	15	13	2	62	24	38	1	1	..
	15—20	*59*	29	30	28	23	5	31	6	25	6	6	..
	20 and over	*261*	152	109	117	109	8	144	43	101	11	11	..
	MUSLIM	**49,912**	**27,286**	**22,676**	**873**	**832**	**41**	**49,039**	**26,404**	**22,635**	**350**	**349**	**1**
	0—5	*7,974*	4,033	3,941	..	..	..	7,974	4,033	3,941	..	..	..
	5—10	*6,769*	3,593	3,176	26	25	1	6,743	3,568	3,175	..	..	..
	10—15	*6,343*	3,433	2,910	67	62	5	6,276	3,371	2,905	7	7	..
	15—20	*4,932*	2,720	2,212	159	151	8	4,773	2,569	2,204	71	71	..
	20 and over	*23,894*	13,457	10,437	621	594	27	23,273	12,863	10,410	272	271	1
	CHRISTIAN	**167**	**100**	**67**	**3**	**2**	**1**	**164**	**98**	**66**	**3**	**2**	**1**
	0—5	*22*	17	5	..	..	..	22	17	5	..	..	..
	5—10	*28*	13	15	..	..	..	28	13	15	..	..	..
	10—15	*31*	13	18	..	..	..	31	13	18	..	..	..
	15—20	*20*	12	8	1	..	1	19	12	7	1	..	1
	20 and over	*66*	45	21	2	2	..	64	43	21	2	2	..

TABLE XIII.—LITERACY

PART B.—DETAILS OF DISTRICTS AND STATES.

District or State.	Religion and Age.	Population. Total. Persons.	Population. Total. Males.	Population. Total. Females.	Population. Literate. Persons.	Population. Literate. Males.	Population. Literate. Females.	Population. Illiterate. Persons.	Population. Illiterate. Males.	Population. Illiterate. Females.	Literate in English. Persons.	Literate in English. Males.	Literate in English. Females.
1	2	3	4	5	6	7	8	9	10	11	12	13	14
CHAMBA.	**ALL RELIGIONS**	**146,870**	**76,059**	**70,811**	**4,610**	**4,269**	**341**	**142,260**	**71,790**	**70,470**	**298**	**294**	**4**
	0—5	*19,863*	9,709	10,154	..	..	..	19,863	9,709	10,154	..	..	..
	5—10	*17,818*	9,018	8,800	115	82	33	17,703	8,936	8,767	3	3	..
	10—15	*16,274*	8,367	7,907	233	183	50	16,041	8,184	7,857	13	13	..
	15—20	*13,422*	6,501	6,921	442	390	52	12,980	6,111	6,869	54	53	1
	20 and over	*79,493*	42,464	37,029	3,820	3,614	206	75,673	38,850	36,823	228	225	3
	HINDU	**134,717**	**69,673**	**65,044**	**4,259**	**3,966**	**293**	**130,458**	**65,707**	**64,751**	**256**	**255**	**1**
	0—5	*17,968*	8,772	9,196	..	..	..	17,968	8,772	9,196	..	..	..
	5—10	*16,198*	8,192	8,006	103	74	29	16,095	8,118	7,977	2	2	..
	10—15	*14,842*	7,622	7,220	213	169	44	14,629	7,453	7,176	12	12	..
	15—20	*12,268*	5,956	6,312	400	357	43	11,868	5,599	6,269	47	47	..
	20 and over	*73,441*	39,131	34,310	3,543	3,366	177	69,898	35,765	34,133	195	194	1
	SIKH	**112**	**63**	**49**	**47**	**34**	**13**	**65**	**29**	**36**	**6**	**5**	**1**
	0—5	*14*	5	9	..	..	..	14	5	9	..	..	..
	5—10	*13*	8	5	2	1	1	11	7	4	..	..	..
	10—15	*15*	9	6	5	2	3	10	7	3	1	1	..
	15—20	*13*	8	5	7	5	2	6	3	3	2	2	..
	20 and over	*57*	33	24	33	26	7	24	7	17	3	2	1
	JAIN	**3**	**1**	**2**	..	..	..	**3**	**1**	**2**	..	..	..
	0—5	..	..	..	..	..	..	..	..	..	..	..	..
	5—10	*1*	1	..	..	..	..	1	1	..	..	..	..
	10—15	..	..	..	..	..	..	..	..	..	..	..	..
	15—20	*1*	..	1	..	..	..	1	..	1	..	..	..
	20 and over	*1*	..	1	..	..	..	1	..	1	..	..	..
	MUSLIM	**10,839**	**5,706**	**5,133**	**259**	**235**	**24**	**10,580**	**5,471**	**5,109**	**26**	**26**	..
	0—5	*1,695*	845	850	..	..	..	1,695	845	850	..	..	..
	5—10	*1,460*	743	717	7	5	2	1,453	738	715	1	1	..
	10—15	*1,296*	675	621	15	12	3	1,281	663	618	..	..	..
	15—20	*1,034*	494	540	30	25	5	1,004	469	535	4	4	..
	20 and over	*5,354*	2,949	2,405	207	193	14	5,147	2,756	2,391	21	21	..
	CHRISTIAN	**94**	**57**	**37**	**31**	**20**	**11**	**63**	**37**	**26**	**9**	**7**	**2**
	0—5	*19*	11	8	..	..	..	19	11	8	..	..	..
	5—10	*14*	8	6	2	1	1	12	7	5	..	..	..
	10—15	*5*	4	1	..	..	..	5	4	1	..	..	..
	15—20	*5*	3	2	3	1	2	2	2	..	1	..	1
	20 and over	*51*	31	20	26	18	8	25	13	12	8	7	1
PATIALA.	**ALL RELIGIONS**	**1,625,520**	**900,597**	**724,923**	**67,667**	**63,306**	**4,361**	**1,557,853**	**837,291**	**720,562**	**6,690**	**6,428**	**262**
	0—5	*245,937*	125,272	120,665	..	..	..	245,937	125,272	120,665	..	..	..
	5—10	*205,724*	110,702	95,022	1,734	1,456	278	203,990	109,246	94,744	77	68	9
	10—15	*198,766*	109,765	89,001	4,211	3,659	552	194,555	106,106	88,449	392	361	31
	15—20	*164,215*	92,052	72,163	8,914	8,084	830	155,301	83,968	71,333	1,328	1,280	48
	20 and over	*810,878*	462,806	348,072	52,808	50,107	2,701	758,070	412,699	345,371	4,893	4,719	174
	HINDU	**621,145**	**340,466**	**280,679**	**36,982**	**35,431**	**1,551**	**584,163**	**305,035**	**279,128**	**3,497**	**3,403**	**94**
	0—5	*95,409*	48,244	47,165	..	..	..	95,409	48,244	47,165	..	..	..
	5—10	*79,010*	42,364	36,646	853	738	115	78,157	41,626	36,531	30	27	3
	10—15	*75,269*	41,507	33,762	2,254	2,031	223	73,015	39,476	33,539	196	184	12
	15—20	*61,855*	34,281	27,574	5,036	4,747	289	56,819	29,534	27,285	681	659	22
	20 and over	*309,602*	174,070	135,532	28,839	27,915	924	280,763	146,155	134,608	2,590	2,533	57
	SIKH	**632,972**	**357,193**	**275,779**	**21,963**	**19,924**	**2,039**	**611,009**	**337,269**	**273,740**	**1,645**	**1,596**	**49**
	0—5	*91,724*	47,386	44,338	..	..	..	91,724	47,386	44,338	..	..	..
	5—10	*77,732*	42,219	35,513	624	495	129	77,108	41,724	35,384	19	17	2
	10—15	*76,513*	42,697	33,816	1,368	1,115	253	75,145	41,582	33,563	105	97	8
	15—20	*64,245*	36,896	27,349	2,665	2,259	406	61,580	34,637	26,943	360	347	13
	20 and over	*322,758*	187,995	134,763	17,306	16,055	1,251	305,452	171,940	133,512	1,161	1,135	26
	JAIN	**3,578**	**1,875**	**1,703**	**684**	**655**	**29**	**2,894**	**1,220**	**1,674**	**35**	**35**	..
	0—5	*612*	300	312	..	..	..	612	300	312	..	..	..
	5—10	*457*	232	225	8	8	..	449	224	225	..	..	..
	10—15	*419*	214	205	28	26	2	391	188	203	1	1	..
	15—20	*365*	184	181	90	83	7	275	101	174	6	6	..
	20 and over	*1,725*	945	780	558	538	20	1,167	407	760	28	28	..
	MUSLIM	**363,920**	**198,945**	**164,975**	**7,769**	**7,122**	**647**	**356,151**	**191,823**	**164,328**	**1,306**	**1,271**	**35**
	0—5	*57,522*	28,985	28,537	..	..	..	57,522	28,985	28,537	..	..	..
	5—10	*48,010*	25,618	22,392	240	209	31	47,770	25,409	22,361	21	20	1
	10—15	*46,091*	25,095	20,996	541	477	64	45,550	24,618	20,932	73	71	2
	15—20	*37,328*	20,463	16,865	1,099	980	119	36,229	19,483	16,746	266	260	6
	20 and over	*174,969*	98,784	76,185	5,889	5,456	433	169,080	93,328	75,752	946	920	26
	CHRISTIAN	**1,449**	**806**	**643**	**235**	**142**	**93**	**1,214**	**664**	**550**	**207**	**123**	**84**
	0—5	*236*	128	108	..	..	..	236	128	108	..	..	..
	5—10	*199*	104	95	9	6	3	190	98	92	7	4	3
	10—15	*181*	95	86	20	10	10	161	85	76	17	8	9
	15—20	*144*	76	68	20	11	9	124	65	59	15	8	7
	20 and over	*689*	403	286	186	115	71	503	288	215	168	103	65

BY RELIGION AND AGE.

PART B.—DETAILS OF DISTRICTS AND STATES.—*continued.*

District or State.	Religion and Age.	Population. Total. Persons.	Total. Males.	Total. Females.	Literate. Persons.	Literate. Males.	Literate. Females.	Illiterate. Persons.	Illiterate. Males.	Illiterate. Females.	Literate in English. Persons.	Literate in English. Males.	Literate in English. Females.
1	2	3	4	5	6	7	8	9	10	11	12	13	14
JIND.	ALL RELIGIONS ..	324,676	176,383	148,293	7,881	7,279	602	316,795	169,104	147,691	1,182	1,030	152
	0—5 ..	*50,837*	25,398	25,439	..	..	..	50,837	25,398	25,439	..	..	..
	5—10 ..	*43,937*	23,481	20,456	233	208	25	43,704	23,273	20,431	29	22	7
	10—15 ..	*42,367*	23,257	19,110	580	509	71	41,787	22,748	19,039	83	66	17
	15—20 ..	*33,070*	18,222	14,848	1,098	969	129	31,972	17,253	14,719	207	175	32
	20 and over ..	*154,465*	86,025	68,440	5,970	5,593	377	148,495	80,432	68,063	863	767	96
	HINDU ..	243,561	131,270	112,291	5,507	5,225	282	238,054	126,045	112,009	685	660	25
	0—5 ..	*38,353*	19,070	19,283	..	..	..	38,353	19,070	19,283	..	..	..
	5—10 ..	*33,457*	17,810	15,647	155	146	9	33,302	17,664	15,638	15	15	..
	10—15 ..	*32,237*	17,598	14,639	411	379	32	31,826	17,219	14,607	50	48	2
	15—20 ..	*24,659*	13,463	11,196	787	725	62	23,872	12,738	11,134	119	112	7
	20 and over ..	*114,855*	63,329	51,526	4,154	3,975	179	110,701	59,354	51,347	501	485	16
	SIKH ..	33,290	19,183	14,107	1,284	1,092	192	32,006	18,091	13,915	217	150	67
	0—5 ..	*4,706*	2,410	2,296	..	..	..	4,706	2,410	2,296	..	..	..
	5—10 ..	*3,995*	2,183	1,812	40	33	7	3,955	2,150	1,805	7	4	3
	10—15 ..	*3,967*	2,239	1,728	94	69	25	3,873	2,170	1,703	19	10	9
	15—20 ..	*3,530*	2,086	1,444	165	122	43	3,365	1,964	1,401	45	28	17
	20 and over ..	*17,092*	10,265	6,827	985	868	117	16,107	9,397	6,710	146	108	38
	JAIN ..	1,613	896	717	247	223	24	1,366	673	693	42	40	2
	0—5 ..	*246*	118	128	..	..	..	246	118	128	..	..	..
	5—10 ..	*207*	111	96	10	7	3	197	104	93	..	..	..
	10—15 ..	*192*	112	80	16	13	3	176	99	77	1	1	..
	15—20 ..	*163*	93	70	31	27	4	132	66	66	8	7	1
	20 and over ..	*805*	462	343	190	176	14	615	286	329	33	32	1
	MUSLIM ..	46,002	24,915	21,087	740	681	59	45,262	24,234	21,028	142	125	17
	0—5 ..	*7,493*	3,774	3,719	..	..	..	7,493	3,774	3,719	..	..	..
	5—10 ..	*6,253*	3,364	2,889	21	19	2	6,232	3,345	2,887	..	..	..
	10—15 ..	*5,951*	3,297	2,654	50	42	8	5,901	3,255	2,646	5	2	3
	15—20 ..	*4,697*	2,570	2,127	109	91	18	4,588	2,479	2,109	30	24	6
	20 and over ..	*21,608*	11,910	9,698	560	529	31	21,048	11,381	9,667	107	99	8
	CHRISTIAN ..	210	119	91	103	58	45	107	61	46	96	55	41
	0—5 ..	*39*	26	13	..	..	..	39	26	13	..	..	..
	5—10 ..	*25*	13	12	7	3	4	18	10	8	7	3	4
	10—15 ..	*20*	11	9	9	6	3	11	5	6	8	5	3
	15—20 ..	*21*	10	11	6	4	2	15	6	9	5	4	1
	20 and over ..	*105*	59	46	81	45	36	24	14	10	76	43	33
NABHA.	ALL RELIGIONS ..	287,574	158,086	129,488	13,720	12,439	1,281	273,854	145,647	128,207	1,349	1,327	22
	0—5 ..	*43,291*	22,063	21,228	..	..	..	43,291	22,063	21,228	..	..	..
	5—10 ..	*36,659*	19,668	16,991	559	431	128	36,100	19,237	16,863	19	17	2
	10—15 ..	*34,772*	19,024	15,748	1,106	905	201	33,666	18,119	15,547	94	91	3
	15—20 ..	*27,342*	15,084	12,258	1,791	1,556	235	25,551	13,528	12,023	245	241	4
	20 and over ..	*145,510*	82,247	63,263	10,264	9,547	717	135,246	72,700	62,546	991	978	13
	HINDU ..	132,348	71,592	60,756	7,664	7,230	434	124,684	64,362	60,322	871	859	12
	0—5 ..	*20,661*	10,492	10,169	..	..	..	20,661	10,492	10,169	..	..	..
	5—10 ..	*17,358*	9,237	8,121	285	242	43	17,073	8,995	8,078	11	11	..
	10—15 ..	*16,170*	8,800	7,370	581	512	69	15,589	8,288	7,301	53	51	2
	15—20 ..	*12,302*	6,675	5,627	1,019	940	79	11,283	5,735	5,548	151	149	2
	20 and over ..	*65,857*	36,388	29,469	5,779	5,536	243	60,078	30,852	29,226	656	648	8
	SIKH ..	97,452	55,262	42,190	4,461	4,003	458	92,991	51,259	41,732	288	279	9
	0—5 ..	*13,510*	6,993	6,517	..	..	..	13,510	6,993	6,517	..	..	..
	5—10 ..	*11,624*	6,350	5,274	172	128	44	11,452	6,222	5,230	4	3	1
	10—15 ..	*11,352*	6,329	5,023	345	280	65	11,007	6,049	4,958	32	31	1
	15—20 ..	*9,406*	5,391	4,015	510	431	79	8,896	4,960	3,936	65	63	2
	20 and over ..	*51,560*	30,199	21,361	3,434	3,164	270	48,126	27,035	21,091	187	182	5
	JAIN ..	309	163	146	100	89	11	209	74	135	14	14	..
	0—5 ..	*49*	22	27	..	..	..	49	22	27	..	..	..
	5—10 ..	*39*	19	20	6	4	2	33	15	18	1	1	..
	10—15 ..	*37*	16	21	11	8	3	26	8	18	2	2	..
	15—20 ..	*26*	17	9	12	11	1	14	6	8	2	2	..
	20 and over ..	*158*	89	69	71	66	5	87	23	64	9	9	..
	MUSLIM ..	57,398	31,027	26,366	1,488	1,111	377	55,905	29,916	25,989	174	173	1
	0—5 ..	*9,071*	4,556	4,515	..	..	..	9,071	4,556	4,515	..	..	..
	5—10 ..	*7,637*	4,061	3,576	95	56	39	7,542	4,005	3,537	3	2	1
	10—15 ..	*7,213*	3,870	3,334	169	105	64	7,044	3,774	3,270	7	7	..
	15—20 ..	*5,608*	3,001	2,607	250	174	76	5,358	2,827	2,531	27	27	..
	20 and over ..	*27,864*	15,530	12,334	974	776	198	26,890	14,754	12,136	137	137	..
	CHRISTIAN ..	66	36	30	5	4	1	61	32	29	2	2	..
	0—5 ..	..	..	..	..	..	..	..	..	..	..	..	..
	5—10 ..	..	..	..	..	..	..	..	..	..	..	..	..
	10—15 ..	..	..	..	..	..	..	..	..	..	..	..	..
	15—20 ..	..	..	..	..	..	..	..	..	..	..	..	..
	20 and over ..	*66*	36	30	5	4	1	61	32	29	2	2	..

TABLE XIII.—LITERACY BY RELIGION AND AGE.

PART B.—DETAILS OF DISTRICTS AND STATES.—*concluded.*

District or State.	Religion and Age.	Population.									Literate in English.		
		Total.			Literate.			Illiterate.					
		Persons.	Males.	Females.	Persons.	Males.	Females.	Persons.	Males.	Females.	Persons.	Males.	Females.
1	2	3	4	5	6	7	8	9	10	11	12	13	14
BAHAWALPUR.	**ALL RELIGIONS** ..	**984,612**	**545,103**	**439,509**	**21,998**	**20,732**	**1,266**	**962,614**	**524,371**	**438,248**	**2,755**	**2,667**	**88**
	0—5 ..	*166,369*	85,666	80,703	..	..	..	166,369	85,666	80,703	..	..	..
	5—10 ..	*132,308*	73,359	58,949	898	777	121	131,410	72,582	58,828	50	45	5
	10—15 ..	*110,187*	63,066	47,121	1,742	1,552	190	108,445	61,514	46,931	140	129	11
	15—20 ..	*84,684*	45,556	39,128	3,071	2,872	199	81,613	42,684	38,929	495	480	15
	20 and over ..	*491,064*	277,456	213,608	16,287	15,531	756	474,777	261,925	212,852	2,070	2,013	57
	HINDU ..	**145,007**	**81,897**	**63,110**	**10,563**	**9,849**	**714**	**134,444**	**72,048**	**62,396**	**1,191**	**1,181**	**10**
	0—5 ..	*22,485*	11,493	10,992	..	..	..	22,485	11,493	10,992	..	..	..
	5—10 ..	*18,179*	9,894	8,285	377	309	68	17,802	9,585	8,217	35	34	1
	10—15 ..	*16,019*	8,956	7,063	745	641	104	15,274	8,315	6,959	69	68	1
	15—20 ..	*14,159*	8,007	6,152	1,320	1,220	100	12,839	6,787	6,052	171	170	1
	20 and over ..	*74,165*	43,547	30,618	8,121	7,679	442	66,044	35,868	30,176	916	909	7
	SIKH ..	**34,896**	**20,000**	**14,896**	**1,274**	**1,197**	**77**	**33,622**	**18,803**	**14,819**	**174**	**172**	**2**
	0—5 ..	*5,927*	3,088	2,839	..	..	..	5,927	3,088	2,839	..	..	..
	5—10 ..	*4,693*	2,629	2,064	46	40	6	4,647	2,589	2,058	1	1	..
	10—15 ..	*4,016*	2,333	1,713	88	77	11	3,958	2,256	1,702	2	2	..
	15—20 ..	*3,302*	1,907	1,395	158	141	17	3,144	1,766	1,378	20	19	1
	20 and over ..	*16,928*	10,043	6,885	982	939	43	15,946	9,104	6,842	151	150	1
	JAIN ..	**12**	**7**	**5**	**5**	**4**	**1**	**7**	**3**	**4**	**2**	**2**	..
	0—5 ..	*3*	2	1	..	..	..	3	2	1	..	..	..
	5—10 ..	*1*	..	1	..	..	..	1	..	1	..	..	..
	10—15 ..	*2*	1	1	..	..	..	2	1	1	..	..	..
	15—20 ..	*1*	..	1	..	..	..	1	..	1	..	..	..
	20 and over ..	*5*	4	1	5	4	1	..	..	..	2	2	..
	MUSLIM ..	**799,176**	**440,054**	**359,122**	**9,974**	**9,576**	**398**	**789,202**	**430,478**	**358,724**	**1,261**	**1,245**	**16**
	0—5 ..	*136,858*	70,509	66,349	..	..	..	136,858	70,509	66,349	..	..	..
	5—10 ..	*108,801*	60,481	48,320	463	420	43	108,338	60,061	48,277	8	8	..
	10—15 ..	*89,460*	51,397	38,063	887	823	64	88,573	50,574	37,999	56	56	..
	15—20 ..	*66,720*	35,362	31,358	1,565	1,498	67	65,155	33,864	31,291	285	283	2
	20 and over ..	*397,337*	222,305	175,032	7,059	6,835	224	390,278	215,470	174,808	912	898	14
	CHRISTIAN ..	**1,054**	**613**	**441**	**180**	**104**	**76**	**874**	**509**	**365**	**126**	**66**	**60**
	0—5 ..	*168*	97	71	..	..	..	168	97	71	..	..	..
	5—10 ..	*127*	70	57	12	8	4	115	62	53	6	2	4
	10—15 ..	*115*	64	51	22	11	11	93	53	40	13	3	10
	15—20 ..	*95*	50	45	28	13	15	67	37	30	19	8	11
	20 and over ..	*549*	332	217	118	72	46	431	260	171	88	53	35

TABLE XIII.—LITERACY BY RELIGION AND AGE.

PART C.—DETAILS OF CITIES AND SELECTED TOWNS.

City or Town.	Religion and Age.	Population. Total. Persons.	Total. Males.	Total. Females.	Literate. Persons.	Literate. Males.	Literate. Females.	Illiterate. Persons.	Illiterate. Males.	Illiterate. Females.	Literate in English. Persons.	Literate in English. Males.	Literate in English. Females.
1	2	3	4	5	6	7	8	9	10	11	12	13	14
LAHORE.	ALL RELIGIONS ..	429,747	274,587	155,160	100,885	81,631	19,254	328,862	192,956	135,906	42,916	37,438	5,478
	0—5 ..	*54,737*	29,190	25,547	..	..	..	54,737	29,190	25,547	..	..	..
	5—10 ..	*43,583*	23,707	19,876	5,133	3,219	1,914	38,450	20,488	17,962	1,008	623	385
	10—15 ..	*42,660*	24,618	18,042	9,337	6,348	2,989	33,323	18,270	15,053	2,678	1,957	721
	15—20 ..	*52,093*	34,748	17,345	16,357	13,144	3,213	35,736	21,604	14,132	7,798	6,880	918
	20 and over ..	*236,674*	162,324	74,350	70,058	58,920	11,138	166,616	103,404	63,212	31,432	27,978	3,454
	HINDU ..	139,125	91,667	47,458	38,729	32,648	6,081	100,396	59,019	41,377	15,795	14,704	1,091
	0—5 ..	*16,667*	8,993	7,674	..	..	..	16,667	8,993	7,674	..	..	..
	5—10 ..	*13,052*	7,178	5,874	1,529	913	616	11,523	6,265	5,258	144	64	80
	10—15 ..	*13,246*	7,853	5,393	3,235	2,290	945	10,011	5,563	4,448	851	679	172
	15—20 ..	*17,874*	12,417	5,457	6,289	5,216	1,073	11,585	7,201	4,384	2,882	2,640	242
	20 and over ..	*78,286*	55,226	23,060	27,676	24,229	3,447	50,610	30,997	19,613	11,918	11,321	597
	SIKH ..	23,477	15,526	7,951	7,344	6,177	1,167	16,133	9,349	6,784	2,651	2,291	360
	0—5 ..	*2,745*	1,409	1,336	..	..	..	2,745	1,409	1,336	..	..	..
	5—10 ..	*2,115*	1,147	968	322	210	112	1,793	937	856	49	21	28
	10—15 ..	*2,040*	1,179	861	572	397	175	1,468	782	686	151	98	53
	15—20 ..	*2,969*	2,029	940	1,183	1,042	141	1,786	987	799	654	607	47
	20 and over ..	*13,608*	9,762	3,846	5,267	4,528	739	8,341	5,234	3,107	1,797	1,565	232
	JAIN ..	791	442	349	304	225	79	487	217	270	136	125	11
	0—5 ..	*129*	67	62	..	..	..	129	67	62	..	..	..
	5—10 ..	*98*	51	47	16	12	4	82	39	43	4	3	1
	10—15 ..	*95*	53	42	32	22	10	63	31	32	11	9	2
	15—20 ..	*106*	66	40	65	49	16	41	17	24	30	28	2
	20 and over ..	*363*	205	158	191	142	49	172	63	109	91	85	6
	MUSLIM ..	249,315	156,486	92,829	45,754	36,776	8,978	203,561	119,710	83,851	17,645	16,059	1,586
	0—5 ..	*33,272*	17,722	15,550	..	..	..	33,272	17,722	15,550	..	..	..
	5—10 ..	*26,681*	14,488	12,193	2,792	1,873	919	23,889	12,615	11,274	550	435	115
	10—15 ..	*25,739*	14,755	10,984	4,874	3,384	1,490	20,865	11,371	9,494	1,269	1,037	232
	15—20 ..	*29,197*	18,986	10,211	7,584	6,017	1,567	21,613	12,969	8,644	3,223	2,930	293
	20 and over ..	*134,426*	90,535	43,891	30,504	25,502	5,002	103,922	65,033	38,889	12,603	11,657	946
	CHRISTIAN ..	16,875	10,368	6,507	8,644	5,736	2,908	8,231	4,632	3,599	6,596	4,195	2,401
	0—5 ..	*1,910*	994	916	..	..	..	1,910	994	916	..	..	..
	5—10 ..	*1,624*	835	789	468	208	260	1,156	627	529	255	97	158
	10—15 ..	*1,528*	771	757	617	251	366	911	520	391	390	131	259
	15—20 ..	*1,936*	1,243	693	1,227	814	413	709	429	280	1,001	670	331
	20 and over ..	*9,877*	6,525	3,352	6,332	4,463	1,869	3,545	2,062	1,483	4,950	3,297	1,653
AMRITSAR.	ALL RELIGIONS ..	264,840	158,985	105,855	39,937	32,643	7,294	224,903	126,342	98,561	12,288	10,485	1,803
	0—5 ..	*34,839*	17,654	17,185	..	..	..	34,839	17,654	17,185	..	..	..
	5—10 ..	*30,983*	16,916	14,067	1,947	1,451	496	29,036	15,465	13,571	322	226	96
	10—15 ..	*29,729*	17,122	12,607	4,011	3,090	921	25,718	14,032	11,686	806	652	154
	15—20 ..	*27,850*	17,546	10,304	6,509	5,128	1,381	21,341	12,418	8,923	2,082	1,745	337
	20 and over ..	*141,439*	89,747	51,692	27,470	22,974	4,496	113,969	66,773	47,196	9,078	7,862	1,216
	HINDU ..	97,837	59,544	38,293	17,706	15,482	2,224	80,131	44,062	36,069	3,953	3,797	156
	0—5 ..	*12,526*	6,312	6,214	..	..	..	12,526	6,312	6,214	..	..	..
	5—10 ..	*11,521*	6,328	5,193	624	495	129	10,897	5,833	5,064	43	39	4
	10—15 ..	*11,164*	6,608	4,556	1,409	1,100	309	9,755	5,508	4,247	165	155	10
	15—20 ..	*10,948*	7,311	3,637	2,759	2,288	471	8,189	5,023	3,166	616	586	30
	20 and over ..	*51,678*	32,985	18,693	12,914	11,599	1,315	38,764	21,386	17,378	3,129	3,017	112
	SIKH ..	32,009	18,721	13,288	6,275	5,094	1,181	25,734	13,627	12,107	2,942	2,895	47
	0—5 ..	*4,142*	2,164	1,978	..	..	..	4,142	2,164	1,978	..	..	..
	5—10 ..	*3,679*	2,075	1,604	300	255	45	3,379	1,820	1,559	97	94	3
	10—15 ..	*3,498*	2,077	1,421	621	529	92	2,877	1,548	1,329	219	211	8
	15—20 ..	*3,179*	2,003	1,176	1,051	931	120	2,128	1,072	1,056	527	520	7
	20 and over ..	*17,511*	10,402	7,109	4,303	3,379	924	13,208	7,023	6,185	2,099	2,070	29
	JAIN ..	604	329	275	132	102	30	472	227	245	25	25	..
	0—5 ..	*105*	52	53	..	..	..	105	52	53	..	..	..
	5—10 ..	*79*	40	39	7	4	3	72	36	36	..	..	..
	10—15 ..	*76*	42	34	17	11	6	59	31	28	2	2	..
	15—20 ..	*71*	44	27	29	21	8	42	23	19	5	5	..
	20 and over ..	*273*	151	122	79	66	13	194	85	109	18	18	..
	MUSLIM ..	132,362	79,324	53,038	15,203	11,668	3,535	117,159	67,656	49,503	5,020	3,521	1,499
	0—5 ..	*17,812*	9,008	8,804	..	..	..	17,812	9,008	8,804	..	..	..
	5—10 ..	*15,460*	8,366	7,094	988	678	310	14,472	7,688	6,784	166	82	84
	10—15 ..	*14,749*	8,289	6,460	1,894	1,419	475	12,855	6,870	5,985	381	259	122
	15—20 ..	*13,391*	8,056	5,335	2,540	1,833	707	10,851	6,223	4,628	864	586	278
	20 and over ..	*70,950*	45,605	25,345	9,781	7,738	2,043	61,169	37,867	23,302	3,609	2,594	1,015
	CHRISTIAN ..	1,819	941	878	596	280	316	1,223	661	562	337	236	101
	0—5 ..	*227*	105	122	..	..	..	227	105	122	..	..	..
	5—10 ..	*220*	96	124	28	19	9	192	77	115	16	11	5
	10—15 ..	*222*	94	128	70	31	39	152	63	89	39	25	14
	15—20 ..	*234*	119	115	127	52	75	107	67	40	68	46	22
	20 and over ..	*916*	527	389	371	178	193	545	349	196	214	164	50

TABLE XIII.—LITERACY

PART C.—DETAILS OF CITIES AND SELECTED TOWNS.

City or Town.	Religion and Age.	POPULATION.									Literate in English.		
		Total.			Literate.			Illiterate.					
		Persons.	Males.	Females.	Persons.	Males.	Females.	Persons.	Males.	Females.	Persons.	Males.	Females.
1	2	3	4	5	6	7	8	9	10	11	12	13	14
MULTAN.	ALL RELIGIONS ..	119,457	68,119	51,338	15,301	13,596	1,705	104,156	54,523	49,633	5,035	4,640	895
	0—5 ..	15,509	7,770	7,739	..	..	..	15,509	7,770	7,739	..	..	..
	5—10 ..	13,820	7,554	6,266	712	568	144	13,108	6,986	6,122	110	77	33
	10—15 ..	13,200	7,436	5,764	1,452	1,208	244	11,748	6,228	5,520	315	263	52
	15—20 ..	12,748	7,340	5,408	2,618	2,323	295	10,130	5,017	5,113	1,017	952	65
	20 and over ..	64,180	38,019	26,161	10,519	9,497	1,022	53,661	28,522	25,139	3,593	3,348	245
	HINDU ..	40,424	22,585	17,839	7,529	6,703	826	32,895	15,882	17,018	2,422	2,326	96
	0—5 ..	5,319	2,698	2,621	..	..	..	5,319	2,698	2,621	..	..	..
	5—10 ..	4,750	2,565	2,185	413	336	77	4,337	2,229	2,108	29	22	7
	10—15 ..	4,587	2,536	2,051	873	731	142	3,714	1,805	1,909	170	156	14
	15—20 ..	4,394	2,568	1,826	1,393	1,238	155	3,001	1,330	1,671	558	539	19
	20 and over ..	21,374	12,218	9,156	4,850	4,398	452	16,524	7,820	8,704	1,665	1,609	56
	SIKH ..	2,960	1,828	1,132	962	813	149	1,998	1,015	983	202	181	21
	0—5 ..	397	212	185	..	..	..	397	212	185	..	..	..
	5—10 ..	320	172	148	29	20	9	291	152	139	5	4	1
	10—15 ..	295	156	139	57	44	13	238	112	126	14	12	2
	15—20 ..	400	259	141	165	140	25	235	119	116	37	31	6
	20 and over ..	1,548	1,029	519	711	609	102	837	420	417	146	134	12
	JAIN ..	424	211	213	91	78	13	333	133	200	14	14	..
	0—5 ..	73	35	38	..	..	..	73	35	38	..	..	..
	5—10 ..	51	25	26	5	2	3	46	23	23	1	1	..
	10—15 ..	48	22	26	6	2	4	42	20	22	..	..	..
	15—20 ..	38	18	20	4	2	2	34	16	18	..	..	..
	20 and over ..	214	111	103	76	72	4	138	39	99	13	13	..
	MUSLIM ..	72,134	41,221	30,913	5,440	5,082	358	66,694	36,139	30,555	1,818	1,773	45
	0—5 ..	9,287	4,603	4,684	..	..	..	9,287	4,603	4,684	..	..	..
	5—10 ..	8,370	4,616	3,754	205	185	20	8,165	4,431	3,734	34	32	2
	10—15 ..	7,988	4,575	3,413	434	397	37	7,554	4,178	3,376	75	72	3
	15—20 ..	7,491	4,203	3,288	916	857	59	6,575	3,346	3,229	336	324	12
	20 and over ..	38,998	23,224	15,774	3,885	3,643	242	35,113	19,581	15,532	1,373	1,345	28
	CHRISTIAN ..	1,823	1,278	545	1,123	813	310	700	465	235	498	281	217
	0—5 ..	171	88	83	..	..	..	171	88	83	..	..	..
	5—10 ..	131	66	65	47	18	29	84	48	36	37	15	22
	10—15 ..	118	54	64	65	25	40	53	29	24	51	19	32
	15—20 ..	258	200	58	111	64	47	147	136	11	72	45	27
	20 and over ..	1,145	870	275	900	706	194	245	164	81	338	202	136
RAWALPINDI.	ALL RELIGIONS ..	119,284	75,971	43,313	27,523	24,769	2,754	91,761	51,202	40,559	12,397	11,158	1,239
	0—5 ..	15,170	7,872	7,298	..	..	..	15,170	7,872	7,298	..	..	..
	5—10 ..	12,217	6,634	5,583	1,247	1,030	217	10,970	5,604	5,366	416	309	107
	10—15 ..	11,673	6,659	5,014	2,139	1,796	343	9,534	4,863	4,671	812	669	143
	15—20 ..	13,453	8,728	4,725	4,175	3,727	448	9,278	5,001	4,277	2,052	1,901	151
	20 and over ..	66,771	46,078	20,693	19,962	18,216	1,746	46,809	27,862	18,947	9,117	8,279	838
	HINDU ..	40,161	24,669	15,492	12,177	11,879	298	27,984	12,790	15,194	4,916	4,901	15
	0—5 ..	5,294	2,781	2,513	..	..	..	5,294	2,781	2,513	..	..	..
	5—10 ..	4,262	2,306	1,956	549	522	27	3,713	1,784	1,929	127	126	1
	10—15 ..	4,047	2,300	1,747	934	890	44	3,113	1,410	1,703	301	299	2
	15—20 ..	4,554	2,818	1,736	1,825	1,767	58	2,729	1,051	1,678	794	790	4
	20 and over ..	22,004	14,464	7,540	8,869	8,700	169	13,135	5,764	7,371	3,694	3,686	8
	SIKH ..	15,532	9,399	6,133	5,355	4,538	817	10,177	4,861	5,316	1,798	1,747	51
	0—5 ..	2,339	1,200	1,139	..	..	..	2,339	1,200	1,139	..	..	..
	5—10 ..	1,782	936	846	256	220	36	1,526	716	810	50	46	4
	10—15 ..	1,798	930	868	514	426	88	1,284	504	780	176	166	10
	15—20 ..	1,809	1,066	743	810	640	170	999	426	573	348	336	13
	20 and over ..	7,804	5,267	2,537	3,775	3,252	523	4,029	2,015	2,014	1,224	1,200	24
	JAIN ..	1,025	563	462	237	231	6	788	332	456	57	56	1
	0—5 ..	153	80	73	..	..	..	153	80	73	..	..	..
	5—10 ..	132	71	61	14	13	1	118	58	60	2	2	..
	10—15 ..	132	73	59	22	22	..	110	51	59	6	6	..
	15—20 ..	97	50	47	26	24	2	71	26	45	11	11	..
	20 and over ..	511	289	222	175	172	3	336	117	219	38	37	1
	MUSLIM ..	55,637	36,732	18,905	5,424	4,936	488	50,213	31,796	18,417	1,476	1,405	71
	0—5 ..	6,550	3,403	3,147	..	..	..	6,550	3,403	3,147	..	..	..
	5—10 ..	5,504	3,039	2,465	223	171	52	5,281	2,868	2,413	48	41	7
	10—15 ..	5,256	3,115	2,141	429	345	84	4,827	2,770	2,057	111	100	11
	15—20 ..	6,165	4,131	2,034	837	741	96	5,328	3,390	1,938	246	229	17
	20 and over ..	32,162	23,044	9,118	3,935	3,679	256	28,227	19,365	8,862	1,071	1,035	36
	CHRISTIAN ..	6,850	4,562	2,288	4,290	3,158	1,132	2,560	1,404	1,156	4,121	3,032	1,089
	0—5 ..	824	404	420	..	..	..	824	404	420	..	..	..
	5—10 ..	528	277	251	204	104	100	324	173	151	188	94	94
	10—15 ..	435	238	197	239	113	126	196	125	71	217	98	119
	15—20 ..	824	661	163	675	554	121	149	107	42	652	536	116
	20 and over ..	4,239	2,982	1,257	3,172	2,387	785	1,067	595	472	3,064	2,304	760

BY RELIGION AND AGE.

PART C.—DETAILS OF CITIES AND SELECTED TOWNS.—*continued.*

City or Town.	Religion and Age.	POPULATION. Total. Persons.	Total. Males.	Total. Females.	Literate. Persons.	Literate. Males.	Literate. Females.	Illiterate. Persons.	Illiterate. Males.	Illiterate. Females.	Literate in English. Persons.	Literate in English. Males.	Literate in English. Females.
1	2	3	4	5	6	7	8	9	10	11	12	13	14
SIALKOT.	**ALL RELIGIONS** ..	**100,973**	**59,894**	**41,079**	**12,054**	**10,987**	**1,067**	**88,919**	**48,907**	**40,012**	**4,844**	**4,145**	**699**
	0—5 ..	*14,970*	7,679	7,291	..	..	..	14,970	7,679	7,291	..	..	..
	5—10 ..	*11,992*	6,577	5,415	695	586	109	11,297	5,991	5,306	310	244	66
	10—15 ..	*11,213*	6,387	4,826	1,292	1,119	173	9,921	5,268	4,653	556	459	97
	15—20 ..	*11,213*	6,910	4,303	2,038	1,820	218	9,175	5,090	4,085	830	690	140
	20 and over ..	*51,585*	32,341	19,244	8,029	7,462	567	43,556	24,879	18,677	3,148	2,752	396
	HINDU ..	**18,644**	**11,098**	**7,546**	**1,790**	**1,406**	**384**	**16,854**	**9,692**	**7,162**	**1,818**	**1,112**	**201**
	0—5 ..	*2,692*	1,421	1,271	..	..	..	2,692	1,421	1,271	..	..	..
	5—10 ..	*2,158*	1,175	983	178	129	49	1,980	1,046	934	140	115	25
	10—15 ..	*2,055*	1,160	895	250	189	61	1,805	971	834	183	155	28
	15—20 ..	*2,082*	1,299	783	248	177	71	1,834	1,122	712	164	126	38
	20 and over ..	*9,657*	6.043	3,614	1,114	911	203	8,543	5,132	3,411	826	716	110
	SIKH ..	**4,931**	**3,338**	**1,593**	**489**	**364**	**125**	**4,442**	**2,974**	**1,468**	**341**	**264**	**77**
	0—5 ..	*570*	282	288	..	..	..	570	282	288	..	..	..
	5—10 ..	*449*	251	198	60	44	16	389	207	182	37	26	11
	10—15 ..	*428*	259	169	89	57	32	339	202	137	53	36	17
	15—20 ..	*641*	477	164	92	63	29	549	414	135	60	45	15
	20 and over ..	*2,843*	2,069	774	248	200	48	2,595	1,869	726	191	157	34
	JAIN ..	**1,570**	**858**	**712**	**154**	**85**	**69**	**1,416**	**773**	**648**	**113**	**65**	**48**
	0—5 ..	*261*	136	125	..	..	..	261	136	125	..	..	..
	5—10 ..	*217*	121	96	18	12	6	199	109	90	14	9	5
	10—15 ..	*189*	104	85	27	17	10	162	87	75	21	14	7
	15—20 ..	*169*	93	76	33	16	17	136	77	59	21	10	11
	20 and over ..	*734*	404	330	76	40	36	658	364	294	57	32	25
	MUSLIM ..	**69,700**	**40,605**	**29,095**	**6,898**	**6,825**	**73**	**62,802**	**33,780**	**29,022**	**2,346**	**2,309**	**37**
	0—5 ..	*10,630*	5,423	5,207	..	..	..	10,630	5,423	5,207	..	..	..
	5—10 ..	*8,569*	4,711	3,858	364	359	5	8,205	4,352	3,853	76	74	2
	10—15 ..	*8,041*	4,598	3,443	807	794	13	7,234	3,804	3,430	228	223	5
	15—20 ..	*7,609*	4,534	3,075	1,183	1,162	21	6,426	3,372	3,054	471	460	11
	20 and over ..	*34,851*	21,339	13,512	4,544	4,510	34	30,307	16,829	13,478	1,571	1,552	19
	CHRISTIAN ..	**6,095**	**3,986**	**2,109**	**2,717**	**2,304**	**413**	**3,378**	**1,682**	**1,696**	**731**	**395**	**336**
	0—5 ..	*808*	414	394	..	..	..	808	414	394	..	..	..
	5—10 ..	*595*	318	277	73	41	32	522	277	245	43	20	23
	10—15 ..	*496*	265	231	117	61	56	379	204	175	71	31	40
	15—20 ..	*707*	506	201	482	402	80	225	104	121	114	49	65
	20 and over ..	*3,489*	2,483	1,006	2,045	1,800	245	1,444	683	761	503	295	208
JULLUNDUR.	**ALL RELIGIONS** ..	**89,030**	**51,119**	**37,911**	**14,028**	**11,607**	**2,421**	**75,002**	**39,512**	**35,490**	**4,262**	**3,823**	**439**
	0—5 ..	*12,416*	6,223	6,193	..	..	..	12,416	6,223	6,193	..	..	..
	5—10 ..	*10,563*	5,682	4,881	736	554	182	9,827	5,128	4,699	130	101	29
	10—15 ..	*10,033*	5,600	4,433	1,545	1,170	375	8,488	4,430	4,058	477	385	92
	15—20 ..	*9,430*	5,765	3,665	2,516	2,022	494	6,914	3,743	3,171	1,032	926	106
	20 and over ..	*46,588*	27,849	18,739	9,231	7,861	1,370	37,357	19,988	17,369	2,623	2,411	212
	HINDU ..	**27,940**	**16,734**	**11,206**	**7,125**	**5,884**	**1,241**	**20,815**	**10,850**	**9,965**	**1,981**	**1,648**	**283**
	0—5 ..	*3,574*	1,814	1,760	..	..	..	3,574	1,814	1,760	..	..	..
	5—10 ..	*3,050*	1,683	1,367	354	267	87	2,696	1,416	1,280	50	37	13
	10—15 ..	*3,073*	1,776	1,297	745	554	191	2,328	1,222	1,106	245	186	59
	15—20 ..	*3,190*	2,136	1,054	1,175	938	237	2,015	1,198	817	501	434	67
	20 and over ..	*15,053*	9,325	5,728	4,851	4,125	726	10,202	5,200	5,002	1,135	991	144
	SIKH ..	**3,003**	**2,148**	**855**	**1,176**	**1,046**	**130**	**1,827**	**1,102**	**725**	**474**	**463**	**11**
	0—5 ..	*323*	177	146	..	..	..	323	177	146	..	..	..
	5—10 ..	*251*	153	98	38	31	7	213	122	91	17	17	..
	10—15 ..	*302*	216	86	129	118	11	173	98	75	55	55	..
	15—20 ..	*447*	352	95	312	283	29	135	69	66	122	121	1
	20 and over ..	*1,680*	1,250	430	697	614	83	983	636	347	280	270	10
	JAIN ..	**1,014**	**515**	**499**	**131**	**100**	**31**	**883**	**415**	**468**	**49**	**45**	**4**
	0—5 ..	*182*	94	88	..	..	..	182	94	88	..	..	..
	5—10 ..	*158*	95	63	21	18	3	137	77	60	12	12	..
	10—15 ..	*134*	79	55	27	21	6	107	58	49	15	14	1
	15—20 ..	*90*	39	51	19	12	7	71	27	44	7	6	1
	20 and over ..	*450*	208	242	64	49	15	386	159	227	15	13	2
	MUSLIM ..	**52,577**	**28,878**	**23,699**	**4,851**	**4,042**	**809**	**47,726**	**24,886**	**22,890**	**1,616**	**1,531**	**85**
	0—5 ..	*7,723*	3,813	3,910	..	..	..	7,723	3,813	3,910	..	..	..
	5—10 .	*6,653*	3,507	3,146	289	225	64	6,364	3,282	3,082	38	33	5
	10—15 ..	*6,110*	3,306	2,804	570	444	126	5,540	2,862	2,678	130	114	16
	15—20 ..	*5,149*	2,859	2,290	861	693	168	4,288	2,166	2,122	359	335	24
	20 and over ..	*26,942*	15,393	11,549	3,131	2,680	451	23,811	12,713	11,098	1,089	1,049	40
	CHRISTIAN ..	**1,533**	**1,187**	**346**	[illegible]	**489**	**130**	**914**	**698**	**216**	**181**	**125**	**56**
	0—5 ..	*121*	56	65	[illegible]	..	..	121	56	65	..	..	..
	5—10 ..	*70*	34	35	6	8	18	44	26	18	12	1	11
	10—15 ..	*54*	25	29	53	24	29	1	1	..	31	15	16
	15—20 ..	*237*	206	31	113	82	31	124	124	..	40	27	13
	20 and over ..	*1,051*	866	185	427	375	52	624	491	133	98	82	16

TABLE XIII.—LITERACY BY RELIGION AND AGE.

PART C.—DETAILS OF CITIES AND SELECTED TOWNS.—*concluded.*

City or Town.	Religion and Age.	Population.									Literate in English.		
		Total.			Literate.			Illiterate.					
		Persons.	Males.	Females.	Persons.	Males.	Females.	Persons.	Males.	Females.	Persons.	Males.	Females.
1	2	3	4	5	6	7	8	9	10	11	12	13	14
AMBALA.	ALL RELIGIONS ..	86,592	51,523	35,069	16,180	13,479	2,701	70,412	38,044	32,368	6,367	5,954	418
	0—5 ..	*10,991*	5,498	5,493	..	..	..	10,991	5,498	5,493	..	..	..
	5—10 ..	*9,458*	5,083	4,375	761	525	236	8,697	4,558	4,139	154	136	18
	10—15 ..	*9,195*	5,135	4,060	1,415	1,030	385	7,780	4,105	3,675	420	383	37
	15—20 ..	*9,558*	5,816	3,742	2,529	2,083	446	7,029	3,733	3,296	1,176	1,118	58
	20 and over ..	*47,390*	29,991	17,399	11,475	9,841	1,634	35,915	20,150	15,765	4,617	4,317	300
	HINDU ..	39,945	23,894	16,051	7,328	6,223	1,105	32,617	17,671	14,946	2,505	2,418	87
	0—5 ..	*4,959*	2,526	2,433	..	..	..	4,959	2,526	2,433	..	..	..
	5—10 ..	*4,269*	2,358	1,911	368	258	110	3,901	2,100	1,801	52	44	8
	10—15 ..	*4,222*	2,426	1,796	706	530	176	3,516	1,896	1,620	193	179	14
	15—20 ..	*4,334*	2,600	1,734	1,085	885	200	3,249	1,715	1,534	448	431	17
	20 and over ..	*22,161*	13,984	8,177	5,169	4,550	619	16,992	9,434	7,558	1,812	1,764	48
	SIKH ..	4,143	2,845	1,298	1,315	1,128	187	2,828	1,717	1,111	402	370	32
	0—5 ..	*403*	199	204	..	..	..	403	199	204	..	..	..
	5—10 ..	*327*	180	147	44	34	10	283	146	137	11	8	3
	10—15 ..	*336*	195	141	92	73	19	244	122	122	35	28	7
	15—20 ..	*613*	447	166	246	211	35	367	236	131	94	84	10
	20 and over ..	*2,464*	1,824	640	933	810	123	1,531	1,014	517	262	250	12
	JAIN ..	1,269	694	575	424	341	83	845	353	492	122	116	6
	0—5 ..	*169*	85	84	..	..	..	169	85	84	..	..	..
	5—10 ..	*145*	72	73	26	19	7	119	53	66	2	2	..
	10—15 ..	*149*	84	65	53	38	15	96	46	50	13	12	1
	15—20 ..	*127*	69	58	59	46	13	68	23	45	25	25	..
	20 and over ..	*679*	384	295	286	238	48	393	146	247	82	77	5
	MUSLIM ..	38,089	21,981	16,108	4,795	4,085	710	33,294	17,896	15,398	1,497	1,457	40
	0—5 ..	*5,172*	2,554	2,618	..	..	..	5,172	2,554	2,618	..	..	..
	5—10 ..	*4,495*	2,370	2,125	246	174	72	4,249	2,196	2,053	51	49	2
	10—15 ..	*4,307*	2,350	1,957	467	347	120	3,840	2,003	1,837	139	134	5
	15—20 ..	*4,063*	2,374	1,689	755	632	123	3,308	1,742	1,566	283	276	7
	20 and over ..	*20,052*	12,333	7,719	3,327	2,932	395	16,725	9,401	7,324	1,024	998	26
	CHRISTIAN ..	3,138	2,103	1,035	2,315	1,699	616	823	404	419	1,839	1,591	248
	0—5 ..	*287*	134	153	..	..	..	287	134	153	..	..	..
	5—10 ..	*222*	103	119	77	40	37	145	63	82	38	33	5
	10—15 ..	*181*	80	101	97	42	55	84	38	46	40	30	10
	15—20 ..	*420*	325	95	384	309	75	36	16	20	326	302	24
	20 and over ..	*2,028*	1,461	567	1,757	1,308	449	271	153	118	1,435	1,226	209
FEROZEPORE.	ALL RELIGIONS ..	64,634	38,884	25,750	12,210	10,126	2,084	52,424	28,758	23,666	4,550	4,164	386
	0—5 ..	*8,233*	4,227	4,006	..	..	..	8,233	4,227	4,006	..	..	..
	5—10 ..	*6,944*	3,704	3,240	769	483	286	6,175	3,221	2,954	173	113	60
	10—15 ..	*6,739*	3,723	3,016	1,235	832	403	5,504	2,891	2,613	337	251	86
	15—20 ..	*7,320*	4,586	2,734	2,020	1,648	372	5,300	2,938	2,362	851	763	88
	20 and over ..	*35,398*	22,644	12,754	8,186	7,163	1,023	27,212	15,481	11,731	3,189	3,037	152
	HINDU ..	26.936	16,119	10,817	5,760	4,719	1,041	21,176	11,400	9,776	1,961	1,821	140
	0—5 ..	*3,343*	1,770	1,573	..	..	..	3,343	1,770	1,573	..	..	..
	5—10 ..	*2,917*	1,588	1,329	397	270	127	2,520	1,318	1,202	79	64	15
	10—15 ..	*2,857*	1,604	1,253	677	493	184	2,180	1,111	1,069	209	180	29
	15—20 ..	*2.961*	1,825	1,136	939	749	190	2,022	1,076	946	402	367	35
	20 and over ..	*14,858*	9,332	5,526	3,747	3.207	540	11,111	6,125	4,986	1,271	1,219	61
	SIKH ..	4,439	2,899	1,540	1,406	1,070	336	3,033	1,829	1,204	428	388	40
	0—5 ..	*466*	267	199	..	..	..	466	267	199	..	..	..
	5—10 ..	*432*	221	211	115	46	69	317	175	142	11	8	3
	10—15 ..	*449*	237	212	178	87	91	271	150	121	37	28	9
	15—20 ..	*565*	394	171	232	179	53	333	215	118	93	78	15
	20 and over ..	*2,527*	1,780	747	881	758	123	1,646	1,022	624	287	274	13
	JAIN ..	511	263	248	162	128	34	349	135	214	56	55	1
	0—5 ..	*73*	37	36	..	..	..	73	37	36	..	..	..
	5—10 ..	*57*	27	30	9	4	5	48	23	25	2	2	..
	10—15 ..	*55*	28	27	12	8	4	43	20	23	5	5	..
	15—20 ..	*51*	30	21	21	17	4	30	13	17	11	11	..
	20 and over ..	*275*	141	134	120	99	21	155	42	113	38	37	1
	MUSLIM ..	28,464	16,760	11,704	3,249	2,813	436	25,215	13,947	11,268	690	681	9
	0—5 ..	*3,851*	1,899	1,952	..	..	..	3,851	1,899	1,952	..	..	..
	5—10 ..	*3,162*	1,669	1,493	170	135	35	2,992	1,534	1,458	21	21	..
	10—15 ..	*3,028*	1,669	1,359	283	216	67	2,745	1,453	1,292	23	21	2
	15—20 ..	*3,240*	1,963	1,277	550	470	80	2,690	1,493	1,197	102	100	2
	20 and over ..	*15,183*	9,560	5,623	2,246	1,992	254	12,037	7,568	5,369	544	539	5
	CHRISTIAN ..	2,942	2,040	902	[illegible]	1,339	237	1,366	701	665	1,397	1,201	196
	0—5 ..	*323*	168	155	..	..	..	323	168	155	..	..	..
	5—10 ..	*235*	122	113	76	26	50	159	96	63	60	18	42
	10—15 ..	*201*	99	102	84	27	57	117	72	45	63	17	46
	15—20 ..	*344*	279	65	271	226	45	73	53	20	241	205	36
	20 and over ..	*1,839*	1,372	467	1,145	1,060	85	694	312	382	1,033	961	72

TABLE XIV.

LITERACY BY SELECTED CASTES, TRIBES OR RACES.

1. The selected castes and the localities for this Table, are the same as those dealt with in Table VIII.

2. Separate figures for Arya, Brahmo and Dev Dharm, which for the purpose of this Table are included among the Hindus, have been printed for British Districts as Table XIV-A in Part III of the Report.

3. In this Table figures for Arya (Vedic Dharm), Brahmo and Dev Dharm are included in those for Hindus, but to illustrate the literacy of those classes, separate figures have been printed as Table XIV-A in Part III of the Report.

TABLE XIV.—LITERACY BY SELECTED CASTES, TRIBES OR RACES.

Serial No.	Caste, Tribe or Race.	Locality.	Population (7 years and over). Total. Persons.	Total. Males.	Total. Females.	Literate. Persons.	Literate. Males.	Literate. Females.	Illiterate. Persons.	Illiterate. Males.	Illiterate. Females.	Literate in English (7 years and over). Persons.	Males.	Females.
	1	2	3	4	5	6	7	8	9	10	11	12	13	14
1	Aggarwal (Hindu) ..	A. C. ..	*280,826*	154,117	126,709	78,888	74,770	4,118	201,938	79,347	122,591	7,151	6,940	211
2	Aggarwal (Jain) ..	A. C. ..	*19,584*	10,359	9,225	6,298	5,744	554	13,286	4,615	8,671	768	751	17
3	Ahir (Hindu) ..	A. C. ..	*173,140*	97,296	75,844	3,109	2,934	175	170,031	94,362	75,669	480	473	7
4	Ahir (Muslim) ..	D. ..	*1,851*	1,012	839	58	52	6	1,793	960	833	10	9	1
5	Arain (Muslim) ..	A. C. D. ..	*1,038,928*	577,253	461,675	36,005	32,082	3,923	1,002,923	545,171	457,752	6,889	6,470	419
6	Arora (Hindu) ..	C. D. ..	*524,582*	285,150	239,432	115,048	101,935	13,113	409,534	183,215	226,319	12,248	11,629	619
7	Arora (Sikh) ..	C. D. ..	*86,805*	47,648	39,157	24,041	19,338	4,703	62,764	28,310	34,454	3,022	2,836	186
8	Awan (Muslim) ..	C. D. ..	*423,693*	228,230	195,463	15,044	13,807	1,237	408,649	214,423	194,226	2,260	2,192	68
9	Bawaria (Hindu) ..	A. C. D. ..	*12,148*	6,425	5,723	150	124	26	11,998	6,301	5,697	11	11	..
10	Bawaria (Sikh) ..	C. D. ..	*12,329*	6,517	5,812	164	147	17	12,165	6,370	5,795	3	3	..
11	Biloch (Muslim) ..	A. C. D. ..	*489,101*	271,073	218,028	6,803	6,423	380	482,298	264,650	217,648	637	620	17
12	Brahman (Hindu) ..	A. B. C. D...	*867,855*	483,169	384,686	141,864	129,189	12,675	725,991	353,980	372,011	22,531	21,763	768
13	Brahman (Sikh) ..	C. D. ..	*5,466*	3,310	2,156	1,604	1,302	302	3,862	2,008	1,854	278	253	25
14	Chamar (Hindu) ..	A. B. C. D...	*545,026*	296,236	248,790	2,769	2,536	233	542,257	293,700	248,557	257	255	2
15	Chamar (Ad-Dharmi) ..	A. B. C. D...	*203,600*	112,273	91,327	2,647	2,500	147	200,953	109,773	91,180	63	58	5
16	Chamar (Sikh) ..	A. C. ..	*124,036*	69,310	54,726	1,686	1,634	52	122,350	67,676	54,674	35	34	1
17	Chhimba (Hindu) ..	A. C. ..	*17,034*	9,452	7,582	685	643	42	16,349	8,809	7,540	59	55	4
18	Chhimba (Sikh) ..	C. ..	*13,728*	7,645	6,083	1,285	1,173	112	12,443	6,472	5,971	73	69	4
19	Chhimba (Muslim) ..	A. C.D. ..	*41,880*	22,780	19,100	848	805	43	41,032	21,975	19,057	87	87	..
20	Chuhra (Hindu) ..	A. B. C. D...	*287,549*	159,104	128,445	2,374	1,977	397	285,175	157,127	128,048	274	236	38
21	Chuhra (Ad-Dharmi) ..	A. C. D. ..	*67,058*	37,271	29,787	364	334	30	66,694	36,937	29,757	12	12	..
22	Chuhra (Sikh) ..	C. ..	*123,268*	67,678	55,590	1,107	997	110	122,161	66,681	55,480	48	46	2
23	Chuhra (Muslim) ..	C. D. ..	*16,886*	9,148	7,738	105	55	50	16,781	9,093	7,688	26	10	16
24	Chuhra (Christian) ..	A. C. D. ..	*26,768*	14,987	11,781	446	348	98	26,322	14,639	11,683	146	106	40
25	Dagi and Koli (Hindu) ..	A. B. C. ..	*149,086*	78,221	70,865	762	726	36	148,324	77,495	70,829	60	58	2
26	Dhobi (Hindu) ..	A. C. ..	*8,254*	4,700	3,554	188	157	31	8,066	4,543	3,523	22	19	3
27	Dhobi (Muslim) ..	A. C. D. ..	*126,939*	69,722	57,217	2,722	2,463	259	124,217	67,259	56,958	253	220	33
28	Faqir (Hindu) ..	C. D. ..	*19,506*	13,232	6,274	3,089	2,917	172	16,417	10,315	6,102	140	140	..
29	Faqir (Sikh) ..	C. ..	*4,029*	2,940	1,089	1,232	1,165	67	2,797	1,775	1,022	29	29	..
30	Faqir (Muslim) ..	A. C. D. ..	*199,647*	110,481	89,166	3,478	3,353	125	196,169	107,128	89,041	160	157	3
31	Gujjar (Hindu) ..	A. B. C. D...	*139,160*	79,756	59,404	1,594	1,514	80	137,566	78,242	59,324	132	132	..
32	Gujjar (Sikh) ..	C. ..	*1,900*	1,037	863	55	53	2	1,845	984	861	6	6	..
33	Gujjar (Muslim) ..	A, B. C. D...	*414,454*	230,375	184,079	9,509	8,903	606	404,945	221,472	183,473	1,358	1,320	38
34	Harni (Muslim) ..	C. ..	*2,636*	1,617	1,019	46	46	..	2,590	1,571	1,019	9	9	..
35	Jat (Hindu) ..	A. B. C. D...	*804,331*	451,072	353,259	16,915	16,121	794	787,416	434,951	352,465	2,288	2,215	73
36	Jat (Sikh) ..	A. C. D. ..	*1,752,202*	1,011,769	740,433	101,455	90,412	11,043	1,650,747	921,357	729,390	12,269	11,939	330
37	Jat (Muslim) ..	A. C. D. ..	*2,298,893*	1,274,578	1,024,315	47,241	44,010	3,231	2,251,652	1,230,568	1,021,084	6,919	6,708	211
38	Jhiwar (Hindu) ..	A. B. C. ..	*100,173*	55,372	44,801	2,183	2,023	160	97,990	53,349	44,641	221	218	3
39	Jhiwar (Sikh) ..	C. ..	*43,645*	23,450	20,195	2,071	1,918	153	41,574	21,532	20,042	133	132	1
40	Jhiwar (Muslim) ..	C. D. ..	*73,927*	40,245	33,682	1,110	1,029	81	72,817	39,216	33,601	127	115	12
41	Julaha (Hindu) ..	A. B. C. ..	*42,110*	22,956	19,154	608	576	32	41,502	22,380	19,122	43	41	2
42	Julaha (Sikh) ..	C. ..	*3,034*	1,659	1,375	211	200	11	2,823	1,459	1,364	..	..	..
43	Julaha (Muslim) ..	A. B. C. D...	*481,193*	264,618	216,575	9,216	8,546	670	471,977	256,072	215,905	804	782	22
44	Kamboh (Hindu) ..	A. C. D. ..	*29,945*	16,648	13,297	1,074	988	86	28,871	15,660	13,211	125	122	3
45	Kamboh (Sikh) ..	C. D. ..	*77,534*	41,662	35,872	3,490	3,121	369	74,044	38,541	35,503	365	358	7
46	Kamboh (Muslim) ..	C. D. ..	*75,868*	41,974	33,894	2,303	2,049	254	73,565	39,925	33,640	361	325	36
47	Kashmiri (Muslim) ..	C. D. ..	*160,497*	91,942	68,555	15,030	12,838	2,192	145,467	79,104	66,363	3,986	3,761	225
48	*Khatri (Hindu)* ..	A. B. C. D...	*373,101*	*209,096*	*164,005*	*108,937*	*91,407*	*17,530*	*264,164*	117,689	146,475	28,333	26,983	1,350
49	Khatri (Sikh) ..	C. D. ..	*43,057*	23,130	19,927	13,868	10,407	3,461	29,189	12,723	16,466	2,871	2,666	205
50	Kumhar (Hindu) ..	A. B. C. ..	*125,588*	68,713	56,875	1,673	1,551	122	123,915	67,162	56,753	163	158	5
51	Kumhar (Sikh) ..	C. ..	*24,966*	13,781	11,185	839	764	75	24,127	13,017	11,110	76	75	1
52	Kumhar (Muslim) ..	A. C. D. ..	*329,339*	180,495	148,844	3,512	3,255	257	325,827	177,240	148,587	319	312	7
53	Lohar (Hindu) ..	A. B. C. ..	*60,728*	33,010	27,718	1,152	1,085	67	59,576	31,925	27,651	69	69	..
54	Lohar (Sikh) ..	A. C. ..	*13,343*	7,208	6,135	1,048	936	112	12,295	6,272	6,023	79	77	2
55	Lohar (Muslim) ..	A. C. D. ..	*189,027*	103,580	85,447	5,709	5,245	464	183,318	98,335	84,983	668	639	29
56	Machhi (Muslim) ..	A. C. D. ..	*244,741*	135,319	109,422	2,538	2,324	214	242,203	132,995	109,208	272	262	10
57	Meo (Muslim) ..	A. ..	*98,353*	53,555	44,798	1,152	1,140	12	97,201	52,415	44,786	59	58	1
58	Mirasi (Muslim) ..	A. C. D. ..	*190,731*	103,317	87,414	4,437	4,206	231	186,294	99,111	87,183	303	292	11
59	Mochi (Hindu) ..	C. ..	*3,843*	2,660	1,183	160	148	12	3,683	2,512	1,171	19	19	..
60	Mochi (Muslim) ..	C. D. ..	*361,075*	199,178	161,897	4,202	3,943	259	356,873	195,235	161,638	304	301	3
61	Mussalli (Muslim) ..	C. D. ..	*311,337*	169,721	141,616	1,133	1,046	87	310,204	168,675	141,529	49	47	2
62	Nai (Hindu) ..	A. B. C. ..	*82,449*	46,037	36,412	2,892	2,711	181	79,557	43,326	36,231	360	356	4
63	Nai (Sikh) ..	C. ..	*31,967*	18,020	13,947	1,939	1,796	143	30,028	16,224	13,804	160	157	3
64	Nai (Muslim) ..	A. C. D. ..	*185,763*	102,027	83,736	3,799	3,534	265	181,964	98,493	83,471	331	322	9
65	Pakhiwara (Muslim) ..	C. ..	*2,400*	1,362	1,038	65	61	4	2,335	1,301	1,034	10	10	..
66	Pathan (Muslim) ..	A. C. D. ..	*276,849*	156,194	120,655	24,949	21,795	3,154	251,900	134,399	117,501	5,816	5,557	259
67	Kanet (Hindu) ..	A. B. C. ..	*250,262*	130,380	119,882	6,367	6,282	85	243,895	124,098	119,797	389	387	2
68	Kanet (Buddhist) ..	B. ..	*4,357*	2,194	2,163	258	258	..	4,099	1,936	2,163	..	..	..
69	Rajput (Hindu) ..	A. B. C. D...	*480,330*	272,372	207,958	39,378	36,126	3,252	440,952	236,246	204,706	5,768	5,608	160
70	Rajput (Sikh) ..	C. D. ..	*38,184*	21,842	16,342	5,226	4,267	959	32,958	17,575	15,383	881	821	60
71	Rajput (Muslim) ..	A. C. D. ..	*1,355,811*	734,715	621,096	56,589	51,542	5,047	1,299,222	683,173	616,049	11,465	10,956	50[illegible]
72	Rathi (Hindu) ..	B. ..	*108,658*	54,732	53,926	3,397	3,324	73	105,261	51,408	53,853	89	89	..
73	Saini (Hindu) ..	A. C. ..	*60,367*	33,779	26,588	2,251	2,145	106	58,116	31,634	26,482	408	404	..
74	Saini (Sikh) ..	A. C ..	*66,215*	35,926	30,289	4,728	4,319	409	61,487	31,607	29,880	732	726	[illegible]
75	Sansi (Hindu) ..	A. C. ..	*20,616*	11,505	9,111	219	194	25	20,397	11,311	9,086	6	6	..
76	Sayad (Muslim) ..	A. C. D. ..	*235,408*	128,002	107,406	31,213	27,693	3,520	204,195	100,309	103,886	6,459	6,183	27[illegible]
77	Sheikh (Muslim) ..	A. C. D. ..	*328,710*	186,755	141,955	43,103	36,934	6,169	285,607	149,821	135,786	10,792	10,178	61[illegible]
78	Sunar (Hindu) ..	A. B. C. D...	*79,469*	43,611	35,858	10,212	9,439	773	69,257	34,172	35,085	686	678	[illegible]
79	Sunar (Sikh) ..	C. D. ..	*20,135*	10,930	9,205	2,924	2,648	276	17,211	8,282	8,929	230	229	[illegible]
80	Sunar (Muslim) ..	C. D. ..	*25,151*	13,724	11,427	1,457	1,326	131	23,694	12,398	11,296	135	117	1[illegible]
81	Tarkhan (Hindu) ..	A. B. C. ..	*118,385*	64,655	53,730	3,042	2,903	139	115,343	61,752	53,591	266	261	[illegible]
82	Tarkhan (Sikh) ..	A. C. D. ..	*128,034*	71,869	56,165	11,924	10,665	1,259	116,110	61,204	54,906	1,809	1,755	5[illegible]
83	Tarkhan (Muslim) ..	A. C. D. ..	*271,390*	149,455	121,935	6,978	6,381	597	264,412	143,074	121,338	722	707	1[illegible]
84	Teli (Muslim) ..	A. C. D. ..	*265,798*	147,428	118,370	3,720	3,469	251	262,078	143,959	118,119	366	357	[illegible]

TABLE XV.

LANGUAGES.

1. Part I, shows the mother tongues of the persons living in the Province. If the mother tongue returned was a dialect it has been included in the language to which it belonged, according to Sir George Grierson's scheme of classification contained in his Linguistic Survey of India.

2. Further detail of languages found in small numbers and lumped together in the main Table appears below:—

Column No.	Languages.	Punjab Province.			British Territory.			Punjab States. A.—Having political relations with the Punjab Government.			Punjab States. B.—Having political relations with the Government of India.		
		Persons.	Males.	Females.	Persons.	Males.	Females.	Persons.	Males.	Females.	Persons.	Males.	Females.
1	2	3	4	5	6	7	8	9	10	11	12	13	14
42 to 44	Ladakhi ..	12	11	1	..	..	..	..	..	..	12	11	1
,,	Kanashi ..	348	170	178	348	170	178	..	..	..	..	..	..
78 to 80	Odki ..	4,952	2,629	2,323	4,952	2,629	2,323	..	..	..	..	..	..
81 to 83	Assamese ..	10	5	5	10	5	5	..	..	..	..	..	..
,,	Bhili ..	2,942	1,655	1,287	4	3	1	..	..	..	2,938	1,652	1,286
,,	Burmese ..	196	87	109	174	77	97	..	..	..	22	10	12
,,	Gondi ..	1	1	..	1	1	..	..	..	..	..	..	..
,,	Khasi ..	1	..	1	1	..	1	..	..	..	..	..	..
,,	Malayalam ..	23	7	16	22	7	15	..	..	..	1	..	1
,,	Oriya ..	128	66	62	106	56	50	21	9	12	1	1	..
,,	Sanskrit ..	21	15	6	21	15	6	..	..	..	..	..	..
96 to 98	Japanese ..	4	2	2	4	2	2	..	..	..	..	..	..
,,	Javanese ..	7	5	2	7	5	2	..	..	..	..	..	..
,,	Malayan ..	3	2	1	3	2	1	..	..	..	..	..	..
,,	Singhalese ..	1	1	..	1	1	..	..	..	..	..	..	..
,,	Syriac ..	1	..	1	1	..	1	..	..	..	..	..	..
,,	Turkish ..	17	12	5	16	11	5	..	..	..	1	1	..
,,	Siamese ..	1	..	1	1	..	1	..	..	..	..	..	..
128 to 130	Danish ..	1	1	..	1	1	..	..	..	..	..	..	..
,,	Dutch ..	1	..	1	1	..	1	..	..	..	..	..	..
,,	Norwegian ..	4	..	4	3	..	3	1	..	1	..	..	..
,,	Russian ..	6	6	..	3	3	..	..	..	..	3	3	..
,,	Spanish ..	6	2	4	6	2	4	..	..	..	..	..	..
,,	Swedish ..	2	..	2	1	..	1	1	..	1	..	..	..
,,	Welsh ..	3	1	2	3	1	2	..	..	..	..	..	..

3. Part II, which is prepared for the first time, shows the number of persons who habitually use some other language subsidiary to their mother tongue.

TABLE XV.—PART I,

Serial No.	District or State.	Population. Persons.	Population. Males.	Population. Females.	Total. Persons.	Total. Males.	Total. Females.	Indian Vernaculars. Vernaculars of the Punjab. Total. Persons.	Indian Vernaculars. Vernaculars of the Punjab. Total. Males.	Indian Vernaculars. Vernaculars of the Punjab. Total. Females.
1	2	3	4	5	6	7	8	9	10	11
	PUNJAB	28,490,857	15,561,194	12,929,663	28,459,378	15,539,866	12,919,512	28,398,058	15,499,686	12,898,372
	BRITISH TERRITORY	23,580,852	12,880,510	10,700,342	23,550,111	12,859,650	10,690,461	23,506,247	12,830,208	10,676,039
	AMBALA DIVISION	4,077,565	2,226,856	1,850,709	4,072,752	2,223,867	1,848,885	4,070,038	2,221,780	1,848,258
1	Hissar	*899,479*	485,690	413,789	899,415	485,647	413,768	899,284	485,564	413,720
2	Rohtak	*805,621*	432,855	372,766	805,586	432,835	372,751	805,491	432,771	372,720
3	Gurgaon	*740,163*	398,513	341,650	739,970	398,417	341,553	739,856	398,346	341,510
4	Karnal	*852,614*	469,870	382,744	852,551	469,829	382,722	852,456	469,759	382,697
5	Ambala	*742,902*	416,411	326,491	739,464	414,114	325,350	738,867	413,709	325,158
6	Simla	*36,786*	23,517	13,269	35,766	23,025	12,741	34,084	21,631	12,453
	JULLUNDUR DIVISION	4,606,446	2,491,638	2,114,808	4,602,167	2,488,642	2,113,525	4,592,696	2,482,799	2,109,897
7	Kangra	*801,312*	415,288	386,024	801,196	415,217	385,979	794,384	411,142	383,242
8	Hoshiarpur	*1,032,187*	551,867	480,320	1,032,150	551,842	480,308	1,032,093	551,803	480,290
9	Jullundur	*943,721*	512,667	431,054	942,416	511,604	430,812	942,239	511,508	430,731
10	Ludhiana	*672,494*	375,560	296,934	671,602	375,183	296,419	670,254	374,381	295,873
11	Ferozepore	*1,156,732*	636,256	520,476	1,154,803	634,796	520,007	1,153,726	633,965	519,761
	LAHORE DIVISION	5,879,075	3,277,661	2,601,414	5,865,439	3,268,486	2,596,953	5,844,056	3,258,172	2,590,884
12	Lahore	*1,378,570*	794,389	584,181	1,369,239	788,178	581,061	1,360,265	781,267	578,998
13	Amritsar	*1,117,120*	621,040	496,080	1,115,724	620,351	495,373	1,108,583	616,218	492,365
14	Gurdaspur	*970,898*	531,935	438,963	970,521	531,751	438,770	967,142	529,081	438,061
15	Sialkot	*979,617*	537,301	442,316	977,306	535,328	441,978	976,754	534,866	441,888
16	Gujranwala	*736,138*	408,606	327,532	736,065	408,562	327,503	735,276	407,854	327,422
17	Sheikhupura	*696,732*	384,390	312,342	696,584	384,316	312,268	696,036	383,886	312,150
	RAWALPINDI DIVISION	3,914,849	2,092,622	1,822,227	3,908,653	2,088,309	1,820,344	3,905,479	2,086,171	1,819,308
18	Gujrat	*922,427*	498,336	424,091	922,216	498,226	423,990	921,677	497,814	423,863
19	Shahpur	*821,490*	445,836	375,654	821,385	445,777	375,608	821,272	445,714	375,558
20	Jhelum	*541,076*	282,714	258,362	540,840	282,575	258,265	540,563	282,400	258,163
21	Rawalpindi	*634,357*	342,771	291,586	629,217	339,138	290,079	627,241	337,860	289,381
22	Attock	*583,960*	306,949	277,011	583,593	306,665	276,928	583,404	306,516	276,888
23	Mianwali	*411,539*	216,016	195,523	411,402	215,928	195,474	411,322	215,867	195,455
	MULTAN DIVISION	5,102,917	2,791,733	2,311,184	5,101,100	2,790,346	2,310,754	5,093,978	2,786,286	2,307,692
24	Montgomery	*999,772*	552,456	447,316	999,554	552,322	447,232	999,354	552,187	447,167
25	Lyallpur	*1,151,351*	630,749	520,602	1,151,190	630,681	520,509	1,149,940	629,926	520,014
26	Jhang	*664,833*	355,671	309,162	664,736	355,611	309,125	664,613	355,493	309,120
27	Multan	*1,174,900*	646,025	528,875	1,173,590	644,920	528,670	1,170,178	642,969	527,209
28	Muzaffargarh	*591,375*	320,674	270,701	591,354	320,661	270,693	590,985	320,488	270,497
29	Dera Ghazi Khan	*520,686*	286,158	234,528	520,676	286,151	234,525	518,908	285,223	233,685
	PUNJAB STATES	4,910,005	2,680,684	2,229,321	4,909,267	2,680,216	2,229,051	4,891,811	2,669,478	2,222,333
	A.—Having Political relations with the Punjab Government.	437,787	229,290	208,497	437,696	229,260	208,436	437,299	228,958	208,341
1	Dujana	*28,216*	14,537	13,679	28,212	14,535	13,677	28,211	14,534	13,677
2	Pataudi	*18,873*	9,922	8,951	18,870	9,920	8,950	18,870	9,920	8,950
3	Kalsia	*59,848*	33,306	26,542	59,848	33,306	26,542	59,784	33,251	26,533
4	*SIMLA HILL STATES*	330,850	171,525	159,325	330,766	171,499	159,267	330,434	171,253	159,181
	Bashahr	*104,389*	51,593	52,796	104,388	51,592	52,796	104,385	51,589	52,796
	Nalagarh	*50,015*	26,635	23,380	50,015	26,635	23,380	50,006	26,628	23,378
	Keonthal	*48,093*	25,734	22,359	48,049	25,724	22,325	47,929	25,637	22,292
	Baghal	*26,352*	13,457	12,895	26,352	13,457	12,895	26,335	13,443	12,892
	Jubbal	*27,172*	14,507	12,665	27,172	14,507	12,665	27,164	14,500	12,664
	Other Simla Hill States	*74,829*	39,599	35,230	74,790	39,584	35,206	74,615	39,456	35,159
	B.—Having Political relations with the Government of India.	4,472,218	2,451,394	2,020,824	4,471,571	2,450,956	2,020,615	4,454,512	2,440,520	2,013,992
5	Loharu	*23,338*	12,326	11,012	23,336	12,325	11,011	23,336	12,325	11,011
6	Sirmoor	*148,568*	82,384	66,184	148,548	82,379	66,169	148,086	82,001	66,085
7	Bilaspur	*100,994*	53,154	47,840	100,994	53,154	47,840	100,991	53,151	47,840
8	Mandi	*207,465*	107,876	99,589	207,280	107,719	99,561	205,358	106,024	99,334
9	Suket	*58,408*	30,851	27,557	58,392	30,841	27,551	58,319	30,813	27,506
10	Kapurthala	*316,757*	171,529	145,228	316,732	171,512	145,220	316,716	171,501	145,215
11	Maler Kotla	*83,072*	45,883	37,189	83,065	45,878	37,187	83,063	45,877	37,186
12	Faridkot	*164,364*	91,163	73,201	164,361	91,162	73,199	161,406	89,501	71,905
13	Chamba	*146,870*	76,059	70,811	146,864	76,055	70,809	144,783	74,936	69,847
14	Patiala } Phulkian States	*1,625,520*	900,597	724,923	1,625,276	900,452	724,824	1,625,101	900,352	724,749
15	Jind } Phulkian States	*324,676*	176,383	148,293	324,630	176,352	148,278	324,601	176,329	148;272
16	Nabha } Phulkian States	*287,574*	158,086	129,488	287,574	158,086	129,488	287,561	158,079	129,482
17	Bahawalpur	*984,612*	545,103	439,509	984,519	545,041	439,478	975,191	539,631	435,560

INDIAN VERNACULARS.

VERNACULARS OF THE PUNJAB.

Punjabi.			*Lahnda or Western Punjabi.*			*Hindustani.*			*Western Pahari.*			*Rajasthani.*			
Persons.	Males.	Females.	Persons.	Males.	Females.	Persons.	Males.	Females.	Persons.	Males.	Females.	Persons.	Males.	Females.	Serial No.
12	13	14	15	16	17	18	19	20	21	22	23	24	25	26	
14,515,090	**8,028,969**	**6,486,121**	**7,378,252**	**3,959,627**	**3,418,625**	**3,988,023**	**2,192,621**	**1,795,402**	**1,690,676**	**882,568**	**808,108**	**613,444**	**315,554**	**297,890**	
12,154,001	**6,713,128**	**5,440,873**	**6,528,325**	**3,492,185**	**3,036,140**	**3,431,393**	**1,893,670**	**1,537,723**	**787,058**	**410,201**	**376,857**	**428,894**	**218,515**	**210,379**	
507,405	**289,936**	**217,469**	**5**	**3**	**2**	**3,182,357**	**1,739,365**	**1,442,992**	**23,921**	**14,408**	**9,513**	**354,877**	**176,828**	**178,049**	
219,718	121,750	97,968	..	..	..	485,772	263,251	222,521	7	6	1	193,747	100,521	93,226	1
526	318	208	..	..	..	804,887	432,393	372,494	6	5	1	41	24	17	2
898	511	387	1	1	..	579,149	322,379	256,770	5	3	2	159,777	75,427	84,350	3
10,430	8,905	7,525	..	..	..	835,784	460,677	375,107	20	13	7	186	131	55	4
264,517	154,620	109,897	4	2	2	471,342	256,858	214,484	1,290	983	307	1,086	705	381	5
5,316	3,832	1,484	..	..	..	5,423	3,807	1,616	22,593	13,398	9,195	40	20	20	6
3,684,755	**2,009,362**	**1,675,393**	**66**	**36**	**30**	**64,372**	**34,352**	**30,020**	**753,849**	**390,055**	**363,794**	**61,433**	**34,129**	**27,304**	
13,137	7,379	5,758	..	..	..	1,247	596	651	753,633	389,933	363,700	147	88	59	7
1,030,016	550,854	479,162	2	2	..	1,655	672	983	107	48	59	53	36	17	8
939,504	509,901	429,603	7	6	1	2,554	1,463	1,091	38	37	1	30	7	23	9
657,682	368,690	288,992	20	14	6	12,208	5,445	6,763	47	18	29	161	129	32	10
1,044,416	572,538	471,878	37	14	23	46,708	26,176	20,532	24	19	5	61,042	33,869	27,173	11
5,463,825	**3,029,545**	**2,434,280**	**257,328**	**140,677**	**116,651**	**108,275**	**72,523**	**35,752**	**3,769**	**2,298**	**1,471**	**2,041**	**1,136**	**905**	
1,268,623	718,736	549,887	464	255	209	84,452	57,256	27,196	650	453	197	802	468	334	12
1,095,569	607,529	488,040	39	22	17	11,309	7,597	3,712	355	272	83	856	449	407	13
960,652	525,375	435,277	2	..	2	3,331	1,805	1,526	2,618	1,490	1,128	32	28	4	14
974,318	533,406	440,912	..	..	..	1,854	956	898	1	1	..	62	34	28	15
575,880	319,150	256,730	156,310	86,451	69,859	1,958	1,382	376	137	76	61	67	59	8	16
588,783	325,349	263,434	100,513	53,949	46,564	5,371	3,527	1,344	8	6	2	222	98	124	17
967,152	**529,008**	**438,144**	**2,843,388**	**1,501,957**	**1,341,431**	**34,077**	**21,313**	**12,764**	**669**	**477**	**192**	**102**	**65**	**37**	
630,545	337,256	293,289	283,031	155,983	127,048	6,872	3,596	3,276	120	75	45	19	17	2	18
231,083	129,309	101,774	576,013	306,269	268,744	9,320	6,307	3,013	120	97	23	35	17	18	19
58,736	33,886	24,850	479,372	246,985	232,387	1,453	939	514	..	..	..	21	14	7	20
27,077	17,746	9,931	582,764	309,382	273,382	14,353	9,169	5,184	414	295	119	1	1	..	21
11,784	6,935	4,849	547,235	285,941	261,294	1,643	1,040	603	1	1	..	2	2	..	22
7,327	3,876	3,451	375,973	197,397	178,576	436	262	174	14	9	5	24	14	10	23
1,530,864	**855,277**	**675,587**	**3,427,538**	**1,849,512**	**1,578,026**	**42,312**	**26,117**	**16,195**	**4,850**	**2,963**	**1,887**	**10,441**	**6,357**	**4,084**	
429,613	245,109	184,504	535,356	285,755	249,601	17,267	10,970	6,297	4,541	2,734	1,807	6,198	3,619	2,579	24
929,787	508,512	421,275	206,764	113,403	93,361	10,310	6,163	4,147	39	19	20	1,729	947	782	25
32,516	19,621	12,895	630,595	334,751	295,844	523	365	158	207	188	19	..	..	..	26
132,664	77,530	55,134	1,013,395	549,228	464,167	12,760	7,730	5,030	1	1	..	1,936	1,494	442	27
3,775	2,387	1,388	584,534	316,466	268,068	1,329	813	516	62	21	41	437	228	209	28
2,509	2,118	391	456,894	249,909	206,985	123	76	47	..	..	..	141	69	72	29
2,361,089	**1,315,841**	**1,045,248**	**849,927**	**467,442**	**382,485**	**556,630**	**298,951**	**257,679**	**903,618**	**472,367**	**431,251**	**184,550**	**97,089**	**87,511**	
46,022	**25,521**	**20,501**	..	..	..	**97,185**	**52,422**	**44,763**	**264,127**	**136,921**	**127,206**	**44**	**23**	**21**	
15	10	5	..	..	..	28,195	14,524	13,671	..	..	..	1	..	1	1
1	1	..	..	..	..	18,869	9,919	8,950	..	..	..	..	..	..	2
10,551	5,847	4,704	..	..	..	49,203	27,388	21,815	..	..	..	26	12	14	3
35,455	**19,663**	**15,792**	..	..	..	**918**	**591**	**327**	**264,127**	**136,921**	**127,206**	**17**	**11**	**6**	4
562	323	239	..	..	..	80	53	27	74,708	37,786	36,922	..	..	..	
29,580	16,051	13,529	..	..	..	47	26	21	20,377	10,549	9,828	..	..	..	
904	670	234	..	..	..	257	175	82	46,038	24,291	21,747	..	..	..	
76	68	8	..	..	..	12	12	..	26,231	13,347	12,884	..	..	..	
266	174	92	..	..	..	73	40	33	26,794	14,261	12,533	..	..	..	
4,067	2,377	1,690	..	..	..	449	285	164	69,979	36,687	33,292	17	11	6	
2,315,067	**1,290,320**	**1,024,747**	**849,927**	**467,442**	**382,485**	**459,445**	**246,529**	**212,916**	**639,491**	**335,446**	**304,045**	**184,506**	**97,016**	**87,490**	
16	8	8	..	..	..	23,320	12,317	11,003	..	..	..	..	..	..	5
11,744	6,576	5,168	..	..	..	24,128	13,802	10,326	111,999	61,410	50,589	155	153	2	6
10,800	5,905	4,895	..	..	..	17	11	6	90,168	47,229	42,939	..	..	..	7
3,435	2,107	1,328	2	1	1	192	111	81	200,804	103,188	97,616	14	5	9	8
779	126	653	..	..	..	13	13	..	57,497	30,656	26,841	..	..	..	9
316,250	171,243	145,007	..	..	..	436	239	197	7	4	3	12	10	2	10
82,794	45,710	37,084	..	..	..	267	165	102	..	..	..	1	1	..	11
156,067	85,973	70,094	..	..	..	4,765	3,170	1,595	..	..	..	572	356	216	12
2,157	1,269	888	2	2	..	48	33	15	140,661	72,562	68,099	1	1	..	13
1,386,328	775,496	610,832	2	..	2	47,772	24,823	22,949	38,306	20,352	17,954	152,591	79,591	73,000	14
66,688	38,246	28,442	..	..	..	257,615	137,875	119,740	37	34	3	231	151	80	15
203,867	114,915	88,952	1	1	..	83,489	43,054	40,435	12	11	1	189	95	94	16
74,142	42,746	31,396	849,920	467,438	382,482	17,383	10,916	6,467	..	..	..	30,740	16,653	14,087	17

Serial No.	District or State.	INDIAN VERNACULARS.														
		VERNACULARS OF THE PUNJAB.														
		Pashto.			*Balochi.*			*Kanauri.*			*Lahuli.*			*Tibetan.*		
		Persons.	Males.	Females.	Persons.	Males.	Females.	Persons.	Males.	Females.	Persons.	Males.	Females.	Persons.	Males.	Females.
1	2	27	28	29	30	31	32	33	34	35	36	37	38	39	40	41
	PUNJAB	**92,554**	**57,186**	**35,868**	**60,985**	**34,292**	**26,693**	**26,067**	**12,039**	**14,028**	**27,335**	**13,788**	**13,547**	**5,272**	**2,861**	**2,411**
	BRITISH TERRITORY ..	**90,020**	**55,312**	**34,708**	**59,804**	**33,634**	**26,170**	**2**	**2**	..	**24,861**	**12,382**	**12,479**	**1,541**	**1,009**	**582**
	AMBALA DIVISION ..	**850**	**744**	**106**	..	..	..	..	..	..	..	..	..	**623**	**496**	**127**
1	Hissar	40	36	4	..	..	..	..	..	..	..	..	..	..	..	..
2	Rohtak	31	31	..	..	..	..	..	..	..	..	..	..	..	..	..
3	Gurgaon	26	25	1	..	..	..	..	..	..	..	..	..	..	..	..
4	Karnal	36	33	3	..	..	..	..	..	..	..	..	..	..	..	..
5	Ambala	612	525	87	..	..	..	..	..	..	..	..	..	16	16	..
6	Simla	105	94	11	..	..	..	..	..	..	..	..	..	607	480	127
	JULLUNDUR DIVISION ..	**2,070**	**1,816**	**254**	**112**	**64**	**48**	..	..	..	**24,861**	**12,382**	**12,479**	**835**	**438**	**397**
7	Kangra	180	160	20	1	1	..	..	..	..	24,861	12,382	12,479	835	438	397
8	Hoshiarpur	150	129	21	110	62	48	..	..	..	..	..	..	..	..	..
9	Jullundur	106	94	12	..	..	..	..	..	..	..	..	..	..	..	..
10	Ludhiana	135	84	51	1	1	..	..	..	..	..	..	..	..	..	..
11	Ferozepore	1,499	1,349	150	..	..	..	..	..	..	..	..	..	..	..	..
	LAHORE DIVISION ..	**8,581**	**6,773**	**1,808**	**158**	**149**	**9**	**2**	**2**	..	..	..	..	**77**	**69**	**8**
12	Lahore	5,128	3,959	1,169	141	135	6	2	2	..	..	..	..	3	3	..
13	Amritsar	451	345	106	4	4	..	..	..	..	..	..	..	..	..	..
14	Gurdaspur	426	312	114	7	5	2	..	..	..	..	..	..	74	66	8
15	Sialkot	518	468	50	1	1	..	..	..	..	..	..	..	..	..	..
16	Gujranwala	920	733	187	4	3	1	..	..	..	..	..	..	..	..	..
17	Sheikhupura	1,138	956	182	1	1	..	..	..	..	..	..	..	..	..	..
	RAWALPINDI DIVISION ..	**59,890**	**33,187**	**26,703**	**190**	**153**	**37**	..	..	..	..	..	..	**6**	**6**	..
18	Gujrat	1,090	887	203	..	..	..	..	..	..	..	..	..	..	..	..
19	Shahpur	5,694	3,713	1,981	7	2	5	..	..	..	..	..	..	..	..	..
20	Jhelum	970	569	401	6	2	4	..	..	..	..	..	..	..	..	..
21	Rawalpindi	2,019	1,256	763	7	5	2	..	..	..	..	..	..	6	6	..
22	Attock	22,634	12,492	10,142	105	105	..	..	..	..	..	..	..	..	..	..
23	Mianwali	27,483	14,270	13,213	65	39	26	..	..	..	..	..	..	..	..	..
	MULTAN DIVISION ..	**18,629**	**12,792**	**5,837**	**59,344**	**33,268**	**26,076**	..	..	..	..	..	..	..	..	..
24	Montgomery	6,289	3,961	2,328	90	39	51	..	..	..	..	..	..	..	..	..
25	Lyallpur	1,307	881	426	4	1	3	..	..	..	..	..	..	..	..	..
26	Jhang	764	564	200	8	4	4	..	..	..	..	..	..	..	..	..
27	Multan	7,554	5,778	1,776	1,868	1,208	660	..	..	..	..	..	..	..	..	..
28	Muzaffargarh	841	568	273	7	5	2	..	..	..	..	..	..	..	..	..
29	Dera Ghazi Khan ..	1,874	1,040	834	57,367	32,011	25,356	..	..	..	..	..	..	..	..	..
	PUNJAB STATES ..	**2,534**	**1,874**	**660**	**1,181**	**658**	**523**	**26,065**	**12,037**	**14,028**	**2,474**	**1,406**	**1,068**	**3,731**	**1,852**	**1,879**
	A.—Having Political relations with the Punjab Government. ..	**306**	**301**	**5**	..	..	..	**26,020**	**12,012**	**14,008**	..	..	..	**3,595**	**1,758**	**1,837**
1	Dujana	..	..	..	..	..	..	..	..	..	..	..	..	..	..	..
2	Pataudi	..	..	..	..	..	..	..	..	..	..	..	..	..	..	..
3	Kalsia	4	4	..	..	..	..	..	..	..	..	..	..	..	..	..
4	*SIMLA HILL STATES* ..	**302**	**297**	**5**	..	..	..	**26,020**	**12,012**	**14,008**	..	..	..	**3,595**	**1,758**	**1,837**
	Bashahr	..	..	..	..	..	..	26,020	12,012	14,008	..	..	..	3,015	1,415	1,600
	Nalagarh	2	2	..	..	..	..	..	..	..	..	..	..	..	..	..
	Keonthal	259	255	4	..	..	..	..	..	..	..	..	..	471	246	225
	Baghal	8	8	..	..	..	..	..	..	..	..	..	..	8	8	..
	Jubbal	..	..	..	..	..	..	..	..	..	..	..	..	31	25	6
	Other Simla Hill States ..	33	32	1	..	..	..	..	..	..	..	..	..	70	64	6
	B.—Having Political relations with the Government of India. ..	**2,228**	**1,573**	**655**	**1,181**	**658**	**523**	**45**	**25**	**20**	**2,474**	**1,406**	**1,068**	**136**	**94**	**42**
5	Loharu	..	..	..	..	..	..	..	..	..	..	..	..	..	..	..
6	Sirmoor	43	43	..	..	..	..	..	..	..	..	..	..	13	13	..
7	Bilaspur	6	6	..	..	..	..	..	..	..	..	..	..	..	..	..
8	Mandi	169	150	19	..	..	..	19	11	8	653	414	239	62	30	32
9	Suket	4	4	..	..	..	..	26	14	12	..	..	..	..	..	..
10	Kapurthala	7	4	3	4	1	3	..	..	..	..	..	..	..	..	..
11	Maler Kotla	1	1	..	..	..	..	..	..	..	..	..	..	..	..	..
12	Faridkot	2	2	..	..	..	..	..	..	..	..	..	..	..	..	..
13	Chamba	31	25	6	1	1	..	..	..	..	1,821	992	829	61	51	10
14	Patiala (Phulkian States) ..	102	90	12	..	..	..	..	..	..	..	..	..	..	..	..
15	Jind (Phulkian States) ..	30	23	7	..	..	..	..	..	..	..	..	..	..	..	..
16	Nabha (Phulkian States) ..	3	3	..	..	..	..	..	..	..	..	..	..	..	..	..
17	Bahawalpur	1,330	1,222	608	1,176	656	520	..	..	..	..	..	..	..	..	..

INDIAN VERNACULARS.																								
			OTHER INDIAN VERNACULARS.																					
Others.			Total.			*Kashmiri.*			*Sindhi.*			*Gujarati.*			*Marathi.*			*Tamil.*			*Telugu.*			
Persons.	Males.	Females.	Persons.	Males.	Females.	Persons.	Males.	Females.	Persons.	Males.	Females.	Persons.	Males.	Females.	Persons.	Males.	Females.	Persons.	Males.	Females.	Persons.	Males.	Females.	Serial No.
42	43	44	45	46	47	48	49	50	51	52	53	54	55	56	57	58	59	60	61	62	63	64	65	
360	**181**	**179**	**61,320**	**40,180**	**21,140**	**21,822**	**15,989**	**5,833**	**11,581**	**6,813**	**4,768**	**2,521**	**1,734**	**787**	**973**	**736**	**237**	**852**	**429**	**423**	**124**	**67**	**57**	
348	**170**	**178**	**43,864**	**29,442**	**14,422**	**19,493**	**14,360**	**5,133**	**2,294**	**1,424**	**870**	**2,382**	**1,640**	**742**	**935**	**717**	**218**	**797**	**397**	**400**	**124**	**67**	**57**	
..	..	..	**2,714**	**2,087**	**627**	**1,234**	**1,099**	**135**	**48**	**24**	**24**	**229**	**141**	**88**	**112**	**81**	**31**	**84**	**57**	**27**	**56**	**36**	**20**	
..	..	..	131	83	48	15	13	2	11	8	3	44	30	14	1	..	1	..	..	..	..	..	..	1
..	..	..	95	64	31	1	1	..	2	2	..	1	1	..	21	18	3	1	1	..	2	1	1	2
..	..	..	114	71	43	..	..	..	2	1	1	33	22	11	26	16	10	..	..	..	47	28	19	3
..	..	..	95	70	25	7	3	4	1	1	..	4	4	..	3	3	..	1	1	..	2	2	..	4
..	..	..	597	405	192	76	48	28	32	12	20	115	64	51	49	34	15	28	26	2	4	4	..	5
..	..	..	1,682	1,394	288	1,135	1,034	101	..	..	..	32	20	12	12	10	2	54	29	25	1	1	..	6
343	**165**	**178**	**9,471**	**5,843**	**3,628**	**2,627**	**1,926**	**701**	**54**	**32**	**22**	**70**	**44**	**26**	**56**	**22**	**34**	**161**	**107**	**54**	**11**	**2**	**9**	
343	165	178	6,812	4,075	2,737	536	466	64	1	1	..	18	14	4	..	..	..	1	1	..	..	..	..	7
..	..	..	57	39	18	19	19	..	2	2	..	2	1	1	3	2	1	3	..	3	..	..	..	8
..	..	..	177	96	81	49	35	14	31	23	8	19	11	8	17	3	14	..	..	..	1	1	..	9
..	..	..	1,348	802	546	1,113	663	450	5	1	4	15	12	3	24	9	15	91	70	21	10	1	9	10
..	..	..	1,077	831	246	916	743	173	15	5	10	16	6	10	12	8	4	66	36	30	..	..	..	11
..	..	..	**21,383**	**15,314**	**6,069**	**13,835**	**9,989**	**3,846**	**940**	**682**	**258**	**908**	**572**	**336**	**663**	**553**	**110**	**378**	**158**	**220**	**47**	**23**	**24**	
..	..	..	8,974	6,911	2,063	5,928	4,763	1,165	811	590	221	274	172	102	541	457	84	161	78	83	8	3	5	12
..	..	..	7,141	4,133	3,008	5,859	3,316	2,543	111	83	28	305	192	113	90	82	8	137	31	106	3	1	2	13
..	..	..	3,379	2,670	709	887	811	76	10	5	5	51	47	4	1	..	1	2	1	1	..	..	..	14
..	..	..	552	462	90	244	235	9	1	..	1	7	4	3	1	..	1	71	46	25	36	19	17	15
..	..	..	789	708	81	649	601	48	3	1	2	27	19	8	29	14	15	1	..	1	..	..	..	16
..	..	..	548	430	118	268	263	5	4	3	1	244	138	106	1	..	1	6	2	4	..	..	..	17
5	**5**	..	**3,174**	**2,138**	**1,036**	**1,540**	**1,107**	**433**	**95**	**33**	**62**	**574**	**456**	**118**	**80**	**45**	**35**	**168**	**72**	**96**	**6**	**5**	**1**	
..	..	..	539	412	127	414	354	60	42	7	35	..	..	..	12	3	9	3	..	3	..	..	..	18
..	..	..	113	63	50	47	21	26	24	16	8	2	2	..	4	2	2	6	5	1	1	..	1	19
5	5	..	277	175	102	118	70	48	1	..	1	39	16	23	1	1	..	..	..	..	..	..	..	20
..	..	..	1,976	1,278	698	902	612	290	19	4	15	522	430	92	33	15	18	145	59	86	5	5	..	21
..	..	..	189	149	40	35	30	5	1	1	..	5	5	..	7	6	1	6	3	3	..	..	..	22
..	..	..	80	61	19	24	20	4	8	5	3	6	3	3	23	18	5	8	5	3	..	..	..	23
..	..	..	**7,122**	**4,060**	**3,062**	**257**	**239**	**18**	**1,157**	**653**	**504**	**601**	**427**	**174**	**24**	**16**	**8**	**6**	**3**	**3**	**4**	**1**	**3**	
..	..	..	200	135	65	70	59	11	22	14	8	102	61	41	2	1	1	..	..	..	..	..	..	24
..	..	..	1,250	755	495	58	52	6	782	409	373	372	267	105	5	2	3	6	3	3	4	1	3	25
..	..	..	123	118	5	105	104	1	13	11	2	..	..	..	1	1	..	..	..	..	..	..	..	26
..	..	..	3,412	1,951	1,461	22	22	..	188	151	37	110	89	21	9	7	2	..	..	..	..	..	..	27
..	..	..	369	173	196	1	1	..	68	28	40	9	7	2	2	..	2	..	..	..	..	..	..	28
..	..	..	1,768	928	840	1	1	..	84	40	44	8	3	5	5	5	..	..	..	..	..	..	..	29
12	**11**	**1**	**17,456**	**10,738**	**6,718**	**2,329**	**1,629**	**700**	**9,287**	**5,389**	**3,898**	**139**	**94**	**45**	**38**	**19**	**19**	**55**	**32**	**23**	..	..	..	
..	..	..	**397**	**302**	**95**	**84**	**64**	**20**	..	..	..	**7**	**3**	**4**	**22**	**9**	**13**	**12**	**7**	**5**	..	..	..	
..	..	..	1	1	..	..	..	..	..	..	..	..	..	..	1	1	..	..	..	..	..	..	..	1
..	..	..	..	..	..	..	..	..	..	..	..	..	..	..	..	..	..	..	..	..	..	..	..	2
..	..	..	64	55	9	1	1	..	..	..	..	..	..	..	..	..	..	..	..	..	..	..	..	3
..	..	..	**332**	**246**	**86**	**88**	**63**	**20**	..	..	..	**7**	**3**	**4**	**21**	**8**	**13**	**12**	**7**	**5**	..	..	..	4
..	..	..	3	3	..	..	..	..	..	..	..	..	..	..	..	..	..	..	..	..	..	..	..	
..	..	..	9	7	2	..	..	..	..	..	..	..	..	..	2	..	2	..	..	..	..	..	..	
..	..	..	120	87	33	67	49	18	..	..	..	..	..	..	2	..	2	12	7	5	..	..	..	
..	..	..	17	14	3	12	11	1	..	..	..	..	..	..	..	..	..	..	..	..	..	..	..	
..	..	..	8	7	1	4	3	1	..	..	..	..	..	..	..	..	..	..	..	..	..	..	..	
..	..	..	175	128	47	..	..	..	..	..	..	7	3	4	17	8	9	..	..	..	..	..	..	
12	**11**	**1**	**17,059**	**10,436**	**6,623**	**2,245**	**1,565**	**680**	**9,287**	**5,389**	**3,898**	**132**	**91**	**41**	**16**	**10**	**6**	**43**	**25**	**18**	..	..	..	
..	..	..	..	..	..	..	..	..	..	..	..	..	..	..	..	..	..	..	..	..	..	..	..	5
4	4	..	462	378	84	107	87	20	..	..	..	3	3	..	..	..	..	..	..	..	..	..	..	6
..	..	..	3	3	..	..	..	..	..	..	..	..	..	..	..	..	..	..	..	..	..	..	..	7
8	7	1	1,922	1,695	227	665	659	6	..	..	..	19	18	1	12	7	5	37	20	17	..	..	..	8
..	..	..	73	28	45	..	..	..	..	..	..	..	..	..	..	..	..	..	..	..	..	..	..	9
..	..	..	16	11	5	..	..	..	9	7	2	1	1	..	..	..	..	..	..	..	..	..	..	10
..	..	..	2	1	1	..	..	..	..	..	..	..	..	..	..	..	..	..	..	..	..	..	..	11
..	..	..	2,955	1,661	1,294	..	..	..	..	..	..	17	9	8	..	..	..	..	..	..	..	..	..	12
..	..	..	2,081	1,119	962	1,456	804	652	..	..	..	..	..	..	..	..	..	..	..	..	..	..	..	13
..	..	..	175	100	75	..	..	..	15	12	3	25	19	6	3	2	1	6	5	1	..	..	..	14
..	..	..	29	23	6	..	..	..	..	..	..	20	17	3	..	..	..	..	..	..	..	..	..	15
..	..	..	13	7	6	..	..	..	..	..	..	6	3	3	1	1	..	..	..	..	..	..	..	16
..	..	..	9,328	5,410	3,918	17	15	2	9,263	5,370	3,893	41	21	20	..	..	..	..	..	..	..	..	..	17

Serial No.	District or State.	INDIAN VERNACULARS. — OTHER INDIAN VERNACULARS. — *Bengali.* Persons.	*Bengali.* Males.	*Bengali.* Females.	*Bhotia.* Persons.	*Bhotia.* Males.	*Bhotia.* Females.	*Eastern Pahari.* Persons.	*Eastern Pahari.* Males.	*Eastern Pahari.* Females.	*Central Pahari.* Persons.	*Central Pahari.* Males.	*Central Pahari.* Females.	*Unclassed (Gipsy).* Persons.	*Unclassed (Gipsy).* Males.	*Unclassed (Gipsy).* Females.	*Others.* Persons.	*Others.* Males.	*Others.* Females.
1	2	66	67	68	69	70	71	72	73	74	75	76	77	78	79	80	81	82	83
	PUNJAB ..	**2,667**	**1,539**	**1,128**	**4,029**	**2,056**	**1,973**	**8,022**	**6,009**	**2,013**	**454**	**343**	**111**	**4,952**	**2,629**	**2,323**	**3,322**	**1,836**	**1,486**
	BRITISH TERRITORY ..	**2,497**	**1,440**	**1,057**	**4,029**	**2,056**	**1,973**	**5,762**	**4,328**	**1,434**	**259**	**220**	**39**	**4,952**	**2,629**	**2,323**	**339**	**164**	**175**
	AMBALA DIVISION ..	**582**	**369**	**213**	..	..	..	**264**	**225**	**39**	..	..	..	..	..	..	**105**	**55**	**50**
1	Hissar	23	13	10	..	..	..	3	3	..	..	..	..	..	..	..	34	16	18
2	Rohtak	27	19	8	..	..	..	15	13	2	..	..	..	..	..	..	25	8	17
3	Gurgaon	4	2	2	..	..	..	1	1	..	..	..	..	..	..	..	1	1	..
4	Karnal	44	32	12	..	..	..	31	22	9	..	..	..	..	..	..	2	2	..
5	Ambala	141	86	55	..	..	..	144	124	20	..	..	..	..	..	..	8	7	1
6	Simla	343	217	126	..	..	..	70	62	8	..	..	..	..	..	..	35	21	14
	JULLUNDUR DIVISION	**184**	**88**	**96**	**4,029**	**2,056**	**1,973**	**2,201**	**1,511**	**690**	**44**	**38**	**6**	..	..	..	**34**	**17**	**17**
7	Kangra	26	14	12	4,029	2,056	1,973	2,176	1,501	675	28	22	6	..	..	..	3	..	3
8	Hoshiarpur	15	5	10	..	..	..	10	8	2	1	1	..	..	..	..	2	1	1
9	Jullundur	32	9	23	..	..	..	5	1	4	..	..	..	..	..	..	23	13	10
10	Ludhiana	65	33	32	..	..	..	10	1	9	9	9	..	..	..	..	6	3	3
11	Ferozepore	46	27	19	..	..	..	..	..	..	6	6	..	..	..	..	..	..	..
	LAHORE DIVISION ..	**1,424**	**831**	**593**	..	..	..	**2,952**	**2,334**	**618**	**130**	**123**	**7**	..	..	..	**105**	**49**	**56**
12	Lahore	902	589	313	..	..	..	194	131	63	98	93	5	..	..	..	57	35	22
13	Amritsar	208	73	135	..	..	..	401	348	53	2	..	2	..	..	..	24	7	17
14	Gurdaspur	124	12	112	..	..	..	2,259	1,763	496	30	30	..	..	..	..	15	1	14
15	Sialkot	177	147	30	..	..	..	6	5	1	..	..	..	..	..	..	9	6	3
16	Gujranwala	9	6	3	..	..	..	71	67	4	..	..	..	..	..	..	..	..	..
17	Sheikhupura	4	4	..	..	..	..	21	20	1	..	..	..	..	..	..	..	..	..
	RAWALPINDI DIVISION	**253**	**120**	**133**	..	..	..	**286**	**206**	**80**	**78**	**52**	**26**	..	..	..	**94**	**42**	**52**
18	Gujrat	15	11	4	..	..	..	44	33	11	..	..	..	..	..	..	9	4	5
19	Shahpur	9	4	5	..	..	..	14	12	2	..	..	..	..	..	..	6	1	5
20	Jhelum	27	17	10	..	..	..	17	17	..	28	28	..	..	..	..	46	26	20
21	Rawalpindi	193	82	111	..	..	..	92	48	44	40	14	26	..	..	..	25	9	16
22	Attock	3	1	2	..	..	..	116	93	23	8	8	..	..	..	..	8	2	6
23	Mianwali	6	5	1	..	..	..	3	3	..	2	2	..	..	..	..	..	..	..
	MULTAN DIVISION ..	**54**	**32**	**22**	..	..	..	**59**	**52**	**7**	**7**	**7**	..	**4,952**	**2,629**	**2,323**	**1**	**1**	..
24	Montgomery	4	..	4	..	..	..	..	..	..	..	..	..	..	..	..	..	..	..
25	Lyallpur	13	11	2	..	..	..	2	2	..	7	7	..	..	..	..	1	1	..
26	Jhang	3	1	2	..	..	..	1	1	..	..	..	..	..	..	..	..	..	..
27	Multan	32	20	12	..	..	..	50	43	7	..	..	..	3,001	1,619	1,382	..	..	..
28	Muzaffargarh	..	..	..	..	..	..	6	6	..	..	..	..	283	131	152	..	..	..
29	Dera Ghazi Khan ..	2	..	2	..	..	..	..	..	..	..	..	..	1,668	879	789	..	..	..
	PUNJAB STATES ..	**170**	**99**	**71**	..	..	..	**2,260**	**1,681**	**579**	**195**	**123**	**72**	..	..	..	**2,983**	**1,672**	**1,311**
	A.—HAVING POLITICAL RELATIONS WITH THE PUNJAB GOVERNMENT. ..	**32**	**23**	**9**	..	..	..	**217**	**187**	**30**	**2**	..	**2**	..	..	..	**21**	**9**	**12**
1	Dujana	..	..	..	..	..	..	..	..	..	..	..	..	..	..	..	..	..	..
2	Pataudi	..	..	..	..	..	..	..	..	..	..	..	..	..	..	..	..	..	..
3	Kalsia	..	..	..	..	..	..	63	54	9	..	..	..	..	..	..	..	..	..
4	*SIMLA HILL STATES* ..	**32**	**23**	**9**	..	..	..	**154**	**133**	**21**	**2**	..	**2**	..	..	..	**21**	**9**	**12**
	Bashahr	..	..	..	..	..	..	3	3	..	..	..	..	..	..	..	..	..	..
	Nalagarh	..	..	..	..	..	..	7	7	..	..	..	..	..	..	..	..	..	..
	Keonthal	11	8	3	..	..	..	28	23	5	..	..	..	..	..	..	..	..	..
	Baghal	3	1	2	..	..	..	2	2	..	..	..	..	..	..	..	..	..	..
	Jubbal	..	..	..	..	..	..	..	..	..	..	..	..	..	..	..	4	4	..
	Other Simla Hill States ..	18	14	4	..	..	..	114	98	16	2	..	2	..	..	..	17	5	12
	B.—HAVING POLITICAL RELATIONS WITH THE GOVERNMENT OF INDIA. ..	**138**	**76**	**62**	..	..	..	**2,043**	**1,494**	**549**	**193**	**123**	**70**	..	..	..	**2,962**	**1,663**	**1,299**
5	Loharu	..	..	..	..	..	..	..	..	..	..	..	..	..	..	..	..	..	..
6	Sirmoor	1	1	..	..	..	..	351	287	64	..	..	..	..	..	..	..	..	..
7	Bilaspur	2	2	..	..	..	..	1	1	..	..	..	..	..	..	..	..	..	..
8	Mandi	16	10	6	..	..	..	996	871	125	177	110	67	..	..	..	..	..	..
9	Suket	1	1	..	..	..	..	72	27	45	..	..	..	..	..	..	..	..	..
10	Kapurthala	1	..	1	..	..	..	3	2	1	1	1	..	..	..	..	1	..	1
11	Maler Kotla	1	1	..	..	..	..	1	..	1	..	..	..	..	..	..	..	..	..
12	Faridkot	..	..	..	..	..	..	..	..	..	..	..	..	..	..	..	2,938	1,652	1,286
13	Chamba	6	5	1	..	..	..	609	303	306	10	7	3	..	..	..	..	..	..
14	Patiala } Phulkian States ..	97	48	49	..	..	..	5	..	5	5	5	..	..	..	..	19	9	10
15	Jind } Phulkian States ..	4	3	1	..	..	..	3	1	2	..	..	..	..	..	..	2	2	..
16	Nabha } Phulkian States ..	4	3	1	..	..	..	..	..	..	..	..	..	..	..	..	2	..	2
17	Bahawalpur	5	2	3	..	..	..	2	2	..	..	..	..	..	..	..	..	..	..

LANGUAGES.—*continued.*

VERNACULARS OF OTHER ASIATIC COUNTRIES AND AFRICA.																		EUROPEAN LANGUAGES.									
Total.			*Persian.*			*Arabic.*			*Chinese.*			*Others.*			*African.*			Total.			*English.*			*Irish.*			
Persons.	Males.	Females.	Persons.	Males.	Females.	Persons.	Males.	Females.	Persons.	Males.	Females.	Persons.	Males.	Females.	Persons.	Males.	Females.	Persons.	Males.	Females.	Persons.	Males.	Females.	Persons.	Males.	Females.	Serial No.
84	85	86	87	88	89	90	91	92	93	94	95	96	97	98	99	100	101	102	103	104	105	106	107	108	109	110	
4,875	**2,714**	**2,161**	**4,000**	**2,158**	**1,842**	**675**	**426**	**249**	**160**	**105**	**55**	**34**	**22**	**12**	**7**	**3**	**4**	**26,604**	**18,614**	**7,990**	**26,204**	**18,356**	**7,848**	**51**	**44**	**7**	
4,661	**2,538**	**2,123**	**3,832**	**2,008**	**1,824**	**667**	**419**	**248**	**123**	**87**	**36**	**33**	**21**	**12**	**7**	**3**	**4**	**26,080**	**18,322**	**7,758**	**25,713**	**18,083**	**7,630**	**50**	**43**	**7**	
87	**49**	**38**	**52**	**32**	**20**	**29**	**14**	**15**	**1**	**1**	..	**5**	**2**	**3**	..	..	..	**4,726**	**2,940**	**1,786**	**4,613**	**2,897**	**1,716**	**5**	**3**	**2**	
4	4	..	3	3	..	1	1	..	..	..	..	..	..	..	..	..	..	60	39	21	60	39	21	..	..	..	1
7	4	3	1	..	1	5	3	2	..	..	..	1	1	..	..	..	..	28	16	12	27	15	12	..	..	..	2
15	10	5	12	8	4	3	2	1	..	..	..	..	..	..	..	..	..	178	86	92	178	86	92	..	..	..	3
24	15	9	23	14	9	..	..	..	..	..	..	1	1	..	..	..	..	39	26	13	37	24	13	..	..	..	4
33	15	18	13	7	6	17	7	10	1	1	..	2	..	2	..	..	..	3,405	2,282	1,123	3,341	2,268	1,073	4	3	1	5
4	1	3	..	..	..	3	1	2	..	..	..	1	..	1	..	..	..	1,016	491	525	970	465	505	1	..	1	6
875	**430**	**445**	**841**	**412**	**429**	**11**	**6**	**5**	**8**	**5**	**3**	**10**	**6**	**4**	**5**	**1**	**4**	**3,404**	**2,566**	**838**	**3,387**	**2,555**	**832**	..	..	..	
4	4	..	1	1	..	..	..	..	3	3	..	..	..	..	..	..	..	112	67	45	105	63	42	..	..	..	7
32	21	11	23	16	7	4	2	2	..	..	..	5	3	2	..	..	..	5	4	1	5	4	1	..	..	..	8
21	13	8	12	10	2	2	..	2	..	..	..	2	2	..	5	1	4	1,284	1,050	234	1,284	1,050	234	..	..	..	9
744	328	416	735	323	412	5	4	1	1	..	1	3	1	2	..	..	..	148	49	99	148	49	99	..	..	..	10
74	64	10	70	62	8	..	..	..	4	2	2	..	..	..	..	..	..	1,835	1,396	439	1,843	1,389	436	..	..	..	11
3,122	**1,689**	**1,433**	**2,502**	**1,289**	**1,213**	**542**	**348**	**194**	**71**	**48**	**23**	**7**	**3**	**4**	**1**	**1**	..	**10,514**	**7,486**	**3,028**	**10,483**	**7,464**	**3,019**	..	..	..	
1,730	1,036	694	1,215	706	509	456	288	168	54	40	14	4	1	3	1	1	..	7,601	5,175	2,426	7,598	5,173	2,425	..	..	..	12
1,184	511	673	1,168	500	668	10	8	2	5	2	3	2	1	1	..	..	..	212	178	34	203	170	33	..	..	..	13
87	64	23	32	24	8	53	39	14	1	..	1	1	1	..	..	..	..	290	120	170	280	117	163	..	..	..	14
32	27	5	20	19	1	9	5	4	3	3	..	..	..	..	..	..	..	2,279	1,946	333	2,275	1,942	333	..	..	..	15
20	16	4	10	10	..	6	4	2	4	2	2	..	..	..	..	..	..	53	28	25	53	28	25	..	..	..	16
69	35	34	57	30	27	8	4	4	4	1	3	..	..	..	..	..	..	79	39	40	74	34	40	..	..	..	17
361	**237**	**124**	**275**	**175**	**100**	**36**	**23**	**13**	**40**	**30**	**10**	**9**	**8**	**1**	**1**	**1**	..	**5,835**	**4,076**	**1,759**	**5,661**	**3,931**	**1,730**	**45**	**40**	**5**	
67	36	31	51	31	20	15	5	10	1	..	1	..	..	..	..	..	..	144	74	70	144	74	70	..	..	..	18
43	25	18	35	17	18	8	8	..	..	..	..	..	..	..	..	..	..	62	34	28	62	34	28	..	..	..	19
27	24	3	12	10	2	7	6	1	1	1	..	6	6	..	1	1	..	209	115	94	204	111	93	..	..	..	20
184	129	55	147	98	49	3	3	..	33	28	5	1	..	1	..	..	..	4,956	3,504	1,452	4,790	3,366	1,424	45	40	5	21
24	12	12	17	10	7	2	..	2	4	1	3	1	1	..	..	..	..	343	272	71	341	270	71	..	..	..	22
16	11	5	13	9	4	1	1	..	1	..	1	1	1	..	..	..	..	121	77	44	120	76	44	..	..	..	23
216	**133**	**83**	**162**	**100**	**62**	**49**	**28**	**21**	**3**	**3**	..	**2**	**2**	..	..	..	..	**1,601**	**1,254**	**347**	**1,569**	**1,236**	**383**	..	..	..	
70	37	33	52	32	20	18	5	13	..	..	..	..	..	..	..	..	..	148	97	51	141	90	51	..	..	..	24
60	27	33	52	22	30	6	3	3	..	..	..	2	2	..	..	..	..	101	41	60	85	35	50	..	..	..	25
22	19	3	4	4	..	15	12	3	3	3	..	..	..	..	..	..	..	75	41	34	75	41	34	..	..	..	26
59	46	13	50	39	11	9	7	2	..	..	..	..	..	..	..	..	..	1,251	1,059	192	1,242	1,054	188	..	..	..	27
5	4	1	4	3	1	1	1	..	..	..	..	..	..	..	..	..	..	16	9	7	16	9	7	..	..	..	28
..	..	..	..	..	..	..	..	..	..	..	..	..	..	..	..	..	..	10	7	3	10	7	3	..	..	..	29
214	**176**	**38**	**168**	**150**	**18**	**8**	**7**	**1**	**37**	**18**	**19**	**1**	**1**	..	..	..	..	**524**	**292**	**232**	**491**	**273**	**218**	**1**	**1**	..	
12	**3**	**9**	**11**	**3**	**8**	**1**	..	**1**	..	..	..	..	..	..	..	..	..	**79**	**27**	**52**	**70**	**26**	**44**	**1**	**1**	..	
..	..	..	..	..	..	..	..	..	..	..	..	..	..	..	..	..	..	4	2	2	3	2	1	..	..	..	1
1	..	1	1	..	1	..	..	..	..	..	..	..	..	..	..	..	..	2	2	..	2	2	..	..	..	..	2
..	..	..	..	..	..	..	..	..	..	..	..	..	..	..	..	..	..	..	..	..	..	..	..	..	..	..	3
11	**3**	**8**	**10**	**3**	**7**	**1**	..	**1**	..	..	..	..	..	..	..	..	..	**73**	**23**	**50**	**65**	**22**	**43**	**1**	**1**	..	4
1	**1**	..	**1**	**1**	..	..	..	..	..	..	..	..	..	..	..	..	..	..	..	..	..	..	..	..	..	..	
..	..	..	..	..	..	..	..	..	..	..	..	..	..	..	..	..	..	..	..	..	..	..	..	..	..	..	
1	..	**1**	..	..	..	**1**	..	**1**	..	..	..	..	..	..	..	..	..	**43**	**10**	**33**	**36**	**10**	**26**	..	..	..	
..	..	..	..	..	..	..	..	..	..	..	..	..	..	..	..	..	..	..	..	..	..	..	..	..	..	..	
9	**2**	**7**	**9**	**2**	**7**	..	..	..	..	..	..	..	..	..	..	..	..	**30**	**13**	**17**	**29**	**12**	**17**	**1**	**1**	..	
202	**173**	**29**	**157**	**147**	**10**	**7**	**7**	..	**37**	**18**	**19**	**1**	**1**	..	..	..	..	**445**	**265**	**180**	**421**	**247**	**174**	..	..	..	
..	..	..	..	..	..	..	..	..	..	..	..	..	..	..	..	..	..	2	1	1	2	1	1	..	..	..	5
12	2	10	..	..	..	..	..	..	12	2	10	..	..	..	..	..	..	8	3	5	7	3	4	..	..	..	6
..	..	..	..	..	..	..	..	..	..	..	..	..	..	..	..	..	..	..	..	..	..	..	..	..	..	..	7
120	117	3	120	117	3	..	..	..	..	..	..	..	..	..	..	..	..	65	40	25	56	31	25	..	..	..	8
16	10	6	..	..	..	..	..	..	16	10	6	..	..	..	..	..	..	..	..	..	..	..	..	..	..	..	9
3	3	..	3	3	..	..	..	..	..	..	..	..	..	..	..	..	..	22	14	8	11	7	4	..	..	..	10
2	2	..	1	1	..	..	..	..	1	1	..	..	..	..	..	..	..	5	3	2	5	3	2	..	..	..	11
..	..	..	..	..	..	..	..	..	..	..	..	..	..	..	..	..	..	3	1	2	3	1	2	..	..	..	12
2	2	..	..	..	..	..	..	..	1	1	..	1	1	..	..	..	..	4	2	2	4	2	2	..	..	..	13
29	23	6	22	18	4	1	1	..	6	4	2	..	..	..	..	..	..	215	122	93	215	122	93	..	..	..	14
2	1	1	1	1	..	..	..	..	1	..	1	..	..	..	..	..	..	44	30	14	42	28	14	..	..	..	15
..	..	..	..	..	..	..	..	..	..	..	..	..	..	..	..	..	..	..	..	..	..	..	..	..	..	..	16
16	13	3	10	7	3	6	6	..	..	..	..	..	..	..	..	..	..	77	49	28	76	49	27	..	..	..	17

TABLE XV.—PART I.—(*concld*).—LANGUAGES.—*continued*.

Serial No.	District or State.	EUROPEAN LANGUAGES.																				
		Gaelic (Scotch).			*Portuguese.*			*French.*			*German.*			*Italian.*			*Flemish.*			*Others.*		
		Persons.	Males.	Females.	Persons.	Males.	Females.	Persons.	Males.	Females.	Persons.	Males.	Females.	Persons.	Males.	Females.	Persons.	Males.	Females.	Persons.	Males.	Females.
1	2	111	112	113	114	115	116	117	118	119	120	121	122	123	124	125	126	127	128	129	130	131
	PUNJAB	95	54	41	51	39	12	82	47	35	30	20	10	26	23	3	42	21	21	23	10	13
	BRITISH TERRITORY	95	54	41	39	32	7	77	46	31	26	19	7	20	17	3	42	21	21	18	7	11
	AMBALA DIVISION	37	2	35	34	29	5	19	1	18	7	3	4	2	2	..	5	3	2	4	..	4
1	Hissar	..	..	..	..	..	..	..	..	..	..	..	..	..	..	..	..	..	..	..	..	..
2	Rohtak	1	1	..	..	..	..	..	..	..	..	..	..	..	..	..	..	..	..	..	..	..
3	Gurgaon	..	..	..	..	..	..	..	..	..	..	..	..	..	..	..	..	..	..	..	..	..
4	Karnal	..	..	..	2	2	..	..	..	..	..	..	..	..	..	..	..	..	..	..	..	..
5	Ambala	32	..	32	4	4	..	14	..	14	4	3	1	1	1	..	5	3	2	..	..	..
6	Simla	4	1	3	28	23	5	5	1	4	3	..	3	1	1	..	..	..	..	4	..	4
	JULLUNDUR DIVISION	..	..	..	..	..	..	13	7	6	..	..	..	1	1	..	..	..	..	3	3	..
7	Kangra	..	..	..	..	..	..	3	..	3	..	..	..	1	1	..	..	..	..	3	3	..
8	Hoshiarpur	..	..	..	..	..	..	..	..	..	..	..	..	..	..	..	..	..	..	..	..	..
9	Jullundur	..	..	..	..	..	..	..	..	..	..	..	..	..	..	..	..	..	..	..	..	..
10	Ludhiana	..	..	..	..	..	..	..	..	..	..	..	..	..	..	..	..	..	..	..	..	..
11	Ferozepore	..	..	..	..	..	..	10	7	3	..	..	..	..	..	..	..	..	..	..	..	..
	LAHORE DIVISION	..	..	..	..	..	..	5	4	1	4	3	1	6	6	..	13	8	5	3	1	2
12	Lahore	..	..	..	..	..	..	2	2	..	1	..	1	..	..	..	..	..	..	..	..	..
13	Amritsar	..	..	..	..	..	..	2	1	1	1	1	..	6	6	..	..	..	..	..	..	..
14	Gurdaspur	..	..	..	..	..	..	..	..	..	..	..	..	..	..	..	7	2	5	3	1	2
15	Sialkot	..	..	..	..	..	..	..	..	..	..	..	..	..	..	..	4	4	..	..	..	..
16	Gujranwala	..	..	..	..	..	..	..	..	..	..	..	..	..	..	..	..	..	..	..	..	..
17	Sheikhupura	..	..	..	..	..	..	1	1	..	2	2	..	..	..	..	2	2	..	..	..	..
	RAWALPINDI DIVISION	58	52	6	3	1	2	39	33	6	13	11	2	8	5	3	..	..	..	8	3	5
18	Gujrat	..	..	..	..	..	..	..	..	..	..	..	..	..	..	..	..	..	..	..	..	..
19	Shahpur	..	..	..	..	..	..	..	..	..	..	..	..	..	..	..	..	..	..	..	..	..
20	Jhelum	1	1	..	..	..	..	1	3	1	..	..	..	..	..	..	..	..	..	..	..	..
21	Rawalpindi	57	51	6	3	1	2	35	30	5	12	10	2	8	5	3	..	..	..	6	1	5
22	Attock	..	..	..	..	..	..	..	..	..	..	..	..	..	..	..	..	..	..	2	2	..
23	Mianwali	..	..	..	..	..	..	..	..	..	1	1	..	..	..	..	..	..	..	..	..	..
	MULTAN DIVISION	..	..	..	2	2	..	1	1	..	2	2	..	8	8	..	24	10	14	..	..	..
24	Montgomery	..	..	..	2	2	..	..	..	..	..	..	..	2	2	..	3	3	..	..	..	..
25	Lyallpur	..	..	..	..	..	..	..	..	..	1	1	..	..	..	..	15	5	10	..	..	..
26	Jhang	..	..	..	..	..	..	..	..	..	..	..	..	..	..	..	..	..	..	..	..	..
27	Multan	..	..	..	..	..	..	1	1	..	1	1	..	1	1	..	6	2	4	..	..	..
28	Muzaffargarh	..	..	..	..	..	..	..	..	..	..	..	..	..	..	..	..	..	..	..	..	..
29	Dera Ghazi Khan	..	..	..	..	..	..	..	..	..	..	..	..	..	..	..	..	..	..	..	..	..
	PUNJAB STATES	..	..	..	12	7	5	5	1	4	4	1	3	6	6	..	..	..	..	5	3	2
	A.—Having Political relations with the Punjab Government.	..	..	..	..	..	..	3	..	3	3	..	3	..	..	..	..	..	..	2	..	2
1	Dujana	..	..	..	..	..	..	..	..	..	1	..	1	..	..	..	..	..	..	..	..	..
2	Pataudi	..	..	..	..	..	..	..	..	..	..	..	..	..	..	..	..	..	..	..	..	..
3	Kalsia	..	..	..	..	..	..	..	..	..	..	..	..	..	..	..	..	..	..	..	..	..
4	*SIMLA HILL STATES*	..	..	..	..	..	..	3	..	3	2	..	2	..	..	..	..	..	..	2	..	2
	Bashahr	..	..	..	..	..	..	..	..	..	..	..	..	..	..	..	..	..	..	..	..	..
	Nalagarh	..	..	..	..	..	..	..	..	..	..	..	..	..	..	..	..	..	..	..	..	..
	Keonthal	..	..	..	..	..	..	3	..	3	2	..	2	..	..	..	..	..	..	2	..	2
	Baghal	..	..	..	..	..	..	..	..	..	..	..	..	..	..	..	..	..	..	..	..	..
	Jubbal	..	..	..	..	..	..	..	..	..	..	..	..	..	..	..	..	..	..	..	..	..
	Other Simla Hill States	..	..	..	..	..	..	..	..	..	..	..	..	..	..	..	..	..	..	..	..	..
	B.—Having Political relations with the Government of India.	..	..	..	12	7	5	2	1	1	1	1	..	6	6	..	..	..	..	3	3	..
5	Loharu	..	..	..	..	..	..	..	..	..	..	..	..	..	..	..	..	..	..	..	..	..
6	Sirmoor	..	..	..	..	..	..	1	..	1	..	..	..	..	..	..	..	..	..	..	..	..
7	Bilaspur	..	..	..	..	..	..	..	..	..	..	..	..	..	..	..	..	..	..	..	..	..
8	Mandi	..	..	..	..	..	..	..	..	..	..	..	..	6	6	..	..	..	..	3	3	..
9	Suket	..	..	..	..	..	..	..	..	..	..	..	..	..	..	..	..	..	..	..	..	..
10	Kapurthala	..	..	..	10	6	4	1	1	..	..	..	..	..	..	..	..	..	..	..	..	..
11	Maler Kotla	..	..	..	..	..	..	..	..	..	..	..	..	..	..	..	..	..	..	..	..	..
12	Faridkot	..	..	..	..	..	..	..	..	..	..	..	..	..	..	..	..	..	..	..	..	..
13	Chamba	..	..	..	..	..	..	..	..	..	..	..	..	..	..	..	..	..	..	..	..	..
14	Patiala (Phulkian States)	..	..	..	..	..	..	..	..	..	..	..	..	..	..	..	..	..	..	..	..	..
15	Jind (Phulkian States)	..	..	..	1	1	..	..	..	..	1	1	..	..	..	..	..	..	..	..	..	..
16	Nabha (Phulkian States)	..	..	..	..	..	..	..	..	..	..	..	..	..	..	..	..	..	..	..	..	..
17	Bahawalpur	..	..	..	1	..	1	..	..	..	..	..	..	..	..	..	..	..	..	..	..	..

TABLE XV.—PART II—BI-LINGUALISM.—*continued.*

Serial No.	District or State.	Number of persons using a Language subsidiary to Punjabi.												Number of persons using a Language subsidiary to Lahnda (Western Punjabi).							
		Total.		*Hindustani.*		*Western-Pahari.*		*Rajasthani.*		*Pashto.*		*Kashmiri.*		Total.		*Hindustani.*		*Rajasthani.*		*Pashto.*	
		Males.	Females.	Males.	Females.	Males.	Females.	Males.	Females.	Males.	Females.	Males.	Females.	Males.	Females.	Males.	Females.	Males.	Females.	Males.	Females.
1	2	3	4	5	6	7	8	9	10	11	12	13	14	15	16	17	18	19	20	21	22
	PUNJAB	84,513	46,764	79,161	41,957	2,050	926	236	141	104	52	2,962	3,688	41,855	24,892	851	865	262	37	4,504	2,060
	BRITISH TERRITORY ..	79,956	35,687	76,012	31,152	680	689	207	111	95	47	2,962	3,688	40,942	24,835	694	839	9	6	4,501	2,060
	AMBALA DIVISION ..	8,977	3,248	3,799	3,180	78	1	99	64	1	3	..	..	3	2	3	2	..	..	..	..
1	Hissar	339	226	239	159	..	..	99	64	1	3	..	..	..	..	..	..	..	..	..	..
2	Rohtak	138	126	138	126	..	..	..	..	..	..	..	..	..	..	..	..	..	..	..	..
3	Gurgaon	370	281	370	281	..	..	..	..	..	..	..	..	1	..	1	..	..	..	..	..
4	Karnal	609	558	609	558	..	..	..	..	..	..	..	..	..	..	..	..	..	..	..	..
5	Ambala	1,616	1,418	1,616	1,418	..	..	..	..	..	..	..	..	2	2	2	2	..	..	..	..
6	Simla	905	639	827	638	78	1	..	..	..	..	..	..	..	..	..	..	..	..	..	..
	JULLUNDUR DIVISION	8,745	4,427	8,261	3,829	370	558	104	35	9	1	1	4	3	..	3	..	..	..	..	..
7	Kangra	426	592	60	30	365	558	..	..	..	..	1	4	..	..	..	..	..	..	..	..
8	Hoshiarpur	37	3	31	3	5	..	..	..	1	..	..	..	..	..	..	..	..	..	..	..
9	Jullundur	736	244	735	241	..	..	..	3	1	..	..	..	..	..	..	..	..	..	..	..
10	Ludhiana	6,069	3,254	6,668	3,254	..	..	..	..	1	..	..	..	2	..	2	..	..	..	..	..
11	Ferozepore	877	334	767	.301	..	..	104	32	6	1	..	..	1	..	1	..	..	..	..	..
	LAHORE DIVISION ..	51,653	24,701	48,523	20,972	199	122	..	..	19	4	2,912	3,603	240	102	14	89	..	..	226	62
12	Lahore	49,233	23,830	46,618	20,608	197	66	..	..	..	..	2,418	3,156	240	102	14	39	..	..	226	62
13	Amritsar	1,213	635	732	132	..	56	..	..	2	..	479	447	..	..	..	..	..	..	..	..
14	Gurdaspur	266	80	251	76	1	..	..	..	11	4	3	..	..	..	..	..	..	..	..	..
15	Sialkot	49	9	37	9	..	..	..	..	..	..	12	..	..	..	..	..	..	..	..	..
16	Gujranwala	471	17	471	17	..	..	..	..	..	..	..	..	..	..	..	..	..	..	..	..
17	Sheikhupura	421	130	414	130	1	..	..	..	6	..	..	..	..	..	..	..	..	..	..	..
	RAWALPINDI DIVISION	14,376	2,743	14,295	2,656	32	6	..	..	..	..	49	81	3,442	1,918	68	7	..	..	3,374	1,911
18	Gujrat	5,374	545	5,333	501	..	..	..	..	..	..	41	44	39	14	..	..	..	..	39	14
19	Shahpur	455	325	455	325	..	..	..	..	..	..	..	..	17	3	4	1	..	..	13	2
20	Jhelum	5,141	1,488	5,125	1,445	11	6	..	..	..	..	5	37	213	29	1	..	..	..	212	29
21	Rawalpindi	1,683	233	1,659	233	21	..	..	..	..	..	3	..	111	92	45	..	..	..	66	92
22	Attock	1,089	136	1,089	136	..	..	..	..	..	..	..	..	1,699	1,486	6	..	..	..	1,693	1,486
23	Mianwali	634	16	634	16	..	..	..	..	..	..	..	..	1,363	294	12	6	..	..	1,351	288
	MULTAN DIVISION ..	1,205	568	1,134	515	1	2	4	12	66	39	..	..	37,254	22,813	606	791	9	6	901	87
24	Montgomery	574	192	532	166	1	2	..	..	41	24	..	..	278	134	269	127	..	..	9	7
25	Lyallpur	151	187	122	162	..	..	4	10	25	15	..	..	50	21	26	5	..	..	24	16
26	Jhang	1	1	1	1	..	..	..	..	..	..	..	..	2	..	2	..	..	..	..	..
27	Multan	409	162	409	160	..	..	..	2	..	..	..	..	288	182	174	112	..	1	113	50
28	Muzaffargarh	70	26	70	26	..	..	..	..	..	..	..	..	171	566	135	547	9	5	26	14
29	Dera Ghazi Khan ..	..	..	..	..	..	..	..	..	..	..	..	..	36,465	21,910	..		..	..	729	..
	PUNJAB STATES ..	4,557	11,077	3,149	10,805	1,370	237	29	30	9	5	..	..	413	57	157	26	258	31	3	..
	A.—Having Political relations with the Punjab Government ..	452	202	317	62	134	140	1	..	..	..	..	..	..	..	..	..	..	..	..	..
1	Dujana	1	..	1	..	..	..	..	..	..	..	..	..	..	..	..	..	..	..	..	..
2	Pataudi ..	..	..	..	..	..	..	..	..	..	..	..	..	..	..	..	..	..	..	..	..
3	Kalsia	21	11	20	11	..	..	1	..	..	..	..	..	..	..	..	..	..	..	..	..
4	*SIMLA HILL STATES* ..	430	191	296	51	134	140	..	..	..	..	..	..	..	..	..	..	..	..	..	..
	Bashahr .. .	58	34	12	..	46	34	..	..	..	..	..	..	..	..	..	..	..	..	..	..
	Nalagarh	39	29	8	..	31	29	..	..	..	..	..	..	..	..	..	..	..	..	..	..
	Keonthal	86	10	86	10	..	..	..	..	..	..	..	..	..	..	..	..	..	..	..	..
	Baghal	2	..	1	..	1	..	..	..	..	..	..	..	..	..	..	..	..	..	..	..
	Jubbal	8	2	8	2	..	..	..	..	..	..	..	..	..	..	..	..	..	..	..	..
	Other Simla Hill States ..	237	116	181	39	56	77	..	..	..	..	..	..	..	..	..	..	..	..	..	..
	B.—Having Political relations with the Government of India.	4,105	10,875	2,832	10,743	1,236	97	28	30	9	5	..	..	413	57	157	26	253	31	3	..
5	Loharu	6	6	6	6	..	..	..	..	..	..	..	..	..	..	..	..	..	..	..	..
6	Sirmoor	57	13	57	12	..	1	..	..	..	..	..	..	..	..	..	..	..	..	..	..
7	Bilaspur	5	9	..	..	5	9	..	..	..	..	..	..	..	..	..	..	..	..	..	..
8	Mandi	187	68	35	14	152	54	..	..	..	..	..	..	..	..	..	..	..	..	..	..
9	Suket	32	7	11	7	21	..	..	..	..	..	..	..	..	..	..	..	..	..	..	..
10	Kapurthala	262	144	252	140	4	..	..	..	6	4	..	..	..	..	..	..	..	..	..	..
11	Maler Kotla	18	12	18	12	..	..	..	..	..	..	..	..	..	..	..	..	..	..	..	..
12	Faridkot	431	8	424	8	..	..	7	..	..	..	..	..	..	..	..	..	..	..	..	..
13	Chamba	1,052	34	9	1	1,043	33	..	..	..	..	..	..	1	..	1	..	..	..	..	..
14	Patiala } Phulkian States.	1,289	10,382	1,257	10,352	11	..	21	30	..	..	..	..	..	..	..	..	..	..	..	..
15	Jind } Phulkian States.	182	39	182	39	..	..	..	..	..	..	..	..	..	..	..	..	..	..	..	..
16	Nabha } Phulkian States.	4	2	4	2	..	..	..	..	..	..	..	..	..	..	..	..	..	..	..	..
17	Bahawalpur	580	151	577	150	..	..	..	..	3	1	..	..	412	57	156	26	253	31	3	..

Serial No.	District or State.	No. of persons using a Language subsidiary to Lahnda (W. Punjabi). Balochi. Males.	Balochi. Females.	Number of persons using a Language subsidiary to Hindustani. Total. Males.	Total. Females.	Punjabi. Males.	Punjabi. Females.	Lahnda (Western Punjabi). Males.	Lahnda (Western Punjabi). Females.	Western-Pahari. Males.	Western-Pahari. Females.	Rajasthani. Males.	Rajasthani. Females.	Pashto. Males.	Pashto. Females.	Kashmiri. Males.	Kashmiri. Females.
1	2	23	24	25	26	27	28	29	30	31	32	33	34	35	36	37	38
	PUNJAB ..	**35,738**	**21,930**	**41,215**	**30,059**	**40,057**	**29,269**	**517**	**434**	**379**	**104**	**124**	**216**	**77**	**23**	**61**	**13**
	BRITISH TERRITORY ..	**35,738**	**21,930**	**33,802**	**25,688**	**32,870**	**25,014**	**312**	**330**	**363**	**96**	**121**	**212**	**75**	**23**	**61**	**13**
	AMBALA DIVISION ..	..	..	**1,508**	**1,098**	**1,208**	**1,001**	..	..	**250**	**51**	**39**	**40**	**11**	**1**	..	..
1	Hissar	..	..	132	121	119	93	..	..	..	..	8	28	5	..	..	..
2	Rohtak	..	..	1	7	1	6	..	..	..	..	..	..	..	1	..	..
3	Gurgaon	..	..	2	..	1	..	..	..	..	..	1	..	..	..	..	..
4	Karnal	..	..	79	64	49	52	..	..	..	..	30	12	..	..	..	..
5	Ambala	..	..	695	661	667	655	..	..	22	6	..	..	6	..	..	..
6	Simla	..	..	399	240	371	195	..	..	228	45	..	..	..	..	..	..
	JULLUNDUR DIVISION..	..	..	**3,483**	**2,613**	**3,328**	**2,500**	**63**	**40**	**21**	**18**	**65**	**55**	**6**	..	..	..
7	Kangra	..	..	51	22	31	4	..	..	20	18	..	..	..	..	..	..
8	Hoshiarpur	..	..	119	397	119	397	..	..	..	..	..	..	..	..	..	..
9	Jullundur	..	..	499	391	499	391	..	..	..	..	..	..	..	..	..	..
10	Ludhiana	..	..	1,206	637	1,204	637	..	..	1	..	..	..	1	..	..	..
11	Ferozepore	..	..	1,608	1,166	1,475	1,071	63	40	..	..	65	55	5	..	..	..
	LAHORE DIVISION ..	..	**1**	**21,981**	**18,027**	**21,868**	**17,821**	**11**	**54**	**51**	**27**	**15**	**112**	**8**	..	**28**	**13**
12	Lahore	..	1	16,549	13,716	16,441	13,514	11	50	47	27	15	112	7	..	28	13
13	Amritsar	..	..	3,250	2,385	3,250	2,381	..	4	..	..	..	..	..	..	..	..
14	Gurdaspur	..	..	311	877	507	877	..	..	4	..	..	..	..	..	..	..
15	Sialkot	..	..	108	253	108	253	..	..	..	..	..	..	..	..	..	..
16	Gujranwala	..	..	600	203	600	203	..	..	..	..	..	..	..	..	..	..
17	Sheikhupura	..	..	963	593	962	593	..	..	..	..	..	..	1	..	..	..
	RAWALPINDI DIVISION..	..	..	**3,737**	**2,361**	**3,646**	**2,352**	**6**	**6**	**41**	..	..	..	**11**	**3**	**33**	..
18	Gujrat	..	..	1,489	1,185	1,489	1,185	..	..	..	..	..	..	..	..	..	..
19	Shahpur	..	..	1,026	667	1,026	666	..	1	..	..	..	..	..	..	..	..
20	Jhelum	..	..	350	186	338	186	..	..	9	..	..	..	3	..	..	..
21	Rawalpindi	..	..	654	170	586	170	2	..	32	..	..	..	1	..	33	..
22	Attock	..	..	167	115	160	113	..	..	..	..	..	..	7	2	..	..
23	Mianwali	..	..	51	38	47	32	4	5	..	..	..	..	..	1	..	..
	MULTAN DIVISION ..	**35,738**	**21,929**	**3,093**	**1,594**	**2,820**	**1,340**	**232**	**230**	..	..	**2**	**5**	**39**	**19**	..	..
24	Montgomery	..	..	1,232	399	1,164	318	40	68	..	..	..	..	28	13	..	..
25	Lyallpur	..	..	1,466	944	1,452	924	14	16	..	..	..	1	..	3	..	..
26	Jhang	..	..	50	8	49	8	..	..	..	..	..	..	1	..	..	..
27	Multan	1	19	248	165	126	62	114	96	..	..	..	4	8	3	..	.
28	Muzaffargarh	1	..	58	34	29	28	25	6	..	..	2	..	2	..	..	..
29	Dera Ghazi Khan ..	35,736	21,910	39	44	..	..	39	44	..	..	..	..	..	..	..	..
	PUNJAB STATES ..	..	..	**7,413**	**4,371**	**7,187**	**4,255**	**205**	**104**	**16**	**8**	**3**	**4**	**2**	..	..	..
	A.—HAVING POLITICAL RELATIONS WITH THE PUNJAB GOVERNMENT ..	..	..	**22**	**48**	**22**	**45**	..	..	..	**3**	..	..	..	..	..	..
1	Dujana	..	..	..	..	..	..	..	..	..	..	..	..	..	..	..	..
2	Pataudi	..	..	..	..	..	..	..	..	..	..	..	..	..	..	..	..
3	Kalsia	..	..	6	11	6	11	..	..	..	..	..	..	..	..	..	..
4	*SIMLA HILL STATES* ..	..	..	**16**	**37**	**16**	**34**	..	..	..	**3**	..	..	..	..	..	..
	Bashahr	..	..	..	..	..	..	..	..	..	..	..	..	..	..	..	..
	Nalagarh	..	..	4	9	4	9	..	..	..	..	..	..	..	..	..	..
	Keonthal	..	..	..	1	..	..	..	..	..	1	..	..	..	..	..	..
	Baghal	..	..	..	..	..	..	..	..	..	..	..	..	..	..	..	..
	Jubbal	..	..	..	..	..	..	..	..	..	..	..	..	..	..	..	..
	Other Simla Hill States ..	..	..	12	27	12	25	..	..	..	2	..	..	..	..	..	..
	B.—HAVING POLITICAL RELATIONS WITH THE GOVERNMENT OF INDIA ..	..	..	**7,391**	**4,323**	**7,165**	**4,210**	**205**	**104**	**16**	**5**	**3**	**4**	**2**	..	..	..
5	Loharu	..	..	..	..	..	..	..	..	..	..	..	..	..	..	..	..
6	Sirmoor	..	..	13	48	4	43	..	..	6	1	3	4	..	..	..	..
7	Bilaspur	..	..	..	..	..	..	..	..	..	..	..	..	..	..	..	..
8	Mandi	..	..	18	6	15	3	..	..	3	3	..	..	..	..	..	..
9	Suket	..	..	5	..	..	..	..	..	5	..	..	..	..	..	..	..
10	Kapurthala	..	..	11	7	11	7	..	..	..	..	..	..	..	..	..	..
11	Maler Kotla ..	..	..	53	53	52	52	..	..	1	1	..	..	..	..	..	..
12	Faridkot	..	..	2,214	373	2,214	373	..	..	..	..	..	..	..	..	..	..
13	Chamba	..	..	2	2	2	2	..	..	..	..	..	..	..	..	..	..
14	Patiala } Phulkian States. ..	..	..	2,547	2,833	2,544	2,833	..	..	1	..	..	..	2	..	..	..
15	Jind } Phulkian States. ..	..	..	431	302	431	302	..	..	..	..	..	..	..	..	..	..
16	Nabha } Phulkian States. ..	..	..	1,020	390	1,020	390	..	..	..	..	..	..	..	..	..	..
17	Bahawalpur	..	..	1,077	309	872	205	205	104	..	..	..	..	..	..	..	..

BI-LINGUALISM.—*continud.*

Number of persons using a language subsidiary to Western-Pahari.						Number of persons using a language subsidiary to Rajasthani.								Number of persons using a language subsidiary to Pashto.						
Total.		*Punjabi.*		*Hindustani.*		Total.		*Punjabi.*		*Lahnda (Western Punjabi).*		*Hindustani.*		Total.		*Punjabi.*		*Lahnda (Western Punjabi).*		
Males.	Females.	Males.	Females.	Males.	Females.	Males.	Females.	Males.	Females.	Males.	Females.	Males.	Females.	Males.	Females.	Males.	Females.	Males.	Females.	Serial No.
39	40	41	42	43	44	45	46	47	48	49	50	51	52	53	54	55	56	57	58	
7,258	**3,336**	**2,350**	**1,447**	**4,908**	**1,889**	**7,764**	**7,420**	**4,396**	**3,804**	**1,775**	**1,356**	**1,593**	**2,260**	**14,383**	**7,613**	**10,410**	**5,623**	**2,063**	**1,504**	
4,722	**2,267**	**2,028**	**1,094**	**2,694**	**1,178**	**3,887**	**4,382**	**2,062**	**1,978**	**237**	**154**	**1,588**	**2,250**	**13,895**	**7,496**	**10,077**	**5,529**	**2,009**	**1,498**	
2,792	**1,091**	**458**	**99**	**2,384**	**992**	**1,515**	**2,293**	**86**	**233**	..	..	**1,429**	**2,060**	**289**	**30**	**67**	**5**	..	..	
3	1	..	..	3	1	1,152	2,203	36	222	..	..	1,116	1,981	21	4	4	2	..	..	1
..	..	..	..	..	..	17	17	..	..	..	..	17	17	8	..	..	..	..	..	2
..	1	..	..	..	1	18	16	..	..	..	..	18	16	17	1	..	..	..	..	3
10	4	..	..	10	4	18	11	..	..	..	..	18	11	23	1	1	..	..	..	4
332	143	141	38	191	105	292	42	50	11	..	..	242	31	217	21	59	3	..	..	5
2,447	942	317	61	2,130	881	18	4	..	..	..	..	18	4	3	3	3	..	..	..	6
310	**166**	**169**	**126**	**141**	**40**	**1,131**	**788**	**1,079**	**715**	..	..	**52**	**68**	**243**	**98**	**151**	**82**	..	..	
290	141	152	104	138	37	1	..	..	..	..	..	1	..	29	4	7	..	..	..	7
7	9	7	9	..	..	11	2	11	2	..	..	..	..	31	8	18	8	..	..	8
1	1	1	1	..	..	3	7	3	7	..	..	..	..	60	10	20	10	..	..	9
2	11	2	8	..	3	48	9	42	9	..	..	6	..	38	21	21	9	..	..	10
10	4	7	4	3	..	1,068	765	1,023	697	..	..	45	68	85	55	85	55	..	..	11
1,421	**920**	**1,266**	**803**	**155**	**117**	**464**	**565**	**408**	**504**	..	..	**56**	**61**	**4,005**	**1,156**	**2,795**	**1,035**	**1**	..	
211	134	149	79	62	55	93	181	87	130	..	..	6	51	2,740	832	1,693	733	1	..	12
243	79	217	17	26	62	236	323	209	313	..	..	27	10	202	73	151	58	..	..	13
894	662	827	662	67	..	25	4	5	4	..	..	20	..	158	63	111	63	..	..	14
..	..	..	..	..	..	..	1	..	1	..	..	..	..	82	12	39	5	..	..	15
70	44	70	44	..	..	28	..	25	..	..	..	3	..	419	91	406	91	..	..	16
3	1	3	1	..	..	82	56	82	56	..	..	..	..	404	85	395	85	..	..	17
126	**41**	**93**	**41**	**33**	..	**12**	**13**	**11**	**13**	..	..	**1**	..	**6,651**	**4,768**	**5,377**	**3,581**	**1,109**	**966**	
49	27	45	27	4	..	..	..	..	..	..	..	..	..	649	198	630	143	..	..	18
42	14	40	14	2	..	11	3	11	3	..	..	..	..	1,212	795	1,193	656	..	1	19
..	..	..	..	..	..	..	7	..	7	..	..	..	..	272	201	262	197	..	..	20
34	..	8	..	26	..	..	..	..	..	..	..	..	..	479	258	413	240	..	2	21
1	..	..	..	1	..	..	..	..	..	..	..	..	..	2,785	2,286	2,741	2,282	..	..	22
..	..	..	..	..	..	1	3	..	3	..	..	1	..	1,254	1,030	138	63	1,109	963	23
73	**49**	**42**	**25**	**31**	**24**	**765**	**728**	**478**	**513**	**237**	**154**	**50**	**61**	**2,707**	**1,444**	**1,687**	**826**	**899**	**527**	
66	40	36	20	30	20	185	129	162	114	16	7	7	8	413	156	293	72	104	67	24
1	2	1	2	..	..	347	396	305	369	12	3	30	24	335	121	290	78	38	27	25
6	3	5	3	1	..	..	..	..	..	..	..	..	..	255	74	255	67	..	..	26
..	..	..	..	..	..	206	177	5	28	198	123	3	26	1,004	714	840	608	88	66	27
..	4	..	..	..	4	16	5	6	2	..	..	10	3	137	65	9	1	106	53	28
..	..	..	..	..	..	11	21	..	..	11	21	..	..	563	314	..	..	563	314	29
2,536	**1,069**	**322**	**353**	**2,214**	**716**	**3,877**	**3,038**	**2,334**	**1,826**	**1,538**	**1,202**	**5**	**10**	**488**	**117**	**333**	**94**	**54**	**11**	
2,392	**462**	**236**	**312**	**2,156**	**150**	**3**	**2**	**2**	..	..	..	**1**	**2**	**40**	**1**	**6**	..	..	..	
..	..	..	..	..	..	..	..	..	..	..	..	..	..	..	..	..	..	..	..	1
..	..	..	..	..	..	..	..	..	..	..	..	..	..	..	..	..	..	..	..	2
..	..	..	..	..	..	..	..	..	..	..	..	..	..	4	..	..	..	..	..	3
2,392	**462**	**236**	**312**	**2,156**	**150**	**3**	**2**	**2**	..	..	..	**1**	**2**	**36**	**1**	**6**	..	..	..	4
437	15	..	..	437	15	..	..	..	..	..	..	..	..	..	..	..	..	..	..	
82	242	81	242	1	..	..	..	..	..	..	..	..	..	1	..	1	..	..	..	
399	20	..	..	399	20	..	..	..	..	..	..	..	..	3	..	..	..	..	..	
33	..	..	..	33	..	..	..	..	..	..	..	..	..	..	..	..	..	..	..	
84	1	3	..	81	1	..	..	..	..	..	..	..	..	..	..	..	..	..	..	
1,357	184	152	70	1,205	114	3	2	2	..	..	..	1	2	32	1	5	..	..	..	
144	**607**	**86**	**41**	**58**	**566**	**3,874**	**3,036**	**2,332**	**1,826**	**1,538**	**1,202**	**4**	**8**	**448**	**116**	**327**	**94**	**54**	**11**	
..	..	..	..	..	..	..	..	..	..	..	..	..	..	..	..	..	..	..	..	5
43	22	..	..	43	22	..	2	..	..	..	..	..	2	6	..	..	..	..	..	6
..	..	..	..	..	..	..	..	..	..	..	..	..	..	4	..	..	..	..	..	7
45	30	43	26	2	4	..	..	..	..	..	..	..	..	20	10	16	3	..	..	8
3	4	3	2	..	2	..	..	..	..	..	..	..	..	..	..	..	..	..	..	9
..	..	..	..	..	..	..	..	..	..	..	..	..	..	..	..	..	..	..	..	10
..	..	..	..	..	..	..	..	..	..	..	..	..	..	1	..	1	..	..	..	11
..	..	..	..	..	..	169	177	169	177	..	..	..	..	2	..	2	..	..	..	12
16	548	7	10	9	538	..	..	..	..	..	..	..	..	5	5	5	3	..	..	13
28	2	24	2	4	..	1,843	1,423	1,842	1,421	..	..	1	2	51	7	18	7	..	..	14
6	..	6	..	..	..	..	3	..	3	..	..	..	..	9	5	9	5	..	..	15
3	1	3	1	..	..	..	..	..	..	..	..	..	..	1	..	1	..	..	..	16
..	..	..	..	..	..	1,862	1,431	321	225	1,538	1,202	3	4	349	89	275	76	54	11	17

TABLE XV.—PART II.—BI-LINGUALISM.—*concluded.*

Serial No.	District or State.	Number of persons using a language subsidiary to Pashto.				Number of persons using a language subsidiary to Balochi.						Number of persons using a language subsidiary to Kashmiri.									
		Hindustani.		*Western-Pahari.*		Total.		*Lahnda (Western Punjabi).*		*Hindustani.*		Total.		*Punjabi.*		*Hindustani.*		*Western-Pahari.*		*Pashto.*	
		Males.	Females.	Males.	Females.	Males.	Females.	Males.	Females.	Males.	Females.	Males.	Females.	Males.	Females.	Males.	Females.	Males.	Females.	Males.	Females.
1	2	59	60	61	62	63	64	65	66	67	68	69	70	71	72	73	74	75	76	77	78
	PUNJAB ..	**1,902**	**477**	**8**	**9**	**6,160**	**4,521**	**6,114**	**4,485**	**46**	**36**	**10,147**	**3,648**	**6,782**	**2,640**	**2,644**	**460**	**704**	**541**	**17**	**7**
	BRITISH TERRITORY ..	**1,804**	**465**	**5**	**9**	**5,953**	**4,180**	**5,907**	**4,144**	**46**	**36**	**9,429**	**3,119**	**6,756**	**2,638**	**2,638**	**459**	**18**	**15**	**17**	**7**
	AMBALA DIVISION ..	**222**	**25**	..	..	..	..	..	..	..	..	**767**	**60**	**2**	**10**	**765**	**49**	..	..	..	**1**
1	Hissar	17	2	..	..	..	..	..	..	..	..	..	..	..	..	..	..	..	..	..	..
2	Rohtak	8	..	..	..	..	..	..	..	..	..	..	..	..	..	..	..	..	..	..	..
3	Gurgaon	17	1	..	..	..	..	..	..	..	..	..	..	..	..	..	..	..	..	..	..
4	Karnal	22	1	..	..	..	..	..	..	..	..	2	..	2	..	..	..	..	..	..	..
5	Ambala	158	18	..	..	..	..	..	..	..	..	6	13	..	6	6	7	..	..	..	..
6	Simla	..	3	..	..	..	..	..	..	..	..	759	47	..	4	759	42	..	..	..	1
	JULLUNDUR DIVISION	**89**	**15**	**3**	**1**	**42**	**36**	..	..	**42**	**36**	**413**	**444**	**224**	**201**	**181**	**228**	**8**	**15**	..	..
7	Kangra	19	3	3	1	..	..	..	..	..	..	30	36	14	21	8	..	8	15	..	..
8	Hoshiarpur	13	..	..	..	41	36	..	..	41	36	12	..	12	..	..	..	..	..	..	..
9	Jullundur	40	..	..	..	..	..	..	..	..	..	14	10	14	10	..	..	..	..	..	..
10	Ludhiana	17	12	..	..	1	..	..	..	1	..	323	370	150	142	173	228	..	..	..	..
11	Ferozepore	..	..	..	..	..	..	..	..	..	..	34	28	34	28	..	..	..	..	..	..
	LAHORE DIVISION ..	**1,207**	**121**	**2**	..	**7**	**1**	**7**	**1**	..	..	**7,685**	**2,447**	**6,035**	**2,262**	**1,632**	**179**	**4**	..	**14**	**6**
12	Lahore	1,044	99	2	..	4	1	4	1	..	..	4,598	1,118	3,204	960	1,377	152	3	..	14	6
13	Amritsar	51	15	..	..	..	..	..	..	..	..	2,285	1,256	2,074	1,238	211	18	..	..	..	..
14	Gurdaspur	47	..	..	..	..	..	..	..	..	..	420	36	391	31	28	5	1	..	..	..
15	Sialkot	43	7	..	..	..	..	..	..	..	..	10	1	10	1	..	..	..	..	..	..
16	Gujranwala	13	..	..	..	2	..	2	..	..	..	300	33	285	29	15	4	..	..	..	..
17	Sheikhupura	9	..	..	..	1	..	1	..	..	..	72	3	71	3	1	..	..	..	..	..
	RAWALPINDI DIVISION	**165**	**221**	..	..	**85**	**6**	**85**	**6**	..	..	**509**	**162**	**442**	**159**	**58**	**3**	**6**	..	**3**	..
18	Gujrat	19	55	..	..	..	..	..	..	..	..	199	28	197	25	2	3	..	..	..	..
19	Shahpur	19	138	..	..	1	1	1	1	..	..	6	5	6	5	..	..	..	..	..	..
20	Jhelum	10	4	..	..	..	3	..	3	..	..	31	33	29	33	1	..	..	..	1	..
21	Rawalpindi	66	16	..	..	..	..	..	..	..	..	243	95	184	95	53	..	6	..	..	..
22	Attock	44	4	..	..	83	..	83	..	..	..	24	1	23	1	1	..	..	..	..	..
23	Mianwali	7	4	..	..	1	2	1	2	..	..	6	..	3	..	1	..	..	..	2	..
	MULTAN DIVISION ..	**121**	**83**	..	**8**	**5,819**	**4,137**	**5,815**	**4,137**	**4**	..	**55**	**6**	**53**	**6**	**2**	..	..	..	..	..
24	Montgomery	16	9	..	8	18	6	18	6	..	..	9	3	9	3	..	..	..	..	..	..
25	Lyallpur	7	16	..	..	..	1	..	1	..	..	13	2	11	2	2	..	..	..	..	..
26	Jhang	..	7	..	..	..	1	..	1	..	..	32	1	32	1	..	..	..	..	..	..
27	Multan	76	40	..	..	7	1	3	1	4	..	..	..	..	..	..	..	..	..	..	..
28	Muzaffargarh	22	11	..	..	..	..	..	..	..	..	1	..	1	..	..	..	..	..	..	..
29	Dera Ghazi Khan ..	..	..	..	..	5,794	4,128	5,794	4,128	..	..	..	..	..	..	..	..	..	..	..	..
	PUNJAB STATES ..	**98**	**12**	**3**	..	**207**	**341**	**207**	**341**	..	..	**718**	**529**	**26**	**2**	**6**	**1**	**686**	**526**	..	..
	A.—Having Political relations with the Punjab Government ..	**33**	**1**	**1**	..	..	..	..	..	..	..	**5**	..	..	..	**5**	..	..	..	..	..
1	Dujana	..	..	..	..	..	..	..	..	..	..	..	..	..	..	..	..	..	..	..	..
2	Pataudi	..	..	..	..	..	..	..	..	..	..	..	..	..	..	..	..	..	..	..	..
3	Kalsia	4	..	..	..	..	..	..	..	..	..	1	..	..	..	1	..	..	..	..	..
4	*SIMLA HILL STATES* ..	**29**	**1**	**1**	..	..	..	..	..	..	..	**4**	..	..	..	**4**	..	..	..	..	..
	Bashahr	..	..	..	..	..	..	..	..	..	..	..	..	..	..	..	..	..	..	..	..
	Nalagarh	..	..	..	..	..	..	..	..	..	..	..	..	..	..	..	..	..	..	..	..
	Keonthal	3	..	..	..	..	..	..	..	..	..	4	..	..	..	4	..	..	..	..	..
	Baghal	..	..	..	..	..	..	..	..	..	..	..	..	..	..	..	..	..	..	..	..
	Jubbal	..	..	..	..	..	..	..	..	..	..	..	..	..	..	..	..	..	..	..	..
	Other Simla Hill States ..	26	1	1	..	..	..	..	..	..	..	..	..	..	..	..	..	..	..	..	..
	B.—Having Political relations with the Government of India.	**65**	**11**	**2**	..	**207**	**341**	**207**	**341**	..	..	**713**	**529**	**26**	**2**	**1**	**1**	**686**	**526**	..	..
5	Loharu	..	..	..	..	..	..	..	..	..	..	..	..	..	..	..	..	..	..	..	..
6	Sirmoor	6	..	..	..	..	..	..	..	..	..	..	..	..	..	..	..	..	..	..	..
7	Bilaspur	3	..	1	..	..	..	..	..	..	..	..	..	..	..	..	..	..	..	..	..
8	Mandi	3	7	1	..	..	..	..	..	..	..	59	6	21	..	1	1	37	5	..	..
9	Suket	..	..	..	..	..	..	..	..	..	..	..	..	..	..	..	..	..	..	..	..
10	Kapurthala	..	..	..	..	..	..	..	..	..	..	..	..	..	..	..	..	..	..	..	..
11	Maler Kotla	..	..	..	..	..	..	..	..	..	..	..	..	..	..	..	..	..	..	..	..
12	Faridkot	..	..	..	..	..	..	..	..	..	..	..	..	..	..	..	..	..	..	..	..
13	Chamba	..	2	..	..	..	..	..	..	..	..	654	523	5	2	..	..	649	521	..	..
14	Patiala (Phulkian States) ..	33	..	..	..	..	..	..	..	..	..	..	..	..	..	..	..	..	..	..	..
15	Jind (Phulkian States) ..	..	..	..	..	..	..	..	..	..	..	..	..	..	..	..	..	..	..	..	..
16	Nabha (Phulkian States) ..	..	..	..	..	..	..	..	..	..	..	..	..	..	..	..	..	..	..	..	..
17	Bahawalpur	20	2	..	..	207	341	207	341	..	..	..	..	..	..	..	..	..	..	..	..

TABLE XVI.

RELIGION.

1. This Table corresponds with Table VI of 1921.

The statement below gives the detail of those persons who described their religion by some unrecognised term. It also shows the religion into which they were thrown in the course of tabulation under the orders of the Census Commissioner for India :—

No.	Religion returned.	Persons.	Males.	Females.	Religion into which they were thrown.	No.	Religion returned.	Persons.	Males.	Females.	Religion into which they were thrown.
1	Achhut ..	21	17	4	Hindu	19	Kabir Dasi ..	41	22	19	Hindu
2	Aipanthi ..	2	2	..	Hindu	20	Kabir Panthi ..	33	20	13	Hindu
3	Ad-Hindu ..	185	106	79	Hindu	21	Kes Dhari ..	4	3	1	Sikh
4	Bala Shahi ..	375	198	177	Hindu	22	Kuchband ..	231	101	130	Hindu
5	Balmiki ..	3,152	1,602	1,550	Hindu	23	Khatik ..	100	54	46	Hindu
6	Bazigar ..	108	62	46	Muslim	24	Mahtam ..	7,896	4,036	3,860	Hindu
7	Bhabra ..	18	..	18	Jain	25	Malang ..	6	5	1	Muslim
8	Bhil ..	35	21	14	Hindu	26	Meghwal ..	12,807	7,135	5,672	Hindu
9	Barrar ..	350	196	154	Hindu	27	Mehtar ..	1	1	...	Hindu
10	Bhangi ..	42	25	17	Hindu	28	Nat ..	137	64	73	Hindu
11	Chamar ..	163	99	64	Hindu	29	Radha Swami ..	1,125	584	541	Hindu
12	Chuhra ..	1,911	1,151	760	Hindu	30	Ram Dasi ..	106	52	54	Sikh
13	Dhai ..	297	164	133	Hindu	31	Sanatan Dharm ..	12	7	5	Hindu
14	Dev Panthi ..	49	33	16	Hindu	32	Sansi ..	25,825	14,030	11,795	Hindu
15	Gagra ..	581	301	280	Muslim	33	Sat Sanghi ..	3	2	1	Hindu
16	Gandhila ..	57	36	21	Hindu	34	Singi Kat ..	2	2	..	Hindu
17	Gurkha ..	1	1	..	Hindu	35	Thori ..	8,270	4,397	3,873	Hindu
18	Jai Kishni ..	3	2	1	Hindu						

2. Vedic Dharm and Brahmo Samaj have been included in the general total of Hindus in this Table but are shown separately in Table XVI-A.

3. Persons who returned themselves as Hindus and at the same time stated they were Jains, Buddhists or Ad-Dharmis, are included in the " Hindu " total, and their number is given below :—

Religion.	Persons.	Males.	Females.
Hindu Jain	526	305	221
Hindu Buddhist	25	12	13
Hindu Ad-Dharmi ..	7,287	4,154	3,133

4. Persons who returned themselves as Jains and at the same time stated they were Hindus, are included in the " Jain " total, and their number is given below :—

Religion.	Persons.	Males.	Females.
Jain Hindus	7,623	4,035	3,588

5. The figures of Christians by sects, sorted for the purpose of India Tables, are given below :—

No.	Sect.	Punjab.			British Territory.			Punjab States.		
		Persons.	Males.	Females.	Persons.	Males.	Females.	Persons.	Males.	Females.
1	Roman Catholic ..	58,206	34,573	23,633	57,153	33,956	23,197	1,053	617	436
2	*Syrian ..	175	125	50	175	125	50	..	..	..
3	Others ..	360,972	197,858	163,114	357,460	195,937	161,523	3,512	1,921	1,591
	Total ..	419,353	232,556	186,797	414,788	230,018	184,770	4,565	2,538	2,027

* Other than Romo-Syrian.

TABLE XVI.—RELIGION.

Serial No.	District or State.	Population.			Hindu.			Ad-Dharmi.			Sikh.		
		Persons.	Males.	Females.	Persons.	Males.	Females.	Persons.	Males.	Females.	Persons.	Males.	Females.
	1	2	3	4	5	6	7	8	9	10	11	12	13
	PUNJAB ..	**28,490,857**	**15,561,194**	**12,929,683**	**8,599,720**	**4,685,705**	**3,914,015**	**418,789**	**228,509**	**190,280**	**4,071,624**	**2,270,946**	**1,800,678**
	BRITISH TERRITORY.	**23,580,852**	**12,880,510**	**10,700,842**	**6,328,588**	**3,465,534**	**2,863,054**	**399,307**	**217,910**	**181,897**	**3,064,144**	**1,703,584**	**1,360,560**
	AMBALA DIVISION	**4,077,565**	**2,226,856**	**1,850,709**	**2,673,215**	**1,462,380**	**1,210,835**	**5,118**	**2,777**	**2,341**	**229,508**	**129,860**	**99,648**
1	Hissar ..	*899,479*	485,690	413,789	583,420	315,578	267,842	9	8	1	55,169	30,542	24,627
2	Rohtak ..	*805,621*	432,855	372,766	655,963	353,935	302,028	..	..	..	596	328	268
3	Gurgaon ..	*740,163*	398,513	341,650	493,174	266,641	226,533	..	..	..	500	281	219
4	Karnal ..	*852,614*	469,870	382,744	565,286	313,117	252,169	5,011	2,719	2,292	16,928	9,692	7,236
5	Ambala ..	*742,902*	416,411	326,491	346,711	195,270	151,441	98	50	48	155,555	88,485	67,070
6	Simla ..	*36,786*	23,517	13,269	28,661	17,839	10,822	..	..	..	760	532	228
	JULLUNDUR DIVISION.	**4,606,446**	**2,491,638**	**2,114,808**	**1,611,677**	**857,486**	**754,191**	**300,274**	**162,544**	**137,780**	**1,126,051**	**624,486**	**501,615**
7	Kangra ..	*801,312*	415,288	386,024	731,215	377,050	354,165	20,883	11,338	9,545	2,396	1,338	1,058
8	Hoshiarpur ..	*1,032,187*	551,867	480,320	414,353	219,303	195,050	111,829	60,899	50,930	173,147	94,652	78,495
9	Jullundur ..	*943,721*	512,667	431,054	155,242	85,469	69,773	113,580	60,948	52,632	249,571	139,154	110,417
10	Ludhiana ..	*672,494*	375,560	296,934	102,441	58,174	44,267	17,720	9,689	8,031	312,829	175,676	137,153
11	Ferozepore ..	*1,156,732*	636,256	520,476	208,426	117,490	90,936	36,262	19,670	16,592	388,108	213,616	174,492
	LAHORE DIVISION	**5,879,075**	**3,277,661**	**2,601,414**	**1,051,818**	**600,644**	**451,174**	**19,484**	**10,818**	**8,666**	**1,108,753**	**618,925**	**489,828**
12	Lahore ..	*1,378,570*	794,389	584,181	258,719	159,112	99,607	1,006	665	341	244,304	137,580	106,724
13	Amritsar ..	*1,117,120*	621,040	496,080	174,392	101,185	73,207	164	101	63	399,951	219,788	180,163
14	Gurdaspur ..	*970,898*	531,935	438,963	249,404	136,160	113,244	6,545	3,566	2,979	178,471	99,724	78,747
15	Sialkot ..	*979,617*	537,301	442,316	206,395	111,853	94,542	26	5	21	94,955	53,996	40,959
16	Gujranwala ..	*736,138*	408,606	327,532	92,762	52,201	40,561	2	2	..	71,595	41,075	30,520
17	Sheikhupura ..	*696,732*	384,390	312,342	70,146	40,133	30,013	11,741	6,479	5,262	119,477	66,762	52,715
	RAWALPINDI DIVISION.	**3,914,849**	**2,092,622**	**1,822,227**	**338,595**	**184,481**	**154,114**	**2,601**	**1,519**	**1,082**	**186,310**	**99,894**	**86,416**
18	Gujrat ..	*922,427*	498,336	424,091	72,346	39,425	32,921	1,010	635	375	59,188	30,795	28,393
19	Shahpur ..	*821,490*	445,836	375,654	88,970	48,641	40,329	1,591	884	707	40,074	22,200	17,874
20	Jhelum ..	*541,076*	282,714	258,362	36,068	19,155	16,913	..	..	..	22,030	11,409	10,621
21	Rawalpindi ..	*634,357*	342,771	291,586	59,485	34,973	24,512	..	..	..	41,265	22,948	18,317
22	Attock ..	*583,960*	306,949	277,011	31,932	16,631	15,301	..	..	..	19,522	10,279	9,243
23	Mianwali ..	*411,539*	216,016	195,523	49,794	25,656	24,138	..	..	..	4,231	2,263	1,968
	MULTAN DIVISION	**5,102,917**	**2,791,733**	**2,311,184**	**653,283**	**360,543**	**292,740**	**71,880**	**40,252**	**31,578**	**413,522**	**230,469**	**183,053**
24	Montgomery ..	*999,772*	552,456	447,316	120,664	69,445	51,219	16,119	9,141	6,978	148,155	82,261	65,894
25	Lyallpur ..	*1,151,351*	630,749	520,602	122,626	71,357	51,269	50,718	28,222	22,496	211,391	117,039	94,352
26	Jhang ..	*664,833*	355,671	309,162	102,924	52,999	49,925	66	40	26	8,476	4,551	3,925
27	Multan ..	*1,174,900*	646,025	528,875	177,102	98,646	78,456	4,927	2,849	2,078	39,453	23,241	16,212
28	Muzaffargarh ..	*591,375*	320,674	270,701	72,577	38,284	34,293	..	..	..	5,287	2,938	2,349
29	Dera Ghazi Khan ..	*491,044*	269,341	221,703	57,217	29,706	27,511	..	..	..	760	439	321
	Biloch trans-frontier tract.	*29,642*	16,817	12,825	173	106	67	..	..	..	..	..	..
	PUNJAB STATES	**4,910,005**	**2,680,684**	**2,229,321**	**2,271,132**	**1,220,171**	**1,050,961**	**19,482**	**10,599**	**8,883**	**1,007,480**	**567,362**	**440,118**
	A.—Having Political Relations with the Punjab Government.	**437,787**	**229,290**	**208,497**	**383,383**	**199,991**	**183,392**	**282**	**155**	**127**	**10,854**	**6,124**	**4,730**
1	Dujana ..	*28,216*	14,537	13,679	22,347	11,650	10,697	..	..	..	1	1	..
2	Pataudi ..	*18,873*	9,922	8,951	15,596	8,227	7,369	..	..	..	1	1	..
3	Kalsia ..	*59,848*	33,306	26,542	28,550	16,085	12,465	282	155	127	9,035	5,121	3,914
4	SIMLA HILL STATES	**330,850**	**171,525**	**159,325**	**317,390**	**164,029**	**153,861**	..	..	..	**1,817**	**1,001**	**816**
	Bashahr ..	*104,389*	51,593	52,796	102,388	50,610	51,778	..	..	..	10	5	5
	Nalagarh ..	*50,015*	26,635	23,380	42,150	22,333	19,817	..	..	..	1,396	752	644
	Keonthal ..	*48,093*	25,734	22,359	46,805	24,885	21,920	..	..	..	93	60	33
	Baghal ..	*26,352*	13,457	12,895	26,013	13,241	12,772	..	..	..	8	6	2
	Jubbal ..	*27,172*	14,507	12,665	26,813	14,311	12,502	..	..	..	9	5	4
	Other Simla Hill States.	*74,829*	39,599	35,230	73,221	38,649	34,572	..	..	..	301	173	128
	B.—Having Political Relations with the Government of India.	**4,472,218**	**2,451,394**	**2,020,824**	**1,887,249**	**1,020,180**	**867,069**	**19,200**	**10,444**	**8,756**	**996,626**	**561,238**	**435,388**
5	Loharu ..	*23,338*	12,326	11,012	20,198	10,717	9,481	..	..	..	2	2	..
6	Sirmoor ..	*148,568*	82,384	66,184	139,031	76,922	62,109	..	..	..	2,413	1,353	1,060
7	Bilaspur ..	*100,994*	53,154	47,840	99,023	52,068	46,955	..	..	..	507	280	227
8	Mandi ..	*207,465*	107,876	99,589	199,935	102,614	97,321	..	..	..	899	612	287
9	Suket ..	*58,408*	30,851	27,557	57,616	30,427	27,189	..	..	..	44	33	11
10	Kapurthala ..	*316,757*	171,529	145,228	54,145	29,590	24,555	10,174	5,444	4,730	72,177	39,729	32,448
11	Maler Kotla ..	*83,072*	45,883	37,189	21,252	11,713	9,539	..	..	..	28,982	16,114	12,868
12	Faridkot ..	*164,364*	91,163	73,201	19,271	11,231	8,040	1,584	890	694	92,880	51,414	41,466
13	Chamba ..	*146,870*	76,059	70,811	134,717	69,673	65,044	537	279	258	112	63	49
14	Patiala (Phulkian States) ..	*1,625,520*	900,597	724,923	621,145	340,466	280,679	2,452	1,310	1,142	632,972	357,193	275,779
15	Jind (Phulkian States) ..	*324,676*	176,383	148,293	243,561	131,270	112,291	..	..	..	33,290	19,183	14,107
16	Nabha (Phulkian States) ..	*287,574*	158,086	129,488	132,348	71,592	60,756	6	6	..	97,452	55,262	42,190
17	Bahawalpur ..	*984,612*	545,103	439,509	145,007	81,897	63,110	4,447	2,515	1,932	34,896	20,000	14,896

TABLE XVI.—RELIGION.—*concluded.*

Jain.			Buddhist.			Zoroastrian.			Muslim.			Christian.			Jew.			
Persons.	Males.	Females.	Persons.	Males.	Females.	Persons.	Males.	Females.	Persons.	Males.	Females.	Persons.	Males.	Females.	Persons.	Males.	Females.	Serial No.
14	15	16	17	18	19	20	21	22	23	24	25	26	27	28	29	30	31	
48,140	**22,962**	**20,178**	**7,753**	**3,770**	**3,983**	**569**	**358**	**211**	**14,929,896**	**8,116,383**	**6,813,513**	**419,353**	**232,556**	**186,797**	**13**	**5**	**8**	
35,284	**18,751**	**16,533**	**5,728**	**2,757**	**2,966**	**546**	**339**	**207**	**13,382,460**	**7,241,612**	**6,090,848**	**414,788**	**230,018**	**184,770**	**12**	**5**	**7**	
21,769	**11,403**	**10,366**	**20**	**15**	**5**	**8**	**7**	**1**	**1,130,398**	**610,770**	**519,628**	**17,527**	**9,643**	**7,884**	**2**	**1**	**1**	
5,988	3,137	2,851	..	..	..	2	2	..	253,784	135,840	117,944	1,107	583	524	..	..	..	1
6,375	3,320	3,055	..	..	..	..	..	..	137,880	72,820	65,060	4,807	2,452	2,355	..	..	..	2
2,665	1,379	1,286	..	..	..	4	3	1	242,357	129,479	112,878	1,463	730	733	..	..	..	3
4,190	2,164	2,026	..	..	.	..	..	..	259,730	141,372	118,358	1,469	806	663	..	..	..	4
2,550	1,402	1,148	6	4	2	2	2	..	230,837	126,913	103,924	7,141	4,284	2,857	2	1	1	5
1	1	..	14	11	3	..	..	..	5,810	4,346	1,464	1,540	788	752	..	..	..	6
5,319	**2,876**	**2,443**	**5,669**	**2,718**	**2,951**	**101**	**66**	**35**	**1,539,145**	**830,920**	**708,225**	**18,210**	**10,592**	**7,618**	..	..	..	
94	46	48	5,663	2,712	2,951	2	2	..	40,483	22,486	17,997	576	316	260	..	..	..	7
1,016	579	437	..	..	..	..	..	..	328,078	174,351	153,727	3,764	2,083	1,681	..	..	..	8
1,379	727	652	..	..	..	70	44	26	419,556	223,611	195,945	4,323	2,714	1,609	..	..	..	9
1,419	765	654	5	5	..	5	4	1	235,598	130,149	105,449	2,477	1,098	1,379	..	..	..	10
1,411	759	652	1	1	..	24	16	8	515,430	280,323	235,107	7,070	4,381	2,689	..	..	..	11
6,144	**3,349**	**2,795**	**17**	**14**	**3**	**216**	**129**	**87**	**3,410,684**	**1,888,696**	**1,521,988**	**281,954**	**155,085**	**126,869**	**5**	**1**	**4**	
1,450	777	673	14	11	3	159	94	65	815,820	464,043	351,777	57,097	32,107	24,990	1	..	1	12
1,272	691	581	..	..	..	42	25	17	524,676	290,387	234,289	16,619	8,862	7,757	4	1	3	13
15	8	7	2	2	..	2	2	..	493,216	268,771	224,445	43,243	23,702	19,541	..	..	..	14
2,236	1,227	1,009	..	..	..	7	4	3	609,633	333,637	275,996	66 365	36,579	29,786	..	..	..	15
1,071	593	478	1	1	..	..	..	..	521,343	287,794	233,549	49,364	26,940	22,424	..	..	..	16
100	53	47	..	..	..	6	4	2	445,996	244,064	201,932	49,266	26,895	22,371	..	..	..	17
1,354	**738**	**616**	**15**	**9**	**6**	**70**	**40**	**30**	**3,362,260**	**1,791,956**	**1,570,304**	**23,639**	**13,982**	**9,657**	**5**	**3**	**2**	
32	18	14	4	1	3	..	..	..	786,750	425,716	361,034	3,097	1,746	1,351	..	..	..	18
14	8	6	1	1	..	..	..	..	679,546	367,879	311,667	11,294	6,223	5,071	..	..	..	19
209	106	103	..	..	..	..	..	..	482,097	251,656	230,441	672	388	284	..	..	..	20
1,077	593	484	9	6	3	65	37	28	524,965	279,287	245,678	7,486	4,924	2,562	5	3	2	21
2	2	..	1	1	..	..	..	..	531,793	279,546	252,247	710	490	220	..	..	..	22
20	11	9	..	..	..	5	3	2	357,109	187,872	169,237	380	211	169	..	..	..	23
698	**385**	**313**	**2**	**1**	**1**	**151**	**97**	**54**	**3,889,973**	**2,119,270**	**1,770,703**	**73,458**	**40,716**	**32,742**	..	..	..	
38	28	10	2	1	1	7	6	1	697,542	381,956	315,586	17,245	9,618	7,627	..	..	..	24
95	66	29	..	..	..	7	7	..	720,996	389,159	331,837	45,518	24,899	20,619	..	..	..	25
..	..	..	..	..	..	20	13	7	552,853	297,801	255,052	494	267	227	..	..	..	26
440	220	220	..	..	..	117	71	46	942,937	515,218	427,719	9,924	5,780	4,144	..	..	..	27
..	..	..	..	..	..	..	..	..	513,265	279,319	233,946	246	133	113	..	..	..	28
125	71	54	..	..	..	..	..	..	432,911	239,106	193,805	31	19	12	..	..	..	
..	..	..	..	..	..	..	..	..	29,469	16,711	12,758	..	..	..	..	..	..	29
7,856	**4,211**	**3,645**	**2,030**	**1,013**	**1,017**	**23**	**19**	**4**	**1,597,436**	**874,771**	**722,665**	**4,565**	**2,538**	**2,027**	**1**	..	**1**	
408	**218**	**190**	**1,308**	**630**	**678**	**1**	**1**	..	**40,845**	**22,071**	**18,774**	**206**	**100**	**106**	..	..	..	
..	..	..	..	..	..	..	..	..	5,863	2,883	2,980	5	3	2	..	..	..	1
105	52	53	..	..	..	..	..	..	3,168	1,640	1,528	3	2	1	..	..	..	2
162	88	74	..	..	..	..	..	..	21,797	11,843	9,954	22	14	8	..	..	..	3
141	**78**	**63**	**1,308**	**630**	**678**	**1**	**1**	..	**10,017**	**5,705**	**4,312**	**176**	**81**	**95**	..	..	..	4
..	..	..	1,301	623	678	..	..	..	674	345	329	16	10	6	..	..	..	
141	78	63	..	..	..	..	..	..	6,315	3,464	2,851	13	8	5	..	..	..	
..	..	..	..	..	..	..	..	..	1,125	765	360	70	24	46	..	..	..	
..	..	..	7	7	..	..	..	..	324	203	121	..	..	..	..	..	..	
..	..	..	..	..	..	..	..	..	350	191	159	..	..	..	..	..	..	
..	..	..	..	..	..	1	1	..	1,229	737	492	77	39	38	..	..	..	
7,448	**3,993**	**3,455**	**722**	**383**	**339**	**22**	**18**	**4**	**1,556,591**	**852,700**	**703,891**	**4,359**	**2,438**	**1,921**	**1**	..	**1**	
18	7	11	..	..	..	..	..	..	3,119	1,600	1,519	1	..	1	..	..	..	5
52	38	14	..	..	..	..	..	..	7,020	4,047	2,973	52	24	28	..	..	..	6
..	..	..	..	..	..	..	..	..	1,458	804	654	6	2	4	..	..	..	7
..	..	..	138	94	44	..	..	..	6,351	4,464	1,887	141	92	49	1	..	1	8
..	..	..	14	8	6	..	..	..	733	382	351	1	1	..	..	..	..	9
27	15	12	..	..	..	..	..	..	179,251	96,240	83,011	983	511	472	..	..	..	10
1,286	699	587	..	..	..	..	..	..	31,417	17,280	14,137	135	77	58	..	..	..	11
550	292	258	..	..	..	..	..	..	49,912	27,236	22,676	167	100	67	..	..	..	12
3	1	2	568	280	288	..	..	..	10,839	5,706	5,133	94	57	37	..	..	..	13
3,578	1,875	1,703	2	1	1	2	1	1	363,920	198,945	164,975	1,449	806	643	..	..	..	14
1,613	896	717	..	..	..	..	..	..	46,002	24,915	21,087	210	119	91	..	..	..	15
309	163	146	..	..	..	..	..	..	57,393	31,027	26,366	66	36	30	..	..	..	16
12	7	5	..	..	..	20	17	3	799,176	440,054	359,122	1,054	613	441	..	..	..	17

TABLE XVII.

RACE, TRIBE OR CASTE.

1. The number of castes for this Table has been reduced to fifty-six. The selection was made with a view to include all the castes, which contributed 4 *per mille* or more to the total population of 1921, the four criminal tribes, Bawaria, Harni, Pakhiwara and Sansi, and the "backward and depressed castes," numbering fourteen in all, five of which, Chamar, Chuhra, Dhobi, Dagi and Koli, and Julaha, also fall under the category of 4 *per mille*, the rest being Bagaria, Dumna, Ghosi, Kahar, Mahtam, Megh, Od, Ramdasia and Sarera. Darzi and Mali, which did not fall under any of the above categories, were also included. Separate figures have also been given for Brahmanic Hindus,' who returned no caste.

2. In some places members of occupational castes, such as *Darzi*, *Chhimba* and *Chhipi*, returned themselves as Tank Kshatrya, and *Lohars and Tarkhans* as Dhiman Brahman. Figures for these two new castes have also been tabulated, and the details of the occupational castes included therein appear in Appendix I to Chapter XII of the Report.

3. In many cases members of certain occupational castes other than those, mentioned in the preceding paragraph, returned a higher caste, and their figures have been included in those of the traditional castes, for instance, Brahman Nai in Nai, Rajput Sunar in Sunar. The details of such figures appear in Appendix II to Chapter XII.

4. The castes of Indian Christian converts have been tabulated on the present occasion.

5. Where members of a caste belong to different religions, separate figures have been given; but where the numerical strength of a caste (for the whole Province) in any one religion falls below 1,000, the figures have been included in the total, with a foot-note to this effect. In order, however, to reduce the number of foot-notes, the figures for the religion with the greatest number of converts have not been detailed by localities, but an asterik indicates the locality and figures can be extracted by subtracting the detail of other religions, given in the body of the Table and in the foot-notes, from the column of "Total". The strength of such castes is. indicated by the table below for the whole Province :—

Caste.	Hindu.		Ad-Dharmi.		Sikh.		Jain.		Buddhist.		Muslim.		Christian.	
	M.	F.	M.	F.	M.	F.	M.	F.	M.	F.	M.	F.	M.	F.
1. Aggarwal	..	..	..	..	..	..	..	..	..	..	22	8	8	6
2. Ahir	..	..	..	..	450	365	1	..	..	..	..	..	17	4
3. Arain	..	..	..	..	40	32	..	..	..	..	..	..	8	12
4. Arora	..	..	..	..	..	..	27	20	..	..	38	50	2	..
5. Awan	..	..	..	..	..	..	..	..	..	..	..	..	4	1
6. Bagaria	..	..	..	..	41	58	..	..	..	..	35	30	..	..
7. Bawaria	..	..	32	24	..	..	..	..	..	..	56	25	..	..
8. Brahman	..	..	..	..	..	..	37	11	1	..	69	46	47	19
9. Chamar	..	..	..	..	..	..	..	..	..	..	..	..	163	132
10. Dagi and Koli	..	..	..	..	350	316	1	..	39	37	15	5	..	..
11. Darzi	..	..	1	..	..	..	..	..	..	..	..	..	..	..
12. Dhobi	..	..	4	..	427	359	..	..	..	..	..	..	..	..
13. Dumna	..	..	20	10	155	173	..	..	..	..	6	2	..	..
14. Faqir	..	..	202	5	..	..	5	5	..	..	..	..	..	..
15. Ghirath	..	..	..	..	105	69	..	..	..	..	102	10	..	..
16. Gujjar	..	..	..	..	..	..	..	..	..	..	..	..	8	2
17. Jat	..	..	..	..	..	..	446	392	..	..	..	..	566	326
18. Jhiwar	..	..	4	1	..	..	..	..	..	..	..	..	2	1
19. Julaha	..	..	421	292	..	..	..	..	..	..	..	..	9	5
20. Kahar	..	..	..	..	..	..	..	..	..	..	..	..	1	2
21. Kashmiri	622	372	..	..	26	7	..	..	..	..	..	..	1	7
22. Khatri	..	..	..	..	..	..	68	37	..	..	63	32	80	14
23. Kumhar	..	..	..	..	..	..	5	4	..	..	..	..	10	4
24. Lohar	..	..	..	..	..	..	5	..	116	119	..	..	1	1
25. Mali	..	..	..	..	341	270	..	1	..	..	..	..	..	..
26. Megh	..	..	35	13	450	364	..	..	..	..	19	11	..	..
27. Meo	47	28	..	..	..	..	..	..	..	..	..	..	..	..
28. Mirasi	..	..	..	..	83	41	..	..	..	..	..	..	90	69
29. Mochi	..	..	116	90	133	64	..	..	..	..	..	..	2	2
30. Nai	..	..	149	70	..	..	2	1	..	..	..	..	85	68
31. Od	..	..	..	..	52	43	..	..	..	..	..	..	..	..
32. Pathan	..	..	..	..	..	..	..	..	..	..	..	..	20	16
33. Kanet	..	..	..	..	284	255	1	..	..	..	1	2	..	..
34. Rajput	..	..	..	..	..	..	171	166	..	..	..	..	258	186
35. Rathi	..	..	..	..	..	1	..	..	..	..	11	6	..	..
36. Ramdasia	..	..	..	..	..	..	..	..	..	..	..	..	2	1
37. Saini	..	..	..	..	..	..	..	..	..	..	64	56	3	..
38. Sansi	..	..	189	195	..	..	..	..	..	..	464	361	..	..
39. Sarera	..	..	45	16	..	..	..	..	..	..	..	..	..	..
40. Sayad	..	..	..	..	..	..	..	..	..	..	..	..	6	5
41. Sheikh	..	..	..	..	..	..	..	..	..	..	..	..	12	10
42. Tarkhan	..	..	..	..	..	..	7	12	10	7	..	..	9	2
43. Teli	..	..	..	..	17	25	..	..	..	..	..	..	..	..
44. Dhiman Brahman	..	..	..	..	335	216	..	..	..	..	..	..	..	..

M = Males. F = Females.

TABLE XVII.—RACE,

Serial No.	District or State.	TOTAL.			AGGARWAL.								AHIR.	
					Hindu.		Sikh.		Jain.		Total.		Hindu.	
		Persons.	Males.	Females.	Males.	Females.	Males.	Females.	Males.	Females.	Males.	Females.	Males.	Females.
1	2	3	4	5	6	7	8	9	10	11	12	13	14	15
	PUNJAB	**25,129,382**	**13,713,697**	**11,415,685**	**191,500**	**161,499**	**917**	**767**	**12,766**	**11,575**	**205,213**	**178,855**	**120,928**	**97,650**
	BRITISH TERRITORY	**20,606,866**	**11,244,518**	**9,362,348**	**125,829**	**105,778**	**511**	**400**	**10,116**	**9,277**	**136,486**	**115,469**	**68,810**	**53,136**
	AMBALA DIVISION	**3,623,743**	**1,977,253**	**1,646,490**	**92,482**	**80,860**	**22**	**12**	**9,192**	**8,465**	**101,717**	**89,342**	**62,934**	**51,367**
1	Hissar	*789,615*	426,071	363,544	28,234	25,634	12	5	2,628	2,439	* 30,875	28,078	5,985	4,743
2	Rohtak	*724,936*	389,294	335,642	20,090	18,088	1	1	2,597	2,366	[1] 22,690	20,455	10,674	8,811
3	Gurgaon	*692,983*	372,855	320,128	13,432	11,742	..	..	1,268	1,194	* 14,702	12,936	44,189	36,486
4	Karnal	*731,576*	403,315	328,261	22,903	19,233	2	..	2,101	1,976	* 25,022	* 21,214	1,027	801
5	Ambala	*653,529*	365,875	287,654	7,549	6,040	7	6	598	490	8,154	6,536	1,042	523
6	Simla	*31,104*	19,843	11,261	274	123	..	..	..	..	274	123	17	3
	JULLUNDUR DIVISION	**4,178,030**	**2,262,842**	**1,915,188**	**22,986**	**18,026**	**308**	**249**	**722**	**694**	**24,022**	**18,977**	**2,804**	**1,065**
7	Kangra	*728,065*	376,689	351,376	266	100	..	..	2	1	268	101	5	5
8	Hoshiarpur	*906,142*	* 488,127	418,015	844	734	..	..	2	..	846	734	2	..
9	Jullundur	*875,725*	476,557	399,168	2,869	2,359	2	3	146	158	[2] 3,023	[2] 2,525	368	222
10	Ludhiana	*636,867*	356,099	280,768	6,045	4,784	12	4	298	275	6,355	5,063	171	51
11	Ferozepore	*1,031,231*	565,370	465,861	12,962	10,049	294	242	274	260	13,530	* 10,554	2,258	787
	LAHORE DIVISION	**4,806,071**	**2,680,655**	**2,125,416**	**8,109**	**5,655**	**67**	**31**	**106**	**76**	**8,285**	**5,762**	**1,429**	**380**
12	Lahore	*1,203,846*	689,437	514,409	3,097	1,757	47	25	60	36	3,204	1,818	940	225
13	Amritsar	*907,869*	506,305	401,564	3,137	2,393	20	6	27	16	* 3,187	2,415	207	61
14	Gurdaspur	*748,065*	409,904	338,161	918	763	..	..	3	3	921	766	17	10
15	Sialkot	*778,048*	428,262	349,786	596	567	..	..	16	21	612	588	103	58
16	Gujranwala	*628,930*	350,511	278,419	83	46	..	..	..	..	83	46	112	10
17	Sheikhupura	*539,313*	296,236	243,077	278	129	..	..	..	..	278	129	50	16
	RAWALPINDI DIVISION	**3,444,031**	**1,834,653**	**1,609,378**	**683**	**434**	**23**	**25**	**52**	**2**	**758**	**462**	**381**	**134**
18	Gujrat	*841,839*	455,064	386,775	49	27	..	..	..	..	49	27	44	17
19	Shahpur	*726,033*	392,142	333,891	21	11	..	..	2	2	23	13	82	25
20	Jhelum	*448,415*	233,241	215,174	59	38	..	..	50	..	109	[2] 39	24	12
21	Rawalpindi	*514,097*	274,804	239,293	529	350	23	25	..	..	552	375	199	59
22	Attock	*517,988*	271,645	246,343	23	8	..	..	..	..	23	8	20	15
23	Mianwali	*395,659*	207,757	187,902	2	..	..	..	..	..	2	..	12	6
	MULTAN DIVISION	**4,554,991**	**2,489,115**	**2,065,876**	**1,569**	**803**	**91**	**83**	**44**	**40**	**1,704**	**926**	**762**	**190**
24	Montgomery	*834,850*	460,781	374,069	858	377	4	1	4	4	866	382	286	75
25	Lyallpur	*1,012,373*	552,697	459,676	518	309	86	82	15	6	619	397	318	74
26	Jhang	*631,442*	339,084	292,358	7	5	..	..	..	..	7	5	10	3
27	Multan	*1,039,101*	570,963	468,138	175	108	1	..	25	30	201	138	148	36
28	Muzaffargarh	*545,094*	294,971	250,123	7	2	..	..	..	..	7	2	..	2
29	Dera Ghazi Khan	*492,131*	270,619	221,512	4	2	..	..	..	..	4	2	..	..
	PUNJAB STATES	**4,522,516**	**2,469,179**	**2,053,337**	**65,671**	**55,721**	**406**	**367**	**2,650**	**2,298**	**68,727**	**58,886**	**52,618**	**44,514**
	A.—HAVING POLITICAL RELATIONS WITH THE PUNJAB GOVERNMENT.	**410,129**	**214,625**	**195,504**	**1,094**	**930**	..	..	**140**	**127**	**1,234**	**1,057**	**5,946**	**5,131**
1	Dujana	24,891	12,887	12,004	56	41	..	..	..	..	56	41	4,154	3,615
2	Pataudi	17,238	9,068	8,170	276	240	..	..	52	53	328	293	1,788	1,513
3	Kalsia	54,164	30,233	23,931	660	601	..	..	88	74	748	675	3	..
4	*SIMLA HILL STATES*	**313,836**	**162,437**	**151,399**	**102**	**48**	..	..	..	..	**102**	**48**	**1**	**3**
	Bashahr	102,244	50,493	51,751	..	..	..	..	..	..	..	..	..	..
	Nalagarh	45,675	24,379	21,296	23	14	..	..	..	..	23	14	..	..
	Keonthal	45,047	24,038	21,009	5	2	..	..	..	..	5	2	..	..
	Baghal	25,022	12,742	12,280	1	..	..	..	..	..	1	..	..	..
	Jubbal	25,457	13,585	11,872	..	..	..	..	..	..	..	..	..	..
	Other Simla Hill States	70,391	37,200	33,191	73	32	..	..	..	..	73	32	1	3
	B.—HAVING POLITICAL RELATIONS WITH THE GOVERNMENT OF INDIA.	**4,112,387**	**2,254,554**	**1,857,833**	**64,577**	**54,791**	**406**	**367**	**2,510**	**2,171**	**67,493**	**57,829**	**46,672**	**39,383**
5	Loharu	20,443	10,778	9,665	461	427	..	..	..	..	461	427	211	159
6	Sirmoor	122,315	67,835	54,480	585	463	..	..	30	12	615	475	33	16
7	Bilaspur	98,189	51,724	46,465	1	..	..	..	..	..	1	..	..	..
8	Mandi	197,263	101,840	95,423	9	..	..	..	..	..	9	..	..	..
9	Suket	54,897	28,997	25,900	18	11	..	..	..	..	18	11	..	..
10	Kapurthala	288,951	156,770	132,181	483	442	7	4	..	..	490	446	15	7
11	Maler Kotla	79,604	44,058	35,546	1,382	1,014	1	1	662	540	2,045	1,555	38	2
12	Faridkot	157,326	87,069	70,257	2,472	1,887	20	27	8	2	2,500	1,916	307	70
13	Chamba	115,043	59,298	55,745	5	1	..	..	..	..	5	1	..	..
14	Patiala (Phulkian States)	1,460,804	809,308	651,496	40,994	35,151	346	311	1,153	1,111	42,493	36,573	27,163	23,046
15	Jind (Phulkian States)	291,788	158,864	132,924	9,517	8,297	2	1	601	462	10,120	8,760	5,314	4,477
16	Nabha (Phulkian States)	269,268	148,300	120,968	7,202	6,199	30	23	56	44	7,288	6,266	13,560	11,606
17	Bahawalpur	956,496	529,713	426,783	1,448	899	..	..	..	..	1,448	899	31	..

Total *Aggarwal* includes *Muslims and :—

TRIBE OR CASTE.—*continued.*

Ahir.				Arain.						Arora.						Awan.		
Muslim.		Total.		*Hindu.*		*Muslim.*		Total.		*Hindu.*		*Sikh.*		Total.		Total *Muslim.*		
Males.	Females.	Males.	Females.	Males.	Females.	Males.	Females.	Males.	Females.	Males.	Females.	Males.	Females.	Males.	Females.	Males.	Females.	Serial No.
16	17	18	19	20	21	22	23	24	25	26	27	28	29	30	31	32	33	
1,389	**1,129**	**122,785**	**99,148**	**691**	**455**	**726,913**	**603,144**	**727,652**	**603,643**	**354,070**	**307,198**	**61,772**	**52,557**	**415,909**	**359,825**	**288,310**	**250,932**	
1,386	**1,097**	**69,921**	**54,433**	**270**	**161**	**622,999**	**517,670**	**623,277**	**517,843**	**315,136**	**275,721**	**59,232**	**50,460**	**374,428**	**326,251**	**285,076**	**248,542**	
22	**13**	**63,079**	**51,491**	**201**	**143**	**26,689**	**22,583**	**26,890**	**22,726**	**1,181**	**1,096**	**1,819**	**1,744**	**3,003**	**2,841**	**373**	**57**	
18	13	[2]* 6,009	[2]* 4,765	7	..	3,302	3,059	3,309	3,059	1,009	947	1,728	1,670	[1] 2,739	[1] 2,618	18	..	1
1	..	[3] 10,678	[3] 8,812	..	..	209	176	209	176	11	8	5	7	16	15	41	4	2
2	..	44,191	36,486	..	..	52	39	62	39	4	2	1	..	5	2	..	..	3
1	..	* 1,124	* 885	175	131	7,632	6,307	7,807	6,438	16	5	17	8	33	13	2	..	4
..	..	* 1,059	* 539	19	12	15,449	12,971	15,468	12,983	118	110	55	45	* 174	155	312	53	5
..	..	[4] 18	[4] 4	..	..	45	31	45	31	23	24	13	14	36	38	..	..	6
30	**13**	**2,882**	**1,113**	**18**	**5**	**155,165**	**132,525**	**155,183**	**132,531**	**14,500**	**12,034**	**3,213**	**2,560**	**17,724**	**14,603**	**17,384**	**13,695**	
..	..	5	5	13	5	448	362	461	367	82	32	12	25	94	57	8	1	7
..	..	* 6	..	2	..	18,666	16,037	18,668	16,037	114	73	85	63	199	136	[1] 5,802	[1] 4,832	8
..	..	368	222	2	..	80,061	70,339	80,063	* 70,340	252	208	97	89	[2] 350	297	8,908	6,811	9
..	..	* 180	* 56	..	..	18,870	14,742	18,870	14,742	299	203	37	31	* 338	* 236	2,015	1,798	10
30	13	[1]* 2,323	* 830	1	..	37,120	31,046	37,121	31,045	13,753	11,518	2,982	2,352	* 16,743	* 13,877	601	253	11
49	**23**	**1,513**	**416**	**22**	**9**	**231,985**	**190,432**	**232,014**	**190,452**	**53,856**	**45,138**	**17,229**	**14,808**	**71,112**	**59,496**	**22,007**	**15,914**	
15	6	[5]* 973	* 236	6	1	76,186	62,030	* 76,199	* 62,041	16,484	13,207	2,950	2,365	[3]* 19,452	[3]* 15,615	5,058	2,567	12
4	..	* 213	* 63	9	5	29,164	23,707	29,173	23,712	8,083	6,773	4,947	4,183	13,030	10,956	1,829	1,242	13
3	4	20	14	7	3	37,998	30,818	38,005	* 30,822	536	372	175	105	711	477	601	507	14
..	..	[6] 112	58	..	..	34,884	28,087	34,884	28,087	4,458	4,160	1,992	1,734	6,450	5,894	12,542	10,085	15
..	..	112	10	..	..	18,262	14,673	18,262	14,673	14,500	12,540	4,324	3,553	18,824	16,093	1,026	814	16
27	13	* 33	* 35	..	..	35,491	31,117	35,491	31,117	9,795	8,086	2,841	2,368	[4] 12,645	[4] 10,461	931	699	17
988	**843**	**1,378**	**986**	**28**	**4**	**30,518**	**25,208**	**30,547**	**25,212**	**57,093**	**52,910**	**14,786**	**13,417**	**71,830**	**66,328**	**230,021**	**206,899**	
8	1	* 53	* 19	11	1	14,541	11,862	* 14,553	11,863	8,211	7,232	5,693	5,241	13,904	12,473	8,727	7,144	18
793	745	* 882	* 777	..	..	12,101	10,092	12,101	10,092	20,372	18,645	3,647	3,171	24,019	* 21,817	42,681	38,658	19
16	23	40	35	..	..	368	213	368	213	2,211	2,183	706	614	2,917	2,797	31,808	29,513	20
40	22	* 240	* 82	16	..	302	206	318	206	2,500	1,725	519	427	3,019	2,152	25,298	21,329	21
111	37	131	52	..	..	90	82	90	82	3,416	3,196	2,623	2,458	[5] 6,040	5,654	[2] 107,111	97,184	22
20	15	32	21	1	3	3,116	2,753	3,117	2,756	20,383	19,929	1,548	1,506	21,931	21,435	14,396	13,071	23
297	**205**	**1,069**	**427**	**1**	**..**	**178,642**	**146,922**	**178,643**	**146,922**	**188,506**	**164,543**	**22,235**	**18,431**	**210,759**	**182,983**	**15,341**	**11,977**	
40	41	* 336	* 138	1	..	52,847	42,379	52,848	42,379	23,236	18,857	8,137	6,864	[6]* 31,384	[5] 25,724	3,246	2,402	24
..	..	318	* 84	..	..	70,616	59,846	70,616	59,846	25,369	20,318	6,860	4,902	* 32,232	* 25,223	4,473	4,023	25
29	15	39	18	..	..	7,463	6,564	7,463	6,564	31,390	30,082	3,241	3,006	34,631	33,088	535	389	26
204	138	352	174	..	..	37,644	29,696	37,644	29,696	61,083	51,406	3,443	3,167	[7]* 64,530	* 54,576	5,148	3,741	27
..	..	..	2	..	..	6,860	5,783	6,860	5,783	25,688	23,642	484	455	26,172	24,097	1,493	1,044	28
24	11	24	11	..	..	3,212	2,654	3,212	2,654	21,740	20,238	70	37	21,810	20,275	446	378	29
3	**32**	**52,864**	**44,715**	**421**	**294**	**103,914**	**85,474**	**104,375**	**85,800**	**38,934**	**31,477**	**2,540**	**2,097**	**41,481**	**33,574**	**3,284**	**2,890**	
..	..	**5,946**	**5,131**	**1**	**2**	**1,719**	**1,405**	**1,720**	**1,407**	**5**	**7**	**3**	**5**	**8**	**12**	..	..	
..	..	4,154	3,615	..	..	..	..	..	..	..	..	..	..	..	..	..	..	1
..	..	1,788	1,513	..	..	..	..	..	..	..	..	..	..	..	..	..	..	2
..	..	3	..	1	2	1,678	1,375	1,679	1,377	3	6	3	5	6	11	..	..	3
..	..	1	3	..	..	41	30	41	30	2	1	..	..	2	1	..	..	4
..	..	..	..	..	..	..	..	..	..	..	..	..	..	..	..	..	..	
..	..	..	..	..	..	24	17	24	17	..	..	..	..	..	..	..	..	
..	..	..	..	..	..	..	..	..	..	2	..	..	..	2	..	..	..	
..	..	..	..	..	..	..	..	..	..	..	..	..	..	..	..	..	..	
..	..	..	..	..	..	..	..	..	..	..	..	..	..	..	..	..	..	
..	..	1	3	..	..	17	13	17	13	..	1	..	..	..	1	..	..	
3	**32**	**46,918**	**39,584**	**420**	**292**	**102,195**	**84,069**	**102,655**	**84,393**	**38,929**	**31,470**	**2,537**	**2,092**	**41,473**	**33,562**	**3,234**	**2,890**	
..	..	211	159	..	..	..	..	..	..	..	..	..	..	..	..	..	..	5
..	..	33	16	..	..	214	155	214	155	1	..	1	4	2	4	..	..	6
..	..	..	..	..	..	24	16	24	16	..	..	1	..	1	..	..	..	7
..	..	..	..	2	..	332	275	334	275	3	3	2	..	5	3	17	3	8
..	..	..	..	..	..	170	168	170	168	..	..	..	..	..	..	..	..	9
..	..	15	7	..	..	29,366	24,757	29,366	24,757	381	320	45	41	426	361	319	269	10
..	..	38	2	..	..	1,191	991	1,191	991	38	26	..	..	38	26	45	13	11
..	..	307	70	..	..	2,435	2,194	2,435	2,194	1,007	799	1,075	841	2,082	1,640	..	..	12
..	..	..	..	..	..	13	8	13	8	7	3	..	..	7	3	11	12	13
3	4	* 27,378	* 23,203	418	292	25,643	21,011	[1] 26,098	[1] 21,333	676	489	703	667	[8] 1,386	1,156	8	12	14
..	..	* 5,342	* 4,493	..	..	2,215	1,762	[2] 2,218	[2] 1,764	22	16	10	11	38	27	2	2	15
..	..	* 13,563	11,606	..	..	2,306	1,858	2,306	1,858	120	94	82	84	202	178	4	..	16
..	28	31	28	..	..	38,286	30,874	38,286	30,874	36,674	29,720	612	444	37,286	30,164	2,828	2,079	17

Total *Ahir* includes *Sikhs and:—

		M.	F.
1.	Jain	1	..
2.	Christian	2	2
3.	,,	3	1
4.	,,	1	1
5.	,,	2	..
6.	,,	9	..

Total *Arain* includes *Christians and:—

		M.	F.
1.	Sikh	37	30
2.	,,	3	2

Total *Arora* includes *Jains and:—

		M.	F.
1.	Muslim	1	1
	Christian	1	..
2.	Muslim	1	..
3.	Muslim	7	39
	Christian	1	..
4.	Muslim	9	7
5.	,,	1	..
6.	,,	9	3
7.	,,	3	..
8.	,,	7	..

Total *Awan* includes:—

		M.	F.
1.	Christian	3	1
2.	,,	1	..

TABLE XVII.—RACE,

Serial No.	District or State.	Bagaria. Hindu. Males.	Hindu. Females.	Total. Males.	Total. Females.	Bawaria. Hindu. Males.	Hindu. Females.	Sikh. Males.	Sikh. Females.	Total. Males.	Total. Females.	Biloch. Total Muslim. Males.	Total Muslim. Females.	Brahman. Hindu. Males.	Hindu. Females.
1	2	34	35	36	37	38	39	40	41	42	43	44	45	46	47
	PUNJAB	1,295	987	1,371	1,075	8,434	7,630	8,440	7,886	16,962	15,565	341,547	283,148	576,735	474,647
	BRITISH TERRITORY ..	1,293	987	1,369	1,075	5,315	4,691	4,542	4,848	9,944	9,087	292,314	242,299	422,561	344,235
	AMBALA DIVISION ..	..	..	..	..	2,736	2,393	235	208	2,971	2,601	4,118	3,764	147,556	119,398
1	Hissar	..		..	..	1,941	1,677	235	208	2,176	1,885	763	648	24,313	20,113
2	Rohtak	..	..	..	..	128	122	..	..	128	122	1,316	1,249	38,300	31,853
3	Gurgaon	..	..	..	..	663	589	..	..	663	589	1,402	1,281	27,191	22,921
4	Karnal	..	..	..	..	..	..	..	..	..	..	617	571	34,726	28,035
5	Ambala	..		..	..	4	5	..		4	5	19	15	20,578	15,507
6	Simla	..	..	..	..	..	..	..	..	..	..	1	..	2,448	964
	JULLUNDUR DIVISION ..	40	18	40	18	1,231	1,126	3,462	3,178	4,710	4,319	1,917	1,584	136,718	122,447
7	Kangra	..	..	..	..	14	5	..	..	14	5	..	..	55,531	53,084
8	Hoshiarpur	..	..	..	..	..	..	..	..	..	..	16	14	41,135	37,300
9	Jullundur	1	..	1	..	1	..	..	..	1	..	96	54	16,431	13,866
10	Ludhiana . ..	..	..	..	..	36	26	256	224	292	250	78	68	12,064	9,687
11	Ferozepore . ..	39	18	39	18	1,180	1,095	3,206	2,954	[1]* 4,403	* 4,064	1,727	1,448	11,552	8,510
	LAHORE DIVISION ..	198	87	210	91	677	593	611	599	1,288	1,192	5,536	4,230	91,786	66,718
12	Lahore	76	41	76	41	596	537	609	599	1,205	1,136	2,877	2,089	22,035	13,139
13	Amritsar	6	5	[1] 9	5	45	14	..	.	45	14	155	112	23,169	15,619
14	Gurdaspur	..	4	..	4	..	..	2	..	2	.	130	80	20,286	17,251
15	Sialkot	..	..	* 9	* 4	..	..	..	..	..	..	18	4	13,042	11,174
16	Gujranwala	42	2	42	2	36	42	..	..	36	42	459	416	8,862	6,584
17	Sheikhupura	74	35	74	35	..	..	..	..	..	..	1,897	1,529	4,392	2,946
	RAWALPINDI DIVISION	160	97	166	101	1	..	..	..	20	9	22,847	19,985	24,416	19,628
18	Gujrat	26	20	* 30	* 24	..	..	..	..	..	..	1,194	971	4,899	4,034
19	Shahpur	96	44	* 98	44	..	..	..	..	* 19	* 9	10,328	8,911	3,679	2,798
20	Jhelum	..	..	..	..	..	..	..	..	..	..	770	697	2,918	2,622
21	Rawalpindi	38	33	38	33	1	..	..	..	1	..	198	85	9,744	7,598
22	Attock	..	..	..	..	..	..	..	..	..	..	754	679	1,634	1,332
23	Mianwali	..	..	..	..	..	..	..	..	..	..	9,603	8,642	1,542	1,344
	MULTAN DIVISION ..	895	785	958	865	670	579	234	363	955	[illegible]	257,893	212,736	22,090	16,054
24	Montgomery	428	343	[2]* 436	343	292	246	174	224	[2]* 504	[2] 494	17,216	14,879	4,258	2,434
25	Lyallpur	2	66	[3] 22	[3] 102	316	274	60	75	376	349	13,526	12,553	7,071	4,777
26	Jhang	..	..	* 1	..	..	..	..	..	* 13	..	13,038	11,460	3,843	3,666
27	Multan	463	376	[4]* 492	[4]* 420	62	59	..	64	62	123	24,167	18,901	4,480	3,190
28	Muzaffargarh	2	.	2	..	..	..	..	..	..	..	65,147	56,153	1,525	1,275
29	Dera Ghazi Khan ..	.	..	..	..	..	..	..	..	..		124,802	98,790	913	712
	PUNJAB STATES ..	2	..	2	..	3,119	2,939	3,898	3,538	7,018	6,478	49,233	40,849	154,174	130,412
	A.—Having Political relations with the Punjab Government. ..	..	..	..	..	177	167	13	12	190	179	16	16	26,604	23,423
1	Dujana	..	..	..	..	126	122	..	..	126	122	..	..	1,080	989
2	Pataudi	..	..	..	..	47	41	..	..	47	41	1	..	1,096	963
3	Kalsia	..	..	..	..	4	4	13	12	17	16	15	16	1,376	1,133
4	*SIMLA HILL STATES* ..	..	..	..	..	..	..	..	..	..	..	..	..	23,052	20,338
	Bashahr	..	..	..	..	..	..	..	..	..	..	..	..	3,206	2,939
	Nalagarh	..	..	..	..	..	..	..	..	..	..	..	..	2,804	2,425
	Keonthal	..	..	..	..	..	..	..	..	..	..	..	..	4,410	3,760
	Baghal	..	..	..	..	..	..	..	..	..	..	..	..	3,574	3,389
	Jubbal	..	..	..	..	..	..	..	..	..	..	..	..	2,210	1,842
	Other Simla Hill States	..	..	..	..	..	..	..	..	..	..	..	..	6,848	5,983
	B.—Having Political relations with the Government of India. ..	2	..	2	..	2,942	2,772	3,885	3,526	6,828	6,299	49,217	40,833	127,570	106,989
5	Loharu	..	..	..	..	22	21	..	..	22	21	..	..	715	617
6	Sirmoor	..	..	..	..	..	..	..	..	..	..	..	..	6,007	4,976
7	Bilaspur	..	..	..	..	..	..	..	..	..	..	..	..	14,056	13,251
8	Mandi	..	..	..	..	..	..	..	..	..	..	3	..	11,524	9,901
9	Suket	..	..	..	..	..	..	..	..	..	..	..	..	3,913	3,447
10	Kapurthala	2	..	2	..	..	..	96	88	96	88	24	19	4,439	3,548
11	Maler Kotla	..	..	..	..	..	..	..	..	..	..	5	..	1,542	1,209
12	Faridkot	..	..	..	..	115	108	1,848	1,664	1,963	1,772	239	227	2,238	1,706
13	Chamba	..	..	..	..	..	..	..	..	..	..	..	..	9,375	8,573
14	Patiala } Phulkian States.	..	..	..	..	700	638	769	738	* 1,470	1,376	692	564	46,147	37,445
15	Jind } Phulkian States.	..	..	..	..	54	40	..	..	54	* 41	150	131	16,452	13,427
16	Nabha } Phulkian States.	..	..	..	..	84	98	33	38	117	136	124	104	8,345	7,088
17	Bahawalpur	..	..	..	..	1,967	1,867	1,139	998	3,106	2,865	47,980	39,788	2,817	1,801

Total *Bagaria* includes *Muslims and :—

		M.	F.
1.	Sikh	3	..
2.	,,	2	..
3.	,,	20	36
4.	,,	16	22

Total *Bawaria* includes *Muslims and :—

		M.	F.
1.	Ad-Dhrami	1	..
2.	,,	31	24

Total *Brahman*.

	M.	F.
1. Buddhist	1	..
2. Muslim	3	..
3. ,,	2	..
4. ,,	18	11
5. { ,,	8	9
{ Christian	1	..

TRIBE OR CASTE.—*continued.*

Brahman.				Chamar.										Chhimba.				
Sikh.		Total.		*Hindu.*		*Ad-Dharmi.*		*Sikh.*		*Muslim.*		Total.		*Hindu.*		*Sikh.*		
Males.	Females.	Males.	Females.	Males.	Females.	Males.	Females.	Males.	Females.	Males.	Females.	Males.	Females.	Males.	Females.	Males.	Females.	Serial No.
48	49	50	51	52	53	54	55	56	57	58	59	60	61	62	63	64	65	
4,156	**2,830**	**581,045**	**477,553**	**366,789**	**318,224**	**139,641**	**116,708**	**87,128**	**71,625**	**1,157**	**948**	**594,828**	**507,637**	**13,466**	**11,493**	**9,846**	**8,052**	
3,575	**2,510**	**426,285**	**346,816**	**246,322**	**214,351**	**135,395**	**113,036**	**33,170**	**28,068**	**1,146**	**947**	**416,196**	**356,534**	**9,442**	**8,229**	**3,768**	**3,164**	
212	**155**	**147,823**	**119,573**	**183,630**	**161,418**	**1,658**	**1,428**	**8,747**	**6,930**	**65**	**37**	**194,220**	**169,920**	**5,341**	**4,582**	**552**	**428**	
5	5	[2]* 24,325	* 20,119	37,611	32,610	8	..	2,828	2,340	13	2	40,460	34,952	2,298	1,984	427	342	1
..	..	* 38,306	* 31,854	34,814	31,525	..	..	3	..	..	..	[1] 34,840	[1] 31,544	1,878	1,687	..	..	2
4	4	[3] 27,197	22,925	41,333	38,726	..	..	..	..	11	7	[2] 41,427	[2] 38,807	369	288	..	..	3
18	16	[4]* 34,763	[4]* 28,063	34,132	28,387	1,600	1,380	200	156	4	1	[3] 35,936	[3] 29,925	323	250	34	22	4
184	130	[5]* 20,779	[5]* 15,648	35,014	29,703	50	48	5,691	4,404	37	27	[4] 40,806	[4] 34,200	467	371	91	63	5
1	..	[6] 2,453	964	726	462	..	..	25	30	..	..	751	492	6	2	..	1	6
558	**428**	**137,303**	**122,904**	**51,099**	**44,655**	**110,486**	**93,514**	**20,880**	**18,463**	**28**	**26**	**182,503**	**156,663**	**8,157**	**2,910**	**1,855**	**1,548**	
10	8	[13] 55,544	[13] 53,096	19,110	18,304	11,327	9,534	129	118	..	..	[5] 30,576	[5] 27,959	1,292	1,132	1	1	7
37	5	41,172	37,305	9,378	8,437	48,452	40,324	931	858	..	..	58,761	49,619	1,043	868	174	164	8
73	36	16,504	13,902	3,779	2,974	44,635	38,443	862	922	9	17	49,285	[6] 42,358	363	503	412	301	9
113	93	* 12,179	* 9,781	7,034	5,368	5,600	4,709	14,087	12,513	2	2	26,723	22,592	148	152	432	375	10
325	286	[7]* 11,904	[7]* 8,820	11,798	9,572	472	504	4,871	4,052	17	7	17,158	14,135	311	255	836	707	11
1,345	**924**	**93,178**	**67,650**	**6,552**	**4,796**	**4,620**	**3,639**	**840**	**504**	**1,037**	**863**	**13,061**	**9,802**	**764**	**581**	**943**	**852**	
364	233	[14]* 22,435	[14]* 13,379	1,581	909	407	200	164	54	277	227	2,429	1,390	82	52	508	539	12
349	257	[8]* 23,529	[8] 15,882	653	411	52	46	101	72	11	20	[7] 818	549	76	29	134	106	13
97	91	20,383	17,342	901	737	1,074	899	218	102	..	..	2,193	1,738	295	217	94	102	14
117	58	13,159	11,232	2,508	2,205	..	7	276	234	749	615	3,533	3,061	290	275	40	43	15
191	158	9,053	6,742	244	117	..	..	26	17	..	..	270	134	..	..	1	..	16
227	127	4,619	3,073	665	417	3,087	2,487	55	25	..	1	[8] 3,818	2,930	21	8	76	62	17
1,195	**765**	**25,625**	**20,397**	**2,170**	**1,458**	**631**	**374**	**307**	**239**	**1**	**..**	**3,109**	**2,071**	**97**	**68**	**28**	**16**	
94	61	[9] 5,004	[9] 4,098	228	108	631	374	21	17	1	..	881	499	8	11	2	..	18
53	32	3,732	2,830	1,604	1,248	..	..	246	187	..	..	1,850	1.435	..	..	..	..	19
174	111	* 3,093	2,633	33	4	..	..	..	..	..	..	33	4	76	45	20	15	20
726	489	10,470	8,087	213	80	..	..	40	35	..	..	253	115	13	12	1	..	21
141	68	* 1,777	[15] 1,401	19	6	..	..	..	..	..	..	19	6	..	..	..	1	22
7	4	1,549	1,348	73	12	..	..	..	..	..	..	73	12	..	..	..	..	23
265	**238**	**22,356**	**16,292**	**2,871**	**2,029**	**18,000**	**14,081**	**2,896**	**1,932**	**15**	**21**	**28,303**	**18,078**	**83**	**88**	**895**	**820**	
115	78	[10] 4,374	2,512	1,014	740	5,108	3,578	615	493	..	13	[9] 6,758	[9] 4,839	21	46	48	37	24
127	149	7,198	4,926	1,158	821	12,247	10,087	1,650	1,353	14	6	15,069	12,267	53	42	339	282	25
1	..	3,844	3,666	287	210	36	23	9	6	..	..	332	239	..	..	..	..	26
22	11	4,502	3,201	329	209	609	393	122	80	1	2	1,061	684	6	..	8	1	27
..	..	1,525	1,275	33	49	..	..	..	..	..	..	83	49	3	..	..	..	28
..	..	913	712	..	..	..	..	..	..	..	..	..	..	..	..	..	..	29
581	**820**	**154,760**	**130,737**	**120,417**	**103,873**	**4,246**	**3,672**	**53,958**	**43,557**	**11**	**1**	**178,632**	**151,108**	**4,024**	**3,264**	**6,078**	**4,888**	
18	**13**	**26,624**	**23,438**	**13,720**	**12,094**	**10**	**7**	**138**	**79**	**3**	**..**	**13,871**	**12,180**	**380**	**318**	**14**	**8**	
..	..	1,080	989	1,226	1,261	..	..	..	..	..	..	1,226	1,261	..	..	..	..	1
..	..	1,096	963	1,164	1,132	..	..	..	..	..	..	1,164	1,132	57	45	..	..	2
17	12	1,393	[11] 1,146	3,609	2,945	10	7	102	63	2	..	3,723	3,015	51	..	11	5	3
1	**1**	**23,055**	**20,340**	**7,721**	**6,756**	**..**	**..**	**36**	**16**	**1**	**..**	**7,758**	**6,772**	**272**	**273**	**8**	**3**	
..	..	3,206	2,939	35	34	..	..	..	..	..	..	35	34	..	..	..	..	
..	..	* 2,806	* 2,426	2,990	2,575	..	..	25	11	1	..	3,016	2,586	140	132	3	8	
..	..	4,410	3,760	642	494	..	..	..	..	..	..	642	494	4	1	..	..	
..	..	3,574	3,389	1,487	1,419	..	..	2	..	..	..	1,489	1,419	84	88	..	..	
..	..	2,210	1,842	9	6	..	..	5	4	..	..	14	10	2	6	..	..	
1	1	6,849	5,984	2,558	2,228	..	..	4	1	..	..	2,562	2,229	42	46	..	..	
563	**307**	**128,136**	**107,299**	**106,697**	**91,779**	**4,236**	**3,665**	**53,820**	**43,478**	**8**	**1**	**164,761**	**138,923**	**3,644**	**2,946**	**6,064**	**4,880**	4
..	..	715	617	1,150	1,093	..	..	..	..	..	..	1,150	1,093	57	42	..	..	5
..	..	[12] 6,008	[12] 4,979	3,177	2,455	..	..	131	89	..	..	3,308	2,544	86	77	..	..	6
1	..	14,057	13,251	6,192	5,512	..	..	12	11	..	..	6,204	5,523	227	202	..	..	7
4	..	[1] 11,529	9,901	6,607	6,462	..	..	58	36	..	..	6,665	6,498	172	139	..	..	8
..	..	3,913	3,447	1,942	1,743	..	..	..	..	..	..	1,942	1,743	..	3	1	..	9
3	2	4,442	3,550	1,481	1,309	3,922	3,378	218	138	..	..	5,621	4,825	58	43	150	143	10
13	6	1,555	1,215	3,783	3,525	..	..	963	867	4	1	4,750	4,393	126	161	117	114	11
36	23	2,274	1,729	1,120	874	29	29	1,008	796	1	..	2,158	1,699	6	5	182	106	12
..	1	9,375	8,574	2,218	2,162	279	258	13	12	..	..	2,510	2,432	22	16	2	2	13
455	258	* 46,603	37,703	39,320	32,931	..	..	44,915	36,258	3	..	84,238	69,189	1,808	1,443	4,563	3,693	14
13	6	16,465	13,433	13,155	11,664	..	..	1,524	1,203	..	..	14,679	12,867	883	690	418	308	15
27	10	8,372	7,098	10,708	9,444	6	..	4,592	3,732	..	..	15,306	13,176	181	125	614	514	16
11	1	2,828	1,802	15,844	12,605	..	..	386	336	..	..	16,230	12,941	18	..	17	..	17

includes* Jains and :—

		M.	F.			M.	F.
6.	Muslim	4	..	11.	Muslim	..	1
7.	,,	22	22	12.	,,	..	1
8.	,,	2	..		Christian	1	2
	Christian	7	6	13.	Christian	3	4
9.	Muslim	9	2	14.	,,	33	5
	Christian	2	1	15.	,,	..	1
10.	Muslim	1	..				

Total *Chamar* includes :—

		M.	F.			M.	F.
1.	Christian	23	19	6.	Christian	..	2
2.	,,	83	74	7.	,,	1	..
3.	,,	..	1	8.	,,	11	..
4.	,,	14	18	9.	,,	21	15
5.	,,	10	3				

Serial No.	District or State.	Chuhra. Muslim. Males.	Chuhra. Muslim. Females.	Chuhra. Total. Males.	Chuhra. Total. Females.	Chuhra. Hindu. Males.	Chuhra. Hindu. Females.	Chuhra. Ad-Dharmi. Males.	Chuhra. Ad-Dharmi. Females.	Chuhra. Sikh. Males.	Chuhra. Sikh. Females.	Chuhra. Muslim. Males.	Chuhra. Muslim. Females.	Chuhra. Christian. Males.	Chuhra. Christian. Females.
1	2	66	67	68	69	70	71	72	73	74	75	76	77	78	79
	PUNJAB	**28,701**	**24,711**	**52,013**	**44,256**	**200,293**	**167,931**	**47,315**	**39,233**	**92,171**	**77,076**	**12,011**	**10,333**	**19,083**	**15,913**
	BRITISH TERRITORY ..	**25,282**	**21,865**	**38,492**	**33,258**	**159,731**	**133,471**	**46,077**	**38,225**	**47,849**	**39,942**	**11,644**	**10,069**	**18,546**	**15,438**
	AMBALA DIVISION ..	**4,212**	**3,711**	**10,105**	**8,721**	**71,615**	**62,943**	**1,085**	**887**	**3,983**	**3,276**	**113**	**64**	**2,946**	**2,818**
1	Hissar	1,063	1,251	3,788	3,577	10,499	9,288	..	..	1,992	1,070	78	51	109	82
2	Rohtak	505	378	2,383	2,065	14,814	14,202	..	..	86	84	4	1	1,700	1,692
3	Gurgaon	15	14	384	302	10,588	10,048	..	..	1	..	..	..	124	143
4	Karnal	2,501	1,996	2,858	2,268	22,020	18,686	1,085	887	135	107	13	8	385	338
5	Ambala	128	72	686	506	12,451	10,112	..	..	1,769	1,415	18	4	610	552
6	Simla	..	..	6	3	1,243	607	..	..	..	..	..	..	18	11
	JULLUNDUR DIVISION ..	**5,736**	**5,015**	**10,748**	**9,473**	**26,425**	**22,088**	**34,656**	**29,494**	**29,423**	**25,024**	**2,141**	**2,010**	**3,143**	**2,646**
7	Kangra	3	..	1,296	1,133	408	264	..	..	1	..	5	..	33	9
8	Hoshiarpur	41	46	1,258	1,078	6,790	5,844	1,533	1,339	225	189	..	..	569	487
9	Jullundur	173	137	948	941	7,391	6,444	12,663	11,191	623	527	40	24	944	857
10	Ludhiana	48	26	628	553	3,188	2,491	2,361	1,743	7,662	6,015	1	..	377	297
11	Ferozepore	5,471	4,806	6,618	5,768	8,648	7,045	18,099	15,221	20,912	18,293	2,095	1,986	1,220	996
	LAHORE DIVISION ..	**10,285**	**9,125**	**11,992**	**10,558**	**46,991**	**37,553**	**1,599**	**1,324**	**10,645**	**8,390**	**6,753**	**5,821**	**7,778**	**6,313**
12	Lahore	4,384	3,958	5,064	4,549	24,291	18,747	..	..	7,017	5,317	6,318	5,471	5,431	4,390
13	Amritsar	2,582	2,290	2,792	2,425	13,793	11,544	..	..	2,720	2,307	4	6	757	642
14	Gurdaspur	708	621	1,097	940	4,166	3,563	10	22	630	515	61	48	606	507
15	Sialkot	115	91	445	409	189	123	..	..	..	..	18	12	756	590
16	Gujranwala	651	477	652	477	701	600	..	..	2	6	19	12	185	160
17	Sheikhupura	1,845	1,688	1,942	1,758	3,851	2,976	1,589	1,302	276	245	333	272	43	24
	RAWALPINDI DIVISION ..	**824**	**708**	**944**	**792**	**3,348**	**1,981**	..	..	**119**	**101**	**240**	**213**	**518**	**380**
18	Gujrat	324	265	334	276	256	144	..	..	..	..	2	3	230	179
19	Shahpur	115	90	115	90	771	495	..	..	55	58	6	4	2	2
20	Jhelum	..	..	96	60	284	160	..	..	17	3	..	..	141	85
21	Rawalpindi	..	..	14	12	1,714	980	..	..	43	29	152	121	..	..
22	Attock	354	329	354	330	285	154	..	..	2	9	7	6	84	66
23	Mianwali	31	24	31	24	38	48	..	..	2	2	73	79	61	48
	MULTAN DIVISION ..	**4,225**	**3,306**	**4,703**	**3,714**	**11,352**	**8,906**	**8,737**	**6,520**	**3,679**	**3,151**	**2,397**	**1,961**	**4,163**	**3,281**
24	Montgomery	1,908	1,542	1,977	1,625	4,352	3,316	2,628	1,796	288	259	8	6	648	403
25	Lyallpur	1,474	1,237	1,866	1,561	5,977	4,849	5,235	4,263	3,227	2,816	283	210	2,782	2,217
26	Jhang	632	363	632	363	125	101	1	..	..	..	..	..	10	8
27	Multan	107	57	121	58	809	578	873	461	164	76	302	232	630	588
28	Muzaffargarh	104	107	107	107	83	49	..	..	..	..	486	385	81	56
29	Dera Ghazi Khan ..	..	..	..	..	6	13	..	..	..	..	1,318	1,128	12	9
	PUNJAB STATES ..	**3,419**	**2,846**	**13,521**	**10,998**	**40,562**	**34,460**	**1,238**	**1,008**	**44,322**	**37,134**	**367**	**264**	**535**	**475**
	A.—Having Political relations with the Punjab Government. ..	6	4	400	330	2,101	1,809	145	120	315	274	..	..	18	8
1	Dujana	..	..	..	..	331	269	..	..	..	..	..	..	..	..
2	Pataudi	..	..	57	45	329	364	..	..	..	..	..	..	..	..
3	Kalsia	5	3	67	8	1,017	831	145	120	311	268	..	..	10	6
4	*SIMLA HILL STATES* ..	1	1	276	277	424	345	..	..	4	6	..	..	8	2
	Bashahr	..	..	..	..	7	8	..	..	..	..	..	..	..	..
	Nalagarh	..	..	143	135	159	149	..	..	..	..	..	..	3	..
	Keonthal	..	..	4	1	97	38	..	..	..	..	..	..	..	..
	Baghal	1	1	85	89	3	4	..	..	..	..	..	..	..	..
	Jubbal	..	..	2	6	..	..	..	..	..	..	..	..	..	..
	Other Simla Hill States ..	..	..	42	46	158	126	..	..	4	6	..	..	5	2
	B.—Having Political relations with the Government of India. ..	3,413	2,842	13,121	10,668	38,461	32,651	1,093	888	44,007	36,860	367	264	517	467
5	Loharu	..	..	57	42	37	25	..	..	..	..	..	..	..	..
6	Sirmoor	..	..	86	77	432	356	..	..	..	..	1	..	7	10
7	Bilaspur	..	..	227	202	28	40	..	..	..	..	..	..	..	..
8	Mandi	..	..	172	139	102	48	..	..	..	..	1	..	..	..
9	Suket	1	..	2	3	14	14	..	..	..	..	..	..	..	..
10	Kapurthala	159	140	367	326	9,937	8,735	234	223	302	273	3	2	420	386
11	Maler Kotla	36	22	279	297	554	432	..	..	253	245	..	..	63	54
12	Faridkot	801	640	989	751	541	472	859	665	9,444	8,002	98	50	27	17
13	Chamba	..	..	24	18	54	38	..	..	..	..	5	5	..	..
14	Patiala (Phulkian States) ..	1,801	1,467	8,172	6,603	17,474	14,701	..	..	27,667	23,273	259	207	..	..
15	Jind (Phulkian States) ..	287	290	1,588	1,288	4,579	3,966	..	..	1,731	1,442	..	..	..	..
16	Nabha (Phulkian States) ..	203	187	998	826	3,398	2,921	..	..	2,790	2,395	..	..	..	..
17	Bahawalpur	125	96	160	96	1,311	903	..	..	1,820	1,230	..	..	..	..

TRIBE OR CASTE.—*continued.*

CHUHRA.		DAGI AND KOLI.				DARZI.								DHOBI.						
Total.		*Hindu.*		Total.		*Hindu.*		*Sikh.*		*Muslim.*		Total.		*Hindu.*		*Muslim.*		Total.		
Males.	Females.	Males.	Females.	Males.	Females.	Males.	Females.	Males.	Females.	Males.	Females.	Males.	Females.	Males.	Females.	Males.	Females.	Males.	Females.	Serial No.
80	81	82	83	84	85	86	87	88	89	90	91	92	93	94	95	96	97	98	99	
370,873	**310,486**	**94,112**	**87,860**	**94,517**	**87,718**	**5,406**	**4,417**	**2,420**	**1,210**	**17,068**	**15,166**	**24,895**	**20,793**	**7,059**	**5,484**	**88,061**	**74,163**	**95,551**	**80,006**	
283,849	**237,145**	**24,867**	**22,957**	**24,979**	**23,075**	**4,558**	**3,659**	**1,757**	**732**	**16,589**	**14,800**	**22,905**	**19,191**	**6,066**	**4,650**	**79,262**	**66,829**	**85,706**	**71,805**	
79,742	**69,988**	**5,534**	**4,503**	**5,534**	**4,503**	**2,665**	**2,198**	**17**	**14**	**714**	**534**	**3,396**	**2,746**	**2,890**	**2,526**	**6,562**	**5,563**	**9,469**	**8,104**	
12,678	11,091	221	147	221	147	668	331	1	..	42	33	411	364	201	174	1,501	1,248	1,702	1,422	1
16,604	15,979	11	6	11	6	606	505	..	..	46	28	652	533	49	45	1,090	1,737	2,039	1,782	2
10,713	10,191	2,627	2,226	2,627	2,226	521	416	..	..	280	199	801	615	1,249	1,182	605	582	1,854	1,764	3
23,638	20,026	30	20	30	20	1,079	881	1	..	118	77	1,198	958	201	192	1,901	1,510	2,162	1,708	4
14,848	12,083	511	318	511	318	83	62	15	14	227	197	325	273	985	832	560	476	*1,562	*1,323	5
1,261	618	2,134	1,786	2,134	1,786	8	3	..	..	1	..	9	3	145	101	5	4	150	105	6
95,788	**81,262**	**18,905**	**18,217**	**18,977**	**18,297**	**1,470**	**1,343**	**546**	**579**	**443**	**482**	**2,460**	**2,404**	**666**	**542**	**3,445**	**2,850**	**4,129**	**3,406**	
447	273	18,797	18,167	*18,854	*18,234	986	925	1	1	4	1	991	927	110	99	82	50	192	149	7
9,117	7,859	23	8	*38	*21	280	279	57	123	213	246	550	648	32	31	1,593	1,322	1,625	1,353	8
21,661	19,043	..	..	..	..	135	97	294	291	153	178	582	566	99	77	1,202	1,061	1,301	1,138	9
13,589	10,546	29	..	29	..	32	17	148	116	10	11[1]	191	144	69	48	325	243	394	291	10
50,974	43,541	56	42	56	42	37	25	46	48	63	46	146	119	356	287	243	174	[1]*617	*475	11
73,766	**59,401**	**351**	**198**	**351**	**199**	**348**	**101**	**282**	**100**	**6,144**	**5,121**	**6,774**	**5,322**	**1,736**	**1,082**	**21,985**	**18,292**	**23,960**	**19,569**	
43,057	33,925	185	142	185	*143	84	27	210	55	1,436	752	1,730	834	1,209	726	3,199	2,118	*4,518	*2,929	12
17,274	14,499	91	26	91	26	40	11	44	18	1,157	984	1,241	1,013	288	183	3,347	2,778	*3,665	*2,985	13
5,473	4,655	39	2	39	2	210	52	..	..	513	481	723	533	11	5	4,298	3,688	*4,314	*3,699	14
963	725	..	..	..	..	8	11	4	3	975	1,043	987	1,057	96	81	5,990	5,445	*6,114	*5,544	15
907	778	36	28	36	28	1	..	17	19	1,719	1,611	1,737	1,630	100	65	3,238	2,742	*3,383	*2,851	16
6,092	4,819	..	..	..	..	5	..	7	5	344	250	356	255	32	22	1,013	1,521	*1,966	*1,561	17
4,225	**2,675**	**76**	**39**	**109**	**74**	**9**	**2**	**874**	**6**	**6,790**	**5,984**	**7,673**	**5,992**	**556**	**432**	**19,199**	**16,939**	**19,822**	**17,436**	
488	326	8	6	8	6	..	..	4	..	1,026	962	1,030	902	12	12	5,146	4,603	5,158	4,615	18
834	559	49	26	[3]*50	[3]29	..	..	..	..	358	251	358	251	7	1	5,162	4,388	*5,177	*4,394	19
442	248	7	7	*10	*12	..	..	5	2	1,303	1,294	1,308	1,296	91	94	2,149	2,067	*2,248	*2,170	20
1,909	1,130	12	..	*35	*27	8	..	862	2	3,437	2,868	4,307	2,870	428	308	794	506	*1,270	*865	21
378	235	..	..	..	..	..	2	3	2	597	540	600	544	16	13	3,475	3,144	*3,494	3,157	22
174	177	..	..	..	..	1	..	..	..	69	69	70	69	2	4	2,473	2,331	2,475	2,335	23
30,328	**23,819**	**1**	..	**8**	**2**	**66**	**15**	**38**	**33**	**2,498**	**2,679**	**2,602**	**2,727**	**218**	**68**	**28,071**	**23,185**	**28,326**	**23,290**	
7,924	5,780	1	..	[4]8	[4]2	1	6	29	20	274	217	304	243	85	13	3,824	3,324	*3,915	*3,343	24
17,504	14,355	..	..	..	..	60	..	9	13	948	720	1,017	733	59	38	3,145	2,571	*3,234	*2,640	25
136	109	..	..	..	..	..	..	..	..	374	888	374	888	2	..	4,579	3,528	4,581	3,528	26
2,778	1,935	..	..	..	..	5	9	..	..	792	736	797	745	68	16	9,389	7,787	[2]9,458	7,803	27
650	490	..	..	..	..	..	..	..	..	67	79	67	79	3	1	5,145	4,295	5,148	4,296	28
1,336	1,150	..	..	..	..	..	..	..	..	43	39	43	39	1	..	1,989	1,680	1,990	1,680	29
87,024	**73,341**	**69,245**	**64,403**	**69,538**	**64,643**	**848**	**758**	**663**	**478**	**479**	**366**	**1,990**	**1,602**	**993**	**834**	**8,799**	**7,334**	**9,845**	**8,201**	
2,579	**2,211**	**31,416**	**30,058**	**31,460**	**30,094**	**94**	**75**	**13**	**14**	**4**	**2**	**111**	**91**	**156**	**125**	**290**	**248**	**446**	**373**	
331	269	..	..	..	..	70	58	..	..	..	..	70	58	9	13	38	47	67	60	1
329	364	..	..	..	..	..	..	..	..	..	..	..	..	1	..	42	61	43	61	2
1,483	1,225	..	..	..	..	9	3	..	..	4	2	13	3	60	49	169	133	229	182	3
436	**353**	**31,416**	**30,053**	**31,460**	**30,094**	**15**	**14**	**13**	**14**	..	..	**28**	**28**	**86**	**63**	**21**	**7**	**107**	**70**	4
7	8	13,048	13,250	[2]13,087	[2]13,287	6	8	..	..	..	..	6	8	1	2	..	..	1	2	
162	149	704	657	704	657	4	5	13	13	..	..	17	18	..	..	18	7	18	7	
97	58	6,437	5,837	6,437	5,837	..	..	..	..	..	..	..	..	24	12	1	..	25	12	
3	4	938	951	[5]939	951	5	1	..	..	..	..	5	1	13	13	..	..	13	13	
..	..	3,415	3,043	3,415	3,043	..	..	..	..	..	..	..	..	..	..	..	..	..	..	
167	134	6,874	6,315	*6,878	*6,319	..	..	..	1	..	..	..	1	48	36	2	..	50	36	
84,445	**71,130**	**37,829**	**34,350**	**38,078**	**34,549**	**754**	**683**	**650**	**464**	**475**	**364**	**1,879**	**1,511**	**837**	**709**	**8,509**	**7,086**	**9,399**	**7,828**	
37	25	..	..	..	..	15	6	..	..	..	..	15	6	7	8	9	17	16	25	5
440	366	16,933	14,372	[6]16,934	14,372	7	..	..	..	1	..	8	..	46	34	18	11	*67	45	6
28	40	1,870	1,621	1,870	1,621	16	11	..	..	1	..	17	11	55	45	..	..	55	45	7
103	48	9,083	9,297	*9,084	9,297	109	136	..	..	6	..	115	136	30	36	4	1	34	37	8
14	14	4,424	4,061	4,424	4,061	..	..	..	..	..	..	..	..	17	24	..	..	17	24	9
10,896	9,619	..	..	..	..	31	24	60	49	234	224	325	297	75	65	868	713	*974	*802	10
870	731	..	..	..	..	12	4	14	10	2	..	28	14	7	..	89	77	96	77	11
10,969	9,200	..	..	..	..	..	..	212	199	113	64	325	263	28	23	18	17	46	40	12
59	43	896	902	896	902	..	..	..	..	..	..	..	..	24	23	2	4	26	27	13
45,400	38,181	4,621	4,091	[1]*4,868	*4,290	323	275	31	27	10	..	364	302	330	279	799	744	*1,148	*1,032	14
6,310	5,408	2	4	2	4	32	32	..	..	23	27	55	59	107	98	556	471	663	569	15
6,188	5,316	..	2	..	2	185	186	264	138	6	7	455	331	44	39	173	212	217	251	16
3,131	2,133	..	..	..	..	24	9	69	41	79	42	172	92	67	35	5,973	4,819	6,040	4,854	17

Total *Dagi and Koli* includes *Sikhs and :—

		M.	F.
1.	Jain	1	..
2.	Buddhist	39	37
3.	Muslim	6	3
4.	,,	7	2
5.	,,	1	..
6.	,,	1	..

Total *Darzi* includes :—

		M.	F.
1.	Ad-Dharmi	1	..

Total *Dhobi* includes *Sikhs and :—

		M.	F.
1.	Ad-Dharmi	3	..
2.	,,	1	..

Serial No.	District or State.	Dumna. Hindu. Males.	Dumna. Hindu. Females.	Dumna. Total. Males.	Dumna. Total. Females.	Faqir. Hindu. Males.	Faqir. Hindu. Females.	Faqir. Sikh. Males.	Faqir. Sikh. Females.	Faqir. Muslim. Males.	Faqir. Muslim. Females.	Faqir. Total. Males.	Faqir. Total. Females.	Ghirath. Hindu. Males.	Ghirath. Hindu. Females.	Ghirath. Total. Males.	Ghirath. Total. Females.
1	2	100	101	102	103	104	105	106	107	108	109	110	111	112	113	114	115
	PUNJAB	**19,658**	**17,517**	**19,839**	**17,702**	**17,198**	**8,747**	**3,372**	**1,383**	**139,930**	**116,603**	**160,702**	**126,743**	**64,239**	**59,815**	**64,446**	**59,894**
	BRITISH TERRITORY ..	**6,788**	**5,769**	**6,893**	**5,867**	**12,044**	**6,380**	**2,781**	**1,148**	**118,568**	**99,264**	**133,598**	**106,752**	**63,219**	**59,023**	**63,426**	**59,102**
	AMBALA DIVISION ..	**89**	**57**	**90**	**59**	**1,210**	**283**	**87**	**37**	**30,867**	**26,569**	**32,164**	**26,889**	**122**	**2**	**122**	**2**
1	Hissar	..	..	..	..	293	53	11	5	2,926	2,507	3,230	2,565	..	..	..	..
2	Rohtak	..	..	..	..	154	7	..	..	4,884	4,090	5,038	4,097	..	..	..	..
3	Gurgaon	..	..	..	..	31	2	..	..	10,423	9,505	10,454	9,507	..	..	..	..
4	Karnal	..	..	..	..	339	85	3	2	5,987	4,973	6,329	5,060	6	..	6	..
5	Ambala	22	8	22	8	385	130	73	30	6,644	5,494	7,102	5,654	39	2	39	2
6	Simla	67	49	*68	*51	8	6	..	..	3	..	11	6	77	..	77	..
	JULLUNDUR DIVISION	**6,294**	**5,373**	**6,397**	**5,452**	**5,778**	**3,614**	**1,282**	**484**	**27,018**	**22,892**	**34,118**	**27,000**	**62,581**	**58,946**	**62,786**	***59,025**
7	Kangra	5,546	4,743	*5,554	[1] *4,751	564	535	..	..	860	695	1,424	1,230	61,998	58,631	[1]*62,199	[1]*58,710
8	Hoshiarpur	748	630	[2] *841	[2] *699	508	260	70	7	8,047	6,947	*8,636	*7,216	442	249	442	249
9	Jullundur	..	..	..	..	1,957	1,541	182	103	8,203	7,258	*10,362	*8,905	137	66	*141	66
10	Ludhiana	..	..	[3] 2	[3] 2	1,378	649	395	201	5,734	4,614	[1] *7,513	[1] 5,469	..	..	..	..
11	Ferozepore	..	..	..	..	1,371	629	635	173	4,174	3,378	*6,183	4,180	4	..	4	..
	LAHORE DIVISION ..	**399**	**324**	**399**	**324**	**3,429**	**1,797**	**1,270**	**554**	**39,858**	**33,689**	**44,722**	**36,040**	**498**	**75**	**500**	**75**
12	Lahore	..	..	..	..	1,143	581	331	174	7,442	5,317	8,916	6,072	281	36	*283	36
13	Amritsar	3	2	3	2	693	379	768	330	7,775	8,756	*9,247	9,465	176	32	176	32
14	Gurdaspur	..	..	..	..	814	441	103	31	6,597	5,607	*7,668	6,079	41	7	41	7
15	Sialkot	396	322	396	322	146	109	16	6	10,345	7,999	10,507	8,114	..	..	..	..
16	Gujranwala	..	..	..	..	153	19	2	3	4,541	3,503	4,696	3,525	..	..	..	..
17	Sheikhupura ..	..	..	..	..	480	268	50	10	3,158	2,507	3,688	2,785	..	..	..	..
	RAWALPINDI DIVISION	..	..	..	**17**	**674**	**198**	**20**	**7**	**5,433**	**4,668**	**6,127**	**4,873**	**4**	..	**4**	..
18	Gujrat	..	..	..	..	57	25	5	..	1,827	1,547	1,889	1,572	..	..	..	..
19	Shahpur	..	..	..	*17	169	34	7	..	1,675	1,262	1,851	1,296	4	..	4	..
20	Jhelum	..	..	..	..	155	53	6	..	638	647	799	700	..	..	..	..
21	Rawalpindi	..	..	..	..	166	74	..	2	938	914	1,104	990	..	..	..	..
22	Attock	..	..	..	..	44	9	..	2	235	176	279	187	..	..	..	..
23	Mianwali	..	..	..	..	83	3	2	3	120	122	205	128	..	..	..	..
	MULTAN DIVISION ..	**6**	**15**	**7**	**15**	**953**	**438**	**122**	**66**	**15,392**	**11,446**	**16,467**	**11,950**	**14**	..	**14**	..
24	Montgomery	..	..	[4] 1	..	257	114	56	9	2,956	2,065	3,269	2,188	14	..	14	..
25	Lyallpur	6	15	6	15	54	28	16	23	5,053	3,964	5,123	4,015	..	..	..	..
26	Jhang	..	..	..	..	243	129	38	25	3,595	2,695	3,876	2,849	..	..	..	..
27	Multan	..	..	..	..	155	54	7	3	2,493	1,689	2,655	1,746	..	..	..	..
28	Muzaffargarh ..	..	..	..	..	154	71	5	6	917	762	1,076	839	..	..	..	..
29	Dera Ghazi Khan ..	..	..	..	..	90	42	..	..	378	271	468	313	..	..	..	..
	PUNJAB STATES ..	**12,870**	**11,748**	**12,946**	**11,835**	**5,149**	**2,417**	**591**	**235**	**21,362**	**17,839**	**27,104**	**19,991**	**1,020**	**792**	**1,020**	**792**
	A.—Having Political relations with the Punjab Government. ..	**1,378**	**1,115**	**1,382**	**1,135**	**90**	**53**	**2**	**1**	**1,220**	**1,031**	**1,312**	**1,085**	**277**	**165**	**277**	**165**
1	Dujana	..	..	..	..	..	..	..	..	151	166	151	166	..	..	..	..
2	Pataudi	..	..	..	..	..	..	..	..	181	139	181	139	..	..	..	..
3	Kalsia	..	..	..	..	19	5	2	1	585	476	606	482	..	..	..	..
4	*SIMLA HILL STATES*	**1,378**	**1,115**	**1,382**	**1,135**	**71**	**48**	..	..	**303**	**250**	**374**	**298**	**277**	**165**	**277**	**165**
	Bashahr	..	..	..	..	2	1	..	..	..	..	2	1	..	..	..	..
	Nalagarh	326	283	*329	*287	10	7	..	..	283	243	293	250	190	159	190	159
	Keonthal	50	24	50	24	16	7	..	..	..	..	16	7	76	4	76	4
	Baghal	268	218	[5] 269	218	3	..	..	..	1	..	4	..	2	..	2	..
	Jubbal	..	..	..	..	10	12	..	..	..	..	10	12	..	..	..	..
	Other Simla Hill States ..	734	590	734	*606	30	21	..	..	19	7	49	28	9	2	9	2
	B.—Having Political relations with the Government of India. ..	**11,492**	**10,633**	**11,564**	**10,700**	**5,059**	**2,364**	**589**	**234**	**20,142**	**16,308**	**25,792**	**18,906**	**743**	**627**	**743**	**627**
5	Loharu	..	..	..	..	..	..	..	..	40	50	40	50	..	..	..	..
6	Sirmoor	2,951	2,487	2,951	2,487	20	9	1	..	191	106	212	115	..	1	..	1
7	Bilaspur	853	756	*855	756	11	3	..	..	30	21	41	24	78	60	78	60
8	Mandi	5,305	5,227	*5,368	*5,292	..	..	..	..	130	87	130	87	623	548	623	548
9	Suket	1,338	1,139	*1,345	*1,141	..	..	..	..	22	28	22	28	..	..	..	..
10	Kapurthala	..	..	..	..	204	163	133	63	3,743	3,303	4,080	3,529	..	..	..	..
11	Maler Kotla	..	..	..	..	314	93	13	5	600	495	927	593	..	..	..	..
12	Faridkot	..	..	..	..	348	136	185	95	548	419	*1,083	650	..	..	..	..
13	Chamba	1,045	1,024	1,045	1,024	1	..	..	..	79	56	80	56	30	18	30	18
14	Patiala (Phulkian States)	..	..	..	..	1,478	190	75	24	9,118	7,185	10,671	7,399	12	..	12	..
15	Jind (Phulkian States)	..	..	..	..	69	..	..	..	1,403	1,159	1,472	1,159	..	..	..	..
16	Nabha (Phulkian States) ..	..	..	..	..	1,675	1,066	157	37	1,492	1,154	3,324	2,257	..	..	..	..
17	Bahawalpur	..	..	..	..	939	704	25	10	2,746	2,245	3,710	2,959	..	..	..	..

Total *Dumna* includes * Sikhs and :—

		M.	F.
1.	Ad-Dharmi	..	2
2.	Ad-Dharmi	20	8
	Muslim	2	..
3.	Muslim	2	2
4.	„	1	..
5.	„	1	..

Total *Faqir* includes * Ad-Dharmis and :—

		M.	F.
1.	Jain	3	5

Total *Ghirath* includes * Sikhs and :—

		M.	F.
1.	Muslim	102	10

TRIBE OR CASTE.—*continued.*

Ghosi.						Gujjar.								Harni.		Jat.				
Hindu.		*Muslim.*		Total.		*Hindu.*		*Sikh.*		*Muslim.*		Total.		Total *Muslim.*		*Hindu.*		*Sikh.*		
Males.	Females.	Males.	Females.	Males.	Females.	Males.	Females.	Males.	Females.	Males.	Females.	Males.	Females.	Males.	Females.	Males.	Females.	Males.	Females.	Serial No.
116	117	118	119	120	121	122	123	124	125	126	127	128	129	130	131	132	133	134	135	
998	**906**	**1,046**	**903**	**2,044**	**1,809**	**96,208**	**74,231**	**2,571**	**2,075**	**283,585**	**237,762**	**382,372**	**314,070**	**2,289**	**1,639**	**547,351**	**444,958**	**1,214,688**	**919,910**	
998	**906**	**1,046**	**903**	**2,044**	**1,809**	**74,008**	**56,090**	**1,864**	**1,489**	**257,700**	**216,916**	**333,580**	**274,497**	**2,085**	**1,470**	**427,248**	**345,298**	**875,426**	**663,606**	
88	**60**	**821**	**730**	**909**	**790**	**53,574**	**40,929**	**891**	**674**	**22,857**	**18,774**	**77,328**	**60,378**	..	..	**350,845**	**289,256**	**67,711**	**49,453**	
7	5	374	342	381	347	4,598	3,687	..	..	2,303	2,075	6,901	5,762	..	..	101,139	84,301	18,813	14,810	1
1	..	208	171	209	171	2,905	2,127	..	..	1,567	1,274	4,472	3,401	..	..	142,764	119,824	83	45	2
76	51	..	..	76	51	20,674	16,341	..	..	302	255	20,976	16,596	..	..	39,668	31,720	193	151	3
..	..	202	178	202	178	13,397	9,622	3	1	4,738	3,505 [1]	18,144 [1]	13,129	..	..	55,076	44,484	4,754	3,328	4
4	4	37	39	41	43	11,989	9,152	888	673	13,798	11,662	26,675	21,487	..	..	12,106	8,412	43,827	31,100	5
..	..	..	..	..	..	11	..	..	..	149	3	160	3	..	..	92	15	41	19	6
423	**389**	**70**	**65**	**493**	**454**	**15,576**	**14,052**	**780**	**726**	**75,378**	**65,932**	**91,735**	**80,711**	**1,143**	**762**	**46,380**	**37,192**	**391,930**	**300,479**	
423	389	..	..	423	389	629	630	..	..	4,960	4,156	5,589	4,786	..	..	5,008	4,542	365	281	7
..	..	..	..	..	..	13,862	13,094	743	699	34,865	31,273	49,470	45,066	362	299	22,896	18,173	49,654	38,609	8
..	..	15	8	15	8	199	76	1	1	10,644	8,741	10,844	8,818	..	..	6,823	5,931	91,663	68,623	9
..	..	55	57	55	57	334	74	36	24	18,169	16,426 [2]	18,540 [2]	16,525	761	449	2,209	1,291	121,190	90,492	10
..	..	..	..	..	..	552	178	..	2	6,740	5,336	7,292	5,516	20	14	9,444	7,255	129,058	102,474	11
470	**444**	**155**	**108**	**625**	**552**	**2,164**	**750**	**48**	**23**	**49,760**	**39,406**	**51,973**	**40,179**	**668**	**463**	**23,315**	**15,335**	**325,711**	**247,004**	
470	444	138	94	608	538	1,320	389	29	20	6,133	3,952 [3]	7,483	4,361	..	..	2,573	929	69,021	53,850	12
..	..	9	8	9	8	150	32	..	..	3,965	2,823	4,115	2,855	11	3	1,185	532	116,194	90,557	13
..	..	..	..	..	..	24	27	..	..	31,607	27,172	31,631	27,199	434	326	2,086	1,414	56,704	43,608	14
..	..	..	..	..	..	84	40	2	..	4,501	3,160	4,587	3,200	223	134	13,911	10,037	38,472	27,158	15
..	..	..	..	..	..	123	14	4	3	1,998	1,250	2,125	1,267	..	..	2,990	2,136	21,415	13,924	16
..	..	8	6	8	6	463	248	13	..	1,556	1,049	2,032	1,297	..	..	570	287	23,905	17,907	17
..	..	..	..	..	..	**609**	**186**	**53**	**47**	**98,420**	**84,021**	**99,082**	**84,254**	..	..	**2,725**	**1,518**	**6,717**	**4,544**	
..	..	..	..	..	..	276	73	4	1	63,652	54,932	63,932	55,006	..	..	1,310	989	1,459	1,263	18
..	..	..	..	..	..	209	31	19	10	1,664	1,146	1,892	1,187	..	..	1,040	390	3,872	2,995	19
..	..	..	..	..	..	29	4	..	..	11,256	9,237	11,285	9,241	..	..	129	69	748	131	20
..	..	..	..	..	..	92	66	30	36	14,719	12,542	14,841	12,644	..	..	131	43	365	112	21
..	..	..	..	..	..	2	2	..	..	7,095	6,147	7,097	6,149	..	..	82	26	218	22	22
..	..	..	..	..	..	1	10	..	..	34	17	35	27	..	..	33	1	55	21	23
17	**13**	..	..	**17**	**13**	**2,085**	**173**	**92**	**19**	**11,285**	**8,783**	**13,462**	**8,975**	**274**	**245**	**3,983**	**1,997**	**83,357**	**62,126**	
..	..	..	..	..	..	654	72	38	6	2,200	1,695	2,892	1,773	215	190	1,611	771	17,803	12,016	24
6	7	..	..	6	7	878	80	22	13	7,265	5,980	8,165	6,073	..	..	1,711	797	54,961	43,891	25
..	..	..	..	..	..	4	1	1	..	582	324	587	325	..	..	22	13	156	101	26
..	..	..	..	..	..	543	20	31	..	1,203	772	1,777	792	59	55	535	339	10,366	6,097	27
11	6	..	..	11	6	6	..	..	..	31	12	37	12	..	..	97	77	37	11	28
..	..	..	..	..	..	..	..	..	..	4	..	4	..	..	..	7	..	34	10	29
..	..	..	..	..	..	**22,200**	**18,141**	**707**	**586**	**25,885**	**20,846**	**48,792**	**39,573**	**204**	**169**	**120,103**	**99,660**	**339,262**	**256,304**	
..	..	..	..	..	..	**4,852**	**3,930**	**309**	**281**	**4,249**	**3,547**	**9,410**	**7,758**	**11**	**11**	**4,805**	**3,856**	**2,978**	**2,182**	
..	..	..	..	..	..	36	25	..	..	..	..	36	25	..	..	1,733	1,443	..	..	1
..	..	..	..	..	..	4	2	..	..	..	..	4	2	..	..	814	710	..	..	2
..	..	..	..	..	..	1,597	1,086	5	2	2,074	1,774	3,676	2,862	11	11	1,815	1,306	2,868	2,124	3
..	..	..	..	..	..	**3,215**	**2,817**	**304**	**279**	**2,175**	**1,773**	**5,694**	**4,869**	..	..	**443**	**397**	**110**	**58**	4
..	..	..	..	..	..	..	..	..	..	55	61	55	61	..	..	3	4	1	..	
..	..	..	..	..	..	2,787	2,445	304	279	1,948	1,586	5,039	4,310	..	..	214	175	84	53	
..	..	..	..	..	..	19	7	..	..	25	3	44	10	..	..	5	5	12	2	
..	..	..	..	..	..	5	7	..	..	30	15	35	22	..	..	132	144	..	..	
..	..	..	..	..	..	..	..	..	..	87	83	87	83	..	..	1	..	..	..	
..	..	..	..	..	..	404	358	..	..	30	25	434	383	..	..	88	69	13	3	
..	..	..	..	..	..	**17,348**	**14,211**	**398**	**305**	**21,636**	**17,299**	**39,382**	**31,815**	**193**	**158**	**115,298**	**95,804**	**336,284**	**254,122**	
..	..	..	..	..	..	42	41	..	..	1	1	43	42	..	..	5,615	5,058	2	..	5
..	..	..	..	..	..	684	502	..	..	761	593	1,445	1,095	..	..	163	81	315	203	6
..	..	..	..	..	..	1,657	1,447	..	..	54	35	1,711	1,482	..	..	734	636	199	166	7
..	..	..	..	..	..	787	761	..	..	631	512	1,418	1,273	..	..	197	174	146	46	8
..	..	..	..	..	..	81	81	..	..	60	50	141	131	..	..	127	146	4	2	19
..	..	..	..	..	..	93	82	64	55	3,828	3,075	3,985	3,212	..	..	630	518	20,436	15,321	10
..	..	..	..	..	..	138	12	..	1	1,311	1,132	1,449	1,145	..	..	222	153	13,301	10,415	11
..	..	..	..	..	..	77	17	1	..	538	452	616	469	179	148	277	99	30,522	24,177	12
..	..	..	..	..	..	..	..	..	..	1,340	1,277	1,340	1,277	..	..	110	78	4	5	11
..	..	..	..	..	..	10,585	8,780	282	219	10,305	7,964	21,172	16,963	14	10	43,124	34,821	206,730	155,842	14
..	..	..	..	..	..	987	626	9	5	310	237	1,306	868	..	..	47,032	40,476	12,869	9,328	15
..	..	..	..	..	..	2,163	1,854	42	25	1,968	1,593	4,173	3,472	..	..	7,396	5,817	38,315	28,582	16
..	..	..	..	..	..	54	8	..	..	529	378	583	386	..	..	9,671	7,747	13,441	10,035	17

Total *Gujjar* includes :—

		M.	F.
1.	Christian	6	1
2.	,,	1	1
3.	,,	1	..

Serial No.	District or State.	Jat. Muslim. Males.	Jat. Muslim. Females.	Jat. Total. Males.	Jat. Total. Females.	Jhiwar. Hindu. Males.	Jhiwar. Hindu. Females.	Jhiwar. Sikh. Males.	Jhiwar. Sikh. Females.	Jhiwar. Muslim. Males.	Jhiwar. Muslim. Females.	Jhiwar. Total. Males.	Jhiwar. Total. Females.
1	2	136	137	138	139	140	141	142	143	144	145	146	147
	PUNJAB	**1,604,628**	**1,336,767**	**3,367,679**	**2,702,353**	**70,006**	**57,875**	**30,701**	**26,982**	**51,627**	**44,313**	**152,840**	**129,172**
	BRITISH TERRITORY	**1,383,009**	**1,155,756**	**2,686,335**	**2,165,051**	**54,029**	**45,403**	**23,105**	**20,949**	**43,595**	**37,742**	**120,735**	**104,096**
	AMBALA DIVISION	**13,210**	**11,130**	**431,834**	**349,897**	**15,068**	**12,416**	**254**	**196**	**656**	**528**	**15,978**	**13,135**
1	Hissar	2,835	2,476	1* 122,796	1 102,093	665	523	113	96	430	371	1,208	990
2	Rohtak	2,163	1,852	2* 145,068	2 121,772	3,953	3,262	9	6	23	14	3,985	3,282
3	Gurgaon	219	214	40,080	32,085	125	131	..	..	..	..	125	131
4	Karnal	1,985	1,612	61,815	49,424	9,917	8,115	65	46	194	126	10,176	8,287
5	Ambala	5,986	4,970	3 61,920	44,482	400	382	67	48	9	12	476	442
6	Simla	22	6	155	* 41	8	3	..	..	..	..	8	3
	JULLUNDUR DIVISION	**56,724**	**47,590**	**495,064**	**385,282**	**17,109**	**14,905**	**5,604**	**5,099**	**14,725**	**12,628**	**37,438**	**32,627**
7	Kangra	159	80	5,532	4,903	5,658	5,230	2	..	14	11	5,674	5,241
8	Hoshiarpur	13,320	11,569	85,870	68,351	4,640	3,890	1,025	886	4,002	3,489	9,667	8,265
9	Jullundur	11,398	9,481	* 109,885	* 84,036	4,669	4,185	1,910	1,791	5,275	4,677	11,854	10,653
10	Ludhiana	13,090	10,868	136,489	102,651	1,818	1,326	2,121	1,997	2,910	2,313	6,849	5,636
11	Ferozepore	18,757	15,592	4* 157,288	* 125,341	324	274	546	425	2,524	2,133	3,394	2,832
	LAHORE DIVISION	**331,026**	**263,697**	**680,208**	**526,181**	**16,789**	**14,485**	**13,066**	**11,987**	**19,654**	**16,951**	**49,515**	**48,425**
12	Lahore	45,464	32,451	* 117,118	* 87,278	1,916	977	3,500	2,936	5,379	4,671	10,795	8,584
13	Amritsar	22,056	17,661	5* 139,454	* 108,760	684	444	4,023	3,866	8,793	7,571	13,500	11,881
14	Gurdaspur	30,378	24,433	* 89,171	* 69,458	6,330	5,728	4,093	4,125	4,935	4,255	1 15,364	1 14,110
15	Sialkot	82,194	65,685	* 134,629	* 102,946	5,462	5,681	690	652	248	239	6,400	6,572
16	Gujranwala	95,680	77,244	* 120,098	* 93,318	1,762	1,250	699	360	19	5	2,480	1,615
17	Sheikhupura	55,254	46,223	* 79,738	* 64,421	635	405	61	48	280	210	976	663
	RAWALPINDI DIVISION	**356,515**	**303,838**	**366,086**	**309,980**	**2,975**	**2,353**	**334**	**378**	**3,663**	**3,173**	**6,972**	**5,904**
18	Gujrat	132,206	108,594	6* 135,087	6* 110,910	2,166	1,880	182	145	568	516	2,916	2,541
19	Shahpur	94,457	79,728	* 99,376	* 83,118	251	138	18	150	470	392	739	680
20	Jhelum	44,278	40,083	* 45,165	* 40,294	128	113	12	5	876	817	1,016	935
21	Rawalpindi	8,437	7,285	8,933	7,440	301	173	78	72	988	748	1,367	993
22	Attock	5,690	4,391	5,990	4,439	81	36	1	2	647	597	729	635
23	Mianwali	71,447	63,757	71,535	63,779	48	13	43	4	114	103	205	120
	MULTAN DIVISION	**625,534**	**529,501**	**713,143**	**598,711**	**2,088**	**1,244**	**3,847**	**3,289**	**4,897**	**4,472**	**10,832**	**9,005**
24	Montgomery	64,394	54,546	* 83,858	* 67,375	727	346	618	542	1,019	1,027	2,364	1,915
25	Lyallpur	100,641	90,234	* 157,389	* 134,967	1,140	783	3,008	2,608	3,593	3,288	7,741	6,679
26	Jhang	89,089	73,667	89,267	73,781	4	4	..	..	51	49	55	53
27	Multan	183,970	156,614	* 195,014	163,050	211	106	197	137	234	108	642	351
28	Muzaffargarh	113,722	93,760	113,856	93,848	6	5	24	2	..	..	30	7
29	Dera Ghazi Khan	73,718	60,680	73,759	60,690	..	..	..	..	..	..	..	..
	PUNJAB STATES	**221,619**	**181,011**	**681,344**	**587,302**	**15,977**	**12,472**	**7,596**	**6,033**	**8,032**	**6,571**	**31,605**	**25,076**
	A.—Having Political relations with the Punjab Government.	**222**	**172**	**8,005**	**6,210**	**222**	**164**	**3**	**2**	**1**	**2**	**226**	**168**
1	Dujana	45	50	1,778	1,493	..	..	..	..	..	..	..	..
2	Pataudi	..	..	814	710	..	..	..	..	..	..	..	..
3	Kalsia	121	92	4,804	3,522	29	21	..	1	1	2	30	24
4	*SIMLA HILL STATES*	**56**	**30**	**509**	**485**	**198**	**143**	**3**	**1**	..	..	**196**	**144**
	Bashahr	..	..	4	4	2	..	..	..	..	..	2	..
	Nalagarh	25	17	323	245	101	85	3	1	..	..	104	86
	Keonthal	13	5	30	12	6	1	..	..	..	..	6	1
	Baghal	2	2	134	146	46	46	..	..	..	..	46	46
	Jubbal	..	..	1	..	4	..	..	..	..	..	4	..
	Other Simla Hill States	16	6	117	78	34	11	..	..	..	..	34	11
	B.—Having Political relations with the Government of India.	**221,397**	**180,839**	**673,339**	**581,092**	**15,755**	**12,308**	**7,593**	**6,031**	**8,031**	**6,569**	**31,379**	**24,908**
5	Loharu	2	..	5,619	5,058	..	..	..	..	..	..	..	..
6	Sirmoor	13	4	491	288	15	11	..	..	..	..	15	11
7	Bilaspur	4	6	937	808	1,096	1,076	..	..	3	1	1,099	1,077
8	Mandi	70	33	413	253	253	271	22	2	1	..	276	273
9	Suket	..	..	131	148	22	8	..	..	..	..	22	8
10	Kapurthala	7,041	5,917	28,107	21,756	839	686	536	475	2,426	2,010	3,801	3,171
11	Maler Kotla	108	94	13,631	10,662	389	308	107	99	476	370	972	777
12	Faridkot	2,826	2,208	33,625	26,484	16	14	110	122	139	116	265	252
13	Chamba	67	48	181	126	183	180	..	..	..	..	183	180
14	Patiala (Phulkian States)	9,851	7,844	7 259,898	7 198,699	9,602	7,268	5,521	4,408	4,251	3,441	19,374	15,117
15	Jind (Phulkian States)	514	334	8 60,582	8 50,273	2,139	1,618	405	277	222	163	2,766	2,058
16	Nabha (Phulkian States)	1,857	1,509	47,568	35,908	1,119	834	828	626	513	468	2,460	1,928
17	Bahawalpur	199,044	162,847	222,156	180,629	82	34	64	22	..	..	146	56

Total *Jat* includes *Christians and:—

		M.	F.			M.	F.
1.	Jain	8	6	5.	Jain	6	..
2.	„	57	51	6.	„	13	8
3.	„	1	..	7.	„	193	192
4.	„	1	..	8.	„	167	135

Total *Jhiwar* includes :—

		M.	F.
1.	Ad-Dharmi	4	1
	Christian	2	1

TRIBE OR CASTE.—*continued.*

Julaha.								Kahar.								Kamboh.				
Hindu.		*Sikh.*		*Muslim.*		Total.		*Hindu.*		*Sikh.*		*Muslim.*		Total.		*Hindu.*		*Sikh.*		
Males.	Females.	Males.	Females.	Males.	Females.	Males.	Females.	Males.	Females.	Males.	Females.	Males.	Females.	Males.	Females.	Males.	Females.	Males.	Females.	Serial No.
148	149	150	151	152	153	154	155	156	157	158	159	160	161	162	163	164	165	166	167	
2 9,017	**24,471**	**2,973**	**2,476**	**331,748**	**280,831**	**364,168**	**308,075**	**35,195**	**27,227**	**4,925**	**4,154**	**9,340**	**7,812**	**49,461**	**39,195**	**20,691**	**16,944**	**54,342**	**47,524**	
19,415	**15,898**	**2,769**	**2,333**	**302,289**	**256,493**	**324,900**	**275,020**	**31,456**	**24,215**	**4,658**	**3,933**	**9,138**	**7,615**	**45,253**	**35,765**	**18,277**	**15,160**	**41,221**	**36,197**	
3,065	**2,349**	**766**	**648**	**15,107**	**12,284**	**18,938**	**15,281**	**22,755**	**17,720**	**2,156**	**1,794**	**461**	**436**	**25,392**	**19,950**	**8,576**	**6,730**	**1,527**	**1,235**	
98	78	1	..	1,440	1,167	1,539	1,245	534	347	6	4	1	4	541	355	78	55	1	..	1
733	575	..	..	734	660	1,467	1,235	1,184	904	..	..	35	39	1,219	943	7	8	..	..	2
94	59	..	..	196	168	290	227	758	685	..	..	..	..	758	685	1	..	..	..	3
1,112	961	139	105	5,225	4,272	6,476	5,338	10,053	7,953	74	34	112	84	10,239	8,091	5,917	4,744	247	182	4
808	589	625	543	7,469	6,002	8,902	7,134	10,188	7,825	2,074	1,736	332	309	12,594	9,870	2,562	1,971	1,279	1,053	5
220	87	1	..	43	15	264	102	38	6	1	..	1	..	[1] 41	6	11	2	..	..	6
13,254	**12,115**	**1,689**	**1,410**	**40,494**	**34,314**	**55,825**	**48,128**	**4,182**	**3,306**	**1,175**	**1,069**	**1,498**	**1,316**	**6,850**	**5,693**	**393**	**282**	**4,316**	**3,774**	
10,407	9,890	153	107	5,254	4,571	15,814	14,568	322	327	1	2	..	..	323	329	6	6	..	..	7
2,447	1,953	1,235	1,070	8,259	6,830	* 12,257	* 10,125	1,458	1,327	440	413	314	231	2,212	1,971	..	..	17	9	8
31	21	208	146	6,775	5,837	1* 7,020	1* 6,011	1,225	976	295	253	285	362	1,805	1,591	283	211	3,000	2,752	9
90	37	49	47	7,241	5,850	* 7,381	5,934	431	269	302	272	193	180	926	721	23	10	33	21	10
279	214	44	40	12,965	11,226	* 13,353	* 11,490	746	407	137	129	701	543	1,584 [2]	1,081	81	55	1,266	992	11
2,132	**953**	**135**	**102**	**104,239**	**86,586**	**106,515**	**87,642**	**3,850**	**2,815**	**1,233**	**973**	**3,100**	**2,993**	**8,183**	**6,781**	**1,165**	**1,130**	**12,153**	**10,956**	
1,432	617	11	14	21,669	17,747	2* 23,118	18,378	744	217	202	65	314	664	1,260	946	924	977	4,738	3,976	12
74	30	31	17	23,487	19,045	23,592	19,092	434	245	170	205	94	38	698	488	208	140	2,512	2,485	13
19	25	60	43	23,922	20,372	24,001	20,440	2,357	1,985	509	410	720	537	3,586	2,932	14	3	37	21	14
87	24	7	9	12,060	10,421	12,154	10,454	163	279	27	17	237	245	427	541	3	3	.	..	15
299	112	2	..	13,134	10,828	13,435	10,940	33	19	1	..	1,230	1,050	1,264	1,069	1	..	6	4	16
221	145	24	19	9,967	8,173	* 10,215	* 8,338	119	70	324	276	505	459	948	805	15	7	4,860	4,470	17
247	**120**	**2**	**4**	**64,604**	**58,334**	**64,857**	**58,458**	**426**	**265**	**45**	**23**	**343**	**253**	**814**	**541**	..	..	**132**	**99**	
52	29	..	1	13,242	11,364	13,294	11,394	67	50	..	..	284	203	351	253	..	..	..	..	18
95	55	2	3	15,001	13,248	* 15,102	13,306	37	25	..	..	23	9	60	34	..	..	111	96	19
45	19	..	..	9,566	9,349	9,611	9,368	192	146	34	19	..	..	226	165	..	..	..	..	20
11	2	..	..	9,983	9,859	9,994	9,861	129	39	..	..	..	..	129	39	..	..	21	3	21
5	1	..	..	11,059	9,840	11,064	9,841	..	..	7	..	36	41	43	41	..	..	..	..	22
39	14	..	..	5,753	4,674	5,792	4,688	1	5	4	4	..	..	5	9	..	..	..	..	23
717	**361**	**177**	**169**	**77,845**	**64,975**	**78,765**	**65,511**	**248**	**109**	**50**	**74**	**3,721**	**2,617**	**4,014**	**2,800**	**8,143**	**6,968**	**23,093**	**20,133**	
369	168	31	35	14,214	12,563	3* 14,622	3* 12,769	71	..	4	6	417	400	492	406	8,113	6,913	11,567	9,819	24
167	92	131	123	15,089	12,008	* 15,402	* 12,226	65	30	7	46	21	14	93	90	15	55	11,100	9,959	25
54	17	1	..	18,942	17,088	18,997	17,105	..	..	..	..	3	5	3	5	..	..	..	..	26
113	78	12	10	18,967	14,246	* 19,095	14,334	107	79	39	22	3,198	2,128	3,344	2,229	15	..	426	355	27
14	6	..	..	8,361	7,144	8,375	7,150	..	..	..	..	44	42	44	42	..	..	..	..	28
..	..	2	1	2,272	1,926	2,274	1,927	..	..	..	..	38	28	38	28	..	..	..	..	29
9,602	**8,57 3**	**204**	**143**	**29,459**	**24,338**	**39,268**	**33,055**	**3,739**	**3,012**	**267**	**221**	**202**	**197**	**4,208**	**3,430**	**2,414**	**1,784**	**13,121**	**11,327**	
1,340	**1,184**	**4**	**3**	**1,991**	**1,646**	**3,335**	**2,833**	**1,125**	**858**	**101**	**92**	**1**	**1**	**1,227**	**951**	**142**	**100**	**205**	**162**	
..	..	..	..	..	..	..	..	2	10	..	..	..	..	2	10	..	..	..	..	1
..	..	..	..	..	..	..	..	54	39	1	..	..	..	55	39	..	..	..	..	2
10	8	..	..	1,704	1,403	1,714	1,411	1,042	788	100	92	1	1	1,143	881	72	38	193	150	3
1,880	**1,176**	**4**	**3**	**287**	**243**	**1,621**	**1,422**	**27**	**21**	..	..	..	..	**27**	**21**	**70**	**62**	**12**	**12**	4
3	6	..	..	..	..	3	6	.	..	..	..	..	..	..	..	..	..	..	..	
80	71	..	..	274	231	354	302	22	20	..	..	..	..	22	20	13	12	5	4	
35	22	..	..	..	..	35	22	..	..	..	..	..	..	..	..	7	10	..	..	
824	785	..	..	..	2	824	787	..	..	..	..	..	..	..	..	15	10	..	..	
1	..	..	..	..	..	1	.	..	..	..	..	..	..	..	..	..	..	..	..	
387	292	4	3	13	10	404	305	5	1	..	..	..	..	5	1	35	30	7	8	
8,262	**7,389**	**200**	**140**	**27,468**	**22,692**	**35,933**	**30,222**	**2,614**	**2,154**	**166**	**129**	**201**	**196**	**2,981**	**2,479**	**2,272**	**1,684**	**12,916**	**11,165**	
10	8	..	..	..	..	10	8	15	24	..	..	..	..	15	24	..	..	..	..	5
65	29	4	1	328	192	397	222	2,043	1,729	11	9	1	..	2,055	1,738	2	..	..	..	6
3,379	3,051	7	2	20	17	3,406	3,070	..	..	..	..	..	..	..	..	..	..	..	..	7
3,092	2,971	4	1	131	103	3,227	3,075	..	..	..	..	..	..	..	..	11	2	..	..	8
468	448	9	2	12	11	489	461	10	24	..	..	..	..	10	24	..	..	..	..	9
4	3	8	7	3,630	3,151	3,642	3,161	149	121	88	66	132	120	369	307	104	85	7,860	7,143	10
16	15	1	..	837	746 [4]	857 [4]	762	24	24	8	8	7	23	39	55	4	2	1	..	11
3	1	..	..	2,626	2,081	2,629	2,082	118	18	..	..	4	3	122	21	1	..	3	3	12
41	36	..	..	789	692	830	728	5	22	..	..	..	..	5	22	..	..	..	..	13
385	277	158	121	9,175	7,651	9,718	8,049	..	..	..	..	..	..	..	..	2,131	1,580	4,829	3,859	14
33	15	8	5	617	553	658	573	..	..	..	..	..	..	..	..	2	2	1	..	15
..	..	..	..	2,292	1,950	2,292	1,950	250	192	59	46	57	50	366	288	17	13	12	2	16
766	535	1	1	7,011	5,545	7,778	6,081	..	..	..	..	..	..	..	..	..	..	210	158	17

Total *Julaha* includes *Ad-dharmis and :—

		M.	F.
1.	Christian	2	2
2.	„	3	..
3.	„	1	2
4.	„	3	1

Total *Kahar* includes :—

		M.
1.	Christian	1
2.	„	..

Serial No.	District or State.	Kamboh. Muslim. Males.	Kamboh. Muslim. Females.	Kamboh. Total. Males.	Kamboh. Total. Females.	Kashmiri. Muslim. Males.	Kashmiri. Muslim. Females.	Kashmiri. Total. Males.	Kashmiri. Total. Females.	Khatri. Hindu. Males.	Khatri. Hindu. Females.	Khatri. Sikh. Males.	Khatri. Sikh. Females.	Khatri. Total. Males.	Khatri. Total. Females.
1	2	168	169	170	171	172	173	174	175	176	177	178	179	180	181
	PUNJAB	**54,471**	**45,610**	**129,504**	**110,078**	**113,759**	**88,126**	**114,408**	**88,512**	**254,289**	**206,562**	**29,366**	**25,746**	**288,816**	**232,391**
	BRITISH TERRITORY	**38,137**	**32,150**	**97,635**	**83,507**	**111,776**	**86,698**	**112,424**	**87,083**	**229,561**	**187,655**	**27,502**	**24,294**	**257,224**	**212,032**
	AMBALA DIVISION	**1,796**	**1,524**	**11,899**	**9,539**	**389**	**139**	**392**	**141**	**5,930**	**4,478**	**551**	**399**	**6,499**	**4,885**
1	Hissar	2	..	81	55	3	5	[1] 4	5	724	508	40	34	[7] 765	[7] 543
2	Rohtak	1	..	8	8	7	4	7	4	270	181	4	6	274	[8] 188
3	Gurgaon	..	..	1	..	..	..	..	..	224	164	..	..	[9]* 230	164
4	Karnal	1,023	878	7,187	5,804	3	..	3	..	696	572	99	73	795	645
5	Ambala	768	646	4,609	3,670	101	77	* 103	* 79	3,637	2,807	385	272	[10]* 4,083	* 3,145
6	Simla	2	..	13	2	275	53	275	53	379	186	23	14	402	200
	JULLUNDUR DIVISION	**4,051**	**3,510**	**8,760**	**7,566**	**5,359**	**4,081**	**5,369**	**4,088**	**43,916**	**35,811**	**2,143**	**1,859**	**46,099**	**37,199**
7	Kangra	..	..	6	6	577	290	* 580	* 291	3,599	2,549	19	29	[1] 3,634	[1] 2,588
8	Hoshiarpur	206	168	223	177	242	196	242	196	11,206	8,806	580	449	11,786	9,255
9	Jullundur	60	34	3,343	2,997	864	796	864	796	13,616	11,454	339	275	13,955	11,729
10	Ludhiana	806	642	862	673	2,563	1,863	2,563	1,863	8,274	6,690	188	150	* 8,464	* 6,842
11	Ferozepore	2,070	2,666	4,326	3,713	1,113	936	* 1,120	* 937	7,221	5,812	1,017	956	[11]* 8,260	[11]* 6,785
	LAHORE DIVISION	**22,715**	**19,094**	**36,033**	**31,180**	**69,550**	**49,477**	**70,128**	**49,842**	**91,804**	**73,587**	**11,957**	**9,724**	**103,850**	**83,349**
12	Lahore	11,016	9,039	16,678	13,992	16,486	9,600	* 16,492	9,600	31,677	23,474	3,430	2,762	[2]* 35,145	* 26,246
13	Amritsar	6,938	6,139	9,658	8,764	16,965	10,464	[2]*17,534	[3]*10,813	24,932	20,575	2,419	1,932	[12]*27,359	[12] 22,513
14	Gurdaspur	923	776	974	800	4,479	3,551	* 4,482	* 3,565	7,372	6,462	936	696	[3] 8,340	[3] 7,175
15	Sialkot	374	291	377	294	16,091	13,782	16,091	13,782	8,332	7,030	1,006	799	[13]* 9,342	* 7,831
16	Gujranwala	346	290	353	294	13,070	10,239	13,070	* 10,241	12,604	10,324	2,755	2,356	15,359	12,680
17	Sheikhupura	3,118	2,559	7,993	7,036	2,459	1,841	2,459	1,841	6,887	5,722	1,411	1,179	[4] 8,305	[4] 6,904
	RAWALPINDI DIVISION	**1,000**	**916**	**1,132**	**1,015**	**32,875**	**30,467**	**32,907**	**30,469**	**48,765**	**42,302**	**9,174**	**9,209**	**57,942**	**51,516**
18	Gujrat	20	7	20	7	15,353	14,384	15,353	14,384	11,564	9,437	1,603	1,737	[14] 13,168	[14] 11,178
19	Shahpur	871	802	982	898	957	784	[3] 958	784	9,362	8,304	837	727	10,199	9,031
20	Jhelum	15	18	15	18	4,891	4,839	* 4,911	4,839	8,318	7,942	1,947	2,504	* 10,267	[15] 10,447
21	Rawalpindi	2	4	23	7	7,680	6,849	[4] 7,691	6,849	9,839	7,186	2,634	2,221	12,473	9,407
22	Attock	28	25	28	25	3,946	3,571	3,946	* 3,573	8,650	8,725	2,078	1,977	10,728	10,702
23	Mianwali	64	60	64	60	48	40	48	40	1,032	708	75	43	1,107	751
	MULTAN DIVISION	**3,575**	**7,106**	**39,811**	**34,207**	**3,603**	**2,534**	**3,628**	**2,548**	**39,146**	**31,977**	**3,677**	**3,103**	**42,834**	**35,083**
24	Montgomery	3,227	2,743	22,907	19,475	454	224	[5]* 459	[5]* 228	4,952	3,737	1,355	1,108	[5]* 6,313	[5] 4,846
25	Lyallpur	2,720	2,163	13,835	12,177	2,743	2,082	* 2,757	* 2,085	9,731	6,031	1,406	1,278	11,137	7,309
26	Jhang	33	20	33	20	129	61	129	* 62	13,771	12,887	423	340	14,194	13,227
27	Multan	2,577	2,164	3,018	2,519	275	164	* 281	* 170	7,947	6,788	445	326	[6]* 8,397	[6]* 7,116
28	Muzaffargarh	18	16	18	16	1	3	1	3	1,279	1,095	32	32	1,311	1,127
29	Dera Ghazi Khan	..	..	..	..	1	..	1	..	1,466	1,439	16	19	1,482	1,458
	PUNJAB STATES	**16,334**	**13,460**	**31,869**	**26,571**	**1,983**	**1,428**	**1,984**	**1,429**	**24,728**	**18,907**	**1,864**	**1,452**	**26,592**	**20,359**
	A.—Having Political relations with the Punjab Government.	**4**	**3**	**351**	**265**	**46**	**28**	**46**	**28**	**741**	**557**	**40**	**18**	**781**	**575**
1	Dujana	..	..	..	..	..	..	..	..	..	..	..	..	..	..
2	Pataudi	..	..	..	..	..	..	..	..	2	3	..	..	2	3
3	Kalsia	4	3	269	191	4	5	4	5	107	90	18	8	125	98
4	*SIMLA HILL STATES*	..	..	**82**	**74**	**42**	**23**	**42**	**23**	**632**	**464**	**22**	**10**	**654**	**474**
	Bashahr	..	..	..	..	..	..	..	..	13	22	..	..	13	22
	Nalagarh	..	..	18	16	..	..	..	..	228	155	14	7	242	162
	Keonthal	..	..	7	10	31	18	31	18	71	33	..	..	71	33
	Baghal	..	..	15	10	..	..	..	..	179	156	..	..	179	156
	Jubbal	..	..	..	..	..	..	..	..	9	3	..	..	9	3
	Other Simla Hill States	..	..	42	38	11	5	11	5	132	95	8	3	140	98
	B.—Having Political Relations with the Government of India.	**16,330**	**13,457**	**31,518**	**26,306**	**1,937**	**1,400**	**1,938**	**1,401**	**23,987**	**18,350**	**1,824**	**1,434**	**25,811**	**19,784**
5	Loharu	..	..	..	..	..	..	..	..	2	..	..	..	2	..
6	Sirmoor	..	..	2	..	..	..	..	..	220	122	9	9	229	131
7	Bilaspur	..	..	..	..	..	..	..	..	847	635	4	..	851	635
8	Mandi	1	..	12	2	226	30	226	30	1,887	1,501	16	5	1,903	1,506
9	Sukot	..	..	..	..	..	3	..	3	225	114	6	2	231	116
10	Kapurthala	1,620	1,390	9,584	8,618	200	173	200	173	4,520	3,707	246	261	4,766	3,968
11	Maler Kotla	3,913	3,182	3,918	3,184	36	24	36	* 25	730	633	23	20	753	653
12	Faridkot	..	..	4	3	144	111	144	111	909	717	192	170	1,101	887
13	Chamba	..	..	..	..	601	516	601	516	788	715	6	3	794	718
14	Patiala (Phulkian States)	6,637	5,274	13,597	10,713	538	415	* 539	415	8,460	6,800	1,052	772	9,512	7,572
15	Jind (Phulkian States)	880	776	883	778	7	11	7	11	256	171	32	16	288	187
16	Nabha (Phulkian States)	2,633	2,276	2,662	2,291	138	93	138	93	1,988	1,686	73	58	2,061	1,744
17	Bahawalpur	646	559	856	717	47	24	47	24	3,155	1,549	165	118	3,320	1,667

Total *Kashmiri* includes *Hindus and :—

		M.	F.
1.	Sikh	1	..
2.	,,	9	5
	Christian	1	7
3.	Sikh	1	..
4.	,,	11	..
5.	,,	4	2

Total *Khatri* includes *Jains and :—

		M.	F.
1.	Muslim	16	10
2.	,,	3	..
	Christian	18	..
3.	Muslim	32	17
4.	,,	7	3
5.	,,	4	1
6.	Muslim	1	1
7.	Christian	1	1
8.	,,	..	1
9.	,,	1	..
10.	,,	2	..
11.	,,	2	1
12.	Christian	3	6
13.	,,	2	..
14.	,,	1	4
15.	,,	..	1

TRIBE OR CASTE.—*continued.*

KUMHAR.								LOHAR.								MACHHI.		MAHATM.		
Hindu.		*Sikh.*		*Muslim.*		Total.		*Hindu.*		*Sikh.*		*Muslim.*		Total.		Total *Muslim.*		*Hindu.*		
Males.	Females.	Males.	Females.	Males.	Females.	Males.	Females.	Males.	Females.	Males.	Females.	Males.	Females.	Males.	Females.	Males.	Females.	Males.	Females.	Serial No.
182	183	184	185	186	187	188	189	190	191	192	193	194	195	196	197	198	199	200	201	
87,769	**74,494**	**19,018**	**15,481**	**228,981**	**194,636**	**335,783**	**284,619**	**40,094**	**34,667**	**9,085**	**7,850**	**130,546**	**111,426**	**179,847**	**154,063**	**171,505**	**143,357**	**8,629**	**6,853**	
69,936	**59,249**	**15,456**	**12,535**	**206,901**	**176,416**	**292,303**	**248,204**	**26,161**	**22,467**	**6,772**	**5,974**	**117,296**	**100,395**	**150,319**	**128,927**	**150,321**	**125,950**	**8,629**	**6,853**	
36,235	**31,484**	**953**	**766**	**8,255**	**6,613**	**45,448**	**38,863**	**12,445**	**10,510**	**245**	**176**	**15,480**	**13,029**	**28,170**	**23,715**	**15,112**	**13,066**	**718**	**520**	
13,534	12,032	544	455	4,728	3,990	18,806	16,477	1,364	1,147	62	52	5,365	4,724	6,791	5,923	3,706	3,140	..	..	1
6,049	5,234	..	..	973	796	7,022	6,030	4,388	3,789	21	23	2,623	2,164	7,032	3,976	3,400	3,036	..	..	2
6,576	5,984	..	..	31	19	6,607	6,003	2,350	1,983	13	10	1,249	1,091	3,612	3,084	5,239	4,536	..	..	3
7,265	6,016	128	108	1,362	967	8,755	7,091	2,635	2,262	93	52	4,499	3,704	7,227	6,018	2,015	1,736	718	520	4
2,780	2,198	281	203	1,160	840	4,221	3,241	1,436	1,158	56	39	1,738	1,344	3,230	2,541	739	613	..	..	5
31	20	..	..	1	1	32	21	272	171	..	..	6	2	278	173	13	5	..	..	6
18,440	**16,345**	**4,500**	**3,796**	**21,263**	**18,511**	**44,173**	**38,652**	**11,621**	**10,443**	**3,941**	**3,631**	**9,310**	**8,082**	**24,961**	**22,246**	**11,170**	**9,350**	**3,094**	**2,274**	
4,196	3,971	62	55	91	19	4,349	4,045	7,329	6,472	5	5	108	95	* 7,531	* 6,062	..	..	..	..	7
2,677	2,402	186	152	2,575	2,276	5,438	4,830	2,801	2,464	1,046	860	1,287	1,160	5,134	4,484	57	42	2,239	1,858	8
1,707	1,415	1,120	1,076	4,832	4,250	7,659	6,741	468	500	892	1,067	2,408	2,120	3,768	3,687	164	135	700	220	9
971	710	877	563	3,169	2,701	5,017	3,974	587	562	1,489	1,289	743	498	2,799	2,349	180	120	..	..	10
8,859	7,847	2,253	1,950	10,596	9,265	21,710	19,062	436	445	529	410	4,764	4,209	5,729	5,064	10,769	9,053	155	196	11
13,077	**9,964**	**8,758**	**6,981**	**74,968**	**62,785**	**96,813**	**79,734**	**1,850**	**1,387**	**2,146**	**1,778**	**43,443**	**36,341**	**47,440**	**39,507**	**43,145**	**35,568**	**849**	**739**	
1,259	397	1,722	1,436	17,476	14,803	* 20,466	* 16,839	213	117	501	386	8,769	6,834	9,483	7,337	15,199	12,729	428	364	12
839	624	4,076	3,070	15,274	13,382	20,189	17,076	36	8	660	609	9,785	8,423[2]	10,482[2]	9,041	5,004	3,987	405	366	13
4,126	3,382	792	747	7,022	5,436	11,940	9,565	1,223	953	838	678	4,140	3,525	6,201	5,156	751	653	..	..	14
4,747	3,931	700	524	9,412	7,877	14,859	12,332	347	299	70	39	8,760	7,647	9,177	7,985	5,238	4,266	..	..	15
739	435	569	527	15,959	13,233	* 17,268	* 14,196	..	..	28	23	7,505	6,272	7,533	6,295	9,396	7,604	..	..	16
1,367	995	899	677	9,825	8,054	12,091	9,726	31	10	49	43	4,484	3,640	4,564	3,693	7,557	6,329	16	9	17
542	**385**	**75**	**41**	**42,245**	**36,678**	**42,862**	**37,104**	**85**	**35**	**74**	**44**	**30,811**	**27,889**	**30,970**	**27,968**	**30,785**	**25,360**	..	..	
114	73	..	..	11,786	9,700	11,900	9,782	25	14	5	2	7,641	6,855	7,671	6,871	9,092	7,244	..	..	18
279	217	59	34	10,831	8,999	11,169	9,250	17	7	32	25	5,115	4,597	5,164	4,629	10,819	8,683	..	..	19
32	21	..	..	4,886	4,564	4,918	4,585	12	1	18	..	4,124	3,769	4,154	3,770	3,237	3,082	..	..	20
93	51	8	2	5,469	5,129	5,570	5,182	26	8	5	4	4,236	3,748	4,267	3,760	1,402	1,047	..	..	21
24	23	8	5	6,012	5,298	6,044	5,326	..	3	..	..	6,799	6,268	6,799	6,271	2,207	1,789	..	..	22
..	..	..	..	3,261	2,979	3,261	2,979	5	2	14	13	2,896	2,652	2,915	2,667	4,028	3,515	..	..	23
1,672	**1,071**	**1,170**	**951**	**60,170**	**51,829**	**63,012**	**53,851**	**160**	**92**	**366**	**345**	**18,252**	**15,054**	**18,778**	**15,491**	**50,109**	**42,606**	**3,968**	**3,320**	
631	370	659	528	11,784	10,732	13,074	11,630	72	35	89	56	3,809	3,265	3,970	3,356	13,914	11,565	2	..	24
815	563	496	409	9,877	8,362	11,188	9,334	56	42	224	256	5,886	4,970	6,166	5,268	7,833	6,489	2	..	25
16	5	1	..	16,879	13,198	16,896	13,203	2	1	..	..	3,110	2,407	3,112	2,408	9,296	8,426	..	..	26
169	112	13	13	13,728	12,584	13,910	12,709	27	14	34	20	3,254	2,646	3,315	2,680	10,431	9,067	666	587	27
39	18	1	1	5,749	5,082	5,789	5,101	3	..	..	..	1,498	1,204	1,501	1,204	3,314	2,746	2,539	2,148	28
2	3	..	..	2,153	1,871	2,155	1,874	..	..	19	13	695	562	714	575	5,321	4,313	759	585	29
17,833	**15,245**	**3,562**	**2,946**	**22,080**	**18,220**	**43,480**	**36,415**	**18,933**	**12,200**	**2,313**	**1,876**	**13,250**	**11,031**	**29,528**	**25,136**	**21,184**	**17,407**	..	..	
1,283	**1,191**	**11**	**8**	**191**	**142**	**1,485**	**1,341**	**2,934**	**2,502**	**35**	**31**	**397**	**305**	**3,393**	**2,867**	**409**	**382**	..	..	
270	266	..	..	..	..	270	266	34	37	..	..	40	34	74	71	177	182	..	..	1
172	183	..	..	..	..	172	183	7	10	..	..	19	7	26	17	77	92	..	..	2
195	149	11	8	177	131	383	288	133	90	8	4	327	255	468	349	122	89	..	..	3
646	**593**	..	..	**14**	**11**	**660**	**604**	**2,760**	**2,365**	**27**	**27**	**11**	**9**	**2,825**	**2,430**	**33**	**19**	..	..	4
147	144	..	..	..	..	147	144	822	734	..	..	..	..	* 849	* 763	..	..	..	..	
144	127	..	..	2	..	146	127	431	336	7	5	3	3	441	344	28	19	..	..	
102	108	..	..	..	..	102	108	461	390	..	..	7	3	408	393	..	..	..	..	
78	68	..	..	12	11	90	79	196	180	4	2	..	..	200	182	..	..	..	..	
17	3	..	..	..	..	17	3	137	125	..	..	..	..	137	125	..	..	..	..	
158	143	..	..	..	..	158	143	713	600	16	20	1	3	730	623	5	..	..	..	
16,550	**14,054**	**3,551**	**2,938**	**21,889**	**18,078**	**41,995**	**35,074**	**10,999**	**9,698**	**2,278**	**1,845**	**12,853**	**10,726**	**26,135**	**22,269**	**20,775**	**17,025**	..	..	
259	208	..	..	..	..	259	208	24	20	..	..	89	76	113	96	23	13	..	..	5
183	93	..	..	1	1	184	94	948	754	1	..	120	91	1,069	845	5	5	..	..	6
532	433	..	..	3	3	535	436	1,400	1,176	6	5	4	..	1,410	1,181	..	..	..	..	7
1,220	1,149	1	..	2	..	1,223	1,149	2,634	2,548	8	11	25	17	2,667	2,576	..	..	..	..	8
172	121	..	..	..	..	172	121	684	738	..	..	..	1	684	739	..	..	..	..	9
509	406	419	372	2,098	1,769	3,026	2,547	70	57	278	261	1,328	1,161	1,676	1,479	1,689	1,538	..	..	10
149	114	40	30	617	506	806	650	172	137	155	122	311	229	638	488	1	..	..	..	11
152	131	199	172	1,285	1,085	1,636	1,388	16	16	13	8	851	811	880	835	1,598	1,347	..	..	12
961	865	..	..	27	15	988	880	940	888	..	..	59	59	999	947	1	..	..	..	13
6,575	5,560	2,529	2,079	7,896	6,707	17,000	14,346	2,394	1,922	1,542	1,227	6,076	5,032	10,012	8,181	315	216	..	..	14
2,695	2,414	95	77	950	754[1]	3,745[1]	3,249	1,151	959	70	59	1,603	1,389[1]	2,829	2,407	..	..	..	..	15
1,259	1,178	231	171	1,174	961	2,664	2,310	536	447	182	136	547	447	1,265	1,030	47	22	..	..	16
1,884	1,382	37	37	7,836	6,277	9,757	7,696	30	36	23	16	1,840	1,413	1,893	1,465	17,096	13,884	..	..	17

Total *Kumbar* includes *Christians and :—

	M.	F.
1. Jain	5	4

Total *Lohar* includes *Buddhists and :—

	M.	F.
1. Jain	5	..
2. Christian	1	1

TABLE XVII.—RACE

Serial No.	District or State.	Mahtam. Sikh. Males.	Mahtam. Sikh. Females.	Mahtam. Muslim. Males.	Mahtam. Muslim. Females.	Mahtam. Total. Males.	Mahtam. Total. Females.	Mali. Hindu. Males.	Mali. Hindu. Females.	Mali. Muslim. Males.	Mali. Muslim. Females.	Mali. Total. Males.	Mali. Total. Females.	Megh. Hindu. Males.	Megh. Hindu. Females.	Megh. Total. Males.	Megh. Total. Females.
1	2	202	203	204	205	206	207	208	209	210	211	212	213	214	215	216	217
	PUNJAB	**19,219**	**17,148**	**7,046**	**6,367**	**34,894**	**30,368**	**39,920**	**31,926**	**6,997**	**6,303**	**47,258**	**38,500**	**12,152**	**10,163**	**12,656**	**10,551**
	BRITISH TERRITORY	**19,219**	**17,148**	**7,020**	**6,341**	**34,868**	**30,342**	**30,530**	**24,262**	**6,987**	**6,280**	**37,744**	**30,728**	**11,988**	**10,016**	**12,487**	**10,396**
	AMBALA DIVISION	**9**	**11**	..	..	**727**	**531**	**29,133**	**23,730**	**84**	**58**	**29,431**	**23,963**	**137**	**112**	**137**	**112**
1	Hissar	..	..	..	..	..	..	6,267	5,421	70	53	*6,429	*5,548	1	..	1	..
2	Rohtak	..	..	..	..	..	..	5,072	4,364	..	..	5,072	4,364	..	..	..	..
3	Gurgaon	..	..	..	..	..	..	5,801	4,803	7	4	5,808	4,807	..	..	..	..
4	Karnal	9	11	..	..	727	531	7,560	5,874	6	1	*7,628	*5,919	..	..	..	..
5	Ambala	..	..	..	..	..	..	4,429	3,268	1	..	*4,490	*3,325	136	112	136	112
6	Simla	..	..	..	..	..	..	4	..	..	..	4	..	..	..	..	..
	JULLUNDUR DIVISION	**7,867**	**7,482**	**424**	**349**	**11,885**	**10,105**	**705**	**294**	**98**	**77**	**809**	**379**	**3**	**1**	**4**	**1**
7	Kangra	..	..	..	..	..	..	19	21	..	..	19	21	3	1	[4] 4	1
8	Hoshiarpur	1,763	1,548	3	7	4,005	3,413	..	..	..	..	..	..	..	..	..	..
9	Jullundur	330	605	..	..	1,030	825	14	..	1	1	15	1	..	..	..	..
10	Ludhiana	1	..	..	..	1	..	21	8	..	..	*26	*16	..	..	..	..
11	Ferozepore	5,773	5,329	421	342	6,349	5,967	651	265	97	76	*749	341	..	..	..	..
	LAHORE DIVISION	**6,598**	**5,517**	**2,389**	**2,034**	**9,836**	**8,290**	**426**	**157**	**123**	**66**	**551**	**224**	**11,693**	**9,759**	**12,133**	**10,111**
12	Lahore	3,645	3,380	1,773	1,603	5,846	5,347	229	80	68	34	*299	*115	76	57	[5]* 82	57
13	Amritsar	1,197	725	3	1	1,605	1,092	96	36	..	..	96	36	50	21	[6]* 66	[6]* 24
14	Gurdaspur	..	..	..	..	..	..	5	..	..	..	5	..	423	341	[1]* 441	* 362
15	Sialkot	63	45	..	..	63	45	9	3	..	..	9	3	11,000	9,233	*11,385	*9,538
16	Gujranwala	..	..	..	..	..	..	81	38	22	17	103	55	12	8	12	8
17	Sheikhupura	1,693	1,367	613	430	2,322	1,806	6	..	33	15	39	15	132	99	[2]* 147	[2]* 122
	RAWALPINDI DIVISION	..	..	**42**	**26**	**42**	**26**	**30**	**7**	**6,242**	**5,585**	**6,272**	**5,592**	**7**	**11**	**32**	**18**
18	Gujrat	..	..	..	..	..	..	12	7	72	55	84	62	..	..	..	..
19	Shahpur	..	..	42	26	42	26	12	..	2	10	14	10	7	..	* 32	* 6
20	Jhelum	..	..	..	..	..	..	..	..	490	676	490	676	..	..	..	..
21	Rawalpindi	..	..	..	..	..	..	..	..	..	..	..	..	..	..	..	..
22	Attock	..	..	..	..	..	..	5	..	5,675	4,841	5,680	4,841	..	11	..	* 12
23	Mianwali	..	..	..	..	..	..	1	..	3	3	4	3	..	..	..	..
	MULTAN DIVISION	**4,745**	**4,138**	**4,165**	**3,932**	**12,878**	**11,390**	**236**	**74**	**440**	**494**	**681**	**570**	**143**	**133**	**161**	**154**
24	Montgomery	3,734	3,243	350	321	4,086	3,564	203	26	30	39	*238	*67	..	..	[7] 1	[7] 1
25	Lyallpur	419	387	7	..	428	387	2	..	7	..	9	..	124	113	[3]* 161	[3]* 133
26	Jhang	..	..	..	..	..	..	1	..	6	..	7	..	..	..	..	..
27	Multan	592	508	3,558	3,302	4,816	4,397	30		378	442	408	490	19	20	19	20
28	Muzaffargarh	..	..	226	300	2,765	2,448	..	48	..	..	..	..	..	..	..	..
29	Dera Ghazi Khan	..	..	24	9	783	594	..	.	19	13	19	13	..	..	..	..
	PUNJAB STATES	..	..	**26**	**26**	**26**	**26**	**9,390**	**7,664**	**10**	**23**	**9,514**	**7,772**	**169**	**147**	**169**	**155**
	A.—HAVING POLITICAL RELATIONS WITH THE PUNJAB GOVERNMENT.	..	..	..	..	..	..	**727**	**611**	..	..	**741**	**622**	..	..	..	..
1	Dujana	..	..	..	..	..	..	69	54	..	..	69	54	..	..	..	..
2	Pataudi	..	..	..	..	..	..	349	313	..	..	349	313	..	..	..	..
3	Kalsia	..	..	..	..	..	..	263	203	..	..	*277	*214	..	..	..	..
4	*SIMLA HILL STATES*	..	..	..	..	..	..	**46**	**41**	..	..	**46**	**41**	..	..	..	..
	Bashahr	..	..	..	..	..	..	..	..	..	..	..	..	..	..	..	..
	Nalagarh	..	..	..	..	..	..	18	20	..	..	18	20	..	..	..	..
	Keonthal	..	..	..	..	..	..	27	19	..	..	27	19	..	..	..	..
	Baghal	..	..	..	..	..	..	..	..	..	..	..	..	..	..	..	..
	Jubbal	..	..	..	..	..	..	..	..	..	..	..	..	..	..	..	..
	Other Simla Hill States	..	..	..	..	..	..	1	2	..	..	1	2	..	..	..	..
	B.—HAVING POLITICAL RELATIONS WITH THE GOVERNMENT OF INDIA.	..	..	**26**	**26**	**26**	**26**	**8,663**	**7,053**	**10**	**23**	**8,773**	**7,150**	**169**	**147**	**169**	**155**
5	Loharu	..	..	..	..	..	..	141	132	..	..	141	132	..	..	..	..
6	Sirmoor	..	..	..	..	..	..	110	66	..	..	110	66	..	..	..	[8] 8
7	Bilaspur	..	..	..	..	..	..	..	..	..	..	..	..	..	..	..	..
8	Mandi	..	..	..	..	..	..	1	..	..	..	1	..	..	..	..	..
9	Suket	..	..	..	..	..	..	..	..	..	..	..	..	..	..	..	..
10	Kapurthala	..	..	10	11	10	11	..	..	..	..	..	..	..	..	..	..
11	Maler Kotla	..	..	..	..	..	..	..	..	..	..	..	..	..	..	..	..
12	Faridkot	..	..	..	..	..	..	43	14	8	..	51	14	..	..	..	..
13	Chamba	..	..	..	..	..	..	..	..	..	..	..	..	168	147	168	147
14	Patiala (Phulkian States)	..	..	..	..	..	..	4,771	3,953	2	23	*4,823	*4,024	..	..	..	..
15	Jind (Phulkian States)	..	..	..	..	..	..	3,074	2,575	..	..	*3,124	[1]*2,601	1	..	1	..
16	Nabha (Phulkian States)	..	..	..	..	..	..	247	215	..	..	247	215	..	..	..	..
17	Bahawalpur	..	..	16	15	16	15	276	98	..	..	276	98	..	..	..	..

Total *Mali* includes *Sikhs and :—

		M.	F.
1.	Jain	..	1

Total *Megh* includes *Sikhs and :—

	Ad-Dharmi. M.	Ad-Dharmi. F.		Muslim. M.	Muslim. F.
1.	2	..	4.	1	..
2.	2	1	5.	5	..
3.	31	12	6.	12	2
			7.	1	1
					8

TRIBE OR CASTE.—*continued.*

Meo.		Mirasi.						Mochi.						Mussalli.		Nai.				
Total *Muslim.*		*Hindu.*		*Muslim.*		Total.		*Hindu.*		*Muslim.*		Total.		Total *Muslim.*		*Hindu.*		*Sikh.*		Serial No.
Males.	Females.	Males.	Females.	Males.	Females.	Males.	Females.	Males.	Females.	Males.	Females.	Males.	Females.	Males.	Females.	Males.	Females.	Males.	Females.	
218	219	220	221	222	223	224	225	226	227	228	229	230	231	232	233	234	235	236	237	
71,633	**61,456**	**610**	**503**	**130,081**	**113,249**	**130,864**	**113,862**	**4,995**	**2,996**	**252,848**	**211,370**	**253,094**	**214,522**	**221,324**	**190,976**	**56,472**	**45,886**	**23,231**	**18,589**	
71,063	**61,012**	**373**	**298**	**114,726**	**100,359**	**115,267**	**100,760**	**4,338**	**2,479**	**236,116**	**197,471**	**240,693**	**200,104**	**206,480**	**178,590**	**43,558**	**35,469**	**16,213**	**13,165**	
67.121	**57,663**	**63**	**59**	**8,723**	**7,813**	**8,786**	**7,872**	**1,054**	**920**	**1,559**	**1,313**	**2,636**	**2,238**	**3**	**2**	**25,244**	**21,284**	**1,013**	**824**	
363	253	33	30	3,262	2,906	3,295	2,936	288	278	1,346	1,113	* 1,649	1,391	..	..	5,847	4,892	371	306	1
115[1]	80	13	7	1,160	1,152	1,173	1,159	40	38	4	2	44	40	..	..	6,922	5,991	..	..	2
66,189[2]	56,971	14	15	1,522	1,344	1,536	1,359	41	29	4	..	45	29	..	..	4,862	4,390	6	11	3
349	285	3	7	1,612	1,432	1,615	1,439	177	138	42	28	219	166	..	..	5,082	4,068	59	40	4
105	74	..	..	1,166	979	1,166	979	447	388	160	170	* 615	563	3	2	2,518	1,916	576	467	5
..	..	..	..	1	..	1	..	61	49	3	..	64	49	..	..	63	27	1	..	6
3,855	**3,240**	**106**	**62**	**17,111**	**15,108**	**17,230**	**15,174**	**633**	**416**	**34,359**	**28,987**	**35,147**	**29,519**	**3,416**	**2,689**	**13,474**	**10,936**	**6,110**	**5,157**	
..	..	2	..	613	473	615	473	9	4	58	47	67	51	..	..	4,106	3,682	..	..	7
18	15	60	20	2,748	2,306	* 2,810	2,326	33	34	8,592	7,310	* 8,679	* 7,376	..	..	4,287	3,413	412	336	8
916	825	..	..	3,776	3,719	3,776	3,719	76	64	9,103	7,935	[1]* 9,205	[1] 8,028	1	..	2,537	2,041	438	327	9
46	22	..	2	3,112	2,453	* 3,114	2,455	83	50	3,716	2,795	3,799	* 2,849	60	37	1,265	974	2,588	2,157	10
2,875[3]	2,378	44	40	6,862	6,157	* 6,915	* 6,201	432	264	12,890	10,900	[2]* 13,397	[2]* 11,215	3,355	2,652	1,279	826	2,672	2,337	11
80	**107**	**141**	**135**	**32,560**	**27,650**	**32,852**	**27,880**	**1,810**	**783**	**63,747**	**52,632**	**65,578**	**53,426**	**21,174**	**17,861**	**3,931**	**2,853**	**7,686**	**6,123**	
..	..	27	5	6,777	5,601	[1]* 6,837	[1]* 5,633	1,072	475	11,497	9,171	[7]* 12,576	[7]* 9,651	1,138	1,079	570	242	2,325	1,779	12
..	..	75	93	6,054	4,967	* 6,147	* 5,073	346	106	14,156	11,780	* 14,509	* 11,891	205	157	632	418	3,298	2,686	13
1	..	21	14	3,683	3,136	[2]* 3,733	[2]* 3,168	29	18	8,726	7,384	[3] 8,757	7,402	4	..	1,519	1,309	1,300	1,048	14
..	..	15	18	4,905	4,480	[3]* 4,958	[3]* 4,511	50	24	7,166	5,883	[8] 7,217	5,907	266	223	566	432	215	148	15
..	..	3	5	6,526	5,477	[4] 6,548	[4] 5,501	109	44	13,327	10,974	13,436	11,018	11,446	8,455	415	288	185	166	16
79	107	..	..	4,615	3,989	[5]* 4,629	[5]* 3,994	204	116	8,875	7,440	[4] 9,083	[4] 7,557	8,115	7,947	229	164	363	296	17
2	..	**6**	**2**	**20,456**	**18,688**	**20,462**	**18,691**	**309**	**181**	**64,925**	**56,702**	**65,241**	**56,887**	**84,319**	**71,154**	**229**	**79**	**73**	**43**	
1	..	..	..	4,859	4,372	4,859	* 4,373	11	11	20,741	17,696	20,752	17,707	26,443	22,022	34	9	2	..	18
1	..	..	..	6,612	6,341	6,612	6,341	6	8	14,012	11,911	* 14,020	11,919	34,858	28,915	79	22	53	39	19
..	..	..	1	2,721	2,499	2,721	2,500	1	..	10,612	9,953	* 10,615	9,953	8,229	7,731	31	14	6	1	20
..	..	..	..	1,868	1,328	1,868	1,328	273	147	6,906	6,009	* 7,182	* 6,160	3,962	3,049	52	24	2	..	21
..	..	..	..	2,129	2,186	2,129	2,186	18	15	8,674	7,504	8,692	7,519	5,587	4,804	19	5	7	3	22
..	..	6	1	2,267	1,962	2,273	1,963	..	..	3,980	3,629	3,980	3,629	5,240	4,633	14	5	3	..	23
5	**2**	**57**	**40**	**35,876**	**31,100**	**35,937**	**31,143**	**532**	**179**	**71,526**	**57,837**	**72,091**	**58,034**	**97,568**	**86,884**	**675**	**317**	**1,331**	**1,018**	
..	..	57	38	6,909	6,352	6,966	6,390	125	54	13,196	10,636	* 13,339	10,690	24,233	21,825	257	120	211	152	24
..	..	..	..	7,944	6,725	* 7,948	* 6,728	208	61	11,735	9,645	11,943	9,706	19,825	17,244	265	140	1,068	825	25
..	..	..	..	7,338	6,183	7,338	6,183	72	..	13,965	11,377	* 14,042	* 11,384	20,634	19,150	12	9	..	1	26
4	1	..	2	8,082	7,433	8,082	7,435	115	56	18,689	14,358	[5] 18,814	[5]* 14,425	24,138	21,522	136	48	52	40	27
..	..	..	..	3,338	2,652	3,338	2,652	4	2	9,630	8,324	9,634	8,326	6,657	5,557	4	..	..	..	28
1	1	..	..	2,265	1,755	2,265	1,755	8	6	4,311	3,497	4,319	3,503	2,081	1,586	1	..	..	..	29
570	**444**	**237**	**205**	**15,855**	**12,890**	**15,597**	**13,102**	**657**	**517**	**16,732**	**13,899**	**17,401**	**14,418**	**14,844**	**12,386**	**12,919**	**10,417**	**7,018**	**5,424**	
22	**10**	**200**	**177**	**275**	**243**	**475**	**420**	**297**	**263**	**126**	**94**	**424**	**357**	..	..	**989**	**759**	**61**	**51**	
..	..	4	4	26	34	30	38	..	..	..	..	..	..	..	..	225	204	..	..	1
22	10	..	..	27	27	27	27	..	..	..	..	..	..	..	..	171	169	..	..	2
..	..	..	..	149	121	149	121	..	..	126	94	126	94	..	..	235	163	56	51	3
..	..	**196**	**173**	**73**	**61**	**269**	**234**	**297**	**263**	..	..	**298**	**263**	..	..	**358**	**223**	**5**	..	4
..	..	78	85	..	..	78	85	7	6	..	..	7	6	..	..	4	2	..	..	
..	..	..	..	34	28	34	28	..	..	..	..	..	..	..	..	236	153	4	..	
..	..	6	4	..	..	6	4	20	19	..	..	20	19	..	..	20	9	..	..	
..	..	..	..	20	12	20	12	..	..	..	..	..	..	..	..	33	34	..	..	
..	..	33	22	..	..	33	22	126	104	..	..	126	104	..	..	3	..	..	..	
..	..	79	62	19	21	98	83	144	134	..	..	* 145	* 134	..	..	62	25	1	..	
548	**434**	**37**	**28**	**15,080**	**12,647**	**15,122**	**12,682**	**360**	**254**	**16,606**	**13,805**	**16,977**	**14,061**	**14,844**	**12,386**	**11,930**	**9,658**	**6,957**	**5,373**	
1	2	..	..	85	82	85	82	..	..	3	2	3	2	..	..	216	158	..	..	5
2	..	8	10	47	31	55	41	1	..	..	..	1	..	..	..	97	59	1	..	6
..	..	..	..	18	16	18	16	..	..	..	..	..	..	..	..	422	355	..	..	7
..	..	..	..	30	10	30	10	1	..	..	..	1	..	..	..	255	258	..	..	8
..	..	..	..	15	17	15	17	..	..	..	..	..	..	..	..	32	26	..	..	9
75	70	..	..	1,244	1,089	[6] 1,246	[6] 1,091	29	14	3,850	3,487	[6] 3,882	3,501	..	..	614	422	210	151	10
..	..	..	..	482	420	482	420	..	4	125	88	125	92	..	..	367	321	124	98	11
102	95	..	..	1,058	895	1,058	895	42	25	1,962	1,726	2,004	1,752	..	..	84	49	814	669	12
..	..	..	..	184	159	184	159	2	2	..	..	2	2	..	..	160	155	..	..	13
45	23	13	4	5,025	4,400	* 5,041	* 4,409	226	167	1,971	1,601	* 2,201	1,768	..	..	5,594	4,459	4,686	3,601	14
18	14	..	..	931	813	931	813	49	34	51	45	100	79	..	..	2,375	2,045	252	181	15
305	230	9	10	1,090	856	1,099	866	10	8	393	381	* 407	* 390	..	..	1,469	1,209	789	610	16
..	..	7	4	4,871	3,859	4,878	3,863	..	..	8,251	6,475	8,251	6,475	14,844	12,386	245	142	81	63	17

Total *Meo* includes :—

		M.	F.
1.	Hindu	2	1
2.	,,	15	8
3.	,,	29	19
4.	,,	1	..

Total *Mirasi* includes *Sikhs and :—

		M.	F.
1.	Christian	26	20
2.	,,	9	13
3.	,,	21	12
4.	,,	19	19
5.	,,	13	3
6.	,,	2	2

Total *Mochi* includes *Sikhs and:—

		M.	F.			M.	F.
1.	Ad-Dharmi	24	29	5.	Ad-Dharmi	10	10
2.	,,	73	50	6.	,,	3	..
3.	,,	2	..	7.	Christian	1	2
4.	,,	4	1	8.	,,	1	..

TABLE XVII.—RACE,

Serial No.	District or State.	Nai. Muslim. Males.	Nai. Muslim. Females.	Nai. Total. Males.	Nai. Total. Females.	Od. Hindu. Males.	Od. Hindu. Females.	Od. Muslim. Males.	Od. Muslim. Females.	Od. Total. Males.	Od. Total. Females.	Pakhiwara. Total Muslim. Males.	Pakhiwara. Total Muslim. Females.	Pathan. Total Muslim. Males.	Pathan. Total Muslim. Females.	Qasab. Total Muslim. Males.	Qasab. Total Muslim. Females.
1	2	238	239	240	241	242	243	244	245	246	247	248	249	250	251	252	253
	PUNJAB	**127,306**	**103,798**	**207,245**	**173,412**	**10,406**	**9,177**	**6,966**	**6,075**	**17,424**	**15,295**	**2,612**	**1,928**	**193,835**	**156,173**	**68,375**	**58,823**
	BRITISH TERRITORY ..	**117,929**	**101,026**	**177,928**	**149,798**	**10,403**	**9,175**	**6,778**	**5,947**	**17,233**	**15,165**	**2,132**	**1,566**	**175,163**	**141,580**	**63,556**	**54,631**
	AMBALA DIVISION ..	**8,136**	**6,965**	**34,393**	**29,073**	**79**	**56**	**3,020**	**2,124**	**3,099**	**2,180**	..	..	**19,642**	**15,903**	**16,783**	**15,152**
1	Hissar	1,666	1,468	7,884	6,666	1	..	222	175	223	175	..	..	3,064	2,372	2,718	2,446
2	Rohtak	563	471	7,485	6,462	1	1	11	3	12	4	..	..	[1] 4,493	[1] 4,237	2,443	2,386
3	Gurgaon	2,408	2,121	7,276	6,522	58	41	58	54	116	95	..	..	3,240	2,772	7,924	7,119
4	Karnal	1,917	1,556	7,008	5,664	19	14	2,704	1,876	2,723	1,890	..	..	4,382	[2] 3,694	3,374	2,900
5	Ambala	1,571	1,348	4,665	3,731	..	..	25	16	25	16	..	..	3,718	2,598	279	265
6	Simla	11	1	75	28	..	..	..	..	..	..	..	..	745	230	45	36
	JULLUNDUR DIVISION ..	**12,623**	**10,400**	**32,355**	**26,563**	**10**	**1**	**330**	**281**	**340**	**282**	**49**	**27**	**13,916**	**11,709**	**5,738**	**5,036**
7	Kangra	49	39	4,155	3,721	..	..	..	..	..	..	..	..	463	536	172	130
8	Hoshiarpur	2,588	2,139	7,287	5,888	..	..	..	..	..	..	..	..	4,457	4,137	2,145	2,141
9	Jullundur	3,646	3,119	[1] 6,769	5,557	..	..	..	..	..	..	6	4	3,138	2,877	1,391	1,114
10	Ludhiana	1,721	1,307	5,574	4,438	3	..	116	103	119	103	37	17	2,152	1,615	918	782
11	Ferozepore	4,619	3,796	8,570	6,959	7	1	214	178	221	179	6	6	[3] 3,706	[3] 2,544	1,112	869
	LAHORE DIVISION ..	**35,176**	**29,352**	**46,875**	**38,396**	**91**	**84**	**1,717**	**1,499**	**1,808**	**1,583**	**1,419**	**1,078**	**40,084**	**28,541**	**8,519**	**6,669**
12	Lahore	5,639	4,663	*8,559	*6,698	21	6	810	657	831	663	176	115	[4] 14,034	[4] 8,274	2,098	1,479
13	Amritsar	4,067	3,399	*7,999	*6,504	..	..	79	74	79	74	19	9	[5] 5,936	[5] 4,220	1,586	1,224
14	Gurdaspur	4,955	4,277	7,774	*6,636	..	..	1	..	1	..	63	31	[6] 10,006	[6] 8,736	823	672
15	Sialkot	8,386	7,411	*9,215	*8,040	..	..	2	..	2	..	711	529	5,420	4,509	1,329	1,048
16	Gujranwala	7,265	5,871	7,855	6,325	56	69	74	62	130	131	309	269	2,591	1,467	1,544	1,251
17	Sheikhupura	4,864	3,731	*5,463	*4,193	14	9	751	706	765	715	141	125	2,097	1,335	1,139	995
	RAWALPINDI DIVISION	**31,710**	**29,613**	**32,013**	**29,735**	**952**	**754**	**141**	**211**	**1,093**	**965**	**77**	**85**	**75,050**	**66,022**	**10,001**	**8,850**
18	Gujrat	8,700	7,829	*8,737	7,838	65	32	8	9	73	41	66	80	[7] 2,653	1,772	834	704
19	Shahpur	6,397	5,608	6,529	5,669	692	517	33	41	725	558	11	5	6,680	4,601	5,400	4,793
20	Jhelum	4,181	4,316	4,218	4,331	..	..	..	..	..	..	..	..	2,456	1,266	745	694
21	Rawalpindi	4,792	3,504	3,846	3,528	..	..	..	..	..	..	..	..	4,325	2,350	198	143
22	Attock	5,128	5,082	5,154	5,090	..	..	..	..	..	..	..	..	[8] 24,069	23,520	508	461
23	Mianwali	3,512	3,274	3,529	3,279	195	205	100	161	295	366	..	..	34,867	32,513	2,316	2,055
	MULTAN DIVISION ..	**30,284**	**24,696**	**32,292**	**26,031**	**9,271**	**8,280**	**1,570**	**1,832**	**10,893**	**10,155**	**587**	**376**	**26,471**	**19,405**	**22,515**	**18,924**
24	Montgomery	5,497	4,582	5,965	4,854	2,452	2,229	1,020	993	[1] 3,524	[1] 3,265	220	139	[9] 4,131	2,277	4,834	4,086
25	Lyallpur	7,197	5,817	8,530	6,782	32	32	328	624	360	656	8	6	4,465	[10] 3,830	3,310	2,824
26	Jhang	5,633	4,608	5,645	4,618	12	8	..	..	12	8	8	10	1,320	991	4,618	3,927
27	Multan	6,638	5,205	*6,828	5,293	4,350	3,784	220	214	4,570	3,998	326	200	8,608	6,021	5,680	4,660
28	Muzaffargarh	3,778	3,173	3,782	3,173	1,274	1,253	2	1	1,276	1,254	25	21	2,325	1,655	2,786	2,348
29	Dera Ghazi Khan ..	1,541	1,311	1,542	1,311	1,151	974	..	..	1,151	974	..	..	5,622	4,631	1,287	1,079
	PUNJAB STATES ..	**9,377**	**7,772**	**29,317**	**23,614**	**3**	**2**	**188**	**128**	**191**	**130**	**480**	**362**	**18,672**	**14,593**	**4,819**	**4,192**
	A.—HAVING POLITICAL RELATIONS WITH THE PUNJAB GOVERNMENT. ..	**231**	**215**	**1,281**	**1,025**	..	..	..	..	..	..	..	..	**1,782**	**1,439**	**669**	**683**
1	Dujana	9	10	234	214	..	..	..	..	..	..	..	..	550	576	366	388
2	Pataudi	5	6	176	175	..	..	..	..	..	..	..	..	228	204	178	197
3	Kalsia	155	138	446	352	..	..	..	..	..	..	..	..	275	256	122	92
4	*SIMLA HILL STATES* ..	**62**	**61**	**425**	**284**	..	..	..	..	..	..	..	..	**729**	**403**	**3**	**6**
	Bashahr	..	..	4	2	..	..	..	..	..	..	..	..	17	19	..	..
	Nalagarh	61	61	301	214	..	..	..	..	..	..	..	..	111	111	..	6
	Keonthal	..	..	20	9	..	..	..	..	..	..	..	..	417	183	2	..
	Baghal	1	..	34	34	..	..	..	..	..	..	..	..	44	17	..	..
	Jubbal	..	..	3	..	..	..	..	..	..	..	..	..	33	12	..	..
	Other Simla Hill States ..	..	..	63	25	..	..	..	..	..	..	..	..	107	61	1	..
	B.—HAVING POLITICAL RELATIONS WITH THE GOVERNMENT OF INDIA. ..	**9,146**	**7,557**	**28,036**	**22,589**	**3**	**2**	**188**	**128**	**191**	**130**	**480**	**362**	**16,890**	**13,154**	**4,150**	**3,509**
5	Loharu	10	11	226	169	..	..	..	..	..	..	..	..	173	156	113	111
6	Sirmoor	60	51	158	110	..	..	..	..	..	..	..	..	218	98	17	16
7	Bilaspur	..	..	422	355	..	..	..	..	..	..	..	..	36	24	4	.
8	Mandi	9	..	264	258	..	..	..	..	..	..	..	..	636	245	9	4
9	Suket	..	..	32	26	..	..	..	..	..	..	..	..	25	17	..	..
10	Kapurthala	1,823	1,526	[2] 2,648	2,099	..	..	..	..	..	..	198	151	602	497	623	528
11	Maler Kotla	173	147	664	566	..	..	..	..	..	..	..	..	821	692	289	314
12	Faridkot	443	399	1,341	1,117	..	..	24	23	24	23	..	..	338	230	211	177
13	Chamba	11	6	171	161	..	..	..	..	..	..	..	..	258	223	12	5
14	Patiala } Phulkian States ..	2,289	1,917	12,569	9,977	..	..	..	..	..	..	..	..	4,241	3,733	..	..
15	Jind } Phulkian States ..	248	209	[3] 2,877	[3] 2,436	3	2	1	..	4	2	..	..	780	796	374	310
16	Nabha } Phulkian States ..	301	239	2,559	2,058	..	..	163	105	163	105	..	..	1,178	1,140	329	260
17	Bahawalpur	3,779	3,052	4,105	3,257	..	..	..	..	..	..	282	211	7,584	5,303	2,169	1,784

Total *Nai* includes *Cheristians and :—

		M.	F.
1.	Ad-Dharmi	148	70
2.	,,	1	..
3.	Jain	2	1

Total *Od* includes :—

		M.	F.
1.	Sikh	52	43

Total *Pathan* includes:—

		M.	F.
1.	Christian	1	1
2.	,,	..	2
3.	,,	3	2
4.	,,	4	1
5.	,,	1	1
6.	Christian	2	5
7.	,,	1	..
8.	,,	3	2
9.	,,	5	..
10.	,,	..	2

TRIBE OR CASTE.—*continued.*

KANET.						RAJPUT.										RATHI.				
Hindu.		*Buddhist.*		Total.		*Hindu.*		*Sikh.*		*Buddhist.*		*Muslim.*		Total.		*Hindu.*		Total.		
Males.	Females.	Males.	Females.	Males.	Females.	Males.	Females.	Males.	Females.	Males.	Females.	Males.	Females.	Males.	Females.	Males.	Females.	Males.	Females.	Serial No.
254	255	256	257	258	259	260	261	262	263	264	265	266	267	268	269	270	271	272	273	
154,909	145,520	2,403	2,439	157,598	148,216	322,692	254,682	28,372	21,940	816	1,033	919,175	802,159	1,271,484	1,080,166	67,256	66,822	67,267	66,829	
39,004	39,874	1,790	1,803	40,822	41,695	225,514	168,914	24,457	18,796	790	1,021	824,904	721,779	1,075,935	910,757	26,154	25,866	26,165	25,872	
5,151	4,602	11	3	5,190	4,623	57,689	41,190	304	169	..	..	157,938	139,552	215,945	180,945	..	..	..	..	
..	..	..	..	..	..	10,245	7,993	22	14	..	..	60,926	53,670	* 71,197	[1]* 61,680	..	..	..	..	1
..	..	..	..	..	..	7,819	6,025	3	6	..	..	19,300	18,326	* 27,124	* 24,369	..	..	..	..	2
..	..	..	..	..	..	13,836	10,842	5	5	..	..	9,312	8,367	23,152	* 19,215	..	..	..	..	3
17	4	..	..	17	4	10,822	7,406	69	67	..	..	41,746	36,599	[2] 52,638	44,072	..	..	..	..	4
1,202	890	..	..	* 1,230	* 907	11,837	7,829	199	97	..	..	26,426	22,528	* 38,466	* 30,459	..	..	..	..	5
3,932	3,708	11	3	3,943	* 3,712	3,131	1,095	6	..	..	..	228	62	[3]* 3,368	* 1,160	..	..	..	..	6
33,853	35,272	1,779	1,800	35,632	37,072	103,583	89,646	6,847	4,252	788	1,021	123,139	107,841	234,424	202,827	26,154	25,866	26,165	25,872	
33,853	35,272	1,779	1,800	35,632	37,072	62,920	55,997	60	29	788	1,021	650	459	* 64,425	* 57,511	26,154	25,866	[2] 26,165	[2] 25,872	7
..	..	..	..	..	..	31,187	27,966	543	383	..	..	26,227	23,213	* 57,983	* 51,582	..	..	..	..	8
..	..	..	..	..	..	3,729	2,356	4,518	2,531	..	..	25,912	22,242	* 34,161	* 27,131	..	..	..	..	9
..	..	..	..	..	..	1,649	898	443	349	..	..	15,736	12,795	* 17,836	[4]* 14,060	..	..	..	..	10
..	..	..	..	..	..	4,098	2,429	1,283	960	..	..	54,614	49,132	[5]* 60,019	* 52,543	..	..	..	..	11
..	..	..	..	..	..	44,480	26,469	8,474	6,807	2	..	156,402	128,067	209,530	161,464	..	..	..	..	
..	..	..	..	..	..	10,392	3,865	2,476	1,856	..	..	46,730	35,324	[6]* 59,745	[6]* 41,148	..	..	..	..	12
..	..	..	..	..	..	5,646	1,920	1,005	700	..	..	27,253	23,379	[7]* 33,914	[7]* 26,008	..	..	..	..	13
..	..	..	..	..	..	19,495	14,561	437	296	2	..	31,026	25,642	50,960	40,499	..	..	..	..	14
..	..	..	..	..	..	6,249	4,530	950	824	..	..	29,588	25,510	* 36,800	* 30,874	..	..	..	..	15
..	..	..	..	..	..	1,440	872	1,496	1,323	..	..	5,656	4,817	* 8,594	* 7,013	..	..	..	..	16
..	..	..	..	..	..	1,258	721	2,110	1,806	..	..	16,149	13,395	19,517	15,922	..	..	..	..	17
..	..	..	..	..	..	6,561	3,735	2,738	2,412	..	..	210,492	198,233	219,808	204,391	..	..	..	..	
..	..	..	..	..	..	1,760	1,620	1,813	1,771	..	..	18,894	17,917	* 22,481	* 21,316	..	..	..	..	18
..	..	..	..	..	..	1,683	1,069	633	479	..	..	24,069	20,400	* 26,387	* 21,949	..	..	..	..	19
..	..	..	..	..	..	915	296	81	31	..	..	39,941	38,072	40,937	* 38,400	..	..	..	..	20
..	..	..	..	..	..	1,676	374	75	32	..	..	108,035	104,383	109,786	104,789	..	..	..	..	21
..	..	..	..	..	..	357	290	88	73	..	..	19,109	17,081	* 19,555	* 17,445	..	..	..	..	22
..	..	..	..	..	..	170	86	48	26	..	..	444	380	662	492	..	..	..	..	23
..	..	..	..	..	..	13,201	7,874	6,094	5,136	..	..	176,933	148,086	196,278	161,130	..	..	..	..	
..	..	..	..	..	..	3,851	2,151	1,082	740	..	..	61,372	51,016	* 66,341	* 53,937	..	..	..	..	24
..	..	..	..	..	..	3,294	1,590	2,185	1,820	..	..	33,292	27,880	* 38,772	* 31,294	..	..	..	..	25
..	..	..	..	..	..	482	407	220	180	..	..	43,338	37,477	* 44,041	38,064	..	..	..	..	26
..	..	..	..	..	..	4,778	3,045	1,103	1,165	..	..	37,686	30,801	* 43,579	35,011	..	..	..	..	27
..	..	..	..	..	..	598	507	1,475	1,207	..	..	642	377	2,715	2,091	..	..	..	..	28
..	..	..	..	..	..	198	174	29	24	..	..	603	535	830	733	..	..	..	..	29
115,905	105,646	613	636	116,776	106,521	97,178	85,768	3,915	3,144	26	12	94,271	80,380	195,499	169,409	41,102	40,956	41,102	40,957	
28,754	26,667	530	593	29,521	27,478	49,481	49,252	52	44	15	9	3,398	3,197	52,954	52,503	..	..	..	..	
..	..	..	..	..	..	340	285	..	..	..	..	1,010	1,092	1,350	1,377	..	..	..	..	1
..	..	..	..	..	..	935	736	..	..	..	..	353	333	1,288	1,069	..	..	..	..	2
4	..	..	..	4	..	346	220	9	4	..	..	1,765	1,599	2,120	1,823	..	..	..	..	3
28,750	26,667	530	593	29,517	27,478	47,860	48,011	43	40	15	9	270	173	48,196	48,234	..	..	..	..	4
1,670	1,812	530	593	2,200	2,405	29,357	30,610	3	2	8	9	24	15	29,392	30,636	..	..	..	..	
6,885	6,579	..	..	[1]* 7,121	* 6,796	284	191	29	27	..	..	103	82	416	300	..	..	..	..	
3,968	3,545	..	..	3,968	3,545	6,467	5,989	9	9	..	..	16	6	6,492	6,004	..	..	..	..	
4	..	..	..	4	..	4,590	4,584	..	..	7	..	39	25	4,636	4,609	..	..	..	..	
6,710	6,035	..	..	6,710	6,035	354	262	..	..	..	..	..	..	354	262	..	..	..	..	
9,513	8,696	..	..	* 9,514	[2] 8,697	6,808	6,375	2	2	..	..	88	45	* 6,906	* 6,423	..	..	..	..	
87,151	78,979	83	43	87,255	79,043	47,697	36,516	3,863	3,100	11	3	90,873	77,183	142,545	116,906	41,102	40,956	41,102	40,957	
..	..	..	..	..	..	128	89	..	..	..	..	103	68	[8] 238	[8] 168	..	..	..	..	5
23,306	18,619	..	..	23,306	18,619	2,893	2,109	3	4	..	..	590	442	3,486	2,555	..	..	..	..	6
11,931	10,824	..	..	[3]* 11,952	[3]* 10,845	5,248	4,492	3	2	..	..	74	69	5,325	4,563	2	2	2	2	7
39,019	38,285	75	37	39,094	38,322	6,037	3,841	16	11	11	3	254	106	6,318	3,961	7,639	8,383	7,639	8,383	8
12,881	11,244	8	6	12,889	11,250	1,510	1,353	..	..	..	..	1	3	1,511	1,356	..	..	..	..	9
..	..	..	..	..	..	1,704	1,207	897	822	..	..	13,088	11,435	15,689	13,464	..	..	..	..	10
12	5	..	..	12	5	128	89	10	6	..	..	2,492	1,978	2,630	2,073	1	2	1	2	11
..	..	..	..	..	..	207	147	287	215	..	..	4,133	3,475	4,627	3,837	..	..	..	..	12
2	2	..	..	2	2	3,467	2,610	1	..	..	..	236	217	3,704	2,827	33,460	32,569	33,460	[1] 32,570	13
..	..	..	..	..	..	17,013	13,652	1,386	1,073	..	..	29,301	24,775	[9] 47,701	[9] 39,503	..	..	..	..	14
..	..	..	..	..	..	3,604	2,856	50	35	..	..	3,683	3,108	[10] 7,430	[10] 6,089	..	..	..	..	15
..	..	..	..	..	..	2,801	2,204	255	208	..	..	4,877	4,287	7,933	6,699	..	..	..	..	16
..	..	..	..	..	..	2,957	1,867	955	721	..	..	32,041	27,220	35,953	29,811	..	..	..	..	17

Total *Kanet* includes *Sikhs and :—

		M.	F.
1.	Jain	1	..
2.	Muslim	..	1
3.	,,	1	1

Total *Rajput* includes *Christians and :—

		M.	F.
1.	Jain	..	1
2.	,,	1	..
3.	,,	1	..
4.	,,	..	2
5.	,,	2	..
6.	Jain	58	54
7.	,,	8	5
8.	,,	7	11
9.	,,	1	3
10.	,,	93	90

Total *Rathi* includes:—

		M.	F.
1.	Sikh	..	1
2.	Muslim	11	6

Serial No.	District or State.	Total Rajput. Hindu. Males.	Hindu. Females.	Sikh. Males.	Sikh. Females.	Buddhist. Males.	Buddhist. Females.	Muslim. Males.	Muslim. Females.	Total. Males.	Total. Females.
1	2	274	275	276	277	278	279	280	281	282	283
	PUNJAB	544,857	467,024	28,656	22,196	3,219	3,472	919,187	802,167	1,496,849	1,295,211
	BRITISH TERRITORY ..	290,672	234,654	24,485	18,814	2,580	2,824	824,915	721,785	1,142,972	978,324
	AMBALA DIVISION ..	62,840	45,792	332	207	11	3	157,938	139,552	221,135	185,568
1	Hissar	10,245	7,993	22	14	..	..	60,926	53,670	*71,197	[1]*61,680
2	Rohtak	7,819	6,025	3	6	..	..	19,300	18,326	*27,124	*24,359
3	Gurgaon	13,835	10,842	5	5	..	..	9,312	8,367	23,152	*19,215
4	Karnal	10,839	7,410	69	67	..	..	41,746	36,599	[2]52,655	44,076
5	Ambala	13,039	8,719	227	114	..	..	26,426	22,528	*39,096	*31,366
6	Simla	7,063	4,803	6	1	11	3	228	62	[3]*7,311	*4,872
	JULLUNDUR DIVISION	163,590	150,784	6,847	4,252	2,567	2,821	123,150	107,847	296,221	265,771
7	Kangra	122,927	117,135	60	29	2,567	2,821	661	465	*126,222	*120.455
8	Hoshiarpur	31,187	27,966	543	383	..	..	26,227	23,213	*57,983	*51,582
9	Jullundur	3,729	2,356	4,518	2,531	..	..	25,912	22,242	*34,161	*27,131
10	Ludhiana	1,649	898	443	349	..	..	15,736	12,795	*17,836	[4]*14,060
11	Ferozepore	4,098	2,429	1,283	960	..	..	54,614	49,132	[5]*60,019	*52,543
	LAHORE DIVISION ..	44,480	28,469	8,474	6,807	2	..	156,402	128,067	209,530	161,464
12	Lahore	10,392	3,865	2,476	1,856	..	..	46,730	35,324	[6]*59,745	[6]*41,148
13	Amritsar	5,646	1,920	1,005	700	..	..	27,253	23,379	[7]*33,914	[7]*26,008
14	Gurdaspur	19,495	14,561	437	296	2	..	31,026	25,642	50,960	40,499
15	Sialkot	6,249	4,530	950	826	..	..	29,588	25,510	*36,800	*30,874
16	Gujranwala	1,440	872	1,496	1,323	..	..	5,656	4,817	*8,594	*7,013
17	Sheikhupura	1,258	721	2,110	1,806	..	..	16,149	13,395	19,517	15,922
	RAWALPINDI DIVISION	6,561	3,735	2,788	2,412	..	..	210,492	193,233	219,808	204,391
18	Gujrat	1,760	1,620	1,813	1,771	..	..	18,894	17,917	*22,481	*21,316
19	Shahpur	1,683	1,069	633	479	..	..	24,069	20,400	*26,387	*21,949
20	Jhelum	915	296	81	31	..	..	39,941	38,072	40,937	*38,400
21	Rawalpindi	1,676	374	75	32	..	..	108,035	104,383	109,786	104,789
22	Attock	357	290	88	73	..	..	19,109	17,081	*19,555	*17,445
23	Mianwali	170	86	48	26	..	..	444	380	662	492
	MULTAN DIVISION ..	13,201	7,874	6,094	5,136	..	..	176,933	148,086	196,278	161,130
24	Montgomery	3,851	2,151	1,082	740	..	..	61,372	51,016	*66,341	*53,937
25	Lyallpur	3,294	1,590	2,185	1,820	..	..	33,292	27,880	*38,772	*31,294
26	Jhang	482	407	220	180	..	..	43,338	37,477	*44,041	38,064
27	Multan	4,778	3,045	1,103	1,165	..	..	37,686	30,801	*43,579	35,011
28	Muzaffargarh	598	507	1,475	1,207	..	..	642	377	2,715	2,091
29	Dera Ghazi Khan ..	198	174	29	24	..	..	603	535	830	733
	PUNJAB STATES ..	254,185	232,370	4,171	3,382	639	648	94,272	80,882	353,377	316,887
	A.—HAVING POLITICAL RELATIONS WITH THE PUNJAB GOVERNMENT. ..	78,235	75,919	288	261	545	602	3,398	3,198	82,475	79,981
1	Dujana	340	285	..	..	..	..	1,010	1,092	1,350	1,377
2	Pataudi	935	736	..	..	..	..	353	333	1,288	1,069
3	Kalsia	350	220	9	4	..	..	1,765	1,599	2,124	1,823
4	*SIMLA HILL STATES* ..	76,610	74,678	279	257	545	602	270	174	77,713	75,712
	Bashahr	31,027	32,422	3	2	538	602	24	15	31,592	33,041
	Nalagarh	7,169	6,770	264	244	..	..	103	82	[8]7,537	7,096
	Keonthal	10,435	9,534	9	9	..	..	16	6	10,460	9,549
	Baghal	4,594	4,584	..	..	7	..	39	25	4,640	4,609
	Jubbal	7,064	6,297	..	..	..	..	..	..	7,064	6,297
	Other Simla Hill States ..	16,321	15,071	3	2	..	..	88	46	*16,420	*15,120
	B.—HAVING POLITICAL RELATIONS WITH THE GOVERNMENT OF INDIA.	75,950	156,451	3,888	3,121	94	46	90,874	77,184	270,902	236,906
5	Loharu	128	89	..	..	..	..	103	68	[9]238	[9]168
6	Sirmoor	26,199	20,728	3	4	..	..	590	442	26,792	21,174
7	Bilaspur	17,181	15,318	23	22	..	..	75	70	17,279	15,410
8	Mandi	52,695	50,509	16	11	86	40	254	106	53,051	50,666
9	Suket	14,391	12,597	..	..	8	6	1	3	14,400	12,606
10	Kapurthala	1,704	1,207	897	822	..	..	13,088	11,435	15,689	13,464
11	Maler Kotla	141	96	10	6	..	..	2,492	1,978	2,643	2,080
12	Faridkot	207	147	287	215	..	..	4,133	3,475	4,627	3,837
13	Chamba	36,929	35,181	1	1	..	..	236	217	37,166	35,399
14	Patiala (Phulkian States) ..	17,013	13,652	1,386	1,073	..	..	29,301	24,775	[10]47,701	[10]39,503
15	Jind (Phulkian States) ..	3,604	2,856	50	35	..	..	3,683	3,108	[11]7,430	[11]6,089
16	Nabha (Phulkian States) ..	2,801	2,204	255	208	..	..	4,877	4,287	7,933	6,699
17	Bahawalpur	2,957	1,867	955	724	..	..	32,041	27,220	35,953	29,811

Total of *Total Rajput* includes *Christians and :—

		M.	F.			M.	F.			M.	F.
1.	Jain	..	1	5.	Jain	2	..	9.	Jain	7	11
2.	„	1	..	6.	„	58	54	10.	„	1	3
3.	„	1	..	7.	„	8	5	11.	„	93	90
4.	„	..	2	8.	„	1	..				

Ramdasia.								Saini.						Sansi.						Sabera.		
Hindu.		*Ad-Dharmi.*		*Sikh.*		Total.		*Hindu.*		*Sikh.*		Total.		*Hindu.*		*Sikh.*		Total.		*Hindu.*		
Males.	Females.	Males.	Females.	Males.	Females.	Males.	Females.	Males.	Females.	Males.	Females.	Males.	Females.	Males.	Females.	Males.	Females.	Males.	Females.	Males.	Females.	Serial No.
284	285	286	287	288	289	290	291	292	293	294	295	296	297	298	299	300	301	302	303	304	305	
6,817	**5,418**	**25,519**	**21,650**	**37,244**	**29,836**	**69,582**	**56,905**	**43,235**	**35,144**	**46,436**	**40,252**	**89,738**	**75,452**	**16,895**	**13,886**	**846**	**392**	**18,394**	**14,834**	**3,760**	**3,262**	
6,528	**5,149**	**24,244**	**20,531**	**36,176**	**28,996**	**66,945**	**54,677**	**38,111**	**31,132**	**40,906**	**35,870**	**79,078**	**67,050**	**14,924**	**12,250**	**841**	**390**	**16,382**	**13,170**	**3,593**	**3,124**	
4,072	**3,224**	..	..	**10,537**	**8,479**	**14,609**	**11,703**	**18,240**	**14,927**	**12,436**	**10,769**	**30,690**	**25,701**	**2,532**	**2,068**	**122**	**86**	**2,657**	**2,157**	..	..	
1	..	..	..	66	9	67	9	951	814	5	4	956	818	760	657	..	..	760	657	..	..	1
151	140	..	..	..	..	151	140	1,565	1,337	8	9	¹ 1,576	1,346	174	165	..	..	174	165	..	..	2
..	..	..	..	..	..	..	..	171	138	..	..	171	138	..	..	..	..	..	..	..	..	3
1,243	1,157	..	..	142	68	1,385	1,225	6,125	4,930	1,709	1,345	* 7,836	6,275	1,326	1,115	..	..	¹ 1,329	¹ 1,118	..	..	4
2,575	1,872	..	..	10,306	8,382	12,881	10,254	9,428	7,708	10,711	9,410	* 20,148	* 17,123	272	131	122	86	394	217	..	..	5
102	55	..	..	23	20	125	75	..	..	3	1	3	1	..	..	..	..	..	..	..	..	6
1,344	**1,212**	**13,220**	**11,347**	**12,756**	**10,288**	**27,320**	**22,847**	**18,174**	**10,970**	**19,396**	**16,864**	**32,594**	**27,851**	**1,014**	**847**	**304**	**227**	**1,412**	**1,183**	**3,452**	**2,984**	
59	47	11	9	29	35	99	91	454	386	6	4	460	390	21	23	..	..	21	23	1,788	1,590	7
259	260	8,603	7,376	3,288	2,683	12,150	10,319	11,058	9,272	11,875	10,365	* 22,943	* 19,640	118	93	..	..	118	² 100	1,642	1,383	8
184	182	2,962	2,445	1,923	1,400	5,069	4,027	1,467	1,190	6,692	5,809	* 8,166	* 7,009	213	135	28	20	³* 321	³ 257	22	11	9
696	620	1,414	1,332	4,986	4,181	7,096	6,133	122	82	339	282	461	364	476	429	148	111	⁴ 638	540	..	..	10
146	103	230	185	2,530	1,989	2,906	2,277	73	40	484	404	* 564	* 448	186	167	128	96	314	263	..	..	11
775	**463**	**3,195**	**2,609**	**9,503**	**7,859**	**13,475**	**10,932**	**6,044**	**4,986**	**5,701**	**4,665**	**11,752**	**9,658**	**8,473**	**6,965**	**47**	**46**	**8,637**	**7,113**	**140**	**139**	
254	99	250	134	8,704	7,443	¹ 9,210	¹ 7,677	256	55	126	41	382	96	1,530	1,145	32	25	* 1,632	* 1,214	..	..	12
259	158	5	15	270	159	534	332	126	55	76	50	202	105	2,160	1,852	8	9	* 2,186	* 1,866	..	..	13
53	88	1,950	1,662	71	83	2,074	1,833	5,101	4,382	3,051	2,456	8,152	6,838	1,235	1,031	..	..	* 1,244	* 1,071	140	139	14
55	28	5	14	277	99	337	141	446	424	62	54	* 515	* 485	427	314	..	..	* 439	* 323	..	..	15
32	9	..	..	37	9	69	18	4	..	..	..	4	..	1,826	1,549	..	..	* 1,830	* 1,551	..	..	16
122	81	985	784	144	66	1,251	931	111	70	2,386	2,064	2,497	2,134	1,295	1,074	7	12	* 1,306	⁵* 1,088	..	..	17
259	**181**	..	..	**1,355**	**1,122**	**1,614**	**1,303**	**54**	**22**	**146**	**126**	**202**	**150**	**1,190**	**947**	..	**1**	**1,332**	**1,049**	..	..	
23	60	..	..	..	..	23	60	3	..	7	11	10	11	795	646	..	..	* 929	* 744	..	..	18
11	..	..	..	1,336	1,114	1,347	1,114	35	10	128	112	163	122	378	298	..	1	* 382	299	..	..	19
20	2	..	..	11	2	31	4	10	6	..	..	10	6	12	3	..	..	* 13	3	..	..	20
197	113	..	..	5	3	202	116	5	..	2	3	* 9	* 5	1	..	..	..	* 4	* 3	..	..	21
5	5	..	..	1	2	6	7	1	6	9	..	10	6	4	..	..	..	4	..	..	..	22
3	1	..	..	2	1	5	2	..	..	..	..	..	..	..	..	..	..	..	..	..	..	23
78	**69**	**7,829**	**6,575**	**2,025**	**1,248**	**9,927**	**7,892**	**599**	**227**	**3,227**	**3,446**	**3,840**	**3,690**	**1,715**	**1,423**	**368**	**30**	**2,344**	**1,668**	**1**	**1**	
7	10	126	116	219	154	352	280	224	45	1,035	1,171	1,259	* 1,220	898	750	..	..	⁶* 1,136	⁶* 941	..	..	24
23	16	6,934	5,868	1,740	1,094	8,697	6,978	98	45	1,650	1,593	* 1,753	* 1,643	240	183	23	30	* 278	⁷* 231	1	1	25
..	..	3	3	13	..	16	3	..	..	..	..	..	..	173	163	..	..	* 181	* 167	..	..	26
13	15	766	588	53	..	832	603	276	137	540	682	* 826	* 827	404	327	344	..	748	* 329	..	..	27
30	28	..	..	..	..	30	28	1	..	2	..	3	..	..	..	..	..	..	..	..	..	28
..	..	..	..	..	..	..	..	..	..	..	..	..	..	..	..	1	..	1	..	..	..	29
294	**269**	**1,275**	**1,119**	**1,068**	**840**	**2,637**	**2,228**	**5,124**	**4,012**	**5,530**	**4,382**	**10,660**	**8,402**	**1,971**	**1,636**	**5**	**2**	**2,012**	**1,664**	**167**	**138**	
44	**32**	..	..	**594**	**476**	**638**	**508**	**1,977**	**1,485**	**191**	**150**	**2,169**	**1,638**	**19**	**16**	..	..	**19**	**16**	..	..	
..	..	..	..	..	..	..	..	..	..	..	..	..	..	..	..	..	..	..	..	..	..	1
..	..	..	..	..	..	..	..	..	..	..	..	..	..	..	..	..	..	..	..	..	..	2
33	23	..	..	593	476	626	499	930	692	180	141	* 1,111	* 836	8	10	..	..	8	10	..	..	3
11	**9**	..	..	**1**	..	**12**	**9**	**1,047**	**793**	**11**	**9**	**1,058**	**802**	**11**	**6**	..	..	**11**	**6**	..	..	4
..	..	..	..	..	..	..	..	..	..	..	..	..	..	..	..	..	..	..	..	..	..	
..	..	..	..	..	..	..	..	1,036	785	10	9	1,046	794	8	6	..	..	8	6	..	..	
9	9	..	..	..	..	9	9	4	1	..	..	4	1	..	..	..	..	..	..	..	..	
..	..	..	..	..	..	..	..	3	5	..	..	3	5	3	..	..	..	3	..	..	..	
..	..	..	..	..	..	..	..	..	..	..	..	..	..	..	..	..	..	..	..	..	..	
2	..	..	..	1	..	3	..	4	2	1	..	5	2	..	..	..	..	..	..	..	..	
250	**237**	**1,275**	**1,119**	**474**	**364**	**1,999**	**1,720**	**3,147**	**2,527**	**5,339**	**4,232**	**8,491**	**6,764**	**1,952**	**1,620**	**5**	**2**	**1,993**	**1,648**	**167**	**138**	
..	..	..	..	..	..	..	..	..	..	..	..	..	..	26	19	..	..	26	19	..	..	5
98	123	..	..	26	26	124	149	465	341	428	415	893	756	..	..	..	..	..	..	..	..	6
..	..	..	..	..	..	..	..	22	14	..	..	22	14	..	..	..	..	..	..	56	46	7
5	..	..	..	10	..	15	..	343	318	4	1	347	319	..	..	..	..	..	..	..	..	8
..	..	..	..	..	..	..	..	..	..	..	..	..	..	..	..	..	..	..	..	..	..	9
..	..	1,275	1,119	160	135	1,435	1,254	502	485	349	264	851	749	135	91	..	..	135	91	5	4	10
47	29	..	..	25	21	72	50	2	2	..	..	* 2	4	162	130	1	2	163	132	..	..	11
100	85	..	..	253	182	353	267	..	..	..	..	..	..	8	10	..	..	8	10	..	..	12
..	..	..	..	..	..	..	..	..	..	..	..	..	..	..	..	..	..	* 9	* 7	106	88	13
..	..	..	..	..	..	..	..	1,717	1,312	4,451	3,472	6,168	4,784	875	750	..	..	875	750	..	..	14
..	..	..	..	..	..	..	..	50	42	105	75	* 159	* 118	154	130	..	..	154	130	..	..	15
..	..	..	..	..	..	..	..	38	13	2	5	* 41	* 20	54	48	4	..	58	48	..	..	16
..	..	..	..	..	..	..	..	8	..	..	..	8	..	538	442	..	..	* 565	* 461	..	..	17

Total *Ramdasia* includes :—

		M.	F.
1.	Christian	2	1

Total *Saini* includes *Muslims and :—

		M.	F.
1.	Christian	3	..

Total *Sansi* includes *Muslims and :—

		M.	F.			M.	F.
1.	Ad-Dharmi	3	3	5.	Ad-Dharmi	..	1
2.	„	..	7	6.	„	98	77
3.	„	74	102	7.	„	—	5
4.	„	14	..				

Serial No.	District or State.	Sarera.				Sayad.		Sheikh.		Sunar.							
		Sikh.		Total.		Total *Muslim.*		Total *Muslim.*		*Hindu.*		*Sikh.*		*Muslim.*		Total.	
		Males.	Females.	Males.	Females.	Males.	Females.	Males.	Females.	Males.	Females.	Males.	Females.	Males.	Females.	Males.	Females.
1	2	306	307	308	309	310	311	312	313	314	315	316	317	318	319	320	321
	PUNJAB ..	**2,175**	**1,972**	**5,980**	**5,250**	**158,395**	**135,828**	**231,516**	**183,107**	**53,763**	**45,263**	**14,052**	**12,019**	**18,576**	**15,982**	**86,391**	**73,264**
	BRITISH TERRITORY ..	**2,143**	**1,946**	**5,781**	**5,086**	**140,949**	**120,971**	**203,653**	**159,470**	**44,376**	**37,917**	**11,533**	**10,014**	**17,354**	**14,956**	**73,263**	**62,887**
	AMBALA DIVISION ..	..	..	..	..	**13,182**	**11,521**	**56,377**	**45,707**	**13,736**	**11,416**	**341**	**306**	**1,055**	**972**	**15,132**	**12,694**
1	*Hissar*	..	..	..	..	*2,143*	*1,870*	*5,810*	*4,655*	*3,690*	*3,233*	*177*	*156*	*281*	*267*	*4,148*	*3,656*
2	Rohtak	..	..	..	..	1,078	927	12,422	10,727	2,970	2,458	..	..	84	87	3,054	2,545
3	Gurgaon	..	..	..	..	2,133	2,046	9,097	7,802	1,707	1,451	..	..	..	..	1,707	1,451
4	Karnal	..	..	..	..	4,237	3,666	11,942	9,404	2,793	2,245	43	39	505	419	3,341	2,703
5	Ambala	..	..	..	..	3,420	2,925	15,519	12,367	2,424	1,897	121	111	185	199	2,730	2,207
6	Simla	..	..	..	..	171	87	1,587	752	152	132	..	..	..	..	152	132
	JULLUNDUR DIVISION ..	**2,132**	**1,937**	**5,627**	**4,936**	**12,185**	**10,579**	**31,811**	**25,084**	**10,563**	**9,372**	**3,088**	**2,640**	**2,029**	**1,787**	**15,680**	**13,799**
7	Kangra	..	2	1,788	1,592	168	127	936	579	1,634	1,497	..	1	10	8	1,644	1,506
8	Hoshiarpur	1,111	950	[1] 2,793	[1] 2,347	2,274	2,060	[1] 3,759	[1] 2,881	2,492	2,328	145	138	237	188	2,874	2,654
9	Jullundur	1,021	985	[2] 1,046	[2] 997	4,075	4,018	7,530	6,414	3,289	2,645	416	318	482	483	4,187	3,446
10	Ludhiana	..	..	..	..	2,201	1,741	9,369	6,937	1,784	1,674	719	617	183	94	2,686	2,385
11	Ferozepore	..	..	..	..	3,417	2,633	10,217	8,273	1,364	1,228	1,808	1,566	1,117	1,014	4,289	3,808
	LAHORE DIVISION ..	**6**	**9**	**146**	**148**	**34,694**	**27,192**	**69,775**	**51,474**	**7,625**	**6,448**	**6,226**	**5,192**	**4,491**	**3,948**	**18,342**	**15,588**
12	Lahore	..	..	..	..	[1] 10,503	[1] 6,591	[2] 33,902	[2] 23,886	539	379	1,891	1,320	1,188	1,013	3,618	2,712
13	Amritsar	..	..	..	..	4,035	3,202	12,561	8,409	884	708	2,568	2,447	293	260	3,745	3,415
14	Gurdaspur	6	9	146	148	4,528	4,062	5,842	4,617	1,442	1,273	498	465	1,305	1,164	3,245	2,902
15	Sialkot	..	..	..	..	7,557	6,838	5,672	4,644	2,495	2,275	279	185	578	571	3,352	3,031
16	Gujranwala	..	..	..	..	4,822	3,870	6,030	4,912	1,516	1,201	429	382	657	484	2,602	2,067
17	Sheikhupura	..	..	..	..	3,249	2,629	5,768	5,006	749	612	561	393	470	456	1,780	1,461
	RAWALPINDI DIVISION ..	..	..	..	..	**47,157**	**43,314**	**24,438**	**20,671**	**7,611**	**6,695**	**1,389**	**1,321**	**4,628**	**4,234**	**13,628**	**12,250**
18	Gujrat	..	..	..	..	12,409	11,352	3,905	3,870	2,128	2,014	128	136	499	443	2,755	2,593
19	Shahpur	..	..	..	..	[2] 7,561	6,536	4,621	4,305	1,748	1,544	69	72	1,446	1,439	3,263	3,055
20	Jhelum	..	..	..	..	7,407	7,425	3,026	2,674	1,768	1,472	287	288	283	331	2,338	2,091
21	Rawalpindi	..	..	..	..	7,920	6,658	7,695	5,151	510	437	424	310	6	32	940	779
22	Attock	..	..	..	..	7,612	7,323	3,514	3,214	679	560	462	497	1,192	893	2,333	1,950
23	Mianwali	..	..	..	..	4,248	4,020	1,677	1,457	778	668	19	18	1,197	1,096	1,994	1,782
	MULTAN DIVISION ..	**5**	..	**8**	**2**	**33,781**	**28,365**	**21,252**	**16,534**	**4,841**	**3,986**	**489**	**555**	**5,156**	**4,015**	**10,486**	**8,556**
24	Montgomery	..	..	..	..	4,968	4,019	3,026	2,074	827	659	165	124	1,430	1,168	2,422	1,951
25	Lyallpur	5	..	[3] 8	[3] 2	4,255	3,597	5,092	3,742	1,186	831	301	407	1,298	991	2,785	2,229
26	Jhang	..	..	..	..	5,474	4,211	3,327	2,655	1,235	1,081	1	1	200	182	1,436	1,264
27	Multan	..	..	..	..	9,183	7,553	6,408	5,202	245	159	21	22	1,438	905	1,704	1,086
28	Muzaffargarh	..	..	..	..	6,077	5,611	1,559	1,297	881	829	1	1	414	411	1,296	1,241
29	Dera Ghazi Khan ..	..	..	..	..	3,824	3,374	1,840	1,564	467	427	..	..	376	358	843	785
	PUNJAB STATES ..	**32**	**26**	**199**	**164**	**17,446**	**14,857**	**27,863**	**23,637**	**9,387**	**7,346**	**2,519**	**2,005**	**1,222**	**1,026**	**13,128**	**10,377**
	A.—HAVING POLITICAL RELATIONS WITH THE PUNJAB GOVERNMENT.	**2**	**4**	**2**	**4**	**379**	**366**	**1,214**	**986**	**689**	**585**	**26**	**28**	**61**	**40**	**776**	**653**
1	Dujana	..	..	..	..	57	37	93	80	89	89	..	..	..	..	89	89
2	Pataudi	..	..	..	..	163	172	155	110	48	53	..	..	..	..	48	53
3	Kalsia	..	..	..	..	65	54	217	187	133	99	24	28	57	39	214	166
4	*SIMLA HILL STATES* ..	**2**	**4**	**2**	**4**	**94**	**83**	**749**	**609**	**419**	**344**	**2**	..	**4**	**1**	**425**	**345**
	Bashahr	..	..	..	..	..	..	211	206	53	53	..	..	..	..	53	53
	Nalagarh	2	4	2	4	54	49	75	53	111	86	2	..	4	1	117	87
	Keonthal	..	..	..	..	8	9	123	88	61	36	..	..	..	..	61	36
	Baghal	..	..	..	..	5	9	4	2	79	78	..	..	..	..	79	78
	Jubbal	..	..	..	..	3	1	66	63	1	..	..	..	..	..	1	..
	Other Simla Hill States ..	..	..	..	..	*24*	*15*	*270*	*197*	*114*	*91*	..	..	..	..	*114*	*91*
	B. HAVING POLITICAL RELATIONS WITH THE GOVERNMENT OF INDIA.	**30**	**22**	**197**	**160**	**17,067**	**14,491**	**26,649**	**22,651**	**8,698**	**6,761**	**2,493**	**1,977**	**1,161**	**986**	**12,352**	**9,724**
5	Loharu	..	..	..	..	49	27	469	472	102	75	..	..	1	1	103	76
6	Sirmoor	..	..	..	..	46	24	494	433	316	177	1	1	4	4	321	182
7	Bilaspur	..	2	56	48	1	..	16	13	193	160	..	..	4	1	197	161
8	Mandi	..	..	..	..	108	14	272	90	326	233	1	..	1	2	328	235
9	Suket	..	..	..	..	6	4	16	6	72	43	..	..	..	..	72	43
10	Kapurthala	30	20	35	24	1,847	1,649	2,042	1,902	428	323	127	97	219	177	774	597
11	Maler Kotla	..	..	..	..	660	450	714	497	363	245	7	5	2	4	372	254
12	Faridkot	..	..	..	..	123	98	496	330	152	51	211	167	10	12	373	230
13	Chamba	..	..	106	88	23	24	756	666	50	32	..	..	..	..	50	32
14	Patiala (Phulkian States) ..	..	..	..	..	4,398	3,717	12,202	10,731	4,517	3,738	1,622	1,314	169	122	6,308	5,174
15	Jind (Phulkian States) ..	..	..	..	..	312	265	2,774	2,357	731	606	96	73	219	237	1,046	916
16	Nabha (Phulkian States) ..	..	..	..	..	480	420	1,643	1,579	789	593	347	268	5	1	1,141	862
17	Bahawalpur	..	..	..	..	9,014	7,799	4,755	3,575	659	485	81	52	527	425	1,267	962

Total *Sarera* includes :—

		M.	F.
1.	Ad-Dharmi	40	14
2.	,,	3	1
3.	,,	2	1

Total *Sayad* includes :—

Christian	M.	F.
1.	5	5
2.	1	..

Total *Sheikh* includes :—

Christian	M.	F.
1.	4	9
2.	8	1

TRIBE OR CASTE.—*continued.*

Tarkhan: *Hindu* Males	*Hindu* Females	*Sikh* Males	*Sikh* Females	*Muslim* Males	*Muslim* Females	Total Males	Total Females	Teli: *Hindu* Males	*Hindu* Females	*Muslim* Males	*Muslim* Females	Total Males	Total Females	Serial No.
322	323	324	325	326	327	328	329	330	331	332	333	334	335	
79,796	**68,159**	**88,857**	**70,746**	**188,366**	**158,582**	**356,545**	**297,508**	**794**	**579**	**188,174**	**156,753**	**188,985**	**157,357**	
56,633	**46,983**	**64,336**	**51,550**	**177,880**	**150,241**	**298,858**	**248,776**	**684**	**473**	**160,640**	**134,818**	**161,341**	**134,811**	
31,661	**26,314**	**1,848**	**1,296**	**6,731**	**5,510**	**40,244**	**33,121**	**299**	**224**	**30,615**	**25,335**	**30,914**	**25,559**	
8,484	6,976	1,139	932	1,299	1,093	10,922	9,001	5	1	8,075	7,082	8,080	7,083	1
8,365	7,287	1	..	385	301	8,751	7,588	27	7	4,943	4,316	4,970	4,323	2
6,436	5,568	2	3	423	334	6,861	5,905	196	160	2,836	2,436	3,032	2,596	3
5,351	4,259	288	189	3,429	2,779	*9,072	*7,228	2	3	8,718	7,000	8,720	7,003	4
2,823	2,143	180	114	1,194	1,003	4,197	3,260	69	53	5,984	4,497	6,033	4,550	5
202	81	238	58	1	..	441	139	..	..	59	4	59	4	6
19,745	**16,864**	**29,955**	**25,679**	**10,486**	**9,126**	**60,186**	**51,669**	**222**	**218**	**33,260**	**28,503**	**33,485**	**28,723**	
8,017	6,827	92	73	58	48	8,167	6,948	199	209	2,860	2,494	3,059	2,703	7
8,373	7,362	4,360	3,624	1,076	931	13,809	11,917	..	..	6,659	5,889	6,659	5,889	8
1,294	1,212	6,105	5,321	2,842	2,689	10,241	9,222	..	1	6,317	5,520	6,317	5,521	9
1,590	1,246	8,126	7,139	402	285	10,118	8,670	2	2	6,737	5,498[1]	6,740[1]	5,501	10
471	217	11,272	9,522	6,108	5,173	17,851	14,912	21	6	10,687	9,102[2]	10,710[2]	9,109	11
4,289	**3,281**	**27,614**	**21,665**	**62,425**	**52,147**	**94,329**	**77,093**	**76**	**23**	**65,348**	**53,985**	**65,436**	**54,024**	
445	142	10,842	8,092	12,875	9,892	24,162	18,126	21	6	21,036	17,164[3]	21,065[3]	17,183	12
62	23	6,257	5,776	7,010	5,970	*13,330	11,769	8	1	14,947	12,283	14,955	12,284	13
2,468	2,048	5,154	4,305	3,632	3,727	11,254	10,080	12	7	10,512	9,101	10,524[4]	9,111	14
1,044	846	2,776	1,535	17,999	15,731	21,819	18,112	1	..	6,714	5,378[5]	6,719	5,378	15
187	171	1,157	960	13,075	10,657	14,419	11,788	23	6	5,576	4,619	5,599	4,625	16
83	51	1,428	997	7,834	6,170	9,345	7,218	11	3	6,563	5,440	6,574	5,443	17
242	**113**	**1,174**	**386**	**51,088**	**43,755**	**52,454**	**44,254**	**33**	**5**	**18,374**	**16,087**	**18,407**	**16,092**	
124	86	98	58	15,568	12,725	15,790	12,869	3	..	5,434	4,562	5,437	4,562	18
62	10	255	167	10,381	8,898	10,698	9,075	..	..	2,170	1,734	2,170	1,734	19
2	5	105	13	7,463	6,962	7,570	6,980	..	..	3,572	3,217	3,572	3,217	20
49	8	480	9	7,452	6,774	7,981	6,791	14	5	2,766	2,529	2,780	2,534	21
3	1	188	118	6,257	5,452	6,448	5,571	16	..	4,390	3,970	4,406	3,970	22
2	3	48	21	3,917	2,944	3,967	2,968	..	..	42	75	42	75	23
696	**411**	**3,745**	**2,524**	**47,200**	**39,703**	**51,645**	**42,639**	**54**	**3**	**13,043**	**10,408**	**13,099**	**10,413**	
167	85	1,232	733	8,817	6,557	*10,217	*7,376	1	..	2,964	2,254	2,965	2,254	24
409	258	2,323	1,682	7,981	7,044	10,713	8,984	35	..	8,264	6,759[6]	8,301[6]	6,761	25
2	1	5	6	8,097	7,257	8,104	7,264	5	2	805	676	810	678	26
117	67	182	102	10,971	9,272	*11,272	9,441	13	1	855	610	868	611	27
1	..	2	1	8,054	6,923	*8,058	6,924	..	..	21	19	21	19	28
..	..	1	..	3,280	2,650	3,281	2,650	..	..	134	90	134	90	29
23,163	**21,176**	**24,021**	**19,196**	**10,486**	**8,341**	**57,687**	**48,732**	**110**	**106**	**27,534**	**22,435**	**27,644**	**22,546**	
3,271	**2,943**	**260**	**192**	**87**	**74**	**3,628**	**3,216**	**2**	..	**1,116**	**899**	**1,118**	**899**	
312	391	1	..	..	..	313	391	..	..	138	112	138	112	1
199	203	..	..	..	..	199	203	..	..	51	40	51	40	2
313	231	216	171	84	70	613	472	1	..	610	495	611	495	3
2,447	**2,118**	**43**	**21**	**3**	**4**	**2,503**	**2,150**	**1**	..	**317**	**252**	**318**	**252**	4
1,104	1,053	..	..	..	..[2]	1,114[2]	1,060	..	..	..	..	..	..	
362	277	5	5	3	4	370	286	..	..	264	206	264	206	
313	269	8	8	..	..	321	277	1	..	..	..	..	..	
1	..	..	..	..	..	1	..	..	..	2	2	2	2	
335	246	..	..	..	..	335	246	..	..	..	..	..	..	
332	273	30	8	..	..	362	281	..	..	51	44	51	44	
19,892	**18,233**	**23,761**	**19,004**	**10,399**	**8,267**	**54,059**	**45,516**	**108**	**106**	**26,418**	**21,536**	**26,526**	**21,647**	
232	255	..	..	1	4	233	259	..	..	110	76	110	76	5
1,261	902	4	..	64	52	1,329	954	..	..	450	368	450	368	6
71	45	..	..	..	..	71	45	..	..	194	141	194	141	7
1,016	1,076	67	23	5	..	1,088	1,099	13	7	121	70	134[7]	82	8
600	664	..	..	..	..	600	664	73	79	11	7	84	86	9
261	220	1,033	897	2,333	2,060	3,627	3,177	..	..	2,251	2,022	2,251	2,022	10
447	413	557	480	23	17	1,027	910	..	..	996	762	996	762	11
42	15	3,166	2,781	325	309	3,533	3,105	..	..	1,891	1,559	1,891	1,559	12
304	262	26	16	..	..	330	278	..	..	60	42	60	42	13
9,787	8,943	14,943	11,770	800	680[1]	25,537[1]	21,405	16	20	15,031	12,281	15,047	12,301	14
3,341	3,117	783	596	202	146	4,326	3,859	2	..	2,230	1,730	2,232	1,730	15
2,116	2,089	2,319	1,831	82	47	4,517	3,967	..	..	2,040	1,668	2,040	1,668	16
414	232	863	610	6,564	4,952	7,841	5,794	4	..	1,033	810	1,037	810	17

Total *Tarkhan* includes *Christians and :—

		M.	F.
1.	Jain	7	12
2.	Buddhist	10	7

Total *Teli* includes :—

		M.	F.			M.	F.
1.	Sikh	1	1	5.	Sikh	4	..
2.	,,	2	1	6.	,,	2	2
3.	,,	8	13	7.	,,	..	5
4.	,,	..	3				

TABLE XVII.—RACE, TRIBE OR CASTE.—*concluded.*

Serial No.	District or State.	Tank Kshatrya. Hindu. Males.	Tank Kshatrya. Hindu. Females.	Tank Kshatrya. Sikh. Males.	Tank Kshatrya. Sikh. Females.	Tank Kshatrya. Total. Males.	Tank Kshatrya. Total. Females.	Dhiman Brahman. Hindu. Males.	Dhiman Brahman. Hindu. Females.	Dhiman Brahman. Total. Males.	Dhiman Brahman. Total. Females.	Caste Nil. Hindu. Males.	Caste Nil. Hindu. Females.
1	2	336	337	338	339	340	341	342	343	344	345	346	347
	PUNJAB	**5,976**	**5,345**	**13,980**	**12,075**	**19,956**	**17,420**	**7,224**	**5,758**	**7,559**	**5,974**	**4,419**	**2,397**
	BRITISH TERRITORY ..	**5,772**	**5,201**	**13,133**	**11,301**	**18,905**	**16,502**	**6,731**	**5,483**	**7,061**	**5,646**	**4,414**	**2,351**
	AMBALA DIVISION ..	**1,307**	**1,054**	**496**	**414**	**1,803**	**1,468**	**4,535**	**3,415**	**4,728**	**3,521**	**814**	**114**
1	Hissar	44	44	67	59	111	103	28	..	28	..	..	..
2	Rohtak	10	14	..	..	10	14	..	16	..	16	33	21
3	Gurgaon	28	29	..	..	28	29	14	10	14	10	60	30
4	Karnal	200	161	12	24	212	185	2	..	2	..	..	..
5	Ambala	994	796	398	327	1,392	1,123	4,428	3,389[1]	4,621[1]	3,495	209	54
6	Simla	31	10	19	4	50	14	63	..	63	..	12	9
	JULLUNDUR DIVISION..	**3,805**	**3,557**	**7,751**	**6,733**	**11,556**	**10,290**	**2,196**	**2,018**	**2,333**	**2,125**	**137**	**128**
7	Kangra	..	..	..	..	..	..	1,113	1,107	1,113	1,107	135	116
8	Hoshiarpur	1,263	1,219	432	352	1,695	1,571	880	800[2]	974[2]	898	..	..
9	Jullundur	1,682	1,637	2,503	2,048	4,185	3,685	197	108[3]	240[3]	117	2	4
10	Ludhiana	650	583	2,196	2,135	2,846	2,718	..	..	..	..	..	..
11	Ferozepore	210	118	2,620	2,198	2,830	2,316	6	3	6	3	..	8
	LAHORE DIVISION ..	**526**	**465**	**4,725**	**4,048**	**5,251**	**4,513**	..	..	..	..	**2,615**	**1,155**
12	Lahore	89	63	992	845	1,081	908	..	..	..	..	155	129
13	Amritsar	146	97	3,105	2,732	3,251	2,829	..	..	..	..	1,263	363
14	Gurdaspur	239	281	486	389	725	670	..	..	..	..	406	279
15	Sialkot	48	24	13	7	61	31	..	..	..	..	181	55
16	Gujranwala	..	..	..	..	..	..	..	..	..	..	599	315
17	Sheikhupura	4	..	129	75	133	75	..	..	..	..	11	14
	RAWALPINDI DIVISION	**38**	**37**	**14**	**10**	**52**	**47**	..	..	..	..	**1,848**	**954**
18	Gujrat	..	..	..	..	..	..	..	..	..	..	737	454
19	Shahpur	38	37	..	..	38	37	..	..	..	..	3	52
20	Jhelum	..	..	14	10	14	10	..	..	..	..	390	322
21	Rawalpindi	..	..	..	..	..	..	..	..	..	..	213	114
22	Attock	..	..	..	..	..	..	..	..	..	..	5	12
23	Mianwali	..	..	..	..	..	..	..	..	..	..		
	MULTAN DIVISION ..	**96**	**88**	**147**	**96**	**243**	**184**	..	..	..	..	..	..
24	Montgomery	70	56	28	2	98	58	..	..	..	..	..	..
25	Lyallpur	26	32	119	94	145	126	..	..	..	..	..	..
26	Jhang	..	..	..	..	..	..	..	..	..	..	..	..
27	Multan	..	..	..	..	..	..	..	..	..	..	..	..
28	Muzaffargarh	..	..	..	..	..	..	..	..	..	..	..	..
29	Dera Ghazi Khan ..	..	..	..	..	..	..	..	..	..	..	..	..
	PUNJAB STATES ..	**204**	**144**	**847**	**774**	**1,051**	**918**	**493**	**325**	**498**	**328**	**5**	**46**
	A.—Having Political relations with the Punjab Government.	**58**	**60**	**35**	**22**	**93**	**82**	**460**	**303**	**465**	**306**	..	..
1	Dujana	..	..	..	..	..	..	..	..	..	..	..	..
2	Pataudi	..	..	..	..	..	..	..	..	..	..	..	..
3	Kalsia	39	43	28	22	67	65	446	303[4]	451[4]	306	..	..
4	*SIMLA HILL STATES* ..	**19**	**17**	**7**	..	**26**	**17**	**14**	..	**14**	..	..	..
	Bashahr	..	..	..	..	..	..	..	..	..	..	..	..
	Nalagarh	..	..	..	..	..	..	..	..	..	..	..	..
	Keonthal	..	..	1	..	1	..	..	..	..	..	..	..
	Baghal	..	..	..	..	..	..	..	..	..	..	..	..
	Jubbal	..	..	..	..	..	..	14	..	14	..	..	..
	Other Simla Hill States ..	19	17	6	..	25	17	..	..	..	..	..	..
	B.—Having Political relations with the Government of India.	**146**	**84**	**812**	**752**	**958**	**836**	**33**	**22**	**33**	**22**	**5**	**46**
5	Loharu	..	..	..	..	..	..	..	..	..	..	..	..
6	Sirmoor	20	9	2	2	22	11	33	22	33	22	..	3
7	Bilaspur	1	..	..	..	1	..	..	..	..	..	..	..
8	Mandi	..	..	..	..	..	..	..	..	..	..	..	..
9	Suket	..	..	..	..	..	..	..	..	..	..	..	40
10	Kapurthala	89	68	423	411	512	479	..	..	..	..	5	3
11	Maler Kotla	28	..	28	12	56	12	..	..	..	..	..	..
12	Faridkot	8	7	359	327	367	334	..	..	..	..	..	..
13	Chamba	..	..	..	..	..	..	..	..	..	..	..	..
14	Patiala } Phulkian States.	..	..	..	..	..	..	..	..	..	..	..	..
15	Jind } Phulkian States.	..	..	..	..	..	..	..	..	..	..	..	..
16	Nabha } Phulkian States.	..	..	..	..	..	..	..	..	..	..	..	..
17	Bahawalpur	..	..	..	..	..	..	..	..	..	..	..	..

Total *Dhiman Brahman* includes :—

		M.	F.
1.	Sikh	193	106
2.	,,	94	98
3.	,,	43	9
4.	,,	5	3

TABLE XVIII.

VARIATION OF POPULATION OF SELECTED TRIBES.

1. This is entirely a new Table and shows the variation in the number of persons belonging to certain castes or tribes for the last five Censuses. The castes are the same as those in Table XVII. For the purposes of locality, the Districts have been grouped as in Table VIII. For the castes, dealt with in this as well as Table VIII, the localities and the figures are the same, but in the case of other castes, figures have been given only for the locality where a sufficient number of persons belonging to these castes are found.

2. In every case the column for total strength of caste includes figures for all religions, but detail has been given for religions contributing 1,000 persons or more.

3. The figures for 1911 and 1921 have been taken from Table XIV of the Table Volumes of the two Censuses in which totals for these localities are available, having been obtained after classification. In other cases the figures have been compiled from the Table XIII of those years which gave details for all the Districts and States.

4. After the Census of 1911, a portion of the Delhi District was added to the Rohtak District and a portion to the Gurgaon District, and the Mianwali District was formed after the Census of 1891, and therefore the figures of previous Censuses in the case of Rohtak, Gurgaon and Mianwali Districts, have been obtained after the necessary adjustment.

5. The figures of 1891, show the total strength of each caste by sex, without a similar detail by religion, and the figures by religion have now been given without a detail by sex. The figures of Aggarwals and Bagarias for the first three Censuses and of Mussallis for the first two, are not available, and in the case of these castes, no variation is shown prior to 1911, and 1901 respectively.

6. The castes sorted separately for the first time, namely, Tank Kshatrya, Dhiman Brahman and Ramdasia have been omitted from this Table.

TABLE XVIII.—VARIATION OF

Serial No.	Tribe and Locality.		Persons.						Variation, Increase+, Decrease—.			
			1931.	1921.	1911.	1901.	1891.	1881	1921 to 1931.	1911 to 1921.	1901 to 1911.	1891 to 1901.
	1		2	3	4	5	6	7	8	9	10	11
1	AGGARWAL, Total	A. C. . .	373.014	349,322	339,494	..	..	..	+23,692	+9,828	..	..
	Hindu	,, . .	347,120	322,019	315,508	..	..	..	+25,101	+6,511	..	..
	Jain	,, . .	24,221	25,784	26,219	..	..	..	—1,563	—435	..	..
2	AHIR, Total	A. C. D. . .	221,897	201,539	201,299	197,805	188,838	165,878	+20,358	+240	+3,494	+8,967
	Hindu	A. C. . .	217,512	197,846	197,096	193,996	184,643	161,521	+19,666	+750	+3,100	+9,353
	Muslim	D. . .	2,308	1,954	2,492	2,109	2,694	2,583	+354	—538	+383	—585
3	ARAIN, Total	A. C. D. . .	1,329,312	1,086,455	973,888	1,003,698	890,264	795,471	+242,857	+112,567	—29,810	+113,434
	Muslim	,, . .	1,328,094	1,084,551	972,804	1,002,175	886,359	791,996	+243,543	+111,747	—29,371	+115,816
4	ARORA, Total	C. D. . .	769,694	707,495	667,943	647,945	603,131	538,465	+62,199	+39,552	+19,998	+44,814
	Hindu	,, . .	658,848	591,230	493,178	582,802	546,629	498,895	+67,618	+98,052	—80,624	+36,173
	Sikh	,, . .	110,713	116,175	174,520	64,982	56,624	36,964	—5,462	—58,345	+109,538	+9,358
5	AWAN, Total	C. D. . .	538,760	439,975	425,450	420,504	389,402	350,848	+98,785	+14,525	+4,946	+31,102
	Muslim	,, . .	538,755	439,975	425,450	420,504	389,402	350,848	+98,780	+14,525	+4,946	+31,102
6	BAGARIA, Total	C. D. . .	2,446	1,619	1,262	..	..	..	+827	+357	..	..
	Hindu	,, . .	2,282	1,537	1,176	..	..	..	+745	+361	..	..
7	BAWARIA, Total	A. C. D. . .	32,508	34,807	32,849	29,112	26,420	22,013	—2,299	+1,958	+3,737	+2,692
	Hindu	A. C. D. . .	16,045	25,517	26,847	27,633	24,401	20,163	—9,472	—1,330	—786	+3,232
	Sikh	C. D. . .	15,858	9,005	6,002	1,275	1,635	1,478	+6,853	+3,003	+4,727	—360
8	BILOCH, Total	A. C. D. . .	624,691	531,084	530,976	466,645	383,138	331,851	+93,607	+108	+64,331	+83,507
	Muslim	,, . .	624,691	531,084	530,976	466,645	382,976	331,851	+93,607	+108	+64,331	+83,669
9	BRAHMAN, Total	A. B. C. D. . .	1,058,598	994,529	985,901	1,077,252	1,069,132	1,040,771	+64,069	+8,628	—91,351	+8,120
	Hindu	A. B. C. D. . .	1,051,382	988,616	976,744	1,064,752	1,062,403	1,020,965	+62,766	+11,872	—88,008	+2,349
	Sikh	C. D. . .	6,564	5,415	8,647	5,016	5,344	5,899	+1,149	—3,232	+3,631	—328
10	CHAMAR, Total	A. B. C. D. . .	1,102,465	1,134,700	1,075,941	1,172,118	1,147,913	1,033,727	—32,235	+58,759	—96,177	+24,205
	Hindu	A. B. C. D. . .	684,963	968,298	909,409	1,089,003	1,029,335	931,915	—283,335	+58,799	—179,504	+59,668
	Sikh	A. C. . .	155,717	161,862	164,110	75,753	106,328	100,014	—6,145	—2,248	+88,357	—30,575
11	CHHIMBA, Total	A. C. D. . .	92,491	120,695	124,090	147,152	141,819	100,448	—28,204	—3,395	—23,062	+5,333
	Hindu	A. C. . .	20,961	37,562	36,455	58,125	63,247	55,396	—16,601	+1,107	—21,670	—5,122
	Sikh	C. . .	16,741	34,129	34,180	28,009	22,507	17,176	—17,388	—51	+6,171	+5,502
	Muslim	A. C. D. . .	53,406	47,136	51,630	59,497	55,218	27,287	+6,270	—4,494	—7,867	+4,279
12	CHURRA, Total	A. B. C. D. . .	681,359	750,596	912,998	1,175,003	1,175,504	1,039,039	—69,237	—162,402	—262,006	—501
	Hindu	A. B. C. D. . .	368,224	693,393	777,821	934,553	859,571	613,434	—325,169	—84,428	—156,732	+74,982
	Sikh	C. . .	157,341	40,345	49,937	21,673	90,321	40,501	+116,996	—9,592	+28,264	—68,648
	Muslim	C. D. . .	22,150	13,678	83,546	216,840	214,419	379,101	+8,472	—69,868	—133,294	+2,421
13	DAGI & KOLI, Total	A. B. C. . .	182,056	165,159	172,269	153,990	167,772	78,559	+16,897	—7,110	+18,279	—13,782
	Hindu	,, . .	181,370	163,750	169,948	153,866	167,578	78,471	+17,620	—6,198	+16,082	—13,712
14	DARZI, Total	A. B. C. D. . .	45,688	38,256	35,508	39,164	36,919	30,190	+7,432	+2,748	—3,656	+2,245
	Hindu	,, . .	9,823	8,178	7,657	9,680	10,218	9,674	+1.645	+521	—2,023	—538
	Sikh	,, . .	3,630	1,587	1,406	716	660	186	+2,043	+181	+690	+56
	Muslim	,, . .	32,234	28,491	26,443	28,739	26,040	20,330	+3,743	+2,048	—2,296	+2,699
15	DHOBI, Total	A. C. D. . .	174,519	163,908	151,566	142,342	139,421	123,767	+10,611	+12,342	+9,224	+2,921
	Hindu	A. C. . .	10,432	11,187	11,812	12,690	14,529	12,867	—755	—625	—878	—1,839
	Muslim	A. C. D. . .	162,044	149,106	135,988	126,419	120,916	103,712	+12,938	+13,118	+9,569	+5,503
16	DUMNA, Total	B. C. . .	32,055	36,669	72,250	53,394	64,046	66,169	—4,614	—35,581	+18,856	—10,652
	Hindu	,, . .	31,707	36,118	70,786	52,465	62,979	65,636	—4,411	—34,668	+18,321	—10,514
17	FAQIR, Total	A. C. D. . .	283,634	270,070	262,511	362,266	300,214	111,995	+13,564	+7,559	—99,755	+62,052
	Hindu	C. D. . .	23,161	20,064	19,407	62,160	59,291	5,211	+3,097	+657	—42,753	+2,869
	Sikh	C. . .	4,484	10,469	14,462	9,856	3,230	607	—5,985	—3,993	+4,606	+6,626
	Muslim	A. C. D. . .	253,969	233,815	224,496	247,328	194,539	104,200	+20,154	+9,319	—22,832	+52,789
18	GHIRATH, Total	B. . .	122,785	117,949	121,107	121,718	118,631	110,507	+4,836	—3,158	—611	+3,087
	Hindu	,, . .	122,505	117,801	120,961	121,553	118,409	110,477	+4,704	—3,160	—592	+3,144
19	GHOSI, Total	A. B. C. . .	3,836	502	2,419	3,012	2,652	2,221	+3,334	—1,917	—593	+360
	Hindu	,, . .	1,887	306	248	271	330	215	+1,581	+58	—23	—59
	Muslim	,, . .	1,949	196	2,171	2,741	2,322	2,006	+1,753	—1,975	—570	+419
20	GUJJAR, Total	A. B. C. D. . .	696,442	627,451	595,958	611,904	600,198	539,251	+68,991	+31,493	—15,946	+11,706
	Hindu	A. B. C. D. . .	170,439	158,998	152,575	151,415	153,773	142,376	+11,441	+6,423	+1,160	—2,358
	Sikh	C. . .	2,321	1,945	3,249	1,229	908	1,138	+376	—1,304	+2,020	+321
	Muslim	A. B. C. D. . .	521,347	465,676	439,198	458,619	444,847	395,353	+55,671	+26,478	—10,421	+13,772

POPULATION OF SELECTED TRIBES:—*continued.*

Variation, Increase + Decrease — 1881 to 1891.	Net variation 1881 to 1931. Increase + Decrease —	Males. 1931.	Males. 1921.	Males. 1911.	Males. 1901.	Males. 1891.	Males. 1881.	Females. 1931.	Females. 1921.	Females. 1911.	Females. 1901.	Females. 1891.	Females. 1881.	Serial No.
12	13	14	15	16	17	18	19	20	21	22	23	24	25	
..	..	201,301	190,127	182,810	..	..	..	171,713	159,195	156,684	..	..	..	1
..	..	187,699	175,577	170,725	..	..	..	159,421	146,442	144,783	..	..	..	
..	..	12,683	13,744	13,879	..	..	..	11,538	12,040	12,340	..	..	..	
+22,960	+56,019	122,761	112,508	112,169	107,858	..	92,490	99,136	89,031	89,130	89,947	..	73,388	2
+23,122	+55,991	120,103	110,252	109,618	105,682	..	89,908	97,409	87,594	87,478	88,314	..	71,613	
+111	−275	1,248	1,005	1,338	1,093	..	1,318	1,060	949	1,154	1,016	..	1,265	
+94,793	+533,841	726,564	593,782	539,155	534,541	..	422,882	602,748	492,673	434,733	469,157	..	372,589	3
+94,363	+536,098	725,840	592,687	538,509	533,687	..	420,982	602,254	491,864	434,295	468,488	..	371,014	
+64,666	+231,229	412,789	381,915	359,601	349,289	..	291,184	356,905	325,580	308,342	298,656	..	247,281	4
+47,734	+159,953	352,791	318,605	266,241	313,103	..	268,403	306,057	272,625	226,937	269,699	..	230,492	
+18,660	+73,749	59,934	63,275	93,240	36,080	..	21,387	50,779	52,900	81,280	28,902	..	15,577	
+38,554	+187,912	287,901	230,768	226,564	221,863	..	182,872	250,859	209,207	198,886	198,641	..	167,976	5
+38,554	+187,907	287,897	230,768	226,564	221,863	..	182,872	250,858	209,207	198,886	198,641	..	167,976	
.	..	1,371	995	754	..	..	..	1,075	624	508	..	..	..	6
..	..	1,295	948	726	..	..	..	987	589	450	..	..	..	
+4,407	+10,495	16,948	18,713	17,481	15,141	..	11,417	15,560	16,094	15,368	13,971	..	10,596	7
+4,238	−4,118	8 420	13,607	14,366	14,306	..	10,428	7,625	11,910	12,481	13,327	..	9,735	
+157	+14,380	8,192	4,969	3,115	700	..	791	7,666	4,036	2,887	575	..	637	
+51,287	+292,840	341,543	289,282	288,813	252,617	..	179,179	283,148	241,802	242,163	214,028	..	152,672	8
+51,125	+292,840	341,543	280,282	288,813	252,617	..	179,179	283,148	241,802	242,163	214,0 28	..	152,672	
+28,361	+17,827	581,045	546,303	544,331	583,309	..	565,270	477,553	448,226	441,570	493,943	..	475,501	9
+41,438	+30,417	576,735	542,822	538,947	573,189	..	554,436	474,647	445,794	437,797	491,563	..	466,529	
−555	+665	3,911	3,192	5,067	2,918	..	3,331	2,653	2,223	3,589	2,098	..	2,568	
+114,186	+68,738	594,828	617,375	585,312	625,206	..	552,449	507,637	517,325	490,629	546,912	..	481,278	10
+97,420	−246,952	366,739	525,643	492,849	581,390	..	498,000	318,224	442,655	416,650	507,613	..	433,915	
+6,314	+55,703	85,446	88,963	91,135	41,343	..	53,882	70,271	72,899	72,975	34,410	..	46,132	
+41,371	−7,957	50,010	66,408	68,533	78,964	..	54,392	42,481	54,287	55,557	68,188	..	46,056	11
+7,851	−34,435	11,338	21,099	20,383	31,554	..	29,847	9,623	16,463	16,072	26,571	..	25,549	
+5,331	−435	9,182	18,821	18,839	15,032	..	9,669	7,559	15,308	15,341	12,977	..	7,507	
+27,931	+26,119	28,696	25,444	28,212	31,781	..	14,549	24,710	21,692	23,418	27,716	..	12,738	
+136,465	−357,680	370,873	409,660	504,020	631,321	..	557,112	310,486	340,936	408,978	543,682	..	481,927	12
+246,137	−245,210	200,293	378,324	429,454	502,905	..	329,161	167,931	315,069	348,367	431,648	..	284,273	
+49,820	+116,840	85,481	22,226	27,758	11,940	..	22,134	71,860	18,119	22,179	9,733	..	18,367	
−164,682	−356,951	11,886	7,323	45,850	115,471	..	202,416	10,264	6,355	37,696	101,369	..	176,685	
+89,213	+103,497	94,408	85,153	88,945	79,889	..	40,494	87,648	80,006	83,324	74,101	..	38,065	13
+89,107	+102,899	94,043	84,415	87,711	79,828	..	40,450	87,327	79,335	82,237	74,038	..	38,021	
+6,729	+15,498	24,895	19,668	18,605	20,494	..	15,767	20,793	18,588	16,903	18,670	..	14,423	14
+544	+149	5,406	4,412	4,194	5 282	..	5,117	4,417	3,766	3,463	4,398	..	4,557	
+474	+3,444	2,420	951	805	419	..	96	1,210	636	601	297	..	90	
+5,710	+11,904	17,068	14,305	13,604	14,793	..	10,554	15,166	14,186	12,839	13,946	..	9,776	
+15,654	+50,752	94,970	88,191	82,319	74,793	..	65,933	79,549	75,717	69,247	67,549	..	57,834	15
+1,662	−2,435	5,824	6,224	6,453	6,795	..	7,020	4,608	4,963	5,359	5,895	..	5,847	
+17,204	+58,332	87,947	79,823	73,653	66,248	..	54,875	74,097	69,283	62,335	60,171	..	48,837	
−2,123	−34,114	16,865	19,772	38,562	27,874	..	34,295	15,190	16,897	33,688	25,520	..	31,874	16
−2,657	−33,929	16,685	19,465	37,784	27,384	..	34,008	15,022	16,653	33,002	25,081	..	31,628	
+188,219	+171,639	158,620	153,059	153,574	208,667	..	63,421	125,014	117,011	108,937	153,599	..	48,574	17
+54,080	+17,950	15,297	13,024	13,719	41,383	..	3,804	7,864	7,040	5,688	20,777	..	1,407	
+2,623	+3,877	3,174	7,592	11,308	7,673	..	453	1,310	2,877	3,154	2,183	..	154	
+90,339	+149,769	138,503	128,508	125,594	134,253	..	57,690	115,466	105,307	98,902	113,075	..	46,501	
+8,124	+12,278	63,284	60,329	62,693	62,727	..	56,912	59,501	57,620	58,414	58,991	..	53,593	18
+7,932	+12,028	63,083	60,251	62,611	62,628	..	56,890	59,422	57,550	58,350	58,925	..	53,587	
+431	+1,615	2,033	291	1,330	1,706	..	1,182	1,803	211	1,089	1,306	..	1,030	19
+115	+1,672	987	182	148	192	..	114	900	124	100	79	..	101	
+316	−57	1,046	109	1,182	1,514	..	1,068	903	87	989	1,227	..	938	
+60,947	+157,191	382,372	344,571	330,285	332,393	..	292,773	314,070	282,880	265,673	279,511	..	246,478	20
+11,397	+28,063	96,208	89,567	86,393	84,213	..	79,612	74,231	69,431	66,182	67,202	..	62,764	
−230	+1,183	1,253	1,137	1,935	694	..	681	1,068	808	1,314	535	..	457	
+49,494	+125,994	283,585	253,424	241,397	247,128	..	212,290	237,762	212,252	197,801	211,491	..	183,063	

TABLE XVIII.—VARIATION OF

Serial No.	Tribe and Locality.		Persons. 1931.	1921.	1911.	1901.	1891.	1881.	Variation. Increase +, Decrease —. 1921 to 1931.	1911 to 1921.	1901 to 1911.	1891 to 1901.
	1		2	3	4	5	6	7	8	9	10	11
21	Harni, Total	C..	3,387	2,988	3,360	3,462	4,157	1,318	+399	—372	—102	—695
	Muslim	,, ..	3,387	2,988	3,360	3,462	4,146	1,318	+399	—372	—102	—684
22	Jat, Total	A. B. C. D...	6,070,032	5,453,747	4,891,060	4,884,285	4,500,340	4,223,885	+616,285	+562,687	+6,775	+383,945
	Hindu	A. B. C. D...	992,309	1,046,396	1,000,085	1,539,574	1,679,177	1,445,374	—54,087	+46,311	—539,489	—139,603
	Sikh	A. C. D...	2,133,152	1,822,881	1,617,532	1,388,877	1,116,417	1,122,673	+310,271	+205,349	+228,655	+272,460
	Muslim	A. C. D...	2,940,819	2,582,495	2,272,176	1,954,849	1,703,895	1,655,235	+358,324	+310,319	+317,327	+250,954
23	*Jhiwar, *Total	A. B. C. D...	370,168	371,418	331,951	450,362	458,702	418,499	—1,250	+39,467	—118,411	—8, 340
	Hindu	A. B. C...	186,673	215,210	213,212	281,591	275,252	258,507	—28,537	+1,998	—68,379	+6,339
	Sikh	C...	59,986	48,456	41,659	25,215	20,192	20,112	+11,530	+6,797	+16,444	+5,023
	Muslim	C. D...	110,960	86,720	69,193	114,285	133,261	114,279	+24,240	+17,527	—45,092	—18,976
24	Julaha, Total	A. B. C. D...	672,243	643,403	626,960	651,800	620,401	593,199	+28,840	+16,443	—24,840	+31,399
	Hindu	A. B. C. ..	51,153	56,593	55,719	52,620	53,707	47,283	—5,440	+874	+3,099	—1,087
	Sikh	C...	3,640	4,272	5,082	5,249	1,911	2,442	—632	—810	—167	+3,338
	Muslim	A. B. C. D...	612,579	579,404	566,057	592,078	563,387	543,020	+33,175	+13,347	—26,021	+28,691
25	Kamboh, Total	A. C. D...	239,365	180,870	171,536	173,780	150,646	129,468	+58,515	+9,334	—2,244	+23,134
	Hindu	A. C. D...	37,465	33,606	32,073	56,158	58,222	52,044	+3,859	+1,533	—24,085	—2,064
	Sikh	C. D...	98,737	64,194	67,912	41,292	34,148	27,497	+34,543	—3,718	+26,620	+7,144
	Muslim	C. D...	96,753	76,829	65,822	70,353	42,014	44,854	+19,924	+11,007	—4,531	+28,339
26	Kashmiri, Total	C. D...	200,066	166,449	175,334	189,878	141,280	149,733	+33,617	—8,885	—14,544	+48,598
	Muslim	,, ..	199,040	166,340	174,812	189,596	140,555	149,623	+32,700	—8,472	—14,784	+49,041
27	Khatri, Total	A. B. C. D...	516,207	452,902	423,704	433,579	418,517	392,413	+63,305	+29,198	—9,875	+15,062
	Hindu	A. B. C. D...	460,851	390,253	335,986	379,042	372,236	353,096	+70,598	+54,267	—43,056	+6,806
	Sikh	C. D...	53,996	61,234	86,454	53,676	49,130	36,076	—7,238	—25,220	+32,778	+4,546
28	Kumhar, Total	A. B. C. D...	620,402	570,158	542,906	561,298	515,331	465,676	+50,244	+27,252	—18,392	+45,967
	Hindu	A. B. C...	156,913	155,879	157,532	184,623	177,491	164,024	+1,034	—1,653	—27,091	+7,132
	Sikh	C...	31,238	24,438	23,435	15,022	12,569	10,704	+6,800	+1,003	+8,413	+2,453
	Muslim	A. C. D...	423,430	383,952	358,298	359,418	323,242	288,131	+39,478	+25,654	—1,120	+36,176
29	Lohar, Total	A. B. C. D...	333,910	322,195	319,847	347,099	323,420	291,506	+11,715	+2,348	—27,252	+23,679
	Hindu	A. B. C...	74,463	83,385	82,204	110,816	110,338	101,190	—8,922	+1,181	—28,612	+478
	Sikh	A. C...	16,460	20,025	34,862	30,455	23,287	24,361	—3,565	—14,837	+4,407	+7,168
	Muslim	A. C. D...	241,576	217,459	201,533	204,377	188,002	164,962	+24,117	+15,926	—2,844	+16,375
30	Machhi, Total	A. C. D...	314,791	280,956	239,702	236,122	196,574	167,882	+33,835	+41,254	+3,580	+39,548
	Muslim	,, ..	314,791	280,956	239,702	235,722	195,021	167,874	+33,835	+41,254	+3,980	+40,701
31	Mahtam, Total	C. D...	64,004	94,325	81,805	82,719	56,982	50,313	—30,321	+12,520	—914	+25,737
	Hindu	,, ..	14,244	19,162	17,512	48,567	26,482	32,539	—4,918	+1,650	—31,055	+22,085
	Sikh	,, ..	36,347	63,322	50,056	19,176	17,536	8,047	—26,975	+13,266	+30,880	+1,640
	Muslim	,, ..	13,413	11,841	14,237	14,976	12,964	9,727	+1,572	—2,396	—739	+2,012
32	Mali, Total	A. C...	72,299	92,933	96,883	105,956	95,989	58,672	—20,634	—3,950	—9,073	+9,967
	Hindu	,, ..	71,015	91,329	94,886	105,016	92,900	57,121	—20,314	—3,557	—10,130	+12,116
	Muslim	,, ..	679	433	881	147	275	117	+246	—448	+734	—128
33	Megh, Total	C...	22,539	30,465	39,549	44,315	41,068	37,373	—7,926	—9,084	—4,766	+3,247
	Hindu	,, ..	21,690	29,808	38,873	44,122	40,364	37,047	—8,118	—9,065	—5,249	+3,758
34	Meo, Total	A...	124,821	111,564	120,752	133,300	115,916	112,568	+13,257	—9,188	—12,548	+17,384
	Muslim	,, ..	124,795	111,563	120,742	133,300	114,736	112,568	+13,232	—9,179	—12,558	+18,564
35	Mirasi, Total	A. C. D...	242,685	232,280	223,093	244,506	230,700	192,107	+10,405	+9,187	—21,413	+13,806
	Muslim	,, ..	241,660	225,164	221,662	220,174	217,522	191,383	+16,496	+3,502	+1,488	+2,652
36	Mochi, Total	C. D...	466,832	429,242	410,977	408,314	384,179	334,034	+37,590	+18,265	+2,663	+24,135
	Hindu	C...	4,600	3,288	2,943	2,130	1,842	87	+1,312	+345	+813	+288
	Muslim	C. D...	461,016	424,792	406,545	405,736	379,192	333,828	+36,224	+18,247	+809	+26,544
37	Mussalli, Total	C. D...	412,295	323,549	309,543	57,367	..	..	+88,746	+14,006	+252,176	..
	Muslim	,, ..	412,295	323,549	309,543	57,367	..	..	+88,746	+14,006	+252,176	..
38	Nai, Total	A. B. C. D...	380,657	360,653	344,845	370,019	371,144	323,703	+20,004	+15,808	—25,174	—1,125
	Hindu	A. B. C...	101,140	106,720	103,303	137,369	143,446	126,794	—5,580	+3,417	—34,066	—6,077
	Sikh	C...	39,157	32,579	32,614	24,144	16,715	20,560	+6,578	—35	+8,470	+7,429
	Muslim	A. C. D...	235,855	218,310	206,189	206,760	195,778	174,584	+17,536	+12,130	—571	+10,982
39	Od, Total	A. C. D...	32,719	28,502	31,690	26,160	22,450	15,652	+4,217	—3,188	+5,530	+3,710
	Hindu	,, ..	19,583	18,282	20,375	17,911	12,316	11,540	+1,301	—2,093	+2,464	+5,595
	Muslim	,, ..	13,041	10,192	11,170	8,174	10,082	4,065	+2,849	—978	+2,996	—1,908

* *Jhiwars* include *Kahars*.

POPULATION OF SELECTED TRIBES.—*continued.*

Variation. Increase +, Decrease —.	Not variation 1881 to 1931.	Males.						Females.						Serial No.
1881 to 1891	Increase + Decrease —	1931.	1921.	1911.	1901.	1891.	1881.	1931.	1921.	1911.	1901.	1891.	1881.	
12	13	14	15	16	17	18	19	20	21	22	23	24	25	
+2,839	+2,069	2,004	1,732	1,787	1,767	..	695	1,383	1,256	1,573	1,695	..	623	21
+2,828	+2,069	2,004	1,732	1,787	1,767	..	695	1,383	1,256	1,373	1,695	..	623	
+276,455	+1,846,147	3,367,679	3,062,543	2,772,579	2,705,982	..	2,348,018	2,702,353	2,391,204	2,118,481	2,178,303	..	1,875,867	22
+233,803	—453,065	547,351	586,332	564,128	859,465	..	806,125	444,958	460,064	435,957	680,109	..	639,249	
—6,256	+1,010,479	1,213,819	1,056,297	950,215	790,167	..	641,058	919,333	766,584	667,317	598,710	..	481,615	
+48,660	+1,285,584	1,604,250	1,418,775	1,257,450	1,055,723	..	900,448	1,336,569	1,163,720	1,014,726	899,126	..	754,787	
+40,203	—48,331	201,801	205,072	183,142	241,157	...	223,991	168,367	166,346	148,809	209,205	..	194,508	23
+16,745	—71,834	102,829	119,016	118,282	151,451	..	138,503	83,844	96,194	94,930	130,140	..	120,004	
+80	+39,874	31,934	26,218	22,645	13,697	..	10,743	28,052	22,238	19,014	11,518	..	9,369	
+18,982	—3,319	39,809	47,287	37,518	60,337	..	60,638	31,131	39,433	31,675	53,948	..	53,641	
+27,202	+79,044	364,168	348,764	340,812	349,122	..	317,507	308,075	294,039	286,148	302,678	..	275,692	24
+6,424	+3,870	27,560	30,482	30,103	27,790	..	24,849	23,593	26,111	25,616	24,830	..	22,434	
—531	+1,198	1,978	2,279	2,800	2,708	..	1,264	1,662	1,993	2,282	2,541	..	1,178	
+20,367	+69,559	331,748	314,094	307,741	317,534	..	291,139	280,831	265,310	258,316	274,544	..	251,881	
+21,178	+109,917	129,391	97,394	94,165	93,333	..	69,832	109,994	83,476	77,371	80,447	..	59,636	25
+6,178	—14,579	20,593	18,586	17,559	30,423	..	28,240	16,872	15,020	14,514	25,735	..	23,804	
+6,651	+71,240	32,610	34,619	37,109	22,290	..	14,953	46,127	29,575	30,803	19,002	..	12,544	
—2,640	+51,899	52,670	40,759	36,582	37,465	..	23,848	44,083	36,070	29,240	32,888	..	21,006	
—8,453	+50,333	112,563	88,990	94,237	96,973	..	80,618	87,503	77,459	81,097	92,905	..	69,115	26
—9,068	+49,417	111,920	88,928	93,953	96,823	..	80,553	87,120	77,412	80,859	92,773	..	69,068	
+26,104	+123,794	283,816	248,257	233,538	238,482	..	220,306	232,391	204,645	190,166	195,097	..	172,107	27
+19,140	+107,755	254,289	215,511	186,442	208,582	..	197,964	206,562	174,742	149,544	170,460	..	155,132	
+13,054	+17,920	28,715	31,937	46,378	29,472	..	20,594	25,281	29,297	40,076	24,204	..	15,482	
+49,655	+154,726	335,783	308,479	295,549	298,415	..	249,346	284,619	261,679	247,357	262,883	..	216,330	28
+13,467	—7,111	84,616	83,863	86,051	98,661	..	87,347	72,297	72,016	71,481	85,962	..	76,677	
+1,865	+20,534	17,206	13,466	13,041	8,080	..	5,903	14,032	10,972	10,394	6,942	..	4,801	
+35,111	+135,299	228,843	207,598	194,253	190,655	..	154,165	194,587	176,354	164,045	168,763	..	133,966	
+31,914	+42,404	179,847	174,528	174,223	184,541	..	156,397	154,063	147,667	145,624	162,558	..	135,109	29
+9,148	—26,727	39,902	45,369	44,767	59,510	..	54,431	34,561	38,016	37,437	51,306	..	46,759	
—1,074	—7,901	8,805	11,048	19,220	16,603	..	13,370	7,655	8,977	15,642	13,852	..	10,991	
+23,040	+76,614	130,333	117,342	109,496	107,755	..	87,950	111,243	100,117	92,037	96,622	..	77,012	
+28,692	+146,909	171,458	151,352	131,026	127,313	..	90,303	143,333	129,604	108,676	108,809	..	77,579	30
+27,147	+146,917	171,458	151,352	131,026	127,094	..	90,295	143,333	129,604	108,676	108,628	..	77,579	
+6,669	+13,691	34,167	50,032	43,602	43,921	..	26,989	29,837	44,293	38,203	38,798	..	23,324	31
—6,057	—18,295	7,911	10,202	9,372	25,265	..	17,429	6,333	8,960	8,140	23,302	..	15,110	
+9,489	+28,300	19,210	33,432	26,384	10,509	..	4,461	17,137	29,890	23,672	8,667	..	3,586	
+3,237	+3,686	7,046	6,398	7,846	8,147	..	3,099	6,367	5,443	6,391	6,829	..	4,628	
+37,317	+13,627	40,059	51,290	53,516	56,918	..	31,435	32,240	41,643	43,367	49,038	..	27,237	32
+35,779	+13,894	39,323	50,398	52,397	56,407	..	30,121	31,692	40,931	42,489	48,609	..	27,000	
+158	+362	400	247	484	64	..	64	279	186	397	83	..	53	
+3,695	—14,834	12,295	16,918	21,706	23,188	..	19,324	10,244	13,547	17,843	21,127	..	18,049	33
+3,317	—15,357	11,818	16,542	21,347	23,060	..	19,104	9,872	13,266	17,526	21,062	..	17,943	
+3,348	+12,253	67,146	60,515	64,119	69,218	..	58,959	57,675	51,049	56,633	64,082	..	53,609	34
+2,168	+12,227	67,129	60,514	64,112	69,218	..	58,939	57,666	51,049	56,630	64,082	..	53,609	
+38,593	+50,578	129,732	124,460	119,657	128,105	..	101,148	112,953	107,820	103,436	116,401	..	90,959	35
+26,139	+50,277	129,147	120,748	118,883	115,448	..	100,779	112,513	104,416	102,779	104,726	..	90,604	
+50,145	+132,798	254,960	231,800	224,701	216,427	..	178,302	211,872	197,442	186,276	191,887	..	155,732	36
+1,755	+4,513	3,081	2,044	1,792	1,270	..	47	1,519	1,244	1,151	860	..	40	
+45,364	+127,188	251,102	229,162	221,986	214,874	..	178,151	209,914	195,630	184,559	190,862	..	155,677	
..	..	221,321	174,061	166,135	30,195	..	..	190,974	149,488	143,408	27,172	..	..	37
..	..	221,321	174,061	166,135	30,195	..	..	190,974	149,488	143,408	27,172	..	..	
+47,441	+56,954	207,245	197,582	189,286	198,172	..	174,080	173,412	163,071	165,559	171,847	..	149,623	38
+16,652	—25,654	55,634	59,238	57,137	74,853	..	68,759	45,506	47,482	46,166	62,516	..	58,035	
—3,845	+18,597	21,741	18,415	18,433	13,083	..	11,301	17,416	14,164	14,181	11,061	..	9,259	
+21,194	+61,271	127,164	118,030	111,952	109,510	..	92,958	108,691	100,289	94,237	97,250	..	81,626	
+6,798	+17,067	17,424	15,202	16,901	13,889	..	8,394	15,295	13,300	14,789	12,271	..	7,258	39
+776	+8,043	10,406	9,782	11,014	9,489	..	6,222	9,177	8,500	9,361	8,422	..	5,318	
+6,017	+8,976	6,966	5,403	5,819	4,379	..	2,148	6,075	4,789	5,251	3,795	..	1,917	

* *Jhiwars* include *Kahars.*

TABLE XVIII.—VARIATION OF

Serial No.	Tribe and Locality.	Persons. 1931.	1921.	1911.	1901.	1891.	1881.	Variation, Increase+, Decrease—. 1921 to 1931.	1911 to 1921.	1901 to 1911.	1891 to 1901.
	1	2	3	4	5	6	7	8	9	10	11
40	Pakhiwara, Total C. . .	3,100	2,801	3,711	3,595	3,674	3,741	+299	—910	+116	—79
	Muslim ,, . .	3,100	2,801	3,711	3,595	3,265	3,741	+299	—910	+116	+330
41	Pathan, Total A. C. D. . .	345,438	261,729	272,547	246,790	221,262	210,613	+83,709	—10,818	+25,757	+25,528
	Muslim ,, . .	345,402	261,729	272,547	246,790	221,236	210,479	+83,673	—10,818	+25,757	+25,554
42	Qasab, Total A. B. C. D. . .	127,198	120,820	117,363	114,158	109,435	92,571	+6,378	+3,457	+3,205	+4,723
	Muslim ,, . .	127,198	120,820	117,363	114,158	109,412	92,571	+6,378	+3,457	+3,205	+4,746
43	Kanet, Total A. B. C. . .	305,814	288,131	403,735	389,645	369,666	345,774	+17,683	—115,604	+14,090	+19,979
	Hindu A. B. C. . .	300,429	282,124	394,649	387,286	366,145	344,813	+18,305	—112,525	+7,363	+21,141
	Buddhist B. . .	4,842	4,609	6,104	1,334	. .	. .	+233	—1,495	+4,770	. .
44	Rajput, Total A. B. C. D. . .	2,351,650	1,853,025	1,566,274	1,784,402	1,747,989	1,648,426	+498,625	+286,751	—218,128	+36,413
	Hindu A. B. C. D. . .	577,374	499,251	358,705	422,592	390,230	350,901	+78,123	+140,546	—63,887	+32,362
	Sikh C. D. . .	49,594	30,013	23,863	17,419	18,598	17,143	+19,581	+6,150	+6,444	—1,179
	Muslim A. C. D. . .	1,718,532	1,320,998	1,181,026	1,342,221	1,335,535	1,276,286	+397,534	+139,972	—161,195	+6,686
45	Rathi, Total B. . .	134,093	118,015	97,763	37,973	100,656	82,957	+16,078	+20,252	+59,790	—62,683
	Hindu ,, . .	134,075	118,000	97,763	37,973	100,619	82,957	+16,075	+20,237	+59,790	—62,646
46	Saini, Total A. C. . .	157,301	120,376	107,759	121,722	120,507	147,183	+36,925	+12,617	—13,963	+1,215
	Hindu ,, . .	74,238	66,359	60,531	101,251	101,967	132,004	+7,879	+5,828	—40,720	—716
	Sikh ,, . .	82,965	52,888	46,846	20,376	17,960	14,458	+30,077	+6,042	+26,470	+2,416
47	Sansi, Total A. C. . .	28,262	17,402	24,439	26,000	22,218	19,929	+10,860	—7,037	—1,561	+3,782
	Hindu ,, . .	26,665	17,090	22,022	23,658	18,246	17,900	+9,575	—4,932	—1,636	+5,412
48	Sarera, Total B. C. . .	11,230	9,873	10,743	9,587	11,366	10,792	+1,357	—870	+1,156	—1,779
	Hindu ,, . .	7,022	8,426	9,391	9,094	10,768	10,209	—1,404	—965	+297	—1,674
	Sikh ,, . .	4,147	1,443	1,322	493	535	517	+2,704	+121	+829	—42
49	Sayad, Total A. C. D. . .	293,313	247,087	239,160	230,802	217,034	200,728	+46,226	+7,927	+8,358	+13,768
	Muslim ,, . .	293,302	247,087	239,160	230,802	217,032	200,706	+46,215	+7,927	+8,358	+13,770
50	Sheikh, Total A. C. D. . .	407,576	244,800	276,687	264,656	287,778	293,606	+162,776	—31,887	+12,031	—23,122
	Muslim ,, . .	407,554	244,800	276,687	264,656	286,305	293,565	+162,754	—31,887	+12,031	—21,649
51	Sunar, Total A. B. C. D. . .	159,655	127,090	155,993	174,628	164,087	145,903	+32,565	—28,903	—18,635	+10,541
	Hindu A. B. C. D. . .	99,026	77,251	100,718	127,111	118,114	108,878	+21,775	—23,467	—26,393	+8,997
	Sikh C. D. . .	25,366	19,067	27,222	18,856	17,236	13,600	+6,309	—8,165	+8,366	+1,620
	Muslim C. D. . .	32,394	28,798	26,153	26,656	26,841	21,335	+3,596	+2,645	—503	—185
52	Tarkhan, Total A. B. C. D. . .	654,053	614,912	637,971	675,361	621,718	564,385	+39,141	—23,059	—37,390	+53,643
	Hindu A. B. C. . .	146,727	161,833	162,305	233,934	215,561	213,070	—15,106	—472	—71,629	+18,373
	Sikh A. C. D. . .	158,446	139,327	180,447	146,904	134,110	113,067	+19,119	—41,120	+33,543	+12,794
	Muslim A. C. D. . .	346,829	312,125	294,677	293,243	270,191	236,440	+34,704	+17,448	+1,434	+23,052
53	Teli, Total A. C. D. . .	339,124	305,122	284,505	309,433	291,513	250,544	+34,002	+20,617	—24,928	+17,920
	Muslim	338,295	304,311	282,850	306,952	284,585	247,964	+33,984	+21,461	—24,102	+22,367

POPULATION OF SELECTED TRIBES.—*concluded.*

Variation. Increase +, Decrease – 1881 to 1891.	Net variation 1881 to 1931. Increase + Decrease –	Males. 1931.	1921.	1911.	1901.	1891.	1881.	Females. 1931.	1921.	1911.	1901.	1891.	1881.	Serial No.
12	13	14	15	16	17	18	19	20	21	22	23	24	25	
–67	–641	1;748	1,529	2,111	1,872	..	2,009	1,352	1,272	1,600	1,723	..	1,732	40
–476	–641	1,748	1,529	2,111	1,872	..	2,009	1,352	1,272	1,600	1,723	..	1,732	
+10,649	+134,825	190,943	143,234	154,424	134,893	..	116,026	154,495	118,495	118,123	111,897	..	94,587	41
+10,757	+134,923	190,923	143,234	154,424	134,893	..	115,915	154,479	118,495	118,123	111,897	..	94,564	
+10,864	+34,627	68,375	63,518	61,542	58,739	..	47,618	58,823	57,302	55,821	55,419	..	44,953	42
+16,841	+34,627	68,375	63,518	61,542	58,739	..	47,618	58,823	57,302	55,821	55,419	..	44,953	
+23,892	–39,960	157,598	148,732	207,160	202,519	..	182,060	148,216	139,399	196,575	187,126	..	163,714	43
+21,332	–44,384	154,909	145,756	202,720	201;321	..	181,553	145,520	136,368	191,929	185,965	..	163,260	
..	+4,842	2,403	2,274	2,903	655	..	..	2,439	2,335	3,201	679	..	..	
+99,563	+703,224	1,271,484	1,004,912	860,368	954,363	..	895,497	1,080,166	848,113	705,906	830,039	..	752,929	44
+39,329	+226,473	322,692	277,966	204,051	232,055	..	196,766	254,682	221,285	154,654	190,537	..	154,135	
+1,455	+32,451	27,933	16,722	13,606	9,661	..	9,807	21,661	13,291	10,257	7,758	..	7,330	
+59,249	+442,246	917,462	708,520	641,083	711,821	..	686,499	801,070	612,478	539,943	630,400	..	589,787	
+17,699	+51,136	67,266	59,705	51,094	19,444	..	43,594	66,827	58,220	46,669	18,529	..	39,303	45
+17,662	+51,118	67,255	59,787	51,094	19,444	..	43,594	66,820	58,213	46,669	18,529	..	39,303	
–26,676	+10,118	85,561	64,991	60,314	65,880	..	79,541	71,740	55,385	47,445	55,842	..	67,642	46
–30,037	–57,766	40,809	35,580	33,907	54,771	..	71,068	33,429	30,779	26,624	46,480	..	60,936	
+3,502	+68,507	44,696	28,960	26,131	11,059	..	8,076	38,269	23,928	20,715	9,317	..	6,382	
+2,289	+8,333	15,500	10,122	13,451	13,963	..	10,850	12,762	7,280	10,988	12,037	..	9,079	47
+256	+8,675	14,628	9,936	12,117	12,777	..	9,785	12,037	7,154	9,905	10,881	..	8,205	
+574	+438	5,980	5,361	5,779	5,083	..	5,582	5,250	4,512	4,964	4,504	..	5,210	48
+559	–3,187	3,760	4,629	5,032	4,832	..	5,271	3,262	3,797	4,359	4,262	..	4,938	
+18	+3,630	2,175	730	724	251	..	273	1,972	713	598	242	..	244	
+16,306	+92,585	157,824	131,755	127,350	119,464	..	105,627	135,489	115,332	111,810	111,338	..	95,101	49
+16,326	+92,596	157,818	131,755	127,350	119,464	..	105,609	135,484	115,332	111,810	111,338	..	95,097	
–5,828	+113,970	227,184	137,550	152,874	142,222	..	157,473	180,392	107,250	123,813	122,434	..	136,133	50
–7,260	+113,989	227,172	137,550	152,874	142,222	..	157,446	180,382	107,250	123,813	122,434	..	136,119	
+18,184	+13,752	86,391	68,980	84,301	93,435	..	78,374	73,264	58,110	71,692	81,193	..	67,529	51
+9,236	–9,852	53,763	42,347	54,893	68,547	..	58,225	45,263	34,904	45,825	58,564	..	50,653	
+3,636	+11,766	13,683	10,335	14,751	10,357	..	7,656	11,683	8,722	12,471	8,499	..	5,944	
+5,506	+11,059	17,440	15,263	13,611	13,632	..	11,377	14,954	13,535	12,542	13,024	..	9,958	
+57,333	+89,668	356,545	337,881	351,774	362,316	..	304,007	297,608	277,031	286,197	313,045	..	260,378	52
+2,491	–66,343	78,979	89,060	89,720	126,196	..	114,478	67,748	72,773	72,585	107,738	..	98,592	
+21,043	+45,379	87,891	77,610	101,013	79,501	..	62,159	70,555	61,717	79,434	67,403	..	50,008	
+33,751	+110,389	188,209	170,078	160,490	155,823	..	126,040	158,530	142,047	134,187	137,420	..	110,400	
+40,969	+88,580	185,077	165,810	156,251	165,347	..	134,024	154,047	139,312	128,254	144,086	..	116,520	53
+36,621	+90,331	184,552	165,288	155,250	164,011	..	132,631	153,743	139,023	127,600	142,941	..	115,333	

TABLE XIX.

EUROPEAN AND ALLIED RACES AND ANGLO-INDIANS BY RACE AND AGE.

1. This Table corresponds with Table XVI of 1921 and is divided into two parts. Part A, shows the distribution by Race and Age periods for the Districts and States of the Province. Part B, gives details for the Cities and Selected Towns only.

2. The statement below gives the Provincial totals of Armenians who have been included among European and Allied Races :—

Sex.	All ages.	0—13	14—16	17—23	24—33	34—43	44—53	54 and over.
Males	2	..	..	..	..	1	1	..
Females	2	..	..	..	1	..	1	..
Total ..	4	..	..	..	1	1	2	..

TABLE XIX.—PART A.—EUROPEAN AND ALLIED

Serial No.	District or State.	TOTAL. Persons.	TOTAL. Males.	TOTAL. Females.	A.—EUROPEAN AND ALLIED RACES (INCLUDING ARMENIANS). (a) British Subjects. All Ages. Persons.	All Ages. Males.	All Ages. Females.	0—13 Males.	0—13 Females.	14—16 Males.	14—16 Females.	17—23 Males.	17—23 Females.	24—33 Males.	24—33 Females.	34—43 Males.	34—43 Females.
		2	3	4	5	6	7	8	9	10	11	12	13	14	15	16	17
	PUNJAB ..	**23,724**	**17,029**	**6,695**	**19,523**	**14,597**	**4,926**	**1,841**	**1,348**	**230**	**226**	**4,198**	**483**	**5,857**	**1,242**	**1,735**	**901**
	BRITISH TERRITORY ..	**22,644**	**16,411**	**6,233**	**19,106**	**14,358**	**4,748**	**1,290**	**1,296**	**224**	**221**	**4,173**	**461**	**5,811**	**1,211**	**1,688**	**873**
	AMBALA DIVISION ..	**4,599**	**2,864**	**1,735**	**3,741**	**2,441**	**1,300**	**419**	**398**	**87**	**76**	**640**	**118**	**793**	**277**	**269**	**224**
1	Hissar	*55*	30	25	18	6	12	..	1	..	..	..	..	..	3	4	3
2	Rohtak	*35*	18	17	18	10	8	2	2	..	..	1	..	2	2	3	2
3	Gurgaon	*171*	81	90	79	41	38	7	7	2	..	4	3	6	12	9	7
4	Karnal	*36*	24	12	27	17	10	1	..	..	1	1	1	4	..	6	3
5	Ambala	*3,321*	2,248	1,073	2,885	2,021	864	339	305	77	64	630	82	723	192	154	129
6	Simla	*981*	463	518	714	346	368	70	78	8	11	4	32	58	68	93	80
	JULLUNDUR DIVISION	**3,161**	**2,473**	**688**	**2,992**	**2,386**	**606**	**181**	**174**	**11**	**34**	**709**	**72**	**903**	**175**	**248**	**92**
7	Kangra	*104*	52	52	69	37	32	6	6	..	..	2	1	11	9	7	9
8	Hoshiarpur	*4*	4	..	2	2	..	..	..	..	..	..	..	..	..	..	..
9	Jullundur	*1,211*	1,027	184	1,171	1,006	165	28	41	1	5	311	21	395	61	157	29
10	Ludhiana	*18*	14	4	16	13	3	5	1	1	..	...	..	2	..	5	1
11	Ferozepore	*1,824*	1,376	448	1,734	1,328	406	142	126	9	29	396	50	495	105	174	53
	LAHORE DIVISION ..	**8,905**	**6,621**	**2,284**	**7,520**	**5,662**	**1,858**	**423**	**517**	**93**	**86**	**1,514**	**182**	**2,507**	**453**	**658**	**325**
12	Lahore	*6,094*	4,349	1,745	4,907	3,488	1,419	224	385	44	68	855	149	1,549	315	412	248
13	Amritsar	*216*	180	36	192	164	28	..	..	35	7	25	6	40	12	64	3
14	Gurdaspur	*229*	109	120	182	83	99	26	30	2	3	5	5	17	24	18	23
15	Sialkot	*2,244*	1,931	313	2,200	1,905	295	162	95	11	7	629	21	898	99	160	49
16	Gujranwala	*67*	36	31	34	20	14	9	5	1	1	..	1	3	3	4	2
17	Sheikhupura	*55*	16	39	5	2	3	2	2	..	..	..	..	..	..	..	..
	RAWALPINDI DIVISION	**4,677**	**3,390**	**1,287**	**3,804**	**2,967**	**837**	**217**	**184**	**29**	**20**	**1,007**	**68**	**1,186**	**269**	**359**	**208**
18	Gujrat	*73*	40	33	49	26	23	4	6	..	1	..	2	9	6	6	5
19	Shahpur	*50*	27	23	49	26	23	..	..	..	..	3	2	11	8	8	11
20	Jhelum	*232*	137	95	184	112	72	23	18	4	7	8	13	28	16	24	10
21	Rawalpindi	*3,866*	2.848	1,018	3,169	2,519	650	166	136	24	12	890	48	1,028	224	289	162
22	Attock	*335*	261	74	289	242	47	8	16	..	..	105	3	106	12	18	11
23	Mianwali	*121*	77	44	64	42	22	16	8	1	..	1	5	5	3	14	4
	MULTAN DIVISION ..	**1,302**	**1,063**	**239**	**1,049**	**902**	**147**	**50**	**28**	**4**	**5**	**303**	**21**	**422**	**87**	**59**	**29**
24	Montgomery	*140*	101	45	89	61	28	14	2	3	..	3	4	13	6	13	6
25	Lyallpur	*70*	37	33	56	29	27	5	5	..	4	1	2	7	4	6	6
26	Jhang	*75*	41	34	2	1	1	..	..	..	..	..	..	..	..	1	1
27	Multan	*985*	868	117	889	802	87	30	21	1	1	298	15	398	25	38	15
28	Muzaffargarh ..	*16*	9	7	5	4	1	..	..	..	..	..	..	2	..	..	..
29	Dera Ghazi Khan ..	*10*	7	3	8	5	3	1	..	..	..	1	..	2	2	1	1
	PUNJAB STATES ..	**1,080**	**618**	**462**	**417**	**239**	**178**	**51**	**52**	**6**	**5**	**25**	**22**	**46**	**31**	**47**	**28**
	A.—HAVING POLITICAL RELATIONS WITH THE PUNJAB GOVERNMENT ..	**54**	**25**	**29**	**34**	**18**	**16**	**4**	**1**	**1**	..	**2**	**2**	**1**	**8**	**4**	**1**
1	Dujana	*4*	2	2	3	2	1	1	..	..	..	..	..	..	1	1	..
2	Pataudi	*3*	2	1	3	2	1	..	1	..	..	..	..	..	..	1	..
3	Kalsia	..	..	...	..	..	..	..	..	..	..	..	..	..	..	..	..
4	SIMLA HILL STATES ..	**47**	**21**	**26**	**28**	**14**	**14**	**3**	..	**1**	..	**2**	**2**	**1**	**7**	**2**	**1**
	Bashahr	*1*	1	..	..	..	..	..	..	..	..	..	..	..	..	..	..
	Nalagarh	..	..	..	..	..	..	..	..	..	..	..	..	..	..	..	..
	Keonthal	*21*	6	15	15	5	10	2	..	..	..	1	1	..	5	..	..
	Baghal	..	..	..	..	..	..	..	..	..	..	..	..	..	..	..	..
	Jubbal	..	..	..	..	..	..	..	..	..	..	..	..	..	..	..	..
	Other Simla Hill States ..	*25*	14	11	13	9	4	1	..	1	..	1	1	1	2	2	1
	B.—HAVING POLITICAL RELATIONS WITH THE GOVERNMENT OF INDIA ..	**1,026**	**593**	**433**	**383**	**221**	**162**	**47**	**51**	**5**	**5**	**23**	**20**	**45**	**23**	**43**	**27**
5	Loharu	*1*	..	1	1	..	1	..	..	..	..	..	1	..	..	..	..
6	Sirmoor	*7*	3	4	4	2	2	..	1	..	..	..	..	..	..	..	..
7	Bilaspur	..	..	..	..	..	..	..	..	..	..	..	..	..	..	..	..
8	Mandi	*141*	92	49	127	79	48	8	15	..	1	10	6	28	9	18	11
9	Suket	..	..	..	..	..	..	..	..	..	..	..	..	..	..	..	..
10	Kapurthala	*6*	3	3	6	3	3	..	..	..	..	..	2	..	..	1	..
11	Maler Kotla	*1*	1	..	1	1	..	..	..	..	..	1	..	..	..	..	..
12	Faridkot	*2*	1	1	2	1	1	..	..	..	1	..	..	..	..	..	..
13	Chamba	..	..	..	..	..	..	..	..	..	..	..	..	..	..	..	..
14	Patiala } Phulkian States ..	*242*	142	100	105	58	47	11	10	2	3	6	2	9	8	10	7
15	Jind } Phulkian States	*116*	63	53	74	42	32	18	12	3	..	3	5	2	2	5	6
16	Nabha } Phulkian States ..	..	..	..	..	..	..	..	..	..	..	..	..	..	..	..	..
17	Bahawalpur	*510*	288	222	63	35	28	10	13	..	..	3	4	6	4	9	3

A.—EUROPEAN AND ALLIED RACES (INCLUDING ARMENIANS)—(*concld*).																					
BRITISH SUBJECTS—(*concld*)				(b)—OTHERS.																	
44—53		54 and over.		All Ages.			0—13		14—16		17—23		24—33		34—43		44—53		54 and over.		
Males.	Females.	Males.	Females.	Persons.	Males.	Females.	Males.	Females.	Males.	Females.	Males.	Females.	Males.	Females.	Males.	Females.	Males.	Females.	Males.	Females.	Serial No.
18	19	20	21	22	23	24	25	26	27	28	29	30	31	32	33	34	35	36	37	38	
875	**440**	**361**	**286**	**576**	**251**	**325**	**33**	**47**	**4**	**8**	**24**	**29**	**70**	**95**	**60**	**77**	**37**	**39**	**23**	**30**	
842	**410**	**330**	**276**	**543**	**228**	**315**	**30**	**47**	**3**	**8**	**22**	**27**	**66**	**93**	**51**	**77**	**35**	**35**	**21**	**28**	
160	**97**	**78**	**115**	**70**	**36**	**34**	**4**	**3**	..	..	**8**	**2**	**13**	**12**	**4**	**9**	**6**	**1**	**6**	**7**	
2	2	..	3	4	1	3	..	..	..	..	..	..	..	2	..	1	1	..	..	..	1
2	1	..	1	2	..	2	..	..	..	..	..	..	..	2	..	..	..	..	..	..	2
8	5	5	4	..	..	..	..	..	..	..	..	..	..	..	..	..	..	..	..	..	3
4	1	1	4	1	1	..	..	..	..	..	..	..	..	..	1	..	..	..	..	..	4
61	43	37	49	31	15	16	2	2	..	..	1	2	8	5	1	5	2	1	1	1	5
83	45	30	54	32	19	13	2	1	..	..	2	..	5	3	2	3	3	..	5	6	6
162	**89**	**77**	**20**	**39**	**13**	**26**	..	**2**	..	**1**	**3**	**2**	**2**	**7**	**3**	**7**	**1**	**8**	**4**	**4**	
7	2	4	5	18	5	13	..	2	..	1	..	2	2	2	1	3	1	2	1	1	7
..	..	2	..	..	..	..	..	..	..	..	..	..	..	..	..	..	..	..	..	..	8
98	7	16	1	..	..	..	..	..	..	..	..	..	..	..	..	..	..	..	..	..	9
..	..	..	1	2	1	1	..	..	..	..	..	..	..	..	..	1	..	..	1	..	10
57	30	55	13	19	7	12	..	..	..	..	3	..	..	5	2	3	..	1	2	3	11
357	**192**	**110**	**103**	**214**	**90**	**124**	**16**	**19**	**1**	**4**	**7**	**17**	**16**	**25**	**25**	**25**	**19**	**24**	**6**	**10**	
308	169	96	85	146	63	83	12	16	..	4	3	10	12	17	19	15	12	15	5	6	12
..	..	..	..	..	..	..	..	..	..	..	..	..	..	..	..	..	..	..	..	..	13
10	7	5	7	25	13	12	2	2	1	..	2	3	2	2	4	4	2	1	..	..	14
37	14	8	10	23	8	15	1	..	..	..	2	4	2	4	1	2	2	4	..	1	15
2	1	1	1	..	..	..	..	..	..	..	..	..	..	..	..	..	..	..	..	..	16
..	1	..	..	20	6	14	1	1	..	..	..	..	..	2	1	4	3	4	1	3	17
122	**64**	**47**	**29**	**149**	**42**	**107**	**2**	**13**	..	**2**	**4**	**4**	**14**	**44**	**16**	**32**	**4**	**5**	**2**	**7**	
3	1	4	2	..	..	..	..	..	..	..	..	..	..	..	..	..	..	..	..	..	18
4	2	..	..	..	..	..	..	..	..	..	..	..	..	..	..	..	..	..	..	..	19
21	8	4	..	11	5	6	1	..	..	..	..	..	..	3	3	3	..	..	1	..	20
86	46	36	27	98	22	76	..	11	..	2	4	4	12	36	4	16	1	5	1	2	21
5	5	1	..	40	15	25	1	2	..	..	..	..	2	5	9	13	3	..	..	5	22
3	2	2	..	..	..	..	..	..	..	..	..	..	..	..	..	..	..	..	..	..	23
41	**18**	**23**	**9**	**71**	**47**	**24**	**8**	**10**	**2**	**1**	**5**	**2**	**21**	**5**	**3**	**4**	**5**	**2**	**3**	..	
13	7	2	3	20	15	5	2	..	..	..	1	..	8	1	2	2	2	2	..	..	24
5	4	5	2	..	..	..	..	..	..	..	..	..	..	..	..	..	..	..	..	..	25
..	..	..	..	48	29	19	5	10	2	1	4	2	12	4	1	2	2	..	3	..	26
22	7	15	3	3	3	..	1	..	..	..	..	..	1	..	..	..	1	..	..	..	27
1	..	1	1	..	..	..	..	..	..	..	..	..	..	..	..	..	..	..	..	..	28
..	..	..	..	..	..	..	..	..	..	..	..	..	..	..	..	..	..	..	..	..	29
33	**30**	**31**	**10**	**33**	**23**	**10**	**8**	..	**1**	..	**2**	**2**	**4**	**2**	**9**	..	**2**	**4**	**2**	**2**	
3	**4**	**3**	..	**6**	..	**6**	..	..	..	..	..	**1**	..	**1**	..	..	..	**3**	..	**1**	
..	..	..	..	1	..	1	..	..	..	..	..	1	..	..	..	..	..	..	..	..	1
..	..	1	..	..	..	..	..	..	..	..	..	..	..	..	..	..	..	..	..	..	2
..	..	..	..	..	..	..	..	..	..	..	..	..	..	..	..	..	..	..	..	..	3
3	**4**	**2**	..	**5**	..	**5**	..	..	..	..	..	..	..	**1**	..	..	..	**3**	..	**1**	4
..	..	..	..	..	..	..	..	..	..	..	..	..	..	..	..	..	..	..	..	..	
..	..	..	..	..	..	..	..	..	..	..	..	..	..	..	..	..	..	..	..	..	
..	4	2	..	..	..	..	..	..	..	..	..	..	..	..	..	..	..	..	..	..	
..	..	..	..	..	..	..	..	..	..	..	..	..	..	..	..	..	..	..	..	..	
..	..	..	..	..	..	..	..	..	..	..	..	..	..	..	..	..	..	..	..	..	
3	..	..	..	**5**	..	**5**	..	..	..	..	..	..	..	**1**	..	..	..	**3**	..	**1**	
30	**26**	**28**	**10**	**27**	**23**	**4**	**3**	..	**1**	..	**2**	**1**	**4**	**1**	**9**	..	**2**	**1**	**2**	**1**	
..	..	..	..	..	..	..	..	..	..	..	..	..	..	..	..	..	..	..	..	..	5
1	..	1	1	..	..	..	..	..	..	..	..	..	..	..	..	..	..	..	..	..	6
..	..	..	..	..	..	..	..	..	..	..	..	..	..	..	..	..	..	..	..	..	7
9	4	6	2	14	13	1	..	..	..	..	..	..	4	1	8	..	1	..	..	..	8
..	..	..	..	..	..	..	..	..	..	..	..	..	..	..	..	..	..	..	..	..	9
..	1	2	..	..	..	..	..	..	..	..	..	..	..	..	..	..	..	..	..	..	10
..	..	..	..	..	..	..	..	..	..	..	..	..	..	..	..	..	..	..	..	..	11
..	..	1	..	..	..	..	..	..	..	..	..	..	..	..	..	..	..	..	..	..	12
..	..	..	..	..	..	..	..	..	..	..	..	..	..	..	..	..	..	..	..	..	13
10	15	10	2	6	5	1	1	..	1	..	2	..	..	..	..	..	..	1	1	..	14
7	4	4	3	7	5	2	2	..	..	..	..	1	..	..	1	..	1	..	1	1	15
..	..	..	..	..	..	..	..	..	..	..	..	..	..	..	..	..	..	..	..	..	16
3	2	4	2	..	..	..	..	..	..	..	..	..	..	..	..	..	..	..	..	..	17

TABLE XIX.—PART A.—EUROPEAN AND ALLIED RACES AND ANGLO-INDIANS BY RACE AND AGE—*continued.*

B.—ANGLO-INDIANS.

Serial No.	District or State.	All Ages.			0—3		4—6		7—13		14—16		17—19		20—29		30—39		40—49		50—59		60—69		70 and over	
		Persons.	Males.	Females.	Males.	Females.	Males.	Females.	Males.	Females.	Males.	Females.	Males.	Females.	Males.	Females.	Males.	Females.	Males.	Females.	Males.	Females.	Males.	Females.	Males.	Females.
1	2	39	40	41	42	43	44	45	46	47	48	49	50	51	52	53	54	55	56	57	58	59	60	61	62	63
	PUNJAB	3,625	2,181	1,444	245	206	164	130	292	200	150	93	142	101	373	265	339	207	237	119	143	65	60	40	36	1
	BRITISH TERRITORY ..	2,995	1,825	1,170	176	143	135	112	257	169	134	73	124	77	303	214	299	173	206	101	116	54	47	37	28	1
	AMBALA DIVISION ..	788	387	401	35	48	32	35	71	80	45	29	19	24	46	67	42	54	45	24	30	18	18	15	4	
1	Hissar	*33*	23	10	3	2	3	..	2	..	..	..	..	1	6	4	4	1	1	2	1	..	3	..	..	
2	Rohtak	*15*	8	7	1	..	..	..	4	3	2	2	..	1	..	..	..	1	1	..	..	..	..	..	..	
3	Gurgaon	*92*	40	52	5	9	8	7	5	8	1	[illegible]	1	4	6	9	7	7	6	2	1	1	..	1	..	
4	Karnal	*8*	6	2	..	..	..	..	..	1	1	..	1	..	1	..	..	..	2	1	1	..	..	..	..	
5	Ambala	*405*	212	193	15	22	11	15	41	45	34	17	13	10	20	28	19	23	26	12	15	9	14	8	4	
6	Simla	*235*	98	137	11	15	10	13	19	23	7	7	4	8	13	26	12	22	9	7	12	8	1	6	..	
	JULLUNDUR DIVISION	130	74	56	9	6	9	6	6	7	2	2	3	3	7	11	12	7	11	7	7	3	4	3	4	
7	Kangra	*17*	10	7	..	..	1	..	2	1	..	1	..	..	..	2	..	2	4	1	2	..	..	..	1	
8	Hoshiarpur	*2*	2	..	..	..	..	..	..	..	..	..	..	..	..	..	..	..	..	..	1	..	..	..	1	
9	Jullundur	*40*	21	19	4	3	4	3	..	2	..	1	..	1	1	3	6	1	3	2	1	1	1	2	1	
10	Ludhiana	..	..	..	..	..	..	..	..	..	..	..	..	..	..	..	..	..	..	..	..	..	..	..	..	
11	Ferozepore	*71*	41	30	5	3	4	3	4	4	2	..	3	2	6	6	6	4	4	4	3	2	3	1	1	
	LAHORE DIVISION ..	1,171	869	302	74	18	47	38	114	25	61	21	72	19	168	52	155	57	89	39	58	17	19	[illegible]	17	
12	Lahore	*1,041*	798	243	70	12	44	31	104	22	61	15	66	18	154	42	137	46	82	29	46	13	19	10	15	
13	Amritsar	*24*	16	8	..	..	1	2	3	..	..	1	3	..	2	4	4	..	..	1	3	..	..	..	..	
14	Gurdaspur	*22*	13	9	..	..	..	..	1	1	..	..	1	1	4	2	3	1	1	3	2	1	..	..	1	
15	Sialkot	*21*	18	3	1	1	2	..	3	1	..	..	1	..	3	1	5	..	2	..	..	..	..	..	1	
16	Gujranwala	*33*	16	17	2	2	..	3	2	1	..	..	1	..	4	3	5	4	2	3	..	..	..	..	..	
17	Sheikhupura	*30*	8	22	1	3	..	2	1	..	..	5	..	..	1	..	1	6	2	3	2	3	..	..	..	
	RAWALPINDI DIVISION	724	381	343	45	56	32	27	50	44	20	19	26	24	71	73	67	47	46	30	17	14	6	7	1	
18	Gujrat	*24*	14	10	3	1	1	3	1	2	2	..	1	..	1	..	2	4	3	..	..	..	..	..	..	
19	Shahpur	*1*	1	..	..	..	..	..	..	..	..	..	..	..	..	..	1	..	..	..	..	..	..	..	..	
20	Jhelum	*37*	20	17	2	2	2	1	2	2	3	2	2	2	4	4	1	..	3	4	1	..	..	..	..	
21	Rawalpindi	*599*	307	292	37	48	25	22	39	37	13	17	23	21	62	64	54	39	31	24	16	12	6	6	1	
22	Attock	*6*	4	2	..	..	..	..	..	..	1	..	..	..	2	1	1	..	..	..	..	1	..	..	..	
23	Mianwali	*57*	35	22	3	5	4	1	8	3	1	..	..	1	2	4	8	4	9	2	..	1	..	1	..	
	MULTAN DIVISION ..	182	114	68	13	15	15	6	16	13	6	2	4	7	11	11	23	8	15	1	9	2	..	2	2	
24	Montgomery	*37*	25	12	3	2	5	2	3	1	3	..	1	1	2	2	7	2	1	..	..	1	..	1	..	
25	Lyallpur	*14*	8	6	..	2	..	..	1	1	..	..	..	1	2	2	4	..	..	..	1	..	..	..	..	
26	Jhang	*25*	11	14	1	3	..	..	4	6	1	..	..	1	..	3	1	1	3	..	..	..	..	..	1	
27	Multan	*93*	63	30	8	8	10	3	7	5	2	1	3	3	7	3	10	4	10	..	5	1	..	1	1	
28	Muzaffargarh	*11*	5	6	1	..	..	1	1	..	..	1	..	1	..	1	1	1	1	1	1	..	..	..	..	
29	Dera Ghazi Khan ..	*2*	2	..	..	..	..	..	..	..	..	..	..	..	..	..	..	..	..	..	2	..	..	..	..	
	PUNJAB STATES ..	630	356	274	69	63	29	18	35	31	16	20	18	24	70	51	40	34	31	18	27	11	13	3	8	1
	A.—Having Political relations with the Punjab Government. ..	14	7	7	1	..	..	..	..	3	..	2	1	1	..	..	2	1	1	..	1	..	..	..	1	..
1	Dujana	..	..	..	..	..	..	..	..	..	..	..	..	..	..	..	..	..	..	..	..	..	..	..	..	..
2	Pataudi	..	..	..	..	..	..	..	..	..	..	..	..	..	..	..	..	..	..	..	..	..	..	..	..	..
3	Kalsia	..	..	..	..	..	..	..	..	..	..	..	..	..	..	..	..	..	..	..	..	..	..	..	..	..
4	SIMLA HILL STATES .	14	7	7	1	..	..	..	..	3	..	2	1	1	..	..	2	1	1	..	1	..	..	..	1	..
	Bashahr	*1*	1	..	..	..	..	..	..	..	..	..	..	..	..	..	1	..	..	..	..	..	..	..	..	..
	Nalagarh	..	..	..	..	..	..	..	..	..	..	..	..	..	..	..	..	..	..	..	..	..	..	..	..	..
	Keonthal	*6*	1	5	..	..	..	..	..	2	..	1	..	1	..	..	..	1	..	..	1	..	..	..	..	..
	Baghal	..	..	..	..	..	..	..	..	..	..	..	..	..	..	..	..	..	..	..	..	..	..	..	..	..
	Jubbal	..	..	..	..	..	..	..	..	..	..	..	..	..	..	..	..	..	..	..	..	..	..	..	..	..
	Other Simla Hill States ..	*7*	5	2	1	..	..	..	..	1	..	1	1	..	..	..	1	..	1	..	..	..	..	..	1	..
	B.- Having Political relations with the Government of India...	616	349	267	68	63	29	18	35	28	16	18	17	23	70	51	38	33	30	18	26	11	13	3	7	1
5	Loharu	..	..	..	..	..	..	..	..	..	..	..	..	..	..	..	..	..	..	..	..	..	..	..	..	..
6	Sirmoor	*3*	1	2	..	1	..	..	..	..	..	..	..	..	..	..	..	1	..	..	1	..	..	..	..	..
7	Bilaspur	..	..	..	..	..	..	..	..	..	..	..	..	..	..	..	..	..	..	..	..	..	..	..	..	..
8	Mandi	..	..	..	..	..	..	..	..	..	..	..	..	..	..	..	..	..	..	..	..	..	..	..	..	..
9	Suket	..	..	..	..	..	..	..	..	..	..	..	..	..	..	..	..	..	..	..	..	..	..	..	..	..
10	Kapurthala	..	..	..	..	..	..	..	..	..	..	..	..	..	..	..	..	..	..	..	..	..	..	..	..	..
11	Maler Kotla	..	..	..	..	..	..	..	..	..	..	..	..	..	..	..	..	..	..	..	..	..	..	..	..	..
12	Faridkot	..	..	..	..	..	..	..	..	..	..	..	..	..	..	..	..	..	..	..	..	..	..	..	..	..
13	Chamba	..	..	..	..	..	..	..	..	..	..	..	..	..	..	..	..	..	..	..	..	..	..	..	..	..
14	Patiala (Phulkian States) ..	*131*	79	52	9	5	7	5	16	6	1	6	8	7	9	5	6	8	9	6	10	3	3	1	1	..
15	Jind (Phulkian States) ..	*35*	16	19	2	2	2	2	4	7	..	1	..	1	3	4	2	..	1	2	2	..	..	..	..	..
16	Nabha (Phulkian States) ..	..	..	..	..	..	..	..	..	..	..	..	..	..	..	..	..	..	..	..	..	..	..	..	..	..
17	Bahawalpur	*447*	253	194	57	55	20	11	15	15	15	11	9	15	58	42	30	24	20	10	13	8	10	2	6	1

TABLE XIX.—PART B.—EUROPEAN AND ALLIED RACES AND ANGLO-INDIANS BY RACE AND AGE.—*concluded.*

A.—EUROPEAN AND ALLIED RACES (INCLUDING ARMENIANS)—(*contd*).

Cities and Selected Towns including Cantonments.	TOTAL.			(a) British Subjects. All Ages.			0—13		14—16		17—23		24—33		34—43	
	Persons.	Males.	Females.	Persons.	Males.	Females.	Males.	Females.	Males.	Females.	Males.	Females.	Males.	Females.	Males.	Females.
1	2	3	4	5	6	7	8	9	10	11	12	13	14	15	16	17
Lahore	6,090	4,347	1,743	4,907	3,488	1,419	224	385	44	68	855	149	1,549	315	412	248
Amritsar	215	179	36	191	163	28	..	..	35	7	25	6	40	12	63	3
Multan	985	868	117	889	802	87	30	21	1	1	298	15	398	25	38	15
Rawalpindi	3,775	2,797	978	3,100	2,476	624	163	130	24	12	887	43	1,018	216	277	153
Sialkot	2,199	1,912	287	2,177	1,895	282	160	92	11	6	629	18	895	96	159	46
Ambala	2,369	1,760	609	2,136	1,653	483	155	151	13	16	582	43	694	134	139	80
Jullundur	1,154	981	173	1,114	960	154	25	41	..	4	286	17	391	59	147	26
Ferozepore	1,684	1,301	383	1,631	1,271	300	126	117	5	28	392	37	481	95	164	46

Cities and Selected Towns including Cantonments.	(a) British Subjects (contd). 44—53		54 and over.		(b) Others—(contd). All ages.			0—13		14—16		17—23		24—33	
	Males.	Females.	Males.	Females.	Persons.	Males.	Females.	Males.	Females.	Males.	Females.	Males.	Females.	Males.	Females.
1	18	19	20	21	22	23	24	25	26	27	28	29	30	31	32
Lahore	308	169	96	85	146	63	83	12	16	..	4	3	10	12	17
Amritsar	..	..	..	..	..	..	..	..	..	..	..	..	..	.	..
Multan	22	7	15	3	3	3	..	1	..	..	..	..	..	1	..
Rawalpindi	73	45	34	25	89	22	67	..	10	..	2	4	4	12	33
Sialkot	33	14	8	10	3	1	2	..	..	..	..	..	..	..	2
Ambala	42	23	28	37	25	11	14	2	2	..	..	..	2	7	5
Jullundur	95	6	16	1	..	..	..	..	..	..	..	..	..	..	..
Ferozepore	50	25	53	12	14	7	7	..	..	..	..	3	..	..	4

A.—EUROPEAN AND ALLIED RACES (INCLUDING ARMENIANS)—(*concld*). (b). Others—(*concld*).

B.—ANGLO-INDIANS.

Cities and Selected Towns including Cantonments.	A (b) Others (concld). 34—43		44—53		54 and over.		B.—Anglo-Indians. All Ages.			0—3		4—6		7—13		14—16	
	Males.	Females.	Males.	Females.	Males.	Females.	Persons.	Males.	Females.	Males.	Females.	Males.	Females.	Males.	Females.	Males.	Females.
1	33	34	35	36	37	38	39	40	41	42	43	44	45	46	47	48	49
Lahore	19	15	12	15	5	6	1,037	796	241	70	12	44	31	104	22	61	14
Amritsar	..	..	..	..	..	..	24	16	8	..	..	1	2	3	..	..	1
Multan	..	..	1	.	..	..	93	63	30	8	8	10	3	7	5	2	1
Rawalpindi	4	13	1	4	1	1	586	299	287	37	47	24	22	38	37	13	17
Sialkot	..	.	1	..	.	..	19	16	3	1	1	2	..	3	1	..	..
Ambala	1	4	..	1	1	..	208	96	112	11	16	6	8	10	23	9	5
Jullundur	..	..	..	..	..	.	40	21	19	4	3	4	3	..	2	..	1
Ferozepore	2	2	..	1	2	..	39	23	16	2	..	1	..	3	2	2	..

Cities and Selected Towns including Cantonments.	17—19		20—29		30—39		40—49		50—59		60—69		70 and over.	
	Males.	Females.	Males.	Females.	Males.	Females.	Males.	Females.	Males.	Females.	Males.	Females.	Males.	Females.
1	50	51	52	53	54	55	56	57	58	59	60	61	62	63
Lahore	65	18	154	42	137	46	82	29	45	13	19	9	15	5
Amritsar	3	..	2	4	4	..	..	1	3	..	..	..	..	..
Multan	3	3	7	3	10	4	10	..	5	1	..	1	1	1
Rawalpindi	22	21	62	62	50	39	31	24	16	10	5	6	1	2
Sialkot	1	.	1	1	5	..	2	..	..	..	..	..	1	..
Ambala	5	3	8	17	10	14	12	7	11	7	11	8	3	4
Jullundur	..	1	1	3	6	1	3	2	1	1	1	2	1	..
Ferozepore	2	1	3	3	3	4	3	2	..	2	3	1	1	1

PROVINCIAL TABLE I.

AREA AND POPULATION OF TAHSILS.

1. The figures of area have been taken from the Revenue Records as survey figures are not available by Tahsils. The totals of these figures, therefore, do not agree with the figures of Imperial Table I which are based on the survey data.

2. The difference, between some of the areas shown in this Table and those given in the corresponding Table of 1921, is due to remeasurement or territorial transfers. The details of transfers whether inter-district or provincial, which affect the areas of Districts, are shown on the fly-leaf to Imperial Table I. Some changes have, however, taken place during the decade inside the Districts, affecting certain Tahsils, as mentioned below :—

a. In the Sialkot District, Zafarwal and Raya have ceased to be Tahsils, while a new Tahsil called Narowal has been formed.

b. In the Sheikhupura District, three new Tahsils, Sheikhupura, Shahdara and Nankana Sahib, have been formed out of the Khangah Dogran and Sharakpur Tahsils, and the area transferred from the Lyallpur District.

c. In the Muzaffargarh District, Sanawan Tahsil has been abolished, while a new Tahsil called Kot Adu has been formed.

d. In Mandi State, Harbhag Tahsil has been abolished, and another called Jogindernagar has been formed.

e. In Suket State, portions have been taken out of Bhal and Karsog Tahsils to form the new Dehar Tahsil.

f. In Kapurthala State, the Bastiat Tahsil has ceased to exist, having been amalgamated with the Kapurthala Tahsil.

g. In Fridkot State, Kot Kapura Tahsil has ceased to exist.

h. In Nabha State, the Tahsil of that name has been added to the Amloh Tahsil ; while Jaitu and Dhanaula Tahsils have been added to the Phul Tahsil of the same State.

i. In Bahawalpur State, Naushehra Tahsil has given place to one named Rahim Yar Khan.

The changes that have altered the area of certain Tahsils are given below :—

FROM WHICH TRANSFERRED.		TO WHICH TRANSFERRED.		Area in square miles.	Notification No.	Date.
District.	Tahsil.	District.	Tahsil.			
Hissar ..	Fatehabad ..	Hissar ..	Hissar ..	258	41- -352 Boundaries, 1—2—4,402	3-4-23
Sialkot ..	Sialkot ..	Sialkot ..	Daska ..	39	41—350—11,207 ..	1-12-22
Sialkot ..	Pasrur ..	Sialkot ..	Daska ..	71	41—350—11,207 ..	1-12-22
Sialkot ..	Zafarwal ..	Sialkot ..	Narowal ..	116	41—350—11,205 ..	1-12-22
Sialkot ..	Raya ..	Sialkot ..	Narowal ..	266	41—350—11,205 ..	1-12-22
Sialkot ..	Pasrur ..	Sialkot ..	Narowal ..	30	41—350—11,205 ..	1-12-22
Sialkot ..	Zafarwal ..	Sialkot ..	Pasrur ..	191	41—350—11,206 ..	1-12-22
Lyallpur ..	Lyallpur ..	Lyallpur ..	Jaranwala ..	188	41—343—950 ..	12-1-23
Lyallpur ..	Jaranwala ..	Lyallpur ..	Samundri ..	10	16,189 ..	31-5-21
Lyallpur ..	Jaranwala	Lyallpur ..	Lyallpur ..	4	41—343—950 ..	12-1-23
Suket ..	Karsog ..	Suket ..	Dehar ..	95	By Durbar Order ..	
Suket ..	Bhal ..	Suket ..	Dehar ..	13	By Durbar Order ..	
Kapurthala ..	Sultanpur ..	Kapurthala ..	Kapurthala ..	4.5	Sadar Order ..	6-12-21
Kapurthala ..	Bholath ..	Kapurthala ..	Kapurthala ..	8	Sadar Order ..	8-4-24
Kapurthala ..	Kapurthala ..	Kapurthala ..	Sultanpur ..	2.5	Sadar Order ..	6-12-21
Kapurthala ..	Bastiat ..	Kapurthala ..	Kapurthala ..	1	Sadar Order ..	6-12-21
Bahawalpur ..	Bahawalnagar ..	Bahawalpur ..	Minchinabad ..	347	By order of Council of Regency.	11-11-22
Bahawalpur..	Minchinabad ..	Bahawalpur ..	Bahawalnagar ..	254	By order of Council of Regency.	11-11-22

PROVINCIAL TABLE I.—AREA AND POPULATION OF TAHSILS.

Tahsil.	Area in square miles.	Number of Towns.	Number of Villages.	Number of occupied houses.	Population 1931 Persons.	Population 1931 Males.	Population 1931 Females.	Population 1921 (both sexes).	Percentage of variation 1921 to 1931.	Percentage of variation 1911 to 1921.	Number of persons per square mile in 1931.
1	2	3	4	5	6	7	8	9	10	11	12
PUNJAB ..	**120,778**	**222**	**50,691**	**5,943,652**	**28,490,857**	**15,561,194**	**12,929,663**	**25,101,514**	**+13·5**	**+5·5**	**236**
BRITISH TERRITORY ..	**91,747**	**177**	**34,630**	**4,894,035**	**23,580,852**	**12,880,510**	**10,700,342**	**20,685,478**	**+14·0**	**+5·7**	**257**
HISSAR DISTRICT ..	**5,184**	**6**	**963**	**177,076**	**899,479**	**485,690**	**413,789**	**816,810**	**+10·1**	**+1·5**	**174**
Hissar ..	1,071	3	221	42,181	213,643	117,331	96,312	190,452	+12·2	+7·5	199
Hansi ..	803	1	129	38,872	192,810	103,468	89,342	177,043	+8·9	+5·4	240
Bhiwani ..	752	1	131	26,504	138,211	73,401	64,810	126,015	+9·7	+5·8	184
Fatehabad ..	919	..	173	29,782	152,259	81,386	70,873	141,621	+7·5	+14·0	166
Sirsa ..	1,639	1	309	39,737	202,556	110,104	92,452	181,679	+11·5	—4·9	124
ROHTAK DISTRICT ..	**2,246**	**7**	**722**	**158,522**	**805,621**	**432,855**	**372,766**	**772,272**	**+4·3**	**+8·0**	**359**
Rohtak ..	517	1	125	40,969	220,803	121,895	98,908	200,939	+9·9	+12·7	427
Jhajjar ..	728	3	255	43,093	228,055	119,840	108,215	213,866	+6·6	+5·9	313
Gohana ..	553	2	115	36,126	177,014	94,044	82,970	175,291	+1·0	+8·8	320
Sonepat ..	448	1	227	37,734	179,749	97,076	82,673	182,176	—1·3	+5·1	401
GURGAON DISTRICT ..	**2,216**	**8**	**1,358**	**157,736**	**740,163**	**398,513**	**341,650**	**682,361**	**+8·5**	**—6·6**	**334**
Gurgaon ..	411	2	210	24,411	119,751	64,656	55,095	111,980	+6·9	—·3	291
Firozpur-Jhirka ..	314	1	231	24,270	108,687	58,181	50,506	98,285	+10·6	—14·2	346
Nuh ..	402	..	258	26,381	124,578	66,947	57,631	112,119	+11·1	—12·8	310
Palwal ..	382	2	186	31,535	144,726	78,814	65,912	131,760	+9·8	—3·5	379
Rewari ..	423	1	289	32,438	158,880	84,205	74,675	147,256	+7·9	—2·5	376
Ballabgarh ..	284	2	184	18,701	83,541	45,710	37,831	80,961	+3·2	—7·0	294
KARNAL DISTRICT ..	**3,146**	**6**	**1,380**	**185,560**	**852,614**	**469,870**	**382,744**	**828,822**	**+2·9**	**+3·5**	**271**
Karnal ..	856	2	385	54,078	247,637	136,357	111,280	232,703	+6·4	+2·6	289
Panipat ..	460	1	168	38,662	173,968	95,492	78,476	173,796	+·1	+1·3	378
Kaithal ..	1,273	1	414	59,157	278,903	153,791	125,112	275,722	+1·2	+9·9	219
Thanesar ..	557	2	413	33,663	152,106	84,230	67,876	146,601	+3·8	—3·4	273
AMBALA DISTRICT ..	**1,870**	**8**	**1,723**	**171,248**	**742,902**	**416,411**	**326,491**	**681,477**	**+9·0**	**—1·4**	**397**
Ambala ..	369	1	292	47,252	202,525	115,006	87,519	187,926	+7·8	—3·8	549
Kharar ..	373	3	375	35,643	155,530	88,560	66,970	142,894	+8·8	+6·5	417
Jagadhri ..	405	2	378	33,064	137,785	76,489	61,296	126,704	+8·7	—9·7	340
Naraingarh ..	436	1	318	26,207	115,460	63,309	52,151	107,798	+7·1	—4·1	265
Rupar ..	287	1	360	29,082	131,602	73,047	58,555	116,155	+13·3	+7·0	459
SIMLA DISTRICT ..	**81**	**5**	**202**	**11,271**	**36,786**	**23,517**	**13,269**	**45,327**	**-18·8**	**+17·9**	**454**
Simla ..	49	5	92	9,310	25,846	18,083	7,763	35,003	—26·2	+26·9	527
Kot Khai ..	32	..	110	1,961	10,940	5,434	5,506	10,324	+6·0	—4·8	342
KANGRA DISTRICT ..	**3,882**	**1**	**713**	**177,159**	**801,312**	**415,288**	**386,024**	**766,065**	**+4·6**	**—·6**	**206**
Kangra ..	422	1	132	26,273	122,527	64,843	57,684	118,374	+3·5	—1·0	290
Dehra ..	495	..	145	29,199	127,251	66,655	60,596	124,638	+2·1	—1·5	257
Nurpur ..	519	..	192	21,440	98,394	55,362	43,032	95,470	+3·1	—4·6	190
Hamirpur ..	590	..	64	39,739	177,199	89,354	87,845	168,504	+5·2	+1·1	300
Palampur ..	521	..	113	32,768	144,516	73,546	70,970	137,052	+5·4	+3·3	277
Kulu ..	1,335	..	67	27,740	131,425	65,528	65,897	122,027	+7·7	—2·2	98
HOSHIARPUR DISTRICT ..	**2,211**	**6**	**2,099**	**233,614**	**1,032,187**	**551,867**	**480,320**	**927,419**	**+11·3**	**+1·0**	**467**
Hoshiarpur ..	509	2	489	60,875	278,829	149,345	129,484	247,196	+12·8	+2·6	548
Dasuya ..	501	2	622	52,126	238,468	128,974	109,494	215,600	+10·6	+3·2	476
Garhshankar ..	511	1	464	60,074	259,403	140,131	119,272	232,772	+11·4	—1·7	508
Una ..	690	1	524	60,539	255,487	133,417	122,070	231,851	+10·2	—·0	370
JULLUNDUR DISTRICT	**1,842**	**8**	**1,210**	**184,728**	**943,721**	**512,667**	**431,054**	**822,544**	**+14·7**	**+2·6**	**703**
Jullundur ..	389	2	402	58,347	347,123	189,533	157,590	289,396	+19·9	+4·1	892
Nawashahr ..	299	3	272	43,002	200,333	108,014	92,319	177,692	+12·7	+4·0	670
Phillaur ..	289	2	223	38,588	190,316	104,710	85,606	164,806	+15·5	+·9	659
Nakodar ..	365	1	313	44,791	205,949	110,410	95,539	190,650	+8·0	+·4	564
LUDHIANA DISTRICT	**1,396**	**4**	**851**	**144,598**	**672,494**	**375,560**	**296,934**	**567,622**	**+18·5**	**+9·8**	**482**
Ludhiana ..	686	1	429	75,708	335,302	185,569	149,733	285,953	+17·3	+10·7	489
Jagraon ..	419	2	165	39,798	204,344	114,589	89,755	164,553	+24·2	+12·2	488
Sambala ..	291	1	257	29,092	132,848	75,402	57,446	117,116	+13·4	+4·4	457

PROVINCIAL TABLE I.—AREA AND POPULATION OF TAHSILS.—*continued.*

Tahsil.	Area in square miles.	Number of		Number of occupied houses.	Population.				Percentage of variation.		Number of persons per square mile in 1931.
		Towns.	Villages.		1931. Persons.	Males.	Females.	1921 (both sexes).	1921 to 1931.	1911 to 1921.	
1	2	3	4	5	6	7	8	9	10	11	12
FEROZEPORE DISTRICT ..	**4,072**	**10**	**1,507**	**236,160**	**1,156,732**	**636,256**	**520,476**	**1,098,866**	**+5·3**	**+14·4**	**284**
Ferozepore ..	680	1	361	51,784	240,326	135,736	104,590	222,355	+8·1	+8·5	353
Zira ..	495	2	344	37,530	176,219	95,083	81,136	166,373	+5·9	+6·9	356
Moga ..	625	1	167	48,343	223,975	121,580	102,395	209,558	+6·9	+9·9	358
Muktsar ..	934	4	318	44,636	224,075	124,094	99,981	209,645	+6·9	+16·4	240
Fazilka ..	1,338	2	317	53,867	292,137	159,763	132,374	290,935	+ ·4	+27·1	218
LAHORE DISTRICT ..	**2,598**	**8**	**1,121**	**290,740**	**1,378,570**	**794,389**	**584,181**	**1,129,839**	**+22·0**	**+13·0**	**531**
Lahore ..	664	3	319	147,606	693,521	420,317	273,204	515,809	+34·5	+17·8	1,044
Chunian ..	1,126	2	465	69,541	329,483	179,769	149,714	294,434	+11·9	+7·8	293
Kasur ..	808	3	337	73,593	355,566	194,303	161,263	319,596	+11·3	+10·7	440
AMRITSAR DISTRICT ..	**1,560**	**5**	**1,036**	**212,771**	**1,117,120**	**621,040**	**496,080**	**929,374**	**+20·2**	**+5·5**	**716**
Amritsar ..	546	4	369	104,484	594,410	338,539	255,871	450,760	+31·9	+6·0	1,089
Tarn Taran ..	597	1	340	68,001	392,256	174,172	148,084	294,465	+9·4	+8·3	540
Ajnala ..	417	..	327	40,286	200,454	108,329	92,125	184,149	+8·9	+·3	481
GURDASPUR DISTRICT ..	**1,827**	**9**	**2,243**	**193,676**	**970,898**	**531,935**	**438,963**	**852,192**	**+13·9**	**+1·8**	**531**
Gurdaspur ..	497	3	656	53,158	263,727	146,215	117,512	234,146	+12·6	+4·3	531
Batala ..	477	2	480	61,846	320,349	175,225	145,124	275,695	+16·2	+2·2	672
Pathankot ..	366	4	402	30,134	139,459	79,191	60,268	129,502	+7·7	—2·0	381
Shakargarh ..	487	..	705	48,538	247,363	131,304	116,059	212,849	+16·2	+1·1	508
SIALKOT DISTRICT ..	**1,569**	**6**	**2,066**	**186,758**	**979,617**	**537,301**	**442,316**	**877,867**	**+11·6**	**+·7**	**624**
Sialkot ..	389	1	586	56,247	308,461	171,517	136,944	266,362	+15·8	+2·5	793
Pasrur ..	378	2	559	44,131	217,055	117,552	99,503	195,111	—11·2	—5·4	574
Narowal ..	408	1	557	45,495	230,980	125,860	105,120	212,627	+8·6	+·8	566
Daska ..	394	2	364	40,885	223,121	122,372	100,749	203,767	+9·5	+2·0	566
GUJRANWALA DISTRICT ..	**2,302**	**7**	**1,219**	**148,857**	**736,138**	**408,606**	**327,532**	**623,581**	**+18·1**	**+3·0**	**320**
Gujranwala ..	936	2	562	72,308	361,000	201,093	159,907	294,567	+22·6	+10·5	386
Wazirabad ..	458	3	254	34,545	163,668	90,345	73,323	146,248	+11·9	—1·8	357
Hafizabad ..	908	2	403	42,004	211,470	117,168	94,302	182,766	+15·7	—3·8	233
SHEIKHUPURA DISTRICT ..	**2,312**	**5**	**1,031**	**135,510**	**696,732**	**384,390**	**312,342**	**634,584**	**+9·8**	**+17·4**	**301**
Sheikhupura ..	880	2	252	58,991	313,978	173,957	140,021	267,674	+17·3	+20·3	357
Nankana Sahib ..	689	1	348	37,882	194,225	106,102	88,123	156,351	+24·2	+10·0	282
Shahdara ..	743	2	431	38,637	188,529	104,331	84,198	210,559	- 10·5	+19·4	254
GUJRAT DISTRICT ..	**2,278**	**5**	**1,440**	**203,660**	**922,427**	**498,336**	**424,091**	**824,046**	**+11·9**	**+4·6**	**405**
Gujrat ..	570	3	512	67,919	316,370	169,520	146,850	295,551	+7·0	—3·0	555
Kharian ..	671	1	508	64,315	275,947	145,900	130,047	250,201	+10·3	—5·7	411
Phalia ..	1,037	1	420	71,426	330,110	182,916	147,194	278,294	+18·6	+27·7	318
SHAHPUR DISTRICT ..	**4,799**	**13**	**973**	**171,922**	**821,490**	**445,836**	**375,654**	**719,918**	**+14·1**	**+11·6**	**171**
Shahpur ..	610	4	246	35,247	155,908	84,277	71,631	137,899	+13·1	- 2·7	256
Khushab ..	2,534	3	161	44,259	193,393	99,077	94,316	168,718	+14·6	- 4·0	76
Bhalwal ..	821	4	276	52,285	246,222	135,960	110,262	220,951	+11·4	+19·6	300
Sargodha ..	834	2	290	40,131	225,967	126,522	99,445	192,350	+17·5	+34·7	271
JHELUM DISTRICT ..	**2,769**	**4**	**884**	**134,222**	**541,076**	**282,714**	**258,362**	**477,068**	**+13·4**	**- 6·7**	**195**
Jhelum ..	889	1	435	46,219	190,594	101,882	88,712	173,122	+10·1	·3·8	214
Pind Dadan Khan ..	876	1	206	39,742	162,214	84,152	78,062	143,338	+13·2	—8·3	185
Chakwal ..	1,004	2	243	48,261	188,268	96,680	91,588	160,608	+17·2	—8·3	188
RAWALPINDI DISTRICT	**2,050**	**2**	**1,170**	**145,093**	**634,357**	**342,771**	**291,586**	**569,224**	**+11·4**	**+3·9**	**309**
Rawalpindi ..	770	1	447	64,819	289,073	166,253	122,820	262,656	+10·1	+5·1	375
Gujar Khan ..	569	..	379	40,987	170,727	87,992	82,735	148,837	+14·7	+·2	300
Murree ..	258	1	106	14,957	69,959	36,361	33,598	60,969	+14·7	+7·8	271
Kahuta ..	453	..	238	24,330	104,598	52,165	52,433	96,762	+8·1	+4·2	231
ATTOCK DISTRICT ..	**4,178**	**7**	**615**	**139,622**	**583,960**	**306,949**	**277,011**	**512,249**	**+14·0**	**—1·4**	**140**
Attock ..	651	4	189	43,149	192,545	103,160	89,385	173,472	+11·0	+7·5	296
Pindigheb ..	1,472	1	139	35,697	143,481	74,704	68,777	120,097	+19·5	— 4·9	97
Talagang ..	1,197	1	86	31,211	127,257	64,813	62,444	108,501	+17·3	- 6·0	106
Fatehjang ..	858	1	201	29,565	120,677	64,272	56,405	110,179	+9·5	—5·2	141

PROVINCIAL TABLE I.—AREA AND POPULATION OF TAHSILS.—*continued.*

Tahsil.	Area in square miles.	Number of		Number of occupied houses.	Population.				Percentage of variation.		Number of persons per square mile in 1931.
		Towns	Villages.		1931.			1921 (both sexes).	1921 to 1931.	1911 to 1921.	
					Persons.	Males.	Females.				
	2	3	4	5	6	7	8	9	10	11	12
MIANWALI DISTRICT	**5,389**	**4**	**398**	**90,462**	**411,539**	**216,016**	**195,523**	**358,205**	**+14·9**	**+4·9**	**76**
Mianwali ..	1,528	1	123	41,430	177,753	93,179	84,574	147,553	+20·5	+6·6	116
Bhakkar ..	3,135	1	213	34,169	164,331	86,868	77,463	147,121	+11·7	+8·9	52
Isa Khel ..	726	2	62	14,863	69,455	35,969	33,486	63,531	+9·3	—6·4	96
MONTGOMERY DISTRICT. ..	**4,461**	**4**	**1,958**	**187,596**	**999,772**	**552,456**	**447,316**	**685,690**	**+45·3**	**+42·3**	**224**
Montgomery ..	1,451	2	508	51,684	322,095	181,205	140,890	193,504	+66·5	+175·9	222
Okara ..	719	1	375	42,574	220,208	121,588	98,620	149,791	+47·0	+120·0	306
Dipalpur ..	955	..	488	45,959	220,456	119,003	101,453	200,978	+9·7	+1·9	231
Pakpattan ..	1,336	1	587	47,379	237,013	130,660	106,353	141,417	+67·6	—3·4	177
LYALLPUR DISTRICT ..	**3,284**	**6**	**1,241**	**201,351**	**1,151,351**	**630,749**	**520,602**	**957,881**	**+20·2**	**+16·2**	**351**
Lyallpur ..	765	1	262	58,780	333,866	185,408	148,458	291,120	+14·7	+9·1	436
Samundri ..	760	1	290	44,260	253,157	137,016	116,141	225,498	+12·3	+13·7	333
Toba Tek Singh ..	1,051	3	422	53,732	304,768	166,401	138,367	262,533	+16·1	+22·3	290
Jaranwala ..	708	1	267	44,579	259,560	141,924	117,636	178,730	+45·2	+23·6	367
JHANG DISTRICT ..	**3,397**	**5**	**981**	**135,537**	**664,833**	**355,671**	**309,162**	**570,559**	**+16·5**	**+8·7**	**196**
Jhang ..	1,332	1	432	55,226	260,307	138,699	121,608	232,570	+11·9	+7·4	195
Chiniot ..	1,016	2	351	52,288	261,140	141,236	119,904	211,188	+23·7	+14·8	257
Shorkot ..	1,049	2	198	28,023	143,386	75,736	67,650	126,801	+13·1	+2·1	137
MULTAN DISTRICT ..	**5,753**	**3**	**1,916**	**238,413**	**1,174,900**	**646,025**	**528,875**	**889,328**	**+32·1**	**+9·3**	**204**
Multan ..	768	1	279	61,172	303,761	169,358	134,403	243,385	+24·8	—6·5	396
Shujabad ..	686	1	143	30,548	147,876	79,901	67,975	132,091	+12·0	—1·7	216
Lodhran ..	1,054	..	324	33,609	163,190	88,476	74,714	125,353	+30·2	—1·9	155
Mailsi ..	1,434	..	532	39,299	189,162	105,102	84,060	113,927	+66·0	—5·5	132
Khanewal ..	978	1	375	39,142	197,774	110,356	87,418	127,131	+55·6	+381·7	202
Kabirwala ..	833	..	263	34,643	173,137	92,832	80,305	147,441	+17·4	+2·5	208
MUZAFFARGARH DISTRICT. ..	**5,561**	**6**	**862**	**128,999**	**591,375**	**320,674**	**270,701**	**568,478**	**+4·0**	**—·2**	**106**
Muzaffargarh ..	911	2	378	38,945	180,105	97,221	82,884	178,579	+·9	—4·5	198
Alipur ..	918	1	181	34,246	162,704	88,418	74,286	146,711	+10·9	+·4	177
Kot Adu ..	1,318	1	160	26,416	117,544	64,728	52,816	108,970	+7·9	+1·2	89
Leiah ..	2,414	2	143	29,392	131,022	70,307	60,715	134,218	—2·4	+4·4	54
DERA GHAZI KHAN DISTRICT ..	**5,428**	**9**	**739**	**104,312**	**491,044**	**269,341**	**221,703**	**469,052**	**+4·7**	**—6·2**	**90**
Dera Ghazi Khan ..	1,452	2	231	42,245	193,713	105,270	88,443	193,789	—·04	+6·0	133
Sanghar ..	1,065	2	166	20,136	88,571	47,669	40,902	84,759	+4·5	—20·5	83
Rajanpur ..	2,019	3	187	22,410	110,856	62,029	48,827	105,008	+5·6	—1·8	55
Jampur ..	892	2	155	19,521	97,904	54,373	43,531	85,496	+14·5	—17·3	110
Biloch Trans-frontier Tract	2,586	..	9	6,862	29,642	16,817	12,825	26,758	+10·8	—6·4	11
PUNJAB STATES ..	**29,031**	**45**	**16,061**	**1,049,617**	**4,910,005**	**2,680,684**	**2,229,321**	**4,416,036**	**+11·2**	**+4·8**	**169**
A.—Having Political relations with the Punjab Government ..	**5,639**	**4**	**2,610**	**95,112**	**437,787**	**229,290**	**208,497**	**408,019**	**+7·3**	**—1·0**	**78**
DUJANA STATE ..	**100**	**1**	**32**	**5,676**	**28,216**	**14,537**	**13,679**	**25,833**	**+9·2**	**+1·4**	**282**
Dujana ..	16	1	2	1,223	5,637	2,886	2,751	5,446	+3·5	+·3	352
Nahar ..	84	..	30	4,453	22,579	11,651	10,928	20,387	+10·8	+1·6	269
PATAUDI STATE ..	**53**	**1**	**40**	**4,040**	**18,873**	**9,922**	**8,951**	**18,097**	**+4·3**	**—7·4**	**356**
KALSIA STATE ..	**192**	**2**	**178**	**13,469**	**59,848**	**33,306**	**26,542**	**57,871**	**+4·3**	**+2·6**	**312**
Chachrauli ..	119	1	109	8,017	35,461	19,731	15,730	32,126	+10·4	—5·8	298
Dera Bassi ..	52	1	57	4,187	18,377	10,245	8,132	17,327	+6·1	+3·7	353
Chirak ..	21	..	7	1,265	6,010	3,330	2,680	7,918	—24·1	+55·0	286
SIMLA HILL STATES	**5,294**	..	**2,365**	**71,927**	**330,850**	**171,525**	**159,325**	**306,718**	**+7·9**	**—1·5**	**63**
BASHAHR STATE ..	**3,837**	..	**85**	**17,066**	**104,389**	**51,593**	**52,796**	**90,366**	**+15·5**	**—3·0**	**27**
Rampur (Bashahr Proper) ..	735	..	29	5,953	34,808	17,850	16,958	31,369	+11·0	—·9	47
Rohru (Bashahr Proper) ..	622	..	27	6,469	40,877	20,700	20,177	34,951	+17·0	—6·0	66
Chini (Bashahr Proper) ..	2,463	..	14	3,797	24,507	10,965	13,542	19,757	+24·0	—1·8	10
Khaneti (Feudatories)	14	..	9	527	2,797	1,368	1,429	2,938	—4·8	+2·9	200
Delath (Feudatories)	3	..	6	320	1,400	710	690	1,351	+3·6	—2·9	467

PROVINCIAL TABLE I.—AREA AND POPULATION OF TAHSILS.—*continued.*

Tahsil.	Area in square miles.	Number of Towns.	Number of Villages.	Number of occupied houses.	Population 1931 Persons.	Population 1931 Males.	Population 1931 Females.	Population 1921 (both sexes).	Percentage of variation 1921 to 1931.	Percentage of variation 1911 to 1921.	Number of persons per square mile in 1931.
1	2	3	4	5	6	7	8	9	10	11	12
NALAGARH STATE ..	**256**	..	**617**	**12,100**	**50,015**	**26,635**	**23,380**	**46,868**	**+6·7**	**—4·8**	**195**
Des ..	126	..	208	7,074	29,546	15,936	13,610	26,990	+9·5	—3·7	234
Pahar ..	130	..	409	5,026	20,469	10,699	9,770	19,878	+3·0	—6·3	157
KEONTHAL STATE ..	**218**	..	**457**	**12,384**	**48,093**	**25,734**	**22,359**	**47,455**	**+1·3**	**+2·7**	**221**
Junga (Keonthal Proper) ..	54	..	110	3,634	12,788	7,153	5,635	13,409	—4·6	+3·6	237
Fagu (Keonthal Proper) ..	42	..	65	1,768	7,495	3,881	3,614	6,931	+8·1	+2·0	178
Rawin (Keonthal Proper) ..	20	..	40	1,156	5,277	2,548	2,729	5,259	+ ·3	—6·5	264
Koti (Feudatories) ..	44	..	10	2,810	8,785	5,030	3,755	9,228	—4·8	+11·7	200
Theog (Feudatories) ..	33	..	169	1,546	6,912	3,613	3,299	6,300	+9·7	—·7	209
Madhan (Feudatories)	9	...	34	931	4,315	2,201	2,114	3,729	+15·7	—4·4	479
Ghund (Feudatories) ..	13	..	17	397	1,963	999	964	2,118	—7·3	+12·2	151
Ratesh (Feudatories) ..	3	..	12	142	558	309	249	481	+16·0	+1·9	186
BAGHAL STATE ..	**124**	..	**416**	**6,145**	**26,352**	**13,457**	**12,895**	**25,099**	**+5·0**	**—3·5**	**213**
JUBBAL STATE. ..	**320**	..	**35**	**5,286**	**27,172**	**14,507**	**12,665**	**25,752**	**+5·5**	**+4·6**	**85**
Babar (Jubbal Proper) ..	32	..	4	694	3,565	1,807	1,758	3,324	+7·3	—7·7	111
Chopal (Jubbal Proper) ..	256	..	17	4,349	22,456	12,101	10,355	21,532	+4·3	+7·5	88
Rawin (Feudatories) ..	7	..	12	186	939	493	446	711	+32·1	—5·1	134
Dhadi (Feudatories) ..	25	..	2	57	212	106	106	185	+14·6	—24·2	8
OTHER SIMLA HILL STATES ..	**539**	..	**755**	**18,946**	**74,829**	**39,599**	**35,230**	**71,178**	**+5·1**	**—1·1**	**139**
Baghat ..	36	..	133	2,810	9,725	5,744	3,981	9,505	+2·3	+8·0	270
Kumharsain ..	90	..	11	2,297	12,781	6,425	6,356	12,227	+4·5	+·1	142
Bhajji ..	96	..	179	5,689	15,413	7,943	7,470	14,263	+8·1	—4·7	161
Mahlog ..	43	..	184	2,012	8,155	4,299	3,856	8,296	—1·7	—4·2	190
Balsan ..	51	..	37	1,464	6,864	3,603	3,261	6,137	+11·8	—1·4	135
Dhami ..	26	..	107	1,150	5,232	2,693	2,539	4,786	+9·3	+6·7	201
Kuthar ..	20	..	6	918	3,760	2,023	1,737	3,841	—2·1	—4·4	188
Kunihar ..	70	..	16	504	2,061	1,035	1,026	1,945	+6·0	—11·9	29
Mangal ..	12	..	15	276	1,248	680	568	1,193	+4·6	—5·8	104
Bija ..	4	..	46	319	994	579	415	943	+5·4	—11·4	249
Darkoti ..	8	..	13	106	331	257	274	610	—13·0	+17·1	66
Tharoch ..	67	..	3	731	4,568	2,521	2,047	4,219	+8·3	—6·1	68
Sangri ..	16	..	5	670	3,497	1,797	1,700	3,213	+8·8	+6·3	219
B.—Having Political relations with the Government of India.	**23,392**	**41**	**13,451**	**954,505**	**4,472,218**	**2,451,394**	**2,020,824**	**4,008,017**	**+11·6**	**+5·5**	**191**
LOHARU STATE ..	**222**	**1**	**70**	**4,193**	**23,838**	**12,326**	**11,012**	**20,621**	**+18·2**	**+10·9**	**105**
SIRMOOR STATE ..	**1,141**	**2**	**965**	**32,204**	**148,568**	**82,384**	**66,184**	**140,448**	**+5·8**	**+1·4**	**130**
Nahan ..	186	2	152	4,456	20,403	11,502	8,901	17,999	+13·4	+1·6	110
Rinka ..	259	..	247	11,646	60,270	33,681	26,589	57,605	+4·6	+·3	233
Pachhad ..	380	..	399	8,506	32,248	17,053	15,195	33,388	—3·4	- 1·0	85
Paonta ..	316	..	167	7,596	35,647	20,148	15,499	31,456	+13·3	+6·2	113
BILASPUR STATE ..	**451**	**1**	**940**	**23,825**	**100,994**	**53,154**	**47,840**	**98,000**	**+3·1**	**+5·3**	**224**
Bilaspur ..	146	1	406	9,541	40,206	21,590	18,616	40,577	—·9	+6·8	275
Ghumarwin ..	305	..	534	14,284	60,788	31,564	29,224	57,423	+5·9	+4·2	199
MANDI STATE ..	**1,202**	**2**	**3,606**	**45,388**	**207,465**	**107,876**	**99,589**	**185,048**	**+12·1**	**+2·2**	**173**
Mandi Sadr ..	202	1	733	10,699	49,412	26,534	22,878	45,755	+8·0	+1·1	245
Jogindar Nagar ..	450	1	1,342	14,379	62,247	34,059	28,188	51,942	+19·8	+ ·4	138
Chachiot ..	350	..	924	7,807	39,894	19,160	20,734	36,259	+10·0	—4·6	114
Sarkaghat ..	200	..	607	12,503	55,912	28,123	27,789	51,092	+9·4	+10·7	280
SUKET STATS ..	**420**	**1**	**87**	**12,634**	**58,408**	**30,851**	**27,557**	**54,328**	**+7·5**	**—1·1**	**139**
Bhal ..	60	1	42	3,647	16,524	8,758	7,766	13,317	+24·1	+3·3	275
Dehar ..	108	..	34	3,022	12,937	7,014	5,923	11,247	+15·0	+·4	120
Karsog ..	252	..	11	5,965	28,947	15,079	13,868	29,764	—2·7	—3·5	115
KAPURTHALA STATE ..	**661**	**8**	**617**	**69,644**	**316,757**	**171,529**	**145,228**	**284,275**	**+11·4**	**+6·0**	**479**
Kapurthala ..	224	1	213	22,883	106,058	57,885	48,173	91,842	+15·5	—5·4	473
Sultanpur ..	175	1	171	15,808	73,959	39,472	34,487	71,185	+3·9	+13·1	423
Phagwara ..	117	1	94	15,332	67,412	36,792	30,620	59,282	+13·7	+3·7	576
Bholath ..	131	..	115	13,420	60,570	32,624	27,946	54,321	+11·5	+25·1	462
Bhunga ..	14	..	24	2,201	8,758	4,756	4,002	7,645	+14·6	+1·3	626

PROVINCIAL TABLE I.—AREA AND POPULATION OF TAHSILS.—*concluded.*

Tahsil.	Area in square miles.	Number of		Number of occupied houses.	Population.				Percentage of variation.		Number of persons per square mile in 1931.
					1931.			1921 (both sexes.)	1921 to 1931.	1911 to 1921.	
		Towns.	Villages.		Persons.	Males.	Females.				
1	2	3	4	5	6	7	8	9	10	11	12
MALER KOTLA STATE	**166**	**3**	**111**	**21,223**	**88,072**	**45,883**	**37,189**	**80,322**	**+8·4**	**+12·9**	**500**
Maler Kotla ..	33	1	18	8,648	32,551	18,258	14,293	34,457	—5·5	+12·9	986
Ahmadgarh ..	59	1	43	5,810	24,293	13,308	10,985	22,761	+6·7	+12·9	412
Fatehgarh ..	74	1	50	6,765	26,228	14,317	11,911	23,104	+13·5	+12·9	354
FARIDKOT STATE ..	**633**	**2**	**171**	**33,168**	**164,364**	**91,163**	**73,201**	**150,661**	**+9·1**	**+15·6**	**260**
CHAMBA STATE ..	**3,216**	**1**	**53**	**30,665**	**146,870**	**76,059**	**70,811**	**141,867**	**+3·5**	**+4·4**	**46**
PATIALA STATE ..	**5,932**	**11**	**3,528**	**343,998**	**1,625,520**	**900,597**	**724,923**	**1,499,739**	**+8·4**	**+6·5**	**274**
Patiala ..	459	2	379	35,735	148,532	86,069	62,463	136,511	+8·8	+1·8	324
Rajpura	304	..	279	22,022	96,881	53,697	43,184	93,210	+3·9	+3·5	319
Sirhind ..	366	2	350	31,069	140,123	78,323	61,800	126,236	+11·0	+7·4	383
Kandaghat ..	344	..	1,057	13,975	55,638	30,333	25,305	54,705	+1·7	—4·4	162
Bhawanigarh ..	490	1	204	26,139	123,155	69,172	53,983	112,195	+9·8	+9·5	251
Sunam ..	486	1	124	26,338	123,596	69,406	54,190	114,071	+8·4	+9·4	254
Dhuri ..	489	..	256	38,802	180,041	100,766	79,275	161,249	+11·7	+9·2	368
Narwana ..	582	..	136	27,482	137,826	75,062	62,764	135,513	+1·7	+12·4	237
Barnala ..	346	2	77	19,959	96,474	53,872	42,602	85,168	+13·3	+7·8	279
Bhatinda ..	868	1	201	38,825	200,704	111,687	89,017	185,652	+8·1	+11·7	231
Mansa ..	622	..	178	29,798	153,461	85,172	68,289	141,182	+8·7	+4·8	247
Narnaul ..	576	2	287	33,854	169,089	87,038	82,051	154,047	+9·8	+ ·1	294
JIND STATE ..	**1,268**	**4**	**439**	**64,327**	**324,676**	**176,383**	**148,293**	**308,183**	**+5·4**	**+13·4**	**256**
Sangrur ..	242	1	97	14,259	70,114	40,415	29,699	60,961	+15·0	+18·9	290
Jind ..	464	2	163	27,858	134,460	72,941	61,519	136,903	—1·8	+13·5	290
Dadri ..	562	1	179	22,210	120,102	63,027	57,075	110,319	+8·9	+10·6	214
NABHA STATE ..	**963**	**6**	**492**	**61,774**	**287,574**	**158,086**	**129,488**	**263,334**	**+9·2**	**+5·8**	**299**
Amloh ..	289	2	232	22,038	95,796	54,309	41,487	87,869	+9·0	+9·8	331
Phul ..	393	3	95	23,646	110,980	61,940	49,040	100,139	+10·8	+6·5	282
Bawal ..	281	1	165	16,090	80,798	41,837	38,961	75,326	+7·3	+ ·7	288
BAHAWALPUR STATE	**7,117**	**4**	**2,372**	**211,462**	**984,612**	**545,103**	**439,509**	**781,191**	**+26·0**	**+ ·1**	**138**
Minchinabad ..	672	..	250	21,840	110,101	59,558	50,543	96,558	+14·0	+18·5	164
Bahawalnagar ..	1,307	1	514	26,093	124,401	70,619	53,782	57,838	+115·1	+19·0	95
Khairpur ..	1,024	..	387	26,393	126,785	69,596	57,189	88,497	+43·3	+ ·8	124
Bahawalpur ..	802	1	257	29,440	121,853	68,690	53,163	98,247	+24·0	—8·1	152
Ahmadpur Sharqi ..	883	1	410	29,057	136,253	75,499	60,754	116,400	+17·1	+4·9	154
Allahabad ..	433	..	118	20,949	92,794	50,440	42,354	90,656	+2·4	+3·9	214
Khanpur ..	499	1	121	20,535	90,534	50,017	40,517	88,201	+2·6	—5·1	181
Rahim Yar Khan ..	743	..	167	20,619	101,883	56,332	45,551	82,659	+23·3	—5·1	137
Ahmadpur Lamma ..	754	..	148	16,536	80,008	44,352	35,656	62,135	+28·8	—19·8	106

PROVINCIAL TABLE II.

POPULATION OF DISTRICTS AND TAHSILS BY RELIGION AND LITERACY.

1. The figures by religion for each Tahsil have been taken from the Village Tables.

2. The figures for literacy by age have been taken from Table XIII.

3. The figures of Hindus have been split up into "Brahmans," "Other Hindus" and "Depressed Classes," which for the purposes of this Table, are *Chamar*, *Chuhra*, *Dagi & Koli*, and *Sansi*. The figures for Ad-Dharmis have been shown separately in columns 14—17, and in order to obtain the total for all Depressed Classes these should be added to columns 10—13.

PROVINCIAL TABLE II.—POPULATION OF DISTRICTS AND TAHSILS BY RELIGION AND LITERACY.

District and Tahsil.	Hindus.												Ad-Dharmis.				Jains.			
	Brahmans.				Other Hindus.				Depressed Classes.											
	No. of Persons.		No. Literate.		No. of Persons.		No. Literate.		No. of Persons.		No. Literate.		No. of Persons.		No. Literate.		No. of Persons.		No. Literate.	
	Males.	Females.	Males.	Females.	Males.	Females.	Males.	Females.	Males.	Females.	Males.	Females.	Males.	Females.	Males.	Females.	Males.	Females.	Males.	Females.
1	2	3	4	5	6	7	8	9	10	11	12	13	14	15	16	17	18	19	20	21
PUNJAB ..	576,735	474,647	129,189	12,675	3,430,931	2,851,967	459,633	54,858	878,039	587,401	5,481	711	223,509	190,280	5,191	554	22,962	20,178	9,701	1,323
BRITISH TERRITORY ..	422,561	344,235	103,050	11,008	2,597,129	2,135,790	387,480	50,335	445,844	383,029	4,180	583	217,910	181,397	5,072	549	18,751	16,533	8,060	1,205
HISSAR DISTRICT ..	24,313	20,113	4,076	309	242,174	205,027	16,563	855	49,091	42,702	195	..	8	1	..	..	3,187	2,851	1,548	110
Hissar ..	4,477	3,400	1,004	78	62,610	50,811	5,774	335	11,098	9,354	63	..	8	..	..	..	862	790	479	65
Hansi ..	7,285	6,013	590	39	59,861	51,375	3,032	85	14,155	12,433	30	..	..	1	..	..	1,330	1,229	629	30
Bhiwani ..	7,641	6,445	1,347	127	45,076	39,670	1,977	242	7,181	6,484	43	..	..	..	..	..	319	333	151	13
Fatehabad ..	1,966	1,704	324	11	36,040	31,181	1,943	39	6,481	5,598	17	..	..	..	..	..	121	109	54	..
Sirsa ..	2,944	2,551	811	54	38,587	31,990	3,837	154	10,176	8,833	42	..	..	..	..	..	505	390	235	2
ROHTAK DISTRICT ..	38,300	31,853	4,136	174	265,822	224,277	16,643	564	49,813	45,898	151	3	..	..	..	..	3,320	3,055	1,364	143
Rohtak ..	10,730	8,202	1,277	81	70,573	55,096	5,322	286	13,362	11,476	40	2	..	..	..	..	784	646	328	52
Jhajjar ..	10,374	9,005	1,525	45	81,935	72,384	5,379	132	13,896	13,604	75	1	..	..	..	..	108	120	49	..
Gohana ..	8,008	6,930	549	3	56,044	48,851	2,428	57	11,483	10,649	18	..	..	..	..	..	1,013	983	427	47
Sonepat ..	9,188	7,716	835	45	57,270	47,946	3,514	89	11,072	10,169	18	..	..	..	..	..	1,415	1,306	560	44
GURGAON DISTRICT ..	27,191	22,921	4,166	256	184,902	152,612	12,748	867	54,548	51,000	258	1	..	..	..	..	1,879	1,286	720	83
Gurgaon ..	4,711	3,931	985	58	38,972	32,005	2,560	247	8,887	8,511	77	..	..	..	..	..	456	449	258	45
Firozpur Jhirka ..	536	412	157	5	6,944	5,756	941	66	5,969	5,388	32	..	..	..	..	..	310	297	158	3
Nuh ..	2,593	2,092	308	12	19,448	15,791	1,410	53	7,513	7,045	22	..	..	..	..	..	63	58	19	..
Palwal ..	8,278	6,924	799	57	41,497	33,644	2,431	157	14,719	13,275	39	1	..	..	..	..	86	63	44	11
Rewari ..	6,249	5,615	1,445	88	53,811	46,263	3,197	190	10,865	10,731	58	..	..	..	..	..	423	385	217	22
Ballabgarh ..	4,824	3,947	472	36	24,230	19,153	2,209	154	6,595	6,050	30	..	..	..	..	..	41	34	24	2
KARNAL DISTRICT ..	34,726	28,035	3,704	232	220,883	175,926	13,911	727	57,508	48,208	105	1	2,719	2,292	6	..	2,164	2,026	1,001	61
Karnal ..	8,987	7,306	1,025	84	60,429	48,308	4,018	260	14,943	12,479	54	..	2,473	2,109	..	..	536	472	254	25
Panipat ..	7,469	5,963	624	48	46,941	37,907	3,049	114	9,724	8,385	17	..	..	..	..	..	1,249	1,188	620	34
Kaithal ..	13,913	11,340	1,235	61	78,085	62,252	4,473	195	21,543	18,276	17	..	..	..	..	..	365	355	125	1
Thanesar ..	4,357	3,426	820	39	35,428	27,459	2,371	158	11,298	9,068	17	1	246	183	6	..	14	11	2	1
AMBALA DISTRICT ..	20,578	15,507	5,732	605	126,444	95,670	15,598	1,887	48,248	40,264	275	14	50	48	6	..	1,402	1,148	731	145
Ambala ..	5,713	3,947	1,079	267	40,367	29,701	6,463	975	13,964	11,657	138	2	..	..	..	..	780	656	388	83
Kharar ..	4,984	3,708	1,345	113	20,658	15,150	3,163	215	4,755	3,373	65	2	1	..	1	..	168	124	100	13
Jagadhri ..	3,397	2,741	685	66	29,628	22,501	2,462	261	17,063	14,630	29	7	..	..	..	..	108	91	53	8
Naraingarh ..	4,064	3,257	758	53	28,179	22,336	2,020	184	10,271	8,784	14	1	..	..	..	..	203	150	101	20
Rupar ..	2,420	1,854	965	106	7,612	5,982	1,490	252	2,195	1,820	29	2	49	48	5	..	143	127	89	21
SIMLA DISTRICT ..	2,448	964	1,144	110	11,288	7,008	3,138	394	4,103	2,855	218	14	..	..	..	..	1	..	1	..
Simla ..	2,075	592	1,015	108	7,534	3,201	2,384	355	2,011	1,634	191	14	..	..	..	..	..	..	..	..
Kot Khai ..	373	372	129	2	3,754	3,802	754	39	1,192	1,221	22	..	..	..	..	..	1	..	1	..

District / Tahsil																				
KANGRA DISTRICT	**55,581**	**53,084**	**12,501**	**626**	**283,183**	**264,823**	**22,157**	**1,836**	**38,386**	**36,758**	**289**	**10**	**11,338**	**9,545**	**109**	..	**46**	**48**	**19**	..
Kangra	3,815	2,901	1,357	64	53,197	48,344	4,336	443	2,034	1,927	16	..	1,070	976	21	..	..	..	..	..
Dehra	9,892	9,555	2,641	155	47,657	43,529	3,753	385	381	246	3	..	5,650	4,753	46	..	..	..	..	..
Nurpur	6,355	5,229	1,119	78	34,284	25,962	1,765	237	1,159	942	7	..	3,301	2,686	23	..	1	..	1	..
Hamirpur	22,041	22,772	3,047	63	54,198	52,667	4,734	274	8,494	8,395	70	4	1,317	1,130	19	..	42	47	17	..
Palampur	8,912	8,231	3,022	141	52,158	51,329	5,252	362	10,512	9,901	111	1	..	..	..	..	..	..	..	..
Kulu	4,516	4,396	1,315	125	41,689	42,492	2,317	135	15,756	15,347	82	5	..	..	..	..	3	1	1	..
HOSHIARPUR DISTRICT	**41,135**	**37,300**	**11,291**	**1,069**	**161,859**	**143,368**	**16,476**	**1,807**	**16,309**	**14,382**	**142**	**11**	**60,899**	**50,930**	**1,846**	**60**	**579**	**437**	**280**	**56**
Hoshiarpur	6,714	5,501	2,774	444	24,606	20,536	4,891	897	2,578	2,205	49	6	20,028	16,909	810	25	278	201	118	18
Dasuya	5,335	4,744	1,567	219	28,897	24,665	2,329	328	2,193	1,810	17	..	11,578	9,565	221	10	152	124	75	28
Garhshankar	7,001	5,842	2,044	114	42,925	36,956	2,749	338	2,934	2,570	10	2	21,982	18,481	657	18	149	112	87	10
Una	22,085	21,213	4,906	292	65,431	61,211	6,507	244	3,601	7,797	66	3	7,311	5,975	158	7	..	..	..	..
JULLUNDUR DISTRICT	**16,431**	**13,866**	**5,339**	**646**	**57,655**	**46,354**	**12,220**	**2,231**	**11,383**	**9,553**	**343**	**137**	**60,948**	**52,632**	**1,049**	**175**	**727**	**652**	**200**	**43**
Jullundur	5,631	4,411	1,883	218	21,411	16,096	6,041	1,244	3,818	3,067	270	123	23,215	19,973	547	138	515	499	100	31
Nawanshahr	4,206	3,732	1,570	218	18,130	15,098	2,831	468	2,897	2,333	25	..	14,777	13,059	239	15	109	67	61	7
Phillaur	4,077	3,558	1,277	175	10,909	9,279	2,087	341	3,683	3,033	44	..	13,149	11,110	158	15	1	2	1	..
Nakodar	2,517	2,165	609	35	7,205	5,881	1,261	178	985	1,120	4	14	9,807	8,490	105	7	102	84	38	5
LUDHIANA DISTRICT	**12,064**	**9,687**	**4,048**	**447**	**35,383**	**26,292**	**9,811**	**1,624**	**10,727**	**8,288**	**657**	**92**	**9,689**	**8,081**	**302**	**12**	**765**	**654**	**297**	**58**
Ludhiana	5,857	4,980	1,518	222	19,471	14,444	5,456	1,141	4,604	3,508	592	91	5,774	4,897	183	3	253	244	85	30
Jagraon	2,644	2,117	1,011	128	7,179	5,327	2,237	321	752	558	8	..	3,915	3,134	119	9	379	297	151	19
Samrala	3,563	2,590	1,514	97	8,733	6,521	2,118	162	5,371	4,222	57	1	..	..	..	..	133	113	61	9
FEROZEPORE DISTRICT	**11,552**	**8,510**	**3,811**	**397**	**85,250**	**65,600**	**18,936**	**2,422**	**20,688**	**16,826**	**218**	**20**	**19,670**	**16,592**	**254**	**13**	**759**	**652**	**388**	**88**
Ferozepore	3,209	2,175	1,286	199	18,370	12,699	5,440	1,025	6,330	5,027	95	3	1,794	1,418	83	..	282	272	138	41
Ziba	1,070	963	397	21	4,619	4,080	1,452	185	439	399	1	..	5,107	4,388	34	..	188	157	106	20
Moga	2,814	2,171	879	53	8,053	6,086	3,210	480	346	297	11	7	3,186	2,705	65	4	16	12	9	2
Muktsar	1,658	1,152	493	42	11,933	9,029	3,339	204	3,045	2,474	13	..	4,364	3,616	31	4	219	167	102	21
Fazilka	2,801	2,049	756	82	42,275	33,706	5,495	528	10,528	8,629	98	10	5,219	4,465	21	5	54	44	28	4
LAHORE DISTRICT	**22,035**	**13,139**	**8,163**	**1,313**	**109,490**	**65,525**	**33,194**	**5,630**	**27,587**	**20,943**	**346**	**53**	**665**	**341**	**15**	**2**	**777**	**678**	**370**	**105**
Lahore	16,840	9,061	7,225	1,242	81,734	43,964	27,772	5,096	9,784	6,019	269	45	659	341	14	2	445	353	225	79
Chunian	2,137	1,632	320	34	16,484	12,809	2,822	368	13,078	10,969	52	2	..	..	..	..	40	39	18	1
Kasur	3,058	2,446	618	37	11,272	8,752	2,600	166	4,725	3,955	25	6	6	..	1	..	292	281	127	25
AMRITSAR DISTRICT	**23,169**	**15,619**	**7,945**	**595**	**61,319**	**43,755**	**15,661**	**2,475**	**16,697**	**13,833**	**154**	**66**	**101**	**63**	..	..	**691**	**581**	**166**	**91**
Amritsar	16,212	9,515	5,553	419	52,155	36,010	13,145	2,135	8,571	6,981	107	62	101	63	..	..	670	562	155	91
Tarn Taran	4,335	3,824	1,704	158	5,250	4,268	1,566	285	5,175	4,390	40	4	..	..	..	..	21	19	11	..
Ajnala	2,622	2,280	688	18	3,914	3,477	950	55	2,951	2,462	7	..	..	..	..	..	..	..	..	..
GURDASPUR DISTRICT	**20,286**	**17,251**	**4,059**	**549**	**109,533**	**90,660**	**11,167**	**1,657**	**6,341**	**5,333**	**56**	**11**	**3,566**	**2,979**	**37**	**28**	**8**	**7**	**3**	**5**
Gurdaspur	3,871	3,182	756	85	18,909	15,126	3,227	447	993	818	22	..	..	..	..	..	2	4	..	2
Batala	4,535	3,767	1,468	109	9,719	7,893	2,737	590	4,164	3,672	23	..	119	52	10	..	2	..	2	..
Pathankot	4,560	3,377	828	131	35,650	27,157	2,658	431	460	233	7	9	3,447	2,927	27	28	4	3	1	3
Shakargarh	7,320	6,925	1,007	134	45,255	40,484	2,545	189	724	610	4	2	..	..	..	..	..	..	..	..
SIALKOT DISTRICT	**13,042**	**11,174**	**2,169**	**239**	**95,687**	**80,726**	**6,990**	**1,178**	**3,124**	**2,642**	**19**	**11**	**5**	**21**	..	..	**1,227**	**1,009**	**212**	**112**
Sialkot	4,361	3,607	730	70	40,631	33,171	2,457	410	1,860	1,604	3	3	5	21	..	..	858	712	85	69
Pasrur	2,514	2,163	608	65	19,431	16,911	1,468	234	703	573	2	1	..	..	..	..	215	148	71	17
Narowal	3,990	3,422	346	43	22,556	19,654	1,241	233	307	251	2	..	..	..	..	..	132	132	46	23
Daska	2,177	1,982	485	61	13,069	10,990	1,824	296	254	214	12	7	..	..	..	..	22	17	10	3

PROVINCIAL TABLE II.—POPULATION OF DISTRICTS AND TAHSILS BY RELIGION AND LITERACY.—*continued.*

District and Tahsil.	HINDUS.												AD-DHARMIS.				JAINS.			
	Brahmans.				Other Hindus.				Depressed Classes.											
	No. of Persons.		No. Literate.		No. of Persons.		No. Literate.		No. of Persons.		No. Literate.		No. of Persons.		No. Literate.		No. of Persons.		No. Literate.	
	Males.	Females.	Males.	Females.	Males.	Females.	Males.	Females.	Males.	Females.	Males.	Females.	Males.	Females.	Males.	Females.	Males.	Females.	Males.	Females.
1	2	3	4	5	6	7	8	9	10	11	12	13	14	15	16	17	18	19	20	21
GUJRANWALA DISTRICT	**8,862**	**6,584**	**2,549**	**482**	**40,532**	**31,683**	**11,208**	**2,499**	**2,807**	**2,294**	**10**	..	**2**	..	..	..	**593**	**478**	**275**	**56**
Gujranwala ..	5,405	4,021	1,780	276	19,143	14,969	5,018	1,195	1,507	1,218	10	..	..	..	..	..	580	466	266	53
Wazirabad ..	2,023	1,630	632	153	8,848	7,056	2,488	656	450	332	..	..	2	..	..	..	12	11	8	3
Hafizabad ..	1,434	933	137	53	12,541	9,658	3,702	648	850	744	..	..	..	..	..	..	1	1	1	..
SHEIKHUPURA DISTRICT	**4,392**	**2,946**	**1,104**	**118**	**29,930**	**22,600**	**7,487**	**1,307**	**5,811**	**4,467**	**47**	**2**	**6,479**	**5,282**	**111**	**1**	**58**	**47**	**28**	**5**
Sheikhupura ..	2,441	1,608	762	46	13,771	10,146	3,179	217	3,379	2,557	11	2	3,893	3,136	84	..	47	43	24	5
Nankana Sahib ..	933	582	237	44	7,905	6,457	2,176	307	1,985	1,595	26	..	2,535	2,085	26	1	1	..	1	..
Shahdara ..	1,018	756	105	28	8,254	5,997	2,132	783	447	315	10	..	51	41	1	..	5	4	3	..
GUJRAT DISTRICT ..	**4,899**	**4,034**	**1,984**	**234**	**33,239**	**27,983**	**9,449**	**1,588**	**1,287**	**904**	**14**	..	**635**	**375**	**38**	..	**18**	**14**	..	**1**
Gujrat ..	1,917	1,823	637	106	12,003	10,401	3,132	791	340	252	1	..	..	..	..	..	13	8	..	1
Kharian ..	1,243	846	495	85	6,575	5,786	2,479	400	222	169	10	..	..	..	..	..	5	6	..	..
Phalia ..	1,739	1,365	852	43	14,661	11,796	3,838	397	725	483	3	..	635	375	38	..	..	..	..	..
SHAHPUR DISTRICT ..	**3,679**	**2,798**	**1,521**	**383**	**42,160**	**35,464**	**13,147**	**2,724**	**2,802**	**2,067**	**69**	**12**	**884**	**707**	**38**	**3**	**8**	**6**	**5**	**1**
Shahpur ..	695	658	411	74	7,882	7,070	2,835	592	352	241	9	1	..	..	..	..	..	1	..	..
Khushab ..	545	499	224	42	7,119	7,157	2,478	643	34	16	..	..	..	..	..	..	..	..	..	..
Bhalwal ..	1,308	989	447	46	13,734	11,602	3,629	465	541	381	9	2	16	16	1	..	..	..	..	..
Sargodha ..	1,131	652	439	221	13,425	9,635	4,205	1,024	1,875	1,429	51	9	868	691	37	3	8	5	5	1
JHELUM DISTRICT ..	**2,918**	**2,522**	**1,284**	**309**	**15,901**	**14,217**	**6,060**	**1,263**	**336**	**174**	**6**	**2**	..	..	..	..	**106**	**108**	**52**	**7**
Jhelum ..	1,100	944	602	77	6,113	4,054	2,616	617	223	119	..	..	..	..	..	..	93	98	52	7
Pind Dadan Khan ..	994	724	408	35	5,908	6,083	1,820	190	100	49	6	1	..	..	..	..	13	5	..	..
Chakwal ..	824	854	274	197	3,880	4,080	1,624	456	13	6	..	1	..	..	..	..	..	..	..	..
RAWALPINDI DISTRICT	**9,744**	**7,598**	**3,475**	**609**	**23,289**	**15,854**	**11,165**	**1,816**	**1,940**	**1,060**	**275**	**16**	..	..	..	..	**593**	**484**	**242**	**15**
Rawalpindi ..	5,132	3,106	2,610	499	21,366	14,302	10,047	1,607	1,676	875	272	16	..	..	..	..	566	463	232	14
Gujar Khan ..	1,717	1,646	464	80	1,249	1,112	520	112	134	113	3	..	..	..	..	..	3	3	..	1
Murree ..	428	372	36	8	409	238	261	23	112	65	..	..	..	..	..	..	..	..	..	..
Kahuta ..	2,467	2,474	365	22	265	202	337	74	18	7	..	..	..	..	..	..	24	18	10	..
ATTOCK DISTRICT ..	**1,634**	**1,332**	**534**	**151**	**14,689**	**13,809**	**4,720**	**920**	**308**	**160**	**30**	..	..	..	..	..	**2**	..	**2**	..
Attock ..	662	420	238	84	4,964	3,876	1,806	489	279	146	27	..	..	..	..	..	2	..	2	..
Pindigheb ..	451	427	81	23	4,995	5,076	1,367	166	2	3	..	..	..	..	..	..	..	..	..	..
Talagang ..	318	292	114	18	3,201	3,421	895	104	4	..	..	..	..	..	..	..	..	..	..	..
Fatehjang ..	203	193	101	26	1,529	1,436	652	161	23	11	3	..	..	..	..	..	..	..	..	..
MIANWALI DISTRICT ..	**1,542**	**1,344**	**621**	**54**	**24,008**	**22,734**	**8,066**	**786**	**111**	**60**	**5**	..	..	..	..	..	**11**	**9**	**8**	**1**
Mianwali ..	507	400	205	37	9,291	8,267	3,642	495	92	45	4	..	..	..	..	..	4	3	2	1
Bhakkar ..	832	744	281	11	12,250	12,208	3,454	199	5	7	..	..	..	..	..	..	..	..	..	..
Isa Khel ..	203	200	75	6	2,462	2,259	970	92	14	8	1	..	..	..	..	..	7	6	6	..

AND TAHSILS BY RELIGION AND LITERACY.—*continued.*

MONTGOMERY DISTRICT	**4,258**	**2,434**	**1,786**	**215**	**58,922**	**43,979**	**12,886**	**1,544**	**6,265**	**4,806**	**88**	**43**	**9,141**	**9,978**	**172**	**4**	**28**	**10**	**19**	..
Montgomery ..	1,812	940	834	103	18,950	13,150	4,430	727	1,769	1,320	61	43	7,286	5,632	139	..	21	6	17	..
Okara ..	939	547	397	44	11,184	7,973	3,032	405	1,689	1,230	11	..	1,252	897	23	2	1	..	1	..
Dipalpur ..	592	388	226	20	9,604	7,964	2,210	125	1,947	1,644	1	..	..	..	..	..	..	..	..	..
Pakpattan ..	915	559	329	48	19,184	14,892	3,214	287	860	612	15	..	603	449	10	2	6	4	1	..
LYALLPUR DISTRICT ..	**7,071**	**4,777**	**2,520**	**456**	**56,911**	**40,639**	**16,943**	**3,084**	**7,375**	**5,853**	**95**	**26**	**28,222**	**22,496**	**999**	**223**	**66**	**29**	**29**	**2**
Lyallpur ..	3,067	2,256	1,254	324	21,303	14,058	7,316	1,854	2,870	1,969	32	18	6,951	5,763	475	133	53	18	26	2
Samundri ..	1,038	627	175	21	11,327	8,656	2,237	125	1,020	821	15	7	5,013	3,946	94	75	..	..	..	..
Toba Tek Singh ..	1,518	947	549	41	15,503	11,553	5,334	895	1,856	1,340	42	1	6,055	4,738	200	15	8	6	2	..
Jaranwala ..	1,448	947	542	70	8,778	6,372	2,056	210	1,629	1,723	6	..	10,203	8,049	224	..	5	5	1	..
JHANG DISTRICT ..	**3,843**	**3,666**	**1,392**	**211**	**48,571**	**45,785**	**13,261**	**3,012**	**585**	**474**	**26**	**10**	**40**	**26**	..	..	..	..	..	..
Jhang ..	1,859	1,980	680	100	20,980	20,595	6,600	2,104	105	68	15	..	..	..	..	..	..	..	..	..
Chiniot ..	1,298	993	502	63	15,879	13,361	4,482	426	323	246	1	..	40	26	..	..	..	..	..	..
Shorkot ..	686	693	210	48	11,712	11,829	2,179	482	157	160	10	10	..	..	..	..	..	..	..	..
MULTAN DISTRICT ..	**4,480**	**3,190**	**954**	**141**	**92,624**	**74,152**	**28,605**	**2,297**	**1,542**	**1,114**	**91**	**28**	**2,849**	**2,078**	**90**	**28**	**220**	**220**	**84**	**13**
Multan ..	1,871	1,261	273	58	29,598	23,744	8,276	972	7	5	..	..	925	650	68	28	211	213	78	13
Shujabad ..	546	471	73	23	10,191	9,048	3,225	248	..	..	..	..	..	..	..	..	1	..	1	..
Lodhran ..	420	343	143	9	13,181	11,408	3,706	69	138	100	3	..	..	..	..	..	..	..	..	..
Mailsi ..	416	269	58	35	13,878	10,265	4,149	293	500	344	76	23	71	42	..	..	2	..	..	..
Khanewal ..	894	532	249	10	15,331	10,437	5,088	570	877	632	12	5	1,847	1,383	22	..	6	7	5	..
Kabirwala ..	333	314	158	6	10,445	9,250	4,161	145	20	13	..	..	6	3	..	..	..	..	..	..
MUZAFFARGARH DISTRICT	**1,525**	**1,275**	**621**	**37**	**36,593**	**32,920**	**10,828**	**584**	**166**	**98**	**3**		..	..	..	..	..	..	..	..
Muzaffargarh ..	399	304	148	30	10,941	9,785	2,627	277	36	25	1	..	..	..	..	..	..	..	..	..
Alipur ..	335	251	106	..	11,232	9,651	3,398	41	107	61	2	..	..	..	..	..	..	..	..	..
Kot Adu ..	299	258	131	3	5,807	5,127	2,343	180	23	12	..	..	..	..	..	..	..	..	..	..
Leiah ..	492	462	236	4	8,613	8,357	2,460	86	..	..	..	..	..	..	..	..	..	..	..	..
DERA GHAZI KHAN DISTRICT. ..	**913**	**712**	**376**	**41**	**28,898**	**26,853**	**8,442**	**762**	**6**	**13**	..	..	..	..	..	..	**71**	**54**	**21**	**4**
Dera Ghazi Khan ..	495	387	247	31	12,570	11,851	3,686	369	6	13	..	..	..	..	..	..	71	54	21	4
Sanghar ..	186	150	51	1	5,279	5,076	1,426	64	..	..	..	..	..	..	..	..	..	..	..	..
Rajanpur ..	131	99	49	8	5,400	4,707	1,789	101	..	..	..	..	..	..	..	..	..	..	..	..
Jampur ..	99	75	29	1	5,540	5,153	1,503	204	..	..	..	..	..	..	..	..	..	..	..	..
Biloch Trans-frontier tract	2	1	..	..	104	66	38	24	..	..	..	..	..	..	..	..	..	..	..	..

PROVINCIAL TABLE II.—POPULATION OF DISTRICTS AND TAHSILS BY RELIGION AND LITERACY.—*continued.*

	SIKHS.				MUSLIMS.				CHRISTIANS				OTHERS.				NUMBER LITERATE.						LITERATE IN ENGLISH	
	No. of Persons.		No. Literate.		No. of Persons.		No. Literate.		No. of Persons.		No. Literate.		No. of Persons.		No. Literate.		Aged 0—15.		Aged 15—20.		Aged 20 and over.			
	Males.	Females.	Males.	Females.	Males.	Females.	Males.	Females.	Males.	Females.	Males.	Females.	Males.	Females.	Males.	Females.	Males.	Females.	Males.	Females.	Males.	Females.	Males.	Females.
	22	23	24	25	26	27	28	29	30	31	32	33	34	35	36	37	38	39	40	41	42	43	44	45
PUNJAB	2,270,946	1,800,678	246,203	39,063	8,116,383	6,813,513	378,742	42,467	232,556	186,797	24,017	11,413	4,133	4,202	585	136	173,971	39,209	190,307	31,051	894,464	92,940	249,003	20,095
BRITISH TERRITORY	1,703,584	1,360,560	211,828	35,485	7,241,612	6,090,848	353,305	40,354	230,018	184,770	23,528	11,065	3,101	3,180	541	129	158,922	36,518	169,647	28,755	768,475	85,440	230,390	19,217
HISSAR DISTRICT ..	30,542	24,627	1,985	109	135,840	117,944	3,877	260	583	524	108	100	2	..	1	..	3,708	453	4,404	321	20,236	969	3,166	125
HISSAR	7,679	6,030	461	25	30,329	25,660	1,545	171	267	267	34	40	1	..	..	..	1,244	217	1,487	133	6,629	364	1,577	59
HANSI	68	33	34	3	20,747	18,251	645	17	22	7	14	3	..	..	..	..	603	41	849	30	3,522	106	455	8
BHIWANI	13	6	13	2	13,114	11,808	416	11	57	64	15	40	..	..	..	..	667	115	622	82	2,673	238	242	34
FATEHABAD	4,385	3,665	312	25	32,348	28,586	427	14	45	30	7	2	..	..	..	..	328	15	461	22	2,295	54	151	3
SIRSA	18,397	14,893	1,165	54	39,302	33,639	844	47	192	156	33	15	1	..	1	..	866	65	985	54	5,117	207	741	21
ROHTAK DISTRICT ..	328	268	90	17	72,820	65,060	4,040	347	2,452	2,355	111	57	..	..	..	..	3,979	293	4,418	244	18,188	768	3,501	114
ROHTAK	172	141	49	11	25,874	23,022	1,756	238	400	325	38	26	..	..	..	..	1,297	149	1,493	129	6,020	418	1,837	93
JHAJJAR	70	61	20	4	13,277	12,836	1,062	60	180	205	15	8	..	..	..	..	1,372	59	1,348	54	5,405	137	931	9
GOHANA	30	16	9	2	17,128	15,222	552	35	338	319	8	2	..	..	..	..	504	31	611	21	2,876	94	225	2
SONEPAT	56	50	12	..	16,541	13,980	670	14	1,531	1,506	50	21	..	..	..	..	806	54	966	40	3,887	119	508	10
GURGAON DISTRICT ..	281	219	56	14	128,479	112,878	4,765	301	730	733	208	155	8	1	3	..	3,536	390	3,520	309	15,868	978	2,867	119
GURGAON	54	39	18	7	11,260	9,851	978	107	316	309	85	25	..	..	..	..	826	112	723	80	3,412	297	817	20
FIROZPUR-JHIRKA ..	4	2	1	..	44,418	38,651	1,150	42	..	..	..	..	..	..	..	..	362	30	365	23	1,712	63	110	..
NUH	4	3	4	3	37,320	32,636	736	14	6	6	2	1	..	..	..	..	411	20	410	11	1,680	52	179	1
PALWAL	25	14	6	..	14,130	11,878	667	45	76	113	46	57	3	1	3	..	556	66	628	70	2,851	192	383	26
REWARI	19	15	15	4	12,731	11,566	807	42	107	100	67	66	..	..	..	..	837	85	926	72	4,043	255	1,037	62
BALLABGARH	176	146	12	..	9,620	8,296	427	51	225	205	8	6	..	..	..	..	544	77	468	53	2,170	119	341	10
KARNAL DISTRICT ..	9,692	7,236	686	79	141,372	118,358	6,426	826	806	663	103	70	..	..	..	.	3,461	405	4,003	387	18,478	1,204	3,935	106
KARNAL	1,564	1,103	166	34	47,211	39,323	2,587	425	214	180	34	31	..	..	..	..	1,132	166	1,289	160	5,717	533	1,493	50
PANIPAT	113	51	36	2	29,836	24,855	1,594	240	160	127	24	14	..	..	..	..	758	95	899	89	4,307	268	974	26
KAITHAL	3,715	2,717	125	10	35,877	29,934	980	117	293	238	34	19	..	..	..	..	890	86	1,067	83	5,032	234	875	16
THANESAR	4,300	3,365	359	33	28,448	24,246	1,265	44	139	118	11	6	..	..	..	..	681	58	748	55	3,422	169	593	14
AMBALA DISTRICT ..	88,485	67,070	8,874	825	126,918	108,924	9,706	1,605	4,284	2,857	2,389	1,108	7	3	3	1	5,461	1,471	6,568	1,103	31,285	3,616	10,743	776
AMBALA	10,172	7,256	1,929	290	41,771	33,151	4,681	753	2,233	1,148	1,718	619	6	3	3	1	2,015	686	2,670	501	12,614	1,803	6,481	431
KHARAR	37,905	28,717	3,069	165	19,013	15,067	1,430	144	1,075	831	583	432	1	..	..	..	1,323	319	1,457	208	6,976	557	1,783	301
JAGADHRI	2,276	1,679	259	58	23,788	19,432	993	52	229	222	30	36	..	..	..	..	501	113	635	94	3,375	281	817	21
NARAINGARH	1,976	1,511	160	29	18,445	15,955	850	42	171	158	5	2	..	..	..	..	477	67	614	66	2,823	198	391	2
RUPAR	36,156	27,907	3,451	283	23,896	20,319	1,752	614	576	498	53	19	..	..	..	..	1,145	286	1,192	234	5,497	777	1,271	21
SIMLA DISTRICT ..	532	228	281	60	4,346	1,464	1,010	125	788	752	510	518	11	3	..	..	649	244	764	169	4,884	808	2,411	402
SIMLA	527	225	278	59	4,278	1,394	1,001	124	758	717	494	499	..	..	..	..	468	227	610	160	4,285	772	2,281	396
KOT KHAI	5	3	3	1	68	70	9	1	30	35	16	19	11	3	..	..	181	17	154	9	599	36	130	6

AND TAHSILS BY RELIGION AND LITERACY.—*continued.*

KANGRA DISTRICT	**1,338**	**1,058**	**371**	**46**	**22,486**	**17,997**	**1,132**	**140**	**316**	**260**	**138**	**125**	**2,714**	**2,951**	**361**	**39**	**4,440**	**630**	**4,659**	**578**	**27,978**	**1,619**	**3,723**	**108**
KANGRA	179	147	72	8	4,488	3,304	320	43	58	85	35	70	2	..	2	..	576	115	838	135	4,745	378	1,148	65
DEHRA	205	228	95	5	2,775	2,282	84	62	5	3	2	2	..	..	..	..	791	94	839	135	4,994	380	368	4
NURPUR	338	264	52	13	9,873	7,914	330	10	25	3	1	..	26	32	..	..	522	113	462	65	2,314	160	501	2
HAMIRPUR	230	161	50	3	3,031	2,670	117	3	1	3	..	2	..	..	..	..	1,016	70	986	69	6,052	210	563	2
PALAMPUR	240	216	71	8	1,602	1,217	178	15	119	72	59	26	3	4	..	..	946	140	1,006	107	6,741	306	769	9
KULU	56	42	31	9	717	610	103	7	108	94	41	25	2,683	2,915	359	39	589	98	528	62	3,132	185	374	26
HOSHIARPUR DISTRICT	**94,652**	**78,495**	**13,443**	**1,412**	**174,351**	**153,727**	**10,461**	**552**	**2,083**	**1,681**	**52**	**58**	..	..	..	..	**9,259**	**1,231**	**8,858**	**981**	**35,874**	**2,813**	**8,478**	**123**
HOSHIARPUR	30,031	25,193	5,486	630	64,674	58,510	4,718	288	436	429	11	39	..	..	..	..	3,406	581	3,251	442	12,203	1,324	3,896	83
DASUYA	19,017	15,997	2,129	222	60,306	51,469	3,037	145	1,496	1,120	19	12	..	..	..	..	1,768	249	1,630	182	5,996	533	1,331	12
GARHSHANKAR	33,213	27,033	4,177	387	31,791	28,165	2,167	102	136	113	17	6	..	..	..	..	2,141	255	2,101	198	7,666	524	1,891	27
UNA	12,391	10,272	1,651	173	17,580	15,583	539	17	15	19	2	1	..	..	..	..	1,944	146	1,876	159	10,009	432	1,360	1
JULLUNDUR DISTRICT	**139,154**	**110,417**	**10,321**	**1,253**	**223,611**	**195,945**	**15,497**	**1,595**	**2,714**	**1,609**	**994**	**220**	**44**	**26**	..	..	**7,720**	**1,317**	**7,539**	**1,294**	**30,704**	**3,689**	**10,074**	**592**
JULLUNDUR	40,150	32,427	2,934	510	92,463	79,793	8,165	1,060	2,286	1,298	922	205	44	26	..	..	3,396	732	3,492	703	13,974	2,094	5,699	557
NAWANSHAHR	34,232	28,260	3,278	353	33,587	29,731	2,158	141	76	39	2	..	..	..	..	..	1,589	271	1,552	249	7,023	682	2,077	17
PHILLAUR	38,871	29,328	2,636	271	33,875	29,175	1,799	121	145	121	51	9	..	..	..	..	1,264	206	1,270	211	5,519	515	1,584	17
NAKODAR	25,901	20,402	1,473	119	63,686	57,246	3,375	273	207	151	19	6	..	..	..	..	1,471	108	1,225	131	4,188	398	714	1
LUDHIANA DISTRICT	**175,676**	**137,153**	**34,572**	**3,013**	**130,149**	**105,449**	**8,813**	**2,062**	**1,098**	**1,379**	**254**	**497**	**9**	**1**	..	..	**9,341**	**2,159**	**9,237**	**1,580**	**40,171**	**4,066**	**11,291**	**708**
LUDHIANA	81,465	65,787	9,179	1,689	67,563	55,041	5,595	1,694	574	831	207	376	8	1	..	..	3,603	1,347	3,818	1,089	15,394	2,810	5,941	648
JAGRAON	60,258	46,281	6,697	975	39,130	31,630	2,168	313	331	411	36	116	1	..	..	..	2,060	637	1,847	374	8,520	870	1,689	26
SAMRALA	33,953	25,085	18,696	349	23,456	18,778	1,050	55	193	137	11	5	..	..	..	..	3,678	175	3,572	117	16,257	386	3,661	34
FEROZEPORE DISTRICT	**213,516**	**174,492**	**15,466**	**2,099**	**280,323**	**235,107**	**9,601**	**1,125**	**4,381**	**2,689**	**1,609**	**380**	**17**	**8**	..	..	**6,792**	**1,874**	**7,465**	**1,261**	**36,021**	**3,409**	**9,708**	**697**
FEROZEPORE	33,166	25,973	3,013	573	69,860	55,587	3,981	501	2,702	1,431	1,402	289	17	8	..	..	1,876	818	2,381	476	11,211	1,337	5,117	448
ZIRA	21,742	17,705	1,322	71	61,477	53,092	1,692	119	441	352	..	..	..	..	..	..	798	95	768	90	3,438	231	564	2
MOGA	78,424	66,182	6,572	937	28,268	24,662	1,047	140	473	280	142	54	..	..	..	..	1,580	481	1,694	361	8,661	834	1,958	140
MUKTSAR	50,332	40,482	2,787	302	52,190	42,790	1,263	101	353	271	39	24	..	..	..	..	1,088	176	1,237	128	5,762	395	779	31
FAZILKA	29,952	24,150	1,742	216	68,522	58,976	1,618	264	412	355	26	13	..	..	..	..	1,450	304	1,385	206	6,949	612	1,290	76
LAHORE DISTRICT	**137,580**	**106,724**	**12,389**	**1,728**	**464,043**	**351,777**	**49,361**	**10,760**	**32,107**	**24,990**	**6,043**	**3,299**	**105**	**69**	**70**	**42**	**13,639**	**5,825**	**17,468**	**3,911**	**78,844**	**13,196**	**42,777**	**5,915**
LAHORE	47,288	33,419	7,858	1,307	243,028	164,859	41,454	9,864	20,438	15,121	5,951	3,031	101	67	69	41	10,895	5,208	14,538	3,467	65,404	12,032	39,535	5,729
CHUNIAN	35,325	28,490	1,884	251	108,822	92,460	3,006	446	3,883	3,315	34	187	..	..	..	..	1,130	396	1,184	258	5,822	635	1,137	125
KASUR	54,967	44,815	2,647	170	112,193	94,458	4,901	450	7,786	6,554	58	81	4	2	1	1	1,614	221	1,746	186	7,618	529	2,105	61
AMRITSAR DISTRICT	**219,788**	**180,163**	**19,922**	**3,297**	**290,387**	**234,289**	**19,711**	**4,012**	**8,862**	**7,757**	**450**	**455**	**26**	**20**	**18**	**8**	**9,364**	**2,472**	**9,857**	**2,041**	**44,806**	**6,486**	**15,499**	**1,923**
AMRITSAR	101,504	81,694	11,274	2,185	156,924	118,901	14,855	3,803	2,376	2,125	322	354	26	20	18	8	6,386	1,929	7,211	1,703	31,832	5,425	13,064	1,882
TARN TARAN	87,908	73,265	6,616	970	69,797	60,885	2,431	140	1,686	1,433	65	75	..	..	..	..	1,881	477	1,662	270	8,390	885	1,635	24
AJNALA	30,376	25,204	2,032	142	63,666	54,503	2,425	69	4,800	4,199	63	26	..	..	..	..	1,097	66	984	68	4,084	176	800	17
GURDASPUR DISTRICT	**99,724**	**78,747**	**7,026**	**728**	**268,771**	**224,445**	**13,892**	**1,277**	**23,702**	**19,541**	**635**	**311**	**4**	..	**2**	..	**6,280**	**1,140**	**5,950**	**955**	**24,647**	**2,471**	**7,072**	**428**
GURDASPUR	35,291	27,124	2,657	202	76,417	62,361	3,984	182	10,732	8,897	275	115	..	..	..	..	1,802	301	1,719	256	7,400	476	2,267	112
BATALA	52,754	42,564	3,457	423	94,069	79,143	5,820	954	9,861	8,033	200	77	2	..	..	..	2,479	556	2,200	437	9,038	1,250	3,140	187
PATHANKOT	2,865	2,143	422	57	31,526	23,872	1,488	83	677	556	124	110	2	..	2	..	717	170	802	164	4,038	518	816	114
SHAKARGARH	8,814	6,916	490	46	66,759	59,069	2,600	58	2,432	2,055	30	9	..	..	..	..	1,282	113	1,229	98	4,171	227	849	15
SIALKOT DISTRICT	**53,996**	**40,959**	**4,407**	**767**	**333,637**	**275,996**	**17,657**	**1,762**	**36,579**	**29,786**	**2,984**	**911**	**4**	**3**	**3**	**3**	**5,648**	**1,349**	**5,808**	**1,010**	**22,985**	**2,619**	**8,333**	**887**
SIALKOT	8,230	5,490	845	207	105,966	85,466	8,988	1,032	9,602	6,870	2,521	632	4	3	3	3	2,367	674	2,570	503	10,695	1,249	4,776	828
PASRUR	11,146	8,270	941	156	76,973	65,691	2,706	207	6,570	5,747	120	81	..	..	..	..	1,038	202	1,060	164	3,818	395	1,217	20
NAROWAL	19,964	15,613	1,210	102	69,317	57,894	2,746	134	9,594	8,154	201	165	..	..	..	..	1,098	218	1,016	138	3,678	344	746	25
DASKA	14,656	11,586	1,411	302	81,381	66,945	3,217	389	10,813	9,015	142	33	..	..	..	..	1,145	255	1,162	205	4,794	631	1,594	14

PROVINCIAL TABLE II.—POPULATION OF DISTRICTS AND TAHSILS BY RELIGION AND LITERACY.—*continued.*

District and Tahsil.	SIKHS.				MUSLIMS.				CHRISTIANS.				OTHERS.				NUMBER LITERATE.						LITERATE IN ENGLISH.	
	No. of Persons.		No. Literate.		No. of Persons.		No. Literate.		No. of Persons.		No. Literate.		No. of Persons.		No. Literate.		Aged 0—15		Aged 15—20.		Aged 20 and over.			
	Males.	Females.	Males.	Females.	Males.	Females.	Males.	Females.	Males.	Females.	Males.	Females.	Males.	Females.	Males.	Females.	Males.	Females.	Males.	Females.	Males.	Females.	Males.	Females.
	22	23	24	25	26	27	28	29	30	31	32	33	34	35	36	37	38	39	40	41	42	43	44	45
GUJRANWALA DISTRICT	**41,075**	**30,520**	**4,806**	**1,254**	**287,794**	**233,549**	**18,564**	**2,228**	**26,940**	**22,424**	**390**	**184**	**1**	..	..	..	**5,230**	**1,653**	**4,864**	**1,239**	**22,708**	**3,809**	**6,376**	**657**
Gujranwala	30,454	22,629	2,691	791	124,601	100,331	6,849	1,407	19,402	16,273	239	117	1	..	..	..	2,725	957	2,540	708	11,588	2,174	3,223	347
Wazirabad	5,910	4,566	1,165	286	67,617	55,298	4,405	607	5,453	4,430	125	62	..	..	..	..	1,374	386	1,318	322	6,131	1,059	1,969	92
Hafizabad	4,681	3,325	950	177	95,576	77,920	2,310	212	2,085	1,721	26	5	..	..	..	..	1,131	310	1,006	209	4,989	576	1,184	218
SHEIKHUPURA DISTRICT	**66,762**	**52,715**	**7,111**	**965**	**244,064**	**201,932**	**8,008**	**300**	**26,895**	**22,371**	**165**	**105**	**4**	**2**	**2**	**2**	**3,498**	**675**	**3,691**	**548**	**16,874**	**1,582**	**3,381**	**154**
Sheikhupura	39,579	31,109	4,178	547	94,953	78,118	3,707	100	15,894	13,304	98	67	..	..	..	..	1,947	224	1,933	183	8,164	577	2,621	68
Nankana Sahib ..	12,629	9,666	1,740	329	77,569	65,672	1,514	106	2,545	2,066	12	9	..	..	..	..	703	189	857	169	4,172	438	731	18
Shahdara	14,554	11,940	1,193	89	71,542	58,142	2,787	94	8,456	7,001	55	29	4	2	2	2	848	262	901	196	4,538	567	629	68
GUJRAT DISTRICT	**30,795**	**28,393**	**10,938**	**2,295**	**425,716**	**361,034**	**16,855**	**1,015**	**1,746**	**1,351**	**124**	**85**	**1**	**3**	..	..	**5,324**	**1,307**	**5,480**	**1,038**	**28,598**	**2,873**	**7,297**	**171**
Gujrat	8,262	7,695	1,566	1,186	146,252	126,097	7,288	671	733	574	65	56	..	..	..	..	2,033	731	1,854	564	8,802	1,516	3,014	115
Kharian	8,370	7,725	3,247	327	129,282	115,356	6,529	210	202	156	..	..	1	3	..	..	1,892	265	1,912	214	8,956	543	1,488	25
Phalia	14,163	12,973	6,125	782	150,182	119,581	3,038	134	811	621	59	29	..	..	..	..	1,399	311	1,714	260	10,840	814	2,795	31
SHAHPUR DISTRICT ..	**22,200**	**17,874**	**7,185**	**3,628**	**367,879**	**311,667**	**14,933**	**1,283**	**6,223**	**5,071**	**222**	**134**	**1**	..	**1**	..	**5,929**	**2,091**	**5,570**	**1,757**	**25,622**	**4,315**	**6,694**	**419**
Shahpur	2,805	2,526	1,144	1,423	72,493	61,091	2,389	361	50	44	3	1	..	..	..	..	953	661	991	741	4,847	1,050	1,284	190
Khushab	2,610	2,577	1,094	621	88,754	84,060	3,704	53	15	7	6	6	..	..	..	..	1,262	313	1,091	228	5,153	824	732	9
Bhalwal	2,809	2,084	841	259	117,228	94,947	4,516	390	323	243	11	9	1	..	1	..	1,565	302	1,454	217	6,436	652	1,725	30
Sargodha	13,976	10,687	4,106	1,320	89,404	71,569	4,324	479	5,835	4,777	202	118	..	..	..	..	2,149	815	2,034	571	9,186	1,789	2,953	190
JHELUM DISTRICT ..	**11,409**	**10,621**	**5,024**	**1,581**	**251,656**	**230,441**	**17,005**	**1,195**	**388**	**284**	**176**	**98**	..	..	..	..	**5,178**	**1,049**	**4,784**	**907**	**19,645**	**2,499**	**4,387**	**306**
Jhelum	4,238	3,065	2,099	588	89,781	80,185	7,325	316	334	247	143	84	..	..	..	..	1,893	363	2,090	322	8,854	1,004	2,000	130
Pind Dadan Khan ..	937	944	414	106	76,165	70,235	3,821	200	35	22	33	14	..	..	..	..	1,043	127	935	118	4,524	301	1,007	35
Chakwal	6,234	6,612	2,511	887	85,710	80,021	5,859	679	19	15	..	..	..	..	..	..	2,242	559	1,759	467	6,267	1,194	1,380	141
RAWALPINDI DISTRICT ..	**22,948**	**18,317**	**9,603**	**3,953**	**279,287**	**245,678**	**24,013**	**1,254**	**4,924**	**2,562**	**3,287**	**1,245**	**46**	**33**	**27**	**13**	**7,958**	**2,041**	**7,978**	**1,501**	**36,151**	**5,379**	**22,629**	**2,339**
Rawalpindi	12,783	9,185	5,915	2,310	119,862	92,394	12,462	987	4,822	2,462	3,238	1,221	46	33	27	13	4,409	1,487	5,169	1,104	25,225	4,076	13,479	1,520
Gujar Khan	6,300	5,848	2,636	35	78,532	73,972	5,361	146	57	41	28	3	..	..	..	..	1,822	104	1,417	56	5,773	217	8,583	180
Murree	475	207	222	837	34,892	32,657	3,406	103	45	59	21	21	..	..	..	..	855	247	610	174	2,481	571	277	636
Kahuta	3,390	3,077	830	771	46,001	46,655	2,784	18	..	..	..	..	..	..	..	..	872	203	782	167	2,672	515	290	3
ATTOCK DISTRICT ..	**10,279**	**9,243**	**4,288**	**1,098**	**279,546**	**252,247**	**9,672**	**1,152**	**490**	**220**	**364**	**105**	**1**	..	..	..	**2,740**	**768**	**2,734**	**589**	**14,136**	**2,069**	**2,879**	**151**
Attock	3,085	2,375	1,386	484	93,770	82,400	4,235	314	307	168	206	78	1	..	..	..	872	369	1,096	253	6,022	827	1,744	123
Pindigheb	1,721	1,459	806	153	67,459	61,769	2,179	741	76	43	55	23	..	..	..	..	734	240	648	193	3,106	673	512	15
Talagang	1,714	1,682	663	145	59,575	57,047	1,183	55	1	2	1	2	..	..	..	..	484	54	447	60	1,925	210	376	10
Fatehjang	3,759	3,727	1,433	316	58,742	51,031	2,075	42	16	7	12	2	..	..	..	..	650	105	543	83	3,083	359	247	3
MIANWALI DISTRICT ..	**2,263**	**1,968**	**835**	**149**	**187,872**	**169,237**	**4,702**	**133**	**211**	**169**	**56**	**32**	**3**	**2**	**2**	..	**1,781**	**286**	**2,166**	**221**	**10,348**	**648**	**2,126**	**46**
Mianwali	1,107	837	436	76	82,027	74,900	2,444	117	148	120	46	23	3	2	2	..	828	208	1,068	139	4,945	402	1,272	37
Bhakkar	780	729	220	16	72,996	63,770	1,239	16	5	5	1	3	..	..	..	..	697	42	767	55	3,731	148	510	2
Isa Khel	376	402	179	57	32,849	30,567	1,019	..	58	44	9	6	..	..	..	..	266	30	331	27	1,672	98	344	7

AND TAHSILS BY RELIGION AND LITERACY.—*concluded.*

MONTGOMERY DISTRICT	32,261	65,894	10,071	1,676	381,956	315,586	10,563	736	9,618	7,627	427	172	7	2	5	..	4,538	925	5,460	874	26,019	2,591	6,223	248
Montgomery	22,961	17,200	3,834	753	123,313	98,716	4,360	462	5,090	3,924	261	113	3	2	2	..	1,946	482	2,212	420	9,780	1,299	2,976	180
Okara	18,093	14,880	2,398	445	84,814	70,137	2,424	132	3,613	2,956	121	46	3	..	2	..	1,065	230	1,260	212	6,084	632	1,330	25
Dipalpur	16,183	13,834	1,596	190	90,551	77,531	1,646	63	126	92	7	3	..	..	..	..	566	56	810	80	4,310	265	604	8
Pakpattan	25,024	19,980	2,243	288	83,278	69,202	2,133	79	789	655	38	10	1	..	1	..	961	157	1,178	162	5,845	395	1,313	30
LYALLPUR DISTRICT ..	117,039	94,352	16,104	2,132	389,159	331,837	19,063	1,985	24,899	20,619	584	222	7	..	4	..	10,168	1,773	10,262	1,823	35,911	4,484	10,187	701
Lyallpur	38,442	31,516	6,059	880	102,114	84,262	7,563	1,342	10,601	8,616	183	99	7	..	4	..	4,210	887	4,390	1,064	14,312	2,701	6,077	631
Samundri	18,226	14,580	2,260	286	96,586	84,254	2,607	192	3,806	3,257	70	11	..	..	..	..	1,161	121	1,371	171	4,926	425	669	21
Toba Tek Singh ..	22,303	18,105	3,370	398	111,319	95,094	6,542	305	7,839	6,584	298	100	..	..	..	..	3,232	481	2,960	378	10,151	896	2,148	30
Jaranwala	38,068	30,151	4,415	568	79,140	68,227	2,351	96	2,653	2,162	33	12	..	..	..	..	1,565	284	1,541	210	6,522	462	1,293	19
JHANG DISTRICT ..	4,551	3,925	1,022	636	297,801	255,052	9,667	1,241	267	227	15	6	13	7	..	..	4,120	1,277	3,890	919	17,373	2,920	2,807	458
Jhang	2,656	2,527	559	523	113,071	96,417	4,115	425	28	21	15	6	..	..	..	..	1,645	682	1,646	543	8,693	1,933	1,156	446
Chiniot	972	654	355	65	122,688	104,601	3,583	710	36	23	..	..	..	..	..	..	1,623	426	1,493	259	5,807	579	1,292	8
Shorkot	923	744	108	48	62,042	54,034	1,969	106	203	183	..	..	13	7	..	..	852	169	751	117	2,873	408	359	4
MULTAN DISTRICT ..	23,241	16,212	4,502	572	515,218	427,719	17,662	695	5,780	4,144	1,104	395	71	46	39	21	5,988	931	7,651	798	39,492	2,461	8,765	508
Multan	3,237	1,746	933	174	132,074	106,152	7,242	464	1,364	586	813	310	71	46	39	21	2,283	486	2,943	351	12,496	1,203	5,101	444
Shujabad	652	545	148	32	68,505	57,905	1,607	23	6	6	..	..	..	..	..	..	566	84	666	65	3,822	177	548	2
Lodhran	1,396	718	189	22	73,317	62,127	1,984	86	24	18	5	6	..	..	..	..	596	38	688	26	4,746	128	590	7
Mailsi	6,655	4,614	929	111	82,909	68,038	1,955	25	671	488	23	3	..	..	..	..	549	72	862	113	5,779	305	660	2
Khanewal	8,861	6,482	1,578	163	78,934	64,972	2,286	52	3,606	2,953	262	76	..	..	..	..	1,158	200	1,444	175	6,900	501	1,435	48
Kabirwala	2,440	2,107	725	70	79,479	68,525	2,588	45	109	93	1	..	..	..	..	..	836	51	1,048	68	5,749	147	431	..
MUZAFFARGARH DISTRICT	2,938	2,349	384	83	279,319	233,946	5,470	218	133	113	24	15	..	..	..	..	1,693	207	2,275	176	18,362	554	1,141	18
Muzaffargarh	536	453	147	64	85,214	72,238	1,525	115	95	79	10	6	..	..	..	..	490	106	648	77	3,320	309	353	3
Alipur	1,078	791	75	10	75,657	63,525	1,205	32	9	7	7	3	..	..	..	..	371	20	569	18	3,853	48	272	3
Kot Adu	955	766	88	9	57,615	46,626	1,480	30	29	27	7	6	..	..	..	..	482	53	597	55	2,970	120	173	7
Leiah	369	339	74	..	60,833	51,557	1,260	41	..	..	..	..	..	..	..	..	350	28	461	26	3,210	77	343	5
DERA GHAZI KHAN DISTRICT.	439	321	66	21	255,817	206,563	6,179	222	19	12	7	3	..	..	..	..	1,500	282	2,324	226	11,267	545	1,920	28
Dera Ghazi Khan ..	110	54	41	19	92,008	76,079	2,321	66	10	5	7	3	..	..	..	..	638	145	704	96	4,981	251	1,208	11
Sanghar	..	..	..	..	42,204	35,676	1,714	92	..	..	..	..	..	..	..	..	280	29	827	43	2,084	85	282	7
Rajanpur	286	229	23	2	56,211	43,792	828	15	1	..	..	..	..	..	..	..	199	24	376	30	2,114	72	145	9
Jampur	43	38	2	..	48,683	38,258	1,221	29	8	7	..	..	..	..	..	..	373	79	401	52	1,981	103	279	1
Biloch Trans Frontier tract.	..	..	..	..	16,711	12,758	95	20	..	..	..	..	..	..	..	..	10	5	16	5	107	34	6	..